W9-BJS-212

Fiscal Administration

ANALYSIS AND APPLICATIONS IN THE PUBLIC SECTOR

Seventh Edition

John L. Mikesell
Indiana University

THOMSON
WADSWORTH

Australia • Brazil • Canada • Mexico • Singapore • Spain
United Kingdom • United States

THOMSON
WADSWORTH

***Fiscal Administration: Analysis and Applications in the Public Sector,* Seventh Edition**
John L. Mikesell

Executive Editor: David Tatom
Development Editor: Jeffrey Goldings
Associate Development Editor: Rebecca Green
Editorial Assistant: Eva Dickerson
Technology Project Manager: Inna Fedoseyeva
Senior Marketing Manager: Janise Fry
Marketing Assistant: Teresa Jessen
Marketing Communications Manager: Nathaniel Michelson
Senior Project Manager, Editorial Production: Paul Wells

Creative Director: Rob Hugel
Art Director: Maria Epes
Print Buyer: Karen Hunt
Permissions Editor: Roberta Broyer
Production Service: Graphic World Publishing Services
Cover Designer: Brian Salisbury
Compositor: Graphic World Inc.
Printer: Thomson/West

© 2007 Thomson Wadsworth, a part of The Thomson Corporation. Thomson, the Star logo, and Wadsworth are trademarks used herein under license.

ALL RIGHTS RESERVED. No part of this work covered by the copyright hereon may be reproduced or used in any form or by any means—graphic, electronic, or mechanical, including photocopying, recording, taping, Web distribution, information storage and retrieval systems, or in any other manner—without the written permission of the publisher.

Printed in the United States of America
1 2 3 4 5 6 7 10 09 08 07 06

Thomson Higher Education
10 Davis Drive
Belmont, CA 94002-3098
USA

Library of Congress Control Number: 2006921608
ISBN 0-495-00740-4

For more information about our products, contact us at:
Thomson Learning Academic Resource Center
1-800-423-0563

For permission to use material from this text or product, submit a request online at **http://www.thomsonrights.com.**
Any additional questions about permissions can be submitted by e-mail to **thomsonrights@thomson.com.**

About the Author

John L. Mikesell is professor of public and environmental affairs at Indiana University–Bloomington and director of the Master of Public Affairs program for the School of Public and Environmental Affairs. He is editor-in-chief of *Public Budgeting & Finance,* the journal cooperatively published by the American Association for Budget and Program Analysis and the Association for Budgeting and Financial Management, and his column on sales taxation periodically appears in State Tax Notes. His work on government finance and taxation has appeared in such journals as *National Tax Journal, Public Budgeting & Finance, Public Finance Quarterly, Southern Economic Journal, Public Administration Review, Public Choice,* and *Journal of Public Budgeting, Accounting, and Financial Management.* He is co-author with John F. Due of *Sales Taxation, State and Local Structure and Administration* (Urban Institute Press). Professor Mikesell has served as chief fiscal economist and chief of party with the USAID Barents Group/KPMG Peat Marwick fiscal reform project with the Government of Ukraine to develop a macroeconomic analysis and budget policy department in the Ministry of Finance and as Moscow-based director for assistance in intergovernmental fiscal relations with the USAID Georgia State University Consortium Russian fiscal reform project. He directed U.S.-Department-of-State-supported public administration partnerships between the School of Public and Environmental Affairs and the Volga Region Academy for Civil Service, Saratov, Russia, and the North West Academy for Public Administration, St. Petersburg, Russia. He has worked on fiscal studies for several states, including New York, Minnesota, Indiana, and Hawaii, has served on the Revenue Forecast Technical Committee of the Indiana State Budget Committee for almost 30 years; has worked as consultant on World Bank missions to the Kyrgyz Republic, Kazakhstan, Azerbaijan, Tajikistan, and Turkmenistan; and has been visiting scholar at the U.S. Congressional Budget Office and at the Department of Public Administration, Erasmus University Rotterdam. He was awarded a David Lincoln Fellowship by the Lincoln Institute for Land Policy in 2005. Professor Mikesell has headed the Association for Budgeting and Financial Management and served on the Board of Directors of the National Tax Association-Tax Institute of America. He holds a BA from Wabash College and MA and PhD in economics from the University of Illinois, where he specialized in public finance and taxation. He is a member of Phi Beta Kappa and received the 2002 Wildavsky Award for Lifetime Scholarly Achievement in Public Budgeting and Finance from the Association for Budgeting and Financial Management.

Preface

Public finance and budgeting is a changing discipline. Ideas, applications, and environments change. Attitudes toward the role of government, ideas about what governments should do, concepts of organizing government decision-making, and views about how governments should finance their operations change. No part of the field remains constant for long, and both neophytes and grizzled veterans have to keep on their toes, because neither the questions nor the answers remain the same. But the age-old questions of how much to allocate for what services and where to obtain the money to finance the allocations remain with us, even if the popular answers to them are different. Indeed, the real veterans see old answers returning as new people enter the field, rediscover the old systems, and proclaim them as new! On top of all the coming and going is the fact that the basic principles of public finance and budgeting do not change, just their application.

This book has stuck to two distinguishing principles through each of its editions. First, a public-affairs student must understand where the money comes from—not just sort of, but really. The statement from an earlier-edition preface continues to be as true at the start of the twenty-first century as it was in the 1980s: "If armies move on their stomachs, then governments certainly crawl on their purses." Students and practitioners who do not understand revenue options, systems, and policies will miss out on much of the fun. And they won't be very useful in many crucial policy discussions. Second, a public-affairs student has not learned much public finance and budgeting if he or she has not run some numbers. Most chapters are followed by questions and exercises that require not speculation or discussion but calculations to get an answer. As in the real world of government finance, life is easier for students who use a computer spreadsheet for many of these exercises—but a paper-and-pencil approach will work just as well.

This edition features materials updated to include the most recent fiscal data available. This includes the path woven by the federal government as it dodges between surplus and deficit and as it applies its performance assessment system in developing the budget. Also, there is somewhat greater attention given to governmental accounting and financial reporting. Finally, several new cases and exercises have been added, some cases have been retired, and the bibliography and list of Internet resources has been expanded and updated.

I would like to thank the reviewers of this edition. Helpful comments were provided by John R. Bartle of the University of Nebraska–Omaha, David Liebschutz of the State University of New York at Albany, Aimee L. Franklin of the University of Oklahoma, and E. Lee Bernick fo the University of Nevada–Las Vegas. I also want to thank Craig Johnson, Robert Kravchuk, and C. Kurt Zorn, my colleagues at Indiana University, for helpful suggestions about topics that could be added and ways that concepts could be explained more clearly. Finally, I want to thank Diana Worman and Karly Wade for secretarial support during the revision.

John L. Mikesell
Indiana University
2006

Contents

About the Author iii

Preface iv

CHAPTER 1 ***Fundamental Principles of Public Finance 1***
Market Failure and the Functions of Government 2
Public Goods 3
Externalities 6
Failure of Competition 8
Privatization 11
Building Social Decisions from Private Preferences 15
Politics, Representation, and Government Finance 19
The Layers of Government 22
Conclusion 24
Questions and Exercises 25
Case for Discussion 26
Case 1–1: Market Interplay, Municipal Utilities, and a Common-Pool Resource 26

PART ONE **Budgeting, Budget Structures, and Budget Reform 29**

CHAPTER 2 ***The Logic of the Budget Process 31***
The Size and Growth of Government Expenditure 32
Budget Process and Logic 38
The Parts of the Public Expenditure/Public Revenue Process 40
A Budget's Traditional Look: The Object-of-Expenditure (or Input) Format 42
Functions of the Budget Process 46
The Budget Cycle 48
Executive Preparation 49
Legislative Consideration 51
Execution 52
Audit and Evaluation 54
Governmental Accounting and Financial Reporting 56
Budgets and Political Strategies 61
The Incrementalist Insight 61
Roles, Visions, and Incentives 62
Strategies 64
Conclusion 69
Questions and Exercises 69
Cases for Discussion 72
Case 2–1: Developing and Using Budget Strategy: The Earth Resources Technology Satellite (ERTS) 72
Case 2–2: Strategies in Defense of the Defense Budget 75

CHAPTER 3 ***Budget Structures and Institutions: Federal and State-Local 79***
The Federal Budget 79
Spending by the Federal Government 80
The Federal Budget Process 82
Fighting Federal Deficits 109
Federal Fiscal Policy 116
State and Local Budgets 118
Spending by State and Local Governments 119
Conclusion 131
Questions and Exercises 131
Case for Discussion 132
Case 3–1: Federal Earmarks and the Battle against Pork 132
Appendix 3–1: An Illustrative State Budget Process: Texas 135
Appendix 3–2: Participatory Budgeting 139

CHAPTER 4 ***Budget Methods and Practices 141***
Preparation of Agency Budget Requests 141
Budget Justification 142
Elements of Cost Estimation 145
Review of Budgets 151
The Executive Budget: The Plan and the Balancing 154
Phantom Balance and Deficit Reduction 156
Managing Budget Execution 161
Internal Controls 165
Audit and Evaluation 167
Conclusion 170
Questions and Exercises 170
Cases for Discussion 177
Case 4–1: Green Felt-Tip Pens, a Tape Recorder, and Embezzlement: Where Did the Budget Process Fail? 177
Case 4–2: Balancing the Chicago Public School Budget 179
Appendix 4–1: Budget Preparation, or How to Be a Budget Analyst 181

CHAPTER 5 ***Budget Classifications and Reform 192***
Alternative Budget Classifications and the Provision of Government Services 193
Traditional Budgets: A Flawed Tool for Decision-making (But Pretty Good for Control and Accountability) 196
Performance Budgets 201
Program Budgets 205
An Illustration of an Expenditure in Alternative Classifications 213
New Performance Budgeting: Focusing on Results/Outcomes 214
Some Challenges for New Performance Budgeting 221
Federal Integration of Performance and Budgeting: Budget and Performance Integration Initiative and the Program Assessment Rating Tool 226
Conclusion 232
Questions and Exercises 233
Cases for Discussion 236
Case 5–1: Following Departmental Lines (and Scores?) 236
Case 5–2: A View of Zero-Based Budgeting 237

Appendix 5–1: Functional Categories of the Federal Budget 240
Appendix 5–2: COFOG 243

CHAPTER 6 *Capital Budgeting, Public Infrastructure Investment, and Project Evaluation 244*
Why Have a Capital Budget? 246
A Capital Budgeting Process 249
Problems in Capital Budgeting 256
Accounting for Time: Discounting and Compounding 258
Cost-Benefit Analysis 263
Elements in Cost-Benefit Analysis 265
Selecting a Discount Rate 271
Decision Criteria 273
Some Special Problems of Cost-Benefit Analysis 277
Conclusion 280
Questions and Exercises 281
Case for Discussion 286
Case 6–1: What Does Cost Mean? 286

***PART TWO* Revenue Sources, Structure, and Administration 289**

CHAPTER 7 *Taxation: Criteria for Evaluating Revenue Options 291*
Taxation in the United States: A Short Overview of the Systems 292
Standards for Tax Policy 298
Equity 300
Adequacy of Revenue Production 309
Collectability 314
Economic Effects 315
State and Local Taxes and Economic Development 318
Transparency 320
Taxes and Externalities 322
Conclusion 324
Questions and Exercises 324
Case for Discussion 326
Case 7–1: Politics and the Protection of Tax Advantages 326

CHAPTER 8 *Major Tax Structures: Income Taxes 331*
Some Background 332
The Argument about Taxing Income 336
For the System of Taxing Income 336
Against the System of Taxing Income 337
Individual Income Taxation 340
Defining Income 340
Adjusted Gross Income 342
Personal Deductions 345
Personal Exemptions 347
Taxable Income 349
Tax Rates 350
Credits 354

Effective Tax Rates 354
Indexation 356
Tax Computation 357
Corporate Income Taxation 357
Dividing the Base 361
Integration with the Individual Tax 362
International Harmonization 364
Payroll Taxation 365
Conclusion 366
Questions and Exercises 367
Case for Discussion 370
Case 8–1: Tax Credits and Government Policy 370

CHAPTER 9 *Major Tax Structures: Taxes on Goods and Services 372*
The Equity Question 378
Selective Excise Taxation 379
Luxury Excises 379
Sumptuary Excises 380
Benefit-Base Excises 382
Regulatory and Environmental Excises 383
Other Excises 383
General Taxes on Goods and Services: Retail Sales and Value-Added Taxes 384
Retail Sales Taxes 387
Exclusion of Producers' Goods 389
Taxation of Services 393
Commodity Exemptions 394
Variation in the State Sales Taxes 395
The Sales Taxes and Internet Commerce: Remote Vendors and Use Taxes 396
Value-Added Taxes 400
Value-Added Tax Features 403
Value-Added Tax versus Retail Sales Tax 406
Conclusion 407
Questions and Exercises 408
Cases for Discussion 409
Case 9–1: Sales Tax and Used Cars 409
Case 9–2: Girl Scout Cookies and the Snack Tax 413

CHAPTER 10 *Major Tax Structures: Property Taxes 415*
Good Tax, Bad Tax? 418
The Arithmetic of Rates, Levies, and Assessed Value 420
Doing Assessments: Standards 423
Doing Assessments: Cycles 426
Doing Assessments: Approaches 427
Doing Assessments: Managing Parcel Data 429
Property Tax Relief Mechanisms 431
Exemptions and Abatements 432
Circuit-Breakers 434
Deferrals 436
Classification 436
Tax Increment Financing 437

Fractional Assessment and Assessment Disparity 439
Limits and Controls 443
Conclusion 448
Questions and Exercises 448
Cases for Discussion 453
Case 10–1: Use-Value Assessment for Farmland: Some Operational Questions 453
Case 10–2: Finding Revenue in Reassessment 455
Case 10–3: Property Taxes and a World-Class House 457
Case 10–4: The Property Tax versus Habitat for Humanity 457

CHAPTER 11 ***Revenue from User Fees, User Charges, and Sales by Public Monopolies 461***
User Fees and Licenses 466
User Charges 468
Advantages of User Charges 470
Limitations of User Charges 472
Charge Guidelines 474
Public Monopoly Revenue: Utilities, Liquor Stores, and Gambling Enterprises 477
Government Utilities 477
Liquor Stores 478
Government Gambling Enterprises: Lotteries and Offtrack Betting 479
Conclusion 483
Questions and Exercises 483
Cases for Discussion
Case 11–1: Entrepreneurial Revenues in State Parks 486
Case 11–2: User Charges for Social Purposes: London Congestion Charge 489

CHAPTER 12 ***Collecting Taxes 492***
Why Do People and Businesses Pay the Tax They Owe? 492
Taxpayer Active or Taxpayer Passive? 494
The Core Functions of Tax Collection 496
Taxpayer Registration/Service 497
Declaration of Assessment 498
Revenue and Taxpayer Accounting 498
Delinquency Control, Compliance, and Collections 500
Audit 501
Appeal or Protest 503
Enforcement 505
Total Collection Cost 505
Conclusion 508
Questions and Exercises 508
Case for Discussion
Case 12–1: The Kursk Tax Inspector 509

CHAPTER 13 ***Revenue Forecasts, Revenue Estimates, and Tax Expenditure Budgets 514***
Revenue Forecast (or Baseline) 515
General Guides for Revenue Forecasts 516

Alternative Methods for Forecasting 518
Univariate Projections and Extrapolations 518
Deterministic Modeling 519
Multiple Regression 520
Econometric Models 521
Microdata Models 522
Choosing the Method 524
Forecasts for the Long Term 526
Wrong Forecasts 527
Revenue Estimating 527
Tax Expenditure Budgets 530
Conclusion 535
Questions and Exercises 535
Appendix 13–1: The State of Minnesota Tax Expenditure Budget: Criteria and Measurement 537

CHAPTER 14 ***Intergovernmental Fiscal Relations: Diversity and Coordination 541***
Correspondence and Subsidiarity 542
What about Economic Advantage from Bigness? 544
Fiscal Disparity 545
Coordination and Assistance: Tax Systems 547
Coordination and Assistance: Grants 551
Categorical Grants 555
Block Grants 558
Revenue Sharing (General-Purpose Fiscal Assistance) 560
States and School Aid 561
Coordination and Assistance: Mandates 563
Conclusion 566
Questions and Exercises 567
Cases for Discussion 567
Case 14–1: It Worked Once, But Would It Work Again? 567
Case 14–2: Correspondence, Subsidiarity, and the Tenn-Tom Waterway 569

PART THREE **Administering Debt, Working Capital, and Pension Funds 573**

CHAPTER 15 ***Debt Administration 575***
Federal Debt 575
State and Local Government (Municipal) Debt 579
Municipal Bonds and the Tax Reform Act of 1986 584
Appropriate Debt Policy 585
The Mechanics of Bond Values 586
Debt Structure and Design 588
Ratings 591
Credit Enhancements 597
Underwriting, Interest Rates, and Ownership 599
Lease-Purchase Finance and Certificates of Participation 605
Conclusion 607

Questions and Exercises 607
Appendix 15–1: General Principles of State Debt Management 610

CHAPTER 16 ***Managing Funds: Cash Management and Employee Retirement Funds 611***
The Cash Budget and Cash Management 612
Elements of Cash Management 614
Accelerating Collections 614
Controlling Disbursements 619
Consolidating Balances 620
Investing Idle Funds 621
Treasury Bills 624
Other Federal-Agency Issues 624
Negotiable Certificates of Deposit 625
Commercial Paper 626
Repurchase Agreements and Reverse Repurchase Agreements 626
State and Local Debt 627
State Investment Pools 627
Money-Market Mutual Funds 628
Keeping Score (Measuring Performance) 628
Managing Public Employee Retirement Funds 628
Critical Issues in Public Employee Retirement Fund Management 635
Conclusion 637
Questions and Exercises 637
Cases for Discussion 638
Case 16–1: Managing Cash for the Sheriff's Interest? 638
Case 16–2: The Underfunded West Virginia Public Employees' Pension Fund 643

Appendix: Some Websites for Fiscal Administration Data and Information 647
Glossary 651
Selected Bibliography 665
Index 675

List of Figures

1–1 The Elements of Nonappropriability 4
2–1 Government Spending in the United States as Percentage of GDP, 1960–2004 35
2–2 Service Delivery and Revenue Systems as Separate Planning Processes 41
2–3 City of Tempe, Arizona: Line Item Budget for the Fire Department, 2004–2005 (Biennial) 43
2–4 Phases of a Budget Cycle 49
2–5 Financial Information for Management 53
2–6 Relationship of Budget Authority to Outlays for 2007 53
3–1 Discretionary Federal Outlays as Percentage of Total Outlays, Fiscal 1962–2005 105
3–2 State and Local Net Lending as Percent of GDP, 1959–2004 130
3A–1 The Biennial Budget Cycle in the State of Texas 137
4–1 An Example of a Budget-Status Report 164
5–1 Flow of Public-Service Provision 194
5–2 Salt Lake City Performance Budget Illustration 203
5–3 Federal Spending by Agency and Function: Multiple Agencies for Functions and Multiple Functions for Agencies 211
5–4 Salary Classification in Traditional, Performance, and Program Budgets 213
5–5 Illustration of New Performance Budget: State of Texas Commission for the Blind 220
5–6 PART Performance Measurement Scoring Illustration, Border Patrol, Fiscal 2006 229
5–7 Illustration of Performance Goals from Department of Homeland Security Performance Budget, Fiscal 2006 231
6–1 Capital Improvement Programming and Budgeting 251
6–2 Compounding 259
6–3 Individual Demand for a Park 268
7–1 Impact, Shifting, and Incidence 305
7–2 Relationships Between Tax Rate and Tax Revenue: The Tax Revenue Curve 310
8–1 Elements of the Federal Individual Tax Structure: How the Flow Works in Calculating the Tax That People Pay 341
8–2 Federal Rate Schedule for 2005: Married Individuals Filing Jointly or Qualifying Widow(er)s 350
8–3 Federal Rate Schedule for 2005: Single Filers 350
8–4 A Portion of the Federal Income Tax Table for 2005 351
9–1 The Flow of Production and Distribution 377
9–2 The Virginia Retail Sales and Use Tax Return 388
9–3 Retail Sales Tax Pyramiding: Typical v. Ideal 390
9–4 Suspending Sales Tax by Certificate 392
9–5 New Zealand Value-Added Tax Return 404
10–1 Parcel Record Card for Residential Property (Structure or Improvement) 430
10–2 Truth in Property Tax Notification: Landover Hills, MD 447
12–1 Illustration of Tax Return Processing Flow 499
15–1 U.S. Federal Debt Relative to GDP (%), End of Fiscal Year 1940–2005 577
15–2 U.S. Treasury Yield Curve, July 29, 2005 590
15–3 Yield of Aaa Municipal and AAA Corporate Debt, End of Year, 1962–2003 591
15–4 A Certificate-of-Participation Arrangement 606
16–1 Cash Balance Through a Year for a Fund 613
16–2 Control for Cash Management: Receipts and Disbursement 615
16–3 Collection and Deposit Float 616
16–4 A Postal Lockbox Collection System 617
16–5 Application of a Concentration Account 621

List of Tables

1–1 Individual Benefits from the Project: Example 1 17
1–2 Individual Benefits from the Project: Example 2 18
1–3 Individual Benefits from the Project: Example 3 18
2–1 Government Spending in the National Income and Product Accounts ($ billions) 34
2–2 Government in Selected Industrialized Countries, 2002 39
3–1 Federal Outlays by Function, 1960–2005 ($ millions) 81
3–2 Highlights of Major Acts Establishing the Federal Budget Process 83
3–3 Major Events in the Federal Budget Process 86
3–4 The Congressional Budget Timetable 89
3–5 Appropriations Subcommittees from the 109th Congress 90
3–6 Mandatory and Discretionary Federal Spending, 1975–2005 ($ billions) 104
3–7 Deficits and Surpluses of the Federal Government from 1940–2005 ($ millions) 110
3–8 State and Local Government Expenditures, 2002–2003 ($ in thousands) 120
3–9 State Budget Cycles 126
4–1 Checklist for Budget Justification 144
4–2 Some Errors or Abuses Sought by Auditors 168
5–1 Alternative Budget Formats and Associated Features 197
5–2 Performance Budget Structure: Commonwealth of Pennsylvania, 2005–2006 206
5–3 Program-Budget Structure in the U.S. Department of Defense 209
5–4 Activities (or Direct Outputs) or Outcomes (or Results) 217
6–1 Selected Questions for a Capital Budget Request 255
6–2 Payback Analysis 276
6–3 Projects with Ranking Criteria Conflict 277
7–1 Government Revenue by Source and Level, Fiscal 2003 ($ millions) 293
7–2 Major Tax Sources Levied by States and Localities, July 2005 295
7–3 Tax Revenue as a Percentage of Gross Domestic Product and as Percentage from Major Taxes, 2001, Countries of the Organization for Economic Cooperation and Development (OECD) 297
7–4 Regressivity, Proportionality, and Progressivity in Tax Systems 303
7–5 Federal Tax Distributions and Effective Tax Rates by Income Quintiles for All Families, 1980–2003 (all in percentages) 306
7–6 Compilation of Selected Long-Term Tax Base Elasticities as Found in Various Tax Studies 313
8–1 Individual and Corporate Income Taxes and Social Insurance Contributions in American Government Finance, Selected Calendar Years, 1930–2004 335
8–2 Distribution of Federal Income Tax Payments and Effective Tax Rates by Income Quintiles for All Families, 2003 (all in percentages) 337
8–3 History of Federal Individual Income Tax Exemptions and Lowest and Highest Bracket Rates 348
8–4 Effective-Rate Impact of a Flat-Rate Income Tax (10 Percent) and a Large Personal Exemption ($1,500 per Person) on Selected Families of Three 356
8–5 An Example of Income Tax Computation 358
9–1 Federal Taxes on Goods and Services (Fiscal Year 2003) 374
9–2 State and Local Taxes on Goods and Services, Fiscal 2003 ($ thousands) 375
9–3 Effective Tax Rates for Federal Excises and Minnesota Retail Sales and Excise Taxes 378
9–4 Standard Value-Added Tax Rate in Countries Around the World, 2005 405
10–1 Property Taxes in U.S. Government Finances, 2002–2003 416
10–2 Property Classifications by Statutory Rates and Assessment Ratios 437
10–3 Tax Increment Financing 438
10–4 Coefficient of Dispersion Calculation 441
10–5 Property Tax Control Structures and Their Impacts 444
10–6 Rate Computations for a Levy Control 446
11–1 State and Local Government Sales Revenues: User Charges and Miscellaneous Revenues, 2002–2003 ($ in thousands) 462

11–2 Federal User Charge Receipts, Fiscal 2005 ($ millions) 465
11–3 Selected Government Services Amenable to Public Pricing 474
11–4 State Lottery Performance, Fiscal Year 2004 ($ in thousands) 481
12–1 Audit Coverage by the Internal Revenue Service by Type of Return (Returns Filed Calendar 2003) 502
12–2 Administrative-Cost Estimates for Major Taxes 507
13–1 Steps in Revenue Forecasting by Multiple Regression 522
13–2 The Twenty-five Largest Tax Expenditures in the Federal Income Tax, Fiscal 2006 Estimated ($ millions) 534
14–1 Tax-Source Separation, 1970, 1994, and 2003: Percentage of Revenue from Tax Collected by Level of Government 549
14–2 Sources of Intergovernmental Revenue ($ millions) 553
14–3 Federal Aid to State and Local Governments 554
14–4 Public School District Revenues by Source of Funds, Percentage of Total 562
15–1 Federal Debt from Fiscal 1940 to Fiscal 2005 578
15–2 Summary of State and Local Indebtedness 2002–2003 582
15–3 Yield by Mergent Municipal Rating Group, 1940–2004 (End of Year) 595
15–4 Credit Ratings by Mergent, Standard & Poor's, and Fitch 596
15–5 A TIC and NIC Computation Worksheet 603
15–6 Distribution of Municipal Debt by Holding Entity (End of the Year) 604
16–1 Sponsors of the Fifteen Largest Public Employee Pension Funds, 2005 629
16–2 National Summary of State and Local Government Employee Retirement System Finances: Fiscal Year 2001–2002 ($ thousands) 632
16–3 Asset Distribution of State and Local Government Employee Retirement Funds (End of Selected Calendar Years) 634

List of Sidebars

1–1 Government Creates a Market for Fishing Rights 7
2–1 Deflating: Dividing between Real and Price Change 36
2–2 Growth Rates and Simple Projections 38
3–1 The First General Appropriation Act 91
3–2 Federal Funds/Trust Funds, On-Budget/Off-Budget, Government Enterprises, Mandatory/Discretionary Relationships 102
3–3 The Biggest Entitlements: Social Security and Medicare 107
4–1 Break-Even Analysis 149
4–2 Ratios and Shares 153
5–1 Activity-Based Costing and Government Budgeting 200
5–2 The Basic Elements of Government Performance and Results Act of 1993 216
6–1 Measuring the Value of Nonmarket Goods 270
6–2 What Discount Rate to Use? 272
6–3 An Application of Net Present Value to Evaluate a Capital Project 275
7–1 The Excess Burden of a Tax—Measuring the Value of Economic Distortion 317
7–2 The Council of Economic Advisers on Externalities and the Environment 323
8–1 Two More Comprehensive Income Measures: Family Economic Income (Treasury) and Expanded Income (Joint Committee on Taxation) 343
8–2 The Earned Income Tax Credit 355
8–3 The Alternate Minimum Tax 359
9–1 Tax-Exclusive and Tax-Inclusive Pricing 386
9–2 The Economic Equivalence of RST and VAT 401
10–1 What the Coefficient of Dispersion Means for Property Tax Bills 443
11–1 Charging Fees: The Federal System 467
12–1 California's ReadyReturn Pilot 496
12–2 Frivolous Appeals 504
13–1 The Congressional Budget Office Approach to Individual Income Tax Forecasting, Fiscal 2001–2011 523
13–2 Preparing Tax Expenditure Estimates 533
14–1 Some Basic Guides for Writing Grant Proposals 557
15–1 Inflation-Indexed Bonds 580
15–2 When Government Finances Go Horribly Wrong 592
15–3 The Costs of Issuing Debt: Sacramento Regional Transit Certificates of Participation 604
16–1 The Value of a Lockbox 618
16–2 Prompt-Payment Discounts 619
16–3 How Treasury Bills Are Auctioned Today 625

To Karen, Elizabeth, Tom, and Dan

CHAPTER 1

Fundamental Principles of Public Finance

Why study public financial administration separately from business finance? Modern public financial administration liberally borrows the tools and concepts of business management. Financial management in business seeks to increase the value of the firm to its owners by judicious allocation and control of its resources. Public financial management uses similar analytic, technical, and managerial tools to allocate and control, but governments differ from private businesses in terms of resource constraints, ownership, and objectives. In particular, governments may tax to enlarge their resources, "ownership" is not clear because many stakeholders share a legitimate interest in government decisions, and the value of government services is neither easy to quantify nor reflected in a single measure (like the sales or profits of a business enterprise). And behind all these differences lies the unique power of government to tax, prohibit, and punish. This capacity to coerce, even in democracies, makes governments different from proprietary businesses and voluntary organizations; the reflection of those differences makes public financial administration distinct from many fundamental practices of business finance. Both sorts of entities are interested in *fiscal sustainability,* that is, the ability to operate over the long term without reducing the standards of life below those currently enjoyed and even to improve that standard.

Many different organizations—private businesses, nonprofit organizations, and governmental agencies—provide the goods and services that we use every day, including both those necessary for life itself and those that make life more enjoyable. Private businesses sell us food and clothing, cars and television sets, and so on: a vast range of commodities that we purchase for survival and enjoyment. The same applies to services: We go to movies run by private companies, travel across the country on privately operated airlines, and hire the neighbor to feed our cats when we go on vacation. All these and many more goods and services are provided under market principles of voluntary exchange: Businesses provide those services to us in exchange for the payment we make to them. No payment, no service. Much the same applies for many nonprofit organizations, like hospitals and social service organizations, that operate on the basis of charges and government contracts. Other services come from voluntary associations or clubs—the services of the county historical museum, the local neighborhood association, or a local youth organization. Their operations are financed by a variety of contributions and fees. Although most voluntary organizations do not require payment before service is rendered, they still need to be paid by someone, voluntarily, in order to survive, because those who provide the resources that are used in providing services (utilities, rents, supplies, etc.) need to be paid for those resources. Finally, we receive services of police departments, school systems, the judicial and regulatory systems, the social safety net, and so on, from governments. But these services are financed differently. Rather than operating from finance by voluntary exchange (market sales) or by voluntary contribution, governments provide goods and services paid by taxes or other revenues raised by law. This revenue comes not from voluntary purchase or contribution, but, even in a democracy, from the operation of a revenue system based on legal requirement for payment, backed, if necessary, by force or threat of force. That is coercion, something we dislike and distrust. In our open and free society, why have a public sector? The reason is that government services are uniquely essential to life: Most countries leave the provision of life's necessities—food, clothing, and usually shelter—to the private sector. But when government fails, the private sector cannot function and citizens are "bereft of even the most basic conditions of a stable existence: law and security, trust in contracts, and a sound medium of exchange."[1] Without a government that does its job in at least some basic areas, the private sector itself cannot properly function.

Market Failure and the Functions of Government

Why can't private businesses selling their products in free markets be relied upon to provide all goods and services that ought to be available? The argument for the efficiency of markets is powerful. The President's Council of Economic Advisors explains: "If markets are competitive and function smoothly, they will lead to prices at which the amount sellers want to supply equals the amount buyers demand. Moreover, the price in any market will simultaneously equal the benefit that buyers get from the last unit consumed (the marginal benefit) and the cost of producing the last unit supplied (the marginal cost). These two conditions ensure efficiency: when they hold in all markets, the Nation's labor and other resources are allocated to producing a particular good or service if and only if consumers would not be willing to pay more to have those resources employed elsewhere."[2] Markets cause the productive capacity of the economy to be used to produce what people want most and

[1]International Bank for Reconstruction and Development/The World Bank, World Development Report 1997, *The State in a Changing World* (New York: Oxford University Press, 1997), 19.
[2]*Economic Report of the President Transmitted to the Congress February 1997* (Washington: U.S. Government Printing Office, 1997), 191.

cause the least possible amount of resources to be used in that production. In a world of limited resources, it is a valuable result.

But there remains an important role for government, even if private markets can deliver most goods and services, and deliver them at low cost. Indeed, there is an important cooperative relationship between healthy government and healthy markets. Markets need government to function efficiently: "Deals must be enforced and fraud discouraged. Without a governmental legal system to guarantee property rights and enforce contracts, corporate organizations and market exchange would be virtually impossible. Anarchy and the free market are not synonymous."[3] Government—at least its protective elements—is necessary if markets are to exist. And governments can obtain important information from market data, use markets as efficient mechanisms for implementing public policy, and acquire goods and services in market transactions to provide government services. The market economy needs government to function properly, and governments need the market economy if they are to serve the public interest.

The role of government, however, extends beyond simply allowing markets to operate, because a system of markets is not always able "to sustain 'desirable' activities or to stop 'undesirable' activities."[4] What makes some services a governmental responsibility? Why can't private action be relied upon to provide police and urban fire protection, primary education, environmental protection, public health, national defense, and so on? Individuals demand these services, and we expect businesses to respond to customer demand in their quest for profit. Why do markets fail, and thereby create an economic need for government?

Public Goods[5]

Some goods will not be supplied in the market or, if supplied, will be supplied in insufficient amounts because of their very nature. The problem comes from two properties: (1) nonexhaustion, or nonrivalry, occurs when benefits of the service can only be shared, meaning that a given quantity of the service can be enjoyed by additional people with no reduction in benefit to the existing population, and (2) inability to exclude nonpayers occurs when benefits cannot be easily limited to those who have paid for the services. The properties reflected in Figure 1–1 distinguish private goods, public goods, and two intermediate kinds of goods—toll goods and common-pool goods.

---

[3]Ibid., 192.

[4]Francis M. Bator, "The Anatomy of Market Failure," *Quarterly Journal of Economics* 72 (August 1958): 351. Public goods are only one type of market failure, but they form the basis for budgeting, taxation, and other parts of fiscal administration. Other failures create the need for government regulation of monopolies; these failures are not considered here.

[5]Some argue that individuals do not recognize their own best interest and that market evaluations made by individuals may be "wrong." In other words, the market underprovides museums, ballets, and symphonies because people do not understand their true value. Therefore, it is argued that these institutions deserve support as merit goods. (Junk food, Saturday morning kids' television, and country music could be viewed as merit bads.) Identifying what is good and what is bad is certainly not scientific (you may disagree with the examples listed here) and ends up in special-interest political battles.

Figure 1–1
The Elements of Nonappropriability

		Exhaustion or Rivalry	
		Alternate Use	Joint Use
		Private Goods	**Toll Goods**
Exclusion	Feasible	Examples: Food, clothing, television sets	Examples: Turnpikes, toll bridges, motion pictures
		Common-Pool Resources	**Public Goods**
	Not feasible	Examples: Aquifers, fishing grounds, petroleum reserves	Examples: National defense, system of justice, vector control

What do these public-good properties mean? When services are nonrival, use of the service by one person does not preclude concurrent full use by others at no additional cost of providing that service. The cost of providing service to additional users, once the service has been provided for someone, equals zero (its marginal cost is zero). Economic efficiency requires that the price paid by the buyer (the value of resources given up by the buyer to make the purchase) not exceed the additional cost of producing the purchased good or service. A private business will charge a price higher than zero, the efficient price, because it cannot afford to do otherwise. Therefore, too little of the good or service will be purchased and consumed, and its price will be too high, compared with quantities and prices in a fully functioning market. When exclusion of those who have not paid for the service is not feasible, a seller could not successfully charge a price; people not paying would receive the service as completely as those who paid. Private goods do not have appropriability problems: One person's use of the good eliminates the possibility of anyone else using it (additional service means extra cost, and sellers charge to cover that cost), and exclusion is feasible. Obviously, the full range of ordinary commodities and services (bread, milk, etc.) are private goods. The only way an individual can receive the benefits from a private good is by paying for it; there are no effects on others, and it is possible to separate payers from nonpayers.

Public goods include national defense, mosquito abatement, pollution control, and disease control. The common characteristics of these services are (1) once they are made available, denial to those who have not paid is impossible (nonexclusion), and (2) any number of people can consume the same good at the same time without diminishing the amount of that good available for anyone else to consume (nonexhaustion, or nonrivalry). Consider mosquito abatement. When a given level of control is provided, all people in the area of control receive the same service. Other people could enter the control district and receive that same service without any additional abatement cost. Many people can simultaneously consume that service, once it has been provided, without diminishing the amount of service available to others (the marginal cost of service is zero), and there is no mechanism to deny service to those not paying for it. Individuals in the service area may value the abatement service differently (reaction to mosquito bites varies among individuals), but all receive the same level of service. This is completely different from the situation with a private good, like a hamburger: When you eat that burger, it is gone and not available for consumption by anyone else—no nonrivalry.

The failure of exclusion is the other public-good characteristic. Within the range of exclusion failure, if someone provides the services, all receive that service. When one structure in an urban area receives fire protection, given the propensity of fires to spread, nearby structures receive protection as well.[6] (The public good is fire protection, not fire fighting; when the equipment is putting out the fire at Smith's house, it is not available to put out the fire anywhere else. Extinguishing Smith's fire, however, provides fire protection equally to many neighbors.) Obviously, there are geographic limits to that range of nonappropriability: Fire protection provided in Bloomington, Indiana, will not extend to the people in Jackson, Mississippi. Within a specific geographic area, however, all receive the service regardless of payment, whether they want it or not. Such is the special monopoly position of governments: Not only are alternative providers unavailable, but residents also do not have the option of not paying for the service because public revenue systems operate independently from service delivery. A governor of Kentucky recognized the difference between operating the state and operating his successful business: "Hell, governing Kentucky is easier than running Kentucky Fried Chicken. There's no competition."[7] Payment regardless of preference or consumption is, of course, a unique feature of government provision.

Toll goods and common-pool goods have one public-good characteristic but not both (as shown in Figure 1–1). Toll goods are nonrival: One person can consume the service to its fullest while not reducing the amount of service someone else may consume. For these goods, however, exclusion is feasible; boundaries can separate payers and nonpayers. Examples include drive-in movies and toll roads: Up to a congestion point, a larger number of people can consume these services without exhausting the service concurrently available to others.

Common-pool goods are goods or services for which exclusion is not feasible, but there are competing and exhaustive uses. Examples include aquifers, oil and gas deposits, and fisheries. There are no normal means of exercising exclusive property rights on the resource, but when used, the resource becomes unavailable for others. Left to private processes, the resource may be rapidly exhausted because it is valuable and is not, in its natural state, subject to normal ownership controls. (First-come-first-served is a normal allocation principle, so getting those resources out of

---

[6]Private firms sell fire protection to individuals in some parts of Arizona. Neighbors are distant and fires seldom spread over desert land, so the service is a private good. Roger S. Ahlbrandt, Jr., *Municipal Fire Protection Services: Comparison of Alternative Organization Forms* (Newbury Park, Calif., and London: Sage Professional Papers in Administration and Policy Studies 03-002, 1973).

[7]The Honorable John Y. Brown, Jr., quoted in *Newsweek* (March 30, 1981).

the ground as quickly as possible is advantageous to any private user—and is why governments frequently intervene in markets for natural resources. That is another element of market failure.) Sidebar 1–1 describes one common-pool resource problem and how government action sought to remedy it.

Externalities

Market transactions between buyer and seller may affect third parties. The consequences may be negative—as with the exhaust fumes from automobiles—or positive—as with the protection provided pregnant women when a boy receives a rubella vaccination—but, either way, that value is unlikely to be fully recognized in the market transaction. For these goods and services, the private return from their consumption is substantial, so the market will not fail to provide. It will not, however, provide at a socially reasonable level.

An attractive (or positive) externality causes the good in question to be underproduced. In the case of the rubella vaccination, those people who are vaccinated receive the benefit of reduced probability that they will contract the disease, a direct benefit to them for which they could be expected to pay. But they also provide protection against the disease to others in that they will not infect others if they themselves do not have the disease. That is a third-party, or external, effect of the vaccination. It is unlikely that everyone considering the vaccination will take full account of these benefits when weighing the advantages of vaccination against the disadvantages (minimal discomfort and some small risk of adverse reaction, time spent and inconvenience met in receiving the injection, and the out-of-pocket price of the service), and some will decide not to be vaccinated. Fewer people would be vaccinated than would be in the best economic interests of society, because of the external benefits from the personal choice about vaccination. Governments require young boys to get rubella vaccinations not simply to protect them—rubella itself is not much worse than a common cold—but because we do not want them to give the disease to a pregnant woman and cause birth defects in her child.[8]

An undesirable (or negative) externality has the opposite effect, an overproduction of the good. Automobile operators choose to pay the operating costs of their cars to enjoy the great personal value of mobility that cars provide, without full attention to the undesirable health and esthetic effects of the exhaust fumes produced by their vehicles or of the congestion delays caused by having many vehicles competing for highway space. Again, this leads to a misallocation of resources:

[8]Public health officials refer to the concept of "herd immunity:" if enough of a population is immunized against an infectious disease, even those without immunization will be protected because any invading germ will not be able to spread. There is no chain of transmission. When the "herd" is sufficiently immunized, those without immunization are able to enjoy free-rider protection. But if overall immunization levels fall below a critical threshold percentage of the population, that protection is gone. Hence, public health officials work to maintain immunization levels even when prevailing incidence of the disease is low, because protection of that "herd immunity" that provides protection for all.

Sidebar 1–1
Government Creates a Market for Fishing Rights

Market failure does not always require direct government provision of a service as a remedy. Sometimes, the government may intervene in ways that create a market where none could exist before. The Council of Economic Advisors provided one example in the *Economic Report of the President* for 1993:

There is no practical way to establish ownership rights of ocean fish stocks. Traditionally, fish have been free for the taking—a common pool resource. Theory teaches that such underpricing leads to overconsumption. In the halibut fisheries off Alaska, fishing fleets caught so many halibut that the survival of the stock was threatened. No single fishing boat had an incentive to harvest fewer fish since the impact on its own future catch would be minimal and others would only increase their take. This is an example of what is known as "the tragedy of the commons."

Officials tried limiting the length of the fishing season. But this effort only encouraged new capital investment such as larger and faster boats with more effective (and expensive) fishing equipment. In order to control the number of fish caught, the season was shortened in some areas from 4 months to 2 days by the early 1990s. Most of the halibut caught had to be frozen rather than marketed fresh, and halibut caught out of season had to be discarded.

In late 1992, the federal government proposed a new approach: assigning each fisherman a permit to catch a certain number of fish. The total number of fish for which permits are issued will reflect scientific estimates of the number of fish that can be caught without endangering the survival of the species. Also, the permits will be transferable—they can be bought and sold. By making the permits transferable, the system in effect creates a market where one did not exist previously. The proposed system will encourage the most profitable and efficient boats to operate at full capacity by buying permits from less successful boats, ensuring a fishing fleet that uses labor and equipment efficiently. Moreover, the transferable permits system establishes a market price for the opportunity to fish—a price that better reflects the true social cost of using this common resource.

The cap-and-trade system for dealing with environmental protection applies a similar approach. Sources of emissions (like sulfur dioxide) are allocated an initial emissions limitation. The entity is permitted to meet the limit by whatever means it chooses (conservation, revised production technology, end-of-pipe controls, etc.), so each will select whatever method is least expensive. But the entity can exceed its limit by purchasing limit caps from other entities—those who have excess cap because of particularly efficient methods for limiting their emissions. By this means, the intended overall emission reduction is achieved at minimal cost to the economy. The market price for emission limits emerges, exactly in the same way as the price for the opportunity to fish was established.

Both are clever ways to employ market-based approaches to deal with problems of initial market failure and achieve an efficient, effective, and low-cost solution.

more car miles traveled than would be the case if their operators based their choices on the full social cost (internal plus external) of using the car.

Governments regularly subsidize or tax to try to correct these market failures caused by externalities.[9] For instance, governments may pay producers or consumers of goods with positive externalities to encourage more consumption of the good in recognition of benefits to third parties. They may also levy corrective taxes to make purchasers and sellers respond to the external damage done by other products. The idea is to make buyers and sellers respond to the external effects of the product, to bring the third-party effect into their decision-making in an economically tangible way.

Failure of Competition

The efficiencies of markets arise from competition among firms. When only a few firms serve a market, those firms may exercise monopoly power to charge prices higher than justified by economic conditions and, thereby, to collect excess profits. Governments watch markets to ensure that barriers do not prevent new firms from entering such markets, because entry of new firms in the industry is the best deterrent to monopoly pricing. And governments strictly police practices that unfairly restrain trade. Sometimes governments choose to regulate industries that, because of cost advantage to larger firms (or increasing returns to scale), seem destined to be dominated by a few large firms (the natural monopoly case). This may be the situation for electrical, telephone, water, and some other utilities, although new technologies (e.g., lower production cost for alternative electricity generators with small production capacity, and diverse telecommunication systems) have opened new competitive options in many such industries. As this occurs, governments have rightly moved from strategies of legalistic regulation of firm operations and the prices they charge to removing barriers to the entry of new firms, thereby allowing competition to allocate resources and establish reasonable prices for products. Nevertheless, expecting private businesses to regulate failures of competition—without the government's prompting—is not reasonable.

Incomplete Markets and Imperfect Information. Governments often intervene in markets when customers have incomplete information about products and there is fear that unfettered market forces will not provide necessary information in a timely fashion. Governments test (or supervise the testing of) new drugs, guard against the sale of hazardous products, establish certain disclosure standards, and so forth. The market may ultimately provide information—but not until after much grief and suffering by the unwary.

Insurance markets can present special problems of adverse selection and moral hazard. *Adverse selection* occurs when insurance purchasers impose higher-than-

[9]When transaction costs are negligible, bargaining between users of resources can internalize external effects and cause an efficient level of output with no more government action (i.e., no taxes, no subsidies, and no prohibitions) than to establish private rights to the use of resources. Ronald Coase, "The Problem of Social Cost," *Journal of Law and Economics* 3 (October 1960): 1–44.

average costs on sellers (in health insurance, for instance, those more likely to purchase insurance are those more likely to need care) or when sellers exclude such potential purchasers (health insurance companies seek to exclude those more likely to require care). It is a particular problem for provision of private prescription drug insurance (or the voluntary Medicare prescription drug benefit program): people vary widely in the extent to which they have high drug expenses, and both high- and low-expense people generally know into which group they fall. The only takers of a plan with premiums that reflect average prescription expenses would be those with high expenses, and, hence, the finances of the plan would be doomed. Insurance sellers rely on having both sets of people in the premium pool. *Moral hazard* is a problem when those with insurance have an incentive to cause the insured event to happen or to be less than diligent in averting the insured event. For example, with health insurance, there is a tendency for people to seek more treatment when the third party, the insurance company, is paying for it.[10] In a case of government failure, federally subsidized flood insurance (premiums for the federal National Flood Insurance Program represent only about 38% of what a full premium would be) makes people more willing to build in floodplains and in coastal areas, thus increasing the loss when the inevitable flood occurs, as with Hurricane Katrina in 2005; and federal bank deposit insurance with coverage to high deposit levels makes people less interested in considering the financial strength of the institutions holding their deposits. Reasoned government intervention involves securing widespread coverage (to prevent adverse selection) and regulating markets to ensure that decision-makers see the accurate cost implications of those choices. Social insurance systems (public pension, health and disability, unemployment, etc.) throughout the world stem from these market problems.[11]

Economic Stabilization. Governments seek to stabilize the macroeconomy, in other words, preventing high unemployment, controlling inflation that could erode purchasing power and distort financial markets, and improving the prospects for economic growth and a higher quality of life. Governments use monetary policy (manipulation of the money supply) and fiscal policies (changes in expenditure and taxation) to correct for these aggregate failures of the market, although there is continuing controversy about the extent to which those policies can make an active improvement in performance. Nevertheless, evidence does indicate that poor government decisions in use of national resources and financing of government programs in a misguided fashion can cause severe economic problems. Central governments worry about the condition of the national economy, whereas subnational units (states, regions, cities, etc.) seek to improve their own particular share of that national economy. And some governments attempt industrial policy, targeted subsidies and tax advantages designed to stimulate particular industries, in the belief

---

[10]Another illustration of moral hazard: There is some evidence that making private automobiles safer has encouraged drivers to be less cautious in their driving.

[11]Another moral hazard: pitchers in the American League do not bat, so they do not face direct retaliation in the batter's box and are thus more likely to throw at opposing batters than are their counterparts in the National League, who do have to bat for themselves. J. C. Bradbury and D. J. Drinen, 2004. Identifying moral hazard: A natural experiment in Major League Baseball. Unpublished manuscript, The University of the South, Sewanee, TN. (Available online at: ddrinen.sewanee.edu/Plunk/dhpaper.pdf)

that they can increase economic growth and reduce unemployment by giving an extra boost to activities destined to be national or even global leaders. Again, the capacity of politicians and government bureaucrats to pick winners better than can markets is decidedly mixed, but that does not stop them from trying as they arrange the public finances. There is also not much evidence to support the idea that subnational government use of targeted tax and expenditure programs can have much of an effect on economic development, but that does not stop the political leaders from trying. The *Economist* succinctly explains why industrial and economic development policy, whether national, state, or local, has such a low success rate: "Neither economists nor emperors can be relied upon to pick winners. The best bet is entrepreneurial trial and error."[12] Government money spent to assist particular industries is, sadly, often badly spent, because even the well-advised government usually guesses wrong. If lawmakers really knew how to do this, would there be poverty anywhere?

Redistribution. Markets distribute products of the economy to those people having resources (talents, properties, etc.), not distinguishing whether those resources were earned, inherited, stolen, or whatever. Those who own the resources get the goods. People with few resources—property or skills—may fall below acceptable living standards and may be destined to a life of poverty in a pure market economy. Governments may correct injustices in the distribution of affluence in society, seeking to improve the conditions faced by the less well-to-do that the market alone would leave them with. Some argue for a degree of redistribution out of a social conscience and a desire for a safety net for all humanity; others argue for a degree of redistribution out of a fear that the poor will revolt, taking property from the affluent. Regardless of motives, most politicians believe that the public wants some protection for the very poor and at least some mild redistribution by the government of the result produced by pure operation of the market. Those concerns are reflected both in government spending programs and in systems for finance of those programs.

Governments employ a variety of different approaches toward redistribution. These include tax structures that levy relatively higher tax burdens on high-affluence households than on low-affluence ones (income taxes that levy higher effective rates on high-income households), direct income payments to low-affluence families (the earned income tax credit), programs that provide assistance services for which only low-affluence families qualify (Medicaid), or programs available to all that low-income families use more heavily (unemployment benefit programs). However, the United States makes less aggressive use of active tax and transfer programs to handle problems of poverty than do other wealthy nations, preferring programs of economic expansion that benefit everyone, trusting that economic expansion will take care of the economic bottom as it benefits the economic top. As a result, the gap between highest and lowest incomes and the level of poverty in the United States is considerably wider than in other wealthy nations.

---

[12]"Finding Your Niche," *Economist,* 21 March 2003: 70.

Privatization

Modern societies argue about where to draw the line between government provision and market provision of goods and services. Many governments have downsized the public sector to achieve efficiency, in the belief that market provision may offer more service options to the public, more flexibility in service response, and lower operating costs. With those possible advantages, it is no surprise that privatization of government operations is an attractive option. After considering the appropriate functions of government, as we did in the last section, it is also reasonable to explore the range for which various forms of privatization may be reasonable.

Privatization encompasses (1) transfer to the private sector of government-owned businesses that operate in goods and services markets that do not have significant market failures, (2) transfer to the private sector of government-owned businesses with natural monopoly power, especially telecommunications and electricity, and (3) contracting out of publicly financed services to private businesses, using service contracts or franchise agreements.[13] This latter variety of privatization is possibly amenable to pure public goods; the former two may be accompanied by government regulation of prices, returns, or other conditions of operation.

Arguments Supporting Privatization. Several logical arguments have been offered in support of privatization.[14] These are three of the most frequently used:

1. **Smaller government.** Some argue for a smaller public sector and fewer public bureaucrats, resulting in a shrunken scope of government, largely as a matter of philosophy. Because governments may spend without producing services (e.g., the check writing of the American Social Security system) and may be deeply involved in the private economy without even spending (e.g., the safety regulations applied to private industry), privatization, while reducing government production, may or may not reduce the size of government or state involvement in the economy. This therefore provides a weak basis for privatization.

2. **Operating efficiency and response to clients.** Governments produce under the political-bureaucratic system of central command and control, often driven from a desire to employ people with minimal attention to the need to at least cover costs of operation. State enterprises frequently lack a hard budget

[13]An excellent analysis of the economics of privatization is John Vickers and George Yarrow, "Economic Perspectives on Privatization," *Journal of Economic Perspectives* 5 (Spring 1991): 111–32.

[14]A recent study of American local government ownership and management of enterprises (gas, electric, and water utilities and public transport) finds that a desire to stem corruption was a major influence in nineteenth-century decisions to make ownership public. Reformers believed that managers of public organizations would have weaker incentives to capture profits for the enterprise from corrupt activities and to risk prison for profits not personally received. The study also suggests that public ownership is likely to create inefficient operation and excessively high government payrolls. (Edward L. Glaeser, "Public Ownership in the American City," *National Bureau of Economic Research Working Paper 8613,* December 2001.) The anti-corruption argument may have continued applicability in privatization discussions in the developing and transition environment, but it is not a clear call.

constraint and, when they operate at a loss, receive a government subsidy to cover it. This situation blunts any incentive for efficient operations. To survive, private businesses must respond to direct customer demand and must constrain prices out of concern for competition from other businesses. That environment drives private business toward operating efficiency (lower production cost) and improved responsiveness to customers, but only if the new private businesses face a competitive business environment. There is no reason to believe that a private monopolist city water company would be more efficient and responsive than a government monopolist city water company serving the same territory under the same regulatory conditions. The cost reduction associated with improved operating efficiency is a frequent objective of government privatizations in the United States. However, a number of studies have found the Veterans Health Administration hospital system to be a better performer than the systems available to other Americans.[15] It is not always the case that a private system will outperform a government one—provided the incentives, direction, and will are strong.

3. **Cash.** Sale of government-operated enterprises may bring revenue to the government. The inflow, assuming a buyer can be found, would occur at sale. Operating profits (or losses) in the future would disappear, although the enterprise would then be subject to the tax system. Unfortunately, many government assets produce no revenue or produce revenue that is less than operating cost. That makes their value extremely low. This is a problem that countries of the former Soviet Union have had to face as they try to move into a market economy. Many state enterprises have high production costs and, even with private ownership, the product will not sell on national or international markets at a price sufficient to cover those costs. Although the old central plans invested heavily in these plants, their privatized value has proved to be low—except in natural resource sectors (oil, gas, etc.). In other environments, the revenues have proved substantial. The cumulative total has been estimated at over $1 trillion through the second part of 1999; the annual flow of privatization proceeds has exceeded $100 billion in the last part of the 1990s.[16]

Other motives behind privatization include lack of appropriate personnel or expertise to perform the service, provide greater operating flexibility, quicken implementation of the program, increase the pace of innovation, and improve quality of service. However, it is important to understand that all government services are not equally susceptible to outsourcing and not all motives will be satisfied in any particular privatization program.

The largest transactions involve formerly nationalized industries under old concepts of the economic role of government or of the need to keep "socially or eco-

---

[15]A number of studies are cited in Phillip Longman, "The Best Care Anywhere," *Washington Monthly,* January/February 2005. With other incentives, the public sector compares badly: Jishnu Das and Jeffrey Hammer, "Money for Nothing: The Dire Straits of Medical Practice in Delhi, India," World Bank Policy Research Working Paper 3669, July 2005.

[16]William L. Megginson and Jeffry M. Netter, "From State to Market: A Study of Empirical Studies of Privatization," *Journal of Economic Literature* 39 (June 2001): 321–89.

nomically significant" industries under state control: telecommunications, petroleum and petrochemicals, gas distribution, automobile manufacturing, electricity generation and distribution, airlines, steel making, and so on.[17] Between 1990 and 2000, 36 percent of privatization proceeds came from telecommunications, 16 percent from power, 15 percent from financial institutions, 10 percent from oil and gas, and 17 percent from other industries.[18] Government operation of these industries has been notoriously bad because of political influences on service decisions (e.g., a city gets served by the national airline because an important politician lives there) and on operations (e.g., the industry is seen as employer of last resort and the resulting bloated payrolls prevent it from ever producing its product at a competitive cost).[19] Governments in the United States have been less active in recent privatization than those in Western Europe, Latin America, Asia, New Zealand, and Australia. Many of the big international privatizations, however, have been in industries never publicly owned in the United States. Privatization of roads, airports, the postal system, schools, and the like raise much more interesting social, political, and economic issues than the state sale of telephone or petrochemical companies.[20]

Production/Provision. The American privatization issue frequently concerns the provision-production dichotomy.[21] Goods and services provided by a government because of market failure need not be produced by that government. Provision means government intervention to ensure availability or, generally, to finance the service; it does not require production by the government. The production choice should be made according to which entity—a government department, a private entity (profit or nonprofit), or another government—would supply the desired quantity and quality of service at least cost to the citizens of the providing government.

The distinction between government and private production and provision can be clarified by example:

1. **Government provision/government production.** The city street department plows the streets after a heavy snowfall. The job uses department managers, department employees, department equipment, and department supplies.
2. **Government provision/private production.** The county hires a private appraisal firm to estimate values of real estate in the county for use in computing

---

[17]The largest of all was the sale of Nippon Telegraph and Telephone by the government of Japan. Share offerings in 1987 and 1988 raised almost $80 billion; the $40 billion offering in November 1987 is the largest security offering in history.

[18]William L. Megginson, *The Financial Economics of Privatization* (New York: Oxford University Press, 2005): 27–28.

[19]National airlines can face difficult political barriers to efficient operations. Keith Johnson and Luca Di Leo, "Alitalia Can't Stanch Red Ink," *Wall Street Journal* (April 21, 2004): A-16. Difficult staff reductions then being proposed would have brought Alitalia down to about 1,100 passengers per employee. That compared with about 9,000 passengers per employee for the competing discount carrier Ryanair.

[20]The pioneer of privatization in the last decades of the twentieth century, Britain, has been unable to fully privatize its coal industry, so apparently technically simple decisions do get muddled by politics and other factors.

[21]It also encompasses application of user-pay concepts, including sale of service and tax payments based on the benefits received from particular government services. These mechanisms, while bringing some market-like principles, do not alter public provision and thus are discussed in the revenue section of this book.

property tax bills. The firm does the work with its managers, employers, equipment, and supplies. Another example: The U.S. Department of Defense hires private firms to provide food and other support services to military units in the field. Outsourcing is almost certainly the most common privatization practiced in the United States.[22] It is a major element in President Bush's management agenda for the federal government, which intends competitive sourcing for federal tasks that are readily available in the commercial marketplace.[23]

3. **Private provision/government production.** A racetrack pays a city for extraordinary traffic control services on race days.

4. **Private provision/private production.** A private manufacturer patrols its factory site with its own security employees.[24] Neighboring properties may receive some protection spillover from this security activity.

Some cities, especially in California, have provided a full range of services entirely by contract. Such an arrangement is called the Lakewood Plan after an early contract city.[25] Production by contract is probably limited more than anything else by the ability to design a contract specifying the service qualities to be delivered. Even parts of the judicial system may be privately produced: California permits litigants to hire private jurists when court congestion or special expertise makes such a procedure attractive to both parties, and private firms have undertaken contractual operation of correction facilities.[26] School districts have similarly chosen private production through vouchers or charter schools.[27] In these systems, the school district provides financing but the educational service is actually produced by another entity.

The production choice should be kept open for possible privatization; the idea of government action is to provide services of desired quantity and quality at the least cost to the economy. When might contracting not be an efficient option? One study suggests that in-house production may be warranted when "(1) there are very few potential suppliers, (2) costs of switching from one producer to another are high, (3) information about the production process and supplier performance is

---

[22]U.S. General Accounting Office, *Privatization: Lessons Learned by State and Local Governments,* GAO/GGD-97-48 (Washington: U.S. Government Printing Office, 1997).

[23]The efforts by the Bush administration to outsource government operations is described in John Maggs, "Compete, or Else," *National Journal* (July 12, 2003): 2228–2237.

[24]Businesses and individuals in the United States spend over twice as much for private security as governments spend on providing public safety. "Welcome to the New World of Private Security," *Economist* (April 19, 1997): 21.

[25]Robert Bish, *The Public Economy of Metropolitan Areas* (Chicago: Markham, 1971), 85.

[26]"California Is Allowing Its Wealthy Litigants to Hire Private Jurists," *The Wall Street Journal* (August 6, 1980); and U.S. General Accounting Office, Private and Public Prisons: Studies Comparing Operational Costs and/or Quality of Service, GAO/GGD-96-158 (Washington: U.S. Government Printing Office, 1996). Correction facilities face an interesting incentive problem: it is against their economic interests to rehabilitate criminals in their care because successful rehabilitation reduces demand for their incarceration services.

[27]Gary Putka, "Baltimore Test of Privatization Gets a Bad Start," *Wall Street Journal* (September 23, 1992). Voucher systems provide families an education grant—a subsidy for purchase of education—which may be spent on services from a variety of producers. Charter schools allow private entities to create schools outside the public system, with finance from public funds. Families pick among schools.

expensive to obtain, and (4) the good or service being provided cannot be clearly defined."[28] In other words, the option would be difficult if contracts would be especially difficult to write and the public would end up being confronted with a monopoly supplier. Otherwise, out-of-government production can be an efficient option.

Privatization of provision is a more difficult problem. For public goods, the market will not function because the private supplier will not charge an efficient price for the service because of nonrivalry and inability to exclude. Business firms provide goods and services because they intend to make money, not for the sheer enjoyment of providing the goods or services. If it is not possible to charge people for the good or service, a business firm will seldom provide it. Furthermore, the price will exceed the cost of providing service to an additional consumer (recall that the additional cost is zero).

The expectation of government provision of public goods is strong, but occasionally governments will provide private goods as well and often do a very bad job of it. Organizational problems, particularly lack of appropriate production incentives, cause high costs, undesirable production strategies, and a bland product designed by an uneasy consensus. Governments provide toll goods (highways, bridges, etc.), and sometimes they do about as well as the private producer would do. But even some toll goods are provided by private businesses. For instance, in France eight public/private joint ventures and one private company operate the toll highway/tunnel system, the most extensive auto toll system in Europe. Evidence indicates that fewer resources will be wasted if government avoids provision of private goods.

Some observers of public fiscal problems have suggested that privatization would relieve pressures on government finances. That is a realistic response if the service being privatized in fact lacks substantial public-good features; one wonders why, in such a case, the government got involved in its provision. On the other hand, to expect private firms to provide public goods at desirable levels is folly. At best, the private firm may be contracted to produce the public good provided (paid for) by the government.

Privatization cannot be a general and complete cure for fiscal problems, no matter how inefficient a troubled government might be. For public goods, efficient private provision cannot substitute for inefficient government provision of public goods. That does not mean that market incentives cannot help, however, in guiding provision by government.

Building Social Decisions from Private Preferences

The logic of moving from individual choice to choices made by society is built on three fairly simple tenets. First, individuals are the best judges of their own well-being and generally act to improve that well-being as they see it. There is no

---

[28]John C. Hilke, *Competition in Government-Financed Services* (New York: Quorum Books, 1992), 8. Why does the federal government run its own printing house, the Government Printing Office? To learn more about mixed motives, see Graeme Browning, "Stop the Presses?" *National Journal* 25 (October 16, 1993): 2483–85.

scientific principle that leads us to reject or accept the judgments made by individuals about their own lives. Dictators or philosopher-kings may accurately make those determinations, but others should not assume that responsibility. Second, the welfare of the community depends on the welfare of the individuals in that community. In other words, communities are made up of people, and community welfare increases only if the welfare of those in the community is improved. From that comes the third tenet, judging the impact of a social action on the welfare of the community. The Pareto criterion, named after a nineteenth-century economist, holds that if at least one person is better off from a policy action and no person is worse off, then the community as a whole is unambiguously better off for the policy.[29] Does a social action harming anyone, despite improving the condition of many individuals, improve the welfare of society as a whole? It cannot be indisputably argued that such an action improves the well-being of society, regardless of the numbers made better off, because the relative worth of those harmed cannot scientifically be compared with those helped. Such a proposed policy would fail the Pareto criterion for judging social action.[30]

With those standards, we can analyze the implications of nonappropriability on public provision. Suppose that only five people would be influenced by construction of a levee to protect a small area from periodic flooding of a river. The cost of that levee is $20,000. Each individual in this community knows the maximum sacrifice that he or she would be willing to make to have that levee as compared to having no levee at all. Presumably it would not be larger than the individual damage avoided by having levee protection. These are the individual benefit numbers in Table 1–1. The levee, we assume, would be a public good: Each individual could use it without diminishing its availability to anyone else in the community, and exclusion of nonpayers is not feasible.

First, would the levee be built without public action, that is, by individual action only? The cost of the levee is $20,000; the most that any single individual (individual D) will pay to get the levee built is $9,000. Thus, the levee would not be produced by any single individual. If the levee only cost $8,500 to construct, however, we suspect individual D would build the levee for his or her benefit, and four other people in the community would receive benefits from the levee without payment. (The four would be *free riders.*) Once the levee is there, it serves all because of its public-good features.[31] The initially presumed construction cost, however, is such that the maximum individual benefit is less than the cost of the project, so the levee will not be built by private action.

Is the levee economically desirable for the community, in the sense that the value of the levee is greater than the resources going into the construction of the

---

[29]Vilfredo Pareto, *Manuel d'Economie Politique,* 2d ed. (Paris: M. Giard, 1927), 617–18.

[30]Benefit-cost analysis, an analytic technique that will be discussed in a later chapter, employs a less restricting and somewhat less appealing rule than the Pareto criterion. This is the Kaldor criterion, which holds that a social action improves community welfare if those benefiting from a social action could hypothetically compensate the losers in full and still have gain left over. Because no compensation need actually occur, losers can remain and the Pareto criterion would not be met.

[31]Voluntary associations (clubs) represent an intermediate option between a government with sovereign powers and individual action. Neighborhood associations offer an example popular in some regions.

Table 1–1
Individual Benefits from the Project: Example 1

Individual	Individual Benefit	
A	8,000	
B	7,000	
C	6,000	*Total cost* = $20,000
D	9,000	
E	6,000	
Total benefit	$36,000	

levee? The social cost, the value of the resources being used in the construction of the levee, equals $20,000. The social benefit of the levee, the sum of the improved welfare of the individuals with the levee, equals $36,000. Because social benefits are greater than social costs, it is a desirable project for the community.[32] A responsive government would act to provide the levee and would raise sufficient funds through the revenue structure to finance the project. If the government levied an equal per-capita tax—a payment based on the coercive power of government rather than the voluntary payment of market exchange—on the community to finance the levee ($4,000 each), all individuals would still be better off with the levee and the tax than without the combination.[33] Government can thus provide a desired service that public-good features prevent private action from providing.

A second example yields additional insights. Assume that the community receives benefits from a project as shown in Table 1–2. The project, possibly a levee in another location, is a public good. The cost of the project is $20,000. Because the sum of individual benefits ($19,000) is less than the cost of the project, the project resources would be worth more in other uses than in the particular use being considered. Suppose, however, that the project decision will be made at a referendum among the people in the community, with a simple majority required for passage. The referendum also includes the method to be used to finance the project: an equal per-capita tax (project cost divided by number of people in the community, or $4,000 per person). If the people in the community vote according to their individual net gain or loss from the project (as computed in Table 1–2), it will be approved (three for, two against). Does voter approval make the project desirable for the community? Not at all, because the project misallocates resources: It consumes resources that would have a greater value in other use. The majority vote may misallocate resources when used for public decisions, as may any technique that does not involve comparisons of social cost and social return.

[32]A small number of people may construct the levee without the full coercion of government. For instance, individuals A, B, and D could form a small property-owners association; the sum of benefits to those three exceeds the cost. These people might privately agree to build the levee for their protection—and benefits would spill over to C and E.

[33]This tax "system" is selected for convenience alone. It is not a "model" or an "ideal" in any sense.

Table 1–2
Individual Benefits from the Project: Example 2

Individual	Individual Benefit	Cost Share	Individual Gain
A	$5,000	$4,000	$1,000
B	5,000	4,000	1,000
C	2,000	4,000	−2,000
D	1,000	4,000	−3,000
E	6,000	4,000	2,000
Total	$19,000	$20,000	

A third example further illustrates the limits of scientific principles in public decision making. Table 1–3 presents individual benefits from a project with a total cost of $12,500 and an equal per-capita tax method of distributing project costs. Total benefits do exceed total cost, so the project apparently represents an appropriate way to use scarce resources, and the project would be approved by majority vote if the people voted according to their individual gains or losses. The project, however, does leave one individual worse off. Is the loss to E less important to the community than the gains of A, B, C, and D? That answer requires a value judgment about the worth of the individuals to society, a judgment with which science and Pareto cannot help. One option would be to distribute costs in exactly the same proportion as individual benefits. That is the approach shown in the last column of Table 1–3. Any project for which total benefits exceed total cost has possible cost distributions from which all will be made better off. There is no redistribution of individual cost from which all will be made better off for projects like that demonstrated in Table 1–2, but choices about situations like that shown in Table 1–3 are difficult. Politicians make such decisions regularly, but not with scientific justification.

One voting rule would ensure that only projects that pass the Pareto criterion could be approved. That rule is unanimity, if we assume that people will not vote

Table 1–3
Individual Benefits from the Project: Example 3

Individual	Individual Benefit	Cost Share	Individual Gain	Individual Share of Total Benefits	Benefit-Based Cost Share
A	$3,000	$2,500	$ 500	15%	$1,875
B	5,000	2,500	2,500	25%	3,125
C	8,000	2,500	5,500	40%	5,000
D	3,000	2,500	500	15%	1,875
E	1,000	2,500	−1,500	5%	625
Total	$20,000	$12,500		100%	$12,500

for policies contrary to their own best interest. This rule is seldom used, because reaching decisions often requires substantial costs. James Buchanan and Gordon Tullock identify two elements constituting the full cost of making a community decision.[34] The first element, the cost of reaching the decision, the "time and effort . . . which is required to secure agreement,"[35] rises as the agreement percentage required for the decision rises. As more of the group must agree on any issue, the effort invested in bargaining, arguing, and discussion normally rises. That investment is a real cost because the effort could have been directed to other uses. The second element, the external costs, or the cost from group "choices contrary to the individual's own interest,"[36] falls as the agreement percentage rises. (These are the costs imposed by a simple majority choice on individuals C and D in Table 1–2. Those costs could have been prevented by requiring a higher vote for approval.) The optimal choice percentage—the lowest combination of the two cost elements—usually would require neither unanimity nor one-person rule because the former has excessive decision costs and the latter has excessive external costs. Certain decisions are more dangerous to minorities (the losers in decisions) than others. For instance, many juries must reach a unanimous verdict because of the very high external costs that juries can place on people. For similar reasons, constitutional revision has high-percentage vote requirements.

Politics, Representation, and Government Finance

Decisions about public spending, raising revenue, borrowing, and so on are not the product of mechanical rationality. They are intensely political and involve personal interests, interest groups, political parties, and the process of representation. Even the clearest preferences of any particular individual are usually filtered through representation, and that one preference becomes part of a vote that may or may not be in the majority whose choice prevails. The many elements that produce a fiscal choice are diverse, but a framework devised by Anthony Downs for exploring the process of representation can help with an understanding of what influences these decisions.[37] He hypothesizes that political parties in a democracy operate to obtain votes to retain the income, power, and prestige that come with being in office. Parties are not units of principle or of ideals but are primarily seekers of votes. A lack of perfect knowledge, however, permeates the system: Parties do not always know what citizens want; citizens do not always know what the government in power or its opposition has done, is doing, or should be doing to try to serve citizen interests. Information that would reduce this ignorance is expensive to acquire. The scarcity of knowledge obscures the path that would lead from citizen preferences to their votes. Neither political parties nor elected representatives know exactly

---

[34]James M. Buchanan and Gordon Tullock, *The Calculus of Consent* (Ann Arbor: University of Michigan Press, 1962), chaps. 6–8.
[35]Ibid., 68.
[36]Ibid., 64.
[37]Anthony Downs, *An Economic Theory of Democracy* (New York: Harper & Row, 1956).

what the voters want, and the voters do not know exactly what the government is up to.

Several consequences for the representative process result. First, some people are politically more important than others because they can influence government action. Democratic government will not treat everyone with equal deference in a world of imperfect knowledge. One person, one vote is the ideal slogan, but it doesn't represent political influence particularly well. Second, specialists in influencing people will appear, and some will emerge as representatives of the people. These individuals will try to convince the government that the policies they support, and that directly benefit them, are good for and desired by the electorate. Information provided by these individuals will be filtered to provide only data consistent with the supported cause. A rational government will discount these claims, but it cannot ignore them. Third, imperfect information makes a government party susceptible to bribery simply because the party in power needs resources to persuade voters to keep it in power. Parties out of power are susceptible as well, but they have less to sell. It is no accident that corruption scandals involve more Republicans when the Republicans are in power and more Democrats when the Democrats are in power. Political influence is a necessary result of imperfect information combined with the unequal distribution of income and wealth in society. Parties have to use economic resources to provide and obtain information.

Lobbying is a rational response to the lack of perfect information, but an important imbalance of interests influences the lobbying process. Suppose a direct subsidy to industry is being considered. This subsidy is of great total value to that industry. The total subsidy paid by taxpayers, of course, exactly equals the subsidy received by the industry. However, each taxpayer bears only a small individual share of that total subsidy. Who will undertake the expense of lobbying on the measure? The industry will, not the taxpayer, because the net benefit of lobbying is positive for the industry (comparing the substantial cost of lobbying with the substantial direct benefit to the industry) and negative for any taxpayer (because the substantial lobbying cost overwhelms the small individual share of the subsidy that could be saved).

These efforts to influence fiscal decisions take two general forms. Traditional lobbying is personal: "Affable men in suits would hang around swarming, sweaty legislative chambers, buttonholing lawmakers as they swaggered through lustrous bronzed doors, whispering in ears, slapping backs, winking knowingly."[38] The lobbyists know the elected representative and have access to them (usually because they can be counted on for contributions and other campaign assistance), know the unelected administrators carrying out public policies, and use these contacts to deliver the message of their clients on issues. Many former legislators and agency administrators—federal and state—develop lucrative careers as lobbyists, using contacts and friendships to help deliver the message of the interests they represent;

[38]Ron Faucheux, "The Grassroots Explosion," *Campaigns and Elections* (December 1994–January 1995). Lobbying state legislators can be crass: "It's one of the accepted rules in the unwritten guide to being a lobbyist. The way to get a lawmaker's ear is to get him a drink first." (Christi Parsons and Rick Pearson, "Springfield Has a Gift for Grab," *Chicago Tribune*, 6 July 1997.)

their value is in their access to the people who remain in government. In one recent example, the member of Congress primarily responsible for the Medicare Prescription Drug Improvement and Modernization Act of 2003 (P.L.108173), an act that provided significant new revenue for the pharmaceutical industry and avoided price constraints on prescription medicines, left Congress for a position as chief lobbyist for brand-name drug companies.[39] Many call this easy mobility between legislative or executive positions and interested private entities "a revolving door," and few believe it to be contributory to fiscal decisions in the public interest. But it is part of the way in which public policies get adopted today.

Grassroots lobbying is the mobilization of constituent action, reflected in letters, phone calls, e-mails, faxes, and other direct contacts to the elected representative. Mass campaigns had great successes in getting civil-rights legislation and in shaping other policies, but communications and information technologies make it much easier to generate what appears to be a groundswell of interest and masses of constituent communications of public policy questions, including those of government expenditure and taxation.

A related influence on representative government is the principle of rational ignorance. Citizen effort to acquire information to cast an informed vote is usually irrational.[40] Although the cost of obtaining information may be low, the expected return from an informed vote is even lower. If others vote in an informed manner, a citizen's uninformed vote is irrelevant because the informed majority choice wins. If others vote in an uninformed manner, a citizen's informed vote is irrelevant because the choice of the uninformed majority wins. In either case, the action of the majority produces the election result, so individual effort to become informed yields no return. Thus, electorate choices produce indivisible benefits or costs. Information gathering to cast informed votes produces no electoral benefits for an individual. That, of course, is a crucial problem in any democratic society. Fortunately, many individuals become informed for other motives, including pure enjoyment. The power of the vote is an important reason why free, high-quality primary and secondary education is so critical for democratic government.

A final important point in the process of representation deals with the intensity of preference. In ordinary voting, there are no methods of representing intensity of preference on particular issues. Each vote has equal weight. In a legislative body, however, the flow of many issues allows legislators to trade a vote on a minor issue (according to that person's preferences) for a vote on a more important one. Trading votes allows adjustments according to intensity of preference. For example, a member of Congress may be particularly interested in the outcome on issue B, but have little concern about issue A. That representative may trade his or her vote on issue A for some other representative's vote on issue B. This process, called *logrolling*, can produce wasteful spending (an irrigation project yielding benefit to a

---

[39]As Robert L. Livingston, former head of the House Appropriations Committee who became president of a lobbying firm, said about lobbying: "There's an unlimited business out there for us." (Jeffrey H. Birnbaum, "The Road to Riches is Called K Street," *Washington Post* 22 June 2005: A1.) K Street in Washington is where the offices of the major lobbyists are located.

[40]Downs, Chapter 18.

small area at great national cost, for instance), but it can also improve the responsiveness of government by ensuring that intense preferences get recognized. Furthermore, the representative process has special devices for protecting the interests of minorities. These do not appear in the general referendum process of choice by direct vote:

> The required majority of those voting (in a referendum) can inflict severe cost on the rest of society with dramatic consequences for the social fabric. Their major disadvantage must emerge from the absence of minority power in the direct legislation system. An initiated referendum has no provision for executive veto, creation of political stalemates in the legislative process, or changed negotiating positions in committees, all vital positions of lawmaking which can serve to protect minorities.[41]

The Layers of Government

In the United States three layers of governments with sovereignty of their own (not a single government) provide public services, levy taxes, and borrow money. Indeed, there are more than 86,000 governments in the United States, counting federal, state, and local entities. Not all nations are governed in this fashion. Some governments are unitary, meaning that a single national government has legislative authority over the entire country. There may be local councils with certain powers, but they function only on the approval of the national government. In many unitary states, local revenue and expenditure programs must be approved by the national government, and a single consolidated financial program (or budget) exists for the entire country. Unitary states include Belgium, France, the Netherlands, Norway, Poland, and many countries of the former Soviet Union (but not Russia). The United Kingdom, historically unitary, is devolving some powers to regional parliaments in Scotland and Wales. Other nations are federal: Subnational governments have considerable autonomous authority to make decisions, including difficult decisions about taxing and spending. In no sense are these subnational units a dependent department of the central government, as they may be in a unitary state. In the United States, states exist as an independent layer of government with full powers (including independent financial authority) and all residual powers.[42] Other important federal states include Argentina, Australia, Austria, Brazil, Canada, Germany, India, Mexico, and the Russian Federation (although recent changes there to reduce sovereign powers of regional and local governments and move them to the national government have moved the nation closer to being a unitary state). In each instance, to understand government finances—spending, taxing, and borrowing—one must understand the intergovernmental structure in the country.

---

[41]John L. Mikesell, "The Season of the Tax Revolt," in *Fiscal Retrenchment and Urban Policy,* ed. John P. Blair and David Nachimaias (Newbury Park, Calif.: Sage, 1979), 128.

[42]The national government under the Articles of Confederation, precursor to the Constitution, lacked the power to tax. Payments from the states proved inadequate, so it is no wonder that it resorted to finance by printing money, which proved to be disastrously inflationary.

In the U.S. federal system, constitutional terms define the elemental financial powers and limits under which the levels function. First, there are powers and limits to national (federal) authority: Article I, Section 8, lists fiscally significant powers. These include the powers

> To lay and collect taxes, duties, imposts and excises, to pay the debts and provide for the common defense and general welfare of the United States; but all duties, imposts and excises shall be uniform throughout the United States.
>
> To borrow money on the credit of the United States.
>
> To regulate commerce with foreign nations, and among the several States, and with the Indian tribes.
>
> To coin money, regulate the value thereof, and of foreign coin, and fix the standard of weights and measures.
>
> To establish post-offices and post-roads.
>
> To raise and support armies, but no appropriation of money to that use shall be for a longer term than two years.
>
> To provide and maintain a navy.

Article I, Section 9, establishes some fiscal constraints:

> No capitation, or other direct, tax shall be laid, unless in proportion to the census of enumeration herein before directed to be taken.
>
> No tax or duty shall be laid on articles exported from any State.
>
> No money shall be drawn from the Treasury, but in consequence of appropriations made by law; and a regular statement and account of the receipts and expenditures of all public money shall be published from time to time.

Of course, legislation and court decisions have, over the years, specifically defined what these powers and constraints mean in practice.

The Constitution similarly identifies, in Article I, Section 10, powers specifically denied the states. Of fiscal significance is the prohibition against coining money. The commerce clause (Article I, Section 8, paragraph 3, listed above) prevents state interference with international commerce and commerce among the states, a particularly significant limit on taxing power and regulatory authority in a global economy. This is referred to as the Commerce Clause, and it plays an important role in many facets of state taxation. A later amendment (Article XIV, Section 1) requires states to follow due process in their actions and to afford equal protection of the law to all within their jurisdictions. These provisions have had substantial impact on service provision in the states, as courts have reminded state and local governments that fiscal processes must meet federal constitutional tests.[43] The federal equal-protection

---

[43]Two examples: Public schools, as examined in Rosemary O'Leary and Charles R. Wise, "Public Managers, Judges, and Legislators: Redefining the 'New Partnership,'" *Public Administration Review 51* (July/August 1991): 316–27; and jails, as examined in Jeffrey D. Straussman and Kurt Thurmaier, "Budgeting Rights: The Case of Jail Litigation," *Public Budgeting & Finance* (Summer 1989): 30–42.

clause has been often copied in state constitutions. The dramatic change in school finance in California generated by the court case *Serrano* v. *Priest*[44] resulted from state constitutional provisions copied after those in the federal law.

The major constitutional provision for states appears in the tenth amendment of the Constitution: "The powers not delegated to the United States by the Constitution, nor prohibited by it to the States, are reserved to the States respectively, or to the people." The states thus have *residual powers.* The Constitution does not need to provide specific authority for a state government to have a particular power: Constitutional silence implies that the state can act in the area in question, thus establishing states as the sovereign "middle layer" in the federal system.

Local governments in the United States typically appear as captive creatures of their states, unless state action has specifically altered that relationship. This principle was defined by Judge J. F. Dillon of Iowa:

> It is a general and undisputed proposition of law that a municipal corporation possesses and can exercise the following powers and no others: First, those granted in express words; second, those necessarily or fairly implied in or incident to the powers expressly granted; third, those essential to the declared objects and purposes of the corporation—not simply convenient, but indispensable. Any fair, reasonable, substantive doubt concerning the existence of power is resolved by the courts against the corporation, and the power denied.[45]

Dillon's rule thus holds that if state law is silent about a particular local power, the presumption is that the local level lacks power. In state-local relationships, state government holds all powers. That is a critical limitation on local government fiscal activity.

Several states have altered Dillon's rule by granting home-rule charter powers to particular local governments. Such powers are particularly prevalent in states containing a small group of large metropolitan areas with conditions substantially different from the environment in other areas of the state. The special conditions of such large cities can be handled by providing them home-rule charter power to govern their own affairs. State law can thus proceed without being cluttered by numerous special enactments for the larger units. When charter powers have been provided, local governments can act in all areas unless state law specifically prohibits those actions. Many times, however, fiscal activities are included in the range of areas that are prohibited under charter powers. Thus, it is better to presume limits than to presume local freedom to choose in fiscal affairs. That presumption is accurate if Dillon's rule applies or if charter powers have been constrained in fiscal activities.

Conclusion

An overview of the basis for government action certainly indicates that government choices made in budgeting and revenue raising will not be simple. Government will

---

[44]Cal. 3d 584, 487 P. 2d 1241, 97 California Reporter 601 (1971).

[45]John F. Dillon, *Commentaries on the Law of Municipal Corporations,* 5th ed. (Boston: Little, Brown, 1911); vol. 1, sec. 237. See *City of Clinton* v. *Cedar Rapids and Missouri Railroad Company* (1868).

be unable to sell its services because these services are nonappropriable (neither excludable nor exhaustible). That means that government will not have normal market tests available to help it with choices.

Governments surely do not want to waste resources—after all, resources are scarce, and most things used by government do have alternative uses—so the benefits to society from government action ought to exceed the cost to society from that action. Determining whether actions really improve the conditions of the community gets complicated, however, when there is no basis for making comparison of the worth of individuals. The Pareto criterion for the welfare of a community does not require interpersonal judgments, but it leaves many choices open to political decision. Despite sophistication and rigor, science and analysis will not provide definitive answers to many government choices. Votes, either on issues or for representatives, will settle many decisions. Direct votes, however, will neither guarantee no wasteful public decisions nor choices that satisfy the Pareto criterion for improving society. They may well cause the imposition of substantial costs on minorities. Some problems of direct choice are reduced when representatives make decisions, but there will remain imbalances of influence and posturing to continue in office rather than to follow clearly defined principles. Lobbying—direct or grassroots—is one way in which some interests obtain extra influence.

Finance in a representative democracy is not simple. Governments should be judged on their responsiveness to public preferences and on their refusal to ignore minority positions. Not all governments can meet those simple standards, and not all budget systems used in the United States do much to contribute to those objectives. The U.S. structure delivers and finances services using three tiers of government—federal, state, and local. Although independent in some respects, there are important mutual constraints. The federal level has powers delimited in the Constitution; the states have residual powers. Local governments—under Dillon's rule—have only powers expressly granted by their states. Some states grant local home rule, giving localities all powers save those expressly prohibited. Few home-rule authorizations are complete, however. Thus, budget and finance functions vary widely across the country.

QUESTIONS AND EXERCISES

1. A community project (a public good) will cost $2,500 and will benefit the five members of the community as follows:

Resident	Individual Benefit ($)	Cost Share ($)
A	800	500
B	800	500
C	300	500
D	350	500
E	450	500

a. Is the project economically feasible?
b. Would the project be approved by a majority at a referendum?
c. Does the project meet the Pareto criterion?
d. If possible, revise the cost shares to allow the project to meet the Pareto criterion and to pass a referendum.

2. Determine for your state the budget and finance constraints that the state places on local government. Does Dillon's rule apply? Do some units have home-rule powers? What is the extent of any such powers?
3. Private businesses have a great interest in quality primary and secondary education because today's students are tomorrow's employees. However, private businesses make limited financial contributions to this sector of education (excluding the taxes they pay to public school systems), even to market-oriented programs like vouchers and charter schools. What do you suppose explains this low contribution level? (Hint: consider what sort of good primary and secondary education might be.)

CASE FOR DISCUSSION

CASE 1–1

Market Interplay, Municipal Utilities, and a Common-Pool Resource

Governments often are surprised by private responses to what appear to be relatively straightforward and sensible public decisions. It should be no surprise that businesses respond to higher prices for their purchases by trying to economize on their use of those more expensive resources. What may be surprising is how these reactions themselves create even more complex problems for the government. In the case described here, the normal business response is particularly interesting because it crosses between the operation of a municipal utility and the exploitation of a common-pool resource. Here is a case from *The Wall Street Journal.*

Consider These Questions

1. Identify the various types of goods (private, public, and in between) involved in this case. What was the primary objective being sought and how was it being financed? Is that financing approach appropriate for the type of good involved?
2. What options might governments in the Boston area have?
3. What would you recommend to prevent further damage?

SOURCE: Wall Street Journal, (20 January 1993), B-1. Reprinted by permission of the *Wall Street Journal,* © 1993 Dow Jones & Company, Inc. All rights reserved worldwide.

City Dwellers Drill for Precious Fluid[1]

As water rates go up, some Bostonians are going down—about 900 feet to find water. Average water and sewer bills in Boston have more than tripled since 1985 to cover costs of cleaning up Boston harbor. To cut their bills, several Boston businesses have recently drilled their own wells.

"It's a very alarming trend," says Jonathan Kaledin, executive director of the National Water Education Council, a Boston-based group that tracks water-project funding issues. As customers "leave the system," those who remain must shoulder higher funding burdens.

If such drilling becomes a trend, it could undermine funding in a number of cities for projects to comply with clean-water laws. New York City water projects, for example, are expected to cost more than $10 billion during the 1990s, according to a recent report by Mr. Kaledin's group.

Boston officials also worry that buildings in the city's Back Bay area, a fill-in swamp, may sink if wells lower the water table. Structures there rest on immersed wooden pilings that "will rot in two or three years" if exposed to air as the water level drops, warns Boston City Councilman David Scondras. City officials, citing over 400 known hazardous-spill sites in Boston, also fret that wells may tap into polluted water.

But the economic arguments for drilling are overwhelming, says Roger Berkowitz, co-owner of Legal Sea Foods, a Boston restaurant chain that recently drilled a well. Its 15,000 gallon-a-day gusher saves the company $2,500 a month by providing water for laundry and other uses. Though it isn't used for drinking, Mr. Berkowitz says, tests show water from the chain's well surpasses Boston's municipal water in purity.

PART ONE

Budgeting, Budget Structures, and Budget Reform

Chapter 2 **The Logic of the Budget Process**

Chapter 3 **Budget Structures and Institutions: Federal and State-Local**

Chapter 4 **Budget Methods and Practices**

Chapter 5 **Budget Classifications and Reform**

Chapter 6 **Capital Budgeting, Public Infrastructure Investment, and Project Evaluation**

CHAPTER 2

The Logic of the Budget Process

The budget process provides the medium for determining what government services will be provided and how they will be financed. It may also help establish how the services will be provided. The basic budgeting problem, simply stated, is the following: "On what basis shall it be decided to allocate *X* dollars to activity *A* instead of activity *B*?"[1] How many dollars should be moved from private businesses and individuals to government and, once moved to government, how much should go to each government activity? Markets for private goods do the allocation invisibly, as prices and profits provide the resource allocation signals in the private sector. The budget process is where those choices get made for government operations, not so quietly and we hope not so invisibly, but definitely politically. When governments tax and spend, making decisions within the framework of the budget process, they are doing for the public section what the private market does for the provision of private goods and services. Each government has some method for making these fiscal choices, although the degree of formality varies widely.

Except for the limited number of town-meeting and referendum decisions, elected representatives make the primary spending and financing decisions. However, in budget preparation and in the delivery of services supported by the budget, nonelected public employees make many crucial decisions. Although these employees enjoy job security and may be less responsive to voters than elected officials, the logic of representative government presumes that such bureaucrats and, indeed, the elected executives and legislators who guide their work, will be responsive to the citizenry.[2]

Governments can operate with a haphazard budget process. However, a system designed with incentives to induce officials to respond to public demands is

[1] V. O. Key, Jr., "The Lack of a Budgetary Theory," *American Political Science Review* 34 (December 1940): 1137.

[2] This is an example of the "principal/agent problem": Bureaucrats and elected officials (agents) are inclined to pursue their own self-interests, which may well differ from the interests for the citizenry (principals). "Participatory budgeting," discussed in a later chapter, provides an alternate and direct channel for getting citizen priorities into the deliberations.

more likely to produce decisions in the public interest, providing citizens with the quality and quantity of desired public services, at the desired times and locations and at the least cost to society. At a minimum, the process must recognize competing claims on resources and should focus directly on alternatives and options. A major portion of the process involves presentation of accurate and relevant information to individuals making budget decisions on behalf of the citizenry. At its best, the budget process articulates the choices of the citizenry for government services (and how those services will be paid for) and manages efficient delivery and finance of those services. Before considering the logic of the budget, however, it is good to understand some basic facts about government expenditure in the United States.

The Size and Growth of Government Expenditure

Government spending can be divided into two primary categories: purchases and transfers. Both purchases and transfers need to be financed (as must interest payments on outstanding government debt, another important spending category) and both entail a government payment, but their impact on the economy differs, so the categories are differentiated in the national economic accounts. Furthermore, transfers and purchases are commonly treated differently by governmental budget processes, as is discussed in some detail in later chapters.

1. **Government purchases** divert productive resources (land, labor, capital, natural resources) from private use by businesses and individuals to government use in the provision of education, national defense, public safety, parks, and so on. Some of this spending pays wages and benefits to government employees, some pays suppliers of items used by these employees in the production of government services, and some pays private entities who have agreed to produce government services under contract. Most of this spending is for the provision of current services, but part of this spending is government investment—the purchase of long-life capital assets like roads, buildings, and durable equipment.[3] In the national income accounting system, this direct provision represents the government contribution to gross domestic product (GDP). In other words, when a city outfits its fire department to provide services during the year, pays its firefighters, or purchases a new fire truck, it will be purchasing from private suppliers. Some purchases will provide services within the year of purchase (consumption) and others will yield services over the longer useful life of the asset purchased (gross investment).

2. **Transfer payments** constitute the other major element of government spending. These payments provide income to recipients without service being

[3]This gross investment—meaning spending to purchase new assets without taking account of the depreciation (wearing out) of the existing capital stock—amounts to a bit more than 10 percent of the U.S. total.

required in return. Such direct payment transfers to individuals include Social Security benefits, unemployment insurance payments, and other cash payments to low-income individuals. These payments amount to almost 40 percent of all current government expenditure in the United States, so they represent an important contributor to the financing requirements of government and an important concern for government operations. The impact on GDP is through spending done by the transfer recipients.

Table 2–1 shows the path of government spending in the United States from 1960 to 2004, following the classification of the national income and product accounts. Figure 2–1 traces government spending as a percentage of GDP over the same period, in total, for transfers, and for government consumption expenditures plus transfers. These data focus on the transfer of resources between private and public sectors, that is, the way in which sectors of the economy claim production of the economy. They do not exactly coincide with the fiscal year, cash-outlay data that later chapters use, but they do make important points needed for the understanding of U.S. government finances.[4]

Current expenditure by all governments in the United States amounts to around 30 percent of the GDP. The government spending share has grown since 1960, when current government expenditure constituted 23.3 percent of the GDP to around one-third from early 1980s to mid-1990s. The 2004 percentage (30.3 percent) is below its recent peak in the first half of the 1990s and back to the level of the early 1980s. The recent pattern is the product of some decline in both transfer payments and government consumption expenditure shares. Much of the growth in earlier years was driven by increases in transfer payments to individuals; even including the period of moderate growth and small decline in the 1990s, the average annual growth rate for these payments from 1960 to 2004 is 9.3 percent, considerably greater than the rate for population, prices, GDP, or other government expenditure categories. Employee compensation as a percentage of current government expenditure of governments was 31.3 percent in 2004, compared with 39.1 percent in 1960, the result of both the changing nature of spending (toward transfers and other nonpurchases) and the inclination toward outsourcing or privatization by contracting out.

The federal component of consumption spending plus gross investment was 37.1 percent in 2004, considerably less than the 57.4 percent in 1960. This decline is largely the result of slow growth in national defense purchases, a slowing that started well before the death of the Soviet Union in 1991. To fight the war on terrorists and the war in Iraq, national defense purchases have increased at an annual

---

[4]The 1995 revision of the national income and product accounts brought significant change in how the accounts treat government expenditure, especially for capital asset purchases. The components in the new structure include the following: Gross government investment includes total government expenditures for fixed assets; government consumption expenditures replaces "government purchases" and includes the estimated value of the services of general government fixed assets, as measured by consumption of fixed capital (as well as the purchases for use in the year); and government consumption and investment expenditures shows the total current-year government contribution to GDP. See Robert P. Parker and Jack E. Triplett, "Preview of the Comprehensive Revision of the National Income and Product Accounts: Recognition of Government Investment and Incorporation of a New Methodology for Calculation Depreciation," *Survey of Current Business* (September 1995): 33–41.

Table 2–1
Government Spending in the National Income and Product Accounts ($ billions)

	1960	1970	1980	1990	2000	2004	Growth Rate Since 1960
Current Expenditures	122.9	294.8	842.8	1872.6	2886.5	3558.6	7.9%
Consumption expenditures	83.3	190.2	465.9	964.4	1417.1	1804.2	7.2%
Current transfer payments	28	76.8	278	586.1	1062.4	1402.4	9.3%
To persons	24.4	71.7	270.8	573.1	1041.6	1373.2	9.6%
Interest payments	10.4	23.1	89.1	295.3	362.8	311.6	8.0%
Government Consumption Expenditure and Gross Investment	111.6	233.8	566.2	1180.2	1721.6	2183.9	7.0%
Consumption expenditures	83.3	190.2	465.9	964.4	1417.1	1804.2	7.2%
Gross investment	28.3	43.6	100.3	215.7	304.5	379.7	6.1%
Federal	64.1	113.5	243.8	508.3	578.8	809.9	5.9%
National defense	53.4	87.6	168	374	370.3	547.9	5.4%
Nondefense	10.7	25.8	75.8	134.3	208.5	262	7.5%
State and local	47.5	120.3	322.4	671.9	1142.8	1373.9	7.9%
Comparison Data							
Compensation of general government employees	48.1	119.4	295.5	608.5	903.2	1113.8	7.4%
Federal	22.6	48.3	102.5	193.9	233.8	305.9	6.1%
State and local	25.5	71.1	193	414.6	669.4	807.9	8.2%
Gross domestic product	526.4	1038.5	2789.5	5803.1	9817	11735	7.3%
GDP Implicit deflator (2000 = 100)	21.041	27.534	54.043	81.59	100	108.237	3.8%
Resident population (April 1, in thousands)	179,323.0	203,302.0	226,542.2	248,718.3	281,423.2	292,952.8	1.1%

SOURCE: U.S. Department of Commerce, Bureau of Economic Analysis, National Income and Product Accounts and U.S. Bureau of Census.

Figure 2–1
Government Spending in the United States as Percentage of GDP, 1960–2004

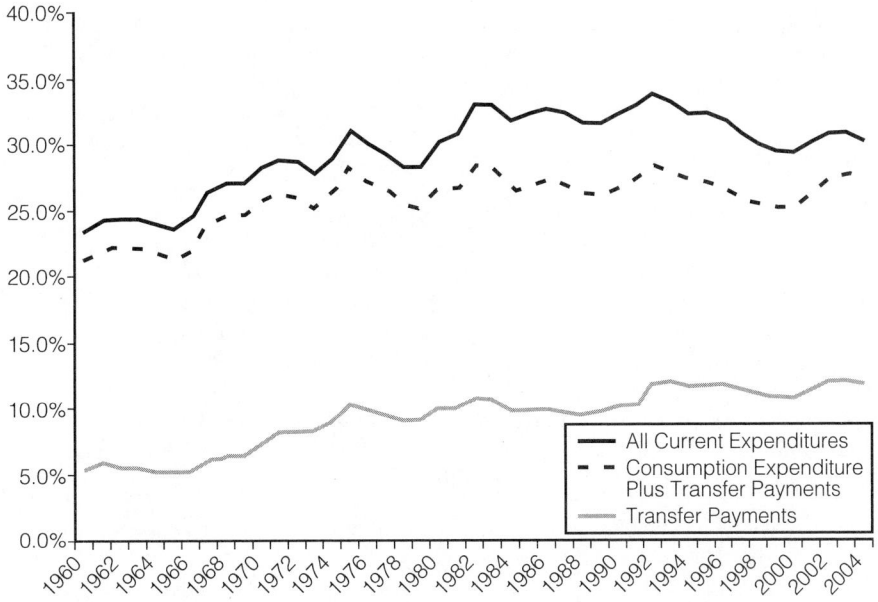

rate of 10.3 percent from 2000 to 2004. However, other federal purchasing did not increase quite as rapidly as did state and local spending in the period: The rate was 7.5 percent for federal nondefense purchasing, compared with 7.9 percent for state and local governments. There has been considerable devolution of responsibility to lower levels of government. Of course, much of federal government total expenditure is for transfer payments, and these rates are considerably greater than other categories.

Special attention should be given to the difference between price and physical effects on purchases. For example, government consumption expenditure plus gross investment—purchases of things and services—increased from $566.2 billion in 1980 to $2,183.9 billion in 2004, an increase of 285.7 percent. That increase resulted from two forces: (1) purchases of more "stuff" (trucks, computers, workers' time, etc.) and (2) payment of higher prices for the items purchased. The total increase encompasses both change in prices and change in physical (real) purchases. Because only the latter represents greater capacity to deliver service, it is important to divide the components of change. Sidebar 2–1 describes the basic mechanics of making price adjustments.

Table 2–1 shows the GDP implicit price deflator, an aggregate measure of price change, to have increased from 54.043 in 1980 (2000 = 100, meaning that 1980 prices averaged 54 percent of their 2000 levels) to 108.237 in 2004, an increase of 100.3 percent. This deflator is a sort of weighted average of the price changes for everything that governments purchase, with weights based on the relative amounts

Deflating $

Sidebar 2–1
Deflating: Dividing between Real and Price Change

The amount of money spent depends on how many items are purchased and what the price of each item is: 400 gallons of motor fuel at $2.10 per gallon means $840 spent on fuel. More money spent does not mean that more things have been purchased if the prices of those things have changed. Fewer things purchased probably means fewer government services can be provided with a given budget. So how can analysts compare real purchasing power of money spent across periods when prices are different? The answer lies in the use of price indexes.

Suppose a set of purchases (commodities and services) cost $100 at 2006 prices, but only $75 at 2000 prices. That means that between 2000 and 2006, prices have risen on average by 33 percent ([100–75]/75, converted to percentage form) or the ratio of 2002 prices to 1999 prices is 1.33, (i.e., 100/75). This ratio of the value of a group of commodities and services in current dollars (or "then-year") to the value of that same group in base-year dollars (or constant dollars) is a price index. If 2000 is the base year, its index would be 100 and the index for 2006 would be 133 (or 33 percent higher than the base year). (The index could also be stated in ratio form. In this case, 2000 would be 1.00 and 2006 would be 1.33.) A price index provides a method for identifying to what extent higher expenditure reflects real change (more items purchased) and price changes (higher prices); the index shows how prices, on average, differ from those in a base year.

Here is an example. From 1994 to 2004, outlays of the federal government rose from $1,461.8 billion to $2,292.2 billion. The composite outlay deflator, using 2000 as base, went from 0.8902 to 1.0917 over that period, indicating that prices paid averaged 22.6 percent higher in the later year. Outlays increased by 56.8 percent; but how much of the increase represented a real change? In constant (base-year 2000) dollars, the outlays equaled $1,642.1 billion (1,461.8/0.8902) in 1994 and $2,099.7 billion (2,292.2/1.0917) in 2004, so the real increase equaled 27.9 percent (2,099.7/1,642.1).

Analysts use many different price indexes, depending on the expenditure category being analyzed; the *Survey of Current Business* from the U.S. Department of Commerce reports many of these, as do other publications. The data used here came from the federal budget. Prices of all items do not change by the same amount. Some go up a lot, some go up a little, some don't change, and some even decrease. All those changes are captured in a single index by computing a weighted average in which the price change for big purchase items counts for more than the price change for small purchase items. Traditional indices have used fixed weight measures: the base year spending patterns establish fixed weight values for computing the averages. This practice creates a problem when there is considerable difference in the amount of price change among items: Purchasers substitute those items whose price has risen less for those items whose price has risen more. The fixed weights become wrong. Analysts now remedy the problem by using a rolling average, or chain weights, instead of fixed base year weights. The system sets the weights by taking the average growth of the current year and the preceding year. Price weights are thus constantly updated for changes in relative prices.

Spending calibrated in prices from one year can be easily converted into prices for another. In the above example, if 1994 were to be the reference year, then 1994 is 1.00 (0.8901/0.8901), and 2004 is 1.2265 (1.0917/0.8901). The ratios can be converted to percentage form by multiplying by 100; either format conveys the same information about prices. The absolute level of the index and the absolute difference between years in the index differ according to the base year used, but the percentage change remains the same across base years. Price indexes and deflated (constant or real) values have meaning only in a relative sense.

spent on the purchase category; the prices of items that relatively large amounts are spent on have greater weight in computing the average. (Deflators are computed for many classes of spending, including various types of government purchases, capital investment, consumption, etc. They are available from various publications of the U.S. Department of Commerce's Bureau of Economic Analysis.) Converting government consumption expenditures plus gross investment to a real basis shows real purchases of $1,047.7 billion in 1980 and $2,017.7 billion in 2004, an increase of 92.6 percent. Thus, the increase in government consumption expenditures from 1980 to 2004 of 285.7 percent resulted from increases of 100.3 percent in prices and of 92.6 percent in physical, or real, purchases.[5] (The increases could also be calculated as growth rates; Sidebar 2–2 shows this method.)

How does the size of the American public sector compare with that of other countries? Table 2–2 reports data for several countries of the Organization for Economic Cooperation and Development. Although the conventions used in these measures do not exactly match those of the national income and product accounts just discussed, the basic logic is comparable and can be interpreted in the same way. Measured by final consumption expenditure, the countries ranged from 28.1 percent of GDP in Sweden to 10.4 percent in Korea; the U.S. value, 15.6 percent, is below the mean of 19.2 percent. As noted previously, purchases do not measure the full extent of public-sector involvement in the economy. Total current government-expenditure percentages range from 27.5 percent of GDP in Korea to 58.3 percent in Sweden. The U.S. percentage, 35.7 percent, is considerably below the mean of 45.1 percent. Among industrialized nations, the United States has a small government component in its national economy.[6]

The nature of these government expenditures—in other words, the kinds of services governments provide—are examined in the next chapter. But it is now

---

[5]The real and price changes do not add to the total change, but they are mathematically related. If $X00$, $X80$, and t are total expenditure in 2000, total expenditure in 1980, and the percentage increase in total expenditure between the years; if $D00$, $D80$, and g are the similar variables for deflated (real or constant dollar) expenditure; and if $P00$, $P80$, and p are similar variables for price levels, then

$$X00 = X80 + (X80 \times t) = X80\,(1 + t)$$
$$D00 = D80 + (D80 \times g) = D80\,(1 + g)$$
$$P00 = P80 + (P80 \times p) + P80\,(1 + p)$$

Total expenditure in 2000 equals real expenditure in 2000 times the 2000 price level:

$$X00 = D00 \times P00$$

Thus, substituting into this equation yields the following:

$$X80\,(1 + t) = D80\,(1 + g) \times P80\,(1 + p)$$

Rearranging terms, we obtain

$$X80\,(1 + t) = D80 \times P80\,(1 + g)(1 + p)$$

Because $X80 = D80 \times P80$, then

$$(1 + t) = (1 + g)(1 + p)$$

One plus the rate of price increase times 1 plus the rate of increase of deflated expenditure equals 1 plus the rate of total expenditure increase.

[6]Governments also interact with the private sector through regulations, legal requirements, and mandates. These effects are difficult to measure, but many would place the United States considerably higher in the league table than its ranking according to government-spending share.

Sidebar 2–2
Growth Rates and Simple Projections

How much has spending, population, income, or some other critical variable grown over the years? Suppose state population increased from 1.8 million in 1990 to 4.5 million in 2000. If population changes at the same rate to 2005, what would be the state population? The compound rate of growth is computed according to the formula

$$r = [(Y/X) \wedge (1/N)] - 1$$

where r = the rate, Y = the end value, X = the beginning value, and N = the number of periods of growth. In this case, the population growth rate would be computed according to the formula

$$r = [(4.5/1.8) \wedge (1/10)] - 1$$

This calculation can be made with the y^x key found on inexpensive pocket calculators:

$y = (4.5/1.8)$ and $x = 1/10$. In this example, $r = 9.6$ percent.

In the example here, population in 2001 would be estimated to equal 4.5 million plus 9.6 percent, or 4.9 million; in 2002, 4.9 million plus 9.6 percent, or 5.4 million; in 2003, 5.4 million plus 9.6 percent, or 5.9 million; in 2004, 5.9 million plus 9.6 percent, or 6.5 million; and in 2005, 6.5 million plus 9.6 percent, or 7.1 million.

The estimate can be made directly according to the formula

$$Y = X(1 + r) \wedge n$$

where the arguments in the formula are as before. In this illustration,

$$Y = 4.5\ (1.096) \wedge 5 = 4.5\ (1.5814) = 7.1$$

This tool is very useful for comparing rates of change over varying time periods and for doing quick projections.

important to learn the general elements of the budget process and the language that applies in fiscal systems.

Budget Process and Logic

The market allocates private resources without a need for outside intervention; price movements serve as a signaling device for resource flows. In the public sector, decisions about resource use cannot be made automatically from price and profit signals because of four special features of government decisions. First, public

Table 2–2
Government in Selected Industrialized Countries, 2002

	Total General Government Expenditure (% GDP)	General Government Consumption Expenditure (% GDP) Final
Australia	37.9	17.8
Austria	51.3	18.4
Belgium	50.5	22.3
Canada (2001)	41.7	19.2
Czech Republic	49.9	20.7
Denmark	55.8	26.3
Finland	50.1	21.7
France	53.5	23.9
Germany	48.5	19.2
Greece	46.8	15.7
Hungary	52.7	23.4
Iceland	46.0	25.5
Ireland	33.3	15.1
Italy	48.0	19.0
Japan	38.2	17.7
Korea (2001)	27.5	10.4
Luxembourg	44.0	17.8
Mexico (2001)	n.a.	11.8
Netherlands	47.5	24.5
New Zealand (1997)	41.8	18.5
Norway	47.5	21.8
Poland	n.a.	18.0
Portugal	45.9	21.2
Slovak Republic	51.0	20.1
Spain	39.9	17.8
Sweden	58.3	28.1
Switzerland (2001)	34.8	11.7
Turkey	n.a.	14.0
United Kingdom	40.7	20.1
United States	35.7	15.6

SOURCE: Organization for Economic Cooperation and Development, *OECD in Figures, 2004 Edition, Statistics on the Member Countries*. Washington, D.C.: OECD, 2005.

goods, the primary service focus of governments, are difficult to sell, and, even where sales may be feasible, nonrevenue concerns may be as important as the cash collected. Consequently, profit can neither measure success nor serve as an incentive to efficient operations. When markets have failed, it is a mistake to try to use simple market information as a first guide for decisions. Second, public and private resource constraints differ dramatically. Whereas earnings and earnings potential constrain spending of private entities, governments are limited only by the total resources of the society.[7] Those resources are privately owned, but governments have the power to tax. There are obviously political limits to tax extractions, but those limits differ dramatically from resource limits on a private firm. Third, governments characteristically operate as perfect monopolies. Consumers of government services cannot purchase from an alternate supplier, and, more important, the consumer must pay whether the good provided is used or not. Again, this makes market-proxy data based on traditional government operations suspect as a guide for resource allocation. And finally, governments operate with mixed motives. In many instances, not only the service provided but also the recipients of the service (redistribution), or the mere fact of provision (stabilization), are important. For example, free school lunches may be provided to improve the living standard of families with schoolchildren or to increase the income of food producers, even though more economical methods may be available to achieve each of these objectives. Accordingly, more may hinge on the provision of a public service than simply the direct return from the service compared with its cost. Because these multiple and mixed objectives cannot be weighed scientifically, the budget process is political, involving both pure bargaining or political strategies and scientific analysis.

The Parts of the Public Expenditure/Public Revenue Process

Government spending must be financed, but, whereas receiving the benefits of a good or service is linked in the private sector to paying for it, in the public sector what the government provides does not determine how its operations will be financed. When a business builds cars, it knows exactly from whom the financing will be received: the people to whom it sells those cars. But when the federal government decides to increase its provision of national defense, it must make another decision: Who will pay? It isn't going to sell the service; there is no link between who receives the service and how it will be financed. In other words, public expenditure and public revenue involve two separate planning processes. Payment for a government service is not a precondition for benefiting from that service; if the mosquito abatement district has seen to its job, both those who pay taxes to the district and those who don't will be free of mosquito bites. The expenditure side of budgeting should set the size of the public sector, establish what is provided, how it is provided, and who gets it. The revenue planning side, on the other hand, determines whose real income will be reduced to finance the provision of the budgeted services. Although the total resources used must equal total resources raised (including both current revenues, borrowing, and, for national governments, creating

[7]Few have dared suggest natural limits to the ability of governments to extract resources from society since Colin Clark's proposition many years ago: "25 percent of the national income is about the limit for taxation in any nontotalitarian community in times of peace." ("Public Finance and Changes in the Value of Money," *Economic Journal* 55 [December 1945]: 380.) That limit was based on zero inflation—so it may not have been truly tested.

new money to spend), the profile of government expenditure does not ordinarily indicate how the cost of government should be distributed. A thoroughgoing benefit-based tax and charge revenue system, as described in a later chapter, would offer an exception, although the range of government services for which such financing would be practical is limited.

Figure 2–2 shows how dollars, resources, and public services logically flow from the revenue system to the procurement process to service delivery. The public procurement process involves exchange transactions (purchase on the open market) and, with few exceptions (eminent domain purchase of property and military draft being two), is economically (but possibly not politically) comparable to procurement by private firms. The unique public-sector features of the flow involve revenue generation and service-delivery decisions, the concerns of the following chapters. Governments devote much of their attention to the part of the budget process that deals with expenditure and service-delivery processes; the next several chapters examine this part of the budget. Revenue planning is examined in later chapters.

The basic communication device of the process is the budget, a government's plan for operation translated into its financial implications. Governments prepare budgets as a means for (1) elaborating executive-branch intentions, (2) providing legislative-branch review and approval of those plans, and (3) providing a control-and-review structure for implementation of approved plans.[8] Governments can also use the budget as a means of communicating their program intentions for the future to the public, although not enough governments think of the budget in such terms, and the public is not accustomed to looking at budgets at all.[9] At the

Figure 2–2
Service Delivery and Revenue Systems as Separate Planning Processes

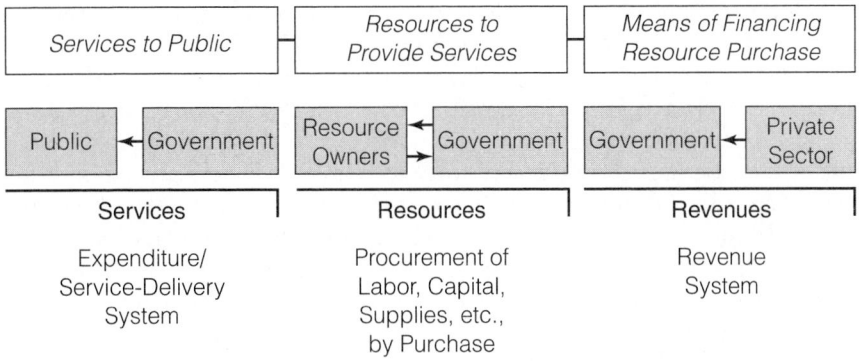

[8]Only appropriation and historical reports of spending and revenue are mentioned in the U.S. Constitution, Article I, Section 9[7]: "No money shall be drawn from the Treasury, but in consequence of appropriations made by law; and a regular statement and account of the receipts and expenditures of all public money shall be published from time to time."

[9]Recent budgets of the U.S. government have been reformulated so that the main volume is intended as a communication device, with colors, pictures, and charts. It is not clear that the public has paid much attention, however.

minimum, the budget includes the expenditure plan, the plan for raising revenue to cover that spending, and a plan for managing any difference between revenue and expenditure.

A Budget's Traditional Look: The Object-of-Expenditure (or Input) Format

The expenditure side of government budgets deals with plans in terms of spending money to deliver services to the public. Logically, the agency develops plans to provide services and estimates the cost of purchasing the resources necessary to execute those plans. In that respect, government operations are similar to those of private business: Resources are acquired and used to deliver a valued output. The public agency's budget is its business plan for the next year, subject to the approval of certain representatives of the people.

The most basic government budgets focus on inputs to the flow of service provision, that is, on the resources—labor, equipment, supplies, and the like—purchased by the government in the course of responding to the demand for service. The object-of-expenditure classification, or line-item budget—the most basic and traditional of budget organizations—reflects that orientation. The budget approved for the fire department of the city of Tempe, Arizona, for 2003/2004 and 2004/2005 illustrates that classification (Figure 2–3). The budget items are for expenditures to be made (purchases) by the department. This format is the basic structure for budget development in that it is the template an agency would use for estimating the cost of carrying out its plan for service. Other budget classifications, to be examined later, begin from some line-item basis.

The budget in Figure 2–3 demonstrates some important features. First, governments develop complete object-classification structures for use across all agencies, but not all agencies will make purchases in all object classes each year. (For instance, this department intends no purchase of computer equipment, object number 7518, in the budget years.) The classification systems will not be the same in different governments, but it is important that consistent classification be used within a single government for tests across agencies and for meaningful aggregation of objects. Second, the budget has been adopted for years 2003/2004 and 2004/2005. It is thus a 2-year, or biennial, budget, rather than a budget for a single year. More is said about this element of budget processes in the discussion of state and local budgeting in a later chapter. However, this biennial approach is relatively common in state and local governments in the United States. Finally, this budget reflects resources intended to carry out plans for 2003/2004 and 2004/2005. The budget display, however, also carries resource information for 2001/2002 and 2002/2003. In budget processes, it is normal to include multiple years in displays, even if the budget is for a single year.

1. **The budget year.** The document focuses on the budget year or years, 2004 and 2005 in this example. These numbers reflect what the agency plans for operations, what it has requested for approval by various stages of review, and

Figure 2–3
City of Tempe, Arizona: Line-Item Budget for the Fire Department, 2004-2005 (Biennial)

City of Tempe

BD08D **06/25/2003**

Departmental Summary by Funds

	Fire Protection	01/02 Actual	02/03 Budget	02/03 Revised	03/04 BASEBUDGET	04/05 BASEBUDGET
6010	Salaries	8,346,420	9,602,825	8,521,675	9,902,142	9,990,174
6011	Wages	5,450	0	0	0	0
6012	Overtime	629,860	754,751	782,100	754,751	754,751
6013	Vacation Pay	569,760	0	498,053	0	0
6014	Sick Pay	290,307	0	518,421	0	0
6015	Holiday Pay	467,779	473,586	439,119	450,000	450,000
6017	Bilingual Pay	2,793	2,400	3,600	3,600	3,60
	Salary & Wages	10,312,368	10,833,562	10,762,968	11,110,493	11,198,525
6120	Fica Taxes	153,956	185,518	152,653	158,820	160,938
6121	Arizona State Retirement	26,815	30,631	27,018	57,217	58,337
6123	Employee Health Insurance	1,006,956	1,156,138	1,160,585	1,339,885	1,478,095
6124	Pub. Safety Ret.-Fire	63,280	76,900	71,174	127,497	128,108
6127	Mediflex Reimbrsd Expens	24,994	89,180	87,550	94,345	100,015
6129	Employee Recognition Program	5,922	0	0	0	0
6132	IRA Expense	83,609	0	0	0	0
6133	Firefighter Cancer Ins	25,200	24,600	24,600	24,600	24,600
6141	Vehicle Allowance Pmts	12,000	12,000	12,000	6,000	6,000
	Fringe Benefits	1,402,733	1,574,967	1,535,580	1,808,365	1,956,094
6201	General Office Supplies	10,529	13,000	8,000	11,000	11,000
6301	Film & Recording Supplies	1,976	2,000	900	1,500	1,500
6305	Uniform Allowance	145,440	177,302	165,000	167,000	167,000
3610	Chemical Supplies	2,185	3,300	1,850	3,000	3,000
6315	Landscaping Supplies	15,450	0	0	0	0
6339	Hazardous Material Suppl	50,240	17,500	17,500	15,000	15,000
6340	Gasoline & Diesel Fuels	154	0	0	0	0
6342	Oil & Lubricants	5,313	0	4,000	0	0
6344	Propane Gas	214	0	0	0	0
6350	Hand Tools	2,397	1,800	1,800	1,800	1,800
6351	Minor Equipment	17,225	22,652	20,064	7,000	7,000
6352	Mechanic Tool Allowance	500	500	500	500	500
6356	Shop Supplies	1,223	900	1,200	900	900
6360	Traffic Control Material	1,995	750	1,100	750	750
6370	Printing & Copier Suppli	3,520	3,000	3,200	3,000	3,000
6401	Building Materials	0	1,000	400	500	500
6404	Special Systems	139	0	0	0	0
6410	Motor Vehicle Parts	45,294	44,000	50,000	44,000	44,000
6415	Communication Equip Part	0	700	628	700	700
6416	Comm. Parts-Telephone	250	700	500	700	700
6420	Oper. & Maint. Supplies	57,215	56,750	53,800	54,000	54,000
6421	SCBA Parts And Supplies	23,982	8,000	10,000	8,000	8,000
6422	Fire Hose & Nozzle	24,251	23,846	23,000	20,172	20,172
6423	Emergency Preparedness	954	1,300	500	1,300	1,300
6505	Books & Publications	7,172	6,000	4,700	5,500	5,500
6513	First Aid Supplies	146,242	140,000	140,000	132,000	132,000
6514	Awards & Decorations	425	500	600	500	500
6599	Miscellaneous Supplies	15,036	7,000	10,000	7,000	7,000
	Materials & Supplies	579,321	532,500	519,242	485,822	485,822
6656	Consultants	5,328	0	1,839	0	0
6659	Testing	4,532	4,800	3,700	4,800	4,800
6672	Contracted Services	213,082	231,105	222,779	231,105	231,105
6675	Software Purchases	1,677	0	0	0	0

(continues)

Figure 2–3
(continued)

City of Tempe

BD08D **06/25/2003**

Departmental Summary by Funds

	Fire Protection	01/02 Actual	02/03 Budget	02/03 Revised	03/04 BASEBUDGET	04/05 BASEBUDGET
6676	Training & Development	1,622	16,413	2,800	3,200	3,200
6677	Hazardous Waste Disposal	1,042	2,700	1,100	1,600	1,600
6690	Medical-Physical Exams	49,780	72,757	65,000	83,570	83,570
6693	Laundry, Uniforms, & Towel	2,216	2,600	2,000	2,600	2,600
6701	Cell Phone Charges	15,378	15,175	22,500	16,417	16,417
6704	Postage	788	500	800	500	500
6716	Membership & Subs	14,487	13,970	13,248	14,833	14,833
6720	Freight, Moving, & Towing	350	0	400	0	0
6753	Outside Printing/Forms	7,066	7,000	7,000	7,000	7,000
6755	Duplicating	1,783	4,000	2,500	4,000	4,000
6810	General Liability Claims	896-	0	0	0	0
6852	Bldg. & Structure Repair	12,566	19,000	23,000	18,000	18,000
6854	Car Wash	1,207	1,500	1,500	1,500	1,500
6856	Equip. & Machinery Repair	44,796	30,500	30,700	30,500	30,500
6906	Equip. & Machine Rental	27,188	26,400	25,360	26,800	26,800
6999	Misc. Fees & Services	776	300	225	300	300
	Fees & Services	404,769	448,720	426,451	446,725	446,725
7008	Maricopa Civil Defense	11,089	13,000	11,773	13,000	13,000
	Other Contrib. & Charges	11,089	13,000	11,773	13,000	13,000
7401	Training & Seminars	38,237	46,335	44,335	38,335	38,335
7402	Employee Mileage Expense	686	0	0	0	0
7403	Travel Expense	12,427	6,700	4,300	3,300	3,300
7404	Local Meetings	4,148	3,000	1,500	1,500	1,500
7405	Recruit Tuitions	4,459	12,000	7,500	10,000	10,000
	Travel & Other Expenses	59,957	68,035	57,635	53,135	53,135
7508	Motor Vehicles	0	484,700	484,700	265,000	265,000
7511	Other Equipment	175,712	165,490	160,257	29,000	29,000
7518	Computer Equipment	859	0	0	0	0
	Capital Outlays	176,571	650,190	644,957	294,000	294,000
8301	Data Processing Services	402,440	360,636	360,636	345,928	351,742
8303	Vehicle Maintenance Cost	72,161	62,906	62,906	76,112	79,126
8304	Worker's Comp. Claims	200,332	184,990	184,990	209,570	209,570
8305	Radio Repair Costs	82,392	72,309	72,309	62,975	63,776
8306	Vehicle Fuel/Oil Costs	65,712	51,372	51,372	45,302	45,302
8307	Communication Cost	87,236	85,779	85,779	88,291	89,413
8308	Eq Maint Cap Outlay Cost	46,419	0	0	46,000	42,000
8313	Risk Management Charges	355,851	255,226	255,226	303,412	310,191
8314	PD False Alarms	900	0	0	0	0
	Internal Service	1,313,444	1,073,218	1,073,218	1,777,590	1,191,120
	TOTAL DEPARTMENT	14,260,252	15,194,192	15,031,824	15,389,129	15,638,421
	Salary & Wages	10,312,368	10,833,562	10,762,968	11,110,493	11,198,525
	Fringe Benefits	1,402,733	1,574,967	1,535,580	1,808,365	1,956,094
	Materials & Supplies	579,321	532,500	519,242	485,822	485,822
	Fees & Services	404,769	448,720	426,451	446,725	446,725
	Other Contrib. & Charges	11,089	13,000	11,773	13,000	13,000
	Travel & Other Expenses	59,957	68,035	57,635	53,135	53,135
	Capital Outlays	176,571	650,190	644,957	294,000	294,000
	Internal Service	1,313,444	1,073,218	1,073,218	1,177,590	1,191,120
	TOTAL DEPARTMENT	14,260,252	15,194,192	15,031,824	15,389,129	15,638,421

what resources will be required for the execution of these plans. These columns are the action items for consideration and legislative approval and, once enacted into law, become the template against which the agency will be held responsible. Some executive budgets will report what the agency requested initially, along with the amount recommended by the executive; this one does not.

2. **The progress-report year.** The budget for 2003/2004 and 2004/2005 will have been considered during the 2002/2003 budget year. The 2002/2003 columns in this budget reports what was budgeted for that year and what the actual result is likely to be for the current year. (Frequently only the likely result for the current year is reported; the figures initially adopted are not reported.) Some budgets, particularly those developed in executive and legislative reviews, also report the amount and percentage of any difference between progress-year and budget-year amounts. This one does not, but you can be certain that those changes were checked by those reviewing the budget.

3. **The final-report year.** This column reports the fiscal figures for the most recently completed fiscal year, 2001/2002 in this illustration. These figures provide a standard for comparison.

4. **Out years.** Some budgets (but not the one in Figure 2–3) also carry figures for out years, or years beyond the budget year in the request cycle.

The federal government now uses the budget year plus four out years in executive budget presentations.[10] The longer horizon reflects a concern with future implications of fiscal decisions, even though specific actions on those figures seldom will be taken in that particular cycle. Nor should those fiscal choices be locked in early; priorities, needs, and fiscal circumstances may well change.

Later chapters explore budgets designed to capture other parts of the flow leading from purchase of inputs to delivery of the services demanded by the citizenry. In particular, budgets can be organized around the activities that agencies undertake or around the outputs or results that the agency provides.[11] Either of these alternative classifications provides greater information for public choices than does the traditional input budget. However, behind any budget format lurks some "grocery list" of inputs that will be needed for the service plan, regardless of the vision or strategy that has produced that plan. Hence, the input classification is the most basic and durable format of all. In many small governments and nonprofit organizations, it is the only classification structure for the budget.

---

[10]The individual department requests, however, reflect only the budget year. The 2003 federal budget ended the 10-year window that had been used since 1997. In the middle of 1996, the Congressional Budget Office started doing 10-year budget estimates. Nobody but politicians and the media took these seriously, particularly the more distant years of the estimating horizon. It is hard enough to get reasonable estimates for the 5 years required in laws establishing budget procedures. Rudolph G. Penner, "Dealing with Uncertain Budget Forecasts," *Public Budgeting & Finance* XXII (Spring 2002): 1–18.

[11]The Tempe budget also categorizes spending by cost centers within each department, so that it can identify the cost of providing each of its primary services to the public, and it provides substantial performance information.

Functions of the Budget Process

Governments exist to provide services. The budget process provides a time for decisions about the services desired by the public and the options available to the government for providing these services. A traditional expectation is that properly working budget processes act to constrain government and to prevent public officials from stealing. Indeed, public budgeting in the United States developed at the municipal level to prevent thievery, pure and simple. Budgets should do that, but they should also do more, particularly in regard to seeing that governments fulfill their appropriate role in delivering the services demanded of them by businesses and individuals through choices made in the democratic process and that resources available to government are reasonably used. The process allocates resources among government activities and between government and private use. The great struggle that the budget process contains is between "needs" and "availability." On the one hand, the resources available to the government are limited by economic conditions and the extent to which the government is willing to apply its fiscal authority to draw revenue from the private economy. On the other hand, agencies and departments of government have commitments and opportunities to deliver services to the citizenry. Long-term fiscal sustainability—the ability of the government to maintain its operations without deterioration of services or dramatic increases in taxation—requires that actual spending be within resource availability. That means continuing tension, because opportunities for service always exceed resource availability. The budget process has to work that out as a part of the agenda for sustainability.[12]

Public financial managers expect budget procedures to (1) provide a framework for fiscal discipline and control, (2) facilitate allocation of government resources toward uses of highest strategic priority, and (3) encourage efficient and effective use of resources by public agencies as they implement public programs.[13] The procedures work through budget planning and development, budget deliberations, budget execution, and audit. The processes of analysis and management apply equally to government and nonprofit organizations, although they are usually more highly developed and more routine in governments.

1. **Fiscal discipline and control.** The expenditure-control function in budgeting involves restraining expenditures to the limits of available finance, ensuring that enacted budgets are executed, and preserving the legality of agency expenditures. The control function—making sure that expenditures agree with the legal intent of the legislature—helps develop information for cost estimates

[12]Many nations have instituted what are called *medium-termexpenditure frameworks (MTEF)* in an effort to provide this balancing of needs and availability over a 3- to 5-year horizon. The MTEF involves development of a top-down (from the central budget office or Ministry of Finance) resource constraint from a macroeconomic model, a bottom-up (from the agencies) estimation of the medium-term cost of delivering services according to current policies, and a reconciliation against government priorities. The framework feeds into the annual budget process to give better responsiveness to national priorities and some greater predictability of funding to agencies.

[13]*Public Expenditure Management Handbook* (Washington, D.C.: The World Bank, 1998), 17.

used in preparation of new budgets and in preserving audit trails after budget years are over.[14] Much of the control comes from within the spending unit, although monitored through the year. A post-expenditure audit is external. Budgeting and appropriating given dollar amounts to purchase given quantities of goods or services simplifies the determination of whether legislative intent has been implemented during the year: Does the agency have resources to meet the appropriation, and were purchases by the agency made according to the appropriation? If the appropriation was for the purchase of 10 tons of gravel, was that gravel actually purchased and delivered? Questions of this simple but critical nature served as the impetus for development of public budgeting.

One of the great challenges of creating a more responsive government may involve restructuring the notion of control. Unfortunately, the definition of accountability in government has remained relatively constant over the past 50 years: "limit bureaucratic discretion through compliance with tightly drawn rules and regulations."[15] If government is to be flexible, responsive, and innovative, narrow control and accountability to the legislature and within the operating agencies almost certainly must change from internal operations to external results.

2. **Response to strategic priorities.** The budget process should work to deliver financing to the programs and projects that are of greatest current importance to the citizenry. Governments face many fruitful opportunities for providing useful services. Their resources are limited, so they must choose, recognizing that their choices both influence and must be influenced by community, state, and national environments. They should not have to work around legal or administrative constraints that protect certain activities, regardless of their relative importance. All resources controlled by the government should be available to respond to the legitimate demands of the country; the competition for those scarce resources ought to be balanced, with outcomes driven by the return from the competing uses, not barriers that hinder allocation of those funds. Budget planning can be used as a decision-making tool for ensuring continuity of activities, developing new programs, and allocating resources among government activities. In developing plans, it is critical, although often difficult, to focus on the services government provides, rather than on the resources governments buy.

3. **Efficient implementation of the budget.** Budgets also serve as a tool to increase managerial control of operating units and to improve efficiency in agency operations. This function focuses on government performance and ought not dwell on inputs the unit has purchased. The important concern is the relationship between the resources used and the public services performed by

---

[14]An audit trail is a sequence of documents—invoices, receipts, canceled checks, and so forth—that allows an outside observer to trace transactions involving appropriated money: when the money was spent and who received it, when purchases were delivered and what price was paid, how the purchases were cared for and used, and how those purchases were finally deposited.

[15]Paul C. Light, *Monitoring Government: Inspectors General and the Search for Accountability* (Washington, D.C.: Brookings Institution, 1993), 12.

the unit. The public budget—as in a private business plan—serves as the control device for the government and identifies operational efficiency. For this purpose, the agency must consider what measurable activities it performs, an often difficult, but seldom impossible, task. The process should induce agencies to economize in their operations, identify the services of greatest importance to the populations they serve, choose best available technologies and strategies for delivering those services, and respond quickly when service demands or operating conditions change. Simple husbandry of inputs or resources purchased by the agency is important, but is not enough.

The budget process should enforce aggregate fiscal discipline, facilitate allocation of government resources to areas of greatest current public priority, and encourage efficient agency operations. Some features that help to realize those promises from the process are (1) realistic forecasts of receipts and other data useful for development of budgets; (2) comprehensive and complete application of the budget system to all parts of the government; (3) transparency and accountability as the budget is developed, approved, and executed; (4) hard and enforced constraints on resources provided agencies, but with considerable flexibility in how agencies may use them in service delivery; (5) use of objective performance criteria for agency and government accountability; (6) reconciliation between planned and executed budgets; and (7) capable and fairly compensated government officials to prevent susceptibility to corruption.[16] The budget must also be forward looking, in the sense that, while being prepared and adopted for the short fiscal period of only a single year or two, it sets the stage for years in the future. Therefore, the public is best served if the budget is formulated within a medium-term economic framework of 4 or 5 years, so that the chances of fiscal sustainablility will be improved.

The Budget Cycle

Recurring (and overlapping) events in the budgeting and spending process constitute the budget cycle. Although specific activities differ among governments, any government that separates powers between the executive and legislative branches shows many of the elements outlined here.[17] The four major stages of the cycle—executive preparation, legislative consideration, execution, and audit and evaluation—are considered in turn. The cycles are in fact linked across the years because the audit-evaluation findings provide important data for preparation of future budgets. The four phases recur, so at any time an operating agency is in different

[16]Ed Campos and Sanjay Pradhan, *The Impact of Budgetary Institutions on Expenditure Outcomes: Binding Governments to Fiscal Performance,* Working Papers Series, Policy Research Department, The World Band (Washington, D.C., 1996).

[17]A parliamentary government would not neatly fit this cycle, because there is no separation between executive and legislative roles—the legislative leader is the chief executive. But the budget still must be prepared and adopted.

phases of different budget years. Suppose an agency is on an October 1 to September 31 fiscal year, and it is March 2007. That agency would be in the execution phase of fiscal year 2007 (fiscal years are normally named after their end year). It would likely be in the legislative-consideration phase of fiscal year 2008, in the preparation phase of fiscal year 2009, and in the audit phase of fiscal 2006 and prior years. Thus, the budget cycle is both continuous and overlapping, as Figure 2–4 illustrates.

The federal fiscal year begins in October; many local governments have fiscal years beginning in January; all state governments except Alabama, Michigan, New York, and Texas start fiscal years in July. The fiscal year in Alabama and Michigan starts in October, New York has an April start, and Texas's is September.

Executive Preparation

Several separate and distinct steps constitute the executive-preparation phase. At the start of the preparation phase, the chief executive instructs all departments and units of government to prepare their agency requests. These instructions (sometimes labeled the "call for estimates") include a timetable for budget submissions, instructions for developing requests, indication of what funds are likely to be available (either in the form of an agency ceiling or in terms of a percentage increase), and overall priority directions from the executive. (For the federal government, these instructions appear in Circular A-11, which is issued by the Office of Management and Budget.) They may also, but not necessarily, provide forecasts of input price increases, service population trends, and so on. An important element in developing the instruction is a forecast of the economic climate and what it means in terms of revenue and expenditure claims on the government. Difficult

Figure 2–4
Phases of a Budget Cycle

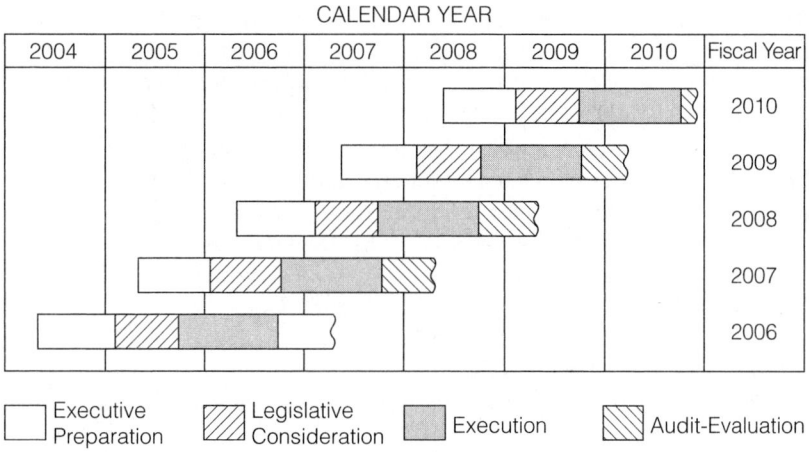

economic conditions usually mean an instruction with limited prospects for expansion of existing programs or the development of new programs, and possibly instructions to reduce spending.

The agency request is built on an agency plan for service in an upcoming year (the agency response to public demands for service) and an agency forecast of conditions in the upcoming year (the group of conditions influencing the agency but not subject to agency control). These forecasts ought to be best estimates of conditions in the future. They are not necessarily projections, or simple extensions, of current conditions into the future. For example, a state highway department request for snow-removal funds would involve a forecast of the number of snowy days and a planned response for handling that snow. For any snow forecast, the agency request will vary depending on how promptly the agency responds to snowfall (after trace snowfall, after 1 inch, after 3 inches, etc.), which roadways will be cleared (arterial, secondary, residential, etc.), and so on. The forecast does not dictate the request. Some agencies build their plans on inputs (the highway department bought 120 tons of road salt last year, so it will request about that amount for the budget year); this approach makes changes in service-delivery methods and practices difficult. The public-service demands will be forecasts, but agency responses will be plans formulated from decisions and forecasts.

An agency develops not only a cost estimate for providing the services it plans to deliver during the upcoming spending period but also a narrative justification for the requests. The estimate and its justification reflect the large number of program decisions the agency has made. The chief executive's budget office gathers the requests made by many operating agencies and consolidates these requests. The budget office reviews budget requests for consistency with the policies of the chief executive, for reasonable cost and logical content, and for total consistency with spending directions. Often there are administrative hearings for reconciliation of an agency request and budget office adjustments. Finally, the executive budget document is transmitted to the legislature for its consideration. Law usually establishes the date of transmission to the legislature, so submission schedules within the administration have to build to that date.

The budget document, or executive budget, incorporates all agency requests into a government-wide request or plan. The requests by the agencies have been accumulated and aggregated according to the policy plan of the chief executive. Some legislative bodies, including the U.S. Congress, propose their own alternative budgets. Agency requests will almost always be reduced by the chief executive to produce an overall executive plan. And, of course, the expectation is that the vision or priorities of the chief executive will dominate the direction of the final plan. As is discussed later, the substantial changes made in agency requests before proposals are seen by the legislature reflect differences in attitudes and service clienteles of the agencies and the chief executive.

The executive budget is a message of policy; the financial numbers on spending, revenues, and deficits or surpluses are driven by those policies. Dall Forsythe, who once served as New York state budget director, emphasizes the point for governors: "If you cannot use the budget to state your goals and move state government in the direction you advocate, you are not likely to make much progress towards those goals."[18] That message applies to any chief executive, whether mayor, president, or prime minister. For the budget process to meet its expectations, the executive presentation for legislative deliberation should (1) be comprehensive (i.e., cover all government revenues and expenditures), (2) be transparent (i.e., present a clear trail from details to aggregate summaries of revenue and expenditure so that the implications of policy proposals and operating assumptions are clear), (3) establish accountability (i.e., clarify who will be responsible for funds, in what amount, and for what purpose), (4) avoid revenue dedications (earmarks) or other long-term commitments that could hinder response to new priorities or problems, and (5) establish as clearly as possible for what public purpose (i.e., desired result, not administrative input) the funds will be spent.

Legislative Consideration

In a government with distinct legislative and executive branches, the budget document is transmitted to the legislature for debate and consideration. The legislature typically splits that budget into as many parts as appropriation bills will ultimately be passed and submits those parts to legislative subcommittees. This consideration usually begins with the lower house of a bicameral legislature. In subcommittee hearings, agencies defend their budget requests, often calling attention to differences between their initial request and what appears in the executive budget. After the lower house has approved the appropriation, the upper house goes through a similar hearing process. When both houses have approved appropriations, a conference committee from the two houses prepares unified appropriations bills for final passage by both houses. The bills are then submitted to the chief executive. Appropriation acts are the outcome of the legislative process. These laws provide funds for operating agencies to spend in a specified fashion in the budget year. The initial requests by the agency reflect the plans of that agency; appropriation converts these plans (or portions of them) into law.

The chief executive normally must sign the appropriation bill before it becomes law, and thus gives operating agencies financial resources to provide services, but not all executives have the same options. Some executives may sign parts of the bill while rejecting others (called *item veto power*); others must approve it all or reject it all, thus returning the bill to the legislature. Most state governors have item veto power, but the president does not. Some observers feel the item veto provides a useful screening of projects that political clout, rather than merit, has inserted in the appropriation bill. Others are skeptical about such power, because of its possible use for executive vendettas against selected groups, legislators, or agencies. Veto powers are discussed in greater detail in the next chapter.

---

[18]Dall W. Forsythe, *Memos to the Governor, An Introduction to State Budgeting* (Washington, D.C.: Georgetown University Press, 1997), 84–85.

Execution

During execution, agencies carry out their approved budgets. Appropriations are spent, and services are delivered. The approved budget becomes an important device to monitor spending activity. Although there are other important managerial concerns during execution, spending must proceed in a manner consistent with appropriation laws. Law typically forbids (often with criminal sanctions) agencies from spending more money than has been appropriated. The Anti-Deficiency Act of 1906 is the governing federal law; similar laws apply at state and local levels and in other countries with well-developed fiscal systems. Spending less than the appropriation, while a possible sign of efficient operation, may well mean that anticipated services have not been delivered or that agency budget requests were needlessly high. Thus, finance officers must constantly monitor the relationship between actual expenditures and planned/approved expenditures (the appropriation) during the fiscal year. Central budget offices (the Office of Management and Budget for the federal government) normally handle the monitoring and release of funds during execution of the budget. Most governments have some preexpenditure audit system to determine the validity of expenditures within the appropriation and some controls to keep expenditures within actual resources available.

Spending is the direct result of appropriations made to carry out the service envisioned in the agency's initial budget plan.[19] However, because expenditures can involve the purchase of resources for use both in the present and in the future, it would generally be incorrect to expect the expenditure to equal the current cost of providing government services. Some of the current expenditure will provide services in later periods. (In simplest terms, part of the road salt purchased this year may be used next year, but much of the difference between expenditure and service cost will be caused by purchase of capital assets, such as buildings, trucks, computers, etc.) The cost of government would equal the amount of resources used, or consumed, during the current period—some resources coming from expenditure in that period and some from previous expenditures. Focus on expenditure thus renders an inaccurate view of the cost of government. Figure 2–5 outlines the flow of transactions and accompanying management information requirements between budget authority and service cost: (1) budget authority provides funding (the appropriation law approves agency Z's plan to publish an information bulletin), (2) obligation occurs when an order is placed (agency Z orders paper from business A), (3) inventories are recorded when materials are delivered (business A delivers the paper to agency Z), (4) outlay occurs when the bill is paid (agency Z pays for the paper), and (5) cost occurs when the materials are used (agency Z prints an information bulletin on the paper).

Some reference to the federal structure may help clarify. Budget authority—provided through appropriation, borrowing authority, or contract authority—allows agencies to enter into commitments that will result in immediate or future

[19]Not all expenditure, however, results from appropriation. This complication is explained later.

Figure 2–5
Financial Information for Management

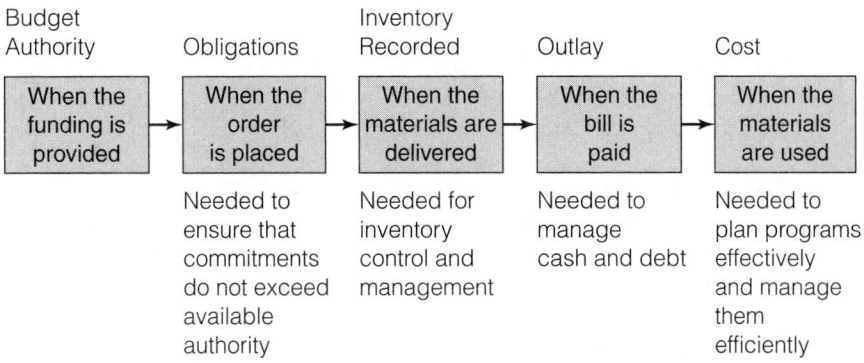

spending.[20] Budget authority defines the upper limit for agency spending without obtaining additional authority. Figure 2–6 illustrates the relationship between budget authority and outlays envisioned in the 2007 federal budget. The budget plans outlays of $2,770 billion. Most of the outlays are based on proposals in this budget ($2,206 billion), but $564 billion (20 percent of the total) is based on unspent

Figure 2–6
Relationship of Budget Authority to Outlays for 2007

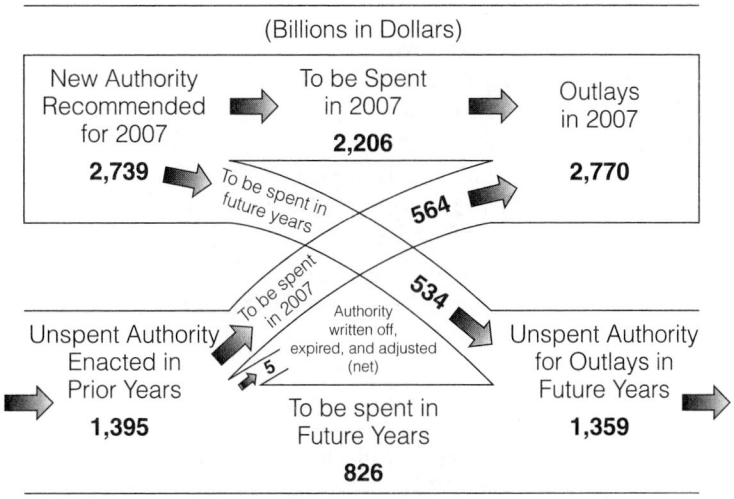

[20]Borrowing authority permits an agency to borrow funds and to spend the proceeds for qualified purposes. Contract authority allows an agency to make obligations before appropriations have been passed.

authority enacted in prior years. Therefore, budget authority in a particular year differs from outlays for the year; outlays may result from either present or previous budget authority.

Operating agencies should have managerial flexibility in the use of funds, allowing them to change the particular mix of inputs they purchase, so long as they can provide the level of service to the public that was envisioned in the adopted budget. Agencies almost certainly know more about new technologies, changes in prices of inputs that could allow cost savings, and emerging problems than does the legislature or the budget agency. Hence, locking agencies to the line-item details of the proposed and adopted budget usually inhibits efficiency and innovation. Ideally, the operating agency should be responsible for budget totals and agency results, not the details of exactly how money was spent (within laws of theft and corruption).

Audit and Evaluation

An audit is an "examination of records, facilities, systems, and other evidence to discover or verify desired information."[21] The audit seeks to discover deviations from accepted standards and instances of illegality, inefficiency, irregularity, and ineffectiveness early enough to take corrective action, to hold violators accountable, and to take steps to prevent further losses. The audit may be internal (in other words, the auditors are subordinate to the heads of the departments being audited) or external (the auditors are outside the structure being audited and, for governments, are ultimately responsible to the citizenry). In general, the auditors verify the assertions made by the audited entity. Information is documented on the basis of a sample of transactions and other activities of the entity—a judgment about purchasing practices, for instance, is made from a review of a sample of transactions, not from an examination of all invoices.

Postexpenditure audits determine compliance with appropriations and report findings to the legislature (or to a judicial body if laws have been violated).[22] At the federal level, the Government Accountability Office (GAO) supervises audits of agencies, although the actual auditing is typically done by agency personnel.[23] States frequently have elected auditors or independent agencies that audit state agencies and local governments. Local governments sometimes have audits done by independent accounting firms as well as by government bodies, although some such governments have not frequently had independent audits.[24]

---

[21]Peter F. Rousmaniere, *Local Governments Auditing—A Manual for Public Officials* (New York: Council on Municipal Performance, 1980), 83.

[22]A preexpenditure audit ascertains the legality or appropriateness of making payment. Such an analysis often occurs, for instance, prior to the delivery of payroll checks.

[23]The international group of audit bodies is the International Organization of Supreme Audit Institutions (ITOSAI). This group establishes international principles of organization and operation of these supreme audit institutions. The GAO is the U.S. member.

[24]Federal general revenue sharing required an audit at least once in 3 years for general-purpose governments receiving such money. The aid program is long gone, but the tradition of regular audits fortunately continues.

Government audits may be classified according to their objectives into two types: financial and performance. Financial audits include financial statement audits, which "determine (1) whether the financial statements of an audited entity present fairly the financial position, results of operations, and cash flows or changes in financial position in accordance with generally accepted accounting principles, and (2) whether the entity has complied with laws and regulations for those transactions and events that may have a material effect on the financial statements;"[25] and financial-related audits, which "include determining (1) whether financial reports and related items, such as elements, accounts, or funds are fairly presented, (2) whether financial information is presented in accordance with established or stated criteria, and (3) whether the entity has adhered to specific financial compliance requirements."[26] These audits test financial records to determine whether the funds were spent legally, receipts were properly recorded and controlled, and financial records and statements are complete and reliable. They concentrate on establishing compliance with appropriation law and on determining whether financial reports prepared by the operating agency are accurate and reliable. The financial audit still must determine, however, whether there has been theft by government employees or their confederates, although this part of the task should be minor because of protections created by controls within the agency (internal controls).

Performance audits similarly encompass two classes of audits: economy and efficiency audits, which seek to determine "(1) whether the entity is acquiring, protecting, and using its resources (such as personnel, property, and space) economically and efficiently, (2) the causes of inefficiencies or uneconomical practices, and (3) whether the entity has complied with laws and regulations concerning matters of economy and efficiency;"[27] and program audits, which examine "(1) the extent to which the desired results or benefits established by the legislature or other authorizing body are being achieved, (2) the effectiveness of organizations, programs, activities, or functions, and (3) whether the entity has complied with laws and regulations applicable to the program."[28] Economy and efficiency audits might consider questions of procurement, safeguarding of resources, duplication of effort, use of staff, efficiency of operating procedures, management to minimize cost of delivering appropriate quantity and quality of service, compliance with laws governing use of resources, and systems for measuring and reporting performance. Program audits emphasize the extent to which desired results are being achieved, what factors might inhibit satisfactory performance, whether there might be lower-cost alternatives for obtaining the desired results, and whether there may be conflict or overlap with other programs. Some states link performance audits with sunset reviews: "a set schedule for legislative review of programs and agencies and an automatic termination of those programs and agencies unless affirmative legislative

---

[25]U.S. General Accounting Office, *Government Auditing Standards,* 1998 rev. (Washington, D.C.: GPO, 1998), 2-1.
[26]Ibid., 2-2.
[27]Ibid., 2-3.
[28]Ibid.

action is taken to reauthorize them. Thus, the 'sun sets' on agencies and programs."[29] States with such legislation typically include a performance audit as part of the preparation for action on agencies or programs eligible for termination.

A simple example may illustrate the focus of each audit. Consider a state highway department appropriation to purchase road salt for snow and ice removal. A financial audit would consider whether the agency had an appropriation for salt purchased, whether salt purchased was actually delivered, whether approved practices were followed in selecting a supplier, and whether agency reports showed the correct expenditure on salt. An efficiency and economy audit would consider whether the salt inventory is adequately protected from the environment, whether the inventory is adequate or excessive, and whether other methods of selecting a supplier would lower the cost. A program audit would consider whether the prevailing level of winter highway clearing is an appropriate use of community resources and whether approaches other than spreading salt would be less costly to the community.

When all audit work is completed, the budget cycle is complete for that fiscal year. In a complementary fashion, the federal inspector-general system in eighteen departments or agencies works within units to identify fraud, waste, or abuse under 1976 and 1978 legislation, and reports findings to department or agency heads and, eventually, to Congress. The system has potential as an adjunct to the audits conducted for Congress by the GAO.

Governmental Accounting and Financial Reporting

Proper accounting and reporting practices make government finances more transparent to constituencies, including public officials, the public, and the investment community. They should improve accountability to the public, including allowing the public to see whether current revenues are sufficient to cover current expenditures; they should make it possible to evaluate the operating results of the government for the year, including determining how financial resources are obtained and how they are spent; and they should help with assessment of the level of services that the government can afford to provide, including supplying information about the financial condition of the government. Important topics in accounting for governments include accounting and reporting standards, use of fund accounting, and the basis of accounting.

Standards. Independent authorities or boards establish the standards (or rules) for accounting and financial reporting; in the United States the Financial Accounting Standards Board (FASB) sets the standards for the private sector and the Government Accounting Standards Board (GASB) sets them for the public sector. Similar bodies do the work in other countries. These standards establish the appropriate

[29]Advisory Commission on Intergovernmental Relations, "Sunset Legislation and Zero-Based Budgeting." *Information Bulletin*, no. 76-5 (December 1976): 1.

practices that the accounting system will implement and allow any interested party to understand the finances of the government and to make certain comparisons of finances across governments. However, the accounts, even when prepared according to recognized standards, are not statements of scientific validity, as anyone even slightly familiar with the Enron experience will understand. At best, they seek fair representation, not unassailable truth.

The accounting system allows the manager to assemble, analyze, and report data for the essential work expected of the budget process. The data must be complete, accurate, timely, and understandable for all public constituencies. The focus of the system is on revenues and expenditures, on financial balances, and on financial obligations of the government. The financial reporting system is expected to provide understandability (reports should be sensible to the general public as well as to experts), reliability (reports should be comprehensive, verifiable, and without bias), relevance (information provided should meet the needs of users), timeliness (reports should be issued shortly after the close of the fiscal year), consistency (the basis should be the same for all transactions and across fiscal years), and comparability (it should be able to compare reports across governments). The accounting system is expected to provide the framework for financial control, but it is also expected to be a ripe source of information to government decision-makers and the public.

The full accounting system combines several elements:

1. **Source documents:** the receipts, invoices, and other original details of transactions.
2. **Journals:** a chronological summary list of all transactions.
3. **Ledgers:** reports at varying levels of detail that present the balance in any revenue, expenditure, or other account.
4. **Procedures and controls:** the forms and instructions for classifying, recording, and reporting financial transactions in the source documents, journals, and ledgers.

Government accounting focuses on cash flows and improved transparency, control, and accountability to constituencies, rather than the profit and loss emphasis of private-sector accounting. This difference brings several normal practices in government accounting:

1. Governments use fund accounting to permit compliance with legal restrictions on the use of revenue and to facilitate strong financial administration of multiple government operations.
2. Debt is segregated. Bonds to be repaid from general financial resources of the government are reported as obligations of the entire government; bonds to be repaid from specific funds are reported as such.
3. The budget of a government is at the heart of its system of "checks and balances." Demonstrating compliance with the adopted budget is a critical part of the accounting and reporting process. In the private sector, budgets are more in the order of an initial flexible plan, not an adopted appropriation law. Nonprofit organization budgets are somewhere in between.

Governments have historically made little attempt to account for fixed assets in their financial records. They built an infrastructure for the operations of general government, but did not account for its condition in their financial records. That meant that any balance sheet of the government's assets did not accurately portray the true financial situation of the government. It did not reflect depreciation and deferred maintenance of these critical assets. Accordingly, financial reports could portray a misleading sense of the condition of the government: Failure to maintain infrastructure eventually adds to the costs of operation, can lead to more borrowing than would be otherwise necessary, can cause previous capital investment to be wasted if not adequately protected, can cause economic development in the community to be impeded because of low-quality government services, and misleads about the total cost of providing services. A new GASB standard—GASB 34—now requires larger governments to account for these infrastructure costs in their accounts, and the standard will eventually extend to all governments.[30] The change is driven by the effort to ensure that governments provide information about the full cost of providing government services, something that the omission of a reflection of cost from the existing infrastructure has prevented in the past.

Funds. In private-sector accounting, a single set of accounts reports all material transactions and details of financial condition. Government accounting segregates funds or accounts because there are legal restrictions on the use of government revenues and on the purposes of government expenditure. Mixing money prevents a clear demonstration of compliance with restrictions. Therefore, distinct funds ("cookie jar accounts") provide the necessary controls.

Governments prepare financial reports in a number of separate funds or accounting entities that are expected to be self-balancing. Generally accepted accounting principles (GAAP) define funds to be interrelated accounts that record assets (revenues) and liabilities (expenditures/obligations) related to a specific purpose. Municipal accounting divides funds into three basic types: governmental funds, proprietary funds, and fiduciary funds, each with subcategories.

1. Governmental Funds
   a. General fund: general revenues to the government, including taxes, fines, licenses, and fees. Most taxes and expenditures are in this fund. There is only one general fund.
   b. Special revenue funds: accounts for operations of government that are supported by dedicated revenue sources—dedicated taxes, fees, or intergovernmental assistance. Transportation trust funds are one example.

---

[30]A symposium in *Public Budgeting & Finance* analyzes the several major implications of the new reporting model produced by Statement 34: Robert S. Kravchuk and William R. Voorhees, The New Governmental Financial Reporting Model under GSAB Statement No. 34: An Emphasis on Accountability;" Terry K. Patton and David R. Bean, "The Why and How of the New Capital Asset Reporting Requirement;" Earl R. Wilson and Susan C. Kattelus, "The Implications of GASB's New Reporting Model for Municipal Bond Analysts and Manager;" John H. Engstrom and Donald E. Tidrick, "Audit Issues Related to GASB Statement No. 34;" and James L. Chan, "The Implications of GASB Statement No. 34 for Public Budgeting," *Public Budgeting & Finance* XXI (Fall 2001).

c. Debt service funds: accounts for payment of interest and repayment of principal due on long-term debt.
d. Capital projects funds: includes resources used for construction and acquisition of capital facilities or major capital equipment purchases. The fund is dissolved when the project is completed.
e. Permanent funds: accounts for resources held in trust, where earnings but not principal may be used for public purposes.

2. Proprietary Funds
a. Enterprise fund: includes the financial records of self-supporting operations, like water or sewer utilities. Accounts for business-type activities of the entity, which are operated for general benefit of the public but are expected to support themselves from their own revenue.
b. Internal service fund: includes the financing of goods or services provided by one agency or department to other agencies or departments of the government on a cost-reimbursement basis, like the operations of a motor vehicle maintenance department.

3. Fiduciary Funds: account for assets held by a government as a trustee for others. Fiduciary funds include (1) pension funds that are used to pay public employees' retirement benefits and (2) trust funds that are used to pay for management of resources and the use of which is usually tightly controlled.

Governments prepare a comprehensive annual financial report (CAFR) that brings together all funds operated under the framework of that government. This report gives a complete overview of finances, prepared according to GAAP, and is critically interesting to those involved in public capital markets.

In a mature fiscal system, an independent auditor prepares an evaluation of government financial operations at the end of the fiscal year. If the auditor renders a so-called "clean opinion," then the way that the government prepared its financial report is considered to have been fair and accurate. Among other things, the auditor's report requires that the agency's statements be prepared according to GAAP. Clean budget processes also bring all government operations together, regardless of the fund structure, in order to preserve the comprehensiveness of public financial decisions.

Accounting Basis: Cash or Accrual. The accounting basis—the method of matching revenues and expenditures over time—may be cash (revenue recorded when cash is received, expenditure recorded when cash payment is completed), full accrual (revenue recorded when earned, expenses recorded when liability incurred), or modified accrual (expenditure recorded when liability incurred, revenues recorded when cash received).

The traditional standard, cash accounting, records money inflows when received and spending when money is disbursed, generally following the flows of the governmental checkbook. Those flows can substantially lag changes in the true condition of the government, and capital assets (buildings, highways, etc.) require a cash payment when they are acquired, but no purchase payments over their many years of useful life. GAAP requires a modified accrual basis for accounting, in which inflows are called revenues, not the receipts of cash accounting, and outflows are called expenditures, rather than the disbursements of cash accounting. The revenue measure requires an estimate of taxes owed but not yet paid; the expenditure measure requires inclusion of purchases for which payment has not yet been made. Expenditure is recorded when liability is recognized, generally meaning when the good or service is delivered to the purchaser and normally well before any check is written to pay for the purchase. GAAP also requires that individual government operations expected to be self-supporting use full accrual accounting, the method of the private sector. In full accrual, outflows, called expenses, are recorded in the period in which benefit is received from the resource.[31]

The accrual basis provides more information for decision makers and for managers, particularly in regard to the distribution of cost over time, and is not susceptible to end-of-year cash manipulations. It has the capacity to place costs properly in the relevant period. Only a handful of national governments around the world prepare financial statements on an accrual basis, although that is the evolving pattern for American state and local governments, and even fewer provide for depreciation of their capital assets in their accounts. The cash basis controls flows of cash and does not distribute cost accurately to periods, but it is less complex than the accrual system and is less subject to fundamental manipulation for impact on financial statements. As *The Economist* summarizes, cash "is far harder to disguise or invent."[32] Either system can be functional, depending on the needs of the entity.

Comprehensive Annual Report. The CAFR is a general-purpose report produced to supply the information needs of public officials, citizens, auditors, and investors. It is expected to be a publicly available document that encompasses all funds and accounts controlled by the governmental entity. It is comprehensive in depth and breadth, reported in sufficient detail to provide full disclosure, and inclusive of all funds and accounts. The report includes three sections: an introductory section that seeks to explain the structure of the government, its nature and scope of activities, and the specific details of its legal environment; a financial section that provides a comprehensive overview of the government's operations and includes an independent auditor's report on the finances; and a statistical section that provides details on government operations and its major financial trends. The CAFR should provide a comprehensive and reliable single source of information about the finances and structure of the government with financial data presented according to generally accepted accounting principles, so that an external observer can understand the situation of that government without having to do additional research on definitions or context.

---

[31]Accrual accounting applies in the preparation of financial reports. Accrual concepts can also be applied in the budget process. Accrual budgeting is used in some countries, including Australia, New Zealand, the Netherlands, and the United Kingdom, and partly used in many more. M. Peter van der Hoek, "From Cash to Accrual Budgeting and Accounting in the Public Sector: The Dutch Experience," *Public Budgeting & Finance* 24 (Spring 2005): 32–45 and Jon R. Blondal, "Issues in Accrual Budgeting," *OECD Journal on Budgeting* 4(No. 1, 2004): 103–119.

[32]"Badly in Need of Repair," *The Economist*, 362 (May 4, 2002): 67.

Budgets and Political Strategies

Budget decisions, both spending and taxing, are intensely political. They do not spin out of an analytic "black box" programmed by purveyors of information technology and program analysis. Presidents, governors, mayors, and other public executives cannot ignore political forces when they develop their fiscal proposals, and legislators certainly do not ignore these forces as they pass budget laws.[33] Understanding the budget process is vital for shaping public policy, and so is the analysis necessary to innovate and implement programs most likely to be in the public interest. But budget proposals do need to be delivered and defended in a political environment: Truth and beauty alone will not save the day. Hence, an understanding of some strategic behavior is important for practitioners of the budget process.

The Incrementalist Insight

The incrementalist concept holds that budgeting is mainly a process of political strategy. It downplays the public-service delivery attitude of models from public finance economics and the attempts at rationality from policy analysis. As outlined by Aaron Wildavsky and Naomi Caiden,

> The largest determining factor of this year's budget is last year's. Most of each budget is the product of previous decisions. The budget may be conceived of as an iceberg; by far the largest part lies below the surface, outside the control of anyone. Many items are standard, simply reenacted each year unless there is a special reason to challenge them. Long-range commitments have been made, and this year's share is scooped out of the total and included as part of the annual budget . . . At any one time, after past commitments are paid for, a rather small percentage—seldom larger than 30 percent, often smaller than 5—is within the realm of anybody's (including congressional and Budget Bureau) discretion as a practical matter.
>
> Budgeting is incremental, not comprehensive. The beginning of wisdom about an agency budget is that it is almost never actively reviewed as a whole every year, in the sense of reconsidering the value of all existing programs as compared to all possible alternatives. Instead, it is based on last year's budget with special attention to a narrow range of increases or decreases. General agreement on past budgetary decisions combined with years of accumulated experience and specialization allows those who make the budget to be concerned with relatively small increments to an existing base. Their

[33]Natural disasters are about as nonpolitical as can be—hurricanes and tornados, for example, are indifferent to political affiliation of their victims. However, research shows that rates of disaster declarations are higher in states of greater electoral importance, the rate of disaster declaration is higher in election years than in non-election years, and states with Congressional representation on the committees with oversight over the Federal Emergency Management Agency receive larger relief payments than states lacking that voice. Even with natural disasters, spending is driven by politics. Molly D. Castelazo and Thomas A. Garrett, "In the Rubble of Disaster, Politicians Find Economic Incentives," *The Regional Economist*, July 2003: 10–11, summarize several studies of disaster declarations and payments.

> attention is focused on a small number of items over which the budgetary battle is fought. Political reality, budget officials say, restricts attention to items they can do something about—a few new programs and possible cuts in old ones.[34]

Dramatic changes in federal expenditure programs, beginning with the end of the Cold War, the Republican Contract with America, the beginning of wars in Iraq and Afghanistan, the Katrina hurricane disaster, and other political changes in the recent past have raised some questions about whether the federal budget process is all as simple as Wildavsky and Caiden claim. But the facts remain that some policies—and resulting expenditure implications—do remain in place over the years; that most spending agencies at all levels of government do begin their new budget development by considering their approved budgets and the changes that should be made to them to adjust to new operating conditions; that budget comparisons in central budget offices, in legislative committees, and in the media are made between the proposed and prior-year budgets; and that the most rational place to get insights about the near future is from the immediate past. Information from looking at incremental change—positive or negative, big or little—ought not be ignored simply because there have been major shifts in the direction of government spending, especially federal. Looking at change is a tool, not a religion, after all. Indeed, some states and many local governments build budgets from percentage increments to the historic budget base (the prior-year budget) in accord with some notion of fair shares to each agency. In many administrative systems, the base is assumed when the next budget cycle begins.

Roles, Visions, and Incentives

Service-delivery choices in the budget process involve several roles, each with different approaches and biases. Participants in the budget process recognize and expect those approaches and are aware of the errors, incentives, and organizational blind spots inherent in each. The major attitude orientations are those of operating agencies, the office of the chief executive, and the legislature. All participants in the budget process seek to provide service to the public without waste. Each, however, works from different perspectives, resulting in differences of incentives and different practical definitions of that objective. A full understanding of the budget process obviously requires recognition of those roles.

1. **Operating agencies.** Operating agencies spend money for the delivery of government services. These agencies focus on the clientele they serve. It is unreasonable to expect an agency to be concerned with services provided by other agencies or to be interested in relative priorities among other agency services. The agency probably is not much concerned with comparisons of service cost with service value. The agency recognizes the value of services it provides to its clients and ordinarily tries to increase those services, regardless of overall

[34]Aaron Wildavsky and Naomi Caiden, *The New Politics of the Budgetary Process,* 3rd ed. (New York: Longman, 1997), 45.

budget conditions of the government. There will be a virtually limitless expanse of service opportunities, many of which go unfunded simply because other uses of public resources are of higher priority to those making fiscal choices. Agencies, however, seldom recognize those competing uses and often complain about their own lack of resources. Large agencies have both operating people who have little direct contact with the budget and budget people who have little direct contact with service delivery. Both groups, however, can be expected to have essentially the same point of view and clientele orientation. Operating agencies usually have identifiable proponents in the legislature—particular people who support the agency in hearings and in committee deliberations—but it is seldom appropriate for the agency to make direct proactive contact with those people in an effort to go around budget decisions made by the chief executive.

2. **Chief executive.** The office of the chief executive, whether that of president, governor, mayor, or whatever, has budget specialists acting on its behalf. The offices have different names (federal: Office of Management and Budget; state: state budget agencies; etc.), but their function and role are the same regardless of name and level. Analysts in that agency conform to the chief executive's priorities, not their own. The analysts pare down requests until total spending is within available revenue. Reductions are typical for items (1) not adequately justified, (2) not closely related to achieving the agency's objective, and (3) inconsistent with the chief executive's priorities. Whereas agencies have a clientele orientation, the chief executive (selected by the entire population) must balance the interests of the total population. Thus, priorities for an individual agency should not be expected to coincide with those of the chief executive because specific client-group priorities seldom match those of the general public. The interests of Corn Belt farmers, for instance, are not the same as those of the general population.

3. **Legislature.** The priorities of elected representatives can be expected to follow their constituents' priorities. Representatives are concerned with programs and projects serving the people who elect them. It is not reasonable to expect representatives to consistently take an overall view of agencies or agencies' programs. Representatives focus on a specific subset of the population, as is the case for operating agencies. Representatives, however, are oriented to a region rather than a specific client group. Most electoral regions do, of course, contain numerous client groups.

Forsythe offers another guide for chief executives in understanding the budgetary vision of legislators: "assume that legislators will apply a simple calculus in reviewing your budget proposals: they will want to take credit for spending increases and tax cuts, and they will want to avoid blame for budget cuts and tax increases."[35] The rule may not work all the time in every legislature—sometimes legislators take an ideological stand that all government is bad and happily cut spending—but

[35]Forsythe, *Memos,* 48.

otherwise it is a reasonable beginning assumption. It is particularly difficult to find legislators in favor of tax increases, especially of broad-based taxes that are not entwined in a complex package. Fiscal responsibility by itself seldom resonates.

Strategies

Budget proposals must be championed within operating agencies to be included in the agency request, within the administration for inclusion in the executive budget, and within the legislature to receive appropriation. A number of strategies, defined by Wildavsky and Caiden as "links between intentions and perceptions of budget officials and the political system that both imposes restraints and creates opportunities for them,"[36] are regularly used in these processes at every level of government and, indeed, in many different countries. They may also be considered devices for marketing and communicating the agency position.

Two strategies are always in use for the support of budget proposals. The first is cultivation of an active clientele for help in dealing with both the legislature and the chief executive. The clientele may be those directly served (as with farmers in a particular program provided by the Department of Agriculture) or those selling services to the particular agency (such as highway contractors doing business with a state department of highways). The best idea is to get the client groups to fight for the agency without having the agency instigate the action when the chief executive proposes the reduction; such instigation would look like insubordination, and the agency might ultimately suffer for it. Agencies unable to develop and mobilize such clientele find defending budget proposals difficult. The media can also deliver the support indirectly, but only with some preparations; agencies normally get coverage because they have bungled something.[37] A strategy can help: "Try to stay in the news with interesting stories that do not put the agency in a bad light and that help you maintain good relations with reporters. Then, when you come close to budget time, you can give them press stories that show how well the agency has done with limited resources, how well its pilot programs are working. Unstated is the premise that with a little more money you could do wonderful things and that if you are cut the public will lose valuable services."[38] The National Aeronautics and Space

---

[36]Wildavsky and Caiden, *New Politics,* 57.

[37]But if the media itself is involved as the agency, it becomes more interesting for mobilizing clientele. For example, in developing the fiscal 2006 appropriation bill for health, education, and labor programs, the House subcommittee proposed a reduction of about one-quarter of funds for the Corporation for Public Broadcasting and to end all funding within 2 years. Public radio and television stations mobilized their listeners to contact their Congressional representatives in a blitz of announcements throughout the nation. The full House voted by a wide margin to restore the funds even as other attractive programs in that bill—like community health care for the uninsured, literacy training for prisoners, maternity group home funding, etc.—were being eliminated. The fifty-seven programs being terminated did not have the capacity to mobilize clientele like public broadcasting did, regardless of their probable value to society. Shailagh Murray and Paul Farhi, "House Vote Spares Public Broadcasting Funds," *Washington Post* 24 June 2005: A6.

[38]Irene S. Rubin, "Strategies for the New Budgeting," in *Handbook of Public Administration,* 2nd ed., ed. James Perry (San Francisco: Jossey Bass, 1996), 286.

Administration (NASA) is a master at using the media to deliver its story through the budget process and serves as a model for any agency interested in learning how the strategy is played. With the exception of some reporters for the national papers of record—*The New York Times, The Washington Post,* and *The Wall Street Journal* in particular—journalists are remarkably uninformed about government finances and are extremely susceptible to manipulation by interest groups and agencies.

A second ubiquitous strategy that an agency may use is developing confidence in the agency among legislators and other government officials. To avoid being surprised in legislative hearings or by requests for information, agency administrators must show results in the reports they make and must tailor their message's complexity to their audience. All budget materials must clearly describe programs and intentions. Strategically, budget presenters must develop a small group of "talking points" that concisely portray their program. If results are not directly available, agencies may report internal process activities, such as files managed or surveys taken. Confidence is critical because, in the budget process, many elements of program defense must derive from the judgments of the administrators, not hard evidence. If confidence has been developed, those judgments will be trusted; if not, those judgments will be suspect.

Contingent strategies depend on the budget circumstances, particularly whether the discussion concerns (1) a reduction in agency programs below the present level of expenditures (the budget base), (2) an increase in the scope of agency programs, or (3) an expansion of agency programs to new areas. Some strategies seem strange or even preposterous; they are used, however, and should be recognized because the budget choices involved are vital parts of government action.[39] It cannot be emphasized enough, however, that strategy and clever rhetoric alone are not sufficient; they matter not at all if the basics of the budget—its logic, justifications, mathematics, and internal consistency—are faulty.

Several strategies are applied as a program administrator responds to proposals for reduction in base (if a program may be terminated or reduced from its existing level of operation). These include the following:

1. **Propose a study.** Agency administrators argue that rash actions (such as cutting their programs) should not be taken until all consequences have been completely considered. A study would delay action, possibly long enough for those proposing cuts to lose interest and certainly long enough for the program administrator to develop other arguments for the program.

2. **Cut the popular programs.** The administrator responds to the proposed reduction by cutting or eliminating (or at least releasing to the news media plans for such action) programs with strong public support. By proposing that the school band or athletic programs be eliminated, for instance, the administrator hopes to mobilize sufficient outcry to ensure no budget cuts. The careful

[39]Important sources on strategy are Aaron Wildavsky, *The Politics of the Budgetary Process,* 4th ed. (Boston: Little Brown, 1984), chap. 3; Robert N. Anthony and David W. Young, *Management Control in Nonprofit Organizations,* 4th ed. (Homewood, Ill.: Irwin, 1988), 459–536; and Jerry McCaffery, *Budgetmaster* (privately printed).

reviewer knows of other activities that are particularly ripe for reduction, so that the political horrors painted by the administrator do not dominate discussion.

3. **Dire consequences.** The administrator outlines the tragic events—shattered lives of those served, supplier businesses closed, and so on—that would accompany the reductions.

4. **All or nothing.** Any reduction would make the program impossible, so it might as well be eliminated.

5. **You pick.** The administrator responds that all agency activities are so vital that agency directors are unable to choose which would be reduced or eliminated if agency funds are cut. Therefore, those proposing the cut should identify the targets, thereby clearly tracking the political blame for the cut and hopefully scaring away the reduction. Anyone proposing a reduction for an agency needs a definite package proposal, in case such a strategy unfolds.

6. **We are the experts.** The agency argues that it has expertise that the budget cutter lacks. The reduction is shortsighted, based on ignorance, and thus should not occur.

Other strategies apply when the agency seeks to continue or augment operations of its existing program:

1. **Round up.** Rounding program estimates—workload, prices, costs, and the like—upward to the next highest hundred, thousand, or million creates substantial slack when consistently done.

2. **"If it don't run, chrome it."** The budget presentation sparkles with data, charts, graphs, and other state-of-the-art management trappings. Much of the material may not relate directly to the decision at hand, and the base data may not be particularly accurate, but the quality of the show aims to overpower weak substance.

3. **Sprinkling.** Budget items are slightly increased, either in hard-to-detect general categories or across the board, after the basic request has been prepared. The layer of excess is spread so thinly that it cannot be clearly identified as padding. If enacted in full, the budget would allow the agency a significant operating cushion. Such a practice may leave no traces at all; however, surpluses might emerge during budget execution.

4. **Numbers game.** Agency administrators may discuss physical units—for example, facilities operated, grants initiated, or acres maintained—rather than the funds requested and spent. The intent is to divert attention from substantially increased spending for each unit.

5. **Workload and backlog.** Administrators often base their request on greater client demands or a backlog of unfilled requests. The argument is reasonable if the workload measure is germane to the agency's function, if the agency is doing something that needs to be done, and if the backlogs are not simply residuals of poor management of existing resources.

6. **The accounting trap.** Either side in the budget process may argue that a proposed expenditure must be made (or is forbidden) because the accounting system controls such transactions. The argument can be politically important. However, accounting systems exist to help management implement policy and to provide information for policy decisions. Policy choices should not be made difficult by the accounting system.

Programs and agencies develop an institutional momentum. To propose a new program, a program that expands the scope of agency operations, entails special challenges because the new program lacks any such momentum. Some budget processes even place new programs in a separate decision structure that considers new programs only after available revenues have covered all requests from existing activities. Other processes cause trouble for proposed programs simply because clients and constituents who could provide political support have not yet developed. Some strategies are characteristic of the new proposal:

1. **Old stuff.** Administrators may disguise new programs as simple extensions or growth of existing operations. When the new operation has developed an institutional foundation (directors, clients, and political allies), it can be spun off into an independent life, having been nurtured through early development by existing agency operations.

2. **Foot-in-the-door financing.** A project starts with a small amount of funding, possibly under the guise of a pilot or demonstration program or as a feasibility study. Modest amounts build each year until the program is operational and has developed a constituency. By the time full costs are identified, it may be more economical to spend more money to finish the task rather than irretrievably abandon the costs sunk into the project. Here is a classic example: In 1991 the Royal Thai Air Force purchased a squadron of F-16 fighters. The military lacked sufficient money to make the purchase, so the planes were purchased without engines. Delivery was scheduled for 1995, which left plenty of time to gather the extra funds. But a new Thai government took office in 1992. Although it wanted to exert control over military spending, its options were to approve more money for the engines or to pay for nonflying (probably undeliverable) airplanes. Rather than get no return from the $560 million spent on airplanes, training, and a new radar system, the purchase was approved—even though the new government sought to constrain military spending and to devote its scarce resources to domestic use.[40]

3. **It pays for itself.** Supporters of new programs sometimes argue that the program will produce more revenue than it will cost. Although many revenue department activities may do just that, the case is made in other areas as well. Examples include arguments made by law enforcement agencies concerning collections of fines and, with growing frequency, by economic development

[40]Cynthia Owens, "And Now They'll Sneak in Orders for Aviation Fuel and Parachutes," *Wall Street Journal,* 28 January 1993, C-1.

departments concerning induced tax collections from economic activity lured by the project.

4. **Spend to save.** Expenditure on the proposal would cause cost reduction somewhere else in the government. The net budget impact would be nil, or even positive, if spending $1 in agency A would allow spending to be reduced by $1 or more either in that agency or somewhere else in government. Whether that claimed spending reduction actually would occur is another argument.

5. **Crisis.** The proposal may be linked to a catastrophe or overwhelming problem—AIDS, economic underdevelopment, homelessness, homeland security, and so on—even though the link may be tenuous, simply because the agency perceives that such proposals are less likely to be reduced.[41] But an agency must use caution because skeptics will question why it did not deal with the problem before it reached crisis proportions.

6. **Mislabeling.** The actual nature of a program may be hidden by mixing it with another, more politically attractive program. Examples abound: Military installations may have blast-suppression areas that look strangely like golf courses; university dormitories or office buildings may have roofs that have seats convenient for viewing events on the football field; the rigid upper-surface covers for the new sewers may support vehicular traffic. These strategies, however, require an essentially supportive environment; all key participants in the budget process must be in agreement on the proposal because budget people remember and make allowances in later years.

7. **What they did makes us do it.** An action taken by another entity may place demands on the agency beyond what could be accommodated by normal management of existing programs. If school libraries were to be closed and teachers continued to assign reference work, local public libraries might argue for new programs to accommodate student requests for assistance. Harsh federal sentencing guidelines for certain classes of drug offenses means that new federal prisons must be built.

8. **Mandates.** Some external entity (courts, a federal agency, the state, etc.) may legally require an agency action that would entail greater expenditure. Rather than rearrange operations to accommodate the new requirement, an agency may use the mandate as an argument for additional funds. The agency may in fact have requested that the external entity issue the mandate as a budget strategy. The approach can be compelling, but analysts need to determine the grounds and authority of the mandate and the extent to which revised op-

---

[41]For many years (at least since 1966), the National Park Service has sought an underground visitors center at the Washington Monument. When the proposal emerged again in 2003, its name had changed from "Washington Monument Visitors Center Plan" to "Washington Monument Permanent Security Improvements." One critic observes: "As soon as you say that it's for security, any project—however questionable—is able to move forward because everyone is afraid that one of these great monuments might be destroyed on their watches. But in reality, [the underground proposal] has nothing to do with security." (Monte Reel, "Washington Monument Dispute Resurfaces," *Washington Post,* August 4, 2003: A01. However, to date, this new strategy has not been effective in producing the visitor center.

erations can accommodate the mandate before simply accepting the argument for an increased budget. The approach also has applications for base expansion and, if the time frame is sufficient, for defense against cuts.

9. **Matching the competition.** Agencies often compare their programs with those operated by others and use the comparison as a basis for adding new programs. (Seldom does the comparison lead to a proposal that some programs be eliminated because similar agencies do not have them.) The argument is also used to expand existing programs.

10. **It's so small.** Program proponents may argue that a request is not large enough to require full review, that its trivial budgetary consequences do not make the review a reasonable use of time. Those who understand foot-in-the-door financing are naturally wary of such arguments and generally respond that smallness makes activities natural candidates for absorption by the agency without extra funds.

Conclusion

Budgets serve as the choice mechanism for allocation of public resources. The flow of budget decisions from plan to expenditure is accomplished in a four-phase cycle involving legislative and executive preparation, legislative consideration, execution, and audit. Although budgets are constructed and approved in a political environment, it is not clear that appropriations are the simple product of adding a small increment to the prior-year appropriation. There is at least some room for attempts at rational choice in budget structures.

QUESTIONS AND EXERCISES

1. The relative size of government has been a continuing public policy concern. Size and growth questions have been important at the state and local levels, as demonstrated by several state referenda to limit federal, state, or local expenditures. Some evidence for those discussions can be drawn from data on trends of spending activity, using information from the Department of Commerce's National Income and Product Accounts and the Census Bureau's Government Finances (annual). Data are available at the Census website (www.census.gov) and the Bureau of Economic Analysis website (www.bea.gov). From those sources, prepare answers to these questions about the size of government in the United States.

   a. Has the public sector grown relative to the private sector? How does the size of the federal government compare with that of state and local government? (A benchmark for comparison is the percentage of GDP or personal income accounted for by the appropriate sector.)

b. Which sectors have grown fastest? Compare growth of the public sector in your state with that of its neighbors and of the nation. Why might a comparison based on expenditure growth differ from one based on employment?
c. Calculate national defense spending as a percentage of total federal government outlays and as a percentage of GDP. Can you identify the impact of the end of the Cold War and the beginning of the Iraq War on these data?
d. Which functions account for the greatest share of federal, state, and local government expenditures? Does the pattern differ much among states?
e. What is the relative significance of local government compared to state government expenditure in your state? (Make the comparison first counting state aid to local government as state expenditure. Then, omit that portion from state expenditure.) How does your state compare with its neighbors and the nation?

2. The following data are from a recent federal budget:

Federal government discretionary outlays ($ billions)

	1998	2004
Defense	270.2	454.1
Nondefense	281.9	441.4
Composite outlay deflator (2000 = 1.00)		
Defense	0.9499	1.1264
Nondefense	0.9623	1.0834

a. Compute the growth rates for defense and nondefense outlays in current-year dollars from 1999 to 2004. Divide that growth into its real and price components.
b. What was the real dollar (2000 = 00) change in defense outlays from 1998 to 2004? Convert the base to 2004 = 1.00 and recalculate that increase. Why might budget strategists try to use one or the other of these two numbers to argue for more or less spending? Are either of the two base years more correct? Explain. Compute and compare the real percentage increases using the two different base years.
c. Suppose prices are expected to change between 2004 and 2008 at the same rate they did between 1998 and 2004. What level of defense and nondefense outlays would leave real purchasing power the same in 2008 as it was in 2004?

3. Identify the strategy represented in each of the following arguments taken from budget discussions:

a. A bill to increase the number of women eligible for Medicaid-funded prenatal assistance in this state would not only save lives but also cut state costs for care of low-birth-weight babies and handicapped children. Studies have shown that every dollar spent on prenatal care reduces long-term healthcare expenditures by $3.38.

b. The change in the Board of Health sanitation position from full-time to part-time will demolish the inspection program. Rather than accept the weakened program, we would prefer that the program be terminated.
c. Faculty salaries at Enormous State University rank seventeenth among eighteen universities with which it competes. Substantial improvements in pay must come in this budget year if major defections are to be prevented.
d. In March, the second of two school-funding referenda failed (by a 2–1 margin) in the Riverside-Brookfield (Illinois) School District. The school board responded by proposing the elimination of the girls' badminton, swimming, and cross-country teams; the boys' soccer, tennis, and wrestling teams; seven additional coaching programs; the cheerleading program; and the Pup-ettes (a pompom squad). A phase-out of the German language program at the school had been started before the failure of the referendum.
e. The Unipacker II will return its full purchase cost in lower labor and maintenance expense within 2 years of initial operation.
f. The elimination of the appropriation to the Massachusetts Arts Council would reduce the budget by $19 million. But this loss of support for administrative staff and for grants to arts groups would be remarkably shortsighted. Arts groups pay taxes to the state in sums aggregating more than four times the amount of the council budget. Therefore, the proposal does not make economic sense for the state.
g. The AIDS education program I have proposed for the biennial budget carries a price tag of only $200,000. This cost represents an absolutely trivial percentage of the $10 billion the state spends each year and will have no impact on the state fiscal crisis. Furthermore, the medical expense to the state associated with even one AIDS case is more than $100,000, so it is the most misguided, mean-spirited, and shortsighted of economies to deny this proposal.
h. The governor proposes major reductions (80% of the $321 million per year program) in state general assistance, a program that provides medical coverage at about $120 per month to its 131,000 recipients (adults with no children or other dependents). This reduction may cost more than the amount it saves if only a fraction of the recipients end up in mental institutions or shelters. For example, keeping one-tenth of the current recipients in the state psychiatric hospital for 90 days would cost more than $200 million, and keeping one-tenth of the recipients in a shelter for 90 days would cost $22 million. The reduction is clearly a false economy.
i. An internal memo leaked to the media said that cuts to the National Weather Service budget in FY 2005 would have a critical impact on its life-saving mission. For instance, ". . . warning lead times will shorten and tornado detection rates will decrease (as will most other NWS performance standards) leading to the troubling and tragic conclusion that there will be unwarranted loss of life." Its operating budget for FY 2005 had been reduced by 2 percent.

If confronted by such arguments, what questions would you raise?

4. The state budget director has asked you to create a medical care cost inflation index to use in evaluation of certain items in the state budget. You are to use

2000 as the base year for your index. If costs have risen at an average annual rate of 4.35 percent since 2000, what is the value of your index in 2006?

CASES FOR DISCUSSION

CASE 2–1

Developing and Using Budget Strategy: The Earth Resources Technology Satellite (ERTS)

Agencies without a specific clientele face special problems in defending their budget requests. A classic illustration of agency strategy appears in the following case, reproduced in its entirety from the *Wall Street Journal.*

Consider These Questions

1. What budget strategies did NASA use in defense of ERTS?
2. At what stage of the budget cycle were the reductions made?
3. How might other agencies use similar approaches? For instance, how might a state university adopt those strategies in dealing with its legislature?
4. Have things changed over the past 25 years? For instance, could such strategies have saved the superconducting supercollider program?
5. What actually has happened with the technology satellite program benefits, compared with the returns promised by its supporters?

How Backers of a Technology Satellite Induced Ford to Overrule His Advisers, Provide Money

By Arlen J. Large

Washington—Frank Moss is an ERTS nut, in a world of people who aren't. So he considers it his duty to spread the gospel about his pet project. It helps that he is a U.S. senator from Utah and chairman of the Senate Space Committee.

Daniel Evans may not be a nut on the subject, but he is an ERTS fan. As governor of the state of Washington, he wrote Senator Moss an unspontaneous letter saying the "Earth Resources Technology Satellite has provided valuable information to both the agriculture and forestry industries and to the state of Washington."

Gerald Ford may not even be an ERTS fan, but he is a friend. Not long ago, he overruled his White House advisers and put $11 million in the new budget to start work on a third ERTS satellite, which will be launched in the fall of 1977.

So some very heavy politicians have been rallying around this little known and unglamorous project of the National Aeronautics and Space Administration. The backstage tugging over the money for the third satellite is the kind of thing that goes on all over town during preparation of a new budget, and it provides a good case study of how budget winners win.

The loser was the president's Office of Management and Budget, which for months had urged that the third satellite be deferred to some future budget. Roy Ash, the just-departed OMB director who was overruled by Mr. Ford, observed with sarcasm that "one must congratulate NASA for its notable job of mobilizing outside opinion" on behalf of the new satellite.

The Show-Biz Problem

However, it would be hard to pin the whole mobilizing effort on the space bureaucrats at NASA. There's something called "the ERTS community"—geographers, foresters, pollution fighters, and land-use planners—that lobbied heavily for the new satellite. For its part, NASA has tried to tackle the show-biz problem caused by the satellite's grating, uncommunicative name. The agency is trying to get people to call it Landsat, but even space officials sometimes forget, and the names are used interchangeably.

The first satellite in the series was shot into polar orbit in 1972. It still is there, but is running down. The second went up last January 22 with similar equipment for looking at the earth in four wavelengths of light and sending images back to ground stations for analysis by computers. Computer-processed pictures are sold by the Interior Department at Sioux Falls, S.D., to anyone who wants to use them to count crops, spot oil, see insect-chewed forests, trace earthquake-producing faults, and do a lot of other things.

All this really turns Senator Moss on, making him a self-admitted "virtual zealot" for these satellites. "ERTS was the first thing I could see where you have a very distinct and obvious applications return," he says. "It's a great example of the benefits coming out of the space program." People who appreciate the down-to-earth value of the ERTS pictures, he says, are more likely to embrace the space agency's loftier doings, such as the exploration of Mars.

The satellite launched last month is expected to work for two years. Congress last year authorized a third ERTS to take its place in 1977. NASA was more than willing to start building it, and so, of course, was General Electric Co., the main contractor for the first two. Plans were made to upgrade the new model with a heat-measuring sensor.

Mr. Ash's OMB, the government-wide spending monitor, demurred. A third satellite shouldn't go up, budget officials argued, until NASA succeeded in developing cameras with sharper vision. Without that, ERTS satellites would never be useful in making good crop-production forecasts, forest surveys, or pollution maps.

The space agency intends to double the sharpness of vision of one of the cameras on the third satellite. The other equipment, officials contend, sees sharply enough on the second and third satellites to undertake a large-scale survey of U.S. wheat production. And with a little practice, space officials think that they will get a better notion of the size of each year's Soviet wheat crop, thus giving a more accurate forewarning of export market demand.

NASA and its allies argued all last year that a third satellite should be on duty in 1977 to take over when the second one dies; otherwise there would be a gap in the data that would discourage picture buyers in "the ERTS community."

The trick was to bring this argument to OMB's attention in an impressive way. An important part of the lobbying blitz was orchestrated on Capitol Hill by Senator Moss and his ally, Arizona's Senator Barry Goldwater.

Letters to the States

Hoping to show that the ERTS community had plenty of political muscle, Senator Moss wrote every governor, asking if state agencies had made use of ERTS and whether the federal government should sell the pictures on a permanent basis.

The senator got replies from 25 governors, plus some top officials in other states. Vermont's Thomas Salmon said ERTS pictures will be used to trace pollution in Lake Champlain. In California, said then-Governor Ronald Reagan, ERTS had helped outline land-use patterns. Missouri's Christopher Bond said the pictures have been used to spot flood-prone areas. Only Delaware's Sherman Tribbitt replied bluntly that the pictures didn't prove useful.

One by one, Senator Moss dribbled the gubernatorial letters in to the Congressional Record in the closing months of last year. "It was like the drop-of-water technique, day by day," he says.

Besides that, Senator Moss waved letters of support from the Society of Photographic Scientists and Engineers, the American Society of Photogrammetry, the Association of American Geographers, the American Forestry Association, and various distinguished professors. Meanwhile, on the scientific seminar circuit, General Electric's people were forever turning up with ERTS displays. Daniel Fink, general manager of GE's space division, preached the need to keep those space photos coming in.

Nevertheless, OMB last December turned down NASA's request to put money for the third satellite, called Landsat-C, into the budget being prepared for the new Congress. Word spread along the ERTS community's grapevine. OMB got letters from the National Academy of Science and the National Academy of Engineering, both quasi-government bodies. Letters came from important scientists.

Appealing the Decision

The budget keepers still said no. Under the rules, an agency can go over OMB's head and appeal directly to the president. So ERTS was kicked around at a meeting between Mr. Ford, Mr. Ash, and James Fletcher, the NASA boss. "It was not a confrontation," Mr. Fletcher insists.

He says his agency kept explaining to OMB that the third satellite didn't represent an "operational," earth-scanning system but would remain an experimental instrument. Then in early January the remaining differences between the two agencies were reduced to an "issue paper" that went to Mr. Ford. The satellite money was approved.

Mr. Ash appeared to see a connection between NASA's victory and a praise-filled article on ERTS in the February issue of *Fortune* magazine. The article portrayed OMB as the villain in trying to block the third satellite, concluding: "To cripple or kill this program after the millions of words spewed out about the coming 'fallout' from space research would certainly be foolhardy."

NASA had indeed been eager for *Fortune* to do the article. "It was Fletcher who put this bug in my bonnet about a year ago," recalls Robert Lubar, the magazine's managing editor. John Donnelly, the agency's assistant administrator for public affairs, also remembers writing Mr. Lubar about the ERTS project. "I tried to plant the seed of an idea for a story I thought was of quite legitimate interest to businessmen," he says. Editor Lubar says that he doesn't remember seeing that letter and that the decision to have the article written was his. Anyway, he says, the February *Fortune* didn't hit the streets until the last week in January, after Mr. Ford had made his decision.

CASE 2–2

Strategies in Defense of the Defense Budget

Once the budget justifications and numbers have been prepared, agencies face the task of marketing the package to the legislature. Conditions vary from year to year; the tactics applicable in one session may not be at all appropriate in the next. The changing approaches are described in the following review of strategies used by Secretary of Defense Caspar Weinberger in selling the budget for fiscal years 1982 through 1986. Recall that these years were the ones immediately before the collapse of the Soviet Union and the defense build-up may have been instrumental in ending the Cold War.

Consider These Questions

1. Identify the budget strategies Weinberger used. Is there a common logic running through them, or is each independent of the others?
2. Would the strategies he used be applicable to the post–Cold War environment? Would the current secretary of defense be able to learn anything by reviewing Weinberger's script? How has the war on terrorism changed the budget environment?
3. To what extent would these strategies be transferable outside the national defense budget?
4. Use the historical statistics section of the most recent federal budget to trace the pattern of defense outlays and budget authority from 1980 through 1989. What pattern do you identify? Compare the patterns there with comparable data for 2000 to the present.

SOURCE: Wall Street Journal (February 20, 1975). Reprinted by Permission of the Wall Street Journal. Copyright 1975 Dow Jones & Company, Inc. All rights reserved worldwide.

Weinberger Finds His Well-Worn Strategies Always Succeed in Blunting Defense Budget Ax

By Tim Carrington

Washington—Defense Secretary Caspar Weinberger has privately referred to his campaign for a bigger defense budget as Kabuki, a highly ritualized Japanese art form in which all movements are tightly choreographed in advance.

Despite the furor surrounding the Reagan administration's push to add $29 billion to the military budget for the next fiscal year, many aspects of the contest seem to follow a set script. And after four years in the fray, the tireless Mr. Weinberger is nothing if not well-rehearsed.

Since President Reagan launched his military buildup, Congress has provided the Pentagon with about 95 percent of the spending authority it has sought. A look at the defense budget debate over the past four years bears out Mr. Weinberger's observations that it's less a political brawl than one of Washington's most stylized dramas. And the past could well foreshadow what happens this year.

1982

In March 1981, Congress granted the Pentagon a startling 20 percent increase, bringing its budget for fiscal 1982 to $216.5 billion, just below the $222 billion the administration sought. However, five months later, Mr. Weinberger faced dissent from within the Reagan administration. David Stockman, director of the Office of Management and Budget, proposed rescinding part of that increase and scaling back the projected military expansion for future years.

The budget chief had just learned that the fiscal 1982 federal budget deficit was likely to rise to $62.6 billion, small in relation to today's deficits of more than $200 billion, but for that time a record. Mr. Stockman recognized that Mr. Reagan's goal of showing a balanced budget by 1984 was in jeopardy, and he considered the defense buildup part of the program.

In staving off Mr. Stockman's assault on the planned buildup, Mr. Weinberger turned to a tactic for which he has since become famous, the chart and easel. The defense secretary's charts, presented in a meeting with the president, showed large soldiers bearing large weapons, which were labeled "Reagan budget." They towered above small soldiers with small weapons labeled "OMB budget." President Reagan went along with the "Reagan budget."

1983

In preparing the fiscal 1983 plan, Mr. Weinberger was again confronted with the budget-slashing demands of Mr. Stockman. The defense chief had many allies within the administration but by now government officials began to refer to the hegemony of the "majority of two," Mr. Weinberger and President Reagan.

With unwavering White House support, the defense secretary shot down an OMB attempt to chop $20 billion from the proposed defense budget, then offered an unusual set of cuts himself. In what became a recurring feature of the budget process, the Pentagon stripped billions from its budget simply by adjusting the inflation assumptions. Weapons programs remained intact.

In defending the budget on Capitol Hill, Mr. Weinberger emphasized "the Soviet threat" and insisted that economic and fiscal concerns shouldn't influence the Pentagon's spending. But deficit concerns were mounting nonetheless and world financial markets were unusually jittery. When the administration sought $257 billion for defense in fiscal 1983, Rep. Joseph Addabbo (D-N.Y.), chairman of the defense appropriations subcommittee, declared that defense is not sacrosanct in the deficit-cutting effort.

In the Senate, Chairman Pete Domenici (R-N.M.) opened Budget Committee hearings with the declaration that "the hemorrhage of the budget deficit must be alleviated." The committee pressed Secretary Weinberger to suggest modest cuts from the proposed Pentagon budget, but the secretary refused. He said he hoped Congress wouldn't be "unwise enough" to reduce the budget request at all.

Congress, while hammering away at the Pentagon to offer up cuts was loath to impose its own set of reductions. When the face-off ended. Congress gave the Pentagon budget authority of $245 billion, $12 billion less than the $25 billion the administration asked for but still 13 percent, or $29 billion, more than it got the previous year.

1984

Preparations of the defense budget for fiscal 1984 brought another confrontation with Mr. Stockman, who demanded that Mr. Weinberger take $11 billion out of his planned $284.7 billion budget.

The Pentagon, expert at protecting weapons programs through what observers call "cut insurance," was ready to meet these demands almost painlessly. Inflation assumptions were lowered, fuel-price calculations adjusted, and some military-construction projects postponed. In addition, a planned pay increase was dropped. In presenting a new budget request for $273.4 billion, Mr. Weinberger declared: "We have reached the bone."

Many legislators expressed outrage at Mr. Weinberger's refusal to consider other cuts despite mounting economic worries over the government's budget deficit. Sen. Don Riegle, a Democrat from badly pressed Michigan, asserted that the United States had a defense secretary "whose basic judgment is dangerous to our country." Mr. Weinberger replied: "You have accomplished your principal purpose, which is to launch a demagogic attack on me in time for the afternoon and evening editions."

The debate had become more rancorous, but the Pentagon's tactics still produced results. When the war of words ended, Congress granted the Pentagon 93 percent of the spending authority it sought—a $262.2 billion budget, up 8 percent, or $20.2 billion from the previous year.

1985

Deficit-reduction efforts in early 1984 centered on making a "down payment" against the deficit in fiscal 1985. After another skirmish with Mr. Stockman, Mr. Weinberger agreed to seek a 15 percent increase that would bring the Pentagon's spending authority to $305 billion.

House Democrats assailed the plan, but as in the past, they wanted Mr. Weinberger to suggest the cuts, rather than slash on their own initiative politically popular military programs in an election year. Mr. Weinberger refused, saying: "We need it all."

Congress didn't give him the full $305 billion he sought but again provided 93 percent of that; it approved a fiscal 1985 military budget of $284.7 billion, up 7 percent, or $19.5 billion, from the previous year.

1986

The contest over the fiscal 1986 budget is following the pattern of early years. Mr. Weinberger called for a 13 percent increase in a budget he said had been "scrubbed" down to the basics. After Mr. Stockman's demands for cuts gathered support from other cabinet members, Mr. Weinberger made accounting adjustments to produce $6.2 billion in reductions.

Further cuts? Mr. Weinberger asserts that the budget he presented is the "bare minimum." When pushed to suggest some cuts, Mr. Weinberger recently resorted to what's called "the Washington Monument strategy"—for "cut my budget and I'll close the Washington Monument" (or something equally visible).

During Senate hearings, the defense secretary warned that if Congress cuts the Pentagon budget, there would be a slowdown in the B-1 bomber project, elimination of two Trident submarines, and cancellation of a multiple-launch rocket system—all considered high-priority programs.

Some participants say the ritual is getting tiring. "It's the same Kabuki dance," says one Senate Budget Committee aide, "but Domenici is getting extremely frustrated with it."

CHAPTER 3

Budget Structures and Institutions: Federal and State-Local

Budgets perform the same functions for choice-making, management, and control, regardless of the entity—government, business, nonprofit—that develops them. The particular institutions and structures that the entity uses, however, are subject to much individuality, sometimes because of real differences in the mission, size, opportunities, and so on, of the entity, but sometimes only because of institutional history ("That's just the way we do it here because that's the way we always have."). In this chapter, we examine the most important federal budget structures and institutions, and then we make some comparisons with similar features of budgeting at the state-local level. We also discuss how each level spends its money.

The Federal Budget

As earlier described, a budget is a financial plan. A government budget, however, reflects choices well beyond those of finance. A congressional agency report makes the point: "Not only is the budget a financial accounting of the receipts and expenditures of the federal government; it also sets forth a plan for allocating resources—between the public and private sectors and within the public sector—to meet national objectives."[1] Budget preparation, discussion, and approval thus must be at the heart of public decision-making. Even in a market economy, the budget represents the basic national economic plan—the chosen mix of public and private sector uses of national resources.

[1]U.S. Congressional Budget Office, *An Analysis of the Administration's Health Proposal* (Washington, D.C.: GPO, 1994), 41.

Spending by the Federal Government

For what does the federal government spend our money? Table 3–1 provides those data for selected years from 1960 through 2005. Most outlays, more than 60 percent, are for human resources, including income maintenance, health, support for the elderly and disabled, and education and training. The largest block in the category, more than 20 percent of all outlays, is for the Social Security system. Much of this human resource expenditure occurs through legal formulas that determine who is eligible and to how much those entitled are eligible. Most elements in this spending category have grown at rates greater than the overall average rate since 1970, and most are expected (or feared) to continue this rapid growth in the future.

National defense was once the predominant interest of the federal government. However, 1961 was the last year in which defense amounted to half or more of federal outlays; it had been over 70 percent for 1942 through 1946, with a maximum of 89.5 percent in 1945, no surprise in light of the expense (and importance) of fighting World War II. The secular decline in the defense share of federal outlays was interrupted for 1981 through 1987. Many believe that this increase, by forcing a reaction from the Soviet Union that its inefficient socialist economy could not support, caused the collapse of the Soviet Union and an end to the Cold War. That defense build-up essentially won a war without firing a shot, undoubtedly the best way to fight battles. There is also an increase in the first years of the twenty-first century, created by the cost of the wars in Iraq and Afghanistan.[2] This increased share remains far below its level of the 1960s and 1970s and, with luck, will not approach those levels again.

Other functional outlays are much smaller parts of the federal total. A particularly high growth rate appears for administration of justice (law enforcement and corrections) but the current share is small. Growth in outlays for health and for Medicare (the federal health program for older people) has been high, and their shares of the total are much larger. Outlays for physical resources, including infrastructure or the federal capital stock, are small in share and not growing as rapidly as totals. Many believe increased public infrastructure investment to be critical for improved standards of living, but the outlay patterns show physical resource growth to be slow. Spending on other functions is both relatively small and slow growing; the rates of increase often have not kept pace with the combined effects of population increase and inflation.

Changing directions is not impossible but, as the incrementalists remind us, difficult to accomplish. The great counterexample of how spending directions can dramatically change, however, is national defense through the past 35 years. Spending shares can change substantially when operating conditions change, no matter what the incremental inertia is. In no way are spending shares replicated year after year, regardless of the external environment.

---

[2]The costs of the Department of Homeland Security are not included as part of National Defense in Federal budget classification. Its spending is in transportation, disaster relief and insurance, and law enforcement functions.

Table 3–1
Federal Outlays by Function, 1960–2005 ($ millions)

	1960	% total	1970	% total	1980	% total	1990	% total	2000	% total	2005	% total	Annual Growth since 1960
National defense	48,130	52.2%	81,692	41.8%	133,995	22.7%	299,331	23.9%	294,495	16.5%	495,355	20.0%	5.3%
Human resources	26,184	28.4%	75,349	38.5%	313,374	53.0%	619,329	49.4%	1,115,481	62.3%	1,586,079	64.2%	9.5%
Education, training, employment, and social services	968	1.0%	8,634	4.4%	31,843	5.4%	37,176	3.0%	53,754	3.0%	97,526	3.9%	10.8%
Health	795	0.9%	5,907	3.0%	23,169	3.9%	57,716	4.6%	154,533	8.6%	250,612	10.1%	13.6%
Medicare			6,213	3.2%	32,090	5.4%	98,102	7.8%	197,113	11.0%	298,638	12.1%	
Income security	7,378	8.0%	15,655	8.0%	86,557	14.6%	148,655	11.9%	253,575	14.2%	345,847	14.0%	8.9%
Social security	11,602	12.6%	30,270	15.5%	118,547	20.1%	248,623	19.8%	409,423	22.9%	523,305	21.2%	8.8%
Veterans benefits and services	5,441	5.9%	8,669	4.4%	21,169	3.6%	29,058	2.3%	47,083	2.6%	70,151	2.8%	5.8%
Physical resources	7,991	8.7%	15,574	8.0%	65,985	11.2%	126,037	10.1%	84,954	4.7%	130,184	5.3%	6.4%
Energy	464	0.5%	997	0.5%	10,156	1.7%	3,341	0.3%	−761	−0.0%	429	0.0%	−0.2%
Natural resources and environment	1,559	1.7%	3,065	1.6%	13,858	2.3%	17,080	1.4%	25,031	1.4%	28,023	1.1%	6.6%
Commerce and housing credit	1,618	1.8%	2,112	1.1%	9,390	1.6%	67,600	5.4%	3,208	0.2%	7,574	0.3%	3.5%
Transportation	4,126	4.5%	7,008	3.6%	21,329	3.6%	29,485	2.4%	46,853	2.6%	67,894	2.7%	6.4%
Community and regional development	224	0.2%	2,392	1.2%	11,252	1.9%	8,531	0.7%	10,623	0.6%	26,264	1.1%	11.2%
Net interest	6,947	7.5%	14,380	7.3%	52,533	8.9%	184,347	14.7%	222,949	12.5%	183,986	7.4%	7.6%
Other functions	7,760	8.4%	17,286	8.8%	44,996	7.6%	60,688	4.8%	113,769	6.4%	141,845	5.7%	6.7%
International affairs	2,988	3.2%	4,330	2.2%	12,714	2.2%	13,764	1.1%	17,216	1.0%	34,592	1.4%	5.6%
General science, space and technology	599	0.6%	4,511	2.3%	5,831	1.0%	14,443	1.2%	18,633	1.0%	23,674	1.0%	8.5%
Agriculture	2,623	2.8%	5,166	2.6%	8,774	1.5%	11,806	0.9%	36,459	2.0%	26,566	1.1%	5.3%
Administration of justice	366	0.4%	959	0.5%	4,702	0.8%	10,185	0.8%	28,501	1.6%	40,019	1.6%	11.0%
General government	1,184	1.3%	2,320	1.2%	12,975	2.2%	10,490	0.8%	12,960	0.7%	16,994	0.7%	6.1%
Undistributed offsetting receipts	−4,820	−5.2%	−8,632	−4.4%	−19,942	−3.4%	−36,615	−2.9%	−42,581	−2.4%	−65,224	−2.6%	6.0%
Total, Federal outlays	92,191	100.0%	195,649	100.0%	590,941	100.0%	1,253,116	100.0%	1,789,067	100.0%	2,472,205	100.0%	7.6%

SOURCE: Executive Office of the President, Office of Management and Budget, *Budget of the United States Government. Historical Tables 2007.* (Washington, D.C.: U.S. Government Printing Office, 2006).

The Federal Budget Process[3]

Expenditure decisions are made through a political process that is governed by a set of laws designed to provide open deliberations about options, ensure accountability and prevent corruption, and provide a mechanism for fiscal control. The budget process is a critical component of public expenditure management. The federal budget process—its practices, timing, and institutions—is the product of both law and tradition. The Budget and Accounting Act of 1921 (the 1921 act), the Congressional Budget and Impoundment Control Act of 1974 (the 1974 act), the Balanced Budget and Emergency Deficit Control Act of 1985 (Gramm-Rudman-Hollings), and the Budget Enforcement Act of 1990 (BEA90) outline the most important features of the process; the structure they establish will be given special attention here.[4] Several highlights of each act, to be examined later in more detail, appear in Table 3–2. Three organizations—the Office of Management and Budget (OMB), the Government Accountability Office (GAO, formerly the General Accounting Office), and the Congressional Budget Office (CBO)—emerged from these laws and constitute the professional budget establishment outside the operating agencies and congressional committees.[5] Each has separate roles, but each office works with agency-budget staff and congressional-committee staff to produce the budgets, appropriations, and expenditures of the federal government.

Federal Budget Organizations. The OMB, part of the Executive Office of the president, was created as the Bureau of the Budget in the 1921 act. (Initially it was part of the Treasury Department but became part of the newly established Executive Office in 1939.) The president appoints the OMB's director, and its staff is expected to carry out the policies of the president. The OMB develops the executive budget by consolidating agency requests for appropriations within the guidelines

---

[3]Executive Office of the President, Office of Management and Budget, *Budget System and Concepts, Fiscal Year* —— (Washington, D.C. Government Printing Office)—a document revised each year—explains the system, process, legal requirements, and concepts used to formulate the president's budget each year. It is available through the Office of Management and Budget website (www.whitehouse.gov/omb/).

[4]A more complete listing would include the following (1) Article 9, paragraph 7 of the U.S. Constitution (quoted previously), which requires appropriation before spending; (2) the Federal Credit Reform Act of 1990 (part of BEA90), which requires budgetary treatment of direct loans and loan guarantees, not on a purely cash basis but on estimated present values (see Chapter 6 for an explanation of present values) of the long-term cost of the loan or guarantee to the government; (3) the Report of the President's Commission on Budget Concepts (Washington, D.C.: GPO, 1967), which, although it has no legal status, remains the only authoritative statement on federal budget accounting; (4) the Chief Financial Officers Act of 1990 which required audited financial statements and increased powers of financial management authorities; and (5) the Government Performance and Results Act of 1993 which required agencies to develop strategic plans, measure performance, and integrate budgeting with performance improvement programs. The rules and procedures for budget execution appear in the Anti-deficiency Act (codified in Chapters 13 and 15 of Title 31, United States Code). Procedures for submission of the president's budget and information to be contained in it are in Chapter 11, Title 31, United States Code.

[5]The GAO became the Government Accountability Office in the GAO Human Capital Reform Act of 2004 (Public Law 108-271). Along with the name change came greater flexibility for the GAO in staffing matters.

Table 3–2
Highlights of Major Acts Establishing the Federal Budget Process

Budget and Accounting Act of 1921 (67th Cong., 1st sess., chap. 18, 47 stat. 20).
Established fiscal year from July 1 to June 30 Supplemental appropriation Bureau of Budget (now Office of Management and Budget [OMB]) General Accounting Office (GAO)
Required President's budget message (first day of session) No direct agency submission of appropriation requests
Congressional Budget and Impoundment Control Act of 1974 (Public Law 93–344)
Established fiscal year from October 1 to September 30 Congressional Budget Office (CBO) House and Senate budget committees
Required Current Services Budget presentation by president (what budget levels would be in the future if no policy changes occur) Congressional Budget Resolution (first and second) Functional classification in president's budget Tax expenditure analysis Rescission/deferral instead of impoundment
Balanced Budget and Emergency Deficit Control Act of 1985 (Public Law 99–177)
Established deficit targets Formula sequestration to enforce targets
Required earlier presidential budget message (first Monday after January 3) No second Congressional Budget Resolution
Budget Enforcement Act of 1990 (Title XIII, Public Law 101–508)
Established mandatory and discretionary spending categories Pay-as-you-go (PAYGO) requirement for mandatory spending categories and revenue provisions Established discretionary spending controls
Required Presidential adjustment of ceilings for sequester Supplemental appropriations be included in controls Supplemental appropriations included in outlay controls, except for wars and dire emergencies.

provided by the president. (Before the 1921 act, departments and agencies made individual appropriation requests; their sole submissions were gathered in an uncoordinated "Book of Estimates" for congressional review.) The OMB usually reduces initial agency requests; an administrative process within the OMB considers protests of these reductions before transmission of the budget to Congress. After appropriation, the OMB meters the flow of spending to ensure that agencies do not spend more than the amount appropriated.[6]

The GAO, a congressional agency created in the 1921 act, holds accountable the operations of federal departments and agencies and is the primary "watchdog" agency for Congress and the American people. As the external audit agent for the federal government, it supervises the accounting done by the executive agencies, but much of its work emphasizes investigations to improve the effectiveness of government. Much audit detail, in fact, is done by the audit staff of the executive agency itself, subject to GAO agreement. The head of the GAO, the comptroller general, is appointed by the president with the consent of the Senate for a single 15-year term; the comptroller general is almost unremovable within term.[7] The current emphasis of the GAO's work is the evaluation of government programs, sometimes at the request of a single member of Congress, sometimes at the request of a committee. Their audit and evaluation is external to the operating agencies of the executive branch.

The CBO, another congressional agency, was established by the 1974 act to provide Congress with staff having expertise similar to that of the OMB, and is the central fiscal support agency of Congress. Before the CBO, there appeared to be an imbalance: The president had a permanent, professional budget staff with well-honed abilities and continuing knowledge about the mechanics and content of the budget; Congress had appropriations committee staff, none of whom maintained a view of the budget as a whole. The CBO provided a permanent, nonpartisan professional staff to supply Congress three basic services: help in developing a plan for the budget (macroeconomic forecasts, baseline budget projections, deficit-reduction options, analysis of the president's budget), help in staying within its budget (cost estimates for bills, scorekeeping or maintaining frequent tabulations of bills that affect the budget, sequestration reports), and help in considering issues of budget and economic policy.[8] The CBO provides assistance, first, to the Congressional Budget Committees; second, to the other fiscal committees (Appropriations, House Ways and Means, and Senate Finance); and third, to other committees and members of Congress. The CBO is rigidly nonpartisan.

Within Congress, most budget work is done in committee, although no tax or expenditure law can be passed without being approved by both the full House and the full Senate. The committees with particularly important roles are the several authorizing committees, the budget committee (in each chamber), the appropriations committee (in each chamber) and its subcommittees, the House Ways and Means

---

[6]Complete studies of the agency appear in Percival Flack Brundage, *The Bureau of the Budget* (New York: Praiger, 1970); and Larry Berman, *The Office of Management and Budget and the Presidency*, 1921–1979 (Princeton, N.J.: Princeton University Press, 1979). Brundage was budget director for President Eisenhower after a career with a national accounting firm.

[7]Two major studies provide a detailed view of the GAO: in *The GAO: The Quest for Accountability in American Government* (Boulder, Colo.: Westview Press, 1979), Frederick Mosher traces the development of the GAO to the end of the 1970s; and Erasmus H. Kolman, ed., *Cases in Accountability: The Work of the GAO* (Boulder, Colo.: Westview Press, 1979) collects several cases that illustrate the kinds of audits or evaluations done by the GAO.

[8]U.S. Congressional Budget Office, *Responsibilities and Organization of the Congressional Budget Office* (Washington, D.C.: GPO, 1993).

Committee, the Senate Finance Committee, and the Joint Committee on Taxation. More about the role played by each of these is discussed later.

Phases in the Federal Budget Cycle. The *executive-preparation-and-submission phase* begins about 18 months before the start of the fiscal year. The president establishes general budget and fiscal policy guidelines, and the OMB works with federal agencies to translate them into agency programs and budget requests. Agencies develop requests according to their own procedures, but with OMB coordination. The OMB collects agency estimates of their planned expenditures for the fiscal year and consolidates these requests. Table 3–3 shows the key dates in the budget cycle, as outlined in the A-11, the primary budget instruction from the OMB. The overall requests are compared with the presidential program objectives, expenditure ceilings set by the president, Department of Treasury revenue estimates, and economic forecasts from the Council of Economic Advisers and the Federal Reserve System.[9] The economic estimates—inflation rate, interest rates, level of unemployment, growth rate of GDP, and so on—are especially important for the federal budget because many budget totals are sensitive to the state of the economy. For example, Congress passes laws that provide for spending dependent on the number of unemployed workers who qualify for assistance, and several programs (most notably Social Security) index spending to inflation. Furthermore, federal revenues are particularly sensitive to economic activity, and, given the considerable amount of federal debt outstanding, total outlays change significantly depending on the rate of interest the federal government must pay on its debt. As a result, the forecast of economic activity can substantially affect the budget's spending and revenue plans. The *budget baseline*—an estimate of the receipts, outlays, and deficits that current law would produce—provides important information to the process by warning of future problems, giving a starting point for formulating the current budget, and offering a "policy-neutral" benchmark against which the president's (and other) budget proposals can be compared[10] without complication from the ways the economy can alter those numbers.

Budget preparation involves continuing communication between the president and officials in the Executive Office of the president (especially OMB) and officials of the departments and agencies regarding policies, programs, and budget implications. What Congress is doing to the budget under consideration and to other legislation is important, as are developments in the execution of the current budget.

---

[9]The Council of Economic Advisors, another part of the Executive Office of the president, provides advice on macroeconomic conditions and overall fiscal policy and on microeconomic issues. *The Economic Report of the President,* which the Council prepares, is an important source document for information and policy discussion. The Federal Reserve System is the American central bank.

[10]The current services budget, one part of the Analytical Perspectives volume of the federal budget, provides a baseline. That volume discusses the baseline concept and its measurement in considerable detail. In general, receipts and mandatory spending (spending that occurs according to a formula, not annual appropriation) are estimated according to current law; funding that must be approved each year is estimated by adjusting the most recently approved appropriation for inflation. The CBO also prepares a budget baseline for its analysis; the CBO baselines have been more widely used in recent years. For an excellent discussion of the problem of defining a baseline, see Timothy J. Morris, "The Uses and Misuses of Budget Baselines," in John F. Cogan, et al., *The Budget Puzzle: Understanding Federal Spending* (Stanford, Calif.: Stanford University Press, 1994), 41–78.

Table 3–3
Major Events in the Federal Budget Process

Major Steps in the Formulation Phase

What Happens?	When?
OMB issues spring planning guidance to Executive Branch agencies for the upcoming budget. The OMB director issues a letter to the head of each agency providing policy guidance for the agency's budget request. Absent of more specific guidance, the out year estimates included in the previous budget serve as a starting point for the next budget. This begins the process of formulating the budget the president will submit the following February.	Spring
OMB and the Executive Branch agencies discuss budget issues and options. OMB works with the agencies to: ▪ Identify major issues for the upcoming budget ▪ Develop and analyze options for the upcoming fall review ▪ Plan for the analysis of issues that will need decisions in the future	Spring and Summer
OMB issues Circular No. A-11 to all federal agencies. This circular provides detailed instructions for submitting budget data and materials.	July
Executive Branch agencies (except those not subject to Executive Branch review) make budget submissions. See section 25.	Fall*
Fiscal year begins. The just-completed budget cycle focused on this fiscal year. It was the "budget year" in that cycle and is the "current year" in this cycle.	October 1
OMB conducts its fall review. The OMB staff analyzes agency budget proposals in light of presidential priorities, program performance, and budget constraints. They raise issues and present options to the director and other OMB policy officials for their decisions.	October–November
OMB briefs the president and senior advisors on proposed budget policies. The OMB director recommends a complete set of budget proposals to the president after OMB has reviewed all agency requests and considered overall budget policies.	Late November
"Passback." OMB usually informs all Executive Branch agencies at the same time about the decisions on their budget requests.	Late November
All agencies, including Legislative and Judicial Branch agencies, enter MAX computer data and submit print materials and additional data. This process begins immediately after passback and continues until OMB must "lock" agencies out of the database in order to meet the printing deadline.	Late November to early January*
Executive Branch agencies may appeal to OMB and the president. An agency head may ask OMB to reverse or modify certain decisions. In most cases, OMB and the agency head resolve such issues and, if not, work together to present them to the president for a decision.	December*
Agencies prepare and OMB reviews congressional budget justification materials. Agencies prepare the budget justification materials they need to explain their budget requests to the responsible congressional subcommittees.	January
President transmits the budget to Congress.	First Monday in February

Table 3–3
(continued)

Major Steps in the Congressional Phase

What Happens?	When?
Congressional Budget Office (CBO) reports to budget committees on the economic and budget outlook.	January
CBO reestimates the president's budget based on their own economic and technical assumptions.	February
Other committees submit "views and estimates" to House and Senate budget committees. Committees indicate their preferences regarding budgetary matters for which they are responsible.	Within 6 weeks of budget transmittal
Congress completes action on the concurrent resolution on the budget. Congress commits itself to broad spending and revenue levels by passing a budget resolution.	April 15
Congress needs to complete action on appropriations bill for the upcoming fiscal year. Congress completes action on regular appropriations bills or provides a "continuing resolution" (a stop-gap appropriation law).	September 30

Major Steps in the Execution Phase

What Happens?	When?
Fiscal year begins.	October 1
OMB apportions funds made available in the budget process and other available funds. Agencies submit apportionment requests to OMB for each budget account by *August 21* or within *10 calendar days* after the approval of the appropriation, whichever is later. OMB approves or modifies the apportionment specifying the amount of funds agencies may use by time period, program, project, or activity.	September 10 (or within 30 days after approval of a spending bill)
Agencies incur obligations and make outlays to carry out the funded programs, projects, and activities. Agencies hire people, enter into contracts, enter into grant agreements, etc., in order to carry out their programs, projects, and activities.	Throughout the fiscal year
Fiscal year ends.	September 30
Expired phase (no-year funds do not have an expired phase). Agencies disburse against obligated balances and adjust obligated balances to reflect actual obligations during the period of availability.	Until September 30, fifth year after funds expire
Agencies continue to record obligations and outlays pursuant to administrative control of funds procedures, report to Treasury, and prepare financial statements.	

SOURCE: Executive Office of the President, Office of Management and Budget, *Preparation and Submission of Budget Estimates.* (Circular no. A-11) (Washington, D.C.: OMB, 2004).
*OMB provides specific deadlines for this activity.

Changes in the economic forecasts for the budget year can also alter budget formulation. From these discussions during budget preparation, agencies submit requests in the fall for OMB review. Most issues are resolved between OMB and the agency (there are OMB hearing examiners), but some require a final policy decision by the president. Transmission of the final document—the president's budget message—occurs no later than the first Monday in February. This document presents the president's program plans, with requests for funds to carry out those plans, for the upcoming fiscal year. That means for the fiscal year beginning on October 1, 2006 (the 2007 fiscal year), the message would be delivered in early February 2006.[11] The final budget is both printed and posted on the OMB website for public disclosure. The president's budget has no legal impact, but it provides the basis for congressional deliberations about providing budget authority, the result of appropriation legislation.

Many months separate the date of the budget message and the end of its fiscal year. Not only can there be economic, international, and social surprises to upset plans, but Congress may not agree with the presidential agenda. Nevertheless, differences between presidential plans and actual spending have been surprisingly small in relative terms. In recent years, total budget outlays seldom differ from the initial executive proposal by more than 2 percent (although that is still a lot of money). In pragmatic terms, this suggests the key role of the executive in aggregate expenditure control. There are, of course, much greater differences in individual programs than appear in these aggregates.

Another product of the long cycle is the phenomenon of lame-duck budgets. A new president not only faces about 9 months of appropriations coming from the previous president and Congress (from inauguration day through October 1) but also a new budget initiated during the term of the prior administration: prior budget instructions, OMB reviews, and so on. The date of the budget message falls just after inauguration day, so not much new perspective can be worked out and any transmission to Congress might be without much real detail.[12]

The *legislative-review-and-appropriation phase* of the federal cycle includes several committee pathways and many political quirks.[13] Table 3–4 indicates the timetable and path of the process through Congress. There are four different committee paths in the congressional fiscal process, each with different responsibilities, focuses, and interests. Each house has authorization (or substantive) committees, an appropriations committee (with its subcommittees), a budget committee, and a financing committee (Senate Finance and House Ways and Means). In the spending

---

[11]Unless the transmission date changes: the 1921 act specified the first day of each regular session; the Budget and Account Procedures Act of 1950 changed the date to within the first 15 days of the session; Gramm-Rudman-Hollings specified the first Monday after January 3; and BEA90 established the current date. Congress and the president have also changed the date by mutual consent.[12]President George W. Bush submitted a general document titled *A Blueprint for New Beginnings: A Responsible Budget for America's Priorities* in April. This is what President Clinton did in February 1993, when he succeeded the earlier President Bush. Karl O'Lessker, "The New President Makes a Budget," *Public Budgeting & Finance* 12 (Fall 1992): 3–18, traces how this revision process has evolved.

[13]The complete details of the legislative consideration phase can be found in Sandy Streeter, *The Congressional Appropriation Process: An Introduction, CRS Report For Congress,* Order Code 97-684 GOV (Washington, D.C.: Congressional Research Service, Library of Congress, 2004).

Table 3–4
The Congressional Budget Timetable

Date	Action
First Monday in February	President submits executive budget to Congress
February 15	Congressional Budget Office submits economic and budget outlook report to Budget Committee
Six weeks after President submits budget	Committees submit views and estimates to Budget Committee
April 1	Senate Budget Committee reports budget resolution
April 15	Congress complete action on budget resolution
May 15	Annual appropriations bills may be considered in the house, even if action on budget resolution has not been completed.
June 10	House Appropriations Committee reports last annual appropriations bill
June 15	House completes action on reconciliation legislation (if required by budget resolution)
June 30	House completes action on annual appropriations bills
July 15	President submits mid-session review of his budget to Congress
October 1	Fiscal year begins

process, the authorization committees set policies and create programs for agencies to carry out. Committees with legislative jurisdiction over subject matter—for example, agriculture—consider (1) enabling, or organic, legislation that creates agencies, establishes programs, or prescribes a function; and (2) appropriation-authorization legislation that authorizes appropriation of funds to implement the organic legislation. The latter may be part of the organic legislation, or it may be separate. There is no general requirement that specific authorization precede appropriation, but there are some requirements and operating rules that make this the usual situation.[14] Some programs require annual authorization; others have authorizations for a set number of years or for an indefinite period. Authorizations usually establish funding ceilings for particular programs, but they do not provide money to carry out those programs. Many authorized programs do not receive any appropriation. During legislative consideration, the president's view on proposed budgetary legislation is communicated, through OMB, in Statements of Administration Policy

[14]In some years there are omnibus appropriation acts that lump what ordinarily would be several separate laws into one.

(SAPs). Negotiations over budget policies and programs continue throughout the appropriation process.

The appropriations committees, working through their subcommittees, develop the appropriation bills that provide funds for federal agency operations. The appropriations committees are not supposed to deal with substantive policy, but often cross that line with clauses such as "Agency X is appropriated $ZZZ million, *subject to* the provision that none of this money shall be used to . . . ." Appropriation subcommittee and authorization committee jurisdictions do not match up: the agencies falling under the jurisdiction of a particular authorizing committee may have appropriations in several different appropriation subcommittees.

Table 3–5 lists the appropriation subcommittees for the house and for the Senate. There are twelve subcommittees in the Senate and ten in the House. For many years there were thirteen matching committees in each chamber, but Congress can juggle its organization as it wishes. For instance, when the Department of Homeland Security was created, subcommittee jurisdictions were shifted to create a

Table 3–5
Appropriations Subcommittees from 109th Congress

Senate (twelve subcommittees):
Agriculture, Rural Development, and Related Agencies
Commerce, Justice, and Science
Defense
District of Columbia
Energy and Water
Homeland Security
Interior and Related Agencies
Labor, Health and Human Services, Education, and Related Agencies
Legislative Branch
Military Construction and Veterans Affairs
State, Foreign Operations, and Related Programs
Transportation, Treasury, the Judiciary, Housing and Urban Development, and Related Agencies
House (ten committees):
Agriculture, Rural Development, Food and Drug Administration, and Related Agencies
Defense
Energy and Water
Foreign Operations, Export Financing, and Related Programs
Homeland Security
Interior, Environment, and Related Agencies
Labor, Health and Human Services, Education, and Related Agencies
Military Quality of Life and Veterans Affairs and Related Agencies
Science, Departments of State, Justice, and Commerce and Related Agencies
Transportation, Treasury, HUD, Judiciary, District of Columbia, and Related Agencies
Plus Legislative Branch—under jurisdiction of full Committee of Appropriations

Sidebar 3–1
The First General Appropriation Act

Here is the first general appropriation act passed by Congress (1789):

> Be it enacted by the Senate and House of Representatives of the United States of America in Congress assembled. That there be appropriated for the service of the present year, to be paid out of the monies which arise, either from the requisitions heretofore made upon the several states, or from the duties on impost and tonnage, the following sums, viz. A sum not exceeding two hundred and sixteen thousand dollars for defraying the expenses of the civil list, under the late and present government; a sum not exceeding one hundred and thirty-seven thousand dollars for defraying the expenses of the department of war; a sum not exceeding one hundred and ninety thousand dollars for discharging the warrants issued by the late board of treasury, and remaining unsatisfied; and a sum not exceeding ninety-six thousand dollars for paying the pensions to invalids. [1 stat. 95]

That is a total of $639,000: $216,000 for civil or administrative governments, $137,000 for defense, $190,000 to retire short-term debt issued by the prior government, and $96,000 for pensions to the disabled. Compare this act with any of the recent regular appropriation acts for a contrast in complexity, length, and money, for instance, the Department of Homeland Security Appropriation Act of 2005 (Public Law 108–334) for $28.9 billion.

homeland security subcommittee within a total of thirteen subcommittees. However, the new arrangement, starting from 2006, has created a different number of subcommittees in the houses and differing jurisdictions for some of those that are there. There will presumably be twelve appropriation bills, but how many will ultimately be passed is not certain. The arrangement may be a transitional one. In any case, the recent trend has been to merge several appropriations bills for eventual passage as a combined, or omnibus, appropriation.

The budget committees develop the congressional budget. The financing committees are Senate Finance and House Ways and Means. These committees have jurisdiction over federal tax and revenue measures, an obviously critical part of government finance, but they also have jurisdiction over spending through the Social Security system, the Medicare and Medicaid structures, unemployment compensation, and payment of debt interest, a span that includes more than half of all federal expenditure. Hence, these committees are extremely important for the finances of the federal government. More about their spending functions is discussed in a later section on entitlements.

Congress does not pass a single federal budget that provides funding to all agencies. The funds are provided through distinct appropriation acts (see Sidebar 3–1), which emerge through the individual appropriations committees. The appropriation subcommittees develop and review the appropriation acts. These subcommittees work with pieces of the president's executive budget that reflect the requests from agencies within their jurisdiction. In this stage of legislative deliberation, elements of agency operation are examined, and agencies make their cases for particular funds in their fiscal plans. Appropriation bills originate in the House.

Traditionally, the bill is approved in the appropriation subcommittee, then by the full appropriations committee, and then by the House before starting a similar flow through the Senate. In recent years, however, Senate appropriation subcommittees have often started hearings before House action is complete. Both House and Senate must approve the bill before it can be transmitted to the president for signature into law.

Congress usually passes appropriations in lump sums to accounts that group related activities together, like "Construction, General." However, there may be "earmarks" that designate some funds for particular purposes (construction in a particular location), usually in committee reports and explanatory statements, rather than in the law itself. Agencies generally regard these notes as binding because they do not want to jeopardize their relationship with Congress in future budget cycles.

Members of Congress covet membership on the appropriations committee because programs and projects of special constituent interest may be developed, expanded, and protected there. All members are selected from geographically specific electoral bases and their constituencies can benefit from location-specific projects—pork-barrel spending or "zip code designated expenditure"—that have scant return to the nation, but bring federal money into the home economy.[15] (Of course, programs that do have a considerable return to the nation have to be situated somewhere, and directing those to the home jurisdiction can be helped by membership on the appropriations committee as well.) Although pork-barrel spending often includes highway projects (the Transportation Equity Act for the 21st Century, H.R. 2400, included 1,850 location-designated projects alone), university institutes and research programs, airports, government office buildings, and the like, no appropriation bill is immune. But what makes particular project "pork" as opposed to being a program that simply happens to be physically in a particular location? Using standards akin to Supreme Court Justice Potter Stewart's statement about pornography (". . . I know it when I see it. . . ." *Jacobellis v. Ohio* [378 U.S. 184 (1964)]), the media can easily identify wasteful government spending, but more careful discussion attempts to hone the concept more precisely. Some common features include the following: the project is created as an earmark (a location-specific line item) in the appropriation bill; the project emerges from a member of Congress rather than from the administrative agency review process; and the project is added to the appropriation bill after the regular hearings and deliberations that produced the bill and without any discussions about the particular project. Many believe that presidential item veto power, to be discussed shortly, would kill the pork; others argue that hard budget ceilings can effectively do the job; some even believe that a bit of pork is useful as a means of lubricating the legislative process. Congressional earmarks

[15]The effectiveness of Robert Byrd as chair of the Senate Appropriations Committee for his home state of West Virginia is legendary, but there are many other successful practitioners as well. For entertaining but troubling examples, see Brian Kelly, *Adventures in Porkland: How Washington Wastes Your Money and Why They Won't Stop* (New York: Villard, 1992). A more scholarly study of appropriations legislation is Richard Munson, *The Cardinals of Capitol Hill* (New York: Grove Press, 1993). Cardinals are the chairs of the appropriation subcommittees. Ronald Utt notes that the pork projects often do not fit the priorities of the recipient locales, Ronald D. Utt, "How Congressional Earmarks and Pork-Barrel Spending Undermine State and Local Decision-making," *The Heritage Foundation Backgrounder,* April 2, 1999, No. 1266.

have been one critical element in the lobbyist influence scandals of 2005–2006. Members of Congress have been accused of inserting special projects into appropriation bills, sometimes in conference committee drafts after all hearings on the appropriations have been conducted, in return for campaign contributions and other favors from lobbyists who represent clients who will gain from those projects. The record shows that earmarks have increased: from 1,439 projects totaling $10.1 billion in 1995, to 4,326 projects totaling $17.7 billion in 2000, to 13,998 projects totaling $27.3 billion in 2005.[16] These violate the expected openness of the budget process and likely result in considerable waste of public resources. But total budget outlays in 2005 were almost $2.5 trillion—the earmarks do not represent a great amount relative to total federal finances.

Before the 1974 act, Congress considered the federal budget only as the several appropriations bills; Congress did not consider the budget as a whole. The budget was fragmented into general administrative department "chunks," and each chunk was considered by a separate appropriations subcommittee. This microlevel budget analysis permitted scrutiny of individual department requests, but it did not permit the overall comparison of revenue, expenditures, and accompanying surplus or deficit. More important, this practice did not permit consideration of government-wide priorities—transportation versus defense, and so on—that effective budget choices require, and there was nothing in the system that balanced the funds added to one department against the need to finance that increase through either more revenue or less spending somewhere else.

The revised process, used initially for the 1977 budget, produced an additional flow through Congress: The appropriations committees work as before, but separate budget committees, with staff assistance from the CBO, draft a budget resolution that encompasses budget levels for 5 years.[17] The resolution presents recommended aggregates for new budget authority, budget outlays, direct loan obligations, primary loan guarantee commitments, revenues, surplus or deficit, and public debt and recommends aggregate revenue change. New budget authority, budget outlays, direct loan obligations, and primary loan guarantees are also divided among twenty categories of government (the major national needs served by the federal government, such as national defense, transportation, agriculture, administration of justice, etc.). The explanatory statement with the resolution allocates budget authority and outlays in functional categories to committees with jurisdiction over programs in the function. The appropriations committees must allocate budget authority and outlays among their subcommittees.[18] Allocations to each House and Senate committee are called 302(a) allocations, after the section in the 1974 Act that provides for them; their allocations to the thirteen subcommittees are called 302(b) allocations.

---

[16]"The Keepers of K Street," *The Wall Street Journal,* January 17, 2006, p. A16. K Street is the street in Washington, D.C., on which the most powerful lobbyists have their offices.

[17]That's the budget year and 4 out years.

[18]Allocations to the appropriations committee are called 602(a) allocations and those to appropriation subcommittees are called 602(b) allocations. The names refer to sections of the 1974 act. The functional categories are the primary purpose the spending serves without regard to the agency or other unit that is responsible for it.

This budget resolution is macrolevel; it does not work from the detailed agency requests, although the budget committees (and their staff) are well-versed with what agencies have in mind and they do receive budget recommendations from each standing committee of Congress as they develop the resolution. The Concurrent Budget Resolution is approved by both houses of Congress in the spring, before the appropriation consideration begins in earnest.[19] The budget resolution does not go to the President for approval, so it does not become law. The deadline for its passage is frequently missed and a few times Congress has approved no budget resolution. The congressional budget provides a template against which the microbudget actions of appropriations committees can be judged for control and constraint. The timetable that Table 3–4 showed for the congressional budget and appropriation process would have Congress complete all appropriations actions before the start of the fiscal year.

There is a final element to the congressional budget process: reconciliation. The 1974 act created reconciliation as a mechanism for getting the year's tax and expenditure policies to coincide with the targets in the congressional budget. It has come to be viewed as the most powerful congressional tool for deficit reduction: Rather than minor, 1-year adjustments to targets, it now entails 5-year instructions to committees for tax or fee increases and for spending cuts. The amounts involved can be large ($496 billion in deficit reduction over 5 years for the reconciliation passed in 1993).[20]

The reconciliation bill can be powerful, if Congress chooses to use its full clout, because (1) the bill gives binding instructions for changes in taxes and spending by formula or for reductions in spending to all committees except for appropriations committees, which are subject to other ceilings; (2) the bill cannot be filibustered, so it requires only a simple majority to be approved in the face of considerable objection; (3) amendments must be germane, and committees cannot add extraneous provisions (both are subject to a 60-vote test in the Senate); and (4) a committee that fails to meet its reconciliation target is subject to a motion to return its report to committee and return with a proposal that meets the target. Furthermore, reconciliation in 1993 and 1997 provided out-year discretionary expenditure ceilings of considerable importance. When the will is present, reconciliation can focus congressional attention on difficult choices about the budget.

The congressional budget process permits Congress to develop its own spending priorities, particularly with the assistance of the CBO, and to consider the appropriate macroeconomic impact for its fiscal actions. Without the congressional budget, the system would have the president responsible for budget aggregates and overall policy plans, and Congress responding to adjust those priorities by moving funds in the appropriation process. The congressional budget process adds a con-

---

[19]The formal Clinton fiscal 1994 budget was the first since the 1974 act received by Congress after it had passed the budget resolution. Appropriation subcommittees start hearings before the resolution.

[20]The reconciliation in 1981 was the medium for implementing President Reagan's economic reconstruction for fiscal 1982 (the 1982 executive budget had originated with President Carter, so this was the best place for President Reagan to revise those plans). The 1993 reconciliation was similarly the medium used by President Clinton.

gressional view on priorities and responsibility for aggregates.[21] Recent failures to pass a budget resolution and expiration of some controls from the Budget Enforcement Act have significantly reduced the Congressional role in budgeting, as opposed to appropriating, however.

After Congress passes an appropriation bill, it must be signed by the president before it becomes law. The president can veto the bill or sign the bill in its entirety. For almost a century and a half, every president has sought the line-item veto, the power to strike individual parts of spending and taxing bills while signing the remaining sections into law. The Line-Item Veto Act (P.L. 104–130, April 9, 1996) revised the Congressional Budget and Impoundment Control Act by granting the president additional power to shape federal finances. For calendar years 1997 through 2004, the president was given power to cancel (1) any dollar amount of discretionary spending authority, (2) any item of new direct spending (roughly, new entitlements), or (3) any limited tax benefit (defined to be a revenue-losing provision with 100 or fewer beneficiaries; the Joint Committee on Taxation was to establish the list of eligible provisions and append the list to the bill sent to the president) within 5 days of signing into law the act containing the item. The president could cancel whole individual amounts in appropriation acts or in the reports accompanying the acts, but could not reduce the amounts. The cancellation required that the president determine that the action would (1) reduce the federal budget deficit (and special controls ensured that this would occur), (2) not impair any essential government function, and (3) not harm the national interest. Congress had the ability to override the cancellation within a 30-day review period.[22] In fiscal 1998 appropriation bills, which were the first approved under the item-veto cloud, President Clinton vetoed seventy-seven items, accounting for about 0.10 percent of discretionary budget authority proposed in those bills. Eighty-seven percent of vetoed items were taken from defense and military construction bills, and Congress overrode the veto of the latter. This was the last use of this power, because in *William J. Clinton, President of the United States, et al.* v. *City of New York et al.* [524 U.S. 417 (1998)], the U.S. Supreme Court ruled that the line-item veto authority departed from the "finely wrought" constitutional procedure for enactment of law. If the president is to have line-item veto power, the Constitution must be amended; the power cannot be provided by simple legislation.

Not all agree that such power would improve government finances. The power can provide the president a tool to prevent pork-barrel and other wasteful spending, but it also gives the president a valuable weapon to punish recalcitrant members of Congress—those who have managed to get on a presidential "enemies list"—by making sure that programs they support receive meager funding. And it cuts the president in on the deal-making that builds appropriations and other pieces

---

[21]Not everyone considers this an improvement. Louis Fisher writes, "By looking to Congress for comprehensive action, the unity and leadership that must come from the President have been unwittingly weakened. Creation of multiple budgets opened the door to escapism, confusion, and a loss of political accountability." "Federal Budget Doldrums: The Vacuum of Presidential Leadership," *Public Administration Review* 50 (Nov./Dec. 1990): 699.

[22]The first use of the line-item veto: three provisions in the 1997 reconciliation laws. See Jackie Calmes and Greg Hitt, "Clinton Uses Line-Item Veto for First Time," *Wall Street Journal,* 12 August 1997, Z-3.

of legislation: the president can assure a congressman's vote on a program by promising not to veto a project dear to the member of Congress. Indeed, the president may be wary of vetoing any pet projects of members of Congress with leadership roles, the people whose support is needed for presidential programs. Many are willing to accept these potential problems for the sake of greater fiscal responsibility and because the president's national constituency probably makes him less controlled by narrow interests than members of Congress. Others regard it as an inappropriate change in the balance of powers between the legislative and executive branches and believe that it carries the potential for great political evil. For now, only congressional action can rescind an appropriation or tax benefit that the president wishes out of a law.

The end dates of the fiscal year presumably set the bounds for the *execution phase,* the third stage of the process. In this period, appropriated monies are spent and public services are provided. The appropriations form the financial plan, placed into law, for the agency during the year. The fact that money is appropriated for a purpose, however, does not automatically and immediately lead to public expenditure. To prevent agencies from exhausting funds before the end of the fiscal year and to use expenditure timing for macroeconomic purposes, the OMB divides total money to agencies into sums for distribution over the year (apportionments), a procedure discussed at greater length in the next chapter. Current law, primarily as defined in the 1974 act, restricts the ability of the president to avoid spending appropriated funds. Historically, appropriations were regarded as maximum authority. The president could spend up to the appropriated amount, but not more. Presidents regularly impounded budget authority, acting on their own, to control spending during budget execution. After the 1974 act, impoundments became subject to congressional review and were divided into two categories: rescissions of budget authority, or permanent cancellation, and deferrals, or temporary withdrawal, of budget authority in the fiscal year.[23] Rescissions proposed by the president must be approved by Congress within 45 days of the proposal. (Congress may also initiate rescissions.) If not approved within the deadline, the funds must be released for expenditure. Deferrals require a message to Congress reporting the action; the deferral may not involve a change in policy but may be justified by a need to provide for contingencies or to achieve savings from changed requirements or operating efficiency. The deferral cannot extend beyond the fiscal year.[24] "Programmatic" delays—when "operational factors unavoidably impede the obligation of budget authority, notwithstanding the agency's reasonable and good faith efforts to implement the program"[25]—do not need to be reported. About one-third of all presidential rescissions have been enacted, both in numbers and in volume, but the success

[23]The events that caused the change are chronicled in Louis Fisher, *Presidential Spending Power* (Princeton, N.J.: Princeton University Press, 1975), especially Chapters 7 and 8.

[24]Congress may enact legislation disapproving a deferral. Under the initial act, either house could prevent the deferral by passing an impoundment resolution. This was ruled to be an unconstitutional legislative veto in *City of New Haven* v. *United States,* 809 F.2d 900 (D.C. Cir. 1987) and was replaced with the current system.

[25]Office of the General Counsel, *Principles of Federal Appropriations Law,* 21.

of proposals has fallen since 1984.[26] However, rescissions in total represent a small share of budget totals or of the deficit. In contrast to most chief executives, the president does have clearly constrained powers of control in budget execution.

The *audit phase* of the federal cycle, supervised by the GAO, formally begins at the end of the fiscal year. Some audit functions, however, do begin during the fiscal year as agencies work to prevent illegal and irregular transactions by various approval stages. In an important sense, the audit phase ensures that everything else in the budget process matters: unless the decisions made elsewhere in the process are carried through, the process is irrelevant. The audit phase determines whether those directions were followed. The GAO reports to the House and Senate Commission on Government Operations.

Budget Authority. The result of congressional deliberations, including passage of identical statutes by both houses and approval by the president of those statutes, is budget authority.[27] This encompasses several authorities to make commitments (obligations) that result in government outlays (or expenditures), either now or in the future. Important types of authority include the following:

1. **Appropriations authority,** the most common authority, permits "federal agencies to incur obligations and to make payments from Treasury for specified purposes."[28]

2. **Contract authority** provides authority for agencies to enter into binding contracts, before the agency has an appropriation to make payments under the contract or in amounts greater than existing appropriations.[29] Eventually there must be appropriations to cover the contracts, and, because the contracts legally commit the U.S. government, Congress has little choice but to provide the appropriation. At one time, contract authority provided a device for "backdoor spending," a way that substantive committees could force the more conservative appropriations committees to accept more aggressive government programs. Now, new contract authority can be provided only to the extent appropriations are also provided for that fiscal year.

3. **Borrowing authority** appearing in either a substantive law or an appropriation act allows an agency to incur and liquidate obligations from borrowed

---

[26]U.S. General Accounting Office, *Impoundment Control Act: Use and Impact of Rescission Procedures (Testimony,* GAO/OGC-99-56) (Washington, D.C.: General Accounting Office, 1999). A much higher percentage of deferrals—99.4 percent of dollars appropriated from 1975 to 1988—have been approved. See Allen Schick, "The Disappearing Impoundment Power," *Tax Foundation's Tax Features* 32 (October 1988): 4.

[27]Federal agencies receive budget authority rather than money to spend. Budget authority gives legal authority to make obligations that require immediate or future outlays. Outlays are payments from the Treasury. The principal reference on budget authority and appropriations is Office of the General Counsel, U.S. General Accounting Office, *Principles of Federal Appropriations Law* (Washington, D.C.: GPO, 1992).

[28]Accounting and Financial Management Division, U.S. General Accounting Office, *A Glossary of Terms Used in the Federal Budget Process* (exposure draft) (Washington, D.C.: GPO, 1993), 21.

[29]Most federal highway programs operate with contract authority. U.S. Department of Transportation, Federal Highway Administration, *Financing Federal-Aid Highways,* Publication no. FHWA-PL-92-016 (May 1992), explains this system.

funds. That authority may involve some combination of borrowing from the Treasury, borrowing directly from the public (selling agency debt securities), or borrowing from the Federal Financing Bank (selling agency securities to it). Again, this authority now is limited to amounts provided in appropriation acts.

4. **Loan and loan-guarantee authority** consists of statutory authorizations for the government's pledge to pay all or part of principal and interest to a lender if the borrower defaults; no obligation occurs until the contingency (default) occurs. Such commitments, after the Federal Credit Reform Act of 1990, now require specified treatment in appropriation acts of estimated long-term costs (defaults, delinquencies, etc.).

5. **Entitlement authority** provides authority "to make payments (including grants and loans) for which budget authority is not provided in advance by appropriation acts to any person or government if, under the provisions of the law containing such authority, the U.S. government is obligated to make the payments to persons or governments who meet the requirements established by the law."[30] Entitlements provide payments according to formula: Social Security, Medicare, Medicaid, and veteran's benefits (pensions and education) are some important examples. Farm price supports fall in this category as well; they were replaced by a firm appropriation for a time. Entitlement spending results not directly from the appropriation process but through the extent to which beneficiaries qualify under the formulas erected in substantive law. Entitlements now fall within the scope of the reconciliation process. As noted earlier, much growth in federal spending comes from this entitlement. In a later section, we examine the nature of entitlements and "mandatory" expenditure in greater detail.

Appropriation is now the checkpoint for most important sources of budget authority, entitlements being the major exception. There are three types of appropriation measures: regular appropriation bills, continuing resolutions, and supplemental appropriations. Regular appropriations come in several durations (periods of legal availability) with different rules attached to each. The traditional appropriation is *annual* (1-year) authority, which provides funds for obligation during a specific fiscal year.[31] Such appropriations usually finance the routine activities of federal agencies; unless specified otherwise, appropriations are assumed to be annual and may not be carried beyond the current fiscal year for obligation later (funds expire). *No-year* appropriations provide funds for obligations with no restrictions placed on year of use. Most construction funds, some funds for research, and many trust fund appropriations have been handled in this fashion. *Multiple-year* appropriations provide funds for a particular activity for several years. General revenue sharing, a program of federal assistance to state and local governments of the late 1970s and

---

[30]GAO, *Glossary*.

[31]Congress may appropriate for less than a full fiscal year. A fiscal 1980 appropriation to the Community Services Administration for emergency energy-assistance grants specified that awards could not be made after June 30, 1980. Congress wanted to help with heating, not air conditioning (Public Law 96-126), but there was a severe heat wave and Congress extended the program to include fans; the appropriation was extended to the full fiscal year (Public Law 92-321).

early 1980s, was funded on that basis to provide greater predictability for the recipients. *Advance* appropriations provide agencies with funds for future fiscal years. This structure is seldom used, although it can facilitate agency planning and has been strongly urged for use in defense-system procurement. *Permanent* appropriations provide funds for specified purposes without requiring repeated action by Congress. To add greater certainty to public capital markets, interest on the federal debt is handled with such appropriations. All but annual appropriations reduce the ability of legislative and executive branches to realign fiscal policy when economic or social conditions change, even though they increase agency ability to develop long-range plans. The trade between control and planning is not an easy one, but responsibility and accountability probably weigh the balance toward annual appropriation, especially in regard to the difficulty of forecasting operating environments many months in advance.

Budget authority not obligated within the time period for which it was appropriated expires and is not held over for future use. Congress may act to extend the availability of funds, either before or after their scheduled expiration, through reappropriation. The federal budget structure counts these funds as new budget authority for the fiscal year of reappropriation.

Two other methods of providing agency funds, in addition to these normal appropriations, should be mentioned. First, a *continuing resolution* allows agencies to function when a new fiscal year begins before agency appropriation laws have been approved for the year. The resolution—an agreement between both legislative houses—authorizes the agency to continue operations. The resolution level may be the same as the prior year, may entail certain increases, or may encompass the appropriation bill as it has emerged from one house of Congress; the resolution may be for part of the fiscal year or for the entire year. Without some action, however, the agency without appropriations could not spend and would not be able to provide services. The congressional budget process establishes a timetable for appropriations that would eliminate the need for continuing resolutions, but that deadline has not always been met. How often are continuing resolutions necessary? In the fiscal years from 1948 through 2006, all thirteen appropriations were signed into law by the first day of the new fiscal year only in 1989, 1995, and 1997—and it was done for 1997 only by rolling six appropriation bills (defense; commerce, justice, state, and the judiciary; foreign operations; interior; labor, health and human services, and education; and treasury) into an omnibus appropriation bill approved on September 30, 1996, just in the nick of time! At the other extreme, all government operations were rolled into an omnibus continuing resolution for fiscal 1987 and fiscal 1988. In fiscal 2003, 2004, and 2005, several appropriation bills were lumped together in a consolidated appropriation because Congress could not agree on them separately and they were finally approved well after the start of the new fiscal year. In 2003, the omnibus appropriation included eleven bills (all but defense and military construction); in 2004, it included seven bills (all but defense, energy and water, homeland security, interior, the legislative branch, and military construction); and in 2005, it included nine bills (all but defense, District of Columbia, homeland security, and military construction). Since fiscal 1996, such omnibus appropriation acts have been the rule, rather than the exception. (However, a full eleven bills were passed for 2006.) And various parts of the government were closed for absence of either appropriation or continuing resolution in the early 1980s and, most recently, at the start of the 1996 fiscal year. The timetable for nicely defined appropriations in place with the new fiscal year is not always met.

Continuing resolutions have many trappings of appropriations, but their continued use raises three special issues. First, the continuing resolution in theory would have few, if any, new programs. A steady pattern of such funding could hinder an agency's program development and response to changing service conditions. Second, the omnibus continuing resolution may partly impede the president's veto power. A veto of an omnibus package could harm the flow of services throughout the government, a consequence the president ordinarily would want to avoid. Third, the omnibus package may tempt members of Congress to add special favors for their constituencies, causing an inordinate number of pet projects, well above those in a smaller appropriation bill more easily open to scrutiny and rejection. The continuing resolution deserves an uneasy life. Many countries have systems of automatic continuing resolutions to ensure that government does not close. Similar programs have been proposed for the federal government, but as yet there has been no agreement on what formula to use.

A second special form of providing funds is the *supplemental appropriation,* an appropriation of funds to be spent during the current fiscal year. (Requests and appropriations are normally for future budget years.) The supplemental may be part of a presidential budget submission or it may be separate. Of the first variety, President Bush's budget message for fiscal 2003, considered during fiscal 2002, contained a request for $1.3 billion in additional 2002 budget authority for the Department of Education to support higher maximum awards for Pell Grants. The new maximum had been approved in the 2002 regular appropriation, but had not been entirely funded there. Typical reasons include the need to (1) cover the cost of programs newly enacted by the legislature, (2) provide for higher-than-anticipated prices or workloads, or (3) cope with surprise developments. The request is for appropriation in addition to funds previously approved by the legislature. Forecasts of operating environments are seldom perfect, so most budget seasons include some supplementals. For example, the terrorist attacks of September 11, 2001, induced an emergency supplemental appropriation for $40 billion—for funds to be spent as required in any fiscal year. Other examples include supplementals to help deal with the Northridge (Los Angeles) earthquake in 1994, flooding in the Dakotas in 1998, and military operations in the 1990s and later. However, emergency circumstances produce supplementals outside the normal cycle.

The Bush administration has chosen to finance the wars in Iraq and Afghanistan almost entirely through supplemental appropriations, leaving these costs out of its regular budget message and adding them through the year. This practice is contrary to accepted budget practice because it hinders the capacity to maintain fiscal discipline and to direct limited resources to areas of greatest national priority. It is as if fighting these wars is an afterthought in finance that must automatically be added to the deficit. It is a good way to cripple the national economy. And supplementals that must pass become a great vehicle for special earmarks: the 2005 military supplement had provisions involving oil drilling, the National Park

Service, a new baseball stadium in Washington, tsunami relief, aid for Palestinians, and emergency watershed protection in Utah attached to it. Of course, supplementals are sometimes necessary because someone made a major mistake. For example, the Department of Veteran's Affairs needed a supplemental appropriation for fiscal 2005 to cover health services for veterans because it based its budget request on demand in fiscal 2002, before the invasion of Iraq and the resulting significant surge in demand for medical treatment for returning service personnel, even though the request was prepared after the war had started.[32]

Spending by the federal government is divided into spending from federal funds, spending from trust funds, spending that is on-budget, and spending that is off-budget. The budget documents also include reports for a number of government-sponsored enterprises whose finances are not included in the budget totals. Sidebar 3–2 describes the nature of these distinctions and what kind of operations fit into the several categories. The distinctions do not help make the process more transparent.

Mandatory and Discretionary Spending. The Budget Enforcement Act of 1990 created two legal categories of federal spending: mandatory and discretionary. Mandatory spending includes outlays that are made according to definitions of eligibility and establishment of benefit or payment formulas, rather than directly through the appropriation process. Table 3–6 shows the major types of mandatory federal spending and divides it into the programs that are *means-tested* (that is, payments are determined by the economic status of the recipient) and those that are *non–means-tested* (transfers made without regard to economic status, but on the basis of other characteristics of the recipient). Social Security, Medicare, and Medicaid constitute the largest components of this spending. Much of the spending comes from the entitlement authority previously described. Congress and the president still control the spending, but they exercise control indirectly by establishing the definitions and rules; when those conditions have been met, however, the government has a legal obligation to pay to the eligible person, corporation, or other entity. The government cannot plead lack of funds or more important uses for its funds. Congress and the president cannot increase or decrease the outlays for a given year without changing the substantitive law that created the eligibility and the payment rules; these rules, not appropriation actions, determine outlay. Because the spending is outside the annual appropriation process, Congress and the president have less capacity to exercise annual control over the spending—a legal checkpoint is gone—and control over total federal spending is lessened. And, as we shall see, those expenditures have taken larger shares of all federal outlays. Mandatory spending also includes offsetting receipts—certain fees and charges that are regarded as negative budget authority and outlay. These receipts are collected from other government accounts or from the public in business transactions (like rents and royalties from oil and gas drilling leases on the Outer Continental Shelf).

Discretionary spending represents the rest of federal spending, the spending that flows through the annual appropriation process and the thirteen appropriation

---

[32]Thomas B. Edsall, "VA Faces $2.6 Billion Shortfall in Medical Care," *Washington Post,* 29 June 2005: A19.

Sidebar 3–2
Federal Funds/Trust Funds, On-Budget/Off-Budget, Government Enterprises, Mandatory/Discretionary Relationships

Federal government finances uses a terminology all its own. Without some general understanding of some of the principal categories, it is impossible to understand what is going on. Outlined here are a few of the most important special terms, with a short description of what each is and why it is significant.

Federal funds (75.5 percent of federal total gross outlays in fiscal 2005): general, special, intragovernmental revolving or management, and public-enterprise revolving funds. *General fund* accounts are financed by undesignated receipts and provided for use by appropriation. *Public-enterprise revolving funds* receive revenues generated by business-type operations with the public, like Postal Service operations, and are available without appropriation for those operations. *Special fund* receipts are designated for specific uses, deposited into separate accounts, and available for use under statutorily prescribed conditions (the Nuclear Waste Fund receives fees from civilian nuclear power operators; funds can be used only for disposal of high-level nuclear waste). *Intragovernmental revolving funds* collect receipts from government agencies selling services to other government agencies. All federal funds are on-budget (see later in this sidebar for meaning).

Trust funds (40.9 percent of federal total gross outlays in fiscal 2005): a budget account that receives specially designated (or earmarked) receipts and has been designated by law as a trust fund. The largest federal trust funds, in terms of receipts, are the Federal Old-Age Survivors Insurance Trust Fund (X), the Federal Hospital Insurance Trust Fund, the Civil Service Retirement and Disability Fund, the Military Retirement Fund, the Federal Supplementary Medical Insurance Trust Fund, the Unemployment Trust Fund, the Federal Disability Trust Fund (X), the Highway Trust Fund, the Foreign Military Sales Trust Fund, and the Railroad Social Security Equivalent Benefit Account. Most lack the fiduciary relationship present in the normal meaning of trust funds: beneficiaries do not own the funds, and Congress may unilaterally alter tax rates, benefit levels, or other features of the program. The shares of the two fund categories do not add up to 100 percent because of interfund transfers.

On-budget and off-budget: The two trust funds marked (X) are legally off-budget. All other trust funds and all federal funds are on-budget (83.7 percent of federal gross outlays in fiscal 2005 were on-budget). Both on- and off-budget operations are in the federal budget. There is currently no particular significance to the distinction.

bills. This spending is for federal programs and the federal bureaucracy. Operations of agencies—the Department of Defense, the Fish and Wildlife Service, the Internal Revenue Service, and so on—fall in the discretionary category. It is a category that is related to the form of the spending, not to its importance to the nation. In other words, being "discretionary" does not mean that the spending is insignificant or that the nation could easily go without the program. It means that the spending goes through the traditional appropriation process and is not automatic. Fees and

Sidebar 3–2
(Continued)

Government-sponsored enterprises: The budget document includes detailed self-reports of financial operations and conditions of several government-sponsored enterprises, although these enterprises are neither on-budget nor off-budget. These enterprises were initiated by the federal government but are classified as private: the Student Loan Marketing Association, the College Construction Loan Insurance Association, the Federal National Mortgage Association, the Banks for Cooperatives and Farm Credit Banks, the Federal Agricultural Mortgage Corporation, the Federal Home Loan Banks, the Financing Corporation (FSLIC), and the Resolution Funding Corporation. The budget document also reports the administrative budget of the Board of Governors of the Federal Reserve System, the independent central bank of the United States. This is neither on-budget nor off-budget, and the system is not a government-sponsored enterprise.

Mandatory and discretionary outlays: categories created by BEA90 and earlier budget agreements. Mandatory outlays result from budget authority provided by law, other than appropriation acts, entitlement authority, and the food stamp program (53.4 percent of total outlay in fiscal 2005). This spending results primarily from benefit programs like Social Security, Medicare, and Medicaid, and results from congressionally established rules for eligibility, benefit formulae, and other standards rather than specific dollar annual appropriations. Baseline projections for this spending assumes that laws and policies remain in place. Mandatory spending also includes offsetting receipts that are recorded as negative budget outlays. These are primarily receipts from the public in business transactions (like rent payments and royalties). Discretionary outlays are provided in annual appropriation acts (39.2 percent in fiscal 2005). Lawmakers decide each year how much to spend in this category. Baseline projections for this spending is assumed to grow with estimated inflation. Net interest is a final federal spending category. This includes interest paid on Treasury securities and other obligations minus interest the federal government collects from various sources (like accounts in commercial banks). The amount depends on the size and maturity of government debt, prevailing interest rates, and the annual surplus or deficit.

SOURCES: U.S. General Accounting Office, *Report to the Chairman, Committee on Government Operations, House of Representatives: Trust Funds and Their Relationship to the Federal Budget* (GAO/AFMD-88–55) (Washington, D.C.: General Accounting Office, Sept. 1988); and Executive Office of the President, Office of Management and Budget, *Budget of the United States Government, Historical Tables, Fiscal Year 2007* (Washington, D.C.: Government Printing Office, 2006).

other charges that are driven by an appropriation action are classified as offsetting collections and offset discretionary spending. Discretionary spending is presumed to be easier to control in the legislative process than is mandatory spending.

Table 3–6 both shows the dramatically different paths that mandatory and discretionary spending have taken over the past 2 decades and identifies the larger mandatory spending programs. Discretionary spending has fallen from 47.5 percent of total outlays in 1975 to 39 percent in 2005. That continues an even longer trend:

Table 3–6
Mandatory and Discretionary Federal Spending, 1975–2005 ($ billions)

	1975	1980	1985	1990	1995	2000	2005	Annual Growth Rate
Important Means-Tested Programs								
Student Loans	0.1	1.4	3.5	4.4	4.4	1	15	18.2%
Medicaid	6.8	14	22.7	41.1	89.1	117	182	11.6%
Food Stamps	4.6	9.1	12.5	15.9	25.6	18	33	6.8%
Child Nutrition	1.5	3.4	3.7	5	7.5	9	13	7.5%
Earned Income Tax Credit	1.4	1.3	1.1	4.4	15.2	27	49	12.6%
Supplemental Security Income	4.3	5.7	8.7	11.5	24.5	31	38	7.5%
Family Support	5.1	7.3	9.2	12.2	18.1	21	24	5.3%
State Children's Health Insurance	0	0	0	0	0	2	5	
Veterans' Pensions	2.7	3.6	3.8	3.6	3	3	*	
Important Non–Means Tested Programs								
Medicare	14.1	34	69.6	107.4	177.1	216	333	11.1%
Social Security	63.6	117.1	186.4	246.5	333.3	406	519	7.2%
Federal Civilian, Military, Veterans and Other Retirement and Disability	18.3	32.1	45.2	59.9	75.2	88	148	7.2%
Unemployment Compensation	12.8	16.9	15.8	17.1	21.3	21	32	3.1%
Deposit Insurance	0.5	−0.4	−2.2	57.9	−17.9	−3.1	n.a.	
Farm Price and Income Supports	0.6	2.8	17.7	6.5	5.8	30	19	12.2%
Social Services	2.9	3.7	3.5	5.1	5.5	4	5	1.8%
Veterans' Benefits	10.2	11	12.9	13.4	18.3	24	*	
General Revenue Sharing	6.1	6.8	4.6	0	0	0	0	−100.0%
Flood Insurance	n.a.	n.a.	n.a.	n.a.	n.a.	n.a.	1	
TRICARE for Life	0	0	0	0	0	0	6	
Universal Service Fund†	0	0	0	0	0	n.a.	6	
Offsetting Receipts	−18.3	−29.2	−47.1	−58.7	−79.7	−78.6	−126	6.6%
Total for Mandatory and Related Programs	151.1	262	401.1	568.1	738.8	951.2	1320	7.5%
Net Interest	23.2	52.5	129.5	184.3	232.1	222.9	184	7.1%
Total Discretionary	158	276.3	415.8	500.6	544.9	614.8	968	6.2%
Defense	87.6	134.6	253.1	300.1	273.6	295	494	5.9%
Nondefense	70.3	141.7	162.7	200.4	271.3	319.9	474	6.6%
Total Outlays	332.3	590.9	946.4	1253.2	1515.8	1789.1	2472	6.9%

n.a.: not available.

*For 2004, included with federal civilian, military, veterans, and other retirement and disability.

†Partly means-tested.

SOURCE: Congressional Budget Office, The Budget and Economic Outlook (various years). Washington, D.C.: CBO.

Figure 3–1
Discretionary Federal Outlays as Percentage of Total Outlays, Fiscal 1962–2005

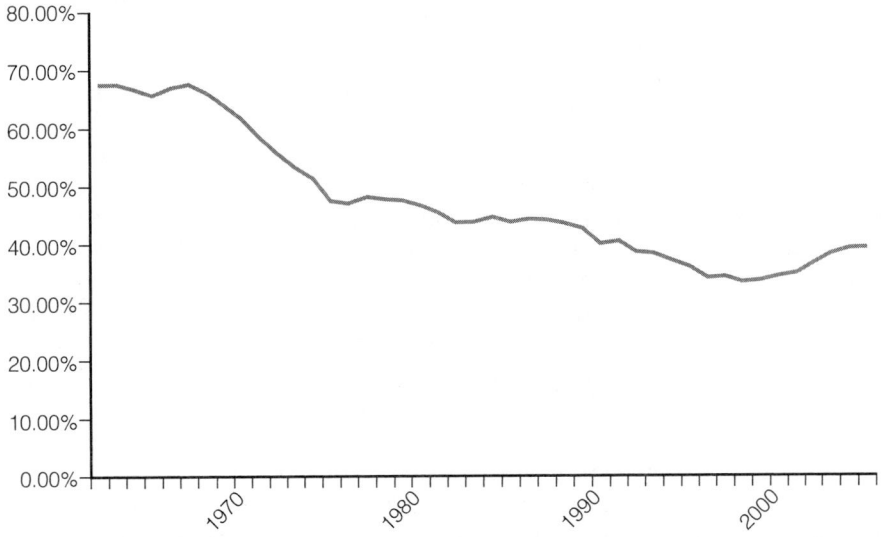

Discretionary spending was almost 70 percent of the total in the 1960s; Figure 3–1 shows the trend. The annual growth rate over this long period for mandatory spending (7.5 percent) is more than a percentage point greater than that for total discretionary spending (6.2 percent) and that compounds to a considerable difference in shares over time. The increase since 2000 for discretionary spending is largely caused by defense spending (wars are expensive), although the nondefense discretionary share is also higher. The net interest share is considerably lower because of low interest rates, not because of reduced debt outstanding.

Two social insurance programs—Social Security and Medicare—are major components of mandatory spending. Social Security, the largest single element of mandatory spending, took up 19.1 percent of total outlays in 1975, and had increased to 21.0 percent in 2005.[33] The aging of the American population guarantees the growth of this outlay. Congress could reduce spending growth by changing the law and increasing retirement age, lowering benefit levels for more affluent retirees, and so on, but without such changes, the spending is predestined. The second largest category is Medicare, the federal health-care program for the elderly. Spending there has gone from 4.2 percent of outlays in 1975 to 13.5 percent in 2004, a large increase caused by higher prices for medical care in general, but also enhancements in program coverage and increases in the number of people who are eligible.

[33]The best single source on entitlement spending is "The Green Book," Committee on Ways and Means, U.S. House of Representatives, *Background Material and Data on Programs Within the Jurisdiction of the Committee on Ways and Means* (Washington: U.S. Government Printing Office). The book is published periodically and includes major entitlements not strictly in Ways and Means jurisdiction.

Neither of these programs is means-tested. That is, all those who meet eligibility standards receive assistance according to a payment formula, regardless of their general affluence; changes in either are closely watched by recipient groups. Any changes would be in the domain of the Finance/Ways and Means Committees, not the annual appropriation process. Both are financed through a trust fund arrangement, by which dedicated taxes on payroll, plus interest income received from investment of trust fund balances are expected to support benefits paid out. More about the financing of these two large entitlements appears in Sidebar 3–3. Other, larger non–means-tested entitlement programs are federal civilian and military retirement programs and unemployment compensation. The long national economic expansion kept unemployment compensation spending low during the 1990s.

A second, but smaller, block of mandatory spending is means-tested; only those with limited affluence are eligible to receive benefits from the program. Medicaid, a program providing medical assistance for low-income people who are aged, blind, disabled, members of families with dependent children, and certain other pregnant women and children, is the largest such program, amounting to 7.4 percent of federal outlays in 2004, and has grown rapidly.[34] Other important programs in the total include: (1) the food stamp program, a program designed to allow low-income households to buy a nutritionally adequate low-cost diet; (2) the earned income tax credit, an income subsidy program for families to encourage work; (3) the supplemental security income program, a cash assistance program for very low-income aged, blind, and disabled people; and (4) family support, the former Aid to Families with Dependent Children, which has now become Temporary Assistance for Needy Families, supported by federal block appropriation to states rather than on an individual entitlement basis. Such means-tested spending constitutes "safety-net spending." The data in Table 3–6 show that, although spending on most means-tested programs has grown more rapidly than has spending on non–means-tested programs, the non–means-tested programs are much larger and create a greater challenge for the budget. In gross budget-control terms, the major financial concern is with the latter programs, especially Medicare and Social Security, the programs for the elderly.

Are Congress and the president powerless to alter the path of mandatory spending? Of course not. Options include (1) capping entitlements (essentially limiting the total amount that can be spent in a program, rather in the manner of ordinary appropriations), (2) making entitlement provisions less generous or at least constraining movements to make them more generous, and (3) making entitlements means-tested (ensuring that only those classified as needy according to a broader measure of affluence receive benefits). And, for the trust-fund entitlements, another prospect is for increasing revenues into the trust funds by either increasing the taxes dedicated for their support or by increasing the income from investment of balances in the funds. The point is that mandatory spending can be controlled; the barrier is political peril.

---

[34]Medicaid is jointly financed by federal and state government. The programs are funded by each of the states within guidelines established by federal legislation.

Sidebar 3–3
The Biggest Entitlements: Social Security and Medicare

The two largest federal entitlement programs—61.6 percent of mandatory spending in fiscal year 2005—are Social Security and Medicare, both social insurance programs systems primarily for the elderly. Social Security, more formally the Old-Age, Survivors, and Disability Insurance (OASDI) Program, provides benefits to retired and disabled workers, their dependents, and survivors that replace income lost to a family by retirement, death, or disability of a worker. It originated with the Social Security Act of 1935, although its coverage and role, as well as many structural features, have changed over the years. Medicare is a national health insurance program for the aged and certain disabled people. Part A Medicare covers inpatient hospital services, post-hospital skilled nursing facility care, home health services, and hospice care, and is available automatically to almost everyone older than age 65. Part B Medicare covers physicians' services, laboratory services, durable medical equipment, outpatient hospital services, and other medical services; payment is generally limited to 80 percent of an approved Medicare fee schedule after the patient has met an annual $100 deductible amount, and the insurance is provided only to those individuals who purchase it. Part D Medicare provides prescription drug coverage through premiums paid to private insurers and general fund subsidies. Social Security and Part A Medicare are financed by payroll taxes paid by workers covered by their program, their employers (roughly 96 percent of the paid workforce), and by a tax on the net annual earnings of the self-employed. Part B Medicare is financed by premiums paid by persons in the program and by general federal revenues. Any fund balances are invested in U.S. Treasury securities to earn interest. Benefits are paid as entitlements; the benefit formulae are determined by Congress, and benefits do not depend on the amount of funds in the respective trust funds.

These programs are reasonable candidates for "self-financing" (or "actuarial funding") schemes associated with social insurance trust funds because of their focus on the elderly. And we also know that conditions of moral hazard and adverse selection make private insurance in old age extremely shaky. With a social insurance system, people must pay into the social insurance fund during their work life and qualify for guaranteed benefits from the fund during that work experience. On retirement, sufficient funds will have accumulated—payments in, plus interest earned—to support pension payments and health insurance coverage for the individual. The life-cycle of the fund is one of accumulation during work years and disbursement during retirement; the fund will be "fully funded" or "actuarially sound" when the system accumulations are sufficient to cover benefits estimated to be owed to system beneficiaries.

Unfortunately, the American social insurance system for too long operated on a "pay-as-you-go" system of finance, wherein people qualified for benefits during their work life, but insufficient money was accumulated to support those benefits on retirement. The scheme worked because it was possible to use revenues collected from the current workforce to support benefits paid to current retirees. But demographic forces create a problem: while there were about five workers for each Social Security recipient in 1960, there are expected to be only about two workers per recipient by 2030—the transfer from worker to recipient cannot be supported any

(continues)

Sidebar 3–3
The Biggest Entitlements: Social Security and Medicare (continued)

more. And the money accumulated in the Social Security Trust Funds rapidly disappears. Payments into the system and interest earned on the accumulation are insufficient to finance the system as people live longer, as "baby-boomers" retire, and as labor-force growth slows—all demographic forces now in place. On top of that is the rapid escalation of health care costs. While the social insurance trust funds, both Social Security and Medicare, have been in surplus for a number of years and have provided a partial cushion against the deficits of the general fund, the cruel truth is that those surpluses are not large enough to cover the benefits being earned by workers.

The economic numbers for both programs are chilling. The trustees of the Social Security system estimate that annual revenue to OASDI will fail to cover annual benefits from 2017 and beyond. From that year, benefits will be paid only by liquidating trust fund assets. That is not the crisis, because that is why trust fund assets have been accumulated. The problem is that those assets will be exhausted in 2041. Of course, those assets are federal fund debt of the U.S. government—so the Federal government will have to raise taxes, borrow more (from some lender other than the Social Security system), or cut Federal fund spending to repay the debt being liquidated by the Social Security system. If the Federal government is unable to repay the debt owned by the Social Security system as it comes due, then the financial problems of the Social Security system will be only one of the fiscal disasters that the country will face; a government that defaults on its debt has big trouble. By 2079, the end of the 75 year forecasting horizon used by the system, Social Security benefits would be 6.4 percent of GDP, against 4.3 percent now. The trustees find an even worse profile for the portion of Medicare financed through its trust fund. Annual revenue already fails to cover annual cost and the trust fund will be exhausted in 2020. Its estimated annual cost in 2079 would be almost 14 percent of GDP, compared with 2.6 percent now.

As with other elements of government finance, the general options are clear: (1) increase current revenues into the system, (2) constrain benefits paid from the system, or (3) increase returns earned while balances are in the system by expanding the investment options available to fund administrators. Of course, making both programs for the elderly a private responsibility is another option, but returning society to pre-1930 conditions, with individuals being solely responsible for their own old age—an environment in which growing old typically meant being forced to move in with family or the county poorhouse—is not an attractive prospect for most Americans. What is clear is that neither the Social Security nor the Medicare problem will go away by itself.

SOURCE: Social Security and Medicare Board of Trustees, *Status of the Social Security and Medicare Programs: A Survey of the 2005 Annual Reports* (Washington, D.C.: Social Security Administration, 2005) and Congressional Budget Office, *Social Security: A Primer* (Washington, D.C.: Congressional Budget Office, 2001).

Fighting Federal Deficits

Federal finances are in deficit when outlays exceed receipts and in surplus when receipts exceed outlays. The federal surplus/deficit record from 1940 to 2005 appears in Table 3–7. The data are presented for a variety of different categorizations. They are the following: (1) the total (or unified) federal surplus/deficit: all receipts less all outlays of the federal government; (2) the federal funds surplus/deficit, which includes all general operations of the federal government (no trust fund operations); (3) the trust fund surplus/deficit, which includes the dedicated revenues operations of the federal government; and (4) off-budget deficit (Social Security, or the Federal Old-Age Survivors Insurance and Federal Disability Trust Funds).[35] The total surplus/deficit is also presented as percentage of GDP to adjust for dramatic differences in the size of the U.S. economy over the years. Until around 1960, the pattern with the unified budget was for mixed years of surplus and years of deficit for the total budget, except during the years of World War II, when huge military expenses relative to the size of the national economy, stretched the financing capacity of the country to the limit. After 1960, the pattern of fluctuation between total surplus and deficit broke down. From 1961 to 1998, Federal outlays exceeded receipts in every year except 1969, when there was a tiny surplus.[36] Within that period, through both economic expansion and economic decline, each year the federal government spent more money than it collected, and hence had to borrow to make up the difference (the Federal debt is the result of accumulated deficits through the country's history). There were unified surpluses from 1998 to 2001.

Federal funds were in surplus in fiscal 2000 for the first time since fiscal 1960, but returned to deficit in fiscal 2001 as a result of the 2001 tax reduction and the recession that started in March 2001. It continues even after the end of the recession because of the continued effects of the tax reduction, increases in discretionary domestic spending, and the wars in Iraq and Afghanistan. Long-term projections of federal finances are always hazardous because Congress and the president can change tax and expenditure policies and render those projections absolutely wrong. The fact that huge projected 10-year surpluses at the end of the twentieth century quickly became huge deficits as far as the eye can see as early as 2002 demonstrates

[35]There has been considerable concern about the finances of the Pension Benefit Guaranty Corporation (PBGC), an entity created by the Employee Retirement Income Security Act of 1974, to ensure that voluntary private pension plans can meet benefit payments, even if the private sponsor of the plan becomes financially unable to make payments. The PBGC is financed by insurance premiums from employers with insured plans; Congress sets the premiums that employers pay. The exposure of the PBGC is huge, exceeding the accumulated premiums it held in 2004 by an estimated $96 billion. But, despite the fact that the Corporation was created under federal law, there is no direct federal exposure: the Corporation receives no general tax revenue, and the federal government provides no guarantees for its program. But does the federal government have an implicit or moral guarantee of PBGC benefits? If so, then when bankrupt private employers like United Airlines turn their underfunded pension plans over to PBGC, the federal government faces even more spending pressures.

[36]Before the late 1990s, the last actual unified surplus (on-budget and off-budget combined) occurred in fiscal 1969 (but budget message planned a deficit); the last planned unified surplus occurred in fiscal 1971 (but actually ended with deficit); the last surplus, counting federal funds/on-budget transactions alone, occurred in fiscal 1960 (planned and actual).

Table 3–7
Deficits and Surpluses of the Federal Government, 1940–2005
($ in millions)

Fiscal Year	Total	Off-Budget	Federal Funds	Trust Funds	Total as % GDP
1940	−2,920	564	−4,045	1,125	−3.0%
1941	−4,941	653	−6,360	1,419	−4.3%
1942	−20,503	830	−22,496	1,992	−14.2%
1943	−54,554	1,041	−57,648	3,094	−30.3%
1944	−47,557	1,178	−51,818	4,261	−22.7%
1945	−47,553	1,167	−52,972	5,419	−21.5%
1946	−15,936	1,028	−19,847	3,910	−7.2%
1947	4,018	1,157	577	3,441	1.7%
1948	11,796	1,248	8,834	2,962	4.6%
1949	580	1,263	−1,838	2,417	0.2%
1950	−3,119	1,583	−3,055	−65	−1.1%
1951	6,102	1,843	2,451	3,651	1.9%
1952	−1,519	1,864	−5,005	3,486	−0.4%
1953	−6,493	1,766	−9,921	3,427	−1.7%
1954	−1,154	1,677	−3,151	1,997	−0.3%
1955	−2,993	1,098	−4,173	1,180	−0.8%
1956	3,947	1,452	1,313	2,634	0.9%
1957	3,412	773	1,657	1,755	0.8%
1958	−2,769	546	−3,017	248	−0.6%
1959	−12,849	−700	−11,271	−1,578	−2.6%
1960	301	−209	791	−490	0.1%
1961	−3,335	431	−4,193	858	−0.6%
1962	−7,146	−1,265	−6,847	−299	−1.3%
1963	−4,756	−789	−6,630	1,874	−0.8%
1964	−5,915	632	−8,588	2,673	−0.9%
1965	−1,411	194	−3,910	2,499	−0.2%
1966	−3,698	−630	−5,165	1,467	−0.5%
1967	−8,643	3,978	−15,709	7,066	−1.1%
1968	−25,161	2,581	−28,373	3,212	−2.9%
1969	3,242	3,749	−4,871	8,112	0.3%
1970	−2,842	5,852	−13,168	10,326	−0.3%
1971	−23,033	3,019	−29,896	6,863	−2.1%
1972	−23,373	2,695	−29,296	5,924	−2.0%
1973	−14,908	338	−25,683	10,774	−1.1%
1974	−6,135	1,063	−20,144	14,009	−0.4%
1975	−53,242	906	−60,664	7,422	−3.4%
1976	−73,732	−4,306	−76,138	2,405	−4.2%
1977	−53,659	−3,726	−63,155	9,495	−2.7%
1978	−59,185	−3,770	−71,876	12,691	−2.7%
1979	−40,726	−1,093	−59,061	18,335	−1.6%
1980	−73,830	−689	−82,632	8,802	−2.7%
1981	−78,968	−5,109	−85,791	6,823	−2.6%

Table 3–7
(Continued)

Fiscal Year	Total	Off-Budget	Federal Funds	Trust Funds	Total as % GDP
1982	−127,977	−7,384	−134,221	6,244	−4.0%
1983	−207,802	−110	−230,874	23,072	−6.0%
1984	−185,367	−98	−218,272	32,905	−4.8%
1985	−212,308	9,222	−266,457	54,149	−5.1%
1986	−221,227	16,688	−283,120	61,893	−5.0%
1987	−149,730	18,627	−222,348	72,618	−3.2%
1988	−155,178	37,087	−252,902	97,724	−3.1%
1989	−152,639	52,754	−276,122	123,483	−2.8%
1990	−221,036	56,590	−341,181	120,145	−3.9%
1991	−269,238	52,198	−380,971	111,733	−4.5%
1992	−290,321	50,087	−386,338	96,018	−4.7%
1993	−255,051	45,347	−355,436	100,385	−3.9%
1994	−203,186	55,654	−298,508	95,322	−2.9%
1995	−163,952	62,415	−263,211	99,259	−2.2%
1996	−107,431	66,588	−222,052	114,621	−1.4%
1997	−21,884	81,364	−147,826	125,942	−0.3%
1998	69,270	99,195	−91,927	161,197	0.8%
1999	125,610	123,690	−87,120	212,730	1.4%
2000	236,241	149,819	1,629	234,612	2.4%
2001	128,236	160,681	−100,513	228,749	1.3%
2002	−157,758	159,659	−360,156	202,398	−1.5%
2003	−377,585	160,833	−555,977	178,392	−3.5%
2004	−412,727	155,234	−605,365	192,638	−3.6%
2005	−318,346	175,265	−555,093	236,747	−2.6%

SOURCE: Executive Office of the President, Office of Management and Budget, Budget of the United States Government. Historial Tables 2007 (Washington, D.C.: U.S. Government Printing Office, 2006).

that principle. Nevertheless, the prospect is for continuing large federal deficits, and they are large enough that some question the fiscal sustainability of the country.

The off-budget (Social Security) surpluses raise a different issue, as the discussion of this entitlement in Sidebar 3–3 indicated. Surpluses in the Social Security Trust Fund (and other trust funds that have accumulations, including those for federal highway finance, Medicare, and so on) are invested in federal fund debt, in the same way that private endowment and pension funds invest their annual surpluses in various interest-bearing assets. Because of the desire that these trust fund assets be entirely secure, federal debt is the only asset the trust funds have been permitted to purchase. The trust fund surpluses are used to finance the federal funds deficit. However, just as is the case with private funds, the debt is owned by the Social Security system and will be used to support the system in years when it is in annual deficit. The problem is that Social Security accumulations are insufficient to finance all anticipated outflows without eventual subsidization from other budgetary resources. The data show the off-budget activity to have been in surplus since the mid-1980s, compared with the near-permanent federal funds deficit. The Social Security (off-budget) surplus gives little reason for satisfaction: the accumulated surplus is intended to finance benefits for the current workforce when those people retire, and actuarial forecasts show that the accumulation will run out in less than 40 years. In other words, the Social Security surpluses are too small to cover the benefit obligations that are being accrued by the current workforces.

To close the deficit when it needs to be closed (during economic decline, the federal government may reasonably intend a deficit as part of a macroeconomic stimulation program) requires the mathematically simple exercise of some combination of increasing receipts or reducing outlays. It is the politics that are complex, because elected officials, Congress and the president, expect the public to object to higher taxes, even to want tax reductions, and to want federal expenditures on programs that provide services. Each tax increase and each expenditure reduction would hit some part of the public, and those interests would object. Running deficits has proven politically much easier than acting to balance budgets or to run surpluses, and no massive national economic catastrophe has occurred, even with the long deficit history. But providing services without taxing to cover their cost gives the public misleading signals and government services seem cheaper than they actually are. So is the harm from deficits worth controlling them? Although the actual economic effects of persistent central government deficits remain a topic of considerable debate among economists,[37] there is no economic argument and probably even no popular sentiment that deficits are acceptable every year. If deficits really do not matter, why bother having taxes? And there certainly is no justification for deficits during economic expansion.

The effects of continuing large deficits are expected to be largely long-term. First, federal deficits threaten long-term economic growth in the nation. In general, national saving (the difference between what is produced and what is consumed in a period of time) may be used to finance investment (increases in the physical productive capacity of the nation) or to accommodate government deficits. Given the overall saving rate, the deficit absorbs savings that otherwise could have been productively invested. Real interest rates rise as extra government borrowing occurs at the expense of financing private projects. That reduces the capital stock, a limiting factor in the output of the nation, thus constraining standards of living. Current deficits harm the future by reducing the nation's long-term economic potential.

Second, effects on international capital markets from the continuing deficit promise to reduce standards of living in the United States. The Council of Economic Advisers outlines the problem:

---

[37]Four good introductions to the deficit argument are Michael Dotsey, "Controversy Over the Federal Budget Deficit: A Theoretical Perspective," *Federal Reserve Bank of Richmond Economic Review* 71 (Sept./Oct. 1985): 3–16; John A. Tatom, "Two Views of the Effects of Government Budget Deficits in the 1980's," *Federal Reserve Bank of St. Louis Review* 67 (October 1985): 5–16; K. Alec Chrystal and Daniel L. Thornton, "The Macroeconomic Effects of Deficit Spending: A Review," *Federal Reserve Bank of St. Louis Review* 70 (Nov./Dec. 1988): 48–60; and Robert Eisner, "Budget Deficits: Rhetoric and Reality," *Journal of Economic Perspectives* 3 (Spring 1989): 73–93.

> When government borrowing or tax increases reduce the supply of available domestic savings, interest rates in the United States tend to rise. Foreign investors take advantage of the higher yields by investing in U.S. assets, either directly, as when a foreign automobile company builds an assembly plant in the United States, or indirectly, by buying debt issued by the government, or the debt or equity of U.S. firms.
>
> Foreign investment in the United States tends to reduce the effect of the deficit (or a current tax increase) on private domestic investment and the capital stock. Whether the government chooses deficit or tax finance, foreign investment in the United States adds to the domestic capital stock. American workers are more productive and earn higher wages when foreign capital augments domestic saving.
>
> Even with foreign capital inflows, however, future generations are still relatively worse off with deficit than with tax financing if the deficit absorbs more saving than a tax increase would have. With deficit financing, foreigners will own more of the U.S. capital stock than with tax financing, and future generations will have to make larger payments to foreign investors (or, equivalently, will enjoy lower payments from foreign debtors).[38]

Thus, the accumulation of debt held outside the U.S. economy will cause reduced domestic standards of living when that debt is serviced. And a surprisingly large percentage of federal debt is in foreign hands: 53.5 percent of privately held debt in September 2005, compared with 20 percent in 1990.[39] Should the United States lose its attractiveness as a safe haven for funds, the foreign dumping of debt holdings would present a great challenge to federal finance and private financial markets.

Third, to the extent the deficit remains a political issue, it constrains the capacity of the federal government to respond to legitimate national concerns. In a deficit-dominated climate, the first reaction to any policy initiative, whether it is national health care reform, welfare reform, or reaction to a severe recession, is not whether a problem exists that the federal government might try to resolve but what the deficit impact of the response might be. Hence, the deficit can place difficult hurdles in the path of important policy debate. And, even with an environment of modest surpluses, a fervent focus on preserving the surplus can hinder response to public problems.

Fourth, deficits could increase the rate of inflation, but that depends on whether the Federal Reserve System (the United States' central bank) "monetizes" the debt. Debt monetization occurs when the Federal Reserve purchases government debt—the product of the deficits—with newly created currency or bank reserves. The increased money supply creates a purchasing force that drives general price levels upward. This is not likely to be a problem in the United States, because the Federal Reserve System is politically independent of the federal government and shows no tendency to monetize deficits. That is also true in most other developed countries, but it definitely was not the case in the early days of the newly independent nations that had been part of the Soviet Union or during the 1980s in several Latin American countries. Deficits there were financed by debt monetization (creating new money

---

[38]Council of Economic Advisors, *Economic Report of the President Transmitted to the Congress,* January 1993 (Washington, D.C.: GPO, 1993), 248–49.
[39]*Treasury Bulletin* (September 2001): 52.

to purchase the debt), and hyperinflation (price increases at triple digit or higher annual rates) was the result.

Finally, continuing deficits bring higher interest obligations in the future. Each succeeding Congress will find a large and usually increasing share of federal resources to be already committed, not to provide services to those paying taxes in that year, but to cover interest on funds spent to provide services in the past. Financing for the current needs of the public gets eaten away by necessity to service the costs of the past. That is not an attractive situation for the public or for the politicians elected to serve the public.[40]

The difficult problem in deficit reduction is that the gain is long-term and the costs are immediate, including both the previously mentioned politics and the danger that higher taxes or reduced expenditure will throw the national economy into recession. How can a long-term, national perspective be reflected against the short-term, home-district perspective of Congress? This is not a simple question. Neither is identifying when the national issues are significant enough to make a small deficit more reasonable than raising taxes or constraining spending to prevent the deficit.

Nobel prize-winning economist Joseph Stiglitz outlines the justification for deficit financing: "The three basic rules of deficit financing are still true: Run a deficit when there is insufficient demand; try to get the biggest bang for the buck—the most stimulation for the economy for each dollar of deficit spending; and try to spend the money in ways which enhance long-term growth and address the country's basic social needs."[41] It is difficult to match this to how the federal government has behaved through much of its recent history, so it is reasonable to expect efforts to patch the system.

The laws establishing the federal fiscal process have been restructured several times to try to control or prevent deficits:

1. **Debt limits.** For decades, the federal government has operated with statutory limits on the amount of debt that could be outstanding. When debt is at the ceiling, no more deficits are possible. These laws have had little, if any, effect because debt limits have regularly increased. For example, the ceiling was $1,490 billion in November 1983; by January 2005, it was $8,184 billion after several intermediate steps, all from congressional action. Furthermore, Congress may choose to classify certain debt as not subject to the limits.

2. **Aggregate budgeting.** The Congressional Impoundment and Budget Control Act of 1974 was thought to induce greater fiscal responsibility because Congress was required to approve a deficit or surplus appropriate to the existing macroeconomic circumstances and to adopt revenue and appropriation laws within that standard. That was the idea of the budget resolution (or the congressional budget itself). No longer would spending increases and tax reduc-

[40]A high ratio of debt to GDP (the result of accumulated deficits over the years) can also be an incentive to allow higher rates of inflation. The inflation causes an increase in the denominator but not the numerator, thus reducing the ratio—but at considerable cost to the economy.

[41]Joseph Stiglitz, "The Parties' Flip-Flops on Deficit Spending: Economics or Politics," *The Economists' Voice I* (Issue 1, 2004): 5. Available online at www.bepress.com/ev/vol1/iss1/art2.

tions be free additions; now they would have to be balanced within the ceilings of the resolution. Shortly after the law was passed, deficits soared.

3. **Targets and Enforcement.** The 1921 act attempted fiscal responsibility by giving the president stronger budget powers; the 1974 act attempted fiscal responsibility by giving Congress stronger budget powers. The Gramm-Rudman-Hollings act took the direct approach. The act established a series of deficit targets that would have led to balance in 1993.[42] The targets were mandatory, and, if violation were forecast at the start of a fiscal year and legislative changes were not made to correct the violation, a sequestration process at the start of the fiscal year reduced spending by formula to restore the target deficit.[43] Discretionary spending was to be cut by the percentage necessary to get the deficit to the agreed legal target, regardless of priorities. Gramm-Rudman-Hollings was, because of its brute force and mindless reductions, intended to be so politically distasteful that Congress would exert extreme caution to prevent a sequester. Three years were sequester-eligible: 1986 (carried out), 1988 (rescinded), and 1990 (replaced by BEA90).

4. **Spending controls, PAYGO, and adjustable deficit targets.** BEA90 revised the control structure. It established dollar limits (caps) on discretionary spending (divided into defense, domestic, and international affairs for fiscal 1991–1993, but combined for 1994 and 1995), enacted a pay-as-you-go (PAYGO) requirement for mandatory spending and revenue legislation, and provided adjustable maximum deficit targets. The discretionary spending ceilings are inflation-adjustable; the deficit ceilings are adjustable for economic (inflation, interest rates, or other economic assumptions) or technical (changed spending concepts) reasons. BEA90 also added supplemental appropriations to the control structure, making sure they counted against either the current year for sequester or the budget year for ceiling calculations.[44] Sequesters could occur if any of the various ceilings were violated. The PAYGO requirement means that revenue reductions or entitlement enhancements must be accompanied by deficit recovery by revenue increase or entitlement reduction. Some observers, reacting to the many adjustments and diffusion of responsibility, have labeled BEA90 as a start toward "no-fault budgeting,"[45] but outlay ceilings do appear to have constrained appropriations until 1998. After that budget year annual adjustments to original statutory caps allowed considerable expansion

---

[42]The 1985 version scheduled balance in 1991, but that date was stretched in the 1987 version. The initial act assigned the enforcement of sequestration orders to the comptroller general. In *Bowsher, Comptroller General of the United States., Appellant* v. *Mike Synar, Member of Congress* (no. 85-1377, 7 July 1986, U.S. Supreme Court), the Supreme Court held that this assignment of powers by Congress to the comptroller general violated the constitutional command that Congress play no direct role in the execution of laws. The 1987 act remedied the problem by assigning the task to the OMB, an executive agency.

[43]Certain spending categories were exempt; remaining spending was split between domestic and defense, and dollar amounts of needed reduction were equally divided between those categories. Because much spending was exempt, the percentage reduction for the remainder would have been great.

[44]Except in the case of supplementals for wars or dire emergencies, emergency supplementals afford a nice loophole for narrow projects.

[45]Richard Doyle and Jerry McCaffery, "The Budget Enforcement Act of 1990: The Path to No Fault Budgeting," *Public Budgeting and Finance* 11 (Spring 1991): 25–40.

of outlays. The Omnibus Budget Reconciliation Act of 1993 extended new ceilings through fiscal 1998, and the Balanced Budget Act of 1997 (P.L. 105–33, the 1997 budget reconciliation) continued ceilings through fiscal year 2002.[46] The discretionary caps and the PAYGO mechanism expired in September 2002.

Will the federal budget—with and without Social Security flows—be in surplus or deficit? A good way to consider the question is by looking at the deficit relative to the national economy and the extra governmental draw that would be required to close the deficit and, ultimately, to service the resulting debts. In the 1950s, the mean deficit relative to GDP was 0.4 percent; in the 1960s, 0.8 percent; in the 1970s, 2.2 percent; in the 1980s, 3.9 percent; in the 1990s, 2.1 percent; and, so far in the twenty-first century, a deficit of 1.2 percent. Strong economic performance (low inflation, low unemployment, and growing incomes) brought good growth of receipts and slower growth in some means-tested entitlement categories; discretionary spending was under BEA control. Indeed, were it not for interest payments on accumulated federal debt, the product of earlier deficits, the overall budget would have been in surplus through the last half of the 1990s. The challenge for the future will be considerable because of the condition of the Social Security and Medicare Trust Funds, the political attractiveness of reducing taxes without accompanying reduction in government services, and the difficulty of keeping discretionary spending, both defense and domestic, constrained.

Federal Fiscal Policy

Economic stabilization (managing the aggregate performance of the economy) is traditionally a federal responsibility. Indeed, two laws, the Employment Act of 1946 and the Full Employment and Balanced Growth Act of 1978 (the Humphrey-Hawkins Act), formally define this macroeconomic stabilization role. The 1946 act, along with establishing the Council of Economic Advisers to assist the president, requires the federal government to use all practical means of "promoting maximum employment, production, and purchasing power" in the U.S. economy. The 1978 act establishes a national policy of full employment, increased real income, balanced growth, a balanced budget, productivity growth, and price stability. Because the federal government traditionally can adjust spending and revenue rates to stimulate or contract the private economy, these responsibilities seem reasonable. Federal policymakers, the president, and Congress view budget manipulations as a stabilization instrument, but the power of discretionary budget policy to stabilize is in some dispute.

Fiscal policy is the use of government decisions on spending and taxing to influence the overall economy.[47] These budget choices also involve delivery of ser-

[46]PAYGO would continue, but without any enforcement mechanism. Other legislation provides caps on highway and mass transit outlays (through 2003) and on conservation outlays (through 2006).

[47]The Federal Reserve System, the central banking authority in the United States, works toward similar macroeconomic objectives through monetary policy.

vices, distribution of wealth and income among regions and groups in the economy, and so on, but the effects at issue here are on aggregate growth, standards of living, unemployment, price levels, and so forth. The influence works through aggregate demand for goods and services in the economy. Spending adds to that demand, either directly when the government purchases something (e.g., when a bridge or reservoir is built or when an airplane is purchased), or indirectly when the government makes a transfer payment (e.g., Social Security) to a person who then buys something with that payment. Taxes subtract from that demand because they remove purchasing power from individuals and businesses. In general, increasing government spending and reducing taxes tends to increase aggregate demand in the economy, at least temporarily, thus increasing the actual level of economic activity.[48] Of course, the process would be reversed if levels of aggregate demand put such pressure on aggregate supply that inflation became a problem.

Both the logical underpinning and the empirical success record for straightforward, discretionary, counter-cyclical fiscal policy—that is, "tweaking" the budget to get the correct amounts of stimulus or contraction to manage the economy—have been severely shaken, however, by revisions in macroeconomic theory, reflections on the empirical record in nondepression applications, slow recognition and response to macroeconomic conditions that could warrant fiscal intervention, and concerns with the long-term consequences of discretionary policy. In particular, the unemployment rate appears to be determined by real factors in the economy, including technological change, labor force composition, the unemployment-compensation system, and so on, and not simply by changes in aggregate demand; the unemployment rate may not respond to aggregate budget-policy manipulations. Thus, the 17.9 percent reduction in federal spending in the first quarter of 1993, the result of defense cutbacks and caps on nondefense discretionary spending from BEA90, meant that people became unemployed, and aggregate economic activity growth was sluggish.[49] Other factors in the economy, however, determine whether unemployed people find new employment quickly and whether economic growth is restored; those other factors, not the path of aggregate government spending and taxing, establish what the aggregate economic results will be. Furthermore, major experiments in counter-cyclical fiscal policy in the 1960s and 1970s (tax cuts in 1964 and 1975 and the 1968 surtax), on closer evaluation, now appear to have had disappointing results.[50] Their effect on GDP seems to have been small, their impact was slow, and their implementation, given the slowness of the budget process and the difficulty of detecting when economic cycles are changing, often occurred after the need for intervention had passed. And there is a significant pragmatic limitation to

---

[48]These macroeconomic relationships are elements in the system brilliantly outlined in John Maynard Keynes, *The General Theory of Employment, Interest, and Money* (London: Macmillan, 1936). An excellent policy restatement of these principles is Charles L. Schultze, *Memos to the President, A Guide Through Macroeconomics for the Busy Policymaker* (Washington, D.C.: Brookings Institution, 1992). An excellent review of modern principles of macroeconomics in N. Gregory Mankiw, "A Quick Refresher Course in Macroeconomics," *Journal of Economic Literature* 28 (December 1990): 1645–60.

[49]Lucinda Harper, "Economy Already Feeling the Impact of Federal Government's Spending Cuts," *Wall Street Journal*, 18 August, 1993, A-2.

[50]Donald W. Kiefer, *Tax Cuts and Rebates for Economic Stimulus: The Historical Record* (Report no. 92-20 S) (Washington, D.C.: Congressional Research Service, Library of Congress, 2 January 1992).

stimulation: increased spending/reduced taxes would add to the fundamental deficit overhang. If this overhang does reduce the national rate of saving and capital formation, then that action would worsen the prospects for future improvements in the American standard of living. Policymakers are reluctant to add further to that burden. Accordingly, discretionary fiscal policy is certainly not regarded with as much respect as it once was. There is evidence, however, that the federal income-tax rebates of 2001 (from the Economic Growth and Tax Relief Reconciliation Act of 2001) provided a considerable boost to consumption expenditure in a way that contributed positively to ending the recession of that year.[51]

The federal budget does, however, include *automatic,* or *built-in, stabilizers* that move in response to changes in the business cycle. These features increase spending and reduce revenue when economic activity lags and do the reverse when activity rises. Because they work within existing law, they do not require identification of a problem or legislative action to put a remedy into place. They function automatically. These stabilizers include progressivity in the income tax (the tax as a share of income rises as income increases, so income tax collections rise more rapidly or fall more rapidly than does aggregate economic activity), and the operation of welfare, food stamps, unemployment compensation, and related systems (payments rise as the economy slows). The automatic stabilizers work to cause deficits to increase when the economy lags and to cause deficits to decrease when the economy grows, without any discretionary fiscal actions.[52] If fiscal policy can stabilize the economy, then these stabilizers are integral remedies that do not need to be legislated and hence can begin corrections without any delays.

State and Local Budgets

Table 3–8 reports expenditure by state and local governments in the United States. States transfer considerable sums to their local governments; this table tallies such spending at the recipient level (which makes the expenditures "direct"). The table also follows the convention of separating general expenditure from expenditures of government-operated utilities and liquor stores and insurance trust systems (unemployment compensation, public employee retirement, etc.). Surpluses from the util-

[51]David S. Johnson, Jonathan A. Parker, and Nicholas S. Souleles, "Household Expenditure and the Income Tax Rebates of 2001," National Bureau of Economic Research Working Paper 10784, Cambridge, Massachusetts: National Bureau of Economic Research, 2004.

[52]Analysts distinguish between automatic and discretionary fiscal impacts through use of the cyclically adjusted budget deficit. (The CBO version is the "standardized employment deficit.") This measure estimates what the deficit would be at a standard level of economic activity. That convention extracts deficit changes that result from the stabilizers and allows cross-year comparisons of discretionary actions. This logic allows one to partition the budget deficit into one element that is cyclical, or created by the condition in the business cycle, and into another that is structural, or reflected in a fundamental imbalance between receipts and expenditure. An Organization for Economic Cooperation and Development analysis across countries estimates the 1993 U.S. deficit at 3.8 percent of GDP, 3.0 percent structural and 0.8 percent cyclical. See "Stripping Down the Cycle," *Economist,* 3 July, 1993, 69.

ities and liquor stores may ultimately support general government operations (or their losses may have to be subsidized); insurance trust operations, especially unemployment compensation, have little direct link to general finances, although general finances of the government do have to maintain employee retirement programs and may need to make up fund shortfalls.[53]

Local government expenditure is dominated by elementary and secondary education, amounting to 40.0 percent of their total spending. Much of this spending is by independent school districts, local governments with a single purpose. However, a number of large cities operate their schools as a municipal department. As is described in a later chapter, a considerable portion of these resources are financed by state aid, but provision remains a critical local concern. No other category amounts to as much as 10 percent of the total, but welfare (4.0 percent), hospitals (5.3 percent), and police protection (5.6 percent) are the largest remaining categories. Categories that have grown rapidly in recent years include corrections, health, air transportation, solid-waste management, and interest payments.

The largest single category of state government spending is for public welfare programs (33.9 percent), and growth in this category has been high as well. The 1996 changes in the federal welfare program, the conversion of Aid for Families with Dependent Children (a federal entitlement to individuals) to the Temporary Assistance for Needy Families (a grant program with conditions that assign responsibility to state governments) place even greater responsibility on states and provide them a great incentive to administer carefully and move people off assistance roles. Medicaid, a federal-state medical program for the poor, is a major component of this category and a major factor in its expansion. Of the other functions, only higher education (17.6 percent) amounts to as much as 10 percent of the total. Larger shares go to highways (9.3 percent), hospitals (4.9 percent), corrections (4.7 percent), and health (3.9 percent); of these, recent growth has been rapid for corrections and health. Although there are major interstate differences, particular problems for state finances emerge from corrections, an area in which both growth of inmate populations and judicial requirements for humane treatment of inmates have increased spending; and from health, especially Medicaid, a program of health care for specific categories of poor people that states operate according to federal guidelines and with both federal and state funding.[54]

Spending by State and Local Governments

The federal government uses a closely defined (but frequently shifting) budget process with narrowly drawn deadlines, regulations, roles, and authority that specify the flow of resources from the germination of an idea for service through the audit of outcomes. Virtually all states and larger localities use the familiar four-phase

---

[53]Surpluses in these trust funds, if invested in government debt, normally are invested in federal rather than state-local debt. Hence, merging them with general state-local operations as is done for federal funds and trust funds at the federal level would not be appropriate.

[54]Jane Sneddon Little, "Medicaid," *New England Economic Review* (Jan./Feb. 1991): 27–50.

Table 3–8
State and Local Government Expenditures, 2002–2003 ($ in thousands)

	State and Local Government Amount[1]	Percent Direct General Expenditure	State Government Amount[2]	Percent Direct General Expenditure	Local Government Amount[1]	Percent Direct General Expenditure
Direct expenditure	2,159,772,278		976,851,809		1,182,920,469	
Direct general expenditure	1,817,512,846	100.0%	781,771,632	100.0%	1,035,741,214	100.0%
Education services:						
Education	621,335,418	34.2%	170,685,136	21.8%	450,650,282	43.5%
Higher education	164,186,932	9.0%	137,348,890	17.6%	26,838,042	2.6%
Elementary & secondary	428,503,200	23.6%	4,690,960	0.6%	423,812,240	40.9%
Other education	28,645,286	1.6%	28,645,286	3.7%	—	
Libraries	8,910,972	0.5%	406,605	0.1%	8,504,367	0.8%
Public welfare	306,462,913	16.9%	265,105,246	33.9%	41,357,667	4.0%
Hospitals	93,174,786	5.1%	38,023,085	4.9%	55,151,701	5.3%
Health	61,703,413	3.4%	30,350,695	3.9%	31,352,718	3.0%
Social insurance administration	5,267,050	0.3%	5,258,083	0.7%	8,967	0.0%
Veterans' services	1,016,563	0.1%	1,016,563	0.1%	—	
Highways	117,695,877	6.5%	72,454,881	9.3%	45,240,996	4.4%
Air transportation (airports)	17,045,966	0.9%	1,564,580	0.2%	15,481,386	1.5%
Parking facilities	1,194,571	0.1%	0	0.0%	1,194,571	0.1%
Sea and inland port facilities	5,874,611	0.3%	1,150,073	0.1%	4,724,538	0.5%
Transit subsidies	443,524	0.0%	175,171	0.0%	268,353	0.0%
Police protection	67,361,388	3.7%	9,860,380	1.3%	57,501,008	5.6%
Fire protection	27,854,042	1.5%	0	0.0%	27,854,042	2.7%
Correction	55,471,298	3.1%	36,937,901	4.7%	18,533,397	1.8%
Protective inspection and regulation	11,592,515	0.6%	7,859,839	1.0%	3,732,676	0.4%
Natural resources	22,808,126	1.3%	17,109,575	2.2%	5,698,551	0.6%
Parks and recreation	31,764,695	1.7%	4,636,036	0.6%	27,128,659	2.6%
Housing and community development	35,275,305	1.9%	4,607,676	0.6%	30,667,629	3.0%
Sewerage	32,539,728	1.8%	1,002,809	0.1%	31,536,919	3.0%
Solid waste management	19,183,332	1.1%	2,692,719	0.3%	16,490,613	1.6%
Financial administration	34,910,963	1.9%	20,627,064	2.6%	14,283,899	1.4%

Judicial and legal	32,460,282	1.8%	14,944,737	1.9%	17,515,545	1.7%
General public buildings	11,951,316	0.7%	3,215,722	0.4%	8,735,594	0.8%
Other governmental administration	19,335,500	1.1%	4,057,986	0.5%	15,277,514	1.5%
Interest on general debt	77,277,119	4.3%	31,294,763	4.0%	45,982,356	4.4%
Miscellaneous commercial activities	366,020	0.0%	312,011	0.0%	54,009	0.0%
Other and unallocable	97,235,553	5.3%	36,422,296	4.7%	60,813,257	5.9%
Utility expenditure	144,593,923		22,404,931		122,188,992	
Water supply	43,260,324		352,719		42,907,605	
Electric power	54,355,187		11,348,630		43,006,557	
Gas supply	5,300,278		9,998		5,290,280	
Transit	41,678,134		10,693,584		30,984,550	
Liquor store expenditure	4,402,018		3,696,515		705,503	
Insurance trust expenditure	193,263,491		168,978,731		24,284,760	
Unemployment compensation	51,546,519		51,410,604		135,915	
Employee retirement	127,197,464		103,048,619		24,148,845	
Workers' compensation	11,224,042		11,224,042		—	
Other insurance trust	3,295,466		3,295,466		—	

SOURCE: U.S. Bureau of Census, Governments Division.

budget cycle. However, it should be no surprise, in light of the great diversity of state and local governments, that there is no one process that all such entities use.[55] Therefore, the process must be learned within the context of the government at hand. The way it works in Wichita may not apply in Altoona, and both governments may have entirely serviceable budget processes. Hence, the discussion about the state and local government budget process can only be general in nature. Justice Louis Brandeis observed in *New State Ice Co.* v. *Liebman,* 285 U.S. 262 (1932), that "it is one of the happy incidents of the federal system that a single courageous State may, if its citizens choose, serve as a laboratory; and try novel social and economic experiments without risk to the rest of the country." And so it is with the budget process. Appendix 3–1 at the end of this chapter describes the budget process in Texas as an example of one system. It has many features common to the federal process but some interesting and significant differences.

State and local budget processes and staffing may be comparable to that of the federal government, except in scope, but many, especially local processes, are remarkably informal. Indeed, there may be no executive budget. Agency heads may submit their requests directly to a legislative body (e.g., a city or county council), without any executive directive for developing those requests. And those local requests, especially for small governments, may be transmitted according to no regular schedule, but simply as agencies run out of funds or encounter new program options. Among states, "the days of agencies having the freedom to request budgets in whatever amounts they see fit are gone, and in their stead are various control mechanisms or types of ceilings that must be observed when requesting funds."[56] That guidance may involve (1) rankings of certain priorities; (2) instructions in regard to allowed program improvements, maintenance of current services, or continuing only minimum services; or (3) specific dollar-level ceilings within which to prepare proposals. State budgets are frequently driven by the baseline (or current services) revenue forecast: the prognosis of revenue available without changing tax rates sets the tone for all that follows in the process. Although the state budget office may be housed in various places (for example, in the governor's office, in a free-standing executive agency, or in a larger department of administration or finance), it provides supervision of the entire process, review of proposals as they are assembled into the budget, and control of the execution of the adopted budget.

Among localities, however, a wide range of practices exists, with and without budget guidance and control. First, many localities continue *Christmas list budgeting,* in which department heads prepare requests without any executive guidance about budget targets or conditions. This practice leads to unrealistic requests that are usually cut without much attention given to programs and priorities. Second, some state and local operating agencies may have elected heads (e.g., a county sheriff); these

---

[55]Some sense of that range is shown in Edward J. Clynch and Thomas P. Lauth, eds., *Governors, Legislatures, and Budgets: Diversity Across the American States* (New York: Greenwood Press, 1991). National Association of State Budget Officers, *Budget Processes in the States* (Washington, D.C.: NASBO, 1999) provides the most complete overview of the structure of each state's budget processes.

[56]Robert D. Lee, Jr. "The Use of Executive Guidance in State Budget Preparations," *Public Budgeting and Finance* 12 (Fall 1992): 29–30.

officials may not feel bound by such directions constraining their proposals in any case. But possibly the most troublesome situation occurs when agency requests go to legislative bodies without executive budget-office review. Agency requests may not have been reviewed by an executive budget office, often because there is no such staff or because the staff is few in number and untrained. Therefore, the requests may arrive for legislative review in inconsistent format, following no particular standards in preparation, with no unifying plan for service delivery, and without screening for technical or presentation errors. In essence, the budget message has been prepared with a stapler only, not according to an analytic template or generally consistent executive vision. Such a system (or nonsystem) swamps the legislative body with details. Members must verify arithmetic and often fall into deliberations about each line item. Rather than consider policy questions, they plunge into the intimate cost estimates of the particular requests and usually exhaust their deliberative time and energy before they reach higher-order questions of program, performance, efficiency, or missions.[57]

Many state and local governments also differ from the federal government in the audit phase of the budget cycle. Although a number of these governments have a public agency serving as external auditor, much in the way that the Government Accountability Office serves Congress, and even have audits performed by staff of that agency, a number have privatized the function by allowing audits to be done under contract with qualified private accounting firms. Their audit procedures are normally those prescribed by some government body, but the work is actually performed by staff of the firm, the firm having been selected according to the normal process for contractual services. So long as audit procedures, audit standards, and audit questions are prescribed and audit firms are qualified before they may bid, there is no particular reason why states need to establish their own version of GAO. States do, however, usually have legislative audit staff who performance audits, program evaluation, and fiscal analysis; this work is kept separate from the financial and compliance audits necessary for control and is less likely to be privatized. In contrast to the recommended model, some states place the audit agency in the executive branch; some states have both an executive and a legislative audit unit.

Executive-Legislative Powers and Functions. The federal budget process has, over the years, created an uneasy and shifting balance of power between the executive and legislative branches of government. The balance that has emerged there does not immediately transfer to state and local government.[58]

First, not all state and local governments have an executive budget in the normal sense, although a budget proposal is prepared. Some states have budgets pre-

---

[57]A good source on the peculiarities of budgeting for local governments is Robert Bland and Irene Rubin, *Budgeting, A Guide for Local Governments* (Washington, D.C.: International City/County Management Association, 1997).

[58]Tony Hutchison and Kathy James, *Legislative Budget Procedures in the 50 States: A Guide to Appropriations and Budget Process* (Denver: National Conference of State Legislatures, 1988) provides an overview of some of the variety found. More recent details from the budget agency perspective may be found in National Association of State Budget Officers, *Budget Processes in the States* (Washington, D.C.: National Association of State Budget Officers, 1995).

pared by the legislature, and others have budgets prepared by the governor and the legislature in a joint budget committee. These joint budgets are difficult to categorize without understanding the details of each state; in some instances they may be truly joint, built by a consensus between the governor and the legislature, but in others the committees may be arranged in such a way that the governor has sufficient votes to guarantee that the budget is an executive budget, regardless of its official title. Some local governments have budgets prepared by professional managers working at the direction of a legislative body. In these governments, there is considerable blurring of the preparation and legislative consideration phases of the budget cycle. Indeed, a council-manager system has, for purposes of the budget, more similarity to parliamentary structure than to the system of separate legislative and executive branches that characterizes our federal and state governments. In many cities, it is common for the council and the mayor to meet before budget deliberations to discuss priorities for the next year. This can be an important contributor to getting a consensus when the budget is actually presented.

Second, state and local government executives often possess extraordinary fiscal powers in regard to expenditure during the fiscal year. Many states do not have year-round legislatures; the body meets in the early months of the calendar year, passes the state appropriations (and other laws), and adjourns for the year. To deal with interim surprises, the governor may have broad impoundment powers—the ability to postpone or cancel expenditures in approved appropriations—and may also be able to spend for certain emergencies without appropriation, although almost always with agreement of some interim legislative committee.[59] These accommodations give governors considerable ability to manage their operations during budget execution. Most state and local governments have allotment processes to control spending through the budget year, with funds parceled out quarterly or, when times are tight, monthly. Unfortunately, some governments have sought to recapture balances not obligated in that control period, thereby eliminating any incentive for agencies to economize.

Third, state and local governments differ in the accommodating mechanisms that provide funds for operations when fiscal years end without new appropriations in place. Some operate with near-automatic continuing resolutions, whereas others provide governors with considerable discretion. Others have no stop-gap option clearly available and are required to shut down if the budget has not been passed by the start of the new fiscal year. A recent occurrence was in Minnesota: all government operations deemed not critical by a district court judge were shut down when no budget was passed before the start of the 2006 fiscal year and the legislature could not agree on any accommodation to continue operations. When the California government was in an impasse during the early months of fiscal 1993, the state made payments by issuing scrip (interest-bearing registered warrants) instead of checks as an interim solution; the scrip could be redeemed for state checks when the appropriation passed. States with part-time legislatures often require that special legislative sessions be called when the constitutionally

[59]The executive may also have substantial contingency funds provided for various emergencies or surprises.

designated regular session ends without a new set of appropriations in place. (Local governments are more likely to have year-round legislative meetings, so the process may become continuous and without year-end crises.) The specific accommodation depends on the institutions and laws of the particular state.

Fourth, because local governments are closest to the people of any tier of government, they are most able to get ordinary citizen input into the fiscal choice processes. It is quite common for cities to integrate citizen hearings and citizen comments into both executive preparation and legislative consideration phases of the budget process. This is input from ordinary citizens, not lobbyists representing interest groups. Such broad opportunity to include individual concerns in budget deliberations would not be feasible at state or federal levels. Appendix 3–2 describes *participatory budgeting,* a formal process for involving citizens in the work of budgeting and for involving traditionally underrepresented people in the system.

And finally, most governors have long-established line-item veto power.[60] Indeed, only five—Indiana, Maine, Nevada, New Hampshire, and Rhode Island—may veto only an entire appropriations bill. Of those governers with line-item veto power, forty may delete funding for a particular line item, and thirty-two may even veto funding for an entire program or agency. Eleven may reduce an appropriation line without full veto.[61] Although specifics of these line-item vetoes vary, all allow the governor to alter the bill approved by the legislature, and sign the remainder into law, with the legislature having the power to override that partial veto.[62]

Budget Features. State and local government budgets show great basic variety. First, budgets may be annual or biennial (Table 3–9 gives a recent tally). At one time, state legislatures usually met only every other year. That meant making appropriations for 2 years in one legislative session. Even as legislative sessions became more frequent, several states continued the biennial budgets so that annual sessions became distinguished between the budget session and the policy session (or, in less-dignified terminology, the correction session).[63] States have generally moved toward annual sessions; local governments have no biennial tradition, probably because they tend to meet throughout each year. In cities, administrators rebudgeting and adjusting the approved appropriations in midyear is a common feature.[64] Some local governments are in rebudgeting-and-appropriating mode almost

---

[60]Louis Fisher, "Line Item Veto Act of 1996: Heads-up from the States," *Public Budgeting & Finance* 17 (Summer 1997): 3–17, reviews state experiences with the line-item veto, including legislative strategies for avoiding the executive control that it might bring.

[61]Hutchison and James, *Legislative Budget Procedures,* 84–85.

[62]The Wisconsin governor has most sweeping line-item veto powers, including the ability to strike words and numbers without much limit, even to the extent of reversing the meaning of the bill (try striking the *not* from "though shalt not commit adultery" to see what that power can do). Until recently, he could veto letters in words, thus permitting a game of legislative anagrams. Governor Tommy Thompson had 457 vetoes in the single 1991–1993 biennial budget bill. Use of the power is illustrated in Dennis Farney, "When Wisconsin Governor Wields Partial Veto, the Legislature Might as Well Go Play Scrabble," *Wall Street Journal,* 1 July, 1993, A-16.

[63]Paula Kearns finds that annual-budget states spend less, other things being equal, than do biennial-budget states. See "State Budget Periodicity: An Analysis of the Determinants and the Effect on State Spending," *Journal of Policy Analysis and Management* 13 (Spring 1994): 331–62.

[64]John P. Forrester and Daniel R. Mullins, "Rebudgeting: The Serial Nature of Budgeting Processes," *Public Administrative Review* 52 (Sept./Oct. 1992): 467–73.

Table 3–9
State Budget Cycles

Annual Budget (29 states)	Biennial Budget
Alabama	Arkansas
Alaska	Arizona*
California	Connecticut
Colorado	Hawaii
Delaware	Indiana
Florida	Kentucky
Georgia	Maine
Idaho	Minnesota
Illinois	Montana
Iowa	Nebraska
Kansas	Nevada
Louisiana	New Hampshire
Maryland	North Carolina
Massachusetts	North Dakota†
Michigan	Ohio
Mississippi	Oregon†
Missouri	Texas
New Jersey	Virginia
New Mexico	Washington
New York	Wisconsin
Oklahoma	Wyoming†
Pennsylvania	
Rhode Island	
South Carolina	
South Dakota	
Tennessee	
Utah	
Vermont	
West Virginia	

SOURCE: Ronald K. Snell, "Annual and Biennial Budgeting: The Experience of State Governments," National Conference of State Legislatures, October 2004. Available online at www.ncsl.org/programs/fiscal/annlbien.htm.
*Biennial budget limited to smaller agencies.
†State enacts a consolidated two-year budget.

all the time, at every meeting of the council or governing board, even though a budget has been passed before the start of the fiscal year.

Second, state and local governments may have a single appropriation law covering all expenditures or may have many appropriation laws. In other words, the legislature may actually pass a complete budget in a sense not traditionally practiced by Congress, or there may really be no budget as ordinarily considered. The range is vast—about one-third of the states typically pass a single appropriation bill, but, at the other extreme, Arkansas passes around 500 appropriation bills.

When there is a single appropriation bill, however, line-item veto power is probably more important for the executive to possess. As is noted in a later chapter, many governments use separate capital budgets. Cities are especially likely to establish multiple appropriation ordinances, one for each fund that the government has established (see discussion of funds in Chapter 2). And, violating the budgetary principle of comprehensiveness, many of these governments do not move monies between funds, despite the appropriateness of directing public resources to the highest priority and greatest public need.

Third, state and local governments historically have passed firm appropriations. They have not passed formula legislation (entitlements), which allow spending to occur at whatever level results from qualifying activities during the year. An exception is the Medicaid program, a federal program for providing medical care for certain low-income families. State assistance to local schools, a program for aiding primary and secondary education, distributes aid according to formula, but state funds ordinarily enter the distribution by appropriation, not vice versa, and the formula may well be underfunded in a particular year. States also do not separate authorizing and appropriating in their legislative processes.

Fourth, state and local governments have historically been unable to accommodate deficits with the easy access to borrowing that the federal government enjoys and, furthermore, the vast majority face statutory or constitutional restrictions against deficit operations. This has induced many to develop rainy-day or budget-stabilization funds to stabilize their finances in an economic downturn, when revenues are likely to decline. Forty-six states now operate such a fund to deal with the problem.[65] Some funds are financed by periodic legislative appropriation, but others are automatic. For instance, when year-to-year real total personal-income growth exceeds a particular threshold, the formula directs a deposit to the fund (so long as the fund is below a critical limit, usually defined in terms of general fund revenue); when that growth falls below another threshold, funds may be withdrawn. Along with providing a degree of stability in finances, properly designed budget-stabilization funds—by reducing perceived default risk on state debt—can reduce the borrowing cost of state debt.[66] Unfortunately, the typical state rainy-day fund is inadequate to mitigate a severe fiscal crisis, as evidenced by the huge budget shortfalls in the first years of the twenty-first century. Local governments are less likely than states to have such stabilization funds. They tend to rely on real property taxes for revenue, and this source is less sensitive to changes in ambient

---

[65]Richard Pollock and Jack P. Suyderhoud, "The Role of Rainy Day Funds in Achieving Fiscal Stability," *National Tax Journal* 34 (December 1986): 485-98 and National Association of State Budget Officers, *Budget Processes in the States* (Washington, D.C.: NASBO, 2002). Somewhat similar budget stabilization funds have been established in some oil-rich countries (Norway, Kuwait, and Kazakhstan, for instance) to insulate against market price shocks and the day when the oil runs out.

[66]There is evidence that the rainy-day funds are something of an illusion. One study indicates that rainy-day funds simply substitute for general fund savings that would have occurred without the rainy-day funds. The evidence is that every dollar deposited into a rainy-day fund increases total savings (rainy-day plus general fund balance) by between $0.44 and $0.49. (Gary A. Wagner, "Are State Budget Stabilization Funds Only the Illusion of Savings? Evidence from Stationary Panel Data," *Quarterly Review of Economics and Finance,* XLIII [Summer 2003]: 213–218.)

economic activity than are the taxes upon which states rely. Local government revenues tend to be much more stable.

Finally, state and local governments often earmark or dedicate portions of some broad revenue sources, like personal income or general sales taxes, to particular narrow uses. For example, a state may earmark a percentage of the state sales tax to primary and secondary education. That would mean that proceeds from that portion of the tax would be tracked to that purpose, regardless of any other needs that the state might have. Around ten states earmark more than one-third of their tax collections to some purpose or another, thereby reducing the ability of the fiscal system to respond to changing public priorities. The average for states is around 20 percent; it is probably somewhat higher for general-purpose local governments. Although there is some possible logic to directing tax and charge revenue directly associated with a public function to that function, in the way that motor-fuel tax collections are frequently dedicated to operation and maintenance of highways, there is no economic sense to locking in general revenue to a specific use; that is a choice that priority balancing in the budget process should make. Not only does it hinder the capacity to respond but it also adds an extra degree of complexity to the fiscal system. Furthermore, revenue is fungible (or easily mixed) in a general-purpose government, allowing easy substitution between uses, while keeping a clear accounting trail to satisfy the requirement for dedication.

Legal Constraints. State and local governments may face extraordinary legal constraints when they make appropriations and other fiscal decisions. Many have legal limitations, statutory or constitutional, on their capacity to tax or to spend. Both limits, taxing and spending, may constrain the size of government and change the manner of finance (strong local limits may, for instance, induce a larger state contribution to joint responsibilities). Some fiscal decisions, like a tax increase or borrowing to build a new school, may be made only after referendum approval, and that vote may require a supermajority. And many state and local governments operate under limitations, or caps, on spending (or revenues to be collected) in the fiscal year; the limit may be linked to personal income, population growth, or inflation. For instance, overall appropriations are limited to the state personal-income growth rate in Oregon and to the combined growth of population and inflation in Alaska.[67] Sometimes the state may be required to refund excess revenues to taxpayers (Colorado, Florida, Louisiana, Massachusetts, Michigan, and Missouri), and sometimes appropriations may be limited to anticipated revenues.[68] Limits, caps, referenda requirements, and supermajorities are common features of state and local fiscal processes; they are not characteristic of the federal government.

State and local governments usually have balanced-budget requirements, a fact often noted when comparisons are made between them and the federal government. That requirement, however, has various meanings across the states, including (1) the governor's proposed budget must be balanced when presented, (2) the

---

[67]National Association of State Budget Officers, Ibid., 39.

[68]Mandy Rafool, "State Tax and Expenditure Limits," *The Fiscal Letter* 18, no. 5 (1996): 4-7. Philip G. Joyce and Daniel R. Mullins, "The Changing Fiscal Structure of the State and Local Public Sector: The Impact of Tax and Expenditure Limitations," *Public Administration Review* 51 (May/June 1991): 240–53.

enacted budget must be balanced, and (3) the budget must be balanced when the year is over. Some states may, within the requirement, carry a deficit into the next year, making the standard much easier to achieve. And the language of the requirements can be interesting. For instance, the Massachusetts constitutional requirement for balance reads as follows: The governor shall submit a budget which shall contain a statement of all proposed expenditures of the commonwealth for the fiscal year, including those already authorized by law, and of all taxes, revenues, loans, and other means by which expenditures shall be defrayed" (*Massachusetts Constitution,* Article LXIII, paragraph 2). By that standard, federal budgets have always been balanced because deficits have been successfully covered by loans! Although requirements usually extend well beyond the state or local general fund to include trust funds, special funds, and funds set up to operate federal programs, they typically do not include capital budgets set up to fund capital improvements (highways, buildings, etc.) and financed by bonded indebtedness (borrowing). One study of state balanced-budget provisions observes that "it is the tradition of balancing budgets, the mindset this tradition creates, and the importance placed on balanced budgets that result in states complying with their requirements."[69] The same probably applies for local governments. And both state and local governments must remain concerned about access to capital markets; profligate behavior will eventually restrict their ability to borrow, and they lack the ultimate backstop of finance by money creation that the federal government has.

State and local governments also typically face limits on their capacity to issue debt, either to finance capital construction (building highways, schools, prisons, etc.) or to cover operating deficits. These limits may involve a requirement that the voters specifically approve the borrowing or dollar limits on debt that can be outstanding, either in absolute terms or in some relationship to the tax base (e.g., constrained to 5 percent of a county's total property tax base). As is described in Chapter 15, governments have devised many legal mechanisms to surmount these obstacles without much difficulty.

State and Local Deficits. Individual state and local governments characteristically do not run large surpluses or deficits. Whether this results from law, tradition, concerns about access to capital markets, or a concern with eventual inability to service accumulated debt (these governments cannot print money, after all, either through printing presses or access to loans from the national central bank) is not clear, but regardless of reason, it remains true even in difficult economic and social times.[70] That does not mean that every state and local government spends no more than it takes in every year or that all state and local governments in total will run a surplus. Figure 3–2 shows the pattern of state and local government net lending (receipts greater than expenditures) and net borrowing (expenditures above receipts as

[69]National Association of State Budget Offices, "State Balanced Budget Requirements: Provisions and Practice," *State Tax Notes* 3 (July 27, 1992): 117.

[70]It may also reflect the limited power of states and localities to practice expansionary fiscal policy. Any stimulus from a tax reduction or an expenditure increase would quickly leak outside the political (and electoral) boundaries of the government. The beneficiaries of the new deficit would be outside the local citizenry.

Figure 3–2
State and Local Net Lending (Borrowing) as Percent of GDP, 1959–2004

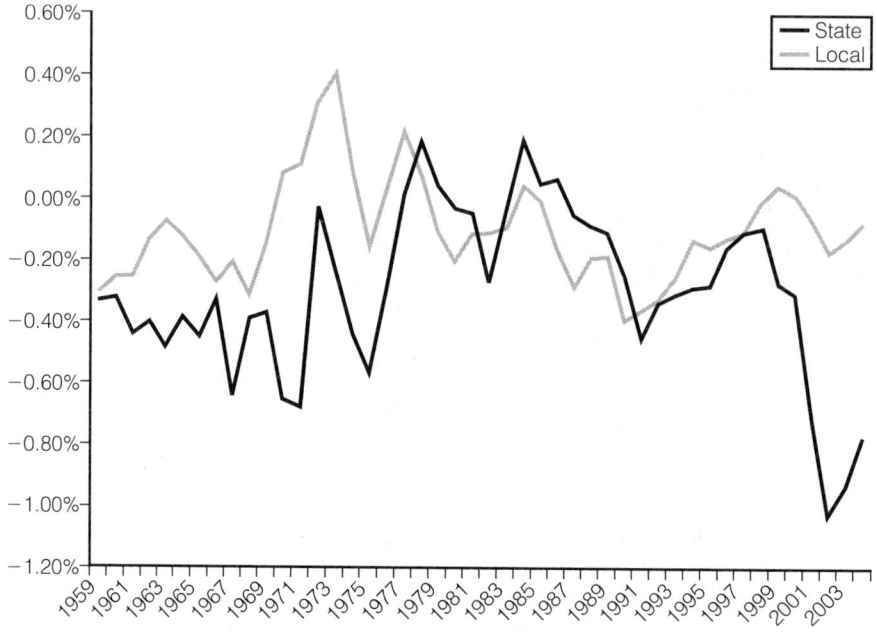

a percentage of GDP, as reflected in the national income and product accounts, from 1959 through 2004.[71] Although there are considerable fluctuations over the years, the difference from zero is always modest. However, since the late 1970s, there has been a general trend toward greater net borrowing, particularly for state government. State borrowing has been at record levels as share of GDP in recent years, although there has been recovery as the 2001 recession—which had a major impact on state government finances—effects diminish. Local net borrowing has usually been lower (or net lending higher) than state net borrowing (net lending) (except in the late 1980s) and local borrowing is lower now.

State and local deficits are considerably lower in total (and in individual units of government) than the federal deficits. There is, within state and local government, a fervent understanding that continuing deficits are not sustainable and there is an expectation that finances will be roughly in balance over time. While recessions (like those in 1973, 1980–1981, 1991, and 2001) increase net borrowing, state and local government finances are expected to recover and move toward a net lending position.

[71]Bruce Baker, "Receipts and Expenditures of State Governments and of Local Governments: New Estimates for 2002–2004 and Revised Estimates for 1990–2001," *Survey of Current Business,* October 2005, 5–10.

Conclusion

The federal government follows a precise budget cycle with clearly defined boundaries between the executive and legislative branches. But the process is in disarray in the middle of the first decade of the twenty-first century. The administration submits budgets that omit major expenditures that are transmitted later in a supplemental request. Two programs that contribute a major share of mandatory expenditure are in severe distress. The congressional budget process functions with no meaningful controls, the appropriation process faces an unclear future, and prospects are for significant deficits throughout the planning horizon. It is not the picture of a government on a sustainable path. State and local processes show great variety: Some are nearly as well defined as that of the federal government, but many are much less formal. Deficits occur but are smaller in aggregate than at the federal level.

Questions and Exercises

1. Use the following federal agencies for this exercise: Fish and Wildlife Service, Forest Service, Bureau of Land Management, Bureau of Reclamation, National Oceanic and Atmospheric Administration, U.S. Geological Survey, Army Corps of Engineers, Environmental Protection Agency, and U.S. Coast Guard. You will be able to locate the answers in the *Budget of the United States Government,* available through the OMB website.

   a. Determine where each agency lies in the administrative structure of the federal government. Is it in an executive department or is it an independent agency?
   b. Determine which of the appropriation subcommittees has jurisdiction over each agency's budget request.
   c. Determine where each agency's operations fall in the functional classification of the budget.
   d. Pick one agency and, for a recent budget year, determine (1) the budget authority and outlays proposed for the agency, and (2) the actual outlays and budget authority for the agency in that year.

2. Identify the congressional committees to which the member of Congress representing your district has been assigned. If the member is on the appropriations committee, identify the subcommittee as well. Try to determine why those committees are interesting to him or her. Thinking about economic interests and major employers in the district is a good start. (Your member of Congress almost certainly has a website that lists his or her committee and subcommittee assignments. Check that first. Another basic source is Congress's own website: http://thomas.loc.gov. It lists all committees and the membership of each. ("Thomas" is for Thomas Jefferson, the spirit behind the Library of Congress.)

3. Identify these key elements of your state budget process:

   a. Does your state have an annual or biennial budget?
   b. What units direct the preparation of the executive budget? (Not all states have an executive budget.)
   c. How many appropriation bills are usually passed?
   d. How much object-of-expenditure detail appears in these bills?
   e. What item veto power, if any, does the governor have?

   The National Association of State Budget Officers provides much of this information in its publication *Budget Processes in the States,* which may be accessed at its website (www.nasho.org).

Case for Discussion

CASE 3–1

Federal Earmarks and the Battle against Pork

Members of Congress work to gain benefits for their home districts by "earmarking" projects into appropriation bills. The Budget Enforcement Act set rigid ceilings for outlays, and the outlay ceilings were translated into amounts available for each appropriations committee. That is no longer the case. Read the article that follows and consider the following questions:

Consider These Questions

1. How was Mr. Daniels being naïve?
2. How would the old system have altered the congressional discussion of the earmarks?
3. How does chairmanship of an appropriation subcommittee give that person power?
4. Are the earmarks identified in the article as wasteful spending? What would be the view of residents of the home districts?

Bush Budget Chief Fails to Cut Capitol Hill's Appetite for Pork—Despite Vow to Clamp Down on Lawmakers, Congressional Earmarks Are Multiplying

By David Rogers.

WASHINGTON—Like a new sheriff in town, White House budget director Mitchell Daniels Jr. rode in last January, vowing to save billions by cracking down on "one time" spending for lawmakers' home-state projects.

A year later, his guns are still holstered, and the number of such congressional "earmarks," to Mr. Daniels's chagrin, is higher than ever. By the time his boss President Bush signed the last of the 13 fiscal-year 2002 appropriations bills earlier this month, the tally had exceeded 7,800—a 20% increase from last year and more than double the level of just two years ago.

"He was kind of naïve," says New York Rep. James Walsh, recalling the first meeting last spring where the House Appropriations Committee's senior Republicans sized up Mr. Daniels.

Naïve? Mr. Daniels doesn't entirely disagree. "When you come around and do your 'Mitch's greatest flops' story, we'll start with earmarks," he told a reporter recently. As for his future tack toward Congress' spenders: "Polite remonstrance."

In fairness, Mr. Daniels is up against a political phenomenon much bigger than the customary favors that grease the wheels of legislation. Congressional members' fierce appetites reflect a changed atmosphere at the Capitol: Pork-barrel politics, once treated as something shadowy, like placing a bet with a backroom bookie, today is done upfront—sort of Congress's equivalent of legalized off-track betting.

Consider the case of Rep. Hal Rogers, a Republican elected in the 1980 Reagan landslide, who this year became chairman of the House subcommittee for transportation appropriations.

With his eye on a possible run for Kentucky governor, Mr. Rogers posted a November news release on the Internet boasting that he secured hundreds of millions of dollars of federal road and airport projects for the state. In his own district, his office takes credit for more than two dozen transportation earmarks valued at $109.3 million this year and says the veteran lawmaker has helped facilitate more than $1 billion for his district government-wide during the past four years.

Not even the Marines can defend themselves. Led by GOP Rep. Jerry Lewis, California's congressional delegation commandeered two KC-130J tankers that the military branch wanted, to fight forest fires. New Jersey Democrats worked with Goldman, Sachs Group Inc. to snag $2 million toward rebuilding a public pier, for ferry service from lower Manhattan to the New York investment bank's future offices in Jersey City, N.J. And the appropriations committees needed six pages of single-spaced type just to list all of the hospitals—backed by members of both parties—seeking a share of money that their local lawmakers had dedicated for construction of additional facilities.

In a bipartisan spirit, the two parties have come to use precise formulas to divide the spoils between them. Staff complain privately that the volume of parochial requests has become a costly distraction from bigger policy issues. But both parties' leaders use the bills as a chance to boost their members' reelection prospects.

The proliferation is obvious in the "Joint Explanatory" reports detailing earmarks, which accompany the 13 spending bills. Take the bill for labor, health and education appropriations: With overall spending for these programs up 50% in the past four years, its accompanying report has doubled in pages during the same period. The Army's account for advanced medical technology tripled in 2001 to $223 million with 44 earmarks, compared with $74.5 million with 15 earmarks the year before.

Given the turnover in Congress, no one seems to remember a time when these practices weren't common. Yet until the mid-1980s, the two biggest domestic-spending bills were managed by two House Democrats, Reps. Edward Boland of Massachusetts and William Natcher of Kentucky, who both resisted earmarks. Even more recently, the Appropriations Committees followed a set of rules that allowed more scrutiny of amendments to the spending bills as they move through Congress. But in the name of speed, Republicans—fighting President Clinton—streamlined the process in such a way that the leadership of both parties and appropriations committees have remarkable flexibility now to add spending and earmarks—regardless of how the House or Senate previously have voted.

The changed approach is illustrated by the history of a health-care-facilities account for the Department of Health and Human Services, a source of federal funds for local hospital construction. In 1985, Mr. Natcher only reluctantly approved $5 million under the program even though the request had come from the more-senior chairman of the full Appropriations Committee, fellow Democrat Jamie Whitten; Mr. Whitten had asked for help to rebuild a medical building that had burned in his Mississippi district.

In contrast, since 1998, funding for the health-facilities account has grown tenfold and the money has been added in a manner that gives most lawmakers no real vote on the increase.

For example, the House allocated no money to the program in its initial bill last fall; the Senate only $10 million. But when House and Senate negotiators met to reconcile their bills, the final compromise that emerged in December provided $311 million and listed page after page of possible recipients.

As a new year of budget writing begins, lawmakers defend the chance to assert their priorities. And history does show, for example, that congressional add-ons proved effective in accelerating development of some of the weapons—such as smart-bomb guidance systems and the Predator reconnaissance aircraft—that have given the United States a huge edge in the war in Afghanistan.

Critics says today's bazaarlike pace—with earmarks as small as $25,000—betrays members' desperation to be more relevant to voters at home. Reps. Boland and Natcher embodied a long-gone past of one-party dominance and strict seniority.

Recent years' switches in party control in both the House and Senate, and the narrow majority margins, have institutionalized earmarking for incumbent protection. At the same time, House Republicans' term limits on their chairmen have forced a major rotation of appropriations subcommittee chiefs, who in turn use earmarks to consolidate their new power.

Going into this year's midterm elections, these pressures will increase. Already there was a nasty fight over how to allocate transportation dollars between two Mississippi incumbents—Reps. Ronnie Shows, a Democrat, and

Chip Pickering, a Republican, who are expected to face each other in November's election due to the state's redistricting.

Democrats surprised the GOP by pumping up funds for Mr. Shows' district, and Rep. Rogers of Kentucky demanded cuts to restore more of a balance with Mr. Pickering. The two sides faced off for hours—until Mr. Rogers ended the showdown by adding millions more dollars for Mr. Pickering's district.

The Marines were less fortunate. Both the House and Senate had included in their Pentagon budgets at least $289 million for the purchase of four Lockheed Martin Corp. C130-J model tankers for the Marines. But when the dust cleared, the funding was cut by almost half. Two of the aircraft—together costing about $148 million—were on their way to help forest firefighters in Western states.

Although surprised, the Corps lives to fight another day. Says a spokesman for the commandant, "We understand that numbers sometimes move around."

Spending Spree: One Man's Share

A sampling of the fiscal 2002 transportation earmarks that senior GOP Rep. Harold Rogers of Kentucky won to fund projects in his homestate

Buses and bus facilities statewide	$15.5 million
Technology at Louisville's airport	$5 million
University of Kentucky transportation academy	$2 million
Improvements to hiking and horse trails	$2.35 million
Straightening Daniel Boone Parkway and improving access to an industrial park	$5.5 million
Roadwork for Country Music Hall of Fame traffic	$2 million

SOURCE: Office of Management and Budget.

APPENDIX 3–1

An Illustrative State Budget Process: Texas

State and local governments apply the standard four-phase budget cycle involving executive and legislative branches of government, but there are many individual characteristics in each application. The differences reflect the particular characteristics of government in the various entities and the differing attitudes of the citizenry regarding the appropriate powers of the executive and legislative branches of government. The state of Texas offers an interesting illustration because there are a number of features that operate somewhat differently from those seen in the Federal process.

SOURCE: Wall Street Journal (January 22, 2002): A22. Reprinted by permission of the Wall Street Journal. Copyright Dow Jones & Company, Inc. All Rights Reserved Worldwide.

The general flow of the preparation and legislative consideration/adoption phases of the biennial Texas budget cycle is shown in Figure 3A–1. (Execution and audit are not shown in the figure; those phases are generally comparable to the federal scheme.) In general, agencies prepare appropriation requests in one year, the legislature passes a General Appropriations Act in the next, and the budget is executed over the next 2 years. And, of course, the cycle continues and overlaps. Notable differences from the federal system are in terms of legislative power, item veto, role of a second elective executive agent (the Comptroller), a single appropriation bill, and constitutional restraints.

Budget Preparation

The process begins with cooperation between the governor and the Legislative Budget Board (LBB), an entity not seen in the federal system. The LBB consists of the lieutenant governor; the speaker of the House; the chairs of Senate Committee on Finance, Senate Committee on State Affairs, House Committee on Ways and Means, and House Committee on Appropriations; two members of the Senate appointed by the lieutenant governor; and two members of the House appointed by the Speaker. The LBB has a permanent staff and is responsible for adopting a spending limit; preparing the general appropriation bill (the budget); preparing agency performance reports; guiding, reviewing, and finalizing agency strategic plans; identifying probable cost of proposed legislation (these are called fiscal notes); and managing transfers among purposes within agencies or among agencies. The LBB provides staff support for the appropriation process during the legislative session: tracking committee decisions, answering committee member inquiries, performing analyses, and providing testimony.

The executive branch is involved through the Governor's Office of Budget, Planning and Policy (GOBPP) (reflecting the governor's policies) and, of course, the agencies that develop their requests for funds according to instructions issued to them. The governor and the LBB develop goals for each state agency to use in developing strategic plans and develop the instructions (Legislative Appropriation Request or LAR instructions) the agencies must use in preparing their appropriation requests. The LARs are submitted to the governor, and hearings are held on those requests in conjunction with the LBB. The governor submits a budget within the first 6 days of the legislative session and delivers a general appropriation bill within 30 days after the start of the session. The governor's budget is often seen as the statement of policy, and the LBB bill is used as the appropriations bill.

The budget is biennial and both legislative and executive branches are involved in preparation of the budget and the strategies upon which it is based.

Legislative Consideration and Adoption

The legislature receives the budget and general appropriation bill. It also receives from the Comptroller of Public Accounts (Comptroller), an elected state official, a *Biennial Revenue Estimate* of funds expected to be received during the budget period. This is important because the Texas Constitution prohibits the legislature from appropriating an amount greater than estimated revenue collections.

Figure 3A–1
The Biennial Budget Cycle in the State of Texas

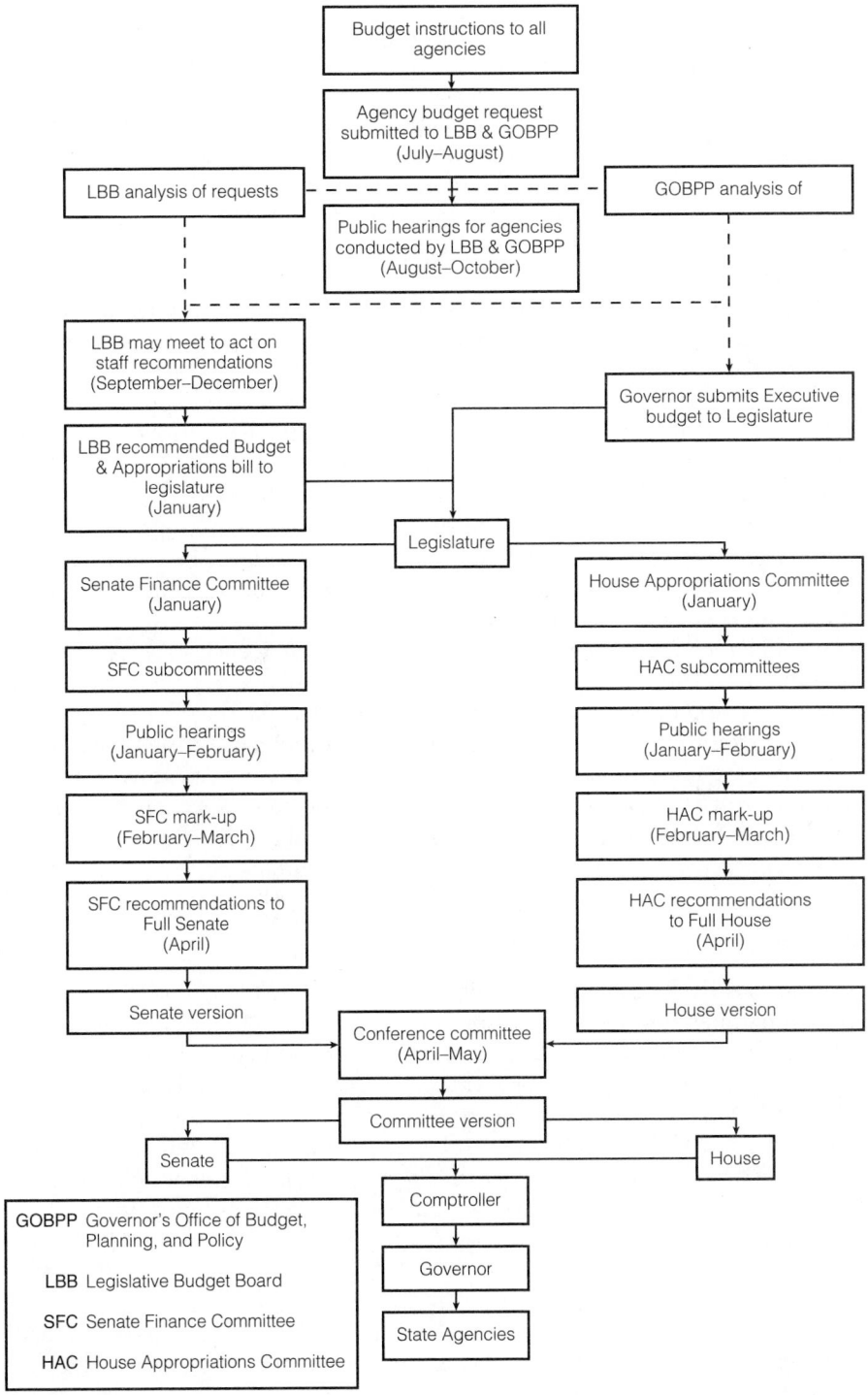

SOURCE: Senate Research Center, Budget 101. A Guide to the Budget Process in Texas (Austin, Texas Senate, 2005).

The two houses of the legislature take turns as the originating chamber for the general appropriations bill and for chairing the conference committee that works out differences between the bills ultimately passed by each house. The House bill goes through the House Appropriations committee; the Senate bill goes through the Senate Finance committee. The general appropriation bill has the following articles: general government, health and human services, education, judiciary, public safety and criminal justice, natural resources, business and economic development, regulatory, general provisions, legislature, savings clause, and emergency clause.

After approval of the appropriations bill, the Comptroller must certify that the state will have sufficient revenue to cover the money approved. In case of an "emergency and imperative public necessity" (Article 3, section 49a of the state's constitution), appropriations may exceed revenue on approval of four-fifths of the membership of each house. Normally, the Comptroller can certify; appropriation bills are not passed if they violate the revenue provision. If the Comptroller does not certify the bill, it returns to the house of origin.

The governor has the power to veto specific items in the appropriation bill. Some agencies have received "lump sum" appropriations, in which case the governor can only veto the entire agency appropriation, not individual components of the agency's appropriation.

Supplemental appropriations are possible when agencies are in danger of running out of funds before the end of a budget period. The legislature may also reduce appropriations during the budget period.

The growth of spending is constitutionally forbidden (Article 8, section 22) to exceed the LBB's official estimate of growth of the state economy. However, spending from dedicated tax revenue is outside the limit. The Constitution also prohibits deficit spending (Article 3, section 49a) and requires that any unanticipated deficit at the end of a biennium must be eliminated in the subsequent budget.

Execution

Execution is by state agencies within the biennium that begins on September 1 of odd-numbered years, subject to monitoring by the LBB and the State Auditor's Office (SAO). The SAO operates under the direction of the Legislative Audit Committee, which consists of the lieutenant governor, the speaker of the House, the chairs of the Senate Finance committee and of House Appropriations and Ways and Means, and a member of the Senate appointed by the lieutenant governor. The LBB is heavily concerned with agency performance objectives.

The governor and LBB have joint authority to transfer funds within or between agencies.

Audit

The SAO, a legislative agency, is the external auditor of state agencies. SAO conducts financial, compliance, and performance audits of agencies and reports its findings to the legislature.

APPENDIX 3–2

Participatory Budgeting

Participatory budgeting is a budget process in which many different stakeholders debate, prioritize, and monitor choices made about public expenditure. Citizens and their local governments, in a process of prioritization and joint decision, together establish the final allocation of public expenditures. The stakeholders are broadly determined to include the general public, poor and vulnerable groups including women, private businesses, organized citizen groups, representative bodies, and, in developing and transition countries, donor groups. The process seeks a wide spectrum of views. The executive still presents the budget proposal to a legislative body, and the legislative body still makes the final choice about putting the budget into law, but the public participates quite formally in the process. It seeks transparency, responsiveness, and broad representation in the budget process.

The participatory influence can be integrated into three stages of the budget process:

1. Budget Preparation. Citizens participate in budget allocation according to priorities they have identified in meetings and workshops.
2. Expenditure Monitoring. Citizens track whether spending is consistent with allocations made in the adopted budget and track the flow of funds to agencies responsible for the delivery of public services.
3. Monitoring Service Delivery. Citizens monitor the quality and quantity of government services relative to the expenditures made for the services.

Main features of the process are the following:

1. Clearly defined regional boundaries within the territory of the government practicing participatory budgeting. In one of the most famous applications, the town of Porto Alegre, Brazil (population 1.4 million), is divided into sixteen regions for citizen meetings. These geographical structures are crucial for decision-making and service monitoring.
2. Open meetings for discussion of thematic issues (Porto Alegre has five areas: transportation; education, leisure, and culture; health and social welfare; economic development and taxation; and city organization and urban development), to decide strategic priorities, to develop action plans, and to monitor current results. Meetings occur both within the regions and according to the thematic issue areas. Priorities from these meetings complement the representative democratic structures. Tens of thousands of people are reported to participate in the Porto Alegre process, vastly more people than

---

SOURCE: House Research Organization, *Writing the State Budget,* State Finance Report No. 79–1, February 4, 2005 (Austin, Texas: Texas House of Representatives) and Senate Research Center, *Budget 101: A Guide to the Budget Process in Texas* (Austin, Texas: Texas Senate, 2005).

ever are involved in any local budget process in the United States (or most other places).

3. An annual cycle of participation, planning, and meeting to regularly involve the citizenry.
4. A budget decision process that brings the priorities in the regions directly into the development and approval of the budget. The Porto Alegre process is particularly focused on the public works section of the budget (or the investment budget).

The process can lead to more responsive and effective government, more equitable distribution of government services, greater consensus among the citizenry regarding government programs, stronger nongovernmental organizations, and improved support for governmental reforms and restructuring. It is particularly aimed at providing a voice for the traditionally underrepresented sections of the population and at control of governmental corruption through openness and monitoring. It is a tool for good governance and effective decentralization of government.

Countries in which some localities practice participatory budgeting include Albania, Brazil, Bolivia, Czech Republic, Canada, Ireland, India, Uganda, the United Kingdom, Romania, and South Africa.

CHAPTER 4

Budget Methods and Practices

Many tasks in the budget cycle can be learned only by dealing nose-to-nose against, and elbow-to-elbow with other participants. However, understanding some methods and perspectives before that first crunch is important. This chapter introduces some methods and activities in each phase of the budget cycle. In particular, it deals with (1) preparation of agency budget requests, (2) review of agency requests, (3) construction of the final executive budget, (4) managing budget execution, and (5) audit.

Preparation of Agency Budget Requests

Operating agencies work from the budget instruction transmitted by the central budget office to develop their operating plans for the year and the budget requests that will accommodate those plans. Ideally, the instructions provide (1) the chief executive's main goals for the people, (2) forecasts of critical operating conditions for the budget year (inflation, service populations, etc.), (3) a format for the budget proposal (usually including prescribed request forms), (4) a schedule to be followed in developing the budget, and (5) some indication of the amount of money that the agency ought to build its budget around (either a ceiling control total or an estimated maximum increase from prior years).

How do the chief executive and central budget office know whether the instructions to agencies should emphasize extreme fiscal constraint, allow modest expansion of existing programs, or permit consideration of sound new programs? Many governments prepare, as a starting point, a preliminary baseline forecast of the surplus or deficit. The baseline provides the projected budget conditions if policies embedded in existing law are maintained.[1] In this analysis, the budget office estimates revenue for the budget year and compares that forecast with the cost of

[1]Establishing exactly what the baseline should entail is not without controversy. See Timothy J. Muris, "The Uses and Abuses of Budget Baselines," in John F. Cogan, et al., eds., *The Budget Puzzle, Understanding Federal Spending* (Stanford, California: Stanford University Press, 1994): 41–78. The argument concerns what exactly current policy should mean.

continuing existing programs at their current level of operations under the conditions expected for the next year (prices, workloads, etc.). In many instances, the simple projection approaches presented in the previous chapter are used, although sometimes more complex forecasting models may be applied. The gap between revenue and expenditure under current law gives a first guidance for the budget instruction: Will agencies be allowed to propose new programs? Will they work under hiring freezes? Will they be constrained in their capacity to request new equipment or to make capital outlays? What sort of ceilings will they face in making their requests? How the chief executive feels about deficits and surpluses and whether that executive is willing to propose revenue increases (tax or charge increases) also shape the instruction.

Within that instruction the agency develops the three important pieces of its budget proposal: (1) a *narrative,* which describes the agency (mostly the same from year to year), indicates its managerial objectives for the budget year and beyond (probably changing from year to year), and is keyed to the agency mission statement; (2) *detail schedules,* which translate the managerial objectives into requests for new agency appropriations; and (3) *cumulative schedules,* which aggregate the new initiatives into existing activities to form the complete request. The presentation also probably includes *workload, productivity,* and *performance measures* for the agency. The workload identifies measurable activities of the agency with historical trends and projections for the future. Productivity relates these workload measures to numbers of personnel. And performance measures identify quantity and quality of service delivered to the public, sometimes including the results of citizen satisfaction surveys.

The most important lesson for the neophyte to learn about budget preparation, and possibly the most surprising, is that description dominates the numbers. The request must describe and justify the plan; the numbers follow from that. Budgeting is logic, planning, justification, and politics, not mathematics or accounting. All three elements are critical because they provide governments the "how much" and "what it does" information needed for successful public decisions. And the whole process begins with the agency's explanation of what it intends for the budget year.

Agency budget documents are likely to include details not just on how money has been and is intended to be spent, but also on agency performance and accomplishments. It is a reasonable expectation that an agency be able to explain what it has done with the money—besides spent it!—and to explain what the public can expect to receive from the planned operations of the agency in the upcoming budget year. This performance information and plans may be embedded as an important element of the budget narrative but, increasingly, the budget proposal has a distinct and identifiable section that deals with performance. Central administrations, legislatures, and the citizenry all seek performance information as they consider budget requests and operating plans of public agencies.

Budget Justification

Program status reports, requests for supplemental funding, supporting explanation for increased staff, budget increases, and so on, require justification for any planned agency action. Well-developed justifications are the key to successful agency budget requests.[2] The standard rules of English prose apply, but there are also several general and specific guidelines for effective budget justifications. The justification must avoid jargon and uncommon and unexplained abbreviations because its audience includes individuals less familiar with the details of the proposed activity than are the operating agency's personnel. Neither budget-agency examiners nor legislators are likely to approve poorly described projects. The justifications must be factual, provide documented sources, and go through ordinary review and revision to produce a polished presentation. Some of the justification may be technical. However, the technical parts cannot overwhelm the rest or be left unexplained.

The justification structure must address the current situation, additional needs, and expected results from honoring the request. One section of the justification should describe the current program in terms of measurable workloads, staffing, funding, or productivity trends. It should briefly and specifically inform the budget examiner of existing conditions, without extraneous detail that might misdirect the examiner's attention. Another section of the justification should describe the additional needs. It must specifically identify additional funds, personnel, and materials needed for the budget activity at issue. The reason for the need must be explicitly developed. The examiner must not have to guess what and why. The request must also indicate what beneficial results will come from granting the request. The details of what belongs in the justification are ordinarily covered in the instructions. Hence comes the basic rule for doing budget justifications: *read the instructions and follow them.*

Common reasons for requesting funds include the following:

1. **Higher (or lower) prices.** Prices of supplies and services needed to maintain agency operations at their existing level may be increasing (or decreasing). For instance, the local electric utility may have received approval for a rate increase during the next year. That could elicit a request for a budget increase to accommodate the increased cost of the service.

2. **Workload.** The clientele served by the agency may increase. To maintain service levels, the agency's budget may need to increase. An agency providing education to children of the homeless, for instance, could argue for a larger budget if the population of such children increases.

3. **Methods improvement.** Administrative changes or innovations can alter the budgets of agencies. An operating unit can become more productive and generate fewer errors if it has more space or if it has more modern equipment. That would require a budget request. Methods improvement can also allow savings, in which case the budget change would be negative. Some improvements may have been mandated, or required by the courts, the legislature, or a higher level of government.

4. **Full financing.** Agencies frequently start new operations at some point other than the start of a fiscal year. Initial appropriations for new operations are

[2]They are also critical for grant proposal writing for public and nonprofit organizations.

thus partial; to cover full operations would require larger appropriations, a change that needs to be described in the agency request.

5. **New services.** New services, enlarged services, improved services, or services to an expanded clientele should be identified and justified. Because new services would not have been previously considered in legislative deliberations, they do require separation in the budget. New services are likely to be closely linked to initiatives in the basic narrative. As with method improvements, some new services may have been mandated.

There may be other categories of justification that would be applied to allow agencies to identify the underlying case for their request. For instance, some federal agencies recognize a judicial restraining order as a separate category. Those noted here, however, are among the most common.

The narrative should describe expected results from the proposal and try to convince the budget office and the legislature of the need for the proposed activity. The narrative should describe the consequences if the requested resources are or are not provided. Because the reviewer will want to know whether partial funding will help, whether critical program objectives will be endangered without funding, whether workload can be backlogged to get around the problem, and what the implications of the request will be for future requests, answers to those questions should be available and defensible. The justification should make a solid case for a realistic increase. There is no reason to spread a justification thin to defend a large increase when a solid case for a smaller increase is possible. Table 4–1 presents a brief checklist for elements to include in a sound justification. An agency should never assume that its request for additional resources, no matter how reasonable it

Table 4–1
Checklist for Budget Justification

Completeness	—Are the major elements (objective of program, magnitude of need, benefits, or accomplishments) covered?
Explicitness	—Are program benefits and related funding increases clearly stated?
Consistency	—Are the statements or data appearing in several places the same or easily reconcilable?
Balance	—Are the most important programs and issues given the most prominence? Do the programs' objectives adequately support the budget level requested?
Quantitative data	—Are quantitative data used appropriately and effectively?
Organization	—Is the material well organized to bring out only the significant matters? Are appropriate headings or titles used? Is introductory or summary material used appropriately?

SOURCE: U.S. Office of Personnel Management, *Budget Presentation and Justification* (Washington, D.C.: GPO, 1982).

may appear to agency staff, will automatically bring more funds. When an agency does not receive its full budget request, the agency cannot complain that it has not been "fully funded." Its legislative masters, the representatives of the citizenry, have not accepted the plan proposed by the agency, but have funded the plan of which it approves.

Budget instructions do not always clearly define what ought to be in a narrative. In that case, explaining (1) what resources the agency wants for the budget year, (2) what it intends to do with those resources, and (3) what good will result from that intention usually suffices.

Elements of Cost Estimation

Estimates of what the cost would be of fulfilling the agency service plan for the budget year may be developed and organized through one or more of the following approaches. First, the cost may be grouped by the organization (branch, section, division, etc.) incurring the cost. The estimates originate in the offices where the costs occur. The costs thus follow the organizational chart. For example, if a city has six organizational units (police, fire, parks, public works, streets, and mayor and council), a cost estimate would be prepared for each unit. The estimates would, of course, entail each unit's planned responses to forecast operating conditions. Second, costs may be grouped by task, purpose, function, or program cost center, or by program outcome group. For instance, program cost centers for a police department might include central administration, the jail, criminal investigations, crime prevention, traffic, training, communication, and records. Each represents an identifiable task for which operating plans and budget cost can be identified. Alternatively, cost may be divided by outcome program: transportation, public safety, environmental protection, etc. Sometimes the organizational breakdown coincides with these task or program breakdowns, but often organizational costs are attributable to several different tasks or programs. Third, the costs may be broken down by object (or economic) class, that is, by the nature of goods and services to be purchased (personnel, utilities, motor fuel, etc.). Agencies organize their cost estimates according to the uniform object classification required and provided by the budget office of that particular government.

The beginning of any budget cost estimation, regardless of eventual focus on department, task cost center, or program outcome, is the object class. This is the basis for estimating resource requirements, regardless of how costs will eventually be organized. Ideally, the agency would determine what it intends to do, determine what resources it needs to do it, estimate the price of those resources, and multiply the price by the number of input units to get a cost total. In routine budget preparation, many of the estimates are based on what the agency has experienced in the recent past ("last year plus 5 percent," for instance). Budget costs occur as agencies acquire resources (personnel, materials, and facilities) to provide public services. Somewhat different estimating techniques apply to each class, with a particular distinction between personnel and nonpersonnel costs.

Personnel Costs: Paying the Staff

Agencies need workers if they are to produce government services or, even if production is contracted out to private firms, to monitor this production by others. Indeed, payments to employees—wages and salaries plus other agreed benefits (pensions, insurance, etc.)—usually represent the largest single component in government agency budget requests and a major element in the total cost of government. For instance, wages and salaries alone amount to around 30 percent of state and around half of local government spending on current operations. A considerable portion of the cost of modern government is determined by compensation paid to employees, even though the wage and salary component of spending has declined through the years as governments provide more services by contract with private firms and by transfer payments.

Wages and salaries. The task is to estimate personnel cost for a budget request: to determine the kind and amount of personal services needed—the time to be spent by employees at work—and then apply prevailing wage and salary rates to compute the total cost. In other words, total personnel cost equals the number of workers in each pay category multiplied by the payment per worker in that category. A standard procedure uses personnel data on individuals in each pay category, adjusted for anticipated movements to the next pay step in the budget year. Thus, if there are fifty people in the Tax Auditor I category with 5 years' experience this year, there will likely be fifty people in the Tax Auditor I category with 6 years' experience next year. The budget estimate for them would be fifty times the annual pay of a Tax Auditor I with 6 years' experience. Governments normally maintain a position management system that charts authorized positions by pay class, which positions are filled and which are vacant, and the pay rate in each class. The system both provides a control over employment and its costs and offers an excellent tool for cost estimation.

The request for payment of staff must be supplemented by lapses that reduce total cost: turnover (retirements, quits, and terminations) with replacement at lower pay grades or nonreplacement, delays in filling vacant positions, and so on. Such lapses may be estimated from experience with the agency workforce. Requests for new personnel ordinarily are based on greater expected workload, on a desire to improve the quality of service, or on new programs. At least at the agency request level, staffing decisions have moved away from regarding government as the employer of last resort, where those unable to find jobs elsewhere can turn, and toward staffing to ensure the agency delivers planned services and achieves its objectives.

But how much should each employee be paid? This question is critical for sound government finances and for the delicate political balance between, on the one hand, the interests of public employees and the groups that represent them and, on the other, the concerns of taxpayers/service recipients who both receive what governments provide and pay the bill for that provision. A reasonable objective in determining pay rates for government finances might be to ensure delivery of government services at least cost to the taxpayer. If employees are overpaid, the taxpayer pays too much for services provided; if employees are underpaid, the taxpayer receives subsidization at the expense of those employees. In practice, pay rates may come (1) from law or tradition, as with the salaries of elected officials, (2) from pay rates established in a civil service classification structure that attempts wage-comparability across position factors, or (3) from collective bargaining agreements.[3] Most governments establish some salaries in each of these way. For example, a city could well have the salaries of the mayor and the members of the council established by state statute, the wages and salaries in most city departments established in a personnel classification system, and the wages of police officers, firefighters, and sanitation workers established in a collective bargaining agreement.

Non-wage-and-salary personnel costs. The total cost of workers includes both direct compensation (wages and salaries) and fringe benefits associated with employment. At least some fringe-benefit payments are included in object classes separate from wage and salary payments, but they must be considered when estimating total compensation and when developing budget estimates. These payments may include payments into public employee pension systems, health and/or life insurance premiums, clothing or uniform allowances, employer Social Security or other payroll tax payments, and so on. Most such benefits are computed by applying formulas, which are established by law, labor contract, or (less frequently now) prevailing practices. Cost is normally driven either by the number of employees (hospital insurance premiums, for example) or the amount paid to employees (e.g., payments into a public employee pension fund based on a certain percentage of wages) and calculation is thus relatively straightforward (although the formulae can sometimes be quite complicated).

Nonpersonnel Costs

Other object costs may be more difficult to estimate than are personnel costs.[4] Nonpersonnel costs are often computed using estimating ratios, as adjusted by recent experience. Much information for the request can be located in prior-year budget materials. Five estimation techniques are frequently used in these computations:

1. **Volume × unit price.** This method is attractive when an identifiable quantity and a single average price are applicable to a relatively high-ticket object class. Candidates for this approach include requests for items such as automobiles or personal computers. These items represent fairly homogeneous categories that can constitute a large share of cost in an object class. If the police department plans to purchase ten new vehicles and the sort of vehicle that would be purchased likely can be purchased for $35,000, the estimated cost of the plan is $350,000.

2. **Workload × average unit cost.** This approach uses recent cost experience with adjustments for inflation and/or productivity changes. For instance, food

---

[3]See Charles A. Pounian and Jeffrey J. Fuller, "Compensating Public Employees," in James Perry, ed. *Handbook of Public Administrations,* 2nd ed. (San Francisco: Jossey-Bass, 1996), for more discussion of pay systems.

[4]See Susan A. MacManus, "Designing and Managing the Procurement Process," in Ibid., for an excellent analysis of the procurement of goods and services.

expenses for a training class could be estimated by such a method (300 trainee days at $20 per trainee day, for a request of $6,000).

3. **Workforce ratios.** Some categories of cost, particularly small categories of miscellaneous costs, can be estimated by relating them to the workforce. For example, office supply expenses for a revenue department district office could be related to the size of staff stationed there. A proposal to hire new police officers may bring with it the need to purchase new police vehicles. (Similar estimates can be made by linking the expense category to the clientele being served by the local office.)

4. **Ratios to another object.** When there is some relationship between certain categories and other resources used in the production process, that expense group can be estimated by use of ratios to the nonpersonnel object class. As an example, a parts inventory for motor vehicles can be linked to the number of vehicles in the motor fleet. Purchase of ten new police vehicles would require some additional costs for operation and repair.[5]

5. **Adjustment to prior-year cost.** Small, heterogeneous cost categories can be estimated by adjusting prior-year lump sums. Prior cost is adjusted to reflect anticipated quality changes in the budget year. This method may be necessary when other means are not feasible or economical, but it lacks the attempted precision of other techniques.

No formula or ratio can be automatically applied without hazard. Cost ratios and other relationships may change if operating methods are altered, prices of inputs change, or production technologies change. All of these change in a dynamic economy, often with great impact on operating cost. Sidebar 4–1 describes break-even analysis, an estimating device often used by managers in public, private, and nonprofit agencies as they develop fiscal plans.

Screening for Errors

Budget estimates must be carefully prepared because the quality of the presentation shapes the impressions that budget analysts (and others) develop about agencies. Analysts are less likely to trust judgments of budget officers who prepare sloppy budget requests. Several simple errors are particularly frequent, although they should never occur.

1. **Instructions Not Followed**: Budgets may not coincide with current budget instructions, budget guidelines, and forms. A budget may be developed using the prior-year budget as a guide, but the submission must coincide with current regulations. Failure to follow instructions produces needless embarrassment and may put the request at extra risk.

---

[5]Sometimes things do not work out well. For instance, a federal judge ordered LaPorte County, Indiana, to remedy chronic jail overcrowding, and the county spent $23 million on a jail renovation and expansion, completed in 2004. Unfortunately, the county did not have enough money to hire additional jailers, so a new wing with space for 200 inmates had to remain empty. Too bad the judge did not order jailers to accompany the jail space.

SIDEBAR 4–1
Break-Even Analysis

Break-even analysis is a helpful tool for certain managerial problems, including budget estimation, subsidy determination, scaling, and the like. Agencies that have sales revenue can make more frequent direct use of the technique, but most managers will find some applications. The technique plots cost against revenues as the quantity of service (output) provided varies. That allows the manager to identify the service level at which service revenue equals service cost (the break-even point) and the required subsidy or contribution (profit) at other operation levels. With the costing model developed here, a budget administrator can easily see how changing demand for a service will influence the agency's spending pace, and that can be useful in both developing a budget request and monitoring spending within budget execution.

The logic of the method is illustrated with this example. Suppose the Smithville Solid-Waste Management Authority has a trash collection fee of $2 per 40-gallon container; that means its revenue in a particular time period will equal the number of containers of trash collected multiplied by $2. Algebraically,

$$TR = P \times Q$$

where TR equals total revenue, P equals price per unit, and Q equals the number of units or service level. Thus,

$$TR = 2Q$$

The authority faces two types of cost, some that are fixed (they do not change with the quantity of service provided, at least within normal service ranges) and some that are variable (the cost increases with the level of service). Authority estimates show the following costs:

Fixed (Annual)	
Administration (staff, utilities, etc.)	$ 35,000
Equipment lease	85,000
Total	$120,000
Variable (Per Container)	
Landfill tipping charge	$1.00
Equipment operation on collection routes (fuel, maintenance, etc.)	0.15
Collection crew payment	0.25
Total	$1.40

An algebraic statement of total cost would be

$$TC = FC + (VC \times Q)$$

(continues)

SIDEBAR 4–1 (continued)

where TC = total cost, FC = fixed cost, and VC = unit variable cost. Thus,

$$TC = 120{,}000 + 1.40Q$$

The authority can now estimate the level of collections at which the operation will break even and, probably more important, the necessary subsidy at actual levels of operation. The break-even service level is the one at which $TR = TC$:

$$2Q = 120{,}000 + 1.40Q$$

The break-even Q is 200,000; collection levels above that will provide a surplus (or contribution) for use elsewhere, and collection levels below that will require a contribution from elsewhere (maybe a tax?) to cover the cost. By substituting the manager's best guess for actual service level into the equation, the actual contribution or subsidy requirement may be estimated. The analysis can also help the manager identify the relative impact of controlling fixed or variable cost in reducing the overall subsidy requirements.

Managers need to recognize the limitations of the analysis, even as they use it. Costs may be difficult to estimate and may not be easily divided into fixed and variable. There may also be cost discontinuities. In other words, certain costs may be fixed up to some production level, but need to increase to support further service production. Service levels almost certainly vary with the price charged, especially with larger price changes. The assumption of linearity can only be seen as a working approximation. The technique, however, remains one of great applicability.

Managers often develop break-even charts to visualize their operations. The charts plot total cost and total revenue against service (or output) levels, as shown here:

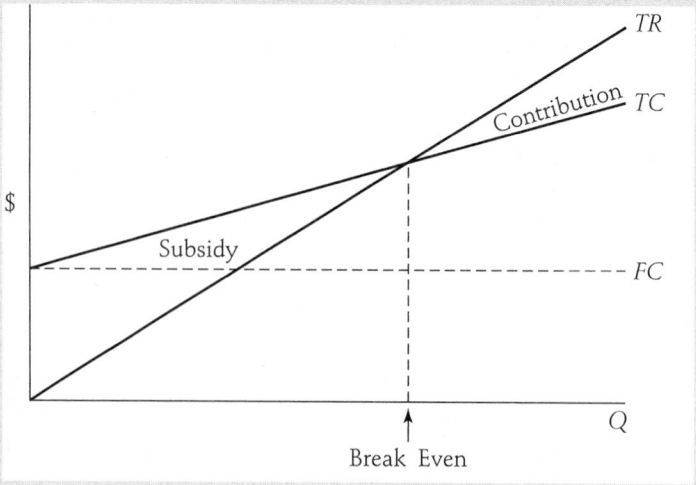

2. **Missing Documentation**: Budget submissions may lack required supplemental documents, or the documents may not be properly identified. Budget examiners seldom give the benefit of doubt to budgets with missing material.

3. **Internal Inconsistency**: Cost-estimate detail columns may not add to totals carried forward in the presentation. One must continuously cross-check to preserve the internal consistency of the budget request.

4. **Math:** The math may not be right. Failure to check all arithmetic can lead not just to professional embarrassment but also to rejected budget requests and to terminated employment. Even spreadsheet calculations need to be verified to ensure that formulae do what is expected and that the formulae are right. The computer does exactly what it is told to do, even when the instructions are wrong.

Review of Budgets

Agency requests are reviewed by a central budget office before proposals are included in the executive budget (and by legislative committees after inclusion in the proposal). The central budget office is working under a total resource constraint—revenue forecast to be available in the budget year, funds to be borrowed during the budget year, and any balances forecast to be available from prior years—and the sum of all executive budget requests must be within that constraint. In almost every circumstance, the sum of requests is more than the money available to spend—so the central budget agency is going to have to reduce some requests. But the budget agency is also concerned that the budget and operating plan finally approved can actually be executed. That means that it may need to add omitted items from some requests if the examiner finds that a program supported by the chief executive cannot be executed with the resources initially proposed by the agency. Furthermore, the budget examiner is less-informed about agency operations than are those in the agency who prepared the budget. That means that the budget must clearly communicate and explain what is in the budget proposal.

How do budget examiners review budgets? Arnold Meltsner has examined budget operations in Oakland, California, in some detail, finding patterns in the way budget analysts review budgets:

> Inexperience in itself forces upon the budget analyst the use of a set of rules of thumb. The analyst first looks at last year's appropriations to identify any significant changes. It is the changes or incremental requests which get his attention. Without going into detail, here is an outline of the rules of cutting:
>
> 1. Cut all increases in personnel.
> 2. Cut all equipment items which appear to be luxuries.
> 3. Use precedent—cut items which have been cut before.
> 4. Recommend repair and renovation rather than replacement of facilities.
> 5. Recommend study as a means of deferring major costs.

6. Cut all non-item operating costs by a fixed percentage (such as 10 percent).
7. Do not cut when safety or health of staff or public is obviously involved.
8. Cut departments with "bad" reputations.
9. When in doubt ask another analyst what to do.
10. Identify dubious items for the manager's attention.

The analyst, by looking for enough items to cut, proceeds until the budget is balanced within the existing revenue constraints.[6]

Beyond those rules of thumb, is there anything that a budget analyst—always less knowledgeable about details of the program under review than those who run the program and always looking for budget reductions—can do? Appendix 4–1, instructions to Oregon budget analysts, gives a good overview of what work must be done and how a budget examiner would proceed with the review task. There are some particular points that must be considered in the analysis.

1. **Policy rationale.** The reviewer must consider what the policy rationale is for the agency's proposal. Among the questions to be considered are these: Is the problem real? Is the problem something that this government should be doing something about? Is the strategy that the agency is proposing likely to be successful? Will the program make any difference? What is the chief executive's view on the policy under consideration?

2. **Arithmetic.** The reviewer must verify the arithmetic used to produce program requests. Errors and overambitious rounding seem to increase requests more often than they reduce them. Remember that spreadsheet formulas do exactly what they have been instructed to do and that the instructions may be wrong. Verify the formulas.

3. **Linkages.** Reviewers should check linkages between justifications and dollar requests. Is there reason to believe that the request will have the expected result, or will things stay about the same, regardless of the money requested? Requests in the latter category are good candidates for elimination, regardless of budget conditions.

4. **Program changes.** The reviewer must determine whether the agency proposes changes in its programs or changed directions in existing programs. If changes are contemplated, they should be consistent with legislative (and executive) intent.

5. **Omissions.** The reviewer must seek omissions from the budget requests. Some years ago, a major university constructed a large center for performing and creative arts but neglected to request money to cover electricity and other utilities needed for its operation. That created significant budget problems during the first year because major reductions had to be imposed on other university activities to cover that utility bill.

6. **Ratios, shares, and trends.** The reviewer must use all resources available for analysis, particularly the prior-year budget and actual expenditure, the cur-

[6]Arnold J. Meltsner, *The Politics of City Revenue* (Berkeley: University of California Press, 1971), 178.

rent-year budget and reported expenditure to date, and the proposed budget. A comparison of these documents can be made without undue trouble, especially since the analyst has been keeping track of the agency through the operating year. The analyst should establish the cause of any deviations from trends apparent in those comparisons. The analyst often computes ratios and shares of cost elements over time and across agencies to identify variances and to raise questions for the agency (Sidebar 4–2 discusses ratios and shares in greater detail). Ratios, shares, and trends seldom answer questions by themselves, but they do frequently open up matters for further inquiry.

Sidebar 4–2
Ratios and Shares

Management guru Peter F. Drucker writes, "A database, no matter how copious, is not information. It is information ore. For raw material to become information, it must be organized for a task, directed toward specific performance, applied to a decision. Raw material cannot do that itself."[1]

Budget documents provide a rich lode of data about agencies, but those data are raw. Budget analysts regularly calculate ratios and shares from that data to convert it into information that might help a decision. For example, it may be interesting to know that East Liverpool spends $400,000 on police salaries, but real insight requires the number to be related to something, often through a ratio or a share. What ratio or share might help, given the considerable array of possible computations that could be made? Here are some fundamental data questions:

1. What period-to-period increase or decrease appears in the categories being examined? What reasons induce the changes, and are they likely to continue in the future?
2. What are the growth rates of elements in the budget totals? Which categories are driving the overall growth, what appears to be causing those patterns, and what are the prospects for the future?
3. What are the shares of individual budget elements in the total? Are particular shares growing rapidly? What are the trends? What components are most significant in the overall budget?
4. How large is the element under consideration, relative to the entity under consideration? Is it big, considering the economy, population, geography, or whatever else may be important?

Ratios and shares do not, by themselves, answer analytic questions, but they can highlight avenues for further inquiry. The analyst spends much time computing them and deducing what additional questions need to be asked. Much of the effort involves comparisons of ratios across units and across time. There will be no "right" value for a particular ratio. Rather, the ratios provide clues that may open avenues of understanding for the analyst and decision-makers.

[1] Peter F. Drucker, "Be Data Literate—Know What to Know," *Wall Street Journal,* 1 December 1992, A-16.

7. **Executive policy.** The reviewer considers the extent to which the agency request coincides with policy directions announced by the chief executive. Those not consistent with that direction are immediate targets for reduction or elimination.

8. **Choices within limits.** The reviewer must understand that resources are finite and choices must be made between worthwhile programs. Government programs to improve adult literacy and programs to reduce fatalities at rural intersections both yield a return that is important for society. But if government resource constraints prevent both programs from being included in the executive budget at the full amount requested by the operating agencies proposing them, a choice has to be made between the two—and there is no common denominator (a social value "converter" between more literate adults and fewer deaths in the country) between the two programs. The choice will be fuzzy, imprecise, and somewhat discomforting. But it is a choice (one of many) that has to be made.

9. **Performance.** The reviewer considers the performance documentation provided by the agency, the extent to which the measures provided are consistent with the mission and goals of the agency, the extent to which accomplishment is appropriate to the budgetary resources available to the agency, and the performance plan related to the budget request of the agency. It is important to consider the extent to which measures are germane to the mission of the agency, and extend beyond just measuring things that are easily measured. Poor performance may, if the work of the agency is sufficiently important to the citizenry, provide a reason for increasing the budget of the agency, rather than for cutting its budget. It is expected that there will be a link between achievement of the performance measures and the implementation of the budget.

The Executive Budget: The Plan and the Balancing

The executive budget document delivers the financial plan for the government, provides a clear statement of the policy vision that shaped those plans, tells the legislature and the public what enactment of the plan would bring, and provide an archive of information about the government and its agencies. It also includes information about operating performance of the government and about the performance plan that is inherent in the financial support that is requested. In all these areas, the message needs to be communicated clearly but concisely; many participants in the process immediately conclude malicious intent for everything that is vague. In other words, the budget should be (1) a policy document, (2) a financial plan, (3) an operations guide, and (4) a device for communicating to the legislature and the public.

The budget, like that delivered to Congress by the president or presented by other executives to their legislative bodies, typically contains four basic elements:

1. **The budget message** is an introduction, from the chief executive, that highlights the major conditions surrounding the budget's preparation (economic conditions, perceived social problems, service priorities, etc.) and the primary changes proposed in the budget. The message sets the tone for the budget ("hard times," "new beginnings and new challenges," "change," "emerging from severe fiscal crisis," etc.); in simple budgets, this may be the only narrative in the entire document.[7] The message is where the executive (president, governor, mayor, etc.) makes a statement about which goals matter to him or her. As Dall Forsythe sums it up: "If you cannot use the budget to state your goals and move state government in the direction you advocate, you are not likely to make much progress towards those goals."[8]

2. **Several summary schedules,** the type and number of which vary by budget, gather the major aggregates planned in the full document. These schedules include both revenue and expenditure categories, each organized by classification schemes seen as important by the government (revenue by source, expenditure by object class, expenditure by organizational unit, expenditure by function, etc.). Schedules ordinarily include the budget-year amounts and comparable figures for the current and most recently completed years.

3. **Detail schedules,** the heart of the budget, explain why the administrative departments seek the money they hope to spend. Estimates may also be presented for several out-years to provide information about long-term trends and impacts on budgets of decisions now and of external developments (e.g., economic or demographic change). The details are presented in at least one and usually more of the following organizational structures: by administrative unit (the department, division, etc., responsible for spending and delivering services), by program or function (type of service delivered), or object of expenditure (input classes to be purchased). Most governments also include a performance plan and report for each agency. These schedules state the actual results in terms of measured indexes for the closed fiscal year and planned accomplishments for the budget year.

4. **Supplemental data** may also be included in the budget document, depending on the information requirements placed on the executive by the legislative body and on the special problems or opportunities encountered by the subject government. Most budgets, including the federal budget, include supplemental tables and displays that are useful and interesting, but have no direct bearing on the key tasks of the budget. Other examples of displays that governments use include detailed historical tables on tax rates, analysis of grant revenue, debt schedules, and special detail on pension and other trust funds.

---

[7]For more about the strategy of that message, see Henry W. Maier, *Challenge to the Cities: An Approach to a Theory of Urban Leadership* (New York: Random House, 1966). Maier was the longtime mayor of Milwaukee.

[8]Dall W. Forsythe, *Memos to the Governor, An Introduction to State Budgeting* (Washington, D.C.: Georgetown University Press, 1997), 84–85.

Building the executive budget from the agency plans requires a serious struggle to get program plans to fit within resources available to the government. Using executive priorities as a guide, the central budget office crafts the budget on behalf of the chief executive by cutting some plans, scaling back other plans, stretching out the pace of programs, and even proposing revenue options to enhance available resources. Controls on filling vacant positions, cuts in supply and equipment purchase proposals, and reduction of inflation adjustments are reasonably uncomplicated mechanisms for dealing with minor imbalances; such adjustments, along with the savings resulting from normal review of agency proposals within the template offered by the chief executive's vision for the future, provide orderly accommodations to resources that "meat-ax" approaches (such as reducing all proposals by a flat percentage, denying all plans for new services, or cutting any proposed increases that exceed a prescribed rate) do not afford. The responsible budget office makes a spending program proposal that can be executed within the funds that the government has for the year.

Phantom Balance and Deficit Reduction

Governments may find it politically convenient or legally necessary to produce a balanced operating budget or to reduce the size of the estimated deficit without changing intended policy or its implementation.[9] Governments have developed a number of pragmatic devices to "cook" budget numbers; many are widely and regularly used to avoid the difficult tasks of actual deficit reduction (increasing actual revenue or reducing actual expenditure).

1. **Rosy scenarios.** Any budget must be constructed with estimates of revenue for the upcoming fiscal year. Phantom budget balances can therefore be developed by using artificially high revenue estimates for that year. Such estimates can be produced by assuming unrealistically high economic activity (state and federal taxes, as well as many local nonproperty taxes, are sensitive to the level of economic activity),[10] impossibly diligent administration of the tax, or by presuming that the link between revenue collections and economic activ-

[9]Richard Briffault, *Balancing Acts, The Reality Behind State Balanced Budget Requirements* (New York: Twentieth Century Fund, 1996), explains that state-balanced budget requirements are not nearly so binding as a casual observer might assume. An operating budget would include the expenditures to be made for services delivered within the year; the resources purchased from the operating budget would largely be used within that year.

[10]There is some evidence that, at the federal level, neither the administration (through the Council of Economic Advisers) nor Congress (through the Congressional Budget Office) exercised as much bias as has been alleged. See Michael T. Belongia, "Are Economic Forecasts by Government Agencies Biased? Accurate?" *Federal Reserve Bank of St. Louis Review* 70 (Nov./Dec. 1998): 15–23. One study of the Office of Management and Budget (OMB) alone concludes, "Contrary to popular belief, the OMB under both political parties has consistently produced unbiased forecasts of the major macroeconomic variables, and unbiased estimates of total receipts. The traditional OMB ethic of neutral competence appears to be alive in its economic forecasts and revenue estimates," (Paul R. Blackley and Larry DeBoer, "Bias in OMBs Economic Forecasts and Budget Proposals," *Public Choice* 76 [July 1993]: 229.)

ity has improved. Local property taxes ordinarily could not be overestimated because rates are set on the basis of assessed value on a prior valuation date (more about this in a later chapter). The estimated revenue can be manipulated, however, by assuming unrealistically low delinquency (or noncollection) levels: if 90 percent of the levy has historically been collected, a budget boost is possible by assuming 95-percent collection. During its fiscal troubles of the late 1970s, New York City apparently got such boosts toward balancing the budget by presuming 100-percent collection, a completely unrealistic basis for budgeting. Similar effects may result from overly optimistic assumptions about intergovernmental assistance from either federal or state sources, or the possibility that some other government or a private organization will assume responsibility for a service previously provided through this budget. Rosy scenarios also can reduce planned expenditures—a healthy (forecasted) economy reduces social program needs and entitlement flows.

2. **One-shots.** An unsustainable revenue boost can be produced by sale of property or other assets held by the government, a "one-shot." As long as that revenue is not viewed as a long-term boost to the fiscal base and the asset is truly no longer needed for government service, the sales may be perfectly reasonable. But this is not always the case. One example was the fiscal 1991 sale by New York State of the Attica Correctional Facility to the state Urban Development Corporation for $200 million (the corporation borrowed $240 million—the difference being administrative costs—with debt service being met by leasing the prison back to the state), a high-cost and transparent scheme to fill a budget hole.[11] Other examples include privatization proceeds, the more profitable of which may bring in substantial revenue in the sale year but mean the loss of profit flows in later years.[12] An eastern state took the one-shot to its ridiculous extreme. A state hospital was declared surplus, was appraised at a handsome value, advertised for sale, and the anticipated revenue from that sale was included in the state revenue estimate. It helped balance a tight budget. But the facility did not sell, so the anticipated sales revenue was included as part of revenue expected for the next budget year! As long as the property remained for sale, the state felt justified in including appraised proceeds as anticipated revenue. Recent presidential budgets have included revenue from the sale of AMTRAK, oil leases in the Artic National Wildlife Refuge, the Naval Petroleum Reserves, competitive sales of the telecommunications spectrum, and so on.[13] The sales have not taken place as planned in the budget presentation; whether gimmick or plan is for others to decide. But Congress is skeptical; revenues from asset sales do not count against official deficit targets. Nor should they. Sale of an asset reduces the financial resources of the government

[11]Elizabeth Kolbert, "Albany's Budget—Balancing One-Shots Will Reverberate for Years to Come," *New York Times,* 21 April 1991, sec. 4, 18.

[12]Privatization is best defended to improve operating efficiency and delivery of service, not as a one-shot revenue enhancer. Currently, the sale or long-term lease of state and local government assets is popular as a means of raising funds for infrastructure development.

[13]Portions of the spectrum have, in fact, actually been auctioned—but not as soon as the revenue started appearing in budgets.

by an amount equivalent to the amount of the sale and should not be treated the same as sustainable operating revenue (like taxes or charges).[14]

3. **Interbudget manipulation.** State and local governments often have capital budgets in addition to and separate from operating budgets. Capital budgets finance purchases of assets with long, useful lives (as is discussed in Chapter 6) and often have no requirement for balance because such long-life assets may logically be financed on a pay-as-you-use basis through the issuance of debt. Some governments have shifted activities that would ordinarily be included in the operating budget to the capital budget to produce the desired balance in the operating budget. For instance, in its fiscal 1992 budget, New York City included an $80 million bond issue to finance the 4-year job of painting 872 city bridges "Yankee Blue," clearly a basic and continuing operating expenditure, but not included in the operating budget.[15] The shift can destroy the logic of the capital budget and, more important, can endanger the capability to finance the government's capital infrastructure.

The federal government currently has no separate capital budget but simply rolls all spending together. Some argue against creating dual federal budgets to prevent such play between documents. Even without dual budgets, there is room to manipulate: the first President Bush's fiscal 1990 budget proposed that a company, the Resolution Financing Corporation (the Corporation), be established to borrow funds to finance assistance for insolvent savings and loan associations. The Corporation, similar in structure to government-sponsored, privately owned enterprises like the Federal National Mortgage Association, would be outside the federal budget (but guaranteed by the federal government for repayment). The money borrowed would be turned over to the federal government to permit the savings and loan bail-out, but the money would—by budget-accounting convention—be a receipt, thus reducing the estimated deficit.[16]

4. **Bubbles and timing.** Deficits may be managed by accelerated collection of revenue to create a cash "bubble" in the year of acceleration.[17] The advantage accrues only in the acceleration year without influencing the fundamental revenue base. The bubble can be duplicated in forthcoming fiscal years only by further accelerating collections, an unlikely possibility. Here is how acceleration can work: Suppose a state requires that vendor collections of sales and use taxes in one month (say, May 2007) be paid to the state by the end of the next month (June 2007). The payment from the vendor then will actually be received by the state early in the next month (July 2007). If the state changes the due date from the end of the month to the 20th, however, the checks will

[14]International standards hold that sales of government-owned assets should be treated as means of financing the deficit, not revenue, because they are asset conversions only, not continuing sources of revenue. For instance, this is the required treatment for privatization receipts from sales of state-owned properties in countries of the former Soviet Union.

[15]John J. Doran, "New York City Comptroller Kills Bonding Plans for Bridge Painting; Cities Mistakes of 1970s," *Bond Buyer,* 16 July 1991, 2.

[16]Alan Murray, "Bush S&L Bailout Creates Illusion of Deficit Cut That Congress Questions But Wants to Believe," *Wall Street Journal,* 22 February 1989, A-16.

[17]In New York State, these accelerations are called "spin-ups."

almost certainly be received by the state in that month, that is, in late June rather than early July. But for a July 1 fiscal-year state, June is the 2007 fiscal year, and July is in the 2008 fiscal year; fiscal 2007 thus receives thirteen months of sales-and-use tax collections. Because a similar schedule applies for 2008 and beyond, each year continues to receive twelve months of collections. Only a return to a slower schedule would leave a fiscal year a month short of revenue. States generally exhausted this device in the 1970s, but many developed another mechanism in the late 1980s with early and prepayment requirements. Well over half of the states require either early payment of collections within the month (e.g., partial payment of May collections in May) or prepayment of estimated collections with reconciliation against actual collections later (estimated May collections paid in May with adjustment against actual collections later) for some major taxes remitted by businesses. The object of each speed-up is the same: to get an extra period of collections in the fiscal year.[18] These manipulations are politically less difficult than raising statutory tax rates and provide added revenue for a problem year through changed revenue flow across fiscal years.[19]

The balance problem may also be concealed by manipulating the timing of expenditure.[20] One approach loads the cost of multi-year programs in later fiscal years rather than in a sequence consistent with normal project-development flow. The low current budget-year request may help achieve balance in that year; the result, however, may well be greater problems in achieving balance in future budget years. A somewhat different method of expenditure manipulation, particularly within a fiscal year, delays payment for purchases made toward the end of a fiscal year until the next fiscal year (and the next year's appropriations). The technique conceals a short-term operating deficit and amounts to short-term borrowing from suppliers across the 2 fiscal years. It obviously reduces funds available for the next year. Unless the imbalance is corrected, similar problems will result in following years, and the operating deficit carryover will expand with time.[21]

---

[18]Acceleration also gives states earlier control of investable funds and protects against possible loss from vendor bankruptcy and the like.

[19]Similar shifts may substitute for ordinary borrowing. For instance, the city of Philadelphia used a property tax provision: businesses willing to pay estimated 1978 taxes along with their 1977 taxes were given a special discount on their 1978 tax bill. See "Early Taxpayers Can Get a Break in Philadelphia," *Louisville Courier-Journal,* 3 April 1977. This shift, however, does reduce aggregate collections, whereas acceleration does not.

[20]For example, in 1980 the city of Chicago, to avoid bank loans in a cash crisis, delayed payments to vendors who regularly did business with the city. The problem emerged because property tax bills were not mailed as scheduled because of a judicial challenge of a homestead exemption program. The city had short-term borrowing authority but feared it was insufficient to cover the shortage. "City May Delay Payment to Suppliers," *Chicago Tribune,* 19 August 1980. Because the taxes were actually levied, there was no borrowing across fiscal years in this instance; the strategy was simply one of cash-flow management.

[21]In 1992 New York City required 2,104 police recruits to begin training at 11:59 P.M. on June 30, the last minute of the fiscal year. These orders met a state requirement for starting the new class in the 1991–1992 fiscal year but deferred required city pension contributions for them ($20 million) until the 1993–1994 fiscal year. Kevin Sack, "Fiscal Footwork Is Fancy in Plan for Police Recruits," *New York Times,* 30 June 1992, B-3.

5. **Ducking the decision.** A balanced executive budget may omit some activities that political pressures would prevent the legislature from excluding. The executive may thus claim a balanced budget (or a smaller deficit), though the hard choices have not been made; appropriations actually made will likely produce a deficit, or proposals will be radically realigned before appropriation. An illustration: Texas requires that its Legislative Budget Board, the body responsible for preparing the budget document for appropriations, submit a balanced budget. In the fall of 1984, after substantial work had been done on the document for presentation to the 1985 session, the state comptroller substantially reduced the official estimate of oil and natural gas tax revenue (a major source of Texas state revenue). The revision occurred just before the board reviewed higher education requests, the last item on its schedule. Rather than alter recommendations for all state agencies, the board opted to balance the budget entirely through reductions in higher education and recommended a 26-percent appropriation decrease. Possibly the board intended to stimulate efficiency in higher education, but it is probably more likely that it was practicing phantom balance. In any case, the legislature made substantial readjustments; virtually all reductions were restored, and some institutions received increases.[22] Another example: The Bush administration omitted any funding to support the wars in Iraq and Afghanistan from its 2006 budget presentation, preferring to use supplemental appropriations (a request for $81.9 billion for those purposes was transmitted on February 14, 2005, just a few days after the budget was presented, and more are likely after the start of fiscal 2006).[23] And this was in a budget presented as one aimed at reducing the deficit.

An artificially balanced budget may even be passed, the legislature relying on supplemental appropriation in the next year to provide required funds. Such proceedings may go largely unnoticed by the media and the citizenry because emphasis traditionally focuses on the budget presentation and consideration, not on what actually happens during the budget year. In a similar fashion, the imbalance may be handled by shifting expenditures normally planned for the early part of the coming budget year into a supplemental request for the current budget year.

6. **Playing the intergovernmental system.** States regularly manage their budget problems by changing the fiscal relationship with their local governments. First, states can assign local governments responsibility for services that have previously been state financed. For instance, highway maintenance is usually a shared state-local responsibility, with certain roads being state and others local. By moving more of the statewide network to the local system, the state can reduce its expenditure requirement. Second, states can reduce the amount of aid they provide local governments. For example, state aid to school districts represents a considerable share of total state spending—about 15 percent of

[22]Lawrence Biemiller, "How the University of Texas, Flexing Its Political Muscle, Foiled Budget Cutters," *Chronicle of Higher Education* 30 (June 19, 1985): 12–15.

[23]David Stout, "Bush Proposes an Ambitious Budget Aimed at Cutting Deficit," *Washington Post* (February 7, 2005).

state expenditure in the United States is for local school-district aid, although there is much variation among the states. By reducing the amount distributed to schools, the state can reduce its budget problem. And third, states can delay appropriated aid payments to local governments, moving expenditure from one state fiscal year to another. When the dates of local fiscal years do not match those of the state year, the change may not even alter the total funds to the localities in their fiscal year, just the timing within their year. Suppose the state is on a July 1 fiscal year and its school districts are on January 1 fiscal year, a common situation in the United States. The state owes school districts twelve monthly aid payments during a year. Suppose that the June payment is made in July rather than June. This saves the state one payment during the first fiscal year, although it still pays the school districts the same amount through their calendar fiscal year. But all these strategies do have considerable potential for moving state fiscal problems to their localities. Indeed, states sometimes simply skip a payment to local governments, allowing the state to handle its fiscal problem while exporting the problem to its localities.

7. **Magic asterisk.** David Stockman, President Reagan's first OMB director, coined the phrase "magic asterisk" to mean budget savings to be identified later, or "whatever it took to get a balanced budget . . . after we totaled up all the individual budget cuts we'd actually approved."[24] Because so much media and public attention is focused on proposed deficits, the fact that the budget provides no clear funding plan gets overlooked. Many times, the asterisk will be linked to "administrative savings," which no one has the foggiest idea about how to achieve. The same kind of unspecified savings appear in many gubernatorial budgets, especially during the first year of office when there is little time between election and budget presentation. The new governor may have almost no idea about how to get some outcome promised in the campaign, but the public still remembers the promise. A magic asterisk permits the desired bottom line and gives the administration some time to figure out how to do it.

Because the last half of the 1990s was a period of good fiscal times for most states, there was little demand for these tricks by those governments. The same was generally true for the federal government. With the start of the twenty-first century, everyone is back to their old tricks with the recession of 2001, new program demands, tax reductions, and so on, threatening with embarrassing new deficits that need to be papered over.

Managing Budget Execution

The appropriations approved by the legislature, not the budget proposed by the executive, determine the amount of funds available for delivery of services during the budget year. This approved budget becomes the standard against which actual

[24]David A. Stockman, *The Triumph of Politics* (New York: Harper & Row, 1986), 124.

operations are controlled, and thus the critical managerial tool in execution, both guiding agency operations and ensuring that spending does not exceed appropriations. The approved budget establishes the control standard; other elements of the execution process measure actual performance against that standard and implement control systems to correct the variance. In practice, systems institute several budget controls:

1. **Preventive controls** are established to block actions that would violate standards. To prevent such violations, some governments establish extraordinary procedures for reviewing planned purchases with price tags that exceed a set limit; the limits tend to be lower when funds are tight. Even more governments apply special pre-audits to establish the appropriateness of payment before checks are written, often requiring approval by multiple independent authorities before spending occurs. (Some of these approvals may represent needless red tape.)

2. **Feed-forward controls** perform diagnostic or therapeutic actions in the spending process. Variance reports may automatically place stop orders on certain accounts when differences between actual expenditures and budgeted expenditures exceed certain levels.

3. **Feedback controls** start corrections into the budget cycle for the future. The comparison between budgeted expenditures and actual expenditures within the fiscal year is important information for those preparing, reviewing, and directing budgets for the next year.

Ordinarily, budgets are approved for an entire fiscal year, but execution of the budget occurs on a day-to-day, week-to-week basis. How can the annual budget establish a control standard for this execution? Well-functioning fiscal systems divide the total budget appropriation to operating units for the year into quarterly (or monthly) allotments by agreement with the central budget office. Suppose the department of streets and storm sewers has an appropriation of $4 million for the fiscal year from January 1 to December 31, and relatively constant expenditure rates are anticipated during the year. An allotment plan adopted by the department and the city budget office could then be as follows:

	Allotment to Quarter	Cumulative Allotments
January 1	$1,000,000	$1,000,000
April 1	1,000,000	2,000,000
July 1	1,000,000	3,000,000
October 1	1,000,000	4,000,000
Total	4,000,000	4,000,000

A comparison of actual expenditure at each quarter's end with the allotment provides an early warning for controlling department activity and preventing overspending or unnecessary underprovision of service. If reports of spending plus commitments to spend (encumbrances) through the end of June exceed $2 million, the activity may be accelerated. The comparison between expenditure plan and spending activity must include both payments made and contractual commitments made that will involve payment later. These latter totals have different titles in different fiscal systems (encumbrances and obligations are two), but regardless of title, they reduce the available spending authority and must be included in the comparison against the plan. Although the accounting system (correctly) would not regard the money as having been spent, the manager must recognize that the budget resource is gone as soon as the commitment occurs.

Service delivery, and hence spending profiles, for many agencies are not spread equally through the year. A typical outdoor swimming pool in the northern United States will be in service during the summer months only, so its operating expenditures concentrate in these months; equal quarterly allotments would not be useful for control and management. Activities that produce uneven expenditure flows during the year (seasonal needs, major capital equipment acquisitions, opening or closing new facilities, etc.) require uneven allotments. The allotment schedule must be consistent with both the approved budget and activity-flow expectations if it is to be useful for control and management.

Comparisons of the allotments and expenditures to date (variances) can suggest (1) areas in which expenditure may have to be curtailed, (2) areas in which surpluses may be available for use against deficits in other areas, (3) patterns that may be helpful in preparation of future budgets, and (4) the possible need to request a supplemental appropriation (funds beyond those initially appropriated for the fiscal year). Some faster-than-allotment spending may simply be accelerated acquisition (e.g., transfer between quarters to take advantage of low prices not anticipated when the budget was prepared). Other spending may imply spending above the approved appropriation. These latter overruns require spending-unit action to control the flow, generally according to budget office direction. Both agencies and finance officers can thus maintain better control of budget execution with these periodic allotment-to-expenditure comparisons. Although the objective of execution is delivery of services to the public, funds must not be spent in a fashion contrary to the appropriation.

Some government units find that there is no special seasonal pattern to their major expenditure categories. Those units may use simple budget-status reports, which compare the percentage of total budget used (spent and obligated) at a particular date with the percentage of the fiscal year expired. If the percentage of budget used exceeds the percentage of year expired, a problem may exist in that portion of the agency operations. Such a budget-status report for a transit agency appears as Figure 4–1. The managerial consequences of this report style are the same as for allotment-expenditure reports. There are dangers, however, in being lulled into inattention by percentages: a small percentage variance in a large budget line can be more disastrous than a large percentage variance in a small line. The analysis of variances should distinguish between those caused by price differences and those caused by different use of resources.

Governments establish special rules within which their agencies may move funds around in response to conditions not foreseen when appropriations were made. At the federal level, *reprogramming* is the use of funds within an appropriation

Figure 4–1
An Example of a Budget-Status Report
Ben Franklin Transit Expenditure Budget Reports as of June 30, 2005

					% Time Expended		50.00
Account Number	Account Name	Budget	Expended	Obligated	Expended and Obligated	Balance	%
	Transportation fund						
100	Operations and maintenance						
41	Operations						
11	Salaries and wages						
01	Salaries and wages—operators	800,000.00	454,671.21		454,671.21	345,328.79	46
02	Salaries and wages—others	109,000.00	46,223.94		46,223.94	62,776.06	42
12	Overtime—operators						
01	Overtime operators	27,000.00	27,690.72		27,690.72	690.722	103
13	Benefits	474,000.00	197,323.60		197,323.60	276,676.40	42
14	Uniforms	10,000.00	4,280.14		4,280.14	5,719.86	43
	Total personal services	1,600,000.00	730,109.61		730,109.61	869,890.39	46
21	Office supplies						
01	Office supplies	10,000.00	1,501.52	125.00	1,626.52	8,373.48	16
02	Copier supplies	2,000.00	547.50		547.50	1,452.50	27
22	Operating supplies						
01	Transfers	5,000.00	990.74	865.20	1,655.94	3,144.06	37
04	Other	2,600.00	2,329.10	29.01	2,358.11	241.86	91
	Total supplies	19,600.00	5,368.06	1,019.21	6,387.27	13,212.73	33
31	Professional services						
04	Other	3,600.00	88.52		88.52	3,511.48	2
05	Janitorial	3,600.00	1,195.73	400.00	1,595.73	2,004.27	44
32	Communication						
01	Radio system	2,000.00	2,850.44		2,850.44	850.442	143
02	Common carrier	300.00	55.93		55.93	244.07	19
04	Other	200.00	865.17		865.17	665.172	433
33	Transportation						
01	Living expenses	2,000.00	579.17		579.17	1,420.83	29
02	Common carrier	500.00	564.77		564.77	64.772	113
03	Personal vehicle mileage	500.00				500.00	
04	Other	500.00				500.00	
14	Advertising						
01	Printer	3,000.00				3,000.00	
35	Printing and binding						
04	Other	5,000.00	2,029.10		2,029.10	2,970.90	41
36	Utilities						
01	Franklin County Public Utility District, one quarter	2,000.00	417.66		417.66	1,582.34	21
01	Cascade Natural Gas, one quarter	2,000.00	600.53		608.53	1,391.47	30
03	Water, one quarter	200.00	144.40		144.40	55.60	72
04	Other, one quarter	200.00	60.58		60.58	139.42	30
05	Heating oil, four quarters	6,000.00	3,605.36		3,605.36	2,394.64	60

account for purposes other than those contemplated at the time of appropriation. Consultation between the agency and the appropriate substantive and appropriation committees of Congress usually precedes the action, which may involve formal notification and an opportunity for disapproval by the committees. *Transfers* move all or part of budget authority in an account to another account or subdivision of an account (e.g., moving funds from Operation and Maintenance to Personnel). Such changes require statutory authority, although some agencies have transfer authority within an established percentage or absolute limits.[25] State and local governments have similar, although often less formal, procedures. Often states establish interim committees to provide needed flexibility during periods of legislative recess, a vital adjustment feature where the legislature meets only periodically.

Internal Controls

Program managers are obviously concerned with delivery of services according to plan. Financial managers are simultaneously concerned with maintaining internal control, defined as the methods and procedures within the agency established to safeguard assets, check the accuracy and reliability of financial and other data, promote operational efficiency, and encourage adherence to the prescribed policies and procedures of the agency.[26] Internal controls represent the first line of defense against fraud.

Some basic steps in establishing internal control include the following:

1. **Provide qualified personnel, rotate duties, and enforce annual leaves/vacations.** This policy ensures capable handling of tasks, and ensures that irregularities can be found when new staff take over tasks on rotation or on temporary assignment. Personnel who are required to work beyond the limits of their capabilities are dangerous because they hold employment more tenuously and are thus more susceptible to requests for inappropriate actions.

2. **Segregate responsibility.** To divide related duties and operating responsibilities among two or more qualified people reduces the chance of error or fraud by providing a check-and-balance on work performed.

3. **Separate operations and accounting.** Divide the responsibilities for operational transactions (purchasing, receiving, collecting, etc.) from maintenance of accounting records to reduce chances for error or theft. Maintain separate reconciliation of transaction records.

4. **Assign responsibility.** This ensures that tasks are performed and that the appropriate party in questioned transactions can be identified.

---

[25]U.S. General Accounting Office, *Budget Reprogramming, Department of Defense Process for Reprogramming Funds,* GAO/NSIAD-86-164BR (Washington, D.C.: General Accounting Office, July 1986).

[26]Paul E. Heeschen and Lawrence B. Sawyer, *Internal Auditors Handbook* (Altamonte Springs, Fl.: Institute of Internal Auditors, 1984), 36.

5. **Maintain controlled proofs and security.** Maintain segregated bank accounts and closely control cash and negotiable documents. Issue sequentially numbered receipts for collections. Make orders only from numbered and controlled standard purchase orders. Make payments only according to standard separate authorizations, require bonding as needed. Require dual signatures on checks. Regularly review and test internal-control systems.

6. **Record transactions and safeguard assets.** Promptly record and accurately classify events and transactions. Limit access to source records and government assets to authorized individuals.

These steps can help implement the internal-control standards of the International Organization of Supreme Audit Institutions, of which the Government Accountability Office is a part: documentation, prompt and proper recording of transactions and events, authorization and execution of transactions and events, separation of duties, supervision, and access to and accountability for resources and records.[27] These control devices can reduce the chances of theft, error, and fraud. Although they offer no protection against poor public choices, they can help ensure that choices get executed as they have been made, for better or worse.

An Intra-Year Cash Budget

A cash budget is a detailed translation of the enacted budget into revenue and expenditure flows through the operating year. It yields a forecast of disbursements, receipts, cash balances, and needs for financing over the budget period, taken at regular points through the year. It is based on likely (or known and controllable) patterns.

1. The pay cycle for employees is known, as are the wage and salary commitments in the enacted budget. From that information, the payment amounts can be forecast through the year.
2. The pattern of payments to suppliers (contractors, utilities, etc.) is established, along with the budgeted amounts of those payments.
3. Large payments—payments of principal and interest of debt or purchases of large equipment—are in the adopted budget and are known in advance. Some large-ticket item purchases may even be controlled within the budget year, so that payment is made shortly after large revenue inflows, not shortly before, to ensure that sufficient cash is on hand without any need for short-term borrowing.
4. Tax and charge revenues are usually driven by regular seasonal patterns. Collections are high in some months and low in others because of the fluctuations of economic activity within the year (high season and low season for some industries, due dates for quarterly payments, etc.). For instance, analysis of data from several recent years might show that sales tax payments received in January are typically 8.5 percent of the annual total. With

[27]Internal Control Standards Committee, International Organization of Supreme Audit Institutions, *Guidelines for Internal Control Standards* (June 1992), 9.

these patterns known, the revenue forecast for the budget year can easily be translated into its likely monthly flow.

The cash budget is helpful to execution of the annual budget because it shows when the government might not have sufficient funds to cover the bills coming due at particular points during the year. That warns when the government might need to arrange a very short-term loan from local banks to tide it over the cash shortage and may allow the government to adjust some flows in or out to avoid the need for such a loan. Preparing such an estimated cash budget is a helpful practice for government fiscal officers. Furthermore, careful estimation of the payment outflows can be helpful in establishing allotment patterns for dividing the annual appropriation for individual agencies.

Audit and Evaluation

When the budget year is over, there are several questions that should be asked. One basic question is whether the budget was executed as it was passed. The adopted budget should reflect priorities for government expenditures and the intentions for funding that spending. If the budget was responsibly developed and became, by legislative action, the legal fiscal plan, then it should be executed intact, subject to emergency changes beyond accommodation within the enacted budget. A first key check is to establish that the executed budget and the adopted budget do coincide. Do the plans reflected in the budget match actual expenditure patterns at the close of the year? And if they do not, have appropriate procedures been followed during execution to make the changes? In other words, the budget law must be followed if the budget process is to be meaningful.

Other questions are asked through the external audit process. Many audits are conducted using a prescribed checklist of steps to establish uniformity in how several different auditors perform a class of audits. Much of the audit focuses on controls built into the systems of the agency. If the internal control/internal audit system operates satisfactorily, the external audit agency need not be concerned with tracing the body of individual transactions because the system produces substantial compliance. The audit does, however, test that system. Accounting controls prevent fraud and waste, ensure the accuracy of operations, ensure compliance with applicable laws, and promote adherence to stated policies (including legislation). The audit determines whether those control systems work. In their audit, examiners look for errors and abuses such as those listed in Table 4–2. Much of the audit employs statistical sampling to permit probabilistic inferences about the extent of error in the total record population. There is seldom reason to scrutinize all records.

Regardless of their relative importance, thefts from the government receive extensive publicity when discovered. Thus, it is worthwhile to review some of the methods that have historically been used to steal from government.

Table 4–2
Some Errors or Abuses Sought by Auditors

Year-end accounting manipulations that push revenues and expenditures from one year to the next
Unrecorded liabilities: commitments to vendors that are suppressed by withholding written agreements and purchase orders from the paperwork system
Overestimation of revenues, to keep down tax rates
Failure to reserve adequately for nonpayment of taxes
Miscalculation of utility, hospital, and other service bills
Unauthorized transfer of funds between appropriation accounts
Recording of grant receipts in the wrong funds
Use of a commingled cash account to disguise use of restricted funds for unauthorized purposes
Failure to observe legal requirements for review and approval of budgets
Failure to compile and submit financial reports to state and federal agencies punctually
Improper computation of state aid claims

SOURCE: Peter F. Rousmaniere, *Local Government Auditing—A Manual For Public Officials* (New York: Council on Municipal Performance, 1980), 10.

Ghosting. Theft through phantom resources—receiving payment for resources not actually delivered—can take several forms. One method, the ghost employee, involves placing on an agency payroll an individual who does not work for that agency. The person receives pay but provides no service. A second method is payment for supplies or services that are not actually delivered. Invoices sent by the firm show delivery, but the agency never receives the supplies or services. A third method is double payment for supplies or services. The services are performed once, but invoices show delivery of two shipments. Each method causes government to pay for resources not delivered, and each artificially increases the cost of public service.

Bid rigging. The procurement fix involves rigging bids on supply contracts. Suppose a section of highway is to be repaved. Potential suppliers would establish beforehand the bid winner and the winning price; other firms would submit noncompetitive bids. Firms would cooperate in the collusion because their turn to win would come on another project. The collusion increases the profits of the firms and increases the cost of government. Government employees may or may not profit from the procurement fix, depending on the arrangements of the scheme.

Honest graft. "Honest" graft uses advance information to produce private profit for the individual employee. The reminiscences of George Washington

Plunkitt, Tammany Hall leader of early twentieth-century New York City, describe the process:

> There's an honest graft, and I'm an example of how it works. I might sum up the whole thing by sayin': I seen my opportunities and I took 'em.
>
> Just let me explain by example. My party's in power in the city, and it's goin' to undertake a lot of public improvements. Well I'm tipped off, say, that they're going to lay out a new park at a certain place.
>
> I see my opportunity and I take it. I go to that place and I buy up all the land I can in the neighborhood. Then the board of this or that makes its plan public, and there is a rush to get my land, which nobody cared particular for before.
>
> Ain't it perfectly honest to charge a good price and make a profit on my investment and foresight?[28]

That profit measures the extent to which the honest grafter, through use of inside information, steals from the public by forcing excess payments for a resource. Honest graft may similarly involve acquisition or establishment of companies to do business with a government. Bid specifications may be written so that company would be the only one qualified. Requirements for the commodity or service would be artificially increased for the enrichment of the government employee.

Diversion. Public assets or the service of employees may be stolen for private use. Office supplies, equipment, gasoline, and so on are as usable for private purposes as for government activities. Public employees may be diverted to private uses, including construction or maintenance projects on property owned by government officials. Employees are sometimes used as workers in political campaigns while on government time—a special illegal advantage of incumbency. These activities involve straightforward stealing because individuals use assets owned by the government without payment. But there are other approaches: poor controls over the use of government credit cards can provide modern thieves a highly effective tool for diverting public assets far beyond the dreams of corrupt public employees of earlier years.

Shoddy material. Because low-quality supplies and materials can generally be delivered at lower cost than can higher-quality supplies and materials, government contract specifications require delivery of quality material. A contractor who provides lower than specified quality (shoddy material) can thus profit at public expense.

Kickbacks. Public officials who have power to select who receives contracts to do business with governments, what banks receive public deposits, and who works for government agencies may profit by arranging for artificially high contract awards or artificial wage payments with a portion of that payment kicked back to the government official. The favored individual or firm receives higher than the appropriate price for the contracted service, and thus is able to profit even after

---

[28]William L. Riordon, *Plunkitt of Tammany Hall* (New York: E.P. Dutton, 1963), 3.

making the payment to the contracting agent. Also, legislators have opportunities to shape appropriation bills to include the goods or services sold by a particular vendor. Sometimes the payment goes to the public official or a relative, or the business purchases something from the official or the legislator at an inflated and highly profitable price. Sometimes the payment is in the form of giving a job to a relative of the official or the legislator. Sometimes the payment assists the finances of the election campaign of that official or of that official's political party; in the language of the politics of the 2000s, the former is "hard money" and the latter is "soft money." Unfortunately, kickbacks and special deals seem to have become an important influence in American politics and policy making.

Conclusion

Budget skills combine techniques that can be taught with a cunning that comes only with experience. The start for all budgets must be a sound understanding of what the agency request intends to accomplish. Without that foundation, no amount of tricks can help much. As in many government operations, the great problem is information—those who have that information and are able to communicate it have greater-than-average success. Beyond that, there are few general truths.

Questions and Exercises

1. The data in the following table present expenditures by object category for the School of Public Affairs at Enormous State University. As with most elite programs at state universities, the school has accepted missions of teaching, research, and service to the university, state, and nation. The operations reported here, however, include only the general fund (tuition and state support); they do not encompass activities financed by private or government contracts or grants.

   Analyze these data as if you were initiating work for the 1993–1994 budget request. You have been warned that total resources may decline by 8 percent.

Category	1988–1989	1989–1990	1990–1991	1991–1992	Estimated Fiscal Year 1992–1993
Academic salaries (full-time faculty)	$1,900,000	$1,981,105	$2,062,114	$2,190,971	$2,683,484
Part-time instructors	$307,462	$273,991	$441,704	$181,518	$173,366
Student academic/ fellowships	$266,117	$248,422	$324,121	$602,463	$669,886

Professional salaries	$325,587	$315,889	$356,074	$494,062	$448,589
Clerical studies	$413,674	$445,983	$470,417	$522,382	$555,350
Wages (part-time workers)	$27,219	$19,744	$24,406	$33,473	$43,299
Group insurance (health)	$174,210	$189,110	$173,143	$225,403	$312,875
Retirement	$619,326	$653,963	$723,261	$791,787	$917,874
Subtotal	$4,033,595	$4,128,207	$4,575,240	$5,042,059	$5,804,723
General supplies and expense	$402,839	$425,141	$460,098	$549,090	$719,504
Travel	$82,718	$97,064	$96,462	$120,600	$134,162
Equipment	$92,112	$32,904	$74,616	$197,844	$367,512
Transfers out				$43,100	$15,000
Subtotal	$577,669	$555,109	$631,176	$910,634	$1,236,178
Total	$4,611,264	$4,683,316	$5,206,416	$5,962,693	$7,040,901

2. The Department of Revenue wants to add more people to the unit that attempts to collect unpaid taxes through telephone contact. What questions would you, as a budget analyst, have after you receive the following request-justification memorandum?

Date: June 19, 200X
Subject: Collection Telephone Pursuit

Currently there are 19 employees working on telephone pursuits on a full-time basis. Each employee can make an average of 25 to 40 phone calls per day. The amount collected by the 19 employees for the past year is $17,858,623. If we could add an automated phone system and increase our staff by 10 full-time employees, we could double the number of phone calls made and increase our collections by 59 percent, or $8,900,000.

3. The following personnel information about the Marshal Fire Department for fiscal year that begins January 1, 200X, is to be used.

Employee Grade	Number in Grade	Salary
Chief	1	$105,000
Shift commander	3	70,000
Firefighter 1	12	39,000
Firefighter 2	26	30,000
Clerical (part-time)	3	15,000

The city is part of the federal Social Security system. For 200X, the city and the employee each pay Social Security payroll taxes of 6.2 percent of all salary paid up to $90,000 per employee to finance federal retirement and disability insurance and 1.45 percent of all salary paid to finance Medicare. The city pays a portion of the cost of health insurance for each full-time employee, an amount equal to $180 per month. Employees on the payroll after June 30, 200X, regardless of hiring date, are part of a new pension system financed by a city payment of 20 percent of the employee's salary and employee payment of

5 percent of the employee's salary on pay received after that date. Payments up to that date were made by state appropriations from state tobacco tax revenue. Full-time employees receive an allowance for uniforms of $750 per year.

Estimate the city's full cost of fire department labor during the 200X fiscal year, assuming no change in staffing. Separate that cost into salary and fringe-benefit components.

4. Write budget requests and justifications for each of the following program conditions. Start your request by categorizing each request as (1) new service, (2) other continuing, (3) workload change, (4) change in service level, (5) price change, (6) full financing, or (7) methods improvement. The program conditions are as follows:

a. The agency sends about 275,000 pieces of mail each year. The postal rate has increased by 5 cents per ounce.

b. The division travel appropriation has been $15,000 per year short of actual expenditure for the last 3 years, after internal transfers of funds.

c. Fifteen account examiners process 115,000 assistance files per year. Client growth estimates indicate that, in the next budget biennium, files will increase to 125,000 in the first year and 130,000 in the second year. (Account examiners' salaries are $3,775 per month plus fringe benefits of 25 percent.)

d. The city council appropriated $18,000 for a program to track down those not paying traffic fines. The program began in the second quarter of the fiscal year and has produced fine revenue far greater than its cost. The legal affairs division wants to continue the program throughout the entire new fiscal year.

e. The division wants to replace the computer workstations for five administrative assistants. Each workstation includes a personal computer, laser printer, and standard office workstation software.

5. The local water utility has maintained records over several years of its monthly purchases of raw water from the state water authority. The monthly averages are shown in the following table.

Assume that the city pays a flat rate per thousand gallons of water purchased and that the fiscal year begins on July 1. Payment is made in the month after use. Prepare quarterly allotments for $8 million appropriated for water purchase.

Gallons (000s)		Gallons (000s)	
January	35,000	July	125,000
February	35,000	August	125,000
March	50,000	September	90,000
April	65,000	October	60,000
May	68,000	November	50,000
June	100,000	December	40,000

6. A progress report for the division of tourism promotion prepared for transactions through March 31 of the fiscal year that runs from July 1 to June 30 shows that the travel account, with a total appropriation of $9,000, has expenditures to that date of $2,500 and encumbrances of $3,500. Because of an important trade fair in May, the allotment distribution for the division had 40 percent of the division budget planned for expenditure in the last quarter of the fiscal year. What is the status of the division's travel account? What managerial actions are appropriate?

7. Analyze this budget justification:

Workload Change—19X5–19X7 Biennial Cost: $84,300

Because of the recognition of new social procedures, our psychometricians are now able to obtain valid test results and scores, enabling our valuators to make sociological recommendations that are realistic and not stereotyped views of battering. Our evaluation professionals, plus specialty counselors with special training, in conjunction with their statewide supervisors, have made great strides in bringing together battered spouses throughout the state. To achieve maximum effectiveness, an additional four counselor teams to be strategically located are essential. This success factor that we have experienced has also brought about an increase in the referral of abused children, which will also require additional case service funds.

a. List the questions you would raise about the justification if you were a budget analyst.
b. Rewrite the justification.

8. A 9-1-1 emergency telephone line provides a single telephone number to be called when help is needed. An operator receives the call and directs police and/or firefighter assistance as needed. The address of the call is displayed on a computer screen, along with other information appropriate to guiding a response. Calls are also recorded, providing full information about the nature of the conversation. In a major metropolitan county, the cost is around $3.6 million per year, after an installation cost of $4.5 million. The system would be financed by a tax of 1.5 percent of the monthly line charge paid to the local telephone company.

Prepare a narrative justification for initiation of such a system.

9. The Public Budgeting and Finance Association is planning its annual conference. The conference hotel has quoted the following prices for services:

Thursday afternoon	Conference facilities rental: $425
	Coffee-break service: $10 per person
	Audiovisual equipment rental: $55
	Evening reception: $25 per person
Friday	Conference facilities rental: $750
	Coffee-break service, morning and afternoon: $15 per person
	Continental breakfast: $15 per person
	Luncheon: $20 per person
	Audiovisual equipment rental: $150

Saturday morning	Conference facilities rental: $375 Continental breakfast: $15 per person Coffee-break service: 10 per person Audiovisual rental: $75

Program materials and marketing would cost about $550. The association charged $130 for each participant last year and would like to use the same price this year.

a. Prepare a break-even chart for the conference and determine the break-even attendance level.
b. Suppose the association wanted to encourage student participation by charging a rate that would cover only the costs directly caused by their attendance. What price would you charge?
c. Prepare a line-item budget for the event if you expect 110 people to attend.

10. Suppose you work for the city budget office. The chief budget officer for the city reports to the staff that revenues are 7.3 percent below the forecast level of $6.8 million for the first 5 months of the budget year. She asks for ideas on what, if anything, should be done to deal with the problem. The city is legally forbidden to borrow to cover operating deficits.

11. The manager of a municipal ice rink is concerned that the flow of patrons will not be sufficient to maintain the long-standing policy of keeping the rink on a self-supporting basis. Revenues come mainly from the hourly rental of ice time (the city has set that at $2.50 per hour per person) and skate rental ($1.50 per pair). The average ice time per patron over the last 3 years has been about 1.5 hours. Approximately half the patrons rent skates. Salaries, scheduled maintenance, and other overhead expenditures amount to $94,500 per year; these costs do not vary with the number of patrons. Costs that vary with the number of patrons (direct maintenance and supplies) are estimated to be $1.80 per patron hour. The number of patrons has been averaging 85,000 per year for the last 3 years. Is the manager right to be concerned?

12. Grantsville is a medium-sized midwestern town, not quite rural, not quite urban, and not quite a willing participant in the twenty-first century. As the new clerk-treasurer, you are eager to bring new aggressiveness to the city administration, so long as none of the "Old Guard" gets mad. You suspect that a non-irritating first step would be the development of a cash plan and short-term investment strategy for the city. You further believe that an appropriate start would be with the four largest funds in the city financial structure: general, parks and recreation, motor vehicle, and cumulative capital. The following data emerge from your search.

Fund Balances for January 1

General fund	$620, 860
Parks and recreation	$ 62,968
Motor vehicle	$102,015
Cumulative capital	$639,611
Revenue Estimates	

Property tax. Collections are received by the city on May 1 and November 1. Because of a discount for early payment, five-eighths of the collections come in the first installment. Delinquency has historically been about 2 percent of the levy.

Levy:

General fund	$2,985,200
Parks and recreation	$ 718,300
Cumulative capital	$ 385,400

Parking meters (general fund). Revenues run about $6 per month, except in September and October (football season), when they run about 5 percent higher, December, when they are about 10 percent higher, and July, when they are about 15 percent lower.

Building permits, inspection fees (general fund). Estimated at $130,000 for the year. The engineer's office transmits collections to you at the end of each quarter. You estimate the seasonal collections as QI, 85.0; QII, 105.0; QIII, 125; QIV, 85.0.

Traffic fines (half to general fund, half to motor vehicle). Estimated at $6,500 per month. The court remits at the end of each month.

Swimming pool admissions (parks and recreation). Estimates are based on prior years.

May	$ 800.00
June	$ 950.00
July	$ 1,750.00
August	$ 2,500.00
September	$ 750.00

Community auditorium rental (parks and recreation). Estimates are based on prior year.

July 4 Freedom Celebration	$ 800.00
Labor Day Customs Show	$1,500.00
Casual rentals (square dances, Rotary, etc.)	$ 150.00/month

State shared tax (motor vehicles). The state department of revenue provides data.

March 31	$114,000
June 30	$125,000
September 30	$115,000
December 31	$113,000

Expenditures, as Appropriated by City Council

Payrolls: Paydays are every other week. The first payday is January 7.

General fund	$95,000 biweekly
Parks and recreation	$15,000

Also, temporary summer lifeguards, playground supervisors, etc., from

May 15 to September 10	$20,000 biweekly
Motor vehicle fund	$10,200 biweekly

Other regular expenditures. Checks to suppliers and other nonemployees are issued only on alternate Thursdays. The first such date is January 13.

General fund	$25,000/disbursement
Parks and recreation	$ 4,000/disbursement

Additional summer payments

(May 10–September 15)	$ 3,000/disbursement
Motor vehicle	$ 7,000/disbursement

Cumulative capital

Bond service due May 15 ($150,000) and November 15 ($125,000)

Special expenditures

General fund: two police cars at $14,500 to be paid for October 1

Motor vehicle fund: Dump truck with sand-salt distributor and snowplow at $34,000 to be paid for October 1

From these data, prepare a complete cash budget for the year and include end-of-year balances. Estimate what amounts are available for investment and what fund shortages will occur. Identify any management strategies to prevent the fund shortages, if possible.

13. Governments and not-for-profit organizations need systems for providing fiscal discipline and control, for directing resources to uses with highest priority of the entity, and for encouraging technical efficiency in use of resources. However, not all such organizations have the same degree of development of these systems of budget and finance, and those with systems do not have them structured in the same way. Select a local government or not-for-profit organization in your area and analyze the budget and finance processes that it employs. This entity may be a local government (a city, a county, a township, a school district, a solid waste district, a library district, etc.) or a not-for-profit organization located in this area. The entity should be chosen because of your interest in the service provided by that entity, and because the entity will cooperate with your review and assessment.

a. Investigate the budget, revenue, and financial management processes and practices of that entity. The topics that should be investigated include, but are not limited to, the following: (a) *budget process*—how the budget developed is, what the cycle is, how decisions are made in developing the budget, what the review procedure is, who adopts the budget, how the process was established, what the style/nomenclature of the budget is, whether processes are transparent, whether there is a separate capital budget and budget process, whether there are extrabudgetary funds or earmarked revenues, whether appropriate internal controls are in place, what the external audit arrangement is, etc.; and (b) *budget analysis*—explore expenditure patterns and trends to the extent possible, analyze inputs and performance results, examine the extent to which the entity operates with fiscal discipline and control.

b. On the basis of your investigation, what do you conclude about the fiscal situation, processes, and procedures of the entity? Be specific. Link your conclusions to the information developed in your analysis. Outline and defend your proposals for reform or restructuring of the entity you have examined.

As you prepare for your review, you may find these references useful: Government Finance Officers Association, *Recommended Budget Practices of the National Advisory Council on State and Local Budgeting* (www.gfoa.org/services/rp/budget/budget-recommended-nacslb.pdf); World Bank, *Public Expenditure Management Handbook* (www1.worldbank.org/publicsector/pem98.pdf); and International Monetary Fund, *Manual on Fiscal Transparency* (www.imf.org/external/np/fad/trans/manual/index.htm).

For the entity you select, you will need to talk with the administrators responsible for the entity's finances, to analyze budget preparation materials, budgets, and annual financial reports, and to examine laws or other documents establishing and governing the entity's framework. You may locate other source materials on some entities (debt rating reports, newspaper stories, etc.).

CASES FOR DISCUSSION

CASE 4–1

Green Felt-Tip Pens, a Tape Recorder, and Embezzlement: Where Did the Budget Process Fail?

The New Hope/Solebury School District serves students in part of Bucks County, Pennsylvania. The county, just north of Philadelphia, has been a peaceful refuge since its colonial beginnings as a stopover on the road between New York and Philadelphia. But modern telemarketing reaches even the quietest parts of the county and can expose even the most straightforward budget-execution tasks to million-dollar fraud.

Consider These Questions

1. What standards of internal control were violated here?

SOURCES: References for this case include Thomas Moore, "A New Scam: Tele-blackmail," *U.S. News & World Report* 108 (June 11, 1990): 51; "An Alert Reader Lends a Hand to the FBI," *U.S. News & World Report* 108 (June 25, 1990): 8; and Joseph A. Slobodzian, "Telemarketer Sentenced in New Hope Scam," *Philadelphia Inquirer* 31 January 1991: B-1.

2. How would you revise financial practices in the district to prevent similar fraud in the future?

3. Compare the roles of internal control and post-audit in the war against waste, fraud, and abuse.

The scam involved the business manager of the district, Kathryn Hock, and American Corporate Supplies, an office-supplies distributor operated as a telemarketer by Marc and Teresa Suckman. The district serves about 825 students, with an annual budget of $6.6 million. Hock, business manager since 1978, had worked her way up from school secretary. Some school board members had questioned her ability to deal with more sophisticated accounting systems and methods and had expressed doubt about her qualifications. She had managed to keep her job, although uneasily. The firm, located in California, made phone calls to prospective purchasers (public, private, nonprofit, it mattered not) around the country offering products at discount. Often the discounts were from artificially inflated prices. Their business was to induce customers to purchase felt-tip pens from them; the scam was that the pens often had not been ordered at all or if ordered were never delivered. Their business was good: along with the school district, victims included an Idaho priest ($66,000), a St. Louis businessman ($40,000), and a Pennsylvania man ($155,000). But the $2 million from the school district apparently was their best.

Hock received a long-distance call from American Corporate Supplies in 1983, offering green felt-tipped pens. Because district teachers had requested the color, she placed an order. The shipment arrived as promised, and she paid the bill.

Through the year, the business manager made more pen orders. Eventually, her contact, William Chester of American Corporate (possibly Suckman), informed her that her good-customer status entitled her to receive a pocket tape recorder, a gift that she accepted. That put Hock in jeopardy, although she did not realize it.

received a gift

After a few weeks, Chester called in regard to filling her back order. There actually was none, but he convinced her that such an order did exist and that she had legal obligation to complete the order. Mr. Chester then proceeded to call one or two times each month to obtain a new order from her.

By April 1984, the district definitely needed no more markers. They had arrived in regular batches, and there was room for little else in the storage closet. Hock tried to stop the flow, but Chester told her that the district had an outstanding balance of $3,547.14 and that she should send a check to close the account. The claim was excessive, Hock objected, but Chester threatened to tell the school board about the gift she had accepted for placing the orders. That would cause her to be fired, so she settled the account and stopped the orders.

Or so she thought. A month later, Chester called again, this time with an outstanding balance of $4,229.53. She again objected, but Chester threatened to inform both the school board and the police, now about the unauthorized payment for goods not received. The stakes for her were higher.

Hock felt in even greater jeopardy and, because of this vulnerability, was going to be called on to provide even greater sums of money. *U.S. News & World Report* describes her response:

Hock knew then she was in deep water. "I was panic-stricken," she says. "I had never come up against anything like this and didn't know how to handle it." She paid that bill, and then another the following month, and dozens more, sometimes three in a month. "Each time he said it would be the final order, but it never was," she says. When the amounts Chester demanded escalated as high as $30,000, she started breaking up the payments with several different checks so they would be easier to hide in the books. She had authority to sign checks and stamp them with the signatures of two board officials. When the canceled checks came back from the bank, she would white out American Corporate Supplies and type in the name of the local fuel oil company and other regular suppliers, inflating their costs. Then she would alter the computerized accounts accordingly.*

This process continued until 1988, when the accumulated overspending had grown so large that Hock could no longer conceal it. She quit in June, just as the district superintendent who had supported her against the skeptical board retired. The new superintendent and business manager soon found discrepancies and performed a special audit. The FBI and the U.S. Attorney received the results, and Hock confessed.

In July 1989, Hock pled guilty to embezzling $2,043,903 from the district; evidence indicated that she kept none of the money but sent it all to Suckman. She was sentenced to 16 months in prison and ordered to pay back the money she had stolen. She cooperated in further investigations to help find the Suckmans. The district had to borrow $1 million to replace the missing funds.

In April 1990, a federal grand jury indicted the Suckmans on thirty-eight counts of transporting stolen securities obtained by fraud, twenty counts of engaging in monetary transactions in criminally derived property, and on single counts of conspiracy to commit interstate transportation of stolen money and securities. Marc Suckman was also indicted on three counts of blackmail. The Suckmans were arrested in Costa Rica, and transported to Philadelphia for trial. They pled guilty shortly before jury selection; Marc Suckman faced up to 6 years in prison and Teresa Suckman up to 4 years and 3 months. They agreed to help in further investigations of telemarketing scams. U.S. District Court Judge James McGirr Kelly ordered restitution (the Suckmans claimed all proceeds had been "dissipated" by high living) and forbade them from working in telemarketing again.

CASE 4–2

Balancing the Chicago Public School Budget

The first day of class in the 411,000-student, 25,700-teacher Chicago Public School system was a week late in 1993, and classes began only under U.S. District Court Judge Charles P. Kocoras's restraining order. The order was necessary because Illinois law requires that school systems have a balanced budget to operate, and the

*Thomas Moore, "A New Scam: Tele-blackmail," *U.S. News & World Report* 108 (June 11, 1990): 51.

Chicago system had a $299 million deficit in its $2.8 billion budget. Judge Kocoras waived the requirement for 10 days, thus allowing the schools to open while the school board and the teachers union negotiated a new contract, and while the state legislature worked to arrange some package of assistance. The board had convinced the judge that if schools were kept closed, it could not fulfill its desegregation obligations.

Consider These Questions

1. What do you think of the proposal outlined here?
2. How are the various interests (schoolchildren, city residents, teachers, the state, etc.) affected by the proposal?
3. What is your reaction to the balanced-budget requirement?
4. What other options might the school system have had?

One of the proposals (supported by Chicago Mayor Richard Daley) to manage the problem for the next 2 years contained the following elements:

Establish concessions from teachers: $75 million annually.

Borrow for the next 2 years: $300 million (total).

Divert contributions to teachers' pension fund: $55 million each year.

Those measures would bring $280 million in deficit reduction each year, close enough to closing the deficit to make everyone happy.

Here are some additional notes about the situation:

Because of early retirements during the summer of 1993, no regular teachers had been laid off, and the school board promised that layoffs would not be used to close the gap.

The Public School Teachers' Pension and Retirement Fund of Chicago was about 82 percent of fully funded, that is, contained sufficient funds that those funds plus interest on them would cover all existing pension obligations. The fund recently increased its annual return assumption to 8 percent.

The state legislature requires annual contributions to the $5 billion pension fund, but the requirement had been suspended before, amounting to about $200 million over the past three years.

The teachers' pension program is a defined benefit program; pensions are paid regardless of amounts in the pension funds.

SOURCES: Complied from Paul G. Barr, "Fund Assets Crucial for School Settlement," *Pensions and Investments* 21 (September 20, 1993); and Jacquelyn Heard, "U.S. Judge May Be Last Hope of Keeping City Schools Open," *Chicago Tribune,* 23 September 1993.

APPENDIX 4–1

Budget Preparation, or How to Be a Budget Analyst

A new budget analyst may well be overwhelmed by the scope and complexity of the task at hand. Nothing can completely prepare one for that first attempt, but most bright, inquisitive, energetic people survive. Here is a memo outlining methods and procedures for analysts in Oregon. Save for references to the particular budget system used there, it could have been written for guidance in any government, and the advice is as fitting today as it was when it was written.

State of Oregon — Interoffice Memo

To: Budget Analysts — Date: June 30, 1982

From: Jon Yunker, Administrator
Budget and Management Division

Subject: Budget Preparation—or—How to Be a Budget Analyst

The Role of the Analyst

Budget analysts are key persons in the development of the governor's biennial budget. While others are responsible for development of the broad program and fiscal policies for the state as a whole, it is the individual analysts who must convert these broad policies to balanced, properly financed programs for assigned agencies. In this regard, several points should be emphasized.

1. You must function as an equal with agency heads or other top agency administrative staff. You are expected to have the maturity necessary to avoid being intimidated by imposing titles, higher-salaried officials, or executives your senior in age. You have a professional assignment and must carry it out with the confidence of a professional.

2. You work primarily for your budget supervisor and the budget and management administrator. Direct relationships with the director, other administrators and staff within the executive department, and governor's assistants are frequently necessary and desirable. However, you should inform the budget and management administrator, in writing, in cases where these contacts will significantly influence your recommendations. All reports submitted to other individuals should be routed through your budget supervisor and the budget and management administrator to ensure that they are fully informed about activities of the division. They are responsible for your actions; make sure you are responsible to them.

3. You must be flexible. Don't busy yourself in work related only to your assigned agencies. State government is too dynamic and interrelated and the central staff too small to allow the luxury of specialists within the division. The analyst must be reasonably conversant with the governor's total program and should be constantly aware of the role a particular assignment plays within it.

During the executive budget preparation season, you will be in an essentially negative posture as far as an agency is concerned. During the legislative session, however, you will be intimately allied with the agency in "selling" approved budget recommendations to the legislature. In some cases, you may be expected to effectively support a program that you originally recommended against.

Responsibilities Prior to Budget Season

The work performed during the budget season represents the culmination of many months of preparation and field work. Prior to receipt of the agencies' request documents, the analyst should be concerned with the following:

1. Budget field work. This phrase simply describes the process whereby an analyst develops a sufficient knowledge of assigned agencies' programs to enable him or her to make informed budget decisions when the time comes. Budget field work may be accomplished in a variety of ways:
   a. Review of items submitted for consideration by the state emergency board.
   b. Execution of special management of fiscal studies affecting your assigned agencies.
   c. Completion of a formal field work program during which you personally visit individual agency activities and discuss them with the person directly responsible for their administration.
   d. Preview of agency budget requests for format and content.

2. Development of the Biennial Budget Preparation Manual. This activity enables the analyst to foresee special problems in format or budget organization which some of his assigned agencies might encounter in meeting executive department requirements. Your knowledge of your assigned agencies enables you to assist in developing budget preparation instructions to be followed by all state agencies. Each analyst must completely understand all instructions included in the manual and supporting documents.

3. An analyst frequently assists agencies in the preparation of their biennial budget requests. It is imperative that the analyst express no opinion about the content or amount, or the ranking of decision packages, to be included in the request. Your role is that of technical advisor on format and compliance with specific budget instructions. You have neither the authority nor the responsibility to advise the agency on what should be requested; you will only assist in ensuring that it is properly presented.

4. As budget season approaches, the analyst should become familiar with the internal procedures to be used by the budget and management division during the biennial budget preparation process. You must learn and understand all significant internal procedures performed by the technical staff to enable you to "track" the budget request and related documents through the entire budget season.

5. Based on your field work and knowledge of the internal procedures, specific deadlines for review of each of your assigned agencies should be established. You cannot spend a disproportionate amount of time on one agency and hope to do an adequate job on the entire assignment. You must assess your assignment and plan your own individual work schedule for that assignment. Keep in mind that time must be spent where the money is—minor, stable, low-cost agencies may be fascinating, but should not take time away from those agencies competing for scarce resources.

When the Budget Request Is Submitted

Don't panic! DON'T PANIC! DON'T PANIC!!!

There will be a few surprises, but generally the request will reflect the same programs you saw during your budget field work. It will look bigger and more complicated than you expected, but bear in mind that it represents all activities of that agency for a two-year period. Several steps are critical at the time of initial receipt of the budget request.

1. Make sure that the budget is given immediately to the coordinating secretary so that internal processing is properly performed. Know where it is at all times.

2. Read the entire budget request. Skim the summary reports and other detailed forms. Read all narrative for content. Study the performance measurement forms. Review previous biennia's performance claims and compare them with what was actually accomplished during that biennium. Finish the job. You will have plenty of opportunities to go back and review various sections, so plow right through the entire request before taking any steps toward detailed analysis.

3. After reading the request, skim the status related to the agency. This will provide you a context in which to assess the programs the agency is proposing to fulfill its legal responsibilities.

4. The analyst should carefully review the objectives and levels of accomplishment upon which the agency has predicated its budget request to make certain they correspond with the agency's statutory responsibilities and executive priorities. These objectives and levels of accomplishment may be modified or augmented by the analysts in the governor's budget to more accurately reflect the executive department recommendations regarding the agency's mission.

5. Identify the major policy issues in the request. A policy issue is a proposed new program or revision in an existing program (either expansion or retrenchment), which represents a significant change in the agency's scope or level of activity.

   The budget analyst must determine which decision packages are major policy issues and if any significant changes are contained in the base budget.

In addition, you must determine if the numerical ranking of decision packages represents a major policy shift.

You should summarize these policy issues (including costs by fund source), develop alternatives, and prepare your recommended course of action. This report, or policy memo, should be submitted through your budget supervisor to the budget and management administrator. This memo will be further distributed to other appropriate members of the executive department.

6. You may also prepare a memo to the budget and management administrator outlining the need for an analysis of a particular portion of a budget request which you will not have time to perform yourself during budget season. In some cases, these analyses can be performed by the management section or by other divisions of the department in time to be considered by you in developing budget recommendations. Their special expertise in the areas of data processing, management analysis, local government relations, personnel administration, or economic analysis can be most helpful to you in arriving at your final recommendations. Bear in mind that they are advising you; the budget recommendations are yours.

   In other cases, the needed analysis will be beyond the capability of the executive department staff to perform during the executive budget season. In these cases, the proposed analysis will be considered as an "item for future study" and held until staff time becomes available. A special form for these memos will be available on which the budget analyst will be expected to enter his or her recommendations as to whether the study should be performed during budget season or deferred as an "item for future study."

7. Review the request for any proposed programs and interagency transfers of funds which affect other state agencies. These proposals should be described and submitted, in writing, to the analyst assigned to the affected agency or agencies. The governor's budget must be internally consistent among agencies.

8. Develop a list of questions about the request you want the agency personnel to answer. . . . You will have many unanswered questions in your mind at this stage (since you are an insatiably curious person), and the easiest way to get answers is to reduce the questions to writing and submit them to the agency. Don't be afraid to ask agency personnel to work for you in this way. You have to do the analysis, but agency personnel can produce needed data for you.

Detailed Analysis

Only after you have read the document and identified the items listed above are you ready to review the request in detail. Once again, don't spend too much time on one agency. Know where all of your assigned budgets are at all times. Detailed analysis should include the following steps:

1. Always contact the agency head first. He or she is responsible for all items in the budget and has the best understanding of how the components interrelate. You should discuss several items during this first meeting:
   a. What approach does the administrator prefer—are you free to meet individually with subordinates on matters in their areas, or does the administrator want to participate in all budget discussions?
   b. What about the role of governing boards or commissions—are they to be involved in the budget review process?
   c. Solicit the administrator's description of the program achievements proposed in the budget request. He or she may have goals or accomplishments proposed in the budget that you missed in your preliminary review.
   d. Explain your personal schedule for review of the request. You may find conflicts which will require revisions in your internal deadlines.

2. Review past approved budgets and Joint Committee on Ways and Means reports and, if possible, talk to analysts previously assigned to the budget. This will acquaint you with past analytical approaches and will highlight executive and legislative decisions of the past few years.

3. Divide the budget into manageable segments. The request may be divided by program or organizational lines—or both. Choose one segment for detailed analysis. Remember that no individual segment should be considered complete until all of your recommendations are prepared.

4. Approach the request with skepticism, not cynicism. Your job is not to justify the request, nor is it to eliminate the agency (usually). All activities of the agency are subject to question, even those most politically popular or well established. It is important to remember that you must not interject your personal philosophy or biases in your review. You deal with facts or clearly understood gubernatorial policy, not emotion.

5. Approach the request with an open mind. You are not responsible for interpreting the governor's political statements or public positions on issues. Don't let the agency tell you that "confidentially, the governor is keenly interested in this program." If he is, you'll find out through normal budget procedures.

6. Don't analyze dollars—analyze programs and decision packages. Dollars are an important item in budgeting. However, it is the program achievements that are budgeted; and the dollars merely provide a common denominator in expressing the resources necessary to provide these programs. Understand the programs and decision packages first, and the dollar levels will follow.

7. When comparing proposed program levels, your base for comparison is the latest legislatively approved level. It is not the agency request. The legislatively approved level will be expressed in both dollar and program

terms in the latest Joint Committee on Ways and Means report. Review the performance of the agency during the first year of the biennium and compare it with the levels approved by the previous legislature. You may find areas where we are actually spending more and accomplishing less.

8. In reviewing the budget, use a zero-based conceptual attitude and consider the following questions:
   a. Is the base budget consistent with the existing approved level?
   b. Does the base budget include expenditures which were originally approved on a "one-shot" or nonrecurring basis?
   c. Are there activities in the base budget which are of lower priority than some proposed expansions, new programs, or decision packages? In an austere budget season, program expansions may have to be financed by offsetting program retrenchment.
   d. Are there activities in the budget request which, for various reasons, should be stopped or could better be performed by a different agency? In these cases, prepare a policy memo outlining the issue. Minor reorganizations can be recommended within the governors budget.

9. In reviewing decision packages based upon increased workload, consider the following questions:
   a. Is the projected workload self-generated? That is, does it represent activity levels controllable by the agency, or does it truly reflect increased demands for service by the public or other beneficiaries?
   b. Is the proposed volume of increased workload consistent with workload patterns of the past few years and supported by adequate justification?
   c. Are the requested levels of staff, support costs, and facilities properly related to the volume of increased workload? Ratios, economies of scale, seasonal peaks and valleys of activities, and the existing capacity to absorb increased workload should be considered.
   d. What is the true program impact of not providing the requested increased volume of service in a particular program?

10. In reviewing program adjustments which have taken place in the interim, consider the following questions:
   a. Was the adjustment approved in the manner and at the level described? (Review emergency board minutes and other relevant documents.)
   b. Was the adjustment intended for continuation into future biennia?
   c. Does the adjustment retain sufficient priority for continuation or was it provided to meet an emergency need which is no longer critical to the agency's program?

11. In reviewing requests for operation of new facilities, consider the following questions:
   a. Has the capital project already been approved, or is it contingent on future executive or legislative action?
   b. What is the latest estimate for the building to come on-line and require operational support?

c. What standards or other empirical justification are available to support the estimated costs to operate the new facilities?
d. What offsetting savings, such as vacation of rental space, are available, and have they been reflected in the request?
e. What effect will the new facilities have on basic programs? Is the agency using the new facility as a smoke screen to go into new programs not fully analyzed? What are the future costs and benefits of these new programs?

12. In reviewing decision packages which constitute program improvements, consider the following questions:
a. What is the true effect or product of the improvement?
b. What are the bases of the request for the improvement—who originated the demand for expanded or improved services?
c. What is the impact of the improvement on existing programs?
d. What criteria were used to develop the staff and support costs of the improvement? Are they valid?
e. Has the improvement been previously requested and denied? If so, on what grounds?
f. Is the improvement consistent with agency objectives?
g. Is the improvement of a higher priority than an existing program or activity?
h. What are the future costs and benefits of the requested improvement?

13. In reviewing requests for new programs, all items listed for program improvements should be considered. In addition, ask the following:
a. Is this the appropriate agency to perform this service? Is the service now being provided by another state agency, other governmental units, or private industry?
b. Are there any revenue sources, such as special fees, available to offset the cost of implementing this program?

14. A note of caution—don't ignore programs simply because no program improvements or new programs are being proposed. The thorough analyst will examine ongoing programs for continued relevance and necessity. This is one of the most lucrative areas of investigation for an economy-minded analyst.

15. Another note of caution—don't get trapped by counting desks—either literally or figuratively. After some frustration in considering the solutions to major social problems, you will be tempted to revert to considering the minor details of bureaucratic operation. Don't yield to the temptation—you'll learn to accept the frustration and maybe even be instrumental in really solving a social problem.

Conversely, do not become so awed by the social issues that you lose sight of your basic purpose—to produce a responsible budget. Don't get lost in the clouds.

16. Still another note of caution—GET ORGANIZED AND STAY ORGANIZED. Know where you've been and know where you are, and where you have to get at all times during the season. If you realize you are becoming disorganized—STOP—get reorganized and then start again.

17. In the course of detailed analysis, you will prepare a variety of memos, worksheets, and other written material. General suggestions.
    a. Keep them neat. Most likely the analyst preparing the budget recommendations will not be responsible for executing that budget. Give your successor a break—and some useful budget files.
    b. Identify your worksheets. Columns of numbers with no headings or other identification are useless to everyone, including the analyst. Each worksheet should be readily identifiable as to content. Date them! Date them! Date them!
    c. Keep your files in an organized manner. Make sure your secretary knows where you keep certain workpapers (such as memos from governor's assistants or other executive department staff). She may need to find something in your absence—and in a hurry.

18. You will never have the time to perform as detailed an analysis as you think is necessary. If you encounter a problem or issue too complex to review in the time available, it may be necessary to prepare a memo recommending an item for future study and move on. This is not a cop-out, but a realistic appraisal of the volume of work which can be done in a limited period of time. Meet your deadlines! Meet your deadlines! Meet your deadlines!

19. Analyze the agency's revenues as well as the expenditures. They matter.

20. After you've completed the detailed analysis of a budget request—step back and "look at the forest." Review the sum of your detailed work to see if the total makes sense and is reasonable.

Preparing the Recommendation

You earn your salary when you tie all of the analytical efforts, alternatives, and mass of data together into one proposed course of action. Remember that you are only recommending. You don't allow or deny. Use these words around an agency and you'll feel rather silly when items are restored at the appeal hearing.

Remember that, even though you are to recommend one course of action, you are also to consider and be prepared to implement various alternatives. Presentation of alternatives is required when forwarding a policy memo, and alternatives can be included in the analyst report. . . .

Although you don't have the authority to include or exclude items in a budget, don't expect your boss to make your decisions for you. You are responsible for your recommendations; and you must be in a position to defend them with hard, objective data. You are telling your superiors what you think they should do—they must also consider other factors in arriving at their decisions.

In developing your specific recommendations, consider the following:

1. Recommendations are transmitted through the analyst report. This document must be a concise, complete summary of your findings. Keep it understandable; don't try to show off your knowledge of agency jargon. Slang and obscure abbreviations have no place in the analyst report.

2. You are displaying a piece of specific analysis, not presenting a discourse on the theory of the agency. All narrative should directly relate to specific recommendations.

3. Don't devote more than a minimum of discussion to items which you have not recommended. If they are significant in size or content, mention them briefly. Otherwise, concentrate your efforts on what you are recommending.

4. The analyst report is an internal document. However, it will be the basic vehicle for transmitting the executive department's recommendations to the agency. Keep it objective. If you have special comments of a confidential nature, attach them as a special memo which can accompany the analyst report through its internal review, or transmit your ideas orally.

5. In developing final recommendations, remember that an unreasonable budget is useless to everyone. You're not paid on a commission of dollars cut from the request. Unrealistically low recommendations place a burden on your superiors to restore the funds. If an agency has erred in preparing its request, you may find yourself in a position where you'll be adding money in a particular area. Don't be alarmed—remember, the goal is a realistic budget.

6. Conversely, your job is to recommend the least amount of money and the least number of positions necessary to support the agency at the recommended program level. Let your superiors make most of the generous gestures to agencies.

7. After you have developed your preliminary recommendations, try them out on the agency administrator. (Even though you may have a big ego, you also are an honestly humble person who realizes he doesn't know everything. Besides, the agency may be able to correct some bad work you've done before someone else uncovers it.)

Agency Appeals

We cannot predict accurately how the various levels of appeal will be handled. There is no question but that agencies generally will appeal the decisions and recommendations of the analyst. These appeals will probably take several forms:

1. The pro forma appeals: These include those agencies which have never accepted the legitimacy of the budget staff and are satisfied only after discussing the budget with the director of the department or the governor.

2. Appeals to correct errors: During the course of a budget season, other analysts (not you) will make some arithmetic or reasoning errors. When the agency discovers these, it has every right to request correction.

3. Emotional appeals: These occur most frequently when the analyst has failed to establish good personal rapport and the agency head is convinced that "he just doesn't understand our problems." Stick to the facts and don't get drawn into personal conflicts. When you lose your objectivity, you lose your usefulness.

4. Objective or "legitimate" appeals: These represent judgments by the agency that your recommendations do not adequately support the programs during the coming biennium. Sometimes the agency will produce supplemental data not made available to you during the course of budget review. The technical word for this is "dirty trick." Most items in this type of appeal, however, deal simply with judgments made by the analyst and questioned by the agency. Be equally objective in analyzing them for your superiors.

In all types of appeals, the analyst is responsible for several actions:

1. Review of the appeal letter and development of specific recommendations with reasons for each item included.

2. Detailed minutes of the proceedings of the appeal hearing.

3. An immediate update of all appropriate documents as soon as the final decisions are made. Draft a letter summarizing the results of the hearing for distribution to the agency and your superiors.

4. Informing the coordinating secretary and technical support section of the results of the hearing so they can update their master summaries.

When the Numbers Are Firm

Don't relax! There is still a lot of work to do. First priority is the final preparation of reproduction copy. Reproduction copy is the narrative and supporting schedules that will be printed in the governor's budget released December 1. Careful editing must be done to ensure that the narrative and fiscal data accurately describe the final budget decisions.

The governor's budget is written primarily for the legislature. It is not the prime working document for the Joint Committee on Ways and Means—that honor belongs to the updated agency request document. The printed budget must be meaningful to the freshman legislator, who has never seen a state budget, and the most experienced member of Ways and Means.

After repro copy has been prepared and all master summaries have been updated, the analyst still has several responsibilities:

1. Edit your working papers. You'll be using them throughout the legislative hearings, so make sure you're not cluttered with excess baggage. Organized, orderly, neat working papers are essential during hearings.

2. Prepare material explaining the budget for your agencies. Additional analyses can be performed and presented in narrative, graphic, or tabular presentations that can be used in orienting the Legislature, selling the budgets to Ways and Means, and informing the public about the proposals.

   The emphasis in these analyses should be on program and decision packages, not dollars. While you should be able to speak very precisely about proposed expenditure levels if asked, don't plan to explain your budgets by accounting for dollars. It's boring—and meaningless.

3. Keep in close communication with your assigned agencies to ensure that they are on schedule in updating their request documents to reflect the governor's recommendations.

4. There are many things not described in this report. A budget season must be experienced before any level of understanding is possible. Hopefully, these comments will provide some help to those analysts about to participate in their first. Good luck!

CHAPTER 5

Budget Classifications and Reform

The budget process discussion in previous chapters has focused primarily on fiscal discipline, an important concern if government operations are to be fiscally sustainable in the long term. But the budget process also matters for choices among government programs and for inducing efficient use of resources within programs. Governments are confronted with many productive uses of resources, but they do not have sufficient resources to do everything that might be seen as desirable. At some point, they have to make choices among good ideas for providing services. To make those choices, government decision-makers need good financial information. The appropriate classification of that information is much of what the budget reforms discussed in this chapter focus on.

Budget processes can help governments allocate public resources, control agency operations, and manage service delivery. Budgets can be clear statements of plans, priorities, performance, and costs as well as the basic template for administrative control. Unfortunately, prevailing practices often impede the full use of budgeting for planning and analysis to guide public choices. Too often, our systems and decision processes cause budget participants to bounce between Oscar Wilde's cynics and sentimentalists, as defined in the exchange between Cecil Graham and Lord Darlington in *Lady Windermere's Fan:*

> Cecil Graham: What is a cynic?
>
> Lord Darlington: A man who knows the price of everything and the value of nothing.
>
> Cecil Graham: And a sentimentalist, my dear Darlington, is a man who sees an absurd value in everything, and doesn't know the market price of any single thing.[1]

The task of the fiscal process must be to avoid the seductions of both cynic and sentimentalist, to understand that reasonable choice entails both value and price, and to recognize that, although good ideas are limitless, resources to finance those good ideas are not.

Traditional budgets have been structured to facilitate spending control, not resource allocation. This emphasis exists largely because public budgeting emerged in

[1]Oscar Wilde, *Lady Windermere's Fan* (London: Methuen, 1908), 134.

a period when the concern was, purely and simply, prevention of theft. Hence, budgets focused on control of resources (or inputs) and little else. Modern governments have moved beyond that stage, but too much of budgeting retains that old preoccupation. Governments provide valued services, so merely keeping a lid on spending is insufficient. Budgets must be seen as more than devices for restraining thieves. Narrow controls almost certainly thwart innovation, constrain capacity to respond to citizen-clients, and increase the cost of service. Decision-makers must control waste and make allocation choices; so budget structures need to facilitate this work.

Logically, the task of budget allocation is simple: Allocate funds among government programs until an additional dollar moved to any program yields an additional return to society equal to the return lost from the program from which that dollar was taken.[2] That is the public-sector equivalent of the familiar resource-allocation rule for profitability in business operations. But the private decision-maker maximizes a clear and measurable objective—profit—and measuring profitable return from several lines of operation is feasible because the standard is clearly calibrated and uniform. Public-sector operations usually (1) have multiple objectives (e.g., subsidized school lunches both feed children and support farm income), (2) have conflicting objectives (e.g., the reservoir needs to be nearly empty to provide flood control and to be nearly full to allow water skiing), and (3) have no standard measure or common yardstick to compare the return from various programs (e.g., the gains from cleaner streams and lakes are not measured in the same units as are reduced traffic fatalities). The beneficiaries of the various programs are not often the same people, so choices among programs cause there to be winners and losers, in violation of the Pareto criterion. Hence, the simple public-program allocation rule, so easy to define, may only be a glimmer in the politics of budget policy. Lawmakers working in the public interest face tough choices, well beyond the complexities a business executive will confront. The budget process is where choices are made among program alternatives. Some budget classifications may make the allocation choices more likely to improve conditions of society.

Alternative Budget Classifications and the Provision of Government Services

Government agencies may be thought of as operating entities that buy resources, use those resources in the performance of certain tasks, and, as a result of performing those tasks, achieve certain results that are valued by society. Budget classification

[2]This rule also applies for a perfectly altruistic nonprofit organization. However, most nonprofit organizations are narrow interest groups, aiming to protect the environment, to ease the plight of the homeless, to care for the indigent sick, and so on. Hence, the budgetary allocation rule for a nonprofit organization is more related to that of a private business than of a general purpose government—allocations among its operations should work toward the particular purpose of the organization, not the competing objectives of society. Otherwise, all tools of public budgeting—budget development, review, adoption, execution, audit, and so on—apply to these entities just as they apply to governments.

schemes may organize and control government expenditure—the total sum paid by agencies for purchases of inputs; for contractual services to be delivered by others; for transfer payments made to individuals, businesses, or other governments; for interest paid on debt outstanding; and so on—in a variety of ways. Figure 5–1 provides a simple outline of service provision. The following explains the terms in that outline:

1. **Inputs.** Inputs are the resources an agency purchases to use in its service delivery operations and are what the agency's budget purchases. A city street department buys resources (asphalt, crushed stone, fuel to operate its equipment, the services of its employees, etc.). The funds in the budget are not inputs; the funds are what the agency uses to purchase the inputs.

2. **Outputs.** Outputs are products or services produced by the agency. With the resources it has purchased, the department undertakes certain tasks or activities (fills chuckholes, resurfaces roadways, etc.). These are "means to an end," not the end itself. Outputs are important for measuring internal operations of the agency but do not indicate the extent to which the agency's purpose is being achieved.

3. **Results or Outcomes.** Because of the activities undertaken, desirable outcomes result (e.g., people and property can move through the city more quickly and safely, with less damage done to vehicles). The measured result or outcome indicates progress by the agency toward achievement of its purposes of improving the economic or social condition of the citizenry. The measures can reflect successful events, occurrences, or conditions, and may also indicate the

Figure 5–1
Flow of Public-Service Provision

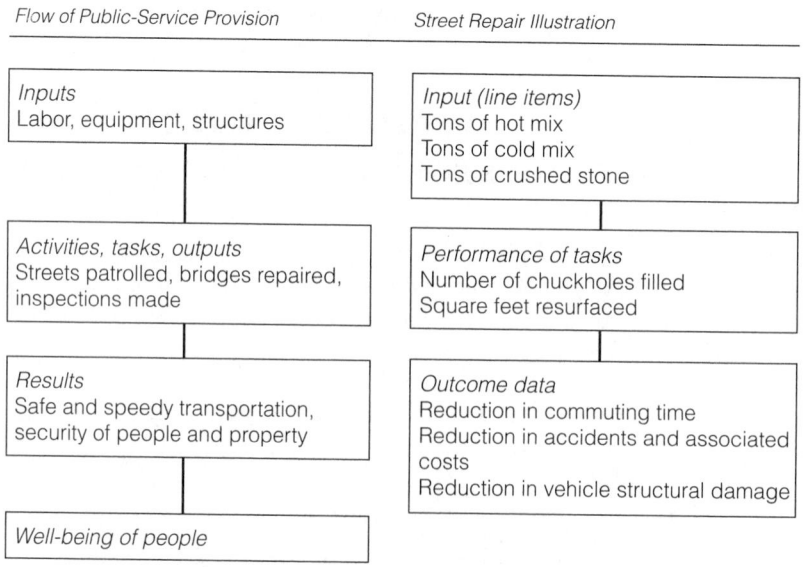

quality of the service being rendered. Consumer satisfaction surveys may play a role in the measurement of outcome performance, particularly in regard to service quality.

4. **Consequences for society.** The outcome improves the standard of life for residents of the city. This is why the agency exists—to improve life for the citizenry.

Government expenditures can be classified for the purposes of planning, analysis, reporting, and control according to several different frameworks. Classifications found in public budgets include the following:

1. **Organizations:** Spending categorized according to the administrative unit (a department or agency, like the city Department of Streets and Roads or national Department of Homeland Security) responsible for delivering services on the basis of the sums appropriated and for using those sums properly. This classification is critical for assigning organizational *responsibility* for delivery of services and *accountability* for public resources.

2. **Items purchased** (line item or object of expenditure): This is grocery list classification. The focus is on what the government buys, either directly from its suppliers or indirectly through transfer-subsidy-loan programs. The input format is basic, traditional, and old. It is the building block for budget cost estimates and provides the focus for the control structures of government operation. This classification emphasizes purchase type: personnel, supplies and equipment, utilities, contractual services, and so on.

3. **Activities or tasks:** Expenditure for tasks performed. This format classifies according to the direct output of government, intermediate product, the activities the government engages in, or the tasks it performs. The classification emphasizes measurable tasks: lane miles paved, pupil class hours taught, prisoners incarcerated, arrests made, tons of solid waste managed, number of border inspections, and so on.

4. **Function, purpose, or program:** Expenditure according to broad public purpose. The orientation is toward the final customer, the people served by the government. Classification would focus on the reasons that the government exists: for example, protection of persons and property or maintaining a healthy citizenry.[3]

Budgets for governments and public organizations mix these classifications in several ways as they attempt to provide information useful for planning the

[3]Budget systems do not use a consistent language in distinguishing between concepts of performance (activity or task) and program (function or purpose). In some budgets, "program" means a service area (like street maintenance) for which a cost center is established; in other budgets, "program" means an outcome group (like safe and speedy transport of persons and property) which can be balanced against other purposes of government. In the discussion here, "what governments do" means task, activity, direct output, or intermediate product, and "why governments exist" means achievement, consumer output, final product, or outcome and program refers to the latter. The distinction is particularly important in examination of municipal budget processes. The two uses of program might be considered "service area programs" and "outcome programs."

utilization of resources, for devising efficient operations of agencies, and for control over use of resources. Most actual budgets are hybrids, but Table 5–1 provides information on some fundamental features of budgets organized by line item, performance of activities, and program. Regardless of how they are organized, budgets also increasingly provide performance measures for each agency, and increasingly these measures attempt to gauge outcomes or results of agency operations, not the activities that the agency is engaged in. Executive agencies, legislators, and the general public are not satisfied with tallies of activities that have characterized such documents in the past, and simply spending appropriations is no longer acceptable as an indicator of accomplishment. Agencies are expected to provide services for the common good and are held accountable for serving the public.

Budget classifications focus on different stages of the expenditure-delivery system, from resources purchased (*line item*) through activities performed (*traditional performance*) to services delivered (*program*). Line-item and performance systems maintain traditional department structures in the organization of expenditure plans; program budgets classify government outputs (or services provided) without regard for the administrative unit charged with service provision. All seek to improve the job done by the government and to keep government operations consistent with the wishes of the citizenry, but their fundamental concerns differ. Line-item budgets have as their foremost concern expenditure control and accountability. Performance budgets seek to improve internal management and cost of services provided. Program budgets emphasize arranging details in a manner to improve decision capacity for rational choice. (See the budget illustration in Chapter 2 for a reminder of the line-item format.)

Traditional Budgets: A Flawed Tool for Decision-making (But Pretty Good for Control and Accountability)

Traditional budget procedures embody several impediments to efficient and effective public management and planning. These include (1) the administrative-department basis for budget requests and appropriation, (2) the short-period concept for costs in budget considerations, (3) the focus on agency inputs rather than services provided outputs or outcomes, and (4) the failure to compare project costs with project benefits. Budget details often take on such bulk that they intimidate inexperienced users and discourage those with limited time from extracting the budgets' policy plans. Unfortunately, legislators—the people who are supposed to review and approve the plans inherent in the budget document—may be just as inexperienced and short of time as the general public. Clear presentation of relevant information is frequently not a strong element in traditional budget documents.

Administrative-department basis. Public decisions require meaningful measurement of the cost of achieving a desired objective. Traditional budget processes, although driven by cost estimates, do not provide that information in a usable format. Budgets are proposed and appropriations are made on an administrative-

Table 5–1
Alternative Budget Formats and Associated Features

Format	Characteristics	Primary Organization Feature	Orientation
Line item	Expenditure by commodity or resource purchased	Resources purchased	Control
Performance	Expenditure by workload or activity Presentation of unit cost by activity	Tasks, activities, or direct output performed	Management
Program	Expenditure by activities serving common public purpose Not limited to single government organization	Achievements, final product, outcome, or consumer output	Planning

SOURCE: Adapted from Edward A. Lehan, *Simplified Governmental Budgeting* (Chicago: Municipal Finance Officers Association, 1981): 79.

department basis, not on the basis of what departments actually intend to achieve. Such categorizations blur the allocation process and impede consideration of alternatives, the essence of resource allocation. Categories of administration—departments of defense, transportation, or justice at the federal level; departments of public works, economic development, public safety, or social services at state-local levels—are too broad for judgments about the appropriate amounts of resources to be allocated to each. Some activities of a particular department may be of extreme importance for social goals, whereas others could be of considerably lower consequence and less significant than activities proposed by other departments. But the traditional budget approach tends to focus on departments, treating all work within them as being of equal contribution to public well-being. An important principle in traditional budgets is that where you are establishes what you get. Departments and even agencies within them include activity conglomerations; some of those activities are related more to the work of other agencies than to the rest of their own agency. The Army Corps of Engineers' work in U.S. rivers or the services of security officers in city park departments offer two examples of work not matching larger titles or primary operations of the larger department. Budgets and appropriations that go through organizational charts complicate identification of the cost of achieving a particular objective because most agencies have multiple outputs. Edmond Weiss notes the "fallacy of appellation . . . the rhetorical act of obscuring the distinction between the name of a budget category and the actual phenomenon generally associated with that name."[4] In short, intelligent resource-allocation decisions are unlikely to emerge from budget considerations based on administrative

[4]Edmond H. Weiss, "The Fallacy of Appellation in Government Budgeting," *Public Administration Review* 34 (July/August 1974): 377.

departments. (Case 5–1 gives a famous illustration of how administrative department classification enters into budget results.)

Budget conventions. Budgets and appropriations to administrative units can conceal the full cost of delivery of government services. For example, cities frequently have departments of public works that are responsible for maintenance of all infrastructure and even for some minor new construction, and may provide employee fringe benefits (pensions, vacation pay, etc.) through the human resources department budget. In this circumstance, identifying the amount the city spends for provision of a city service—like parks and recreation or police protection—would require analysis of the operations of the primary department but also analysis of some spending of these other departments that have no immediately visible link to that agency's role. This violates the transparency standard for government operations and lessens the utility of the budget document in making public choices.

Single-year basis. Traditional budgets are developed and considered on a single-year basis without developing cost profiles over time. Appropriation decisions usually cover a single year of agency operation[5]—an appropriate period for fiscal control—even though many activities proposed by an agency have significant future cost implications. The single-year cost is often little more than a program down payment with many installments ahead. Reasonable decision-making requires that the total cost of a project be examined, not just the single-year cost. Because data with so full a scope are seldom a part of the budget process, budget choices must be made without appropriate information. The federal process now displays the budget year plus 4 out years; because few appropriation decisions lock in choices for full program life, the impact on decision processes is not clear. (The detailed department-by-department presentations from which the appropriation committees work includes only the single budget year.) The out years can contain much mischief when governments try to prove their fiscal conservatism by showing how they will control deficits—in the future. Nevertheless, good-faith attempts to identify future (out-year) cost implications of choices made now are necessary for reasonable budgetary deliberations.

Input orientation. Reasoned choice requires a comparison among alternative methods of reaching a desired objective. The input orientation of traditional line-item budgets blocks operational vision and traps agencies into conventional operations.[6] Agencies traditionally build budgets from existing input combinations. The agencies lock themselves into "normal" operating techniques and overlook alternative methods and legislatures appropriate into definite line items. Public agencies and legislatures focus on what they buy (inputs) to the near exclusion of what they provide (services or outputs). Ordinary reviews emphasize changes in the objects of expenditure—that is, the personnel to be hired (or fired) and their pay grades, changes in the pay of current staff, and the supplies and equipment to be purchased. An input orientation produces the following logic: if the price of gaso-

---

[5]Some governments have biennial budgets, but these are essentially single-year budgets times two. Only by accident will the complete cost of a project be captured in a biennial budget.

[6]David Osborne, "Escaping from the Line-Item Trap," *Governing* 5 (September 1992): 69.

line increases by 25 percent, agency operation requires a 25 percent increase in the appropriation for those purchases. Otherwise, the agency must cut back its services.

This logic implies that the objective of the agency is the purchase of given amounts of specific inputs. A budget process should induce consideration of alternative production strategies to economize the use of resources that have become more expensive—are there ways of accomplishing the agency mission that do not use as much gasoline? Seldom is there but a single way to provide a service, and budget processes need to consider alternatives, especially when the price of some inputs has increased dramatically. Reviewers too infrequently consider the public services to be provided with these inputs or the alternative combinations of inputs that could produce those services. Legislatures too often expect appropriations to be spent on exact line-item templates, without managerial flexibility to deliver service. A simple analog to traditional budgeting would be a baker who purchases flour, milk, and sugar without considering either the number of cakes, cookies, breads, and so on, to be sold or alternative recipes for their production. That would be a silly way to run a business, and it is a silly way to run a government. How is it possible to make reasonable choices between programs that offer different services to the population when the budget presentations and discussions focus on what the government agencies will be buying? It isn't a responsible way to make decisions across government agencies, and it isn't a responsible way for agencies to make decisions about their internal operations.

These physical input requirements are selected before any cost estimation and without reference either to alternative production methods or to the programs sacrificed if a particular choice is made.[7] Indeed, some governments treat final appropriations to input class so rigidly that agencies, faced with a burdensome series of approvals should they adjust to changed operating conditions during the budget year, choose to do nothing. The language of the appropriation law defends them against the need to respond to the legitimate service demands of the public.

The question of value. The toughest but most fundamental problem of all is that public decisions must weigh the cost of public programs against their worth to society. The line-item costs in traditional budgets are financial, out-of-pocket costs. They exclude social costs not directly paid; they reflect financial transactions, not the value of opportunities not chosen; and they do not distinguish between sunk and incremental costs of actions. Thus, the cost data presented may not be quite right for making decisions. A number of governments have experimented with activity-based costing (ABC) as a way to improve their decisions. Sidebar 5–1 discusses this approach. Yet budget costs are often all decision-makers consider. The

[7]William Niskanen, Gordon Tullock, and others point out that agency administrators have individual incentives to spend as much as possible (conduct any project at the highest feasible cost). See Gordon Tullock, *The Politics of Bureaucracy* (Washington, D.C.: Public Affairs Press, 1965); and William A. Niskanen, Jr., *Bureaucracy and Representative Government* (Chicago: Aldine, 1971). Whether the budget-maximizingbureaucrat is an accurate reflection of reality has been empirically argued many times over the years. One recent answer ("no") appears in Julie Dolan, "The Budget-Minimizing Bureaucrat? Empirical Evidence from the Senior Executive Service," *Public Administration Review* 62 (January/February 2002): 42–50.

Sidebar 5–1
Activity-Based Costing and Government Budgeting

Many government decisions need information about the cost of services provided. ABC, initiated in the late 1980s in the private sector and extended to public and nonprofit agencies about a decade later, offers a system for organizing input cost data to help with program and operational choices.

ABC assigns cost to products or processes according to the resources they consume. It seeks to move accounting data from its traditional input organization (personnel, supplies, contractual services, etc.) to organization according to output, service provided, or project. The idea became popular initially as a way to allocate indirect (overhead) costs to manufacturing, then was applied to services sold by businesses. Finally the approach has been extended to government operations, not with an eye to the private-sector concerns about pricing or gauging profitability of a product line, but rather with the intent of improving operational efficiency by cost control and identifying opportunities for economical contracting out of public-service production. It seeks clear assignment of cost to each government activity without cross-subsidization of one activity by another.

Traditional cost accounting focuses on the product as the consumer of resources. Cost is measured according to the number of direct labor or machine hours in production or material dollars consumed. It is a "volume-based" cost system. Overhead is added according to some allocation factor or factors linked to direct use of resources in production. ABC, on the other hand, traces costs to activities (entering data, processing reports, maintaining equipment, etc.) and then to products (or services) according to the product's use of the activities in its production process. In skeletal form, ABC has three steps:

1. Define cost categories (salaries, materials, travel, utilities, etc.)
2. Identify key processes and principal activities associated with each and estimate activity costs for each. First-stage cost allocations assign costs from resource categories to activity centers.

needed comparison between cost and program value, vital to intelligent resource allocation, is not a regular component of budget processes, because the value of programs delivered is seldom reported or formally considered. Without such regular comparison, poor public decisions are likely. Public decisions based only on program cost—either because costs are remarkably high or affordably low—will not consistently lead to a wise use of scarce resources; neither would consideration based solely on project worth to the exclusion of cost. A society with scarcity must require consideration of worth against cost, if only in the sense of considering how society would be poorer in the absence of the service. Regardless of whether worth is easily measurable, no choices are possible solely on a cost basis. Budget people must avoid the blind spots of both cynic and sentimentalist. Unfortunately, the traditional budget does not provide important information for choice.

Sidebar 5–1
(continued)

3. Assign costs by activity to appropriate categories, that is, services or products produced. Second stage cost allocations assign costs from activity centers to products or services.

In the language of ABC, resources used are linked to activities by "resources drivers" and activities are linked to costs by "cost drivers." In application, some costs are calculated by detailed record keeping and some are calculated by an allocation cost driver, that is, distributed or allocated according to some reasonable basis. The degree of precision required depends on how material the cost, how significant the service, and the extent to which the costing might distort incentives for efficient operations.

There are limits to the utility of full-blown ABC to government decision-making. First, cost recovery is not an important concern for most government services. Accurate cost estimates may be interesting as an intellectual and philosophical exercise, but may not mean much for actual public choice. Second, precise allocation of overhead cost, the primary advantage promised for ABC, matters for decisions only if those costs can be avoided. Marginal or incremental costs—those costs that can be avoided by making a particular choice—are critical for decisions about what services will be provided and what services will not. These costs change as a result of the decision matter, but much of government overhead is independent of service choice. Effort toward the precise allocation of such costs therefore yields little extra value to the decision process because the service is not being sold and extent of cost recovery is not relevant.

If services are being financed on a charge basis, however, ABC will be extremely useful for guiding pricing decisions and choices about service provision. Better identification and measurement of avoidable cost can be an important aid to improved decision-making in all aspects of government.

Performance Budgets

The principal idea behind performance budgets of all varieties is that putting performance information alongside budget numbers will improve public decisions. Performance budgets emphasize agency-activity performance objectives and accomplishments, not the purchase of resources. Budgets present the cost of performing measurable accomplishment units during the budget year, so the budget process has the dual role of providing funds and establishing performance objectives. Performance budgeting dates to the mid-1910s in New York City; similar efforts continue in state and local governments to the present.[8] The primary impact of performance budgeting on the service-delivery process, however, dates from the first Hoover Commission (Commission on Organization of the Executive Branch of the Government) report of 1949.[9]

The performance budget concept entails certain shifts in thinking from that of the traditional line-item budget.

1. Budget information should be organized in terms of activities (repairing roads, planting trees, treating patients, teaching students, making arrests, etc.) rather than in terms of individual line items only.
2. Activities should be measured, costs should be identified for these activities, and efficiency in performance of these activities should be evaluated.
3. Performance should be monitored by comparing actual cost and accomplishment against the planned levels for each agency.
4. Although the performance measures would ordinarily not be "end products" of government, the activities ideally should be associated with these beneficial results or outcomes. In modern terminology, these performance measures are on the order of "means to end" rather than being the end themselves.

The performance classification promises better services at lower cost from more accountable officials; improved legislative review as attention and debate shift away from issues of personnel, salaries, supplier contracts, and the like, toward activity issues more related to how resources are used; and decentralized decision-making, allowing top management to concentrate its attention on policy matters. Classification of requests follows the activities of the agency, not the inputs it purchases. Performance budgets link costs with activities. This linkage permits unit-cost comparisons across agencies and over time within agencies to emphasize improvements in operating efficiency.

Figure 5–2 further illustrates the performance classification. It includes performance-budget material for snow removal from the 1981–1982 Salt Lake City budget, a historic document noted for its faithfulness to the performance concept. Note the following elements:

1. **The demand section** defines the expected operating environment for the budget year, with prior- and current-year levels for comparison.
2. **The workload section** establishes how the operating unit intends to respond to expected demand by allocation of staff time.
3. **The productivity section** presents the cost per activity unit that emerges from the budgeted costs. This is the special identifying feature of full performance budgets. Most budget documents will not, for instance, allow easy identification of either historic or proposed costs of dealing with snow

[8]U.S. General Accounting Office *Performance Budgeting: State Experiences and Implications for the Federal Government* (GAO/AFMD-93-41) (Washington, D.C.: Government Printing Office, 1993) surveys these experiences.

[9]Commission on Organization of the Executive Branch of the Government, *Budgeting and Accounting* (Washington, D.C.: U.S. Government Printing Office, 1949).

Figure 5–2
Salt Lake City Performance Budget Illustration

Public Protection — Traffic Regulation

Program: Snow Removal — Department: Public Works

Program Description: To remove snow and ice from city streets for safe travel during inclement weather conditions.

	Program Operating Expense			
Resource Requirements	1979–1980 Actual	1980–1981 Budget	1980–1981 Estimated	1981–1982 Recommended
Personnel/personal services	19.5/$279,318	16.9/$325,358	11.25/$190,618	4.7/$111,975
Operating and maintenance supplies	39,081	48,300	29,763	47,720
Charges and services	61,774	193,169	111,864	199,379
Capital outlay	0	17,596	12,570	0
Work order credits	(212)	0	0	0
Total	$379,961	$584,423	$344,815	$359,074
Program Resources				
General fund	$379,961	$584,423	$344,815	$359,074
Total	$379,961	$584,423	$344,815	$359,074

Program Budget Highlights

The 1980–1981 budget indicators had an over allocation of man hours in the snow and ice program which have been rectified by mid-year adjustments and are now correctly reflected in the 1980–1982 request. During 1980–1981, a study was conducted analyzing the past five winters. It was obvious as a result of this study that our projections for the 1980–1981 budget year were unrealistic, so we reassigned employees' time to other programs causing other program expenditure levels and personnel allocations to rise.

Performance Objectives

1. To review "scale" of snow fighter program.
2. To develop an expanded U.D.O.T. and S.L.C. responsibilities exchange where practical.
3. To evaluate an "exceptional storm" emergency backup system.

Performance Review	1979–1980 Actual	1980–1981 Budget	1980–1981 Estimated	1981–1982 Recommended
Demand				
1. Lane miles of priority snow routes	400	400	460	460
2. Inches of snowfall	63	68	45	68
3. Storms requiring crew mobilization	15	19	16	19
4. Storms requiring salt only	7	10	10	10
5. Storms requiring snow plowing	8	9	6	9
Workload				
1. Man hours salting streets	n.a.*	12,640	1,000	2,060
2. Man hours plowing streets	n.a.	18,960	1,400	3,090
3. Tons of salt applied	7,410	8,000	4,900	8,000

(continues)

Figure 5–2
Salt Lake City Performance Budget Illustration (continued)

Performance Review	1979–1980 Actual	1980–1981 Budget	1980–1981 Estimated	1981–1982 Recommended
Productivity				
1. Cost/priority lane mile	962	1,418	874	765
2. Average cost/storm	25,663	29,864	25,138	18,513
Effectiveness				
1. Vehicle accidents in which snow and ice are a contributing factor	253	250	135	250
2. Complaints received	49	50	35	50

*n.a. = Not available.

removal after a snowstorm; the performance classification does because it links costs to measured units of activities. Even budgets with cost centers identified within departments will not provide answers to those sorts of questions.

4. **The effectiveness section** shows the unit's performance against criteria that indicate whether the unit is accomplishing its intended objectives. This is important because one avenue to low cost is to reduce quality of service—one pickle slice fewer per hamburger will reduce the cost of producing hamburgers by millions of dollars in a national restaurant chain, and the same goes for government services.

The performance structure has some special implications. First, the budget can become a powerful tool for management responsibility and accountability. In that structure, budgeting must be a central management responsibility because activity levels and their costs are specifically presented in a document that guides agency operation. Operating supervisors can no longer permit separate budget personnel to prepare budget requests because they become detailed operating plans for the budget year.[10] Many agency managers do not like the performance-budgeting concept because it exposes the agency operating details (demand estimates, workload trend, etc.) to the scrutiny of external observers—like taxpayers and legislators. Second, legislatures must change their review and appropriations procedures from traditional line-item reviews to agency-activity reviews. The legislature may feel uncomfortable considering something other than objects of expenditures, particularly where there is no apparent linkage to revenue and budget balancing and when the activities may be difficult to measure or relate to what the citizenry really wants. Third, a performance budget can make a management-by-objectives program easier to operate. The objectives would be the performance measures (activities) appearing

[10]Traditional budgets are operating plans as well, except they do not contain identifiable operating objectives. That addition provides the new constraint on the agency.

in the budget. Performance and budget attainment can thus be monitored through the fiscal year.

The performance budget hinges on the quality of its performance measure and a legislative-executive consensus that those measures are the proper ones for agency attention. Some performance measures may be misleading or irrelevant, despite the fact that they can be measured and reported. Audit quality, for instance, may be more important than simply the number of audits conducted. The number of audits could well be the performance measure, however, simply because it is more easily quantified. And if the Department of Parks and Recreation is going to be responsible for maintaining flower beds, then it will need to define a standard flower bed for calculation of unit costs. Furthermore,the performance budget does not ask whether the performance being measured is the service the public actually wants. And, of course, there is no necessary consideration of alternate ways to do a particular task. The drive to lower a government's unit cost of performance should induce development of improved methods, not sacrifice the unit's quality—but the technique is not geared to handle that problem.

Curiously enough, advocates of performance budgeting come from two ends of the political spectrum. Some public officials see performance budgets as a way to justify their contributions to the community and possibly to expand their budgets. Others see performance budgets as a tool to expose waste and, hence, a guide for expenditure reduction that would permit tax cuts.

The performance-budget structure does not question whether objectives are appropriate or a service is worth its cost of production. Performance budgets consider whether the activity is being done at low cost; they do not consider whether the activity is worth doing. And that brings up the Achilles heel of performance budgets: they are extremely expensive to develop. Unless the government really will use them as an integral part of public management and decision-making, they are not likely to be a worthy use of government resources.

Program Budgets

The program-budget format organizes proposed expenditure according to consumer output or contribution to public objectives.[11] Programs are constructed on the basis of their contributions to those objectives without regard to administrative organizations responsible for delivery of the particular service. In essence, the program format requires the government—and agencies in the government—to identify what products or services it provides and then to organize its budget requests and budget execution along those product or service lines. The format redirects focus from the expenditure object (the things that the government purchases) to the

[11]These programs are linked to fundamental missions. In recent years, some jurisdictions have started to identify service areas (like street cleaning) of government agencies as programs. That obviously creates some confusion in discussion of budget structures.

subject of that expenditure (the services to society that the government provides) and it breaks down the administrative boundaries between government agencies. A complete program budget combines services that contribute to a similar objective so that competition for funds occurs among real alternatives, contrary to the style of an ordinary budget, in which agencies or departments compete for funds, as do service units within agencies or departments. Similar service units may receive different treatment simply because different agencies house them. In a program budget, similar service units compete with each other, not with dissimilar programs housed in an administrative agency.

Program budgeting defines the goals of an agency and classifies organizational activities contributing to each goal. To focus competition for resources on objec-

Table 5–2
Program Budget Structure: Commonwealth of Pennsylvania, 2005–2006

EDUCATION: The goal of this program is to ensure that funds for education are spent on proven practices that will boost student achievement. This Commonwealth program supports the Administration's goal to Build a World Class Public Education System.

Some Agencies involved: Departments of Education, Revenue, Public Welfare, and Labor; Higher Education Assistance Agency; Tax Equalization Board; etc.

PROTECTION OF PERSONS AND PROPERTY: The goal of this Commonwealth program is to provide an environment and a social system in which the lives of individuals and the property of individuals and organizations are protected from natural and man-made disasters and from illegal and unfair actions. This Commonwealth program supports the Administration's goal to Ensure the Safety of Our Citizens as well as the goal to Protect Our Natural Resources.

Some Agencies involved: State Police; Departments of Banking, Corrections, Military Affairs, State, Environmental Resources, Agriculture; Emergency Management Agency; Milk Marketing Board; Insurance Commission; etc.

HEALTH AND HUMAN SERVICES: The goals of this program are to ensure access to quality medical care for all citizens; to support people seeking self-sufficiency; to provide military assistance; and to maximize the capacity of individuals and families to participate in society. This Commonwealth program includes activities that support the Administration's goal to Increase Access to High Quality Health Care.

Some Agencies involved: Departments of Aging, Health, Public Welfare, Agriculture, Labor and Industry, Military Affairs, Transportation, etc.

TRANSPORTATION AND COMMUNICATION: The goal of this program is to provide a system for the fast, convenient, efficient and safe movement of individuals, cargo, and information within the Commonwealth that is interfaced with a national and international system of transportation and communication. This Commonwealth program supports the Administration's goal to Create Jobs and Build a Vital Economy through the establishment of a first-rate infrastructure.

Some Agencies involved: Department of Transportation.

RECREATIONAL AND CULTURAL ENRICHMENT: The goal of this program is to improve the quality of life in Pennsylvania's urban, suburban, and rural communities. This Commonwealth program supports the Administration's goals to Protect Our Natural Resources and Create Jobs and Build a Vital Economy.

tives and alternative programs for achieving objectives, items are grouped by end product, regardless of the agencies' functions. The program structure identifies agency products; it does not focus on the inputs used by the agency. Table 5–2 illustrates the program-budget classifications used by the commonwealth of Pennsylvania. Notice that the format classifies by service provided to the public rather than by individual department (several services would in fact be provided in more than one department), input purchased, or department activity. The structure seeks a final product orientation. The Direction and Supportive Services (Pennsylvania) classification is normal in program budgets; those functions provide unallocatable inputs to the provision of the other services. The Pennsylvania display shows that many agencies contribute to several programs and that most programs include operations of more than one agency.

Table 5–2
(continued)

Some Agencies involved: Departments of Conservation and Natural Resources and of Education; Historical and Museum Commission; Fish and Boat Commission; Public Television Network; Council on the Arts; etc.

RETRAINING AND CREATING JOBS: The goal of this program is to retain and create family-sustaining jobs through tax cuts; provide capital, technology, marketing, and support services to employers; and provide support and guidance to communities for their development and economic growth.

Some Agencies involved: Departments of Community Affairs, Education, Environmental Resources, Labor and Industry, Revenue; Auditor General; Housing Finance Agency; etc.

ECONOMIC DEVELOPMENT: The goal of this program is to invest public resources to create jobs for Pennsylvanians. This Commonwealth program supports the Administration's goal to Create Jobs and Build a Vital Economy as well as the goal to Boost the Skills of Our Workers.

Some Agencies involved: Department of Community and Economic Development; the Pennsylvania Economic Development Financing Authority; the Infrastructure Investment Authority; Auditor General; and Departments of Education, Labor and Industry, and Revenue.

DEBT SERVICE: The goal of this Commonwealth program is to provide sufficient financial resources necessary to meet the timely payment of Commonwealth debt obligations.
Agency involved: Treasury.

DIRECTION AND SUPPORTIVE SERVICES: The goal of this Commonwealth program is to provide an efficient and effective administrative support system through which the goals and objectives of the Commonwealth programs can be attained. This Commonwealth program supports the Administration's goal to Deliver Greater Value and Efficiency in Government through activities of centralized agencies to support this goal.

Some Agencies involved: Governor's Office; Executive Offices; Auditor's Office; Legislature; Treasury; Civil Service Commission; Departments of Revenue and General Services; State Employees' Retirement System; etc.

NOTE: Some agencies have activities that are included in more than one program.
SOURCE: Governor's Office of the Budget, *2005–2006 Executive Budget, Commonwealth of Pennsylvania* Harrisburg, Pennsylvania: Commonwealth of Pennsylvania, 2004.

Program budgeting requires careful definition of programs, an exercise in taxonomy that is the essence of such budgets. Although a good understanding of government operations is vital for program classification, the logical criteria for program design provided by Arthur Smithies are generally helpful:

1. **Facilitate comparisons.** Design programs so that they "permit comparison of alternative methods of pursuing an imperfectly defined policy objective."[12] If there are competing ways of reducing some social problem, make certain they end up in the same program. That breakdown can clarify issues for analysis.

2. **Include complementary resources.** Programs must include complementary components that cannot function separately. Thus, health programs require physicians, nurses, physical facilities, and the like in appropriate proportions, and those elements must all be in the program.

3. **Recognize the unallocable.** When one part of a government serves several other parts of that government, separate supporting service programs may be needed. Thus, centralized electronic data processing, personnel administration, and so forth may permit operating economies that would not be possible if each agency handled them separately. These activities can be handled as programs, even though their outputs are not government objectives (e.g., the Direction and Supportive Services program in Pennsylvania).

4. **Multiple structures.** Governments may need overlapping program structures to achieve their objectives. Many revenue departments, for instance, have structures arranged both functionally and geographically. That approach appears when both national and regional (or statewide) objectives are important.

5. **Recognize long-term activities.** Some activities involving research, development, or long-term investment may be considered separate subprograms because of the long time span over which the expenditures take effect. Uncertainties preclude reasonably reliable estimates of resource requirements beyond short portions of their lives.

It can be assumed that all government activities seek to improve the general welfare. Program budgeting's goal is to identify the components of that broad objective so that choices can be made among those components and among alternative approaches to their achievement.

Program construction is the identifying feature, but program budgets often include other elements. First, budget time horizons expand beyond an annual appropriation to the program's lifetime. Although appropriation remains annual, decision-makers are presented the total program cost, not simply a down payment. Second, steps in preparation induce agencies to consider alternate operating methods and to propose only those that require the least cost to achieve the desired results. Because agency administrators traditionally have incentives toward larger budgets for prestige or advancement, such steps are difficult to enforce. Third, program budgets often include some cost-benefit analysis of the resource use of proposed

---

[12]Arthur Smithies, "Conceptual Framework for the Program Budget," in David Novick, ed. *Program Budgeting,* 2nd ed. (New York: Holt, Rinehart & Winston, 1969), 42.

TABLE 5–3
Program-Budget Structure in the U.S. Department of Defense

Mission (program)
Strategic forces
General-purpose forces
Intelligence and communications
Airlift and sealift
Guard and reserve forces
Research and development
Central supply and maintenance
Training, medical, other general personnel activities
Administrative and associated activities
Support of other nations
Special operating forces
Appropriation title
Military personnel (including retired pay)
Operation and maintenance
Procurement
Research, development, testing, and evaluation
Military construction
Family housing
Revolving and management funds
Departments within Defense
Navy
Army
Air Force
Defense agencies, Office of Secretary of Defense, Joint Chiefs of Staff
Defense-wide

programs.[13] Programming combines costs for achieving particular objectives, so an important piece of the data needed for cost-benefit analysis is provided.

All these elements appeared in the federal planning-programming-budgeting system (PPBS) experiment, applied initially to the Department of Defense in 1961, expanded to other federal agencies in 1965, and officially terminated in 1971. Elements of that system remain in budget frameworks of many federal agencies and of many state and local governments.[14] The Department of Defense continues with a formal system, as shown in Table 5–3, renamed in 2003 the Planning Programming

[13]Cost-benefit analysis is discussed in Chapter 6.

[14]See Allen Schick, *Budget Innovation in the States* (Washington, D.C.: Brookings Institution, 1971), for a review of state use of program and performance structures. About thirty-five states have implemented modified PPBS at one time or another.

Budgeting Execution System (PPBES). The system provides a link between the missions or programs of the Department of Defense and the departments within Defense charged with delivery of those missions.

The functional classification required by the 1974 Congressional Budget and Impoundment Control Act provides a program format for federal expenditures that appears in the congressional budget resolution and in the president's budget, alongside the administrative, line-item classification. The functions frequently include more than a single department (the national defense function, for instance, encompasses activities of Defense and Energy Departments) and departments may have activities in more than a single function. The federal functional classifications are described in Appendix 5–1. Appendix 5–2 presents the United Nations classification of functions of government (COFOG), a functional classification that applies to services provided by all levels of government, not just the national functions of Appendix 5–1. This classification, because of its breadth, provides a good thinking template for any government developing a functional classification for its operations, and it serves as the basic template for making comparisons of government operations across countries.

As is characteristic of program budgets, the Federal functional classification cuts across agencies so that decision-makers may think about use of public resources to the advantage of the citizenry without regard for organizational boundaries. Figure 5–3 shows the extent to which functions are distributed to agencies and the extent to which agencies support multiple functions in the U.S. government. A Government Accountability Office (GAO) report describes the situation for fiscal 2003:

> Sometimes there is a "match" between a function and a department—for example, the Department of Transportation is associated almost exclusively with the Transportation function (400) and over 80 percent of spending within the Transportation function (400) is by the Department of Transportation. Sometimes, however, there is an imbalance between the importance of an agency in a mission area and the importance of the mission area within the department. For example, while almost all obligations in the Agriculture function (350) are by USDA [U.S. Department of Agriculture], that function represents only about 41 percent of the spending by the department. Over 40 percent of USDA's obligations are for the Income Security function (600).[15]

One classification focuses on resource allocation choices for the Federal government; the other focuses on establishing responsibility and accountability. Barring a reorganization to make functions (or programs) and agencies match, the sort of dual classification with a crosswalk between the two is critical for getting all that is expected from the budget process. Without an easy, quick, and understandable crosswalk, the function or program format yields numbers that are not usable by

[15]U.S. Government Accountability Office, *Federal Budget: Agency Obligations by Budget Function and Object Classification for Fiscal Year 2003,* GAO-04-834 (Washington, D.C.: GAO, 2004). The numbers in parentheses refer to function numbers in the classification system.

Figure 5–3

Federal Spending by Agency and Function: Multiple Agencies for Functions and Multiple Function for Agencies

	Budget function[a]																		
	National Defense (050)	International Affairs (150)	General Science, Space, and Technology (250)	Energy (270)	National Resources and Environment (300)	Agriculture (350)	Commerce and House Credit (370)	Transportation (400)	Community and Regional Development (450)	Education, Training, Employment, and Social Services (500)	Health (550)	Medicare (570)	Income Security (600)	Social Security (650)	Veterans Benefits and Services (700)	Administration of Justice (750)	General Government (800)	Net Interest (900)	Number of functions charged by agency
Executive branch																			
Department of Agriculture		●		●	●	●	●		●		●		●				●		9
Department of Commerce					●		●		●	●									4
Department of Defense	●	●			●						●		●		●		●		7
Department of Education										●						●			2
Department of Energy	●		●	●													●		4
Department of Health and Human Services										●	●	●	●				●		5
Department of Homeland Security	●				●			●	●		●		●			●	●		8
Department of Housing and Urban Development							●		●				●			●			4
Department of Justice	●	●														●			3
Department of Labor	●									●	●		●		●		●		6
Department of State		●			●								●						3
Department of Transportation	●							●											2
Department of Veterans Affairs															●				1
Department of the Interior					●				●	●	●						●		5
Department of the Treasury		●			●		●	●	●		●		●			●	●	●	10
Environmental Protection Agency					●														1
Executive Office of the President		●					●										●		3
General Services Administration							●										●		2
Independent Agencies	●	●		●	●	●	●	●	●	●	●		●		●	●	●		14
National Aeronautics and Space Administration			●					●		●									3
National Science Foundation	●		●																2
Nuclear Regulatory Commission				●															1
Office of Personnel Management											●		●				●		3
Postal Service							●												1
Small Business Administration							●		●										2
Social Security Administration													●	●	●				3
Number of executive agencies charging this function	8	7	3	4	9	2	9	5	8	7	9	1	11	1	5	6	12	1	
Judicial Branch													●			●			2
Legislative Branch		●					●			●		●	●			●	●		7
Number of agencies charging this function		1					1			1		1	2			2	1		
All	8	8	3	4	9	2	10	5	8	8	9	2	13	1	5	8	13	1	

SOURCE: U.S. Government Accountability Office, *Federal Budget: Agency Oblications by Budget Function and Object Classification for Fiscal Year 2003,* GAO-04-834 (Washington. D.C.: GAO. 2004) budget decision-makers, and choices continue to be made in the familiar setting of the traditional budget. That problem contributed heavily to the demise of the earlier federal PPBS. Computer spreadsheet and database programs make translation between classifications—from function or program to administrative-agency accounts, for instance—almost instantly possible.

Three problems with program budgets require special attention. First, many public services contribute to more than one public objective, and the best programmatic classification for them is not always apparent. Whatever choice is made will emphasize one set of policy choices at the expense of another. For example, federal expenditures on military academies might be attributed to higher-education elements or to defense objectives. The placement of that expenditure establishes which analysis it faces, so placement must depend on the most important current issues raised by the expenditure. It should be apparent that any long-maintained program structure produces the bureaucratic blindness associated with continued examination of the same issues from the same approach. Furthermore, difficult interrelationships among public programs remain. Thus, highway transportation activities may influence urban redevelopment or complicate environmental protection. These interrelationships can baffle any budget navigator.

Second, cost estimates for programs may be less meaningful for public decisions than imagined. There is no scientifically defensible method for allocating substantial joint agency costs or administrative overhead costs. Because most agencies work with several programs, many resources used by an agency are shared and not are clearly attributable to a single program. Furthermore, public decisions require concern for social implications—not simply money out of pocket—but program budgets still focus on agency cost alone. Thus, the program-cost data are unlikely to be directly usable for decision-making.

Third, programs cannot entirely displace departments to deliver all expectations from the budget process. This is because responsibility and accountability for performance and for funds must be assigned to an organizational unit. Programs cannot be accountable; departments (and the people in them) can. Hence, fiscal discipline, in the final analysis, requires a budget and appropriation structure beyond that provided by a program format.

Finally, program budgets may have little impact on decisions. Legislatures, lobbyists, and government departments have experience with the traditional budget format. Participants know where their allies are located and the location is in a department. All are familiar with that construction and have developed general guidelines for its analysis. New presentations require new guidelines and extra effort by all. Unless the major participants in the budget process actually want the improved presentation, it will be ignored in favor of the format to which they are accustomed.

A budget can be made more useful for decision-making without recategorizing all expenditure activities. Arranging budgets according to services or groups of services benefiting citizens or addressing some stated need can be a considerable improvement. Many modern budgets now are hybrids, bringing program and performance information together.

An Illustration of an Expenditure in Alternative Classifications

The difference that classification system makes may be shown in a simple illustration carried through in Figure 5–4. How might the salary of a teacher employed in a state correctional facility appear in traditional-, performance-, and program-budget formats? With a traditional budget, that salary would appear as a part of the personnel (wage and salary) line of the state Department of Corrections budget. It would thus compete for funds, in the first instance, within that department. Money received could well depend on how the governor and legislature viewed the overall prison system. If that budget were classified according to performance, that expenditure would appear as part of the cost of achieving a target number of departmental instruction hours. Again, competition for resources would be with other activities of that department. It would be distinguished, however, from activities not related to instruction. A program structure might classify that expenditure as a part of a human-developmentprogram, separating the expenditure from its link to incarceration and causing it to be considered with training and education activities. The salary expenditure is the same dollar amount, but the different budget classifications require different treatment to accommodate different budget purposes. The budget classification undoubtedly would influence the questions asked about the expenditure and, possibly, the size of its appropriation.

Figure 5–4
Salary Classification in Traditional, Performance, and Program Budgets

Morris Hall is employed by the Green Valley Correctional Facility as a teacher in the basic literacy program. His salary is $25,000 per year. Where would Mr. Hall's salary appear in different budget classifications? Follow the asterisk (*).

Traditional	Performance	Program
Department of Corrections	Department of Corrections	Human Resource Development
Green Valley Correctional Facility	Activity: Adult literacy	Service: Adult literacy
Personnel	Personnel*	Local
Director	Supplies	State facilities*
Clerical	Cost per student instructional hour	Service: Vocational education
Guards		
Instructors*	Activity: Incarceration	Protection of Persons and Property
Supplies and equipment		
Contractual services	Department of Highways	Provision of Safe and Speedy Transportation
Jackson State Correctional Facility		
Department of Highways		
Department of Education		

New Performance Budgeting: Focusing on Results/Outcomes

New performance budgeting continues the effort to move budget processes from an input focus to a focus on results or outcomes.[16] Traditional performance budgeting, as noted previously, attempts to budget according to the direct outputs or activities of government agencies. But these outputs are not the real reason for government's existence. Some illustrations are as follows:

1. **Public health agencies** should seek to vaccinate against childhood diseases not to get high vaccination counts but to reduce infant mortality and other consequences of those childhood diseases. The objective is healthy children, not lots of children having been run through a vaccination line.
2. **A manpower development agency** should be tested according to numbers of people placed in improved jobs that they keep, not according to how many people went through the job-training program.
3. **An environmental protection agency** should seek to improve ambient environmental conditions, which might not be associated with numbers of regulatory actions.

The idea of new performance budgeting is that the societal goal, the outcome or result, is what matters for government performance, not the direct output or activity of the agency. And certainly it is not what the government purchases (its inputs) that matter for the good of the citizenry. New performance or results-oriented budgeting intends to reorient the focus toward these outcomes. It is intended to be an approach to evidence-based decision-making. Coincidentally, the results a government achieves are probably of more interest to the citizenry than is internal government operations, no result orientation may be a way to get the public more involved in government.

The new performance/results-oriented budget logic is comparable to that of the private sector—auto companies manufacture cars to make a profit, not to buy materials to use in making cars (the focal point for traditional government budgets) nor even simply to sell cars, and satisfy their stockholders according to the size of that profit. The new performance budgeting looks toward the *result,* or *outcome,* of agency operations and accordingly tests agencies on results, not on how results are attained (i.e., not on input use or operational management). Its performance, result, or outcome orientation flips the input control focus of traditional budgets on its head. The ideal results-oriented performance budget would, following the pattern of private business, have sparse details on what the agency would purchase—the line-items would not be controlled—because control would be on what services the agency would provide. Agencies might have some focus on operational

[16]The logic of new performance budgeting appears under many different names, including entrepreneurial budgeting, results-oriented budgeting, mission budgeting, and outcome-based budgeting, among others.

outputs or tasks, for example, caseloads or miles of highway patrolled, but that would be for internal management, not for indicating agency performance success. Agencies would identify the outputs and outcomes to be produced by their programs, set performance targets and make budget requests based on that performance, and be accountable for those results without micromanagement of inputs or operations.

Of important influence on the development of performance budgeting was the "reinvention" movement. As David Osborne and Ted Gaebler write, "Cynicism about government runs deep within the American soul."[17] To break this cynicism, they propose a results-oriented budget system, so that lawmakers and the public would focus on the desirable services that government provides, thereby reinventing the entire thought process.[18] The system would hold governments accountable for results, would not appropriate to agencies for inputs, would reward agencies for cost-saving and entrepreneurial efforts to serve their clients (including shedding service responsibility if private provision or production were appropriate), and would take a long-term perspective in strategy development, cost analysis, and planning.[19] By focusing on results, governments could become more responsive to the interests of the citizenry; by allowing greater flexibility, governments could become more entrepreneurial and efficient in service delivery.

New performance budgeting integrates information on government outcome performance into the budget process and involves these principles:

1. **Objectives/strategic plan.** The agency should state what it is trying to accomplish that matters for the citizenry. In part, the agency develops a strategic plan (Sidebar 5–2, an outline of the Government Performance and Results Act of 1993 [GPRA], shows the requirements for federal agency strategic plans), but it must also consider why it exists in the first place. Annual performance plans and annual budgets are to be linked to the strategic plan, but the thinking about existence (and its justification) comes first.[20] The strategic plan should show how the agency intends to achieve results.

2. **Performance measures.** From that strategic plan must be developed measures that will gauge progress toward meeting these objectives. Performance measurement should provide the connection between the strategic plan and the results. The measures, however, are not to focus on agency activities, but

---

[17]David Osborne and Ted Gaebler, *Reinventing Government, How the Entrepreneurial Spirit Is Transforming the Public Sector* (Reading, Mass.: Addison-Wesley, 1992), xv.

[18]Osborne and Gaebler call the system "expenditure control budgeting:" The city council gives operating departments an expenditure limit; the council monitors departments against performance outcomes, not spending lines; and the council abstains from micromanagement of department operations. Departments may receive "profit sharing," in that they get to retain part of any end-of-year savings against the expenditure limit. *Reinventing Government,* 119–22.

[19]Critics correctly point out that what Osborne and Gaebler recommend is far from new. See Charles T. Goodsell, "Reinvent Government or Rediscover It?" *Public Administration Review* 53 (January/February 1998): 85–87. But it is difficult to complain about their conclusions about the failings of many traditional budget processes.

[20]The National Aeronautics and Space Administration states that the goal of the Space Science Program is to "chart the evolution of the universe from origin to destiny." Performance measures would likely not be easy to spin from this goal.

Sidebar 5–2
The Basic Elements of Government Performance and Results Act of 1993

GPRA seeks to reduce inefficiency and ineffectiveness in government programs by directing attention to agency performance and results. The act has three important elements:

A. Multi-year Strategic plans (3- to 5-year) that identify the fundamental mission of the agency, the general goals that would be used to accomplish the mission, and resource requirements consistent with the mission. Strategic plans are to be updated at least every 3 years. The act provides for the following required parts of the strategic plan:

> "(1) a comprehensive mission statement covering the major functions and operations of the agency;
> (2) general goals and objectives, including outcome-related goals and objectives, for the major functions and operations of the agency;
> (3) a description of how the goals and objectives are to be achieved, including a description of the operational processes, skills and technology, and the human, capital, information, and other resources required to meet those goals and objectives;
> (4) a description of how the performance goals included in the plan required by section 1115(a) of title 31 shall be related to the general goals and objectives in the strategic plan;
> (5) an identification of those key factors external to the agency and beyond its control that could significantly affect the achievement of the general goals and objectives; and
> (6) a description of the program evaluations used in establishing or revising general goals and objectives, with a schedule for future program evaluations." (Section 306 of Chapter 3 of Title 5 of *United States Code*)

B. Annual Performance plans that drive day-to-day operations. The plans include objective, quantitative, and measurable performance goals, measurable indicators to determine whether programs are meeting goals, and a summary of funding and staffing resources being used to achieve the goals.

C. Annual Performance Reports to be made 6 months after the end of the fiscal year to relevant committees and subcommittees for evaluating the agency record. The report is based on achievement of planned measurable performance indicators.

The intent was that these performance activities would link into a performance budget process.

on the agency's broader societal consequences. Budget processes focus on inputs (the resources purchased by the agency) or direct outputs (the agency's activities on tasks); the performance budget measures outcomes (the results or the extent to which agency activities have their intended effect). Executive budgets would include these planned performance standards, as would the approved appropriations. Table 5–4 illustrates the activity (direct output) to outcome shift and provides illustrations for several basic governmental functions. Some performance measures can be observed from existing social, economic, demographic, or health status data, but some may require new tests or surveys

Table 5–4
Activities (or Direct Outputs) or Outcomes (or Results)

The Congressional Budget Office highlights the difficult issue of measuring performance outcomes.

One of the most difficult tasks in measuring government performance is that of deciding on terminology. The concept of inputs is fairly easy to understand, and these measures do not differ very much from one program to another. In general, inputs represent the raw materials, such as personnel, building materials, and office equipment, that go into the delivery of government services. There is considerably more confusion between outputs and outcomes. In general, in order to be classified as an outcome measurement, the assessment must present information that enables the policymaker to determine how well a particular program is operating in relation to its goals. Measures of output, however, focus on the amount of work accomplished or on the quality of the processes used to accomplish that work.

Outputs are sometimes treated as ends in themselves. But the question of whether the work is done is very often distinct from the question of whether the work is achieving a particular purpose. For this reason, if the purpose of measuring performance is evaluating the results achieved by a program, outcome measures are superior to output measures.

The following table gives some examples of outcomes (or results) and direct outputs for a number of governmental functions.

Fire Department
Activities: inspections performed, fire calls answered, arson investigations performed, hours of education programs offered, property value protected in service area

Outcomes: ISO fire insurance rating, dollars of fire losses, number of fire-related injuries and fatalities, number of traffic accidents during fire runs, number of reported and unreported fires

Police Department
Activities: hours on patrol, responses to calls for assistance, crimes investigated by category, number of arrests

Outcomes: deaths, injuries, and property losses from crime, crime clearance rate

Elementary and Secondary Education
Activities: instructional days, students promoted or graduated

Outcomes: test score results, parent/student satisfaction ratings, percent of graduates employed

Public Health
Activities: number of persons served, number of vaccinations given, number of restaurant inspections, training program days

Outcome: mortality rates, morbidity rates, cases of infectious disease by category

Public Welfare
Activities: number of clients, number of clients according to types of assistance provided

Outcomes: former clients leaving welfare status

Solid Waste Management
Activities: waste collected and processed, residences served

Outcomes: proportion of streets rated as clean, incidence of vector-borne disease, citizen satisfaction rating, achievement of environmental standards

(continues)

Table 5–4
Activities (or Direct Outputs) or Outcomes (or Results) ***(continued)***

Tax Department
Activities: returns processed, processing times, delinquency rates

Outcomes: overall compliance rate, taxpayer complaint rates, measured uniformity of treatment of taxpayers

Environmental Protection and Management
Activities: permits granted, inspections performed

Outcomes: percent of state residents living where air meets government ambient air quality standards, percent of groundwater that meets drinking water standards, release and generation of solid waste as percent of baseline year

Municipal Sanitation
Activities: tons of refuse collected, miles of road cleaned, number of residential and commercial customers served

Outcomes: evaluation of street cleanliness measured by periodic visual investigation, citizen satisfaction surveys, general indicators of public health

Juvenile Justice
Activities: number of children in juvenile justice system, numbers by type of placement and variety of offense, worker caseload

Outcomes: juvenile justice recidivism rates, juvenile justice system clients leaving system for school or employment

to gauge performance.[21] Agencies face greater pressure in the budget process to show improvement in their performance results. And the focus is intended to be on performance outcomes, not performance outputs—not the number of passengers subjected to search by the Transportation Safety Administration, silver-haired grandmothers, infants, and all, but whether flying is safer from terrorist threats.

There are five critical principles in selecting outcome performance measures:

a. External focus. The measure should relate to the client or customer, not to internal procedures of the agency.
b. Truly measurable. It should be possible to gauge success or failure and whether performance is improving, deteriorating, or staying the same. Data from third parties are best, to avoid the danger of agency manipulation, and any client-satisfaction surveys should be done by third parties.

[21]The Health Care Financing Administration uses three principles to guide its national performance measurement strategy: measures should be consumer driven, measures and the collection tools used to obtain them should be in the public domain to assure broad access (and validation), and content and collection of measures should be standardized. These would be useful guides for any performance measurement process.

c. Outcome based. It should measure service delivery to the citizenry rather than impact within the entity.
d. Significance. The measurement should encompass the full scope of agency work so that a complete idea of success is portrayed.
e. Manageable. The number of measures should be no greater than necessary to cover the scope of agency operations. There should be no danger of user overload. For the integration of performance measurement and budgets, cost must be tied to performance, and the capacity for good costing is not limitless.

3. **Flexible execution.** Agencies, after appropriations are received, would be responsible for service delivery. They would not be constrained by the narrow control of how resources get used during budget execution (the details of spending) that is the hallmark of traditional accountability. Accountability would focus on outcomes, not expenditures. Both executive and legislative branches would need to agree on places and measures (points 1 and 2) for this flexibility. Agencies might also be allowed to retain at least some portion of unexpended funds for use in upcoming fiscal years, rather than following the traditional practice of having unspent funds returned to the general treasury, so that agencies would not face the "use it or lose it" choice.[22]

4. **Reporting.** At the end of the year, agency reports emphasize service outcomes with their financial reports. Audit and evaluation emphasize outcomes and de-emphasize details of how money was spend. Ideally, agencies would have received lump-sum appropriations, without any itemization about how the money is to be spent, so the resources utilization plan against which actual use would be tested would be largely aggregate in any case. The federal Chief Financial Officers Act of 1990 requires financial officers to develop and report *systematic measures of performance* for their agencies. At the state-local level, the Governmental Accounting Standard Board (GASB) seeks to have annual financial statements to include a *service efforts and accomplishments* (SEA) report. Both emphasize performance measurement in terms of outcomes.

The new performance budgeting brings features from both old performance- and program-budget formats. The attention to result or outcome shares the focus of program budgeting. The new format, however, does not pretend to cross agency lines to gather similar programs administratively housed in different organizations. The attention to performance measurement is common with old performance budgeting. That older measurement, however, concentrated on tasks, activities, or direct outputs, whereas the new attempts an outcome focus. In an important sense, the new approach melds ideas from older classification efforts.

Early and influential applications of new performance budgeting came at the local level: Sunnyvale, California; Dayton, Ohio; and Phoenix, Arizona, were among the leaders. Among the states, Missouri, Texas, Louisiana, and Virginia were early to make extensive use of performance information to shape budget

[22]A strong internal control structure is necessary if agencies are to have greater flexibility over their finances. A strong control structure frees auditors to focus on performance, rather than financial, issues.

office decisions and operations; most other states use performance measures to support internal management (budget implementation or execution) but do not use the measures more widely. Performance measures for individual agencies appear in the budget documents of well over half the states and many cities, although the extent to which responsibility and control focuses on these measures, as opposed to the input categories, is generally limited.[23] Systems often continue to measure direct outputs (or activities), not outcomes.

The state of Texas has gone as far as any government in integrating outcome performance into budget planning, adoption, and execution. Figure 5–5, a portion of the appropriation act providing funds for the state Commission for the Blind, illustrates the way in which this integration has occurred. This appropriation is part

Figure 5–5
Illustration of New Performance Budget: State of Texas Commission for the Blind

	For the Years Ending August 31, 2004	August 31, 2005
A. Goal: Independent Living To assist Texans who are blind or visually impaired to live as independently as possible consistent with their capabilities.		
Outcome (Results/Impact): Percent of Consumers Whose Dependent Living Risk Was Diminished	98%	98%
A.1.1. Strategy: Independent Living Skills To provide a program of developing independent living skills.	$2,356,320	$2,652,390
Output (Volume): Number of Consumers Served	4,730	4,890
Efficiencies: Average Cost per Consumer Served	552	600
A.2.1. Strategy: Habilitative Services For Children To provide habilitative services to blind and visually impaired children.	$2,579,469	$2,637,629
Output (Volume): Number of Children Receiving Habilitative Services	3,062	2,946
Efficiencies: Average Cost per Child Served	933	990
A.2.2. Strategy: Blindness Education Blindness Education, Screening and Treatment Program.	$619,928	$619,928
Total, Goal A: Independent Living	$5,555,717	$5,909,947

SOURCE: State of Texas, *General Appropriations Act, 2004–2005 Biennium*

[23]Melkers and Willoughby find that all but three states require strategic planning regarding agency mission, goals, and objectives, and a process that requires measurable data on program outcomes. See "The State of the States: Performance-Based Budgeting Requirements in 47 out of 50," *Public Administration Review,* 58 (January/February 1998): 66–79.

of Article II Health and Human Services of the Act. The Commission has three goals identified in the act: Independent Living (presented here), Maintain Employment (for the blind and visually impaired), and Indirect Administration. Each goal has its own appropriation, and attached with the appropriation are outputs, outcomes, and strategies, all shown in the figure. In the performance logic, (a) the goal sets forth what the agency plans to achieve, (b) the output establishes performance measures to count services provided by the agency (with unit cost information to gauge technical efficiency), (c) the outcome sets a measurable target (diminished risk of dependent living for the client population) in meeting the goal, and (d) the strategy which indicates the actions to be taken by the agency in meeting the goal. The appropriation establishes funds to be used by the agency and an expectation of performance to be expected from those funds. Because Texas uses a biennial budget process, all data are for 2 years.

The federal government has been slower, but there are strong currents toward performance budgeting approaches.[24] The Chief Financial Officers Act of 1990 requires financial officers of federal agencies to develop and report systematic measures of performance for their agencies and, even stronger, the GPRA (Public Law 103-62) directs agencies to develop strategic plans, to measure their performance, and, at least tentatively, to work toward performance budgets. In this context, performance budgeting means the process of linking results to budget levels, not the cost of activities in the traditional performance budgets.[25]

Some Challenges for New Performance Budgeting

Moving the budgetary focus away from an input orientation seems to be getting it right for making public decisions. Nevertheless, there are some crucial concerns in this important transition:

1. **The need for agreement on what is to be accomplished.** What agencies are supposed to do is not always clear. Managers have to respond to elected executives, legislative bodies, and the general public. And programs often have multiple and conflicting objectives and disagreements about the relative importance of the objectives. Without strong consensus about agency objectives, establishing performance measurement and budget systems based on those measures will be difficult, and legislatures will continue to insist on riders to constrain agency operations. Furthermore, there has to be agreement on the need to spend the money necessary to measure performance. Measurement is a nagging problem. An evaluation of the Next Steps Initiative, a program in Britain to hold agency heads directly accountable for agency performance in exchange for greater flexibility in operation, noted that deciding what to measure is a challenge:

> [P]erformance measures frequently focus on what agencies can measure, rather than on what is most important in assessing performance. For example, on enforcement agency

[24]Other countries have moved more rapidly than the U.S. government in performance-oriented budget reform. The leaders include Australia, Canada, Great Britain, and New Zealand.

[25]U.S. General Accounting Office, *Performance Budgeting, Past Initiatives Offer Insights for GPRA Implementation,* GAO/AIMD-97-46 (Washington, D.C.: General Accounting Office, 1997).

had established a performance measure to count the total number of enforcement actions. However, the agency had no information about how many infractions actually occurred, so the agency did not know to what extent, if at all, its enforcement actions contributed to reducing illegalities. Further complicating the determination of what to measure is the fact that some targets, such as efficiency and quality, may even be in conflict with one another, requiring a careful balance.[26]

As a pilot agency under GPRA, the Internal Revenue Service (IRS) developed strategic goals and performance measures to guide their operations. The IRS sought to increase its collection performance to at least 90 percent of total taxes due through a mix of increased voluntary compliance and enforcement. It also sought public satisfaction with conduct of the IRS in terms of ethical behavior, fairness, and uniformity of application of tax laws. The agency proceeded with aggressive pursuit of these objectives, and soon congressional hearings showed dissatisfaction with zealous efforts to improve compliance and media accounts of taxpayer harassment. The IRS abandoned its performance measures.[27] Now it is working with "balanced measures" to guide its work: customer satisfaction (provide accurate and professional services to internal and external customers in a courteous, timely manner), employee satisfaction (create an enabling environment for employees by providing quality leadership, adequate training, and effective support services), and business results (generate a productive quantity of work in a quality manner and provide meaningful outreach to all customers). With these measures, it is hard to know that the IRS is actually a tax collection enterprise! So much for the value of precision in defining missions, goals, and performance, at least for tax collectors.

Experience with new performance budgeting has taught that all stakeholders—the executive branch, the legislature, the citizenry, and community leaders—need to accept the measures through an open discussion process. Where feasible, citizen discussions can be helpful as part of a movement toward greater transparency in government.

2. **Performance budgets do not cross agencies.** Outcome measures give minimal guidance in comparisons among agencies, in other words, in answering the traditional budget allocation question "how much to agency A, and how much to agency B?" There is no standard performance measure or yardstick that makes sense for all agencies, the causal link between agency effort and performance outcome differs dramatically among agencies, and the ease of measuring outcomes varies widely among agencies. The results orientation can give guidance within each department, but government budgets have to allocate between departments, not just within. For example, results orientation in Transportation and results orientation in Natural Resources does not help with

[26]J. Christopher Mihm, "Performance-Based Organizations, Lessons from the British Next Steps Initiative," Testimony before the Subcommittee on Government Management, Information and Technology of the House Committee on Government Reform and Oversight, GAO/T-GGD-97-151 (Washington, D.C.: GPO, 1993).

[27]Brian Friel, "IRS Learns Results Act Lesson," *GovExec.com Daily Briefing,* 16 September 1998. (www.govexec.com/dailyfed/0998/091698b1.htm)

resource allocation choices between Transportation and Natural Resources—and failure to achieve results in Transportation is as likely to signal a need for better management of existing resources in Transportation as it is to signal a need for a reduction in those resources. Simply taking funds from agencies that fail to meet performance targets and giving the funds to those that do makes no sense. Suppose, for instance, that the Department of Homeland Security did not meet its targets while the National Endowment for the Arts (NEA) did. Would it be reasonable to move funds between agencies on that basis? Or would it be reasonable to continue to pay attention to basic national priorities, which likely still rank homeland security above the programs of the NEA? Should funds for homeland security decrease, or should they increase, based on the missed performance target?

3. **Cost must be tracked.** Government accounting systems need to provide cost information that can be linked to outputs or activities that generate particular outcomes. Decisions need appropriate measures of outcomes that can be linked outputs that track to appropriate measures of input (or resource cost). Even with better tracking, including the use of ABC, a fair amount of the cost of government—policy formation, information technology, general administration, for instance—is not associated with any particular activity and cannot fairly be assigned.[28] And some costs are fixed and will not be reduced if a program is reduced or eliminated. Will the cost of having the mayor around be reduced if the curbside recycling program, toward which the mayor devoted some time, is eliminated?

4. **Responsibility without control.** Agencies find results-oriented goals to be difficult to accept because they correctly understand that many measured performance outcomes may be outside their control. They do not want to be held responsible for objectives that they can only influence. They prefer to focus on activities or outputs because these can be controlled. Until agencies, budget offices, legislatures, and the public can come to an understanding on what results agencies can really be responsible for, the movement toward results orientation will be slow. For example, diligent effort by a local job-development agency can control the number of trainees run through its seminars, but many environmental conditions—especially overall economic conditions—determine how many of those graduates end up in lasting employment. Great effort by local schools may produce dismal educational results if parents and the community do not cooperate in the learning process. Agencies are reluctant to be responsible for objectives that they cannot fully control. And no participants in the process are likely to pay much real attention to measured performance unless they have an incentive to do so, that is, unless budget decisions are actually made on the basis of the performance outcome measures.

5. **Trust and no micromanagement.** New performance budgeting requires a different relationship between operating agencies and the legislatures. If the

[28]Retirement, health insurance, capital expenditure, and similar costs can and should be tracked to their source agency programs. But this involves better tracking, not allocation of the unallocable.

agency is to be flexible in its service delivery and to be responsible for results instead of input use, then the legislature must leave it alone. It cannot dictate which installations it is to close (the Defense Department and Congress, for instance, do not agree on which military bases—inputs to the provision of national security—are redundant to national security at the level envisioned in recent appropriations) and cannot place other restrictions on how the agency uses its resources. Those are input-oriented requirements, the antithesis of a results orientation. Some financial controls need to be relaxed and agencies need the flexibility to reallocate funds freely. It is sometimes suggested that, because elected officials find micromanagement hard to resist, they ought not be provided line-item expenditure information at all. It is not at all clear that the advantages of flexibility can accrue unless there is considerable trust between branches of government.

6. **Refocused Audit.** Audit can no longer focus on financial detail. Agencies would be responsible for the sum appropriated, but the detailed use of those appropriations, within the normal laws of financial propriety, would no longer be an oversight concern. Attention would be directed to performance measurement, achievement of outcome expectations, and audit of the performance measurement and reporting process, not to the details of how money was spent. However, the need for accountability means that the appropriation must be made to the agency—ideally, agencies would be accountable for appropriated sums of money and for agreed performance measures, but for no other expenditure details.

7. **Information Overload.** When performance measurement becomes an element in the budget process, large quantities of information are produced. Experience in the states shows that decision-makers become overloaded with the details and find it difficult to locate what would be useful to them. This potential overload means that it is critical to have a distillation process to outline and summarize the most important elements for the decision-makers. And an effort must be made to limit the measures that are collected and reported to a manageable and useful number. This again supports the need for stakeholder agreement on what performance measures count as accomplishments. Not only does it focus the discussion but it also reduces information overload.

8. **Outcome Measurement.** In practice, outcome measurement is not easy for all governmental agencies, and many units eventually resort to output, not outcome, indicators. Frequently, client satisfaction surveys are part of the measurement process to gauge the quality of service provided.[29] In general, an outcome orientation increases the administrative expense, because some outcome measures are unlikely to emerge from the normal flow of agency operations.

---

[29]Some governments, both in the United States and internationally, conduct citizen "report card" surveys of satisfaction of particular public services. Along with being an element in performance budget processes, they also contribute to campaigns for more open governance, accountability, and control of corruption.

Every agency dreads the prospect of more data collection. And there are questions of interpretation. For instance, are lower findings on tax audits to be taken as evidence of audit agency negligence or of the taxing authority's diligence in inducing taxpayers to pay without audit? Are low arrest rates evidence of little crime or poor police work?

Perhaps the most basic concern of all, however, is the need for honest measurement. When appropriations are at stake, the performance measures are critical, and when the measures are self-reported, the danger of manipulation is high. In this circumstance, an external verification of reporting is necessary. In Texas, the State Auditor's Office does periodic reviews to determine whether agencies have adequate systems for collecting performance measures and whether measures are reported accurately.[30] Not all reports are accurate. For example, outstanding outcome performance in some Texas school districts in the late 1990s to early 2000s appears to have been the product of data manipulation, rather than actual performance.[31] When unaudited, self-reported information becomes high-stakes for agency budgets and for administrators of agencies, the danger of data manipulation becomes great.

There is much optimism about what can be gained from the new performance budgeting and the focusing of budget decisions on results. But experience indicates a need for some wariness. The PPBS experiment in the 1960s and the zero-based budget (ZBB) system of the 1970s (see the discussion of ZBB in Case 5–2) were results-oriented systems, as were various efforts at establishing Management by Objective (MBO) systems in government.[32] None brought lasting systematic reform in how governments budget, although each experiment left some positive residual. The new results-oriented budget focus has brought revisions in how all levels of government develop and present their budgets, vastly greater attention to measurement, testing, and citizen satisfaction surveys, and, most important, greater focus on outcomes or results. Whether much will change, in terms of real government performance and allocation of budget resources, remains an open question. As Hilton and Joyce observe, ". . . the development of better performance and cost information can itself spur greater attention to performance, even in places where an input focus has been ascendant. Transparency concerning the relationship between funding and results can shine a light on practices that result in failing to allocate resources toward desired societal ends."[33]

---

[30]U.S. Government Accountability Office, *Performance Budgeting: States' Experience Can Inform Federal Efforts,* GAO-05-215 (Washington, D.C.: U.S. GAO, 2005).

[31]Michael Dobbs, "Education 'Miracle' Has a Math Problem," *Washington Post* 8 November 2003: A1; and Diana Jean Schemo and Ford Fessenden, "Gains in Houston Schools: How Real Are They?" *New York Times* 3 December 2003.

[32]U.S. General Accounting Office, Performance Budgeting, Past Initiatives Offer insights for GPRA Implementation, GAO/AIMD-97-46 (Washington, D.C.: General Accounting Office, 1997).

[33]Rita M. Hilton and Philip G. Joyce, "Performance Information and Budgeting in Historical and Comparative Perspective," in B. Guy Peters and Jon Pierre, eds., *Handbook of Public Administration* (London: Sage Publications, 2003), 411.

Federal Integration of Performance and Budgeting: Budget and Performance Integration Initiative and the Program Assessment Rating Tool

The objective of an integration of performance measurement and budgeting has been a major element of President George W. Bush's agenda to improve the management and performance of the federal government. This agenda has built upon GPRA requirements to create the Budget and Performance Integration (BPI) initiative that has shaped the federal budget process since the fiscal 2003 budget. That document claimed to move toward reporting on the relative effectiveness of federal spending and to link program performance to spending levels. "It asks not merely 'How much?'; it endeavors to explain 'How well?'"[34] Although GPRA had agencies developing strategic plans and annual plans, they were not integrated into the budget. BPI seeks to take the next step. Overall, the initiative has a results orientation and a zero-based philosophy, and expects federal programs to bear the burden of proof in demonstrating that they are achieving results in the most effective and efficient way. The specific objectives of the BPI initiative are, as outlined in the fiscal 2006 budget, an "increasing accountability, effectiveness, and efficiency—implementing plans designed to improve the management and performance of programs; (b) investing in high pay-off or high priority activities—focusing on programs that can achieve demonstrably greater results for the same or less cost; and (c) improving program design—developing, enacting, and implementing legislative or other proposals to fix flaws identified through the Program Assessment Rating Tool (PART) that impede performance."[35] It seeks to link requested resources to strategic and programmatic outcomes, to shift focus from expense items to resource allocation based on program goals and measured results, to identify full costs of program activities to link them to goals, and, overall, to move beyond inputs and outputs to outcomes.

A critical element of the President's Management Agenda (PMA) is to make the federal government more results oriented. Overall, there are five key management initiative areas in the PMA: strategic management of human capital, competitive sourcing, improved financial performance, electronic government, and budget and performance integration. The areas are scored according to a "red-yellow-green" indicator system, in an effort to collapse a number of complex judgements into a single factor for more straightforward decision-making. "Green" means the agency has fully achieved all goals for the particular initiative, "yellow" indicates intermediate achievement, and "red" means that the agency has at least one deficiency. The idea of the scorecard is to hold agencies accountable.[36]

---

[34]Executive Office of the President, Office of Management and Budget, *Budget of the United States Government, Fiscal 2003* (Washington, D.C.: U.S. Government Printing Office, 2002): 5.

[35]Executive Office of the President, Office of Management and Budget, *Analytical Perspectives, Budget of the United States Government, Fiscal Year 2006* (Washington, D.C.: U.S. Government Printing Office, 2005): 2.

[36]Since the scorecard system was introduced with the fiscal 2003 budget, the number of green indicators has increased significantly (among the twenty-six departments and independent agencies, the tally went from one green in financial management and no greens in budget and performance integration in fiscal 2003 to eight greens in financial management and nine greens in budget and performance integration for fiscal 2007. "Getting to green" is a concern of all agencies.

The system establishes the criteria for the scores on each indicator. For "Budget and Performance Intergration," the indicators for an agency "red" are the following:

> Senior agency managers do not have a regular process for considering financial and performance information when making decisions regarding the management of Agency programs;
>
> Strategic plans contain too many goals and objectives to provide a clear focused statement of Agency priorities. Performance measures included in annual budget and performance documents do not meet the standards of the PART;
>
> Performance appraisal plans do not link to agency mission, goals, and outcomes, effectively differentiate between various levels of performance, or provide consequences based on performance;
>
> Does not have a systematic way to estimate the full cost of achieving performance goals reported in budget and performance documents; OR
>
> Agency does not consistently use PART ratings to justify funding requests, management actions, and legislative proposals. More than 50 percent of agency programs receive a Results Not Demonstrated rating for more than two years in a row.[37]

The indicators for an agency "green" are the following:

> Senior agency managers meet at least quarterly to examine reports that integrate financial and performance information that covers all major responsibilities of the Department. Agency demonstrates improvement in program performance and efficiency in achieving results;
>
> Strategic plans contain a limited number of outcome-oriented goals and objectives. Annual budget and performance documents incorporate measures identified in the PART and focus on the information used in the senior management report described in the first criterion;
>
> Has performance appraisal plans and awards programs for all SES [Senior Executive Service] and managers, and more than 60 percent of agency positions that effectively link to agency mission, goals, and outcomes; hold employees accountable for results appropriate to their level of responsibility; differentiate between various levels of performance; and provide consequences based on performance. The agency is also working to include all agency employees under such systems;
>
> Reports the full cost of achieving performance goals accurately in budget and performance documents and can accurately estimate the marginal cost (+/– 10 percent) of changing performance goals;
>
> Has at least one efficiency measure for all PART ed programs; AND
>
> Uses PART evaluations to direct program improvements, and PART ratings and performance information are used consistently to justify funding requests, management actions, and legislative proposals. Less than 10 percent of agency programs receive a Results Not Demonstrated rating for more than two years in a row.[38]

---

[37]Scorecard Standards (www.whitehouse.gov/results/agenda/standards.pdf)
[38]*Ibid.* There are similar indicators for each of the other four management initiatives.

The indicators are clearly driven by a desire to integrate outcome performance in the development and review of budgets. They also are concerned about the extent to which credible linkages are made between funding and performance and about including all costs for programs. Developing true and full costs for programs involves two principal efforts: making sure that agency account structures are aligned with the programs of the agency, and making sure that agency costs include pension and retiree health benefits (and, eventually, capital asset and support service costs). The performance elements are critically driven by PART.

The Office of Management and Budget (OMB) developed PART to produce the performance to budget link and to answer the critical performance question. Each program that a department operates is subject to PART evaluation according to four weighted sections: Program Purpose and Design (20 percent weight), Strategic Planning (10 percent), Program Management (20 percent), and Program Results/Accountability (50 percent). The score in each section is based on answers to a number of key questions about the program. The scoring questions for Strategic Planning follow.

Strategic Planning

Does the program have a limited number of long-term performance measures that focus on outcomes and meaningfully reflect the purpose of the program?

Does the program have ambitious targets and time frames for its long-term measures?

Does the program have a limited number of specific annual performance goals that can demonstrate progress toward achieving the program's long-term goals?

Does the program have baselines and ambitious targets for its annual measures?

Do all partners (grantees, sub-grantees, contractors, cost-sharing partners, and other government partners) commit to and work toward the annual and/or long-term goals of the program?

Are independent evaluations of sufficient scope conducted on a regular basis or as needed to support program improvements and evaluate effectiveness and relevance to the problem, interest, or need?

Are budget requests explicitly tied to accomplishment of the annual and long-term performance goals, and are the resource needs presented in a complete and transparent manner in the program's budget?

Has the program taken meaningful steps to address its strategic planning deficiencies?[39]

Each question is answered "yes" or "no," with a brief explanation of the answer and a short presentation of the evidence upon which the answer is based. The set of answers to these questions, again weighted, becomes the score for the section and thus the score for the overall program is developed. Figure 5–6 shows the scor-

[39]These questions, plus those from the other sections of PART, may be found in Executive Office of the President, Office of Management and Budget, *Analytical Perspectives, Fiscal Year 2006* (Washington, D.C.: U.S. Government Printing Office, 2005): 17–18.

Figure 5–6
PART Performance Measurement Scoring Illustration, Border Patrol, Fiscal 2006

		Section Scores				Rating
Program:	Border Patrol					
Agency:	Department of Homeland Security	1	2	3	4	Results Not
Bureau:	Bureau of Customers and Border Protection	100%	63%	86%	47%	Demonstrated
Types(s):	Direct Federal					
2.7	Are Budget requests explicitly tied to accomplishment of the annual and long-term performance goals, and are the resource needs presented in a complete and transparent manner in the program's budget?	Answer: NO		Question Weight: 12%		
Explanation:	Border Patrol resource requests are tied to the annual and long-term performance goals of the program as required by OMB Circular A-11 in the preparation of the annual budget to Congress.					
Evidence:	Agency budget requests to OMB. Border Patrol requests funding in direct support of its National Strategic Plan. Funding is required for implementation each phase of the strategy. Resources require the deployment of additional personnel, surveillance systems (cameras and sensors), tactical infrastructure and equipment. These areas are often specifically line itemed by Congressional language for funding of the Border Patrol's program needs. Reports to Congress on Border Patrol hiring and status of ISIS program spending. ISIS deployments occurred as planned in the financial report. Border Patrol met hiring goals as approved by Congress with the appropriated funds. Budget requests for Border Patrol activities do not make clear the impact of funding on expected performance and do not report all direct and indirect costs needed to attain performance results. We still maintain that the Budget requests for Border Patrol do not make clear the impact of funding on expected performance. They also do not report direct and indirect costs.					

ing, explanation, and evidence for one question concerning strategic planning for border patrol, part of the Bureau of Customs and Border Protection, an agency in the Department of Homeland Security from the fiscal 2006 process.

The answers here regarding linking budget and performance depend on the program budget submission by the Department of Homeland Security. Its program budget submission to Congress identifies seven Strategic Goals:

1. **Awareness:** Identify and understand threats, assess vulnerabilities, determine potential impacts and disseminate timely information to our homeland security partners and the American public.
2. **Prevention:** Detect, deter, and mitigate threats to our homeland.
3. **Protection:** Safeguard our people and their freedoms, critical infrastructure, property and the economy of our nation from acts of terrorism, natural disasters, and other emergencies.
4. **Response:** Lead, manage, and coordinate the national response to acts of terrorism, natural disasters, and other emergencies.
5. **Recovery:** Lead national, state, local, and private sector efforts to restore services and rebuild communities after acts of terrorism, natural disaster, or other emergencies.
6. **Service:** Serve the public effectively by facilitating lawful trade, travel, and immigration.

7. **Organizational Excellence:** Value our most important resource, our people. Create a culture that promotes a common identity, innovation, mutual respect, accountability, and teamwork to achieve efficiencies, effectiveness, and operational synergies.[40]

For each Strategic Goal, there is a discussion of Objectives, Means, and Strategies, followed by presentation of Performance Goals associated with the objectives. Explicit measures for gauging accomplishment are then presented for previous fiscal years, current year, and the budget year, along with the costs associated with the Performance Goal. Figure 5–7 illustrates this for a Homeland Security Performance Goal that has U.S. Customs and Border Protection as its lead organization.[41]

PART scores are reported for each agency and each program, and they become one factor in developing the president's budget proposal. They are intended to give insights into how the federal government can improve what it does for the citizenry. They are also intended to generate program improvements through recommendations made in the PART process.

Much of the process, despite seeking outcomes, remains performance oriented according to internal standards, not according to successes in delivering for the American citizenry. PART and its components directly apply to work by agency managers and OMB staff. And, although Congress receives performance documentation at both the authorization and appropriation levels, those ideas have not yet been reflected in appropriation bills. The president's budget presentation looks more like a glossy corporate annual report with colors and pictures—with a good dose of marketing spin—than a document for budget and finance geeks (who quickly move to the *Analytical Perspectives, Appendix,* and *Historical Tables* volumes for what they care about), but whether this public display makes much of an impact on the public or the media is unclear at best. However, the integration initiative has moved the focus of budget development aggressively toward attention to agency performance in ways it never has been focused before. A GAO study of this federal performance budgeting effort found OMB and agency officials in support of the results orientation with greater attention to strategic plans and results, more complete information on the association between budget and performance, and greater agency flexibility and incentives for efficiency and effectiveness. However, some agencies saw some greater complications for resource management, and congressional appropriations committee staff objected to the loss of object class and workload information with the new presentations.[42] The system also provides an almost overwhelming number of measures and scores, making it difficult to track down the ones that matter most for the common good of the citizenry.

For the system to have its desired results on government decisions and management, both Congress and the executive branch must agree on information flows

---

[40]U.S. Department of Homeland Security, *Performance Budget Overview, Fiscal Year 2006, Congressional Budget Justification* Available online at www.dhs.gov/interweb/assetlibrary/Budget_PBO_FY2006.pdf.

[41]Notice that, strictly speaking, some measures are more of the nature of outputs than outcomes. This is normal for the reality of outcome oriented budgets.

[42]U.S. Government Accountability Office, *Performance Budgeting: Efforts to Restructure Budgets to Better Align Resources with Performance,* GAO-05-117SP (Washington, D.C.: GAO, 2005).

Figure 5–7
Illustration for Performance Goals from Department of Homeland Security Performance Budget Fiscal 2006

Performance goal: Improve the targeting, screening, and apprehension of high-risk international cargo and travelers to prevent terrorist attacks, while providing processes to facilitate the flow of safe and legitimate trade and travel.

Measure: Compliance rate in the Air Passenger Environment (percent of travelers compliant).	Fiscal Year	FY 2003	FY 2004	FY 2005	FY 2006
	Target	None	99.2%	99.3%	99.2%
	Actual	None	99.2%	N/A	N/A
Measure: Compliance rate in the Vehicle Passenger Environments (percent of travelers compliant).	Fiscal Year	FY 2003	FY 2004	FY 2005	FY 2006
	Target	None	99.9%	99.9%	99.9%
	Actual	None	99.9%	N/A	N/A
Measure: Number of pounds of cocaine seized (thousands of pounds at the ports of entry).	Fiscal Year	FY 2003	FY 2004	FY 2005	FY 2006
	Target	None	77.8	43.1	43.6
	Actual	None	44.6	N/A	N/A
Measure: Number of pounds of marijuana seized (thousands of pounds at the ports of entry).	Fiscal Year	FY 2003	FY 2004	FY 2005	FY 2006
	Target	None	873.8	743	750
	Actual	None	652.8	N/A	N/A
Measure: Advanced Passenger Information System (APIS) Data Sufficiency Rate. (Percent)	Fiscal Year	FY 2003	FY 2004	FY 2005	FY 2006
	Target	None	94.2%	99.1%	99.2%
	Actual	None	98%	N/A	N/A
Measure: International air passengers in compliance with agricultural quarantine regulations (percent compliant).	Fiscal Year	FY 2003	FY 2004	FY 2005	FY 2006
	Target	None	97%	97%	97%
	Actual	None	97%	N/A	N/A
Measure: Border vehicle passengers in compliance with agricultural quarantine regulations (percent compliant).	Fiscal Year	FY 2003	FY 2004	FY 2005	FY 2006
	Target	None	96%	96.4%	96.4%
	Actual	None	96.0%	N/A	N/A
Measure: Number of pounds of heroin seized (thousands of pounds at the ports of entry).	Fiscal Year	FY 2003	FY 2004	FY 2005	FY 2006
	Target	None	3.9	3.5	3.5
	Actual	None	2.8	N/A	N/A
Measure: Number of foreign mitigated examinations by category.	Fiscal Year	FY 2003	FY 2004	FY 2005	FY 2006
	Target	None	None	10,000	14,000
	Actual	None	2416	N/A	N/A
Measure: Percent of worldwide U.S. destined containers processed through Container Security Initiative (CSI) ports.	Fiscal Year	FY 2003	FY 2004	FY 2005	FY 2006
	Target	None	None	68%	78%
	Actual	None	48%	N/A	N/A
Measure: Compliance rate for Customs-Trade Partnership Against Terrorism (C-TPAT) members with the established C-TPAT security guidelines.	Fiscal Year	FY 2003	FY 2004	FY 2005	FY 2006
	Target	None	None	98.0%	98.0%
	Actual	None	None	N/A	N/A
Measure: Average CBP exam reduction ratio for Customs-Trade Partnership Against Terrorism (C-TPAT) member importers compared to Non-C-TPAT importers.	Fiscal Year	FY 2003	FY 2004	FY 2005	FY 2006
	Target	None	None	3.5 times less	3.5 times less
	Actual	None	None	N/A	N/A
Measure: Percent of sea containers examined using Non-Intrusive Inspection technology (NII).	Fiscal Year	FY 2003	FY 2004	FY 2005	FY 2006
	Target	None	5%	5%	5.25%
	Actual	None	5.2%	N/A	N/A
Measure: Percent of truck and rail containers examined using Non-Intrusive Inspection (NII) technologies.	Fiscal Year	FY 2003	FY 2004	FY 2005	FY 2006
	Target	None	10%	10%	10.25%
	Actual	None	26.2%	N/A	N/A
Program: Border security inspections and trade facilitation at POE's.	$ Thousands	None	2,206,493	2,269,685	2,396,306
Lead organization: United States Customs and Border Protection	FTE	None	14,985	15,456	15,585

DHS strategic objectives supported and % allocation of activities: 2.1 – 21% 2.2 – 21.0% 2.3 – 21.0% 6.4 – 37.0%

and how the system will work. Although the president is charged with developing and executing the budget, no programs are put in place and no funds are available for delivery of programs unless Congress approves them. Currently, Congress lags behind the executive branch in integrating performance information in its budget work. The test of the system is the extent to which deliberations about the way public programs work to achieve national goals is reshaped. The integration of performance information into the budget process will not remove controversy and debate from choices about government expenditure because the issues are about competing uses for limited resources and different people have different priorities. But none can doubt the importance of the effort and that the effort can help inform the discussions.

Conclusion

Budget classifications away from the traditional try to improve the rationality of budget choices. None provide the complete solution to the budget problem—it is wrong to expect any system to provide judgments that must be made by people. Each system, however, tries to organize information so that decision-makers can make choices in a reasonable fashion. Each system arranges information in a more usable way than do traditional budgets and, in varying degrees, seeks to increase the decision-makers' flexibility. People will continue to make budget decisions, and that is appropriate; the useful organization of information and the erection of reasonable organizational incentives are the roles of budget systems.[43] Each of the structures described here can represent significant improvements over the traditional, line-item, administrative-unit structure—if executive, bureaucratic, and legislative branches choose to use them. Reluctance to participate on the part of any group can doom any structure. And there is no magic bullet that will replace budget judgment and budget politics with science. Furthermore, government officials are not likely to find for agency evaluation a pubic sector equivalent to the easily definable, measurable, and widely accepted indicators of performance that private-sector profitability comparisons afford. What budget classification reform can accomplish is the provision of performance data and other information when political decisions are made. Performance itself will not and should not determine the allocations.

---

[43]Embedded in most efforts to reclassify and reform government budgeting is the assumption that there is a clear understanding of the link between government spending and results or outcomes. This confidence is misplaced if it is cast too broadly. In the government-service area subjected to the greatest amount and intensity of study, primary and secondary education, Eric Hanushek's extensive and intensive review of 147 separately published studies leads him to the conclusion that "there is a consistency to the results: there appears to be no strong or systematic relationship between school expenditures and student performance. This is the case when expenditures are decomposed into underlying determinants and when expenditures are considered in the aggregate." Eric A. Hanushek, "The Economics of Schooling: Production and Efficiency in Public Schools," Journal of Economic Literature 24 (September 1986): 1162.

Chapter 5 Questions and Exercises

1. The following sections are narrative from the 1973–1974, 1974–1975 budget request for the South Carolina Department of Social Services. They are part of a nicely prepared and presented line-item budget that requests funds for organizational units.

   Goals

   In our opinion there are only two reasonable goals for any governmentally supported welfare or social service agency—these are (1) to assist the citizenry in achieving through self-sufficiency a living standard which eliminates the need for public support and (2) to meet the needs for societal service within society and the family unit without the public provision thereof.

   Means of Achieving These Goals

   These are generational goals. It is not feasible this year or this decade to achieve "self-sufficiency" for aged, blind, or disabled adults or dependent children who have insufficient income to provide the basic necessities of life. Further, as technological changes occur the demand for unskilled labor decreases. It becomes increasingly difficult for an illiterate or semi-educated person to obtain employment paying wages sufficient to enable him/her to support the family. But the basic sexual drive remains, and children are born into families or to women who probably did not want them and have no means to support them. Many of them see no books, papers, or pencils until school. There is little or no home training or "push" for achievement in school. And the cycle repeats itself.

   It seems to us that the means of achieving the stated goals are as follows:

   a. Social and moral guidance through churches, civic groups, and other interested parties. It can only be effective when it comes through peer groups—outside forces can encourage and guide but cannot force acceptance.
   b. Family planning to assure that no unwanted child is conceived. We are of the opinion that family limitation is a personal matter, but we also believe that most persons will gladly accept assistance in this regard, and few have any desire to bring additional children into a deprived setting.
   c. Adequate nutrition and medical care to the prospective mother to assure, insofar as possible, a mentally and physically healthy baby.
   d. Adequate "preschool" training for socially deprived children to enable them to enter school on a level comparable to that of other children. We support the Department of Education's continuing emphasis on kindergartens, but we also believe that this preschool training should be for the "whole" child and thereby be comprehensive in social services to enable both the child and his/her family to integrate into society.
   e. Adequate and enforced educational opportunities and standards. Illiterate high school graduates may end up on welfare rolls. Many children should

be directed to vocational opportunities which do not require a high level of academic achievement.

f. Adequate scale of living and housing distributed so that "pockets" of persons living on welfare do not form, thereby giving people a sense of belonging to society and a desire to contribute thereto, and thus eliminating the "welfare" mentality, if indeed such exists.
g. Adequate medical care so that physical deficiencies and disease can be detected early and treated, thereby contributing a healthy individual to society and maintaining him therein.
h. Adequate varied job opportunities so that the individual can be productive.
i. Adequate industrial safeguards, highway standards, and public safety enforcement, to reduce the occurrence of accidental disability.
j. Adequate employer pensions and health insurance plans to provide for an adequate living standard upon retirement, and medical care treatment during and after retirement.

Objectives

Many of the objectives of the department have been stated in the "means" section. Also, over many of the means this department has no control. The following list of objectives are those which we feel are more urgent in alleviating current conditions and assisting in moving toward the stated goals.

a. Provision of adequate means of living to those persons in South Carolina unable to provide such for themselves.
b. Provision of "protective services" to those adults and children who are unable to fend for themselves. Neglect of older and disabled adults, abuse and neglect of children should not be tolerated. Our social service program is geared toward these persons now but much additional work needs to be done.
c. Provision of adequate medical care to these persons.
d. Provision of family planning services to those individuals willing to accept such services.
e. Provision of comprehensive social services in a fashion which will prevent dependency and/or encourage persons to become self-sufficient. Such services include but are not limited to early childhood development (including day care), emergency homemaking assistance, transportation, adoptions, counseling, foster care, assistance in obtaining information or aid from other groups, locating suitable housing, developing community aid resources, self-support services, etc.
f. Provision of prenatal medical care to unwed mothers.

From this information, prepare a program budget classification for the department.

2. Refer to question 1 from Chapter 4. What alternate budget-classification systems for the School of Public Affairs at Enormous State University are possible? Identify (a) the measurable performance activities, programs, and outcomes for which the school might be responsible; (b) the budget classifications you would prescribe for each; and (c) the problems you would encounter in assigning spending to the categories.

3. The new mayor of a midwestern city has developed a list of administration goals and objectives for the city. They are the following: (a) establish effective government by incorporating improved information systems and management practices; (b) improve intergovernmental cooperation for more effective, cost-effective service delivery; (c) build public support for administration priorities through two-way communication; (d) make timely investments in roads, utilities, sewers, parts, and alternative transportation systems to encourage responsible growth and sustain a healthy economy; (e) maintain and improve the city as a place where people can live and work without fear; (f) protect the community's natural assets and enhance environmental quality; (g) work to improve the economic health of the city in an equitable manner for all citizens; (h) support and facilitate access to basic social services for all citizens; (i) establish a customer-driven city workplace; and (j) maintain and improve park services and facilities. Use this statement to structure (a) a program budget format and (b) a new performance budget format for the city. For the latter, identify measurable performance indicators.

4. The U.S. Coast Guard has five central missions: search and rescue, preservation of national marine resources, enforcement of federal laws at sea, ship safety in American waters, and national defense. The first of these is recognized as its main job, but dealing with pollution and preserving marine resources takes the largest share of its budget.

An article in *The Economist,* commenting on a 1999 budget request presentation by Admiral Robert Kramek (the request was for $2.77 billion), proclaimed:

> . . . he dwelt on something rare in the armed services: results. In the past four years, he proudly informed the legislators, the Coast Guard has saved 20,000 lives and $9.3 billion in property, seized 370,000 pounds of illicit drugs, interdicted (or assisted) 75,000 foreigners trying to enter America, reported 64,000 cases of marine pollution and checked 59,000 fishing boats for possible catch violations. 'We're a model of better government at least cost,' said the Admiral. "The Coast Guard: Keeping All Channels Open," *The Economist,* 12 [September 1998], 28–29.)

Discuss and answer the following questions:

a. Did Admiral Kramek provide outcomes, as envisioned by mission or results oriented performance budgeting? Explain your answer.
b. From what you understand to be the Coast Guard mission, what sort of performance measures would you propose for use by the agency?
c. How could we test whether Admiral Kramek is right when he asserts that the Coast Guard is delivering "better government at least cost?"
d. What budgetary strategy is the admiral using and what questions would you prepare for Admiral Kramek if you were on the staff of the appropriation subcommittee considering his request?

5. Select a governmental agency or a nonprofit organization. From documents available to you (budgets, financial reports, mission statements, legislation, media reporting, etc.) and your general knowledge about that entity, do the following: (a) identify the inputs used by the entity (personnel, contractual services, etc.), (b) identify the activities or outputs produced by the entity, and (c) identify the measurable performance outcomes of that entity. What new data systems (testing, sampling, surveying, etc.) might be necessary to produce the outcome measures? What environmental influences outside the easy control of the entity are important in shaping those measured outcomes? What budget classification system or systems does the entity currently use in its budget processes?

Cases for Discussion

CASE 5–1

Following Departmental Lines (and Scores?)

This selection illustrates the budgetary impact of being in the right department at the right time, when traditional budget structures are being used. It requires no additional comment.

Spending for B1s and MXs Is Rising, So the Tubas Got an Increase, Too

By Richard L. Hudson

Washington—Military spending is going up. So spending for military bands is going up. What could be more natural?

It isn't fair, say outraged partisans of the arts, to spend more money on Sousa oompahs when spending for genuine classical music is being cut. They note balefully that the National Endowment for the Arts has been targeted by the administration for a 50 percent budget cut this year, to $77 million, while the Army, Navy, Air Force and Marine bands are in line for a 2 percent increase, to $89.7 million.

The discrepancy has arts hawks in Congress seething. "There are three full (military) bands in the Washington area, and each of them has a larger budget than the National Symphony Orchestra," says Rep. Fred Richmond, a New York Democrat and a leading congressional Medici. "I don't think it's fair," he says, that civilian arts should suffer while military music prospers.

Noncombat Troops

Such cries draw a sympathetic audience among legislators worried about Pentagon "waste." One is Republican Sen. Mark Hatfield of Oregon, whose Appropriations Committee scrutinizes defense spending. He recently lambasted the military brass for budgeting bands, historians, museum curators, and 1,605 "recreation specialists and sports technicians," all of whom "contribute little or nothing to our military strength."

Democratic Rep. Dan Glickman of Oklahoma calls the band budget "a sacred cow that has waded" through prior spending debates with insufficient scrutiny.

Preserving Morale

"It looks like everybody's trying to chop our heads off," complains an Army band official, Sgt. Major Donald Young. The bands "wave the flag" and "stir patriotism," he says. A Pentagon spokesman says the 5,355 military-band members are needed to help lure recruits, preserve morale at foreign bases, and burnish the military image.

It remains to be seen if critics of the military band buildup can torpedo Mr. Reagan's plans to raise funding. But arts lobbyists say the sniping has at least helped protect the arts endowment from the full 50 percent cut pushed by the White House. The Senate last Tuesday backed a 25 percent cut, and the House approved a token 1 percent reduction.

The critics aren't denying that a good military band plays a rousing tune. It does, says Representative Richmond. But "it's sure as heck not the National Symphony."

CASE 5–2

A View of Zero-Based Budgeting

When Jimmy Carter became president in 1976, he brought to the federal government a budgetary system that he had used while governor of Georgia some years before. His ZBB system was intended as an orderly device for reallocating public resources to areas of greatest social need, a noble intention.[1] The idea was that each agency had to defend its budget in its entirety every year, with no presumption that the agency would receive at least its prior-year appropriation. Budget deliberations were to involve the full proposed appropriation. By that means, the government was to become more flexible, eliminate low-yield programs, improve governmental effectiveness by forcing administrators to consider their entire operations annually, and simplify shifts of government resources in response to changed demands without the need for government reorganizations. The scheme kept the familiar line-item, departmental organization format, but government managers were required to prepare *decision packages* at varying levels of funding for their operations, with indications of what would be produced for the public at each level of funding. The decision packages were expected to include operating data—workload information,

---

SOURCE: Wall Street Journal, 9 November 1981. Reprinted by permission of the *Wall Street Journal,* © 1981 Dow Jones & Company, Inc. All Rights Reserved Worldwide.

[1]Executive Office of the President, Office of Management and Budget, *Zero Base Budgeting,* Bulletin no. 79-9 (April 19, 1977), provides a full description of the federal version of ZBB.

performance data, etc.—appropriate for making choices. Administrators throughout the government would then rank the decision packages for units for which they were responsible and those ranked packages would flow up the bureaucracy until the departments used them to build their full budget proposal. Ultimately, the chief executive would make the final decision on which of the decision packages get into the budget proposal. The system did not survive beyond the Carter presidency, although some state and local governments retained elements of the system for many years. *Target-based budgeting,* a close relative, continues in several jurisdictions: central budget offices establish a budget target for each budget unit and budget units develop two budgets, one for the target and one for additional resources.[2]

The following article appeared in the *Wall Street Journal,* just as the ZBB system was adopted for federal budget preparation.

Consider These Questions

1. Why did Professor Anthony (a member of the Harvard Business School faculty) view ZBB as a fraud?
2. In this application, could a "fraud" still serve a useful purpose?
3. In what ways was the ZBB experiment similar to and different from PPBS and BPI of the Bush II administration?

Zero-Base Budgeting Is a Fraud

By Robert N. Anthony

Zero-base budgeting is supposed to be a new way of preparing annual budgets, which contrasts with the current way, which is called incremental budgeting. Incremental budgeting, it is correctly said, takes a certain level of expenses as a starting point and focuses on the proposed increment above that level.

By contrast, if the word "zero" means anything, it signifies that the budgeting process starts as zero and that the agency preparing the budget request must justify every dollar that it requests.

There is only one recorded attempt to take such an approach to budgeting in a government organization of any size. In 1971, the governor of Georgia hired a consultant to install such a system. He did so because of an article the consultant had written for *Harvard Business Review*.

A casual reader of that article could easily get the impression that the author had successfully installed a zero-based budgeting system in a large industrial company. A more careful reader would learn that the author had installed a system in certain staff and research units of that company, comprising an un-

[2]Robert K. Goertz, "Target-Based Budgeting and Adaptations to Fiscal Uncertainty," *Public Productivity and Management Review* 16 (Summer 1993): 425–29. Some of the ZBB logic similarly appears in *decremental budgeting,* an approach to greater flexibility through imposing request-reduction constraints on managers. See Jerry McCaffery, "Revenue Budgeting: Dade County Tries a Decremental Approach," *Public Administration Review* 41 (January 1981): 179–89. Continued use of ZBB by federal agencies is reviewed in Stanley B. Botner, "Utilization of Decision Units and Ranking Process in Budgetary Decision-Making by Federal Departments and Agencies," *Government Accountants Journal* 33 (Fall 1984): 18–23.

specified fraction, but less than 25 percent of the company's annual expenditures, and that the judgment that the system was a great success was entirely the author's and based on a single year's experience.

Anyway, the consultant started to work for the state of Georgia. He was well-intentioned and probably sincere in his belief that it is possible to prepare and analyze a budget from scratch. This belief did not last long. Well before the end of the first budget cycle, it was agreed that expenditures equal to approximately 80 percent of the current level of spending would be given only a cursory examination and that attention would be focused on the increment.

Thus, even before one go around of the new system, the "zero" benchmark was replaced by 80 percent. Moreover, amounts above this floor were in fact "increments" despite the claim that the process is the opposite of incremental budgeting. Eighty percent is a long way from zero and increments above 80 percent are just as much increments as increments above some other base. To put it bluntly, the name zero-based budgeting is a fraud.

Facts Don't Support

The facts don't even support the glowing reports about what happened with respect to the amounts above the 80 percent. In 1974, thirteen heads of Georgia departments were interviewed, and only two went so far as to say that zero-base budgeting "may" have led to a reallocation of resources. (The whole idea of budgeting is to allocate resources.) None of thirty-two budget analysts reported that the system involved a "large" shifting of financial resources, and only seven said it caused "some" shifting. Twenty-one said there was no apparent shifting, and four were uncertain.

People experienced in budgeting know that zero-based budgeting won't work. Basically, the idea is that the entire annual budget request is to be broken down in "decision packages." These packages are to be ranked in order of priority, and budget decisions are made for each package according to the justification contained therein and its relative priority ranking. There are several things wrong with this approach.

Most important is that large numbers of decision packages are unmanageable. In Georgia, there were 11,000 of them. If the governor set aside four hours every day for two months he could spend about a minute on each decision package, not enough time to read it, let alone analyze the merits. If he delegated the job to others, the whole idea of comparing priorities is compromised.

In the Defense Department, whose budget is 30 times as large as Georgia's, top management makes budget judgments on a few hundred items, certainly not as many as a thousand.

Even if the numbers of decision packages were reduced to a manageable size, it is not possible to make a thorough analysis during the time available in the annual budget process. In a good control system, basic decisions are made during the programming process, which precedes the budget process. And the annual budget process is essentially one of fine tuning the financial plan required to implement these decisions during the budget year; there is not time to do anything else.

In zero-based budgeting, there is no mention of a programming process. The assumption evidently is that program decisions are made concurrently with budget decisions. This simply can't be done in an organization of any size; there isn't time.

Experience also shows that the idea of ranking decision packages according to priority doesn't work. Such rankings have been attempted from time to time in government agencies, as far back as 1960. They have been abandoned. Honest agency heads will admit that program priority is influenced by the amount of funds likely to be available, rather than the other way around. If they are less than honest, they will deliberately structure priorities so that essential or politically popular decision packages are given low priority, knowing they will probably be approved and that their approval will automatically constitute approval of packages listed as having a higher priority. Only quite naive people would not expect this to happen.

The budget process is not primarily a ranking process. It is primarily the fine tuning of an approved program. The worth of programs can't be determined by reading words on a two-page form. Judgments about new programs are based on discussions with people involved, in which words on paper play some but not a dominant part. The budget analyst has a whole set of techniques for squeezing water out of budget requests for continuing programs; reading "decision packages" is not one of them.

Compared with the antiquated budget process which Georgia had at the time, zero-based budgeting was probably an improvement—almost any change would have been. Compared with the procedures that already are used in the federal government, it has nothing of substance to offer. The new parts are not good, and the good parts are not new.

Nevertheless, zero-based budgeting is rapidly becoming a highly prestigious term. I think there is a way of capitalizing on this prestige so as to give impetus to improvements in the budget process that really need to be made.

First, by a slight change in wording, the push behind the phrase might be transferred to a process called "zero-based review." This is an extremely valuable part of the control process. It is used by some agencies, but it is not widely used in a systematic way. It should be made systematic and extended throughout the government.

APPENDIX 5–1

Functional Categories of the Federal Budget

The functional classification arranges budget resources so that budget authority and outlays, loan guarantees, and tax expenditures can be related to the national needs they address. The congressional budget resolutions establish bud-

---

SOURCE: Wall Street Journal, 27 April 1977. Reprinted by permission of the *Wall Street Journal,* © 1977 Dow Jones 7 Company, Inc. All Rights Reserved Worldwide.

get targets for each function, and the president's budget presents the functional classification along with the classification by administrative unit.

According to the Budget of the U.S. Government, Fiscal Year 1986, these criteria are used in assigning activities to functions:

A function must have a common end or ultimate purpose addressed to an important national need. (The emphasis is on what the federal government seeks to accomplish rather than the means of accomplishment, what is purchased, or the clientele or geographic area served.)

A function must be of continuing national importance and the amounts attributable to it must be significant.

Each basic unit of classification (generally the appropriation or fund account) is classified into the single best or predominant purpose and assigned to only one subfunction. However, when an account is large and serves more than one major purpose, it may be subdivided into two or more subfunctions.

Activities and programs are normally classified according to their primary purpose (or function) regardless of which agencies conduct the activities.

The functional classification of federal spending follows:

Functional Categories	Subfunctional Categories
National defense (050)	Department of Defense-Military (051)
	Atomic energy defense activities (053)
	Defense-related activities (054)
International affairs (150)	International development and humanitarian assistance (151)
	International security assistance (152)
	Conduct of foreign affairs (153)
	Foreign information and exchange activities (154)
	International financial programs (155)
General science, space, and technology (250)	General science and basic research (251)
	Space flight, research, and supporting activities (252)
Energy (270)	Energy supply (271)
	Energy conservation (272)
	Emergency energy preparedness (274)
	Energy information, policy, and regulation (276)
Natural resources and environment (300)	Water resources (301)
	Conservation and land management (302)
	Recreational resources (303)
	Pollution control and abatement (304)
	Other natural resources (306)
Agriculture (350)	Farm income stabilization (351)
	Agricultural research and services (352)
Commerce and housing credit (370)	Mortgage credit (371)
	Postal service (372)
	Deposit insurance (373)
	Other advancement of commerce (376)

Transportation (400)	Ground transportation (401)
	Air transportation (402)
	Water transportation (403)
	Other transportation (407)
Community and regional development (450)	Community development (451)
	Area and regional development (452)
	Disaster relief and insurance (453)
Education, training, employment, and social services (500)	Elementary, secondary, and vocational education (501)
	Higher education (502)
	Research and general education aids (503)
	Training and employment (504)
	Other labor services (505)
	Social services (506)
Health (550)	Health care services (551)
	Health research and training (552)
	Consumer and occupational health and safety (554)
Medicare (570)	Medicare (571)
Income security (600)	General retirement and disability insurance (excluding social security) (601)
	Federal employee retirement and disability (602)
	Unemployment compensation (603)
	Housing assistance (604)
	Food and nutrition assistance (605)
	Other income security (609)
Social security (650)	Social security (651)
Veterans benefits and services (700)	Income security for veterans (701)
	Veterans education, training and rehabilitation (702)
	Hospital and medical care for veterans (703)
	Veterans housing (704)
	Other veterans benefits and services (705)
Administration of justice (750)	Federal law enforcement activities (751)
	Federal litigative and judicial activities (752)
	Federal correctional activities (753)
	Criminal justice assistance (754)
General government (800)	Legislative functions (801)
	Executive direction and management (802)
	Central fiscal operations (803)
	General property and records management (804)
	Central personnel management (805)
	General purpose fiscal assistance (806)
	Other general government (808)
	Deductions for offsetting receipts (809)
Net interest (900)	Interest on the public debt (901)
	Interest received by on-budget trust funds (902)
	Interest received by off-budget trust funds (903)
	Other interest (908)
Allowances (920)	Varies by year

Undistributed off-setting receipts (950)	Employer share, employee retirement (on-budget) (951) Employer share, employee retirement (off-budget) (952) Rents and royalties on the Outer Continental Shelf (953) Sale of major assets (954) Other undistributed offsetting receipts (959)

A recent GAO report discusses the functional classification in greater detail: *Budget Function Classifications: Origins, Trends, and Implications for Current Uses,* GAO/AIMD-98–67, February 1998.

APPENDIX 5–2

COFOG

The United Nations classification of functions of government (COFOG) divides the major service commitments accepted by governments as follows:

- General Public Service (legislative, executive, fiscal management, public debt service, etc.)
- Defense
- Public Order and Safety (police services; fire protection; courts; prisons)
- Economic Affairs (general economic, commercial, and labor affairs; agriculture, forestry, fishing, and hunting; fuel and energy; mining, manufacturing, and construction; transport; communications)
- Environmental Protection (waste management; waste water management; pollution abatement; protection of biodiversity and landscape)
- Housing and Community Amenities (housing development; community development; water supply; street lighting)
- Health (medical products, appliances, and equipment; outpatient services; hospital services; public health)
- Recreation, Culture, and Religion
- Education
- Social Protection (sickness and disability; old age; survivors; family and children; unemployment; housing)

Data in these program or functional categories provides a good basis for making international comparisons and a good start for developing the framework for a program budget.

CHAPTER 6

Capital Budgeting, Public Infrastructure Investment, and Project Evaluation

Capital expenditures purchase assets—physical properties—that are expected to provide services for several years; the outlay will yield benefits in the future without having to repeat the purchase. Public capital assets, also called infrastructure, become inputs into private economic production. The Congressional Budget Office (CBO) writes, "The production and distribution of private economic output depends on public transportation and environmental facilities including highways, mass transit, railways, airports and airways, water resources, and water supply and wastewater treatment plants."[1] All these fit directly into production processes yielding *private* goods and services. Roads, sewers, and transportation systems have become part of the competition between states and localities for new industrial and commercial development, so a sound system of infrastructure finance represents a crucial factor for regional economic growth. But public infrastructure also enters into production processes that deliver *public* services: elementary and secondary school buildings, park and recreation areas, state hospitals, administrative complexes, jails and police facilities, fire stations, the defense establishment, and so on, and these are critical for society as well. Therefore, for both private and public production of the nation's goods and services, the public capital stock is important.[2]

[1]U.S. Congressional Budget Office, *How Federal Spending for Infrastructure and Other Public Investments Affects the Economy* (Washington, D.C.: GPO, July 1991), x.

[2]Capital budgeting is an important topic in private finance, but it is focused narrowly on applications of the time value of money and net present value (NPV) calculations. Those applications also are important for the public sector and are covered at length in this chapter. However, because public organizations have multiple objectives and priorities, not the single profitability standard of the private entity, there are procedural as well as calculation issues that must be considered.

Capital expenditure choices can have considerable future impact, so special care is appropriate in these decisions.[3] Furthermore, the price tag on most of these items tends to be high, and purchases typically occur at irregular intervals. For those reasons, both public and private entities prepare and maintain a capital budget separate from the current service expenditures in an operating budget. Some argue that the separate budgets can help achieve the "golden rule" of government finance: match current revenue to spending on current services, but borrow to support capital spending and thereby maintain the net worth of the public sector.[4] That is the basic principle of long-term fiscal sustainability, the test of whether citizens in the future will be able to at least maintain the standard of living enjoyed by citizens in the present. A distinct capital budget can focus decisions, facilitate financial planning, smooth tax rates over time, and regularize the provision of projects that (1) have long life (10 or 15 years), (2) have a high price tag relative to the resources of the governing unit, and (3) are nonrecurrent.[5]

Capital budgeting integrates physical and financial planning. That combination has not always been found in the provision of government capital assets:

> During one phase of development of municipalities, there was a tendency to consider the capital improvement program as the exclusive domain of the Public Works Department. It was assumed that since capital improvements were largely in the nature of construction projects, the planning was of an engineering nature. After all the planning was complete, then a price tag could be established and proper plans made for the obtaining of funds necessary to carry out the program.[6]

That simple engineering approach seems primitive today because urban mobility and socioeconomic change can render facilities obsolete in a handful of years; the requirements of intergovernmental relationships complicate many financial arrangements; and many governments operate near their legal, economic, or political fiscal limits. Because the link between capital and operating resources in delivery of services is so clear, capital asset programs are too important to be engineering choices. Thus, the designers of a facility must integrate their plans with the social, economic, financial, and political environment. In fact, that environment will almost certainly be of greater consequence to the capital expenditure profile than the construction plans. The capital budget process establishes the formal mechanism for consideration and adoption of construction plans within prevailing constraints. This chapter describes government capital budgets and introduces cost-benefit analysis, a powerful tool that can help inform capital budget and other public choices.

---

[3]Human capital and research and development spending also contribute to long-term economic growth, so this attribute is not unique to capital spending. See U.S. General Accounting Office, *Choosing Public Investments,* GAO/AIMD-93-25 (Washington, D.C.: GPO, July 1993). But teachers and researchers expect to be paid year after year, so spending to pay them is considerably different from spending to build a bridge.

[4]Measured annual deficits in support of additions to the real public capital stock would not violate sound financial practices.

[5]In developing and transition countries, what is essentially the capital budget is called the development budget.

[6]Morris C. Matson, "Capital Budgeting—Fiscal and Physical Planning," *Governmental Finance* 5 (August 1976): 42.

Why Have a Capital Budget?

A budget process helps decision-makers select between individual projects for funding while keeping expenditures within a total resource constraint. Maintaining two different budgets certainly seems to complicate an already complex process. For capital budgets to be defensible, they must make a substantial contribution to improved fiscal choice. That contribution can be substantial for state and local government, but the advantage to the federal government, which presently has no separate capital budget, is less clear, although many believe this to be a way to protect federal investment spending by clearly distinguishing between spending with single-year return and spending with returns for the future.

First, separate consideration can improve both the efficiency and equity of providing and financing nonrecurrent projects with long-term service flows. These projects serve the citizenry, for good or bad, for many years beyond the year of purchase. Separate consideration in a budget when deficits may be financed and annual balance is not required provides important opportunities to improve equity between generations and among local citizenry pools. In other words, the spending program in a capital budget can be covered either by revenue raised currently (current taxes, charges, grants, etc., a "pay-as-you-go" system) or by borrowing on the promise to repay from future revenues (or "pay-as-you-use" system). This is consistent with the "golden rule" of government finance, because the borrowing is to cover the acquisition of long-life capital assets. The spending in the capital budget must be covered (the money is raised from current revenue or debt sources), but the budget need not necessarily be balanced (total expenditure equals current revenue). The general standard is that operating budgets typically must be balanced; capital budgets, financed. The inequity of the "pay-as-you-go" approach is apparent: if a local government project with a 30-year service life is constructed and paid for this year, no construction cost will be incurred during the remaining life of the project. Anyone entering the area taxpaying pool after the construction year (by moving into the area or by growing up) may receive project service without appropriate contribution. This inequity does not occur if the project is paid for over its useful life. Handling high-price, long-life projects through a debt-financed capital budget has strong equity advantages. Furthermore, the use of capital budgets can improve decision efficiency. In a combined budget, big-ticket investment looks expensive relative to consumption (operating expenditures), even though the true cost of that investment (its depreciation or its "wearing out") occurs over many years. Separate consideration can avoid that bias and improve the chances for more reasonable responses to service demand.[7] Dual budgets—a balanced operating budget

[7]Lennox Moak and Albert Hillhouse suggest that governments having financial trouble may find that identifiable capital projects are more easily postponable than are expenditures for operating agencies. A separate capital budget can improve the chances for preserving capital projects when the operating budget is under great pressure. See Moak and Hillhouse, *Concepts and Practices in Local Government Finance* (Chicago: Municipal Finance Officers Association, 1975), 98. Cities regularly use capital spending reductions as a means of dealing with difficult fiscal conditions. See Michael A. Pagano, "Balancing Cities' Books in 1992: An Assessment of City Fiscal Conditions," *Public Budgeting and Finance* 13 (Spring 1993): 28.

and a financed capital budget—can thus make important improvements in the equity and efficiency of providing projects and producing long-term service flow.

Second, capital budgets can stabilize tax rates when individual capital projects are large relative to the tax base of the host government. If a city with a tax base of $1.5 billion decided to construct a $150 million water reservoir, it would undoubtedly be dissuaded if it were required to collect sufficient revenue for construction in 1 year. The cost would be 10 percent of the total city tax base, hardly leaving enough tax capacity for police and fire protection, street operation, and so on. However, the reservoir may have a service life of 50 years or more. It is reasonable, then, to divide the construction cost over the service life, thus reducing the burden on the tax base each year and, accordingly, preventing the dramatic fluctuation in tax rates that would result from financing the project in the construction year. The case for a regular capital budget process is strong whenever projects are large enough to significantly influence tax rates. However, the entire capital budget need not be debt-financed to maintain stable tax rates; recurring capital outlays should be financed from current revenue, as is discussed in Chapter 15.

Third, the special reviews of capital budgeting are appropriate because capital projects are permanent—mistakes will be around for many years. Kenneth Howard describes the problem:

> If a new state office building is built today, it will stay there for a long time. Everybody may know by next year that it is in the wrong place, but not much can be done about moving it then. Perhaps it is disrupting the development of a downtown business district; perhaps it is affecting traffic flows and parking facilities in a most undesirable way; or perhaps its location makes it psychologically, if not geographically, far removed from certain segments of the population. Whatever these effects may be, they are real, and they will endure awhile. They should be anticipated to the fullest extent possible before the project is undertaken.[8]

The capital budget reviews will not prevent all mistakes, but they can reduce costly errors. Those reviews and associated planning processes can produce the orderly provision of public capital facilities to accommodate economic development. Thus, the capital budget process serves to reduce errors both of commission and omission in public infrastructure construction.

Finally, capital budgets are valuable tools for managing limited fiscal resources, particularly in light of the special care required to plan activities that necessitate long-term drains on those resources. Items in this budget tend to be "lumpy." A capital budget provides a mechanism to smooth out peaks and valleys, regularize construction activity in an effort to avoid local bottlenecks that can delay projects and inflate their costs, avoid excessive drains on the tax base when projects must be paid for, and balance spending with the resources available within political, economic, and legal tax and debt limits. Thus, the capital budget is an important resource management tool: "The capital budget . . . provides a vehicle for financial planning and for the regulation of local tax rates. It thus contributes to financial

---

[8]S. Kenneth Howard, *Changing State Budgeting* (Lexington, KY: Council of State Governments, 1973), 241.

solvency, and at the same time assures that over a period of years needed improvements will be constructed."[9] The states are almost evenly divided between those legislatures receiving executive capital budget requests in a separate budget document and those receiving requests with the operating budget. There is no separate capital budget or capital budgeting process at the federal level.

The reasons supporting a separate capital budget are strongest for local and state governments. They are less strong at the federal level. First, critics of a federal capital budget fear that a separate capital budget would create a bias toward deficit spending or, more accurately, add to the existing bias that is apparent in the historical record. The danger is that all items potentially definable as investment (and politicians love to refer to every dollar spent for anything as "investment"), whether the addition contributes to physical or human capital, would be inserted into a debt-financed capital budget, even if the spending were recurring. It is much easier for the federal government to borrow than to tax, so this extra incentive is dangerous. Second, the federal government is so large that no single infrastructure project is likely to influence tax rates. Although a careful physical inventory and planning for estimated demand conditions are helpful, scheduling of projects to control tax rates is of little practical consequence. Large projects may, however, create "spikes" in budget authority to individual agencies—but that does not make a case for the smoothing that a capital budget process might create for the federal government as a whole. Third, the federal government does not need the careful project financing planning inherent in capital budgeting to preserve its debt rating. The federal government has, after all, the ultimate power of printing money to cover deficits, and capital project financing is not a factor in the federal credit rating. Fourth, skeptics say that another budget would simply provide federal bureaucrats and lawmakers with another way to conceal fiscal conditions. Adding operating/capital to the existing on-budget/off-budget, federal fund/trust fund complications doesn't contribute to fiscal transparency and would likely muddle citizen understanding even more, even as it satisfies fiscal purists. Thus, the gains from capital budgeting at lower government levels, particularly local, may not be translated to a similar federal case.

The federal budget has included outlays and budget authority for federal investment—outlays that yield long-term benefits—in a section on federal investment expenditure for more than half a century. The coverage is included in the *Analytical Perspectives* volume of the budget.[10] Outlays are divided into (1) physical investment (construction and rehabilitation, purchase of major equipment, and purchase or sale of land and structures), (2) conduct of research and development, and (3) conduct of education and training.

Outlays are further categorized by broad functional classes within those divisions. Major acquisition proposals are specifically identified by agency. Agency proposals for capital asset investment are expected to

---

[9]Jesse Burkhead, *Government Budgeting* (New York: Wiley, 1963): 205.

[10]Executive Office of the President, Office of Management and Budget, *Analytical Perspectives, Budget of the United States Government, Fiscal Year 2007* (Washington, D.C.: GPO, 2006), 53–64. However, the investment program is not extended beyond the budget year.

> demonstrate a projected return on the investment that is clearly equal to or better than alternative uses of available public resources. Return may include: improved mission performance in accordance with measures developed pursuant to the Government Performance and Results Act; reduced cost; increased quality, speed, or flexibility; and increased customer and employee satisfaction.[11]

Investments are subject to PART review as the budgets are developed.

The budget and the budget process, however, remain unified, in that there is no other separation between capital and operating spending. Agencies develop operating and capital projects in the same budget cycle, Congress reviews proposals and makes appropriations without distinguishing between the two sorts of spending,[12] and there are no separate rules for the finance of capital as opposed to operating programs. Agency appropriations include budget authority for both operations and capital projects on the same basis. The budget process attempts to achieve full appropriation for long-term, large-ticket capital projects (e.g., the International Space Station) by a combination of current and advance appropriations. Up-front funding for the full cost allows Congress to control spending at the time of commitment. However, it requires agencies to bear that cost in the annual budget, even though returns will accrue over the long life of the project and the cost may absorb a considerable portion of discretionary spending.[13] The scope of the presentation in *Analytical Perspectives* includes many recurrent, non–capital asset purchases, and it does not establish separation and protection of capital asset decisions in the process.

A Capital Budgeting Process

The capital budget process seeks to constrain the financial impact of capital asset acquisition on the overall budget while delivering the infrastructure needed to satisfy the citizenry's public-service demands. Formal capital budget processes operate in many different ways, using various terms, steps, and the sequencing of those steps, and function separately from the process producing the annual (operating) budget, although they obviously do merge. The process described here amalgamates processes from several different state and local governments for illustration;

---

[11]Executive Office of the President, Office of Management and Budget, *Planning, Budgeting and Acquisition of Fixed Assets*, Circular A-11, part 3 (Washington D.C.: Office of Management and Budget, 1997): 305.

[12]A Government Accountability Office (GAO) study reports that federal capital project requests provided to the appropriate House and Senate committees do not always identify the total cost of proposed projects (funding has been sought in increments, not total), have not always identified funds already spent on the project, and have often provided scant descriptions of the nature of the project. U.S. General Accounting Office, *Budget Issues: Agency Data Supporting Capital Funding Requests Could Be Improved*, GAO-01-770, (Washington, D.C.: U.S. Government Printing Office, June 2001).

[13]U.S. Government Accounting Office, *Budget Issues: Budgeting for Federal Capital*, GAO/AIMD-97-5 (Washington, D.C.: GPO, November 1996), offers a good review of capital investment practices of the federal government, and the problems that they create.

most existing systems can easily be identified with this outline. The processes are concerned with selecting capital projects from the multitude of possible alternatives, timing expenditure on the projects selected, and fitting capital projects into the overall financial program of the government. The politics of capital projects can be complicated because each project is at a known and specific location and will likely have specific impacts on the area surrounding it, some desirable (a new park) and possibly some not (a new incinerator). This focuses citizen interests in ways far beyond concerns about, for instance, social programs or police protection, which have general impact. Figure 6–1 provides a rough view of the financial flow in the process that links a multi-year capital improvement plan, the capital budget for the current year, and the operating budget in a comprehensive expenditure program for the year.

The capital budget typically becomes an element of the annual budget, either as a section of the overall budget or as a separate capital budget document. The capital budget should have cost estimates (requests) for all infrastructure projects that are proposed, including both the proposed investment cost and its implications for the operating budget. The budget usually goes through the normal legislative review and enactment requirements that any expenditure program would face and, once approved, spending follows the same internal and external control mechanisms as faced by any public expenditures. The future years of the capital budget may or may not be appropriated when the facility proposal is first considered, and the government may or may not honor future capital expenditure requirements as later components of the plan are proposed. Executives and their priorities change, as do legislatures. One would hope that an approved capital budget does not include facilities so repugnant as to bring their cancellation when legislatures and chief executives change, but later governments do not always feel bound by decisions made by their predecessors.

A fully developed capital budget process functions separately from the process for the annual budget, although they obviously do intersect in the final states of the cycle. There are several steps in the process: inventory of capital assets, development of a capital improvement plan (CIP), development of a financing plan, and implementation of the capital budget. The capital budget process seeks to constrain the financial impact of capital asset acquisition on the overall budget while delivering the infrastructure needed to satisfy the citizenry's public service demands.

Capital asset inventory. Governments need to start their infrastructure development programs with a good assessment of the existing situation. The necessary information base would include an inventory of the capital facilities owned by the government with these data for each facility: (1) its age, (2) an assessment of its condition, (3) its degree of use, (4) its capacity, and (5) its replacement cost. Such an inventory can help the government estimate needs for renewal, replacement, expansion, and retirement of its existing capital stock. It can also contribute information for the repair and maintenance portion of the operating budget. The level of detail for the inventory and degree of accompanying analysis varies by the significance of the facility to the operations of the government.

The capital improvement plan (CIP). Choices about infrastructure investment are driven by the perceived consequences of facility failure, the recurring ben-

Figure 6–1
Capital Improvement Programming and Budgeting

Capital-Improvement Program

	Projects ($000s)			
Year	Fire Station	Library	Sewer Expansion	Park
2007	185	0	15	15
2008	10	0	20	0
2009	0	20	30	0
2010	0	100	50	0
2011	0	0	75	0
2012	0	0	40	0

Capital Budget

Projects for 2007	($000s)
Fire station	185
Sewer expansion	15
Park	15

Operating Budget

	($000s)
Personnel costs	640
Supplies and equipment	140
Other	20
	800

Capital Expenditures	*Operating Expenditures*
$215,000	*$800,000*
Total Expenditures	
$1,015,000	

efits from the facility, the cost and financial impact of the project, and citizenry attitudes toward the facility. A capital improvement plan identifies capital expenditure projects appropriate for the next 6 years or so. That list is proposed by government agencies and, sometimes, private organizations; each project proposal includes a justifying narrative and cost data. These project proposals are screened by a government-wide planning department or a similar body to evaluate costs, locate interrelationships, and establish initial priorities. Some decisions can be guides by established service goals of the community. For instance, if a local government has certain fire protection standards it wants to achieve for all properties in its jurisdiction, and it cannot achieve that goal because of infrastructure limitations, then this unmet standard can shape an element of the investment plan.[14]

This screening is particularly concerned with scheduling: projects should be timed to avoid waste (the new sewers should be put in before the streets are resurfaced), predetermined program emphases should be implemented, and projects that can be postponed should be identified.[15] Part of this priority review may be linked to a community (or state) master plan—a long-term (10- to 25-year), broad-gauge estimate of community growth encompassing estimated needs for public improvements and controls on private use of property. Because long-term forecasts of social, demographic, and economic behavior are so inaccurate, that plan should not be taken too seriously as a guide to actions if the government intends to base its operations on what people want, as opposed to the schemes of politicians and bureaucrats.

The capital program ordinarily is developed in agencies, but with central oversight and coordination. Governments are becoming especially concerned that capital investment program outcomes contribute to overall government goals. The final capital improvement program has a segment scheduled for each year of its multi-year span. The capital budget proposal for the year includes current year expenditures from the capital improvement program.

An analysis of project costs and time schedules in the CIP ordinarily show a need for reprioritization of projects. Because priorities change across the years, the plan should be revised annually to create a rolling multi-year investment plan. The plan should include the time schedule and estimated costs for all projects in the plan. Such a multi-year plan should help the government manage its limited financial resources, induce the government to manage toward more cost-effective approaches to infrastructure development, and assist with prudence in the financial management of infrastructure acquisition.

Financing plan/long-term financial analysis. The government must keep its infrastructure development program within its financial capacity. The limit to its capacity depends on several factors, including the government's operating expenditure level, the fundamental revenue capacity of the government, any revenues produced by the infrastructure facility itself, the extent to which other governments or private entities will share the cost of the infrastructure facilities or of their operation, and the debt structures and instruments available to the government. Any impact of the facility on recurring expenditures of the government must be part of the financial analysis; facilities can either reduce or increase the operating expenditures of a government.

This part of the process coordinates a financial analysis of the government with the facility additions envisioned in the capital improvement program. This interrelationship is vital because of the long-term fiscal commitments that such facilities

---

[14]A good guide for developing facilities plans is Alan Walter Steiss, *Strategic Facilities Planning, Capital Budgeting and Debt Administration* (Lanham, Md.: Lexington Books, 2005).

[15]Moak and Hillhouse, *Concepts and Practices in Local Government Finance,* 104–105.

involve. Just as a poorly conceived physical structure can disrupt a city for many years, a poorly conceived financing approach can disrupt that city's fiscal condition. Finance officers must examine the present and anticipated revenue-and-expenditure profile to determine the financial cushion available for new projects. Particularly important are the status of existing debt issues (Will any debt issues be retired soon? Will funds be available to meet contractual debt service—principal and interest—payments? Are there needs for extra funds for early bond retirement?), estimated growth profile of the tax base, and potential for new revenue sources. This fiscal profile, year-by-year, may then be related to the priority list of projects, again scheduled by years. In this analysis, fiscal officers usually consider the financing alternatives available for specific projects (special assessments for sidewalks, user charges for water utilities, state or federal aid for highways, etc.), and further reports will have financing sources attached to projects. Choices also need to be made about whether to finance by borrowing (general or limited obligation bonds), by use of capital reserve funds (special funds accumulated over time for future capital spending), or from current sources (pay-as-you-go financing). Some projects may involve a public–private partnership, and the private financial support is important in making choices. From those considerations, the project list is revised in preparation for its insertion into the annual budget process.

Implementation of the capital budget. The capital component for the annual budget—infrastructure investment—must be prepared, either to be transmitted separately or as an element of the operating budget. Cost estimates for projects need to be prepared with greater precision than was sufficient for the capital plan, and justifications must be developed in the format prescribed for that budget cycle. The financial analysis may indicate that the full project schedule can remain intact for the year, but more often fiscal conditions require choices to fit a proposal to the scarce available resources.

A number of priority systems are possible. These include priorities based on (1) functional areas, such as natural resources, higher education, transportation, or assistance for local government projects; (2) problem severity, such as the health and safety of the population, critical maintenance of facilities, facility improvements, and new construction; (3) status of support, such as governor's priorities, agency priorities, legal or federal mandate, and passage of referenda; or (4) a formal scoring system according to ranked criteria.[16] Realistically, the priorities of the chief executive (governor or mayor) have to play an important role in making the choices, and the interests of the legislature cannot be ignored. Many states provide no clear ranking, but there does continue to be some preference for maintaining existing facilities against new construction. And concern for public health and safety is usually important—as are court orders. Other projects may be evaluated with cost-benefit analysis, as described later in this chapter.

Evaluating projects for the capital budget is not a simple task, because the decisions intertwine economic, political, and social forces. An Urban Institute study

---

[16]National Association of State Budget Officers, *Capital Budgeting in the States,* preliminary draft (Washington, D.C.: National Association of State Budget Officers, April 1997). The participatory budgeting process outlined in Appendix 3–2 provides one approach to making these decisions.

identified a number of criteria that were important in evaluations done by local governments:

1. Fiscal impacts, including capital, operating, and maintenance costs; revenue effects; energy requirements; and legal liability
2. Health and safety effects on both the citizenry and government employees
3. Community economic effects on the tax base, employment, incomes of people and business, and neighborhoods
4. Environmental, aesthetic, and social effects on the quality of life in the community
5. Disruptions and inconvenience created during the work on the project
6. Distributional effects across age and income groups, neighborhoods, business and individuals, people with and without automobiles, and people with and without disabilities
7. Feasibility in terms of public support, interest-group opposition, special federal or state permitting procedures, consistency with comprehensive plans, and legal questions
8. Implications of deferring the project to a later year
9. Amount of uncertainty and risk with regard to cost and other estimates, technology, and the like
10. Effects on relationships with other governments or quasi-governmental agencies that serve the area
11. Effects on the cost or impacts of other capital projects[17]

The extent to which these concerns matter differs across types of projects—a new jail raises different questions than a sewage-treatment plant, for instance. Furthermore, evaluation signals may conflict for particular projects. But these are the kinds of questions that apply when evaluating such choices. Table 6–1 identifies several standard questions that budget examiners raise. Because capital projects are place-specific, political pressures can be intense. Some projects are desirable and can become parts of pork-barrel trading and rewards; others may be unattractive and subject to considerable protest from residents of the host locality. For example, controversy surrounds proposals for both a new community college and a nuclear waste storage facility.

The projects surviving agency and executive cuts become the capital budget section of the annual budget. The document usually provides a distribution of projects by function and agency, shows prior and estimated future costs of the project (initial appropriations may well have been annual—each year's construction plan requires a new appropriation), and summarizes sources of financing (type of debt, aid, etc.). The capital improvement program thus feeds the capital budget proposal for the next year, subject to revisions produced by the environmental conditions and the legislative process. The projects are reviewed by the legislature and some-

[17]Harry P. Hatry, "Guide to Setting Priorities for Capital Investment," *Guides to Managing Urban Capital,* vol. 5 (Washington, D.C.: Urban Institute, 1984), 716.

Table 6–1
Selected Questions for a Capital Budget Request

What evidence is given of need for the project, and what happens if the project is not funded?
What benefits are claimed for the project and how convincing are those claims?
What plans have been developed for the project?
Can the project wait for another year?
How sensitive is the justification to changed circumstances: population growth or decline, major technological change, decline or increase in service demand, change in government structure, actions of other governments or businesses, etc.?
Is the capital cost comparable with experience on similar projects here and elsewhere?
Are all costs included in the request: fees, equipment, insurance, etc.?
What are the operating costs for the life of the project, are they reasonable and affordable, and could project redesign allow savings?
Can the project be financed elsewhere (by the private sector, by another government, or through a cooperative arrangement)?
What other options are available: renovation, remodeling other facilities, lease, etc.?
What financing options are appropriate: current account, general obligation bonds, revenue bonds, lease-purchase agreement, etc.?

times are substantially modified. When projects are approved, provision must also be made in the operating budget for operation and maintenance of the completed facility. A new civic arena will not be usable if the operating budget has no money for its interior lighting.

Total government expenditure includes both the operating expenditures from the operating budget and capital purchases from the capital budget. Operating expenditures are normally financed by current revenue (taxes, grants, charges, etc., collected in the current year). If operating expenditures are financed by borrowing instead of by current revenue, the current-period expenditures must be paid in the future, along with necessary interest. Thus, that future period will bear the costs of both current and past operating expenditures; the overhang from previous years can severely restrict the capacity to provide necessary services. That is why the operating portion of the budget needs to be balanced as a requirement for long-term fiscal sustainability.

Capital budget transactions, however, involve isolated acquisitions of long-life assets. These purchases may be handled either on a pay-as-you-go basis, paying for the project out of current revenues at the time of the expenditure, or on a pay-as-you-use basis, borrowing to finance the expenditure with debt-service payments made from revenues raised through the useful life of the project. In the full capital budget, projects usually are financed by both current and debt funds.[18]

In terms of the comprehensive budget, the revenue that must be generated in any budget year equals the operating budget plus a capital project component. The latter equals capital items purchased without debt plus the *debt-service* requirements (interest and repayment of principal) on borrowing for capital items purchased in prior years. Those debt costs would ideally approximate a depreciation charge for capital assets acquired in the past; serial bonds (bonds in a single project issue that are to be paid off at various dates through the life of the project) can provide a rough approximation of that cost distribution.

Executing the capital budget. The final step in the capital budget process is execution of projects for which funds have been appropriated. Special attention must be given to (1) the rules (bidding, procurement, etc.) under which contracts can be issued, (2) controls to keep project work on schedule, so that facilities will be completed as planned, and (3) monitoring to keep project cost within budget. A full capital asset management program also requires a scheme for financing routine maintenance and upgrading of capital assets (not as politically attractive as building new facilities) and a system for keeping a current inventory of capital assets.

Problems in Capital Budgeting

As is always the case with mechanisms to help make public decisions, there are problems in applying capital budgeting. First, the capital improvement/capital budget process assumes a continuous cycle of reappraisal and revaluation of project proposals. The cycle is necessary because the world changes, causing substantial changes in the value of public projects. Unfortunately, many processes assume established priorities to be unchangeable, even in the face of different project costs and different project demands. As Howard points out, "Too often cost fluctuations do not generate a reassessment of priority rankings; original rankings are retained despite the fluctuations."[19] In a related manner, the time a project has spent in the priority queue sometimes establishes its priority rank; all old project proposals have higher rankings than any new ones. That approach makes no sense because time alone does not improve the viability of a marginal project. Indeed, items entering the priority queue some years before may, by the time they reach the funding point, have outlived their usefulness or may have been superseded by adjustments made by people and markets. The project may have gone unfunded for many years because sensible people in the administration understood that the project would be a bad use of money. The passage of time has not made it any better. Again, the problem can be resolved by maintaining reviews of projects in the capital improvement program.

[18]In a system like that used by the federal government, high-ticket projects may be divided into parts for inclusion in agency annual budget requests and appropriations.
[19]Howard, *Changing State Budgeting*, 256.

Second, questions may arise about which projects or programs belong in the capital budget because, in the strictest sense, more than capital assets provide future benefit flows. Planning and zoning departments, educational institutions, training programs, and so on, all provide benefits that extend beyond the year in which the service expenditure is made. Most generally, however, these activities would properly be excluded from the capital budget because spending for them is recurrent, not single-year. Furthermore, most processes include established dollar-size limits for capital budget treatment: A $1,000 personal computer, with a useful life of 5 years, would be part of the operating budget, whereas an $18,500 automobile, with a useful life of 4 years, would be in the capital budget. Dollar limits differ, but some limit usually is encountered. Such arbitrary rules are a common factor in any decision process.

Third, availability of funds can distort the priority ranks. As Howard observes, "Despite the fact that how a project is financed does not change the need for it, there is a strong tendency for differences in the availability of capital outlay funds to skew priority decisions."[20] The appropriate approach in establishing final priorities should involve a general comparison of the cost of the project with the project's return to the community—the money's source doesn't matter in this comparison. Some projects can get favored treatment, however, because earmarked funds are available (a special tax creates a fund pool that can be spent only on one class of project), because they produce revenue that can be pledged to repayment of revenue bonds without identifiable tax burden or the need to satisfy restrictions placed on general debt, because federal or state assistance is available for particular projects, or because a private partner is contributing something to the project. The purpose of many grants is to bend local priorities (and partnership arrangements), so that influence is excusable. The other influences, however, are inappropriate and show why most analysts oppose such fiscal constraints.

Fourth, capital budgeting can unduly and uneconomically favor the use of debt finance. Borrowing to purchase capital assets may not always be desirable. For instance, items that are purchased regularly and in considerable numbers—vehicles used by a larger city government, for instance, or buses for a large school district—may be more economically purchased on a regular-flow basis, even though the purchase of individual vehicles would appear to be a good candidate for debt finance. Furthermore, debt-financed capital budgets can add to inflationary pressures during strong economic expansion, when government finances are robust and legislatures feel good enough about fiscal prospects to respond to pent-up demand for infrastructure. To put long-life assets in a capital budget can create a strong temptation to debt finance, even when sound economic management would suggest that their purchase should be paid from current revenues.

Finally, there is a standard problem in all public decisions: establishing priorities. How do items get into the capital budget? Cost-benefit analysis, examined in a later section, gives some assistance, but as with operating programs, there are no unambiguous answers. Projects that the elected chief executive is interested in always have a good shot at being included.

---

[20]Ibid, 256.

Accounting for Time: Discounting and Compounding

The costs and benefits of most public projects, particularly those long-life, high-price projects proposed in a capital budget, seldom occur in any single year. More often than not, an initial capital expenditure is made in one year and both operating cost and program returns accrue over a long project life. In that event, special attention must be given to the timing of the flows, recognizing that a return available only at some point in the future has less value than an equal return available now.

The approach for comparing such impacts on personal, business, and public finance is discounting, a process of converting a stream of returns or costs incurred over time to a single present value. The present value accounts for both the absolute size and the timing of impacts of a proposed action. It applies the concept of time value of money.

Why is a payment of $100 received 1 year from now not equivalent to $100 received now? If inflation's erosion of purchasing power and the uncertainty of the future seem to make the answer obvious, assume that the $100 is certain to be received and has been adjusted for price-level changes: The reason for discounting is related neither to inflation nor to uncertainty. The reason is simply that the $100 available now can yield a flow of valuable services (or interest) throughout the year. Or, even more to the point, the private market tells us that people must be compensated if they sacrifice current use of resources for future use. At the end of the year, the holder could have $100 plus the flow received from use of the $100 during the year. Therefore, $100 now has greater value than does $100 received at the end of the year. As the date of receipt is more distant, the present value of a given dollar amount is lower: the flow of services between now and then would be greater.

Although the principle of time value applies to any resource or service, the mechanics are most often done using market-exchange equivalents (dollar values) of those returns, and the analysis uses investment for interest as the earned service flow. Thus, $\$X$ available now (the principal) becomes $\$X$ plus $\$X$ times the rate of interest (the principal plus interest earned on that principal) at the end of 1 year. The mechanics of discounting are easier to understand after working through the more familiar process of compounding. Suppose the appropriate rate of interest is 5 percent; if $1,000 is invested today, it will accumulate to $1,050 by the end of the year. Thus,

$$\$1{,}050 = \$1{,}000 + (\$1{,}000 \times 0.05)$$

or

$$\text{Amount at end of year} = \text{Original principal} + \text{Interest earned}$$

Algebraically, if r = rate of interest, PV = the present amount, and FV_1 = the amount at the end of a year, then

$$FV_1 = PV + PVr \text{ or } FV_1 = PV(1 + r)$$

Where FV_1 equals the original principal (PV) plus accumulated interest ($PV \times r$)

Many policy and management questions involve multiple-year decisions in which the returns are permitted to compound over several years. In other words, the principal plus accumulated interest is reinvested and allowed to accumulate. An example is calculation of the amount to which $1,000 would have accumulated at the end of 5 years with 5 percent annual interest. Figure 6–2 shows annual account balances. There is an easier way, however, to compute compound interest. Using the symbols previously introduced for values now and values at the end of a year,

$$FV_1 = PV(1 + .05) = PV(1.05).$$

At the end of the second year, the account balance would increase from interest earned:

$$FV_2 = FV_1(1.05) = PV(1.05)(1.05) = PV(1.05)^2.$$

The same increase from interest earned occurs at the end of the third year:

$$FV_3 = FV_2(1.05) = \{[PV(1.05)](1.05)\}(1.05) = PV(1.05)^3.$$

For the fourth year,

$$FV_4 = FV_3(1.05) = \{[PV(1.05)](1.05)\}(1.05)(1.05) = PV(1.05)^4.$$

Figure 6–2
Compounding

Initial Deposit, $1,000	Interest Earned (interest rate × previous balance)	Account Balance
End of year:		
1	$50.00	$1,050.00
2	52.50	1,102.50
3	55.13	1,157.63
4	57.88	1,215.51
5	60.78	1,276.29

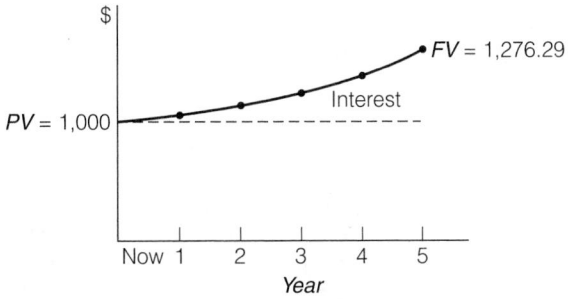

The same process applies regardless of the number of years. In general, if PV = the present amount, r = the appropriate interest rate, n = the number of periods of compounding, and FV_n = the account balance at the end of the periods,

$$FV_n = PV(1 + r)^n.$$

From the previous example,

$$FV_n = 1{,}000(1.05)^5 = 1{,}276.28$$

Financial contracts often provide for compounding more frequently than once a year. The compounding formula can easily be adjusted to allow for semiannual, quarterly, or any other regular frequency-of-interest payment. For example, suppose interest is paid twice a year. With an annual rate of 10 percent, that system would mean 5 percent interest is paid for the first half of the year and 5 percent is paid for the second half of the year. Thus, principal plus interest amounts at the end of the half-years would be:

$FV_1 = PV(1.05)$ (balance at end of one half-year)
$FV_2 = PV(1.05)^2$ (balance at end of two half-years)
$FV_3 = PV(1.05)^3$ (balance at end of three half-years)

and so on. Thus, at the end of n years,

$$FV_n = PV(1.05)^{2n}.$$

In general, if interest is added x times per year and other definitions are as before,

$$FV_n = PV\left[1+\left(\frac{r}{x}\right)\right]^{2n}$$

Discounting simply adjusts sums to be received in the future to their present-value equivalent, the amount that will accumulate to that future sum if invested at prevailing interest rates. Recall that FV, the accumulated balance at the end of 1 year, equals $PV(1 + r)$, the balance at the start of the year multiplied by 1 plus the rate of interest. That formula can be rearranged to become:

$$PV = \frac{FV_1}{(1+r)}$$

The amount PV invested at interest rate r will grow to FV_1 by the end of the year.

Suppose $1,000 will be received at the end of 1 year (FV = 1,000). If the interest rate that could be earned is 5 percent, what sum today (PV) would accumulate to $1,000 by the end of the year? That present value emerges from operation of the present-value formula:

$$PV = \frac{\$1,000}{(1+0.05)} = \$952.38$$

That means that $952.38 now, plus 5-percent interest earned for 1 year ($952.38 × 0.05) equals $1,000: the present-value equivalent of $1,000 received at the end of 1 year when the available prevailing interest rate is 5 percent is $952.38. That prevailing rate is called the discount rate.

What happens if the return is received more than 1 year into the future? The same logic of adjusting for interest that could have been earned still applies, but the computations look messier because the interest earned would compound. In other words, interest earned during the first year would earn interest in the second year, and so on through the years. The general formula for compounding, $FV_n = PV(1 + r)^n$, can be rearranged in the same way that the single-year compounding formula was to produce the general present-value formula

$$PV = \frac{FV_n}{(1+r)^n}$$

where PV = the present-value equivalent, FV_n = a value received in the future, r = the discount rate, and n = the number of years into the future that the sum is received. For example, $800 received 10 years in the future, assuming a 10-percent discount rate, would have a present value of $800/(1 + r)^n$, or $308.43.

Projects yielding dramatically different returns over time can and must be compared using this technique. Suppose an agency has two projects under consideration. Each costs $1,900 (all occurring at the present), but the profile of returns from the projects differs substantially:

Received at End of Year	Project A	Project B
1	1,000	480
2	300	480
3	1,000	480
4	0	480
5	0	480

Neither project lasts beyond the fifth year. Which project yields greater net benefits? Recognize that simple addition of returns—$2,300 for project A and $2,400 for project B—is not appropriate because the timing of those returns is not the same.

A fair comparison requires that both streams be converted to their present-value equivalents. Suppose that prevailing interest-rate conditions indicate that resources should earn a 10-percent return. Ten percent is then a reasonable discount rate to use, with the following results:

Received at End of Year	Discount Factor	Project A Return ($)	Discounted ($)	Project B Return ($)	Discounted ($)
1	$1/(1.1) = .909$	1,000	909	480	436
2	$1/(1.1)^2 = .826$	300	248	480	396
3	$1/(1.1)^3 = .751$	1,000	751	480	360
4	$1/(1.1)^4 = .683$	0	0	480	328
5	$1/(1.1)^5 = .621$	0	0	480	298
Total	Present Value		1,908		1,818

Under those conditions, the present value of project A is $1,908 and of project B, $1,818. Of the two projects, only A has a value exceeding its cost.

What would happen if 3 percent were the appropriate discount rate? As the following table shows, the present value of both would be above the cost of the project:

Received at End of Year	Discount Factor	Current ($)	Discounted ($)	Current ($)	Discounted ($)
1	$1/(1.03)^2 = .971$	1,000	971	480	466
2	$1/(1.03)^2 = .943$	300	283	480	453
3	$1/(1.03)^3 = .915$	1,000	915	480	439
4	$1/(1.03)^4 = .888$	0	0	480	426
5	$1/(1.03)^5 = .863$	0	0	480	414
Total	Present Value		2,169		2,198

In fact, project B now has a present value greater than project A, because returns in the future make greater contributions to present value when the discount is lower. Choice of the appropriate discount rate clearly matters for public decisions—an artificially high or low rate can lead to wasteful choices.

Analysts sometimes compare alternatives by determining what discount rate would cause the present value of projects under consideration to be equal. Thus, the present value of projects A and B would be the same at a rate around 4 percent. If the rate is above that level, A is better; if below, B is better.

In many situations, the income stream to be discounted may be constant for several years. For instance, a new maintenance garage might reduce costs by $20,000 per year for 25 years, and that cost savings is to be compared with the construction cost of the garage. The flow in each year could be discounted back to the present; a quicker approach entails use of an annuity formula to compute the present value of the income stream in a single computation. If S equals the amount of the annual flow and other variables are as previously defined,

$$PV = \frac{S}{r}\left[1-\left(\frac{1}{1+r}\right)^{n}\right]$$

All rules about more frequent compounding (quarterly, semiannually, monthly) apply in this formula as well. In the example here, the present value of those maintenance garage cost savings if $r = 10$ percent would equal

$$PV = \frac{20{,}000}{.10}\left[1-\left(\frac{1}{1.1}\right)^{25}\right] = \$181{,}541$$

This formula is used later in bond pricing (Chapter 15).[21]

These basic principles of discounting and compounding are the building blocks of most financial analysis. Not only are they used in capital budgeting decision-making but, as is seen in later sections, they are critical for cost-benefit analysis, debt administration, fund investment, and tax policy. An understanding of the time-value concept is essential to become fully functional in government finance.

Cost-Benefit Analysis

Because society cannot afford to waste its scarce resources, judging whether a particular program is worth its cost is a constant problem in public-program choice. Cost-benefit analysis provides a way of organizing information about a program under consideration so that priorities may be reasonably established.[22] A private

[21]This formula can also be used to determine the mortgage payment (principal and interest) needed to pay off a loan, and is often used by engineers to convert a capital cost into an annual cost equivalent (annualization). In the formula, change *PV* (present value of the flow) to *P* (amount of the loan) and solve for *S* (the periodic payment):

$$S = \frac{P * r}{\left[1-\left(\frac{1}{1+r}\right)^{n}\right]}$$

For example, the monthly principal and interest for an $80,000 mortgage taken for 20 years at a 7-percent interest rate would be computed as follows:

$$S = \frac{80{,}000 * \frac{0.07}{12}}{\left[1-\left(\frac{1}{1+\left(\frac{0.07}{12}\right)}\right)^{12*20}\right]} = 620$$

[22]One source for more complete coverage of cost-benefit analysis is Edward M. Gramlich, *Benefit-Cost Analysis of Government Programs,* 2nd ed. (Englewood Cliffs, N.J.: Prentice Hall, 1990).

firm considers a major project (say, the purchase of a new delivery truck to replace an older, smaller one) and compares the anticipated increase in revenue from the new truck with the anticipated increase in costs. If the revenue exceeds cost, the purchase of the truck is a wise use of the firm's scarce resources; if not, the purchase is unwise.

Cost-benefit analysis is the government analog to that process of private capital budgeting. Governments can use the tool for assistance in making decisions as diverse as purchasing information technology systems, modernizing vehicle fleets, developing water resource projects, developing communicable disease control programs, and building new highways and bridges. It has also been used to evaluate the worth of numerous government regulations.[23] For capital budget purposes, however, cost-benefit analysis is similar to decision-making processes used by private firms: The analysis estimates whether the gain to society (benefit) from the project is greater than the social sacrifice (cost) required to produce the project. If so, the project is worthwhile; if not, the project is not worthwhile. Worthwhile projects improve economic conditions in that worthwhile projects direct resources where their use provides a greater return than would alternative uses.

Skeptics point out that what characterizes the public decision process is political bargaining, not an exercise in rational consideration by nonpolitical administrators.[24] So what service can cost-benefit analysis provide? First, the analysis augments the political influence of underrepresented potential beneficiaries and identifies the position of cost bearers. A display of costs and benefits makes it more difficult for the unrepresented to be ignored in political bargaining. In some instances, it can be a valuable weapon (for either side) in the "it pays for itself" budget strategy. Second, economic efficiency—the guiding force of cost-benefit analysis—is but one of several public goals. Even though a decision may not be based primarily on those grounds, the potential gain sacrificed in the selection of a particular public policy is important information. Third, cost-benefit analysis forces public decision-making to focus on the value of competing alternatives. Valuation and the accompanying process of competing priorities are the keys to sound decision-making, so cost benefit analysis directs attention to vital questions.

The cost-benefit logic is not limited to complex projects; it can be particularly useful in more narrow public-management decisions about alternative methods of accomplishing a particular task. Among the applications are repair-replace and lease-purchase decisions, fuel conversion, modernization choices, and data-processing equipment acquisitions. In these decisions, the objective is simply to perform a task at least cost, often when one option involves a capital expenditure and others do not.

---

[23]"Best practices" for preparing economic analysis of regulatory actions are presented in Executive Office of the President, Office of Management and Budget, *Economic Analysis of Federal Regulations Under Executive Order 12866* (Washington, D.C.: Office of Management and Budget, 1996).

[24]Federal water resource projects have one of the longest histories of cost-benefit applications. Even here, Eric Schenker and Michael Bunamo indicate that these projects are strongly influenced by purely political factors when examined across regions in the United States. See "A Study of the Corps of Engineers' Regional Pattern of Investments," *Southern Economic Journal* 39 (April 1973): 548–58.

Elements in Cost-Benefit Analysis

Five steps make up formal cost-benefit analysis: (1) categorizing project objectives, (2) estimating the project's impact on objectives, (3) estimating project costs, (4) discounting cost and benefit flows at an appropriate discount rate, and (5) summarizing findings in a fashion suitable for decision-making.[25] The content of the analysis varies according to the project considered; the following discussion focuses on common elements and their application in selected situations.

Project objectives. The project analysis should identify the project's benefits. What desirable results will happen because of the project? The relationship between the project and the objective must be traceable to establish a sound foundation for the analysis. The following are some examples: A rapid transit system could increase travel speed (saving time for travelers), reduce accident costs, and reduce private-vehicle operation costs; a water project might reduce flood damage, provide water for residential and other use, and improve effluent dilution for water-quality management; a new fire station may reduce operating costs of an older facility and reduce prospective fire loss in a service area; a word processing system may reduce labor costs, material costs, and filing expenses. The analysis must focus on the factors that are different in the options under consideration. Nothing can be gained by examination of factors that are not changed by the decision. The principle seems too simple to matter, except that much policy argument takes place about elements that will not change regardless of the choice selected.

This simple example illustrates some elements of the necessary incremental logic. Suppose a town is contemplating a newspaper-recycling project; its garbage truck will be fitted with a rack to collect bundles of newspapers along the collection route. Cost and revenue estimates prepared by the town clerk appear in the following list:

	Annual Cost
Labor (one extra worker to gather and process papers)	$14,000
Purchase and installation of rack (1-year useful life)	400
Apportioned share of truck operation and maintenance	1,500
Apportioned share of Public Works Department administrative expense	2,000
Total	$17,900
	Annual Revenue
980 tons of paper at $15 per ton	$14,700
Annual Loss (or Required Subsidy)	($3,200)

Although the estimates are consistent with accounting principles that require each activity to bear its share of entity-operation cost, the conflict is with the

[25]The Office of Management and Budget provides in Circular A-94 an instruction guide to preparing cost-benefit analyses for the federal government: Executive Office of the President, Office of Management and Budget, *Circular A-94 Revised (Transmittal Memo No. 64)*, 29 October 1992.

incremental principle: Only costs or revenue that change with a decision should be considered in making the decision. In the preceding example, there is nothing logically wrong with estimates of revenue, labor cost, or rack cost: None of those would exist without the recycling, so they are incremental to the decision. There are problems, however, with the administrative, operational, and maintenance cost figures: Will any of these costs be different because of the recycling program? If not (which is probably the case), they should be excluded in making the decision. When the adjustment to incremental reasoning is made, the program actually will subsidize the general government ($300 incremental revenue over incremental cost), rather than require subsidization. And there may be further gains if costs of the traditional waste-management operation are reduced because newspapers are no longer in the stream going to the landfill.

Benefit estimation and valuation. A Senate guide to water-project evaluation defines benefits as "increase or gains, net of associated or induced costs, in the value of goods and services which result from conditions with the project, as compared with conditions without the project."[26] The same logic applies to any project. Thus, the analyst must estimate for the life of the project both physical changes from the project and the value of these changes. No single method applies for all projects: Specific techniques used to estimate benefits of a personnel-training project would not be the same as those used in water projects. Regardless of the project, however, the decision must be made from estimates, not facts. Facts in economic or social relationships can be only historical. Present decisions cannot change what has already happened, and what will happen can only be estimated. The analysis must proceed with best estimates; it cannot be paralyzed by lack of complete information because complete information is only available when it is too late to decide.

An initial step estimates the physical size of the project's expected change. Sometimes a controlled experiment on a sample can estimate probable effects before resources are committed to the entire program. For instance, the state of Virginia estimated the likely benefits of reflectorized motor vehicle plates by comparing accident frequency among a random sample of cars equipped with these plates with frequency in the remainder of the population.[27] The controlled experiment results could be used to estimate accident reduction from reflectorized plates for the entire state.

Controlled experiments, however, are seldom possible. More often, models developed from the social, physical, or engineering sciences are used to estimate that change. For water-resource projects, hydrological models can yield estimates of the influence of reservoirs, canals, and channelization on water flows and levels. From that information, the effects on navigation, probability of flooding, water supply, and so on, can be derived. Gravity models from economic analysis and marketing

---

[26]U.S. Senate, *Politics, Standards and Procedures in the Formulation, Evaluation and Review of Plans for Use in Development of Water and Related Land Resources,* 87th Cong., 2nd sess., May 1962, S. Doc. 97.

[27]Charles B. Stoke, *Reflectorized License Plates: Do They Reduce Nighttime Rear-End Collision?* (Charlottesville: Virginia Highway Research Council, 1974). Drivers were not told and could not control the type of plates they received. The plates did not make a difference in the incidence of such collisions.

can indicate likely drawing power of various public facilities. Trip-generation models can suggest traffic flows from transportation facility changes. Any model allows the analyst to apply evidence from other environments to predict the results of projects under consideration, so that these changes can be valued: Analytical models are the key to linking government inputs to government outputs. Harold Hovey describes the importance of models:

> To analyze any program . . . requires a model, which describes the relationship between what we put into the activity (inputs) and what we expect to get out of it (outputs). Good models explain what exact relationships are, not just that a relationship exists . . . To require that the model be made explicit is one of the greatest potential contributions of systematic analysis to government. An explicit model can be studied, criticized, evaluated, and improved. Too often, decisions are made without explicit models. The result can never be better than if the model is explicit, it can frequently be worse.[28]

When the project's impact has been estimated, the worth of its benefits must then be gauged. Such valuation permits comparison of project cost to project returns and helps establish whether the undertaking increases the net well-being of the region. Money values are used, not to glorify money but to provide a common yardstick to compare how individuals value the project with how they value the resources used by that project. For example, one million tons of concrete applied to highway construction may prolong by 1 year the useful life of 5,000 automobiles; resources of one type are used to save resources of another type. Will the community be better off with that use of its scarce resources? A direct comparison is impossible because units being measured (cars and concrete) are not the same. Our only meaningful alternative is to estimate the relative value individuals place on cars and concrete: How much general purchasing power are individuals willing to give up to acquire each? Those purchasing-power units provide the measuring standard.

The particular valuation approach depends on the project, but the task is always easiest when values can be connected to a private market, that is, when the public good being considered is an intermediate good. For instance, river-navigation projects may reduce shipper costs: The estimated difference between costs of river shipment and costs of the cheapest available alternative can indicate the value of an increased volume of shipping. The value of employment-training projects can best be estimated from differences in anticipated pre- and post-project incomes of trainees. Many capital expenditure items purchased by governments may reduce operating costs, in which case those savings are the primary benefit from the project.[29]

---

[28]Harold A. Hovey, *The Planning-Programming-Budgeting Approach to Government Decision-Making* (New York: Praeger, 1968), 23.

[29]The public value of a National Football League (NFL) franchise has been estimated by real property rents in NFL cities compared to cities without a franchise. Gerald Carlino and N. Edward Coulson, "Compensating Differentials and Social Benefits of the NFL," *Journal of Urban Economics* 56 (June 2004): 25–50. A cost-benefit analysis of government subsidies to NFL franchises (mostly stadium subsidies) working from this benefit calculation suggests that they may be a good investment for cities.

For some projects, however, outputs are not linked to goods or services sold in private markets: The output is desired for its own sake (relaxation in a city park), not because it contributes to another production process. In other words, these outputs are final products, as opposed to the intermediate products that contribute to the production of a private good.[30] When the government product or service is a final product, or when prices of marketed commodities change as a result of the project, a different approach is used. That approach is the estimation of *consumers' surplus*—the difference between the maximum price consumers would willingly pay for given amounts of a commodity and the price that the market demands for the commodity (which would be zero for public services provided at no direct charge). The underlying logic of consumer surplus is relatively simple, although its application is anything but simple: Points along an individual's demand curve for a product or service represent the value the person places on particular amounts of the product in question. The individual would voluntarily pay a price up to the level on the demand curve rather than not have the product. He or she would not pay more, so the price on the curve represents the individual's valuation of the product.

Figure 6–3 is a representation of an individual's demand for visits to a park; for ten visits to the park, the maximum that individual would pay is $5. If the price actually charged is above $5, the individual would visit fewer times (if at all); if the price is below $5, the individual receives a consumer surplus—the consumer receives the service at less than the price he or she would have willingly paid. Consumer surplus then equals the difference between the maximum price the individual would have paid less the price he or she actually pays multiplied by the number of units purchased. If the price were zero (the park has no admission charge), the total consumer surplus here would be

$$(\$10 \times 5) + (\$5 \times (5) + (\$2 \times 5) + (\$1 \times 5) = \$90.$$

That is the entire area under the demand curve for the service.

Figure 6–3
Individual Demand for a Park

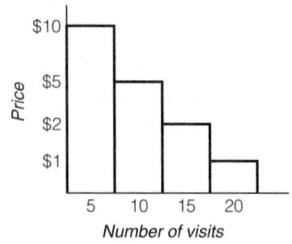

[30]Richard A. Musgrave, "Cost-Benefit Analysis and the Theory of Public Finance," *Journal of Economic Literature* 7 (September 1969).

Public services are seldom sold, so how is it possible to consider quantities demanded as a function of price? The demand curves are constructed by recognizing that implicit prices must be paid to use even free services. Individuals must bear the cost of getting from where they live to the free facility; this cost is the implicit price. User-pattern analysis allows estimation of a demand curve. Use (quantity demanded) usually is greater by those who are closest to the facility (travel cost, or implicit price, is lower), following the configuration of a conventional demand curve.[31] Estimating consumer surplus is not without problems, but it really is the only reasonable technique for that class of public services. Contingent valuation, as described in Sidebar 6–1, provides another approach to estimating the demand for a pure public good.

Estimating project costs. A project's resource cost estimate includes construction cost and operating cost for the life of the project. Obviously the preparation of these estimates requires the close cooperation of engineers and accountants skilled in costing, particularly if heavy public-work facilities are involved. The analyst must recognize, however, that the important cost for society is the opportunity cost of the resources used in the project: "By the opportunity cost of a decision is meant the sacrifice of alternatives required by that decision . . . [O]pportunity costs require the measurement of sacrifices. If a decision involves no sacrifices, it is cost free."[32] The cost that matters for decisions is the value of paths not taken, the true cost of any decision. That complication can produce three types of cost-estimate adjustments based initially on resource purchase prices. First, ordinary project cost estimates include only private or internal costs. Many public projects, however, can create undesirable effects on others, or negative externalities. Examples include the damage done to surrounding properties by pollutants produced by a municipal incinerator or the traffic delays created when streets are blocked by construction of a government office building. These are costs inflicted on parties outside the market transaction, but the costs are just as real to society as wages or payment for construction materials. These adjustments are made using the same indirect methods applied in benefit estimation—these impacts are, logically, negative social benefits.

Second, adjustments are appropriate if the project uses completely unemployed resources or resources for which there is no alternative use. If such is the case, there is nothing sacrificed in consuming those resources in the project being considered. Thus, the actual social opportunity cost of the resource to the project is zero, not the financial cost involved in paying the resource's owner. For that reason, it may be sensible to undertake programs in areas with massive unemployment when that program ordinarily would not be economically justifiable: Putting the idle resources to work adds a desired product without economic loss.

Third, many public projects use property already owned by the government. Property acquisition brings no out-of-pocket cost; when sites for a new highway,

---

[31]An interesting application of the technique to estimate benefits from visits to historical sites using the consumer-surplus approach is Richard J. Cirre, *Estimating User Benefits from Historic Sites and Museums* (Ithaca, N.Y.: Program in Urban and Regional Studies, Cornell University, 1977).

[32]William Warren Haynes, *Managerial Economics* (Plano, Tex.: Business Publications, 1969), 32.

Sidebar 6–1
Measuring the Value of Nonmarket Goods

The nonappropriability feature of a public good prevents direct measurement of the market value of that good. Market value emerges from the independent decisions of buyers and sellers in exchange transactions. Nonappropriability means that sellers cannot charge an appropriate price to cover the cost of resources needed for service provisions and buyers will not pay a price sufficient to reflect the full social value of the service. Where transactions do occur, they cannot be expected to reflect the social value of the service.

So is there a way in which market-type valuation information can be obtained for a pure public good? The Council of Economic Advisers in its 1993 *Economic Report of the President* describes one approach that has been used.

> Since a public good is not traded on a competitive market, the market cannot assign it a price based on its value. Measuring the benefits public goods provide is problematic. One method is to infer the value of public goods from actual markets or observable economic behavior. For example, to estimate the value people put on scenic beauty, economists may measure the effect of scenic beauty on actual real estate prices. The value that people put on a park may be reflected in the amount of time and money that they spend to visit and use it.
>
> The contingent-valuation method (CVM) uses public opinion surveys. A polltaker asks people to estimate the amount they would be willing to pay to maintain or create a certain public good or the amount they would require to compensate for its loss. Advocates of the CVM argue that it can generate reliable estimates of value in cases where it is impossible to make inferences from actual markets or behavior, and in principle, it takes into account the fact that some people value a good more highly than others do.
>
> However, the CVM also has generated considerable criticism. For example, those surveyed do not actually have to pay the amount they report, a factor that can lead to overstatements. Responses are sensitive to the way questions are posed. (In one case, the estimated value of protection from oil spills changed by a factor of 300 when polltakers asked additional questions before eliciting this value.) CVM results can be inconsistent. (For example, one CVM study showed that people were willing to pay more money to clean up small oilspills than to clean up both small and large spills.) In many cases, CVM results cannot be verified except by another CVM study.
>
> These problems are exacerbated when the CVM is used to estimate the value of goods that are abstract, symbolic, or difficult to comprehend. One study showed that if the CVM were used to estimate the value of saving whooping cranes from extinction, resulting estimates might be as high as $37 billion per year (more than the Federal Government spends each year on education and Head Start programs). Finally, even if all the problems of the CVM could be resolved, care must be taken to ensure that it is not used to analyze policy in a one-sided way. For example, a proposed program to protect whooping cranes might put people out of work. The $37 billion figure could be cited by those who claim that the benefits of the program exceed its costs. But opponents of that view could undertake a CVM study of their own asking people how much they would be willing to pay to protect these jobs.

A valuation by CVM will not be perfect, but it certainly is preferable to ignoring these nonmarket impacts—which generally amounts to assuming that they have no value.

SOURCE: Executive Office of the President, Council of Economic Advisors, *Economic Report of the President, Transmitted to Congress January 1993* (Washington, D.C.: U.S. GPO, 1993), 209.

incinerator, and so forth, are being compared, the site using public property has the lowest financial cost. The real social cost of that site for the proposed project is the site's value in its existing (or other possible) use. What does the community lose if the site is selected for the new use? There is no justification for valuing already-owned properties at zero. Furthermore, the amount paid for the resource (its historical cost) may not be a usable guide. For example, if a municipality invests $1.5 million in a new incinerator plant that will not burn the refuse mix generated by the city, the value of the plant clearly is less than $1.5 million and, unless there is some salvage value for the facility, approximates zero.

Decisions have to be based on alternatives sacrificed and opportunities forgone. Amounts paid in the past (historical costs) have no necessary bearing on cost in present decisions. Options now establish the cost that matters for current choices.

Selecting a Discount Rate

Public projects usually create a flow of costs and returns that span several years. Therefore, both streams must be converted to present value for comparison; discounting is necessary. There is, however, no single discount rate that is immediately obvious as the appropriate rate for analysis.[33] Market imperfections and differences in risk cause a broad spectrum of interest rates in the economy. Two important alternatives for discounting are the cost of borrowed funds to the government (the interest rate the government must pay) and the opportunity cost of displaced private activity (the return that private resources could earn). There are conditions under which either may be appropriate.

The cost of borrowed money provides the closest analog to private-project analysis—it is an interest rate that presumably must be paid by a borrower. Because most public programs are ultimately financed by tax revenues, use of the rate at which a government can borrow would not necessarily direct resources to their best-yield uses. Absence of default risk on (federal) government debt makes that rate abnormally low. Allocation using that rate would pull resources away from higher-yielding private activities to prospectively lower-yield public use. Sidebar 6–2 describes the different philosophies and rules in the federal government. For state and local governments, the borrowing rate could be particularly misleading because the exclusion of interest on most state and local debt from federal income tax allows these governments to borrow at well below the market rate.[34] Public authorities that generate revenue from sales of products or services might use that rate because it estimates the market attitude toward the prospects of the

---

[33]The Federal Reserve discount rate is the interest rate at which the Federal Reserve will make loans to banks that are members of the Federal Reserve System. Although this rate is published as the discount rate, it is not appropriate for discounting or compounding in financial management.

[34]An individual in the 35-percent federal tax bracket would receive the same after-tax rate of return on a taxed corporate bond yielding 15 percent as on an untaxed municipal bond yielding 9.75 percent, calculated by subtracting the tax that would be owed on that 15 percent rate to get the net after-tax rate, that is, $(15 - .35(15)) = 9.75$.

Sidebar 6–2
What Discount Rate to Use?

The big three of federal government finance—Office of Managament and Budget (OMB), GAO, and CBO—all do discounting in consideration of capital expenditure programs, lease-purchase decisions, regulatory reviews, valuation of assets for sale, and so on. But the discount rates they use are not the same. Here is a quick summary of their rates.

The OMB establishes the discount policy for almost all executive agencies in its Circular No. A-94. The current base case analysis prescribes a real discount rate of 7 percent, a rate to approximate the marginal pretax rate of return on average private sector investment in recent years. There are exceptions to that base policy. Water project analysis uses a rate based on the average yield during the previous fiscal year on interest-bearing marketable securities of the United States, which have terms of 15 years or longer to maturity. Cost-effectiveness analysis with constant-dollar costs should use the real Treasury borrowing rate on marketable securities of comparable maturity to the period of analysis and lease-purchase analysis of nominal lease payments should use the nominal Treasury borrowing rate on marketable securities of maturity comparable to the period of analysis. Internal Federal investments that either increase Federal revenue or decrease Federal cost should generally use the comparable maturity Treasury rate.

The GAO uses a discount rate based on the average nominal yield of marketable Treasury debt with maturity between 1 year and the life of the project, with benefits and costs in nominal terms. The same rate applies for all evaluation uses; the GAO endorses sensitivity analysis.

The CBO uses the real yield of Treasury debt and estimates that rate to be 2 percent with a sensitivity analysis of 2 percentage points to test variability. Asset valuation uses comparable private sector interest rates.

SOURCES: Randolph M. Lyon, "Federal Discount Rate Policy, the Shadow Price of Capital, and Challenges for Reform," *Journal of Environmental Economics and Management* 18 (March 1990), Part 2; and Office of Management and Budget, *Circular A-94 Revised (Transmittal Memo No. 64),* (29 October 1992).

enterprise. Even here, however, the interest excluded from income taxes complicates the analysis.

The return that could have been achieved in displaced private spending is generally more appropriate for the logic of cost-benefit analysis (an analysis aimed at discovering actions that increase the welfare of the community). It is a rate the analyst must estimate—there is no defined interest rate. William Baumol lucidly expresses the essential argument:

> If the resources in question produce a rate of return in the private sector which society evaluates at *r* percent, then the resources should be transferred to the public project if

that project yields a return greater than r percent. They should be left in private hands if their potential earnings in the proposed government investment is less than r percent.[35]

The problem is to estimate what the rate of return would have been on these displaced resources, because that is the opportunity cost a public project must exceed if it is not to misallocate community resources. In general, this rate can be estimated according to the formula

$$P = k_1 r_1 + k_2 r_2 + \ldots + k_n r_n$$

where

P = rate of return on displaced resources (the project discount rate)
k = fraction of project cost extracted from a particular sector (usually the percentage of total taxes collected from it)
r = return on investment in a particular private sector
n = number of private sectors with displaced resources

This weighted average provides a workable estimate of the private opportunity cost of the displaced resources and the resulting discount rate is applied to the estimated benefit and cost flows.[36]

Decision Criteria

The final stage in project analysis applies a decision criterion to the discounted cost and return flows to summarize the economic case for the project. The summarization can either identify whether a project is economically justifiable or establish rankings among projects to be fitted into a limited budget. Two criteria often used are the benefit-cost ratio (BCR, the present value of benefits divided by the present value of costs) and the NPV of the project (the present value of benefits less the present value of costs). If B = project benefit, C = project cost, r = the appropriate discount rate, t = the year in the life of the project, and T = the life of the project, then

$$NPV = \sum_{t=1}^{T} \frac{(B_t - C_t)}{(1+r)^t}$$

[35]William J. Baumol, "On the Discount Rate for Public Projects," in Robert H. Haveman and Julius Margolis, eds., *Public Expenditures and Policy Analysis,* (Chicago: Markham, 1970), 274.
[36]When the time span for the consequences is very long—hundreds of years, as would be the case for certain environmental policies—it is extremely difficult to identify an appropriate discount rate. The long-term ramifications may be huge, but disappear at any normal discount rate. Some options are proposed in Paul R. Portney and John P. Weyant, eds., *Discounting and Intergenerational Equity* (Washington, D.C.: Resources for the Future, 1999).

and

$$BCR = \frac{\sum_{t=1}^{T} \frac{B_t}{(1+r)^t}}{\sum_{t=1}^{T} \frac{C_t}{(1+r)^t}}$$

The test of economic efficiency requires NPV greater than 0 or BCR greater than 1: If the test is met, resource use for the project will increase economic well-being because alternative use of those resources would produce a lower return for the community. Application of these criteria ignores politics, desires for wealth redistribution, regional problems, and other important concerns, but both NPV and BCR capture the economics of the project. Sidebar 6–3 gives a simple illustration of a capital project evaluated according to the principles of cost-benefit analysis.

Two additional measures sometimes proposed should be mentioned briefly. These are the payback period and the internal rate of return. The payback-period method divides the estimated net annual flow of project returns into the capital cost of the project to obtain the number of years it would take to fully recover (pay back) the capital cost. Thus, if $2,000 is the net annual return from a project with a capital cost of $8,000, the payback period is 4 years. The shorter the period, the more attractive the project. This measure is defective in that it ignores both the time profile of returns (proceeds available only late in project life are valued as if equal to earlier returns) and proceeds received after the payback point. For example, consider the projects in Table 6–2. By payback-period reasoning, the project ranking (best to worst) would be A, B, C. If a discount rate of 10 percent were appropriate, the NPV of A = 2,909, of B = 909, and of C = 1,292. Crude payback periods are simply not generally reliable as a project guide.[37]

The internal-rate-of-return method seeks the interest rate that would equate the present value of benefits with the present value of the costs. That return is compared with the discount rate: The project passes the economic efficiency test if its rate of return is higher than the discount rate. Computation of an internal rate of return may be illustrated using the data for project C in Table 6–2. The internal-rate-of-return (R) is the rate that causes the stream of net benefits in the future to exactly equal the present capital cost:

$$10{,}000 = \left(\frac{3{,}000}{(1+R)}\right) + \left(\frac{4{,}000}{(1+R)^2}\right) + \left(\frac{7{,}000}{(1+R)^3}\right)$$

R may be computed only by successively trying values of R until the value for the right side equals the left side. The computations are relatively simple in this instance

[37]However, a recent study of Canadian municipalities found a distinct preference for the payback approach in doing capital budgets, in spite of its clear deficiencies. Yee Ching Lillian Chang, "Use of Capital Budgeting Techniques and an Analytic Approach to Capital Investment Decisions in Canadian Municipal Governments," *Public Budgeting & Finance,* 24 (Summer 2004), 40–58.

Sidebar 6–3
An Application of Net Present Value to Evaluate a Capital Project

A major university hosted a nationally televised football game toward the end of its unsuccessful season, and the field was in such poor condition that alumni from around the country called to complain about the poor image it gave their alma mater. The university must replace the field. It has two alternatives: a conventional sod field or a synthetic turf called Astro Play. The Astro Play would cost $446,000 to install, requires no annual maintenance, and can be used for 12 seasons. The sod field would cost $110,000 to replace, will last 3 seasons, and requires an annual maintenance cost of $20,000 in each non-replacement year. Suppose that 5 percent is a reasonable discount rate. What is the NPV of installing the turf?

The NPV of installing Astro Play is computed by comparing the NPV of costs over the 10 year period for the two field options. The NPV of the cost of the sod field would equal the benefit from installing the synthetic surface because it is these costs that would be avoided with the Astro Play. The cost of Astro Play simply equals its installation cost because there are no other costs through its useful life.

The flow of costs from the alternatives, the appropriate discount factor [$(1.05)^n$ where n = years since initial installation], and the discounted costs of the alternative are as follows:

	Cost of Sod Field ($)	Discount Factor	Present Value of Sod Field Cost ($)
Beginning	110,000	1.00	110,000
Year 1	20,000	1.05	19,047.62
Year 2	20,000	1.103	18,140.59
Year 3	110,000	1.158	95,022.14
Year 4	20,000	1.216	16,454.05
Year 5	20,000	1.276	15,670.52
Year 6	110,000	1.340	82,083.69
Year 7	20,000	1.407	14,213.63
Year 8	20,000	1.477	13,536.79
Year 9	110,000	1.551	70,906.98
Year 10	20,000	1.629	12,278.27
Year 11	20,000	1.710	11,693.59
Total			479,047.86

The NPV of installing Astro Play equals the difference between discounted benefits and discounted costs. Discounted benefits equal $479,047.86; discounted cost equals $446,000. The NPV equals $33,047.86 and the benefit-cost ratio equals 1.074.

The football team may still lose, but the cost-benefit analysis indicates that it should be playing on the synthetic turf to save the university some money. And it will look good while losing!

Table 6–2
Payback Analysis

		Annual Net Benefits (End of Year)			
Project	Capital Cost ($)	Year 1 ($)	Year 2 ($)	Year 3 ($)	Payback Period
A	10,000	10,000	0	0	1 year
B	10,000	9,000	1,100	0	1+ years
C	10,000	3,000	4,000	7,000	3+ years

(the solution is $R = 16.23$ percent), but iterations involving flows over many years are tedious. Fortunately, computers can be programmed to do the work, and internal-rate-of-return calculations are standard features of good personal computer spreadsheet programs and of many electronic calculators.

However, the present-value methods are "simpler, safer, easier, and more direct,"[38] because they can be adapted to use multiple discount rates during investment life, they avoid the problem of multiple internal rates of return that can emerge in computing internal rates, and they do not require additional tests to determine the validity of a computed rate of return. If conditions are right, however, internal rate of return will give the same results as present-value (or BCR) computations.

Project analysis may require not just an evaluation of the economics of a number of projects but also selection of particular projects from several alternatives. Two ranking indexes are available: ratios of benefit to cost and NPV.[39] Project rankings are often the same with either criteria, but sometimes—especially when project sizes are substantially different—the ranks are different. Which ranking should apply: that produced by NPVs or the ratio of benefit to cost?

Table 6–3 presents the discounted cost and benefit data for two capital projects. If $500 is to be budgeted, should project A or project B be undertaken? Project B has a higher NPV, whereas project A has the higher BCR. Each criterion supposes particular facts about the projects. Ranking by BCR assumes that either project can be increased in any proportion without changing the return relationships. In the present comparison, ranking by BCR presumes that project A can be expanded 3 1/3 times its present size at the same benefit rate ($667), yielding a NPV of $167. That expansion must be technically and economically possible if ratios are to guide the decision. Ranking by NPV presumes that the alternative investment streams are the size indicated, without the possibility of changing project size at the same BCR.

In many situations, of course, neither presumption is met entirely. When such is the case, the decision must rely on a comparison of present value of benefits from the use of available funds in feasible combinations of all project sizes. If the

[38]Harold Bierman, Jr., and Seymour Smidt, *The Capital Budgeting Decision* (New York: Macmillan, 1975), 57.

[39]The ratio of excess benefit to cost (benefit minus cost, divided by cost) provides no additional information because project ranks are the same as with the BCR: $B/C = [(B - C)/C] + 1$.

Table 6–3
Projects with Ranking Criteria Conflict

Project	Cost ($)	Benefit ($)	NPV ($)	BCR
A	150	200	50	1.33
B	500	600	100	1.20

analysis attempts to determine economically feasible projects, not allocation within a fixed budget, either method will be satisfactory: If NPV is positive, the BCR will be greater than 1. Conflict emerges only with rankings. In public-project analysis, the difficult questions involve estimating benefits, costs, and discount rates; conflict between criteria seldom is the concern. More often than not, knowing how a project stands according to either criterion is enough.

Some Special Problems of Cost-Benefit Analysis

Multiple objectives. Cost-benefit analysis provides information about the economic impact of projects. Overall economic impacts, however, may not be the sole or even the most important objective of some programs, particularly those concerned with redistributing income. If redistribution is important, benefits received by some groups in society will be more important than benefits received by others. Market values do not measure this objective, so benefit values would need explicit adjustment to encompass redistribution concerns.

Normal cost-benefit analysis accepts all portions of the economy as equal; who gains and who loses does not matter. It accepts the hypothetical compensation criterion of theoretical welfare economics: A public decision will be regarded as sound if those gaining from a public action receive sufficient benefits to compensate any losses, with some surplus gain remaining.[40] The principle ignores distribution of gains and losses across society and can be defended by these arguments: (1) Changes affecting income distributions can be viewed as negligible;[41] (2) public investment is neither a proper nor an effective tool for redistribution, and other fiscal policies can easily correct for any investment-related maldistribution; or (3) many projects over time will have benefits randomly distributed, causing the overall effect to average out at no redistributional change. On these grounds, distribution effects can be ignored with some theoretical justification. The view has been growing, however, that such treatment assumes way too much.

Two general techniques have emerged to deal with this distributional concern. Some analysts have allowed for distribution effects by weighting benefits according to a measure of the societal importance of the recipient. Benefits received by

[40]J. G. Head, "The Welfare Foundations of Public Finance Theory," *Rivista di Diritto Finanziaro e Scienza Della Finanze* 24 (September 1965): 379–428.
[41]Otto Eckstein, *Water Resource Development* (Cambridge, Mass.: Harvard University Press, 1958), 36–37.

meritorious groups (those society wants to help) count more than benefits received by others. Selection of weights is obviously a problem. Burton Weisbrod has applied weights derived from past public project decisions that have not followed strict cost-benefit rankings.[42] This approach does not, however, attack the problem of how the distribution should be changed but weighs analysis in the historical pattern. Besides, this pattern may simply reflect the clout of congressional delegations, not the relative importance of certain groups in society. John Krutilla and Otto Eckstein approach the problem by using marginal rates of federal taxation as weights, assuming that these rates roughly measure the importance of redistribution to society.[43] The technique does focus directly on the income distribution, but it too has political pressure problems. Furthermore, it ignores the difference between statutory rates (those quoted in the tax law) and effective rates (those applicable after loopholes). And whenever the tax structure changes, the evaluation of all projects would need to be revised. Does that make sense? Other approaches would apply specific weights specified by the analyst. All bend the general rule that the analyst be an impartial observer in the analytic process. Decision-makers may not recognize (or accept) the value system assumed by the analyst.

An alternative, the display technique favored by Roland McKean, would supplement general cost and benefit totals with a tabulation of how costs and benefits are divided among the population.[44] Many distributions, such as income, age, race, sex, and geographic area, could be important: By providing such a display, the analyst need not weight the social importance of groups. Decision-makers could supply their own weights to each recipient group as desired. The number and type of displays provided would not likely be the same for all projects. If the analyst's goal is to provide information for decision-makers and consumers and not to yield conclusive, social-maximizing decisions, such displays seem a prerequisite.

Valuing projects that save lives. A sticky problem occurs when public projects seek to reduce the loss of human life, as with transportation safety, cancer research, nutrition education, or fire protection. Life or death can rest on government allocation of resources to particular projects. Those decisions are distasteful, but they have been and will continue to be made. The real question is whether decision-makers know what they are assuming about that value. Any decisions that deny resources to activities that have a lifesaving element have implicitly placed a value on life: They imply that the value is less than the cost of the rejected activity. Is that implicit value reasonable?

A number of methods, none flawless but some with stronger logical foundation than others, have been proposed to value lifesaving. Historically, the first was average life-insurance face-values outstanding, under the logic that this was a value on loss of life that individuals placed on themselves. The obvious problems are that individuals buy life insurance for varied motives, including some that have

---

[42]Burton A. Weisbrod, "Income Redistribution Effects and Benefit-Cost Analysis," in Samuel B. Chase, ed., *Problems in Public Expenditure Analysis* (Washington, D.C.: Brookings Institution, 1968), pp. 177–222.

[43]John V. Krutilla and Otto Eckstein, *Multiple-Purpose River Development* (Baltimore: John Hopkins University Press, 1958).

[44]Roland McKean, *Efficiency in Government Through Systems Analysis* (New York: Wiley, 1958), 131–33, 208, 242.

nothing to do with death potential (e.g., forced saving) and that individual holdings vary substantially by family characteristics. These influences render insurance values generally inappropriate for this use.

A second technique, the human capital or earnings-loss method, views the human as something equivalent to a machine. Thus, the value of a life saved is estimated at the present value of lifetime earnings less subsistence cost through the work career of the individual. This computation equals, it is alleged, the contribution of the individual to the economy—the lost earnings potential of the victim—and is the value of a life saved. There are questions both about what earning pattern to use and whether that narrow production view truly gauges the social worth of an individual. This approach is now seldom used.[45] Most people would be willing to pay more than their lost earnings to avoid death or injury—so governments using such measures probably spend less on life and injury saving programs than their public would prefer.

The third technique, willingness to pay, assesses what people would pay for reduced risk to life, and then uses that estimate to calculate the value of a whole statistical life. A number of occupations (logging, off-shore drilling, etc.) have greater death risks than other occupations with similar skills. The wage premiums necessary to recruit workers to high-risk occupations provide an estimate of the value of life in the labor market. Thus, lifesaving values emerge directly from the choices made by individuals. There are some logical questions about this method—for one, the values may be artificially low because those jobs apparently appeal to individuals whose attitudes toward risk are different from those of others (they may actually enjoy extreme danger)—but it apparently gives the soundest estimates generally available.[46]

Government decisions do generate implicit values for lifesaving every time one project alternative is accepted and another is rejected.[47] That valuation cannot be avoided. Cost-benefit analysis must ensure that these valuations are conscious and consistent. It can hope for little else.

Cost-benefit analysis and politics. Cost-benefit analysis can supply decision-makers with valuable information about government activities. The analysis can estimate whether a particular project improves the efficiency of resource allocation. Supplemental displays, where relevant, can indicate a project's distributional impact across income classes, regions, races, genders, and so forth.

The relationships and variables in the computations are estimates based on assumptions made by the analyst. Those making project choices must know what

---

[45]A close variant is reportedly used in military pilot safety decisions; the value used is the cost of training a replacement. Safety-feature costs are balanced against that value estimate. Should this make military aviators a little nervous? Also, the judicial system uses this approach in wrongful death cases: One element in the awards to families is the estimated net discounted lifetime earnings of the victim.

[46]A pioneering work is W. K. Viscusi, "Wealth Effects and Earnings Premiums for Job Hazards," *Review of Economics and Statistics* 60 (August 1978): 408–16. Estimates can also be developed from contingent valuation surveys asking people what they would be willing to pay for reduced risk of death of injury.

[47]Some government decisions also involve saving human lives in the future. Should there be a discount rate for human life? One study suggests that Maryland households consider six lives saved 25 years in the future of equal value to one life saved today (this is about a 7.5-percent discount rate). See Maureen L. Cropper and Paul R. Portney, "Discounting Human Lives," *Resources* (Summer 1992): 1–4.

those assumptions are and how the analysis would differ under other reasonable assumptions. At a minimum, the public decision-maker must comprehend the structure of cost-benefit analysis to safeguard against deception from self-interested parties.

Public choices are political. No computerized, sterile analysis can substitute. Cost-benefit analysis is, however, an invaluable information tool and merits expansion as such, despite its possible weaknesses and potential misuses. As Krutilla has observed,

> Since the alternative is not to retire to inactivity but, rather, to reach decisions in the absence of analysis, we may take some comfort from the belief that thinking systematically about problems and basing decisions on such analysis are likely to produce consequences superior to those that would result from purely random behavior.[48]

Conclusion

Public capital infrastructure contributes to both private and public production. Crumbling roads and bridges, inadequate sewers and outmoded sewage-treatment plants, antiquated schools and public buildings, levees that leak or are too low, low-capacity airports, and so on, can have considerable national impact; so governments need to attend to the public capital stock and the capital investment that renews and expands that stock. Capital budgets, providing a separate review for capital as opposed to current expenditures, establish a process for making choices about the development or replacement of long-life assets such as those just noted. Special concern is warranted because capital investment choices now can influence the quality of life for many years into the future.

Most capital projects involve payments now, when infrastructure is constructed, with a flow of services coming in the future, through the long, useful life of the project. Discounting provides a mechanism for converting these future impacts into their present equivalents. In general, discounting provides a means of converting flows occurring at different times into a standard equivalent and is an important cornerstone of analysis of debt and investments.

Many public projects, including those involving capital investment, involve the use of one sort of resource (concrete to build a highway) to obtain a different return (a saving of travel time with the new highway). Cost-benefit analysis provides a technique for organizing information for the evaluation of public programs when the resources used in the program are dissimilar from the return received from the program. The analysis uses microeconomic market evaluations of the worth of resources and program results.

---

[48]John Krutilla, "Welfare Aspects of Benefit-Cost Analysis," *Journal of Political Economy* 69 (July 1961): 234. Not all public officials see cost-benefit analysis in the same way; refer to the perspectives of analysts, guardians, and spenders in Anthony Boardman, Aidan Vining, and W. G. Waters, "Costs and Benefits through Bureaucratic Lenses: Example of a Highway Project," *Journal of Policy Analysis and Management* 12 (Summer 1993): 532–55.

CHAPTER 6 QUESTIONS AND EXERCISES

1. Roachdale has a population of 32,000, more or less. Several of its important features appear on the map. The city eagerly awaits the full operation of the Intercontinental Widget plant early in 20X3. Although the plant has few employees now, it will have a workforce of around 900. The plant has caused a shift in city population to the south. Many people are moving to the Wonder Hills subdivision (45 percent developed now), although a good number are located along SR4 outside of town.

The data presented here, along with department-project proposals, should be used to prepare a capital improvement program for the years 20X0 to 20X4 and a capital budget for 20X0. Financial conditions suggest that the city will be unable to pay more than $900,000 for capital investment in any year, so one part of the exercise requires that priority criteria be established if all requests cannot be included in the budget.

The city has two special capital asset problems. First, the main sanitary sewer at Westside Elementary School near the Red River has suffered structural failure and must be replaced. Second, the SR4 bridge over Red River is unsafe. The bridge replacement will take 2 years. During the first year, traffic will have to be detoured.

City department heads have proposed the following projects:

Streets, Roads, and Bridges

SR4 bridge replacement: 20X0, $350,000; 20X1, $250,000 (costs are totals)

Street upgrading, Wonder Hills subdivision: 20X0, $600,000; 20X1, $50,000; 20X2, $20,000.

Street sign replacement—20X0 to 20X9, $18,000 per year (high visibility, breakaway signs)

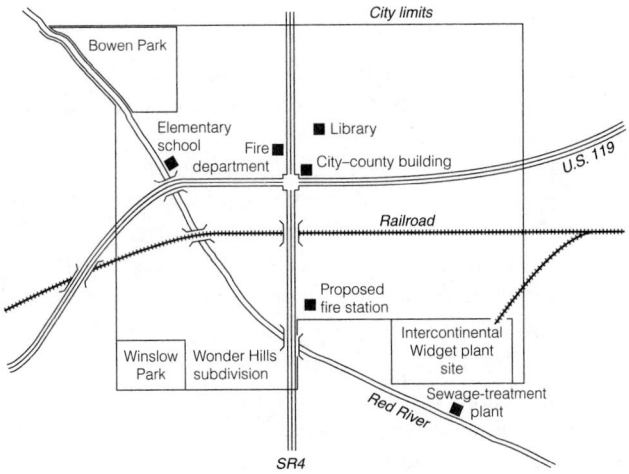

Parks and Recreation

Bowen Park pool: 20X0, $300,000 (construction of new above-ground aluminum pool)

Winslow Park recreation complex: 20X1, $525,000; 20X2, $125,000; 20X3, $300,000; 20X4, $300,000; 20X5, $85,000 (pool, ice skating rink, baseball diamonds)

Libraries

Air-conditioned building: 20X0, $45,000; 20X1, $20,000

Water and Sewer

Water-line upgrading, Wonder Hills: 20X2, $725,000

Storm-sewer installation, Wonder Hills: 20X3, $850,000

Sanitary-sewer replacement (structural failure): 20X0, $150,000

Fire Department

New fire substation: 20X3, $450,000; 20X4, $65,000

Fire equipment: (a) pumper (main station)—20X0, $25,000, (b) pumper, hook and ladder (substation)—20X0, $130,000

2. My son informed me that a comic book I purchased for 10 cents in 1948 is worth $55 today. What has been the average annual compound rate of return on that valuable asset? (See Chapter 2.)
3. Dr. Rubin has $10,000 to invest for 3 years. Two banks offer a 3-percent interest rate, but bank A compounds quarterly and bank B compounds semiannually. To what value would his money grow in each of the two banks?
4. A time-sharing condominium firm offers prizes to people who visit their project and listen to a marketing presentation. One prize was a $1,000 savings account. Unfortunately, the account would not be available for 45 years and required that the winner pay an initial service fee of $55. If one put $55 in an investment account, what annual compound rate of return would cause that sum to reach $1,000 in 45 years?
5. The Penn Central Railroad has not paid local taxes since 1969, under federal bankruptcy court protection. Some years later, the court required Penn Central to offer municipalities a choice of two payment options to clear this liability. (Penn Central has been absorbed by Conrail, so there were no future tax liabilities involved.) The choices were (a) immediate payment of 44 percent of total liability or (b) immediate payment of 20 percent of the liability, 10 percent paid at the end of each of the next 3 years, and 50 percent paid at the end of 10 years. Which alternative would you recommend to a municipality and why?
6. "A logical estimate of the current opportunity cost to the community of destroying the Parris-Dunning house (a structure built in the early 1800s and lived in by an early governor of Indiana) for construction of a traffic corridor in Bloomington, Indiana, could be prepared by using the formula $C_p = C_o(1 + r)^n$, where C_p = current opportunity cost, C_o = the original construction cost of the

house, r = the appropriate interest rate available on investments over a period, and n = the number of years between construction and the present." Do you agree? Explain.

7. Two public infrastructure projects have the economic profiles that follow:

	Option A			Option B		
Year	Capital Cost ($)	Operating and Maintenance Cost ($)	Benefits ($)	Capital Cost ($)	Operating and Maintenance Cost ($)	Benefits ($)
1	2,000,000	0	0	2,500,000	0	0
2	1,000,000	10,000	0	500,000	50,000	750,000
3	500,000	70,000	120,000		100,000	750,000
4		90,000	600,000		100,000	750,000
5		90,000	800,000		100,000	750,000
6		90,000	800,000		100,000	750,000
7		90,000	800,000		100,000	750,000
8		90,000	800,000		100,000	750,000
9		100,000	800,000		100,000	750,000
10		100,000	500,000		100,000	300,000

Use these data to compute for each (a) the NPV at discount rates of 10 and 5 percent, (b) the BCR at the same rates, and (c) the internal rate of return. Describe the facts about the projects that would dictate which criterion is appropriate and indicate which project is preferable under each circumstance.

8. The narrow gravel road to Jehnzen Lake is open only for the summer months. At present the county spends $750 per mile each year to prepare the road for summer traffic and another $150 per mile for maintenance during the period in which it is open. A "permanent" road could be constructed at a cost of $10,000 per mile; the county would have to spend $800 per mile for maintenance (patching, etc.) only every 5 years through the 30-year life of the road. Prospects for the area suggest that the road would have to be relocated at the end of that period. If 8 percent is a reasonable discount rate, which option is less costly? What discount rate would cause the two alternatives to have the same cost in present-value terms?

9. The irrigation system a farmer uses cost $10,000 8 years ago. It will last another 25 years without additional investment. With that system, he produces crops valued at $3,000 per year at a cost of $1,000 per year. A new system would cost $15,000 to install, but would increase production to $7,000 per year. Operating cost would be $2,500 per year. The farmer would have to refurbish the new system twelve years after installation at a cost of $5,000. Assume that investment in the new system occurs at the start of the first year, that revenue and operating cost occur at the end of each year and do not change over the 25 years, and that both systems have a salvage value of $1,000 at the end of 25 years. Assume a 6-percent discount rate. Should the farmer replace his existing system?

10. "When the Nuclear Regulatory Commission wanted to consolidate its 10 buildings in the Washington area into a single headquarters, the GSA (General Services Administration) calculated the annual rent required at $15 million and the construction cost at $113 million, for a building with a 20-year useful life" (Monica Langley, "Government's Staggering Leasing Expense Stirs Debate on Whether to Rent or Buy," [*Wall Street Journal* 4 September 1982]). Compute the NPV of the lease expense at a discount rate of 8.0 percent. Assume a 20-year building life. How does it compare with the cost of construction?

11. What problems involving cost-benefit analysis appear in the following statements?

a. A public power project uses a discount rate of 8.5 percent, the after-tax rate of return for electric utilities in the area.

b. Evaluation of a new municipal fire station uses a discount rate equal to the rate at which the city can borrow long-term funds.

c. Evaluation of a new four-lane highway to replace an older two-lane highway shows saved travel time for truckers and for private vehicles, the value of increased gasoline sales, and increased profits of trucking firms.

d. A cost-benefit analysis of removal of architectural barriers for disabled people from commercial buildings produced these benefit estimates for a 202,000-square-foot shopping center: economic benefit during 50-year useful life of center (1975–2024) = $4,537,700 cumulative gross revenues from leasable area. (This increase in gross revenue per year attributable to new accessibility to disabled people is calculated by multiplying gross revenues per year by the ratio of disabled to nondisabled people in the area. The estimate is based on gross revenue per leasable area experienced nationally in 1969, brought forward to 1975 by the rate of consumer price index increase, and extended through the 50-year life of the building according to the compounded rate of growth in sales revenue experienced by community shopping centers, 1966–1969. A 7-percent discount rate is employed.)

12. *The Chronicle of Higher Education* (Oct. 21, 1981, and Jan. 20, 1982) reported that the Kent State University athletic and alumni associations, in an effort to stimulate attendance at its homecoming football game, had sponsored an appearance at the game by the Dallas Cowboy Cheerleaders. For that game, 21,053 tickets were sold, compared to 7,186 the year before. A letter to the *Chronicle* editor sometime later questioned the sexist overtones of the promotion and wondered whether the event had been profitable.

"The *Chronicle* article did not say whether revenue from the 52 percent increase in ticket sales offset the cost of bringing 32 cheerleaders from Dallas," a cost that the writer estimated to be about $13,000. An official of the university provided information that the athletic department paid $5,000 toward the travel expenses, with another $5,000 provided by outside donors. Further, gate receipts were $23,902. Another letter to the editor, 6 weeks later, provided a "rudimentary" cost-benefit analysis:

If one makes the assumption that the 52-percent increase in ticket sales represented a 52-percent increase in dollars from ticket sales, and the university realized $23,902 in gate receipts at the game, it is simple to conclude that previous gate receipts amounted to $15,725.

Since the Dallas Cowboy Cheerleaders cost a total of $10,000, $5,000 of which was paid by the athletic department and $5,000 provided by outside donors, a total of ($10,000 – [23,902 – 15,725]) = $1,823 was lost on the stunt.

Now, it's true that the university only paid $5,000 to recoup $8,177 in gate receipts, but they may also have otherwise been able to use the outside donation for some other (more educational) purpose, and thus would have been better off soliciting the funds for some other endeavor.

a. How does this analysis differ from cost-benefit analysis?
b. Rework the analysis of financial effect, making any necessary corrections and taking full account of the principle of opportunity cost.

13. Highway departments and airports need some substance that will melt ice from roads and runways so that traffic may continue to flow safely when winter storms hit. Here are some options that are available:

Road salt costs about $30 per ton, and it works fast. More than 10 million tons are spread each year in the United States. It is corrosive to concrete, asphalt, and metal, thus eating road, bridges, and car bodies. It contaminates drinking water and kills trees and plants. Studies suggest that this damage costs from $600 to $1,000 per ton of salt to correct.

Calcium magnesium acetate, a commercial deicer, is made from limestone and vinegar. It costs about $650 per ton and takes about 15 minutes longer than salt to melt large ice patches. It usually lasts somewhat longer. Scientists think it may actually do some good for soil and plant life, and it is not corrosive.

Contrast financial cost and social cost involved with using these products. Which cost should be used for government decision-making? Why?

14. Philip Morris, the tobacco company, presented to the government of the Czech Republic an economic analysis that concluded that smoking was good for government finances. As reported in the *International Herald Tribune*, ". . . the net economic benefit of smoking there was about 5.82 billion koruna ($147.1 million) in 1999. The report put the company's argument starkly: 'Our principal finding is that the negative financial effects of smoking—such as increased health care costs—are more than offset by positive effects such as excise tax and value-added taxes collected on tobacco products.' The monetary estimate of benefits was based on the fact that the average smoker dies 4.3 years to 5.23 years earlier than a nonsmoker and is therefore less of an economic drain." (Lee Dembart, "Critics Assail Philip Morris Report on Smoking," *International Herald Tribune* (18 July 2001). The report estimates the following:

Income/reduced costs from smoking (million Czech korona)	
Savings from earlier mortality (housing, pensions, health care)	1,192
Customs duties collected	353
Corporate income tax	747
Value added tax	3,521
Excise tax	15,648

Smoking-related public finance costs (million Czech korona)	
Fire-induced costs	49
Lost income from earlier mortality	1,367
Public finance costs from work absences	1,667
Second-hand smoke-related health-care costs	1,142
Smoking-related health-care costs	11,422

How does this analysis differ from cost-benefit analysis? What comments do you have on the analysis?

CASE FOR DISCUSSION

CASE 6–1

What Does Cost Mean?

Air travel to England through Heathrow or Gatwick, the airports serving London, can be complicated and slow. Projections done in the 1960s indicated that those airports would be unable to handle future traffic loads. A commission was established to recommend sites for a third London airport. (The concern was where to locate the airport, not whether the airport was needed. Thus, the effort was a cost-effectiveness analysis, not a cost-benefit analysis.) The case presented here, reproduced from the *Wall Street Journal,* provides an interesting illustration of the problems created in valuing public losses and gains. (As a postscript, a third London airport has not been built, and none is currently under serious consideration.)

Consider These Questions

1. What problems do you see with valuation according to fire insurance values?
2. What is wrong with the antiquarian's approach?
3. Can you propose an alternate approach?

Fight Over an Old Church Raises a Tough Question

What's in a number? It seems inevitable that corporations will try to assign numerical values to elusive social values, but in so doing they may run a risk of absurdity.

Professor C. West Churchman, professor of business administration at the University of California, gives an example from the search for a site to build a third airport to serve London. One spot under serious consideration would have required demolishing the 12th-century Norman church of St. Michael's in the village of Stewkley.

It was disclosed that a cost-benefit analysis had calculated in monetary terms just what would be lost by tearing down St. Michael's. The calculation had used the face value of the fire insurance of the church—the equivalent of a few thousand dollars.

When the calculation was made public, an outraged antiquarian wrote to the London Times to urge another, perhaps no less plausible, method of calculation: Take the original cost of St. Michael's (perhaps 100 pounds sterling or about $240), and assume the property grew in value at a rate of 10 percent a year for 800 years. That would put the value of St. Michael's at roughly one decillion pounds. A decillion is a one followed by 33 zeroes.

St. Michael's was spared after a public outcry arose. But to Professor Churchman it was striking how glibly either side could pin a numerical value on the church. "Only a modicum of plausibility is needed to convince people that the numbers represent reality," he says. "I don't think the need is for more numbers at all. The need is for justifying the numbers"—for some rationale that "tells us what difference the numbers make."

SOURCE: Wall Street Journal, 9 December 1971. Reprinted by permission of the *Wall Street Journal* (c) 1971 Dow Jones & Company, Inc. All Rights Reserved Worldwide.

PART TWO

Revenue Sources, Structure, and Administration

Chapter 7 **Taxation: Criteria for Evaluating Revenue Options**

Chapter 8 **Major Tax Structures: Income Taxes**

Chapter 9 **Major Tax Structures: Taxes on Goods or Services**

Chapter 10 **Major Tax Structures: Property Taxes**

Chapter 11 **Revenue from User Fees, User Charges, and Sales by Public Monopolies**

Chapter 12 **Collecting Taxes**

Chapter 13 **Revenue Forecasts, Revenue Estimates, and Tax Expenditure Budgets**

Chapter 14 **Intergovernmental Fiscal Relations: Diversity and Coordination**

CHAPTER 7

Taxation: Criteria for Evaluating Revenue Options

Governments collect most of their revenue by exercising their sovereign power to collect coercive payments—taxes—rather than by selling products or services. These coerced payments differ from prices in that they purchase no specific good or service. Their faithful payment does serve to keep the taxpayer out of trouble with the tax collectors, but, with few exceptions, if neighbors pay enough to finance a government service, then what the individual pays (or doesn't pay) has no impact on the level of service that person will receive. Neither are these payments voluntary contributions offered through some sense of civic duty. They are amounts established in a political process that erects a structure of laws—tax statutes and administrative regulations—to determine how the collective cost of government services will be distributed among elements of the market economy. Some services can, indeed, be sold, and a later chapter discusses the conditions under which such systems are feasible. However, governments exist, in large measure, to provide services when the private market has failed or may be expected to fail to provide those services in sufficient quantity or quality, if at all. Attempts to sell public goods would be ineffective, so taxes are the answer.

The tax may be structured to have quasi-market effects—particularly in regard to distributing the cost to those using a service most heavily, and to inducing those consuming or producing a product that inflicts uncompensated costs on others to recognize those impacts in their decisions—but the tax remains an involuntary payment to support collective provision of certain goods and services, not a price for services rendered. Nevertheless, the power to finance by coercion reflects a faith in government that allows government to step in when markets fail and is central to government operations. Once-notorious bank robber Willie "The Actor" Sutton allegedly said, "I rob banks because that's where the money is." The following chapters emphasize taxes because, for most general-purpose governments, that's where the money is.

Taxation in the United States: A Short Overview of the Systems

Governments in the United States collect most of their own-source general revenue from taxes on income, purchases or sales, or property ownership or transfer, as Table 7–1 shows.[1] For all governments, 75.4 percent of own-source general revenue came from taxes. Revenue from charges and from miscellaneous sources (these include lotteries, interest on invested funds, royalties, etc.) play a relatively small role in the finance of general government. Special revenue, shown at the bottom of the table, includes the substantial collections from the payroll tax that funds the federal insurance trust system. This federal payroll tax, mostly for Social Security, is the second largest revenue producer among all sources at all levels; only revenue from the federal individual income tax is greater. But this payroll tax revenue is not directly available for general government.

The table reflects a distinct separation of revenue sources by level of government, although there are no national laws that assign particular taxes to particular levels of government, in contrast to the practice in many nations. The federal revenue system is not diversified among tax bases. The federal government relies predominantly on income taxes, individual and corporate, for revenue—64.4 percent of total general revenue from the individual income tax and 10.7 percent from the corporate income tax—and raises about as much from these two taxes as state and local governments raise from all taxes combined. The federal individual income tax is, by a good margin, the most productive of all the taxes; indeed, it produces more money than any tax levied by any other government in the world. Federal dominance in income taxation is even greater because the payroll tax for Social Security amounts to a second federal income tax for individuals receiving only wage and salary income and for the self-employed. Indeed, for lower-income households, payments for this payroll tax far exceed the amounts paid in federal individual income tax.

The federal government levies no general sales tax, a rarity among economically developed countries. There is no fundamental "catch" or legal barrier that prevents the federal government from levying such a tax, but these taxes are a major source for state and local governments and this heavy reliance has created political resistance each time the federal government has considered invading that territory, as it did periodically throughout the twentieth century, and continues to consider to the present. The federal government does, however, collect sales taxes on selected commodities, like motor fuels and alcoholic beverages, and on certain imported products (customs duties). The amounts collected from these taxes pale in

[1]Own-source general revenue excludes (1) revenue from intergovernmental aid and (2) revenue from liquor stores, utility operations, or insurance programs (e.g., Social Security or unemployment compensation). The first exclusion leaves own-source revenue; the second, general. These distinctions do not reflect laws that restrict certain revenues for certain uses (earmarking). For instance, most states earmark motor-fuel tax revenue for highway use. The division used here and in census data would consider that revenue to be general and not in the special category.

Table 7–1
Government Revenue by Source and Level, Fiscal 2003 ($ millions)

					Share of Total Revenue from Source (%)			
	All	Federal	State	Local	All	Federal	State	Local
Revenue	4,440,953.46	2,004,662.00	1,295,658.82	1,140,632.64				
Total General Revenue	3,383,850.21	1,231,684.00	1,112,349.02	1,039,817.19	100.0%	100.0%	100.0%	100.0%
Intergovernmental revenue*	778,218.02	—	361,617.05	416,600.97	23.0%		32.5%	40.1%
From federal government	389,263.57	—	343,307.80	45,955.77	11.5%		30.9%	4.4%
From state government	370,645.20	—	—	370,645.20	11.0%			35.6%
From local government	18,309.25	—	18,309.25		0.5%		1.6%	
General Revenue Own Sources	2,614,632.20	1,231,684.00	750,731.98	632,216.22	77.3%	100.0%	67.5%	60.8%
Taxes	1,973,892.76	1,034,921.00	548,990.87	389,980.89	58.3%	84.0%	49.4%	37.5%
Property	296,683.19	—	10,470.51	286,212.68	8.8%		0.9%	27.5%
Individual income	993,106.02	793,699.00	181,932.51	17,474.51	29.3%	64.4%	16.4%	1.7%
Corporate income	163,246.06	131,877.00	28,384.47	2,984.59	4.8%	10.7%	2.6%	0.3%
Customs duties	19,862.00	19,862.00	—	—	0.6%	1.6%		
General sales and gross receipts	229,222.30	—	184,596.71	44,625.59	6.8%		16.6%	4.3%
Selective sales and gross receipts	176,088.26	67,524.00	89,214.51	19,349.75	5.2%	5.5%	8.0%	1.9%
Motor vehicle licensing	17,379.05	—	16,009.47	1,369.58	0.5%		1.4%	0.1%
Estate and gift	28,644.30	21,959.00	6,685.30	—	0.8%	1.8%	0.6%	
Severance	5,321.56	—	5,321.56	—	0.2%		0.5%	
Other taxes	44,340.02	—	26,375.83	17,964.19	1.3%		2.4%	1.7%
Current charges†	431,781.43	162,221.00	106,356.92	163,203.51	12.8%	13.2%	9.6%	15.7%
Institutions of higher education	66,831.36		59,391.62	7,439.74	2.0%		5.3%	0.7%
Hospitals	68,926.70		24,131.11	44,795.59	2.0%		2.2%	4.3%
Postal Service fees	67,752.00	67,752.00			2.0%	5.5%	0.0%	0.0%
Sewerage	28,209.88			28,209.88	0.8%			2.7%
Medicare Part B premiums	28,466.00	28,466.00			0.8%	2.3%		
Miscellaneous general revenue	199,958.01	34,542.00	95,384.19	70,031.82	5.9%	2.8%	8.6%	6.7%
Total Special Revenue								
Utility revenue	103,050.09		12,517.95	90,532.14				
Liquor store revenue	5,338.19		4,517.99	820.20				
Insurance trust revenue‡	948,714.98	772,978.00	166,273.86	9,463.12				

SOURCE: U.S. Bureau of Census, Governments Division and Budget of the U.S. Government.

*Duplicative intergovernmental transactions are excluded.

†Federal offsetting collections and receipts from the public.

‡Includes: old age, survivors, disability, and health insurance contributions; unemployment compensation, employee retirement, worker's compensation, and other insurance trust revenues.

comparison to those from the federal income taxes—just 7.1 percent of federal general revenue.

The federal government collects no property tax. The U.S. Constitution makes the adoption of a federal property tax politically difficult because it requires apportionment of any direct tax: "No capitation, or other direct, Tax shall be laid unless in Proportion to the Census or Enumeration herein before directed to be taken" (Article I, Sec. 9[4]). What that means is this: A state with one-twentieth of the national population would have to pay one-twentieth of the tax. To produce that apportionment, a federal tax would require high tax rates in poor states and low rates in wealthy states. Any state-by-state difference in federal tax rates would be politically impractical, and to have rates inversely related to state wealth would add an extra degree of difficulty, as the writers of the Constitution surely knew. In his economic analysis of the Constitution, Charles Beard sums up: "Direct taxes may be laid, but resort to this form of taxation is rendered practically impossible, save on extraordinary occasions, by the provision that they must be apportioned according to population—so that numbers cannot transfer the burden to accumulated wealth."[2] The framers of the Constitution, no matter what their many liberal virtues, were generally rich men who appeared not to want to have national taxes placed on their wealth by the masses.

A reasonable question at this point is, what are direct and indirect taxes? Richard Musgrave suggests the possibilities:

> Some have suggested that (1) indirect taxes are taxes which are shifted [i.e., the real burden is borne by someone other than the one paying the tax to the government], and others that (2) they are taxes which are meant to be shifted. Still others hold that (3) they are taxes which are assessed on objects [or privileges] rather than on individuals and therefore not adaptable to the individual's special position and his taxable capacity; or finally (4) that they are simply taxes which are not on income. While (3) is probably the most useful criterion, this is not the place to resolve this terminological matter. It is evident, however, that under most criteria, the classification of certain taxes is far from clear-cut.[3]

Fortunately, the difference has little economic importance, although it can complicate the legal constraints surrounding the tax. For instance, in addition to the constitutional provision previously noted, some states specify certain rate structures or collection processes that differ according to whether the tax is direct or indirect—so there must be determinations about the particular tax in question. If Professor Musgrave is not up to resolving the issue, then there is not likely to be a generally accepted resolution to the question; governments do not all agree. The lack of a definition periodically provides a good income for tax lawyers attacking some tax provision or another according to whether the particular tax in question qualifies as direct or indirect.

In comparison with the federal government, the revenue systems of state and local governments are broadly diversified, as demonstrated in the view of state

---

[2]Charles A. Beard, *An Economic Interpretation of the Constitution of the United States* (New York: Macmillan, 1935), 215.

[3]Richard A. Musgrave, *Fiscal Systems* (New Haven, Conn.: Yale University Press, 1960), 173.

and local revenue collections in Table 7–1.[4] The three levels of government combined, although forming tax policies independently, manage a tax system split between income, property, and sales taxes. Table 7–2 presents further information on these structures by indicating the number of states that use the major tax bases and contain localities using these bases. State revenue systems tend to have a balance between bases, far greater than the income dominance of the federal system or property dominance for local systems. State governments apply income taxes (forty-one states levy broad individual income taxes; forty-four states tax corporate income), but their aggregate collections do not approach federal government collections. Several states, however, do receive more revenue from income taxes than from any other source. State income taxes often mirror federal taxes. In fact, state

Table 7–2
Major Tax Sources Levied by States and Localities, July 2005

Tax	States Using the Tax	States with Localities Using the Tax
General Property	Thirty-seven states plus D.C. Exceptions: Colorado, Connecticut, Delaware, Hawaii, Idaho, Iowa, New York, North Carolina, Oklahoma, South Dakota, Tennessee, Texas, and Utah.	All fifty states.
General Sales	Forty-five states plus D.C. Exceptions: Alaska, Delaware, Montana, New Hampshire, and Oregon. Many Alaskan municipalities and boroughs levy general sales taxes.	Thirty-five states plus one authorized.
Individual Income	Forty-one states plus D.C. Exceptions: Alaska, Florida, Nevada, New Hampshire, South Dakota, Tennessee, Texas, Washington, and Wyoming. New Hampshire and Tennessee levy taxes on dividend and interest income.	Twelve states plus two authorized.
Corporate Income	Forty-four states plus D.C. Exceptions: Michigan, Nevada, South Dakota, Texas, Washington, and Wyoming. Michigan levies a single business tax (a modified value-added tax) and Texas levies a corporate franchise tax.	Six states.
Motor Fuel	All states plus D.C.	Thirteen states.
Cigarettes	All states plus D.C.	Eleven states.
Alcohol Beverages	All states plus D.C.	Seventeen states.

SOURCES: Federation of Tax Administrators; U.S. Bureau of Census, *Census of Governments 2002;* and John L. Mikesell, "General Sales, Income, and Other Nonproperty Taxes," in J. Richard Aronson and Eli Schwartz, eds., *Management Policies in Local Government Finance,* 5th ed. (Washington, D.C.: ICMA, 2004).

[4]Intergovernmental revenue (grants and contracts are netted out across governments in Table 7–1). Therefore, there are no net grants for all government: one grants, one receives, and net is zero for government as a whole.

tax returns often copy information directly from the federal return in computing state liability, and state tax authorities rely heavily on the efforts of the federal government in enforcing their taxes. A number of cities levy local income taxes, but in many cases the taxes are limited to coverage of employee payroll, not taxes on income for all sources. About 3,500 local governments levy local income taxes, but only 900 of these are outside Pennsylvania.

Taxes on goods and services, general and selective, are the largest single source of state revenue, and states are the largest overall users of that source.[5] All states receive revenue from sales or gross receipts taxes, and only five (Delaware, New Hampshire, Montana, Oregon, and Alaska) do not use a general sales tax. Around 6,400 local governments levy general sales taxes as well; they are second only to property as a local tax source. Although the sales tax shows no sign of eclipsing the property tax in overall local importance, in some communities it is the major tax-revenue producer. Contrary to the local income tax, which is typically administered locally, local sales taxes are usually administered by the state government in conjunction ("piggybacked") with the state tax. The U.S. Constitution prohibits states and their subdivisions from levying customs duties, which are taxes levied on imported goods.

The property tax remains the major own-source revenue producer for local government. Despite continued popular attacks on the tax, it remains the predominant local tax, possibly because it is the only major tax generally within the means of independent local administration and capable of fine statutory-rate differences between geographically small jurisdictions. A number of state governments levy their own general property tax but its significance in state finances is modest, although it was the dominant state source before the Depression of the 1930s.

How does the tax structure in the United States stack up against that in other industrialized countries? Some comparisons are possible from the data in Table 7–3. Among the countries in the Organization for Economic Cooperation and Development (OECD), the U.S. tax burden as a percentage of Gross Domestic Product (GDP) is toward the bottom, 28.9 percent here against an OECD average of 36.9 percent.[6] Looking at shares of that total by tax source, the United States makes heavier use of taxes on personal income (42.3 percent of the total for the United States, compared with 26.5 percent for the OECD), heavier use of other taxes, mostly property (11.8 percent against a 9.7 percent OECD average), lighter use of taxes on corporate income (6.5 percent against 9.4 percent), and much lighter use of goods-and-service or sales taxes (16.1 percent against 31.3 percent OECD average). Our Social Security contributions are close to the average. This point may bear repeating: Among the industrialized nations of the world, the United States is a low-tax country. That does not mean that certain economic activities or individuals are not competitively or inequitably disadvantaged by American tax systems.

---

[5]In recent years, the individual income tax and the general sales tax have traded off as the largest single source of state tax revenue. From 1947 to 1997, the general sales tax was the largest source but was replaced by the individual income tax from 1998 to 2002. It returned to its position as largest producer in 2003 and 2004.

[6]These data include operation of national social insurance systems and aggregate all levels of government.

Table 7–3

Tax Revenue as a Percentage of Gross Domestic Product and as Percentage from Major Taxes, 2001, Countries of the Organization for Economic Cooperation and Development (OECD)

		Tax Revenue of Main Taxes as Percentage of Total Taxation				
	As % GDP	Personal Income	Corporate Income	Social Security Payroll	Goods and Services	Other
Australia	30.1	40.8	14.9	0	29.1	15.3
Austria	45.4	22.9	6.9	29.1	27.1	14
Belgium	45.8	31.6	7.9	28.7	24.6	7.1
Canada	35.1	37.1	10	14.3	24.7	14
Czech Republic	38.4	12.5	11	39	30.5	7
Denmark	49.8	52.7	6.3	4.5	32.2	4.4
Finland	46.1	30.5	10.6	24.8	29.4	4.6
France	45	17.7	7.6	33.9	25.2	15.5
Germany	36.8	27.1	1.7	37	28.8	5.4
Greece	36.9	14.7	9.2	26.4	37.9	11.8
Hungary	39	19.6	6.1	29.4	38.7	6.3
Iceland	36.5	39.8	3.2	8.1	41.5	7.4
Ireland	29.9	29.7	12.1	13.8	37.3	7
Italy	42	25.9	8.6	25.6	25.6	14.2
Japan	27.3	20.1	12.7	33.9	19	14.4
Korea	27.2	14.1	12.3	18.2	39.6	15.7
Luxembourg	40.7	17.7	18.3	24.4	26.6	13.1
Mexico	18.9	28		17	51.5	3.5
Netherlands	39.5	16.3	10.4	28.6	30.7	13.9
New Zealand	33.8	42.9	11.3	0	35.5	10.3
Norway	43.3	24.2	21.7	19.2	31.3	3.5
Poland	33.6	23.6	5.8	30.2	35.8	4.5
Portugal	33.5	17.9	10.8	25.4	40	5.8
Slovak Republic	32.3	10.8	6.8	35.1	33.2	14.1
Spain	35.2	19.6	8.1	30.7	29.3	12.4
Sweden	51.4	31.9	5.7	29.2	25.1	8.1
Switzerland	30.6	32	10.2	23.6	23.2	11
Turkey	36.5	21.3	6.6	17.8	38.7	15.7
United Kingdom	37.3	30.2	9.5	16.4	31.3	12.6
United States	28.9	42.3	6.5	23.3	16.1	11.8
European Union Average	41	25.8	8.9	25.3	30.1	10
OECD Average	36.9	26.5	9.4	23.1	31.3	9.7

SOURCE: Organization for Economic Cooperation and Development, *OECD in Figures, 2004 Edition* (Paris: OECD, 2005).
NOTE: Mexican corporate and individual income taxes are combined.

But the U.S. tax burden is, on average, low in relation to that of generally comparable countries.[7]

Standards for Tax Policy

Jean-Baptiste Colbert, finance minister in Louis XIV's court before the French Revolution, is alleged to have succinctly summed up the task of financing government: "The art of taxation consists in so plucking the goose as to obtain the largest amount of feathers with the least possible amount of hissing."[8] Taxation based on power alone is an excellent device for inflicting costs on minorities, but power so used is inconsistent with leadership and is likely to produce policies that trade long-range damage for quick political gain.

Most people prefer taxes to be paid by someone else because an individual's payment of a tax ordinarily has no influence on whether a public service is available. Former Senator Russell Long (D.-LA) elucidated a major principle of tax politics some years ago: "Don't tax you, don't tax me, tax that fellow behind the tree."[9] That principle, combined with a public that is not familiar with tax structure and tax effects, renders pure public opinion a hazardous standard for revenue choice. Indeed, robbing Peter to pay Paul is an almost certain way to get Paul's vote. But attention to opinion may guide approaches through which otherwise desirable changes may be implemented and may identify desirable changes that must await a beneficial political climate. Case 7–1 demonstrates how politics and lobbying matters in the design of tax structures in the United States.

Economists George Break and Joseph Pechman describe the fundamental principle behind the evaluation of tax policy: "The primary goal of taxation is to transfer control of resources from one group in the society to another and to do so in ways that do not jeopardize, and may even facilitate, the attainment of other economic goals."[10] Those transfers include (1) shifts of purchasing power among groups in the private sector and (2) shifts of control over purchasing power from the private sector to the public sector. A tax intends to move resources away from private use and will by itself harm the private sector; tax policy seeks to achieve that shift with the least possible economic or social harm. Without this concern for minimizing harm, any revenue would be about as good as any other, and tax policy

[7]Compared with the industrialized nations, developing countries tend to have lower tax burdens, greater reliance on consumption as opposed to income taxes, and greater reliance on corporate as opposed to personal income taxes. Vito Tanzi and Howell H. Zee, "Tax Policy for Emerging Markets: Developing Countries," IMF Working Paper WP/00/35 (Washington, D.C.: International Monetary Fund, 2000).

[8]H.L. Mencken, ed., *A New Dictionary of Quotations on Historical Principles from Ancient and Modern Sources* (New York: Knopf, 1942), 1178.

[9]Thomas J. Reese, "The Thoughts of Chairman Long, Part I: The Politics of Taxation," *Tax Notes* 6 (February 27, 1978): 199.

[10]George F. Break and Joseph A. Pechman, *Federal Tax Reform, The Impossible Dream?* (Washington, D.C.: Brookings Institution, 1975), 4.

would not be a significant element in public decisions. In other words, tax policy is about damage control.

When public goods are financed, the tax must not be voluntary. Otherwise, rational actions of nonpayers—who could fully enjoy the service provided without financial payment—would keep the system from producing expected revenue. Regardless of other attributes, a tax may be distinguished from other ways of raising revenue by its *compulsory* nature: If one possesses the tax base, one pays the tax regardless of whether one uses the services provided by the taxing unit. Absence of voluntarism distinguishes taxes from the user charges—recreation admissions, tolls, and so on—that many governments collect. The tax is neither a price for service received nor a voluntary contribution. Furthermore, governments do not rely on "fair-share" contributions because fairness is susceptible to widely different individual definitions, particularly what one's own fair share would be.

Criteria for judging taxes and tax systems have been proposed by many observers, but there has been a substantial conformity between those standards. The grandfather of evaluation standards appears in *The Wealth of Nations* (1776), as Adam Smith proposes four classic maxims that should guide taxation in a market-based economy:

> I. The subjects of every state ought to contribute towards the support of the government, as nearly as possible, in proportion to their respective abilities; that is, in proportion to the revenue which they respectively enjoy under the protection of the state.
>
> II. The tax which each individual is bound to pay ought to be certain and not arbitrary. The time of payment, the manner of payment, the quantity to be paid, ought all to be clear and plain to the contributor, and to every other person.
>
> III. Every tax ought to be levied at the time or in the manner, in which it is most likely to be convenient for the contributor to pay it.
>
> IV. Every tax ought to be so contrived as both to take out and to keep out of the pockets of the people as little as possible, over and above what it brings into the public treasury of the state.[11]

Although the language of those standards has changed over the years and emphasis has shifted with the development of a more complex economy, modern reform still concerns essentially the same issues. Whether the deliberations involve the 1986 federal tax reform in the Reagan administration, the 1993 Clinton economic plan, design of a tax system for a newly independent nation, the Bush 2001 tax reductions, the 2005 Bush tax reform panel,[12] or a state tax study, attention will

---

[11]Adam Smith, *An Inquiry into the Nature and Cause of the Wealth of Nations,* Modern Library edition (New York: Random House, 1937), 777–79.

[12]The President's Advisory Panel on Federal Tax Reform was charged with transmitting to the Secretary of the Treasury revenue neutral reform options that would "(a) simplify Federal tax laws to reduce the costs and administrative burdens of compliance with such laws; (b) share the burdens and benefits of the Federal tax structure in an appropriately progressive manner while recognizing the importance of home-ownership and charity in American society; and (c) promote long-run economic growth and job creation, and better encourage work effort, saving, and investment, so as to strengthen the competitiveness of the United States in the global marketplace." In regard to the last concern: the President may not trust the operation of the free market in terms of growth and job creation, but hopes to use the tax system to intervene in a non-neutral fashion. (Executive Order 13369, President's Advisory Panel on Federal Tax Reform, January 7, 2005.)

be directed to some translation of the basic criteria: equity, economic efficiency effects, and collection cost/simplicity (cost to government and impact on taxpayer), plus revenue consequences. Recent proposals for tax restructuring have brought renewed concern for transparency, the modern translation of the need for taxes to be certain and not arbitrary, with clear political responsibility when they are levied. Even though transparency is an important concern in the good governance movement, in terms of taxation, it dates back to 1776 Scotland.

Equity

Given that a government seeks to raise a specific amount of money, how should the revenue burden be distributed? Of course, our answer will be "fairly" or "equitably," but what does that really mean? Two general equity standards are available: (1) according to taxpayers' benefits from or usage of the public service (*benefits received*) and (2) according to taxpayers' capabilities to bear the burden (*ability to pay*). The approach chosen must finally be partly philosophic and partly pragmatic.

The logic of the benefits-received approach is an appealing complement to the exchange economy for private goods.[13] In this quasi-market arrangement, individuals would pay for a public service if and only if they benefit from the public service, and payments should be higher for those who receive greater benefits. When governments sell services—that is, apply user charges (or public prices)—then only those who benefit must pay, assuming that the service has no considerable external benefit, in which case charge finance is suspect because nonpayers gain. (More is said about this in a later chapter.) Tax structures can be benefit-based as well, if there is some tax that will cause tax payments to align closely with benefits received from a government service. One example might be a motor-fuel tax financing highways: the more a person uses highways, the more motor fuel used, and the more motor fuel tax is paid on the fuel purchases, so those with heaviest use of the facility make greatest payment. If the individual benefits, he or she pays an amount consistent with that benefit; if not, he or she does not pay. There are neither the wasteful oversupplies of public services that can result when a service's price is artificially low nor the equally wasteful underprovision when prices are too high. A taxpayer receiving 1 percent of the benefits of a public service would pay 1 percent of the cost of providing that service; there will be no cross-subsidization among taxpayers. The user pays for the service; the nonuser does not bear the burden.

Not only will fiscal cross-subsidization from nonusers to users be prevented, but revenue production may help guide the allocation of government resources, and the benefit basis may override anti-tax sentiment among the citizenry. People may accept a tax on hunting ammunition, for instance, if proceeds are used for wildlife habitat development. Unfortunately, before tax revenue flow can tell us

[13]How might benefits be measured? The logically correct measure would be the value of the service to the individual. Failing that, less-satisfactory measures include the cost of rendering the service to the beneficiary, the insurance value of the property protected, or, according to Adam Smith's criteria, the amount of income earned by the individual.

about the demand for a service, there must be close complementarity between the tax base and the governmental activity, a situation not often occurring.[14] The link between motor-fuel taxes and use of roads previously noted is a good example of such complementarity. In these instances, the tax becomes a proxy for a price paid for consumption of the government service.

Problems prevent wholesale application of a benefits-received approach, as even the staunchest supporter of a social contract version of government recognizes. For one thing, pure public goods, by their very nature, provide no divisible exchange in the public-good transaction. Any "purchaser" will buy benefits for others. Furthermore, modern governments typically try to redistribute—providing services directly aimed at transferring affluence from one group to another. In this circumstance the benefits-received approach fails: the objective of the action is subsidization, not exchange. When circumstances of measurement and redistribution do not prohibit, however, the benefits-received approach has strong logical support.

The benefits-received philosophy implies that for every particular mix of government services provided, there is a different appropriate distribution of the cost of government: Identify who benefits, and those people are the ones who should pay. A different mix of services implies that different people should pay. On the other hand, the ability-to-pay approach eschews the market-exchange philosophy and argues that, regardless of services, those most capable of bearing the cost of government should bear the greatest amount of that cost.

The logic of the ability-to-pay principle is that appropriability (and its absence) makes public services and private goods fundamentally different, and only the latter are susceptible to market approaches to payment for services. The decision to provide public services can be considered separately from the choice of financial-burden distribution, so the distribution may be set according to concepts of fairness or equity. Unfortunately, scientific tools do not provide the analytic resources to establish fair distribution. If individual satisfaction levels could be measured and compared, tax systems might be designed to yield revenues for public use at least-satisfaction loss to society. There remains no calibration method, so a scientific distribution of financial burden seems beyond reach. Distribution is a matter of political opinion and political power, within ethical limits that may or may not shape the political process, not a matter of establishing what is scientifically correct.

Application of the ability-to-pay approach has two decision elements: selecting an ability-to-pay measure and choosing the way tax payments should vary with that measure. The appropriateness of alternative ability measures varies with the level of economic development. In an agrarian society—for instance, eighteenth-century America—an effective measure of ability to pay might be property ownership, particularly of land, buildings, carriages, and cattle. Modern conceptions that lean toward current income—the corporate form of business enterprise, the development of complex debt forms, and the importance of intangible values in total wealth—make gross property values an unreliable measure of ability to pay. Therefore, most

[14]Earmarking a portion of a general tax—dedicating a particular share of the state sales tax for support of public education, for instance—provides no evidence of preferences for that service, so the practice cannot be justified on the basis of improving information for public decisions.

public discussion about ability to pay concentrates on income as the appropriate measure. A more comprehensive measure would encompass net wealth as well (possibly using the annuity formula introduced in Chapter 6 to convert accumulated wealth into an estimated annual flow) because both income and wealth figure into an individual's real affluence. Others argue, as we shall see in a later chapter, that consumption by households is a superior index to income.[15] Exactly which index should gauge ability-to-pay is not an entirely settled issue, despite the tendency toward annual income in most popular discussions.

The second choice is the extent to which households with different abilities should pay different taxes. Suppose current income has been selected as the appropriate measure of ability to pay. A household with $100,000 income presumably should pay more tax than a household with $50,000 income. Should the payment by the higher-income household be twice that of the other, more than twice, or less than twice? In other words, should the distribution of income after tax be different from the distribution of income before tax and, if so, in favor of what income group should redistribution occur? This equity decision is an important element of social policy. It is, however, significant only for the ability-to-pay approach; it is not a factor for a true believer in the benefits-received approach.

Horizontal and vertical equity. Equity in tax-payment distribution has both horizontal and vertical components. Horizontal equity—what might also be called "equal justice"—considers equal treatment of taxpayers who have equal capability to pay taxes: If two taxpayers are equivalent in all relevant aspects, but one taxpayer pays significantly more tax, the tax structure lacks horizontal equity. Such a condition may emerge when taxes vary by individual taste and preference, as with taxes levied on commodities that are used by a narrow segment of the population or when some sectors of the economy have extra access to schemes that can reduce their tax liability.[16] It may also occur when tax administration is haphazard or capricious or when the task at hand is particularly challenging. For instance, property tax valuation practices may cause houses of apparently similar market value to bear considerably different tax burdens.

An obvious problem here is defining equivalent taxing units: The behavior that creates the observed horizontal equity, for example, the family's taste for taxed luxury items, may itself be regarded as evidence of elevated taxpaying capability. In sum, the concept of horizontal equity may have problems in application, but the principle is strong. Equal treatment, after all, is a principle implicit in the equal-protection requirements of the U.S. Constitution: In a property tax case, the U.S. Supreme Court explained ". . . the constitutional requirement is the seasonable attainment of a rough equity in tax treatment of similarly situated property owners."[17] The logic extends to other taxes.

---

[15]For a defense of the consumption view, see Nicholas Kaldor, *The Expenditure Tax* (London: George Allen and Unwin, 1958).

[16]For example, the 1986 federal tax reform act sought to improve horizontal equity by reducing the availability of tax shelters available to the daring, slick, or cagey investor.

[17]*Alleghency Pittsburgh Coal Company* v. *County Commission of Webster County, West Virginia* 109 S. Ct. 633 (1989).

Vertical equity concerns the proper relationship between the relative tax burdens paid by individuals with different capabilities to pay taxes. The comparison is among unequals, and the question is, by how much should tax payments differ? No scientific guides indicate what the proper differentiation might be, but most would argue that those with more capacity should pay more tax. This simple observation, however, provides minimal guidance for tax policy. What needs to be determined further is whether the tax structure should be proportional, progressive, or regressive.

Table 7–4 illustrates the three distributions, assuming a simple community with only two taxpayers, one of high income and the other of low income. Each distributes a tax burden of $10,000 between the taxpayers. The vertical-equity concept gauges the relationship between income and effective rates (tax paid divided by the relevant affluence measurement; the examples here use current income). A tax structure is *regressive* if effective rates are lower in high-ability groups than in low (effective rates fall as ability rises), *progressive* if effective rates are higher in high-ability groups than in low (effective rates rise as ability rises), and *proportional* if effective rates are the same in all groups (effective rates remain constant as ability

Table 7–4
Regressivity, Proportionality, and Progressivity in Tax Systems

Regressive System ($10,000 Total Tax)

Taxpayer Income ($)	Share of Pretax Income (%)	Tax Paid ($)	Effective Tax Rate (%)	Share of Posttax Income (%)
20,000	20	3,000	15	18.9
80,000	80	7,000	8.75	81.1
100,000	100	10,000		100.0

Proportional System ($10,000 Total Tax)

Taxpayer Income ($)	Share of Pretax Income (%)	Tax Paid ($)	Effective Tax Rate (%)	Share of Posttax Income (%)
20,000	20	2,000	10	20
80,000	80	8,000	10	80
100,000	100	10,000		100.0

Progressive System ($10,000 Total Tax)

Taxpayer Income ($)	Share of Pretax Income (%)	Tax Paid ($)	Effective Tax Rate (%)	Share of Posttax Income (%)
20,000	20	1,200	6	20.9
80,000	80	8,800	11	79.1
100,000	100	10,000		100.0

rises). Effective-rate behavior distinguishes whether the high-income taxpayer is paying relatively more, relatively less, or the same in relation to income as is the low-income taxpayer. That determines the extent to which the tax structure redistributes affluence in the society. Notice in the table that the proportional structure leaves the shares of post-tax income exactly as the shares were before tax, the regressive structure improves the share of the high-income taxpayer, and the progressive structure improves the share of the low-income taxpayer. These patterns of redistribution reflected in the effective rate patterns are the essence of vertical equity. What society wants the tax system to do in regard to redistribution establishes whether public policy should seek progressive, proportional, or regressive tax structures, and that is an ethical judgment.

At one time, public finance scholars sought scientific support for the redistribution caused by progressive rate structures through reference to diminishing marginal utility of income: those with more affluence gain less satisfaction from income (increments to affluence) than do those with less affluence. Thus, total utility loss to society to obtain a given amount of revenue would be minimized by applying higher tax rates to those with greater affluence. The diminishing-marginal-utility-of-income argument has not been provable and may be wrong, so progression remains unscientific.[18] There continues, however, a general feeling that tax systems should not do great relative harm to the less affluent.

Table 7–4 also illustrates measurements that do not reliably indicate whether a structure is progressive or regressive. For instance, a comparison of total tax paid by high- and low-income groups does not produce meaningful information about vertical equity. For each structure here, the high-income taxpayer pays more tax, despite the dramatic differences in relative burden. Therefore, simply comparing total taxes paid by income groups does not distinguish the regressivity/progressivity/proportionality of the tax structure. Neither does a comparison of the proportion of total taxes paid by an income group with that group's proportion of total population. In the example, the highest-income taxpayer represents half of community population, and the regressive tax structure causes that taxpayer to pay 70 percent of community taxes, so that comparison is not useful. If the tax base per taxpaying unit is unequal among income groups (as it certainly must be), proportional, regressive, and progressive taxes all cause high-income groups to pay a disproportionately high share of taxes and low-income groups, a low share relative to share of the population. Thus, effective-rate comparisons or their logical equivalents are the only reliable guide to vertical equity of a structure.

Who really pays? Estimating who bears the burden of taxes is important for both reasoned discourse and political argument. The work is complicated because the entity legally required to pay any tax may be able to shift some or all the real burden elsewhere. In the language of tax analysis, the *impact* or statutory incidence may not coincide with the *incidence* of the tax because *shifting* has occurred.

---

[18]See Walter J. Blum and Harry Kalven, Jr., *The Uneasy Case for Progressive Taxation* (Chicago: University of Chicago Press, 1953).

Figure 7–1
Impace, Shifting, and Incidence

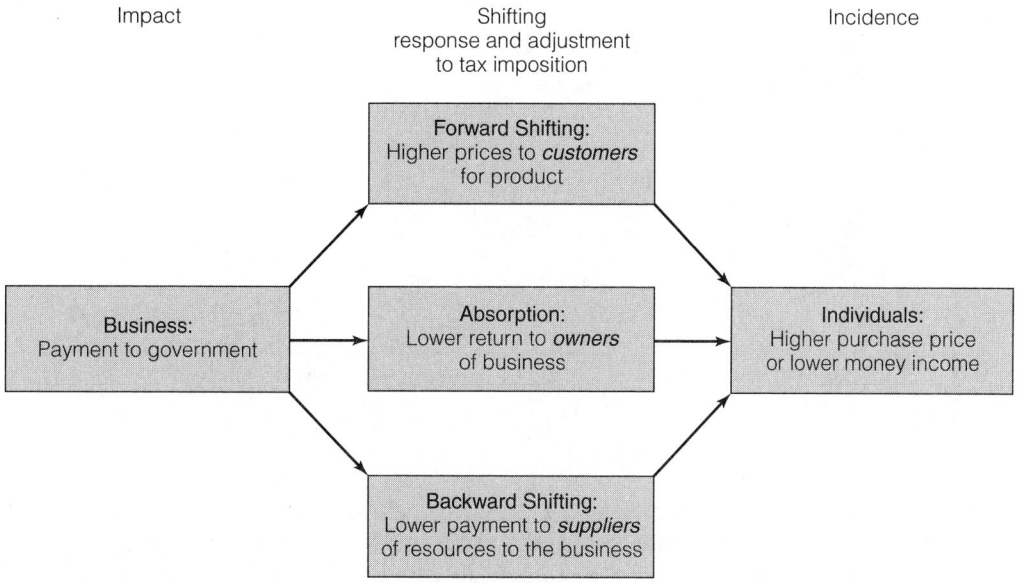

The incidence question most often involves taxes with impact on businesses, like taxes on corporate net income, business property, or employee payroll. As illustrated in Figure 7–1, a business may respond in three ways to a tax:

1. *Forward Shifting:* The business increases its prices to reflect the tax.
2. *Backward Shifting:* The business reduces the price it pays to owners of the resources it purchases, including the wages paid workers, the prices paid suppliers of raw materials, and so on.
3. *Absorption:* The business may return a lower profit to its owners.

What actually occurs depends on the form of the tax, that is, whether the tax is levied on net profits, sales, or property, and on the market conditions the firm faces, but it can be expected to respond in whatever fashion leaves its owners with greatest profit after tax.[19] It will not automatically respond by increasing prices because buyers will respond to the higher prices by purchasing less, and the profit lost from

[19]The responses are carefully analyzed in Richard A. Musgrave, *The Theory of Public Finance* (New York: McGraw-Hill, 1959), Chapter 13; and in Joseph E. Stiglitz, *Economics of the Public Sector,* 3rd ed. (New York: W. W. Norton, 2000), Chapters 18, 23, and 27. Another good source: Executive Office of the President, Council of Economic Advisors, *Economic Report of the President Transmitted to Congress February 2004* (Washington, D.C.: U.S. GPO, 2004), Chapter 4 "Tax Incidence: Who Bears the Tax Burden?"

Table 7–5
Federal Tax Distributions and Effective Tax Rates by Income Quintiles for All Families, 1980-2003 (all in percentages)

	1980			1985			1990		
Quintile	Income Share	Tax Share	Effective Tax Rate	Income Share	Tax Share	Effective Tax Rate	Income Share	Tax Share	Effective Tax Rate
Lowest	5.7	2	7.7	4.8	2.3	9.8	4.6	1.9	8.9
Second	11	7	14.1	10.1	7.2	14.8	10	6.8	14.6
Third	15.7	13.3	18.7	15.2	13.2	18.1	15.1	12.6	17.9
Fourth	22.1	21.3	21.5	21.9	21.3	20.4	21.6	20.7	20.6
Highest	45.8	56.3	27.3	48.6	55.8	24	49.5	57.9	25.1
Top 5%	20.7	28.7	30.8	23.4	28.4	25.4	24.3	30.6	27
Top 1%	9.1	14.2	34.6	11.5	14.8	27	12.1	16.2	28.8

SOURCE: Congressional Budget Office, *Historical Effective Federal Tax Rates: 1979 to 2003.* Available online at www.cbo.gov/ftpdocs/70xx/doc7000/12-29-FedTaxRates.pdf

those sales may be greater than the tax recovered from the price increase. No matter how the business responds, however, the business tax reduces the real income of individuals, either by causing customers to pay higher prices, causing workers or other resource owners to receive lower income for what they sell to the firm, or leaving owners of the firm with lower profits. For example, the payroll tax to finance Social Security has two shares, one paid by the employer and one paid by the employee. Some analysts argue that both components reduce the real income of the employee: the payroll tax paid by the employer represents wages, salaries, and fringe benefits that would have been paid to the employee in the absence of the tax. The employer knows about the payroll tax and adjusts wages downward to cover that tax. Hence, the real burden, or incidence, of this share, along with the employee share, is on the employee. Or another example: the landlord pays property tax on his or her rental units. However, over time, the landlord adjusts the rents upward to accommodate that property tax. The incidence of the tax rests on the renter.

Two important principles about tax incidence are often forgotten in political discussions. First, laws may define tax impacts, but market forces determine incidence; *to legislate incidence is about as effective as legislating against snowfall.* Second, all taxes are ultimately borne by individuals. Businesses serve as conduits of burdens to people, either as buyers, as sellers, or as owners. The shifting process is not easy to sort out, but its determination is necessary to identify the vertical equity of a tax.

In order to illustrate the application of vertical equity analysis, Table 7–5 displays effective tax rates for federal taxes across families, arrayed by income-group quintiles, to permit some comparability across time and place in selected years from 1980 to 2003. The table is calculated to include all taxes levied by the federal government; more individual attention will be given them in later chapters. The distribution in Table 7–5 makes these incidence assumptions: (1) Families who pay the tax bear the burden of the individual income tax (no shifting); (2) social insur-

Table 7–5
(Continued)

1995			2000			2003		
Income Share	Tax Share	Effective Tax Rate	Income Share	Tax Share	Effective Tax Rate	Income Share	Tax Share	Effective Tax Rate
4.6	1.3	6.3	4	1.1	6.4	4.2	1	4.8
9.7	5.8	13.4	8.6	4.8	13	9.1	4.5	9.8
14.9	11.4	17.3	13.5	9.8	16.6	14.4	9.9	13.6
21.3	19.3	20.5	19.6	17.5	20.5	20.9	18.6	17.7
50.2	61.9	27.8	54.8	66.6	28	52.2	65.7	25
25.1	35.4	31.8	30.7	41.4	31	27	38.7	28.4
12.5	20.1	36.1	17.8	25.5	33	14.3	22.6	31.4

ance tax burden is allocated to employee compensation (employer share shifted backward, no shifting of employee share); (3) excise taxes are paid by individual consumers in higher prices (forward shifting); (4) corporate income tax is paid by families (half shifted back to employees, half shifted to stockholders).[20] Notice that the impact or statutory incidence of these taxes does not always fall on the individuals who bear the final burden or incidence. For instance, product producers usually are responsible for paying the federal excise taxes, but the incidence analysis assumes that the taxes are shifted forward in higher product prices.

The distribution is progressive through the years, with rate differences between the highest quintile and the lowest somewhat greater in 2003 than in 1980. The effective rate paid by the highest income earners is lower in 2003 than it was in 1980, but the decline is greater for the lowest quintile. The table also shows the share of pre-tax income received and the share of federal tax borne in each quintile; as is characteristic of a progressive distribution, the share of tax is greater than the share of pre-tax income for higher-income groups and the reverse for lower-income groups.[21]

[20]The Joint Committee on Taxation and the Department of Treasury believe the corporate income tax to be borne entirely by capital income, so their estimates show greater progressivity than those presented here. For a description of the allocation approach used by the staff of Congress's Joint Committee on Taxation, see *Methodology and Issues in Measuring Changes in the Distribution of Tax Burdens,* JCS-7-93 (Washington, D.C.: GPO, 1993).

[21]Because individuals face different economic conditions and make different economic choices over their lifetimes, they are not always taxed in the same way and by the same taxes. Some economists have tried to estimate the lifetime incidence profile of tax system and its elements, moving away from the traditional annual focus. See, for example, Don Fullerton and Diane Lim Rogers, *Who Bears the Lifetime Tax Burden?* (Washington, D.C.: Brookings Institution, 1993). A study that looks at burden over a longer time horizon appears in Congressional Budget Office, *Effective Tax Rates: Comparing Annual and Multiyear Measures* (Washington, D.C.: CBO, 2005).

More on business and individual shares. Analysts occasionally estimate the relative share of taxes paid by businesses and individuals, especially at the state and local levels of government, as a guide to tax policy. Business taxes usually include taxes on business property, corporate net income taxes, business gross receipt taxes, corporate franchise taxes, miscellaneous business and occupation taxes, licenses, severance taxes, document and stock transfer taxes, and the like. Taxes on individuals include property taxes on residences and household personal property, individual income taxes, retail sales taxes, and selective excise taxes. Special classification problems arise with taxes on agricultural property (what portion of a farmer's property tax bill is individual, and what portion is business?), unincorporated business income (the business is taxed through the individual income tax system), and sales tax paid on business purchases. Those complexities, however, can usually be resolved by allocations based on a sample of taxpayers.

Of course, the burden of taxes levied on businesses ultimately falls on individuals, even if the tax is collected initially from business. Those engaged in transactions with the business as its customers, suppliers, employees, or owners bear the tax. So why tax the business separately from taxing those people directly? Much of the answer is pure politics—lawmakers prefer the fiction that by taxing businesses they are sparing individuals the burden of paying for government services. But there are a couple of reasons that have some logical support. First, there is an economic reason: the business tax may charge the business for costs they generate but otherwise would not take account of when deciding what, where, and how to produce. In other words, a carefully designed business tax may make the business recognize the cost of otherwise unpriced inputs used in production. The most important costs involved are the cost of services provided by government to the business—public safety, civil court system, and so on—and environmental damage caused by production of goods and services (air, water, and soil pollution). In both of these instances, the business tax can provide signals about resource use to the operators of the business, thus improving the utilization of resources in the economy. Second, it may be more effective and less costly to use the business as a conduit of burden to individuals than to collect directly from the individuals. For example, collection of a retail sales tax indirectly through vendors who add the tax to the price of goods that they sell is much more efficient than trying to collect a comparable tax from purchasers directly after the sale has been made.[22] As far as the owners of a business are concerned, probably more important than the share of taxes paid by business is the amount of those taxes that cannot be readily shifted to suppliers or to customers—the taxes that, under existing market conditions, reduce the return received by owners of the business.

State and local governments are interested in relative business-individual shares, however, for reasons other than equitable burden distribution (or the politically important fact that tax paid by business has a more hidden burden on individuals—politicians are less fervent believers in transparency than are fiscal

[22]For a good discussion of the idea of business taxation, see Thomas F. Pogue, "Principles of Business Taxation: How and Why Should Businesses Be Taxed?" in W. Bartley Hildreth and James A. Richardson, eds. *Handbook on Taxation,* (New York: Marcel Bekker, 1999): 191–203.

analysts). In many instances, the individuals ultimately bearing the burden of business taxes live out of state.[23] A higher business share thus means that a greater amount of state and local government costs are exported to nonresidents. That exporting is politically attractive, even if the extent of exporting attempted may not always be logically justified. Although those businesses do receive services provided by the host community, the appropriate amount of payment is always subject to dispute between businesses and the government. Furthermore, states must take care that out-of-state businesses are not treated more harshly than are domestic businesses, because differential treatment would violate the commerce clause of the U.S. Constitution.[24]

The capability to use taxes with the initial impact on business to export the cost of government to nonresidents, however, does have an important limitation. Taxes may adversely affect the competitive position of business in the state. If tax structures designed to export cost to nonresidents place local business at competitive disadvantage relative to out-of-state competitors, the state economy may suffer. Therefore, tax-share data must be tempered with evaluation of the overall tax level in the competitive states (all of a very low total tax burden would have less influence on competitive position than would a moderate share of a very high total tax burden), but the concern with competitive balance does influence the quest for cost exporting. Thus, states frequently trade the desire to export government cost for a competitive balance for local firms.

Adequacy of Revenue Production

A tax levied for revenue is worthwhile only if it can generate meaningful revenue at socially acceptable rates.[25] Some taxes may be levied for reasons other than revenue—punitively high rates to stop an undesirable activity or taxes applied simply to keep track of a particular activity—but revenue is the prime objective of most taxes. How much revenue will a tax yield and how does yield change when a government changes the effective rate applied to a particular tax base? Tax yield (R), or total collections, equals the tax rate (t) times the tax base (B): If the resident income tax rate is 1 percent and resident income equals $200 million, then tax yield equals $2.0 million. That is the simple accounting relationship for tax revenue. If the tax rate were quadrupled, to 4 percent, the yield would quadruple as well, to $8.0 million. The tax-revenue equation $R = t \times B$ is graphed in Figure 7–2 as the straight line from the origin (no revenue is produced when the tax rate is zero): There is a linear relationship between the effective tax rate and the yield from the base. Tax-rate changes produce additional revenue in proportion to the rate change: A 10-percent increase in rate will yield a 10-percent increase in revenue, and so on.

---

[23]Note that certain individual taxes may be substantially exported in special circumstances: for example, residential property taxes in second-home communities, and lodging taxes in tourist areas.

[24]"The congress shall have Power . . . to regulate Commerce with foreign nations and among the several States and with the Indian Tribes" (Article 1, Sec. 8[3]). Differential treatment by a state involves a power reserved to Congress.

[25]Recall that Adam Smith did not include revenue production among this maxims.

Figure 7–2
Relationships Between Tax Rate and Tax Revenue: The Tax Revenue Curve

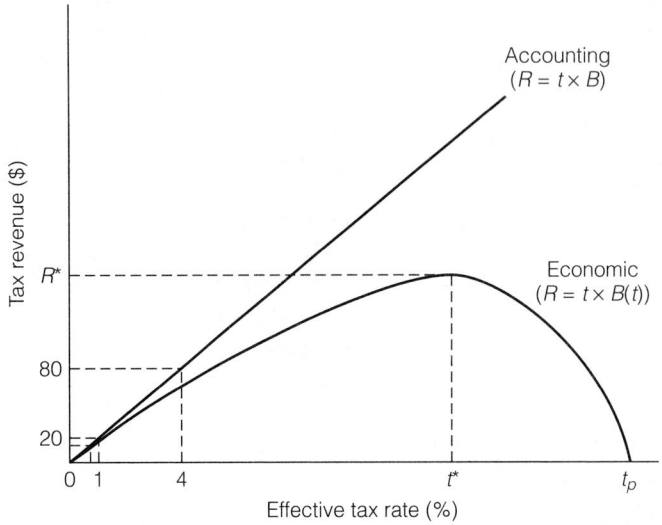

This accounting relationship, however, ignores the economic response by individuals and businesses who now face a different tax rate, and that response will cause the tax base to differ from what it was at the old rate. In other words, the tax base itself is determined in part by the effective tax rate levied against it: If the resident income tax rate increases to 4 percent, resident income will not be $200 million. As Robert Inman explains, ". . . the increase in the tax on resident's income might well cause residents to work less as their incomes are taxed or even cause wealthier families to leave the taxing jurisdiction. . . ."[26] Similar economic responses to tax-rate changes also apply for other taxes. Furthermore, higher rates provide greater returns from various "fiddles" to illegally remove operations from the tax system. Therefore, the economic relationship between effective rate and revenue yield is not linear but allows for change in the tax base that the changed tax rate will cause. In Figure 7–2, the economic response to the higher tax rate causes actual yield to be less than shown from the linear relationship. The economic relationship considers first the negative rate-to-base effect (the base as a function of rate or $B(t)$) of a rate increase and then estimates yield by multiplying this adjusted base by the rate ($t \times B(t)$). That causes the economic relationship to differ from the accounting relationship in revenue yield estimates and in Figure 7–2.[27]

[26]Robert P. Inman, "Can Philadelphia Escape Its Fiscal Crisis with Another Tax Increase?" *Federal Reserve Bank of Philadelphia Business Review* (Sept./Oct. 1992): 7.
[27]One analysis of rate revenue curves for each tax in a state: Michael L. Walden, "Dynamic Revenue Curves for North Carolina Taxes," *Public Budgeting & Finance,* (Winter 2003), 49–64. None of the state taxes had rates that pushed state beyond the revenue peak.

Figure 7–2 portrays a maximum yield (R^*). This peak measures the maximum economic yield from that tax base. Further tax-rate increases from t^* will cause declining yield as the revenue loss from the tax-induced decline in the base overwhelms the additional yield from the higher rate.[28] The profile of this rate-revenue curve would depend on how responsive the particular tax base is to the effective tax rate. At lower rates and for small relative changes, change impacts may well approximate the accounting relationship. But the economic relationship cannot be ignored for larger changes and, especially, when the tax is being applied to a geographically small region or when avenues for avoidance are easy (e.g., close to borders). Several efforts have been made to estimate what this economic relationship actually looks like for various taxes, and tax policy has sometimes been made on the basis of assertions about its configuration. President Reagan's 1981 tax reductions were based in part on the view, argued most effectively by Arthur Laffer (after whom the rate-revenue curve has popularly been named) that federal personal income tax rates were above t^* and hence the rate reduction would help close the budget deficit by increasing tax revenue. Laffer was by no means the first to note the possibility. John Maynard Keynes wrote in 1933: "Nor should the argument seem strange that taxation may be so high as to defeat its object, and that, given sufficient time to gather the fruits, a reduction of taxation will run a better chance, than an increase, of balancing the budget."[29] Careful analysis has shown yields to have been reduced by the Reagan reductions, however.[30] Tests for local taxes usually show actual rates to be below t^*, but not always.[31]

Yield can be a difficult practical problem—before reaching the limits of economic capacity—when state restrictions limit local fiscal autonomy. For instance, a state may establish a special district to provide services financed only from a single excise tax base or may impose restrictive property-tax-rate ceilings on local governments. These limits can create considerable revenue adequacy problems. In most instances, however, there are political constraints to use of tax bases that bind before the problem of absolute capacity binds.[32]

---

[28]Carrying the analysis further, there would be a rate so high (t_p) that the taxed activity would cease and there would be no revenue produced.

[29]"The Means to Prosperity," reprinted in *Essays in Persuasion: The Collected Works of John Maynard Keynes,* vol. IX (London: Macmillan, St. Martin's Press, 1972), 338.

[30]Donald Fullerton, "On the Possibility of an Inverse Relationship Between Tax Rates and Government Revenue," *Journal of Public Economics* (October 1982), 3–22. Influences of changing the top marginal rate—the tax highest-income people pay on additional income—on revenue are far less clear. See Robert J. Barro, "Higher Taxes, Lower Revenues," *Wall Street Journal* (9 July 1993), A-10.

[31]Studies revealing in actual rate to be below t^* include the following: for city property taxes, Helen Ladd and Katharine Bradbury, "City taxes and Property Tax Bases," *National Tax Journal* 41 (December 1988); local sales tax, John L. Mikesell and C. Kurt Zorn, "Impact of the Sales Tax Rate on Its Base: Evidence from a Small Town," *Public Finance Quarterly* 14 (July 1986); Long Island school districts, Robert Inman, "Micro-fiscal Planning in the Regional Economy: A General Equilibrium Approach," *Journal of Public Economics* (April 1977); and state sales taxes, Gerald E. Auten and Edward H. Robb, "A General Model for State Tax Revenue Analysis," *National Tax Journal* 29 (December 1976): 422–35. The rate was shown to be above t^* in: for New York City business taxes, Ronald Grieson, William Hamovitch, Albert Levenson, and Richard Morgenstern, "The Effect of Business Taxation on the Location of Industry," *Journal of Urban Economics* (April 1977); and for Philadelphia city taxes, Inman, "Micro-fiscal Planning."

[32]There is no reason for any government to identify and use its maximum revenue capacity. That would mean the government seeks to maximize its budget, and that almost never be in the public interest. t^* represents the maximum yield, not the optimum yield.

Another capacity problem is that of fiscal disparity. Not all regions in a country or localities within a region have equal tax-base endowments. For instance, some regions contain important commercial centers or valuable natural resources, whereas other regions have no revenue base of any consequence. To the extent that these regions must finance government services from their own revenue sources, the poorer areas and the people who live in them are at a considerable disadvantage. This disparity question is examined in greater depth in Chapter 14 with discussions of intergovernmental horizontal fiscal balance.

Adequacy also considers revenue patterns across both cyclical (short-run) and secular (long-run) time dimensions. Efforts to manage the national economy have not eliminated economic fluctuations, particularly in states and smaller economic regions, some of which periodically suffer from episodes of unemployment approaching depression levels. Government functions continue during depressed economic activity and may grow because of social tensions in these periods. A revenue source with good cyclical adequacy remains reasonably stable during periods of declining economic activity. Such stability is vital for state and local governments because they lack the borrowing flexibility and money-creating powers that can accommodate federal deficits. In general, taxes on corporate profits are particularly unstable because of the volatility of that base. Some states historically were reluctant to rely on corporate taxes for that reason. Property taxes have considerable stability, except for delinquency problems during deep depressions (including localized economic collapse). General sales taxes are somewhat less stable than individual income taxes, probably because business equipment purchases constitute a sizable share of the former tax base.

Revenue stability, however, is a problem for government when economic growth continues with little interruption. Demand for many government services increases more rapidly than the increase in economic activity. The demand pattern can be examined using the income elasticity of service expenditure, an estimate of the percentage increase in expenditure that will result from each 1 percent increase in income. Those services for which expenditure increases more rapidly than does income have an income elasticity greater than 1. An increase in income of 1 percent generates an increase in government spending greater than 1 percent. Governments lacking revenue sources with similar growth characteristics face the prospect of increased debt, increased tax rates (or new taxes), or unmet demand for government services. Each of these options is politically unpleasant, so there is a general preference for responsive taxes, taxes whose revenue increases more rapidly than does income (the revenue elasticity or the elasticity of the tax base with respect to income exceeds 1). Table 7–6 reports income elasticities by individual tax bases as found in several recent tax studies.[33] Because the exact structure of each tax differs to some degree from government to government, and these differences influence

[33]These elasticities are typically computed from a time-series regression of the form in $\ln B = a + b \ln Y$, where B is the tax base analyzed, Y is the measure of economic activity, and b is the income elasticity of the tax. Other influences on the base—for instance, statutory-tax-rate changes—may also be included as independent variables. Sometimes analysis is done of *tax buoyancy*. This analysis considers tax yield (base times tax rate) rather than just the tax base.

Table 7–6
Compilation of Selected Long-Term Tax Base Elasticities as Found in Various Tax Studies

	Low	High	Median
Personal income tax (41 states)*	0.809	3.983	1.604
Retail sales tax (44 states)*	0.339	1.365	0.781
Corporate income tax (nine studies)†	0.72	1.44	1.1
General property tax (twelve studies)†	0.34	1.41	0.87
Motor-fuels tax (50 states)‡	1.091	0.478	0.739
Tobacco tax (eight studies)†	0.00	0.54	0.26

SOURCES: *Donald Bruce, William F. Fox, and M. H. Tuttle, "Tax Base Elasticities: A Multi-State Analysis of Long-run and Short-run Dynamics" (University of Tennessee, processed, September 2004) Available online at http://web.utk.edu/~dbruce/bruce.fox.tuttle.elasticities.pdf.
†ACIR (Advisory Commission on Intergovernmental Relations), *Significant Features of Fiscal Federalism, 1976-1977, Vol. 2, Revenue and Debt* (Washington, D.C.: GPO, 1977), 254.
‡John H. Bowman and John L. Mikesell, "Recent Changes in State Gasoline Taxation: An Analysis of Structure and Rates," *National Tax Journal* 36 (June 1983): 174–176.

performance of the tax, the table provides elasticity ranges as well as the median. Overall, the individual income tax show greatest responsiveness (caused both by rate graduation and sensitivity of the base), whereas motor-fuel and tobacco taxes—generally applied on a specific (volume or unit) basis rather than on a value (volume times price) basis—have the least responsiveness. The general sales tax is in an intermediate position. The property tax elasticity estimates are probably artificially high because some studies did not separate the revenue effects of increased property tax rates, so the elasticity result is not purely the outcome of automatic base growth.[34] Because responsive taxes may not be stable, the appropriate choice for adequacy over time depend on whether problems of growth or problems of decline are most likely and whether the government has access to debt markets and the ability to raise rates during periods of economic decline.

So what does income elasticity mean for a state government? Suppose that private economic activity is increasing at a rate of 10 percent annually. If that state has a personal income tax with typical base elasticity (from Table 7–6), personal income tax revenue would generally be increasing at a rate of 16.04 percent annually without any increase in tax rates. If the state happened to rely upon a general property tax, revenue from that tax would generally be increasing at a rate of 8.7 percent annually. This difference in elasticity can significantly influence the fiscal performance of the government. High elasticities can insulate the government in a growing area from having to increase tax rates; low elasticities can bring perpetual fiscal crises.

[34]A study that extracts both rate changes and general reassessments of property found a property-tax-base elasticity of 0.27 in one state (Indiana). This measurement is more comparable to those reported for sales and income tax bases because it extracts all statutory and administrative sources of base change. See John L. Mikesell, "Property Tax Assessment Practice and Income Elasticities," *Public Finance Quarterly* 6 (January 1978): 61.

Collectability

A tax must be collectable at reasonable cost to society. Resources used in the collection of revenue provide no net service to society: the revenue, not its collection, is valuable. Efficient collection "avoids complex provisions and regulations; multiple filing and reporting requirements; and numerous deductions, exclusions, and exemptions. The more complicated the tax system, the greater the costs of taxpayer compliance. A less-complicated system of taxation enables understanding of the law and enhances public confidence in the system. From the government's perspective, complexity increases the costs of administration, and frequent changes to tax laws prohibit effective fiscal planning."[35] A complicating influence is the fact that complexity is usually the product of well-intentioned efforts to correct some perceived inequity in the tax system or to improve some element of how the system impacts economic incentives. The complications allow policy-makers to achieve other goals of tax policy. There is, indeed, a demand for complexity and with that complexity comes increased costs of compliance and of administration. The quest for tax simplicity is an excellent applause line in political speeches, but the public rather likes tax complications that reduce their tax liability. Therefore, improving collectability in the real world of tax restructuring requires a delicate balancing of other objectives of tax policy.

In general, taxes and tax provisions should be designed to keep total collection cost as low as possible within the constraint of satisfactory equity and economic impact. Unfortunately, there are frequently trade-offs. For instance, taxes on payrolls represent the income tax format with least collection cost: collection is made by employers (there are far fewer of them to keep track of than there are employees, and the return from one employer can cover many employees), the problem of checking on interest and dividend income is avoided, and special questions about rents and capital gains do not arise. Unfortunately, self-employed individuals and those with interest, dividend, rental, and capital gain income tend to be more affluent than those receiving only payroll income. Thus, the tax that is simple to administer has equity problems. As a rule, collection complexity with broad-based taxes (property, sale, and income) results from attempts to improve the equity of the particular tax. That is the critical and difficult trade. Narrow-based taxes, particularly selective excises, often simply cannot be collected at low cost and are good candidates for elimination.[36] The resources used in their collection can be more profitably used in administration of other taxes. A more detailed analysis of the tax-collection process, along with collection costs, appears in Chapter 13.

---

[35]David Brunori, "Principles of Tax Policy and Targeted Incentives," *State and Local Government Review* 29 (Winter 1997): 53.

[36]Some excise taxes function to compensate for social costs associated with use of particular products or services.

Economic Effects

Taxes change the way people and businesses behave, often with considerable consequence to economic activity from those distortions. It is important to design tax structures and their administration so that they are not needlessly harmful to the economy. There is a difference of opinion as to whether taxes can be expected to do more than simply produce revenue and cause as little economic harm as possible. Some argue that a tax should be neutral in its effect: market systems can be trusted to function well without intervention, so the most one should expect from a tax is that it disturbs the marketplace as little as possible. The 1986 federal tax reform, for instance, sought to establish a "level playing field" for types of economic endeavors. In other words, the tax should ordinarily be neutral: economic behavior should be the same with a particular tax in place as it would have been without the tax. Others argue that a tax should have favorable economic effects: the outcome from market operations can be improved by using tax incentives to alter private behavior in some desired fashion. That means that the tax structure should be used to try to improve on the results from the market.[37]

Regardless of one's view about the appropriateness (or even the possibility) of trying to improve on the results from the market with such distortion, it is clear that taxes do influence economic behavior and that influences differ among taxes. Taxes can have important effects on economic activity, and tax incentives—good and bad—are part of tax policy discussions. Whenever a tax produces a difference in the return that can be gained between two or more competing economic activities, individuals and businesses can be expected to respond toward the alternative leaving a greater after-tax return. Individuals and businesses change their behavior in response to a tax, but the reaction depends on how the tax is structured, not just its absolute level. Furthermore, the response can come in anticipation of a change in the tax, the response may differ according to whether the tax is believed to be permanent or temporary, and the response increases as individuals and businesses have more time to make adjustments to the tax.

Here are a number of different choices that a tax wedge—the difference between before and after tax prices, payments, or rates of return—can create, along with some examples of the effect:

1. **Work versus leisure.** High taxes on extra income earned may induce workers to choose more leisure time instead of working more hours. Working overtime is less attractive if governments tax away a very high percentage of income earned from that overtime, for instance. Suppose that, of each $100 of overtime pay that a worker earned, the government taxed away $80. Do you suppose workers would choose to work as much overtime as they would if the tax were only $15?

[37]How tax structure may induce (or discourage) development in poor countries is exhaustively reviewed in the excellent survey by Robin Burgess and Nicholas Stern, "Taxation and Development," *Journal of Economic Literature* 31 (June 1993): 762–830.

2. **Business operations.** Firms should not be induced to organize business practices—production techniques, type of business organization, distribution or marketing system, and so forth—on the basis of tax provisions. Thus, a state property tax on business inventory held on a particular date can induce firms to ship inventory out of state on that date for return later. Suppose that Indiana levies a tax of 10 percent of the value of automobiles on the showroom floor on March 1 and that the tax does not apply to automobiles owned by private owners. Do you suppose that auto dealers would have special sales events to reduce their inventory just before the tax day?[38]

3. **Shopping, purchases, and business location.** High tax rates on goods—cigarettes, liquor, or retail sales in general, for instance—in some states induce their residents to purchase those items from nearby states with lower taxes and lower prices and these and other taxes may change where entrepreneurs set up their businesses. Do you suppose that New York City residents, facing a sales tax rate of 8.375 percent on their purchases, might drive to New Jersey, where the rate is no higher than 6 percent, to purchase some appliances and other high ticket items?

4. **Personal management.** Because travel expense to professional conventions can be subtracted from income subject to the federal individual income tax, such conventions may be held in resort locations. Those attending can thus combine vacation and business while reducing their tax obligation. Also, tax provisions can influence how people prefer to be paid. If, for instance, payments received as fringe benefits are not taxed as income, then employees will prefer more of their compensation in that form, rather than in taxable wages and salaries. If your employer can purchase health insurance for you, paying $6,000 per year for that insurance and that compensation to you is not taxed, or if your employer can pay you an extra $6,000 per year, fully taxable, and then you have to purchase your own health insurance, which option would you prefer?

5. **Productive investment and financial portfolios.** Investment may be expected to be influenced by the after-tax rate of return and by tax-induced rate of return differentials between sorts of enterprise. Furthermore, high-income entities may direct investable funds to municipal bonds yielding tax-free interest rather than to other productive investment, the return on which would be taxed.

6. **Savings.** Taxes can distort the decision to save by making consumption postponed to the future (savings) more expensive than equivalent consumption in the present. The influence can be on personal decisions to save and on business decisions to retain or distribute earnings to business owners.

---

[38]Historically, newspapers have been published in broadsheet rather than tabloid format because in 1712 Britain introduced a stamp tax on newspapers per sheet of newsprint. Papers responded by increasing the size of their pages to reduce the amount of tax that they would owe. Bigger sheets, fewer pages, lower tax. The traditional size spread globally and only recently have newspapers started reducing the size of the sheets.

Sidebar 7–1
The Excess Burden of a Tax—Measuring the Value of Economic Distortion

Economists identify two components of the total burden of a tax. These are the *tax burden,* the payment made by the taxpayer to the government, and the *excess burden* (also called the deadweight loss or welfare cost), a measure of the economic distortion caused by the tax. The excess burden is the loss created by changes in producer and consumer decisions that the tax produces. In general, economists expect that free choice by producers and consumers will direct resources to those activities yielding the best return for society and that consumers will use their purchasing power to acquire those goods giving them the greatest satisfaction. Imposing the tax yields revenue to the government—the tax burden—but it also normally causes a reduction in the amount of the subject of the tax (a commodity or an input) sold. That reduction in units sold brings the deadweight loss: those now-unsold units were bringing satisfaction to the purchaser above the price the purchaser was paying and a return to the seller above the price the seller was receiving (otherwise neither buyer nor seller would have made the exchange). This market loss is above the tax paid to the government. Indeed, we don't worry much about the tax burden—if the government is budgeting wisely, the use of the resources by the government will yield a return above that which could have been earned in the private market.

The idea of excess burden can be illustrated in a simple example. Suppose Fred ordinarily buys three compact disks (CDs) per month at a price of $15 each (spending a total of $45 per month). The government now imposes a new CD tax that adds $3 to the price of each disk. Fred concludes that $18 per disk is simply too much to pay and no longer buys CDs. The government collects no tax revenue from Fred (his tax burden is zero) and he now has $45 per month available to spend on other things.

Does Fred bear any burden from the tax? Certainly he does, under the assumption that he was making well-informed, free choices before the imposition of the tax. The tax has caused him to move from his preferred use of that $45 to the purchase of something else, a less desirable (to Fred) option. We know it is less desirable to him, because he rejected it before, choosing to buy the CDs instead. Fred loses the satisfaction from the CDs and switches to a less preferred use of his money. This loss is called the excess burden by tax analysts.

That governments should avoid excess burden in structuring their tax systems is an application of the general principle that government should avoid doing things that are economically stupid. If the private market is managing its basic role of allocating resources, then the tax system should leave it alone as much as possible.

There are many other examples of each distortion. Overall, taxes should not discourage private employment or economic activity more than the minimum needed to extract resources for government operation. Undesirable distortions should be minimized because they cause a waste of productive resources, lower rates of economic growth, and lower national living standards.

Sidebar 7–1 explains excess burden, a measure used in the analysis of distortion. The example in Sidebar 7–1 provides a worst-case scenario: The tax yields no revenue (from Fred) but does create an economic burden (the value lost from the distorted consumer choice). The efficiency objective in tax policy seeks to yield necessary revenue (the tax burden) while keeping economic distortion (the excess burden) as low as possible. And, although the illustration is of consumer choice, there is a similar concern with minimizing producer distortions as well. In general, excess burden can be reduced by (1) keeping tax rates low (a good reason to have broad tax bases), (2) by avoiding different tax rates on similar products, similar uses for competing productive resources, or similar ways of earning an income, and (3) avoiding taxes in markets where buyers or sellers react substantially to changes in price.

State and Local Taxes and Economic Development

State and local governments are keenly interested in the impact that their taxes might have on economic development and, particularly, on jobs. They are cautious about raising rates, they compare their taxes with their neighbors, and they make tax concessions to bring businesses into their markets. Competition for industry among the states, within states, and now with the rest of the world is fierce and can serve as a powerful force for keeping these governments efficient and responsive to the service demands of their citizenry. State and local governments really want to manipulate their fiscal systems to influence business location, employment, and physical investment; market-oriented politicians seem perfectly willing to manipulate market forces if it might mean more for their electorates.[39]

But do taxes really have much impact? Non-tax influences on business profitability (access to markets, availability of usable business sites, levels of production cost, availability of a good-quality workforce and other resources, etc.) vary so much between prospective locations that they could swamp the effect of taxes. The question has been argued for decades and it is far from settled now. The evidence does seem to indicate the following:

[39]In *Cuno* v. *Daimler Chrysler* (No. 00-7247, October 19, 2004), the U.S. Court of Appeals for the Sixth Circuit ruled that Ohio's corporate investment tax credit for new manufacturing equipment and machinery violated the Commerce Clause of the U.S. Constitution because state taxpayers who invested in Ohio received the credit but state taxpayers who invested outside Ohio did not. That would hinder free trade between states. That is exactly what the state intended, of course—to bias the decision of the corporation toward expansion in Ohio. Although praised by some as the first step in stopping inefficient tax bidding among the states that distorts the operations of the free market, its exact implications are not clear and some may be adverse to sound tax policy and contrary to established legal principles. Some incentives were not ruled unconstitutional in the decision; states continue with their development-chasing as if nothing has happened, Congress has legislation in process to overturn the decision, and the case is being appealed to the Supreme Court. However, the Supreme Court has made it clear in various decisions that the Commerce Clause does not prevent a state from competing for interstate businesses, nor does it prevent states from designing competitive tax systems. Previous cases have involved challenges by out-of-state taxpayers, challenging unfair assessment of a state tax that is designed to benefit in-state businesses. *Cuno* is different because it comes from in-state businesses challenging a tax benefit they did not receive. It is unclear what the eventual impact of the *Cuno* decision will be on state tax incentive practices. The U.S. Supreme Court should rule on the case in 2006.

First, tax levels have a small effect on interregional location of economic activity. For any particular state, the extent to which its overall tax level differs from the level of states with which it competes matters to a degree but almost certainly less than publicized. And specific tax provisions can make certain lines of business unattractive in a state or locality. The effect of total tax burden on total economic activity is certainly smaller than the impact of particular tax provisions on particular industries.

Second, taxes have a much larger effect on economic outcomes within a region. In other words, the effect of tax differences on location choice between Louisville and Cincinnati is much greater than between Louisville and Phoenix. Within a region, tax differences are likely to be determining because many other factors—climate, access to resources and markets, and so on—are generally the same.

Of course, the tax influence is only part of the story. Taxing governments use the proceeds to finance public services, some working to enhance the attractiveness of the jurisdiction to business enterprise. Education, highways and transportation, and public safety services seem to be important, but the evidence is substantially less clear than for tax influences.[40]

State and local governments also use various special provisions or narrow tax incentives—targeted abatements that forgive property taxes on new industrial development for specified periods, enterprise zones in which state or local taxes do not apply, deductions or credits for making certain types on capital investment or for hiring certain categories of employees, and so on—that provide exceptional treatment within a general tax to a limited number of taxpayers as an inducement for development. The argument against such exceptions to standard tax policy is strong.

When the business climate of a state becomes so problematic that tax laws need to be changed routinely to attract business, the practice may be a symptom of problems with the tax system itself and a signal that systematic tax reform might be a more useful approach. In effect, tax reform treats existing and new firms equally, and responsible reform also systematically accounts for any tax revenue lost due to reform. Sound tax and fiscal policy probably obviates many of the tax perks that businesses seek.[41] Tax analysts are in general agreement that the best tax policy for economic development is a broad base, low-tax-rate strategy that makes business tax climates more attractive to all firms and less discriminatory among types of business activities.

Getting elected officials to follow a policy of designing a tax structure that is economically attractive to all, as opposed to being laden with special exceptions to entice some particular footloose business or to relieve taxes paid by a particular industry, is a difficult task, however. The problem is that the geeky guy tinkering in his mother's garage is about as likely to come up with what truly transforms the economic prospects of a region as are the bureaucrat-approved scientists working

---

[40]Ronald C. Fisher, "The Effects of State and Local Public Services on Economic Development," *New England Economic Review* (Federal Reserve Bank of Boston) (March/April 1997): 53–66.

[41]Michael Wasylenko, "Taxation and Economic Development: The State of the Economic Literature," *New England Economic Review* (Federal Reserve Bank of Boston) (March/April 1997): 49.

at firms designated by the state as engines of economic growth. And that geek could have gotten going even faster if he hadn't been burdened by paying his share of the taxes forgiven those firms. Attempts at "good discrimination" in taxation have an excellent chance of being about as harmful as unintended ordinary discrimination.

Transparency

The revenue system in a market democracy should be transparent in its adoption, in its administration, in its compliance requirements, and in the amounts that must be paid because democracy requires that the people know who is responsible for public actions, including what goes on with the taxes they must pay. Transparency is critical for good governance in a democracy.

1. **Adoption.** Tax laws should be adopted in an open legislative process. The electorate needs to know the origin of tax proposals—who is introducing the legislation and who is voting for it—and their implication for the distribution of the cost of government. There should be a clear and accessible hearing process for receiving public input on legislative proposals. Unfortunately, just as appropriation earmarks slip into spending bills, the same technique gets used by lawmakers to insert tax provisions into tax bills. And, for the security of contracts, tax laws should not be changed retroactively, in the sense of changing the tax treatment of transactions that already have occurred.[42] There should be consistency between various elements of the tax system and there should be reasonable certainty about how a change in the tax law will change the distribution of tax burden.

2. **Administration.** Tax payments should be based on objective and explicit criteria that should be apparent to all and should appear to be fair to all. Taxpayers should have easy access to tax procedures and those who administer them. The tax should not be subject to individual negotiation on a taxpayer-by-taxpayer basis and payments should be based on an impersonal and uniform application of the tax law, not the judgments—particularly negotiable judgments—made by a tax bureaucrat. Regulations should be developed in a predictable process, should be reasonably derived from the tax statutes, should operate without special treatment for particular taxpayers, and should be understandable, at least in broad terms, to all taxpayers. Taxpayers must also know the process for appeal and what standards may be used to appeal their tax obligation, must be confident that the appeal will be judged fairly, and must be certain that the authorities will not seek revenge on anyone filing an appeal.

---

[42]One exception on retroactivity is that when a bill is in preparation it may establish a particular date upon which the law will be effective for certain transactions, even though the law has not yet passed on that date. That helps reduce the delay of transactions based on a desire to get more favorable treatment (or the acceleration to avoid harsher treatment) from the changed law.

3. **Compliance requirements.** How the tax is to be calculated should not be a mystery to current and potential taxpayers. Each taxpayer should understand how the tax he or she is paying is determined, how changes by the taxpayer would change the tax, and what filing responsibilities are. The meaning and effect of different provisions of the tax should be easy to trace and to understand. Everyone should be given full information about all rules and regulations governing economic transactions so all potential competitors can base their decisions on an accurate assessment of potential costs, returns, and market opportunities.

4. **Amount of payment.** Each taxpayer should know how much tax he or she is paying (hidden taxes are not likely to allow sound choices to be made about the scope of government) and should know to what government payment is being made. If taxpayers do not see the tax or believe that the tax is being paid by somebody else, they may believe that the government service has no cost, which is unlikely to produce good fiscal choices. A combined tax bill for several governments (for instance, a property tax bill with a payment that will be divided between a city, a county, and an independent school district) is convenient for collections but not so good for ensuring that each government's tax actions are clearly understood by taxpayers. However, gauging this standard is not always easy: Is a sales tax (either a retail sales tax or a value-added tax) with a requirement that customers receive receipts separated stating the tax paid and the tax rate on each transaction more transparent in terms of knowing the amount of tax paid than an individual income tax collected through periodic withholding by the employer with a summary filing at the end of the year? The payments and tax rate are obvious through the year for the former, but the taxpayer has almost no idea of what total payment to the government is, whereas with the latter, the taxpayer may have no running idea but knows precisely the tax paid at the end of the year. The electorate needs to know the cost of government—but which cost is more relevant? What we do know is that making taxpayers believe that taxes paid by businesses somehow involve no tax payment by individuals is fiscally dishonest.

A tax structure that is not transparent, at least in its broad outlines, is likely to be seen as unknown and probably unfair, can hide significant inequities in the treatment of taxpayers in its confused application, is subject to "rigging" to the advantage of those people in power, and opens the tax authority to the presumption—often accurate—that bribes might be taken and deals may be struck.

Some argue that tax structures can create "fiscal illusions" that conceal from the public the actual budgetary cost of government, allowing politicians to behave irresponsibly and probably causing government expenditure to be higher than a fully informed citizenry would prefer. Evidence of this influence, if any, is far from clear, partly because it is difficult to define what a completely transparent tax structure is and then to calibrate how actual systems differ from that ideal, and partly because it is difficult to specify how nontransparency might alter fiscal behavior. However, it is difficult to see how tax structures that make it difficult for the public to understand taxes and to identify the cost of public programs can possibly contribute to the objectives of an open, democratic government.

Taxes and Externalities

An important exception to the ordinary standard of neutrality for tax efficiency occurs when private actions create important negative external effects—that is, when production or consumption by one person or firm causes adverse real consequences on some other person or firm. Market forces induce producers and consumers to react to prices that they pay, and they can be expected to economize on the use of goods and services that must be paid for. The impacts on others are outside the market, so producers and consumers watch out for these external interests only out of the goodness of their hearts—a motive often less compelling or reliable than others. (Sidebar 7–2 provides more about the logic of externalities.)

Governments may respond to this problem in many different ways, including but not limited to regulations, subsidies, tradable pollution rights, or taxes.[43] Taxes applied under this argument do not seek neutrality in the ordinary sense of staying clear of pure market outcomes; rather, they intend to change private actions so that external effects directly and predictably enter the decision calculus. The market is then allowed to respond to consumer demand and to obtain production at least cost, but with both buyer and seller economically aware of (not just morally sensing) the external effects of their actions. Indeed, the tax makes the cost now internal to the decisions of both buyers and sellers. These taxes designed to have environment-friendly effects are sometimes called green taxes.

Two types of tax instruments can be applied:[44]

1. **Emission taxes.** These instruments, often called Pigovian taxes after a British economist who proposed them long ago,[45] apply a tax per unit of measured pollution output. They require direct measurement if they are to have their desired incentive effect and ordinarily apply to only one emission type at a time. They apply at the last link in the production-distribution chain to those emitting the substance into the environment. Unlike charges, these taxes bring no expectation that the payer receives anything in return, except that he or she is not treated as a lawbreaker.

2. **Indirect taxes on goods or services.** These taxes apply to goods or services, the production or consumption of which causes environmental damage.[46] Taxes on the use of fossil fuel or ozone-depleting chemicals, for example, discourage processes using them and encourage the quest for alternatives. They do not directly tax the discharge with undesirable external effect, but they seek to discourage the discharge indirectly. Portions of the energy tax (a BTU base) proposed in 1993 were of this nature, through application of higher rates on

[43]For greater detail, see J. B. Opschoor and H. B. Vos, *Economic Instruments for Environmental Protection* (Paris: Organization for Economic Development, 1989).

[44]Governments may also provide subsidies through the tax system, as with special credits offered to businesses that purchase certain pollution-control equipment.

[45]A. C. Pigou, *The Economics of Welfare* (London: Macmillan, 1920).

[46]Organization for Economic Cooperation and Development, *Taxation and the Environment: Complimentary Policies* (Paris: OECD, 1993).

Sidebar 7–2
The Council of Economic Advisers on Externalities and the Environment

In the *Economic Report of the President for 1994,* the Council of Economic Advisers describes the concept of externalities and how they change conclusions about the workings of the market, especially when environmental effects are involved.

> The notion of tradeoffs is among the most fundamental in economics: nothing is free; everything has an opportunity cost. In private markets, tradeoffs are handled automatically, as consumers choose among alternative goods and services, and producers choose among alternative inputs. Prices guide these decisions. Tradeoffs involving the environment cannot be made so easily, however, because use of the environment is generally unpriced. As a result, firms and individuals, in their marketplace decisions, do not always make the best tradeoffs from the standpoint of society as a whole. The effects of failing to price environmental goods and services are examples of externalities. . . .
>
> An externality, or spillover, is a type of market failure that arises when the private costs or benefits of production [or consumption] differ from the social costs or benefits. For example, if a factory pollutes, and neither the firm nor its customers pay for the harm that pollution causes, the pollution is an externality. In presence of this negative (harmful) externality, market forces will generate too much of the activity causing the externality, here the factory's production, and too much of the externality itself, here the pollution. In the case of beneficial externalities, firms will generate too little of the activity causing the externality, and too little of the externality itself, because they are not compensated for the benefits they offer. . . .
>
> To remedy market failures and induce the market to provide the efficient level of the externality-causing activity, the private parties involved in the activity must face the full social costs and benefits of their actions. Policy-makers may employ a variety of tools to accomplish this result, such as taxes, user fees, subsides, or the establishment or clarification of property rights.

The economic approach to undesirable externalities is, in general, not to ban the activity producing the externalities but rather to adjust the trades between buyers and sellers so that the full social effects, not just the private effects, of transactions are felt by parties to the transaction. Taxes (and charges) represent one avenue for causing recognition of these external impacts.

SOURCE: Economic Report of the President, Transmitted to the Congress, February 1994 (Washington, D.C.: Government Printing Office 1994): 179–180.

certain fossil fuels. Most industrialized countries levy motor-fuel taxes at rates much higher than in the United States, partly as an environmental measure designed to discourage emissions of the greenhouse gases associated with internal combustion engines. Because these taxes, unlike those levied in the United States, are not earmarked for highway construction and maintenance, they unambiguously aim to reduce use of motor vehicles.

Governments also identify particular products or services that seem undesirable and use taxes to discourage their production or consumption. Examples include a Canadian federal tax on automobile air conditioners (an extra inducement to convince automobile purchasers to skip an accessory that reduces fuel economy) and the U.S. gas-guzzler tax (a tax applied to vehicles that do not meet prescribed fuel-economy ratings). Some other examples of green taxes include higher taxes on leaded than on unleaded motor fuel in a number of countries, taxes on batteries in Sweden, a Belgian tax on disposable razors, and taxes on emissions of carbon dioxide in Denmark, Finland, the Netherlands, Norway, and Sweden.[47] The taxes intend to distort ordinary market choices by making polluters face the true (internal plus external) costs of their actions.

Conclusion

The number of handles available to governments seems almost without end. In general, the many possible handles eventually translate into taxes on incomes, taxes on ownership and ownership exchange, and taxes on purchase or sales. Taxes require an involuntary payment; they are not collected for services received on a normal exchange basis. Because of separation of service receipt and payment, it is possible to evaluate taxes on the basis of planning criteria. Those criteria are equity (vertical and horizontal), adequacy, collectibility, transparency, and economic effects.

Chapter 7 Questions and Exercises

1. Patterns and structure of revenue for state and local government are important policy concerns because they establish the distribution of the burden of public-service provision. Revenue revision can only begin with a clear understanding of where revenue policy leaves the state and its localities now and what available options have not been selected. Furthermore, it is useful to understand what conditions are like in surrounding areas. Evidence for such discussions can be drawn from sources like the Department of Commerce's Survey of Current Business (monthly); the Census Bureau's Census of Governments (quinquennially), Governmental Finances (annually), State Tax Collections (annually), and City Finances; and state tax handbooks published annually by Research Institute of America (RIA) and Commerce Clearing House (CCH). From those and similar sources, prepare answers to these questions about the revenue system in your state:
   a. How does the burden of state, local, and state-local taxation in your state compare with that of the nation and region? (Comparisons are often made as percentages of state personal income and per capita.) Data on state and local tax collections for each state are available at the website of the U.S. Bureau

[47] "Taxes for a Cleaner Planet," *The Economist,* 28 (June 1997): 84.

of Census (www.census.gov); look under the section labeled "Government." How does the local share of state and local taxes compare?

b. Prepare an estimate of the relationship between business and individual tax shares for your state. Where are there allocation problems?

c. How rapidly have state and local taxes grown in your state during the past 5 years? Is that faster or slower than growth in state personal income and the rate of inflation? Have there been tax increases (decreases) affecting that growth?

d. What are the major revenue sources used by governments in your state? How does relative use of those sources compare with the nation and the region? Does your state have any major taxes not common to other states (severance, business and occupation, local income, etc.)? Are some typical taxes not used?

2. The Joint Committee on Taxation of the United State Congress estimates that the highest 1 percent of income earners paid 33.6 percent of total federal individual income tax collected in calendar year 2000. What does this information tell about progressivity or regressivity of the federal income tax? Explain.

3. Not-for-profit organizations lack the authority to levy taxes for support of their programs and must finance their operations from a variety of revenue streams. Some are commercial and operate largely from the sale of goods or services, others are charitable and operate with various sorts of donated support, and others combine revenue from a variety of sources. Select a not-for-profit organization in your area and analyze its revenue resources. The entity should be chosen because of your interest in the service provided by that entity and because the entity will cooperate with your review and assessment.

a. Analyze the revenues received by the entity (taxes, charges, donations, etc.—provide disaggregated data), examine trends and shifts, determine whether sources are sensitive to general economic conditions, explore limits and controls that the entity may face, review process by which revenue decisions are made. You should pay particular attention to the division of revenues from use of endowment, charges for services, and annual donations. To what extent does the entity employ the principle that those using services must pay (an analogue to the benefits-received principle in taxation)? In light of the purpose of the entity, to what extent is payment for service appropriate?

b. Examine how the entity manages fund development, that is, money raising. Is it self-administered or does another entity administer the system, possibly by contract? Are protective controls properly in place? What are the costs associated with this activity?

c. On the basis of your investigation, what do you conclude about revenues available to the entity? Do you have recommendations for reform and restructuring? Be specific. Link your conclusions to the information developed in your analysis.

Case for Discussion

CASE 7–1

Politics and the Protection of Tax Advantages

The federal tax system is used to provide encouragement for certain business activities. Just as some members of Congress support expenditure programs that are important to their constituencies, so too do those representatives protect these tax advantages. The following article shows how the political system works to preserve subsidies in the tax system.

Consider These Questions

1. What is "corporate welfare" and how does it differ from other forms of welfare?
2. Why might a business prefer a subsidy embedded in the tax code as opposed to receiving direct financial support from the government?
3. What political lessons can be learned from the episode?

How Cash, Caucuses Combine to Protect a Fuel on the Hill

By Jackie Calmes

Washington—This should have been the year in which the nearly 20-year-old tax subsidy for ethanol, a gasoline additive typically made from corn, finally was scrapped—or so its foes expected.

Robert Dole, the self-professed "Senator Ethanol," had left Congress. Archer-Daniels-Midland Co., the nation's biggest ethanol producer and among its biggest political contributors, had been humbled by a guilty plea to price-fixing charges and shareholder unrest.

Environmentalists had soured on the product and President Clinton's economic advisers had long been unenthusiastic. Congress's investigative arm, the General Accounting Office, questioned its merits. The subsidy made nearly every hit list of "corporate welfare." Indeed, it topped the short list of Texas GOP Rep. Bill Archer, whose oil state produces a rival fuel additive made from natural gas, and who heads the House Ways and Means Committee from which all tax laws must come.

Potent Blend

But the ethanol subsidy, which has cost more than $7 billion to date and will last until 2000, survived this year's tax-bill debate and nearly was extended further into the 21st century. That could yet happen before the year is out.

The fuel subsidy lives on, thanks to a potent blend of Cornbelt politics, campaign cash and Iowa's presidential caucuses. Its survival also illustrates the power of special-interest politics. Getting a narrow tax break into the tax code is hard enough; getting it out can be even harder. In this case, an obscure regional product has made friends in the highest places—including the Democratic president and vice president, plus the Republican speaker of the House—so that targeting ethanol proved too much even for the powerful Ways and Means chairman.

Its longevity, says GOP Sen. John McCain of Arizona, "is a cautionary tale about what happens to quote-unquote temporary subsidies around here. They never go away."

Yet Rep. Archer wasn't pessimistic when this year's ethanol saga began March 13. The nattily dressed chairman stood before Capitol Hill reporters to launch his antisubsidy campaign.

Never mind that he had failed two years earlier. He was back. Mr. Dole wasn't and he had new ammunition—a study ordered from the GAO that punctured claims the subsidy was good for the economy, the environment and energy independence. The study concluded: "Without the incentives, ethanol fuel production would largely discontinue."

Populist Issue

The subsidy is "highway robbery," Mr. Archer intoned as members from both parties nodded nearby. "I'm pleased to report that there is bipartisan and widespread support for our actions."

The fight was on. Some Archer staffers had opposed reviving the issue and provoking Cornbelt Republicans. Others were gung-ho to attack. But there had been no debate: Mr. Archer himself decided to charge forward. The pro-business congressman from a tiny Houston House district hated the very term "corporate welfare." But his party was determined to seize the populist issue. Also, Mr. Archer had to find revenue savings to offset big GOP tax cuts; what better time to attack a subsidy he hated? Besides, Texas producers of the gas-based fuel additive aren't subsidized.

As Mr. Archer drafted a tax package prior to his committee's June vote, he met occasionally with Speaker Newt Gingrich. The speaker had promised to give chairmen more leeway after his strong-arm rule of prior years. But he made ethanol an exception. He advised Mr. Archer several times not to tamper with it, yet Mr. Archer clearly planned to forge ahead.

Blunt Talk

At a last meeting in his inner sanctum near the Capitol Rotunda, Mr. Gingrich was blunt: "The House is not going to be the place that kills ethanol."

He had several concerns: the fate of the tax bill, the survival of his House majority and, ultimately, his own ambitions. The GOP's cherished tax-cut bill faced an uncertain vote, since Republicans had only a narrow House majority; defecting farm-state members could doom it. Voting for a bill with an anti-ethanol provision could be political suicide—for them and perhaps for the GOP majority. As for the future, Mr. Gingrich is pondering the next presidential race.

And as presidential wannabes all know, you can't easily get there without first tramping through the cornfields prior to Iowa's early nominating caucuses. "Nobody is going to have a chance in Iowa if they're not on the right side of ethanol," says Gov. Terry Branstad, a Republican.

Spawned in 1978 by the Mideast oil shocks, the ethanol subsidy was intended as a short-term incentive for alternative fuels. Later clean-air laws were expected to boost demand and make long-term subsidies unnecessary. The subsidy gives gasoline blended with ethanol a 5.4 cents-a-gallon reduction in the federal gas tax of 18.3 cents—equal to 54 cents per gallon of ethanol, since most gas blends contain one-tenth ethanol. Through 1995, that cost the federal highway trust fund, which receives proceeds from gas taxes, $7.1 billion. The tax break goes to blenders, but creates product demand benefiting producers and farmers.

"The point is to have a renewable, clean-burning fuel that makes us energy-independent," says Sen. Charles Grassley, an Iowa Republican. Yet while ethanol reduces carbon monoxide in winter, it adds to summer smog. "Environmentally, ethanol is very much a mixed bag," says Dan Becker, a Sierra Club director who monitors global warming and energy issues. "It takes more energy to make a gallon of ethanol than the energy you get when you burn it. It ain't a renewable fuel."

Supporters originally expected rising oil prices to let ethanol be priced competitively with gasoline without government props. Instead, oil prices remain low. Today, ethanol—available mostly in Cornbelt states because of distribution problems—accounts for less than 1% of U.S. fuel consumption and the GAO says that share won't increase even if the subsidy survives another two decades.

Yet by early June, the White House also came to ethanol's defense—just as the Archer committee began work.

Benefit for Producers

Early in his presidency, Mr. Clinton's economic advisers had opposed ethanol subsidies, without success. "I never have thought there was any economic policy justification for these subsidies," says Laura D'Andrea Tyson, who held senior first-term economic posts. "There were anticipated environmental benefits and they proved to be nonexistent. So the only benefit is for the producers."

But the president has been pro-ethanol since his 1992 Iowa campaign days. Now his vice president and would-be heir, Al Gore, trumpets the disputed environmental benefits. (In Congress, Mr. Gore's potential Democratic rival, House Minority Leader Richard Gephardt of Missouri, is one of ethanol's biggest cheerleaders.)

Even so, the Clinton team's lack of enthusiasm was evident on June 10 when Treasury Secretary Robert Rubin went on PBS television's "The News Hour With Jim Lehrer." After first interviewing Mr. Archer, Mr. Lehrer turned to the secretary: "How about eliminating the subsidy for ethanol?"

"I'm not sure what I think on that at this point, Jim," he replied. "As Mr. Archer said, it was originally designed for a particular purpose. I think we could probably go either way on that."

Iowa's Democratic Sen. Tom Harkin responded to this heresy the next day by having an aide protest to the White House. Mr. Rubin admitted his gaffe, and Chief of Staff Erskine Bowles checked with the president and vice president. As one senior administration official puts it, "The vice president's office made it very clear what our position is."

Soon after, Mr. Rubin issued a one-sentence statement favoring a subsidy extension through at least 2005. It was read into the record when tax-bill writers of the Ways and Means committee turned to ethanol the following day.

Special Attention

Mr. Archer's tax package included a provision reducing the subsidy, limiting ethanol production and reaffirming its year 2000 cutoff. In early evening, however, Iowa Rep. Jim Nussle introduced an amendment to kill that provision. By his count, he would win by one vote. But Mr. Archer then announced he was breaking with his practice of keeping silent on members' amendments: "I believe that this one deserves particular attention."

When the chairman so speaks, his Republicans listen; he influences what special requests survive in a tax bill. Now Mr. Archer was saying that ethanol producers were "leading farmers . . . into a dead alley" for an additive that is neither viable nor beneficial, when farmers could thrive by selling corn for food and feed. He denied doing Big Oil's bidding; that industry, he noted, includes ethanol blenders who get the tax break.

When the roll was called, three Republicans switched to the chairman's side—including Nevada Rep. John Ensign, who had spoken for the Nussle amendment only minutes before. The three votes tipped the scale. Mr. Archer won, 21–17.

Mr. Nussle wasn't the only disappointed party. Mr. Gingrich had counted on the committee to keep the subsidy alive. Now he had to step in.

To prod Mr. Gingrich a bit, about 15 farm-state Republicans called on the speaker. Don't worry, he reassured them; his Rules Committee would delete the Archer provision from the tax bill before a full House vote. But Pennsylvania Rep. Phil English, a Ways and Means Republican who opposed the subsidy, angrily sought his own meeting with Mr. Gingrich. The speaker was brief: If ethanol was attacked, he told Mr. English, some Midwestern Republicans could lose their seats.

The Rules Committee included special wording in its rule for debating the tax bill. When the House approved the rule, it in effect deleted the Archer provision without separate consideration.

"Ethanol Queen"

The story then took a bizarre turn. Emboldened ethanol forces went on the offense in the Senate, where rural states enjoy disproportionate influence. When the Finance Committee drafted its own tax bill, it included a Grassley amendment extending ethanol subsidies through 2007 at a cost of $3.8 billion. A chief backer was Sen. Carol Moseley-Braun, a Chicago Democrat who needs votes from rural downstate Illinois—home to Archer-Daniels-Midland's Decatur headquarters—in her tough re-election fight next year. She keeps a pink hat labeled "Ethanol Queen" in her office.

In Senate debate, Sen. McCain tried to kill the extension. He lost 69–30, thanks, he says, to the Senate's rural tilt, its back-scratching ethic ("You support my subsidy and I'll support yours") and the desire "to subsidize thousands of corn growers—and Archer-Daniels-Midland." However chastened it might be by legal problems, ADM divided nearly $1 million between the two parties during the last election cycle, according to the watchdog Center for Responsive Politics.

And there was the presidential-caucus dynamic. Sen. Grassley was surprised by support from GOP Sen. Phil Gramm, who has presidential hopes. The wry Texan told him, "I've got corn growers in my state, but I also have friends in Iowa." Having caught flak from corn growers in 1996, Sen. Gramm is, in Gov. Branstad's words, "an ethanol convert."

In the final act, House and Senate leaders, and the administration, negotiated their tax bill differences in July. In closed-door conferences, Mr. Archer found himself no longer fighting to kill the subsidy but to prevent its extension.

At one point, Sen. Grassley was invited into the speaker's Dinosaur Room, so-named for the prehistoric bones in one corner, and the folksy farmer pleaded for the subsidy. After he left, GOP leaders looked at Mr. Archer. Senate Majority Leader Trent Lott proposed an extension to 2004.

"No," said Mr. Archer.

"2003?" Sen. Lott asked.

"No," Mr. Archer replied.

Presidential Support

Still, ethanol backers weren't giving up. Days later, as Mr. Clinton boasted to the nation's governors at Las Vegas's Mirage Hotel that a budget-balancing deal was in hand, Iowa Gov. Branstad gambled that time remained to secure an extension.

Collaring the president, he implored, "We need you to weigh in." Mr. Clinton made a note and "assured me that he was very supportive," Mr. Branstad says. A senior Clinton aide relayed the concern to White House negotiators, still haggling with Republicans over such final details.

The negotiators already knew the administration stance; the problem was Mr. Archer. The extension had to be shelved, yet it was hardly the victory the Texan had envisioned back in March. The ethanol subsidy survived, without limits on benefits or production.

Less noticed in the bipartisan celebration of final budget-and-tax compromise, Mr. Clinton and Mr. Gore each issued statements vowing to push again for extension this fall. "By now," Mr. Clinton said, "all Americans should be aware of the important role ethanol plays in cleaning our air and in providing economic development for rural America." Mr. Gore added: "We can't let this crucial program go by the wayside."

Mr. Gephardt, meanwhile, that very weekend was posing before tall corn on an Iowa farm, pledging his support for an extension.

Mr. Archer says he will keep fighting, but ethanol forces predict they will prevail. Sen. McCain resignedly concurs: "I don't have a shred of doubt in my mind that they will win over time."

SOURCE: Wall Street Journal, 8 August 1997. Reprinted by permission of the *Wall Street Journal* (c) 1997 Dow Jones & Company, Inc. All Rights Reserved Worldwide.

CHAPTER 8

Major Tax Structures: Income Taxes

Because governments rely on taxes as the ultimate source of funds to buy resources for use in service delivery, understanding the structure of taxes is important. Although governments make different choices as to how to structure their taxes, a common logic and language defines tax bases and the manner in which rates are applied to the chosen base. Furthermore, there are common issues of tax design that arise wherever a particular base is considered. In this chapter and the following two chapters, we examine the general nature of the three predominant tax bases: income, spending on goods and services, and property. Taxes on income and spending typically apply to current transaction values; property taxes apply to the value of holdings, not transactions. In many respects, that difference makes property taxes more difficult to administer, although growth of the underground economy—economic activity "off the books," or outside traditional accounting records—has complicated operation of the other two taxes in recent years.

There is one important point to emphasize at the outset: All taxes labeled income (or sales or property, for that matter) do not operate in the same fashion, and statements about the yield response, collectability, equity, or economic effects of a particular tax must carefully define what the structure of the tax actually is. Income might generally be defined as the money or other gain received over a period of time by an individual, corporation, or other entity for labor or services rendered or from property, natural resources, investments, operations, and so on. But governments differ in what particular receipts are selected for taxation, how those receipts are manipulated to become the tax base, and what structure of rates apply to that base. Because of those tax-policy options, general statements about burden distribution can be hazardous. For example, the federal individual income tax has a generally progressive burden distribution because statutory rates increase as income is higher and because the tax applies to a broad measure of income; many local income taxes have a generally proportional or slightly regressive burden pattern because they often levy flat rates on a base limited to wages and salaries alone. Not all income taxes have progressive burden distributions; it depends on the structure of the particular tax.

Governments apply taxes to the income of individuals and/or corporations.[1] Unincorporated business (partnership, proprietorship) income is ordinarily taxed through the individual income tax. Wage and salary income (payrolls) and income of the self-employed are taxed both by the regular individual income tax and by separate taxes to finance the social insurance system (Social Security, unemployment compensation, etc.). Individual income tax yield is much greater than that of corporate income taxes, so greater attention is focused on the former. Many of the structural elements of individual taxation also apply to the corporate form as well; many other corporate tax questions are too arcane for coverage here. One important issue to which there may be no answer will be considered: How should corporate income taxes be related to the income tax of individual corporate stockholders?

Some Background

Before the Civil War, the federal government relied on excises (customs, duties, liquor taxes, etc.) and tariffs on imported goods to finance its limited activities. War, however, was too expensive to finance with that revenue alone. The northern states enacted an income tax in 1861 (3 percent on all incomes of more than $800 per year) to help finance their war expenditure, but the law was so unclearly structured that it was not put into effect. An income tax passed in 1862 was enforced; it applied an initial rate of 3 percent and a top rate of 5 percent on incomes of more than $10,000. It expired in 1872, having raised about $376 million (about 20 percent of internal revenues produced during the period).[2]

There remained an important legal question. As Chapter 7 noted, the U.S. Constitution requires federal direct taxes to be apportioned among the states, but it was not clear whether an individual income tax was legally direct or indirect.[3] If the tax were direct, it would have to be divided among the states according to population, and each state's share then raised from its population according to income. A state

[1]A corporation is an entity created by a government (state or federal) and empowered with legal rights, privileges, and liabilities of an individual, separate and distinct from those held by the individuals who own the entity. Owners have liability limited to their investment in the corporation. A growing number of states now allow limited-liability companies, a business form taxed like a partnership (business income is fully distributed to the owners for taxation and is not taxed separately at the business level) and easier to establish than a corporation, but with the liability limits of a corporation.

[2]Harold M. Groves, *Financing Government* (New York: Holt, 1939), 153–55.

[3]Corporate income taxes were never regarded as direct taxes on individuals and thus were never subject to apportionment. The federal corporate tax began some years before the federal individual income tax that is in place now.

with lower per capita income would have to apply higher income tax rates than would a state with higher per capita income. The U.S. Supreme Court held in *Springer* v. *United States* (102 U.S. 586 [1880]) that the income tax was, for purposes of the Constitution, indirect and hence valid. By the time of the ruling, the tax was no longer in force, so the ruling had minimal immediate importance.

In 1894 the federal government again enacted an individual income tax, this time in a package with reduced tariffs. The low-rate tax (2 percent of income above $4,000) affected only a small portion of the population, but it was challenged on constitutional grounds. This time, the U.S. Supreme Court, in *Pollock* v. *Farmer's Loan and Trust* (157 U.S. 429 [1895] and 158 U.S. 601 [1895]), ruled that the income tax was direct and hence subject to apportionment. Therefore, the tax was unconstitutional and could not be collected. The decision left the federal government with no broad-based revenue source to finance the increased international role the nation was taking in the early part of the twentieth century.[4]

How could the lawmakers swallow federal income taxation? In 1909, President William Howard Taft agreed to accept an "excise" on corporate net income (which did not require an amendment to enact) if Congress would propose an amendment for a national individual income tax. Both the amendment and the excise quickly passed. Getting approval of the necessary number of states for the amendment to be approved took longer, but when Wyoming became the thirty-sixth state to ratify the Sixteenth Amendment (1913) the revenue problem was resolved: "The Congress shall have power to lay and collect taxes on incomes, from whatever source derived, without apportionment among the several States, and without regard to any census or enumeration." That provided the financial base for defense and, eventually, an expanded federal role in domestic affairs.

The 1913 income tax applied a normal rate of 1 percent on incomes in excess of $3,000 ($4,000 for married persons) with a top surtax rate of 6 percent (a combined rate of 7 percent) on incomes above $500,000. Moreover, the tax was not paid by the multitudes: Only about 1 percent of the population had income sufficient to be liable for the tax.[5] There were 357,598 returns filed (so few that the Bureau of Internal Revenue audited them all), with an average tax of $78. Only with the advent of the Second World War did the tax become a mass tax as the level of income at which the tax started to apply fell to levels earned by many people. In 1939, 7.6 million returns were filed to yield $1,028.8 million in that fiscal year; by 1945, the number of returns had increased to 49.9 million to yield $19,034.3 million.[6] Until 1944,

---

[4]How desperate was the federal government for revenue at the turn of the twentieth century? So desperate that it even applied a tax to chewing gum.

[5]Richard Good, *The Individual Income Tax,* rev. ed. (Washington, D.C.: Brookings Institution, 1976), 3. There was a problem in the initial law. It applied the tax to "lawful income." Congress soon amended the law to remove the word "lawful," thus clearing up definitional problems and opening up additional enforcement powers. It should be pointed out that gangster Al Capone was sent to prison for tax evasion, not other crimes. The change in the tax law undoubtedly helped stop his villainy.

[6]U.S. Bureau of Census, *Historical Statistics of the United States, Colonial Times to 1970, Bicentennial Edition,* Part 2 (Washington, D.C.: Government Printing Office, 1975), 1107, 1110.

collections from the corporate income tax had exceeded those from the individual income tax in all years but 1934 and 1937; from 1944 onward, individual income tax collections have always exceeded those from the corporate income tax. This represents an important watershed in how the federal government was to be financed. Withholding of individual income tax from wages began in 1943, thus dramatically simplifying the collection process and permitting application of the tax to the general population.

The third, and newest, portion of the federal income tax structure consists of the payroll taxes that support most of the social insurance system. These narrow-base taxes on wage and salary income and certain income from self-employment may legally be imposed on the employer, on the employee, or shared between employer and employee; most analysts suspect that the economic incidence is on the employee, regardless of who is responsible for sending payment to the government. The shifting logic is simple: the employer knows that paying a certain wage to the employee will require an accompanying payroll tax payment to the government. Why wouldn't the employer take account of that payment when deciding how much to offer employees and how many employees to hire? These taxes now support the Social Security system (old age, disability, and survivor's income support), Medicare (health insurance for the elderly), and unemployment compensation. The Social Security and unemployment compensation taxes began with the Social Security Act of 1935; the Medicare tax began with amendments to that act in 1965. For many lower income individuals and families, their social insurance payroll tax liability amounts to more than the amount of individual income tax owed.

The individual and corporate income taxes and the payroll taxes on wages and salaries are the dominant government revenue source in the United States. Table 8–1 reports the pattern from 1930 to 2003. In 2004, individual income taxes yielded $1,025.8 billion, corporate income taxes yielded $258.9 billion, and receipts for the social insurance system (largely payroll taxes to for Social Security, Medicare, and unemployment compensation) produced $822.2 billion, 65.6 percent of the $3,208.2 billion in current receipts to all governments.[7] Revenue from individual and corporate income taxes increased dramatically as a share of gross domestic product (GDP) with the need to finance World War II, but fell modestly when the war ended. The share was from 11.5 to 13.5 percent of GDP until 2000, when it jumped to 15 percent. It has now fallen to a post-WWII low of 10.9 percent, although all post-WWII shares are well above pre-WWII levels. The percentage increased a bit in the 1990s, the product of somewhat higher rates and great prosperity of high-income individuals. When social insurance taxes are added in, the share of all government revenue is more than 60 percent and somewhat less than 20 percent of GDP. This latter percentage has been generally increasing for 50 years.

---

[7]Bureau of Economic Analysis, *National Income and Product Accounts* (www.bea.gov).

Table 8–1

Individual and Corporate Income Taxes and Social Insurance Contributions in American Government Finance, Selected Calendar Years, 1930–2004

	1930	1935	1940	1945	1950	1955	1960	1965	1970	1975	1980	1985	1990	1995	2000	2004
Individual and Corporate Income Taxes as % of:																
All Government current receipts	19.0%	16.2%	24.1%	57.6%	54.6%	55.6%	49.9%	47.9%	46.8%	44.0%	47.3%	41.6%	42.2%	42.4%	47.1%	40.0%
Gross domestic product	2.1%	2.3%	3.9%	13.3%	12.3%	13.0%	12.7%	12.0%	12.9%	11.8%	13.5%	12.0%	12.4%	12.7%	15.0%	10.9%
Income Taxes Plus Social Insurance Contributions as % of:																
All government current receipts	19.0%	16.2%	33.7%	62.6%	60.8%	63.4%	60.8%	59.7%	61.5%	62.7%	66.8%	63.4%	64.5%	64.6%	68.2%	65.6%
Gross domestic product	2.1%	2.3%	5.5%	14.4%	13.7%	14.8%	15.5%	15.0%	17.0%	16.9%	19.1%	18.2%	19.0%	19.3%	21.7%	18.0%

SOURCE: Bureau of Economic Analysis, *National Income and Product Accounts.*

NOTE: Social Insurance Contributions include employer and employee shares of Social Security and Unemployment Insurance payroll taxes.

The Argument about Taxing Income

For the System of Taxing Income

Many regard an income tax as a fair and reasonable source of revenue because of the nature of the base and the method of its administration—and it certainly is productive. Why do many believe that the income tax is a satisfactory source?[8]

Equity—measuring ability. Income is an important measure of a taxpayer's capacity to bear the cost of government.[9] Economic well-being is significantly determined by current income. An exception is the person with substantial wealth and minimal current income, so a better measure could include current income and net wealth converted into an income equivalent, but such logic does not appear in income tax codes. Current income remains for most people the most reliable single indicator of relative affluence.

Equity—adjustability. The income tax can be made to account for individual taxpayer conditions (family size, infirmities, special economic circumstances, etc.). This offers a unique advantage: Any tax not based on individual filing will not easily be adjusted to such conditions. For instance, a package of cigarettes is taxed regardless of the economic status of the purchaser. Adjustments when a tax return is filed can allow a more equitable distribution of burdens by recognizing family circumstances that restrict tax-bearing capacity. Table 8–2 shows the pattern of the federal taxes on income as they are distributed across quintiles of household income, taking full account of likely shifting of taxes paid by a business on individuals. The pattern is of considerable progressivity of individual and corporate income taxes, even through to the highest-income taxpayers. Broad-based income taxes can be made progressive and lawmakers do tend to follow through on the opportunity. However, the social insurance taxes—Social Security and unemployment compensation—based on payrolls, with flat or even declining rates, no adjustment for economic circumstances, and no coverage of income from capital ownership (particularly dividends, interest, and rent) show a regressive pattern of effective rates at higher income levels. So adjustability to taxpayer conditions can produce a progressive tax pattern and can be difficult for other tax formats. Table 8–2 shows that 56.6 percent of total individual income tax paid was paid by 5 percent of the population, the highest income earners in the nation. This reflects an extreme concentration of income in the United States, a concentration that has increased significantly

[8]For many years the U.S. Advisory Commission on Intergovernmental Relations conducted a nationwide survey to discover what tax Americans viewed as the least fair. The federal income tax or the local property tax was always seen as the least fair. In the last poll (1994), 27 percent viewed the federal income tax as the worst, compared with 28 percent of the local property tax. As in previous surveys, respondents viewed the state income tax as the least unfair (7 percent). This is an interesting finding, given that the state income taxes are virtually all linked copies of the federal income tax, although at lower rates. U.S. Advisory Commission on Intergovernmental Relations, *Changing Public Attitudes on Governments and Taxes 1994* (Washington, D.C.: Advisory Commission on Intergovernmental Relations, 1995).

[9]Recall that some also regard individual income as a measure of the benefits that a person receives from government.

Table 8–2
Distribution of Federal Income Tax Payments and Effective Tax Rates by Income Quintiles for All Families, 2003 (all in percentages)

	Individual Income Tax		Corporate Income Tax		Social Insurance Tax	
Quintile	Tax Share	Effective Tax Rate	Tax Share	Effective Tax Rate	Tax Share	Effective Tax Rate
Lowest	−2.9	−5.9	0.6	0.3	4.1	8.1
Second	−1.1	−1.1	1.6	0.4	9.9	9.1
Third	4.6	2.7	4.3	0.6	15.7	9.2
Fourth	14.6	5.9	6.1	0.6	25.4	10.3
Highest	84.9	13.9	85.8	3.4	44.7	7.2
All	100	8.5	100	2.0	100	8.4
Top 5%	56.6	17.8	73.2	5.5	15.0	4.7
Top 1%	34.6	20.6	55.5	8.2	3.9	2.3

SOURCE: Congressional Budget Office, Historical Effective Federal Tax Rates: 1979–2003. Available online at www.cbo.gov/ftpdocs/70xx/doc70000/12-29-FedTaxRates.pdf.
NOTE: Income equals comprehensive household income, which includes all cash income (taxable and exempt), taxes paid by businesses, employee contribution to 401(k) retirement plans, and value of income paid in kind.

in the past few years. High-income households have done very well, both absolutely and relative to how middle- and lower-income households have done.

Yield. A broad income base permits significant revenue at socially acceptable rates, and the growth of that base keeps pace with general economic activity. Governments with income taxes need not seek rate increases as often, or apply such high nominal rates, to keep up with growing public demand for services as may governments with narrower bases or bases with lower elasticity to economic growth.

Base breadth. The resource distortion with the general income tax may be less than with narrower bases.[10] The distortion question, however, is far from clear in the comparison across taxes. Many provisions of existing income taxes do certainly influence the economic behavior of individuals in investment, housing, compensation packages, and so on. To the extent that breadth permits a low rate, there are clearly efficiency and equity advantages.

Against the System of Taxing Income

Many others argue that the income tax system has horrible flaws and that it should be fundamentally changed. Indeed, it is often argued that consumption is a far better base for distributing the cost of government than is income. What are the elements of that argument?

[10]Income taxes may distort work and investment decisions made by individuals and businesses. Thus, the resources-distortion basis for general income taxation is unclear at best. Economists seek an "optimal tax," that is, one minimizing total distortions. See Joel Slemrod, "Optimal Taxation and Optimal Tax Systems," *Journal of Economic Perspectives* 4 (Winter 1990): 157–78.

Transparency and compliance. The individual income tax is so complicated that it violates the transparency standard. Taxpayers do not understand the system, its provisions are so arcane as to be beyond the comprehension of all but the very few experts, the electorate sees little association between tax paid and the work of government, and some privileged individuals use loopholes (or tax preferences) designed in the backrooms of congressional committees to avoid paying their fair share of the tax. Billions of taxpayer hours are spent on complying with the tax, but, in spite of all the attention it gets, only a tiny fraction understand how the system works and the withholding process conceals how much individual taxpayers actually pay. In 2005 the individual income tax law contains more than a dozen retirement planning schemes with a confusing array of rules and regulations, at least nine separate preference programs for encouraging education spending, an earned income tax credit (EITC) program for low-income workers so complicated that 72 percent of those claiming the credit paid a tax preparer to complete their returns, and a second tax structure that penalizes taxpayers for qualifying for certain legal tax preferences.[11] The majority of people have a paid preparer do their taxes (55.4 percent of returns in 2002), so the citizenry really doesn't know much about what goes on in determining their liability.[12] In terms of seeing the burden, people are more aware of their tax refund at the end of the year than how much their tax liability is. Simplification would make the tax more transparent and would reduce its collection costs. Complexity was one of the most important problems with the existing federal income taxes reported to President Bush's Advisory Panel on Federal Tax Reform in 2005.

Administration and Compliance. The income tax system is expensive to collect. The annual operating cost of the Internal Revenue Service (IRS) exceeds $9.7 billion and deals with more than 130 million individual income and over 6 million corporate income tax returns, and the cost that state and local governments incur in collection of their income taxes adds even more to the total. A number of critics maintain that, even with this expenditure, the IRS is poorly administered, not particularly helpful when taxpayers request assistance, and abuses its powers to inspect individual and business records. The administrative cost per dollar collected is small—currently reported as less than 50 cents per $100 collected. But this cost is only the tip of the iceberg. The cost to taxpayers of complying with the tax law is at least ten times that of the cost of administration.[13] And that is only the dollar cost, with no accounting of the mental pain individuals endure as they struggle to complete their tax returns as the filing deadline approaches each year.[14]

---

[11]Testimony of Nina E. Olsen, National Taxpayer Advocate, to the President's Advisory Panel on Federal Tax Reform, March 3, 2005.

[12]Data from Tax Statistics from the Statistics of Income Division of the Internal Revenue Service (www.irs.gov/taxstats).

[13]Marsha Blumenthal and Joel Slemrod, "The Compliance Cost of the U.S. Individual Income Tax System: A Second Look After Tax Reform," *National Tax Journal* 45 (June 1992), 185–202.

[14]And it isn't getting easier. The IRS is required by the Paperwork Reduction Act to estimate the time required to complete each component of the tax and report those times in its taxpayer instructions. In 1988, completion of a standard return with itemized deductions and reported interest and dividends was estimated to require 15.1 hours for a taxpayer; in 2004, the same forms were estimated to require 20.5 hours. That is not a victory for simplicity. The need for other forms significantly increased the filing time.

Economic effects. Critics argue that the income tax has adverse effects on the long-term prosperity of the American economy by discouraging saving and investment. The argument is that income taxation distorts the choices that people make between how much income they consume in a year against how much they save for future spending because the tax applies to interest earned on the savings. By capturing part of the return from "waiting" to consume in the future, the tax distorts the choice between present consumption and future consumption with the distortion toward present consumption. Accordingly, saving (delayed consumption) is reduced. This matters for economic growth, because saving ultimately provides the basis for increased capital stock, which provides a foundation for economic growth. And the effect can be even worse under our multiple income tax structure, because returns to investment may be taxed once under the corporate income tax and then again under the individual income tax when the shareholder receives those corporate earnings.

Economic distortion. Provisions in the tax structure provide varying reliefs and punishments to different sectors of the economy. Some industries, businesses, and individuals end up facing higher effective tax rates on their capital investment and on their productive labors than do others. That causes economic resources to move because of tax advantages, rather than moving according to market forces that reflect consumer demand, resource prices, and production technology. This brings considerable economic loss to the nation and decay in the competitive position of American businesses in the world economy.

Equity. Many people believe that the income tax distributes the cost of government unfairly. The distribution is, overall, progressive. A good number believe that rates should be about the same for everyone, and a many others believe that the tax should be more progressive than it is now. But very few believe that people in similar economic circumstances should pay dramatically different effective tax rates, simply because of the way they arrange their economic affairs, either from fortunate accident or clever assistance from tax advisors. And there is evidence that access to "loopholes" or tax preferences is not uniformly distributed through the economy. This maldistribution strikes many people as a patently unfair violation of horizontal equity. The costs avoided by some have to be taken up by the rest. And it is unquestionably the case that the income tax extracts higher payments from high income earners, in comparison to the rest. While this may appear equitable, it does pose a penalty on success, and reward for success and the quest for this reward is what produces efficient allocation of resources in a market economy. Is it equitable to penalize those people who are successfully doing what the market economy commands? And there is something of a mirror-image issue: data for 2002 show that 5,650 U.S. taxpayers whose income exceeded $200,000 in that year paid no federal income tax and only 728 of that group paid income tax to any foreign government.[15] Something seems inherently inequitable about that as well, but it is in the system.

---

[15]David Cay Johnston, "In 2002, More Wealthy People Paid No Tax," *New York Times,* (3 July 2005), A-1. The major reason—taxpayers (non-taxpayers would be a better term) received income from interest paid on tax-exempt state and local government bonds.

Overuse. The distortions and inequities of any tax become more significant as the tax is heavily used. Problems that are minor irritants when tax rates and burdens are low can become severe when the tax is high. Businesses and individuals find it worthwhile to invest more effort to avoid paying the tax by restructuring their affairs and by hiding operations that would subject them to a tax; at lower rates, such efforts are not worth the expense. Differences in tax between individuals and businesses have little significance when the tax is low, but discrimination becomes a major issue when the tax is high. The economic value of distortions from a tax rises more rapidly than the tax rate and more rapidly than revenue from the tax. Even if the income taxes were otherwise sound in design, their extremely heavy use in the U.S. revenue system could be reason for seeking tax alternatives, even if the taxes were not to be replaced. Greater balance among tax sources might relieve pressure created by the dominance of the income tax, especially in the federal tax system.

Individual Income Taxation

The following sections examine the logical construction of the federal individual income tax and some issues in its design. Because most states link their income tax to the federal tax, understanding the federal structure, its concepts, and its terminology is important for all levels of finance. For instance, some states use federal adjusted gross income (AGI) or taxable income as the initial computation point for their income tax. Some states even define their income tax as a specified percentage of federal liability. Only a few local governments tie their income taxes to the federal system, typically indirectly by linking to their state tax; most use independent and much narrower income measures, often payroll. These local structures are usually extremely simple. Figure 8–1 provides a schematic overview of the federal structure (as later sections describe) and captures the structural heart of the federal revenue system.

Defining Income

Tax statutes do not define income, but list transactions that produce income for tax purposes. Items on the list include wages, salaries, interest, stock dividends, rents, royalties, and so on. There is no general definition for use in cases of doubt. (Instructors usually receive a copy of this book at no charge: Would its value be income for them? Would it depend on whether they sell the book when the semester ends?) Tax lawyers earn healthy incomes in part because of their efforts to structure transactions that give their clients more money to spend, but legally do not cause income as far as the tax laws are concerned. Many analysts favor the Haig-Simons income definition as a standard. The version proposed by Henry Simons

Figure 8–1
Elements of the Federal Individual Income Tax Structure: How the Flow Works in Calculating the Tax That People Pay

Total income*
minus
Adjustments
equals
Adjusted gross income.
minus
Standard deduction or itemized deductions
and
Personal exemptions
equals
Taxable income.
apply
Rate schedule or tax tables to calculate
Tax.
minus
Credits
equals
Total tax.
minus
Withholding and other payments
equals
Tax refund or tax due.

State income taxes typically use Adjusted Gross Income, Taxable Income, or Tax as the starting point for calculating their income taxes. Therefore, elements of the federal tax structure are important for understanding the state taxes as well. States may add their own special routines in calculating their taxes.
*The Internal Revenue Code does not include as income some flows that may appear to be income under comprehensive measures. These exclusions are not part of total income on the tax return, although some—like interest received on tax exempt bonds—may need to be reported.

defines personal income for tax purposes as "the algebraic sum of (1) the market value of rights exercised in consumption and (2) the change in the value of the store of property rights between the beginning and the end of the period in question."[16] In other words, income equals the value of consumption plus any increase in net wealth during the year.

This definition can yield results that differ from application of existing tax law, as three examples illustrate. Suppose Mr. Smith owns shares of a corporate stock that increase in value by $10,000 during the year, but he does not sell the stock during the year. The Haig-Simons concept views that as income: this increase in

[16]Henry C. Simons, *Personal Income Taxation: The Definition of Income as a Problem of Fiscal Policy* (Chicago: University of Chicago Press, 1938), 50. A similar concept appears in Robert M. Haig, "The Concept of Income—Economic and Legal Aspects," in R. Haig, ed. *The Federal Income Tax* (New York: Columbia University Press, 1921), 7.

Smith's net wealth adds to his total potential command over the economy's resources. The existing tax system would not tax that gain; the system taxes such gains only as they are realized—that is, when the higher-value stock is actually sold, not when the return accrues.[17] Second, suppose Ms. Jones lives in a home that she owns. She thus consumes the services provided by that structure. These services are a part of Jones's consumption and would be part of Haig-Simons income. The current system taxes no such imputed incomes, thus providing a significant incentive for purchase of assets that produce noncash returns to the owner. Third, suppose Mr. White's great aunt gives him $50,000. That clearly increases his net wealth (or permits increased consumption), so it would be part of Haig-Simons income. Because the transaction occurred without any work by White, however, the current system does not regard that payment as part of income. It could be taxable under the gift tax, but White's aunt's economic circumstance, not his, would determine that tax liability.[18]

Policy analysts, both inside and outside government, typically use broad affluence measures for distributional analysis and for thinking about how the tax base might be revised. Sidebar 8–1 describes expanded income and family economic income, measures in the spirit of the Haig-Simons concept that Congress and the Treasury Department use in analyzing the distribution of tax burden and in considering changes in the AGI tax base.

Adjusted Gross Income

AGI is the tax-law measure of aggregate tax-bearing capacity. Because the philosophy of income taxation is that the tax should apply to net income, not gross receipts, the AGI includes, along with the listed salaries, wages, rents, dividends, and interest received by an individual, returns from individual business operation after deducting that business's operating costs. But there are adjustments made to total income before applying elements of the tax structure to calculate liability. First, adjustments are made for alimony payments made (such contribute to the recipient's well-being and are taxed as part of that person's income, not that of the one who pays). Second, certain expenses associated with job-related moves and some business expenses are subtracted. It is always difficult to distinguish between relocation associated with earning an income and relocation associated with personal preference; the logic of taxing net income suggests that the former should be subtracted (moving for employment represents a cost of earning that income) and the latter should not (that moving expense is a result of a lifestyle or consumption choice). There is no simple, clear, logical line, so the error is made on the side of encourag-

[17]Not all national tax systems regard all capital gains as income, and not all American policy analysts agree that the U.S. approach makes sense, in terms of equity or economic efficiency. See Bruce Bartlett, "Slaying a Pair of Cap Gains Villains," *Wall Street Journal,* (10 June 1993), A-20. Current law taxes gains as realized, but at a preferential (lower) rate.

[18]That means the tax on the gift to White (who has an annual income of $5,000) is the same as the tax on the aunt's similar gift to his brother (who has an annual income of $60,000). Same aunt, same gift, same tax—regardless of the recipient's economic status.

Sidebar 8–1
Two More Comprehensive Income Measures: Family Economic Income (Treasury) and Expanded Income (Joint Committee on Taxation)

Ideal income concept has many possible operational definitions. The tax-code definition of AGI does not meet the needs of being consistent over time, as Congress redefines what the tax system will or will not cover, or of capturing the full scope of taxpayer affluence during the year. The U.S. Treasury Department and the Joint Committee on Taxation have devised their own broader measures of income for use in their distributional studies. The Office of Tax Analysis in Treasury developed family economic income for use in analysis developed before the 1986 tax reform to approximate the concept of income as consumption plus change in real net worth in the year. Because it is independent of prevailing tax law, it provides a strong basis for examining the effects of major tax changes. The Joint Committee uses a more conservative concept, that of expanded income. It sticks more closely to tax-return data than does the Treasury concept, but it also is broader than AGI.

Family Economic Income

Family Economic Income combines income and taxes paid of related family members in a single economic unit. The measure starts with AGI reported on the tax return and then adds:

1. An estimate of unreported income.
2. Deductions for tax-sheltered retirement accounts such as Keogh, 401(k), Individual Retirement Account programs, and taxed employer pension contributions plus interest and dividends from those investments. Included are the employer contributions to accounts.
3. Social Security income that is not already taxed and cash assistance and other welfare investments, including the cash value of food stamps.
4. Employer-provided health benefits and other fringe benefits. The cost of fringe benefits generally amounts to about 35 percent of an employee's salary.
5. Imputed net rent is the estimated amount of money a homeowner would earn if he or she rented the house, minus the money spent on mortgage interest, property taxes, property-upkeep expenses, and an allowance for property depreciation.
6. Annually accrued capital gains on stocks, business, land or a house—for instance, the amount your home increased in value this year.
7. Inflationary losses of lenders are subtracted, and gains of borrowers are added.
8. The increase in value of a life insurance policy.
9. Interest on tax-exempt bonds.

Expanded Income

Expanded income is narrower and follows the existing tax law more closely. The concept starts with AGI and then adds:

1. Tax-exempt interest
2. Workers' compensation
3. Nontaxable Social Security benefits
4. Excluded income of U.S. citizens living abroad
5. Value of Medicare benefits in excess of premiums paid
6. Minimum tax preferences
7. Employer contributions for health plans and life insurance
8. Employer share of payroll taxes
9. Corporate tax payments imputed to individual holders of corporate equity

ing mobility. Third, adjustments are made to encourage certain activities by individuals—the deduction of Individual Retirement Account and other personal retirement plan payments to encourage private retirement saving, the student loan interest deduction to reduce the cost of borrowing to pay for education, and deductions to reduce the cost of private provision of health insurance.[19]

Net proceeds from some transactions simply do not show up in AGI but appear to be income by both popular and Haig-Simons concepts.[20] Among the exclusions are interest received from certain state and local government bonds, certain transfer payments (e.g., welfare payments, most Social Security benefits, and food stamps), many fringe benefits received by employees from their employers (particularly pension and health plans), income from savings placed in life insurance, and gifts or inheritances. The value of fringe benefits received from an employer is taxable unless the law explicitly excludes the benefit from the tax, as is the case for many important benefits (services provided at no additional cost to the employer, certain employee discounts, working-condition benefits, etc.). The practical scope of the remaining untaxed fringe benefits is extensive. The system does not include unrealized capital gains and excludes imputed incomes. Most federal and state-local distributional analysis uses some larger measure of ability (like those in Sidebar 8–1), rather than simple AGI to maintain a consistent measure of economic capacity. The impact of these exclusions can be huge. For instance, the exclusion of employer-provided health insurance is the largest single federal health subsidy for the non-elderly.

Several exclusions seem reasonable, particularly those directed to low-income individuals: it is not sensible to assist individuals because of their poverty and then tax away part of that assistance. Some assistance categories, however, are not limited to the poor—that is, they are not need-based, and eligible recipients may have sizable income from other sources. Thus, if one desires to apply tax according to net well-being, there is a case for including retirement pay, Social Security, unemployment compensation, and similar payments not strictly conditioned on current income or wealth. Unemployment compensation is now fully taxable; other related flows may be taxable in certain circumstances.[21]

The exclusion of interest received on state and local government debt historically stems from the principle of reciprocal immunity, that the federal government cannot destroy state or local governments (and vice versa). Because "the power to tax involves the power to destroy," the federal government historically did not tax instruments of state and local government.[22] The exclusion represents an important

---

[19]Similar provisions to encourage certain activities may also appear in the itemized deductions. However, only taxpayers not opting for the standard deduction receive the benefit of these deductions. The impact of providing relief as an adjustment, rather than as a deduction, is therefore much greater. For instance, changing the preference for charitable contributions from an itemized deduction to an adjustment would significantly increase the number of taxpayers able to take advantage of the preference.

[20]Some federal tax preferences were subjected to an alternate minimum tax (AMT) in the Tax Reform Act of 1979 and continued by the 1986 law, but some exclusions remain.

[21]The link between income earned by those receiving Social Security benefits and those benefits within the tax system is troublesome for incentives. Earning income can cause more of Social Security benefits to be taxable and can cause loss of benefits, leaving little, if any, net return from work.

[22]*McCulloch* v. *Maryland*, 4 Wheat, 316 L.Ed. 579 (1819), is the source of John Marshall's famous "power to tax" quote. The reciprocal immunity doctrine, however, is enunciated in *Collector* v. *Day*, 11 Wall, 113, 20 L.Ed. 122 (1871).

subsidy to state and local governments because it allows these governments to borrow at interest rates below current market rates. To demonstrate the influence of this exclusion, suppose an individual pays 35 percent of any additional income as federal income tax. A tax-exempt municipal bond paying 5.2 percent yields the same after-tax income as would a taxable bond paying about 8 percent.[23] Thus, the state or local government borrower automatically receives an interest subsidy through the federal tax system, allowing that government to borrow at artificially low rates. These bonds have been a favorite avenue of tax avoidance for higher-income individuals, and the value of interest subsidization to state or local government must be balanced against the damage done to tax system equity by the exclusion.

Any suspicion that the nondiscriminatory taxation of interest on state and local bonds might be unconstitutional was eliminated in the 1988 U.S. Supreme Court decision in *South Carolina* v. *Baker:* "The owners of state bonds have no constitutional entitlement not to pay taxes on income they earn from state bonds, and states have no constitutional entitlement to issue bonds paying lower interest rates than other issuers."[24] So the provision remains as a valuable federal subsidy, a subsidy especially important to state and local governments and aggressively defended by them because it is received at their own control. The Tax Reform Act of 1986 dramatically reduced the scope of such borrowing, however, as Chapter 15 describes.

Personal Deductions

Personal deductions adjust the measured ability to pay the tax to the circumstances of the individual taxpayer. Personal deductions may improve the tax's horizontal and vertical equity by allowing individuals with such deductions to subtract them from the AGI and hence lower their tax base. Personal deductions may also encourage taxpayers to do things they might not otherwise do because of the tax savings that may result.

There are, logically, three types of spending that the itemized personal deductions identify as reducing the taxpayer's capacity to bear the tax below that of others with similar incomes. First, some expenditures are largely outside the control of the household and reduce ability to share in covering the cost of government. Currently in this category (philosophies and coverage change with tax code revisions) are deductions for medical and dental expenses above 7.5 percent of AGI, losses from casualty or theft above 10 percent of AGI (less $100), and state and local income and

---

[23]The taxable bond at 8 percent would leave the investor 65 percent (100 percent minus 35 percent) of its yield after tax. Thus, 8 percent times 65 percent equals 5.2.

[24]*South Carolina* v. *Baker, Treasury Secretary of the United States,* 485 U.S. 99, LEJ 2d 592, 108 S. Ct. South Carolina sued because it objected to a Tax Equity and Fiscal Responsibility Act of 1982 provision that requires identification of owners of such bonds. Before that requirement, states could issue "bearer bonds"—whoever presented the bond received the periodic payments, no questions about ownership were asked. They were popular with tax evaders, for money laundering, and with organized crime. The Court volunteered more answers than the state and local governments would have wished.

property taxes. In each instance, individuals—presumably through little fault of their own—must bear these special expenses that more fortunate individuals do not incur. Thus, an adjustment of measured tax-bearing capacity is permitted.[25]

Second, some expenditures are deductible because the federal government has decided that private spending in those areas should be encouraged by reducing the after-tax cost of those actions. Thus, charitable contributions are directly deductible. This spending is optional (not like state taxes or medical bills), but the federal government seeks to encourage contributions. Interest paid on home mortgages (first and second homes) is similarly deductible as an important encouragement to home ownership, a matter of considerable importance to individuals who have borrowed to purchase homes.[26]

Finally, some deductions are needed to maintain the principle that the tax apply to net incomes, not gross receipts. In this category are expenses associated with moving to a new job and certain job-related expenses (education expenses needed to maintain or improve skills on the present job, union dues, work uniforms, research expenses for a college professor, occupational taxes, etc.). The latter group, combined with some miscellaneous deductions (tax-preparation fees, fees associated with earning income from investments, etc.), are deductible only to the extent they exceed 2 percent of AGI. Gambling losses are fully deductible, but only up to the amount of winnings.

The attempts at "netting" produce some interesting policy choices because it is difficult to distinguish between costs of earning income and personal consumption. For example, commuting expenses apparently are a cost of earning an income: If one does not get to work, income is not earned. This expenditure, however, results from choice of residence (commuting expense can be reduced by choosing to live closer to the point of employment) and is thus a consumption choice. To change this approach would provide a further incentive to urban sprawl. Moving expenses incurred to follow a changed place of employment, on the other hand, are considered a cost of earning income and are subtracted from income to obtain the tax base (as an adjustment, not as a deduction). The assumption is that such expenses are necessary for the job, not expenses from consumer choices. Of course, many people seek jobs elsewhere because they prefer a different climate, different cultural activities, and so on—personal consumption choices, not costs of employment—but our tax system chooses to err in favor of enhancing labor mobility.

Each policy choice in designing the tax was made because it seemed to improve the equity or efficiency of the system. Because each provides greater tax

---

[25]Until the 1986 Tax Reform Act, state and local sales taxes were also deducted. The American Jobs Creation Act of 2004 reinstated state and local sales tax deductibility for 2004 and 2005, but taxpayers have the choice of deducting either these taxes or state and local income taxes, not both. Income tax deduction was a way of providing coordination between income taxes at the two levels, particularly necessary when the federal marginal rate was extremely high. Restoration of sales tax deductability was designed to give a tax reduction to states with high state-local sales taxes but no income tax.

[26]Other personal interest payments—credit card, automobile, education, installment, or signature loans—were fully deductible before the 1986 tax act. And the 1997 tax reconciliation act made interest paid on certain student loans again deductible (but only for individuals with incomes up to $40,000 and for couples with incomes up to $60,000). Student loan interest now is an adjustment, subtracted in calculating adjusted gross income, even for those not itemizing deductions.

relief to high income taxpayers (a charitable deduction of $100 has an after-tax cost of $65 to an individual in the 35-percent bracket and a cost of $85 to someone in the 15-percent bracket), there is a special incentive for such individuals to arrange their affairs so that their expenses fit into these deductible categories. Thus, professional meetings are timed to double as vacations, consumer loans are converted to home equity (mortgage) loans, and so on. As a result, these provisions can reduce the overall progression of the tax system and distort economic behavior. The system works to reduce this impact by applying a phase-out of several itemized deductions—each dollar of deduction is reduced by 3 percent for taxpayers whose AGI exceeds a limit; to add some extra complexity to the system, this phase-out is currently scheduled itself for phase-out.

Not all taxpayers, however, use the personal deductions. Since the early 1940s, an optional standard deduction has permitted individuals to subtract from their AGI base a specified deduction amount, regardless of itemized totals, and for tax-year 1998, about 70 percent of total tax filers chose the standard deduction, rather than itemizing. This deduction eliminates the need for keeping records of deductible expenses. The initial idea was to make the tax simpler for the many people who became taxpayers for the first time during the Second World War as effective rates for lower-income classes rose dramatically. Furthermore, the optional deduction for people without a high total of itemized deductions may have some psychological advantage.

The standard deduction has gradually increased over time and is now indexed to increase with inflation; from 1987 to 2005, for instance, it increased from $2,540 to $5,000 for a single person. The standard deduction for taxpayers filing joint returns is $10,000. Unless taxpayers have itemized deductions totaling more than that amount, they will not choose the itemized deduction route; homeownership with the accompanying mortgage interest payment and local property tax typically creates the threshold to make itemization pay. When all taxpayers have a general deduction, however, tax rates must be higher for everyone to generate a given amount of tax revenue, diluting the relief for the deserving and the undeserving alike.

Personal Exemptions

The tax law allows an exemption for each person in a taxpaying unit—the taxpayer, the taxpayer's spouse, and dependents (certain members of the household who are supported by the taxpayer, usually the taxpayer's children)—plus extra exemptions if the taxpayer or spouse is blind or older than age 65. The exemption is a flat amount for each exemption claimed—$3,200 in 2005. The exemption serves to adjust tax payment for size of the taxpaying unit, adds some progressivity to the effective rate pattern, and works to remove many low-income households from the tax system. Table 8–3 traces the history of personal exemptions since the inception of the tax. The structure provides greater relief for those in higher tax brackets, so the system provides that taxpayers above a certain AGI level will reduce personal

Table 8–3
History of Federal Individual Income Tax Exemptions and Lowest and Highest Bracket Rates

	Personal Exemption ($)				
Year	Single	Married	Dependents	Lowest Rate (%)	Highest Rate (%)
1913–1915	3,000	4,000	—	1	7
1916	3,000	4,000	—	2	15
1917	1,000	2,000	200	2	67
1918	1,000	2,000	200	6	77
1919–1920	1,000	2,000	200	4	73
1921	1,000	2,500	400	4	73
1922	1,000	2,500	400	4	56
1923	1,000	2,500	400	3	56
1924	1,000	2,500	400	1.5	46
1925–1928	1,500	3,500	400	1.125	25
1929	1,500	3,500	400	0.375	24
1930–1931	1,500	3,500	400	1.125	25
1932–1933	1,000	2,500	400	4	63
1934–1935	1,000	2,500	400	4	63
1936–1939	1,000	2,500	400	4	79
1940	800	2,000	400	4.4	81.1
1941	750	1,500	400	10	81
1942–1943	500	1,200	350	19	88
1944–1945	500	1,000	500	23	94[c]
1946–1947	500	1,000	500	19	86.45
1948–1949	600	1,200	600	16.6	82.13
1950	600	1,200	600	17.4	91
1951	600	1,200	600	20.4	91
1952–1953	600	1,200	600	22.2	92
1954–1963	600	1,200	600	20	91
1964	600	1,200	600	16	77
1965–1967	600	1,200	600	14	70
1968	600	1,200	600	14	75.25
1969	600	1,200	600	14	77
1970	625	1,200	625	14	71.75
1971	675	1,350	675	14	70
1972–1978	750	1,500	750	14	70
1979–1980	1,000	2,000	1,000	14	70
1981	1,000	2,000	1,000	13.825	69.125
1982	1,000	2,000	1,000	12	50
1983	1,000	2,000	1,000	12	50
1984	1,000	2,000	1,000	11	50
1985	1,080	2,160	1,080	11	50
1986	1,080	2,160	1,080	11	50
1987	1,900	3,800	1,900	11	38.5
1988	1,950	3,900	1,950	15	33
1989	2,000	4,000	2,000	15	33

Table 8–3
(continued)

	Personal Exemption ($)				
Year	Single	Married	Dependents	Lowest Rate (%)	Highest Rate (%)
1990	2,050	4,000	2,050	15	33
1991[i]	2,150	4,300	2,150	15	31
1992	2,300	4,600	2,300	15	31
1993	2,350	4,700	2,350	15	39.6[j]
1994	2,450	4,900	2,450	15	39.6
1995	2,500	5,000	2,500	15	39.6
1996	2,550	5,100	2,550	15	39.6
1997	2,650	5,300	2,650	15	39.6
1998	2,700	5,400	2,700	15	39.6
1999	2,750	5,500	2,750	15	39.6
2000	2,800	5,600	2,800	15	39.6
2001	2,900	5,800	2,900	10	39.1
2002	3,000	6,000	3,000	10	38.6
2003	3,050	6,100	3,050	10	35.0
2004	3,100	6,200	3,100	10	35
2005	3,200	6,400	3,200	10	35

SOURCE: SOI Bulletin.
NOTES: From 1948, additional exemption for taxpayers blind or older than 65 years; for 1921–1923, married exemption was $2,000 if net income was more than $5,000; for 1944–1963, there were maximum effective rate limitations; for 1971–1981, lower maximum marginal rate on earned income; in addition to exemptions, $30 per capita credit in 1975 and $35 credit (or 2% of first $9,000 taxable income) in 1976–1978; indexation began in 1985; phase out of exemptions for persons with high income began in 1988; limit on itemized deductions for high income taxpayers began in 1991.

exemptions by 2 percent for each $2,500 or part thereof by which AGI exceeds that threshold. The provision itself is presently subject to a phase-out.

Taxable Income

Taxable income results from subtracting personal deductions, either itemized or standard, and personal exemptions from AGI. It is the base to which the tax-rate structure applies. The elemental identity of taxation is that tax yield equals tax base times tax rate. Therefore, a given tax yield may be generated through many different base and rate combinations, some involving narrow-based definitions (many deductions, exclusions, and exemptions from the Haig-Simons or other general income concepts) and high-rate structures; some involving broad-based definitions (few deductions, exclusions, and exemptions) and low-rate structures.

An important trend in federal taxation, particularly shown in the 1986 Tax Reform Act and somewhat eroded by the Revenue Reconciliation Act of 1993, has been a movement toward the broader-based lower-rate option. This has been done in the belief that lower rates at the decision margin do less to discourage investment and work effort than do higher rates, that broader bases leave fewer protected pockets that could harbor economic activity profitable only because of tax provisions, and that broad coverage is less likely to engender horizontal inequity.

Tax Rates

Federal individual income tax rates increase in steps as income increases. At each step, the rate applicable to additional income is slightly higher than the rate on lower income. Figures 8–2 and 8–3 present recent tax-rate schedules for single and married taxpayers; Figure 8–4 gives one portion of the tax tables that filers are directed to use in computing their tax liability. (Higher-income taxpayers use the rate schedules for calculation of amounts.) The rate schedule is graduated upward with marginal rates (the percentage taxed from each additional dollar of taxable income) of 10, 15, 25, 28, 33, and 35 percent. A single individual with taxable income of $85,000 would thus have part of that income taxed at 10 percent, part at 15 percent,

Figure 8–2
Federal Rate Schedule for 2005: Married Individuals Filing Jointly or Qualifying Widow(er)s

If Taxable Income Is:	Then Tax Is:
$0–$14,600	10% of the amount over $0
$14,600–$59,400	$1,460 + 15% of the amount over $14,600
$59,400–$119,950	$8,180 + 25% of the amount over $59,400
$119,950–$182,800	$23,318 + 28% of the amount over $119,950
$182,800–$326,450	$40,916 + 33% of the amount over $182,800
$326,450 and above	$88,321 + 35% of the amount over $326,450

Figure 8–3
Federal Rate Schedule for 2005: Single Filers

If Taxable Income Is:	Then Tax Is:
$0–$7,300	10% of the amount over $0
$7,300–$29,700	$730 + 15% of the amount over $7,300
$29,700–$71,950	$4,090 + 25% of the amount over $29,700
$71,950–$150,150	$14,653 + 28% of the amount over $71,950
$150,150–$326,450	$36,549 + 33% of the amount over $150,150
$326,450 and over	$94,728 + 35% of the amount over $326,450

Figure 8–4
A Portion of the Federal Tax Table for 2005

If line 43 (taxable income) is—		And you are—			
At least	But less than	Single	Married filing jointly *	Married filing separately	Head of a household
		Your tax is—			
83,000					
83,000	**83,050**	17,754	14,086	18,113	16,254
83,050	**83,100**	17,768	14,099	18,127	16,266
83,100	**83,150**	17,782	14,111	18,141	16,279
83,150	**83,200**	17,796	14,124	18,155	16,291
83,200	**83,250**	17,810	14,136	18,169	16,304
83,250	**83,300**	17,824	14,149	18,183	16,316
83,300	**83,350**	17,838	14,161	18,197	16.329
83,350	**83,400**	17,852	14,174	18,211	16,341
83,400	**83,450**	17,866	14,186	18,225	16,354
83,450	**83,500**	17,880	14,199	18,239	16,366
62,500	**83,550**	17,894	14,211	18,253	16,379
83,550	**83,600**	17,908	14,224	18,267	16,391
83,600	**83,650**	17,922	14,236	18,281	16,404
83,650	**83,700**	17,936	14,249	18,295	16,416
83,700	**83,750**	17,950	14,261	18,309	16,429
83,750	**83,800**	17,964	14,274	18,323	16,441
83,800	**83,850**	17,978	14,286	18,337	16,454
83,850	**83,900**	17,992	14,299	18,351	16,466
83,900	**83,950**	18,006	14,311	18,365	16,479
83,950	**84,000**	18,020	14,324	18,379	16,491
84,000					
84,000	**84,050**	18,034	14,336	18,393	16,504
84,050	**84,100**	18,048	14,349	18,407	16,516
84,100	**84,150**	18,062	14,361	18,421	16,529
84,150	**84,200**	18,076	14,374	18,435	16,541
84,200	**84,250**	18,090	14,386	18,449	16,554
84,250	**84,300**	18,104	14,399	18,463	16,566
84,300	**84,350**	18,118	14,411	18,477	16,579
84,350	**84,400**	18,132	14,424	18,491	16,591
84,400	**84,450**	18,146	14,436	18,505	16,604
84,450	**84,500**	18,160	14,449	18,519	16,616
84,500	**84,550**	18,174	14,461	18,533	16,629
84,550	**84,600**	18,188	14,474	18,547	16,641
84,600	**84,650**	18,202	14,486	18,561	16,654
84,650	**84,700**	18,216	14,499	18,575	16,666
84,700	**84,750**	18,230	14,511	18,589	16,679
84,750	**84,800**	18,244	14,524	18,603	16,691
84,800	**84,850**	18,258	14,536	18,617	16,704
84,850	**84,900**	18,272	14,549	18,631	16,716
84,900	**84,950**	18,286	14,561	18,645	16,729
84,950	**85,000**	18,300	14,574	18,659	16,741

and part at 25 percent. Only part of his or her income would face the 25 percent rate, but if he or she earned an extra $100, after tax, only $75 would be retained. This marginal rate is critical in economic choices. The average tax rate he or she would pay is substantially less than 25 percent. In a graduated rate schedule, all taxable income is taxed at the lowest rate, with decreasing portions of the total base taxed at each increasing rate.[27] In terms of revenue impact, changes in the bottom rate are most important, and those in the highest rate are least important—in 1998, the 15-percent rate produced 37.9 percent of federal income tax revenue, whereas the highest rate (36.9 percent at that time) yielded 16.3 percent.[28] All taxable income goes through the lowest rate; relatively little goes into the highest rate. An increase in the top marginal rate may have great political significance and adverse disincentive effects without adding as much to total tax collections as might be expected.

In comparison with the recent past, the rate structure consists of fewer rate brackets (fourteen before the 1986 tax reform) and a lower top-rate bracket. Few returns characteristically have been filed by taxpayers paying any tax at the highest marginal rate (although that has changed dramatically in the last decade), but the history of these rates provides an interesting profile of political attitudes, incentives at the margin, and room for state-local taxation of the income base. Table 8–3 provides that history from 1913 through 2001 for individual rates.

In some years, the highest marginal rates have been well above 70 percent. Those high rates may harm the national economy without adding much revenue. For example, a person in the 70 percent bracket, a person with considerable income, would face this sort of choice: "I can work a bit more and earn an additional $1,000, of which $700 will be paid to the federal government (and some probably will be paid to state and local income taxes as well) and $300 I can keep for myself. I can use that extra time for rest and relaxation. Or I can hire tax advisers to try to structure that additional $1,000 so I won't have to pay so much tax." Two of these alternatives do not contribute much to the national economy, but, given the after-tax return to the individual, many people would select them. That is an important influence behind tax structuring to raise necessary revenue and achieve the desired degree of progressivity without high marginal rates. In designing tax structures, it is useful to think about what tax wedge—the tax-created difference between the total paid by the buyer and the net received by the seller—has been created. A high wedge on the margin of decision causes distortions and invites strategies (legal and illegal) to keep from paying tax.

The average rate (tax liability divided by taxable income) always lies below the marginal rate (the increase in tax liability resulting from $1 additional income). With that structure, an individual will never have greater after-tax income by hav-

[27]The Federal income tax system now has a recapture system to remove the impact of the lowest tax bracket for high-income taxpayers, an extra complication in the system.

[28]David Campbell and Michael Parisi, "Individual Income Tax Rates and Tax Shares," *SOI Bulletin* (Spring 2001): 32–33.

ing less income. The percentage of income going to federal tax increases as income rises, but the absolute income left over will not decline.[29]

But the tax rates are more complicated than just the graduated rates shown in Figures 8–2 and 8–3. First, as noted previously, most states (and many localities) levy their own income taxes, applying supplemental rates to federal AGI, taxable income, or the federal tax itself. Each adds another layer to the rate paid, although state returns are filed separately from the federal. The combined rate cannot be simply found on a rate schedule; it has to be added up, sometimes with allowances made for differences in statutory coverage between federal and state taxes.

A second complication results because not all income is taxed under the same rate. Some countries apply detailed schedular rate systems, in which different sorts of income—wages, interest, or earnings from a business—are taxed at different rates. The federal government taxes income from realized capital gains—increase in value of a capital asset between time of acquisition and time of sale—at preferential rates. Long-term capital gains and dividend income is taxed at 5 percent for those in the 10- and 15-percent brackets, and at 15 percent for those in higher brackets. Such schedular systems create an economic distortion favoring the lower-taxed flows and encourage conversion of flows that normally would be received as ordinary income to capital gains income. Not only would the incentive distort economic resources, it would also require extra administrative effort to police shelter schemes established to exploit the difference. It represents a clear violation of normal principles of tax policy as it complicates, distorts, and makes the system less certain and transparent. Special treatment of long-term capital gains is supported, however, by concerns about the unfairness of taxing gains that are nominal (inflation) but not real (purchasing power), about the danger of capital being locked in to current holdings (no capital gains tax applies when heirs receive appreciated assets when an estate is settled),[30] and about the possible chilling effect of the tax on saving and investment.

Not all income taxes are levied with graduated rates. At the present time, six states levy flat-rate income taxes and several countries, particularly in a number of new democratic states of Eastern Europe, also apply such rate structures.[31] The idea of such structures is to reduce the complexity of the tax for compliance and administration and to prevent the distortions that upwardly graduated rates can produce. In these systems, any progressivity in effective rates is produced by other structural features, not through graduation of the legal rates.

---

[29]That may not necessarily be the case when effects from government benefit programs are added in, however. For an illustration, see Mary Rowland, "When Working Isn't Worth It," *New York Times,* (26 September 1993), F-15.

[30]This is called "step up in basis." For eventual capital gains tax purposes, the value of the inherited asset becomes the value at the time of inheritance, not the value at which the asset was purchased. This increase in value from purchase to inheritance therefore escapes the income tax system.

[31]The impact of Russia's implementation of a flat-rate tax, replacing a graduated-rate tax, is analyzed in Clifford G. Gaddy and William G. Gale, "Demythologizing the Russian Flat Tax," *Tax Notes International,* (March 14, 2005), 983–988. This is significant because some American commentators have erroneously pointed to this experience as evidence of that moving from graduated- to flat-rate structures boosts economic activity and possibly even tax revenue.

Credits

Tax credits, direct forgiveness of tax owed, are a powerful device for stimulation of private activities. The credit amount reduces tax liability by an amount exactly equal to the credit; it does not reduce the tax base, as is the case for exemptions or deductions, so its tax-reducing impact is not filtered through the rate structure. Therefore, the tax reduction from a given credit is the same for taxpayers in all rate brackets; deductions and exemptions, on the other hand, have greater tax-reducing impact for those in higher tax brackets.[32] But because credits reduce taxes directly, they produce greater revenue loss than do equivalent deductions or exemptions, an important concern for most governments.

Credits have been used over the years to induce political contributions, installation of energy-saving mechanisms, capital investment, and home purchase, to cite some recent federal system examples. Current credits are provided for families with children, for certain college tuitions, for child- and dependent-care expenses, for the elderly and disabled, and for certain adoption expenses. Furthermore, the federal system provides a credit for low-income workers (the EITC), as described in Sidebar 8–2, a credit defined as a percentage of earned income that substantially relieves taxes for the working poor. State income taxes similarly employ credits to support desirable activities, choosing the power and evenness of support from credits against the substantial revenue loss they produce.

Effective Tax Rates

The statutory, or nominal, rates appearing in the rate schedule, of course, are not the same as the effective rates. Analysis of the income tax system usually is conducted by looking at the relationship between taxes paid and AGI, the federal tax system equivalent of net income, or one of the broader measures in the Haig-Simons tradition. This rate is the average effective rate. The statutory rates are reduced substantially by the operation of tax provisions removing individual income from the base (adjustment, deductions, exemptions, and exclusions) and forgiving tax owed (credits). These elements can be regarded as the work of tax loopholes or as the work of tax policy designed to correct inequities or to encourage socially desirable behavior. Table 8–4 illustrates how a relatively generous exemption by itself can convert a flat statutory rate into progressive effective rates. In essence, the large exemption works to create progressive effective rates because the exemption provides greater relief *relative to* family income to the lower income family—$4,500 is a much more significant portion of total income for Family C than for Family A (or B). That translates into a much greater impact on the effective rate. The impact on vertical equity works with any rate structure—the personal exemptions make the

[32]A number of federal credits and other tax preferences are reduced in stages as income increases; there are about twenty different phase-out ranges and calculation methods. All add complexity and uncertainty to the system, presumably in the name of targeting relief and social engineering.

Sidebar 8–2
The Earned Income Tax Credit

The federal EITC provides needy families with financial assistance while it gives a positive incentive for work among the lower-paid members of society. It aids these people without the need for a special welfare bureaucracy and appears to reach a higher percentage of those eligible than does any other income support program, possibly because it avoids any stigma associated with programs that more specifically identify the recipients. It also avoids the major work disincentives that some welfare programs have when earning additional income causes countervailing loss of welfare benefits. Quite simply, assistance is provided through the individual income tax system with fully refundable tax credits given to those who qualify. Here is how the Council of Economic Advisers described the operation of the EITC in the 1994 *Economic Report of the President:*

> The earned income tax credit is often thought of as a type of negative income tax, but in fact it is more complicated than that. The EITC has three ranges: a "credit range" in which it functions like a wage subsidy, a "plateau" in which it has no marginal effect, and a "phaseout" range in which the credit is paid back as earnings rise. . . .
>
> To illustrate, when the increases enacted in 1993 are fully effective (in 1996), the credit will work as follows for a family with two or more children. (Less generous schedules apply to one-child and childless families.) As earnings rise from zero to $8,425 (all dollar figures are in 1994 dollars), the EITC will provide a 40 percent wage subsidy, so that each $100 of additional earnings will net the family $140. The maximum credit is $3,370, which is therefore reached when earnings hit $8,425. The credit will then be constant as earnings rise from $8,425 to $11,000. Beyond $11,000, however, the family's tax credit is reduced 21 cents for each extra dollar earned. Benefits are thus exhausted when earnings reach $27,000.

Clearly, the EITC provides a marginal work incentive in the credit range (unlike a negative income tax), a marginal disincentive in the phaseout range, and neither in the plateau. However, to the extent that labor supply decisions involve whether or not to work, rather than how many hours to work, the credit provides a positive work incentive to all recipients.

In fiscal 2004, the EITC provided $42 billion in benefits. That amount was more than provided through Temporary Assistance for Needy Families (TANF), what is thought of as America's foundation public welfare program, the Food Stamp program, and the Supplemental Security Income Program, three of the most important income security programs functioning through the spending side of the fiscal system. More than half of EITC payments go to families below the poverty line. The program has been of particular benefit to families at the bottom of the income ladder and represents a significant component in the economic safety net, even though administered through the tax system.

SOURCE: Council of Economic Advisors, *Economic Report of the President, Transmitted to the Congress, February 1994* (Washington, D.C.: Government Printing Office, 1994), 51.

Table 8–4
Effective-Rate Impact of a Flat-Rate Income Tax (10 Percent) and a Large Personal Exemption ($1,500 per Person) on Selected Families of Three

	Before-Tax Income ($)	Taxable Income ($)	Effective Tax ($)	Exemption ($)	Rate (%)
A	20,000	4,500	15,500	1,550	7.75
B	10,000	4,500	5,500	550	5.5
C	5,000	4,500	500	50	1.0

progressivity of an upward graduated tax structure even greater. But there is a downside: the net tax saving from a given exemption amount, for instance $1,000, is greater for a taxpayer in the 35-percent tax bracket than for a taxpayer in the 10-percent bracket. This provides an argument for giving certain relief in the form of credits rather than exemptions—the net tax saving with a credit is the same, regardless of the tax bracket of the recipient—or for adopting a flat statutory rate system.

One little-observed feature of the federal income tax is the large number of tax filers who do not owe any tax liability. In the 2003 tax year, 31.8 percent of tax returns—over 41 million returns—had no tax liability. And the number of Americans who did not owe income tax was even higher because around 15 million individuals earned some income but not enough to be required to even file a return. When all dependents represented on the filed returns are added in, around 120 million people or 40 percent of the total population is estimated to be legally outside the income tax net because of credits, deductions, or low income.[33] When this tally is placed against the concentration of individual income tax payments in the upper categories of the income distribution shown previously in Table 8–2 (56.6 percent of individual income tax collections come from the top 5 percent of taxpayers and 34.6 percent from the top 1 percent), the extent to which the system revenue depends on a small pool of taxpayers is apparent. Of course, the upper-most income recipients have done extremely well, and that is the primary reason for the concentration of payment—but is it good for sound democratic decision-making for the payment for public services to be so concentrated and for so many to have no liability?

Indexation

When a tax structure has many upward graduated brackets, as the federal structure did until the 1986 tax act, a phenomenon known as bracket creep can occur during high inflation. Suppose a family has an AGI of $28,000, pays a tax of $3,300, and is in the 15-percent marginal tax bracket. In 2 years, its income has increased to, say, $33,600 (a 20-percent increase), but the cost of living has increased by 20 percent as

[33]Patrick Fleenor and Scott Hodge, "Number of Americans Outside the Income Tax System Continues to Grow," *Tax Foundation* (processed), (June 9, 2005).

well, so its real income has not changed. The family would, however, pay tax on that higher money income even though its living standard has not really changed, and that income is subject to a higher marginal bracket. Thus, it might now pay $4,300, an increase of tax liability of more than 20 percent because of the upward rate graduation. And, of course, the real value of personal exemptions and standard deductions decrease as well.

This graduation has historically helped stabilize the economy, accelerating tax collections during inflation to provide a macroeconomic brake, and slowing tax collections during recession to provide a macroeconomic stimulus without legislative action. During the long economic expansion of the 1980s, governments raised substantial revenue without statutory-rate increases simply by letting growth, real and inflated, carry taxpayers into higher-rate categories.

Indexation removes the effect of bracket creep. An annual adjustment changes personal exemptions, standard deductions, and/or bracket starting points to allow for impacts of inflation that increase income but not purchasing power. A number of states have systems of indexation; the federal income tax has indexed exemptions, standard deductions, and bracket points since 1985.

Tax Computation

The nature of income taxation can best be understood by working the mechanics of the tax. Table 8–5 provides an illustration of such a manipulation. It applies the general schematic of the federal income tax to demonstrate deductions and exemptions, as well as the computation of average, marginal, and average effective-tax rates. But that is not quite everything for the taxpayer. There is an alternate minimum tax (AMT) computation that might mean extra tax to be paid. AMT is described in Sidebar 8–3.

Corporate Income Taxation

The corporation net income tax applies to the net earnings of incorporated businesses, following the theory that the legal person created by incorporation creates an economic entity with tax-bearing capacity separate from the owners (shareholders) of that business.[34] The tax applies to total corporate profit as defined by the accounting system and the tax law, including both earnings retained by the firm and

[34]Business income is not the same thing as corporate income. Many businesses, including many that are highly profitable, are not legally organized as corporations. These other businesses, such as sole proprietorships and partnerships, pay tax through the individual income tax structure. Also, certain corporations, because of the manner in which they are organized, are treated by the tax system like partnerships. All these are "pass through" entities: their income is not taxed at the business level, but is "passed through" to the owners of the business for taxation on their individual returns. As might be expected, these entities are a popular way for organizing businesses.

Table 8–5
An Example of Income Tax Computation

Mr. and Mrs. Gross have one dependent child. Their total income is $142,500. They also received income from municipal bonds of $7,500, but this money is not included as part of total income. They have adjustments of $12,000 from student loan interest, educator expenses, and Individual Retirement Account contributions, so their adjusted gross income equals $130,500. They have itemized deductions of $12,500 (property tax, state income tax, and mortgage interest paid). Because this amount exceeds the standard deduction for which they would qualify ($10,000), they use the itemized deduction for the filing. Each exemption is $3,200. Mrs. Gross's employer has withheld (prepaid) $24,230 of their tax liability. They file a joint return.

Computing Taxable Income:

Adjusted Gross Income = $130,500
- Less itemized deductions ($12,500)
- Less personal exemptions (3 × $3,200 = $9,600)
- Taxable income = $108,400

Computing Tax Liability:

From Tax Rate Schedule for Married Filing Jointly (Figure 8–2):
- Tax Liability for those with taxable incomes from $59,400 to $119,950 equals $8,180 plus 25% of the amount over $59,400 or $8,180 + .25 (108,400 – $59,400) = $20,430
- Tax Refund equals $24,230 less $20,430 = $3,800

Some Important Tax Indicators:

Average Rate = Tax/Taxable Income = $20,430/$108,400 = 18.8%
Average Effective Rate = Tax/(Taxable Income + Adjustments + Exclusions) = $20,430/($108,400 + $12,000 + $7,500) = 16.0%
Marginal Tax Rate = Change in Tax/Change in Taxable Income = 25% (from the brackets)

---

those paid in dividends to the stockholder. Although the tax lacks the personal exemptions and deductions found in the individual tax, it does allow deductions of charitable contributions (to encourage corporate generosity) and ordinary and necessary costs of operating the business. Because the individual income tax encompasses dividends in its tax base, dividends could be taxed at both the individual and corporate levels. That means that the U.S. tax system treats corporations and their investors as separate entities and causes an extra tax burden on distributed, as opposed to retained, profits. It puts an extra burden on income from capital.

The federal corporate income tax rate is 35 percent on income over $18.3 million. There are lower rates (starting at 15 percent) provided as a concession to small enterprises, but most taxable corporate income hits the highest rate. Profits of the corporation are really the profits of its owners. The lower rates for corporate income would be sensible only if the income of its shareholders would quality for the

Sidebar 8–3
The Alternate Minimum Tax

The United States has two tax systems. The regular system encompasses the standard individual and corporate income taxes, but there is a separate system, the AMT system, that is designed to ensure that corporations and individuals with substantial income do not exploit tax preferences provided in the tax law to avoid significant tax liability. The AMT system requires the taxpayer to do two distinct calculations of tax liability, one for the regular system and one for the AMT.

The AMT was enacted in 1969 with the intent that it be an add-on tax to insure that the few high-income individuals who otherwise would pay no tax would pay at least something. These individuals were not tax cheats but were simply taking advantage of various tax preferences that Congress had adopted to encourage certain economic behavior or to relieve certain inequities.

The AMT process for individual taxpayers is the following.

1. The taxpayer calculates tax liability according to the regular law.
2. The taxpayer calculates AMT liability by adding preferences (personal deductions and exemptions) and adjustments to regular taxable income, subtracting the special AMT exemption, and computing AMT liability using a simple rate structure (only two rates: 26 and 28 percent).
3. The taxpayer compares tax liabilities under the two systems and, after making proper allowance for credits, pays whichever is higher.

The AMT is simpler than the regular income tax: there are fewer tax preferences to keep track of and the rate structure has fewer brackets. The added complexity is caused because the taxpayer has to do two tax calculations: the regular income tax and the AMT. And the taxpayer can't easily know ahead of time which income tax he or she will be subject to.

The AMT was intended initially to reach high-income taxpayers but its net now catches many middle-income taxpayers. The reasons are simple: the regular income tax is generally indexed for inflation and the AMT is not, and recent tax cuts have significantly reduced the regular income tax for many taxpayers. Inflation brings higher income, the regular income tax adjusts its provisions upward to keep tax burdens from rising simply because of inflated incomes, but the AMT thresholds remain based on price and income levels of the late 1960s. Hence, more and more people find that their income status throws them into the AMT net. And these people still are not tax cheats. What sort of tax avoidance behavior causes people to fall prey to AMT? The people most likely to have AMT liability are those paying high state and local property and income taxes, those with large families, those with high miscellaneous deductions, and those running businesses with large operating losses. It is hard to believe that these people should be hit with an extra income tax liability, but that's the way the law works.

So why doesn't Congress get rid of the AMT? Quite frankly, it hardly can afford to. AMT revenue in 2004 was $15 billion, and making that sum up when lawmakers are reluctant to pass any provisions that generate extra revenue would be extremely difficult. And it gets worse: in 2012, it is estimated that the AMT will produce more money than the regular income tax.

(continues)

Sidebar 8–3 (continued)

Critics point to increased taxpayer compliance burdens, higher IRS administrative cost, redistribution of tax burdens among taxpayers, and denial to taxpayers of entirely legal tax incentives that Congress intended to provide. For a huge number of taxpayers, it requires a second calculation of tax liability with no revenue flowing to the government—the worst sort of tax program. Similar arguments also apply to the corporate AMT.

Some observers have suggested a way out. The AMT by itself is simpler than the individual income tax. Why not repeal the regular income tax and change the name of the AMT to the income tax? That would allow taxpayers to make fewer calculations, to keep fewer records, and to reduce their need for costly tax advisors. In other words, if you can't slay the dragon, why not convert it into domestic livestock?

lower rate, which, given the concentration of corporate ownership among higher-income households, does not make sense. Indeed, corporate rate graduation provides an incentive for splitting businesses into separate entities to gain the tax advantage from the lower rates. While the federal structure does have graduated rates, the threshold for the highest rate is rather low, so distortions from this are probably limited.

Determining taxable profit for any business, but particularly an infrastructure-intensive corporation, requires some formula for translating the purchase price of long-life capital equipment and structures into cost for a particular year. The cost of the infrastructure is part of the cost of making the product, but how much of the lumpy cost ought to be assigned to (or recovered in) any particular year? Ideally, the depreciation schedule should provide a "deduction profile over time that mimics the profile of the asset's true economic depreciation."[35] As the asset wears out, a comparable chunk of its purchase price would be subtracted from what would otherwise be profit of the firm. Because there is no administratively feasible way to track actual depreciation for every asset, tax systems adopt arbitrary depreciation rules that define the useful life of broad asset classes and the speed with which the purchase's price of the asset can be recovered over that life. Many recovery schemes are possible, but one common rule is *straight-line,* a method under which an equal portion of cost is recovered in each year of the asset's life. Thus, if the asset life is 10 years, then 10 percent of asset cost is deductible each year. Other systems allow faster recovery of cost (*accelerated depreciation*), that is, larger deductions in early years of life and smaller deductions in later years. Fastest of all would be to allow expensing, in which all the cost is deducted in the year of purchase. Faster depreciation is often proposed as a means for increasing capital investment

[35]Dale Chua, "Depreciation Schedules," in Parthasarathi Shome, ed., *Tax Policy Handbook* (Washington, D.C.: International Monetary Fund, 1995), 136.

and, hence, economic growth. Whatever the system, however, the depreciation rules are critical for determining the profit to be taxed.

Dividing the Base

Also critical for taxing the profits of international businesses is the price that a foreign owner charges its U.S. branches for supplies, services, or inventory. If the price is unduly high, U.S. profit is understated, and therefore corporate profit tax paid in the United States is artificially low. Multinational firms are frequently accused of establishing internal prices in such a way that high profits appear only in countries with low corporate-profit taxes. Thus, *transfer-pricing rules* (the rules establishing what internal prices are allowed) are critical in establishing corporate liability. If the transfer price is high, profit is increased for the subsidiary where the shipment originates; if the transfer price is low, profit is increased for the subsidiary where the shipment ends up. The profit all ends up with the company owning the subsidiaries, but the total profit tax—part paid to the originating country and part paid to the destination country—differs depending on what the transfer prices are. And there is evidence that multinational corporations do manage to report more of their profits where corporate tax rates are lower.[36]

Fairness of profit distribution suggests that the transfer prices should approximate the prices that would be charged in a transaction between unrelated companies, but that is not always simple to establish. An approach that is increasingly popular for multinational companies is the *advance pricing agreement,* in which the tax authority and the company agree on what pricing approach the company will employ in calculating its profits, thereby avoiding the danger that the approach will be disallowed on audit and thus bring fines and other sanctions. Unfortunately, such agreements are time-consuming and may make the system a bit overly individualized in its application.

At the state level, only Michigan, Nevada, South Dakota, Texas, Washington, and Wyoming do not currently have corporate income taxes roughly patterned after the federal tax, and the state taxes do create some special problems.[37] Foremost is the complication created because corporations conduct business in more than one state and often in more than one country. Some income may be clearly defined as originating from property or other assets in a single state, but much cannot be so identified. For instance, a particular corporation may have retail outlets in forty-five states, warehouses in nine states, and factories in two states. How much of that firm's profit should be taxable in any one state? To handle the problem, each state with a corporate income tax has adopted its own income *apportionment*

[36]When a U.S. corporation repatriates income from a foreign subsidiary it controls, it must pay a tax equal to the difference between the U.S. corporate tax rate and the rate applicable in the foreign country. For 2005, the American Jobs Creation Act of 2004 created a holiday during which repatriated profits would be taxed only at a rate of 5.25 percent. As would be expected, federal corporate profit tax collections for 2005 increased dramatically as businesses took advantage of this one-shot window.

[37]Michigan uses instead a single business tax, roughly a form of value-added tax (see the next chapter).

formula to determine how much of the total profit earned by a multistate corporation it will tax. States employ formulae that involve the share of total corporate sales in the state, the share of total corporate property in the state, and the share of total corporate payroll in the state. (Of course, the corporation must be conducting a minimum amount of business in the state in order to be taxable by the state; this contact is referred to as having *nexus* with the state.) One approach is the three-factor formula, in which the shares are equally weighted: If state A has 50 percent of the firm's total property value, 25 percent of the firm's total payroll, and 60 percent of the firm's sales, that state would apply its corporate tax rate to 45 percent [(50 + 25 + 60)/3] of the firm's total profit. Other states use the same three factors, but give double weighting to the sales factor, whereas yet others use only sales in the formula.[38] States are migrating toward formulae that give greater emphasis to sales in comparison to property or payroll in an effort to favor corporations with production facilities in their borders (having production facilities means property and employees, but does not bring an allocation of profit for state taxation if these factors are not in the apportionment formula). In other words, the attempt is to improve the competitive position of the state by shifting factors from those that reflect the origin of economic activity (payroll and property) to those that reflect the destination (sales). States see this change toward heavy weight on the sales share as part of their economic development effort.[39] There is no clearly correct formula for apportionment, of course, but having production facilities in a state certainly requires the state to deliver some services to the business. That is the logic behind having the non-sales factors in the formula. Because many states lack sufficient audit staff to verify the factor computed by all corporate filers, they must accept the calculations done by many corporations. This problem of profit apportionment makes local corporate income taxes extremely difficult for compliance and enforcement.

Integration with the Individual Tax

A major question in the structure and operation of the corporate income tax is whether it reduces the real income of the stockholders of the corporation, produces higher prices for the corporation's products, or causes the real income of labor and other resources used by the corporation to be lower. Neither theoretical nor empirical evidence is clear. This uncertainty is troublesome because the corporate income tax is the third largest source of federal revenue, and that revenue would be difficult to replace from other sources. Problems with the corporate income tax, however,

---

[38]The U.S. Supreme Court, in a case involving Moorman Manufacturing Company, upheld the Iowa formula that uses only sales. See "New Flexibility on Business Tax Granted State," *Wall Street Journal,* (16 June 1978). The problem was that, by having states use a variety of differing apportionment formulae, an unlucky multistate business could find that it paid state corporate income tax on more 100 percent of its total profits. And more lucky businesses could pay tax on less than 100 percent of their profits. Corporations do face inequitable treatment by states.

[39]Austan Goolsbee and Edward L. Maydew, "Coveting Thy Neighbor's Manufacturing: The Dilemma of State Income Apportionment," *Journal of Public Economics* 75 (2000), 125–43, measures the impact of the apportionment factor on manufacturing employment in a state.

must be considered. There is the problem of equity. If corporation stockholders bear the tax, why should dividend income be taxed more heavily than other sources of income? Furthermore, because not everyone within a particular income group receives dividend income, the special tax on corporate income—as translated through to stockholders—obviously violates the equal-treatment-of-equals rule for appropriate tax-burden distributions. The corporate income tax, however, does fill a gap: without it, the portion of corporate income not distributed would go untaxed.[40] In addition, the corporate income tax probably increases the progressivity of the system because dividend income tends to be more concentrated in higher-income groups. At the state level, the corporate income tax allows the state to extract compensation for benefits that the state provides to corporations whose owners may be largely out of state.

The major problem with the current corporate income tax, however, is its effects on savings and real investment. The corporate income tax probably constitutes a double tax on dividends, and thus reduces the rate of savings, with undesirable effects on capital formation. And it certainly influences choices by corporate executives between finance by debt (interest payments to bondholders are deductible) or by equity (dividend payments to shareholders are not deductible). Those capital-formation effects add to the productivity problems of the nation, so some change might be appropriate.

Many of the undesirable economic and equity effects would be reduced if individual income and corporate income taxes were integrated either partially or completely to mitigate the extra tax the two systems place on distributed corporate profit. Complete integration would treat the corporation in the same way as partnerships. The tax would not apply to corporate income at all, but the owners of the corporation would be taxed according to their proportionate shares of dividends and retained earnings. That treatment would eliminate the traditional difficulties with the corporate income tax, but it would create some additional sticky issues.[41] Those issues are as follows:

1. The tax would apply to income not realized. Individuals would be taxed according to income received as dividends and on income that the corporation retains. There is some question whether this would encourage greater corporate payout of earnings and thus might even lower the rate of real investment.

2. Many holders of corporate stock are tax-exempt entities (e.g., pension funds). Under this integrated structure, those entities would not pay individual income tax on their dividends and retained earnings, and there would be no collection of tax at the corporate level either. How could that revenue loss be replaced?

3. Sizable amounts of U.S. stocks are held by foreign entities. How would that income be treated? What country would be entitled to tax those U.S. dividends

[40]It may increase the market value of corporate stock and create capital gain income when the stock is sold.

[41]R. Glenn Hubbard, "Corporate Tax Integration: A View from the Treasury Department," *Journal of Economic Perspectives* 7 (Winter 1993): 115–32.

and retained earnings? And if it were a country other than the United States, how would that federal revenue loss be made up?

4. Corporations do not have single classes of stock. Corporations frequently have common stock, preferred stock, and possibly other varieties of equity-ownership representations. How would corporate income be divided equitably among those various classes of stock?

The alternate approach is partial integration. Partial integration would provide relief only on the share of corporate earnings that are distributed as dividends, either by giving some special credit to dividend recipients to account for the corporate income tax already paid on the flow or by applying the corporate income tax only to undistributed corporate profit. That relief would cut tax collections substantially, and there is the fear that it would appear to be an unwarranted tax break for business. Those two factors have kept interest in such reform low, although there is a revival in connection with the relatively slow growth rate of the U.S. economy and the slow rate of capital formation that has worked to produce that slow growth.[42]

International Harmonization

As economic activity becomes more globalized, many of the economic development struggles that have gone on for decades within countries have moved to international scope. One particularly important discussion involves whether corporate income taxes should be harmonized within a trade area, like the European Union, or whether competitive differences should be permitted. This has become an issue in the European Union because of dramatically different attitudes toward corporate income tax rates across its member countries. Rates are above 35 percent in, for instance, Germany and Italy but below 20 percent in Ireland and several of the countries added to the EU in 2004, including Poland, Slovakia, Latvia, and Hungary. This creates a strong fear of movements in international investment to take advantage of higher after-tax rates of return driven by the lower tax rates. The lower rates are not some sort of accident. They are the product of national economic strategies designed to boost economic growth driven by private investment—and evidence, particularly from Ireland, suggests that the strategy can make an important contribution.

Here is the dilemma: To what extent should countries be permitted the flexibility to compete on the basis of their corporate tax system and to what extent should fiscal competition be restrained, thus letting economic activity flow internationally

[42]Countries of the Organization for Economic Cooperation and Development (OECD) follow several different schemes for mitigating the extra tax. Some eliminate the extra tax at the corporate level by full deduction of dividends paid at the corporate level (Greece and Norway) and some eliminate at the individual level by giving full credit for tax paid by the corporation (Australia, Finland, Germany [partial], Italy, New Zealand). Others reduce the extra tax by lower rates on distributed profits, partial deduction of dividends paid, or partial credit for corporate tax on dividends received (Germany [partial], Iceland, Spain, Sweden, France, Ireland, United Kingdom, Austria, Denmark, Japan, Portugal). Belgium, Luxembourg, the Netherlands, Switzerland, and the United States do not provide accommodation.

in response to non-fiscal resource forces? Is fiscal competition unfair? Or is fiscal competition healthy? The debate continues to flourish without any clear resolution.

Payroll Taxation

Besides the broad-based individual and corporate income taxes, there are also narrow taxes on payrolls or wage and salary income alone, either levied on the employer or the employee.[43] Because they are collected from the employer, they are easier to enforce than are broader taxes based on filings by income recipients. These taxes include those levied by the federal government on employer and employee for the support of the Social Security system and for Medicare, those levied by federal and state governments on employers to support the unemployment compensation system, and earned-income taxes levied on employee wages and salaries by some local governments.[44] Most believe the real burden of these taxes, regardless of legal impact, is largely on the employee. When labor markets permit, employers simply adjust their compensation packages to account for the payroll tax to which they know they will be liable.

The payroll taxes have several peculiarities. First, they are narrow and exclude income forms more likely to be received by higher-income individuals, including interest, dividends, capital gains, and so on. That exclusion increases the likelihood that the tax will treat low-income people more harshly than high-income people. Moreover, people with roughly the same income would pay different amounts of tax according to the kinds of income. Therefore, these are both vertical- and horizontal-equity questions.

Second, the federal and state payroll taxes for the social insurance system have unusual statutory rate patterns. Taxability begins with the first dollar earned, and, except for the Medicare tax, the tax rate falls to zero on income above some maximum level earned in the year. That means the marginal rate structure is graduated downward, and for individuals above the maximum, the average rate falls as income rises. Because the tax applies with the first dollar earned, the payroll tax burden is more than that of the individual income tax for many low-income workers. For 2005, the federal tax supporting Social Security applied at a rate of 6.20 percent on the employee and 6.20 percent on the employer, but only the first $90,000 of earnings were taxed. The rate supporting Medicare is 1.45 percent on both employer and employee and there is no limit on the base. Therefore, the tax paid for a person earning $10,000 would be $1,530 (15.3 percent of total pay), whereas the tax paid by a person earning $100,000 would be $14,060 ($11,160 for Social Security—12.4 percent of the maximum taxable wage base of $90,000—plus $2,900 for

[43]Payroll taxes are also common in other countries.

[44]A good overview of the social insurance taxes appears in Committee on Ways and Means, U.S. House of Representatives, *1996 Green Book, Background Material and Data on the Programs within the Jurisdiction of the Committee on Ways and Means* (Washington, D.C.: Government Printing Office, 1996).

Medicare—the 2.9 percent rate applied to the full $100,000). The average rate on earnings is 14.06 percent for the higher-income person, and 15.3 percent for the person with lower earnings. As earnings increase, the average rate decreases.

The payroll tax financing the unemployment compensation system has federal and state components. The federal tax rate is 6.2 percent on earnings to $7,000, paid by the employer. However, if a state has an approved unemployment compensation system (and all fifty do), then up to 5.4 percent of the state rate is a full credit against the federal liability, leaving a net federal rate of 0.8 percent. States may have a taxable wage base higher than the federal limit (forty-one do). States also can levy rates on employers that differ from the 5.4 percent standard based on the unemployment experience rating of the firm: those with fewer layoffs pay lower tax than do those with more layoffs.[45] The idea is to encourage employers to stabilize their labor force while financing the unemployment compensation system.

Finally, the federal and state taxes are all earmarked. That is, their revenues are dedicated to finance only particular social insurance benefits. Because these benefits tend to be more valuable to lower-income individuals, the public generally accepts the unusual features of these taxes. Nevertheless, they do contribute to labor-market incentive effects by adding to the wedge between what employers pay and what employees retain. The funds generally are in overall surplus; investments of accumulated balances help support the U.S. government bond market.

Conclusion

The income tax has been the heart of the federal revenue system from the early years of the twentieth century, providing sizable revenue for global responsibilities and domestic programs. For more than 60 years, the individual income tax has been the dominant source, although the payroll taxes for social insurance have become almost as significant in overall finance. Corporate income taxes now play only a small role in finances. Individual income taxes also make a major contribution to the finances of state governments. While achieving progressivity, the income taxes do have problems of economic inefficiency, horizontal inequity, expensive collection, and failure of transparency. Corporate and payroll taxes raise considerable revenue, but they offer difficult challenges of equity and efficiency. There are enough preferences inserted in the income tax system to raise the belief that lawmakers have lost sight of the fact that the fundamental purpose of the system is to raise money to support government operations.

[45]Rates can range from zero (sixteen states) up to 10 percent (three states). Three states also tax the employee.

CHAPTER 8 QUESTIONS AND EXERCISES

1. Identify the important elements of the income tax in your state: What governments levy the tax, does the tax apply to individuals and corporations, how is the tax linked to federal income taxes, are the rates graduated, and is the tax indexed?
2. A midwestern state aids its institutions of higher education by giving a credit against its income tax equal to 50 percent of any gift to such institutions (subject to a limit of $50 credit per person). Two residents of that state, Mr. Blue (in the 15-percent federal tax bracket) and Ms. Jones (in the 35-percent federal tax bracket), each contribute $100 to an eligible state university.
   a. How much will state tax liabilities of each change as a result of their gifts?
   b. State income tax payments and contributions to charitable organizations (such as universities) are both currently deductible from the base used to compute federal tax liability. How much will federal tax liability change for Mr. Blue and Ms. Jones as a result of their contributions?
   c. Considering both changes in federal and state tax liability, what is the net after-tax cost of Mr. Blue's and Ms. Jones's gifts? (*Hint:* Subtract the changes in state and federal liability from $100.)
   d. Suppose the state program changed from a credit to a deduction. If the state tax rate were a flat 3 percent, how much would state liability for Mr. Blue and Ms. Jones change?
   e. From the previous computations, which approach (credit or deduction) do you suppose universities in the state would favor? Why?
3. Mr. Brown is in the 10-percent federal income tax bracket and wants to invest $8,000 in interest-earning assets. Mr. Black is in the 35-percent bracket and wants to invest $15,000. The current rate on a typical high-quality tax-exempt municipal bond is 5 percent and on a similar quality corporate bond is 6.5 percent. You are the financial adviser to both. Which investment would you recommend to each individual?
4. The Millers, a family of three filing joint returns, have the following information to prepare their federal income tax. Use the current federal tax forms (available at the local IRS office) to make your computation.

Salaries	65,000
Interest income, corporate bonds	1,000
Interest income, municipal bonds (issued in 1984)	1,500
State and local income taxes	800
Real estate taxes	750
General sales taxes	750
Home mortgage interest	3,350
Credit card interest	500
Cash contributions to charities	250
Interest on education loans	500
Hospital and doctor expenses	1,500

Compute the following:

a. Adjusted gross income
b. Taxable income
c. Tax
d. Average tax rate
e. Average effective-tax rate
f. Marginal tax rate

5. Ms. Busch has gathered these data about her finances:

Salary	92,000
Taxable interest received	2,500
Total itemized deductions	8,000

The personal exemption is $3,200. The standard deduction for a single filer is $5,000. Use the rate schedule in Figure 8–2 to compute the following:

a. Her tax
b. Her average effective-tax rate
c. Her average tax rate
d. Her marginal tax rate
e. Her accountant discovers a previously omitted personal deduction of $800. By how much does her federal tax liability fall with that addition?
f. Amazingly enough, the accountant now discovers a $250 credit omitted from previous calculations (but after discovering the $800 in part d). By how much does her federal tax liability fall because of this credit?

6. A proposed state income tax would require individuals with income of $15,000 or less to pay no tax, and those with incomes above $15,000 to pay a tax of 10 percent only on the part of their income tax that exceeds $15,000.

a. Could an individual pay an average tax rate of 7.5 percent under this system?
b. Could an individual pay an average tax rate of 10 percent under this system?
c. What average and marginal tax rates would individuals with these income levels face: $10,000, $20,000, $40,000, and $150,000?

Explain each of your answers and provide examples to justify your conclusions.

7. The Ukrainian tax system in late 1990s had several components. The personal income tax (calculated and paid on a monthly basis) had these brackets:

zero	if income was below one NTM
10%	for income from one NTM + 1 KBV to five NTM
20%	for income from five NTM + 1 KBV to ten NTM, plus the tax on five NTM
30%	for income from ten NTM + 1 KBV to fifteen NTM, plus the tax on ten NTM
40%	for income from fifteen NTM + 1 KBV to twenty-five NTM, plus the tax on fifteen NTM

50% for income above twenty-five NTM, plus the tax on twenty-five NTM.

KBV, karbovantsi; NTM, non-taxed minimum.

The NTM was 1,400,000 KBV (one U.S. dollar was worth about 180,000 Ukrainian KBV). In September 1995, the average monthly salary was 9 million KBV. Use of NTM provides an easy way of adjusting the entire tax structure for the impact of inflation.

The employer paid payroll taxes at these rates: 37 percent to the social insurance fund, 12 percent to the Chernobyl fund, and 2 percent to the employment fund. Employees also pay 1 percent to the employment fund.

a. Analysts calculate the tax wedge—defined to be the difference between what the employer must pay to hire an employee and the amount that the employee receives net of all taxes as a percentage of the employee's net—in examining the nature of tax systems. Compute the total tax wedge for a worker at the average monthly salary, at twice the average, and at five times the average.
b. Compute the average effective tax rate and the marginal tax rate for a worker at the three salary levels from part a.
c. Comment on the likely incentive effects of this tax structure.

8. The Bartonia Company manufactures grommets in Georgia and sells them directly to industrial customers in Georgia, Florida, and South Carolina. The company's profit for last year was $15,000,000. The company has its manufacturing plant and headquarters in Georgia, it has warehouses in South Carolina and Florida, and sales forces in each state. Here are some of its financial statistics:

	Payroll	Property	Sales
Georgia	5,000,000	35,000,000	6,000,000
South Carolina	1,000,000	5,000,000	13,000,000
Florida	500,000	400,000	1,000,000
Total	6,500,000	40,400,000	20,000,000

a. Suppose each state uses a simple three-factor apportionment formula. What share of company profit would each state tax?
b. Make that same calculation, but suppose each state double weights the sales factor.
c. Make the calculation with each using only the sales factor.
d. Assume now that Georgia adopts the single sales factor and the other states use double-weighted sales.
e. Assume now that South Carolina adopts the single sales factor and the other states use double-weighted sales.
f. Explain why manufacturing firms in some state have pressed for use of the single sales factor? Why have nationwide business organizations not made this switch an issue?

Case for Discussion

CASE 8–1

Tax Credits and Government Policy

Tax credits are a popular mechanism for support of many activities. They give the public a choice about how their tax payments are used, and that choice is entirely voluntary. Taxpayers can, in essence, direct their tax payments to particular programs that interest them the most.

The state of Arizona provides such a tax credit program for the support of school districts. The details of the program are outlined in the article that follows.

Consider the following questions:

1. Is this tax credit program consistent with the fundamental principles of tax policy?
2. What are the advantages and disadvantages of using a credit rather than a deduction for this sort of program?
3. Are there revisions to the program that could retain advantages without the significant problems you have identified?

Wealthy schools get most tax-credit funds

Anne Ryman
The Arizona Republic
Dec. 27, 2004, 12:00 AM

NORTHEAST VALLEY—Schools in wealthier areas of the northeast Valley continue to generate the most education tax-credit donations, a trend that disturbs an advocate for fair education policies.

Tax-credit money must be spent on extracurricular programs under state law. The more money a school generates, the more it can spend on such activities as after-school clubs and field trips.

"It's really a case of the rich getting richer," said Tim Hogan, an attorney who has fought all the way to the U.S. Supreme Court for equal funding in Arizona schools.

Hogan said the state should consider changing the system so it's fairer to schools in less-wealthy areas.

One example: Desert Mountain High School in north Scottsdale took in nearly a half-million dollars in 2003, while Coronado High School in south Scottsdale brought about $60,000.

From "Wealthy Schools Get Most Tax-Credit Funds" by Anne Ryman, *The Arizona Republic,* December 27, 2004. Used with permission. Permission does not imply endorsement.

The disparities are even greater between some school districts. Donations in the 8,800-student Isaac Elementary School District in central Phoenix totaled $30,850, while one 596-student school in northeast Phoenix, Desert Shadows Elementary, raised about the same amount.

Hogan said parents can't be faulted for donating to their children's schools. But he said the state should consider changing the tax-credit system so schools in lower-wealth areas can share more funding.

Hogan is unsure what the solution is, but it could include giving greater tax incentives for donations to schools in less-wealthy areas.

Taxpayers can donate up to $200 individually or $250 per couple to the public school of their choice. The donation can be claimed as a state tax credit, meaning it is subtracted from the amount of taxes owed.

Last year, the Scottsdale Unified School District generated $1.7 million, which was the second-highest in Maricopa County behind Mesa Public Schools with $4.5 million. The Paradise Valley Unified School District had the third-highest donations with $1.3 million.

Donations to individual schools varied widely. Tonalea Elementary School in south Scottsdale reported $10,825, while Kiva Elementary in wealthier Paradise Valley had nearly five times that much.

School district officials recognize the disparities among schools, and they say there is no easy solution.

Parents typically want to give to their child's school, said Bob Flach, the Scottsdale district's chief financial officer.

Flach said that if the tax credit were higher, more parents would consider giving a portion to other schools. As it is, the current $250 limit per couple doesn't go that far at a school, he said.

Flach said people also may not realize they can split their $250 tax-credit donations among schools.

Although public schools are closed for winter break for the rest of December, people can still make tax-credit donations by mailing their checks to schools. Checks must be postmarked by Dec. 31.

CHAPTER 9

Major Tax Structures: Taxes on Goods and Services

Governments in the United States collected more than $454 billion from taxes levied on goods and services in 2004.[1] Federal excises and customs duties yielded $90 billion—far behind the collections from individual income, Social Security payroll, and corporate income taxes. State and local sales and excise taxes generated $364.4 billion, in total the most significant base for these governments. As pointed out in an earlier chapter, however, American reliance on goods and services levies, the consumption base overall is less than that in most industrialized democracies.

Taxes on goods and services have several desirable features as a part of a revenue system. First, they can provide considerable revenue when they apply to a broad base, thus allowing diversification from other tax bases. A range of alternative tax bases can be important because heavy use of any tax is likely to bring out all of its worst efficiency and equity problems. Second, the consumption taxes provide a means for extracting payment from individuals with high economic capacity and low current income, including those who have successfully evaded the income tax or are living off of inherited wealth. If the income tax cheat enjoys an elegant lifestyle with purchases from honest vendors, some tax is collected when purchases are made. Third, some taxes on goods and services may function as quasi-prices to collect for social costs or to act as surrogates for charges for certain government services. Finally, some argue that consumption taxes can have important desirable production effects because they tax according to what people take from the economy (consumption), not according to what of value they add to the economy (income), and because they encourage saving. Indeed, consumption taxes distribute the cost of government according to the individual's own assessment of what private goods and services he or she can afford to purchases. That's how the cost of producing private goods gets distributed, after all, so why shouldn't the same distribution concept apply to the cost of government services as well?

Goods and services taxes may be general or selective, specific or ad valorem, single stage or multistage, for general or earmarked purposes, legally applied to the

[1]Bureau of Economic Analysis, U.S. Department of Commerce, *National Income and Product Accounts.*

buyer or the seller, and all these varieties appear in the slate of goods and services taxes that governments now levy. Before considering the taxes in detail and the special issues each may involve, here is a quick summary of some structural distinctions:

1. **General or Selective.** A general sales tax applies to all transactions at a level of economic activity, except for certain listed exemptions (e.g., a sales tax applied to all sales at retail except those of food). A selective sales tax (commonly called an excise tax) applies only to enumerated transactions (e.g., a lodging tax applied to room rentals for 30 days or less).

2. **Specific or Ad Valorem.** A specific tax (or unit tax) applies only to the number of physical units bought or sold (e.g., a motor-fuel tax might be 50 cents per gallon of fuel). An ad valorem tax applies to the value (number of units times price per unit) of the transaction (e.g., a lodging tax of 10 percent of the hotel bill).

3. **Multistage or Single Stage.** A tax may apply every time a transaction occurs (multistage tax) or only at one stage in the production-and-distribution process (single-stage tax). The taxed stage may be at the manufacturer level, at the wholesaler or distributor level, or at the retail level. A multistage tax would apply at more than one of these points of exchange.[2]

4. **General Fund or Earmarked.** Excise taxes often are earmarked to special funds for expenditure only on specific purposes, as opposed to being collected for the general purposes of government. For example, most motor-fuel tax revenue collected by American states goes into special funds for highway-associated expenditure. Unfortunately, such fund earmarking creates rigidity in the budget process, and revenue flows into these funds may not reflect need for public services.[3] Only if revenue going to the fund reflects demand for the service financed by the fund does earmarking make a positive contribution. That can happen when purchase of the taxed item is complementary to use of the government service, that is, when there is a close relationship between purchase of the taxed item and consumption of the government service.

Tables 9–1 and 9–2 present an overview of general and selective goods or service tax collections to federal, state, and local governments. In the tables, the selective excises are divided into four main groups: (1) sumptuary excises applied "to control the consumption of items that are considered immoral or unhealthy,"[4]

---

[2]Governments have occasionally levied gross receipts (turnover) taxes that apply at a low statutory rate on all business activities, and such taxes are sometimes still proposed. They harm economic competitiveness, distort across types of businesses, are hidden and significantly understate their actual effective rate (probably why some states have recently considered them), and are grossly inequitable. See Charles E. McLure, Jr., "Why Ohio Should Not Introduce a Gross Receipts Tax—Testimony on the Proposed Commercial Activity Tax," *State Notes* (April 18, 2005): 213–15. Ohio ignored his wise advice and passed the tax anyway. The state will be sorry.

[3]The revenues may also simply substitute for other government resources that would have been provided even without the dedicated tax. Because revenues are fungible, it is difficult to ensure that money supports only the dedicated purpose.

[4]Sijbren Cnossen, *Excise Systems, A Global Study of the Selective Taxation of Goods and Services* (Baltimore: Johns Hopkins University Press, 1977), 8.

Table 9–1
Federal Taxes on Goods and Services (fiscal year 2003)

	Total ($ thousands)	Percent Federal Receipts (except Social Insurance)
Transportation		
Truck, trailer, and semi-trailer chassis	1,608,208	0.15%
Tires	403,892	0.04%
Aviation fuels	797,873	0.07%
Motor fuels	32,813,893	3.07%
Fuel used commercially on inland waterways	111,058	0.01%
Transportation of persons by air	6,185,415	0.58%
Use of international air travel facilities	1,452,015	0.14%
Tax on heavy vehicle use	911,445	0.09%
Diesel fuel used by trains	162,654	0.02%
Transportation of property by air	455,209	0.04%
Environmental		
Ozone-depleting chemicals	15,293	0.00%
Gas guzzler	126,685	0.01%
Sumptuary		0.00%
Alcoholic beverages	8,470,199	0.79%
Tobacco products	15,433,159	1.44%
Other		
Luxury passenger vehicles*	65,162	0.01%
Coal	517,531	0.05%
Certain vaccines	179,009	0.02%
Telephone and teletypewriter services	5,809,503	0.54%
Private foundation investment income	267,721	0.03%
Firearms and ammunition	193,420	0.02%
Sport fishing equipment	97,986	0.01%
Tax on policies issued by foreign insurers	292,897	0.03%
Total excise collections	69,490,000	6.50%
Total customs duties and fees	19,862,000	1.86%
Total excises and customs	89,352,000	8.36%

*Expired, January 1, 2003.
SOURCE: SOI Bulletin (Spring 2005) and Budget of the U.S. Government.

(2) transport excises potentially defensible as proxy service charges for transportation facilities, (3) environmental excises levied "to improve efficiency in the use of resources"[5] by causing recognition of damage associated with the taxed product, and (4) miscellaneous excises that have been applied for reasons that include the capture of extraordinary taxpaying capacity (the recent federal luxury excises) and

[5]Ibid., 9.

Table 9–2
State and Local Taxes on Goods and Services, Fiscal 2003 ($ thousands)

	Total ($)	Share of Total Tax Revenue (%)	State ($)	Share of Total Tax Revenue (%)	Local ($)	Share of Total, Tax Revenue (%)
Sales and gross receipts	337,786,567	36.0%	273,811,221	49.9%	63,975,346	16.4%
General sales and gross receipts	229,222,301	24.4%	184,596,707	33.6%	44,625,594	11.4%
Selective sales and gross receipts	108,564,266	11.6%	89,214,514	16.3%	19,349,752	5.0%
Sumptuary						
Alcoholic beverage	4,756,547	0.5%	4,398,717	0.8%	357,830	0.1%
Tobacco products	11,806,700	1.3%	11,482,064	2.1%	324,636	0.1%
Pari-mutuals	*		302,110	0.1%	*	
Amusements incl. gaming	*		4,485,261	0.8%	*	
Transportation						
Motor fuel	33,378,664	3.6%	32,269,077	5.9%	1,109,587	0.3%
Miscellaneous Public utilities	21,014,692	2.2%	10,557,058	1.9%	10,457,634	2.7%
Insurance premiums	*		12,522,736	2.3%	*	
Other selective sales	37,607,663	4.0%	13,197,491	2.4%	7,100,065	1.8%

* Data for local governments for this tax category are unavailable, but total amounts are small.
SOURCE: U.S. Bureau of Census, Governments Division.

the lure of taxing the nonresident (lodging taxes). State yields, combining selective and general taxes, are more than triple the amount of federal excises and almost four times the amount of local general and selective excises. Most of the revenue comes from the "traditional" excises on tobacco products, alcoholic beverages, and fuels. In the worldwide context, these are the "big three" excises in terms of revenue production.

Selective excise revenues tend to grow slowly. Because many have specific rates, their yields do not pick up the effects of increasing prices, and substantial revenue increases require higher statutory rates. When rates have not increased, the share of total revenue from the excise tends to decline. Governments sometimes preserve the administrative ease of specific rates (enforcement officers need only track the items, not their value) while protecting revenue amid inflation by means of automatic adjustment formulae of various types. For instance, some countries of the former Soviet Union define excise and import duty rates in terms of the "euro" (the monetary unit of the European Union), rather than their local currency. That protects against both inflation and exchange rate deterioration with no need for regular changes in the tax law. Excise revenue can also be vulnerable to tastes and preferences of the population—for instance, in the United States, cigarette tax revenue has declined dramatically as fewer people smoke.

Almost half of state tax revenue in the United States (and an important amount of major city revenue) comes from taxes on consumption, either from general sales taxes or selective excise taxes. General sales tax revenue is much greater, producing about one-third of all state tax revenue. Mississippi and West Virginia imposed the first general sales taxes during the early 1930s when existing state revenue sources (predominantly property taxes) were unable to finance state spending of the period. The retail sales taxes (RST) got many states through the Great Depression—they could produce revenue even when the property tax failed—and the taxes quickly spread to almost half the states before World War II. These sales taxes were the largest single source of state tax revenue from 1947 until 1998, when their yield was surpassed by that from individual income taxes (until 2003, when the RST returned to the top position). The RST bailed state governments out of fiscal crisis during the Great Depression and financed the significant expansion of state government activities in the years after World War II. Many local governments levy general sales taxes as well, and revenue from these taxes is second only to the property tax in overall significance to local governments.

Selective excises are also widespread among state and local governments, but far less productive. All states levy at least one selective excise, the most common being taxes on motor fuels, tobacco products, alcoholic beverages, public utilities, and insurance premiums. Excise taxes on gaming, part of the amusement excise category, are significant in a few states (more than half a billion dollars in Nevada, Illinois, and Indiana), but their effect is minor in aggregate.[6] Many local governments levy selective excises as well, with public utility taxes being most productive.

Items or services for consumption typically pass through several stages of production, each performed by a separate economic unit, as they go from raw material to the product desired by the user. Figure 9–1 outlines that flow, from the extraction of raw materials to use by that customer. Between each stage there is an exchange transaction, a buyer and a seller, and at each transaction, a consumption-based tax may apply. Some taxes are designed to apply at more than one level of the flow, as is the case with gross-receipt (turnover) taxes and value-added taxes (VATs). Other taxes apply at only one stage of the flow: manufacture, wholesale, or retail. Unless special allowances have been made in structuring the tax (as is described later in the discussion about VATs) single-stage, retail-level taxes cause the least economic damage associated with the revenue they raise.

There are three reasons why single-stage taxes, especially retail, are preferred. First, price increases from tax paid by the customer will likely equal the amount received by the government. Multistage and pre-retail taxes tend to pyramid or cascade. For example, any manufacturer-level tax paid would be part of the cost seen by the wholesaler—that is, if the wholesaler buys garden tractors from a manufacturer for $1,500 plus a 10 percent excise, the wholesaler would undoubtedly see its unit cost as $1,650. When selling the tractor to a retailer, the wholesaler would add

[6]These are revenues from casino excises (taxes on gross receipts, number of gaming devices, or admissions) and are distinct from taxes collected on profits earned by the casinos or on their property and from the profits states receive from lotteries they operate.

Figure 9–1
The Flow of Production and Distribution

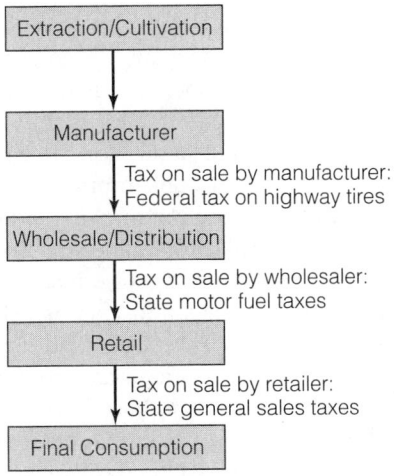

a markup percentage to that cost—say, 50 percent—to a charge of $2,475 ($1,650 plus 50 percent of the $1,650) to the retailer. The same markup process works for the retailer. When the customer finally purchases the tractor, that 10-percent excise would have increased the price of the tractor by more than $150—the price of the product would increase by more than the tax that the government receives. A single-stage retail tax would not have that impact. Second, multistage taxes strike with each market transaction (purchase and sale). Integrated firms (e.g., those that manufacture, wholesale, and retail) have fewer such transactions and hence lower tax embedded in product cost.[7] Single-stage application (particularly at retail) eliminates that effect. Third, retail application cause no incentive for the production process to move to a stage of trade above the point taxed to reduce the base to which the tax applies. In general, the more total product value produced after the tax is levied, the lower the tax. Retail application leaves no point for escape.

The retail application, however, does requires some greater administrative effort because there are more retailers than there are manufacturers or wholesalers and hence more taxpayers for tax administrators to track. Many selective excises levied by both federal and state governments—motor fuel, tobacco products, alcoholic beverages, etc.—are collected at the manufacturer or distributor level because of those economies. These taxes are usually applied on a specific basis for ease of enforcement—the amount paid for the product at the point of taxation does not determine how much tax is owed. It is the physical units alone that determine liability.

[7]Integrated firms move the product through stages of production, but these are bookkeeping transactions within the firm, not sales and purchases, so they are not taxable.

The Equity Question

A difficult policy issue for consumption taxation is that of dealing with vertical equity. Evidence from many studies done at many different times and many different environments shows that consumption spending is higher as a share of household income for lower-income households than it is for higher-income households. This is true for total consumption, and it is also true for categories of expenditure. This creates an equity problem for taxes on consumption: the effective tax rate (consumption expenditure times the statutory tax rate divided by household income) is higher for low-income households than for higher-income ones. The distribution of the tax burden is regressive. Table 9–3 shows effective rate evidence for federal excises and for the Minnesota retail sales and excises. This is the pattern that is typically found in analysis of virtually all excises and it raises a difficult issue in taxation. Consumption expenditure is regarded as a reasonable base for distributing the cost of government and consumption-based taxes are effective producers of substantial revenue. But the distribution pattern is regressive. Lawmakers must do a balancing act between the revenue productivity of such taxes and the equity issue.

These taxes also raise horizontal equity issues. Consumers have varying tastes and preferences in terms both of overall consumption and consumption of particular items. That variation in consumption pattern within household-income groups creates variation in effective tax rates borne by households simply based on preferences. Therefore, on top of the vertical equity questions that consumption-based

Table 9–3
Effective Tax Rates for Federal Excises and Minnesota Retail Sales and Excise Taxes

		Minnesota State Consumption Taxes (2004)	
	Federal Excise (2003)	Retail Sales Tax	State Excises
Lowest Quintile	2.30%	5.9%	1.9%
Second Quintile	1.40%	4.1%	1.1%
Third Quintile	1.10%	3.4%	0.8%
Fourth Quintile	0.90%	3.1%	0.7%
Highest Quintile	0.50%	2.3%	0.3%
Top 5%	0.40%	2.0%	0.2%
Top 1%	0.30%	1.1%	0.1%

Sources: 2005 Minnesota Tax Incidence Study (Revised April 27, 2005) and Congressional Budget Office, *Historical Effective Tax Rates: 1979–2003.*

taxes raise, there are also horizontal fairness problems as well. The extent to which these issues matter for policy depends on the reason for levying the tax. When revenue is the principal reason, the policy questions are greatest. But, as later sections describe, not all selective excises are levied purely for the revenue they generate and for those non-revenue excises, the equity issues are somewhat less pressing.

Selective Excise Taxation

Selective excises apply differential tax treatment to particular products or services, causing those purchasing or selling them to bear greater tax burden than general measurements of tax-bearing capacity (income, wealth, or total consumption) would otherwise indicate. Although these excises yield revenue—seldom enough to be a major factor for general government operations—their major attractiveness often lies on other grounds or with other special purposes. Indeed, their intent is often discriminatory, to try to charge people for the social cost of their actions. When that is the plan, selective excises could be judged effective, at least partly, on the basis of nonrevenue effects, not collections.[8]

Luxury Excises

Governments levy luxury excises on goods or services whose purchase is deemed to reflect extraordinary taxpaying ability. They attempt to distribute the cost of government to those best able to pay, so luxury excises may be evaluated on normal revenue-policy standards. If the luxury excises raise substantial revenue, they may ease rate pressure on other taxes; seldom does that happen. Such excises have been applied to jewelry, furs, entertainment, services, and the like. Recent federal luxury excises have applied to expensive aircraft, automobiles, yachts, furs, and jewelry; all but that on automobiles were repealed in 1993, and the automobile tax ended in 2003.[9]

The objections to luxury excises are several. First, such taxes distort producer and consumer choices: because the tax establishes a difference between the resource-cost ratios in production and the price ratios to which consumers respond, there is unnecessary loss of economic welfare in the economic system.[10] Purchasers

[8]The best general discussions of selective excises are Cnossen, *Excise Systems* and Sijbren Cnossen, ed., *Theory and Practice of Excise Taxation, Smoking, Drinking, Gambling, Polluting, and Driving* (Oxford, U.K.: Oxford University Press, 2005).

[9]These taxes applied only to the amount of the transaction above a particular threshold.

[10]John A. Tatom, "The Welfare Cost of an Excise Tax" *Federal Reserve Bank of St. Louis Review* 58 (November 1976): 14–15.

and sellers change their behavior because of the tax, and that brings an economic loss to them. They aren't behaving the way they would like to because of the tax. Second, and pragmatically more important, the tax distributes burdens on the basis of personal preferences for the taxed items. The tax imposes higher effective rates on people within an income class who have high taste for the taxed commodities or services. Furthermore, low-income people buy the taxed items; there are few products with no low-income purchasers. Third, there are administrative problems with these excises. Because retailers would have difficulty separating the sales of the taxed luxury items from other sales, these excises typically apply to the manufacturer or wholesaler level. They thus fall prey to the objections to any nonretail levy.[11] But another administrative problem emerges in the definition of the taxed commodity. For example, a handful of states tax soft drinks, but what is a soft drink?[12] Are powdered-drink mixes, imitation orange juice, flavored waters, bottled chocolate drink, and so forth to be taxed? Is low-alcohol beer a soft drink? How is a concentrate, sold to be mixed with water, to be equated for tax purposes with bottled drinks? In each case, a difficult administrative problem in interpreting and applying the tax may well be handled only by separate, brand-name determinations, a process that is time-consuming for the tax-department rule makers.

Even though luxury excises can have considerable political appeal, they are not strong elements of a revenue system. Revenue growth for most luxury excises is low, largely because their specific nature does not allow capture of price effects. They do yield some revenue, although at considerable collection cost, and who but industry lobbyists will stand up for luxury purchases? How important is the revenue? In fiscal 1992, the last year before repeal of the federal luxury excises on boats, aircraft, jewelry, and furs, these excises produced $29 million, a year in which the federal individual income tax alone generated more than $475 billion.[13] As taxes levied for revenue purposes, luxury excises do not measure up.

Sumptuary Excises

Sumptuary excises seek to discourage excess consumption of items considered unhealthy or unsafe, both for the consumer and for the public as a whole. The best examples are taxes on tobacco products and alcoholic beverages: the prices paid to producers do not reflect the social cost of product use and abuse in terms of damage to health, property, and families.[14] The tax may charge for these external disec-

---

[11]The recent federal luxury excises were at the retail level. They created problems because they applied only on prices above a threshold, an extra complication for compliance recordkeeping and enforcement.

[12]Is this an example of a luxury excise? Probably so—it doesn't make much sense as anything else and very little sense as a luxury excise, either.

[13]"Selected Historical and Other Data," *SOI Bulletin* 16 (Winter 1996–1997): 167.

[14]One study estimates that a much higher excise on beer would have dramatically reduced the number of young drivers killed in automobile accidents (1,660 lives saved between 1982 and 1988). See Michael Grossman, Frank J. Chaloupka, Henry Saffer, and Adit Laixuthai, "Effects of Alcohol Price Policy on Youth," *National Bureau of Economic Research*, Working Paper No. 4385 (1993).

onomies to compensate society in ways not attainable by the market. (The taxes may also have moral overtones and are sometimes labeled "sin taxes;" along with tobacco and alcoholic beverage taxes, special taxes are also applied to gambling activities, and these taxes may be considered sumptuary as well.) Taxes on alcoholic beverages and tobacco products are among the oldest taxes in the United States; indeed, an early test of the new central government was the Whiskey Rebellion (1794)—a violent challenge to a federal excise.

Demand for items subject to these excises is relatively insensitive to price, particularly in the short-term, so consumption seldom changes much with imposition of the tax. Legislatures do not propose truly prohibitive tax rates because they want tax revenue—a curious balancing between discouraging harmful activity and maintaining revenue flow from the activity. Increases in sumptuary excise rates generally elicit minimal protest from consumers, although sellers complain about illegal (nontaxed) competition. Bootlegging is a continual problem; one enforcement procedure uses stamps applied to units on which tax has been paid at the manufacturer level. The tax is collected early and enforcement agents need only look for the stamp to verify that tax has been paid. Sizable rate differences among states swamp control structures with evasion.[15]

But, within limits, these excises do raise revenue with minimal public protest. Complaints normally come from producers rather than consumers, and legislators are usually wary of overt support for those interests, unless the producers are concentrated in the legislator's home district. The importance of producer politics is demonstrated by the fact that state cigarette taxes have historically been lowest in the states where tobacco production is economically important.

There are three primary objections to sumptuary excises. First, the demand for the products taxed is often highly price-inelastic, so the tax has little short-term effect on the amount of the product purchased. It may divert consumption from desirable or beneficial activities to pay the tax. (The extreme example sometimes quoted by lobbyists is the alcoholic who fails to buy milk for his children because of the tax he pays on liquor.) Responses to higher taxes increase as producers and consumers have time to adjust, however. Second, the absolute burden of these taxes may be particularly heavy on low-income families and may even involve higher effective tax rates on lower-income families. The tax is applied, after all, on the basis of personal preferences, so the teetotaling millionaire pays less liquor tax than the whiskey-drinking laborer. Third, a problem results from the specific (not ad valorem) nature of these excises. Even though that basis is logical, because any social cost involved would be related to the amount of consumption, not its value, it does discriminate against lower-priced brands and those who purchase them. If the tax is $10 per gallon on distilled spirits, the effective rate is much higher on liquor sold for $6 per fifth than on liquor sold for $10 per fifth. This is a special problem if users of the lower-priced brands come from low-income groups. Furthermore, the specific nature of the tax obscures the actual ratio of the tax to the net price, which frequently turns out to be high.

---

[15]For a review of the problem, see Advisory Commission on Intergovernmental Relations, *Cigarette Tax Evasion: A Second Look,* Report A-100 (Washington, D.C.: ACIR, 1985).

Benefit-Base Excises

Benefit-base excises, primarily transportation-related taxes, operate as a quasi price for a public good.[16] Highway use normally involves consumption of motor fuel, so a tax on fuel purchase approximates a charge for the use of the highway. These taxes allocate cost to road users and have been less expensive to administer than direct user charges (tolls) for streets, roads, and highways. The motor-fuel tax thus operates as a surrogate for price. It does have difficulties for the truck-to-car relationship because differences in incremental costs of providing highways are difficult to calibrate and relate to motor-fuel use, but the system functions to generally distribute cost of operating the highways to those more heavily using the highways.[17] For a benefit-base levy to be possible, there must be strong complementarity between the taxed commodity and the public good being financed. The motor-fuel tax provides one of the rare instances of such a relationship.

There are additional questions: whether motor-fuel tax revenues should be segregated for highway construction and maintenance only, whether these funds should be spent for all transportation (mass as well as highway), and whether motor-fuel tax revenue should receive the same budget treatment as other revenue, with no earmarking for transportation. These questions are not yet answered, but if revenues from the gasoline tax do not go to transportation projects, then they are probably subject to the complaints made against luxury excises. They sacrifice their benefit-base logic and must be evaluated on ability-to-pay grounds. On the other hand, if revenue from the gasoline tax goes exclusively to highways, there is a substantial bias for highways in the total transportation system. In most European countries, motor-fuel taxes are high, revenues are not dedicated to use for highways, and the taxes are considered part of an environmental strategy to make travel by automobile less attractive relative to mass transportation, not as part of a user-pays strategy for financing highways.

The benefit-base logic of highway or motor-fuel taxes suggests that the tax should be specific because the number of units of motor fuel used is related to the use of the service. At the same time, however, the specific nature of the tax means that, in times of inflation, there are significant pressures placed on the motor-fuel tax fund because of highway operation and construction cost increases. Some states have attempted to avert the need for legislated rate increases by tying the specific tax rate to the prevailing price of gasoline, so that as the price of gasoline is higher, the specific gasoline tax rate is higher.[18] This strategy has not succeeded over the long run because episodes of declining prices brought significant decreases in revenue and price fluctuations brought major revenue instability. Linking the rate to a general inflation index or road-operation and maintenance costs shows greater permanent promise.

---

[16]The federal logic of certain excises as user charges is discussed in Chapter 11.

[17]Alternative power sources, such as electricity, create a problem.

[18]An extensive review of state gasoline tax problems and of variable-rate structures can be found in John H. Bowman and John L. Mikesell, "Recent Changes in State Gasoline Taxation: An Analysis of Structure and Rates," *National Tax Journal* 36 (June 1983): 163–82.

Regulatory and Environmental Excises

Excises may be applied to improve resource use efficiency, much like the intent of the sumptuary excises, but without the moral or ethical overtones and without the explicit revenue objectives of the sumptuary taxes. Regulatory excises do such things as tax pollutants (the taxes on ozone-depleting chemicals) or penalize automakers not producing fuel efficient automobiles (the gas guzzler tax). They reflect the ideas that the polluter must pay and that particular actions should be discouraged or penalized. As described in Chapter 7, they seek to make buyers and sellers cognizant of the full social cost of their actions. The United States is far behind Europe in the use of "green taxes" designed to explicitly make the polluter pay for the cost that pollution imposes on others. Some proponents of environmental excises have argued that there is a "double dividend" from such taxes. First, the imposition of the tax corrects for the external and unpriced damaging impact of the pollutant. Second, the revenue generated by the tax can be used to replace other taxes that distort efficient operations of the economy. Thus, the tax can provide two desirable impacts for the economy, not just one.

The big question: how high should the environmental tax rate be? Europeans are more willing to use the market to get corrections made and to collect information from market responses to adjust the tax rates. Americans continue to insist on the outmoded command and control mechanism of regulations and restraints than to set appropriate environmental tax rates and then let the market function.

Other Excises

There are some other miscellaneous excises, as well. Selective excises on imported items (customs duties) are often levied for revenue and to protect local producers during development. Excises may also be narrowly applied to finance research or trade promotion activities, as with agricultural commodity excises functioning through marketing boards or lodging excises used to promote tourism. Particularly narrow excises are often dedicated to a particular purpose, as with the federal vaccine injury compensation fund financed by an excise on certain childhood disease vaccines or the federal excise on fishing equipment that supports sportfish restoration programs. Across all the selective excises, however, the basic criteria for success include "large sales volume, few producers, inelastic demand, ready definability, and no close substitutes unless these can be included in the base."[19] Few selective excises meet all the criteria.

---

[19] Cnossen, *Excise Systems*, 9.

General Taxes on Goods and Services: Retail Sales and Value-Added Taxes

Consumption represents an alternative to income as a general basis for distributing the cost of government among elements of the private economy. Many people believe that making a switch from heavy reliance on taxes on individual and corporate income would be good public policy. There are two main elements in this argument:

1. Increase economic growth: a switch from income to consumption as a tax base ". . . will reduce the difference between the pre- and post-tax return to saving that encourages taxpayers to consume rather than to save, so saving will be encouraged by the change and the growth path of the economy may subsequently move upward."[20] Future consumption (in other words, saving) is not penalized in comparison with current consumption. The higher saving improves rates of capital formation, labor productivity, and standards of living.

2. Improve fundamental equity: consumption represents a fundamentally more equitable way for assigning shares of the cost of government than does annual income: ". . . each individual [measures tax capacity] for himself when, in the light of all his present circumstances and future prospects, he decides on the scale of his personal living expenses. Thus a tax based on actual spending rates each individual's spending capacity according to the yardstick which he applies to himself."[21] Using the amount that the individual believes that he or she can afford in purchases of private goods and services as the standard for distributing a major share of the total cost of government would seem to be appropriate for financing government in a market economy.

A general consumption tax may be administered either directly, through administrative systems that follow more or less the same filing and collection structures as the current income tax, or indirectly, through a sales tax following either the multistage collection scheme of the VAT or the single-stage collection scheme of the RST. The three administrative systems are economically identical ways of taxing consumption.

A direct consumption tax uses the fact that, by definition, individual income less personal saving equals consumption. Therefore, if a household had income of $75,000 and saved $35,000 in the year, then its consumption was $40,000 and that base can be taxed accordingly.[22] No government currently uses such a system, possibly because of some questions about defining and reporting savings, but, because of the several provisions in the federal income tax system that provide preferences

[20]S. Cnossen and C. Sanford, *Taxing Consumption* (Paris: Organization of Economic Cooperation and Development, 1988), 32.
[21]Nicholas Kaldor, *An Expenditure Tax* (London: Allen and Unwin, 1955), 47.
[22]One careful analysis of such a system: Laurence S. Seidman, *The USA Tax: A Progressive Consumption Tax* (Cambridge, Mass.: MIT Press, 1997). The flat tax proposals of the 1996 election cycle and later were also driven in part by a desire to move toward consumption taxation.

for saving (the many retirement savings programs, provision for medical saving accounts, provisions for tax-preferred saving for education expenses, etc.), the current federal tax is often described as a hybrid income-consumption tax, rather than a pure income tax. Some proponents of consumption taxation argue that the easiest and least disruptive way to transform the federal system into a pure consumption tax would be to dramatically broaden the preferences of savings already in the system. In other words, a direct tax would build on existing foundations in a manner that would be impossible for an indirect approach.

There are two alternative systems for collecting an indirect and transaction-based (i.e., on individual purchases or "over the counter" rather than through individual filing) general tax on consumption. The forms are the RST and the VAT. The RST is the American format.[23] The VAT is the format used by virtually all central governments in the industrialized world, including all members of the Organization for Economic Cooperation and Development (OECD) except the United States, all countries of Latin America, all countries of the former Soviet Union, and all countries that would like to join the European Union (it is a membership requirement). The formats are not necessarily mutually exclusive; for instance, Canadian provinces levy RST, whereas the federal government levies a VAT (called the goods and services tax).[24] Statutory rates for these tax may be quoted on either a tax-inclusive or a tax-exclusive basis. Sidebar 9–1 explains the difference and shows how to switch between the two methods.

Both taxes can apply a general, uniform tax on household consumption with minimal distortion of production and consumption choice, but they differ in how each accomplishes that end and, in practice, differ in the extent to which they are general, uniform, and non-distorting. The U.S. RST applies to household consumption by taxing only the last stage of the full production-distribution process. Tax that otherwise would be applied on earlier purchases is suspended through a system of exemption certificates. The VAT applies to each transaction in the full production-distribution process, but, in usual application, every purchaser except the final customer has tax refunded through credits for tax the business has collected on its sales. Thus, when they are functioning properly, both systems relieve tax on all transactions but the last—the one to the final household customer; the difference between the two taxes lies in the administrative mechanism. Both mechanisms are described in detail later because they are at the essence of each tax and are the distinguishing feature between the two taxes.

In contrast to direct taxes, indirect taxes are extremely difficult to personalize for the individual circumstances of the taxpayer. In other words, a direct tax, administered through a periodic filing procedure, can be adjusted for such factors as size of the taxpaying unit and particular events that have befallen the taxpayer during the

---

[23]The sales tax is also used in some African countries, Indian states, and local governments in some countries of the former Soviet Union. For a few years it was an important revenue source for regional governments in the Russian Federation.

[24]In three provinces, the Canada Customs and Revenue Agency administers the Harmonized Sales Tax, a tax that includes both provincial sales tax and national value added tax. In Quebec, the provincial agency administers both provincial and national taxes. And in other areas with a provincial tax, administration of the taxes is separate.

Sidebar 9–1
Tax-Exclusive and Tax-Inclusive Pricing

Many Americans traveling in Europe are surprised to find that no sales tax is added to their purchases, just as Europeans visiting the United States are surprised when tax is added to their purchases. Both transactions include sales tax, but the RST tradition is for tax-exclusive pricing ("separate quotation")—adding the tax at the cash register—whereas the VAT tradition is tax-inclusive pricing—including tax in the sticker price. There are exceptions—for instance, some European hotels and car rental agencies quote prices without VAT and add the tax on final purchase, and American vending machines usually sell at tax-inclusive prices. Nevertheless, it is normal for American RSTs to be added at the cash register and for European VATs to be included in prices. Neither treatment is required by the logic of either tax, although tax laws often make the requirement.[1]

Tax laws may quote rates on either a tax-exclusive or tax-inclusive basis, but conversion between the two styles is simple. If TE is the tax-exclusive rate in percent and TI is the tax-inclusive rate in percent, then the relationship is as follows:

$$TI = TE/(100 + TE)$$

and

$$TE = TI/(100 - TI)$$

Therefore, a tax-exclusive VAT rate of 20 percent is equivalent to a tax-inclusive rate of 16.7 percent. A tax-inclusive VAT rate of 15 percent is equivalent to a tax-exclusive rate of 17.6 percent.

Which tax is less transparent? Neither VAT nor RST paid on a purchase need be hidden. Cash register receipts in many European stores include at statement of how much VAT was paid on the total purchase, just as cash register receipts in the United States include a statement of sales tax paid. The only difference: the U.S. receipt includes the sales tax as part of the calculation of how much is owed, and the VAT receipt includes VAT paid as a separate display after the total payment. American politicians who charge that the VAT is a hidden tax either haven't traveled much outside the United States or haven't bothered to look at receipts they have been given for European purchases. Or maybe someone else is paying their way. It is far easier to know how much personal income tax you have paid through the year than to know your total payments of either RST or VAT, however, because you do have to file an income tax return at the end of the year.

[1]When the American states were adopting sales taxes in the depths of the Great Depression of the 1930s, retailer organizations demanded separate quotation laws so that they would not be blamed for the price increases that would come with addition of the taxes. On the other hand, when Russia permitted regional sales taxes in the late 1990s, the national enabling law required that the sales taxes be included in listed prices, following the tradition of their VAT.

filing period. An indirect tax collected on a transaction by transaction basis is impersonal and cannot easily be adjusted for those sort of conditions because it is applied without an effective way to make allowance for who is doing the purchasing. There may be allowances for the particular transaction (a preferential rate for food, for instance), but that rate will be the same for all purchasers, regardless of their circumstances. This inability to target and limit makes preferences provided in an indirect tax less efficient because taxpayers in all sorts of circumstances have access to them.

Retail Sales Taxes

American RSTs share three common features. All are ad valorem taxes "imposed upon the sales, or elements incidental to the sales, such as receipts from them, of all or a wide range of commodities;"[25] all have a system for suspending tax on items purchased for resale; and all encourage separate quotation of the tax in each transaction (in other words, the tax is added at purchase rather than being included in the price on the shelf and tax thus collected is excluded from gross receipts upon which the tax is levied). The taxes—levied by all states but Alaska, Delaware, Montana, New Hampshire, and Oregon and by thousands of local governments—yield something over one-third of total state tax revenue, and rank second to the property tax for local governments, something more 10 percent of tax revenue.[26]

In early 2006, state tax rates ranged from 2.9 percent (Colorado) to 7 percent (Mississippi, Rhode Island, and Tennessee). Twenty-one states levied rates of 6 percent or higher. Piggybacked local rates for city, county, and transit or other special districts add to the total rate in many parts of the country. For instance, in New York City, the rate of 8.375 percent applied on retail purchases combines a 4-percent state rate, a 4-percent city rate, and a 0.375-percent Metropolitan Commuter Transportation District rate. In Chicago, state plus local rates equal 9 percent. Payment to the state is made by the vendor; returns like that in Figure 9–2 from Virginia cover all such transactions for a specified period (quarter, month, year). This state includes local tax as well; in this state, local taxes are state administered. The vendor has, through the reporting period, been collecting tax on each of its many sales; this return accumulates all those transactions for transmission to the government. Reporting on the return begins with total sales of the vendor and sales that are not taxed are subtracted to obtain taxable sales. The amount of sales tax that is owed comes from reported taxable sales.

More often than not, computation of RST owed on an individual transaction by multiplying sales price times the tax rate yields fractional cents: a selling price of $1.65 multiplied by a 5-percent tax rate yields a tax of 8.25¢, an amount not

[25]John F. Due, *Sales Taxation* (Urbana: University of Illinois Press, 1957), 3.
[26]The standard reference on general sales taxation is John F. Due and John L. Mikesell, *Sales Taxation, State and Local Structure and Administration,* 2nd ed. (Washington, D.C.: Urban Institute, 1994).

Figure 9–2
The Virginia Retail Sales and Use Tax Return

Form ST-9
Doc ID 109
Virginia Retail Sales And Use Tax Return
For assistance call: ***(804) 367-8037***

For Period Ending	
Due Date	

0000000000 1019104 000000

Account Number	Locally
Name	
Address	
City, State, ZIP	

I declare that this return (including accompanying schedules and statements) has been examined by me and to the best of my knowledge and belief is true, correct and complete.

Signature Date Phone Number

Va. Dept. of Taxation ST-9 W (Rev. 5/05)

1 **Gross Sales**	1	
2 **Personal Use**	2	
3 **Exempt State Sales & Other Deductions**	3	
4 **Total Taxable State Sales & Use**	4	

(a) Item & Rate	(b) Taxable Amount			(c) Tax
5 **State** Food (See above.)			5	
6 **State** General (See above.)			6	
7 **Local** (1%)			7	
8 **Total State Tax** [Line 5(c) plus Line 6(c)]			8	
9 **Dealer's Discount**			9	
10 **Net State Tax Due** [Line 8 minus Line 9]			10	
11 **Total State & Local Tax Due** [Line 10 plus Line 7(c)]			11	
12 **Penalty**			12	
13 **Interest**			13	
14 **Total Amount Due** Check here if paid by EFT ☐				

Do not write in the space at right

collectible with current U.S. coinage. States and merchants handle that problem by using bracket systems to define the tax to be collected in exact cents for any transaction. If the brackets are based on rounding from the major fraction rule (half cent or more, round up; less than half a cent, round down), collections from accumulated individual transactions through the reporting period will almost exactly equal total taxable sales times the statutory rate. Some states define vendor liability to be the tax rate multiplied by total taxable sales, regardless of the amount the brackets produce from individual transactions. The vendor keeps (or makes up) any differences between what the brackets generate and tax liability; that difference is called breakage. Some states have required that vendors remit the amount of collections produced by the brackets. Historically, states have done this because they have the brackets rigged to generate slightly more than the statutory sales tax rate. National compliance simplification movements are working against these exact collection remittance rules.

Two special evaluation standards apply to sales tax structures: uniformity and neutrality.[27] The first standard holds that the tax should produce a uniform tax on consumer expenditures. Thus, the structure should ease shifting to ultimate consumers, it should apply at a uniform rate to all consumption expenditures unless there is reason otherwise, and it should apply to the amount actually paid by the consumer. Second, to avoid loss of economic efficiency, the tax should not create competitive disturbances among types of distribution channels, methods of doing

[27]Due, *Sales Taxation*, 351–52.

business, or forms of business organization. Choices should not be distorted because of the tax. Figuring out how to get sales taxes to be uniform and neutral—and as fair, revenue-productive, and collectible as possible—is not a simple task. The next sections on coverage of non-retail transactions, the problem of equity exemptions, taxability of services, and treatment of interstate transactions demonstrate that.

Exclusion of Producers' Goods

Business purchases are a tempting target for taxation. The overall RST base is greater when business purchases are included, so a given statutory tax rate raises more revenue when business purchases are taxed and a large piece of the tax burden is hidden to most individuals. These purchases are hardly consumption in any economic sense, but the lure of revenue without higher statutory rates is attractive: such purchases constitute an estimated average of around 40 percent of state sales tax bases.[28] If businesses must pay tax on inputs to their business operations (raw materials, supplies, utilities, machinery and equipment, structures, etc.), their costs are higher. Consequently, prices are higher, but customers are unable to detect the embedded effect of the producer sales tax on prices, a clear violation of the transparency standard, as well as a source of economic distortion. If producers' goods are not excluded, the tax is not a uniform percentage of consumer expenditures (some consumption items require use of more producers' goods than others), the tax affects choices among methods of production (it makes capital more expensive), and it may delay the replacement of old equipment by increasing the after-tax price of new equipment. Furthermore, the firm has an incentive to produce goods for its own use, rather than purchasing the goods, because their internal cost of production is not subject to sales tax. Thus, producers' goods should be excluded from the tax for reasons of economic efficiency, equity, and to avoid thwarting industrial development.

States have developed two general standards for business-purchase exemption: the component-part, or physical-ingredient, and the direct-use rules.[29] The former rule regards an item as being resold and hence not taxable if it becomes a physical ingredient or component part of a good that is itself being sold (flour sold to a bakery, or gasoline tanks sold to a lawnmower manufacturer). If the good does not become a physical part of the product, then its sale is taxed as a retail sale. The business purchasing the item is regarded as the final consumer of the item, even though it is becoming an input into another product. This rule predominates probably because it leaves a larger tax base, although it also is somewhat easier to administer.

---

[28]Raymond J. Ring, Jr., "Consumers' Share and Producers' Share of the General Sales Tax," *National Tax Journal* 52 (March 1999), 79–90; and Robert Cline, John Mikesell, Tom Neubig, and Andrew Phillips, "Sales Taxation of Business Inputs: Existing Tax Distortions and the Consequences of Extending the Sales Tax to Business Services," *State Tax Notes*, XXXV (February 14, 2005), 457–70.

[29]Daniel C. Morgan, Jr., *Retail Sales Tax, An Appraisal of New Issues* (Madison: University of Wisconsin Press, 1964), Chapter 2.

The direct-use rule exempts both physical ingredients and machinery and equipment used in the production process (a stamping machine that forms lawnmower gasoline tanks or an oven in a bakery). This rule produces a smaller tax base, but the base comes closer to consumer expenditures. No existing sales tax, however, is limited exclusively to final consumption expenditure.

What happens when business purchases are not excluded from the sales tax? Figure 9–3 illustrates how pyramiding works and what its impact is. The figure contrasts a typical state sales tax with an ideal sales tax. The difference between the taxes: the ideal sales tax applies only to sales to the household consumer, and the typical sales tax applies to some business input purchases, as well as to consumer sales. In the ideal case, all input purchases by businesses are exempt from tax; in the typical case, purchases by the business of inventory for resale and purchases in the direct manufacturing process are exempt, but other business purchases are taxed. In this example, there are three businesses: a computer manufacturer, an appliance manufacturer, and an appliance retailer. The computer manufacturer sells computers to the retailer and to the appliance manufacturer. Some of the computers sold to the appliance manufacturer are for administrative work and some of the computers sold to the appliance manufacturer are used in the production process. The state applies a sales tax rate of 5 percent to taxable sales. In the typical case, the flow of business generates $58,000 in sales tax revenue from $1,000,000 of sales to households—the effective tax rate is 5.8 percent, compared with the statutory rate of 5 percent. The extra rate results because $160,000 in computer sales to the manufacturer and to the retailer were taxed; the cost of those computers to the

Figure 9–3
Retail Sales Tax Pyramiding: Typical v. Ideal

	Sales by:			Sales Tax (5% Statutory)	
Sales to:	Computer Manufacturer	Appliance Manufacturer	Appliance Retailer	Typical*	Ideal†
Appliance manufacturer					
Computers used in production line	50,000			0	0
Computers used in administration	150,000			7,500	0
Appliance retailer					
Computers used in administration	10,000			500	
Appliances		800,000			
Household consumer			1,000,000	50,000	50,000
Total sales tax paid				58,000	50,000
Effective tax rate paid				5.8%	5%

*Exempts purchases of inventory for resale and purchases for use in production process.
†Exempts business purchases.

business are going to be embedded in the final price of the product, so the value of those computers is being taxed twice—once when the business purchases them and again when the products of those businesses get sold to the household consumer. This is sales tax pyramiding.

There are problems with sales tax pyramiding. First, products purchased by households bear differing effective sales tax rates, depending on the way in which products are produced. Those involving more inputs that are subject to tax when businesses purchase them have higher rates than those produced without those kinds of purchases. This distorts consumer and business behavior. Second, businesses have an artificial incentive to vertical integration. In the previous example, a firm that made both computers and appliances would have an economic advantage because its appliance branch could obtain administrative computers without facing any sales tax, while a firm that was not integrated would need to pay sales tax when it purchased computers on the open market. Third, businesses in states that have limited exemptions for business purchases are at distinct disadvantage in interstate and international competition; they face higher costs of production because of the tax paid on their purchases. Finally, the statutory or advertised sales tax rate understates the true sales tax rate. This violates an important transparency standard—taxpayers need to see what tax they are actually paying. In spite of the attractiveness of hidden taxes to politicians, it is still difficult to see why lawmakers would want to accept the economic disadvantages of taxing business inputs.

RST remove transactions from tax by suspending collection on those transactions. Figure 9–4 illustrates a suspension certificate from the Indiana RST; certificates of this sort are critical to the operation of the tax. When a business purchases an item or group of items that are for an exempt purpose, such as buying inventory for resale or acquiring production equipment, it provides the seller with such a certificate. That allows the seller to make the sale without collecting the tax. Sales are assumed to be taxable unless a certificate justifies that the tax not be collected. The accumulation of such sales during a reporting period is reported on the seller's return (see line 3 in Figure 9–2); deducted sales of otherwise taxable items need to be ultimately documented by certificates provided by the purchaser when tax authorities audit the business. States may have a wide variety of such certificates, depending on the range of exempt purchases in the state law. In general, U.S. sales taxes remove pre-retail transactions from the tax by a system of time-of-sale exemption certificates that suspend collection of the tax. The certificate in Figure 9–4 removes purchases by governments and nonprofit organizations from the sales tax as well.

One enforcement problem in sales taxation is fraudulent use of the exemption certificate, for example, if a business owner presents the certificate to suspend sales tax on purchase of a computer that will be used at home rather than in an exempt business use. Notice the reminder at the bottom of the certificate that it is only to be used for exempt purchases. It is the responsibility of the vendor to make a good-faith effort to verify that the certificate is properly used before exempting the purchase. If the vendor errs, the revenue is probably lost.

The American states are stingy in exempting pre-retail purchases. They exempt items purchased for resale, component parts of items for resale, and goods used directly in production. Many producer goods (fuel, fixtures, tools, furniture, machinery,

Figure 9–4
Suspending Sales Tax by Certificate

Form ST-105
State Form 4965 R3/ 5-05

Indiana Department of Revenue
General Sales Tax Exemption Certificate

Indiana registered retail merchants and businesses located outside Indiana may use this certificate. The claimed exemption must be allowed by Indiana code. Exemption statutes of other states are not valid for purchases from Indiana vendors. **This exemption certificate can not be issued for the purchase of *Utilities*, *Vehicles*, *Watercraft*, or *Aircraft*.** Purchaser must be registered with the Department of Revenue or the appropriate taxing authority of the purchaser's state of residence.

Sales tax must be charged unless all information in each section is fully completed by the purchaser. Purchasers not able to provide all required information must pay the tax and may file a claim for refund (Form GA-110L) directly with the Department of Revenue.

Section 1 (print only)

Name of Purchaser _____

Business Address _____ City _____ State _____ Zip _____

Purchaser must provide minimum of one ID number below.*

Provide your Indiana Registered Retail Merchant's Certificate TID and LOC Number at shown on your Certificate..... _____ – _____
TID# (10 digits) LOC# (3 digits)

If not registered with the Indiana DOR, provide your State Tax ID Number from another State..... _____ _____
State ID # State of Issue

***See instructions on the reverse side if you do not have either number.**

Section 2

Is this a ☐ blanket purchase exemption request or a ☐ single purchase exemption request? (check one)

Description of items to be purchased. _____

Section 3

Purchaser must indicate the type of exemption being claimed for this purchase. (check one or explain)

☐ Sales to a retailer, wholesaler, or manufacturer for **resale** only.

☐ Sale of manufacturing machinery, tools, and equiptment to be used directly in direct **production**.

☐ Sales to **nonprofit organizations** claiming exemption pursuant to Sales Tax Information Bulletin #10. (May not be used for personal hotel rooms and meals.)

☐ Sale to persons predominately (51% or more of total sales) engaged in **public transportation** - provide USDOT#. _____
A person or corporation who is hauling under someone else's motor carrier authority, or has a contract as a **school bus operator**, must provide their SS# or FID# in lieu of a State ID# in Section #1.

☐ Sale to persons, occupationally engaged as farmers, to be used directly in production of **agricultural** products for sale.
Note: A farmer not possessing a State Business License# may enter a FID# or a SS# in lieu of a State ID# in Section #1.

☐ Sales to a **contractor** for exempt projects (such as public schools, government, or nonprofits).

☐ Sales to **Indiana Governmental Units** (agencies, cities, towns, municipalities, public schools, and state universities).

☐ Sales to the **United States Federal Government** - show agency name. _____
Note: A U.S. Government agency should enter its Federal Identification Number (FID#) in Section #1 in lieu of a State ID#.

☐ Other - explain. _____

Section 4

I hereby certify under the penalties of perjury that the property purchased by the use of this exemption certificate is to be used for an exempt purpose persuant to the State Cross Retail Sales Tax Act, Indiana Code 6-2.5, and the item purchased is not a utility, vehicle, watercraft, or aircraft.

I confirm my understanding that misuse, (*either negligent or international*), and/or fraudulent use of this certificate may subject both me personally and/or the business entity I represent to the imposition of tax, interest, and civil and/or criminal penalities.

Signature of Purchaser _____ Date _____

Printed Name _____ Title _____

The Indiana Department of Revenue may request verification of registration in another state if you are an out-of-state purchaser.
Seller must keep this certificate on file to support exempt sales.

and equipment) often remain in the base, despite the clear logic for excluding them. Taxing these acquisitions makes business investment less attractive, puts American business at a cost disadvantage in international competition, and makes the effective tax rate differ across types of consumption, but legislatures are reluctant to follow the logic of the tax to appear to remove the tax from business—even though the business is almost certain to transmit the cost to its individual customers.

Taxation of Services

Most state sales taxes, although applying generally to retail purchases of tangible personal property, apply only selectively to purchases of services. The taxes usually tax the lease or rental of tangible personal property (motor vehicles, videotapes, cement mixers, etc.), the rental of transient accommodations, and some utility services; only about half the states even tax the repair, installation, or maintenance of tangible personal property that they tax, let alone tax other varieties of service purchases made by households.[30] These omissions show a secular vulnerability in the sales tax base. In 1965, 59 percent of personal consumption expenditure was of goods; by 2004 that share had fallen to 42.6 percent.[31] A base quite serviceable in a goods economy may be hard-pressed to yield adequate revenue at tolerable statutory rates in a more service-oriented economy.

Taxing services on the same basis as goods can close a horizontal-equity gap, allows more revenue at any statutory rate, may improve vertical equity, and may improve secular adequacy of the tax. It would even reduce some compliance problems, as some businesses would no longer need to segregate sales of goods from sales of service in their billing and bookkeeping processes (auto-repair businesses would not need to distinguish between parts and labor, for instance). Why aren't services taxed more widely? Initial objection to taxing services was that the tax on services is a tax on labor income. Of course, labor constitutes much of the production cost of tangible personal property, so the argument lacks merit. A more important reason for exempting services is the frequent absence of a clear line between the worker-client relationship and the worker-employer relationship (e.g., an accountant doing personal tax returns versus an accountant working for a business firm). The latter, a producer-good relationship, should not be taxed. Furthermore, some services—medical and possibly legal, for instance—possibly should not be taxed as a matter of social policy. Consumers purchasing these services have enough trouble as it is without adding the sales tax to their bill.

The pragmatic difficulty of taxing services is not surprising, even though the theory is sound. Politically, many types of services are sold by businesses with well-developed professional associations (accountants, barbers, lawyers, realtors, etc.) and those associations strive diligently to keep their services outside the sales

---

[30]John L. Mikesell, "Sales Tax Coverage for Services—Policy for a Changing Economy," *Journal of State Taxation* 9 (Spring 1991): 31–50.

[31]U.S. Department of Commerce, Bureau of Economic Analysis, *National Income and Products Accounts*. Larger changes appear when *business* purchases of services are included in the analysis.

tax. The problem is not just that these sellers may find adding the sale tax to their bills mathematically challenging. They do understand that adding the tax would have some negative impact on their sales and that dealing with the tax would add to their administrative costs. Only a few states apply broad coverage of consumer services, but the realities of modern society cause extension to many services to be virtually inevitable. The difficult problem is to avoid taxing services sold almost exclusively to businesses; these are politically attractive targets, under the false impression that somehow applying a tax to a business avoids having the cost of government borne by the people.

Commodity Exemptions

RSTs typically exempt some items of tangible property that are clearly household consumption expenditures. The most frequently exempted items are food for at-home consumption (more than half the states) and prescription drugs (all but one state). There is a logical reason for these exemptions based on the standard evaluation criteria for taxes. Purchases of these items constitute a higher percentage of the income of low-income families than of high-income families. Excluding them from the tax base gives low-income families greater relief relative to their incomes than it does for high-income families, so the impact is to make the tax less regressive. The reduction of the effective tax rate on income is greater for low- than for high-income families. Hence, excluding the items improves the vertical equity of the tax. However, their exclusion makes the sales tax more difficult to collect (the state must define what items are exempt, stores selling both food and taxed items must maintain segregated accounting records, and audits are more complex) and the tax rate must be higher to yield a given amount of revenue on the smaller base (food constitutes around one-third of a prospective sales tax base).[32] Eight states (Connecticut, Massachusetts, Minnesota, New Jersey, New York, Pennsylvania, Rhode Island, and Vermont) have extended commodity exemption to purchases of clothing under the apparent logic of exempting a necessity from the tax base. Unfortunately, clothing expenditures are less concentrated among low-income groups than is the ordinary sales tax base, so the exemption provides about four and one-half times more relief to the highest quintile of families compared to the lowest quintile, does not improve vertical equity of the tax, causes effective rates within income classes to vary according to relative tastes for clothing, complicates compliance and administration, and causes higher rates for given revenues.[33]

---

[32]The distinctions for commodity exemptions can be maddening (as well as expensive to operate). This illustrates the problem: in Illinois, whether a shave cream is considered a medicine (and some are) determines whether its purchase is taxed at a rate of 1 percent or 6.25 percent. The same rate differences apply between types of bottled water and between juices and juice-beverages, according to whether they are considered food. More work for the conscientious vendor, more work for the tax authorities, possible distortion of consumer and producer choice, and confusion for the public. How can this be good public policy?

[33]John L. Mikesell, "Exempting Clothing from the Sales Tax: The 'Supply Side Message' from the New York Tax Holiday," *State Tax Notes* (March 17, 1997): 835–38.

Five states (Idaho, Kansas, Oklahoma, South Dakota, and Wyoming) provide an RST credit or rebate as an alternative to commodity exemption for controlling sales tax regressivity. Rather than provide exemption for all purchasers of selected commodities, the credit systems return a fixed sum to taxpayers at year's end, usually equal to estimated payment of sales tax on food purchases by individuals in the lowest-income class. If the prevailing sales tax rate is 4 percent and per capita food purchases by individuals in the under-$15,000-annual-income class are about $10,000, the amount returned would be $400. Return of $400 to all individuals—either by rebate application or as a credit on a state income tax return—would effectively eliminate the sales tax on food purchases by very low-income purchasers. The rebate amount would not increase, however, as food consumption increased through the higher-income classes. (High-income people spend more on food than do low-income people; the food exemption works because the percentage of income spent on food declines with higher income.) The rebate concentrates assistance where assistance is most needed and eliminates the need for vendors to account for taxed and exempt sales. Overall, the rebate effectively reduces (or even eliminates) regressivity at a lower loss of revenue than commodity exemption. The rebate requires that individuals file returns with the state and that the state make cash payment to individuals, but these would seem small disadvantages relative to the other efficiencies of the device. Canada provides a quarterly payment to low-income individuals and families for the national Goods and Services Tax to accommodate tax that would have been paid on food purchases. There is a similar refund program for provincial sales taxes. The food purchase rebate/credit system allows better targeting of the relief to those in need, thereby getting greater reduction in regressivity per dollar of tax revenue lost and reducing the fiscal impact of the relief provided.

Commodity exemptions (1) narrow the tax base, thereby reducing the case that can be made for the sales tax as a means of general consumption taxation and requiring a higher statutory rate to yield a given amount of revenue; (2) increase the probability that family sales tax burden will differ according to individual tastes and preferences for consumption items; (3) reduce the stability of the revenue base in the face of a business downturn (household consumption on nondurables tends to be less influenced by recessions than is spending on household durables); and (4) complicate administration and compliance by requiring sorting between taxed and exempt. Nevertheless, legislators find them popular with the electorate; they create the illusion that responsibility for the cost of government is being avoided, rather than being distributed to the public in less transparent ways.

Variation in the State Sales Taxes

The states that levy RSTs do not apply the tax to the same transactions. They vary in the exemptions they provide for household consumption expenditure (food, clothing, non-prescription medicines, motor fuels, magazines, etc.), the extent to which they include service purchases in the tax base, and the degree to which they exclude purchase of business inputs from the tax base. The result of these variations is that the breadth of the tax base differs dramatically across the states. A given statutory sales tax rate yields significantly different revenues from one state to another because of these structural differences. In fiscal 2003, the ratio of the sales tax base to state personal income in the five states with broadest bases was 70.7 percent, compared with a ratio of 27.6 percent for the five states with the narrowest bases, the result of the differing choices that lawmakers in the two states have made about including transactions in the tax base. That means that each percentage point of statutory sales tax rate is 2.6 times more productive in the broad-base states than in the narrow-base states.[34] The structure of the base is critical for revenue yield; the broader the base, the more revenue can be produced from a given rate, and the evidence is that states with broader bases do tend to levy lower statutory sales tax rates.

It is important to remember that, while there is an American model for sales taxation that states and localities follow, there is no single template for these taxes. The structures are established by state lawmakers, and each state is different in how it chooses to structure its own sales tax. The same principle applies in Canada, the only other country making significant use of the RST, where all but one province levies the tax. With the exception of three maritime provinces that have chosen to harmonize their sales taxes with the federal goods and services tax (the Canadian VAT), the provinces structure their taxes independently and not according to a national standard. In the United States and Canada, subnational governments generally levy RST, but these governments do not use a common structure for these taxes.

The Sales Taxes and Internet Commerce: Remote Vendors and Use Taxes

All states levy use taxes on the storage, use, or consumption of taxable property on which the sales tax has not been paid (in fact, some state laws call them "compensating use taxes" for that reason). The tax may not have been paid because the purchase was made in a jurisdiction without a tax on the item (e.g., an oriental rug brought back from Turkmenistan for use in Chicago) or because the purchase was made in interstate commerce (e.g., purchase of a computer from an Internet vendor). The rules governing interstate commerce (based on the commerce clause of the U.S. Constitution) do not allow either the origination or destination state to levy a sales tax on such interstate business; however, the destination state may impose the use tax on the purchase after it has come to rest.[35] The use tax serves to protect both the state sales tax base and local vendors against sales tax-free competition. And protection, not direct collections, really is the primary objective; use tax

[34]John L. Mikesell, "State Retail Sales Tax Burdens, Reliance, and Breadth in Fiscal 2003," *State Tax Notes*, 33 (July 12, 2004): 125–31.

[35]The U.S. Supreme Court case *Henneford* v. *Silas Mason Co., Inc.*, 300 U.S. 577 (1937) upheld the Washington state use tax. The tax was on the privilege of use after interstate commerce was complete and did not interfere with interstate commerce itself.

collections seldom constitute as much as 10 percent of combined sales and use tax collections.

The use tax problem is with enforcement. Transaction taxes—like the sales tax—can best be collected through vendors, in other words, as indirect taxes, rather than as direct taxes from purchasers. There are far fewer vendors than purchasers for tax authorities to track, and vendors have far greater recordkeeping and accounting capacity than household purchasers. Trying to administer a tax on individual transactions as a direct tax would be virtually impossible.[36] But that is the expectation for most retail activity subject to the use tax, including Internet sales. The key to enforcing any tax applied to individual transactions is getting vendors registered as tax collectors on behalf of the tax administration and the Constitutional standard for requiring vendors to register is "physical presence" in the taxing state, as prescribed by the U.S. Supreme Court in *National Bellas Hess v. Department of Revenue* (386 U.S. 753 (1967)) and reaffirmed in *Quill v. North Dakota* (112 S Ct 1904 (1992)). The Commerce Clause of the U.S. Constitution prohibits states from placing "undue burden" on interstate commerce and frivolous registration requirements on remote vendors surely would be considered such a burden. For every jurisdiction in which the vendor is registered, it would need to know the rate and base structure in order to collect the tax—and it would need to know that for the thousands of taxing local jurisdictions, not just the forty-five sales tax states plus the District of Columbia. A vendor selling nationwide would need to know them all, and vendors selling via the Internet might get an order from anywhere. The Court sought to provide with physical presence a "bright line" standard for firmly establishing when an enterprise would be required to bear the compliance responsibilities of becoming a tax collector. Only vendors with physical presence in a state may be required by that state to register as collectors for its sales and use taxes. If the vendor is physically there, it is not an undue burden for it to learn about the sales and use tax system in place in the jurisdiction.

The situation can be explained by reference to three classes of purchases and how the commerce clause of the U.S. Constitution requires that they be handled by state sales and use taxes:

1. **Purchases made from a local storefront**. A local storefront—a store in your local shopping mall—must register with its state as a tax collector and must remit tax from purchases made from that store. That collection requirement includes both purchases taken with the purchaser or delivered within the state. Physical presence, registration required. If the purchase is delivered to another state by a common carrier (postal service, package delivery firm, etc.), the sale is in interstate commerce and the storefront state cannot apply its sales tax. If the storefront uses its own delivery trucks, it has physical presence.

2. **Purchases made from a remote vendor with physical presence in the state**. A remote vendor—Internet seller, mail-order firm, telemarketer, home

[36]Most states do try to collect use tax directly from individuals, with varying degrees of rigor. For instance, some states provide use tax reporting on their individual income tax return, but revenues are modest. See John L. Mikesell, "Administering Use Tax as Direct Collection Through Income Tax Reports," *State Tax Notes*, 13 (May 26, 1997), 1603–1606.

shopping channel, store in another states, etc.—with some physical presence, not necessarily a retail storefront, in the state must register with that state as a tax collector and must remit tax on purchases made for delivery into that state. The presence might be its delivery trucks, a warehouse, or a repair facility. However, the tax is a compensating use tax that the vendor is collecting and remitting on behalf of the purchaser. Example: The purchaser orders from the remote (out-of-state) vendor, but the remote vendor has some physical presence in the purchaser's state. The remote vendor must collect use tax for the purchaser's state. Physical presence, registration required.

3. **Purchases from a remote vendor without physical presence**. A remote vendor without physical presence may not be required to register as a use tax collector. (Voluntary registration is permitted.) Purchasers owe use tax on their purchases, as in the immediately preceding instance, but they are expected to remit the tax on their purchases directly, rather than through the vendor.[37] No physical presence, registration not required.

How does a state collect its use tax? Some out-of-state vendors collect use tax on sales made in the state, either because they have some physical presence in the state (e.g., some catalog vendors also have retail or outlet stores, so they must register and collect in states with those stores) or because they have chosen to register and collect voluntarily. Some use tax is collected when the purchaser registers the item with the state of use, as with a motor vehicle or a boat. Some use tax is collected on audit, when state officials check a taxpayer's record and discover major purchases made out-of-state without payment of tax. And some use tax is voluntarily reported by the purchaser, either on special returns or on a convenience line added to the state's individual income tax return.

The fact of the matter is that states do not presently have any completely successful mechanism for enforcing use tax on purely interstate sales, like those from mail-order catalogs, telemarketing, Internet sales, etc., and this is extremely worrisome in terms of fairness of the tax and long-term revenue productivity. States would like to require registration by firms with a significant economic presence in the state—as a way to protect their in-state retailers from tax-free competition and to protect their tax base—but Congress has not yet been convinced of the reasonableness of this effort. States need to develop a way to make registration and collection by remote vendors simple and cheap, in other words, to make it something other than an undue burden in the eyes of Congress.

---

[37]The problem is primarily one of purchases *made* through the Internet (or other remote vending formats) and delivered through conventional means (postal service, delivery firms, etc.) and not of purchases *delivered* through the Internet. Only purchases subject to digitization can currently be delivered by electronic means and that is a small component of the possible tax base. Furthermore, many such purchases are not taxable, even if purchased from a local storefront, because they are not tangible personal property—part of the general failure of state sales taxes to keep up with economic change. Some multistate businesses have established Internet subsidiaries that are separated from the regular storefront operations of the business. There is an ongoing argument whether presence of a storefront establishes a registration requirement for the Internet subsidiary.

What states have developed is the Streamlined Sales Tax Project (SSTP). Many states are cooperating on a sales tax streamlining project to simplify and reduce the compliance burden on remote vendors, in order that Congress would allow required registration. States that participate in the project do not adopt a common sales tax base, but they do agree to certain unified sales tax conditions to make it easier for a remote vendor to comply with any sales and use tax responsibilities. In general, the SSTP provisions are these:

1. When a state permits local governments to levy sales taxes, those local taxes must be state administered, must apply to the same base as the state tax, and must all use the same tax rate.
2. States must use standard definitions for certain exemptions and exclusions. Important definitions include those for food, drugs, clothing, and tangible personal property. The agreement does not require that the items be exempt, but if they are, the definition must follow standard lines.
3. States must participate in an online sales and use tax registration system that covers registration in all agreement states. A firm needs to register only once to be registered in all participating states.
4. The agreement provides three sales and use tax remittance options: a certified service provider acts as the firm's agent in all sales and use tax functions; the firm uses a certified automated system to handle tax calculation, remittance, recordkeeping, and reporting; or the firm does compliance itself according to a performance standard acceptable to each agreement state. Compliance is paid under each option.
5. States adopt a variety of other changes in how taxes are calculated to make compliance easier. For instance, the state must use brackets consistent with major fraction rounding, the state may not limit the amount of tax due on a particular transaction, the state must require statewide consolidated returns for multiple location vendors, and so on.

The agreement also establishes a system of self-governance, in particular, in terms of deciding whether a state sales and use tax law is consistent with the requirements of the streamline agreement.

Why have the states voluntarily surrendered a portion of their fiscal sovereignty? It is a pragmatic decision. The states see remote vendors as an important challenge to the survival of the sales tax base, in terms of equity to local vendors and in terms of loss of sales tax base, particularly as commerce through the Internet grows. By streamlining their sales taxes, they hope to convince Congress that compliance with sales and use taxes by remote vendors will no longer be an undue burden to interstate commerce and that Congress will then revise the physical-presence rule. They hope to require registration of remote vendors as tax collectors and restore the competitive balance between local and remote vendors. It represents a calculated gamble by the states, and the result remains unclear.

Value-Added Taxes

A VAT provides an alternate mechanism for taxing consumption.[38] In contrast to the U.S. RST, however, the tax applies to the increment in value at each stage of the production and distribution process, rather than applying only at the final (retail) stage. The VAT sets the world standard for general consumption taxation, but not in the United States. In the United States, the VAT over the years has been proposed as a means of financing the social insurance system in place of or in addition to the payroll tax, as a way to stimulate saving and investment through reducing reliance on income taxation, as an avenue to stimulating exports, as a replacement for the property tax as a means for financing primary and secondary education, and as a revenue source that might unify state fiscal systems. But none of the arguments have yet been strong enough for lawmakers to act.

The value added tax (or goods and services tax as it is called in, for instance, Canada and Australia) provides a simple but sophisticated way of taxing consumption expenditure. It is collected by businesses on their sales of goods and services to their customers. Each business in the flow of production and distribution from manufacturer to retailer charges VAT on its sales and, in remitting payments to the taxing authority, is permitted to subtract from this amount the VAT that it paid on its purchases.[39] Invoices showing VAT paid must be available to support the VAT credits taken on the return and credit is provided immediately for tax on all business purchases, including capital goods. Businesses of all types must be registered as VAT collectors in order to get the credits, so there will be more firms registered under a VAT than under an RST, in which only retailers need to register. The result of offsetting tax paid on purchases against tax collected on sales is to impose the tax on value added (sales less purchases) at each stage of production-distribution. The final consumer—the household—is not a business, has no sales through which VAT paid may be reimbursed, and thus bears the tax. It is multistage, but it does not pyramid because the tax applies only to the value added at each transaction, not to the total receipts of the transaction, and businesses are reimbursed for the tax that they have paid on their purchases. Why is the VAT equivalent to an RST? The RST applies to the total value of the product (the purchase price at retail), levied at the last stage of the production-distribution process; the VAT applied to the value added at each stage of the process and the accumulation of these increments equals the total value of the product.[40] Sidebar 9–2 outlines the basic math that shows how the two taxes are economic equals.

The logic of a VAT can be demonstrated with a simple illustration. Remember in this example that the business is both a taxpayer (on its purchases) and a tax col-

[38]An excellent reference is Alan A. Tait, *Value-Added Tax: International Practice and Problems* (Washington, D.C.: International Monetary Fund, 1988). The tax may also be designed to approximate an income tax, but the consumption variety predominates.

[39] The tax on the total value of its sales less the tax on the total value of its purchases equals the tax on the value that the business adds. Hence, it is a VAT. A tax on the value of its sales only is a gross receipts or turnover tax.

[40]Value added by a firm is also equal to the total amount the firm pays to factors of production (rent to land, wages and salaries paid to employees, interest to capital, and profit to entrepreneurial activity). The VAT base could thus alternatively be calculated by adding these payments—as is done with the Michigan single business tax and the New Hampshire tax on business enterprise.

Sidebar 9–2.
The Economic Equivalence of RST and VAT

An ideal RST and an ideal VAT are economically the same, just administered in a different fashion. Here is an explanation of the logic behind this equivalence. Assume the following economic chain: an extractor who sells to a manufacturer who sells to a wholesaler who sells to a retailer who sells to a final customer. Notice that one entity's sales are another entity's purchases: for example, the product that represents sales by the wholesaler is the product that is the purchases of the retailer.

Let t = the VAT or RST rate, S = sales or purchases, the subscripts $_{e, m, w, r}$ indicate whether the sales is by extractor, manufacturer, wholesaler, or retailer, and R = total revenue collected in the production and distribution chain.

RST: the ideal RST applies only to the final retail sales to the household customer. All sales between businesses are not taxed via use of the suspension certificate. Therefore, revenue from the RST equals:

$$R = t\,S_r$$

VAT: The ideal VAT applies to value added at each transaction in the production and distribution chain. In other words, it applies to the difference between sales made by the business entity less purchases from other business entities. Therefore, revenue from the VAT equals:

$$R = t(S_e - 0) + t(S_m - S_e) + t(S_w - S_m) + t(S_r - S_w)$$

or

$$R = tS_e + tS_m - tS_e + tS_w - tS_m + tS_r - tS_w = tS_r$$

This expression reflects two VAT facts: (a) before the final sale to the household consumer, the purchases of one business are the sales of another business, and (b) VAT paid by a business on its purchases will be refunded from the VAT it collects on its sales.

Conclusion: Although the two taxes are administered in significantly different ways, the two taxes apply to the same final base and will yield equal revenue from a common statutory rate. The VAT accumulates through the stages of production and distribution to be a tax on all household consumption.

[1]For a more extensive comparison of the retail sales and value added taxes, see John L. Mikesell, "Is the Retail Sales Tax Really Inferior to the Value-Added Tax?" in W. Fox and Murray, ed., *The Sales Tax in the 21st Century* (Westport, Conn.; Greenwood Press, 1997).

lector (on its sales). However, the tax that the business pays gets reimbursed (credited or refunded) in the tax that it collects on its sales. Suppose a 10-percent rate applies in a hypothetical production-distribution process that gets a wool sweater to a customer.[41]

[41]This illustrates the credit-invoice method of collection, as used in European-style VATs. The subtraction method, an alternate collection approach, would have businesses subtract purchases from sales and pay tax on the difference, without using invoices and credits. Zero rating, removing certain consumption categories from tax by taxing it at a rate of zero, does not work well, however, with the subtraction method.

1. A farmer sells wool to a textile company for $20, collects $2 in tax ($20 times 10 percent), and sends the $2 to the government. (The farmer's value added equals sales less purchases, that is, 20 minus 0 equals 20.) The textile company receives the wool, for which it has paid $20 plus $2 tax, or $22, and a statement showing that it paid $2 in VAT.

2. The textile company sells the yarn that it spins from the wool to a sweater manufacturer for $50. (Therefore, its value added equals sales minus purchases or $50 minus $20 equals $30.) The company collects $5 in tax from the manufacturer and sends the government $3 plus the receipt showing $2 already paid when purchasing the wool. The textile company keeps the $2 and is now fully reimbursed for the VAT it paid when it purchased the wool. The sweater manufacturer has the yarn, for which it has paid $50 plus $5 tax, or $55, and a receipt for $5 VAT paid.

3. The sweater manufacturer knits a sweater and sells it to a retailer for $90 (its value added, $90 minus $50 equals $40). The manufacturer collects $9 in tax from the retailer and sends the government $4 plus the receipt showing $5 already paid when purchasing the yarn. The retailer has the sweater, for which it has paid $90 plus $9 tax, or $99, and a receipt for $9 VAT paid.

4. The retailer sells the sweater to a final customer for $200 plus $20 VAT (the value added by the retailer, $200 minus $90 equals $110). The retailer sends the government $11 plus the receipt showing $9 already paid when purchasing the sweater from the manufacturer. The customer has the sweater and has paid $200 plus $20 in VAT or $220. But, in contrast to the businesses in the production-distribution chain, the customer has no avenue to refund through the next transaction because the customer is the final link in the chain. The final customer, the household, pays the tax and the tax paid equals 10 percent of the value of the purchase.

There are, of course, many transactions going on in each of these businesses, but the basic principle of removing the tax from business purchases by refund remains the same. The tax does not pyramid because each business in the chain both pays the tax on its purchases and then receives a refund when it collects tax on its sales. The tax is not embedded in its operating cost. Notice in the example that the value of the sweater at the end ($200) equals the sum of values added at each stage of production (20 plus 30 plus 40 plus 110 equals 200), that each cash payment to the government equals the tax rate times value added at that stage (2, 3, 4, 11), and that the sum of payments equals the VAT rate times the final value of the sweater. The result is thus equivalent to applying a 10 percent RST to the value purchased by the final customer.

VAT accounting can be quite simple for a business. Think about the scheme in this fashion. The business has two boxes. In one box goes all the invoices for purchases during the month, with each invoice showing the amount of the purchase and the amount of VAT paid on the purchase. In the other box goes all the invoices for sales during the month, with each invoice showing the amount of the sale and the amount of VAT collected on the sale. When it is time to do the VAT return at the end of the month, the business owner (1) goes to the purchase record box and tallies all purchases made and the tax paid on those purchases, (2) goes to the sales record box and tallies all sales made and the tax collected on those sales, (3) subtracts total purchases from total sales to get value added during the month, and (4) subtracts total tax paid on purchases from total tax collected on sales to figure the amount of VAT to send to the government. It can get more complicated if the legislature wants to add exemptions or preferential tax rates, but that is how the process works. Figure 9–5 shows what a value added tax return looks like; this is the return for New Zealand goods and service (VAT) tax. Here is the basic structure of the return. The business reports its total sales on line 5 and the total includes VAT that has been collected on these transactions. The business subtracts sales on which it has not collected VAT (in RST terminology, these would be considered exempt sales but VAT terminology refers to these sales as zero-rated, as in subject to a zero tax rate). The resulting total on line 7 is divided by 9 to produce the total VAT collected by the business. How does that make any sense? The statutory VAT rate is 12.5 percent. This is the tax-exclusive rate. Its tax-inclusive equivalent, from Sidebar 9–1, would equal TE/(100 + TE) or 12.5/112.5 or 0.111. The reciprocal of 0.111 equals 9, so the amount of tax in the total equals 0.111 times the total or 9 divided by the total. Dividing by 9 is the equivalent of multiplying the tax-inclusive total sales by the tax-inclusive tax rate to obtain the amount of tax. This calculation produces line 10, total VAT collected. The next steps involve total purchases, which includes VAT paid on the purchases. Again, the purchase total is divided by 9, as above, to identify the amount of VAT paid. Finally, line 15 is the difference between VAT collected and VAT paid—and that difference is paid if collections are higher and is refunded if payments are higher. The return calculation works through exactly like the simple system of a box with receipts showing VAT collections and a box with receipts showing VAT payments, with a netting of the two boxes on a periodic basis.

Value-Added Tax Features

VATs are typically levied by national governments, and those governments rely heavily on revenue from these taxes. As a result, statutory VAT rates are usually much higher than typical RST rates. Table 9–4 displays the standard VAT rate for a number of countries around the world. Rates of 20 percent are common, though there are higher rates. Indeed, countries of the European Union are required to levy a minimum rate of 15 percent, and most levy even higher rates. Because the VAT plays such an important role in their revenue systems, high rates are necessary. (Individual income tax reliance is lower as a result.) Many countries also levy special preferential rates on some purchases (food, medicines, etc.) to reduce the regressivity of the tax, and others levy special higher rates on certain luxuries as they attempt to combine excise effects with the general consumption tax. These multi-rate systems make both compliance and administration more difficult. VAT systems assign zero-rating to goods or services they want to relieve entirely from tax; that relieves the purchaser from tax and allows the seller to have any tax it might have paid be refunded.

Figure 9–5
New Zealand Value-Added Tax Return

Inland Revenue
Te Tari Taake

Goods and services tax return

Goods and Services Tax Act 1985

Please use the *GST guide (IR 375)* to help you complete this return, or phone us on 0800 377 776.

GST 101
March 2005

Registration number 1

Period covered by the return

from 2 to

This return and any payment are due

If your correct **postal** address for GST is **not** shown above, print it in Box 3. 3

If your correct daytime phone number is **not** shown here, print it in Box 4 4 Area code Telephone number

Goods and services tax on your sales and income

Total sales and income for the period (including GST and any zero-rated supplies)	5	$
Zero-rated supplies included in Box 5	6	$
Subtract Box 6 from Box 5	7	$
Divide the amount in Box 7 by nine (9)	8	$
Adjustments from your calculation sheet	9	$
Add Boxes 8 and 9. This is your **total GST collected** on sales and income.	10	$

OFFICE USE ONLY
Operator code
Corresp. indicator
Payment attached
Return cat.

Goods and services tax on your purchases and expenses

Total purchases and expenses (including GST) for which tax invoicing requirements have been met, excluding any imported goods	11	$
Divide the amount in Box 11 by nine (9)	12	$
Credit adjustments from your calculation sheet	13	$
Add Box 12 and Box 13. This is your **total GST credit** for purchases and expenses.	14	$
Print the difference between Box 10 and Box 14 here	15	$

Declaration
The information in this return is true and correct and represents my assessment as required under the Tax Administration Act 1994.

Signature

Date

If Box 14 is larger than Box 10 the difference is your GST refund

If Box 10 is larger than Box 14 the difference is GST to pay

Has payment been made electronically? Yes No

(Tick one)
Refund
GST to pay

Inland Revenue
Te Tari Taake

Payment slip

GST 700

Registration number

Return for the period ending

This return and any payment are due

Amount of payment 16 $

Use the envelope provided to post the top copy of both your return and payment slip, and any cheque payment. **Keep the bottom copy for your records.**

Copy your total from Box 15 to Box 16 and include any late payment penalties for this period only.

Table 9–4
Standard Value-Added Tax Rate in Countries Around the World, 2005

Country	Rate	Selected Other Countries	Rate
Members of OECD			
Australia	10	Algeria	21
Austria	20	Argentina	21
Belgium	21	Brazil	multiple rates
Canada	7	Chile	19
Czech Republic	19	China	17
Denmark	25	Columbia	16
Finland	22	India	12.5
France	19.6	Indonesia	10
Germany	16	Kazakhstan	15
Greece	19	Kenya	15
Hungary	25	Latvia	18
Iceland	24.5	Malaysia	10
Ireland	21	Morocco	20
Italy	20	Peru	19
Japan	5	Philippines	10
Korea	10	Russia	18
Luxemburg	15	Slovenia	20
Mexico	15	South Africa	14
Netherlands	19	Thailand	7
New Zealand	12.5	Ukraine	20
Norway	25	Venezuela	15
Poland	22	Vietnam	10
Portugal	19		
Slovak Republic	19		
Spain	16		
Sweden	25		
Switzerland	7.6		
Turkey	18		
United Kingdom	17.5		
U.S.A.	no tax		

SOURCE: Deloitte Touche Tohmatsu, *Global Indirect Tax Rates*

VAT exemptions do not work in the same way that RST exemptions do. An exemption relieves the seller from collecting the VAT on its sales, but it does not relieve the seller from paying tax on its purchases. There are no purchase suspension certificates in the VAT. For exempt goods and services, the seller of the service is treated like the consumer of its purchases. In general, with the VAT, businesses do not want their product to be exempt; by being registered vendors of taxed goods or services, they have a mechanism for refund of the VAT that they pay on their purchases. Without that registration, they pay the tax without refund. Unless the business purchases very little from other businesses (certain service providers would be an example), so that very little of its operating cost is covered by the VAT, it will much prefer to be selling a taxed rather than an exempt product.

The typical VAT system does not require small businesses to register as VAT collectors. For example, the registration threshold for 2005 in the United Kingdom is £60,000; any business with annual gross receipts (turnover) below that sum is not required to register as a VAT collector. That relieves them of VAT compliance responsibilities and reduces administration cost for Her Majesty's Customs and Revenue, the United Kingdom's VAT collectors. Of course, that business would not be able to get VAT it paid on business input purchases refunded. Because this threshold is relatively high, the United Kingdom permits businesses to voluntarily register as VAT collectors. Countries have different policies in regard to both size of threshold and voluntary registration, but some threshold is common. The country loses revenue from the value added by these smaller firms, but reduced compliance and administrative costs are seen as making it a worthwhile loss.[42]

Value-Added Tax versus Retail Sales Tax

The VAT is undoubtedly the global choice for general consumption taxation. Why might VAT be more desirable than an RST?[43] First, the VAT might help if tax evasion and a lack of vendor cooperation are problems. The VAT induces purchasers to require a documented receipt for vendors for taxes paid because the tax payments shown on those receipts are used to pay part of the taxes the purchasers will owe when they make sales. The VAT does not administer itself, but it certainly encourages a good trail of invoices for the audit process. The tax authorities have to make sure that VAT collections actually end up in the treasury and that VAT claims are not fraudulent, the fact that the tax is collected at each transaction in the production-distribution chain means that revenue is collected, even if some businesses cheat. The RST, on the other hand, puts all its collection eggs in one basket—if the retailer cheats, all revenue is lost.[44] Nevertheless, European experience shows that businesses still cheat, for instance, by claiming credit for VAT not actually paid, and that businesses are still delinquent in payment, so the tax authorities continue to have a job to do.[45] But VATs with high statutory rates have been successfully collected in countries with historically bad compliance environ-

---

[42]Charities usually must pay VAT when they make purchases, but seldom have a mechanism for having their payments refunded. One of the few exceptions: Canada does provide a rebate of half the goods and services tax that charities pay.

[43]For a more extensive comparison of the RST and VAT, see John L. Mikesell, "Is the Retail Sales Tax Really Inferior to the Value-Added Tax?" in W. Fox and M. Murray, eds., *The Sales Tax in the 21st Century* (Westport, Conn.; Greenwood Press, 1997), 75–87.

[44]Furthermore, the RST puts the burden of judging whether the tax should be suspended or collected on the vendor. But the vendor is almost certainly keenly interested in making a sale and could be willing to sacrifice revenue rightfully owed the state, by failing to deny a doubtful suspension certificate, in order to make the sale. The VAT requires payment of tax—which may be recovered by a business making a successful claim to the revenue department.

[45]Henry J. Aaron, ed., *The Value-Added Tax, Lessons from Europe* (Washington, D.C.: Brookings Institution, 1981).

ments. Most observers agree that traditional RSTs cannot be successfully administered at statutory rates much higher than 10 percent. If a government intends to levy high statutory rates, for instance, in an effort to replace national income taxes, experience teaches that the VAT is the only feasible choice.

Second, countries are able to remove VAT from international trade and international competitiveness considerations. The chain of tax documentation produced by the VAT makes this extraction simple—the exporter requests refund of VAT paid at the time inventory is exported and the importer must pay VAT at the time inventory is brought into the country. That levels the tax comparison between foreign and domestic products within the country and removes the VAT from prices of goods the country is selling on world markets. This sort of adjustment is not possible with other general taxes.[46] Indeed, under the rules of the World Trade Organization, only an indirect tax like the VAT can be adjusted at borders in this fashion. There is no way to remove RST embedded when pre-retail purchases are taxed from export prices, so there is an international competitive problem. A VAT levied at the subnational level would have issues regarding the administration of cross-border credits or rebates, although they could be handled in one way or another (Brazil illustrates how subnational VATs could work, although not perfectly). Subnational RSTs are clearly quite feasible; this may be the best level of government for application of such taxes.

Third, the VAT comes closer to being a general consumption tax than does the RST. The VAT provides more complete exclusion of business purchases than does the RST because the credit-refund device politically seems less like a special break for business than does the exemption certificate. Furthermore, the VAT achieves more general coverage of services. The RST exempts a considerable portion of household consumption expenditure and taxes a considerable portion of business purchases of inputs. Legislatures simply seem unable to accept the idea that exemption of business purchases represents the proper design of the tax base, not an unfair tax advantage to business. Legislatures seem more accepting of the VAT idea of having businesses pay on purchases, but refund on their sales, thus permitting the VAT to more closely work as a general consumption tax. Therefore, at higher statutory rates, the VAT is substantially less likely to do damage to economic development prospects and infrastructure investment than is the RST.

Conclusion

Taxes on goods and services are at the heart of state revenue systems, an important contributor to local revenue system, but are relatively unimportant for U.S. federal finance. Though questions of structure persist for each base, there is no doubt concerning the serviceability of these taxes. The case for general sales taxes is much stronger than it is for the selective excises as a general revenue source. The key

[46]Some suspect that flexible exchange rates may eliminate any impact of the VAT on international trade patterns.

problem with consumption taxation remains regressivity; no perfect solution exists. VATs and RSTs provide two alternative formats for collecting a tax on general consumption. Although the RST provides an important foundation for state and local revenue systems in the United States, it has significant adverse equity and economic effects. VATs provide an alternate with better economic performance and these taxes are widely used throughout the world as the mechanism of choice for national general consumption taxation.

CHAPTER 9 QUESTIONS AND EXERCISES

1. Identify the important elements of sales taxation in your state. What governments levy general and selective sales taxes? Identify the following for the RST: What commodity sales are exempt? Are services taxed? What is the nominal rate? What are the brackets? Does your state provide sales tax credits? In regard to selective excises: What selective excises are used? How are their bases defined? What rates apply?

2. It has been proposed that the Foundation for Preservation of the American Badger (*taxidea taxus*) be provided a sales tax exemption for its purchases and for its annual sales of "Badger Booster" cookies. Please analyze according to the general principles of tax policy.

3. The Bureau of Labor Statistics' Consumer Expenditure Survey: 1995 gives the following data:

		Average Annual Expenditure	
Income Category of Family	Average Income Before Taxes ($)	Alcoholic Beverages ($)	Tobacco ($)
Lowest quintile	6,305	118	204
Second quintile	16,114	193	242
Third quintile	28,242	230	327
Fourth quintile	44,753	350	307
Highest quintile	89,011	617	278

Analyze the likely vertical equity of selective excises on alcoholic beverages and tobacco products.

4. A bottle of wine has about three times the alcoholic content of the same volume of beer. If alcohol is the component of these beverages that merits taxation, the specific tax rate for wine should be around three times the specific tax rate on beer. Perform this ratio test for the rates applied in a state (or nation) of your choice. What might account for divergence from this ratio?

5. The text worked the logic of a VAT through a production-distribution process from a farmer to the final customer. Work the same process through with a 10-percent turnover or gross receipts tax. Assume that value added at each stage is

the same as before, but that no credit for prior tax paid is provided and that each sales price equals tax-inclusive cost of purchases, plus value added at that stage, plus the 10-percent tax. Compute the final price paid by the consumer and the effective tax rate as a percentage of total value added. Make the same computation, assuming the sweater manufacturer and the retailer merge (i.e., there is no taxable sale in this exchange).

6. Vendors at Municipal Stadium sell their wares at prices that include the city, state, and transit district sales taxes; the total of these taxes is 8.25 percent when added to prices that do not include the sales tax.
   a. Convert this 8.25-percent tax-exclusive sales tax rate into its tax-inclusive equivalent rate. (Hint: use the method outlined for VAT calculations.)
   b. A vendor has receipts (including sales tax) at a game of $15,325. What sales tax must the vendor remit to the tax authorities?

7. Several states have declared sales tax holidays, in which the state does not collect sales tax on certain items for a short period of time. In most instances, the holiday has been for clothing and the period has been a week or ten days in August, the idea being to give a "back-to-school" discount as families get ready for the new year. Analyze the idea of such holidays according to yield, equity, administration and compliance, and economic impact.

CASES FOR DISCUSSION

CASE 9–1

Sales Tax and Used Cars

Large amounts of total sales and use tax collections typically result from sales of automobiles. The sales tax in each transaction is often substantial, so gains from avoidance or evasion can also be large. As a result, states often devise special taxes to replace the ordinary sales tax on such purchases. The Kentucky automobile usage tax considered in the following excerpt from an article in the *Louisville Courier-Journal* is such a tax.

Consider These Questions

1. How is the tax supposed to be computed? What variants do the dealers use? How are dealers alleged to profit?
2. Does the tax base coincide with the standard used in evaluation of sales taxes? Explain.
3. Can you propose a system better able to eliminate abuses?
4. Kentucky collected sales tax on the original sale of most cars sold by used car dealers. Should there be any tax at all on their resale by used car dealers? Explain.
5. How does your state base sales tax on such transactions?

Probe Finds Some Dealers Overcharging in Used Car Sales Taxes

By Larry Werner

A major investigation by the attorney general's Consumer Protection Division into Kentucky's retail automobile industry has uncovered instances of "substantial" overcharging of consumers on the sales tax for used cars.

The investigation, which could result in thousands of dollars in refunds for the state's used car buyers, has angered the powerful Kentucky Automobile Dealers Association (KADA), which is claiming that the attorney general has embarked on a "fishing expedition" to harass legitimate businessmen.

To this, Attorney General Ed W. Hancock replied: "If we are (fishing), we've got the right bait, I would say."

What the attorney general's investigators are looking for are deviations by the dealers from the method of charging sales tax set out in Kentucky Revised Statute 138.450, the state officials said.

According to that statute, the 5 percent sales tax must be assessed on the "retail value given in the automotive reference manual prescribed by the Department of Revenue" after deducting "a trade-in allowance equal to the value of the vehicle taken in trade."

The "automotive reference manual prescribed by the Department of Revenue" is the "National Automobile Dealers Association (NADA) Official Used Car Guide."

The statute also says that the trade-in allowance, which is sworn to by the seller on the bill of sale, shall not exceed "the fair market value of the vehicle taken in trade." Although the law doesn't spell out what the "fair market value" of the trade-in is, an attorney general's opinion has defined it as "in the area of" the NADA book value.

The attorney general's investigation has been aimed at the practice of certain dealers' charging used car buyers more sales tax than is remitted to county clerks for payment to the state. There are several ways in which this is done, according to Hancock and [Assistant Attorney General Robert] Bullock.

One method of overcharging the sales tax is outlined by former Asst. Atty. Gen. David R. Vandeventer in a memo to KADA on the investigation.

"For example, by charging the consumer 5 percent of the lot sale price for a used car and remitting 5 percent of the NADA guide book if, as usual, the sale price exceeds the NADA guide price."

Hancock and Bullock explained that if a dealer charges 5 percent of the sales price to the consumer and then gives the county clerk only 5 percent of the lower NADA book value, the dealer is "pocketing" illegally obtained income.

In other cases, they said, dealers seemed to be simply charging the consumer a "lump sum" for sales tax regardless of the NADA book price of the car. When the bill of sale is registered with the county clerk, they said, the proper sales tax is calculated and paid.

For example, a dealer might be charging buyers a uniform $150 for sales tax. But if the NADA price on the car is $2,500, only 5 percent of that amount—or $125—is paid to the county clerk, resulting in a $25 bonus for the dealer.

Hancock and Bullock emphasized that this "lump-sum" method of charging sales tax also results in undercharges in cases where the actual amount of tax due exceeds the lump sum charged the buyer.

In other cases, Hancock said, the investigators have been unable to determine how dealers have arrived at the sales tax they have charged buyers.

"In some instances, there seems to have been no rhyme or reason to the basis for the tax charged," Hancock said. "You can't tie it into any computation."

Bullock and his staff have been visiting auto dealers and asking to see both purchase orders—which are filled out at the time the sale is made—and the bills of sale that are registered with the county clerks.

In many cases, Bullock said, the sales tax figure on the purchase order—which is the amount of tax the buyer paid to the dealer—exceeds 5 percent of the "total" price that is recorded on the bill of sale and on which the tax paid by the dealer is based.

Examples provided by the attorney general's office included:

1. A case in which the purchase order indicated that $93.40 was charged the consumer, but in which the bill of sale indicated only $70 was paid by the dealer to the county clerk.
2. A case in which the purchase order indicated that $75 sales tax was paid by the consumer, but in which the bill of sale indicated only $39.15 was paid by the dealer to the county clerk.
3. A case in which the purchase order indicated that $143.75 was charged the consumer for sales tax and other incidental fees, but in which the bill of sale indicated only $62.50 was paid by the dealer to the county clerk.

Hancock and Bullock suggested that consumers who have purchased used cars since June 16, 1972, check to see if they have been overcharged for sales tax.

They said this is done by checking the amount of sales tax listed on the purchase order. This should amount to 5 percent of "total" purchase price listed on the "motor vehicle bill of sale" that is sent to the purchaser by the county clerk.

The "total" listed on the bill of sale is equal to the "average retail as shown in NADA Book," less the trade-in value of the car. These figures are listed on the bill of sale in a section entitled "Used Vehicles Valuation of Motor Vehicle for Computation of Usage Tax."

Hancock said the Consumer Protection Division was alerted to the overcharging practice by a former credit manager for a Kentucky dealer.

In a February 22 letter from Hancock to attorneys for KADA, Hancock states that the investigation was begun last November by members of the consumer division staff.

"After bringing it to my attention, I suggested that they contact representatives of KADA, for the purpose of asking for their help in investigating this matter . . . ," Hancock's letter states.

However, after Bullock met with the KADA board of directors on December 18 and requested assistance from the trade association, KADA reported to Bullock's staff that the members of KADA "would be opposed to such cooperation and, therefore, no cooperation would be given. . . . " the letter says.

Used Vehicles—Valuation of Motor Vehicle for Computation of Usage Tax (KRS 138.450 & 138.460)

Passenger Cars

1. Average retail as shown in NADA Book	$2000.00
2. Less trade-in per KRS KY. Registration No.	600.00
3. Total	1400.00
Cash-delivered price of vehicle	1868.00
Sales tax	93.40
Documentary fee	15.50
Total cash-delivered price	$1976.90

The illustration above contains segments of a bill of sale and a purchase order on an actual used car sale in which the Kentucky attorney general's office detected an overcharge on sales tax. On top is a section of the bill of sale that lists the $1,400 "total" on which the 5 percent sales tax is computed for payment by the dealer to the county clerk. The "total" is arrived at by subtracting the trade-in allowance from the "book value" of the car being purchased. The correct tax due is $70 ($1400 × .05). However, as the purchase order pictured on the bottom shows, 5 percent of the "cash delivered price of the vehicle" before subtraction of the trade-in allowance, or $93.40, was paid by the consumer to the dealer.

The "cooperation" requested of KADA by the attorney general's office was that the trade association ask each of its members to supply the Consumer Protection Division with "complete sets of records on every sale during July and August 1973," according to Vandeventer's memo to KADA.

Vandeventer states in his memo that this would enable the consumer agency to determine whether overcharging was going on and which dealers were doing it.

When KADA refused cooperation, Hancock said, "There was no choice left to me but to authorize the investigation on a dealer-by-dealer basis."

When asked about KADA's alleged refusal to cooperate with the investigation, KADA president [Ernie] Bates said:

"I told Mr. Bullock we can't give him authority to come into a man's place of business and let him go fishing around for a mistake this man has made."

Bates added:

"We don't condone in any case any overcharging or undercharging of the automobile usage tax. It's a pretty complicated thing to compute. Surprisingly enough, there are a lot of people who don't understand it. There have probably been some mistakes made on it. I think they (dealers) are probably computing it to the best of their ability."

Bates said it is his opinion that "Mr. Bullock went on a fishing expedition in Mr. Jones' case, and he has no law to back him up."

Hancock said: "As far as his (Bates) saying there's no law behind us, that's going to be up to the court to decide. As far as saying, 'There's nothing wrong, but you can't see the records,' that's about like (President) Nixon saying, 'There's nothing wrong, but you can't have the tapes.'"

CASE 9–2

Girl Scout Cookies and the Snack Tax

State sales taxes often exempt purchases of food purchased for at-home consumption to help relieve the regressivity of the tax. But that exemption causes a substantial loss of revenue. Furthermore, some people question the nutritional value of certain items exempted under the food label and doubt the wisdom of losing revenue in a tax structure to provide relief to such purchases. In difficult fiscal times in the early 1990s, a few states sought additional revenue by narrowing the food exemption, particularly by removing some of these questionable categories from the exempt list. These new laws and their enforcement have produced policy problems testing the resolve of the legislators and tax administrators.

In the 1991 legislative session, Maine passed a package of tax changes designed to increase revenues by $300 million annually. (Total tax collections in fiscal 1990 were $1,560.9 million.) The changes included higher income taxes, an increase in the state sales and use tax rate from 5 to 6 percent, and a revision to remove snack food from the "sales of grocery staples" category then exempt from the state sales and use tax. The new law was estimated to yield $10 million annually.

The new law taxed snack food, as defined by the legislature:

14-C. "Snack food." Snack food means any item that is ordinarily sold for consumption without further preparation or that requires no preparation other than combining the item with a liquid; that may be stored unopened without refrigeration, except that ice cream, ice milk, frozen yogurt and sherbet are snack foods; that is not generally considered a major component of a well-balanced meal; and that is not defined in this section as a grocery staple. "Snack food" includes, but is not limited to, corn chips, potato chips, processed fruit snacks, fruit rolls, fruit bars, popped popcorn, pork rinds, pretzels, cheese sticks and cheese puffs, granola bars, breakfast bars, bread sticks, roasted nuts, doughnuts, cookies, crackers, pastries, toaster pastries, croissants, cakes, pies, ice cream cones, marshmallows, marshmallow creme, artificially flavored powdered or liquid drink mixes or drinks, ice cream sauces including chocolate sauce, ready-to-eat puddings, beef jerky, meat bars and dips. (36 Maine Revised Statutes © 1752 [1992])

SOURCE: Louisville Courier Journal 27 March 1974, C1. Copyright © 1974. *The Courier Journal.* Reprinted with permission.

The lawmakers soon discovered that the expansion of the sales and use tax base had some unexpected consequences, particularly in regard to the finances of Girl Scouts. Two councils, the Abnakin and Kennebec, served about 19,500 girls in Maine and 60 to 65 percent of their revenues came from cookie sales. Because neither council was qualified to purchase inventory for resale as a registered retailer, then charging sales tax on each transaction, the councils now had to pay tax on their cookie purchases. That amounted to around $58,000, or almost 2 percent of cookie revenue (they paid tax on the wholesale price of about 80¢ per box).

The two councils responded differently to the new tax. Abnaki raised their cookie prices from $2.25 to $2.50, but sales fell 7 percent from the prior year. Kennebec lacked sufficient time to react, so had to absorb about $40,000 in cookie losses. But neither council thought the new tax was fair. Jo Stevens, executive director of the Abnaki Council, voiced the general view: "We're not selling groceries. We're raising charitable contributions."

The joint Taxation Committee was generally sympathetic. Its co-chair, Sen. Stephen Bost, said, "We had not intended as a committee to include . . . Girl Scouts in the snack tax." But proposed legislation to exempt Girl Scouts and related organizations (including the pre-popped popcorn sold by Boy Scouts) would cause a revenue loss of around $175,000 annually—and the state had no clear way to make it up. (Incidentally, candy had been taxed for some time, but candy sales by school groups and parent-teacher organizations are exempt.)

What should Maine do? Here are some options: (1) do nothing—the tax is working as it should; (2) direct the Bureau of Taxation to rewrite the instruction; (3) repeal the snack tax; (4) exempt sales and purchases by the Girl Scouts and similar organizations; (5) require the Girl Scouts to register as retail merchants, buy their cookies using the resale exemption, and collect sales tax on their cookie sales; and (6) exempt sales and/or purchases by all youth or charitable organizations. (You may think of other possibilities.) Use the standards for revenue-policy evaluation (yield, fairness, economic effect, and collectability) to test options and provide a recommendation. Explain which approach is most consistent with the logic of sales taxation. Which parties would have an interest in the eventual outcome of the discussion? What is your overall view of the snack tax, without respect to the Girl Scout issue?

SOURCE: Data and quotations from "Scouting and Tax Relief," State Government News 35 (April 1992), 33.

CHAPTER 10

Major Tax Structures: Property Taxes

Annual taxes on property in the United States yield over $296 billion each year for state and local governments. That considerable yield is substantially less than the total from either income or consumption bases, and much less than states collect from those bases, but the tax on real property—roughly 90 percent of the total—is the lifeblood for fiscal independence of local governments. As Glenn Fisher points out: "There are no taxes capable of financing our current system of local governments that can be locally levied and administered, except the property tax."[1] They are unpopular with the electorate, with enlightened and craven politicians alike, and with some academic observers—but they endure because they produce reliable, stable, independent revenue for the governments closest to the people, and there is no clearly superior alternative for providing local fiscal autonomy. Property taxes of various designs are levied throughout the world, although governments in the United States and Canada raise relatively more of their tax revenue from them than is the case elsewhere. Because of their utility for providing a source of revenue subject to local control, they are an important element in fiscal decentralization programs in many countries of central and eastern Europe.

Property taxes were once the primary tax for both state and local government finance. Indeed, as recently as 1932, property taxes produced almost three-quarters of all state and local tax revenue and 92.5 percent of local government tax revenue.[2] But in the depths of the Great Depression, much property tax could not be collected from farmers, businesses, and individuals who had lost their usual sources of income, and states began to develop transaction-based taxes on goods and services,

[1]Glenn W. Fisher, *The Worst Tax? A History of the Property Tax in America* (Lawrence, Kans.: University Press of Kansas, 1996), 210.

[2]U.S. Bureau of Census, *Financial Statistics of State and Local Governments: 1932 (Wealth, Public Debt, and Taxation)* (Washington, D.C.: GPO, 1935). The federal government has levied property taxes twice, in 1798 and in 1813. The taxes were apportioned among the states, as required for direct taxes by the Constitution. See Dall W. Forsythe, *Taxation and Political Change in the Young Nation, 1781–1833* (New York: Columbia University Press, 1977).

especially retail sales taxes and motor-fuel excises. These new taxes offered high yield and greater reliability—not to mention their less harsh enforcement mechanisms (enforcement of uncollected property tax on a house or farm, for example, meant seizure and sale of that property)—and state governments especially financed their post–World War II responsibilities with more nonproperty tax revenues. Local governments overall continue a heavy reliance on the property tax, although large cities in some states make significant use of other options.

Table 10–1 offers an overview of property tax reliance in the United States. Although states obtain only 2 percent of their tax revenue from these levies, local governments collect almost three-quarters of their tax revenue from it. Independent school districts rely more heavily on the property tax than any other type of government, raising 96 percent of their tax revenue from that source in the 2002–2003 fiscal year. Only in Alabama, Georgia, Iowa, Kentucky, Louisiana, Missouri, Nebraska, Pennsylvania, and Tennessee do school district nonproperty taxes yield as much as 3 percent of total tax revenue—but the significance of school district general sales, personal income, and payroll taxation has been rising in recent years.[3] Because schools receive substantial intergovernmental aid, mostly from their states, the share of all their revenue from the property tax is much lower (around 35 percent), but they still receive more than 40 percent of all property tax collected. Cities and counties both receive more than 20 percent of property taxes, but cities rely somewhat more heavily on nonproperty taxes than do counties. Despite the continuing unpopularity of the property tax, property tax collections have grown at a compound rate of over 4.5 percent annually from 1992–1993 to 2002–2003.

Table 10–1
Property Taxes in U.S. Government Finances, 2002–2003

	Total ($ millions)	% of General Revenue	% of Tax Revenue	Share of Property Tax Revenue (%)	Growth Rate Since 1992–1993
State and Local Governments	296683.2	16.8%	31.6%	100.0%	4.6%
States	10470.5	0.9%	1.9%	3.5%	3.0%
Local Governments	286212.7	27.5%	73.4%	96.5%	4.6%
Counties	65777.9	24.5%	69.5%	22.2%	n.a.
Municipalities and Townships	83316.2	25.1%	55.9%	28.1%	n.a.
School Districts	126136.3	34.3%	96.2%	42.5%	n.a.
Special Districts	10982.2	11.2%	71.9%	3.7%	n.a.

SOURCE: U.S. Bureau of Census, Governments Division.
n.a., Data not available.

[3]Data from U.S. Bureau of the Census Governments Division.

Property taxes are the closest approximation to annual wealth taxes currently levied in the United States.[4] They are not, however, true net-wealth taxes because they typically exclude some types of wealth (e.g., personal property owned by individuals); they apply to gross, not net, wealth (e.g., the debt against a house or car is seldom completely subtracted from taxable value); and they may apply twice to certain wealth forms (some states tax both the value of corporate stock and properties owned by the corporation). To the extent that the taxes do reach wealth holdings, they may add an element of redistribution from rich to poor otherwise missing from the tax structure.[5] Because they apply to accumulated wealth, not income, they may also have less effect on work and investment incentives than do income taxes. They are not based, however, on values from current transactions (as is usually the case for income and sales taxes), so the tax requires a value-estimation procedure (assessment). That procedure is the primary weakness of property taxation.[6]

Property taxes cannot be simply summarized. As Richard Almy observes,

> In the United States, "the" property tax is composed of fifty-one separate state level property tax systems, each subject to numerous legal and extralegal local variations and each changing in some fashion over time—through constitutional revision, enactment of statutes and ordinances, changes in administrative procedures, court decisions and changes in the capabilities of tax administration.[7]

In most states, real property is assessed by local assessors, subject to state rules and regulations and, to varying degrees, state supervision and evaluation of the work that has been done.

Property within the scope of taxation may be either real or personal. *Real property* means real estate, realty, or land and improvements on that land. It encompasses soil and things permanently fixed to it by nature (trees, crops, grass, water, minerals, etc.) or by people (buildings, fences, etc.). Real property may also include air rights, the space above that land, but only when that space is actually used. *Personal property* includes everything that can be owned that is not real property. The category includes machinery and equipment, jewelry, automobiles, inventory, household furnishings, stocks and bonds, and much more. Personal property generally is more

---

[4]There are federal, state, and local *transfer* taxes, however. The federal estate tax is the most widely known, although it produces only modest revenue (1.2 percent of total receipts in 2001). In spite of the fact that it is paid by very few estates (fewer than 1.3 percent of estates are covered by the tax because of large exclusions before the tax begins to apply) and is highly progressive in burden, it is extremely unpopular. Because much of the money actually taxed by the estate tax represents unrealized capital gains that have not been taxed by the income tax, the tax fills a gap in the fiscal system and does not represent a double tax on income. Nevertheless, a small group of holders of great inherited wealth is likely to get the tax entirely abolished. See Michael J. Graetz and Ian Shapiro, *Death by a Thousand Cuts: The Fight over Taxing Inherited Wealth* (Princeton, N.J.: Princeton University Press, 2005) for the drama.

[5]One fact of American society is that wealth is significantly more concentrated than income. The wealthiest 1 percent of the population owns about 30 percent of wealth in the economy, whereas the top 1 percent of income earners receive 20 percent of total income. See Javier Diaz-Gimenez, "Dimensions of Inequality: Facts on the U.S. Distribution of Earnings, Income, and Wealth," *Federal Reserve Bank of Minneapolis Monthly Review* 21 (Spring 1997): 3–21.

[6]The tax may have development and redevelopment disincentives as well, depending on its structure.

[7]Richard Almy, "Rationalizing the Assessment Process," in George Peterson, ed., *Property Tax Reform* (Washington, D.C.: Urban Institute, 1973), 175.

easily moved than real property, but there is no general dividing line between the types. Each government develops its own definitions and distinctions, usually resorting to lists of property types to make borderline distinctions.[8] The distinction is crucial because some governments tax personal property more heavily than real property, whereas others exempt certain personal property. The personal-property share of the locally taxable property base is small, only around 10 percent on national aggregate, but it is much higher in a handful of states; many states exempt personal property entirely from the property tax base.[9]

Another distinction is between tangible and intangible personal property. *Tangible personal property* is property held for its own sake, including cars, machinery, inventories of raw materials and finished products, and household items. *Intangible personal property* is property valued because it represents an ownership claim on something of value; intangible properties include stocks, bonds, and other financial assets. Property taxes vary widely in the extent to which they apply to these properties. Many types of tangible personal property are both difficult to locate and, once located, difficult to value (what is the value of a 10-year-old television set or the old sofa where the cat sleeps, after all?); intangible personal property can often be easily valued, but may be difficult to locate. Sometimes intangible property is exempt by law, sometimes by local practice. Seldom is taxation complete.[10]

Good Tax, Bad Tax?

Academicians and tax analysts like property taxes more than do politicians, the media, and most of the general public. Property tax advocates believe that real property taxation is synonymous with fiscal autonomy for local government. There are no broad-based revenue options that are as well suited for local use as is this tax. If local governments do not have access to a property tax, then they are almost certainly destined to become fiscal wards of their state. There simply is no satisfactory tax option available for local use to replace the lost property tax revenue. Local fiscal autonomy means local property taxation. The specific advantages of the tax for local finance are significant:

1. The base is immobile, so the tax can be administered without fear that it will escape a local jurisdiction before the tax is collected.
2. The tax is stable, so it will not drop dramatically when the economy dips into recession.

---

[8]One interesting problem concerns the treatment of mobile homes—are they real or personal property? States use rules including permanency of foundation, presence of wheels or axles, highway licensing, and so forth, but there is no general division.

[9]John L. Mikesell, "Patterns of Exclusion of Person Property from American Property Tax Systems," *Public Finance Quarterly* 20 (Oct. 1992): 528–42.

[10]John H. Bowman, George E. Hoffer, and Michael D. Pratt, "Current Patterns and Trends in State and Local Intangibles Taxation," *National Tax Journal* 43 (December 1990): 439–50.

3. The tax rate can vary within small geographic areas to support even the smallest local governments.

4. The services typically supported by local property taxes provide direct protection to real property (fire and police protection, for instance) or contribute to making real properties valuable (high quality local schools, for instance). The property tax is a charge for these services.

5. The property tax base associated with industrial development provides a way of compensating those living around the property for the inconvenience (noise, traffic, pollution, etc.) associated with such activity.

6. Property taxes are visible, and the decisions made about them are close at hand, thus bringing people directly into the fiscal process, as should be the case in a democracy.

7. Many decisions made by local government have a direct impact on the value of real property. A property tax gives the government a direct stake in the quality of those decisions, while leaving property ownership, management, and allocation in private hands.

Furthermore, the tax does get at the owners of extremely valuable properties, including owners who have managed to avoid being taxed as their income was received, a particularly important contribution in countries with porous application of income taxes, either because of poor administration or because of generous tax preferences.

Popular opinion does not hold property taxes in such high regard, and politicians regularly build their campaigns on anti-property tax platforms. What is wrong with the taxes? There are several main complaints.

1. Property taxes are seen as regressive. Some state studies do generally show that the effective property tax rate does decline as income is higher. The degree is, however, usually not as great as with sales taxes. But the standard view among economists holds that the basic property tax is progressive: ownership of land and capital are concentrated among high-income households, so the burden of the tax is progressive.[11] Abnormally high property taxes in a locality may behave like selective excises, but the normal tax likely is progressively distributed. In spite of the evidence, the belief that shapes the political discussion is the regressivity opinion.

2. Property taxes are horizontally inequitable. The effective property tax rate varies substantially across properties of similar value and property tax borne by

[11]Wallace E. Oates, "An Overview and Some Reflections," in Wallace E. Oates, ed., *Property Taxation and Local Government Finance* (Cambridge, Mass.: Lincoln Institute for Land Policy, 2001). There are three primary views of property tax incidence: the "traditional view" that the property tax is shifted to consumers in the form of higher housing prices, the "benefit view" that concludes that the property tax is simply a charge for services provided by local government, and the "new or capital tax view" that argues that the tax is a distortionary tax on the use of capital within the local jurisdiction. See George R. Zodrow, "The Property Tax as a Capital Tax: A Room with Three Views," *National Tax Journal* LIV (March 2001), 139–56. Only the traditional view would cause the property tax to be significantly regressive.

families of similar affluence also differs significantly. The former is the result of how property taxes are structured and administered; the latter is the result of differing household preferences for property ownership. There is much evidence of this horizontal disparity problem.[12]

3. Local property taxes create a scattered pattern of fiscal affluence and fiscal poverty. Some localities have great endowments of property values (those with manufacturing facilities, for instance) and some have minimal property tax values. That creates great disparity in the type and quality of public services that the localities can afford to provide their citizenry and this fiscal disparity can be quite inequitable. The problem can be particularly acute when primary and secondary education is driven by local property tax endowment. These issues are discussed at greater length in Chapter 14.

4. Property tax burdens can be shockingly high for people living in areas with increasing property values and can become difficult for people with low incomes. Long-time residents of an area that has suddenly become trendy can experience sudden increases in their property tax bills because of the unexpected increase in value of their properties and those bills can confront them with difficult choices.

5. A property tax can significantly reduce the prospects for economic development by reducing the after-tax rate of return that can be earned from building productive facilities or refurbishing deteriorated properties. With upgrading comes higher values, which causes higher tax bills, thus reducing the return from development.[13]

The Arithmetic of Rates, Levies, and Assessed Value

Most tax rates change only with special legislative action—they are the portion of the fiscal system that is most strictly incremental, in the sense of small changes made to a permanent base. That is the case, for example, with state sales taxes and state and federal income taxes. Property tax rates are typically set, however, as a part of the annual budget process with rate setting as the climax to the process establishing how much will be spent. The rate in most circumstances must be annually readopted at a level sufficient to yield enough revenue to balance the operating

[12]And there are some systematic problems with the horizontal disparity. For example, Harris finds that majority-minority neighborhoods are assessed at higher effective ratios than are residents of majority-white neighborhoods. Lee Harris, "Assessing Discrimination: The Influence of Race in Residential Property Tax Assessments," *Journal of Land Use and Environmental Law,* 20 (Fall 2004).

[13]The development disincentive can be reduced by adopting a dual rate property tax in which the undeveloped value of land is taxed at a higher rate than the improvements constructed on the land. Ideally, the tax would be applied only to the land value, thus removing the development disincentive entirely. A number of American cities have experienced good development results from such dual rate systems. Wallace E. Oates and Robert M. Schwab, "The Impact of Urban Land Taxation: The Pittsburgh Experience," *National Tax Journal,* 50 (March 1997), 1–21.

budget and to cover current costs of servicing debt obligations (interest to be paid plus any maturing principal). This rate setting uses the following data:

1. **Planned Expenditure:** The total of approved (or proposed) expenditure plans (*E*) included in the appropriation act or ordinance.
2. **Estimated Nonproperty Tax Revenue:** The estimate of revenue from nonproperty tax sources, including miscellaneous charge and fee revenue, revenue from nonproperty taxes (sales or income), grants, and so on (*NPR*). Part of this revenue may be guaranteed state payments, but much will be forecasted.
3. **The Levy:** The property tax levy (the amount of revenue the government plans to collect from the property tax), or approved spending less nonproperty tax revenue (*E* minus *NPR*).
4. **Net Assessed Value:** The net assessed value (*NAV*) in the taxing unit, as established at the standard assessment date for the jurisdiction, equals the base on which the property tax will be levied. Assessed value itself may be a statutorily defined fraction of the value initially appraised by the property assessor.

The levy ($E - NPR$), net assessed value (*NAV*), and the property tax rate (r) are related in the formula

$$r = (E - NPR)/NAV.$$

This relationship applies for each unit levying the property tax. Some units may face limits on levies or may need to raise set sums to cover contractual debt service, others have constrained rates, and others have considerable freedom to establish what rate is necessary to balance their budgets. But regardless of the conditions, the formula links those terms and applies to each government using the tax.[14] For example, suppose a village appropriated $95,000 for the 2007 fiscal year (January 1 to December 31, 2007), estimated that it would receive $15,000 from nonproperty tax sources during that fiscal year, and had the net assessed value of $1.75 million on March 1, 2006 (the assessment date). In that village, the property tax rate for 2007 would be 4.58 percent, or $4.58 per $100 of assessed value. A parcel valued at $8,000 for tax purposes would have a 2007 property tax bill of $366.40, possibly payable in equal installments due in May and November of 2007. This rate setting process goes on for each of the several local governments serving an area (for instance, the county, cities, school districts, special districts, etc.), each independently, as if the other jurisdictions do not exist.

The actual property tax bill received by a property holder is like a layer cake of rates imposed by each jurisdiction in which the property is physically located; for instance, $4.58 for the village, $1.22 for the county, and $3.25 for the school district, with a total rate of $9.05 on the net assessed value of the property. Another property located in the same county would face a somewhat different set of rates if it were not in the village (or in a different village) and in a different school district.

---

[14]Joseph K. Eckert, ed., *Property Appraisal and Assessment Administration* (Chicago: International Association of Assessing Officers, 1990), 20.

The property holder will ordinarily make one payment to cover all the taxes; a single property tax collector (possibly a county treasurer) collects and disburses to each taxing unit. Each of those taxes would have been set in the same way that the village rate was set, but each done independently.[15]

There is normally a separation of function in property tax administration. The property assessor is responsible for determining the taxable value of parcels in the jurisdictions, the local governing bodies determine the amounts to be raised for their budgets from the property tax, a clerk or auditor calculates the statutory property tax rate for each jurisdiction, and the treasurer collects the tax owed on each parcel and distributes the collections to the proper governments.

These legal (or advertised) tax rates cannot be directly compared across governments. For instance, suppose that the combined rate in one city is $10.00 per $100 of net assessed value and the rate in another city is $15.00 per $100 of net assessed value. Would it be reasonable to assume that a property worth $100,000 in the second city would face a tax bill that is 50-percent higher than would a property of equivalent value in the first city? The legal rate is 50-percent higher, but we cannot be certain that the two properties of equal market value would be assessed at the same level by the property assessor. To make the comparison, we must adjust the legal or statutory tax rate for differences in the assessment ratio, the ratio between the value of the property as established in the assessment process and its market value (the price at which a willing buyer and a willing seller would reach agreement on a sale). As we shall see in the next sections, not all property tax systems define the value for tax purposes to be full market value, and not all property tax assessors are equally adept at hitting the legal assessment target. Therefore, to compare property taxes, it is necessary to adjust legal tax rates for differences in assessment ratios to look at effective property tax rates. The effective property tax rate (*ETR*) on a parcel of property equals the property tax (*T*) divided by the market value of the property (*MV*):

$$ETR = T/MV.$$

The property tax equals the legal tax rate (*r*) multiplied by the assessed value of the property (*AV*):

$$T = r \times AV$$

so the effective tax rate equals the statutory tax rate multiplied by the assessment ratio (the ratio of assessed to market value):

$$ETR = (r \times AV)/MV = r \times (AV/MV)$$

In the previous example, if the assessment ratio were 100 percent in the first city and 50 percent in the second, the effective tax rate would be higher in the first

[15]A government may, of course, see the computed rate, worry about the consequences, and revise the amount of levy it chooses to raise.

($10.00 per $100) than in the second ($7.50 per $100), the reverse of the legal rates. Comparisons across jurisdictions—and even across properties in a single jurisdiction—absolutely require consideration of assessment ratios!

Doing Assessments: Standards

Property taxation requires a basis for distributing the tax burden among property holders. Because the tax base includes property holdings (accumulated asset values) rather than current flow of property sales during the year, values must be estimated.[16] This estimation—or assessment—determines what the tax value is for each property parcel and, by aggregation, the total tax value of the government; it is the heart of the property tax system. When a reassessment changes property values for tax purposes, some properties pay a higher share of the tax burden and others a lower share, compared with shares before reassessment. This adjustment of tax payments to more closely match perceived capability to pay the tax—as measured by property value—is the objective of assessment.

What is the standard for property appraisal? The most widely used standard is market value: "Market value is the cash price a property would bring in a competitive and open market."[17] This hypothetical exchange, the same concept used by banks, insurance companies, and other institutions to determine a property's worth, assumes that (1) markets have adequate time to function, (2) no undue pressure is exerted on either buyer or seller, (3) both parties are well informed about the parcel at sale, and (4) the transaction is at arm's length.[18] Actual transaction prices—that is, what someone just paid for a property—may provide information about market value, but they are not necessarily that value, both because those conditions may not be met and because the price may include sale of something in addition to the parcel itself.[19] Market value, internationally recognized in both public and private finance, is a standard with the same meaning everywhere, a meaning that is

[16]The current value approach to establishing the tax base is used in the United States and Canada, but other approaches are used. The United Kingdom, for instance, bases tax on the annual rental value of land and buildings ("rates"). Other countries use land or building area as the base. Joe Eckert, *Property Appraisal and Assessment Administration* (Chicago: International Association of Assessing Officers, 1990), 7.

[17]Ibid., 35.

[18]House appraisals for mortgage lending is increasingly done through automated systems using computer models provided by Fannie Mae (Federal National Mortgage Association) and Freddie Mac (Federal Home Loan Mortgage Corporation) to quickly estimate values for mortgage loans. These appraisals cost much less than traditional in-house appraisals. They are done by mining databases that list selling prices for homes in the neighborhood and comparing those properties with the one being appraised. Freddie Mac and Fannie Mae operate as financial intermediaries by acquiring, packaging, and then securitizing mortgages originated by various entities. The appraisals are done primarily to test the reasonableness of the proposed transaction price for the appraised property—to verify that the property being purchased has sufficient value to protect the lender if the loan goes bad—and are less concerned with great accuracy. But the principles are consistent with other appraisals, including for property tax purposes. Patrick Barta, "Lenders Tout Home Appraisals by Computer; Human Appraisers Demur," *The Wall Street Journal*, 20 July 2001, B1, B3.

[19]Such additions may include, for instance, some personal property or some special financing from the seller.

not linked to any particular tax law, legal system, or government structure. Although value estimates are hypothetical, they can be tested against actual transactions and can be challenged on an objective basis.[20] As is described shortly, a few states in the United States do not use market value as the statutory standard, but it is the assessment basis most widely used.

Within market-assessment systems, there often are special exceptions for certain property groups, often agricultural land. An ordinary appraisal assumes that a prospective buyer may put the newly acquired property to a different use—that is, the farmland close to the growing city might be developed into a shopping center, an apartment complex, or a housing subdivision, or a single-family residence near a university might be converted into apartments or offices. That potential for different use might indeed be a principal influence on market value. *Current-use assessment*, however, assumes that the buyer would continue the same use of the parcel. For most parcels, there would be no difference between market and current-use assessment because there is but trivial chance that a market-driven prospective buyer would change how the property is used. The difference can be important where markets are changing with urban or other development and expansion. Generally, the idea is to protect existing property holders from the tax implications of the higher values of the properties and prevent tax-induced conversion away from agriculture and open-space uses.[21]

A few states legally require some general assessment standard other than market value.[22] One such alternative standard is the *acquisition value* or assessment-on-sale system required in California by Proposition 13 (1978), required for homestead property in Florida by the 1992 referendum that approved Amendment 10, and introduced in Michigan with the revision of school finances in 1994. In this system, properties are revalued for tax purposes only when they are sold and then at the new transaction price.[23]

This structure of reassessment only on sale disrupts the property market (because prospective buyers would face a different property tax than would the prospective seller), creates a property record substructure of sales without recorded

---

[20]If a property assessed for $75,000 sells for $300,000, we can be reasonably certain that it was assessed at considerably less than current market value. Therefore, current market value estimates are testable and hence refutable.

[21]John H. Bowman and John L. Mikesell, in "Assessment of Agricultural Property for Taxation," *Land Economics* 64 (February 1988): 28–36, find use-value assessment to improve the uniformity of property assessment. But many studies question the effectiveness of such laws in influencing land use, their primary objective. See, for example, David E. Hansen and S. I. Schwartz, "Landowner Behavior at the Rural-Urban Fringe in Response to Preferential Taxation," *Land Economics* 51 (November 1975): 34–54.

[22]Assessment may also be done with uniform application of an administrative formula, not the standard estimation of a value, as the target. It is virtually impossible for a property owner to know whether his or her parcel is over- or under-assessed in the system, because the owner cannot tell the extent to which the formula has been properly applied to other parcels. If the owner's parcel is properly assessed and other parcels are under-assessed, then the owner is over-assessed in the system. But the only test the owner has, save for reassessing all parcels in the taxing unit, is to verify application of the formula to his or her parcel.

[23]Both California and Florida apply across-the-board adjustment increases, but realignments between parcels occur only when parcels exchange hands. Allen Manvel noted the precipitous decline in assessment quality produced by that system. See "Assessment Uniformity—and Proposition 13," *Tax Notes* 24, (August 27, 1984): 893–95.

deeds as individuals seek to avoid the property tax adjustments that would accompany a recorded sale, and causes similarly situated properties to pay widely different property tax. This last problem is especially difficult because it directly conflicts with assessment uniformity, the primary concern of the assessment task. Indeed, in a 1989 case involving the assessment of coal properties in West Virginia, the U.S. Supreme Court unanimously held that valuation of some properties at their recent purchase price when similar parcels are valued on earlier assessments violates the equal protection clause of the Fourteenth Amendment of the U.S. Constitution. Chief Justice Rehnquist wrote, in a classic statement of the horizontal equity standard that ". . . the constitutional requirement is the seasonable attainment of a rough equality in tax treatment of similarly situated property owners."[24] In that case, the plaintiff's property, because more recently purchased, was assessed at values eight to thirty-five times the value of comparable neighboring property, and nothing was bringing the assessments closer together. But the assessor followed this procedure contrary to the state law. It was, as the Court labeled it, an "aberrational enforcement policy."

A test of acquisition-value assessment as the legal state standard came from California in *Nordlinger* v. *Hahn*.[25] Stephanie Nordlinger found that, when she purchased a house in the Baldwin Heights neighborhood of Los Angeles County, the accompanying reassessment on acquisition brought a 36-percent increase in property tax, from $1,247.40 to $1,701 per year. She later discovered she was paying about five times more in taxes than some of her neighbors who owned comparable homes within the same residential development. For example, one block away, a house of identical size on a lot slightly larger than the petitioner's was subject to a general tax levy of only $358.20 (based on an assessed valuation of $35,820, which reflected the home's value in 1975 plus the up-to-2 percent per year standard inflation factor). The general tax levied against her modest home was only a few dollars less than that paid by a pre-1976 owner of a $2.1 million Malibu beachfront home.

Nordlinger believed this pattern to be both patently unfair and contrary to constitutional requirements for equal protection. The state, however, disagreed, arguing that the system represented a rational system of classification because there was a legitimate state interest in allowing longer-term owners to pay a lower tax than newer owners of property: (1) to avoid taxing property holders on unrealized gains on their properties and possibly taxing people out of their homes, (2) to ensure predictability of tax payments for property owners, and (3) to achieve revenue stability for local governments. The Supreme Court, while showing considerable sympathy for Nordlinger's argument and noting that most of these state objectives could have been better achieved through other means, chose to accept that there was some rational basis for the system—despite its undesirable effects, including dramatic differences in property tax paid by similarly situated individuals. Furthermore, evidence indicates that Proposition 13 did induce homeowners and renters to

---

[24]*Allegheny Pittsburgh Coal Co.* v. *County Commission of Webster County, West Virginia,* 190 S. Ct. 633, decided Jan. 18, 1989.

[25]*Stephanie Nordlinger, Petitioner* v. *Kenneth Hahn, in His Capacity as Tax Assessor for Los Angeles County,* 112 S. Ct. 2326.

stay put and avoid higher tax rates than they would face when buying new properties: from 1970 to 2000, the average tenure for owners and renters in California increased by slightly more than 1 year and slightly more than three-quarters of a year, respectively, relative to comparison states.[26] Ordinarily, reduced mobility is regarded as an impediment to economic growth and, hence, regarded as undesirable public policy in market-driven economies. The Court found that there was a rational basis for the assessment scheme and, in contrast to the West Virginia situation, the acquisition value system was constitutional.

Two other valuation standards are worth noting. These are an area-based assessment, in which the tax is driven exclusively by the size of the property, and a formula-based or cadastral assessment, in which the assessment is driven by the application of a legal formula that uses physical attributes (e.g., size, design, location, soil type, etc.) of each property. The test of a cadastral assessment is not whether it approximates a certain value, but whether the physical attributes have been correctly recorded and whether the formula has been accurately applied to them. These systems are usually applied in situations in which there are few reliable market transactions of the property being taxed, as in developing countries or in countries transitioning from centrally planned to market economies.

Doing Assessments: Cycles

The assessment cycles that governments in the United States use fall into three general categories: *mass cyclical assessment, segmental assessment,* and *annual assessment.* With mass cyclical assessment, all properties in a taxing jurisdiction are valued for tax purposes in a particular year; that value does not change until the next scheduled mass assessment, except for new construction, demolition, or change in use of a property. States prescribe mass cyclical assessment at intervals ranging from 2 to 10 years. Examples include Iowa (2 years), Maine (4 years), Minnesota (4 years), and Connecticut (10 years).[27] Some states explicitly indicate that a physical inspection of real property will be made with the reassessment. Many jurisdictions that operate under a mass cyclical assessment system choose to contract the reassessment with a private appraisal firm so that they do not face great changes in staffing between normal and reassessment years.

Segmental assessment is a procedure by which a specified fraction of real-property parcels in a jurisdiction is reassessed each year, moving through the assessing unit in sequence. Thus, if a 3-year cycle is used, one-third of the properties in the area are reassessed each year, with all properties reassessed in 3 years. The last-valued taxpayers can complain about the inflation in their valuations, which is absent from earlier-valued parcels, but administrative convenience and the fact

---

[26]Nada Wasi and Michelle J. White, "Property Tax Limitations and Mobility: The Lock-in Effect of California's Proposition 13," National Bureau of Economic Research Working Paper 11108, February 2005. Available online at www.nber.org/papers/w11108.

[27]U.S. Bureau of the Census, *Census of Governments 1992,* Vol. 2, *Taxable Property Values, No. 1 Assessed Valuation for Local General Property Taxation* (Washington, D.C.: GPO, 1994), D-1–D-3.

that all parcels take their turn as last valued has preserved the method. Examples include a 3-year cycle in both Maryland and Cook County, Illinois.[28] Idaho requires that 20 percent of property in each assessment class be appraised each year.

The final system is annual assessment, a process that assumes updated values for all real property parcels each year. Computers and modern information management systems make such reappraisals possible, but an annual physical inspection and inventory of all parcels, the traditional mark of reassessment, is unlikely. More often than not, annual valuation employs the physical characteristics of properties as identified in earlier parcel inventories with new value weights applied to those characteristics and a realignment of the significance of neighborhood location to keep up with changing markets. For instance, in earlier years, a fireplace might have added $1,000 to the value of a house; this year, it is estimated to add $1,800. Or, after adjusting for other charges, properties in one area may have values altered by 1 percent, whereas in other areas the change may be 2 percent. In that fashion, new value estimates emerge from old physical feature data. Of course, annual reassessment can become no reassessment if last year's forms are simply recopied or if all parcels have values increased by a flat factor of, for example, 3 percent.[29] That process destroys the equity of the property tax because no adjustments are made for properties whose value has either fallen or increased. The fiction that properties are reassessed annually prevents any meaningful realignment of parcel values.

Modern information management systems, often involving geographical information systems, make good quality annual updates feasible and equitable, so long as there is process transparency, careful monitoring of changes in real estate markets, and an appeal process that property owners can navigate without great difficulty.

Doing Assessments: Approaches

Assessment is a technical process, and each system has distinct peculiarities. There are, however, three general approaches to estimating real property values employed in various mixtures in state and local systems; all are offshoots of private property appraisal techniques used by realtors, banks, and others needing estimates of value. The techniques are (1) the market data or comparable sales approach, (2) the income approach; and (3) the cost or summation approach.[30]

---

[28]In Cook County, the cycle through reassessment works like this: 2004, reassess City of Chicago; 2005, reassess southwest suburbs; 2006, reassess northwest suburbs; 2007, reassess City of Chicago; and so on. See John E. Petersen and Kimberly K. Edwards, "The Impact of Declining Property Values on Local Government Finances," *Urban Land Institute Research Working Paper Series*, Paper 626 (March 1993): 49.

[29]Not all housing values go up, and not all values in a market area move together. In the Boston area, "sales of single-family homes in the upscale town of Wellesley fell 2.2 percent in 1992, with an increase in the median sales price of 8.6 percent. In nearby Malden, a lower-middle-class town, single-family home sales grew 8.3 percent, but median prices fell 2 percent" Christopher J. Mayer, "Taxes, Income Distribution, and the Real Estate Cycle: Why All Houses Do Not Appreciate at the Same Rate," *New England Economic Review* (May/June 1993): 40. Uniform adjustments in assessments can not substitute for reassessment in improving fairness. The larger the area included, the greater the disparity in changes in value, so standard value adjustments may be feasible in small, but not large, areas.

[30]Eckert, *Property Appraisal,* Chapters 6–13.

1. **The market-data,** or *comparable sales,* **approach** estimates value of a subject parcel by comparing it with similar properties that have recently been sold. The approach uses information directly produced by the market about how property owners and prospective owners value properties. Of course, the approach requires a number of actual transactions in order for meaningful comparisons to be made. It does not work for unique properties because it requires property transactions involving properties similar in economically relevant details.[31] A reasonably good comparison is usually possible for residential property (there are many three-bedroom, split-level houses with about 2,500 square feet of living space in most cities, after all, and some have probably sold recently), but uniqueness can create a virtually impossible problem for most commercial or industrial parcels and some residential parcels.

2. **The income approach** converts the future returns from ownership of a parcel into their present-value equivalent to estimate the amount a willing and knowledgeable investor would pay for the future income flow. Application of the approach requires an estimate of the gross return from holding the parcel, the expenses associated with holding the parcel, and a rate at which the resulting net annual return would be capitalized into a current-value equivalent. In practice, an estimated annual income stream is converted into current value with a capitalization rate derived from market observation that reflects the prevailing relationship between a single year's net operating income and total property value. (Recall the discounting of future income flows to their present value in Chapter 6.) The approach is most attractive for estimating the value of income-producing properties (apartments, stores and offices, agricultural land, parking lots, etc.). On the market, how many multiples of net annual return are being paid for such properties? That comparison provides the value estimate.

3. **The cost or summation approach** estimates value by adding the depreciated cost of improvements on a parcel to the estimated land value of the parcel. The land value is normally estimated from either sales comparison or from income capitalization, the previously noted approaches for general valuation. The approach typically determines the cost of constructing a standard (average) grade structure at a particular date (with the labor and materials prices of that time, using the prevailing technology, and in the size and type as the subject property). That cost is adjusted to account for nonstandard construction materials and workmanship, either higher or lower than standard. To that cost is added extra features not found in the standard unit, such as extra bathroom fixtures, fireplaces, central air conditioning, and so on, for residential units; escalators, sprinkler systems, vaults, etc., for commercial units; and cranes, elevators, air handling systems, and so on, for industrial units. The "new cost" improvement value is calculated by either of two conceptual methods:

a. *Reproduction cost,* the cost of constructing an exact replica of the building at current prices. The building would have the same materials, construction

[31]Estimates using forms of regression analysis implicitly use sales comparisons, but the approach is also used without regression equations.

standards, design, workmanship, and all deficiencies and obsolescence of the subject building.

b. *Replacement cost,* the cost of constructing a building having equivalent utility to the subject building at current prices: The building would be built with modern materials and using current standards and design but would have the same utility as the existing building. (Replacement cost may ignore the cost of structural elements in the building that provide no utility—e.g., the unused second story of a warehouse could be ignored in costing the building.)

Both reproduction and replacement should reasonably lead to the same value estimate through logically different adjustments for *accumulated depreciation.* In general, that accumulated depreciation can be from physical wear and tear from elements, and may be curable (primarily from deferred maintenance) or incurable (correction expenses would be enormous and impractical), from functional obsolescence due to lack of utility or desirability in property design (inadequacy or absence of features and super adequacy or presence of nonuseful features), or from economic obsolescence due to changes external to the property (changes in the neighborhood). The depreciation estimate would vary, depending on whether "new cost" was estimated on reproduction or replacement concepts.

The three approaches to estimating value are alternatives, but each has special strengths. The income approach is best used for properties bought and sold largely on the basis of income production—office buildings, apartments, motels and hotels, and some types of land. The cost approach, although applicable to most improvements, is especially suitable for special or unique properties that are seldom exchanged on the market (for instance, a purpose-built manufacturing facility) and properties that generate no income (for instance, a public museum). It also, along with the income approach, is vital for use-value assessment. The market-data approach applies in any circumstance for which a sufficient number of reliable transactions occur. Market-data and cost approaches are particularly amenable to the requirements of mass reassessment. Each would be tested by the extent to which the value estimate it generated matches the price received in a voluntary, arm's length, knowledgeable exchange of a parcel.[32]

Doing Assessments: Managing Parcel Data

The parcel inventory data (its physical identifier), the valuation technique, and value estimates are maintained either in electronic record image files or on parcel record cards. Figure 10–1 presents such a property record card: One side describes

[32]Another special case for assessment involves public utility and transportation properties. These properties are usually assessed by the state government, rather than by local assessors, and the value of the properties is calculated as an operating unit and divided among local jurisdictions by formula, rather than having the value calculated on a property in place basis.

Figure 10–1
Parcel Record Card for Residential Real Property (Structure or Improvement)

OCCUPANCY	STORY HEIGHT	ATTIC	BSMT	CRWL
1 SING. FAMILY	2.00[ ]	0 NONE	0 NONE	0
2 DUPLEX		1 UNFINISH	1 1/4	1
3 TRIPLEX	2 BI-LEVEL	2 1/2 FIN	2 1/2	2
4 4-6 FAMILY	3 TRI-LEVEL	3 3/4 FIN	3 3/4	3
		4 FINISHED	4 FULL	4
0 ROW-TYPE				

CONSTRUCTION TYPE			BASE	FLOOR	FNSH LIV	VALUE
1 FRAME/ALUMINUM		1	1804	1.00	1804	41100
2 STUCCO		1	1344	2.00	1344	22900
3 TILE						
4 CONCRETE BLOCK						
5 METAL						
6 CONCRETE	---			ATTIC		
7 BRICK	---		1620	BASEMT		12500
8 STONE	---			CRAWL	----	
9 FRAME W/MASONRY						

ROOFING				TOTAL BASE	76500
ASPHALT SHINGLES		X		ROW-TYPE ADJUSTMENT	100%
SLATE OR TILE				SUB-TOTAL	76500
				UNFIN. INTERIOR [-]	
METAL				EXTRA LIVING UNITS [+]	
FLOORS	B	1	2	D C	
EARTH				REC ROOM [+]	1900
SLAB	X			FIREPLACE [+]	1600
SUB & JOISTS		X	X	NO HEATING [-]	
				AIR CONDITIONING [+]	3500
WOOD				PLUMBING [+/-]	
PARQUET				TF: _____ -(5X( )]=	
TILE	X			_____ X400	
CARPET		X	X	NO PLUMBING [-]	
UNFINISHED	X			[+/-]	
INTERIOR FINISH	B	1	2	SUB-TOTAL, ONE UNIT	83500
PLASTER/DRY WALL	X	X	X	SUB-TOTAL, UNITS	
PANELING				GARAGES & CARPORTS [+/-]	4000
FIBERBOARD				EXTERIOR FEATURES [+]	5200
				[+/-]	
UNFINISHED	X			SUB-TOTAL	92700
ACCOMMODATIONS				GRADE/DESIGN FACTOR	105%
NUMBER OF ROOMS			8	C+1	
BEDROOMS			4	REPRODUCTION COST	97340
FAMILY ROOMS			1		
DINING ROOMS					

OTEN

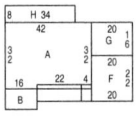

PARCEL 010-05300-00
CARD 1 OF 1

ID	DESCRIPTION	AREA
A	2SFR/B(16R-2U-22R 2D-4R-32U-42L-32D)	1300
B	1SFR/S(10D-16R-10U -16L)	160
C	EFP(6D-22R-6U-22L)	132
D	1SFROH/(2D-22R-2U-22L)	44
E	1SFR/S(6D-4R-6U-4L)	24
F	2CFRG(20R-22U-20L-22D)	440
G	1SFR/B(20R-16U-20L -16D)	320
H	WDDK/CONCP(8U-34R-8D-34L)	272

IMPROVEMENT FEATURES

COMMENTS

SUMMARY OF IMPROVEMENTS

			ID	USE	STRY HGHT	CNST TYPE	GRADE	YEAR CONST.	YEAR REMOD.	COND	NEIG	SIZE OR AREA	BASE RATE	FEATURES	ADJ. RATE	REPRODUCTION COST	PHYS DEPR	REMAINDER VALUE	OBS. DEPR	TRUE TAX VALUE
REC ROOM	TYPE	2		DWELL				1977		AV	AV					97340	20	77870		77900
	AREA	600																		
FIREPLACE	STACKS	1																		
	OPENINGS	1																		
HEATING & AIR COND																				
CENTRAL WARM AIR		X																		
HOT WATER/STEAM																				
HEAT PUMP																				
NO HEAT (GRAVITY/WALL/SPACE)																				
CENTRAL AIR CONDITIONING		Y																		
PLUMBING	CNT	TF																		
PLUMBING BASES	1	5																		
FULL BATHS																				
HALF BATHS																				
KITCHEN SINKS																				
WATER HEATER																				
EXTRA FIXTURES																				
TOTAL		5																		
NO PLUMBING																				

APPRAISER/DATE/CONTACT: 03/01/89

DATA COLLECTOR/DATE: LISTED 8-3-88 BY ADR

SUPPLEMENTAL CARD IMPROVEMENT TOTAL

TOTAL TRUE TAX IMPROVEMENT VALUE: 77900

the land and the factors used in its valuation; the other side does the same for the structure. The values on such records for all parcels in the jurisdiction, when summed, constitute the property tax base for the taxing unit; the record information similarly is used for computation of individual tax bills from that rate, after subtracting whatever exemptions may be applicable for the holder of the parcel. Some systems include a photograph of the property in the file.

Where physical parcel cards are maintained, they are usually filed according to the order that one would encounter the properties when going down the street. That is convenient for building records in a reassessment and for making comparisons of properties in a neighborhood. Note that the record includes the physical descriptions of structures and land that would easily translate into either market-data or cost assessment. Parcel records for commercial and industrial properties

Figure 10–1
Continued (Land)

PARCEL	0100530000	OWNERSHIP	TRANSFER OF OWNERSHIP — CARD 1
COUNTY	MONROE COUNTY		DATE
TAX BILL NUMBER	0100530000		03/23/77
DISTRICT	10 SALT C		
MAP NUMBER			
SECTION & PLAT	7.01	SE NE 7-8-1E 40.00A	
ROUTING NUMBER	6.000		
PROPERTY CLASS	101 AGR		
HOMESTEAD CREDIT	Y		
USER KEY	SE NE 7-8-1E 40.00A		
PROPERTY ADDRESS	8900 LAMP ROAD		
NEIGHBORHOOD CODE	.339079E-19		
DET. SOIL ID NUMBER	0100530000		

TOPOGRAPHY		PUBLIC UTILITIES		STREET OR ROAD		NEIGHBORHOOD	
	LEVEL	X	WATER	X	PAVED		IMPROVING
	HIGH		SEWER		UNPAVED	X	STATIC
	LOW		GAS		PROPOSED		DECLINING
X	ROLLING	X	ELECTRIC		SIDEWALK		BLIGHTED
	SWAMPY		ALL		ALLEY		

VALUATION RECORD

ASSESSMENT DATE		03/01/89								
REASON FOR CHANGE		REVALUATI								
TRUE TAX VALUE	LAND	11000								
	IMPROVEMENTS	77900								
	TOTAL	88900								
ASSESSED VALUE	LAND	3670								
	IMPROVEMENTS	25960								
	TOTAL	29630								

LAND DATA AND COMPUTERS — MEMORANDUM

LAND TYPE	SOIL ID	MEASURED ACREAGE	PROD FACTOR	BASE RATE	ADJUSTED RATE	EXTENDED VALUE	INFLUENCE FACTOR	TRUE TAX VALUE
9		1.000		6200		6200		6200
4	BDB	1.330	77	495	381	510		510
4	WMC	9.330	60	495	297	2770		2770
6	BKF	8.000	50	495	248	1980	00-80	400
6	BU	1.330	64	495	317	420	00-80	80
6	WMC	20.000	60	495	297	5940	00-80	1190
	LAND TOT	39.99						4950

Parcel Acreage	39.99		
81 Legal Drain NV [-]			
82 Public Roads NV [-]			
9 Homesite(s) [-]	1.000		
TOTAL ACRES FARMLAND		38.99	
True Tax Value	4950		
Measured Acreage	39.99		
Average True Tax Value/Acre		124	
TRUE TAX VALUE of FARMLAND		4830	
Homesite(s) Value [+]	6200		
Classified Land Value [+]			
TOTAL TRUE TAX LAND VALUE		11000	

LAND TYPE
F Front Lot
R Rear Lot
1 Primary Ind/Comm. Site
2 Secondary Ind/Comm. Site
3 Undeveloped
4 Tillable
5 Non-Tillable
6 Woodland
7 Other Farmland
71 Farm Buildings
72 Water
8 Ag Support
81 Legal Drain
82 Public Road
9 Homesite
CF Classified Forest
RL Riparian Land
WH Wildlife Habitat

PROPERTY CLASS AGRICULTURE
100 Vacant Land
101 Cash Grain/General Farm
102 Livestock other than Dairy or Poultry
103 Dairy Farms
104 Poultry Farms
105 Fruit & Nut Farms
106 Vegetable Farms
107 Tobacco Farms
108 Nurseries
109 Greenhouses
120 Timber
199 Other Agricultural Use
200 Mineral

INFLUENCE FACTORS
10 Occasional flooding
11 Severe flooding
0 Other

REMODLING	Amount	Date
Exterior		
Interior		
Kitchen		
Bath Facilities		
Plumbing System		
Heating System		
Electrical System		
Extensions		

normally include more data about the characteristics of the property and its operations. Parcel cards are increasingly being maintained electronically, often as a part of a geographical information system that overlays many sources and uses of information about land and properties.

Property Tax Relief Mechanisms

Governments provide a number of different systems of relief from property tax payment. They may involve reductions in the tax base, preferential tax rates, or direct credit of tax owed. The relief may be provided because of the (1) character of the owner, (2) the type of property, or (3) how the property is (or is going to be) used. Most programs are established by state legislation for all localities in the state, even though most property tax revenue goes to local government. Some state programs do allow some local choice about granting the relief.

Exemptions and Abatements

Property tax systems almost always include provisions that subtract a portion of assessed value from the taxable holdings of certain individuals or institutions. Thus, if an individual holding property with assessed value of $8,500 qualifies for a veteran's exemption of $1,500, that person's tax bill would be computed on a net assessed value of $7,000. The exemption reduces the tax base; it is not a direct credit against tax owed. In most instances, the exemptions are additive, so if a parcel holder qualifies for exemption because of age and veteran status, for example, the property tax base would be reduced by the sum of both exemptions.

Exemptions may be granted to certain individuals or institutions, or they may be granted to certain types of property. In the first group are exemptions granted conditional on ownership: (1) government property (federal, state, or local, and foreign government property not used for commercial purposes); (2) property held by religious, educational, charitable, or nonprofit organizations; and (3) residential property through homestead, veteran's, mortgage, or old-age exemptions. The second group includes preferential incentives intended to induce favored activities without regard for the otherwise taxable nature of the property holder. These include exemptions for economic development (new plants or equipment), pollution-control facilities, or land maintained in an undeveloped, natural state. Closely related are abatements, negotiated contracts between a locality and a parcel holder, under which some share of assessed value are not taxed for an agreed-on period of time. The share may vary over time, bringing the parcel gradually into the tax system. The negotiations are normally arranged to induce developers to undertake projects they would not otherwise have done. Whether abatements actually have that effect is not entirely clear. In most environments, to abate the tax on certain properties means that properties without abatement in the taxing unit pay higher tax to support government services; other taxpayers, not the government offering the abatement, bear its cost.

Individuals qualify for many different classes of exemption. Some of the more important classes used by states (in terms of size of value) are homestead, veteran's, and old-age exemptions. Homestead exemptions allow homeowners a given assessed value base before any property tax bill is levied against property. Veterans' and old-age exemptions provide similar partial exemption from the tax. These exemptions can dramatically reduce the base on which the tax can be applied. Nationwide, the partial exemptions reduced gross locally assessed property values by 3.6 percent in 1991. However, the loss of value exceeded 10 percent in several states: Alabama (12.3), Florida (14.1), Hawaii (13.4), Idaho (15.0), Indiana (10.6), and Louisiana (27.5).[33] The redistributions of the cost of government are not trivial.

---

[33]U.S. Bureau of the Census, *Census of Governments 1992*, XI, 1, 2.

Such exemption programs are politically popular because of their apparent tax savings and burden redistribution, but they have a number of important problems. First, the programs usually have a statewide purpose, but because property taxes primarily support local government, the revenue consequences are local. They may become a way for state legislatures to win favor with the electorate without losing state revenue. Abatements are locally arranged, but one government (e.g., a city) may contract away a property tax base important to another locality (e.g., a school district). Second, the programs do not focus tax relief on the needy. All people falling into the specific categories (e.g., homeowners or veterans) receive aid regardless of their specific needs because there is no income or means test for receipt of exemption. Despite trials and tribulations, homeowners probably are better off than renters, and not all homeowners are equally well (or poorly) situated. Third, if the exemption program is sufficiently widespread, as in the case of general homestead exemption programs, the effect may be substantially higher property tax rates to recover lost revenue. For properties not completely exempted from the base, actual relief may be more psychological than real because the owner pays a higher rate on a smaller base, with about the same total tax bill. Fourth, individual exemption programs ordinarily do not reach renters, many of whom are much less affluent than are property owners. This must be seen as an inherent defect in the structure of exemption programs.

Exemptions also apply to selected types of commercial and industrial property.[34] The exemption for a parcel may be complete and permanent, or it may abate all or a portion of property tax for a specific period of time. It may also exempt portions of an otherwise taxable parcel, such as pollution-control equipment or solar-energy equipment. Some areas also provide special exemption for rehabilitated property. The idea is to stimulate economic activity of particular types at defined locations. Evidence suggests things other than property taxes—particularly accessibility to markets, resource availability, transportation networks, and environmental amenities—are much more significant in determining the location of commercial and industrial facilities. Thus, the expected return from such exemptions is low. An even greater problem than low return from the exemption, however, may be the effect on existing property in the area if the incentive works. New industries create a demand for public services (police protection, fire protection, planning, etc.), and new people in the area will likely demand more services than can be covered by the residential tax base they bring. With the new industrial property exempt, those costs must be borne by the existing tax base. This system is, at best, discriminatory and, at worst, may eliminate some marginal businesses. Those properties not qualifying for the exemption face artificially high property tax rates because of the assistance provided the new arrivals.

A final exemption group includes properties that are fully exempt because of the religious, government, educational, or charitable nature of the owner. An accurate estimate of the total amount of the potential tax base removed by these exemptions is not available because where the law requires assessment of these properties,

---

[34]The best general source of information on these programs is Steven Gold, *Property Tax Relief* (Lexington, Mass.: Heath, 1979). Unfortunately, it is severely out of date.

officials do not devote much effort on properties that yield no tax revenue. Observers maintain that the taxes forgiven are substantial. The revenue loss is a particular problem because such properties are unequally distributed among localities. Cities or counties with major state installations (e.g., universities and state parks) can be particularly affected: They must provide for the peak and special service demands created by users of that facility without the power to include that facility in the tax base. Thus, taxpayers of that locality must subsidize the citizenry of the state. The problem is reduced somewhat when exemptions are conditioned on both ownership and use of the facility (a university classroom building may be exempt, but not a university-owned hotel), but the dual requirement is neither universal nor applied without interpretation problems. The federal government does make in-lieu-of-property-tax payments to state and local units hosting certain federal installations, but states seldom provide similar relief to their local governments. As is discussed in a later chapter, local user charges may well be an attractive option in such instances.

Circuit-Breakers

Property tax exemptions to individuals fail to target property tax relief to those individuals most in need. That problem can be reduced by conditioning property tax assistance on individual income levels, as done by property tax circuit breakers. Residential-property circuit breakers, used by twenty-nine states and the District of Columbia, pinpoint relief of property tax overload (defined in terms of the ratio of property tax payment to current family income) through integration of the local property tax and the state individual income tax structure.[35] The taxpayer reports, on his or her income tax return, the amount of property tax paid for the year. The property tax paid is compared with the taxpayer's income. If the ratio of property tax to income is excessive as defined in the circuit-breaker law (an "overload"), the state returns some portion of that excess to the individual as an addition to income tax refund, a reduction in income tax owed, or a direct cash payment. Thus, the circuit breaker reduces the property tax overload at state expense.

Critical structural elements for circuit breakers include age restrictions, income definition and limits, renter status, and benefit formulas. Many programs limit overload relief to the elderly, at least partly to reduce program cost. Elderly individuals, however, may be especially susceptible to overload because the property tax bill on property they accumulate during their work careers does not fall as their income falls with retirement. The property tax bill that was reasonable in relation to salary may consume an excessive chunk of the pension. The circuit breaker can reduce the need for forced sale and can ease retirement. Nonelderly low-income homeowners, however, may face similar overloads as well, particularly in the early years

[35]Steven D. Gold and David S. Liebschutz, "State Tax Relief for the Poor," *State Tax Notes* 10 (May 6, 1996): 1397–1404.

of home ownership or when a family income earner becomes unemployed. Exclusion of these homeowners may not be fair, but it does reduce the cost of the overall program.

Income limitations for the circuit-breaker program are another design question. States do not provide circuit-breaker formula relief to all, but rather impose income ceilings beyond which the system does not apply. And income definitions are not all the same. The ceilings reduce program cost and concentrate assistance on lower-income people. For these purposes, however, income must be defined more broadly than federal or state taxable income to include nontaxed retirement income sources. If it does not, individuals who are reasonably well off because of pension, Social Security, and other nontaxed incomes would qualify, reducing aid available for the truly unfortunate.

Renters pose a third design issue, under the assumption that they bear a portion of the property tax burden on units they occupy—that is, if the property tax is partially shifted forward. A circuit breaker limited to homeowners would provide renters no assistance, even though many renters are much less affluent than the poorest homeowners. Renter relief, where given, presumes a property tax equivalent as a specified percentage of rent paid. The share is not scientifically determined because analysts have been unable to estimate the extent (if any) to which property tax is shifted to renters. With reasonable income limits, however, the program can be seen as a part of general assistance, regardless of property tax conditions.

The final design element is the choice between threshold and sliding-scale relief formulas. The former approach defines a threshold percentage of income as the overload level. Property tax payments above that overload level are subject to partial relief. Relief computation follows the formula

$$R = t(PT - kI),$$

where

R = relief to be provided (subject to a lower limit of zero),
t = the percentage of the overload that is relieved,
PT = property-tax payment,
k = the overload threshold percentage, and
I = family income.

Suppose a family has an income of $12,000 and pays property tax of $900. If it lives in a state that defines the overload threshold as 5 percent and grants 60-percent overload relief, the family would receive circuit-breaker relief of $180. Some states further reduce their cost by increasing the threshold percentage as income increases—a further effort to economize and focus aid.

The second formula is the sliding-scale approach. In this formula, relief is computed as a percentage of property tax payment with the percentage falling as family income increases:

$$R = z \times PT$$

Where z is the percentage of property tax relieved for the income class and R and PT are as previously defined. Unless the relief percentage falls to zero at high incomes, all taxpayers receive assistance under this approach, so it is more like general property tax relief than the specific relief of the property tax overload. It does differ, however, from general property tax relief in that (1) there is usually an upper limit to circuit-breaker relief available to a parcel holder, (2) taxpayers must file to obtain this relief, (3) only homes occupied by the owner receive the circuit-breaker relief (although some states extend the assistance to farm property), and (4) relief is conditioned on income of the property owner.

Circuit breakers are flexible and easily administered in conjunction with the state income tax. Circuit breakers improve property tax equity by targeting relief to those in greatest need and, furthermore, are financed from state, not local, revenue. They provide no incentive, however, for improved property tax administration and may encourage greater use of local property taxes as some property tax costs are shifted to the state.

Deferrals

An additional relief device applicable to the special property tax problems of certain property owners—notably the elderly, disabled, those with limited income, and farm owners on the fringe of developing areas—is tax deferral. With this mechanism, individuals whose property values have risen dramatically through no fault of their own are permitted to pay tax on the basis of old values, with records kept on the difference between that payment and what it would have been at full property value. That difference is deferred to a later time, but not forgiven. In the case of the agricultural property, it is collected when the farmland converts to a different (higher-value) use. In the case of the elderly individual, the deferred tax becomes a claim against that individual's estate.

These recaptures can be complete or partial, and interest may or may not be charged; state approaches vary. The tax deferral relieves special property tax burdens without creating the problems that circuit breakers and special exemptions can often create. Deferrals can relieve without special subsidization—a rare combination in tax policy.

Classification

Nineteen states and the District of Columbia, structure their property tax to apply different effective rates to different types of property: Their tax rates are classified, rather than uniform.[36] Classification assumes that certain property classes have

[36]U.S. Bureau of Census, *Census of Governments 1992,* IX and Richard R. Almy, "Property Tax Policies and Administrative Practices in Canada and the United States," *Assessment Journal* (July/August 2000): 41–57. Cook County, Illinois, also uses a classified tax (the rest of the state does not). These taxes still presume uniformity within property classes. The equal-protection clause permits such separation of property into classes and assignment of different tax burdens to each class, as long as the divisions are not arbitrary or capricious.

superior taxpaying capability than other classes and should pay higher effective property tax rates. Tax-bearing capability, however, varies dramatically within classes, often to a greater extent than variation between classes. In other words, there are affluent and not-so-affluent homeowners, prosperous and poor farmers, and profitable and bankrupt businesses. The classification systems, however, treat each ownership class or property type as if all units in that class were alike. Furthermore, the classification basis is more likely to be based on political clout or the expected ease of shifting the tax to someone else than any reasonable basis for allocating appropriate tax burdens.

Classification can be accomplished by either variation in assessment ratios or variation in statutory rates; most states employ different assessment ratios. Each method can produce the same effective-rate pattern, as Table 10–2 shows. Classification by statutory-rate variation is more straightforward, transparent, and interferes less with the assessment process. If classification is to be adopted, that approach is preferable, although it is used only in Massachusetts, Minnesota, West Virginia, and the District of Columbia.

Tax Increment Financing

Cities and counties often seek to encourage economic development within their boundaries. In property taxation, such enticement often means tax exemptions or abatements to remove otherwise taxable property from the tax rolls. Property tax payments made by the benefited facility are thereby reduced; local governments serving that facility either receive less property tax revenue or replace the lost proceeds by adjusting their statutory rates upward on the other taxable properties in their jurisdictions. If all works well, the fiscal impacts of the relief will be bearable because the fruits of economic development, by reducing social expenditure demands and increasing taxable base, will restore the finances of the localities.

Tax increment financing (TIF) offers an alternative for supporting economic development in targeted, usually blighted, areas. A TIF program "largely freezes the assessed valuation of all property parcels in a designated area (the TIF district) for a specific period of years. Property taxes levied in this frozen tax base continue to

Table 10–2
Property Classifications by Statutory Rates and Assessment Ratios

	Rate Classification			Ratio Classification		
Classes of Property	Statutory Rate ($)	Assessment Ratio (%)	Effective Rate ($)	Statutory Rate ($)	Assessment Ratio (%)	Effective Rate ($)
Owner-occupied housing	2.00	50	1.00	4.00	25	1.00
Farms	1.00	50	0.50	4.00	12.5	0.50
Commercial and industrial	4.00	50	2.00	4.00	50	2.00
Public utilities	8.00	50	4.00	4.00	100	4.00

accrue to local taxing bodies, but taxes derived from the increases in assessed values (the tax increment) resulting from new development are used to pay for infrastructure needs and development expenditures in the TIF district. Thus, TIF serves as a geographically targeted tax, expenditure, and regulatory inducement to a specific location."[37] In logic, the public capital infrastructure needed for a private development project would be self-financed from property taxes from the project. Here is how the scheme could work. Suppose a large manufacturing plant wants to build on a site that lacks certain critical infrastructure normally provided by local government (roads, storm and sanitary sewers, water, etc.). A sponsoring local government could borrow to finance the improvements with payment of debt service (principal and interest) coming from the property tax proceeds from the increased property tax base. Table 10–3 illustrates the general idea of a TIF. If property assessments before development totaled $5 million, taxing units would receive tax proceeds on that base as usual. As assessments rise with development, say, to $8 million, property tax collections on that higher base, regardless of the government levying the tax rate, will be diverted to service the infrastructure debt: property tax on $5 million to the overlapping local governments and property tax on $3 million (the increment) to service the debt that allowed the infrastructure making the development feasible.

TIFs have proven popular with industry and development officials, but they often irritate other local officials, especially those operating schools, because the transfer of revenue can seriously strain the finances of general government. Also, use of TIF revenues is so uncontrolled in some jurisdictions that they can be returned to developers to recoup costs not related to improving the public infrastructure around the project—something like a tax "kickback."

Table 10–3
Tax Increment Financing

	Assessed Value ($)	Tax Rate ($/$100)	Yield to Overlapping Governments ($)	Yield to TIF ($)
Base (predevelopment)	5,000,000	8.00	400,000	0
Year 1	6,000,000	8.10	405,000	81,000
Year 2	7,000,000	8.15	407,500	163,000
Year 3	8,000,000	8.15	407,500	244,500
Year 4	8,000,000	8.20	410,000	246,000

TIF, Tax increment financing.

[37]Joyce Y. Man, "Introduction," in Craig L. Johnson and Joyce Y. Man, eds., *Tax Increment Financing and Economic Development: Uses, Structures, and Impact* (Albany, N.Y.: State University of New York Press, 2001), 1. Some states have included nonproperty taxes in the TIF as well, although this is not common.

Fractional Assessment and Assessment Disparity

The heart of the property tax is assessment, the determination of property value for distributing total tax burden. As previously described, tax law may or may not value property at current market value (what most people understand to be the meaning of "what is its value?" or "what is it worth?"). Even where assessment ties to current market value, prevailing assessment practices may cause substantial difference between market and assessed values. For example, according to the 1982 Census of Governments, the national median-area assessment rate (assessed value to market value) for single-family (nonfarm houses) was 36.9 percent in 1981 (an assessment ratio of 0.369).[38] State median-area rates ranged from a high of 86.8 percent in Idaho to a low of 0.6 percent in Vermont.[39] Much to the chagrin of tax analysts, the Census of Governments no longer reports any data having to do with market value, so we cannot tell whether national performance has improved or deteriorated since then. Many states do collect the data as part of their performance evaluation programs, but the information is not comparable across states.

Under normal circumstances, the overall assessment rate has little impact on absolute property tax burdens because assessment levels can be counteracted by differences in the statutory tax rate. For instance, suppose a municipality seeks $5 million from its property tax and that the market value of taxable property is $80 million. If the assessment rate is 100 percent, a property tax rate of $6.25 per $100 assessed value will yield the desired revenue. If the assessment rate is 50 percent, a property tax rate of $12.50 per $100 assessed value will produce the desired levy total. Low assessment rates produce compensating statutory-rate adjustments.

Fractional assessment, meaning assessment at less than full market value, creates inequities and other complications, not inadequate revenue.[40] First, low assessment rates increase the likelihood of unfair individual assessments because an individual parcel holder will probably be unaware of any over-assessment. Suppose the legal assessment standard is one-third of market value, but the prevailing practice is 20 percent. If a parcel worth about $40,000 is assessed at $10,000, an unwary owner would believe that he or she has a favorable assessment: The tax assessor has valued the property far below the market value and, should the parcel owner know about legal standards, even below the one-third value standard. In fact, the parcel is over-assessed—a 25-percent assessment compared with the prevailing 20 percent—so the parcel bears an artificially high effective-tax rate. Unless the parcel owner has knowledge about the ways of property taxation, he or she will never

---

[38]The single-family, nonfarm home is used as a benchmark for assessment evaluation because almost every assessing district contains several parcels of that class and that grouping tends to be more homogeneous than other property types. Furthermore, markets for such properties usually have many transactions in comparison periods.

[39]U.S. Bureau of the Census, *Census of Governments 1982,* Vol. 2, *Taxable Property Values and Assessment—Sales Price Ratios* (Washington, D.C.: GPO, 1984), 50.

[40]Rigid statutory rate ceilings, however, may combine with fractional assessment to create revenue constraints more severe than intended by the law.

realize the inequity.[41] As John Shannon puts it, "The lower the assessment level, the larger becomes the administrative graveyard in which the assessor can bury his mistakes."[42]

Second, fractional assessment can make state-imposed property-tax rate ceilings and debt limits linked to assessed value more restrictive than intended. Many states permit local government debt levels to be no higher than, say, 2 percent of total local assessed value. If assessment rates are artificially low, for instance, assessment at 20 percent of value rather than at 50 percent, that limit becomes artificially restrictive and creates extra incentive to avoid those debt limits. Furthermore, the practice can cause uneven distributions of any state property tax rate across local areas with differing assessment rates. The effective state property tax rate is higher in areas with high assessment rates than in other areas. Finally, state grant assistance, especially aid to local school districts, is frequently distributed in formulas keyed to local assessed value: the lower the assessed value in an area, the greater the amount of state aid. Fractional assessment can obviously distort that distribution, so states typically develop equalization multipliers to get assessed values to a common assessment level for aid purposes: If an area has an assessment rate of 25 percent and the statewide standard is 50 percent, its assessed value would be doubled for aid formula calculations. These equalization multipliers may or may not be applied to individual parcel values for computing tax bills. If rates are flexible and all parcels in a taxing area receive the same multiplier, the process makes no difference.

The major difficulty with fractional assessment occurs, however, when assessment rates of parcels within a taxing area differ. When this occurs, as it does to some extent in all systems, the effective tax rate is no longer uniform, and similarly situated properties bear different property tax burdens because of the assessment system. Thus, if property A is assessed at 30 percent of value, and property B is assessed at 20 percent, a property tax of $10 per $100 of assessed value translates into an effective rate of $3 per $100 on property A and $2 per $100 on property B. No tax should be so capricious. Unfortunately, property taxes do show such dispersion in operation. The coefficient of dispersion (CD) measures the extent of dispersion (or the absence of uniformity) in assessment ratios and hence the extent to which effective property tax rates vary within a taxing unit. The CD—the average percentage by which individual assessment rates deviate from the median assessment rate—equals

$$CD = \left[\frac{\sum_{i=1}^{n} |A_i - M|}{n} \div M \right] \times 100$$

[41]There is an extra pitfall in the process. The legal standard is 33⅓ percent; the parcel is valued at 25 percent. Some appeal mechanisms suggest that the appropriate action is an increase in assessed value to the legal standard. That is not however, the view of the U.S. Supreme Court: See *Sioux City Bridge Co.* v. *Dakota County,* 260 U.S. 441, 43 s. Ct. 190, 67 L. Ed. 340 (1923).

[42]John Shannon, "Conflict between State Assessment Law and Local Assessment Practice," in Richard W. Lindholm, ed., *Property Taxation—USA* (Madison: University of Wisconsin Press, 1969), 45.

A_i = the assessment ratio for an individual property parcel,
M = the median assessment ratio for all parcels sampled, and
n = the number of parcels in the sample.[43]

If assessment ratios of individual properties are clustered closely around the median ratio, the CD is low, and assessments are relatively uniform. If individual ratios vary widely from the median, the CD is high; properties are not uniformly assessed, and the property tax burden is not fairly distributed among taxpayers. Table 10–4 illustrates CD computation. The CD of 17.3 means that the average parcel is assessed 17.3 percent above or below the median assessment ratio. In practical terms, it means that equally situated properties pay substantially different effective tax rates. In the previous example, the owner of property D pays an effective tax rate 87.5 percent higher than the rate paid by the owner of property C, simply because of lack of uniformity in the assessment process. The higher the CD, the greater the difference of effective rates in the jurisdiction.[44]

Fluctuations in property market conditions make it impossible to maintain completely uniform assessment ratios. However, the International Association of Assessing Officers does prescribe clear standards for uniformity as measured by the coefficient of dispersion. For single-family residential properties, "The COD for single-family and condominiums should be 15.0 or less. In areas of newer or fairly similar residences should be 10.0 or less."[45]

Table 10–4
Coefficient of Dispersion Calculation

Parcels	Assessed Value ($)	Market Value ($)	Assessment Ratio	Absolute Dispersion
A	15,000	30,000	0.50	0.10
B	20,000	30,000	0.67	0.07
C	8,000	20,000	0.40	0.20
D	30,000	40,000	0.75	0.15
E	15,000	25,000	0.60	0.00
Total	88,000	145,000		0.52

Median assessment ratio = 0.60
Sum of absolute dispersion = 0.52
Average absolute dispersion = 0.104
Coefficient of dispersion = 17.3

[43]The CD is the average absolute deviation from the median divided by the median, then multiplied by 100.
[44]Analysts also examine whether the pattern of inequity correlates with property value by computing the intra-area price-related differential, or PRD. The PRD equals the mean assessment ratio in the jurisdiction sample divided by the ratio of the sum of all assessed values in the jurisdiction sample to the sum of all sales prices in that sample. A ratio over 1.00 suggests higher-value parcels are relatively under assessed; a ratio below 1.00 suggests higher-value parcels are relatively over assessed. Underassessment of higher-value properties is often a problem.
[45]"IAAO Standard on Ratio Studies," *Assessment Journal* 6 (September/October 1999), 60.

Many states conduct annual assessment/sales ratio studies. These studies perform three important functions. First, the state uses these results to equalize assessed values (i.e., ensure that properties are valued according to the same standard) for use in aid distribution to local governments, for application of a state property tax rate, for equity when local tax rates extend beyond one assessing jurisdiction, and for calculation of local government debt limits. Without such equalization, there is an incentive for competitive underassessment to shift costs to other areas. Second, the studies give property owners a better idea as to whether their property assessment is generally consistent with that of other taxpayers. The property holder knows that an assessment of $36,000 on a house worth about $120,000 is no bargain if the assessment study shows the mean ratio in the community to be 20 percent; without the ratio study, the holder might celebrate good fortune rather than appeal. Finally, the ratio studies are necessary for evaluation of the work done by property tax assessors. A high CD, in particular, means considerable horizontal inequity in the distribution of the tax burden. A coefficient of 25 means that the average property pays property tax that is 25 percent lower or higher than it would if all properties were assessed at the same ratio. Sidebar 10–1 illustrates the significance of the CD measure for property tax uniformity. Illinois is one state that takes assessment quality seriously. Assessment/sales ratio studies are prepared annually and assessors qualify for a pay bonus if they meet a standard defined in terms of median assessment ratio and CD.[46]

The property tax rate, defined statutorily as the same for all property, differs substantially as it applies to parcels of equal market value because of administration of assessment. When assessments are not uniform, comparable properties pay dramatically different property taxes and there are large differences in effective property taxes paid. A high CD means big differences in assessment ratios and big differences exist in effective rates paid by comparable property.

A number of studies have tried to identify what might improve the uniformity of property tax assessment. Evidence shows higher uniformity results where assessment ratios are high, reassessments are frequent, assessment personnel are full-time and specifically trained, assessment technology is available (tax maps are current, computer-assisted mass appraisal is used, building permit and deed transfer data are available, etc.), and formal relief mechanisms are available (circuit breakers, use-value assessment, etc.). Size of assessing district, use of contract appraisal firms, and whether assessors are elected or appointed seem not to matter much. Uniformity is greater when property tax rates are higher, presumably because more is at stake. But much of actual performance depends on local property market and economic conditions.[47]

---

[46]See Illinois Department of Revenue, *Findings of the 1994 Assessment/Sales Ratio Study,* PTAX-1007 (R-11/96) (Springfield, Ill.: State of Illinois, 1996).

[47]John H. Bowman and John L. Mikesell, "Improving Administration of the Property Tax: A Review of Prescriptions and Their Impact," *Public Budgeting and Financial Management* 2 (November 2, 1990): 151–76.

Sidebar 10–1
What the Coefficient of Dispersion Means for Property Tax Bills

The CD measures the extent to which assessment ratios (assessed value divided by selling price) of property parcels recently sold differ from uniformity. If all parcels were assessed at the same ratio, then the effective property tax rate—the property tax owed divided by the value of the property—would all be the same (the rate would be uniform) and the CD would be zero. As there are differences in assessment ratios, the CD rises. The implications of this disparity, or lack of uniformity, can be demonstrated in a simple illustration.

An analysis of 5,639 sales of single-family residential properties in Marion County (Indianapolis), Indiana during calendar 1999 showed that the median assessment ratio (assessed value divided by the selling price) was 19.5 percent and that the CD was 47.4. That means that the average house was assessed at 47.4 percent above or below 19.5 percent of its market value as measured by its recent selling price. In these data obtained from Indiana State Board of Tax Commissioners sales disclosure forms, the median selling price was $87,000.

What do these data tell us about the property tax bill and the effective property tax rate paid by the typical property?[1] In Marion County in 1999, twenty-nine properties sold for $87,000 exactly. The assessed value of these properties ranged from $11,243 to $22,087. The combined statutory property tax rate was around $10.00 per $100 assessed value in much of the county, so the property tax bill for these properties which sold for $87,000 ranged from $1,124 to $2,208—simply because the assessor estimated a different taxable value for the properties. The uniform $10.00 statutory rate becomes an effective tax rate that ranges from $1.29 to $2.54 per $100 of value. The CD gives a measure of how large, in general, this degree of assessment disparity is, and the CD here is quite high. The higher the CD, the greater the variation in effective property tax rates.

In Indiana, the property tax rate is supposed to be uniform, the same for all properties and in the law it is. However, if we look at how the property tax applies to economically equivalent properties, we see great differences in the property tax paid and, accordingly, in the effective property tax rate [property tax divided by market value] applied to the parcels. The difference is created by lack of uniformity in assessment, measured by the CD.

[1]Effective property tax rates are normally calculated relative to market value of the property rather than relative to income of the property holder because the tax is based on the property (in rem) and not on who owns it. Distributional analysis may link owners and their income to properties, but that is a set of questions different from the success of achieving uniform and unbiased assessments of property parcels.

Limits and Controls

Extraordinary tax-rate limits and controls—beyond the normal process of rate setting—establish a special structure for property tax operation. A categorization of controls appears in Table 10–5. A number of the special controls date from the

Table 10–5
Property Tax Control Structures and Their Impacts

Type of Limit	Example	Impact on Property Tax Rate	Impact on Property Tax Levies	Impact on Expenditures
Legal limit on statutory property tax rate	Cities limited to rate of $5.00/$100 assessed value.	Same ceiling rate statewide.	Levy can increase as assessed value increases or with rate increase for jurisdictions not at legal limit.	Same as levies, plus possible increases from other revenue sources.
Property tax Rate freeze	Cities limited to statutory rate applied in 2005.	Ceiling rate varies across state.	Levy can increase only as assessed value increases.	Same as above.
Property levy limit	Cities' 2007 levy cannot exceed 105% of 2006 levy.	Depends on change in assessed value.	Constrained to limit.	Depends on access to nonproperty tax revenues.
Expenditure limit	Cities' 2007 appropriations cannot exceed 108% of 2006 appropriations.	Depends on change in assessed value and on change in other revenues.	Depends on access to nonproperty tax revenues.	Constrained to limit.
Assessed value increase limit	Assessed value of any property (or properties) in city may not increase by more than 5% in 2007, regardless of reassessment result.	Depends on regular rate calculation.	Depends on local budget process/ rate calculation.	Depends on local budget process.
"Truth in taxation"/full disclosure	Cities announce impact of new assessed values on tax levy if rates maintained, what rate reduction would maintain old tax levy, proposed new tax rate, and call for publicinput on their decisions.	Depends on regular rate calculation.	Depends on local budget process/ rate calculation.	Depends on local budget process.

SOURCE: Daniel Mullins and Bruce Wallin, "Tax and Expenditure Limitations: Introduction and Overview," *Public Budgeting & Finance*, 24 (Winter 2004): 2–15.

1970s, although several have more lengthy heritages. The "tax revolt," especially Proposition 13 in California and related referenda in other states from 1978 through 1980, was partly the product of high and rising effective property tax rates on owner-occupied housing. The rising taxes were created by, among several forces, demands for local public service, limited access to nonproperty tax sources, waste in local government, and special exemptions provided other property types. A large part of that rebellion, however, surely reflected irritation with government in general and the feeling of powerlessness to do anything about federal or state taxes—those taxes rose without any statutory-rate increase for which elected representatives were clearly responsible. The property tax was another matter: The rate would normally vary each year, so it presented an ideal focal point for those concerns. It became the lightning rod for government finance nationwide during the periods of taxpayer discontent.

Property taxes have been subject to extraordinary limitations at least since the Great Depression of the 1930s. Those limits, however, traditionally controlled local statutory tax rates by state law, either in statute or constitution. These controls on the tax rate appeared ineffective as assessed values increased dramatically, both in total and for individual property parcels, during the high-inflation 1970s. Governments could adopt statutory property tax rates no higher than those of the prior year and within the statutory limit and obtain dramatically increased revenue because of the higher assessed values. Property owners whose parcels had been reassessed would face increased property tax bills at the controlled property tax rate. Thus, controls on statutory rates, whether through a statutory rate limit or a rate freeze, seemed powerless as constraints on either local governments or property tax bills.

The approach taken in the 1970s was the levy or expenditure limit, which capped total dollars, not the rate applied to the tax base. That approach does constrain the growth of government activity and prevents increases in assessed value from being automatically translated into higher tax collections and higher tax bills for parcels with increased assessment.[48] With a levy freeze, a general assessed-value increase will require a reduction in tax rates. For example, suppose a control law permits 5-percent levy growth from one year to the next, and that assessed value increases by 8 percent. Rate computations might look like those in Table 10–6. With this control structure, property tax levy ceilings dominate the budget process: Maximum growth in the levy establishes the budget size, and total budget requests must keep within the limit. As soon as assessed-value figures are known, property tax rates can be computed because law establishes the total levy. The only unknown is the manner in which the total is appropriated among operating units. In this case, the budget total is not made up of its operating components, rather, the

[48]Some states have systems that require a rollback of statutory tax rates when property is reassessed, with provision allowing higher property tax collections if formally approved. These provisions are called truth-in-taxation or full disclosure laws; rather than rigidly control property taxes, these laws try to open the property tax budget to public scrutiny.

Table 10–6
Rate Computations for a Levy Control

Budget Year	Assessed Value ($)	Levy ($)	Property Tax Rate ($)
1	5,000,000	250,000	5/100
2	5,400,000	262,500	4.86/100

budget total is divided among the operating components, and one extra dollar provided one agency is truly a dollar not available to any other agency. The total budget cannot expand to accommodate any additions.

Limits of the 1970s were obviously more stringent than the earlier rate controls.[49] They led local governments to adopt a consistent set of responses. First, governments reacted by trying to get other governments or nonprofit organizations to take over services the controlled governments had been providing. If the approach succeeds, the service in question are provided, but the controlled government retains the previously committed resources for other activities. Second, governments have sought increased intergovernmental aid (grants, shared taxes, etc.) to continue services without the use of increasingly scarce local resources. This search is particularly intense to finance mandated services, that is, services the government provides largely because it has been required to do so by another government. If that government both restricts taxing powers and mandates new expenditure, the intergovernmental strain is especially intense. The quest for grants is particularly accelerated when spending from such revenue is placed outside any control structure, as is often the case. Finally, governments search for charges and nonproperty tax revenues outside the limits. In some instances, the charges are merely disguised property taxes (e.g., fire- or police-protection fees based on property characteristics), but they can be welcome additions that improve both the efficiency and the equity of service finance. Expanded use of legitimate charges is in fact the most attractive side effect of the new limitation movement.

Another approach limits the growth in assessed value. In this case, when properties are reassessed, the increase in value cannot exceed a particular percentage. Over time the full increase in valuation is permitted, but it is gradual. It does not otherwise have an impact on the property tax process. It is primarily a control over reassessment shock and the danger that local governments will not adjust their statutory rates when the increase in assessed value hits their financial system.

A final approach to controlling property tax increases, but without the direct constraints previously noted, is the "truth in taxation" or full disclosure requirement. This is a system that requires local governments to call attention to the fact that assessed values have increased and that their property tax levies will increase unless they reduce their statutory property tax rates to allow for the higher assessed values. An illustration of a "truth in taxation" notification appears in Figure 10–2. It

[49]The exception is for governments experiencing assessed-value decline. A levy control for these units permits the accommodating rate increases that rate control does not.

Figure 10–2
Truth in Property Taxation Notification: Landover Hills, Maryland

THE TOWN OF LANDOVER HILLS
NOTICE OF PROPOSED
REAL PROPERTY TAX INCREASE

The Mayor and Town Council of the Town of Landover Hills proposes to increase real property taxes.

1. For the tax year beginning July 1, 2005, the estimated real property assessable base will increase by 4.6% from $55,462,950 to $57,988,056.

2. If the Town of Landover Hills maintains the current tax rate of $0.4800 per $100 of assessment, real property tax revenues will increase by 4.6% resulting in $12,120.00 of new real property revenues.

3. In order to fully offset the effect of increasing assessments, the real property tax rate should be reduced to $0.459, the constant yield tax rate.

4. The Town is considering not reducing its real property tax rate enough to fully offset increasing assessments. The Town proposes to adopt a real property tax rate of $0.4800 per $100 of assessment. This tax rate is 4.6% higher than the constant yield tax rate and will generate $12,120.00 in additional property tax revenues.

A public hearing on the proposed real property tax rate increase will be held at 6:45 p.m. on Friday, June 17, 2005 at the Landover Hills Town Hall, 6904 Taylor Street, Landover Hills, Maryland 20784. The hearing is open to the public and public testimony is encouraged. Persons with questions regarding this hearing may call 301-773-6401 for further information.

warns citizens that the property tax base has increased and, unless the statutory tax rate is reduced by the stated amount, that more property tax revenue will be available for the locality's budget. The public is then provided an opportunity to voice its opinion of what is being proposed for the property tax. The idea is to bring more transparency into the rate setting process and to allow for public response in fiscal decisions. Similar increases in the tax base, of course, occur with taxes on income and consumption but there are no laws requiring such "truth in taxation" notifications for them.

Conclusion

Almost by default, the property tax is the predominant tax source for local government. Though property taxes represent an opportunity to tax accumulated wealth not offered by levies on other bases, that advantage is overshadowed by haphazard and capricious assessment of the tax base. Because the tax applies to values defined by applying regulations, not values from market transactions, assessment is troublesome and requires special attention. Most problems with the property tax, outside of valuation, can be largely resolved by circuit breakers, deferrals, and the like. It would be unfortunate if the advantages of the tax were sacrificed solely because of unwillingness to improve administration. The advantages of the property tax for local government finance are several. The base is visible, easily attached in an enforcement action, and physically immobile. The tax can be administered at a leisurely pace and the rate can be adjusted to a fine degree. Those supporting a considerable degree of fiscal independence for the government closest to the people should consider how important the real property tax is to this independence.

CHAPTER 10 QUESTIONS AND EXERCISES

1. Identify these elements of the property tax in your state: Who assesses property? Are some types assessed locally and some types by the state? What valuation standard is used? When was the latest reassessment of real property? Is personal property taxed? What classification system (if any) is used? What circuit-breaker type (if any) is used? Does the circuit breaker extend beyond residential property owned by the elderly?

2. Why is the acquisition value or assessment-on-sale assessment system sometimes called the "Welcome Stranger" assessment system?

3. Knightstown has a property tax base with an appraised value consisting of $142,000,000 of taxable real property and $78,000,000 of taxable personal property. The assessment ratio is 50 percent. Exemptions for the elderly reduce assessed value by $3,000,000. The city has a planned budget of $3,500,000 and expects to receive $750,000 in nonproperty tax revenue.

a. Compute the statutory property tax rate.
b. Compute the effective property tax rate.
c. The Smith family lives in Knightstown. Their property has an appraised value of $42,000. What is their city property tax bill?

4. Central County includes five townships (Nixon, Reagan, Davis, Greasy Creek, Navaho) and one city (Booneville). It is served by two independent school districts: Seagram United (Davis and Greasy Creek Townships) and Yeltsin Consolidated Schools (Nixon, Reagan and Navaho Townships). Each government in the county levies a property tax to finance its activities, although Booneville has also enacted a local earned income tax (it is expected to yield $750,000 in the next year). Property tax rates are applied to assessed value, defined to equal 50-percent fair cash value. Local unit tax rates fully overlap.
The county assessor reports the following fair cash values for units within the county:

Nixon Township	$69,535,000
Reagan Township	$35,000,000
Davis Township	$23,720,000
Greasy Creek Township	$15,922,000
Navaho Township	$27,291,000
Booneville (Davis Township)	$88,450,000
Booneville (Greasy Creek Township)	$75,392,000

The township value data are for the area outside of any city or town that resides in the township. Values within a city must be added to obtain the township total.

Planned Expenditure by Taxing Units

The following presents the amounts that each taxing unit has budgeted to spend in the next year:

Central County	$3,428,000
Booneville City	$4,539,000
Nixon Township	$99,000
Reagan Township	$150,000
Davis Township	$250,000
Greasy Creek Township	$175,000
Navaho Township	$83,000
Seagram United Schools	$6,350,000
Yeltsin Consolidated Schools	$3,800,000

Questions

a. Set the property tax rate for each taxing unit. Report each rate in dollars per $100 assessed value.

b. The Knight family owns property with a fair cash value of $120,000 in the Davis portion of Booneville. Prepare an itemized tax bill for them.
c. Suppose the current market value of Knight's property is actually $225,000. What is their actual assessment ratio? What effective total property tax rate do they pay?
d. There are 1,800 students in the Seagram United School District and 600 students in the Yeltsin Consolidated Schools. How many dollars per pupil would a tax rate of $1 per $100 of assessed value yield in each district? Explain the significance of this comparison.
e. A factory with an estimated fair cash value of $12 million may be built in Navaho Township. If the factory has no impact on spending by any local government and there are no other changes in the county assessed values, what total property tax bill would the factory face?
f. Suppose the county undergoes a general reassessment that doubles the assessed values of every taxing unit and that state law forbids any taxing unit from increasing its property tax levy, by more than 3 percent. (The factory from question e, sadly enough, ends up in Mexico, so there is no impact from its value.) Assume that the property owned by the Knights (as above) doubles in assessed value and that the city, county, and school districts increase their levies by the maximum allowed, but that there is no increase in levies by any township. What is their new property tax?

5. The state owns 16,500 acres of state forest land in a county. Forest and untilled open areas (the kind of land largely within the boundaries of the state forest) are valued at $180 per acre on average when in private ownership. Assessed value is one-third of that value. The forest area is in two townships of the county; 60 percent is in a township with a tax rate of $1.72 per $100, and the remainder is in a township with a rate of $1.64 per $100. According to the aid formula for compensating local governments containing substantial amounts of untaxed state property, the county receives in-lieu-of-property-tax payments of $18,000 per year for division among the affected taxing units of the county. Is the state payment about right in comparison to the equivalent property tax the land would bear? Explain.

6. Mr. and Mrs. Woodward, an elderly couple with no dependents, have taxable source income of $7,000 and $4,000 income from Social Security. The state income tax is imposed at 3 percent on taxable income (equal to taxable-source income less $500 per person). They own property assessed at $18,000 (current market value of $45,000) and are subject to a property tax rate of $5/$100 assessed value. They each receive an old-age property tax exemption of $500. They are eligible for the state property tax circuit breaker. The relief threshold is 6 percent of total money income; 25 percent of any overload is returned by the state in an income tax credit. Maximum relief paid is $600 per couple.
a. What property tax would they pay without circuit-breaker relief?
b. For how much circuit-breaker relief are they eligible?
c. What is their state income tax liability after circuit-breaker relief?

7. There have been complaints about assessment practices in Garfield County. Each of the three townships in the county assesses property independently, using an elected assessor. State law dictates that assessed value equal one-third of market value; the state constitution contains a clause requiring uniform property tax rates. The state agency of which you are an employee judges assessment quality in counties, recommends multipliers to produce overall balance among townships, and can recommend general reassessments where needed.

You have obtained a random sample of assessed values and selling prices of the residential properties that have sold during the last quarter in the county. All prices are arm's-length transactions, none involve special financial arrangements, and none involve substantial amounts of personal property. Table A presents these data.

a. Prepare a preliminary opinion of assessment quality in Garfield County. Compute all important statistics.

b. The Garfield County Board of Equalization wants multipliers to get each township assessed-value/market-value (AV/MV) ratio up (or down) to the state-required one-third ratio. What multipliers would you apply in each township? Will the application of these multipliers increase or reduce measured equality of assessment in each township? What would their impact be on measured equality in the county?

c. Total property tax rates by township are as follows:

Buchanan Township	$6.15 per $100 AV
Arthur Township	$6.00 per $100 AV
Coolidge Township	$5.75 per $100 AV

What properties pay the highest and lowest nominal tax rates?

What properties pay the highest and lowest effective tax rates?

8. The following data are for the town of Paragon in the fiscal year starting January 1, 2008:

Budgeted town expenditures	$18,000,000
Estimated revenue from grants, fees, and licenses	$6,000,000
Assessed value of property	$142,000,000

a. What is the town property tax rate in dollars per $100 of assessed value?

b. The Wooden family has property with a fair cash value of $45,000. The assessment ratio is one-third. The family is entitled to a mortgage exemption of $1,000. That is taken against assessed value. What is their property tax bill from Paragon?

c. Suppose that for 2009 properties in Paragon are not reassessed but new construction increases total assessed values by 5 percent. The state institutes a levy control, allowing 2009 levies to increase by 6 percent over their 2008 level. Nonproperty tax revenue is estimated to be $6.5 million. What is the maximum 2009 property tax rate permitted, what is the maximum town expenditure, and what property tax bill would the Wooden family face?

Table A

Parcel	Assessed Value ($)	Selling Price ($)
Coolidge Township		
1-1	30,190	120,745
1-2	39,060	201,500
1-3	66,690	372,000
1-4	13,830	86,800
1-5	39,720	207,700
1-6	23,550	232,500
1-7	16,650	91,450
1-8	45,870	85,870
1-9	32,910	114,390
1-10	21,060	107,725
1-11	19,740	71,300
1-12	28,620	122,450
1-13	13,920	77,190
1-14	20,370	114,700
1-15	19,290	94,550
Arthur Township		
2-1	14,190	71,750
2-2	59,700	54,250
2-3	19,390	52,500
2-4	20,160	134,750
2-5	19,260	100,625
2-6	19,420	94,500
2-7	14,220	77,000
2-8	19,840	54,250
2-9	11,760	68,250
2-10	19,720	64,750
2-11	14,010	61,250
2-12	13,350	94,850
2-13	11,370	87,500
2-14	17,920	44,530
2-15	11,310	91,000
2-16	18,790	54,250
2-17	15,360	99,750
Buchanan Township		
3-1	53,440	249,600
3-2	34,880	180,000
3-3	22,720	114,000
3-4	52,320	218,400
3-5	13,600	60,000
3-6	13,840	72,000
3-7	20,160	94,400
3-8	27,400	144,000
3-9	32,720	167,600
3-10	14,320	82,000
3-11	18,360	87,500
3-12	20,200	132,000
3-13	21,880	116,000

d. Suppose that for 2010 properties in Paragon are not reassessed but that new construction increases total assessed value by 9 percent. The state enacts a new property tax control: The 2010 rate can increase by $1.80 per $100 over the 2009 level. Nonproperty tax revenue is estimated to be $6.75 million. What is the maximum town property tax rate permitted, what is the maximum town expenditure, and what property tax bill would the Wooden family face?

9. A Review Question: What performance outcome measures would you propose for a revenue department charged with all responsibilities for administration of the real property tax? Would its outcome measures differ from those appropriate for an individual income tax? Explain.

CASES FOR DISCUSSION

CASE 10–1

Use-Value Assessment for Farmland: Some Operational Questions

The state of Kentucky provides a special-assessment basis for farmland for the property tax. In essence, such land is valued not at current market value, the standard there for other property, but at its agricultural-use value. The following article, excerpted from the *Louisville Courier-Journal,* describes problems with that special treatment.

Consider These Questions

1. Why did the state prescribe a special-assessment basis for farmland?

2. What valuation approach would the proposed agricultural assessment process use? Why not one of the other two?

3. How did the process become a loophole? Was that surprising?

4. Can you find a computational error?

Panel Tries to Decide How to Define Farmland and How to Assess It Fairly

By James R. Russell

Frankfort, KY—A legislative subcommittee struggled yesterday to assure farmers that they won't be taxed off their land and to close loopholes for the rich hobby farmer.

But two basic questions remain unanswered: What is farmland, and how do you assess it?

"Some people," said state Senator John M. Berry Jr. (D-New Castle), "are receiving the benefits of farmland assessments who don't deserve it, and we're trying to protect those people who are trying to make a living out of it (farming)."

And Revenue Commissioner Maurice P. Carpenter, who sat in the subcommittee meeting, added: "Frankly, I think some (farm assessments) are too high, but we took it on ourselves to implement the constitutional amendment and many PVAs (property valuation administrators) are using their own judgments, and you can imagine that out of 120 counties, what you'll come up with."

Carpenter also said, "I believe that there are no pure agricultural sales anymore—there's an investment thought in all of them."

And therein lies the problem. The constitutional amendment, passed in 1969 and implemented by the 1970 Kentucky General Assembly, made special provisions for assessing agricultural land. Its intent was to prevent farmland from being taxed for anything other than agricultural uses, as long as it was indeed a farm.

The amendment supposedly protected farmers from artificially high land values caused by speculators, developers, weekend hobby farmers and sideline investments by wealthy professional people.

The intent of the amendment is not being carried out, Berry said yesterday, noting that fair market value based on comparable sales is being used to assess farmland. And that defeats the purpose of earlier constitutional and legislative efforts.

The "income producing capability" of farmland should be the basis for tax assessment, members of the subcommittee agreed. "And we need a law to require that it be used to determine the value of farmland," Berry said.

Working over a rough bill daft yesterday, agricultural land was defined—tentatively—as 10 contiguous acres, including improvements which are necessary to produce farm income. The residence would not be included in this portion of the farm assessment.

The draft also would define farmland as yielding at least $1,000 per year during the two years immediately preceding the tax year. For horticultural land, the requirements are the same, except only five acres are needed to qualify.

Tentatively—and apparently very tentatively—value would be figured this way:

Each year on January 1 the University of Kentucky College of Agriculture would determine a five-year average net farm income per acre on each county and give that information to the Department of Revenue.

The Revenue Department would "capitalize the new farm income per acre at a rate equal to the average interest cost for money during the previous five years." (Thus, if the average interest rate were 8 percent and the average per acre net income were $40, the land value would be $320 per acre.)

This information would be sent to the county PVAs, who would multiply the average net farm income per acre by the number of acres in a farm.

But because a county can have farmland ranging from excellent to poor, the local PVA will have discretionary power to adjust the average net farm income figure to coincide with the individual farm.

This adjustment would be determined by a number of factors, including the type of land—tillable, pasture, woodland—and the land's fertility and its risk of flooding.

But the business of getting a true picture of land value through a formula of income-producing capability is still complex and unresolved.

CASE 10–2

Finding Revenue in Reassessment

Consider These Questions

1. According to the standard criteria, how is this assessment system doing?
2. What sort of city program would you develop?
3. What information would you gather, and how would you use it?
4. Where would you get your information?
5. What political factors must be considered?
6. What would you emphasize about the program?
7. How would you handle inquiries from the press?

The city of Western Hills is an extremely wealthy suburb with a population of approximately 40,000. It is primarily a "bedroom community" in that most workers residing in Western Hills commute 7 miles to downtown Adel, which is a major industrial center of the mideastern United States. Both cities are in Steele County.

Since Western Hills has long been considered a prestigious place to live, settlement came early, and the city is currently 95 percent developed. This development is primarily single-family dwellings with very few retail establishments. The community borders Adel and is otherwise surrounded by other suburbs. Consequently, there is almost no chance of substantial new growth.

During the past half-century, Western Hills has prided itself on its good municipal government. The city operates under the council-manager system, and the current manager has served for the past 15 years. His municipal staff is primarily young, well trained, and experienced. The finance director is competent.

SOURCE: Louisville Courier-Journal (June 13, 1975), A-5. Copyright (c) The Courier-Journal. Reprinted with permission.

Western Hills receives half of its revenue from the property tax. The specific breakdown follows:

Source	Total Revenue (%)
Real estate tax revenue	50
Earned income tax	20
Transfers from other governments	15
Interest licenses, fees, service charges, etc.	12
Real estate transfer tax (1% of the sale price; all sales must be reported for proper deed transfer)	3

The city council, city manager, and finance director are concerned with the lack of growth in the city's assessed valuation. The reason for their concern is illustrated in the following table:

	Total Assessed Valuation ($)	Increase in the Fiscal Year Consumer Price Index (%)
19X1–X2	158,400,493	5.7
19X2–X3	159,444,545	2.5
19X3–X4	159,705,525	4.1
19X4–X5	165,573,670	7.4
19X5–X6	165,250,000	12.6 (estimated)

This table indicates that the consumer price index is increasing at a substantially faster pace than the city's assessed valuation. With Western Hills' heavy reliance on the real estate tax, that could result in severe financial constraints.

Further investigation shows that the tax mileage for the 19X5–19X6 budget was increased from 13.15 mills to 16.15 mills. (A mill is 1/10th of a cent. The rates are mills per dollar.) (The state ceiling is 20 mills per dollar of assessed value.) The state department of revenue reports a CD for single-family housing of 22.0 and a median assessment sales price ratio of 39.8 for Steele County; data for Western Hills are unavailable.

Western Hills is not suffering from any form of urban blight. Instead, property values seem to be increasing. Real estate agents maintain that Western Hills is still the place to live in the Adel area, and home prices have been increasing accordingly.

The county performs the assessment function for all units of government. Each parcel of property is reassessed every third year. The current market value is the assessment standard; by law, assessments are required to be at 50 percent of that value. Any property that sells is immediately revalued on the basis of that price, regardless of the reassessment cycle. The county assessor's office tries to do a good job, but it lacks skilled workers. The entire county assessment system is not likely to radically change; the assessors apparently will cooperate in any city program.

The city manager and finance director will provide reasonable funds for a program designed to improve the city fiscal structure. Temporary summer employees (college students) are available.

CASE 10–3

Property Taxes and a World-Class House

Consider These Questions

1. What approaches may apply in this assessment question and what problems do they have?
2. What is your view of the assessment system briefly outlined here?
3. What help does the asking price for the rental property give the assessor?

Ross Perot owns an 8,264-square-foot house with four fireplaces and five baths on more than 25 acres of land in North Dallas. His estate also has a 5,327-square-foot rental house with 2.2 acres he purchased about 1988. This parcel has been for sale for about a year, with an asking price of $1.2 million. In 1992 Dallas Central Appraisal District assessed the main house and land at $12,279,600 and the rental property at $1,220,340. (Those had been the assessment levels for 3 years.) For 1993 the values were $11,870,550 and $1,200,000 in recognition of declining residential property values in Texas. The district does use full market-value assessment in its appraisals but does often estimate values by area rather than conduct detailed assessments of each parcel.

The district received 65,000 assessment protests in 1993, one of them being from Mr. Perot. He had not protested in earlier years, but comparable sales in the neighborhood led him to conclude that his properties were over-assessed. After the initial hearing, his assessment was reduced by $96,100; he filed suit for further reduction in state district court, the normal avenue to continue the appeal. Following routing procedure, assessing officials will inspect and appraise the property; that is the normal approach to beginning negotiations.

CASE 10–4

The Property Tax Versus Habitat for Humanity

The real property tax is based on property values, not the income of holders of the real estate. As the story reported here demonstrates, this situation can create some difficult issues when real estate values are increasing rapidly.

SOURCE: This case assembled from Scott McCartner, "There is One Thing We Can Be Sure Of: It's a World-Class House," *Wall Street Journal,* 2 September 1993, B-1; Anne Beilli Gesalman, "Perot Sues Over Home Appraisal," *Dallas Morning News,* 1 September 1993, 25-A; and Steven R. Reed, "Perot Files Suit to Lower Taxes on His Estate," *Houston Chronicle,* 2 September 1993, 29.

Analyze the situation described here. Is there a property tax problem that a government needs to deal with? If so, what options are available? What legal changes might be appropriate? What do you recommend?

Burned by the Boom in N.Va. Real Estate Soaring Property Taxes Overwhelm Habitat for Humanity Homeowners

By Annie Gowen

Kesha James still remembers walking through the freshly painted rooms of her Habitat for Humanity house for the first time, making plans for the leather couch she would buy, and the piano and the canopied bed for her three little girls.

Today, the couch is still a dream. The living room is in ruins because of a plumbing leak she can't afford to fix. She took a second job and works seven days a week but is still afraid she might lose her house.

Her modest mortgage isn't the problem; it's rising property taxes that keep her up nights. Her little house in Alexandria has more than doubled in value since it was built in 1999 and is now worth a half-million dollars, forcing her monthly house payment, which includes real estate taxes, up from $515 to $954 in the past 18 months—chiefly because of higher taxes.

"It's not fair. It doesn't make any sense," said James, 29, sitting at her cheerful kitchen table, her youngest daughter curled up in her arms. "Alexandria is my home. . . . I don't want to leave."

Asked when her last day off was, she can't remember.

Rising property values across the region have put the squeeze on taxpayers, but the bite has been especially acute for owners of Habitat for Humanity homes in Northern Virginia. In some areas, their homes have doubled and tripled in value in the past three years.

At least a dozen of the 47 Habitat homeowners in Northern Virginia pay more in property taxes and insurance than they do to pay off their mortgages, according to Karen Cleveland, executive director of the Northern Virginia arm of the housing nonprofit group. It is part of an international group that builds homes with volunteers and sells them to low-income buyers.

"The rising property taxes have truly made it almost impossible for them to stay in their homes," Cleveland said. "We're saying, 'Help us to make it appropriate so our homeowners are paying what is fair for them.' "

Soaring home values are also a growing concern for the owners of 19 Montgomery County Habitat for Humanity homes, most of them in Silver Spring and Rockville, program officials said. Tax caps and a five-year tax abatement program for new Habitat owners in the District have kept costs in the city and the Maryland suburbs from rising as steeply as they have in Virginia.

"We're expecting them to have problems," said Carol Casperson, executive director of D.C. Habitat for Humanity, which has renovated 150 homes and low-income co-ops across the city. She noted that a Habitat house that sold on 54th Street NE for $99,000 in the fall was recently assessed at $186,000.

In recent months, Habitat for Humanity of Northern Virginia has launched a campaign to persuade localities to provide tax relief for their homeowners. It is arguing that the Habitat homes shouldn't be assessed at market rates because deed restrictions prevent their owners from selling the homes for profit or getting home equity loans until the 20-year mortgages are paid. If Habitat homeowners sell their homes before 20 years are up, they must sell them back to Habitat for the amount they cost—$80,000 to $120,000 in most cases, Cleveland said, which is the restricted value.

The campaign has had some success in Fairfax County, where assessors granted several appeals last year. They resulted in a reduction of up to a 50 percent in some cases, Cleveland said.

In recent days, Alexandria city employees have begun examining restrictions on the deeds of eight Habitat homes to see whether similar tax relief can be provided, said Cindy Smith-Page, director of the city's real estate assessment office.

But talks with real estate assessors have not yet begun in Arlington County, where owners of eight properties have had values triple in the past three years.

"To be honest with you, I'm a little concerned," said Ronnie Watson, 42, who was able to buy a cozy Arlington duplex in 2000 after he and his teenage son spent months in a homeless shelter and a rat-infested apartment. "We are living paycheck to paycheck."

He has to work overtime as a meter reader to pay their basic bills, he said. Anything extra—such as his son's yearbook and cap and gown for his coming graduation from Washington-Lee High School—is a stretch. Watson is praying that his house payment, already up from $363 to $442 in recent months, won't top $500.

"That's a whole lot to me," he said.

Kesha James had never known a home until she and her new husband, Ian Roger James, 35, moved into their townhouse in Old Town in 1999. They had poured more than 500 hours of "sweat equity" into the project, helping build it, working alongside Habitat volunteers putting up siding and painting. They were able to buy the house—then appraised at $190,000—with a zero-interest mortgage, for $90,000.

James, a District native, had grown up shuttled among relatives by her widowed mother, who struggled with a gambling addition.

She ended up in an Alexandria homeless shelter in 1997 with her first child, Kaya, now 9, after fleeing an abusive relationship. A social worker there was impressed by James's flinty determination to keep taking classes at Strayer University even while living in the shelter. She urged James to apply for the Habitat house.

By then she was with Roger James and the couple had two more children, so having a house seemed like a miracle. Once they were settled, she even bought the piano she had dreamed of, a $300 used upright.

Things were happy for a long time, but 18 months ago the monthly payments started rising fast, as home values in Northern Virginia exploded, doubling since 2000.

There was less and less money for such things as Girl Scouts and dance club for her daughters, things she desperately wants them to have. She was working full time for a homeless advocacy group in Arlington, making $28,000 a year. She added Saturday and Sunday overnight shifts as a monitor at a homeless shelter to bring in extra money. School fell by the wayside.

Her husband started saying maybe the house wasn't such a good idea. One day last fall, they had another fight about money.

"I said, 'Roger, why don't you just leave?' " James recalled. "I'd said that before and nothing had happened, but this time he said, 'I think I'm going to get my own place.' And then I was thinking, 'What have I done?'"

He decamped to Pennsylvania near Hagerstown, leaving James to struggle with her mortgage payments and the girls, although he visits frequently. She pays $954 a month in house payment, $493 of that for taxes and insurance. If the city can't provide a tax break, her payment is expected to increase another 30 percent in July.

James said her husband wants the family to reunite up north, but James wants to stay in her house.

"That's my house I helped build," she said. "I put my heart and soul into it, so I'm going to fight."

SOURCE: Washington Post 14 February 2005, A-1. © 2005 The Washington Post Company.

CHAPTER 11

Revenue from User Fees, User Charges, and Sales by Public Monopolies

Governments normally collect revenue through their sovereign taxing power to define the payment owed without any connection to the value of any public product or service received by the taxpayer.[1] But there are some goods and services that governments sell, which potential buyers may purchase or not, according to their individual tastes, preferences, and affluence. Impacts on others from those purchases are so small that provision is not a public problem. In these instances, revenue to finance these services can be raised without the brute force and compulsion of taxation, but through voluntary exchange. And governments also license the privilege to undertake certain activities, limiting payment only to those engaging in the controlled activities. This privatization of finance occurs while public provision of the service itself continues. There is almost certainly a wide territory that governments should explore for such financing that relieves the general revenue system by requiring specific "customers" to pay for the services they receive.

Sales revenue can be tantalizing for governments. By appearing to behave like a private business, government leaders can blunt some critics of tax-and-spending politics; although the sums involved may be relatively small in the full scheme of public finance, the revenues do make a contribution possibly without facing public revulsion to higher taxes. But most important, public prices may improve both the efficiency of resource allocation and equity in distributing the cost of public services. They do make the government behave more like a private business.

[1]Civil forfeiture, a controversial tool now widely used by law enforcement officials, operates as a tax, in that revenue arises from application of the system of laws. Police agencies have no more special right to these proceeds than does the Internal Revenue Service (IRS) have a special claim to its individual income (or other) tax collections.

Table 11–1

State and Local Government Sales Revenues: User Charges and Miscellaneous Revenues, 2002–2003 ($ in thousands)

	State & Local Total ($)	% Total	State Total ($)	% Total	Local Total ($)	% Total	Counties Total (%)
General revenue from own sources plus Utility and liquor store revenues	1,482,336,468	100.00%	767,767,912	100.00%	714,568,556	100.00%	169,614,617
Taxes	938,971,754	63.34%	548,990,867	71.50%	389,980,887	54.58%	94,702,466
Charges and miscellaneous general revenue	434,976,439	29.34%	201,741,108	26.28%	233,235,331	32.64%	70,973,490
Current charges	269,560,428	18.18%	106,356,917	13.85%	163,203,511	22.84%	50,927,101
Education	78,522,007	5.30%	60,214,863	7.84%	18,307,144	2.56%	2,485,608
Institutions of higher education	66,831,362	4.51%	59,391,624	7.74%	7,439,738	1.04%	1,360,938
School lunch sales (gross)	6,074,010	0.41%	18,511	0.00%	6,055,499	0.85%	581,088
Hospitals	68,926,691	4.65%	24,131,106	3.14%	44,795,585	6.27%	20,219,940
Highways	8,502,629	0.57%	5,350,911	0.70%	3,151,718	0.44%	498,223
Air transportation (airports)	12,758,630	0.86%	870,608	0.11%	11,888,022	1.66%	1,996,032
Parking facilities	1,448,631	0.10%	0	0.00%	1,448,631	0.20%	109,411
Sea and inland port facilities	2,930,095	0.20%	808,936	0.11%	2,121,159	0.30%	218,376
Natural resources	3,017,634	0.20%	2,160,399	0.28%	857,235	0.12%	0
Parks and recreation	7,342,012	0.50%	1,202,478	0.16%	6,139,534	0.86%	1,065,479
Housing and community development	4,589,371	0.31%	564,915	0.07%	4,024,456	0.56%	190,924
Sewerage	28,236,940	1.90%	27,062	0.00%	28,209,878	3.95%	3,320,386
Solid-waste management	11,559,395	0.78%	415,963	0.05%	11,143,432	1.56%	3,794,274
Other charges	41,726,393	2.81%	10,609,676	1.38%	31,116,717	4.35%	17,028,448
		0.00%		0.00%		0.00%	
Miscellaneous general revenue	151,634,184	10.23%	81,602,364	10.63%	70,031,820	9.80%	20,046,389
Lottery net proceeds	13,781,827	0.93%	13,781,827	1.80%			
Interest earnings	58,316,949	3.93%	29,730,088	3.87%	28,586,861	4.00%	8,926,764
Special assessments	5,808,240	0.39%	305,755	0.04%	5,502,485	0.77%	1,624,308
Sale of property	1,773,033	0.12%	608,249	0.08%	1,164,784	0.16%	220,089
Other general revenue	99,517,789	6.71%	64,740,099	8.43%	34,777,690	4.87%	9,275,228
		0.00%		0.00%		0.00%	
Utility revenue	103,050,084	6.95%	12,517,945	1.63%	90,532,139	12.67%	3,521,896
Water supply	34,736,304	2.34%	178,486	0.02%	34,557,818	4.84%	2,941,849
Electric power	53,938,073	3.64%	10,634,200	1.39%	43,303,873	6.06%	167,562
Gas supply	5,390,996	0.36%	12,418	0.00%	5,378,578	0.75%	28,838
Transit	8,984,711	0.61%	1,692,841	0.22%	7,291,870	1.02%	383,647
		0.00%		0.00%		0.00%	
Liquor store revenue	5,338,191	0.36%	4,517,992	0.59%	820,199	0.11%	416,765

SOURCE: U.S. Bureau of Census Governments Division.

Table 11–1
State and Local Government Sales Revenues: User Charges and Miscellaneous Revenues, 2002–2003 ($ in thousands) (continued)

% Total	Municipal & Township Total ($)	% Total	Special District Total ($)	% Total	School District Total ($)	% Total
100.00%	293,510,937	1	93,419,074	100.0%	158,023,928	100.00%
55.83%	148,928,396	50.74%	15,263,885	16.3%	131,086,140	83.0%
41.84%	86,728,158	29.55%	48,595,895	52.0%	26,937,788	17.0%
30.03%	58,303,536	19.86%	38,958.472	41.7%	15,014,402	9.5%
1.47%	807,134	0.27%	0	0.0%	15,014,402	9.5%
0.80%	272,316	0.09%	0	0.0%	5,806,484	3.7%
0.34%	372,466	0.13%	0	0.0%	5,101,945	3.2%
11.92%	6,635,213	2.26%	17,940,432	19.2%	0	0.0%
0.29%	1,248,485	0.43%	1,405,010	1.5%	0	0.0%
1.18%	5,864,781	2.00%	4,027,209	4.3%	0	0.0%
0.06%	1,267,742	0.43%	71,478	0.1%	0	0.0%
0.13%	932,157	0.32%	970,626	1.0%	0	0.0%
0.00%	0	0.00%	857,235	0.9%	0	0.0%
0.63%	3,829,148	1.30%	1,244,907	1.3%	0	0.0%
0.11%	1,652,721	0.56%	2,180,811	2.3%	0	0.0%
1.96%	19,941,847	6.79%	4,947,645	5.3%	0	0.0%
2.24%	6,363,372	2.17%	985,786	1.1%	0	0.0%
10.04%	9,760,936	3.33%	4,327,333	4.6%	0	0.0%
0.00%		0.00%		0.0%		0.0%
11.82%	28,424,622	9.68%	9,637,423	10.3%	11,923,386	7.5%
5.26%	10,739,395	3.66%	5,932,640	6.4%	2,988,062	1.9%
0.96%	2,613,256	0.89%	1,264,921	1.4%	0	0.0%
0.13%	704,060	0.24%	240,635	0.3%	0	0.0%
5.47%	14,367,911	4.90%	2,199,227	2.4%	8,935,324	5.7%
0.00%		0.00%		0.0%		0.0%
2.08%	57,450,949	19.57%	29,559,294	31.6%	0	0.0%
1.73%	22,545,479	7.68%	9,070,490	9.7%	0	0.0%
0.10%	27,771,906	9.46%	15,364,405	16.4%	0	0.0%
0.02%	4,357,558	1.48%	992,182	1.1%	0	0.0%
0.23%	2,776,006	0.95%	4,132,217	4.4%	0	0.0%
0.00%		0.00%		0.0%		0.0%
0.25%	403,434	0.14%	0	0.0%	0	0.0%

Three different sorts of "private" revenue to government are discussed in this chapter:

1. **User fees** derived from government sale of licenses to engage in otherwise restricted or forbidden activities.
2. **User charges**, or prices charged for voluntarily purchased, publicly provided services that, although benefiting specific individuals or businesses, are closely associated with basic government responsibilities.
3. **Fiscal monopoly** and utility revenues that the government receives from exclusive sale of a private or toll good or service. These proceeds include revenue from government-operated utilities, state liquor stores, and state lotteries.[2]

Tables 11–1 and 11–2 present recent sales data for U.S. governments. These receipts are modest in comparison with those from taxation and that is not surprising. The principal economic reason for governments is, after all, market failure, and that implies that prices will not function properly. Pricing often simply is not feasible and not desirable, and that is what the revenue patterns reflect. Nevertheless, collections from market transactions play an important role in government finance and their role is likely to continue to increase for reasons both of political pragmatism and from the quest for improved governmental efficiency.

Charges amount to 13.85 percent of general revenue states raise; adding the revenues from state lotteries, liquor stores, and utilities increases the percentage to around 26 percent.[3] Charges by state institutions of higher education are the single largest source of such revenue. Localities have more opportunity for charge revenue because they provide more individual beneficiary services than do other governments; they produced 22.84 percent of revenue raised by local governments in 2003. Adding utility revenue increases the percentage to 32.64 percent. Charge revenue from hospitals, sewerage, and water and electric utilities are particularly important to the local revenue totals. Because tax alternatives available to local government are often tightly controlled by their states, these governments have special incentive for seeking out charge revenues. But even these governments seldom exhaust possibilities for charging. Among the types of local governments, charges are most important for counties (hospitals) and special districts (hospital and electric utilities). For municipalities, water, electric, and sewerage charges are the most important, although overall charge reliance is less than for counties and special districts.

The federal scheme for reporting charge revenue is somewhat convoluted. In federal budgetary accounts, most charge revenues are called offsetting collections or offsetting receipts, and they do not appear in tallies of federal revenue. These are payments for goods and services sold to the public and include such charges as

---

[2]Some countries have operated fiscal monopolies on tobacco products, matches, salt, sugar, caviar, and playing cards. See Sijbren Cnossen, *Excise Systems, A Global Study of the Selective Taxation of Goods and Services* (Baltimore, Md.: Johns Hopkins University Press, 1977), 84–98. They offer an alternate to excise taxation, although there are other issues involved in the choice.

[3]The Government Finances Division of the Census Bureau reports user charge and utility revenue on a gross basis, without offset for production or acquisition cost. Lottery revenue reported as part of the miscellaneous revenue category is included on a net basis.

Table 11–2
Federal User Charge Receipts, Fiscal 2005 ($ millions)

Corps of Engineers: Harbor maintenance fees	1,048
Department of Commerce: Patent and trademark, fees for weather services, and other fees	1,596
Department of Defense: Commissary and other fees	8,934
Department of Health and Human Services: Food and Drug Administration, Centers for Medicare and Medicaid Services, and other fees	1,377
Department of Homeland Security: Border and Transportation Security and other fees	2,044
Department of State: Passport and other charges	1,605
Department of Treasury: Sale of commemorative coins and other fees	1,550
Department of Veterans Affairs: Medical care and other fees	1,938
Securities and Exchange Commission: Regulatory fees	1,665
Department of Agriculture: Crop insurance and other charges	1,880
Department of Defense: Commissary surcharge and other charges	1,090
Department of Energy: Proceeds from sale of energy, nuclear waste disposal, and other charges	4,709
Department of Health and Human Services: Medicare Part B insurance premiums and other fees	39,854
Department of Homeland Security: Customs, immigration, and other fees	6,196
Department of Interior: Recreation and other fees	5,584
Department of Labor: Insurance premiums to guaranty private pensions and other fees	2,519
Department of Veterans Affairs: Veterans life insurance and other charges	1,682
Office of Personnel Management: Federal employee health and life insurance fees	10,298
Postal Service: Fees for postal services	68,504
Tennessee Valley Authority: Proceeds from sale of energy	7,806
Outer Continental Shelf receipts and other collections	6,146
Total User Charges	185,222

SOURCE: Executive Office of the President, Office of Management and Budget, *Analytical Perspectives, Budget of the United States Government, Fiscal Year 2007* (Washington, D.C.: U.S. GPO, 2006).
NOTE: Only categories exceeding $1,000 million are separately identified.

those for postal services, for admissions to national parks, for sale of public lands, for oil extraction royalties from the Outer Continental Shelf, for sale of commemorative coins, and so forth. Table 11–2 identifies some of the more significant revenue producers. The largest sums came from postal services and insurance premiums for optional Medicare coverage. Total collections—$185 billion—represent a modest sum in comparison with the total federal receipts of over $2 trillion in fiscal 2005.

Most federal charge revenues are treated differently from tax revenues in that they are deducted from gross outlays of a particular agency, rather than being counted as part of government receipts. For offsetting collections, the charges are credited directly to the account from which they will be spent and, usually, may be spent without further legislation. As an example, the postal service may use its charge revenue to finance its operations without annual appropriation. For offsetting receipts, the charges are offset against gross outlays, but are not credited directly to expenditure accounts.[4] Because of this offsetting process, the regular budget displays understate to some degree both total government spending and collections from the public. But the amounts are small in the overall tally of government operations.

User Fees and Licenses

Governments levy a number of user fees that have some features of public prices but reflect the revenue-raising potential of the rule of law rather than voluntary exchange in the private market. (As described in Sidebar 11–1, terminology in the federal budget broadens the user-charge concept to include narrow-base taxes.) They are not user charges or public prices, even though these fees may share some equity and fiscal advantages of prices. Their yield to states in 2004 amounted to more than $39 billion, with slightly less than half the total from motor vehicle and motor vehicle operator licenses. Over $10 billion came from state corporate licenses.[5]

License taxes imposed to regulate specific activities for the benefit of the general public (e.g., massage parlor licenses, hunting licenses, and licenses associated with the ownership or operation of motor vehicles) offer one example. A license tax is a fee—flat rate, graduated by type of activity, related to business receipts, or whatever—levied by a government as a condition for exercise of a business or nonbusiness privilege. Without the license, one or more governments forbid the activity. The license is a necessary condition for operation, but it does not "purchase" any specific government service. It may thus be distinguished from a user charge, which may be avoided if any individual or firm chooses not to purchase the supplied item or service and the payment of which entitles the individual or firm to a commodity or service, and from fees that are indirectly related to particular privileges.

The license tax must also be distinguished from franchise fees. The latter (1) involves contracts detailing rights and responsibilities of both franchisee and the issuing municipality, (2) entails a requirement to service the entire population in the servicing area, and (3) brings a presumption of rate and quality of service regulation. A license simply permits a holder to undertake an activity otherwise forbidden and involves no contractual or property rights.[6] In general, franchises are

[4]Executive Office of the President, Office of Management and Budget, *Analytical Perspectives: Budget of the United States Government, Fiscal Year 2002* (Washington, D.C.: U.S., GPO, 2001), 8–10. This offsetting process provided a way around BEA90 outlay controls.

[5]U.S. Bureau of Census, Governments Division.

[6]Charles S. Rhyne develops this logic further in *Municipal Law* (Washington, D.C.: National Institute of Municipal Law Officers, 1957), 655.

Sidebar 11–1
Charging Fees: The Federal System

Most federal revenue comes from taxes that have no relation to any benefits received by the person paying the tax and that are not related to any particular service provided by the government. That is the case with the broad-base taxes on income and payrolls that constitute the great majority of federal revenue. User fees, however, can be appropriate and are feasible when the government can deny use of service to nonpayers or when the government can prohibit activities by nonpayers. Also, as described in Chapter 9, some narrow-base excises can serve to allocate costs to those using certain government services or cause private entities to recognize the social implications of their actions.

The Congressional Budget Office calls both these fees and narrow taxes user charges and divides them into four classes:

1. User fees are payments for goods or services sold or rented by the government, voluntarily purchased, and not generally shared. They include natural-resource royalties, tolls, insurance premiums, leases and rentals, revenue from sales of resources, fees from use of federal land, admission to federal parks, charges for postal service, and permits or licenses not associated with regulation.
2. Regulatory fees are payments based on government authority to regulate particular businesses or activities that stem from the sovereign powers of the government. They include regulatory and judicial fees; fees from immigration, passport, and consulate services; Customs Service fees; fees for testing, inspecting, and grading; fees for patent, trademark, and copyright services; and licenses through regulatory programs.
3. Beneficiary-based taxes are levied on bases correlated with the use of particular government services (the good or service taxed and the public service are close complements). They include the transportation-related excises (highway, airway, inland waterway, and harbor) and the excises on fuel and equipment associated with boating safety programs.
4. Liability-based taxes are levied for the purpose of abating hazards, discouraging damaging activities, or compensating injuries. They include excises on certain chemicals that are dedicated to the Hazardous Substance Trust Fund, taxes on certain fuels dedicated to the Leaking Underground Storage Tank Trust Fund, taxes on crude oil dedicated to the Oil Spill Liability Trust Fund, taxes on domestically mined coal dedicated to the Black Lung Disability Trust Fund, and taxes on childhood-disease vaccines dedicated to the Vaccine Injury Compensation Trust Fund.

Revenues in the first two groups can be particularly attractive under the BEA90 control structures because they may be offsetting collections—that is, they are netted against a particular budget outlay. Congressional committees can thus meet outlay ceilings by adding fees rather than cutting programs.

SOURCE: U.S. Congressional Budget Office, *The Growth of Federal User Charges* (Washington, D.C.: GPO, 1993).

provided in very limited numbers, whereas licenses are made available to virtually all applicants.

The definitions usually do not differentiate between licenses for revenue and for regulation. Both varieties are based on the inherent authority of a state to exercise all elements of police power. States delegate this power to municipalities by constitution, statute, or city charter grant. Revenue and regulation motives may often be hopelessly entangled. Nevertheless, a tentative separation can be suggested: A license ordinance that does not require inspection of the business or articles sold or fails to regulate the conduct of the business in any manner is a pure revenue license, particularly if license applications are never denied. If such controls apply or if licenses are difficult to obtain (not just expensive), the license is regulatory. The distinction may not always be clear. Some states require that license charges be reasonably related to the cost of issuing, policing, or controlling the thing or activity being licensed. When that stipulation applies, it is especially important to review cost and adjust charges frequently.

Both user charges and fees attempt to relieve burdens placed on the general-revenue system by extracting greater contribution from service beneficiaries, but the former more closely resembles private-enterprise pricing.[7] Fees can compensate government for extra costs incurred in providing special services to identifiable entities or for administrative paperwork done for individuals. Thus, governments often apply fees for traffic direction or crowd control and charge fees for many legal filings. Fees, however, seldom involve the direct sale of a good or service but involve payment for some privilege granted by government. The exercise of that privilege may cause government to incur a cost that the fee seeks to recoup in part or in total.

User Charges

User charges can induce production and consumption efficiency while gauging citizen preferences and demand for government services. User charges can function only when activities financed have two necessary conditions: benefits separability and chargeability. These are the features absent from pure public goods (see Chapter 1); the further a good or service departs from publicness and the closer it approximates a private good, the more feasible are user charges.

First, user charges are feasible when identifiable individuals or firms, not the community as a whole, benefit from the service. Services to a narrow segment of

[7]In recent years, many communities have adopted *exactions*, in-kind or financial payments, on real estate developers as a condition for permits, access to public facilities, and so on. Development for impact fees are one type of exaction. See Alan A. Altshuler and Jose A. Gomez-Ibanez with Arnold M. Howitt, *Regulation for Revenue* (Washington, D.C./Cambridge, Mass.: Brookings Institution/Lincoln Institute for Land Policy, 1993).

the community financed by general revenues provide an opportunity for that segment to profit at the expense of others. Those using the service benefit, but pay no more than similarly situated citizens who do not benefit. A user charge prevents that systematic subsidization. If recipients of benefits cannot be identified, or if the community in general benefits, a user charge is neither feasible nor desirable. Thus, charges for elementary education would be inappropriate, but charges would be desirable for an adult auto mechanics course. Relying on voluntary provision in the first instance would be foolish: Milton benefits if his neighbor's children receive an elementary education because they help choose his government, they read traffic signs, they go on welfare less often, and so on. In the latter instance, the mechanic does help the community, but that help is for a fee: If Milton's car is repaired, he pays the bill—there are no uncompensated community benefits. However, governments too often lose their resolve to be entrepreneurial adherents to the user-pays principle when they give away costly services to businesses in the name of economic development.

Second, user charges require an economical method for excluding from service benefits those who do not pay for the service. If exclusion cannot be accomplished, the charge cannot be collected. Furthermore, resource-allocation gains are greatest if service use can actually be metered, as with water meters, toll booths, and the like, so that heavy users pay more than light users, and any user pays more than nonusers. Some discretion is needed here, however, because everything that can be gauged may not be worth gauging: Use of city streets could be metered using the tollgate technology of turnpikes and toll bridges; however, the costs involved, including the time waiting in lines, make that option untenable.[8] Administrative cost—measuring customer service use (metering), calculating charges according to service cost, and billing and collecting computed charges—and compliance cost must not be excessive. Many services can, however, be gauged and controlled by meters, fences, turnstiles, decals, and the like. Others may be indirectly measured—many cities gauge residential sanitary-sewer use by water use, a reasonable proxy for volume in the drain. (Industrial use is more difficult to gauge because there is a problem with quality of the discharge in addition to quantity.) Without enforceable charge barriers, user charges are inappropriate.

Charges are particularly appropriate when substantial waste would occur if the individually identifiable service were unpriced. Such would undoubtedly result if, for instance, water were provided through property tax financing. Under that system, efforts to economize on water use would yield the individual consumer no direct return. Payments for water would be determined by property holdings, not the amount of water used. Usage would be much inflated. Investment in supply

[8]Electronic tags (like EZ Pass in the northeastern United States) on automobiles are being used on some toll facilities to reduce collection costs for frequent users. See "High-Tech Helps Highways to Hustle," *Wall Street Journal* (8 May 1989), C-1. Germany uses a global positioning satellite system for charging truck tolls (16 cents per kilometer for trucks weighing over 12 tons) on its autobahns. Billing goes to a data center or drivers may pay manually at roadside terminals. A private company (Toll Collect GmbH) operates the collection system for the German government. Microwave sensors are used for collecting tolls in Austria and some other European countries.

facilities would have to be abnormally great, and artificially expanded amounts of water would have to be treated. Appropriate user charges could substantially reduce water waste and total water-supply cost.[9]

Advantages of User Charges

User charges have four advantages beyond the naked pragmatism of additional revenue for government functions. These advantages include both the important efficiency effects of appropriately designed charge structures and improved equity from direct pricing. First, user charges can register and record public demand for a service. Suppose a city is considering supporting extensive summer softball leagues for adults. If these leagues are financed by user charges (either team sponsors or individual participants), the city receives important information for choices about service type, quality, and quantity. Without a user charge, there would be continual—and inconclusive—debate about program advisability and structure. But as rural philosopher Kin Hubbard observed: "Nothing will dispel enthusiasm like a small admission charge."[10] The charge offers a conclusive test of demand for the service. Furthermore, a program that, through user charges, covers its provision cost is not likely to be eliminated and will not burden other government activities. Not incidentally, citizens who do not want the service do not have to receive it and do not have to pay for it. A user-charge system not only provides a tangible way for citizens to register their preference for particular services but also provides some funds for providing those services.

Those extra funds can be a problem, however, when the charge does not cover all incremental costs of the service. During periods of tight finances, decision makers are tempted to expand revenue-generating activities, often reasoning that any revenue will help with the fiscal problem. Unfortunately, such expansion can actually increase the total subsidy required for that service and worsen the overall budget condition. For example, a city may expand its summer tennis instruction program because it generates $25 per person in revenue. If recreation department costs increase by $30 per person enrolled in the program, the expanded revenue produced actually increases any city deficit.[11]

Second, the user charge can dramatically improve financing equity for selected services. If the service is of a chargeable nature, its provision by general tax revenues undoubtedly subsidizes the service recipient group at the expense of the general taxpaying public. User charges can obviously prevent that problem. Less obvious but equally significant are two related equity problems that user charges can

---

[9]By charging higher prices during periods when capital facilities, such as highways or airports, are heavily congested, usage may be redistributed, and need for new construction may be reduced.

[10]Quoted in *Forbes*, (21 October 1985): 216.

[11]The program may still be worth expanding, even if the charge does not cover the cost of providing the service. That would depend on the social benefits, if any, that extend beyond the participants paying the direct charge. The point here is that such a program should not be expanded because of *revenue* considerations.

reduce: the problems created by nonresident service recipients and by tax-exempt entities. Many urban services, particularly cultural and recreational, can easily be used by anyone in the region. General revenue financing permits a subsidy to any nonresident consumer; a user charge prevents that subsidy. It is a simple and direct way to reduce burdens placed on one government by citizens of neighboring governments. A user charge also provides a mechanism for obtaining financial support from tax-exempt institutions. Many cities, for example, finance refuse collection with property tax revenue. Charitable, religious, or educational institutions exempt from property tax would contribute nothing to finance refuse collection, even though they receive the service, whose cost must be borne by general taxpayers. If, however, refuse collection were financed by user charges, that cost shifting would not occur. Just as these entities must pay for gasoline purchased from a private firm, they would pay the refuse-collection charge: Tax exemption does not exempt institutions from paying for goods or services bought on the open market. For both nonresidents and exempt institutions, the user charge allows governments to extract revenue from entities outside their tax network; if they use, they must pay.

Third, a user-charge program may improve operating efficiency because agency staff must respond to client demand. Agencies usually operate with funds obtained from and justified to a legislative body. That justification elaborates needs as estimated by the agency staff and is defended according to performance criteria established by the agency staff. Those agencies with the best bureaucratic expertise—the ones best able to prepare convincing budget justifications and apply the strategies of the budget process described in previous chapters—are the ones most likely to receive appropriations. User-charge finance, however, requires a shift to preferences articulated directly by customers. The agency must provide services that are desired by consumers, or it will fail the financial test for survival. It cannot define what clients should want in its budget defense; it must provide the services clients actually will purchase.

Finally, a user charge may correct cost-and-price signals in the private market. Suppose a manufacturing plant places extraordinary demand on traffic control in a neighborhood. That special demand requires additional police officers at a handful of intersections in that area during shift changes at the factory. The way the plant operates thus produces substantial extra costs for the community. If the plant must pay for the extra traffic-control costs its operations require, its management has a direct financial incentive to consider whether its current operating pattern (with attendant traffic-control charges) is cost-effective. The plant's management may decide that lower peak-flow traffic produced by staggered shifts, van pooling, subsidies for mass-transit use, and so on (and no traffic-control charge) is less expensive. The user charge makes the decision-making unit recognize and respond to the true social cost of its action. In the example cited, without the user charge, the additional traffic-control costs the plant nothing; no one can be expected to conserve a resource that appears to be free. The same logic applies in the application of effluent charges to the discharge of environmental pollutants.

In summary, user charges make the public recognize that the services provided are not costless. The public can choose whether it wants the service and, if so, how much to purchase. People may save money by economizing on the service, and receiving the service does not place costs on others. In charge-financed areas, the government has an excellent gauge of what services the public wants and is willing to pay for.

Limitations of User Charges

User charges cannot generally substitute for taxes to finance government services because many public services—in fact, most services provided by most governments—simply do not fit the requirements for user-charge financing. First, activities that have substantial benefits extending beyond the principal recipient are not candidates for user-charge financing. Basic fire protection in an urban area could not, for example, be considered for user-charge financing because fire tends to spread; extinguishing a fire in one building protects surrounding units. Thus, protection financed by one individual automatically protects others; nonpayers are not excludable, so the service cannot be financed by charges. There is a corollary to the external-benefit problem: The ability to charge for particular services can distort agency decision making. Thus, a high school football team receives magnanimous resources because gate receipts are sizable (even though unlikely to cover even a decent percentage of the program's cost), whereas the girls' volleyball team gets hand-me-downs. The question for resource allocation is contribution to the purposes of the community (or social benefits); simple cash flow should not be the determining factor in such an instance.

Second, services may intentionally subsidize low-income or otherwise disadvantaged recipients. Charges for these services could be counterproductive.[12] Beneficiaries should not pay if the service has welfare elements. In a related fashion, some have argued that user charges in general are unfair because they often produce a regressive-burden pattern, taking a larger percentage of a low-income consumer's income than from higher-income consumers.[13] That argument is not a convincing attack on user charges for several reasons. For one thing, low-income families not using the service clearly are better off with the user-charge system—no charge to be paid and no tax paid to subsidize the service used by others. Furthermore, tax-financing devices may have a more regressive burden than user charges, even if the service is widely used by disadvantaged citizens. Local revenue systems often are very regressive, so it is not unlikely that a shift to user charges could reduce regressivity. Finally, it may be possible to design "payability" tests for the charges because the services are received by identifiable individuals.[14] Suppose a city charges an admission fee to swimming pools: Benefits are primarily individual (to the swimmer and family), prices can be enforced using fences and turnstiles (safety

[12]There are, of course, more efficient ways of redistributing income in society than providing government services. But once that method is selected, it should not be thwarted by charges.

[13]Willard Price, "The Case Against the Imposition of a Sewer Use Tax," *Governmental Finance* 4 (May 1975): 38–44.

[14]Selma J. Mushkin and Charles L. Vehorn coined the "payability" phrase in "User Fees and Charges," *Governmental Finance* 6 (November 1977): 46.

requires access control, regardless of financing technique), and overcrowding may otherwise result when children are dumped at the facility for "free" babysitting. Charge opponents argue that free pools are a significant recreation option for low-income families; a charge would harm that redistributive function. Charges, however, can function equitably and efficiently if disadvantaged families receive season passes at no cost or if pools located in low-income areas are free while charges apply at other pools. In general, protection of the disadvantaged should not be an excuse for subsidizing the well-to-do.

Third, some charges, though technically feasible, may be expensive to collect. Spending a considerable share of the revenue raised in collecting that revenue is not likely to be a wise use of agency resources. The high cost suggests a degree of publicness making the appropriateness of the charge itself questionable.

Fourth, there are important political issues when a tax-supported service is proposed for shift to charge financing. The charge may face considerable public resentment based on the view that, having paid taxes, the person is entitled to the public service without any additional payment. Although this agreement is roughly the same as arguing that, because you purchased bread, the store should provide meat for the sandwich at no charge, it does often accompany shifts toward charge finance. But, in addition to public opposition, there is frequently bureaucratic resistance. Service providers understand that moving from tax finance to a user charge means that, for the client, the service price is increased from zero (though there are costs of providing the service, those costs are borne by other parts of the fiscal system, with no difference in payment according to use) to some positive amount (the price). This change will ration out some use of the service, a change that goes against the attitudes of public officials. Both service providers and clients tend to offer a unified opposition to user charges in all but fiscally distressed environments. But the fact that service use may decline when a charge is imposed or raised is not a flaw of the charge but simply what one expects from downward-sloping demand curves in a market economy—that is, at any given time people will voluntarily purchase more units at a low price than at a higher price.

Finally, there is the ultimate reality in user charge finance that those who do not pay need to be denied service and this is often unpopular. If the water or electric bill is not paid, service needs to be shut off for the charge system to be effective, even though the service is necessary. The charge is intended to raise money and to regulate use of the service and, for it to have the intended effects, delinquent accounts cannot be tolerated. Unfortunately, enforcement can be painful and inevitably brings forth stories in the media and from some politicians of the crisis that enforcement causes for some low-income and elderly people. The government adopting an aggressive program of user-charge finance has to understand that enforcing the charges against delinquent customers has the potential for bad publicity and needs to accept that before it adopts the policy.[15] And it needs some sort of safety net or lifeline program to deal with the toughest cases. However, if the delinquents are not

[15]An aggressive program against delinquent water users in Atlanta caused one-quarter of city water customers there to face shutoff. The city had lax enforcement before the new program. Ariel Hart, "Atlanta Shutting Off Water as It Tries to Collect $35 Million Overdue," *New York Times*, (3 November 2004).

successfully pursued, then the cost of providing them service is borne by others—including low-income and elderly customers who do not cheat on their bills. That isn't fair at all.

Charge Guidelines

Governments differ in the extent to which they charge for services, partly because of the different services they provide (e.g., national defense, welfare, and highway patrol are hardly priceable) and partly because of political attitudes toward pricing public goods. Outside those constraints, there are some guides for user-charge preparation and manipulation. Any service showing the features described earlier (individual benefit, susceptibility to excluding nonpayers, and an absence of redistributive elements) are reasonable candidates for user-charge financing. The short list in Table 11–3 provides some options. Selma Mushkin and Richard Bird nominate for charge (1) household-support functions (water, refuse collection, sewerage), (2) industrial-development support (airports, parking, special police or fire services, etc.), (3) "amenities" (specialized recreation facilities, cultural facilities, etc.), and (4) services provided to tax-exempt entities.[16] The list and its classification

Table 11–3
Selected Government Services Amenable to Public Pricing

Special police work	Service for stadium or auditorium events, alarm servicing
Parking	Garage, meters
Solid-waste management	Collection, disposal
Recreation	Golf courses, tennis courts, swimming pools, park admissions, concessions, rescue insurance, instruction
Health and hospitals	Ambulance charges, inoculations, hospital rates, health insurance premiums
Transportation	Transit fares, bridge and highway tolls, airport landing (departure fees, hangar rentals), lock tolls
Education	Rentals of special books, equipment, or uniforms, college or technical school tuition, facility rentals, special training programs for individual businesses.
Resource management	Surveys, extension service inquiries, tree nursery and development stock, livestock-grazing fees, mineral royalties
Sewerage	Treatment, disposal
Utilities	Water, electric, gas, transit
Other	Licensing for use of institution name, miscellaneous special services provided an individual household or business.

[16]Selma J. Mushkin and Richard M. Bird, "Public Prices: An Overview," in S.J. Mushkin, ed., *Public Prices for Public Products* (Washington, D.C.: Urban Institute, 1972), 8–9.

should give ample direction. Anytime the service is to an identifiable household or business and there are no discernable external impacts of the service, the service belongs on the candidate list.

Some governments—often in response to property tax limits, controls, or freezes—have applied general police- or fire-protection charges based on the value of property protected. These are not true user charges because they are not voluntary; they are simply an escape mechanism around the tax limitations. Assigning service costs in relation to a property's physical characteristics, according to an estimate of how those characteristics produce demand for a service, has greater logical appeal but should not be considered a true user charge because it cannot be voluntary. Because unchecked fires in urban areas will spread, voluntary decisions about purchasing fire protection are untenable. Protection for one unit protects its neighbors, and an unprotected unit endangers its neighbors. Thus, these financing devices must be structured as taxes (nonvoluntary), but they are taxes based on a concept other than the ability of an economic unit to afford the designated tax burden. The burden of financing that municipal service is allocated among economic units according to the physical attributes of those units that require service cost to be incurred. As such, fire-protection fees could have desirable development effects: they could provide owners of structures an extra financial reward for installing private fire-control devices (smoke alarms, sprinklers, fire walls, etc.) in older units, and could also cause owners of particularly deteriorated structures to raze them. The fees, of course, would not be related to firm profitability: Some marginal businesses housed in deteriorated, high-fire-risk structures could face substantial fees. On the whole, however, a rigid structure of fire-risk fees could significantly accelerate the process of structural modernization and, over time, could reduce the total cost of fire protection, even though fire-risk fees are not user charges.

When a government decides that a particular service can be financed by a user charge, the appropriate level of that charge must be determined. That determination is not simple. Frederick Stocker reports: "Evidence suggests that pricing policies used by municipal governments are often fairly unsophisticated, perhaps understandably so in light of the difficulty of determining price elasticities, marginal costs, distribution of benefits and other things that enter into economic models of optimal pricing."[17]

The municipality, however, may get some guidance from fairly simple concepts about service costs.[18] In particular, the government should separate its service costs into two categories: (1) costs that change as a result of the service being provided

---

[17]Frederick D. Stocker, "Diversification of the Local Revenue System: Income and Sales Taxes, User Charges, Federal Grants," *National Tax Journal* 29 (September 1976): 320.

[18]Paul Downing maintains that an appropriately designed user charge would have three components: a portion that reflects short-run production costs and varies with output consumed, a portion that reflects plant and equipment costs (possibly allocated as an individual's share of its designed capacity), and a portion based on the cost of delivering the service to a specific customer location. The first portion may vary by the time of day, depending on whether the system is at peak utilization. If so, the charge would be increased. These principles are particularly important for utility operation. See Downing's "User Charges and Special Districts," in J. Richard Aronson and Eli Schwartz, eds., *Management Policies in Local Government Finance* (Washington, D.C.: International City Management Association, 1981), 191–92.

(incremental cost) and (2) costs that do not change with service provision. The latter includes any cost that would continue, regardless of decisions concerning that service, and thus can be disregarded in the charge analysis. Prices need to be based on market conditions—that is, on demand for the service being sold—and on the offerings of competitive providers of that service. The prospective purchaser is not driven by what it costs the municipality to produce the service, so the municipality is not able to determine what price it should charge from its costs.[19] A knowledge of cost, however, lets the municipality understand to what extent the particular service, after allowance for revenue from the price charged for the service, contributes to or must be subsidized by the remainder of government finances. A price that recovers the incremental cost of providing a particular service means that the provision of that user-charge-financed service does not burden other functions of government.[20] Prices above that level are possible, subject to the demand for the service and the government's desire to use surplus to support other government activities.

How can the government arrive at a reasonable price for the services it has chosen to sell? Setting prices is often an uncomfortable and unfamiliar activity for governments and the task is made more complicated by a shortage of adequate market information and by political complexities. Sometimes the government may find similar services being sold by private firms and can use this market information as a guide for setting its own prices. Sometimes there may be no similar service being sold, and the government may decide to set its price at some markup of its incremental cost. In either case, the initial price will probably need to be adjusted up or down as customer response provides the government with more information about what their preferences really are and as government agencies get better insights into how their operating costs change as the amount of service provided varies. And the government almost certainly will learn from the political response when it moves certain services from tax finance to charge finance. However, decisions are not permanent: There is no reason why the government cannot experiment with various prices for its services to determine their effect on the amount of service purchased and on net revenue to the government. There is no special economic virtue in maintaining stable prices, although it may be politically more convenient.

A final consideration about user charges concerns their method of application. Alfred Kahn writes, in an analysis of public-utility pricing, "The only economic function of price is to influence behavior. . . . But of course price can have this effect on the buyer's side only if bills do indeed depend on the volume of purchases. For this reason, economists . . . are avid meterers."[21] A similar principle applies to user

---

[19]A good analysis of government price setting appears in Chapter 8 of David L. Rados, *Marketing for Non-Profit Organizations* (Boston: Auburn House, 1981). Peter F. Drucker calls *cost-driven pricing* one of "The Five Deadly Business Sins" in *Wall Street Journal,* (21 October 1993), A-22.

[20]James Johnson has identified six elements in existing municipal sewerage-service charges: water use (a volume proxy), flat charges, number of plumbing fixtures used by the customer, size of water meter or sewer connection, property characteristics (assessed value, square footage, front footage), and sewage strength. Water use is the most frequently encountered user-charge element. See James A. Johnson, "The Distribution of the Burden of Sewer User Charges under Various Charge Formulas," *National Tax Journal* 22 (December 1969): 472–85.

[21]Alfred E. Kahn, "Can an Economist Find Happiness Setting Public Utility Rates?" *Public Utilities Fortnightly* (January 5, 1978): 15.

charges. Buyer behavior will not change unless changes in behavior will influence payments owed. If a refuse-collection customer pays $25 per year for that service, regardless of whether two or fifteen trash cans are collected per week, the customer cannot be expected to change the number of trash cans set out for collection. A charge sensitive to usage, however, does induce behavioral changes by some customers. To obtain the full benefits of user-charge financing, then, the service must be metered and made usage-sensitive. Dividing estimated total costs by the number of entities served and presenting a bill to each entity does not produce the desired effects of public prices.

Public Monopoly Revenue: Utilities, Liquor Stores, and Gambling Enterprises

Government power to own and operate business enterprises, to sell private goods, is extensive, although contrary to the global wave of privatization. Government ownership is the exception, not the rule, in the United States. Whenever a public interest is identified that competitive pressures cannot handle, the normal approach in the United States is to regulate the private firm, not for government to own and operate the enterprise. A government official seeking public ownership of a private business has not paid sufficient attention to the lessons from the collapse of the Soviet Union.

Government Utilities

Some services are widely provided by municipal utilities, especially in water supply, electric power, intra-city transit, and gas supply.[22] The great majority of cities with a population over 5,000 are serviced by municipal water utilities. However, municipal electric-power systems, usually distributors of power produced by others, operate mostly in small communities. Gas supply is predominantly through private ownership. Intra-city transit has made something of a resurgence with the failure of private transit systems, but the public systems have been as unprofitable as their private predecessors. Table 11–1 reported the extent to which state and local governments generated utility revenue in fiscal 2003. In the tradition of census statistics, utilities report gross revenues; they do not net out expenditures made by the utility in producing the service sold to generate that revenue. In fact, expenditures in the utility categories often exceed the revenue taken in by the utility. When

[22]Solid-waste management, a candidate for utility finance, is typically managed within general government or by a special district if not provided by a private firm.

that happens, the government may have to subsidize the operation of the utility, or the deficit must be financed.

Why should a municipality choose to operate a utility rather than allow a private firm to do it? Surely government can better allocate its time to more pressing public concerns than to focus on the mundane questions of utility management. Motivation is, not surprisingly, usually mixed. In some instances, the governing body believes that it can use utility-operation profits to subsidize the operations of the general government. In fact, some decades ago, some cities could boast of being tax-free towns, because of profits from electric-utility systems. That era has passed, however, and the best that one could hope for is some assistance from the utility to the city, not a fiscal bonanza.[23]

In other instances, the government owner may be more interested in keeping the price of the service as low as possible, perhaps even providing the service at less than cost. That policy requires some subsidization of the utility by the sponsoring government. This practice can be politically appealing—the low-cost service can be an important element in reelection strategy—and may be supported by a desire to encourage economic development, but the government decision-makers must be certain that other important city services are not shortchanged by subsidizing the utility. Otherwise, the practice can contribute to the city's fiscal decay. However, experience suggests that, compared to private owners, government operation may be less greedy in pricing, but probably not more efficient in producing the service.

Liquor Stores

Seventeen states maintain another and radically different sort of monopoly: the operation of liquor stores. In these states, some if not all alcoholic beverage sales are made in the state-owned stores. The state establishes a markup over inventory cost sufficient to cover its operating cost as well as to return a profit for other state operations. In some instances, the state will also add an excise to the price. Table 11–1 reported liquor store revenues, again following the census practice of not netting out cost. In contrast to the utility case, however, liquor stores return a profit to their parent governments. Only in New Hampshire, a state with neither general sales nor individual income taxes, do these profits make more than a negligible contribution to state finances (in 2003, liquor store sales exceeded liquor store expenditures by $48 million, compared with total state general revenue of $4,566 million).[24]

---

[23]Cities can move costs to the utility operation by charging the utility for services rendered it by city government (charges for the mayor, the city council, use of space in the municipal building, etc.) or by getting free utilities for city operations, if direct payments are difficult or legally restrained.

[24]U.S. Bureau of Census, Governments Division.

Government Gambling Enterprises: Lotteries and Offtrack Betting

In 2003 the total gross gambling revenue in the United States exceeded $72.8 billion.[25] Such a pool of money offers an attractive revenue opportunity for governments, but it also creates social and moral concerns about evils that gambling might bring. That ambivalence appears in how governments respond to gambling. As *The Economist* keenly headlined, "That's So Wicked We'll Do It Ourselves:"

> They restrict its availability; they subject it to high taxes; and they keep the promotion of some forms of it to themselves. Their defense is the same nearly everywhere: gambling is basically a bad thing, so you should have tight rules to ban or restrict it; where it is permitted, it should be discouraged by high taxes; even so, the profits will be huge, so the state should run some gambling itself.[26]

States selectively allow pari-mutuel gambling on certain events (horse racing, greyhound racing, jai alai, and, in Nevada, other sporting events),[27] casinos (either land-based or on riverboats), bingo, card rooms, and lotteries. State revenue normally flows from taxes on these activities, through the regular income, property, and sales tax structures and through selective excises or licenses directly on operators or applicants for licenses to operate. The gambling excises may be on the number of admissions (a tax on each person going on a riverboat, for instance), on the total amount wagered in the establishment, or on the number of tables or other gaming devices in the establishment. Casinos offer strong competition for other gambling formats, being identified as an important factor in the demise of some horse and greyhound racetracks and in slower lottery revenue growth—even some decreases—in several states. State revenues from casinos are unstable, driven as they are by private management decisions and competitive forces in the gaming market, are cyclically sensitive to national and regional economies, and are expensive to collect. Furthermore, except possibly for play at destination resorts, casino gambling appears to be distributed regressively.[28]

Seldom do U.S. governments actually operate the gaming facilities, preferring to leave the business to private operators who specialize in those activities and limiting

---

[25]"2003 Gross Gambling Revenue by Industry and Change from 2002," prepared by Christiansen Capital Advisers, Inc. (Available online at www.cca-i.com, accessed August 24, 2005). The distribution of the total handle: casinos, 39.4 percent; lotteries, 27.4 percent; pari-mutuels, 5.2 percent; Native American reservation games, 23.1 percent; card rooms, 1.2 percent; bingo, 1.5 percent; charitable games, 2.1 percent; legal bookmakers, 0.2 percent; and Internet gambling, 7.8 percent.

[26]That's So Wicked We'll Do It Ourselves," *Economist,* 11 April 1992, 24.

[27]The pari-mutuel system is one in which those backing the winner divide, in proportion to their wagers, the total pool bet, after a percentage has been removed by those conducting the event. Some lottery games are pari-mutuel as well.

[28]Ranjana G. Madhusudhan, "Betting on Casino Revenues: Lessons from State Experiences," *National Tax Journal* 49 (September 1996): 401–12. Casinos may also reduce state sales tax revenue. See Jim Landers, "The Effect of Casino Gambling on Sales Tax Revenues in States Legalizing Casinos in the 1990s," *State Tax Notes* 38 (December 26, 2005): 1073–83.

the government's role to regulation and collecting taxes.[29] There are two exceptions. Offtrack betting may have state (or local, in New York City) government proprietors in some places, and state-operated lotteries have become a standard component of state fiscal systems. Government-operated offtrack betting has seldom been particularly profitable and has not spread beyond the northeast quadrant of the nation, although private operations are common at casinos and race tracks. Lotteries merit some additional attention because they are state-operated, have spread throughout the nation, and produce more net revenue for states than other gambling activities, although casino excise collections are larger in some individual states. The spread of state lotteries in the 1980s—when they became a standard element in state government fiscal operations—probably paved the way for public acceptance of casinos and pari-mutuel gaming in the 1990s.

In 1964 New Hampshire initiated the first state lottery since the demise of the corrupt Louisiana lottery in 1894. New York followed in 1967, but proceeds in both were disappointing. Greater success came with better merchandising and attention to customer tastes, the approach pioneered by New Jersey in 1970, to generate remarkable revenue totals and substantial public excitement. That approach featured "(a) lower priced tickets; (b) more frequent drawings; (c) more numerous outlets; (d) numbered tickets in lieu of recording purchasers' names and addresses; (e) somewhat better odds; and (f) energetic promotion."[30] By 2004, forty states and the District of Columbia operated lotteries.[31] Table 11–4 indicates the lottery revenue generated in 2004, a tiny amount in comparison with taxes, but larger than some user-charge categories.

There are five general lottery formats:

1. **Passive.** The customer receives a prenumbered ticket with a winner selected at a periodic drawing. This type has largely been superseded by other games.
2. **Instant.** The player buys a ticket and rubs off a substance to reveal whether the ticket is a winner. A few states offer a video-terminal version of the game, creating a product much like casino slot machines.
3. **Numbers.** The player selects a three- or four-digit daily number and places a bet on an online computer terminal regarding whether the number will be drawn.

---

[29]Casinos operated by Native American tribes, a special type of government, are obviously an exception, although even here, outside management has been the rule. Tribe members are, however, developing expertise for a more active role. The U.S. Supreme Court in *California* v. *Cabazon Band of Mission Indians* [480 U.S. 202 (1987)] effectively removed all existing restrictions on gambling on Native American reservations, thereby transforming a small and isolated activity often limited to bingo halls into a growth industry. The congressional response, the Indian Gaming Regulatory Act of 1988, specifically authorized casino gambling on Indian reservations, established a regulatory framework for this gambling, and created the National Indian Gaming Commission to oversee the industry. The great expansion of Native American casino gaming emerged under this system; the largest casino in the world is a Native American casino. More than half the states host at least one Native American casino.

[30]Frederick D. Stocker, "State Sponsored Gambling as a Source of Public Revenue," *National Tax Journal* 25 (September 1972): 437.

[31]Not included is the special state-sanctioned, privately operated statewide lottery for charities in Alaska.

Table 11–4
State Lottery Performance, Fiscal Year 2004 ($ in thousands)

	Year of First Play	Ticket Sales	Net to State	Net as % Own-Source General Revenue	Net as % Ticket Sales	Administrative Cost as % of Ticket Sales	Administrative Cost as % of Net Proceeds
Arizona	1981	342,081	108,019	0.90%	31.58%	9.87%	31.25%
California	1985	2,768,477	1,045,771	1.00%	37.77%	5.66%	14.98%
Colorado	1983	407,175	133,348	1.29%	32.75%	7.69%	23.47%
Connecticut	1972	909,593	283,930	2.14%	31.22%	9.60%	30.76%
Delaware	1975	379,386	283,915	6.94%	74.84%	11.14%	14.89%
Florida	1988	2,901,719	1,042,283	2.61%	35.92%	4.65%	12.95%
Georgia	1993	2,376,271	783,572	4.10%	32.97%	4.73%	14.34%
Idaho	1989	101,366	25,892	0.73%	25.54%	10.60%	41.48%
Illinois	1974	1,572,457	542,137	1.68%	34.48%	3.59%	10.42%
Indiana	1989	668,920	200,815	1.22%	30.02%	4.72%	15.72%
Iowa	1985	195,231	53,470	0.68%	27.39%	13.99%	51.06%
Kansas	1987	211,531	70,034	1.02%	33.11%	9.80%	29.59%
Kentucky	1989	680,125	196,312	1.69%	28.86%	6.56%	22.73%
Louisiana	1991	311,085	121,838	1.00%	39.17%	6.26%	15.98%
Maine	1974	188,975	42,567	1.01%	22.53%	15.65%	69.50%
Maryland	1973	1,395,408	466,209	2.85%	33.41%	9.99%	29.90%
Massachusetts	1972	4,375,585	1,153,902	4.81%	26.37%	1.67%	6.35%
Michigan	1972	1,841,381	684,874	2.07%	37.19%	3.09%	8.30%
Minnesota	1990	345,915	82,598	0.46%	23.88%	6.54%	27.40%
Missouri	1986	742,476	219,274	1.70%	29.53%	5.17%	17.50%
Montana	1987	34,649	9,166	0.36%	26.45%	19.63%	74.22%
Nebraska	1993	92,608	19,395	0.39%	20.94%	22.25%	106.24%
New Hampshire	1964	226,282	73,720	2.20%	32.58%	6.81%	20.91%
New Jersey	1970	2,065,672	795,852	2.81%	38.53%	3.54%	9.18%
New Mexico	1996	138,446	35,956	0.58%	25.97%	12.51%	48.18%
New York	1967	5,491,844	1,959,181	3.35%	35.67%	4.12%	11.55%
North Dakota	2004	0					
Ohio	1974	2,154,715	600,915	1.95%	27.89%	12.89%	46.23%
Oregon	1985	1,609,515	195,860	2.04%	12.17%	16.45%	135.16%
Pennsylvania	1972	2,162,359	837,349	2.41%	38.72%	0.89%	2.29%
Rhode Island	1974	1,309,355	278,436	7.90%	21.27%	0.55%	2.60%
South Carolina	2002	883,058	290,877	2.74%	32.94%	4.52%	13.72%
South Dakota	1987	140,659	116,565	6.99%	88.87%	3.53%	4.26%
Tennessee	2004	0					
Texas	1992	3,487,925	1,063,053	2.31%	30.48%	10.21%	33.51%
Vermont	1978	86,986	20,099	0.81%	23.11%	10.69%	46.28%
Virginia	1988	1,262,359	422,235	1.94%	33.45%	10.53%	31.49%
Washington	1982	481,439	120,266	0.66%	24.98%	13.64%	54.62%
West Virginia	1986	673,789	520,456	8.22%	77.24%	4.46%	5.78%
Wisconsin	1988	449,045	140,578	0.82%	31.31%	7.41%	23.68%
U.S. Total		45,465,862	15,040,719				
U.S. Mean				2.33%	33.82%	8.31%	30.49%

SOURCE: U.S. Bureau of Census Governments Division, *2004 Annual Survey of Government Finances,* January 2006.

4. **Lotto.** This is a pari-mutuel game in which the player selects a group of numbers out of a larger field of possible selections (e.g., six of a possible forty-four). If no ticket has been sold for the particular group of numbers picked in the weekly drawing, the amount not won rolls over to the next week. Top-prize money can grow rapidly, producing multimillion-dollar prizes. The lotto games may be offered by a single state or by multistate groups (like those operating the Powerball or MegaMillions games in the United States). Lotto produces more revenue than the other products currently offered.

5. **Keno.** This is a casino-type game in which a player can make a variety of bets, involving long or short odds and large or small prizes, on the selection of numbers from a large field. Play is virtually continuous, with many draws during the day. Play is in sites, often bars, connected to a statewide system.

Lotteries appear to be a painless, voluntary, and enjoyable approach to government finance. What are their limitations? Some answers may be deduced from Table 11–4. First, lottery proceeds, although large in several states, contribute but a small amount to overall state finances. In a few states, the lottery contributes more than 5 percent of state own-source general revenue, but the national share across all lottery states is only 2.3 percent. These amounts are not sufficient to provide either significant tax relief or support for crucial state functions. If a state has important fiscal imbalance, a lottery is unlikely to correct it. Second, lottery revenue is expensive to produce. Both security and advertising are crucial for lottery success; neither is cheap, and the advertising seldom reveals the real chances of winning. If evaluated on roughly the same basis as would be a tax, the ratio of administrative cost to net proceeds to the state, not including commissions of 5 or 6 percent of sales paid directly to lottery vendors, was 30.49 percent. Even though there is no compliance cost to add in for the lottery, advertising, security, and commission costs are much greater than collection cost for taxes. Third, lottery proceeds are subject to considerable change from year to year, making them an unstable base for financing. Lottery sales have an extremely high elasticity to state income. One estimate indicates a 3.9 percent increase in sales for each 1 percent increase in state personal income. That response is tempered by response to the state unemployment rate. Apparently lower prospects of employment in the economy make the small but real change of the lottery jackpot more attractive for households.[32] Fourth, evidence suggests that low-income families spend a higher percentage of their income on lottery tickets than do high-income families, thus producing a regressive-burden distribution. Although it is a voluntary burden, it does remain a burden that makes distributive correction by other parts of the tax or expenditure system more difficult.[33]

Finally, Charles Clotfelter and Philip Cook raise a fundamental question about state lotteries that is even more important than their fiscal implications: "The lot-

[32]John L. Mikesell, "State Lottery Sales and Economic Activity," *National Tax Journal* 47 (March 1994): 170.

[33]Some have suggested that lotteries can cut into the profits of gambling operated illegally. Unfortunately, lotteries typically offer worse odds than do illegal operations, do not offer regular gambling on credit, and report large winnings to tax authorities, so the competition presented by state systems is not likely to be effective.

tery business places the state in the position of using advertising that endorses suspect values and offers deceptive impressions instead of information."[34] Should this line of business be something that states operate, regardless of the money?

Lottery proponents note that profits are often dedicated to the support of important and valuable state programs, especially education. The revenue, however, is fungible, leading to the possibility that the lottery profits going to the dedicated program will simply substitute for other budget resources that would have gone to the program anyway. One analysis done of the Illinois lottery's support for education speaks directly to the point: ". . . lotteries which are designated to support education, in all likelihood, do not. Further, there is no reason to believe that other specific programs designated as lottery fund recipients are any more likely to be truly supported by the lottery funds."[35] Money mixes in government operations and dedication to useful purposes do not ordinarily change the basic points in the case for or against lotteries as an element in government finances.

Conclusion

Public prices can be an attractive alternative to tax financing. Public prices avoid citizen resistance to taxes and can improve both equity in finance and service provision efficiency. Of the various government levels, cities currently make greatest use of user charges in the United States. User charges have the advantage of voluntarism not found with taxes, but only services with some considerable degree of benefit separability and chargability are reasonable candidates for user-charge financing. Basic services provided by government usually lack those features. Most governments could increase their user-charge revenues, but seldom can true user charges (not disguised taxes) consitute a major portion of financial support. A similar conclusion is warranted for municipal utilities and state liquor monopolies; it is not clear why, if a governent operates such facilities, it would not seek roughly the same objectives as a private owner. Lotteries in recent years have produced, relatively speaking, more public attention and acclaim than revenue.

CHAPTER 11 QUESTIONS AND EXERCISES

1. The Fernwood Wastewater District—at the gentle insistence of both state and federal agencies—is changing methods of financing the operating and maintenance costs of its system. Presently, all users of the system (residential, commercial,

[34]Charles T. Clotfelter and Philip J. Cook, *Selling Hope* (Cambridge, Mass.: Harvard University Press, 1989), 249.

[35]Mary O. Borg and Paul M. Mason, "The Budgetary Incidence of a Lottery to Support Education," *National Tax Journal* 41 (March 1988): 83.

agricultural, industrial, etc.) pay for the system by a property tax; payments to the district are assigned according to individual holdings of property value. If a car wash constitutes 0.0001 of total property in the district, the car wash pays 0.0001 of the operating and maintenance cost of the system. The proposed effluent-charge system would assign cost on the basis of estimated toxic-waste quality and quantity introduced into the system. The structure could easily be applied because a federal agency has data on the amount and type of waste that production and consumption processes generate annually, based on national data. These data would then be used to assign an annual effluent charge to each user, based on the total costs of the district.

How do the two systems differ in terms of incentive to reduce wastewater quantity and toxicity?

2. The following describes the manner in which a public library sets its nonresident library card fee: The South Bend Public Library issues free library cards to anyone residing or paying property taxes within the boundaries of Center, Clay, Greene, German, Liberty, Portage, or Warren Townships of St. Joseph County, Indiana—those townships that provide property tax support to the public library. For those who do not reside or pay property taxes within any of these townships, the South Bend Public Library offers an annually renewable nonresident fee card. The annual fee for this card is equal to approximately the annual property taxes paid for library services by the average household within the library's taxing district. At its January 1984 board meeting, the board of the library trustees passed a resolution to set this fee on a schedule approximating the cost per family in the library's service area, as indicated in the following formula:

Divide the library budget by the population to obtain average cost per capita. Then multiply that average cost by the average number of persons per household. The result is the cost per family in the service area.

With a budget of $3,153,753, a population of 168,000, and an average number of persons per household of 2.7 in the latest census, the cost per family came to $50.00.

Some other details about the area for your use:

- In the most recent census, the seven townships paying property tax to the library constituted almost 69 percent of St. Joseph County's population; in the prior budget year, those townships made up 70 percent of the county's property-tax base.
- The card is required to check out books from the library. One can consult available materials in the library without a card.
- The property-tax base includes farm, residential, commercial, industrial, utility real estate, and personal property owned by businesses.
- A large share of total library cost is independent of year-to-year circulation.

Operating information for all public libraries (each operated by an independent library district) in the county are found in this table.

	Registered Borrowers	Total Circulation	Total Books	Total Periodicals	Total Operating Income ($)	Operating Income—Property Tax ($)	Percent of Operating Spending on		
							Personal Services	Library Materials	Supplies
Mishawaka	20,116	299,519	111,760	240	617,446	486,882	51.6	19.5	2.7
New Carlisle	4,630	28,110	25,026	98	70,086	57,039	50.3	19.6	1.9
South Bend	64,546	1,434,789	323,631	386	1,967,760	1,623,839	54.0	16.0	2.4
Walkerton	1,077	22,071	18,009	28	21,776	17,505	52.9	14.2	2.2

a. Does the method of computing the charge produce a figure roughly equal to the property tax paid for the library service by the typical resident of the tax-paying townships?
b. Is the computation likely to approximate the user charge that would emerge from the principal of efficient charging?
c. Is the charge likely too low or too high for efficiency? Who loses, in your estimation?
d. Can you suggest an alternative financing structure?

3. In mid-1985, the U.S. Customs Service proposed a user-charge system for partial support of its services. The system would charge $2 for every arriving passenger on an international flight, $0.25 for passengers arriving by train from a foreign destination, and $2.50 for arrivals by boat. Fees to inspect airplanes would be $32 and to check passenger and freight carriers, up to $397. The customs system currently is financed by general revenue.

Does the proposal seem reasonable? Discuss its logic, advantages, and disadvantages.

4. Here is a list of miscellaneous revenue sources received by governments. Categorize them as best you can as (1) user charge, (2) license tax, (3) franchise fee, or (4) fiscal monopoly using the standards established in the chapter.[1] Explain your logic.

a. A fee for disposal of used tires
b. A fee to reserve books at the library
c. A charge for processing the arrest of a convicted drunk driver
d. A charge for emergency services required when a driver causes an accident through negligence
e. A charge by the fire department to pump water from basements flooded by a downpour
f. A fee for the services of a probation officer
g. A fee for reviewing developer's plans
h. A fee for police response to a malfunctioning alarm system
i. A charge for ball-field use by the youth athletic league

[1]Most of these examples have been taken from Penelope Lemov, "User Fees, Once the Answer to City Budget Prayers, May Have Reached Their Peak," *Governing* (March 1989): 24–30.

j. Admission to the city zoo
k. A mandatory fee for municipal garbage collection
l. A charge for use of the city municipal garbage collection
m. A charge for yacht owners who dock at the city marina
n. Fees for a summer daycamp run by the city parks department

5. Due City has decided to shift municipal garbage-collection financing from the property tax to user charges. Describe some ways in which such a system could be implemented. Make certain that your system is primarily one of user charge, not a disguised tax.

6. The odds against selecting the winning lotto number are extreme. The formula

$$N = (c!)/[r!(c - r)!]$$

provides the number of possible winning numbers (N), where c equals the range of numbers possible and r equals the number from that range to be selected, against which the player has one chance of selecting. For example, for the popular 6/44 games, the possible winning numbers could come from

$$N = (44!)/[6!(44 - 6)!] = 44!/[6! \times 38!] = 7{,}059{,}052$$

different possibilities. Thus, the odds of picking the winning series are 1 in 7,059,052. Because the pari-mutuel pool is carried over from game to game until it is won, the lotto jackpot can reach truly remarkable levels, $40 million in one instance. As the jackpot rises, the expected value of the ticket rises as well: Expected value = Probability of winning × Size of payoff. The rising jackpot brings increased lotto sales to the state as well.

a. Compare the probable effects on the jackpot size and likelihood of having a winner in the first week of play of a 5/36 and a 6/44 lotto game.
b. Discuss the strategic issues, including the revenue flow to the state and the likely player, involved in choosing between those games. Would the strategy differ according to whether the state lottery was old or new? According to what neighboring lotteries were doing?
c. A bumper sticker proclaims the following: "Lotteries are a tax on people who are bad at math." Do you agree?

CASES FOR DISCUSSION

CASE 11–1

Entrepreneurial Revenues in State Parks

Park managers in many states have faced difficult financial choices. Although state government financial conditions have been generally comfortable, budgets for parks have not kept pace with aspirations for development, expansion, and, sometimes even maintenance. At the same time, Americans flock to parks and nature areas in huge numbers. Entrepreneurial park managers have seen this popularity with people—as opposed to popularity with state politicians—to be an opportunity for revenue. The article that follows discusses how some of them have seized this opportunity.

Consider These Questions

1. Why do states operate parks at all? In light of the discussion in the case, couldn't the parks be completely privatized by sale to private operators? Isn't that the ultimate direction that the quest for "entrepreneurial revenue" is heading?
2. If parks are owned and operated by the state, why shouldn't all park revenue be included in the state budget and subject to full state financial control?
3. What ought to determine, as a matter of state policy, what should and should not be sold by the park?

Meet the New Entrepreneurs: State Parks

By Terzah Ewing

Dwindling budgets and growing maintenance backlogs are forcing state parks to become entrepreneurs.

In Ohio, campers unwilling to buy or haul their own gear into the wilds can rent cots, coolers, cookstoves and tepees at the parks. Even recreational vehicles are available. "All you have to do is bring your clothes and a fishing pole, and you're ready to go," boasts Ohio Parks Chief Glen Alexander, whose office came up with the "rent-a-camp" idea.

With more states allowing their facilities to fatten their budgets with proceeds from such entrepreneurial efforts, parks are experimenting with programs designed to attract more visitors, reduce their dependence on state money and improve their overall financial viability. California's facilities have been touted on television by actor Clint Eastwood, while the Texas system now boasts a glossy mail-order catalog offering Stetson hats, silver earrings and limestone paperweights.

The marketing strategies aren't a panacea. In California, a pioneer in such efforts, state parks still rely on government funding and special taxes for 40% of their operating budgets. In some cases, the programs also face opposition and skepticism from environmental groups, such as those that last year lobbied the U.S. Senate to defeat a bill that would have allowed the National Parks Foundation to form fund-raising alliances with private corporations.

But many parks administrators believe they don't have any choice but to pursue profits on their own. Park attendance is up, but overall state-park budgets have fallen by an estimated 22% since 1980, while funds for capital improvements and maintenance have dropped 68%, according to the Political Economy Research Center, a think tank in Bozeman, Mont., devoted to free-market environmentalism. Entrepreneurial fund raising is "the wave of the future for state parks and someday national parks," says Donald Leal, the center's senior associate.

In Ohio's case, the effort appears to be working. Park revenue—including user fees—have climbed to $21 million from about $12 million when Mr. Alexander took over as chief six years ago. Meanwhile, park-generated funds now account for about 41% of the agency's annual budget, up from about 23%. "We try to analyze each revenue-producing facility and see what's best for it," says Mr. Alexander, who holds a master's degree in business from the University of Chicago. "We make decisions based strictly on the numbers."

In New York, Parks Commissioner Bernadette Castro has taken another approach. Last fall, she announced a $2 million alliance with Coca-Cola Co., whose products are now the official soft drink, Olympics-style, of the state's park system. Over time, its soft drinks will be phased in as the exclusive sodas sold in the parks.

She has also persuaded local Saturn dealerships to donate $250,000 of playground equipment for three parks in return for small signs at each facility advertising their donation. "I could never afford to put that amount of taxpayer money into playgrounds," she says.

Under an "entrepreneurial budget system" pioneered by Texas in 1993, parks can keep as much as 35% of the revenue that they generate beyond a targeted amount set at the beginning of each fiscal year. Moreover, if a park spends less money than its budget allows, it can pocket the difference for the following year. In the past, individual parks kept none of the revenue they generated for their own use.

The program, which is being studied by other states, has exceeded expectations at places like Inks Lake State Park in the hills of central Texas. The park has been allowed to keep $92,000 of the $1.8 million in total revenue that it has booked since the program began three years ago.

Inks Lake manager Paul Kisel has begun trekking to the distant Rio Grande Valley to recruit visitors to his park from among the hordes of nomadic retirees from the North who descend on the state in their RVs in the winter. Closer to home, he has organized "buy one night, get one night free" promotions at campsites and relentlessly experimented with goods at the park store to come up with the most profitable lines of soda, aspirin and bait.

"If I had known back in college I'd be worrying about profit-and-loss statements, I'd have double-majored in business," says Mr. Kisel, who has degrees in forestry and criminal justice.

Sherry Cummings, 54 years old, who visited Inks Lake last month with her husband, daughter and grandson, applauds the park's efforts. "We like to go to parks that offer things," she says. "The new paddleboat rides are great. When you come with kids, it's nice to know there's more to do than just walk on trails."

Of course, implementation of the new budgeting and marketing programs hasn't always gone perfectly. Texas parks are still plagued by a backlog of critical repairs—including antiquated sewer systems—while the number of park visitors continues to grow, further straining resources.

Meanwhile, amid a devastating drought that lowered the level of many lakes and rivers last summer, Texas parks brought in only $19.3 million in revenue in fiscal 1996 instead of the $23 million projected. As a result, not all parks earning their keep under the entrepreneurial budget system have been paid the revenue they earned.

Mr. Kisel says the parks agency owes Inks Lake $71,000 in back revenue and has yet to sign a contract continuing the program into fiscal 1997. "It's taken some of the wind out of the staff's sails this year," he says.

Despite the growing pains, park officials insist the programs—and the accompanying glitzy marketing—are here to stay. "The spirit of the entrepreneurial budget system won't ever go away, even if the existing program does," says Mike Crevier, director of revenue management for the Texas parks. "We can't go back to the old way," he adds. "State money just isn't there anymore."

CASE 11-2

User Charges for Social Purposes: London Congestion Charge

Consider These Questions:

1. How is this charge system different from simply adding a new annual license charge to all motor vehicles in the London area? Why might this approach be more effective at getting at congestion?
2. Does the logic of the charge depend on how the revenue from the charge is used? Explain.
3. Pick a large city with which you are familiar, Los Angeles, Boston, New York, Moscow, or any other. Would a congestion charge system be sensible there? What are the political or economic barriers to applying a congestion charge in a selected city?

At the beginning of the twenty-first century, traffic in the center of London moved about as quickly as it did in the horse-and-buggy era. The 200,000 or so cars and trucks that entered the city center made their way down narrow and winding streets that were laid out in the Middle Ages. Congestion was so bad that any small mishap brought traffic from its normal slow crawl to a complete stop. Total gridlock hung as an impending threat over the city every day.

The traditional engineering approach—providing more lanes for traffic—was not possible. All the properties in the congested space were occupied by buildings, including many of historic importance. Even if solving the problem with wrecking crews and bulldozers were technically feasible, voters were unlikely to accept the considerable tax burden this approach would involve. And the city was reluctant to use a regulation approach—like permitting cars access only on alternate days, based on license plate numbers.

SOURCE: Wall Street Journal (11 February 1997). Reprinted by permission of the *Wall Street Journal* (c) Dow Jones & Co., Inc. All rights reserved worldwide.

The mayor of London, Ken Livingstone, developed a radical approach built on the principles of basic microeconomics: a congestion charge of 8 pounds per day for driving in the eight square miles of London. Drivers entering the congested area would normally take no account of the fact that their presence had the effect of slowing the progress of other travelers. The charge was intended to make them aware of this impact. When implemented in February 2003 the system used 816 special video cameras at 400 points around the city center that scanned rear license plates of vehicles entering the zone between 7 AM and 6:30 PM each working day, the peak congestion period. Drivers who had not already purchased a permit paid the charge by phone, via the Internet, or in shops and garages. Each evening the system compared those who had entered against those who had paid—and charged double if the charge was not paid by 10 PM, and even more if not paid by midnight.

The congestion charge was intended to make drivers pay attention to the cost they imposed on others—slowed traffic—when they added their vehicles to the mass of metal choking London streets. When drivers must bear this cost, many decide that the trip can be postponed to a less congested time, canceled, or can be undertaken on public mass transport (bus or train) rather than by private vehicle, because the full cost of the trip was greater than the value of the journey. The hope was that the number of vehicles entering the center would fall by 15 to 20 percent, thus allowing travel at speeds faster than horse-and-buggy. After paying for the cost of the control equipment, all profit was earmarked for transportation system improvements.[1]

Critics had several complaints in addition to the skeptical view that the system was technologically untested and certain to fail. The criticisms included:

1. the concern that the fee put greater burden on low income than high income vehicle owners and was thus inherently unfair;
2. the fear that people would be forced off the roads and onto the bus and train system, creating a crisis there;
3. the complaint that the scheme amounted to charging the public to use public property; and
4. the argument than so many people would be discouraged from entering the charge area that there would be a devastating collapse of economic activity there.

What has been the result of the charges? It is too early to know the long-term effects, but measurements show that traffic congestion in the charge area has fallen by 30 percent (as measured by delay per kilometer traveled), traffic entering the charge zone is down by 18 percent, and 90 million pounds are being generated yearly from the charges, with the bulk of the revenue going to

[1]The U.S. Embassy demanded exemption for the tolls for its approximately 700 London employees, arguing for diplomatic tax immunity. London was not impressed, pointing out that a user charge is not a tax.

improve London bus services. There have been erroneous billings and a new scam has developed: people locate cars of the same make, model, and color of their own and produce a phony license plate with that car's number so that the owner of the other car receives the bills and fines, based on photographic evidence of that car violating the charge controls. And there have been considerable impacts outside the charge zone as drivers divert around the charge zone, creating congestion where there was none before, and as drivers park at the charge zone border to take public transportation for the rest of their travel. But the experiment is seen as an overall success: national politicians who opposed the idea before it was implemented have now started to refer to the congestion charges as a transportation success worth replicating elsewhere and the person who devised the specifics of the system in London resigned to undertake a new career designing similar systems for other cities.

SOURCES: "Congestion Charging: Ken Livingstone's Gamble," *The Economist,* February 15, 2003: 51–53; Glenn Frankel, "Toll Zone Put to Test in Divided London," *Washington Post* (February 17, 2003): A2; and Transport for London, *Central London Congestion Charging, Impacts Monitoring, Third Annual Report,* (April 2005) Available online at www.tfl.gov.uk/tfl/cclondon/pdfs/ThirdAnnualReportFinal.pdf.

CHAPTER 12

Collecting Taxes

Most government revenue comes from taxes, not prices the government charges for products or services. And businesses and individuals would rather not pay taxes because, by and large, the amount of government services anyone receives is independent of the tax that person or business pays. With few exceptions, if the neighbors pay enough to finance a public service, then the taxpayer (or nontaxpayer, as the case may be) is able to receive the service as well. How much tax the individual pays has no bearing on the level of service that individual receives. That disconnection creates a tension for the tax administrator and, ultimately, for the public agencies that must live within the revenue raised by the tax system. Paying tax keeps the taxpayer out of trouble with the tax collectors, but it purchases no specific public service. In a market economy, businesses and individuals are used to the principle of exchange that says, crudely, "You get what you pay for." But that principle is inoperative in the tax system financing public services. The tax is the law and the tax collectors enforce the "application of the rules of collection to a tax base,"[1] not the collection of prices charged for services rendered.

Why Do People and Businesses Pay the Tax They Owe?

Noncompliance means lost revenue, a distribution of the cost of government that differs from that intended in the tax law, and competitive advantage for those who cheat. What can governments do to preserve compliance? To answer that question requires a consideration of why individuals and businesses actually pay their taxes. Unfortunately, there is much uncertainty about the answer. Enforcement has traditionally been considered within the economic model of the compliance gamble:

[1]John L. Mikesell, "Administration and the Public Revenue System: A View of Tax Administration," *Public Administration Review* 34 (1974): 651.

The taxpayer compares the expected gain from evasion (not paying) with the expected gain from substantial compliance (paying) and chooses whichever gain is larger. As the probability of being caught rises or the severity of punishment if caught increases, compliance increases, because the expected net gain from cheating declines. Revenue authorities adjust penalty rates and the probability of detection (audit coverage) to reduce the expected net gain from evasion. Analysts have less confidence in the model than they once did. James Alm captures the new view: ". . . the real puzzle is 'Why is there so little cheating?' . . . most people [in the United States] pay most of their taxes most of the time, even though the chances of detection are quite small and the penalties on evasion are also extremely light."[2]

Why people pay their taxes remains something of a mystery, but evidence does seem to support the following observations about compliance:

1. **Withholding works.** Even withholding on wage and salary income can be evaded, but usually the mechanisms leave a trail that attracts attention (electronically) of the tax authorities. Reporting of payments—for instance, when banks report to the tax authorities the interest they have paid their depositors—helps, but not as much as does withholding. If a third party neither withholds tax from the payment nor reports that the payment has been made, then the recipient is less likely to comply with tax laws. Furthermore, collecting from fewer sources is easier—an enforcement visit to a single employer can cover wage and salary payments for hundreds of employees—and the visibility of the reports helps induce taxpayers to comply.

2. **Exaggerated consequences.** Taxpayers overestimate the probability of detection (the number of accounts actually reviewed) and the severity of punishment for violators. Tax authorities enjoy a compliance halo because taxpayers perceive much higher chances of getting caught and far greater consequences than are actually the case.

3. **Low rates.** When marginal tax rates are low, the gains from evasion are low and usually aren't worth the effort and cost. In other words, evading a 25-percent tax is more worthwhile than evading a 1-percent tax on comparable tax bases. When the evasion payoff is lower, so is the rate of evasion.

4. **Consensus on government.** A general consensus about what government is spending its money for and on the need to use taxes to raise that money reduces evasion. People grudgingly pay their taxes because they agree, by and large, with the system.

5. **Complexity hurts.** The more complicated, frustrating, and seemingly unfair the tax is seen to be, the less likely it is that taxpayers will comply fully with the tax.

6. **Tradition.** An institutional tradition of paying taxes, whether we like them or not, reduces evasion. The tradition in the United States is to complain about taxes, rather than not to pay. Not all countries are so fortunate.

---

[2]James Alm, "Explaining Tax Compliance," in Susan Pozo, ed., *Exploring the Underground Economy* (Kalamazoo, Mich.: Upjohn Institute, 1996), 103.

Tax administrators devise strategies that balance deterring noncompliance with penalties and sanctions and encouraging compliance through more positive means (instruction and assistance). In recent years, the focus has moved in the direction of the latter approach, what Joel Slemrod describes as "an emphasis on the 'carrot' for compliance rather than the 'stick' for noncompliance."[3] Indeed, this shift is reflected in the Internal Revenue Service's (IRS's) Compliance 2000 project, an effort to increase general compliance levels to at least 90 percent in the first decade of the twenty-first century—voluntary compliance rates for the individual income tax have been mired at slightly above 80 percent for years, without any evidence that stiffer penalties, higher audit coverage, or other heavier applications of the "stick" make much difference. The IRS estimates that in 2001 it collected between 83.4 and 85 percent of total taxes due, a rate slightly below its performance rate of 85.1 percent when it did a similar performance study in 1988.[4] The new strategy stresses nonenforcement efforts (education and assistance) to correct unintentional noncompliance while reserving enforcement for intentional noncompliance, especially in problem market segments identified by district offices. Not only is compliance important for the revenue it produces, it also is important that individuals and businesses not have economic advantage over their neighbors and competitors based on cheating and dishonesty. The compliance effort is important to protect the honest taxpayer.

Noncompliance problems are not limited to income taxes. Sales and use tax enforcement data show that businesses do not voluntarily remit all the tax that is owed, that taxpayers with greater opportunity to reduce liability do so, and that there is no easy way to combat this noncompliance. But much of the problem is driven by the tax laws themselves. Matthew Murray explains the problem: "The problem has far less to do with reporting procedures, tax returns, and cross verification, than with ambiguities in sales and use tax laws themselves. Insofar as exempt and use tax provisions remain intact, ambiguities will remain that will lead to inadvertent and intentional noncompliance activity."[5] The laws create much of the problem; simplification and better instruction, not enforcement, offers considerable advantage in collection.

Taxpayer Active or Taxpayer Passive?

Not all tax-collection systems use the same combination of duties assigned the taxpayer and tasks done by the tax authorities in producing revenue. "Taxpayer passive" systems require tax collectors to do most of the work (and bear most of the

[3]Joel Slemrod, "Why People Pay Taxes: Introduction," in Joel Slemrod, ed., *Why People Pay Taxes: Tax Compliance and Enforcement* (Ann Arbor, Mich.: University of Michigan Press, 1992), 7.

[4]Internal Revenue Service, *Understanding the Tax Gap,* FS-2005-14, March 2005. The estimates are based on a random sample of audits done to research compliance levels and to identify areas in which additional enforcement should be directed.

[5]Matthew Murray, "Sales Tax Compliance and Audit Selection," *National Tax Journal* 48 (December 1995): 527.

cost) of raising revenue: For instance, real property taxes typically require that the government maintain property records, compute the tax base, calculate the tax bills for each parcel of property, distribute the bills on a timely schedule, collect payments as they arrive, manage appeals and protests coming from the assessments, and so on, while the property owner need only verify what the tax collector has done, decide whether to protest, and then pay the bill. The total cost of tax collection with this system is almost exclusively what the government spends in administering the law.

"Taxpayer active" systems privatize much of the collection effort, that is, impose most of the collection responsibility on the private taxpayer: For instance, the American income tax requires the individual taxpayer to "supply all relevant information, compute the tax base, calculate the tax, and pay the tax, or some installment of it, when he files his return,"[6] while the tax collector distributes forms, verifies taxpayer reports, and manages revenue flows. The tax administrators aim to induce voluntary taxpayer compliance, rather than to collect the tax directly, with this sort of administrative system.[7] When the system is functioning properly, most revenue comes without direct administrative action, and the bulk of collection cost is the expenses of taxpayer compliance, not government administrative cost. Less than 2 percent of total revenue collected by the IRS comes from enforcement actions; the vast majority comes from voluntary compliance.

Neither collection system is always best, and most taxes could be administered with different mixes of taxpayer and tax collector responsibilities. The approach selected for a particular tax should reflect prevailing economic conditions, compliance environments, and technologies to best pass the tax policy criteria described earlier. For example, not all individual income taxes place as much responsibility on the taxpayer as does the U.S. system. In various degrees, income tax agencies in such countries as Great Britain, Germany, and Japan have used information on taxpayer filing status, number of children, and employee compensation to compute tax and handle collections only through withholding, a "return-free" system. Those receiving only that employer-reported compensation and interest or dividends reported by the payer file no tax return.[8] And some people argue that a self-assessment system for real property would do no worse than the current taxpayer passive system. Sidebar 12–1 illustrates how the formats can be converted with the ReadyReturn example in California; many other income taxes could be similarly converted.

---

[6]Carl S. Shoup, *Public Finance* (Chicago: Aldine, 1969), 430.

[7]Value-added taxes collected under the credit-invoice structure have sometimes been called taxes that administer themselves. That is not accurate. Tax officials must devote the normal amount of resources to policing divisions between business and person use, verifying statements of creditable taxes, watching for bogus invoices, controlling delinquency, and so on.

[8]Great Britain now uses a system of self-assessment, a switch they refer to as "privatization." U.S. General Accounting Office, *Internal Revenue Service: Opportunities to Reduce Taxpayer Burden Through Return-Free Filing,* GAO/GGD-92-88BR (Washington, D.C.: GAO, 1992).

Sidebar 12–1
California's ReadyReturn Pilot

An experiment in California illustrates how tax compliance formats—taxpayer active or taxpayer passive—can be converted. For tax year 2004, the California Franchise Tax Board (FTB), the agency responsible for administering the state individual income tax, gave a pilot group of 51,850 taxpayers the opportunity to forgo the traditional return preparation process. These are returns for which the FTB had wage and withholding information from employers with single taxpayers who claimed only the standard deduction. On the basis of that information, the FTB could calculate tax liability and whether refund or additional payment would be needed. The pilot group was a sample of the nearly 3 million Californians with the simplest returns out of 14 million resident taxpayers.

Taxpayers in the ReadyReturn program received by mail an invitation to participate in the program and a filled-in tax return done by the FTB on the basis of information the FTB had about the taxpayer. The taxpayer could then (1) accept the return as prepared, (2) make modifications in regard to filing status, changed address, claim tax credits, or add income information, (3) go to the FTB ReadyReturn website to e-file or modify and e-file, or (4) ignore the ReadyReturn and file the conventional way. The important point about the program: it had the potential for dramatically reducing the filing burden for participants but it did not reduce their filing options in any way in comparison with the traditional system. They could file the ReadyReturn by mail or electronically, or they could ignore the whole thing.

By mid-June 2005, 5,594 ReadyReturns had been e-filed and 4,692 ReadyReturns had been paper filed, almost 20 percent of the taxpayers who had been invited to participate in ReadyReturn filing had done so. Because of reduced processing errors, lower cost for compliance, and general satisfaction with the program, FTB intends to extend the program in the future.

SOURCE: State of California Franchise Tax Board, *ReadyReturn Pilot Preliminary Study Results* (Sacramento, California: Franchise Tax Board, 2005).

The Core Functions of Tax Collection

The core functions of tax collection—taxpayer registration and service; declaration or assessment; revenue and taxpayer accounting; delinquency control; audit; enforcement; and appeal or protest—"have been essentially constant since at least biblical times."[9] Technologies have changed, but they are the standard necessary steps involved in moving from the tax laws that governments have enacted to getting money in the public treasury.

[9]John A. Baldwin, "Evolving Taxpayer Information Systems," *State Tax Notes* 10 (April 8, 1996): 1105.

Taxpayer Registration/Service

Tax collectors need (1) an up-to-date roster (or master file) of those to whom returns, information, and assistance on tax responsibilities should be distributed and from whom tax reports and payments may be expected and (2) a system of identifying many taxable flows to particular taxpayers. The U.S. individual income tax identifies taxpayers with the number used in the Social Security system. Employers, financial institutions, and others making payments link the payment to the individual with this number. Other economic entities—corporations, trusts, and so on—have separate taxpayer identification numbers for their activities. States typically use the federal number for their income tax payers, but often use unique registration numbers for their other taxes (sales and use, excises, etc.). For real property taxes, much of the master file work is keyed to the parcel listing (assessment roll), which is an inventory of real property by ownership, description (dimensions and specific location), and value. The inventory list may be on cards, on microforms, or in machine-readable form (tape or disk); federal and state revenue systems use computer-accessible files, as do most local governments. The inventory of eligibles provides the foundation for administering any tax structure. A government without such an inventory has no basis for delinquency control and probably administers a system of contribution, not taxation.

For taxpayer active systems like those used in the United States for individual income or retail sales taxes, the registration master file provides a distribution list for tax returns and a master for comparing returns received against returns expected as the starting point for delinquency control. For taxpayer passive systems, the master file is a guide and checklist for the work of the tax authorities, as well as a master for comparing payments received against payments expected. For many taxes that businesses file, for example, retail sales and value-added taxes, tax authorities provide forms specifically for each taxpayer, with preprinted name, address, taxpayer identification number, and their scannable equivalents. These preprinted forms improve processing flow and provide an additional delinquency check.

Taxpayer active taxes (or taxes with privatized collection) place considerable compliance requirements on taxpayers, so tax authorities need to explain those requirements. Taxpayer service—assistance, education, and so forth—provides a critical input to the collection process. Voluntary compliance is higher, regardless of enforcement effort by the tax authorities, if taxpayers understand what they are supposed to do to comply. But many American taxpayers use paid preparers to handle their federal income tax obligations. For tax year 2004, 60.35 percent of all returns were done by a paid preparer, including 20.5 percent of 1040EZ returns, the simplest of them all.[10] Taxpayers have a distinct inclination to contract out their compliance responsibilities.

---

[10]Internal Revenue Service, *Tax Year 2004 Tax Payer Usage Study* (Report Number 14). Available online at www.irs.gov/pub/irs-soi/04tp14tb.xls.

Declaration or Assessment

All major taxes except those on real property require a periodic taxpayer declaration of tax liabilities from market transactions. The declaration tabulates taxable activity—retail sales, income earned, and so on—during the reporting period, calculate tax liability from those activities, and pay tax owed. Returns are required at intervals ranging from annually to weekly, depending on the tax involved and, often, on the size of payment expected (large-tax payers must file returns more frequently than do small-tax payers). Many filers of returns with substantial liability must make payment electronically, giving the government quick and certain use of funds. Indeed, some tax authorities require advance payment for certain taxpayers—for example, a number of states require prepayment of sales tax by the largest vendors—with reconciliation of any over- or underpayment on subsequent returns.[11] Frequent reports even out the cash flow to government and keep taxpayers from having to make large lump sum payments at the end of a longer period.

Property taxes follow a different pattern because they apply to an estimated stock value at a particular date, not to a periodic flow. Valuing the tax base is not a process of tallying a flow of transactions, and that makes good-quality property tax administration an extremely difficult task. Property tax authorities appraise parcels in the taxing unit according to the legal assessment standard. Actual transactions may be some help, but there will be no recent transaction evidence for most properties. Tax authorities use these tax assessment records for property parcels, linked to property location in overlapping taxing jurisdictions, to compute tax owed and send bills to owners on the basic tax roll of all parcels. The individual property owner has no recordkeeping or tax calculation responsibilities; the tax is taxpayer passive in its administration. Hence, many details of the tax can be complex, given its operation by specialists, although it is important that results be transparent to the public and challengeable by the property holder. Property taxes are usually paid in semiannual installments, although some jurisdictions prescribe quarterly payments and some retain annual payments.

Revenue and Taxpayer Accounting

Tax authorities have two accounting tasks as they receive returns and payments: (1) revenue accounting, which entails the deposit, recording, and distribution of payments to appropriate accounts, and (2) taxpayer accounting, which includes the posting of return information to files kept on individual taxpayers. Figure 12–1 illustrates the tax return flow in which these tasks are accomplished in a traditional sys-

[11]Tax stamps or decals offer an entirely different administrative structure. In this system, the taxed item—cigarettes, soft drink, alcoholic beverage, matches, and so on—cannot be legally sold if the product does not have the appropriate stamp affixed to it. Manufacturers or distributors purchase the stamps for the tax authorities (a form of prepayment) and place them on the product going to that jurisdiction. Enforcement personnel police the tax by checking to see whether the product has a tax stamp placed on it. Because of its simple and transparent enforcement process, the stamp system is particularly useful in primitive or hostile compliance climates.

tem. Tax authorities usually prefer electronic transmission of returns and payment for reasons of speed and accuracy of entry and easy storage of reports. The IRS accommodates e-filing of individual income tax returns, as do the states. Some states even provide Web-based software for preparation and filing of returns to make e-filing extremely easy. In revenue accounting, tax authorities deposit payments and distribute revenues to proper government accounts. This task seeks precise recording of funds and immediate control and deposit of remittances to ensure that collections are not misdirected or stolen and to give fund managers immediate control of investable resources.

Taxpayer accounting, done in the same flow as revenue accounting, posts information on the taxpayer's return to that taxpayer's master file.[12] Basic taxpayer

Figure 12–1
Illustration of Tax Return Processing Flow

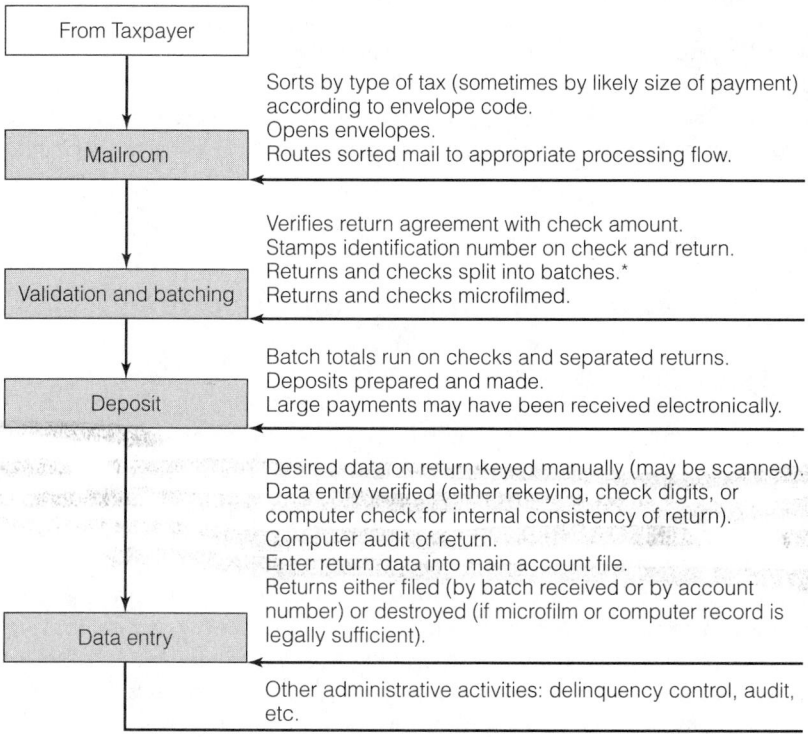

*A batch is a group of documents (usually 50 or 100) that goes through the processing together. For record control each item has a batch and item number stamped on it.

[12]Returns themselves may be kept in batches as they have come to processing (in which case taxpayer master files need to include a record number indicating where the return is filed), kept in an account file, or discarded as soon as an image of the return has been captured.

information—identification number, name, address, prior return information, and so forth—are in the file; information from the new return is posted for purposes of delinquency control, audit selection, statistical analysis, and reporting. Return information captured in the process—deductions, exclusions, and so on—varies by tax administration and by tax, but amounts owed and remitted are the basic data entered. Accurate taxpayer accounting guides eventual enforcement efforts (filing history tells the collections unit which returns are likely to be most productive and, hence, which should be pursued first), provides a basis for selecting accounts for audit, and maintains files for distribution of returns for the next reporting cycle.

Taxpayer accounting is different for the real property tax. Tax officials maintain records for parcels at particular geographic locations and periodically update those records for changes in physical features and ownership. Assessors monitor building permit and zoning activity and conduct periodic inventories of all properties for general updating of records and assessments. This record may also include the history of selling prices for the parcel.

Revenue accounting and taxpayer accounting are normally done in centralized processing centers, although the centers may be distributed geographically for political reasons (the return flow can require a considerable workforce) or to reduce the flow burden on any one location; both tasks are sometimes done on contract with private businesses. Basic processing, accounting, and file development for the federal individual income tax occurs at ten IRS service centers distributed around the country.

Delinquency Control, Compliance, and Collections

Tax authorities compare returns received against the master file of tax eligibles to determine which accounts are delinquent; those eligibles are contacted to obtain returns and, ultimately, any tax due. The delinquency may involve (1) tax owed by the taxpayer directly, as with the personal income tax or real property tax; (2) tax owed by the taxpayer, but collected from others, as in the case of sales tax owed by a retail vendor; or (3) taxes that the entity is expected to remit on behalf of other taxpayers, as in the case of individual income withholdings of an employer. Tax authorities monitor the latter two sorts of delinquency with particular care, because the delinquency can signal business problems, and, if the account is not pursued quickly, the business may have disappeared, leaving nothing to satisfy tax liabilities that have been prepaid to the business. Because some payments are simply in slow transit (the check really is in the mail), authorities have to balance protection of the tax base from a quick delinquency run against the unnecessary expense from action against accounts simply delayed in the flow. Initial account contacts are often done by a computer-generated letter driven by the comparison of returns received against returns expected. Later contacts may be in person, may be done by contracted private collection agencies, and may involve legal action, but mail and telephone contacts clear most delinquencies. The IRS has historically been much slower to begin pursuit of delinquencies than have state revenue departments.

Electronic file management systems often manage delinquent account contacts. The system selects accounts for contact, based on probable risk to the revenue system, records the results of each communication with the taxpayer, and monitors the agency-taxpayer relationship, including negotiated progress payments, until the account returns to good standing.

Audit

Audit seeks to ensure substantial taxpayer compliance with the tax law, in other words, to make certain that taxpayers are paying the amount of tax dictated by the tax law, and thereby to protect the fully compliant taxpayer against the clear competitive advantage that those paying too little would gain, whether that gain comes from computational accident, confusion about the law, or an effort to cheat. How the audit works varies between taxpayer passive and taxpayer active collection schemes. Where collection is taxpayer passive, the audit assesses the performance of tax administrators. For instance, in a typical real property tax system, audit would evaluate whether tax assessors have appraised properties according to the legal standard, usually uniformity against market value. The audit tests the work of tax administrators, not whether particular taxpayers have complied with the tax law. By correcting the errors of the administrators, whether occurring through mistake or malice, the audit realigns the distribution of tax burdens to what the law intended.

Where collection is taxpayer active, audit seeks to induce voluntary compliance and to protect honest taxpayers. The audits recover revenue, but the induced effect on voluntary compliance should be many times greater than these direct collections. Tax collectors do not have sufficient resources to examine each taxpayer account in detail, so most taxpayers understand that the probability of audit is relatively low. Hence, the audit agency task is one of inducing compliance in returns that are not audited. As Norman Nowak notes, "The auditing of the taxpayer's books is the usual means whereby respect for the tax service in finding and punishing evasion is developed. On the effectiveness of this function hinges the percentage of tax evasion that each country will have."[13] Table 12–1 provides 2003 federal data on audit coverage. Coverage is greater for higher-income individuals and for individuals whose income is outside the withholding system for wages and salaries (sole proprietorships and farmers). Audit coverage for the corporate income tax is much higher than for the individual income tax. A low- to moderate-income taxpayer receiving most of his or her income from wages or salary is extremely unlikely to be audited by the IRS. Less is known about audit coverage of state taxes. However, in the early 1990s, seven states had sales tax audit coverage of 3 percent or more, a consensus ideal for sales tax audit coverage, whereas twelve states audited fewer than 1 percent of their accounts.[14]

---

[13]Norman D. Nowak, *Tax Administration in Theory and Practice* (New York: Praeger, 1970), 68.
[14]John F. Due and John L. Mikesell, *Sales Taxation, State and Local Structure and Administration*, 2nd ed. (Washington, D.C.: Urban Institute Press, 1994), 237–39.

Table 12–1
Audit Coverage by the Internal Revenue Service by Type of Return (Returns Filed Calendar 2003)

	Returns Filed	Returns Examined	Percent Covered
United States, Total	**173,345,622**	**1,081,134**	**0.62**
Taxable Returns:			
Individual Income Tax	130,134,277	1,007,874	0.77
Nonbusiness Returns:			
Form 1040A, TPI under $25,000	33,694,530	168,887	0.5
All Other Returns:			
Less than $25,000	19,512,708	245,470	1.26
$25,000–$50,000	31,100,008	135,041	0.43
$50,000–$100,000	25,616,486	113,944	0.44
$100,000 or more	10,927,511	151,969	1.39
Business Returns:			
Schedule C returns by size TGR:			
Less than $25,000	2,946,685	92,855	3.15
$25,000–$100,000	3,645,094	53,477	1.47
$100,000 or more	10,927,511	151,969	1.39
Schedule F (farm) returns by size of TGR:			
Less than $100,000	341,689	3,140	0.91
$100,000 or more	248,422	4,003	1.61
Corporate income returns	2,394,271	17,097	0.71
Small corporations:			
No balance sheet returns	317,109	1,193	0.38
Balance sheet returns by total asset size:			
Less than $250,000	1,369,250	2,784	0.2
$250,000–$1,000,000	408,392	1,462	0.36
$1,000,000–$5,000,000	185,876	1,223	0.66
$5,000,000–$10,000,000	29,652	632	2.13
Large Corporations			
Balance sheet returns by total asset size:			
$10,000,000–$50,000,000	30,616	2,864	9.35
$50,000,000–$100,000,000	7,488	965	12.89
$100,000,000–$250,000,000	7,761	1,308	16.85
$500,000,000 or more	11,018	4,386	39.81
Estate tax returns			
Total	87,114	6,455	7.41
Size of gross estate:			
Less than $1,000,000	16,087	793	4.93
$1,000,000–$5,000,000	64,843	4,019	6.2
$5,000,000 or more	6,184	1,643	26.57
Excise tax returns	844,532	12,560	1.49

SOURCE: Internal Revenue Service, *Data Book 2004,* Publication 55B. (Washington, D.C.: IRS, 2005). Form 1040A is a short form (simple) return. TPI, Taxpayer positive income; TGR, total gross receipts.

Because so few accounts are audited, great care must be taken in selecting those for examination. Accounts may be selected for audit for three general reasons: to obtain direct revenue, to induce voluntary compliance, and to measure administrative effectiveness. Substantial revenue can be obtained in audits because taxpayers misinterpret complex tax laws, and administrators are often tempted to select accounts solely on revenue production. That practice typically leads to audit of the same accounts over and over, because the same accounts remain large and complex. Such predictability can reduce voluntary compliance by other accounts. Thus, accounts can appropriately be selected to gain notoriety for the audit, a process that could reduce direct audit recovery somewhat but should improve voluntary collections by deterring taxpayer evasion. Finally, some accounts may be randomly selected for audit, partly to induce voluntary compliance, partly to evaluate the success of tax administration, and partly to improve the criteria used for the selection of returns for audit. Even the simplest selection techniques yield productive audits because audit coverage is typically so low and because most taxes are so complex that even conscientious businesses have doubts about how much tax is actually owed.

Appeal or Protest

Tax statutes typically contain many uncertainties (gray areas), some because the legislature erred, and some because the legislature wanted to leave technical specifics to the tax administrators. Because they help clarify these uncertainties, appeals and protests play a valuable role in the lawmaking process. Property tax appeals, however, typically occur at a different point in the administration flow than do appeals of other taxes. The valuation of the property tax base is appealed because that is the sole point ordinarily open to objection. Accordingly, property tax appeal follows valuation and comes before computation of liabilities and collection. Appeal after the taxpayer receives a property tax bill is ordinarily too late. Other taxes are appealed on the basis of either a proposed tax payment or after the payment is made.

Appeals assure nondiscriminatory application of the tax system, work toward the achievement of an equitable tax system, and finish the development of the rules of collection applied to the legislated tax base. In general, more specific tax legislation reduces the scope for taxpayer protest. But greater specificity frequently makes the tax structure less impersonal, more complex, and more likely to discriminate unfairly. Appeals and protests in balanced and open hearings can correct oversights and protect the general public. Clear administrative regulations can prevent some appeals, but it is not economical to attempt to resolve all issues in the tax statute or when regulations are initially promulgated. This is especially true when technological and economic change is dramatically altering the nature of commerce. A smooth appeals process, usually proceeding from an informal hearing within the tax department, to a formal hearing in a special hearing division of the tax department, to a hearing in a specialized tax court, and finally to the regular court system,

Sidebar 12–2
Frivolous Appeals

Taxpayer appeals help clear up uncertainties about application of the tax law. However, not all issues that a taxpayer might raise about the federal income tax (or any other tax, for that matter) are uncertain, even though some tax protesters continue to assert them. They have been settled in many cases over the years and neither the IRS nor the court system take nonpayment based on those issues lightly. Here are some of the frivolous tax arguments that some tax advisors still try to sell the unwary:

1. The filing of a tax return or the payment of the tax is voluntary.
2. Wages, tips, and other compensation received for personal services are not income or that payment in Federal Reserve Notes does not represent income.
3. Taxpayer is not a "citizen" of the United States and thus is not subject to federal income tax, is not a "person" as defined by the Internal Revenue Code and hence not subject to federal income tax, or the "United States" consists only of the District of Columbia, federal territories, and federal enclaves and the taxpayer does not live in any of those.
4. Taxpayer can refuse to pay income tax on religious or moral grounds by invoking the First Amendment, the tax represents a "taking" in violation of the Fifth Amendment, filing returns violates the protection against self-incrimination of the Fifth Amendment, compelled compliance with federal income tax law represents involuntary servitude in violation of the Thirteenth Amendment, the Sixteenth Amendment was not properly ratified so the individual income tax is unconstitutional, and the Sixteenth Amendment does not authorize a nonapportioned federal income tax.
5. The IRS is not an agency of the federal government, the return violates provisions of the Paperwork Reduction Act, African Americans can claim a special tax credit as reparation for slavery and other oppression, and taxpayers are entitled to a refund of Social Security taxes paid over their lifetime.
6. Communications to the taxpayer have not been signed by the Secretary of Treasury.
7. The Tax Court has no authority to decide legal issues.
8. Revenue Officers are not authorized to seize property or IRS employees lack credentials or have improper identification badges.

The Tax Court imposes various civil and criminal penalties when such frivolous arguments are introduced as defense of a taxpayer's actions.

SOURCE: Internal Revenue Service, *The Truth About Frivolous Tax Arguments.* Available online at www.irs.gov/pub/irs-utl/frivolousarguments-3-14-2005.pdf. This source also cites the settled cases that refute the contention made in the argument.

helps to ensure that laws are applied uniformly and economically and that gray areas of tax law are clarified with due speed. However, not all issues about a tax are unsettled, and tax administrations are unlikely to treat protests over settled issues with much charity. Sidebar 12–2 describes some of the favorite "frivolous arguments" used to attempt nonpayment of the federal income tax.

Enforcement

Enforcement is the last resort for the tax system, the action taken when other remedies have not produced payment of tax due. Most taxpayers do not reach this step. Enforcement of sales and income taxes involves action against the income or wealth of the taxpayer: seizing and selling assets, attaching wages, attaching individual or business bank accounts, padlocking businesses, and so on. Real property taxes are, however, traditionally enforced by action against the property on which the tax is levied, not the owner of the property. The enforcement remedy is sale of the property. Because tax sales are politically unattractive, many governments are understandably reluctant to conduct such sales. As a consequence, areas of older cities may contain substantial blocks of property that no one clearly owns because of substantial delinquent taxes. If assessment systems do not keep up with neighborhood decline, and if tax sales are infrequent, the delinquent taxes may even exceed the property's current market value. This orphan property thus adds to the general decline of already depressed areas as it becomes a haven for derelicts, a deteriorating eyesore, and a constant fire hazard.[15]

Even though voluntary compliance or the regular operation of the administrative structure yields the most revenue in a normal tax system, tax payment cannot become a freewill offering. Recalcitrant filers must face appropriate penalties to keep the honor of the system. Enforcement protects the tax structure and preserves the competitive balance for honest taxpayers by its extraordinary sanctions when other remedies have not collected the tax due. Enforcement is the stick lurking behind voluntary compliance. There are strong protections against unwarranted enforcement actions, both within the tax administrative system and in the courts. Enforcement actions are rare and not taken lightly.

Total Collection Cost

The total cost of tax collection includes both the cost incurred by the government in administering the tax and the cost incurred by taxpayers and their agents in satisfying the tax's legal requirements (excluding tax actually paid). Because both components of collection cost use resources, neither can be ignored. Although a tax agency may reduce its budget problems by shifting greater collection cost to individuals (as with requiring individuals to pick up return forms from revenue agency offices instead of mailing them to everyone on the tax roll), there is no reason to believe that such practices reduce collection cost. In fact, loss of specialization and economies of scale may actually cause total collection cost to increase. The decision

[15]There is evidence that, when rates charged to delinquent properties fall below prevailing interest rates, property owners use delinquency as a cheap credit source. See Larry DeBoer and James Conrad, "Do High Interest Rates Encourage Property Tax Delinquency?" *National Tax Journal* 41 (December 1988): 555–60.

focus is properly on collection cost, the combination of administrative and compliance activities.

Combined costs are particularly critical when comparing real property taxes and the major nonproperty taxes. The nonproperty taxes are largely taxpayer administered: The individual or firm maintains records of potential taxable transactions, tabulates the tax base, computes appropriate liability, and makes payments at appropriate times. Government agencies concentrate on partial coverage audits, not direct agency collection, to ensure substantial compliance with the law. The taxpayer bears the bulk of total collection cost. Administration for voluntary compliance would have low administrative cost and higher compliance cost.

The real property tax, on the other hand, does not depend on voluntary compliance. A government agent maintains parcel records, values these property parcels for tax distribution, computes the liability for each parcel, and distributes tax bills to parcel owners; the taxpayer is passive. Moreover, when overlapping units of government (city, county, special districts, school district, etc.) levy property taxes, the taxpayer typically receives a single bill for all property taxes. This reduces compliance cost even further. Unless the taxpayer appeals an assessment, payment is the only taxpayer activity. In the normal scheme, total collection cost equals administrative cost. Thus, comparing the cost of administering a real property tax with the cost of administering a nonproperty tax is not appropriate.

Table 12–2 presents administrative cost data for a selection of taxes levied by a variety of governments. Because most revenue agencies administer more than one tax and in fact undertake some nonrevenue functions, the joint cost-allocation problem makes completely accurate cost estimates impossible. The data here must thus be viewed as simply estimates prepared through reasonably consistent allocation schemes. None of these broad-based taxes show administration costs much above 1 percent of revenue produced. In comparison, the cost of administering a high quality property tax system has been estimated at around 1.5 percent of collections, substantially more than the cost estimates presented for other broad-based taxes.[16]

There is, however, a critical distinction between the property tax and other major taxes. That difference is the extent to which voluntary compliance generates revenue with minimal direct government action. For the major nonproperty taxes, most revenue comes from taxpayer actions alone; relatively little of the total comes from enforcement, audit, or related revenue-department actions. For example, 2 percent of total Michigan collections, 4.5 percent of California sales and use-tax collections, 5 percent of total Arizona revenues, and 1.69 percent of IRS collections come from direct enforcement actions, including audits, penalties and interest, and delinquency collection.[17] Taxpayers—not government agencies—bear the bulk of the total collection costs (recordkeeping, return preparation, accounting and legal fees, etc.). Those compliance costs vary substantially among taxpayers, and estimates are hazardous. It is not unreasonable to expect that, for most taxpaying

[16]Ronald B. Welch, "Characteristics and Feasibility of High Quality Assessment Administration," in IAAO, ed., *Property Tax Reform*. (Chicago: International Association of Assessing Officers, 1973), 50.
[17]These data come from the same sources as the data in Table 12–2.

Table 12–2
Administrative-Cost Estimates for Major Taxes

	Administrative Costs as a Percentage of Revenue
Income tax	
Colorado (individual and corporate)	0.5
Michigan (individual)	0.64
Michigan (single business tax)	0.42
U.K. individual income, capital gains, and national insurance tax	1.5
U.K. corporate income tax	0.52
General sale and use tax	
California	0.70
Colorado sales	0.3
Colorado use	0.2
Idaho	0.8
Mississippi	1.0
North Carolina	0.68
North Dakota	0.5
South Dakota	0.41
Washington	0.7
Other taxes	
Federal luxury excises	0.3
Twelve OECD value-added taxes	0.32–1.09
GAO estimates for 5% broad U.S. value-added tax	1.2–1.8
Taxes administered by IRS	0.48
Arizona taxes	0.61
California alcoholic beverage	0.68
California cigarette tax	1.13
California motor vehicle fuel tax	0.64
Colorado alcoholic beverage	5.1
Colorado cigarette and tobacco	0.6
Colorado gaming tax	10.1
Colorado mileage and fuels	1.8
Colorado death and gift	0.1
Idaho taxes	1.06
U.K. major excises	0.25
U.K. value-added tax	1.03

SOURCES: Internal Revenue Service, *Data Book 2004,* Publication 55B. (Washington, D.C.: IRS, 2005); Sijbren Cnossen, "Administrative and Compliance Costs of the VAT: A Review of the Evidence," *Tax Notes International* 8 (June 20, 1994); Colorado Department of Revenue, *Annual Report, 2004* (Denver: Colorado Department of Revenue, 2005); Michigan State Treasurer, *Annual Report, 1977–78* (Lansing: State Treasurer, 1980); California State Board of Equalization, *Annual Report, 2003–2004* (Sacramento: State Board of Equalization, 2005); John F. Due and John L. Mikesell, *Sales Taxation* (Washngton, D.C.: Urban Institute, 1994); U.S. General Accounting Office, *Annual Report on Tax Related Studies* (GAO/GGD-93-68) (Washington, D.C.: GAO, 1993); U.S. General Accounting Office, *Value Added Tax: Costs Vary with Complexity and Number of Businesses* (GAO-GGD-93-78) (Washington, D.C.: GAO, 1993); Cedric Sanford et al., *Administrative and Compliance Costs of Taxation* (Bath, U.K.: Fiscal Publications, 1989); Arizona Department of Revenue, *2004 Annual Report* (Phoenix: Department of Revenue, 2005); Idaho State Tax Commission, *Annual Report 2003* (Boise: Idaho State Tax Commission, 2004).

OECD, Organization for Economic Cooperation and Development; GAO, Government Accountability Office; IRS, Internal Revenue Service.

units, compliance cost is several times as large as administrative cost. For instance, Joel Slemrod and Nikki Sorum have estimated that the compliance cost of federal and state income taxes is between 5 and 7 percent of total tax revenue.[18]

For the property tax, however, administrative cost is virtually the only cost of collecting the tax. After allowance for the difference between taxpayer active and taxpayer passive characteristics, the real property tax does not appear to be an unduly expensive tax to collect. Relative cost of collection—compliance plus administration—does not appear to be a deterrent to better-quality administration. To summarize, a comparison of administrative costs across taxpayer active and taxpayer passive tax systems does not provide useful information for public-policy consideration. The focus must be on total collection cost.

Conclusion

Tax collection usually requires effort by both the taxpayer (compliance cost) and the collecting government (administrative cost). Both elements are true cost to society; government decisions must not ignore either portion. For the major nonproperty taxes, in fact, voluntary compliance—effort by the taxpayer—produces far more revenue than does direct government collection and enforcement. That points out the predominant objective of direct collection—not revenue for itself, but rather protection of the voluntary compliance system.

CHAPTER 12 QUESTIONS AND EXERCISES

1. Pick a state or national government that has responsibility for collecting taxes. Determine the organizational structure of the tax authority. What are the administrative functions of the tax authority? Does the tax authority maintain district offices? If so, where are these district offices, what is their role, and what is the processing flow for returns received by the authority? What administrative functions should be contracted out to private businesses and what functions should not? What is the distribution of responsibilities between the central office and district offices? What changes in that distribution are possible?

2. The Republic of Megalomash is a small, poor country that is still struggling to escape its legacy as a European colony. It has a measured unemployment rate of about 35 percent, the poor live mainly in urban slums or in the countryside, the rich keep most of their savings in offshore bank accounts in the Cayman Islands, and at least 40 percent of total economic activity is in the underground

[18]Joel Slemrod and Nikki Sorum, "The Compliance Cost of the U.S. Individual Income Tax System," *National Tax Journal* 39 (December 1984): 461. An extensive catalog of compliance-cost estimates appears in Francois Vaillancourt, "The Compliance Cost of Taxes on Businesses and Individuals: A Review of the Evidence," *Public Finance/Finances Publiques* 42, no. 3 (1987): 395–430.

economy. The Megalomash coast is long with many natural harbors and the national coast guard is completely ineffective at controlling smuggling. The Republic has relied on loans from the International Monetary Fund (IMF) to finance its budget, but the IMF now requires that the country increase its total tax revenues (individual and enterprise income taxes, a national sales tax collected at the wholesale level, excises on tobacco, alcoholic beverages, and motor fuels, and customs duties) to 25 percent of gross domestic product (GDP). The Republic now collects only 12 percent of GDP. The government that tried to raise tax rates 3 years ago was thrown out of office in election that followed after extensive rioting. In addition to other problems, tax inspectors supplement their poor pay with bribes that almost certainly amount to almost as much money as actually shows up in the Republic's treasury.

Prepare a report for the IMF in which you analyze the nature of the economy and identify the implications of its structure for tax collection. Outline how you would propose to meet the IMF condition for further loans.

3. Would total tax collections be an acceptable performance indicator or outcome measure for a tax collection department?

4. Your assignment in the legislative analysis division of a government is to evaluate the budget request of the tax administration authority. You are expected to focus on performance outcomes of the agency, rather than just the narrow processes or internal activities of the agency. Your task: propose (1) outcome or final results for this tax collecting agency and (2) processes or activities of the agency that you would use in evaluating its performance. Would the measure differ according to whether the tax being collected is taxpayer active or taxpayer passive? Explain why each measure you suggest would be important, identify what activity measures go with each of the major stages of revenue administration, and what problems you would encounter in doing the measurement.

CASE FOR DISCUSSION

CASE 12–1

The Kursk Tax Inspector

Countries in transition from authoritarian, centrally planned government toward market-oriented democracies have endured many difficulties, but one of the most persistent has been with creation of tax structures and tax administrations that are both productive and consistent with the new economic and political system. The Russian Federation has been no exception. Despite considerable technical assistance from many donors, the Russian tax system remained inequitable, a producer of great economic inefficiency, and fertile ground for corruption. But it is improving.

The following newspaper story reports a visit to one of Russia's regions and illustrates many of the problems in the tax structure and its administration. You should be able to analyze it on the basis of your understanding of the process of tax administration and the nature of tax policy developed in this and earlier chapters on taxation.

Your analysis should (1) identify the problems of tax structure and administration illustrated in the story and (2) propose reforms that would mitigate the problems that you have identified.

Some background notes may help as you read the story:

a. Kursk oblast is southwest of Moscow, on the border with Ukraine. *Gubernia* is the old name for an oblast, dating from before the 1917 Revolution.

b. The Russian Federation is divided into eighty-nine subjects (or independent regional governments). One type of subject is an oblast.

c. The Federation Ministry of Taxation is responsible for collecting all taxes in the Russian Federation, regardless of whether the tax is technically national, regional, or local. All the tax inspectorate employees are federal employees, although they receive considerable support from regional and local governments. The Ministry objective, gradually changing as smaller private enterprises become a larger portion of the total economy, is to audit all businesses each year. It also has been Ministry policy for the same inspectors to visit the same enterprises in the audit cycle to allow full exploitation of the inspector's expertise gained in earlier visits.

d. A rouble has 100 kopeks. In May 1998, one U.S. dollar was worth about 6.2 roubles; in March 1999, it was worth about 23 roubles. In mid-2001, the rate was about 29 roubles per dollar.

e. About Russian cars: A Moskvich (literally, "Son of Moscow") is made in the Moscow region, is relatively inexpensive, and not noted for its reliability. Reportedly the purchaser of a new Moskvich must take the engine and transmission apart on the kitchen table, then carefully and properly reassemble each if the car is to survive. A Zhiguli (a Lada produced for the domestic market) is made in the Samara region and is probably more reliable than the Moskvich. There are businesses that reassemble these cars when they are purchased new; seldom is it done in one's own apartment.

f. In Soviet times, it was normal for the employer to provide housing for its employees.

Tax Collectors See Extortion as Part of the Job

By Igor Gamayunov

Our rattling Moskvich was cutting across the empty fields of Kursk gubernia, dipping from time to time into clear grooves. We were several kilometres away from the Pristen city centre when the driver nodded in the direction of a wooded ravine built up with mansions constructed from silicone bricks.

"Here is our main local destination 'The Valley of the Destitute,'" the driver said.

Our car belonged to the prosecutor's office in the neighbouring region, where I was on a business trip. The driver, of course, knew everything about local life.

"You see that two-story cottage with the iron roof?" he asked. "It was built for the head of the local tax inspectorate, apparently with public funds. But the house is her property."

We drove closer along the crunch gravel.

"She herself is now in prison, and they're supposed to confiscate the house," he added.

The mansion was luxurious, with a spacious garage, on whose metal gates was written in chalk: "The Nikitins." We were getting ready to leave when a Zhiguli pulled up. Out came a lean, thirty-something man, who looked at us warily and introduced himself. He turned out to be the son of the jailed tax chief. Next out of the car came a woman with a three-year-old child. She smiled politely and invited us in for tea. But we were in a hurry.

"They live in Moscow," the driver explained as we turned onto the highway. "They spend the summers here. They're rich! The son also has a privatized apartment in Pristen, which he rents out."

The next day, in Kursk, at the oblast prosecutor's offices, I took a look at the material from the Nikitina criminal case. It turns out that she, as head of the Pristen state tax inspectorate, made a decision to improve the housing conditions of her employees, eight of whom were still waiting for living quarters. She decided to build housing using money from the tax inspectorate's social development fund. True, the fund was not rich. But there was a well-known method of replenishing it: If tax inspectors find mistakes in the records of the enterprises and shops they are auditing, 10 percent of the penalties levied for those mistakes are legally remitted to the tax inspectorate's social development fund.

The only problem was that experienced accountants began to make fewer mistakes. So Nikitina instructed her employees to get the rough drafts of their records and find the mistakes there. If necessary, enter incorrect figures yourselves, she instructed them, and correct them later. That will replenish the fund. The employees became flustered, thinking: "Falsification." But Nikitina let it be known in no uncertain terms that whoever refused would be fired. Given how difficult it is to find work in a small town, they decided to go along. Nikitina's scheme proved successful—her eight employees got housing. And when they had collected around a half billion roubles, Nikitina, in the name of the tax inspectorate, cut a deal with contracting firms to build a two story house.

The inspectorate's employees quickly figured out who the lucky beneficiary was—Nikitina herself.

They felt not only swindled, but dragged through the mud. With their hands, Nikitina had cheated the state while building herself a royal palace with

160 square metres of floor space. In order to formally have the right to expanded floor space, she had registered her son and daughter-in-law, residents of Moscow, as part of her family. She then privatized the residence.

Nikitina also liked to make the rounds of the shops, particularly those that had been cited for underpaying taxes. The owner of one of these, the Yug shop, had asked Nikitina to lower the shop's tax penalties in exchange for "favours." The penalty was lowered to a symbolic amount.

Exactly one day after it was paid, Nikitina arrived at the shop and, without ceremony, asked for her favour. The owner made a grand gesture, saying: "Pick for yourself." Nikitina glanced at the green velour and took two cuts of four metres each. Following that visit, Nikitina frequently returned to the shop. If she needed a suit to be made or a dress for her daughter, it was done—naturally, for free.

Then Nikitina, preparing for a vacation in the United States, panicked: How will she look in front of the American people? So she hurried back to the shop, whose owner went to Moscow and brought her back a jacket and skirt made from stone-washed silk. Nikitina also demanded pocket money for her trip, but the owner, exhausted from the seemingly endless extortion, could only come up with half the sum Nikitina demanded. (To get the rest, Nikitina went to another shop that owed her a favour.)

According to the Yug shop's owner, the sum total of her favours to Nikitina exceeded what she owed the state in taxes and penalties by several times. She cursed the day she had cut a deal with Nikitina. As soon as the story about Nikitina privatizing her mansion came to light—followed by news of the whole chain of bribes she had extracted—the shop owner, along with the other entrepreneurs caught on Nikitina's hook, began to give evidence against her.

If only the Nikitina case had been an exception. In the Ileksk region of Orenburg oblast, business people were similarly fleeced by Maria Proskuryakova, also head of the local tax inspectorate. Only she brought her son, Yevgeny, in on the scheme. He was a specialist on the Ileksk administration's committee for quality and the protection of consumers' rights. The mother-and-son act worked this way: Yevgeny went to businesses to carry out inspections accompanied by his mother's subordinates. Upon uncovering violations, the young Proskuryakov would invite the accused for a face-to-face conversation, during which time he would launch an all-out attack. The merchant would surrender and bring Proskuryakov everything he asked for—food, dishes, money, imported household appliances.

As with Nikitina in Kursk, the Proskuraykovs were blinded by their own greed and impunity. They could not stop, and kept going back to the same shops over and over again, extracting nightmarish payments.

Racketeers acting in the name of the tax authorities prey not only on merchants, but on many others, even the heads of factories. Their behavior is not surprising given that the state already grabs 80 kopeks from every rouble, and the tax mean already feel themselves accomplices in robbery and thus freed from moral responsibility. What is more, given the insane tax system, practically everyone evades taxes. Thus the state's tax racketeers see almost every Russian as a swindler from whom it is no sin to extort money. Practically all these collusions take place outside the sphere of legality.

Our lawmakers have been battling over a new tax code for more than a year now, while the tax organs transmute into bandit structures, making a living from an open racket.

SOURCE: The Moscow Times (17 March 1999). Reprinted by permission of *The Moscow Times.*

CHAPTER 13

Revenue Forecasts, Revenue Estimates, and Tax Expenditure Budgets

Reliable and trusted revenue predictions provide the foundation for fiscal discipline and for the adoption of an executable public budget. Participants in the budget process need to know how much money the revenue system will yield in the budget period, first as it exists, and then with proposed changes. For fiscal transparency, budget participants also need to know the cost of carrying out budget programs through tax system preferences. The predictions are never certain because private economic behavior is not certain, and if the private economy—the source of government revenue in a market economy—is uncertain, so too will be revenue yield. But best available predictions are necessary for developing the budget, for preparing long-term fiscal profiles, for understanding the implications of fiscal decisions being considered, and for short-term cash-flow forecasting. Financial management without trustworthy revenue predictions is not meaningful.

Three distinct revenue prediction tasks play a prominent role in public finance: the revenue *forecast* (or baseline), revenue *estimates* (or fiscal notes or scores), and *tax expenditures*. Approaches, methods, and skills required, as well as organizational responsibility for their preparation, typically differ, although the tax-collecting agency—the tax service, treasury, or revenue department—is the repository of basic data used in each. However, the tax collectors (mostly accountants and lawyers) likely do not have the appropriate technical staff (mostly economists and statisticians) to develop the models and procedures necessary for the predictions, but the collectors serve as a conduit of expert data to those preparing the predictions. Official forecasts and estimates may come from executive budget agencies, legislative fiscal staff, or consensus groups representing both the legislature and the executive. Of course, there are many interest groups, lobbyists, consultants, and so on, who devise their own forecasts and estimates of varying trustworthiness for their clients and distribute them to whomever in government will pay attention.[1]

[1]Many of these consultants started out as government fiscal staff, so their predictions can be of excellent quality. But many numbers created by interest groups are so tinged with self-interest as to be worthless.

Revenue Forecast (or Baseline)[2]

The revenue forecast predicts the *revenue baseline,* meaning the forecast of what revenue will be collected in the budget period under current law. It is driven by forecasts of economic, demographic, administrative, and other structural conditions in the tax-collecting environment, but it assumes no change in tax policy as represented in the current tax laws. At the federal level, the Office of Tax Analysis in the Department of Treasury prepares revenue forecasts that the Office of Management and Budget (OMB) uses in development of the president's budget, whereas the Congressional Budget Office (CBO) prepares baseline forecasts for the budget and other Congressional fiscal committees.[3] These forecasts drive executive budget development, advise the budget committees of Congress as they develop the budget resolution, and form the basis for the midsession reviews by the OMB and CBO. States organize their revenue forecasting in many different patterns. Some assign the task to a single executive agency; others develop a consensus forecast from a joint executive-legislative body (often with formal inclusion of independent experts); and a few develop separate legislative and executive forecasts.[4] Because revenue forecasts can become political tools, there can be considerable advantage to an open, consensus forecast process. Local revenue forecasts for all but the largest governments tend to be informal, simply done in the budget or finance office. Revenue forecasts are often a controversial part of the state and local budget process. However, they seldom are subject to much dispute at the federal level.

Revenue forecasts are made using several different approaches; seldom will all revenues collected by a government be forecast by exactly the same approach. The more important formal approaches in current use include (1) extrapolation or projection, (2) deterministic models, (3) multiple regression equations, (3) econometric equation systems, and (4) microsimulation from taxpayer data files. All but the first are "cause-and-effect" approaches that try to link economic, demographic, or other influences to revenue sources, then exploit that linkage to forecast revenue. Each method has its appropriate uses in the revenue forecast environment; all are ultimately time-series estimates because they consider revenue flows across years, quarters, months, or weeks into the future.

Some forecasts are heavily judgmental or nearly subjective, based on the personal experience, intuition, and guesswork of public-finance staff from the revenue department, budget or finance agency, or legislative fiscal committees. These intuitive estimates can be devastatingly accurate and immensely useful, particularly in a consensus estimation process in which judgments from multiple "old hands" are condensed into a single forecast and not released separately. These judgmental

---

[2]An excellent basic source on general techniques of forecasting is "Chapter 5: Forecasting Techniques," *The Economist Numbers Guide, The Essentials of Business Numeracy* (London: Profile Books, 1997), 92–119.

[3]U.S. Congressional Budget Office, *The Economic Budget Outlook: An Update,* and Office of Management and Budget, *Mid-Session Review of the 1994 Budget* (Washington, D.C.: GPO, 1993), for example.

[4]For an excellent overview of how governments in the United States, forecast and estimate, see Marilyn Marks Rubin, J.L. Peters, and Nancy Mantell, "Revenue Forecasting and Estimation," in W. Bartley Hildreth and James A. Richardson, eds., *Handbook on Taxation* (New York: Marcel Dekker, 1999), 769–99.

forecasts are particularly important for use with sources yielding relatively small amounts of revenue that can be subject to major fluctuations caused by institutional or administrative factors; certain intergovernmental transfers and development impact fees offer two examples of sources in which such insights can be especially helpful. If administrative factors can produce major changes in revenue flows, then having the experience from the "old hands," who have seen almost everything play out at least once before, can be crucial to getting those impacts correctly in the forecast.

General Guides for Revenue Forecasts

Before discussing each method in some detail, there are several general points about revenue forecasting that need to be highlighted. The first and most fundamental principle is that the forecaster must understand the tax being forecast, how it is administered, and the procedures that generate collection data. It is folly to try to forecast the state insurance tax, for instance, if you do not fully understand the nature (structure and administration) of that tax; having what you believe to be a consistent series of collections data for the tax is not enough. Novice revenue forecasters usually underestimate the problems involved in developing a consistent data series for each tax to be forecast. Messy little transactions (changes in tax law, failure to properly record receipts for an unspecified period, failure to open mail bags at the end of a fiscal year, changes in filing or revenue-processing schedules, loss of revenue reports, inconsistent revenue accounting, etc.) confuse almost every revenue series, causing the revenue estimator to spend many hours to obtain a clean and consistent data series. Many possible adjustments can remedy problems with independent variables, including the decision to substitute some other variable to drive the forecast, but estimation based on incorrect, misunderstood, or inconsistent revenue data is nearly hopeless. Furthermore, the forecast is always subject to sabotage, usually accidental, through a repeat of the episodes that messed up the initial data.[5] These problems haunt every revenue forecaster.

Second, the cleaned revenue series to be forecast should be plotted in a simple graph against time. An examination of the graph offers insights into the forecasting task (expansion or decline? large change or small? smooth changes or considerable fluctuations?) and identifies important questions (When were there large increases or decreases in revenue and what caused the changes? Are the overall patterns consistent with general forces in the regional or national economy?). Additional plots, sometimes against time and sometimes against independent variables ("causes") thought to influence the revenue flow, can be helpful throughout the forecasting process as tests of logic and of strength of relationship.

---

[5]Some revenues are subject to a degree of control by program administrators. For instance, state lotteries can manipulate the introduction of new games, payout rates, or advertising programs and so influence at least the timing of net proceeds to government. Therefore, revenue forecasters must give great deference to what their administrators forecast for their operations—an irritated lottery director can make external forecasters look inept.

Third, openness in forecasting is a virtue. Both legislative and executive branches occasionally seek artificially high or low revenue estimates as a part of a political budget strategy to increase or reduce expenditure. An open and transparent process prevents such manipulation. The general public seldom wins when several different revenue estimates are strategically unveiled during budget sessions. A wrong consensus forecast used by all in crafting a budget leads to more responsible budget development and adoption than does a process with many competing estimates from executive and legislative branches, from each political party, or from factions within parties—even if one of the competitors happens to be absolutely correct. Most huge forecast errors on the high side, except when the business cycle turns unexpectedly (and downturns are difficult to predict accurately), turn out to be the result of political manipulation designed to create phantom revenue needed to close a budget gap. An open, consensus forecast prevents that problem. State and local government forecasts (and estimates) tend to be more openly prepared than are those in the federal government.[6] Historically, political manipulation of revenue forecasts have been more common at state and local levels than at the federal level.

Fourth, the approach selected often depends on the tasks to be served by the model. If one seeks revenue forecasts for the annual budget process, the multiple regression approach ordinarily yields good results. If one needs to divide annual revenues into amounts expected within the year (quarterly or monthly), univariate analysis may be appropriate. If one seeks the impact of a structural change, in the economy or in the demographic character of the population, microsimulation may be more appropriate. If estimates are needed for long-range plans, trend extrapolations—sometimes adjusted for guesses about structural changes—are as good as anything. In summary, no single approach is ideally suited for all revenue forecasting tasks.

Fifth, individual revenue sources normally are forecast separately. It would be extremely unusual, for instance, to forecast general fund revenue for a state as a single aggregate, instead of adding forecasts of each individual revenue source to obtain the total. Different sources respond to different factors, and they should be separately examined. Furthermore, compensating errors in the separate source forecasts can cause the total forecast—the one upon which the budget is based—to be closer to the actual revenue.

Finally, revenues need to be monitored carefully and on a regular schedule against the forecast. A single month's variation, though potentially troublesome, can disappear later in the fiscal year, and comparisons between year-to-date actual and estimated revenues are more helpful than the comparison for a single month. However, the record needs to be continuously evaluated to maintain control of overall government finances. That performance becomes important information for the development of future revenue forecasts.[7] Monitoring through the year usually involves comparisons of revenue collected in months or quarters against shares of

---

[6]Thomas F. Field, "Transparency in Revenue Estimating," *Tax Notes*, (January 17, 2005): 329–61.

[7]Useful standards for revenue estimation are presented in National Association of State Budget Officers/Federation of Tax Administrators, *Good Practices in Revenue Estimating* (Washington, D.C.: National Association of State Budget Officers, 1989).

annual totals collected in comparable periods in previous years. At the close of the fiscal year, the success of the forecast needs to be evaluated to permit improvements in future outcomes. Where "cause-and-effect" models are used, variances from the actual need to be divided into (1) the part caused by errors in forecasting the cause(s), (2) the part from errors in the model, and (3) the part attributed to legislative changes that make the tax for which the forecast was prepared different from the one that produced the revenue.[8]

Alternative Methods for Forecasting

The problem in revenue forecasting is not to find a method for doing the forecast. It is selecting from among the many alternatives the method or methods that are most likely to produce a satisfactory forecast for the problem at hand. Lots of approaches are available, but which ones will work best for the current forecast? And the approaches often give considerably different results when applied to a particular assignment.

Univariate Projections and Extrapolations

Forecasters do projections and extrapolations because they can be quick, inexpensive, done without much data, and accurate enough for some assignments. These forecasts, through complex or simple means, extend past patterns of the revenue into the future. They make no explicit effort to model a cause-effect relationship between some economic or other force and the revenue being forecast. This presents a problem for most tax forecasters: They want to understand causal influences in the revenue system and so do their legislative and executive agency bosses. The need to understand causes is particularly great when the forecaster must explain a revenue shortfall.

Both simple and complex univariate methods share a common feature: Only past revenue data are used to forecast future revenue data (e.g., sales tax collection data for the last 15 years are used to forecast sales tax collections for the budget year and the out years). No other economic, demographic, social, or cultural variables are involved.

One method is a simple time series extrapolation or regression against time. These extrapolations may be by (a) constant increments (collections increased by $5,000 in each of the last 5 years, so they are estimated to increase by $5,000 this year); (b) constant percentage change (collections increased by 5 percent in each of the last 5 years, so they are estimated to increase by 5 percent this year); (c) simple growth models using the average annual compounding formula developed in

---

[8]In other words, suppose the retail sales tax (S) was forecast to be related to personal income (I):

$$S = 389.7 + 0.782I$$

Actual collections could differ from forecast collections because (1) an error was made in the personal income forecast or (2) the forecast relationship between personal income and retail sales did not hold. Legislative changes are a shock from outside the model.

Chapter 2; and (d) linear or nonlinear time trends in which revenue for the budget year is estimated as an arithmetic function of time ($R = a + bt$) or as a logarithmic function of time ($\ln R = a + bt$), where R equals collections from the revenue source and t equals a time index, choosing between the trends according to which is judged most likely to produce a reasonable estimate. Many local governments use these approaches because they lack the data on the local economy requisite for developing more complex cause-and-effect models. States often use the approach for minor revenue sources when improved estimates make no consequential impact on the overall fiscal pattern. Everybody uses them when there are insufficient data or insufficient time for other methods.

Another simple univariate short-term forecasting approach that can be usable in periods of general stability is the moving average technique. A moving average forecast operates with the following procedure:

$$R_{t+1} = (R_{t-1} + R_{t-2} + R_{t-3} + \ldots + R_{t-j})/N$$

where R_{t+1} = revenue for the forecast period, R_{t-1} to R_{t-j} = actual revenue for previous periods included in the average, and N = the number of periods used in calculating the average. For instance, a forecast of motor vehicle license revenues in 2008 might be prepared during 2007 as the average of actual revenues in 2006 (the most recent year for which actual data are available), 2005, and 2004. The forecaster selects the number of periods according to an expectation about how many will keep the forecast error to a minimum—in general, fewer periods when there have been recent significant fluctuations and more in periods of general stability.

Other univariate approaches work with auto-regression techniques, more complex moving average approaches (the Box Jenkins auto-regressive integrated moving average model being one example), and various smoothing techniques (spreadsheet programs usually offer several alternatives). The applicability of the more sophisticated techniques is limited by the need for lengthy data series; revenue forecasting seldom has data series that extend for long periods without considerable shocks from change in the fundamental structure of the tax. Again, revenue forecasters do use these techniques for causal variables entering their models.

Deterministic Modeling

Deterministic models use a preestablished formula (or "rule of thumb") that "ought" to forecast revenue. In other words, there should reasonably be a link between gross domestic product (GDP), personal income, or some other broad economic aggregate and tax revenue; the forecast results from multiplying that aggregate by the formula coefficient for that particular source. For instance, data from several countries show the value-added tax (VAT) to yield, on average, 0.37 percent of GDP for each percentage point of tax rate.[9] The forecaster could use that ratio to develop a rough forecast of VAT yield from a forecast of GDP—possibly developed itself by application of a simple guess about annual growth rates. Forecasters

[9]Vito Tanzi and Parthasarathi Shome, "A Primer on Tax Evasion," *IMF Staff Papers* 40 (December 1993): 823. This is sometimes called "Cnossen's Rule."

working in data-scarce environments regularly use such approaches in developing budget numbers. Such conditions may occur, for example, when the revenue source is relatively new and there are insufficient data for meaningful statistical modeling (fitting equations makes little sense when there are only two or three data points), when the national economic environment is too unstable for the results of statistical modeling to be usable with confidence (in countries undergoing transition from centrally planned to market economies, for instance), or when data are of insufficient reliability to make statistical modeling meaningful. Many longer-term forecasts use such approaches, not because of a shortage of historical data, but because secular change is likely to alter any relationship that formed a model based on those data.

Multiple Regression

The multiple regression model, the most widely encountered forecasting device, forecasts revenue as a function of one or more independent variables determined outside the revenue model. Each equation used to estimate a revenue source is independent of the others. For instance, a state might forecast quarterly retail sales tax collections with an equation like the following one that was estimated from an ordinary least-squares regression program:

$$ST = -5.523 + 0.926\,PI - 0.034\,P - 0.773\,R + 0.022\,Q1 + 0.011\,Q2 + 0.032\,Q3$$

Where

ST = retail sales tax collections for the quarter in logarithmic form,

PI = state personal income in logarithmic form, lagged one quarter,

P = the inflation rate measured as percentage change in the GDP deflator in logarithmic form, lagged one quarter, and

$Q1$, $Q2$, and $Q3$ = categorical dummies to indicate the quarter of the year (sales tax revenues being subject to seasonal variation through the year).[10]

The economic data are lagged because allocation processes are such that economic activity in one period generates tax revenue that is received by the government in the next period. In other words, there is a mismatch between when the taxable activity occurs and when the collections from that activity show up in the state treasury. The lagged economic data account for that mismatch. Of course there are several different ways to measure economic activity that is producing the sales tax revenue, including gross state product, GDP, and national personal in-

[10]Because tax collections, personal income, and tax rate are in logarithmic transformation, the coefficients in the equation are interpreted as elasticities. That is, the estimating equation shows that a 10-percent increase in personal income produces a 9.3-percent increase in tax collections, and that a 10-percent increase in the statutory tax rate produces only a 7.7-percent increase in tax collections. This evidence is consistent with the idea that the retail sales tax grows more slowly than the economy and that rate increases do have a negative impact on the tax base—but that this tax is not on the downward sloping side of the rate—revenue curve. The forecasting equation is for Indiana with data from third quarter 1977 through first quarter 2005.

come. Each of these measures has some logical attractiveness as a drive force for forecasting state sales tax revenue. The forecaster will almost certainly experiment with each of these possible measures until he or she settles on the one that seems most likely to reliably track the actual path of tax revenue. The forecaster also experiments with lags of different lengths and with other formats for the relationship as well.

Forecasts for the independent or causal variables, personal income and the inflation rate in this example, come from analytic and forecasting work outside the tax equations. To use this approach, estimates of the independent variable must be available for the forecast period: An estimating equation for sales tax collections that uses a stock market index, for instance, will not be usable if the necessary index is not available until three-quarters of the way through the budget year, because, for budget preparation, the revenue estimate has to be presented well before the start of the budget year. Dummy variables offer an approach to allowing for the influence of unusual qualitative experiences in the past—2 years in which budget constraints prohibited any out-of-state audits, a tax amnesty, or a period in which the regulations for certain sales tax exemptions differed from those currently in effect are examples.

The equation estimated by multiple regression ordinarily is selected based on the extent to which estimates from the equation coincide with actual revenue collections in prior years. Because many alternative specifications yield similar fit to historic data (several specifications will be almost indistinguishable in terms of normal tests of goodness of fit and forecast error), trial predictions (simulations or "out of sample forecasts") for earlier years are also prepared: Suppose data are available for 1960–2005 and a forecast is being prepared for the 2007 budget year (the estimate is being prepared during 2006). Possible equations can be developed from 1960 to 2004 and test "predictions" made for 2005. The equation coming closest to the known 2005 result is selected.

Ordinarily, separate equations are prepared for each major revenue category to allow for different responses to changes in independent variables. That is, equations are developed for individual income tax, corporate income tax, retail sales tax, and so on, rather than simply for all tax revenue. Careful application of multiple regression models should produce overall predictions within 1 to 3 percent of actual collections. Table 13–1 illustrates the basic steps in preparing a regression-based forecast.

Econometric Models

Econometric models estimate revenue within a simultaneous system of interdependent equations that express theoretical and empirical relationships between economic and fiscal variables.[11] These models are particularly important when revenue

[11]The independent variables used in the multiple regression approach (possibly state personal income or U.S. GDP) often are the product of larger econometric models of the region of the nation. State and local governments obtain these estimates from numerous sources, including proprietary economic forecasting companies, universities, committees of technical advisers, and government economists.

Table 13–1
Steps in Revenue Forecasting by Multiple Regression

Step 1. Developing Economic Forecasts
- a. Select or develop national, regional, and state economic models.
- b. Make reasonable assumptions (or scenarios) about critical variables (national policies, demographic trends, etc.).
- c. Use assumptions and models to forecast economic activity.

Step 2. Predict the Revenue Base
- a. Devise methodology to translate economic activity forecast into the revenue base.
- b. Apply methodology to predicted economic activity to yield the forecast base.

Step 3. Estimate Tax Liability: Apply Rates to Forecast Base

Step 4. Adjust for Timing and Structure
- a. Adjust tax liability flow to match the fiscal year and lags between liability and payment.
- b. Accommodate legislative changes in the tax structure.

sources are not truly independent (as when the state personal income tax allows a deduction for the state sales tax) and may provide useful insights into the way state economies operate and the way in which they respond to external shocks. Economists generate forecasts from the system of equations by putting current values of key variables into the models and working them through the estimating equations. As a practical matter, however, states have generally found that the revenue predictions from econometric models are not much more accurate than the estimates that multiple regression models produce and the regression models are less expensive and have smaller data requirements.[12] But, overall, these models provide highly reliable forecasts of most major macroeconomic variables, particularly real GDP, inflation, and unemployment. Interest rates, exchange rates, and stock prices are another matter, however.

Microdata Models

The Office of Tax Analysis of the U.S. Treasury, the CBO, and many states use microsimulation from sample data files for tax forecasting (and for estimating the effect of tax changes as well).[13] Sidebar 13–1 describes the steps in the CBO's fore-

[12]C. Kurt Zorn, "Issues and Problems in Econometric Forecasting: Guidance for Local Revenue Forecasters," *Public Budgeting & Finance* 11 (Autumn 1982): 100–10.

[13]A federal approach is described in Howard Nester, "The Corporate Microdata File Employed by the Office of Tax Analysis," *Proceedings of the National Tax Association-Tax Institute of America* 70 (1977): 293–306; and James M. Cilke and Roy A. Wyscarver, "The Individual Income Tax Simulation Model," in U.S. Department of Treasury, Office of Tax Analysis, *Compendium of Tax Research* 1987 (Washington, D.C.: GPO, 1987). The microsimulation model developed for New York State is described in T.N. McCarty and T.H. Marks, "The Use of Microsimulation Models for Policy Analysis: The New York State Personal Income Tax," *Proceedings of the Eighty-Sixth Annual Conference on Taxation of the National Tax Association* (1994): 179–85.

Sidebar 13–1
The Congressional Budget Office Approach to Individual Income Tax Forecasting, Fiscal 2001–2011

Step 1.

Begin with a sample of 1998 tax returns.

"Age" the sample to match

- Projected demographic changes (such as in population and employment).
- Projected incomes based on the CBO's macroeconomic projections (such as for wages, interest, and dividends), outlay projections (for program benefits), and other projections (such as for capital gains and retirement income).

Result: the projected tax base for 1999 through 2011.

Step 2.

Apply the tax calculator (a mathematical formula that represents the calculations required by the tax structure), incorporating

- Tax law parameters.
- CBO's macroeconomic projection of the consumer price index.

Result: projected tax liabilities on individual income tax returns for 1999 through 2011.

Step 3.

Adjust projected tax liabilities for consistency with actual collections of owed taxes in 1998 through 2000.

Result: projected collections liabilities for 2001 through 2011.

Step 4.

Convert projected liabilities into fiscal year payments by

- Breaking down liabilities by type of payment.
- Applying recent experience in the timing of payments.
- Adjusting for recent legislation not incorporated in step 2, and
- Adding fiduciary taxes and back taxes.

Result: projected tax payments for fiscal years 2001 through 2011.

SOURCE: Congressional Budget Office, *Description of CBO's Models and Methods for Projecting Federal Revenues* (Washington, D.C.: CBO, 2110), 8.

casting method for its 10-year baseline projection of the federal individual income tax. In general, microdata approaches start with a computer file of tax-return data from a sample of taxpayers. Tax calculator models use this file to forecast how economic activity expected in the budget year tracks into its impact on the taxpayers in the sample. A computer program figures the tax liability for each taxpayer in the sample, the effect within the sample is expanded to the entire population it represents, and the result is the forecast of tax revenue for the new budget year. Full microsimulation models use the same files as the simpler tax calculator models, but they allow the underlying tax return to vary as taxpayers react to changes in tax policy.[14] The approach is particularly valuable in the analysis of policy changes, but it can also be employed in regular forecasting. Much effort is involved in selecting and preparing the microfile, so uses beyond the forecast improve the economic viability of such an effort. As is discussed later, the microfile is extremely helpful in fiscal note preparation: estimating the revenue consequences of legal changes in the tax structure. However, data in the microfile need to be refreshed as return years go by and modified when new tax provisions are enacted; the sampling must be a continuing process.

Choosing the Method

Revenue forecasts need methods that predict well enough to satisfy the requirements of those developing, adopting, and executing budgets and that can be explained to the satisfaction of executive and legislative tax and budget policymakers. They almost always use a combination of the several forecast approaches to predict the revenue baseline for the executive or legislative budget. In revenue forecasting, the ultimate choice would be whichever produces estimates closest to final yield, but that is something the forecaster finds out after the year is over, too late to be a guide. Among the factors that may enter into the choice of method are:

1. **The resources that are available.** The tools of cause-and-effect estimation—computers, software, and data analysts—have come within easy reach of every government with reliable electric supply. The resources that may not be available are sufficient time to perform the tasks necessary to prepare and test more complex estimating formats and the data necessary to employ some approaches. For example, microsimulation approaches require complex data files on a sample of taxpaying entities; the approach cannot be contemplated unless the government has devoted the time and money to develop the files. Some governments simply choose to do forecasting on the cheap and do pretty well most of the time. No matter how much money is spent, nobody forecasts downturns very well.

[14]For revenue forecasting, tax calculator and full microsimulation models are not distinguishable in operation: There are no policy changes in the baseline revenue forecast.

2. **The materiality of the forecast.** How critical is an error in the forecast being made? If the revenue source constitutes but a small amount of the total, it is a poor use of analytic resources to devote much effort to forecasting it. A huge error in a small revenue source will have vastly smaller importance to budget execution than a small error in a huge source.

3. **The availability of historic revenue data.** Unless a long data series is available to test relationships under a considerable variety of economic and other environments, trying to create a reliable causal model is not likely to be productive. Indeed, an inadequately clean historical series can be a problem for more complex projection models themselves.

4. **The availability and quality of causal data.** A forecasting model with excellent statistical properties does not provide usable forecasts if causal data needed for the forecast period are not available or if the available forecasts of them are unreliable. For instance, a regression equation may show a strong and reliable relationship between corporate profits and state corporate profits tax collections. Unless there is a good forecast of corporate profits available, this equation is useless for the revenue forecast.

5. **The time period of the forecast.** Long-term forecasts—the years beyond the out-years—will be done with cruder approaches than will budget-year forecasts. Technological, political, and economic forecasts are not terribly reliable in the longer term and a revenue forecast based on "cause-and-effect" models cannot rise above problems in forecasts of the causes.

6. **The "explainability" of the forecast.** A forecast number is not enough. There must be a story that goes with it for the budget director, the legislative fiscal committees, and the media. "Black boxes" have difficulty surviving the first shaky episode.

These forecasts establish the amount of current revenue that will be available to spend during the fiscal year. For many governments, their presentation is an event of considerable importance because it sets the tone for the deliberations that produce appropriations to operating agencies. Although there is no standard template for such presentations, they frequently are organized according to the following format:

1. **A Look Back:** a review of the forecast for the last budget year and why it was wrong;
2. **The Future Environment:** a prognosis of economic conditions for the next year for the nation and, for subnational government forecasts, for the state or local economy that will drive the revenue being forecast;
3. **The Approach:** an explanation of the general approach being used for the forecast; and
4. **The Forecast:** the forecast itself, divided among the major revenue sources.

The presentation normally has charts and tables as appendices accompanying the actual forecast document.

Forecasts for the Long Term

Governments develop longer-term, multiyear revenue (and expenditure) outlooks that extend beyond the annual budget horizon. These prediction tasks vary widely in their sophistication, depending on the term for which they are prepared and on their intended use. They may be prepared, for instance, (1) to guide a city as it prepares an infrastructure development program that fits within likely revenue resources, (2) to show a credit-rating agency what revenue flows might be during the term of a loan to a state or local government, (3) to let planners know the probable financial implications from some major development (a theme park or a truck assembly plant, for instance) in the community, (4) to inform the public or oversight boards what the prospects are when a local government is on the brink of a severe financial emergency, (5) to inform the legislature and the executive what the longer-term implications are of the financial program that the government has in place or might be considering, or (6) as an element in a medium-term economic framework for the development of government policies within available revenues. Revenue predictions for the out years have been particularly important for federal budget resolutions, especially as deficits turned to surpluses and lawmakers began discussion about new spending and tax reduction programs to get rid of the projected surpluses (which they decisively did). Longer-term outlooks can also be used to trace the likely impacts of demographic developments on finances.[15] These outlooks are vital for the development of Social Security and Medicare programs, in which present revenues are expected to finance benefits paid many years in the future.

The longer the outlook, the less sophisticated should be the method—because of the great imprecision associated with economic, political, demographic, and technological factors that shape underlying forecasts. However, methods are generally the same as those used for budget-year revenue forecasts, although more attention has to be given to estimating the longer-term economic, demographic, and structural trends that themselves will drive the revenue flows, and huge uncertainties cloud the process. And many are prepared using deterministic formulae ("rules of thumb") taken from experience in other jurisdictions. Medium-term forecasts—3, 5, or even 10 budget "out years"—done by the CBO and similar bodies to identify the impact of policy changes, demographic drift, macroeconomic conditions, and so on are done with considerable care to understand links and to identify policy options and are of considerable quality and value. The distant out-year forecasts are important only as a part of political drama.

Longer forecasts are usually not tested against actuals, in the way that budget-year estimates are, and they are replaced by shorter-term forecasts when budget-year choices are being deliberated. Indeed, they often cannot be so tested, because they have served their purpose as warning devices and the dangerous practices have been corrected. Seldom should the predictions be expected to provide great precision; they can, however, assemble information to help with difficult choices

[15]An excellent example of such an outlook study: Congressional Budget Office, *The Budget and Economic Outlook: Fiscal Years 2006 to 2015* (Washington, D.C.: GPO, 2005).

and to cause policy changes that keep the projected result from occurring. Longer-term predictions may provide a range of forecast values because of the considerable uncertainty involved; however, forecasts for preparation of the annual budget need to be single numbers.

Wrong Forecasts

The future is uncertain and errors in revenue forecasts are bound to happen. Forecasting is particularly difficult when the economy is going into or coming out of recession, but errors occur in more stable times as well. Perfection is not the standard against which any revenue forecasting method should be tested. The appropriate test is the accuracy of other feasible forecasting approaches, and there is evidence that formal forecasting methods are better than simple rules of thumb.[16] If another forecasting method that can be adopted within available resources can produce more accurate results for the budget, then it should be used. But it undoubtedly will be wrong eventually. The test can never be perfection, just better than feasible alternatives and not subject to political bias. As Nobel-prize-winning economist Kenneth Boulding would say, "All forecasts are wrong, including this one."

Revenue Estimating

Revenue estimating (called scoring in the federal system, tax costing in the United Kingdom, and preparation of fiscal notes in many states) gives the government a prediction of how revenue will change from the baseline if a new law is passed or administrative processes change. The revenue estimate is the difference between receipts under current law and receipts under a proposed change in the law. Governments need to know what the fiscal impact will be of legislation that is being deliberated, especially revenue measures being considered. How much would revenue increase if the personal exemption in the income tax were reduced by $100, or how much would revenue fall if a certain class of business asset purchases could be expensed (subtracted from income immediately) rather than depreciated (subtracted from income over the estimated life of the asset)? The pay-as-you-go (PAYGO) requirement in the federal budget system demanded these estimates, most states have prepared such fiscal impact notes for many years, and reports from the Senate Finance and House Ways and Means Committees have carried these estimates since the 1974 Congressional Budget and Impoundment Control Act.[17] The Office of Tax Analysis of the Department of Treasury prepares the executive branch

[16]Stephen K. McNees, "An Assessment of 'Official' Economic Forecasts," *New England Economic Review* (July/August 1995): 13–23.

[17]The revenue-impact estimating method used by Congress is described in Joint Committee on Taxation, *Overview of Revenue Estimating Procedures and Methodologies Used by the Staff of the Joint Committee on Taxation* (JCX-1-05, February 2, 2005).

revenue estimates.[18] From the legislative side, the Joint Committee on Taxation scores all tax legislation and the CBO scores tariffs and user charges (along with spending proposals). The CBO incorporates these estimates from any legislation that passes into its 10-year baseline forecast. For states, fiscal notes attached to revenue proposals often come from legislative fiscal staff, although they may also come from the state budget agency or the state tax department.

Revenue estimates often must be rough because existing data sets do not categorize information that follows the same lines as does the proposed legislation. For instance, the revenue loss from a sales tax exemption for grass seed purchases by homeowners in blighted urban areas would be a difficult estimate because neither sales tax collection or household spending data are tracked to that detail by geographic areas. However, even when only developed as a rough approximation, the estimates provide an important discipline for the budget process. They estimate the change in the baseline. Federal estimates normally are for 5 years; state estimates may be much shorter.

These estimates usually are prepared from a sample of existing returns, supplemented with additional data sources as necessary. In effect, they represent microsimulations, although at widely varying degrees of sophistication—the work of the Office of Tax Analysis uses an extremely complex model created from a large sample of individual tax returns, whereas estimates in a state legislative service bureau may be extremely informal. The returns give information about transactions currently reported in the tax system and, to the extent the new provision changes those reported lines, can provide a basis for the estimate. But not all proposed changes will be to transactions on those reports. Therefore, there usually needs to be information taken from outside the tax system.

There is continuing political debate about the protocol to be used in preparation of revenue estimates. Three systems are identifiable:

1. **Completely static estimation/scoring.** This approach assumes that the change in the tax law will have no impact on taxpayer behavior or on the level of economic activity. The estimate assumes that taxpayers will not alter their behavior in the face of the new tax structure. The estimate is based on tax return data, plus supplemental data about taxpayers that may be necessary to estimate the new tax base for each return, and a tax calculator that computes the tax paid on each return under both the baseline law and the proposed changed law. For example, a static estimate of changing the capital gains tax rate would use capital gains reported on each tax return and recalculate the tax at the new rate instead of at the rate under existing law. Adding all returns gives the impact estimate. Revenue estimators usually use this approach when they have no basis at all for estimating the degree of taxpayer response to a change in the tax law. In the absence of trustworthy data, tax professionals prefer the fiscally conservative approach to their estimates.

2. **Static estimation/scoring.** The static approach that revenue estimators normally employ is to recognize that taxpayers do respond when the tax law

[18]Emil M. Sunley and Randall D. Weiss, "The Revenue Estimating Process," *Tax Notes*, 51 (June 10, 1991): 1299–1314.

changes. In other words, it is not entirely static. The approach recognizes that taxpayer behavior will shift in response to the incentives added or subtracted by the tax law and, as a result, the tax base with the new law will differ from what it would have been under the old law. The behavioral effects may include shifts in timing of transactions, changes in portfolio holdings, shifts in consumption, use of tax planning and avoidance strategies to reduce liability, changes in work effort, and so on, all impacts that would involve microeconomic behavior. For instance, (1) a higher tax on cigarettes will cause fewer cigarettes to be sold, (2) a lower capital gains tax rate will induce businesses and individuals to realize capital gains that would otherwise have been deferred and to convert ordinary income to formats judged to be capital gains, and (3) a new tax credit for college tuition will induce more students to attend college—so static estimates of revenue from these tax proposals would need to be adjusted for these effects. In these instances, simple use of historical data on cigarette consumption, capital gains, and college tuition would not be entirely sufficient to produce the estimate. The problem is that the effects are difficult to gauge because the data required may be unavailable and the size of taxpayers' response (the demand and supply elasticities) are unknown. Revenue estimates at the federal level and in most states do include these microeconomic impacts when estimating or scoring tax law changes when there is a way to include them. And there is no meaningful debate among professionals that such adjustments are appropriate. The greatest barrier is always the extent to which there is a firm and reliable basis for making the behavioral adjustments.

3. **Dynamic estimation/scoring.** Dynamic scoring adds the impact on revenue from changes in outputs, interest rates, or other macroeconomic elements. The static estimates work under an assumption of fixed total economic activity (GDP or gross state product). Dynamic scoring seeks to add to the estimate the effect of any change in total economic activity on tax collections. In other words, a tax reduction may have a macroeconomic impact on aggregate economic activity, inflation, interest rates, and so on, and these effects will cause the tax bases to differ from what they would have been without the tax reduction and any resulting change in tax revenue should be included in the estimate. The static estimate, even one that includes the effects of microeconomic changes, thus overstates the amount of the revenue cost from the tax reduction. For instance, the reduced capital gains tax rate may increase aggregate economic activity, and that will cause more tax to be collected from several federal taxes, all of which would be included as part of the estimated impact of the tax reduction. Federal estimates traditionally have not included a macroeconomic component, largely because of considerable uncertainty about whether effects exist and the great cost of systematically trying to find out what the effects are, although the CBO has recently developed some dynamic estimates (they do not change the traditional estimates by very much).[19] Furthermore,

[19]Congressional Budget Office, *Analyzing the Exonomic and Budgetary Effects of a 10 Percent Cut in Income Tax Rates* (Washington, D.C.: CBO, 2005). Depending on assumptions, as much as one-third of the revenue lost from the reduction might be made up in a decade. The cut would not pay for itself.

> there is the added problem of guessing what the Federal Reserve monetary response would be to any fiscal program with considerable macroeconomic impact. The legislatures in a number of states do require that estimates include macroeconomic effects, however. Much of the argument about including the macroeconomic component in revenue estimates centers around political efforts to make the official revenue loss estimate of reduced tax rates or enhanced tax preferences lower than it would be with only static and microeconomic components included. Evidence does indicate that use of dynamic scoring makes only a small difference in the estimates. The dream of self-financed tax reductions, that is, tax cuts that pay for themselves with increased tax revenue, is not supported by the evidence.[20]

Although revenue forecasts are keenly watched and tested against actual revenue collections, revenue estimates are seldom judged for accuracy. Even the federal government, with its great concern and staffing for measuring and evaluating performance, seldom evaluates scoring. A CBO report states: ". . . it is generally not possible to assess the accuracy of past revenue estimates of enacted legislation. Most legislative provisions are part of a large mix of changes, and identifying the revenues associated with a particular provision is impossible. Often, subsequent legislation obscures the effect of previous actions."[21] The estimate matters when the legislation is being considered—particularly when there are limits like those of PAYGO that constrain how much fiscal change is permitted in a year—and then it is typically forgotten and not tested against actual data. Usually, nobody knows whether the estimates turned out to be right or wrong.[22] Federal battles have usually been about tax estimates, not forecasts.

Tax Expenditure Budgets

The Congressional Budget and Impoundment Act of 1974 defines tax expenditures to be "revenue losses attributable to provisions of the federal tax laws which allow a special exclusion, exemption, or deduction from gross income or which provide a special credit, a preferential rate of tax, or a deferral of tax liability." The tax expen-

---

[20]Expenditure proposals have macroeconomic effects that can be at least as large as tax reductions. However, the strongest proponents for dynamic scoring of tax provisions have not made an argument for extending the principles to the spending side of the budget.

[21]Congressional Budget Office, *Projecting Federal Tax Revenues and the Effect of Changes in Tax Law* (Washington, D.C.: CBO, 1998), 1.

[22]But sometimes wrong estimates can be exciting. For instance, in 2000, Arizona offered a large tax advantage for propane-burning motor vehicles. The estimate was for lost revenue of $3–$10 million dollars. Part of the way through the first year, lost revenue appeared to be around $420 million: the person doing the estimate did not see an error in writing the legislation that effectively made the program open-ended and miscalculated exactly how attractive the program would be. (Jim Carlton, "If You Paid Half Price for that new SUV, You Must Be in Arizona—With Big Rebates to Car Buyers, Clean-Air Law Cleaned Out the State's Coffers Instead" (*Wall Street Journal*, 26 October, 2000): A1.

diture budget, an accumulation of the estimates of revenue lost through these preferences, thus reflects the dual nature of every tax system and the conflicting nature of provisions in the system: Some provisions are in the tax system to implement traditional tax policy and should be judged according to the criteria of taxation, whereas others intend to favor certain economic activities or to relieve personal hardships and should be judged according to budget policy criteria.

A tax expenditure is equivalent to having the taxpayer pay the tax that would be owed without the special provision and simultaneously receiving a government grant equal to the amount of tax in that provision. A direct expenditure and a tax expenditure are comparable because both provide a benefit to a recipient and reduce public resources available for other uses. However, they look different politically. As Eugene Steuerle points out, tax expenditures "allow politicians to appear to be reducing the size of government (reducing taxes) while actually increasing it (increasing spending)."[23] This represents gross hypocrisy and a clear violation of fiscal transparency. The tax expenditure concept and the tax expenditure budget is a tool for adding transparency.

The development of a tax expenditure budget is "a classification exercise: dividing the provisions of the tax system into a benchmark or norm and a series of deviations from that norm."[24] But what is normal? The practical problem is deciding what components are part of the *benchmark* and what components represent the *deviations* from the norm that constitute a tax preference to be measured by the tax expenditure budget. By classifying most of the tax system as part of the norm, the size of the tax expenditure is reduced. Conversely, by defining the norm narrowly, more provisions in the law become suspect and the tax expenditure budget is large.

Because there are so many specific translations of tax concepts into tax structures, any tax-expenditure budget demands a careful explanation of what normal means. For instance, the normal federal income tax definition used by the Joint Committee on Taxation, called the *normal tax* baseline, is not the same as the *reference tax law* baseline that the administration uses. Therefore, the two sets of tax expenditure estimates will not be the same. As the federal budget describes the two:

> The normal tax baseline is patterned on a comprehensive income tax, which defines income as the sum of consumption and the change in net wealth in a given period of time. The normal tax baseline allows personal exemptions, a standard deduction, and deductions of the expenses incurred in earning income. It is not limited to a particular structure of tax rates, or by a specific definition of the taxpaying unit.
>
> The reference tax law baseline is also patterned on a comprehensive income tax, but in practice is closer to the existing law. Reference law tax expenditures are limited to special exemptions in the tax code that serve programmatic functions. These functions correspond to specific budget categories such as national defense, agriculture, or health care. While tax expenditures under the reference law baseline are generally tax expenditures under the normal tax baseline, the reverse is not always true.[25]

---

[23]Eugene Steuerle, "Summers on Social Tax Expenditures: Where He's Wrong . . . or at Least Incomplete," *Tax Notes* 89 (December 18, 2000): 1639.

[24]Organisation for Economic Cooperation and Development, *Tax Expenditures: Recent Experiences* (1996): 9.

[25]Executive Office of the President, Office of Management and Budget, *Analytical Perspectives, Budget of the United States Government, Fiscal Year 1998* (Washington, D.C.: GPO, 1997).

The normal tax defines the ideal or standard tax, the tax that follows the textbook concept of what structure would assign shares of the cost of government in a way consistent with the logic of the tax. It starts with a fundamental principle (notice the track from the Haig-Simons comprehensive definition of income here) and allows some appropriate adjustments (the Joint Committee makes more than does the Treasury) to define "normal" or "reference." Differences from that definition constitute tax expenditures. If the structure now in place were to be considered "normal," then there would be no tax expenditures. Therefore, getting the standard right is vital for making meaningful estimates of tax expenditures.

Existing federal tax expenditures encourage selected economic activities (investment, housing, municipal borrowing, support of charities, etc.) or reduce taxpayers' liability in special circumstances (deduction of medical expenses, casualty-loss deduction, etc.). (Sidebar 13–2 describes the general process for making the estimates.) Estimates by both Congress (the Joint Committee on Taxation) and the president (Department of Treasury) are a regular part of the executive budget and other presentations.[26] Table 13–2 presents estimates of the twenty-five largest tax expenditures for fiscal 2006 according to the Treasury. Estimates also are prepared on a regular, although not always annual, basis in about thirty of the states.[27] Appendix 13–1 describes the criteria and measurement principles that Minnesota uses.

Tax policy is generally predisposed against tax expenditures—assuming the normal structure is rationally designed—because the differential provisions distort business and household decisions, because their implementation complicates the tax system, because they continue without regular evaluation and legislative approval, because they are open-ended in amount, and because they are not transparent in enactment, in delivery of benefits, or in overall magnitude.[28] These same features make them attractive to special interests—who frequently prefer them to direct cash assistance—they are hidden (absent a tax expenditure budget), permanent, and open-ended. However, not all tax expenditures are bad; conducting some budget policy through the tax system may be a sensible, quick, inexpensive, and feasible approach in comparison with other alternative approaches (e.g., direct expenditure or regulation) to achieving a particular objective. There is no need to establish an administrative structure to operate tax expenditure assistance, and the tax expenditure may reach a wider population of beneficiaries than would a free-standing program that requires special application.

The critical stage in development of a useful tax expenditure budget is that of defining the normal tax, that is, deciding what basic tax policy is. This question is

---

[26]They may be in revenue- or outlay-equivalent terms. The latter estimates the dollar amount of direct spending that would provide taxpayers the net benefits equaling what they receive from the tax expenditure.

[27]An analysis and evaluation of state tax expenditure budgets appears in John L. Mikesell, "Tax Expenditure Budgets, Budget Policy, and Tax Policy: Confusion in the States," Public *Budgeting & Finance*, XXII (Winter 2002): 34–51, and John L. Mikesell, "The Tax Expenditure Concept at the State Level: Conflict between Fiscal Control and Sound Tax Policy," *Proceedings of the Ninety-fourth Annual Conference on Taxation of the National Tax Association* (2001). The states in general fail to clearly identify the normal structures upon which their tax expenditure estimates are based.

[28]At the Federal level, tax expenditures also face fewer legislative check points because House Ways and Means and Senate Finance serve as both authorizing and appropriating committees for tax legislation.

Sidebar 13–2
Preparing Tax Expenditure Estimates

The Joint Committee on Taxation makes 5-year tax expenditure estimates each year. The following provides their short description of what they do.

> The tax expenditure estimates in this report are based on Congressional Budget Office and Joint Tax Committee staff projections of the gross income, deductions, and expenditures of individuals and corporations for calendar years 2000–2005. These projections are used to compute tax liabilities for the present-law baseline and tax liabilities for the alternative baseline which assumes that the tax expenditure provision does not exist.
>
> Internal Revenue Service (IRS) statistics from recent tax returns are used to develop projections of the tax credit, deductions, and exclusions that will be claimed under the present-law baseline. These IRS statistics show the actual usage of the various tax expenditure provisions. In the case of some tax expenditures, such as the earned income tax credit, there is evidence that taxpayers are not claiming all of the benefits to which they are entitled, while others are filing claims that exceed their entitlements. The tax expenditure estimates in this report are based on projections of actual claims under the various tax provisions, not the tax benefits to which taxpayers are entitled.
>
> Some tax expenditure estimates are based partly on statistics for income, deductions, and expenses for prior years. Accelerated depreciation is an example. Estimates for this tax expenditure are based on the difference between tax depreciation deductions under present law and the deductions that would have been claimed in the current year if investments in the current year and all prior years had been depreciated using the alternative (normal tax law) depreciation schedule.
>
> Each tax expenditure is estimated separately, under the assumption that all other tax expenditures remain in the tax code. If two or more tax expenditures were estimated simultaneously, the total change in tax liability could be smaller or larger than the sum of the amounts shown for each item separately, as a result of interactions among the tax expenditure provisions.
>
> Year-to-year differences in the estimates for each tax expenditure reflect changes in tax law, including phaseouts of tax expenditure provisions and changes that alter the definition of the normal tax structure, such as the tax rate schedule, the personal exemption amount, and the standard deduction. Some of the estimates for this tax expenditure report may differ from estimates made in previous years because of changes in law and economic conditions, the availability of better data, and improved estimating techniques.

SOURCE: Joint Committee on Taxation, *Estimates of Federal Tax Expenditures for Fiscal Years 2001–2005* (Washington, D.C.: GOP, 2001), 13–14.

currently under debate at the federal level. Recent federal budgets, to stress that the current federal income tax is actually a sort of hybrid income–consumption–tax, have added tax expenditure estimates under a consumption tax normal base. Of course, that causes a different pattern of tax expenditures than under the traditional income base norm. In particular, the several tax provisions providing preferences for saving are no longer tax expenditures. The most obvious of these are the several exclusion for pension contributions shown in Table 13–2. When the normal tax is consumption, they would become components of the normal base. This illustrates why a clear consensus on normal tax policy must be reached before the tax expenditure budget can have any practical meaning or utility for policy discussions. If

Table 13–2
The Twenty-five Largest Tax Expenditures in the Federal Income Tax, Fiscal 2006 Estimated ($ millions)

Provision	Amount
Exclusion of employer contributions for medical insurance premiums and medical care	125,690
Deductibility of mortgage interest on owner-occupied homes	76,030
Net exclusion of pension contributions and earnings: Employer plans	51,050
Net exclusion of pension contributions and earnings, 401(k) plans	48,140
Capital gains exclusions on home sales	36,270
Deductibility of non-business state and local taxes other than on owner-occupied homes	34,620
Child credit	32,810
Deductibility of charitable contributions, other than education and health	32,550
Exclusion of net imputed rental income on owner-occupied homes	29,720
Step-up basis of capital gains at death	28,760
Capital gains (except agriculture, timber, iron ore, and coal)	28,370
Exclusion of interest on public purpose state and local bonds	26,610
Exclusion of interest on life insurance savings	24,070
Social Security benefits for retired workers	19,770
Deductibility of state and local property tax owner-occupied homes	14,830
Net exclusion of pension contributions and earnings: Keough plans	9,980
Deductibility of medical expenses	9,140
Expensing of research and experimentation expenditures (normal tax method)	7,920
Deferral of income from controlled foreign corporations (normal tax method)	7,440
Net exclusion of pension contributions and earnings: Individual Retirement Accounts	7,310
Exclusion of worker's compensation benefits	5,940
Earned income tax credit	5,423
Deduction for U.S. production activities	5,420
Exception from passive loss rules for $25,000 of rental loss	4,750
Self-employed medical insurance premiums	4,330

SOURCE: Executive Office of the President, Office of Management and Budget, *Analytical Perspectives, Budget of the United States Government, Fiscal 2006* (Washington, D.C.: U.S. GPO, 2005).

you cannot agree on the basic tax policy, then doing a tax expenditure budget is hardly worth the effort.

A properly drawn definition of a benchmark or normal structure provides a defense *against* arbitrary and capricious tax policy. Most fiscal experts would agree with the Surrey and McDaniel conclusion: "unless attention is paid to tax expenditures, a country does not have its tax policy or its budget policy under full control."[29] The same message applies for American state governments. Without a proper tax expenditure budget, a government has no gauge of the extent to which its revenue system is being used for nonrevenue purposes.

[29]Stanley S. Surrey and Paul R. McDaniel, "The Tax Expenditure Concept and the Legislative Process," in Henry J. Aaron and Michael J, Boskin, eds., *The Economics of Taxation* (Washington, D.C.: Brookings Institution, 1980), 124.

Conclusion

Revenue prediction, a portion of administration particularly vital for budget preparation, has three significant divisions: forecasting collections in future fiscal years, estimating the impact of proposed changes in tax law, and calculating revenues currently sacrificed by existing elements of the tax law. The former activity normally produces excellent accuracy (1- to 3-percent error) when professionally done and when the forecasts are not politically driven. Errors are usually greater when the country enters a recession. Revenue estimates are important to let policymakers know what the fiscal cost of their policies is likely to be. Tax expenditure budgets tally the revenue effects of provisions in existing tax laws. The practice of revenue prediction, especially forecasting and estimating, has a high degree of art mixed the quantitative science in its real world application.

CHAPTER 13 QUESTIONS AND EXERCISES

1. A state intangibles tax is levied on the holders of intangible personal property in the state. The tax base is market value of the item of property on the last day of December; for most taxpayers, intangible holdings in December establish tax due by April 15 of the next year (paid with the annual income tax return). Tax rates have been 0.0025 percent, but a phase-out of the tax begins in calendar year 2007. In that year, the rate will be 0.00233 and in the following year, 0.00217.

   Fiscal year (July 1–June 30) collections for the tax from 1999 through 2005 follow, along with estimates previously prepared for fiscal 2006 and 2007 and calendar-year data on state personal income. Both income and collections are in millions.

Year	Collections ($)	Personal Income ($)
1999	15.6	26,158
2000	17.8	27,776
2001	15.7	29,816
2002	17.1	33,206
2003	16.6	37,132
2004	18.4	41,487
2005	22.2	46,279
2006 (forecast)	18.0	n.a.
2007 (forecast)	18.5	n.a.

n.a., Not available.

Estimate revenue from the tax for fiscal years 2007, 2008, and 2009, using any method that is appropriate. (An independent commission has estimated state personal income for the 3 years to equal $52,660 million in 2007, $59,800 million in 2008, and $67,500 million in 2009.) Describe the method you used and indicate why it is better than other alternatives available.

2. Does your state develop a tax-expenditure budget? Does it prepare fiscal-impact statements? What agency does this work? How are revenue forecasts prepared for the budget process?
3. A state in the southeastern region of the United States operates state liquor stores. Prices at the stores are set in the following fashion: Add 41 percent to the wholesale price at which the system acquires the product. To that is added an excise of $8.10 per case. The state sold roughly 36 million cases. The state, however, increases the excise rate to $9.10 per case, and a tentative revenue estimate shows that excise revenue will increase by $36 million. The state economist objects: "The demand for liquor is inelastic, so sales will be relatively insensitive to a tax increase. Therefore, revenue will increase by more than $36 million." What is your reaction to this objection?
4. Revenue estimates are sometimes at the mercy of the administrative process. Suppose you are developing estimates of corporate income tax collections for a state. In your review of historical data, you find that a large but quantitatively imprecise amount of collections were moved from one fiscal year to another because overlapping vacation schedules caused the collections' mailroom to shut down in the last 2 weeks of a recent fiscal year. How might you handle this problem in preparing your estimate, both in perfecting the historical data and in delivering your estimate?
5. Your state plans to adopt a tuition tax credit for college students. How would you estimate the revenue impact of this provision? How would the decision to use static, microeconomic feedback, or dynamic approaches influence your estimate?
6. When the Soviet bloc broke up in the early 1990s, the Republic of Vardar declared its independence. As the country established a monetary system, democratic processes, and a controlled fiscal system, the early problems of hyperinflation, unemployment, and declining standards of living slowly subsided. In late 1997 the country initiated a personal income tax, heavily dependent on taxes withheld by large employers on wages and salaries, but still broad in coverage. The country has been collecting about 30 percent of its tax revenue from that tax, although a law passed in 2000 is expected to reduce personal income tax collections by 25 percent in the short term. The lower tax rates are expected to stimulate economic activity and to encourage business to move from the shadow to the official (taxpaying) economy, so some of the revenue loss will ultimately be recovered. The Ministry of Finance forecasts collections of 7,789,000.0 thousand markka (MK) for 2001. Data on tax collections are reported below.
   a. From this information, would you advise the Ministry to revise its 2001 forecast? Explain.
   b. What factors may influence the patterns you see in the data?
   c. What other issues would you pursue in addition to the data presented here?

Collections are in MK thousand.

	1998	1999	2000	2001
January	668,534.0	625,149.1	559,070.9	714,981.0
February	782,026.6	754,396.9	874,000.0	575,115.0
March	738,856.7	811,506.7	988,047.2	583,592.0
April	826,622.9	880,075.8	916,030.7	586,743.0
May	678,031.1	756,507.9	800,876.8	
June	736,974.5	831,054.5	940,975.1	
July	824,343.7	978,485.6	967,098.4	
August	668,708.8	743,718.4	841,267.5	
September	766,271.3	898,210.0	874,308.1	
October	759,679.8	846,494.2	887,091.4	
November	742,371.5	847,950.2	936,090.7	
December	984,911.2	1,259,467.1	1,204,961.7	

APPENDIX 13–1

THE STATE OF MINNESOTA TAX EXPENDITURE BUDGET: CRITERIA AND MEASUREMENT

The Minnesota Department of Revenue prepares a tax expenditure budget on a 2-year cycle, delivering it on the off-year from submission of the governor's biennial budget. The following description of the criteria the department uses for identifying a tax expenditure and then for measuring it comes from the 2004–2007 edition.

Tax Expenditure Criteria

The preparation of this tax expenditure budget involves more than simply listing every exemption, deduction, credit, and so on, that is contained in the tax system. A conceptual framework governs the preparation of the report. Each provision is evaluated, not subjectively according to its purpose or effectiveness, but objectively against a list of criteria. Every effort is made to eliminate value judgments.

Seven criteria have been established to determine if a provision is a tax expenditure. Some of the criteria are taken directly from the authorizing statute; some are based on concepts used in the preparation of federal tax expenditure reports; and others are based on what is believed to be a logical application of the tax expenditure concept. A provision must meet all the criteria in order to be a tax expenditure.

A provision is a tax expenditure if it:

- has an impact on a tax that is applied statewide,
- confers preferential treatment,
- results in reduced tax revenue in the applicable fiscal years,
- is not included in the budget as an expenditure,
- is included in the defined tax base for that tax,
- is not subject to an alternative tax, and
- can be amended or repealed by a change in state law alone.

The first four criteria are based on the statute requiring the tax expenditure budget.

The tax expenditure budget is required by statute to include every state tax and any local tax that is applied statewide. A local tax imposed pursuant to a special law is not included in the report.

Preferential treatment is a key concept in determining tax expenditures, and a key word in the authorizing statute is "certain." Minnesota Statutes, Section 270.067, Subd. 6(1) (italic emphasis added):

> "Tax expenditure" means a tax provision which provides a gross income definition, deduction, exemption, credit, or rate for *certain* persons, types of income, transactions, or property that results in reduced tax revenue.

If a provision is not preferential, it is not a tax expenditure. For example, the personal exemption for the individual income tax is not preferential because each person receives the same amount of exemption. Likewise, the graduated rate structure of the individual income tax is not a tax expenditure because each taxpayer with the same amount of tax base pays at the same rate.

In the statute quoted above, a requirement is that the provision ". . . results in reduced tax revenue." A provision that would otherwise qualify is not considered a tax expenditure if it is not being used or is not likely to be used during fiscal years 2004–2007.

The federal law (Congressional Budget Act of 1974, Public Law 93-344) that requires a list of tax expenditures to be included with the federal budget includes in its definition of tax expenditures ". . . provisions of the Federal tax laws which allow . . . a deferral of liability." Although the Minnesota law does not mention deferral of liability, this concept has been adopted in the preparation of the report.

A deferral of liability involves the time value of money and affects primarily the individual income and corporate franchise taxes. A deferral can result either from postponing the time when income is recognized for tax purposes or from accelerating the deduction of expenses. In the year in which either of these is done, taxable income is lower than it would be otherwise, although an adjustment may be made in a future year. The effect of the deferral of liability is similar to as an interest-free loan for the taxpayer.

Some provisions of tax law are similar to tax expenditures, but they are already included on the spending side of the budget. Many of the property tax relief provisions fit this pattern. For Minnesota budget purposes, income tax revenues are reduced by the total amount of refundable credits. Therefore these credits are included in this report.

The tax base for each tax must be clearly defined so that exceptions to that base can be identified. Some tax provisions help to define the base; others are exceptions to the base. Each chapter introduction includes an explanation of the defined tax base for that tax. The tax base for each tax is the conceptual framework used for this report and is not necessarily the same as an ideal tax base. The determination of the tax base includes a review of the statutes, history of the tax, and other pertinent literature.

In some instances, one tax may be imposed in place of another tax, and it would not be reasonable for a taxpayer or activity to be subject to both taxes. Therefore, the exemption from one tax is not considered a tax expenditure if the alternative tax is imposed. However, if a taxpayer can elect to be taxed under an alternative tax that is lower, then the alternative tax provision is considered to be a tax expenditure, measured as the difference between the two taxes.

The application of the alternative tax concept for this report was limited to these situations:

- The income from taconite and iron mining is subject to the occupation tax in lieu of the corporate franchise tax.
- The purchase of a motor vehicle is subject to the separate motor vehicle sales tax (Chapter 5) in lieu of the general sales and use tax (Chapter 4).
- The solid-waste management taxes are imposed in lieu of the general sales tax.
- A number of taxes are imposed in lieu of the general property tax, including the motor vehicle registration tax and the taconite production tax.
- Noncommercial aircraft are taxed under the aircraft registration tax, whereas commercial air flight property is taxed under the air flight property tax.

The biennial budget contains only items that can become law upon action by both houses of the Minnesota Legislature and the Governor. Likewise, the tax expenditure budget contains only items which can be changed or repealed by the concurring actions of the Legislature and the Governor. Therefore, provisions that are contained in the Minnesota Constitution, federal law, or the U.S. Constitution are not included in the tax expenditure budget.

Measuring the Fiscal Impact of Tax Expenditures

The fiscal impact of a tax expenditure is intended to measure what is being "spent" through the tax system on that one provision. It is not necessarily the same as the amount of revenue that would be gained by repeal. This distinction is important.

For the tax expenditure budget, each provision is estimated in isolation, and other provisions in that tax and in other taxes are held constant. The secondary impact of that provision on other provisions is not taken into account. Because the estimates measure the impact of the provision as it exists and not what would happen if it were repealed, no change in taxpayer behavior is assumed.

In contrast to the tax expenditure estimates, estimating the repeal of a provision would take into account interactions within a tax or between taxes and may include changes in taxpayer behavior. If two or more provisions in a tax were repealed at the same time, the combined impact of repealing the provisions would be estimated, rather than estimating each provision separately.

The methodology used to estimate tax expenditures can produce misleading results if the estimates for two or more provisions are combined. Depending upon the situation, the combined impact of two or more provisions could be more or less than the total of the provisions estimated separately.

When two or more tax expenditures in a tax overlap, it is important to understand how this situation is treated in the tax expenditure estimates. When one provision is estimated, other provisions are assumed to remain unchanged.

The sales tax exemptions for food and for school district purchases illustrate this point. When the exemption for food is estimated, purchases by school districts would still be exempt and are not included in the estimate. When the exemption for purchases by school districts is estimated, purchases of food are excluded. Therefore purchases of food by school districts are not included in either estimate. If the two exemptions were repealed together, the estimate of repeal would include the overlap and would be larger than the sum of the two exemptions estimated separately.

The estimates for provisions that result in the deferral of tax are the net impact for that year. For example, the expensing of depreciable business property is estimated for a given year as the net of accelerated deductions taken that year and deductions not taken because they were expensed in an earlier year.

The precision of the estimates varies with the source of the data and with the applicability of the data to the tax expenditure provision. Data from Minnesota tax returns were used whenever possible. Other sources included federal tax expenditure estimates, data from federal tax returns, and numerous other sources of data for Minnesota and the nation.

SOURCE: Tax Research Division, Minnesota Department of Revenue, State of Minnesota Tax Expenditure Budget, Fiscal Years 2004–2007 (St. Paul: Minnesota Department of Revenue, 2004).

CHAPTER 14

Intergovernmental Fiscal Relations: Diversity and Coordination

Federal, state, and local governments provide and finance public services in the United States, sometimes independently, sometimes cooperatively. Governments of each level are selected by their own electorates and no government level functions as a regional department of another. Even though the localities add up to the state and the states add up to the nation, the balance of choices differs among localities in a state and among states in the nation. Because of that diversity of choice, state and local governments have an important role in providing and financing government services. That includes the power to spend, as well as the responsibility to raise revenue adequate to support that spending.

Completely independent operation of these levels would, most argue, produce unacceptable results. Such a posture would undoubtedly leave the public without desired and affordable services, inflict severe burdens on some unluckily placed individuals and businesses, and leave some lower-level governments in chronic fiscal crisis. Those problems create the importance for fiscal interrelationships among governments.[1]

Subnational governments allow fiscal diversity and choices about which government should provide which services. Although the federal government continues as sole government provider of national defense and postal services, other significant government functions are divided among federal, state, and local governments. State and local governments are dominant for the services of public safety (police, fire, and protective regulation), education (primary, secondary, and higher), recreation and culture, and transportation (highways, air, water, and urban mass transit).

States and localities can adjust both levels and types of government services they provide as they respond to the preferences of a heterogeneous population.

[1]Not all federations are characterized by the degree of political independence between federal and regional governments that characterizes the United States. For instance, Russia and India have systems in which regional chief executives are selected in a process that gives considerable control and influence to the national chief executive, rather than the free election of state governors that is the practice in the United States.

Maintaining service responsibility at state and local levels almost certainly means great diversity in what services are provided and how they are financed. It may also bring economies in service provision as jurisdictions compete to keep the cost of government service affordable. Centralization would mean greater uniformity and possibly more secure financing. And centralization makes for clear governmental responsibility: with only a single government, there would not have been the competitive finger pointing to identify which government was responsible for mishandling the response to hurricane Katrina. What establishes the level that should have primary responsibility for providing particular services, and how should intergovernmental financing be arranged? To what extent should diverse provision be constrained or coordinated? And to what extent should subnational governments expect to receive revenue from the central government, as opposed to being required to raise the revenue they spend from their own taxing powers?[2]

Correspondence and Subsidiarity

The critical factor in identifying the level of government that should provide a public service is the range of benefit spillover. A structure of governments "in which the jurisdiction that determines the level of provision of each public good includes precisely the set of individuals who consume the good" satisfies the *correspondence principle* in defining geographic boundaries and government size.[3] Making the spillover area and the decision unit coincide concentrates government attention on the important matters and prevents the problems that occur when beneficiaries do not pay for a service.

To analyze intergovernmental systems, one can define by use of the correspondence principle a hierarchy of public services by the geographic extent of primary spillovers. A completely private good would have no spillovers; no distortions result from permitting private individuals to decide on the provision of purely private goods. Public goods and services, however, yield external benefits over areas of widely different geographic range. For instance, a neighborhood park benefits a small community of households around it, benefits from basic police and fire protection spill beyond the neighborhood to a broader local community, interregional mobility causes benefits from primary and secondary education to extend to whole regions, whereas the benefits of national defense and international relations extend to the entire nation (and beyond). Correspondence offers a rule for assigning responsibilities to governments: Expenditure and service responsibilities should be aligned with the benefit areas for each government service. Therefore, services

[2]Among countries of the Organization for Economic Cooperation and Development, Canada and the United States are the leaders in terms of expecting regional and local governments to raise their own revenues. Julia Darby et al., "Fiscal Consolidation and Decentralization: A Tale of Two Tiers," *Fiscal Studies,* XVI (No. 2, 2005): 173.

[3]Wallace E. Oates, *Fiscal Federalism* (New York: Harcourt Brace-Jovanovich, 1972), 34.

whose benefits do not spill beyond the local community should be locally provided, services that benefit a number of communities should be state provided, and services that benefit the entire county should be nationally provided. Failure to match spillover range and provision range, at least in general terms, can produce substantial misallocations in resources, overspending for some services, underspending for other services, poorly served citizens, badly managed service delivery, and poorly structured revenue systems.

There is a second general principle in assigning responsibility for government services, the principle of *subsidiarity*. The principle is that governmental responsibility for a function should be at the lowest level of government that can deliver the function efficiently. Jorge Martinez-Vazquez explains why:

> Because subnational governments are closer to the preferences and needs of taxpayers, they are more likely than the central government to deliver services that local residents want. And, to the extent that preferences for public services differ, efficiency will lead to (indeed, will require) diversity among subnational jurisdictions. Reliance (to the extent possible) on locally imposed taxes to finance subnational expenditures internalizes the costs of providing these services and leads residents in turn to demand more accountability from public officials. When the beneficiary pays, there is greater efficiency and responsibility in government decision-making.[4]

Subsidiarity brings devolution, moving government responsibility to lower levels of government. The devolution trend "is largely a reflection of the political evolution toward more democratic and participatory forms of government that seeks to improve the responsiveness and accountability of political leaders to their electorates, and to ensure a closer correspondence between the quantity, composition, and quality of publicly provided goods and services and the preferences of recipients."[5]

Efforts for Congress to shed responsibility, for the United Kingdom to give more power to Scotland and Wales, for division of responsibilities between the European Union and its component nations, and for efficiently rebuilding governments in the former Soviet Union are all driven by the dual principles of subsidiarity and correspondence in deciding which government will do what so that governments serve the people most effectively and efficiently.

A mismatch between spillover range and government jurisdiction can distort the use of public resources. Suppose a city can construct a local sports complex that would cost $1 million with only $50,000 of its own resources, the difference being financed by the federal government. The city would reasonably behave as if the full cost of the project is $50,000, even though the project uses $1 million of resources. If the project has minimal beneficial impact beyond the city, there is no significant spillover that federal financing corrects. Thus, the lack of correspondence causes the city to behave as if $1 million of resources have a value of only $50,000. Had the city been required to finance the project itself, it would have been unwilling to pay

---

[4]Jorge Martinez-Vasquez, "Expenditures and Expenditure Assignment," in Christine I. Wallich, ed., *Russia and the Challenge of Fiscal Federalism* (Washington, D.C.: The World Bank, 1994), 99.
[5]Teresa Ter-Minassian, "Decentralizing Government," *Finance and Development* (September 1997): 36.

the $1 million if the project did not return at least $1 million in benefits to the community. When the correspondence principle is not followed, wasted resources are likely.

But broad financing can also correct misallocations from spillovers. Consider a situation in which city A's sewage-treatment plant dumps partially treated waste into a river. That river flows past city B, which draws river water for the municipal water utility. The more complete the sewage treatment by city A, the less the water-treatment costs for city B, and the more attractive is the river to the residents of city B. The primary beneficiaries of city A's water treatment are residents of city B. Without some intervention by a geographically larger government—assistance designed to relieve city A of treatment-plant expense incurred primarily for the benefit of those downstream—socially desirable actions probably would not be undertaken. City A's decision would be made by comparing returns to its residents (only a small portion of total returns) against the full cost of the complex. In this case, federal (or state) financing of a large share of project cost is justified. That financing would allow city A to pay only to the extent its residents receive benefits, whereas federal (or state) taxpayers pay for returns received by outsiders.

What about Economic Advantage from Bigness?

Correspondence and subsidiarity imply relatively small size for providing many government services, subject only to the problems of externalities for some services. But that ignores the possible unit-cost advantage of larger governments. Economies of scale, in the sense used in government finance, exist if the cost per person served decreases as the size of the service unit increases.[6] In other words, the cost per person of delivering a given level of fire protection would be smaller for a 100,000-person service district than for a 10,000-person service district. The scale advantage may also reflect an advantage of joint consumption: Up to a congestion point, the total cost of providing additional service does not rise as more people are served, so the cost per unit declines with size. In other words, if the operating cost of an agency is $1,000,000, expanding the population served from 50,000 to 60,000 reduces unit cost from $20 per person to $16.67per person—assuming, of course, no associated increase in that operating cost. If such scale economies exist, then governments can economize by growing and consolidating, regardless of the advantages the correspondence principle tells us are available in getting small units to better capture citizen preferences.

[6]From microeconomic theory, economies of scale occur in production when doubling all inputs—a double plant size, in other words—more than doubles output: "Because larger scale permits the introduction of different kinds of techniques, because larger productive units are more efficient, and because larger plants permit greater specialization and division of labor, the long-run average cost function declines, up to some point, with increases in output." Edwin Mansfield, *Microeconomics*, 7th ed. (New York: Norton, 1991), 199. In analysis of government services, the focus is commonly on population served and per capita cost, rather than on cost per unit of product.

There are two problems with the general idea that larger governments operate more economically. First, empirical evidence shows there to be few traditional state and local government services that show economies of scale, except at the very smallest population sizes. Economies of scale do exist for capital-intensive services such as water supply, wastewater treatment, electricity, and gas distribution; however, for services such as police and fire protection and primary and secondary education, unit cost seems not to vary much over a wide range of operating scales. That would be expected for most labor-intensive services.[7] In other words, the cost per person of delivering the service is pretty much the same for a small government provider as it is for a large government delivering the same service. Cost economies from bigness do not stand in the way of achieving the advantages of correspondence and subsidiarity from smallness.

Second, economies of scale refer to the conditions of production only. Size of government matters only if production and provision of the service are necessarily joined. If production by an external contractor is feasible, then scale economies are of no particular importance for determining size for provision decisions. Just as households need not be large enough to actually build an automobile at low cost in order to buy an inexpensive car, neither do governments need great size to provide service at an attractive price.[8] They may deal with larger governments, form cooperative supply arrangements with other small governments, or contract with private businesses for service provision, depending on the circumstances. Therefore, even where there are cost advantages from large size, those advantages are from *producing* the service. Smaller units, designed under the principles of correspondence and subsidiarity, can make the provision decisions and contract with larger units for production, thereby gaining the best of large size for production and small size for purchase.

Fiscal Disparity

Another complication in intergovernmental service-delivery questions is disparity between regions. Some parts of a country or state are likely to be more affluent than others. Within the United States, per capita income of states ranges significantly—from an average of $24,650 in Mississippi and $25,725 in Arkansas to an average of $45,398 in Connecticut and $41,801 in Massachusetts in 2004.[9] And within each state, some localities have residents with considerably greater affluence

[7]Roy W. Bahl and Walter Vogt, *Fiscal Centralization and Tax Burden: State and Regional Financing of City Services* (Cambridge, Mass.: Ballinger, 1975), 13–14.

[8]There may be economies of scope: A single firm may produce more than one product more cheaply than if each product were produced by a separate firm. In this environment, there may be economies associated with having one government provide several services, rather than having separate governments providing each.

[9]U.S. Department of Commerce, Bureau of Economic Analysis. Per capita income in the District of Columbia was $51,803.

than do others. Although resident incomes and affluence do not immediately translate into taxes, similar differences occur in the tax base available to governments.[10] If fiscal resources differ among governments, otherwise equally situated individuals will have considerably different access to public services because of the relative affluence of their government.

The property tax provides a simple demonstration. Suppose Smith and Jones each own houses assessed at $10,000 for the property tax. Smith lives in a community with a property tax base of $40,000 per pupil in its public schools; Jones lives in a community with a property tax base of $20,000 per pupil. If a quality education uses resources costing $1,500 per pupil, Smith's community need levy only a property tax of $3.75 per $100 assessed value to meet that cost. Jones's community would require a tax of $7.50 per $100. When both communities spend the same amount per pupil, the Jones's property must pay twice as much as the Smith's property for the same quality education ($750 versus $375). Thus, services rendered from a given tax rate—or level of *tax effort*—is be greater where the capacity endowment is greater. Because there often is a mismatch between need for government services and capacity to finance those services, higher governments intervene by providing various fiscal assistance. Higher-level governments can use their tax systems to raise revenue and then distribute that revenue to lower levels, using that distribution to even out the disparities in fiscal capacity between those lower levels. As is discussed later in this chapter, state governments are particularly concerned with disparity problems as they affect local school finances.

Fiscal disparity can be particularly acute between cities and their suburbs. In any metropolitan area, some parts are considerably more prosperous than others and the distribution of the local government tax base may not be related well to where the needs for local government services are greatest. Localities with a revenue-rich economic base—for instance, a regional shopping center or an auto-sales mall for local sales tax communities or an electric-generating plant or a major industrial plant for real-property tax communities—can have huge fiscal affluence without much population at all; workers and shoppers generating that revenue base live in many other locations in the metropolitan area, and where they live is where the need for schools, police and fire protection, park and recreation, and other local services is. A small number of local governments use *regional tax-base sharing* of the property tax to assist with the disparity problem (as well as to reduce competition among local governments for new base-rich development). In these plans, a portion of commercial and industrial property assessment growth is pooled—the Minnesota Twin Cities program for seven counties captures 40 percent for the pool—to provide revenue for all the localities. A portion of local fiscal indepen-

[10]An effort to calibrate total fiscal capacity and compare it with actual effort is the Advisory Commission on Intergovernmental Relations' representative tax systems: Advisory Commission on Intergovernmental Relations, *1988 Fiscal Capacity and Effort* (M-170) (Washington, D.C.: ACIR, 1990). The representative tax system estimates how much revenue a jurisdiction would raise if it applied typical (national average) tax rates to the major tax bases; an index of that representative yield is the capacity estimate. Robert Tannenwald and Nicholas Turner, "Interstate Fiscal Disparity in State Fiscal 1999," Federal Reserve Bank of Boston Public Policy Discussion Paper, No. 04-9, estimates per capita tax capacity in Nevada to be 1.74 times as great as that in Mississippi, clearly demonstrating the disparity issue.

dence is surrendered for the common good of the metropolis and to smooth the tax spikes between localities that certain economic activities can produce. But the sharing concept has critics as well: Economic developments that are particularly rich in tax base are often not desirable neighbors, bringing noise, smells, traffic, and so on. That extra tax base—which can be used to enrich local services or to reduce local tax rates—may be a way of compensating the host community for those factors. Fiscal disparity can also be great between urban and rural areas.

Coordination and Assistance: Tax Systems

Governments can tailor their revenue structures to provide mutually beneficial financial and administrative assistance. Such assistance, although not bringing new resources into a government, may improve access to the existing revenue base and may be arranged with minimal interference to local autonomy. The two general classes of revenue relationship are (1) relief in tax-base use and (2) assistance with revenue administration and compliance.

Revenue relief includes deductions and credits granted the taxes of one unit in tax computations made for another unit. Both are important, but they work differently and have different clout. Deductibility reduces the tax base for one governmental unit by the amount of tax paid to a supported government. For example, the federal individual income tax currently permits deduction of selected state and local taxes from the federal base. Not only does that free tax capacity for the lower units, but it also serves to induce adoption of deductible taxes. The power of deduction can be demonstrated: Suppose a taxpayer is in the 35-percent federal tax bracket. If his or her state income tax increases by $100, the taxpayer's net tax burden increases by only $65 because deducting that state tax reduces his or her federal liability by $35. The deduction rewards state and local governments that use deductible taxes by making their net cost to taxpayers less.[11] Of course, the coordination effects are not extraordinarily strong (states continue to use nondeductible taxes), and deductibility does not equalize wealth between lower units.

A stronger device is the tax credit, an arrangement in which the tax levied by one government unit acts as full or partial payment of the liability owed to another government. One of the best examples is the federal tax on transfer at death: Payments under a qualifying state tax act as an 80-percent credit of liability owed on the federal tax.[12] This creates an almost overwhelming incentive for state governments to adopt the tax at least up to the maximum credit limit. The credit involves revenue loss for the government unit that grants the credit, and the credit does not

[11]In the pre-1964 tax-reduction period—when marginal rates were as high as 91 percent—deductibility prevented taxpayers from encountering marginal rates above 100 percent.

[12]Death taxes (estate and inheritance) are levied on the value of property transferred to another at the property owner's death. The transfer must be gratuitous, not in payment for services rendered. Estate taxes apply at the benefactor level; inheritance taxes apply to the heir. The federal taxes are being phased out, leaving states in a quandary.

alter the basic distribution of resources among states or localities: Affluent units remain affluent, and poor units remain poor. In general, the credit involves substantial implicit control of the lower government unit by the higher government unit.[13]

Deductions and credits create a curious effect for state (or local) tax reductions—the loss of state tax revenue when such a tax is cut is greater than the increase in disposable income available to its taxpayers. The other beneficiary is the federal government. Estimates suggest, for instance, that federal income tax revenue increased by between $1 billion and $1.7 billion in 1979 as a result of California's Proposition 13 property tax reduction.[14] Every state or local program to reduce property or income taxes, under the current federal tax law, brings more federal tax revenue.

Deducting and crediting lower-level taxes frees resources for lower-level use and provides incentive for using "approved" tax forms. Both can have considerable coordinating potential. Deductions and credits do not assist lower government levels with administration and do not reduce the burden of complying with multiple-government taxes encountered by businesses and individuals.

Another set of revenue tools can assist with that part of the intergovernmental fiscal problem. These devices include source separation, cooperative administration, coordinated tax bases, tax supplements, and centralized administration, arrayed in order of high to low amounts of lower-level government involvement in operations.

Separation of tax sources prevents tax overlapping. Vertical overlapping occurs when governments at different levels (say, federal and state) apply a tax to exactly the same base; horizontal overlapping occurs when more than one government at the same level (say, two different states) applies a tax to the same base. Overlapping may not only produce the nuisance of multiple taxpayer filings but also may distort economic activity. If each level of government were guaranteed an exclusive use of particular tax bases, the vertical-overlap problem would be effectively eliminated.

Table 14–1 presents the record on source separation over the past 30 years. In 1970 local government dominated the property tax source, as it has for as long as reliable records are available. The federal government has been, for all practical purposes, excluded from that source by the Constitution. State government once obtained a large portion of its revenue from property taxes (e.g., 40 percent of state revenue in 1922 came from general property taxes).[15] Overall, the state role was small relative to that of local government. As state expenditures increased, state governments resorted to revenue sources other than the property tax. Little has changed in the pattern of use of property taxation over the past quarter century.

---

[13]The power of the credit can be easily shown. Property can be transferred on death or during the benefactor's life. There are federal death and gift taxes, but the credit applies only to the former. Only Nevada has no state death tax, but only fifteen states apply gift taxes.

[14]Report to the Comptroller General of the United States, *Will Federal Assistance Be Affected by Propositions 13?* GGD-78-101 (Washington, D.C.: General Accounting Office, 1978). Some state income taxes provide a tax deduction for federal income tax paid. Taxpayers in those states found that the federal income tax rebates of 2001 were taxable under the state income tax because their deduction for federal income tax paid was lower.

[15]Bureau of the Census, *Wealth, Public Debt, and Taxation: 1922. Taxes Collected Compiled as a Part of the Decennial Report on Wealth, Public Debt, and Taxation* (Washington, D.C.: GPO, 1924), 12.

Table 14–1
Tax-Source Separation, 1970, 1994, and 2003: Percentage of Revenue from Tax Collected by Level of Government

	Federal			State			Local		
	1970	1994	2003	1970	1994	2003	1970	1994	2003
Reliance of levels of government on tax sources									
Taxes on property	0	0	0	2.3	2.2	1.9	84.9	74.8	73.4
Taxes on individual and corporate income	84.4	87.6	89.4	26.9	38.3	38.3	4.2	5.7	5.2
Taxes on sales or gross receipts	12.5	9.6	6.5	56.8	49.8	49.9	7.9	15.0	16.4
Other taxes	3.1	2.8	4.0	14.0	3.2	9.9	3.0	0.4	5.0
Distribution of tax sources by level of government									
Taxes on property	0	0	0	3.5	4.3	4.9	96.8	95.7	96.5
Taxes on individual and corporate income	89.4	81.3	80.0	9.4	17.0	18.2	1.2	1.7	1.8
Taxes on sales or gross receipts	37.6	25.0	16.7	56.1	62.3	67.6	6.3	12.7	15.8
Other taxes	36.6	65.3	36.2	53.9	33.9	47.1	9.4	2.7	16.7

SOURCE: Government Finance Division, U.S. Bureau of Census and Executive Office of the President, Office of Management and Budget, *Historical Tables, Budget of the United States Government, Fiscal year 2005* (Washington, D.C.: U.S. GPO, 2004).

The source remains distinctly for local use but local governments are reducing their reliance on it.

The federal government nearly monopolized the income base in 1970: Of the total individual and corporate collections, 89.4 percent were at the federal level. The highest federal marginal rate on individuals was 70 percent at that time, so neither states nor localities were much inclined to add any tax to that rate, even though very few individuals would have been subject to such punitive rates. The highest federal marginal rate now is only about half that high, making state-local income taxes more attractive. By 2003 the federal share of income taxes had fallen about 9 percentage points (to 80.0 percent), the state share had risen around 9 percentage points (to 18.2 percent), and the local share had increased to 1.8 percent. Federal dominance in income taxation continues, but source separation is not nearly so complete as it was three decades earlier.

The pattern of sales and gross receipts tax separation is less easily summarized. The federal government collected a lower share (37.6 percent) in 1970 than did states (56.1 percent); local use was minimal (only 6.3 percent). In the years since, the federal share from selective excises (taxes on motor fuel and alcoholic beverages constitute over half of such revenue) has fallen by half; state governments have increased their use of general-sales taxes; and local governments have added both general-sales and selective-excise taxes. State use dominates at 67.6 percent, the federal share has fallen to 16.7 percent, and the local share has doubled to 15.8

percent. There has never been a federal general consumption tax of any sort, although there have been periodic attempts to levy a value-added tax and, recently, a national retail sales tax. Either would be a movement away from base separation and would complicate state use of the base.

Governments show little taste for source separation as a response to vertical-coordination problems; all want access to the "better" sources, regardless of how that may confuse tax administration, compliance, and transparency of the levy. Only sources viewed rightly or wrongly as inferior (like the property tax) are likely to be happily shed by any level of government. Although source separation would be orderly, most governments would prefer expanded revenue options.

Fortunately, there are coordination mechanisms that accommodate more than one level of government using a single tax base. These include (1) cooperative administration, (2) coordinated tax bases, (3) tax supplements, and (4) centralized administration.[16] *Cooperative administration* involves continuous contact and information exchange among taxing units. Sales tax administrators may inform their peers when a firm is found to be violating tax laws in a manner that would generate liability in other states. Income tax administrators may exchange information about audits. The Internal Revenue Service (IRS) may inform a state about audit findings for an individual living in that state. Business tax administrators may exchange information about contractors who should be registered to pay taxes in other states. Coordination is weak but profitable for the administering parties: Work done by one administration can generate revenue for another with little or no additional work. Base, rates, and rate structures need not coincide among governments for this cooperation, but all governments can gain from the exchange. Indeed, every state in the United States links its income tax administration closely to the work of the IRS and relies heavily on IRS enforcement.

With *coordinated tax bases,* one government links its tax to some point in the tax structure of another government. For example, several states key their individual income tax to federal adjusted gross income, and a number of localities begin their local sales tax ordinances with definitions taken from their state sales tax. Other elements of the tax may differ from that point—different exemptions, rate patterns, rate levels, and so on—but the higher- and lower-level taxes have important common elements. The links reduce taxpayer-compliance problems (one set of records can be used for both taxes, and some of the computations need not be replicated) and simplify administration across governments. However, substantial differences between the taxes reduce the gains in both compliance and administration.

Tax supplements provide more coordination, either through applying a lower-level rate on the base used by the higher level (many state sales taxes have supplements added by localities) or applying a lower-level rate that is a percentage of tax paid to the higher level (a few states define their income tax to be a percentage of federal liability). This method dramatically reduces compliance requirements for taxpayers and cuts administration expenses when the supplementing unit refrains

[16]George Break, *Financing Government in a Federal System* (Washington, D.C.: Brookings Institution, 1980), 34.

from adding extra features. Few government units can refrain from at least a few changes, and each change cuts the savings to taxpayers.

The final coordination system is *central administration* of a "piggyback" tax: A lower-government unit applies its own rate to the tax base used by a higher-government unit. Full piggybacking would have the higher unit doing all administrative and enforcement work—the taxpayer reports on a single form to the higher unit, which records for and remits collections to the lower unit. Lower units must adopt the tax to receive revenue (it is not simply a system of tax sharing), but they cannot select a base different from that used by the higher unit. Administrative economies are possible with single-unit administration, and the taxpayer can comply with multiple obligations at one time. Supplemental tax rates, however, do not permit a redistribution of resources among lower units. Most local sales taxes piggyback on their state sales tax—often, the local tax return consists only of some extra lines on the state sales tax return—and local income taxes in Maryland, Indiana, and Iowa are similarly supplements to the state return. Most local income taxes, however, are not related to either federal or state taxes. States that continue a state property tax do apply them to the locally administered base, a rare example of piggybacking from state to local.[17] Piggybacking obviously provides considerable economy in collection, but at the cost of transparency in taxation. Taxpayers seldom know, without considerable checking, which government is levying which tax on them.

Coordination and Assistance: Grants

Grants transfer spending power (command over resources) from one government to another. In a multilevel governmental relationship, like that between the federal government and the states or between a state and its localities, grants can compensate governments for benefit spillovers to nonresidents, reduce the problems created by fiscal disparity, encourage programs of special national merit, reduce special problems associated with regional economic decline, and induce governments toward management reform as a condition for receiving aid.[18] In other words, they can have a purpose in a federal system, beyond simply using the supposedly stronger revenue administration capacity of the higher level to raise money for the lower level.

There is a classic conflict between the donor and the recipient in transfer systems, a conflict that can never be entirely resolved. The donor government raises

[17]In Canada, the federal government administers provincial individual and corporate income taxes and some provincial sales taxes are harmonized with the national goods and services (value-added) tax for federal collection. In Quebec, provincial authorities administer the national goods and service tax along with the provincial retail sales tax.

[18]U.S. General Accounting Office, *Federal Grants: Design Improvements Could Help Federal Resources Go Further,* GAO/AIMD-97-7 (Washington, D.C.: GPO, 1996). A number of local governments instituted external financial audits for the first time because that was a condition to receive federal revenue-sharing funds.

the revenue, bearing whatever political burdens may be associated with the revenue function. The recipient government gets any political benefits associated with service delivery. Because the recipient did not have to raise the money, might it be likely that the funds will be mismanaged or misallocated? To prevent such carelessness (or worse), the donor seeks controls, or "strings," on the use of the funds. The recipient government, of course, views the situation differently. The granting government is less familiar with local conditions, needs, and priorities. Any controls make service delivery more difficult and reduce the ability to provide needed services. The controls that the donor seeks to ensure accountability are viewed by the recipient as barriers to effective response.

A significant amount of the money spent by state and local governments comes from assistance provided by other levels of government. The general pattern of intergovernmental aid between 1971–1972 and 2001–2002 appears in Table 14–2. In 2001–2002, 31.5 percent of state revenue and 40 percent of local revenue was assistance in the form of grants from other levels of government. Aid to states was mostly from the federal government (94.7 percent in 2001–2002), and aid to localities was mostly from their states (89.2 percent). Among local governments, aid is particularly vital to school districts; they received 56.9 percent of their general revenue from aid in 2001–2002, with 95.7 percent of that coming from states. States receive a somewhat increased share of revenue from aid in 2001–2002 compared with 1971–1972 (from 28.4 percent to 31.6 percent), but there are considerable changes in aid shares for local governments. Reliance has fallen for cities (32.9 percent to 29.8 percent) and for counties (42.1 percent to 38.4 percent), but risen considerably for school districts (45.0 percent to 56.9 percent). The important increase in aid to schools comes from state government, for reasons that are discussed later in this chapter.

The flows of federal aid to state and local government have recently increased. As Table 14–3 shows, aid rose through the late 1970s to the mid-1980s to more than 20 percent of total state-local general revenue, but then fell as the environment became what John Shannon called "fend-for-yourself federalism," one in which governments spending money were expected to raise that money.[19] Recent real (and percentage) increases have been driven by what the federal budget classifies as outlays for state and local government aid for payments to individuals, including Medicaid and certain welfare programs, through which state administrative agencies distribute federal assistance. That category now constitutes almost two-thirds of the total.[20] Aid for regular state and local programs, the "Other" class in Table 14–3, is dramatically less than during the 1970s. A considerable amount of the capi-

[19]John Shannon, "The Return to Fend-for-Yourself Federalism: The Reagan Mark," *Intergovernmental Perspective* 13 (Summer–Fall 1987): 34–37. The United States expects subnational governments to raise a considerably greater share of the money spent than do most other nations, including the major federal states (Australia, Canada, and Germany)—it always has, and probably always will.

[20]Medicaid provides medical assistance for low-income people who are aged, blind, disabled, members of families with dependent children, and certain other pregnant women and children. States establish their own coverage rules, scope of benefits offered, and amounts paid for services, all within guidelines established by the federal government. The federal government then pays a portion of the total spent by the state, according to an annually adjusted rate that ranges between 50 and 83 percent, the rate inversely related to state per capita income. This is a categorical formula grant program.

Table 14–2
Sources of Intergovernmental Revenue ($ millions)

		Intergovernmental Revenue			
	Total General Revenue	Total	From Federal	From State	From Local
1971–1972					
State	98,632	27,981	26,791	—	1,191
Local	105,243	39,694	4,551	35,143	—
Cities	34,998	11,528	2,538	8,434	556
Counties	23,652	9,956	405	9,252	299
School districts	39,256	17,653	749	16,471	433
1991–1992					
State	608,804	169,928	159,068	—	10,861
Local	579,083	217,996	20,107	197,890	—
Cities	175,116	49,474	8,103	37,380	3,992
Counties	148,367	55,292	3,243	49,663	2,386
School districts	198,320	107,160	1,354	103,084	2,722
1996–1997					
State	815,442	230,859	215,839	—	1,020
Local	747,030	287,003	28,768	258,235	—
Cities	222,190	62,851	11,699	45,932	5,220
Counties	191,271	71,751	4,890	64,007	2,854
School districts	257,342	141,974	1,762	137,246	2,966
2001–2002					
State	1,062,305	335,423	317,581	—	17,842
Local	995,856	398,497	42,953	355,544	—
Cities	285,545	85,114	15,201	62,405	7,508
Counties	256,684	98,648	7,539	86,759	4,349
School districts	350,793	199,544	3,632	191,145	4,767
Rate of Change, 1971–1972 to 2001–2002 (%)					
State	8.2	8.6	8.6	—	9.4
Local	7.8	8.0	7.8	8.0	—
Cities	7.2	6.9	6.1	6.9	9.1
Counties	8.3	7.9	10.2	7.7	9.3
School districts	7.6	8.4	5.4	8.5	8.3

SOURCE: U.S. Bureau of Census, Governments Division.

tal investment aid comes through trust funds supporting highways and airports. In terms of government function, virtually all federal aid comes through four categories: health, income security, education, and transportation, as Table 14–3 shows. Growth in Medicaid spending is particularly important for the increase and it is the largest single federal grant program to state and local government.

Both federal and state governments operate intergovernmental assistance programs. Many problems and structural features are common to both. The federal

Table 14–3
Federal Aid to State and Local Governments

Fiscal Year	Federal Outlays for Grants to State-Local Governments ($ billions constant 2000)	Percent Grants for			Percent of Grants by Function				Federal Aid as % State-Local General Revenue
		Individuals	Capital Investment	Other Purposes	Transportation	Education	Health	Income	Security
1960	39	30.8	43.6	25.6	42.7	7.5	3	37.5	13.7
1965	56.7	29.8	42.7	27.5	37.6	9.6	5.7	32.2	14.9
1970	105.3	31.8	25.8	42.4	19.1	26.7	16	24.1	16.7
1975	157.7	30.4	16.5	53.1	11.8	24.4	17.7	18.8	20.6
1980	192.6	33.2	20.2	46.7	14.2	23.9	17.2	20.2	21.7
1985	163.1	46	21	33	16.1	16.1	23.1	26.3	17.8
1990	172.1	56.1	18.9	24.9	14.2	16.1	32.4	27.2	16.1
1995	247.9	63.6	17.5	19	11.5	13.7	41.6	25.9	19.6
2000	284.7	64.1	17.1	18.8	11.3	12.9	43.9	24.1	18.9
2005	347	65.5	14.4	20.2	10.2	13.4	46.4	21.3	n.a.

SOURCES: Bureau of Census, Governments Division and Executive Office of the President, Office of Management and Budget, *Historical Tables: Budget of the United States Government, Fiscal Year 2007* (Washington, D.C.: U.S. GPO, 2006).
n.a., Data not available.

grant system has included three types of assistance: (1) categorical grants, (2) block grants, and (3), from 1972 through 1986, general revenue sharing.[21] The last is a type of general fiscal assistance, a more common element of state to local grant programs. There is much hybridization of grant styles, making clear classification difficult. However, the great preponderance of federal grant programs—measured in both numbers and in outlay totals—are for categorical grants.[22]

State aid systems have some elements similar to the federal systems, although each state has its own peculiar mix. State grants to general-purpose local governments (mostly cities and counties) have always been for relatively broad purposes. The grants sometimes distribute earmarked percentages of certain state taxes. In a later section, we examine state aid to schools, a major component of total state aid.

Categorical Grants

Categorical grants finance specific and narrowly defined programs, usually limited to spending for certain activities, such as constructing a wastewater-treatment plant or paying salaries of special education teachers. Such aid seeks to induce the recipient government to behave in a fashion other than the way it would behave without the aid. The grants encourage recipient governments to shift expenditures to particular functions or to guarantee provision of certain recipient government services in a manner consistent with national interest. In these areas, narrow local interest and national interest presumably do not coincide. The grant changes the returns as seen by the recipient to make certain activities more attractive—the federal share makes the aided activity cheaper for the lower-level government—so that recipient actions coincide with national interest.

Categorical grants may be:

1. **Formula,** in which aid is distributed among eligible governments according to a legislatively or administratively determined formula. Formula elements may include population, population in certain demographic categories, per capita income, unemployment, energy use, housing categories, fiscal capacity, program performance, highway lane miles, or other measures. For example, the Dingell-Johnson Sport Fish Restoration Program (Federal Aid in Sport Fish Restoration Act of 1950) distributes funds to state fish and wildlife agencies according to a formula that includes the state share of land and water area, miles of coastline, and of paid fishing license holders.[23]

2. **Project,** in which aid is distributed at the discretion of the administrator for particular projects. These grants are usually awarded on a competitive basis

[21]The federal government also assists state and local governments through credit, either directly via loans and advances or indirectly through loan guarantees.

[22]Advisory Commission on Intergovernmental Relations, *Characteristics of Federal Grant-in-Aid Programs to State and Local Governments: Grants Funded FY 1995,* M-195 (Washington, D.C.: ACIR, 1995), 3.

[23]U.S. General Services Administration, *Catalog of Federal Domestic Assistance* (Washington, D.C.: GPO, 1997): 357–58.

from applications made to support a particular proposal from a state or local government (or other entity).

3. **Project/formula,** in which aid is distributed at the discretion of the administrator within constraints set by a formula that limits amounts awarded in a state. For instance, the National Recreational Trails Funding Program (16 U.S.C. 1261) supports specific trail project proposals, within a statutory formula: 50 percent of funds are allocated equally among states and 50 percent are allocated according to off-road recreational fuel use in the state.[24]

These grants may have *matching* provisions that require the recipient to spend a specified sum for each dollar spent by the federal government in the grant (match can often be in-kind contribution to a program, e.g., office space, rather than in cash) or *maintenance of effort* provisions that require the recipient to continue a specified level of spending in a specific area to receive the federal funds and to use the funds to supplement, not supplant, spending.[25]

Project grants—about 70 percent of all categorical grant programs, but considerably less than half of total categorical aid outlay—are the realm of the grants person, the individual assigned by many state and local governments and nonprofit agencies to manage the quest for external assistance. (Formula and reimbursement categories plus the block and revenue-sharing assistance examined later do not require competitive application.) This person becomes familiar with the activities of federal agencies and private foundations (state governments tend not to use project grants) and watches available funding announcements published in sources such as the Federal Register and the Catalog of Federal Domestic Assistance (OMB/General Services Administration). When project requirements and the activities of the government coincide, the manager prepares a project proposal. The funding-agency awards go to proposals evaluated as best according to legislative and regulatory constraints. Decisions are based on the extent to which the proposal responds to the requirements presented in the funding advertisement, the extent to which the proposer demonstrates ability to carry out the project, and other factors such as the creativity or novelty of the project approach or the possibility that results may be used elsewhere. Selection criteria and weighting among factors is usually published with program announcements. Skeptics stress the significance of noncompetitive, political factors in some assistance programs, however. These are the earmarked or pork-barrel projects described in an earlier chapter. Sidebar 14–1 outlines basic rules for writing a grant proposal to a governmental or nongovernmental donor.

One peculiarity of the categorical grant must be recognized. For the recipient, the grant is most valuable if it supports an activity the recipient was going to undertake even without the assistance. In that case, there is minimal disruption of local interest, and resources are released for use in accord with local priorities. For the

[24]Ibid., 506.

[25]Evidence indicates that about sixty cents of each federal grant dollar substitutes for state funds that would have been spent anyway. U.S. General Accounting Office, *Federal Grants*, GAO/AIMD-97-7, 2.

Sidebar 14–1
Some Basic Guides for Writing Grant Proposals

Most federal assistance to state and local governments is provided on a noncompetitve basis for particular programs, as is virtually all state aid to their local governments. However, some assistance is awarded competitively to particular projects on the basis of grant proposals, as are awards from foundation and other nongovernmental organizations. Although grant writing is more art than science, there are a few simple steps that can assist in grant proposal preparation.

1. Read the materials provided by the granting entity with great care. Often the information comes in the form of a "request for proposals" (RFP) and the instructions included there are to be followed scrupulously. The RFP indicates deadlines for submission (which, for federal agencies and most other donors, are rigidly enforced), instructions for submission, format and style for the submission, and a description of the kind of projects than can be proposed. The proposed project must fit the intent and guidelines of the competition. If it doesn't, then writing the proposal is just a waste of time.
2. Write the proposal in the language of the RFP. The proposal should use exactly the same terminology, key phrases, concepts, and so on that the RFP uses. One grantsperson has described this as "writing the RFP back to the agency." This approach is effective in part because the people who wrote the RFP are likely to be evaluating the proposals and seeing their own words coming back is a nice form of flattery. Besides, they are experts in the area being supported and this degree of consistency is only logical. If you can't use the terminology of the RFP in what you are proposing, then probably this isn't the right grant competition for the project you have in mind.
3. Keep in contact with the granting entity. Unless there are rules that forbid advance contact, you should let the agency know that your proposal will be coming and you should find out as much about the agency's interests as you can. Part of this work involves studying proposals that have been funded by the agency in the past, if they are available for public inspection, so that you can get hints about what might be sensible in your project and how successful projects have been structured. Even if full proposals are not available, you should be able to obtain brief abstracts, and these can be helpful as you develop your proposal. Many grant competitions have "no contact" periods after the submission deadline. You may not contact the agency about your proposal after that date and you must take care not to cross the line and have your proposal ruled ineligible by accident.
4. Follow the traditional guidelines for preparing budget requests (review the relevant sections of Chapter 4) in your proposal because, after all, a budget request and a grant proposal are exactly the same in logic. The proposal must describe what is intended in the project, what resources will be necessary, what funds are requested, and what results of the project are expected—just as with a fully developed agency budget request. The RFP frequently specifies a format for the submission and it usually specifies a particular budget classification structure and certain standards for the budget. These requirements need to be followed to make the proposal eligible for consideration.
5. Agencies frequently enter into negotiations about the proposal after the first review of competitors. To receive a call for further information or for revisions of your proposal is usually a good sign because it means that your proposal has passed the first set of tests and the chances that your proposal will be funded are very good.

Grant proposals, even for good projects, are not always successful. Following these simple steps can improve the likelihood that a strong project—and some not-so-strong ones—will receive support.

donor, the grant is most powerful when it supports activities not ordinarily undertaken at levels consistent with the donor's interest. Thus, there is some divergence of interest between recipient and donor in a well-designed categorical grant.

Critics of the categorical grant system emphasize three particular difficulties. First is the administrative complexity of the categorical grant system. In an effort to ensure that federal policy objectives are met as nearly as possible by the recipients, federal programs establish elaborate control mechanisms to monitor and shape actions taken by the recipient. Systems usually have different planning, application, reporting, and accounting requirements—none of which coincide with those ordinarily used by the recipient government. Not only are these controls an irritation, but they also divert state and local resources to the administrative process.

A second criticism is the program overlap and duplication that has emerged in the federal grant system. Complexity means that some communities do not participate, leaving their residents less well served than would be desirable. Other local governments aggressively seek funds, producing extraordinary assistance for their residents. Government may even use funds from one program to meet another program's matching requirements, thus thwarting the intention of matching to stimulate local expenditure.

Third, critics complain that categorical grants distort local priorities. Although grant requirements try to reflect national interests, the distortion may exceed the level justified by the traditional spillover-of-local-action argument. Furthermore, the aid may not be reliable. Aid may be eliminated after a few years, leaving state and local governments with program responsibility but no resources. The combination of these criticisms has been instrumental in movement toward block assistance and calls for a return to general-purpose assistance.

Block Grants

Block grants are usually distributed to general-purpose governments (categorical grants often go to special-purpose governments or nongovernments) according to a statutory formula to finance activities in a broad functional area. Recipients have considerable discretion in how to spend the money. Among the features of federal block grants are that "aid is authorized for a wide range of activities within a broadly defined functional area; recipients have substantial discretion to identify problems, design programs, and allocate resources; administrative, fiscal reporting, planning, and other federally imposed requirements are limited to those necessary to ensure that national goals are being accomplished; and federal aid is distributed on the basis of statutory formula with few, if any, matching requirements and, historically, spending has been capped."[26] Federal block grants support programs that include health (Community Mental Health Services, Prevention and Treatment of Substance Abuse, Maternal and Child Health Services, Preventive Health and

[26]U.S. General Accounting Office, *Block Grants: Issues in Designing Accountability Provisions,* GAO/AIMD-95-226 (Washington, D.C.: General Accounting Office, 1995), 4.

Health Services), crime control (Local Law Enforcement, Juvenile Accountability Incentive), community development (Community Development), social services (Social Services, Child Care and Development, Low-Income Home Energy Assistance, Community Services), aid for the needy (Temporary Assistance for Needy Families), and emergency management (Emergency Management Performance).[27] The largest single surge of conversion from categorical to block grants in terms of programs involved was in the Omnibus Reconciliation Act of 1981 (P.L. 97–35), when fifty-seven categoricals were consolidated into nine block grants (social services; home-energy assistance; community development; elementary and secondary education; alcohol, drug abuse, and mental health; maternal and child care; community services; primary health care; and preventative health and health services). Federal welfare reform, through the Personal Responsibility and Work Opportunity Reconciliation Act of 1996 (P.L. 104–193) added welfare to the list of block aid to states by replacing Aid to Families with Dependent Children (AFDC), a formula entitlement paid to states for distribution to needy mothers and children, with a multiyear fixed appropriation block grant to states for support of the welfare programs. The appropriated amount is distributed among states by a formula based on money each state received for programs it replaced in the higher of fiscal 1994, fiscal 1995, or the average of fiscal 1992–1994. State programs must be within certain federal standards and states must achieve certain performance goals to continue to receive the funds.

The Advisory Commission on Intergovernmental Relations (ACIR) maintained that block grants with "well-designed allocation formulas and eligibility provisions" could:

1. Provide aid to those jurisdictions having the greatest programmatic needs, and give them a reasonable degree of fiscal certainty.
2. Accord recipients substantial discretion in defining problems, setting priorities, and allocating resources.
3. Simplify program administration and reduce paperwork and overhead.
4. Facilitate interfunctional and intergovernmental coordination and planning.
5. Encourage greater participation on the part of elected and appointed generalist officials in decision-making.[28]

Block grants should not be expected to stimulate new recipient-government initiatives and should be confined to activities for which a broad consensus already exists. Block grants are not designed to bend local choices in a direction more consistent with national interest or to cause local government units to change their operating methods. They may replace groups of similar categoricals that have already established strong local clienteles. But critics complain that block grants, especially community development block grants, usually aid affluent as well as poor communities, and some funds get used in ways that would stretch congressional intentions.

---

[27]Plus special block grants for Native Americans.

[28]Advisory Commission on Intergovernmental Relations, *Characteristics, op. cit.,* (1995), 24.

Revenue Sharing (General-Purpose Fiscal Assistance)

The third variety of federal grants is revenue sharing, a formula distribution with few or no restrictions on the use of funds provided.[29] The federal revenue-sharing program, started in 1972, used a formula to distribute multiyear appropriations to states and general-purpose local governments. The funding approach—appropriation rather than a share of certain taxes—provided some greater certainty of aid during the appropriation's life (unforeseen changes in federal revenue did not influence distributed shares), but the funds had to be appropriated again when the appropriation period expired. The program was the primary source of the increase in the federal share of state and local general revenue in 1975 and 1980 that was shown in Table 14–3. Each renewal raised questions about the program's continuation; the entire program was excluded from the 1986 budget. Similar (and older) state tax-sharing programs typically dedicate a given share of selected taxes (e.g., 1 percentage point of the state sales tax rate) to a local-aid formula.

Revenue sharing distributed funds according to a formula that combined population, percentage of urban population, tax effort, income tax effort, and per capita income to define the appropriate shares. State governments initially received one-third of revenue-sharing funds but were gradually removed: The 1980 extension of the program discontinued the share for any state not giving up categorical grants equal to the allocation received, and, as noted previously, the state share ended entirely in 1983. Local general-purpose governments (cities, counties, Native American governments, townships, etc.) continued receiving aid through the life of the program. Checks were sent to each eligible government without application and with only minimal restrictions concerning use (there had to be a publicized appropriation process, there could be no discrimination in hiring or compensation, funds could not be used for grant matching, use had to be subject to external financial audit, etc.).

Although federal revenue sharing ended at the national level in 1986, such programs continue as an important feature of several state fiscal systems, including those of Michigan, Alaska, Louisiana, Florida, Maine, and Wisconsin. The distributions are sometimes of dedicated shares of particular taxes and sometimes of specific appropriations. The distributions are by formula and the funds are for general use by the recipient government with few if any controls. When these distributions are on a per capita basis, they reduce fiscal disparity to an extent because the per capital amount provides greater relative assistance to lower-capacity areas than to higher-capacity ones. High-capacity areas pay more into the state aid pool than they receive in return.

Programs of revenue or tax sharing can strengthen local spending power and reduce intergovernmental disparities (the great differences in fiscal capacity that exist among governments at the same level across the nation or within a state). Such pro-

[29]Although they are not general, the federal government does have a few shared taxes, levied at the federal level for formula distribution to state government for specific use. The most significant of these support the highway and airport and airway trust funds. These funds do have to be appropriated, however; they are not automatically distributed to states.

grams would not shape local priorities to make them more consistent with national interest because of the lack of controls placed on the assistance. They would not be particularly effective as a way to aid disadvantaged groups because advantaged and disadvantaged tend, with few exceptions, to live in the same political jurisdictions. General aid to the jurisdiction can improve capacity to provide services (or reduce taxes with no change in services) for anyone, and probably the advantaged will do better because they usually have greater political clout. Revenue sharing should not be expected to achieve the targeting and revision of public action that categorical programs can produce. Revenue sharing can reduce fiscal disparity among governments and strengthen the expenditure capability of government units with constrained taxing powers.

Tax-sharing programs from central to subnational governments are a common feature of the finances of many countries, including both unitary and federal systems and many countries of the former Soviet Union, but not the United States. In these programs, the central government adopts a tax, for instance, an individual income tax, and establishes what share of collections will be assigned regional or local governments, for instance, 25 percent. In this example, 25 percent of individual income tax collected in each region or locality is distributed to that government. Fiscal choices are made centrally, but a share of the tax accrues to the lower-tier government.

States and School Aid

Primary and secondary education in the United States has traditionally been a local responsibility, either of independent school districts or, in some larger cities, of city governments. That arrangement allows local decision making and control, so that choices can be made by governments close to the families affected most by the schools. But state governments have ultimate responsibility for the provision of education; state constitutions contain education clauses that require the state to provide statewide systems of education that are "equitable," "thorough and efficient," "adequate," "general and uniform," and so forth.[30] Local finance seems likely to violate the idea of a "statewide" system because local fiscal capacity (the local tax base) per pupil—and thus access to educational resources—varies widely among districts. Not all school districts are created equal, so how can the education that they provide be considered equitable across the state? How can this state-provided system

[30]Earlier concerns with equal-protection violations of the U.S. Constitution were resolved in favor of the states in 1973. See *Rodriguez* v. *San Antonio Independent School District,* 411 U.S. 1 (1973). Recent challenges have involved state constitutional requirements. Some of the challenges have brought increased school spending, but some appear to have caused spending to be less than would otherwise have been expected. See Robert L. Manwaring and Steven M. Sheffrin, "Litigation, School Finance Reform, and Aggregate Education Spending," *International Tax and Public Finance* 4 (May 1997): 107–27. Only Delaware, Hawaii, Mississippi, Nevada, and Utah have not have a lawsuit over such school finance issues. Jennifer Carr and Cara Griffith, "School Finance Litigation and Property Tax Reform: Part I, Litigation," *State Tax Notes* (June 27, 2005): 1015.

of education be accommodated with local control when localities have significant differences in preferences for schooling and in fiscal resources to fund those schools?

There are no simple answers to the dilemma, but one response has been an increased state role in public school finance (Table 14–4). The trend shows an expanding state role in finance, from 30.3 percent of total revenues in 1940 to 49.0 percent in 2002–2003, and a falling local role, 68.0 percent to 42.7 percent. (The federal role is greater as well, increased from 1.8 percent to 8.4 percent, but still small.) But 2002–2003 state shares do vary widely, from 34.1 percent in South Dakota to 90.1 percent in Hawaii.[31] Local school finance remains almost exclusively a matter of property taxation (96 percent of school tax revenue), whereas state finances are usually balanced between sales and income taxes and provide an opportunity for state-aid systems to offset disparities in resources between local districts.

School-aid systems that states use are remarkable for their complexity as legislators seek to balance local control, state responsibility, and protection for their home districts. It should be no surprise that distribution formulas combine various philosophies, but there are three general systems that have been devised to distribute basic state aid:[32]

1. **Flat grants, general and categorical.** In a few states, every school district receives the same dollar amount per pupil from the state. There is no distinction between high-affluence and low-affluence districts. Some aid may be distributed according to types of students or to finance certain categories of expenditure (such as student transportation on a bus-mile basis).

2. **Foundation grants.** The foundation programs, used in about three-fourths of the states, aid in direct proportion to the number of students and inversely

Table 14–4
Public School District Revenues by Source of Funds, Percentage of Total

School Year	Federal	State	Local
1939–1940	1.8	30.3	68.0
1949–1950	2.9	39.8	57.3
1959–1960	4.4	39.1	56.5
1969–1970	8.0	39.9	52.1
1979–1980	9.8	46.8	43.4
1989–1990	6.1	47.2	46.6
2002–2003	8.4	49.0	42.7

SOURCES: U.S. Department of Education, National Center for Education Statistics, Digest of Education Statistics 1992 (Washington, D.C.: 1992), table 148, and Government Finance Division, U.S. Bureau of Census, Public Education Finance. Available online at ftp2.census.gov/govs/school/03f33pub.pdf.

[31]Government Finances Division, U.S. Bureau of Census, *Public Education Finance: 1992–93*, GF/93, No. 5 (Washington, D.C.: GPO, 1995).

[32]Katherine L. Bradbury, "Equity in School Finance: State Aid to Local Schools in New England," *New England Economic Review* (Mar./Apr. 1993): 25–46.

with local property tax base per pupil. Aid per pupil to a district equals the difference between the per-pupil foundation spending level (the amount of expenditure the state determines to be the minimum acceptable) and the per-pupil revenue the district would collect by applying the statewide target tax rate to the district tax base. States usually require the district to spend at least the foundation amount to receive aid.

3. **Guaranteed tax base (or percentage equalizing).** These formulas provide aid to districts to make up the difference between what the district tax rate raises on the district tax base and what the district tax rate would raise if applied to a guaranteed tax base. Therefore, without regard to actual district affluence per pupil, all districts will raise the same tax per pupil from a given tax rate. Actual aid systems may add other factors, such as adjustments for differences in operating costs between districts, for service to special client populations, or to prevent substantial aid loss from year to year. The elements in a state formula may change often, as may the money the state puts into state aid. Many states create hybrids that distribute total aid according to more than one logical system.

States generally are uncomfortable with state school-aid systems. A considerable amount of state revenue has to be raised for school support, and many critics question whether its distribution satisfies the responsibility that states have for seeing to the provision of this service. Local control and state responsibility are real concerns that no system has fully resolved.

Coordination and Assistance: Mandates

A mandate is a constitutional provision, a statute, an administrative regulation, or a judicial ruling that places an expenditure requirement on a government. That requirement comes from outside the government forced to take the action.[33] A state government can mandate local spending, the federal government can mandate either state or local spending, and the judiciary—the branch of government outside the normal budgeting and appropriation flow—can mandate spending at any level. Mandates are like the operating restrictions that governments place on private industry to regulate workplace safety, environmental quality, and so on. Indeed, some costly mandates are simply extensions to government of these regulations of the private sector.[34] Much concern about mandates emerges at the local level

[33]Advisory Commission on Intergovernmental Relations, *State Mandating of Local Expenditures* (Washington, D.C.: ACIR, July 1978), 2. *Gideon* v. *Wainwright*, 372 U.S. 335 (1963), and *Argersinger* v. *Hamlin*, 407 U.S. 25 (1972), illustrate two court mandates.

[34]In *Garcia* v. *San Antonio Metropolitan Transit Authority*, 105 S. Ct. 479, 27 W.H. 65 (1985), the Supreme Court held that the federal Fair Labor Standards Act of 1938, mandating standards for overtime pay and minimum wages, applied to state and local government. The cost implications are substantial. In *Monell* v. *Department of Social Services of the City of New York*, 436 U.S. 658 (1978), the Court eroded the idea of sovereign immunity by extending the right of citizens to sue a government for negligent acts of its employees.

because these government units typically lack the size needed to respond flexibly to external expenditure shocks (few individual mandates would be sufficiently large, relative to overall expenditure, to significantly disrupt the federal government) and lack the revenue options available to other levels. States also express considerable concern for mandated cost, even as they place such cost on their localities.[35]

Mandates seek to cause governments to behave in some manner other than the way they would ordinarily behave. This changed behavior can be directed either toward (1) services and programs or (2) inputs used (normally, personnel). Examples of the former include such things as hours libraries will be open, provision of special education by local schools, jail-condition standards, water temperature in hospitals, provision of legal defense for indigents, and accessibility of facilities to all. Input-use mandates encompass required compensation levels, resources acquired, input quality and/or quantity, and the conditions under which the input will be employed. All potentially change the cost of providing any given level of service. Examples include states determining local welfare-department salaries; required employee training; required funding for pension systems; required participation in unemployment insurance or workers' compensation systems; and regulation of wages, hours, and working conditions. Several of this latter group are simply extensions of requirements applied to private employers.

Beyond the mandates, there are many other state controls on local government action because states establish the "rules of the game" for localities: election frequency, budget and finance structures, permissible forms of government, due process definitions, and so on. Many of these standards cause extra expenditure, but we accept them as reasonable costs of an informed democracy. Rules of the game, however, are often designed to reduce local government costs by limiting competition among local units, restricting direct democracy initiatives and official elections, constraining elected officials' salaries, or defining tax processes on a statewide basis. They are clearly of a different nature than the earlier group of mandates. Other interventions determine tax-burden distribution as the scope of local taxation is defined (e.g., residential electricity may be removed from the local sales tax base). Furthermore, these controls, along with controlling the rules of the game, are best considered with the home-rule issue and the balance between local power and state sovereignty.

The case for mandates has two logical elements. First, the benefit of a lower-unit action (or the cost of inaction) may spill beyond the lower unit's boundaries. For example, an irresponsible action by one government can reduce that unit's expenditures (and the taxes paid by those in that unit) while harming residents of adjacent governments; the state government may mandate service levels to prevent damaging innocent bystanders. Second, the legislature or the judiciary may view statewide uniformity as essential. The state may require equal expenditure per unit

[35]Governments also pick up restrictions as a result of accepting grants from federal or state governments. Grant controls create fewer logistical problems than ordinary mandates: The recipient government accepts obligations as a condition of accepting the funds. There is no compulsion to enter the system. The advisory commission on Intergovernmental Relations describes the major federal mandates in *Federal Regulation of State and Local Governments: The Mixed Records of the 1980s* (Washington, D.C.: ACIR, 1993).

for schools, sanitation, and so on, to prevent individuals from having low-service levels solely because of their residence. Expenditure correction thus is mandated.

Against these arguments for mandates are strong countercases. First, many argue that the mandating government unit should be responsible for financing the mandate. The mandate can become a political tool for the higher government unit while the lower government unit bears the burden of finance—a condition not conducive to careful decision making. Second, mandates can threaten other government programs. If limits constrain a government's ability to raise revenue, mandates for certain expenditures can endanger the provision of other desirable services. Third, mandates are characteristically enacted without cost awareness. Although the mandate's result may be desirable, the cost of its achievement may be excessive, particularly when compared with the return from other uses of government resources. Mandates seldom are imposed in an environment favorable to cost-benefit comparisons. This is particularly true when mandates emerge from the judiciary. More than half the states estimate the cost of state mandates to localities, but there is seldom any effort to identify the cost to the government units that must finance the expenditures. Finally, mandates restrict fiscal autonomy. Mandates are clearly an uneasy companion to home rule.

For decisions about mandates, the appropriate comparison would appear to be whether the resource cost created by the mandate is worth the return generated by the mandate. Inflicting costs on other units may not be a likely way to generate that comparison. Some suggest that mandates without financial assistance sufficient to cover their costs are a violation of intergovernmental fair play. Others point out that governments do not finance mandated activities for private firms or individuals (minimum-wage requirements, safety regulations, etc.); therefore, although, mandates may raise questions of appropriate governmental roles, they do not necessarily require accommodating fiscal transfers.

Concerns about cost imposed on state and local governments lead Congress to pass the Unfunded Mandates Reform Act of 1995 (UMRA, Public Law 104–4) in order "to end the imposition, in the absence of full consideration by Congress, of federal mandates on state, local, and tribal governments without adequate federal funding." Rather than prohibiting mandates or requiring that mandates be financed, the Act requires that the cost of mandates on subnational governments be explicitly identified by Congress before it approves a mandate.

The Act has three critical elements:[36]

1. **The Act defines** mandates to be "any provision in legislation, statute, or regulation that would impose an *enforceable duty* on state, local, or tribal governments or the private sector, or that would reduce or eliminate the amount of funding authorized to cover the costs of existing mandates." The definition includes direct requirements for state and local spending, provisions that preempt use of certain revenue sources by subnational governments, and reductions in

[36]Congressional Budget Office, *An Assessment of the Unfunded Mandates Reform Act in 1997* (Washington, D.C.: U.S. GPO, 1998).

federal aid that defrays subnational government costs of complying with existing federal mandates.

2. **The Act assigns** the Congressional Budget Office the task of informing congressional committees when their bills contain federal mandates. When the total direct costs of mandates in a bill exceed $60 million for governmental mandates in any of the first 5 fiscal years in which the mandate is effective, CBO must estimate those costs (if feasible) and the committees must publish these mandate statements. The CBO statement also assesses whether the bill provides funds to cover the costs of any new mandate.

3. **The Act provides** an enforcement mechanism. Neither house of Congress may consider legislation that contains mandates unless the bill has a CBO statement about costs of mandates and provides direct spending authority or authorization for appropriations sufficient to cover the costs. However, the provision is not self-enforcing—a member of Congress must raise a formal objection for the requirements to be applied. A majority of the body can pass the mandate anyway, but the provision guarantees debate on the mandate, should any member so wish.

The UMRA controls exclude certain types of mandates, including those preventing discrimination, establishing conditions of grants, and preempting state and local authority to regulate or provide services that do not carry state or local fiscal implications. The exclusion of grant conditions allows the federal government to continue its influence within the realm of state and local affairs. However, new grant conditions or funding caps for eleven entitlement grant programs, such as Medicaid, are defined as mandates under the Act if state and local governments lack authority to adjust these changes.

From the effective date of the Act in January 1996 through 2004, the CBO reported that fifty-eight bills proposed in Congress included intergovernmental mandates over the $50 million threshold (inflation adjusted to $60 million in 2004), but only five became law.[37] Whether this congressional restraint has been a result of the Act is unknown. However, laws with smaller mandates have been passed. And state and local governments note that nothing has been done about the existing mandates.

Conclusion

Multiple levels of government provide public services in the United States. That diversity allows greater individual choice, but service delivery cannot be entirely uncoordinated because of two factors: intergovernmental spillovers and fiscal imbalance. Spillovers occur when an action by one government has an impact (good or bad) on its neighbors. Intergovernmental intervention can induce governments

[37]Congressional Budget Office, *A Review of CBO's Activities in 2004 Under the Unfunded Mandates Reform Act* (Washington, D.C.: U.S. GPO, 2005).

to allow for those external effects. Imbalance emerges because fiscal capacity is unevenly distributed across the nation and within states. Without an intergovernmental response, some individuals will be unduly penalized by the public sector simply because of where they live.

Those intergovernmental problems can be reduced by three varieties of coordination: revenue adjustments (relief, administrative assistance, source separation, or coordinated use of a single base), grants (categorical, block, or revenue-sharing), or mandates. The devices together help retain the advantages of multilevel government without some associated problems.

CHAPTER 14 QUESTIONS AND EXERCISES

1. Your state constitution almost certainly contains an education clause. What does the clause say? How might it be used (or how has it already been used) to challenge the system of financing local schools?
2. Mundane County wants to develop an old railroad right-of-way into a hiking and bicycling trail. Examine the *Catalog of Federal Domestic Assistance* (it has a website that is easy to find) to determine whether federal aid might be available for the project. What critical points would need to be in the application to improve chances for its success? The *Catalog* has a guide to developing and writing grant proposals that is quite useful.
3. Which of the governmental functions listed in the United Nations Classification of Governmental Functions (Appendix 4–2) would normally be work for the central government, and which would normally be assigned to subnational governments?

CASES FOR DISCUSSION

CASE 14–1

It Worked Once, But Would It Work Again?

The following selection appeared in the *Wall Street Journal.* No questions about it are necessary.

The Squirrel Memo

Many releases and handouts that cross newspaper desks each day could be offered as prime exhibits for hiking the postal rates on unsolicited mail. But occasionally there's gold in them thar hills, and we offer as evidence a recent item from the news bureau of Washington and Lee University in Lexington, Virginia.

It seems that one Frank Parsons, assistant to the university president, was struggling with a lengthy application for federal funds to be used in building the university's proposed new library. Among other things, HEW wanted to know how the proposed project "may affect energy sources by introducing or deleting electromagnetic wave sources which may alter man-made or natural structures or the physiology, behavior patterns, and/or activities of 10 percent of a human, animal or plant population." The questions go on and on. But you get the idea.

Assistant Parsons plugged away, dutifully answering as best he could. And then he came to the section on animal populations, where he was asked to list the extent to which the proposed library would "create or precipitate an identifiable long-term change in the diversity of species within its natural habitat."

"There are some 10 to 20 squirrels living, or appearing to live, in the site proposed for the new library," he wrote. "Some trees that now provide either homes or exercise areas for the squirrels will be removed, but there appear to be ample other trees to serve either or both of these purposes. No major food source for the squirrels will be affected. It is likely that the squirrels will find no difficulty in adjusting to this intrusion. . . . They have had no apparent difficulty in adjusting to relocations brought on by nonfederally supported projects."

To the question of whether the proposal will "create or precipitate an identifiable change in the behavior patterns of an animal population," he assured HEW the squirrels and such would have to make some adjustments but "it will be difficult to tell if they're unhappy about having to find new trees to live in and sport about."

Eventually the application was shipped off to Washington, and lo and behold, before long HEW official Richard R. Holden actually wrote the president of the school. He said: "Perhaps bureaucracy will tremble, but I salute Washington and Lee University. . . . The mountain of paperwork which confronts me daily somehow seemed much smaller the day I read about the squirrels in Lexington. May they and your great university coexist in harmony for many, many years." As copies of the correspondence zipped throughout federal agencies, with all the speed of a confidential memo destined for Jack Anderson, bureaucrats from all over telephoned their congratulations to the "squirrel memo man."

We're still not sure exactly what lesson is to be drawn from all this. Our initial reaction was surprise that anyone actually reads these exhaustive applications, and even now we're undecided whether that's cause for comfort or dismay. Yet while we never doubted that HEW possessed a sense of humor—indeed, we've gotten some of our biggest laughs from proposals emanating from the vicinity of 330 Independence Ave., S.W.—it's nice to know that an occupational devotion to red tape has not completely eroded the agency's ability to laugh at itself.

SOURCE: Wall Street Journal, October 24, 1974. Reprinted with permission of the *Wall Street Journal,* © 1974 Dow Jones & Company, Inc. All rights reserved worldwide.

CASE 14–2

Correspondence, Subsidiarity, and the Tenn-Tom Waterway

Consider These Questions

1. According to the principle of subsidiarity, should the Tenn-Tom have been a federal, state, or local project?
2. If principles of subsidiarity and correspondence had been followed, is it likely that the waterway would have been built?
3. Is the Tenn-Tom a good use of public funds? Explain your position, whichever it may be.
4. What budget strategies do the supporters of the project appear to have employed? Could they have been as effective if the waterway were state financed instead of federally financed?

Geography

The Mississippi River provides a natural waterway—with significant help from locks and other government assistance along the way—through the central United States to the Gulf of Mexico at New Orleans. But for two hundred years some have dreamed of a cut-off further east—a waterway linking the Tennessee River and the Tombigbee Rivers to the Gulf at Mobile, Alabama, a short-cut to the sea for industrial cities of the North and a remedy for chronic unemployment in the areas through which the waterway would pass. In the French colonial era, the leaders of Mobile proposed a canal and towpath link to the Tennessee, but the King of France thought it extravagant. In the 1870s, the idea surfaced again, as a way to allow the year-round shipping on the Tombigbee that sandbars prevented during low-water season. The full waterway would provide a shorter route for cargoes passing through the Ohio River system from the direction of Louisville, Cincinnati, Pittsburgh, and beyond. The trip would be shorter, the nation's economy would be stimulated, and thousands of new jobs would be created.

Congress

The U.S. Congress authorized the project in 1946, but construction of the 234-mile waterway did not begin until 1972.[1] It opened for business in 1985, stretching from the Tennessee River immediately above the Yellow Creek port in northern Tishomingo County to the Demopolis lock connecting to the Tombigbee River, which empties into the Gulf at Mobile, Alabama. For any cargo heading to the Gulf of Mexico from the east, the system of ten locks,

[1]In the federal budget process, public infrastructure spending must be first authorized (or approved as a matter of government policy) and second appropriated (or provided funds, usually in 1-year blocks to the agency responsible for the project). The authorizing process is not concerned with budgets and financing, so there are far more infrastructure projects authorized than actually constructed.

dams, and ten man-made lakes in the states of Alabama and Mississippi reduced the trip by 235 miles. The project—five times longer than the Panama Canal—was the largest civil works ever undertaken by the U.S. Army Corps of Engineers, the primary public works agency of the federal government.

The Tenn-Tom Waterway had strong supporters in the U.S. Congress. It was the grand plan of powerful Southern politicians who steered the public work project through Congress in the 1970s and 1980s. While the project was under consideration and construction, the chairman of the House Appropriations Committee, the committee that must approve all federal appropriations, was Jamie Whitten of Mississippi, the member of Congress representing the part of northeastern Mississippi through which the waterway would flow. Chairman Whitten said, "Everything is in someone's district. I've got the position in Congress I most want. It doesn't mean you can run [the Appropriations Committee]. It just means you've got the first say."[2] And the chair of the House Appropriations Subcommittee on Energy and Water, the subcommittee through which all waterway development projects must go, was Tom Bevill of Alabama. But even these friends didn't provide complete political insulation. In 1981, when Congress threatened to stop funding, floodlights were installed on the waterway so that digging could continue through the night, getting the project so close to completion that its supporters could argue that to stop the canal would be a horrible waste of public funds.

The Numbers

U.S. Army Corps of Engineers estimates in the late 1970s showed a cost-benefit ratio of 1.2 to 1, based on a construction cost of $1.6 billion and $250 million that would be necessary for maintenance during the 50-year useful life of the waterway. For these estimates, the Corps followed the requirements of the Water Resources Development Act of 1974 and used a discount rate of 3.25 percent, the rate for federal borrowing. A rate estimated for tax funds would have been around 6.625 percent and the cost-benefit ratio would then have fallen to 0.64 to 1. Construction cost of the waterway finally amounted to $1.992 billion, compared with the initial appropriation estimate of $323 million (and only $117 million when the project was authorized). Its maintenance cost is now around $22 million per year.

Operations

Doubts expressed during development of the waterway about the generosity of other parts of the analysis have proven accurate. The U.S. Army Corps of Engineers estimated that the waterway would move 27.3 million tons of cargo in its first year of operation, eventually expanding to 40 million tons. However, actual traffic has proven to be much less. In 1993, 7.6 million tons of cargo was shipped; in 1988, when a drought made transport difficult on the Mississippi difficult, 10 million tons were shipped. In general shippers preferred the free-

[2]David Rogers, "Rivaling Cleopatra, A Pork-Barrel King Sails the Tenn-Tom," *The Wall Street Journal,* 31 May 1985, p. 1.

flowing Mississippi to the west and there have been few new industrial plants springing up along the waterway. The major products shipped on the waterway have been wood products (especially wood chips) and logs (about half the traffic), followed by coal. None of these are high-value, time-sensitive products for which speedier transit is critical. Indeed, transit via the Tenn-Tom appears to be more expensive than using the Mississippi because of the many locks and narrow path of the Waterway.[3]

[3]S. Chang and P.R. Forbus, "Tenn-Tom Versus the Mississippi River," *Transportation Journal XXV* (Summer 1986).

PART THREE

Administering Debt, Working Capital, and Pension Funds

Chapter 15 **Debt Administration**

Chapter 16 **Managing Funds: Cash Management and Employee Retirement Funds**

CHAPTER 15

Debt Administration

Federal, state, or local government debt results when that government borrows from an individual or institution. Borrowing changes the pattern of purchasing power between the lender and the borrower: The lender forgoes purchasing power now for the promise of repayment later, and the borrower receives purchasing power now with an obligation for repayment later. The bond representing that debt is a long-term promise by the borrower (bond issuer) to the lender (bondholder) to pay the bond's face amount (or par value or the principal of the loan) at a defined maturity date and to make contractual interest payments until the loan is retired.[1] The borrower is committed to debt service—interest payments as required plus periodic repayment of the principal—through the life of the loan.

Government debt results from (1) covering deficits (annual expenditures greater than annual revenues), (2) financing capital-project construction, and (3) covering short periods within a fiscal year in which bills exceed cash on hand. Not all governments borrow for the same set of reasons; in particular, the causes of the debt of the federal government are not the same as those behind the debt of state and local governments.

Federal Debt

The federal government's debt is the product of war finance, attempts to stabilize the nation's macroeconomy (i.e., to deal with problems of unemployment and

[1]Some governments, notably the British, have sold obligations with no maturity, but paying interest in perpetuity. Holders of these securities, called consols, may retrieve principal by sale to another investor. Another variation: Some debt is sold on a discount basis; the difference between what is paid for the debt instrument by the lender and the amount repaid by the borrower constitutes the interest. Short-term obligations—typically sold on a discount basis—are called bills and notes.

slow growth),[2] and miscellaneous political disputes that have caused expenditures to exceed receipts. As the General Accounting Office (GAO) explains:

> The federal deficit . . . is the difference between total federal spending and revenue in a given year. To cover this gap, the government borrows from the public. Each yearly deficit adds to the amount of debt held by the public. In other words, the deficit is the annual amount of government borrowing, while the debt represents the cumulative amount of outstanding borrowing from the public over the nation's history. . . . [Each year] the federal government pays only the interest costs of its debt. The principal is paid off when bonds come due. The cash to pay the principal comes from additional borrowing; hence the debt is "rolled over" or refinanced. To reduce its debt, the government would need to run a budget surplus and use the surplus funds to pay off the principal of maturing debt securities.[3]

There are two important measures of federal debt: *Gross debt* that equals all federal debt outstanding and *debt held by private investors* that equals all federal debt except that held by federal accounts and the Federal Reserve System. Figure 15–1 traces both measures of the federal debt since 1940, each as a percentage of gross domestic product (GDP) to accommodate the considerable difference in the size of the economy over those years. Debt rose dramatically—equaling 122 percent of GDP in 1946—as a consequence of financing World War II. From that peak, the percentage fell almost continuously until the mid-1970s—reaching a low of 34 percent in 1974—as economic growth was greater than the rate of increase of the debt. Occasional surpluses sometimes even allowed debt to be retired. There was a plateau period from the mid-1970s to the early 1980s, followed by an increase until the mid-1990s. From then until the first years of the new century, the debt-to-GDP ratio fell, but the recent record has been one of an increasing relationship as the brief era of budget surpluses ended.

Details on the federal debt appear in Table 15–1. Debt held by private investors is an impressive number—more than $3.8 trillion in 2005—but not as large as the gross federal debt—more than $7.9 trillion. The amount of debt in private-investor hands depends on accumulated federal deficits (gross public debt), monetary policy actions by the Federal Reserve that involve purchase and sale of federal debt, and federal trust funds' investable cash balances. Privately held debt excludes federal debt owned by elements of the federal government, leaving debt that represents a net requirement for resource transfer to private holders as the debt is serviced.

---

[2]Management of the federal debt, including the mechanics of issuing new debt, is intimately connected to decisions about and implementation of national monetary and fiscal policy. A good history of the federal debt and how it has been managed is Donald R. Stabile and Jeffrey A. Cantor, *The Public Debt of the United States: Historical Perspective, 1775–1990* (Westport, Conn.: Praeger, 1991). Most of the federal debt has been issued by the Treasury, but a small amount, less than 1 percent of total federal debt held by the public, has been issued by agencies directly (Tennessee Valley Authority, Corporation, Architect of the Capitol, National Archives, Federal Housing Administration, etc.). This agency debt has little practical difference from the rest and is included with federal totals. Office of Management and Budget, *Budget of the United States Government: Analytical Perspectives, Fiscal Year2006* (Washington, D.C.: Government Printing Office, 2005): 250–52.

[3]U.S. General Accounting Office, *Federal Debt: Answers to Frequently Asked Questions*, GAO/AIMD-97-12 (Washington, D.C.: GPO, 1996), 13–16. The exception is the rare years in which there is a federal surplus rather than the persistent deficit.

Figure 15–1
U. S. Federal Debt Relative to GDP (%), End of Fiscal Year 1940–2005

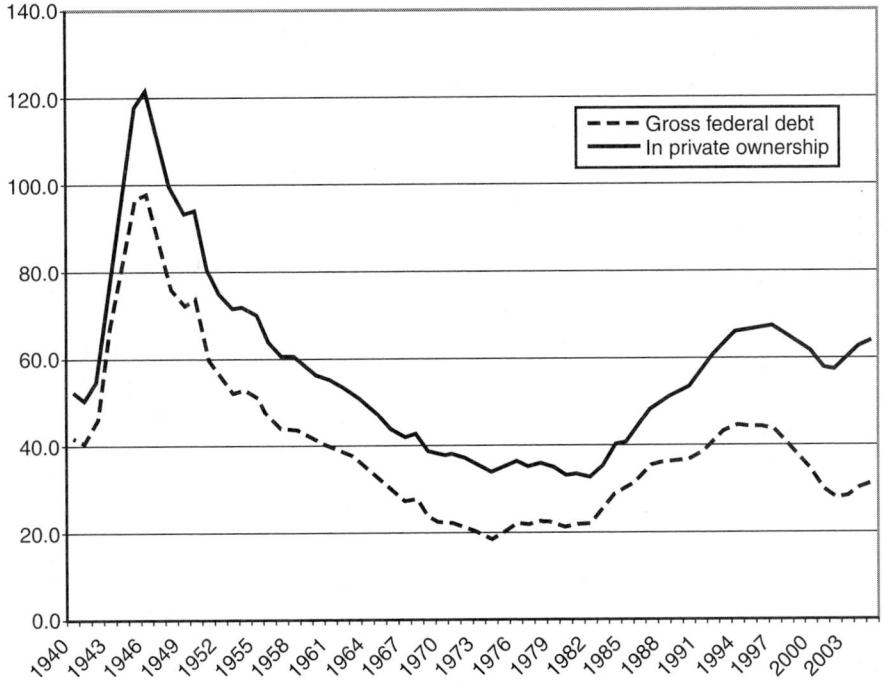

Federal agency or trust fund accounts held roughly half of federal securities in 2005. They acquire the debt in their cash-management programs—what safer (and more politically neutral) place to invest surplus funds than in U.S. Treasury debt?—so this debt is not a net claim on federal government resources. The Federal Reserve system conducts monetary policy by sale and purchase of federal debt, so these transactions to change the supply of money in the economy also influence the amount of debt in private hands. Because the Federal Reserve Banks legally must return to the U.S. Treasury sizable portions of interest received and because they are, at least loosely, government agencies, their holdings—just below 10 percent of the total in 2005—do not represent an outside claim on the government. For most analytical purposes, it is the debt held by private investors—that debt outside federal agencies, federal trust funds, and Federal Reserve Banks—that is the major concern for federal debt policy. The share of the debt that is privately held—the share that represents a net requirement for resource transfer outside government—declined throughout the 1990s, to 49 percent in 2004 from around 68 percent in 1990.

One notable change in historic pattern is the new importance of foreign and international ownership of the federal debt. Until the mid-1970s, foreign ownership of the federal debt was small, considerably less than 10 percent of the total privately held debt. However, those holdings quickly jumped to around 20 percent in

Table 15–1
Federal Debt from Fiscal 1940 to Fiscal 2005

End of Fiscal Year	Gross Debt ($ millions)	Gross Debt as % GDP	Debt Held by Private Investors ($ millions)	Debt Held by Private Investors (% GDP)	Average Maturity
1940	50,696	52.4	40,314	41.6	
1945	260,123	117.5	213,390	96.4	
1950	256,853	94.1	200,692	73.5	
1955	274,366	69.5	203,009	51.4	
1960	290,525	56.1	210,317	40.6	
1965	322,318	46.9	221,678	32.3	
1970	380,921	37.6	225,484	22.3	3 yr 8 mo
1975	541,925	34.7	309,707	19.8	2 yr 8 mo
1980	909,041	33.3	591,077	21.7	3 yr 9 mo
1985	1,817,423	43.9	1,337,454	32.3	4 yr 11 mo
1990	3,206,290	55.9	2,177,147	38.0	6 yr 1 mo
1995	4,920,586	67.2	3,230,264	44.1	5 yr 4 mo
1996	5,181,465	67.3	3,343,149	43.5	5 yr 3 mo
1997	5,369,206	65.6	3,347,826	40.9	5 yr 5 mo
1998	5,478,189	63.5	3,262,917	37.8	5 yr 10 mo
1999	5,605,523	61.4	3,135,719	34.4	6 yr 0 mo
2000	5,628,700	58.0	2,898,391	29.9	6 yr 2 mo
2001	5,769,881	57.4	2,785,480	27.7	6 yr 1 mo
2002	6,198,401	59.7	2,936,235	28.3	5 yr 6 mo
2003	6,760,014	62.4	3,257,327	30.1	5 y5 1 mo
2004	7,354,673	63.7	3,595,203	31.1	4 yr 11 mo
2005	7,905,316	64.3	3,855,869	31.4	4 yr 10 mo

the mid-1970s and have expanded since then. At the end of fiscal 2005, 53.5 percent of privately held federal debt was in foreign and international investor ownership. Repayment of that portion of federal debt cannot be casually dismissed with "we owe it to ourselves." Servicing that debt transfers resources from U.S. taxpayers to foreign bondholders, a condition with substantially different standard-of-living implications for the United States than service of internal debt. As long as foreign entities build up dollar reserves in international trade and world investors regard U.S. government debt as yielding a high return without significant risk of political upheaval, such investment will continue.[4]

Table 15–1 shows that the federal debt tends to have a short term to maturity, averaging 4 years and 10 months at the end of fiscal 2005. That is a reflection of the

[4]Bond purchases are made by our major trading partners; those countries are the ones with individuals and institutions having dollars to invest. In June 2005, the major shares of Treasury securities in international ownership were the following: Japan (34.0%), Mainland China (12.2%), United Kingdom (7.0%), Caribbean Banking Centers (5.4%), Taiwan (3.6%), Germany (3.06%), and Korea (3.0%). Other countries held less than 3 percent of the total. (Source: U.S. Treasury/ Federal Reserve Board. Available at www.ustreas.gov/tic/mfh.txt.)

fact that the federal government has historically borrowed to finance its continuing deficits, not to finance long-life capital projects. The maturing has lengthened in recent years, from its low point of 2 years and 8 months at the end of 1975, but is much shorter than the post–World War II maximum of 10 years and 5 months at the start of 1947.[5] The relatively short maturity combines with the substantial federal debt to create a continued federal presence in debt markets, either refinancing maturing debt or financing new cash needs. But interest rates tend to be lower for short-term than for long-term loans, so maturity shortening can reduce interest cost of serving the debt. Although some federal debt is sold directly to the public, most is sold through a small group of primary security dealers who acquire the debt at auction for resale to investors. Yields are normally established at those auctions at fixed nominal levels. As Sidebar 15–1 describes, the U.S. Treasury has recently started selling securities with inflation-indexed returns to investors.[6]

State and Local Government (Municipal) Debt

State and local government debt has similarly grown rapidly since the early 1970s, from $175.2 billion in 1972 to $1,812.7 billion in 2003. This debt, the product of borrowing by states, counties, municipalities, townships, school districts, and special districts as shown in Table 15–2, is all called municipal debt, distinguishing it from corporate or federal issues. The preponderance of this debt is long term. That differs radically from the federal debt. Furthermore, municipal debt is typically issued for construction of identifiable, long-life assets. Some purposes are indicated in Table 15–2, which shows the heavy state-local debt emphasis on education and utilities; substantial portions are also for private purposes, as is explained later. Such an identification of purposes, of course, would not be possible for federal debt.

The state-local debt figures distinguish between full-faith-and-credit debt and nonguaranteed, or limited-liability, debt. Full-faith-and-credit obligations "have an unlimited claim"[7] on the taxes (and other revenues) of the issuing unit; nonguaranteed-debt issues lack that assurance and are sold on the basis of repayment from particular revenue sources only. Because public-debt purchasers (the individuals and institutions lending the money to state-local governments) regard the claim on all tax resources as offering greater likelihood that bond principal and interest

[5]*Treasury Bulletin* (March 1989); 32. In late 2001, the Treasury stopped selling 30-year bonds, historically the benchmark bond in many financial markets, with intention that the longest Treasury bond would have a 10 year maturity. However, increases in the federal debt that needed to be financed brought the 30-year bond back in 2005.

[6]The process through which the Treasury borrows is described in Kenneth D. Garbade and Jeffrey F. Ingber, "The Treasury Auction Process: Objectives, Structure, and Recent Adaptations," *Current Issues in Economics and Finance, Federal Reserve Bank of New York,* 11 (February 2005).

[7]Roland I. Robinson, "Debt Administration," in. J. Richard Aronson and Eli Schwartz, eds., *Management Policies in Local Government Finance* (Washington, D.C.: International City Management Association, 1975), 23.

Sidebar 15–1
Inflation-Indexed Bonds

Conventional bonds repay the bondholder the principal of the loan plus a contracted interest rate; an inflation-indexed bond repays the principal adjusted for inflation plus the contracted interest rate applied to that adjusted principal. That prevents the purchasing power of the investment from being eaten away by unexpected price increases. Price increases in the economy will be matched by higher payments from the indexed bond—so holders of indexed bonds are not hurt by inflation. Their real rate of return is protected.

A number of governments, including those of Israel, the United Kingdom, Australia, Canada, Sweden, Mexico, Argentina, and New Zealand, have sold such bonds. The U.S. Treasury offered its first index bonds in January 1997—$7 billion of 10-year bonds with a 3.45 percent coupon rate—with the intent for quarterly auctions of more such bonds. In contrast with conventional bonds, the principal is adjusted before each semiannual payment to reflect any change in the Consumer Price Index since the issue of the bond. By that adjustment, the real return from the bond remains the same for the bondholder—and the U.S. Treasury knows the real, but not the nominal, cost of this debt. These are now referred to by Treasury as Treasury Inflation-Protected Securities (TIPS).

Jeffrey Wrase of the Federal Reserve Bank of Philadelphia provides a comparison of payments for conventional and indexed bonds:[1]

> Consider a 10-year conventional nominal bond and a 10-year inflation-indexed bond. Each bond is purchased at its face, or principal, value of $1000. Although Treasury notes and bonds provide semiannual payments, the bonds in this example are assumed to provide annual coupon payments. Each coupon payment on a conventional bond is the coupon rate stated on the bond times the principal. Each coupon payment on an indexed bond is the coupon rate times the indexed principal. The indexed principal is simply the beginning principal of $1000 scaled up through time at the rate of inflation. We'll assume that the coupon rate on the indexed bond is 3 percent, and that actual inflation over the 10-year horizon turns out to be a steady 2 percent, equal to expected inflation, and that the coupon rate on the conventional bond is 5.06 percent so that its expected real rate of return equals the coupon rate on the indexed bond.
>
> A schedule of nominal and real values of payments on the bonds is given below. The real values give the purchasing power of the nominal payments. For example, suppose a given item today cost $1. With 2 percent inflation, at the end of the year the same item will cost $1.02, and $1 will purchase .98 (1/1.02) units of the item. So, $50.60 received at the end of year 1 from the nominal bond will purchase 49.61 units.

[1]Jeffrey M. Wrase, "Inflation-Indexed Bonds: How Do They Work?" *Federal Reserve Bank of Philadelphia Business Review* (July–August 1997): 5.

payments will be made on time, full-faith-and-credit debt bears a lower interest rate than does equivalent nonguaranteed debt. (Later sections suggest why many governments use nonguaranteed debt, despite its higher cost.) Long-term state government debt is almost three-quarters nonguaranteed; long-term local government debt is somewhat more heavily full faith and credit. Short-term debt at both levels is almost completely full faith and credit.

Sidebar 15–1 (Continued)

As the schedule of payments shows, the nominal value of the conventional bond's principal stays fixed. The real value is eroding through time because of inflation. When received at maturity, the $1,000 principal can purchase 820.35 units of the good. In contrast, when the bond was first purchased, that $1,000 could buy 1000 units. The payment schedule also shows how the fixed nominal payment of $50.60 per year on the nominal bond has a smaller real value over time because of inflation. Note that for the indexed bond, the real values of the principal and interest payments are preserved for the life of the bond. As the principal gets scaled up, so, too, does the nominal coupon payment to preserve the real return of 3 percent. The indexed bond pays less interest than the nominal bond each year, but that is offset by its larger payment of principal at maturity.

Schedule of Payments

	Conventional Bond				Indexed Bond			
Year	Nominal Value of Principal	Real Value of Principal	Nominal Interest Payment	Real Value of Interest Payment	Nominal Value of Principal	Real Value of Principal	Nominal Interest Payment	Real Value
1	$1,000	980.39	$50.60	49.61	$1,200.00	1,000	$30.60	30
2	$1,000	961.17	$50.60	48.64	$1,040.40	1,000	$31.21	30
3	$1,000	942.32	$50.60	47.68	$1,061.21	1,000	$31.84	30
4	$1,000	923.85	$50.60	46.75	$1,082.43	1,000	$32.47	30
5	$1,000	905.73	$50.60	45.83	$1,104.08	1,000	$33.12	30
6	$1,000	887.97	$50.60	44.93	$1,126.16	1,000	$33.78	30
7	$1,000	870.56	$50.60	44.05	$1,148.69	1,000	$34.46	30
8	$1,000	853.49	$40.60	43.19	$1,171.66	1,000	$35.15	30
9	$1,000	836.75	$50.60	42.34	$1,195.09	1,000	$35.85	30
10	$1,000	820.35	$50.60	41.51	$1,218.99	1,000	$36.60	30

Total Nominal Receipts: $1,506
Real Value of Principal at Maturity: $820.35
Total Nominal Receipts: $1,554.07
Real Value of Indexed Principal at Maturity: $1,000

Nonguaranteed debt is outside limits frequently placed on municipal government debt by state statute or constitution. Interest on such debt is, however, eligible for the same exclusion from federal taxation received by municipal debt. That creates a logical inconsistency: In order to invoke tax immunity, the agency that issues those bonds must show that they are the obligations of a state or subdivision. However, in order to provide that they are revenue bonds and not subject to the

Table 15–2
Summary of State and Local Indebtedness 2002–2003 ($ thousands)

Description	State and Local Government Amount	State Government Amount	Local Government Amount	County Government Amount	Municipal and Township Government Amount	Special District Government Amount	School District Government Amount
Debt outstanding	1,812,666,705	697,929,028	1,114,737,677	210,892,766	456,647,553	225,308,926	221,888,432
Short-term	40,469,575	16,133,156	24,336,419	3,869,799	9,326,078	1,629,546	9,510,996
Long-term	1,772,197,130	681,795,872	1,090,401,258	207,022,967	447,321,475	223,679,380	212,377,436
Full faith and credit	675,469,843	179,372,361	496,097,482	74,445,871	178,497,363	37,792,752	205,361,496
Nonguaranteed	1,096,727,287	502,423,511	594,303,776	132,577,096	268,824,112	185,886,628	7,015,940
Long-term debt by purpose							
Public debt for private purposes	431,361,173	267,277,642	164,083,531	69,686,351	57,899,577	36,497,603	—
Education	362,034,544	105,855,516	256,179,028	15,057,786	22,363,848	6,379,958	212,377,436
Utilities	238,408,191	36,116,328	202,291,863	9,604,963	95,336,107	97,350,793	—
Other	740,393,222	272,546,386	467,846,836	112,673,867	271,721,943	83,451,026	—

SOURCE: U.S. Bureau of Census, Governments Division.

usual debt limitations, the agency must show that they are not the obligations of any such unit.[8]

Creating and defending the appropriate distinctions is the source of substantial income for bond counsel, legal firms that specialize in issuing opinions on the legality of debt issues, the security of pledge for repayment, and the tax-exempt status of issues. The convenience and savings of having the debt interpreted both ways is usually worth the price. Much revenue-bond debt is issued by public authorities, entities with public powers that operate outside the normal constraints placed on government. Governments form authorities to build a public project (bridges, power projects, highways, etc.) and pay off bonds used to finance the construction with charges from users; the authorities seldom have taxing authority. The authority may or may not go out of existence when the bonds are retired.[9] (Special entities created for lease-purchase finance are discussed later.)

Table 15–2 provides extensive detail on the nature of local government debt. Three features are particularly noteworthy. First, municipalities are the largest users of debt markets, in total and for both full-faith-and-credit and nonguaranteed sectors of the market. Second, special districts are heavy users of nonguaranteed debt. Many special districts (waste management, transit, water, etc.) are established on a semicommercial basis in that they collect charges from their customers and lack a tax base for guarantee. Third, school districts are heavy users of full-faith-and-credit debt. School districts traditionally have not been operated from user charges (there are strong public policy reasons for providing primary and secondary education at no direct cost to patrons), so they lack project revenue to support borrowing and must repay from tax and intergovernmental aid revenue. They are the sole sources for repayment, so full-faith-and-credit issues must be the primary mechanism for debt finance for schools. They do establish, however, separate building corporations that issue debt to finance construction with repayment guaranteed by leases charged to a school district, as is discussed later.[10]

The municipal bond market is dominated by revenue bond debt. This nonguaranteed debt was only 38 percent of all state and local long-term debt outstanding in 1960. The market has continuously shifted toward nonguaranteed debt to allow governments to avoid legal restrictions placed on general obligation debt, and to allow revenue-producing projects to float on their own debt. However, the trend is somewhat troubling for older, large cities: "The economic advantage of cities lies in making the marginal maintenance and repair expenditures that can keep the basic elements of their present infrastructure in adequate working order."[11] Nonguaranteed bonds are not easily adapted to generate financing for reconstruction or maintenance, so the shift indicates special problems for those cities. If the infrastructure (streets, water and sewage systems, etc.) is not maintained, the economic advantage

---

[8]B. U. Ratchford, "Revenue Bonds and Tax Immunity," *National Tax Journal* 7 (March 1954): 42.

[9]For a fascinating view of public authority operation, see Robert Caro, *The Power Broker: Robert Moses and the Fall of New York* (New York: Vintage Books, 1975), Chapter 28.

[10]These building corporations are outside normal fiscal limitations—"off the books" in a manner similar to entities associated with Enron and other private businesses.

[11]George E. Peterson, "Capital Spending and Capital Obsolescence—The Outlook for Cities," in Roy Bahl, ed., *The Fiscal Outlook for Cities* (Syracuse, N.Y.: Syracuse University Press, 1978), 49.

of new cities becomes overwhelming. Debt is not, however, the complete answer to public infrastructure deterioration; much work on maintenance is recurring and should be part of operating financing.

Municipal Bonds and the Tax Reform Act of 1986

The federal income tax adopted in 1913 specified that interest on state and local government bonds would be exempt. The reasoning apparently reflected the doctrine of intergovernmental tax immunity reflected in the 1819 decision *McCulloch* v. *Maryland* (4 Wheat, 316, 4 L.Ed. 579) stating that "the power to tax is the power to destroy" and furthered in the 1871 *Collector* v. *Day* (11 Wall. 113) case finding that the federal government could not tax state judicial officers' salaries. Indeed, the 1895 *Pollock* v. *Farmers Loan & Trust Company* (157 U.S. 492) decision that the income tax would require apportionment as a direct tax also ruled on a provision that would have included state and local debt interest in the base: "The tax in question is a tax on the power of the states and their instrumentalities to borrow money, and consequently repugnant to the Constitution." Therefore, the constitutional principle appeared clear.

There were economic impacts and equity effects, however, that soon muddied the issue.[12] Because interest payments on municipal bonds were not subject to tax, municipalities could borrow at artificially low interest rates. That created the possibility of capital-market distortions between taxed and tax-exempt activities and certainly caused lost federal revenue. Furthermore, as marginal tax brackets rose over the years, interest payments that were not subject to federal tax became more attractive to high-income taxpayers as a safe avenue for tax avoidance. That avoidance reduced the progressivity of the federal system, along with reducing federal revenue. And after Mississippi (1936) introduced industrial development bonds (IDBs), a mechanism whereby a tax-exempt borrower constructed a plant for a private firm and serviced the debt with lease payments from the firm, the distortion problems became especially troubling. Some controls on exempt bonds were inevitable.

Although controls on the bonds started with limits on IDBs in 1968, the most dramatic changes came in the 1986 Tax Reform Act.[13] The law distinguishes between two municipal-debt categories: private activity (taxable) and public purpose (tax-exempt). The law and regulations putting the categories into effect are complex; here is a simplified version: (1) Private-activity and taxable bonds pass the private-business-use and private-loan tests.[14] The bond issue is in this category if

---

[12]For an excellent analysis of the equity and efficiency problems of the municipal-bond market, see two articles by Peter Fortune: "The Municipal Bond Market, Part I: Politics, Taxes, and Yields," *New England Economic Review* (September/October 1991): 13–36; and "the Municipal Bond Market, Part II: Problems and Policies," *New England Economic Review* (May/June 1992): 47–64.

[13]The control legislation is chronicled in Robert L. Bland and Li-Khan Chen, "Taxable Municipal Bonds: State and Local Governments Confront the Tax-Exempt Limitation Movement," *Public Administration Review* 50 (Jan./Feb. 1989): 42–48.

[14]*Bond Buyer 1997 Yearbook*. Such bonds can tap foreign capital markets because of the higher yield that the absence of federal tax advantage requires.

(a) more than the greater of 5 percent or $5 million of bond proceeds are used for loans to nongovernment entities (the private-loan test) or (b) more than 10 percent of the bond proceeds are used by a nongovernment entity in a trade or business and more than 10 percent of the debt service is secured by or derived from payments from property used in a trade or business (private-business-use test).[15] (2) Public-purpose and tax-exempt bonds are issued by a state or its political subdivision in registered form and do not pass these tests. Passing these tests would ordinarily not be a good thing for the borrower, in terms of likely interest costs.

Certain private-activity bonds, however, can be tax-exempt. Allowable uses include multifamily rental housing; publicly owned airports; publicly owned docks and wharves; publicly owned nonvehicular mass-commuting facilities; hazardous-waste disposal facilities; sewage- and solid-waste disposal facilities; some student loans; some water, electric, and gas utilities; and some other categories.[16] The annual volume of such bond issues, however, is subject to a state cap of the greater of $50 per capita or $150 million.[17] How states allocate the amounts is their choice. Furthermore, state and local governments may choose to sell their debt in taxable markets; indeed, $183 billion taxable municipal bonds (5.3 percent of the total) sold in 1996.

The 1986 act clearly reduced the scope of future tax-exempt borrowing. Furthermore, a 1988 Supreme Court ruling in *South Carolina v. Baker* (56 USLW 4311), a case testing whether state and local governments could be required to issue bonds only in registered form, held that the Constitution does not prevent applying the federal income tax to state and local debt interest.[18] As the federal government seeks revenue and reform of its revenue system, municipal bond interest, even for clear public purpose debt issues, will continue to be one option for base broadening. The preference provided municipal borrowing is a policy choice, not a necessary constitutional requirement.

Appropriate Debt Policy

Borrowing provides funds to acquire resources for current public use. The debt from that borrowing must be repaid, with interest, in the future. Therefore, borrowing commits future budgets. Because of the contractual rigidity, debt must be

---

[15]Some state and local governments do regularly use these hybrids (taxable municipal securities). Such issues can be attractive to foreign investors.

[16]The development impact of small-issue IDBs appears doubtful. See U.S. General Accounting Office, *Industrial Development Bonds: Achievement of Public Benefits Is Unclear,* GAO/RCED-93-106 (Washington, D.C.: General Accounting Office, 1993).

[17]Private-activity bonds for airports, docks, wharves, and solid-waste facilities are outside the cap; certain public-purpose bonds (parts earmarked for private activities costing more than $15 million and private portions of advance refunds) are included in the cap.

[18]Bonds had been issued as bearer bonds (whoever presents the bonds receives interest and principal owed, no questions asked) or as registered bonds (the owner is explicitly named). There was concern that such bonds were being used to launder illicit incomes and to evade gift and estate taxes. The Tax Equity and Fiscal Responsibility Act of 1982 limited tax-exempt status to registered issues alone. The case challenged that provision; the state did not expect the extra comment on tax-exempt status in general. See Bruce F. Davie and Dennis Zimmerman, "Tax-Exempt Bonds After the South Carolina Decision," *Tax Notes* (June 27, 1988): 1573–80.

issued with care: Improper use can disrupt the lives of those paying taxes and expecting services in the future. Debt-service costs can impair the ability of the borrower to operate normally. The fundamental rule of debt policy is: do not issue debt for a maturity longer than the financed project's useful life. If the debt life exceeds useful life, the project's true annual cost has been understated, and people will continue to pay for the project after the project is gone. If the useful life exceeds the debt period, the annual cost has been overstated, and people will receive benefits without payment. The timing-of-payment question is particularly significant across generations and, at the local level, across a citizenry that is frequently changing.[19]

Long-term borrowing can be appropriate for long-life capital facilities. Economic growth requires expanded public-capital infrastructure, often before any associated expansion of public revenue. A strong case can be made for using debt for these projects: The future revenue stream will be adequate to service debt expansion, to borrow a concept from corporate finance. Some governments, however, have elected to employ pay-as-you-go financing, paying for capital facilities only from current-year operating surpluses. Such a policy can produce both inefficiency and inequity. First, with population mobility, users would not pay an appropriate charge for those facilities. Those in taxing range would pay when the facility is built; they may not be there when the facility for which they have paid is actually providing services. Second, the high single-year ticket price of a major project may discourage construction, even when the project is sound and feasible. Third, pay-as-you-go financing can produce substantial tax-rate instability, with artificially high rates during the construction phase and artificially low rates during operation. Such instability is unlikely to help development of the local economy. Furthermore, debt financing produces annual debt-service charges that are fixed by contract. Therefore, when the area tax base grows, the tax rate required for debt service for a project will decline over time.

Debt commits resources for extended periods and can be misused by public officials who seek to postpone the cost of public actions. Potential for misuse, however, does not preclude debt financing, but it does mean that debt needs to be issued with caution. When properly handled, debt is an appropriate financing medium. In fact, strict pay-as-you-go can be as unsound as careless use of debt. Both financing methods can be appropriate tools in the fiscal arsenal. Appendix 15–1 illustrates a debt policy with the principles of debt management endorsed by the New York state comptroller.

The Mechanics of Bond Values

Bond sales represent transactions in which a lender exchanges payment to a borrower now for the contractual promise of repayment plus interest at a later date. The bond contract specifies the interest the borrower will pay the lender for using

[19]Temporary cash needs should be covered by short-term borrowing liquidated within the fiscal year. Carrying short-term cash borrowing across a fiscal year (rolling over) would violate the fundamental principle.

the money, typically with a semiannual interest payment. This stated or nominal return on a bond is its coupon rate, the percentage of par value that will be paid in interest on a regular basis. Thus, a 5-percent coupon rate means that the bond pays $50 interest per $1,000 face value.[20] The yield on a bond may differ substantially from the coupon rate because the current value of the bond itself may differ from the face value. The bond contract, however, states a coupon rate and face value to be redeemed at maturity.[21] Bond calculations thus employ the time value of money, compounding, and discounting techniques discussed in Chapter 6. Recall that

$$FV_n = PV(1 + r)^n$$

and

$$PV = FV_n/(1 + r)^n$$

where

FV_n = a value received in the future,
PV = a value received now,
r = the market rate of interest, and
n = the number of years.

The current bond price equals the present value of cash flow to which the bondholder is entitled (return of principal plus interest). Therefore,

$$P = \sum_{i=1}^{m} \frac{F \times c}{(1+r)^i} + \frac{F}{(1+r)^m}$$

where

P = the market value or current price of the bond,
m = the number of years in the future until maturity of the bond,
F = the face value of the bond,
C = the coupon rate of the bond, and
r = the market interest rate available on bonds of similar risk and maturity.

The first term of the formula requires computing the present value of a constant stream of returns in the future, so the annuity-value formula (Chapter 6) provides a

[20]Municipal bonds are normally issued in denominations of $5,000 face value, even though coupon discussions use the smaller face value. Small denomination bonds ("minibonds") are sometimes sold. Lawrence Pierce describes an issue from Virginia Beach, Virginia, in "Hitting the Beach and Running: Minibonds," *Government Finance Review* 4 (Aug. 1988): 29.

[21]For a bond purchaser, the yield-to-maturity is the total annualized return earned on a bond if it is held to maturity. It includes both the coupon and any difference between the amount paid for the bond and its face received on redemption by the borrower. A bond may be zero coupon, in which case the yield is the difference between the amount paid initially and the amount ultimately received back.

quick valuation method. For a bond with semiannual interest payments, the first term—the value of the coupon flow—would be computed using ($2m$) instead of m and ($r/2$) and ($C/2$) instead of r and C.

To illustrate, suppose a Stinesville Water Utility bond matures in 15 years, pays an 8-percent coupon semiannually, and has a face value of $5,000. The market rate currently available on comparable bonds is 6 percent. The holder receives an interest payment of ($F \times C$)/2, or $200, each six months for 30 periods ($m/2$). At the end of those 30 periods, the holder will receive back the $5,000. The bond price emerges from the formula

$$P = \sum_{i=1}^{30} \frac{(5{,}000 \times 0.08)/2}{\left(1 + \frac{0.06}{2}\right)^{i}} + \frac{5{,}000}{(1+0.06)^{15}}$$

$$= 3{,}920 + 2{,}086 = 6{,}006$$

It is obvious that the value of a bond can change, causing capital gain or loss for its holder, as market interest rates vary. The value of the Stinesville bond will be higher than computed here if the market rate is less than 6 percent and lower if the market rate is above 6 percent. The change would not cause a cash loss or gain for an individual holding the bond to maturity but would change the return for anyone selling it early.

Debt Structure and Design

After the decision to borrow has been made, a number of debt-structure decisions remain. They are considered here, along with some institutional detail about municipal-bond markets.[22] Characteristics should ideally be designed to ensure least-cost marketability of the issue, simplify debt management, and provide appropriate cost signals to fiscal decision makers.

One initial decision involves the type of security and its term to maturity (i.e., the period for which the money will be borrowed). Markets respond differently to full-faith-and-credit bonds than to revenue bonds. The greater security behind full-faith-and-credit debt typically causes a lower interest rate to be paid on that offer-

[22]The federal government constantly borrows to accommodate the continuing deficit and refinancing of maturing debt. Decisions about debt maturity are driven not by the life of particular capital projects but by concerns of economic management. A longer term (Treasury bonds, notes) relieves financial markets of the regular disruptions that occur when maturing debt is refinanced but may interfere with private long-term capital investment. A shorter term (Treasury bills) usually reduces the average initial interest rate on the debt but requires more frequent financing, probably will cause higher ultimate interest cost, and may make inflation more difficult to control. These are radically different concerns from those in the municipal market. Federal debt, an important medium for cash-management programs, is discussed further in Chapter 16.

ing. Revenue bonds may be desired, however, because of legal restrictions placed on the full-faith-and-credit debt[23] or because revenue debt provides a good way to allocate costs to the project's users. For instance, a city may enter capital markets to obtain funds for pollution control equipment for a private electric utility. There is no logic to full-faith-and-credit finance here: Charges paid by utility customers should be the sole source of debt service.

Debt maturity should roughly coincide with project life to ensure that the project will be paid for and the debt liquidated before replacement or major repair is required. This maturity-matching principle prevents debt financing for operating expenditures and permits those financing an improvement to receive its benefits. Debt-service costs along the project's life roughly represent a rental (or depreciation) charge. The facility users pay charges or taxes to cover those annual costs. The total charge can thus more accurately reflect the service's annual cost, including both capital and operating costs.

A bond issue, for example an issue with 30 years' overall maturity, can be either term or serial. A term issue would have all bonds in the issue timed to mature at the end of 30 years. Funds to repay principal would be obtained through the bond issue's life (along with interest charges along the way) and placed into a sinking fund maintained by the bond issuer. At maturity, sinking-fund accumulations would be sufficient to repay the principal. A serial issue contains multiple maturities in a single issue. Thus, some bonds would be for a 30-year term, some for a 20-year term, and so on. (Issuers often seek to maintain constant total annual debt service—interest plus retirement of maturing bonds—through the length of an issue by gradually increasing the volume of bonds maturing through the life of the issue.) Portions of the project cost would be paid through the overall term of the issue. The serial issue may improve marketability of many municipal issues. Thin secondary markets for municipal debt cause most purchasers of that debt to hold the bond to maturity.[24] With serial issues, the issuing government can sell its debt to purchasers with funds available for several different periods of time. Either term bonds with sinking funds or serial bonds spread a project's financing over the life of the project and provide financing on a pay-as-you-use basis.

Debt maturity plays an important role in determining what the issue's ultimate interest cost will be because there is a relationship between the debt's term of maturity and the interest rate required. This relationship, the term structure of interest rates, is influenced by economic conditions at the time of borrowing and is often, but not always, upward sloping (the longer the term to maturity, the higher the interest rate required to borrow for that period of time) because borrowers must

---

[23]Full-faith-and-credit may be limited to a maximum total amount for the jurisdiction, to a maximum percentage of the jurisdiction's tax base (usually assessed value), or by a requirement that voters approve the debt at a referendum. Revenue-bond debt generally escapes all these limits. Limits are reported by state in tables 61–63 of Advisory Commission on Intergovernmental Relations, *Significant Features of Fiscal Federalism, 1976-77, Vol. 2, Revenue and Debt* (Washington, D.C.: ACIR, 1977).

[24]Corporate-bond purchasers can purchase a bond with reasonable assurance that the bond can be sold to another person if funds are needed prior to maturity; a strong secondary market exists. Thus, these bonds are ordinarily not serial.

Figure 15–2
U.S. Treasury Yield Curve, July 29, 2005

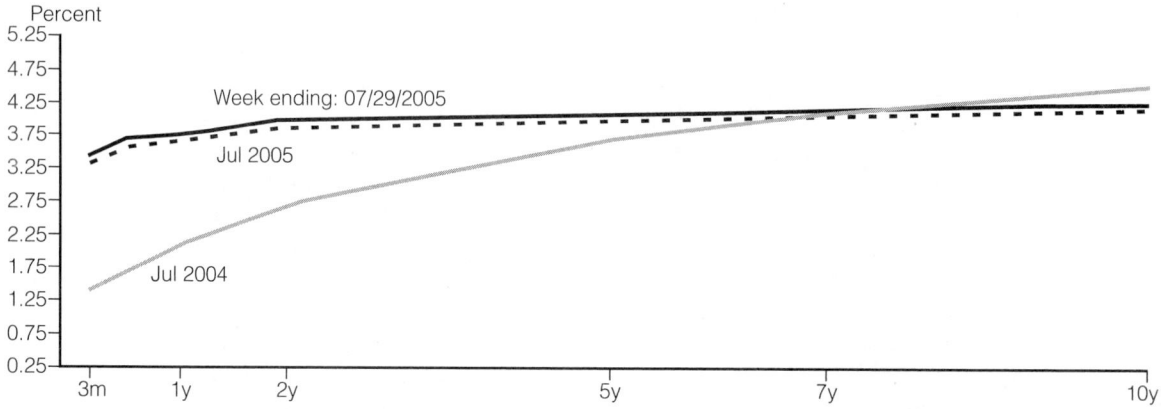

compensate investors for locking up their resources for a longer period. (The yield curve is called *inverted* when long-term rates are lower than short-term rates.) Expectations about the future of interest rate conditions and the economy, especially expectations about inflation, determine the curve's shape at any time.[25] Figure 15–2 illustrates the term structure of the yield curve for U.S. Treasury securities at mid-2005 (the yield curve here is upward sloping, or ascending, but flattens at longer maturities). It is flatter than it was a year earlier. A similar yield curve can be constructed for any security, such as municipal bonds of a standard quality. Rates for municipal and corporate securities tend to move together with market conditions, as shown in Figure 15–3.

Municipalities can protect themselves from being locked into high borrowing costs for long periods. A *call provision* in a debt issue allows the borrower to repay debt before the normal maturity. The borrower usually refunds the debt, or borrows to cover the repayment, at the lower interest rates prevalent at the time of the refunding. If interest rates fall sufficiently before the first call date, the municipality may use advance refunding—borrowing at the lower interest rate and using the proceeds to cover debt service until the call date allows the initial issue to be entirely replaced.[26] Of course, possibility of a call reduces an issue's attractiveness to lenders, so issues with such a provision must compensate the investor (a call premium above face value) to permit marketability of the original issue.

---

[25]When inflation is expected to be mild, the purchasing power of debt repayments in the distant future will be closer to the same as purchasing power given in the initial loan. Interest rates do not need to compensate for purchasing power loss and hence are lower in money terms. See Peter A. Abken, "Inflation and the Yield Curve," *Economic Review* 78 (May/June 1993): 13–30.

[26]Proceeds of advanced refunding will be invested. The U.S. Treasury provides special securities for this purpose (since 1972) to prevent violation of arbitrage restrictions (municipalities cannot borrow tax exempt while lending on ordinary markets).

Figure 15–3
Yield of Aaa Municipal and AAA Corporate Debt, End of Year, 1962–2003

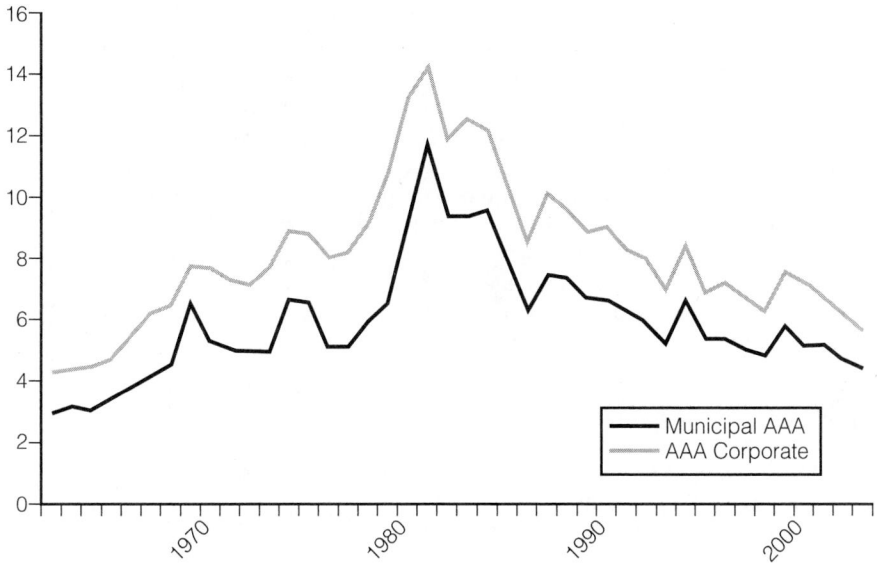

Ratings

When risk (the chance of loss of principal and interest) is greater, lenders demand a higher return for their loans. Therefore, risk is important to both borrowers and lenders and, in bond markets, commercial rating firms assess the risk of particular bond issues. Because the assumption of risk must be compensated by higher returns to lenders, this assessment of risk will be critical in determining the interest rate paid by the borrowing government. Ratings also allow governments to sell on larger capital markets because they convert bonds issued by a locality into a commodity; all bonds with the same rating carry the same estimated risk. Credit risk is low because defaults in the United States are rare, although less rare for revenue bonds issued by public authorities than for full-faith-and-credit bonds issued by general purpose governments. Defaults by the latter are usually linked to major economic recession, flagrant fiscal mismanagement, or unresolved political disputes. Because capital markets have long memories, governments want to avoid "a reputation-based loss of access to future loans."[27] That makes general purpose governments especially reluctant to miss scheduled debt service. (As Sidebar 15–2 describes, default is only one way in which government finances can go wrong.)

[27]William B. English, "Understanding the Costs of Sovereign Default: American State Debts in the 1840's," *American Economic Review* 86 (March 1996): 272.

Sidebar 15–2
When Government Finances Go Horribly Wrong

Scarcity is *the* economic problem: In the real world, resources are not and have never been sufficient to cover all human wants. Hence, choices must be made from among the many different ways that those scarce resources could be used. The problem is logically the same for families, businesses, or governments. Having to cut, stretch, and fiddle with finances can be trying and irritating, but it is a normal consequence of human existence in this world and does not constitute fiscal crisis. Economic and fiscal choice cannot be avoided. In the realm of government, those choices may involve higher taxes or reduced services, neither of which are necessarily markers of something particularly wrong with the government. Indeed, the government may function with an operating deficit for the year—which will mean use of prior accumulated surpluses or borrowing on the basis of prospects for the future. That is not ordinarily a recommended strategy, but obviously it happens—as we know from operations of the federal government.

The process of fiscal choice can, however, go badly wrong, sometimes through economic or social misfortune, sometimes through incompetence or malevolence, sometimes through a stubborn unwillingness to make tough choices, and often through a combination of these causes. At the worst, governments may face or consider default, repudiation, receivership, or bankruptcy as an outcome of fiscal crises that cannot be managed by tough manipulation of finances to reduce spending or to increase revenue. The terms are often carelessly used in public discussion; they do have different meanings and different consequences. All are, for American general-purpose governments, extremely rare.

1. *Default.* A government defaults when it does not meet a scheduled payment of principal or interest on a debt issue. Widely publicized defaults in the municipal securities market over the past few decades include New York City and Cleveland in the 1970s and the Washington Public Power Supply System in the 1980s. In the New York case, the issuer defined the episode to be a "technical default," because it unilaterally announced a slower-than-contracted payment schedule. Bondholders may not have appreciated the distinction. Most defaults are of small issues by special-purpose districts, often involving industrial development projects. The 1978 Cleveland default was the first general obligation bond default since the Great Depression. Some defaults are permanent, as with that of the Washington Public Power Supply System bonds; some defaults are only temporary, as with New York City and Cleveland. Bondholders may be protected from the economic consequences of default by bond insurance purchased by the issuer. The default may occur without any discernible impact, at least in the short term, for those receiving services from the defaulting government, but the impact is felt when the government proposes to borrow again and faces higher interest rates because of the market reaction to the earlier default.

2. *Repudiation.* Repudiation occurs when the borrower announces that it will make no more principal or interest payments on debt, that it will no longer recognize that debt as a liability. This action is rare; bond markets have long memories and a government that has repudiated debt will have difficulty borrowing again. Some American states repudiated debt issued in the first half of the nineteenth century to finance canals, roads, railroads, and other internal improvements. Some of the projects were absolutely scandalous and money almost certainly was stolen by both government and private thieves. However, these repudiating governments faced premium interest rates on their borrowing well into the twentieth century because the capital markets remembered that experience.

Sidebar 15–2
(Continued)

The bond market effects even cross radical changes in government. For instance, questions about payments on Russian tsarist debt issued in France from 1822 to 1914 complicated Russia's entry into international bond markets in 1996. A French bondholders' association (Association Francaise des Porteurs d'Emprunts Russes) kept rating agencies informed and warned prospective investors. Eventually the governments of Russia and France reached an agreement for at least partial payment of that old debt and the new Russian government was able to enter the market.

3. *Receivership*. A government enters receivership when an appointed third-party manager takes control of operations of the government. The receiver, appointed by a superior government or by a court, has the responsibility to protect the assets of the unit and to meet legitimate demands made by those owed money by the government. States often appoint receivers or trustees to manage the finances of local governments in great jeopardy; for instance, Massachusetts appointed a receiver to take over the management of the city of Chelsea in the face of major financial irregularities, including alleged theft of city funds and properties, discovered there. School districts in California have also been placed in receiverships by the state. State control boards—in which states take over financial operations of particular localities (usually cities)—behave something like receiverships. Examples include the Pennsylvania Intergovernmental Cooperation Authority (for Philadelphia in 1991, Pittsburgh in 2004, and several smaller jurisdictions since the state created the oversight law in 1987), the Miami Financial Emergency Oversight Board in 1996, the Buffalo Fiscal Stability Authority (2003), and the New York State Financial Control Board (for New York City, 1975). Washington, D.C., lost most of its fiscal independence to a congressionally appointed board in 1997, for similar reasons.

Courts may also appoint receivers for public entities, although less frequently than for private firms or nonprofit organizations. In 1986, the Wayne County Circuit appointed a receiver to operate the city of Ecorse, Michigan, after suits by Detroit Edison, the Detroit Water and Sewerage Department, and others for nonpayment of bills. The receivership, apparently the only instance of such judicial intervention into general government, ended in 1990 without having been fully tested by the judicial system. Receivers may well dramatically change the services supplied by the government and possibly the taxes it levies, so the population almost certainly will see a difference from the experience. About twenty states have provisions for state assistance and control for municipalities in fiscal distress.

4. *Bankruptcy*. Governments enter bankruptcy by a formal filing with a federal court under Chapter 9 of the federal bankruptcy code. The court then protects the government from financial claims while the government develops a plan under which it can pay a large share, but usually not all, of its financial obligations. The bankruptcy aims to ensure that the government can continue to provide services to its citizenry and retain its assets. In contrast to individual or corporate bankruptcies, governmental bankruptcies can only be voluntary. That is, they cannot be forced by creditors. After the 1991 effort by Bridgeport, Connecticut, to declare bankruptcy, Congress changed the bankruptcy code to require specific state authorization before a municipality may file for bankruptcy.

Bondholders are superior creditors, so debt service ordinarily flows on schedule (besides, the government wants continued access to municipal capital markets), but other contractual obligations may not be met. For instance, wages and salaries may be reduced from the previously agreed-to levels. Government bankruptcy is rare, usually involving smaller special districts, not general-purpose governments.

Three firms—Mergent (formerly Moody's Investors Services), Standard & Poor's (a subsidiary of McGraw-Hill, Inc.), and Fitch Investors Service/ICBA—prepare most creditworthiness opinions in the municipal market.[28] Mergent/Moody's has been doing municipal ratings since 1919; Standard & Poor's since 1940; Fitch has only recently undertaken municipal rating, but has been in the market since 1913. These agencies, for a fee paid by the bond issuer, prepare an opinion of the borrower's credit quality (for full-faith-and-credit issues) or of the particular bond issue (for revenue-bond issues). These rating opinions are widely distributed to the investment community and are used nationally to form portfolio strategies. The agencies also prepare "sovereign credit ratings," the ratings for central government debt, as international debt markets have grown; U.S. federal government debt has been generally regarded as fully secure and has been the standard against which risk is judged.[29] An issue without a rating seldom sells on national markets, but issues can be unrated if local markets will buy them. Notice in Table 15–3 that a full percentage point or more often separates highest grade (Aaa) and lower grade (Baa) investments, although the spread has been less since the 1980s. Grades lower than investment grade fare less well because many financial institutions are forbidden to hold speculative, lower-rated securities. Table 15–4 relates the ratings definitions of the three services and suggests the general risk factors associated with each rating.

The precise manner in which borrowing-unit characteristics contribute to a rating is not estimable and is proprietary. Statements by the rating firms identify four sorts of factors that are important in their reviews and evaluations of creditworthiness:

1. **The Economy.** The economy in which the issuing unit operates is important. A strong and growing economy brings a strong revenue base for servicing the debt. That reduces the credit risk of the issue.

2. **Debt.** Debt history and the debt position of the issuing unit are important. A high debt burden and high debt service requirements in relation to government resources raise questions about the credit risk of the issue. Plans for retiring the debt, the maturity structure in relationship to the project being financed, and any prior defaults are also reviewed.

3. **The Government.** The investigation considers the degree of professionalism shown by the issuing government, the capacity of administrators, and the quality of the full budget process (audits, documents, appropriations, controls, etc.), and the quality of governmental financial reports. Delays in approving budgets are not regarded as a favorable factor.

---

[28]The Securities and Exchange Commission (SEC) identifies these firms as those whose ratings will be used in valuing bond assets of SEC-registered brokers and dealers. A fourth firm, Duff and Phelps Credit Rating Company, specializes in ratings for water and public power systems, commercial development, toll roads, airports, and education-facilities financing and does sovereign credit ratings, especially in emerging markets. It has narrower focus than the other three.

[29]Richard Cantor and Frank Packer, "Sovereign Credit Ratings," *Current Issues in Economics and Finance* (June 1995): 1–6. Had the federal government not met its debt service requirement during the 1995–1996 period during which it was constrained by a statutory debt ceiling, its rating would have been damaged for decades, with considerable extra cost to American taxpayers. Similar problems emerged in the summer of 2002.

Table 15–3
Yield by Mergent Municipal Rating Group, 1940–2004 (End of Year)

	Aaa	Aa	A	Baa
1940	1.56	1.78	2.11	2.60
1945	1.11	1.27	1.62	1.91
1950	1.42	1.60	1.92	2.17
1955	2.29	2.46	2.81	3.25
1960	3.12	3.35	3.60	4.03
1965	3.39	3.47	3.60	3.78
1970	5.21	5.33	5.60	5.80
1972	4.91	5.04	5.19	5.39
1974	6.65	6.81	7.14	7.50
1975	6.50	6.94	7.78	7.96
1976	5.07	5.50	6.42	6.73
1977	5.07	5.23	5.46	5.79
1978	5.91	6.01	6.51	6.76
1979	6.50	6.69	6.89	7.42
1980	9.44	9.64	9.80	10.64
1981	11.70	12.16	12.60	13.30
1982	9.34	9.85	10.24	10.80
1983	9.34	9.58	10.08	10.29
1984	9.54	9.88	10.19	10.45
1985	7.98	8.31	8.64	9.05
1986	6.28	6.48	6.84	7.24
1987	7.45	7.74	7.97	8.42
1988	7.35	7.44	7.56	7.76
1989	6.71	6.81	6.86	7.03
1990	6.63	6.82	6.96	7.10
1991	6.32	6.43	6.52	6.65
1992	5.91	6.03	6.14	6.27
1993	5.18	5.27	5.44	5.69
1994	6.62	6.59	6.73	7.17
1995	5.40	5.43	5.53	5.66
1996	5.38	5.47	5.54	5.68
1997	5.02	5.06	5.11	5.16
1998	4.82	4.90	5.04	5.17
1999	5.83	5.92	6.08	6.25
2000	5.11	5.18	5.27	5.85
2001	5.18	5.22	5.39	5.81
2002	4.70	4.76	4.96	5.57
2003	4.41	4.54	4.67	4.97
2004	4.35	4.47	4.61	4.91

SOURCE: Mergent Municipal and Government Manual (New York: Mergent, 2005).

Table 15–4
Credit Ratings by Mergent, Standard & Poor's, and Fitch

Mergent	Symbol
Best quality, smallest degree of investment risk; referred to as "gilt edge"	Aaa
High quality; smaller margin of protection or larger fluctuation of protective elements than Aaa	Aa
Upper-medium grade, adequate security of principal and interest; some susceptibility to future risk	A
Medium grade: neither highly protected nor poorly secured; adequate present security but may be unreliable over any great length of time	Baa
Speculative elements; not well safeguarded; very moderate protection of principal and interest, over both good and bad times	Ba
Lack characteristics of desirable investment	B
Poor standing; may be in default, danger to principal or interest	Caa
Speculative in high degree; default or other marked shortcomings	Ca
Lowest-rated class; extremely poor prospects of ever attaining any real investment standing	C
Standard & Poor's	**Symbol**
Prime: obligation of highest quality and lowest probability of default; quality management and low-debt structure	AAA
Higher grade: only slightly more secure than prime; second lowest probability of default	AA
Upper-medium grade: safe investment; weakness in local economic base, debt burden, or fiscal balance	A
Medium grade: lowest investment security rating; may show more than one fundamental weakness; higher default probability	BBB
Lower-medium grade: speculative noninvestment-grade obligation; relatively low risk and uncertainty	BB
Low grade: investment characteristics virtually nonexistent	B

4. **Financial Analysis.** The investigation covers fund balances, trends in revenues and expenditures, adequacy of the revenue base, vulnerability to new liabilities (pension requirements, etc.), adequacy of financial planning, and so on.

Accumulations of report summaries are published annually as a guide to investors.

Revenue-bond analysis is primarily concerned with the enterprise's revenue potential and the legal protection of bondholders in the bond resolution's covenants. There is little concern with the government because there is no precedent requiring bailout of revenue bonds. For instance, in two well-publicized incidents, neither the city of Chicago nor the state of West Virginia prevented default of associated revenue-bond issues (Chicago Skyway and West Virginia Turnpike).[30] No government intervened to assist the Washington Public Power Supply System in its

[30]The finances of the Chicago Skyway have been straightened out and the city was able to lease the Skyway to a private Euro–Australian firm for $1.82 billion dollars in 2004.

Table 15–4
Credit Ratings by Mergent, Standard & Poor's, and Fitch (continued)

Standard & Poor's	Symbol
Vulnerability to default: timely payment dependent on favorable business, financial, and economic conditions	CCC
Debt subordinated to senior debt with CCC rating	CC, C
Debt on which no interest being paid	Cl
Payment in default	D

Fitch	Symbol
Investment grade of highest quality: extraordinary ability to pay, unlikely to be affected by reasonably foreseeable events	AAA
Investment grade and high quality: strong ability to pay	AA
Investment grade and good quality: strong ability but more vulnerable to adverse changes in economic conditions and circumstances	A
Investment grade and satisfactory quality: adequate ability	BBB
Low investment grade and speculative: ability not strong and likely to be affected by adverse economic conditions	BB
Highly speculative: lightly protected over life of bond	B
Characteristics could lead to default	CCC
Minimal protection: default seems probable	CC
Actual or imminent default	C
Default and in arrears	DDD, DD, D

NOTE: Mergent designates with 1 those bonds in Aa, A, Baa, Ba, and B groups with the strongest investment attributes (i.e., Aa1). A plus or a minus attached to an S&P rating indicates upper or lower segment of the rating category. Mergent Con. (2) indicates security depends on completion of some act or fulfillment of some condition; rating in parenthesis notes probable statute when condition fulfilled. Fitch uses plus or minus in ratings from AA to B.

$2.25 billion default from 1983. Thus, revenue-bond analysis presumes the project must stand on its financial merits.

Credit Enhancements

Credit enhancements may reduce the interest rates that a municipal borrower must pay by adding a third-party guarantee that debt service will be paid when due. These guarantees reduce the risk associated with the bond, enabling the borrower to issue at a lower interest rate. Three such guarantees should be noted: (1) state-credit guarantees, (2) bank letters of credit, and (3) municipal-bond insurance. Each adds the credit strength of the guaranteeing entity to that of the borrower to one extent or another.

The state-credit guarantees are an "explicit promise by the state to a local unit bondholder that any shortfall in local resources will automatically be assumed by the state. In its strongest form, a state guarantee places the full faith and credit of the state behind the contingent call on state funds."[31] The guarantees may take the form of a state insurance fund into which local issuers make premium payments, the program may guarantee only portions of debt service, the guarantee may not automatically pledge the full faith and credit of the state, or there may be other conditions placed on the backing. In the final analysis, the guarantee can hardly be stronger than the state's finances. That fact, plus the many different shades of the guarantee, make generalizations about this form of third-party credit strengthening particularly hazardous.[32]

A second form of guarantee is the bank letter of credit (LOC), "an unconditional pledge of the bank's credit to make principal and interest payments of a specified amount and term on an issuer's debt. The LOC may be valid even in cases of issuer default, in effect acting as a guarantee of the debt."[33] The LOC may provide a source of liquidity to the municipality, but it can also provide the municipality with the creditworthiness of the bank issuing the LOC. Thus, if the bank has an AAA rating, the LOC held by a municipality with a much lower rating would normally allow the municipality the benefits of that higher rating. The fee for the LOC typically is charged annually. Meaningful LOC guarantees require cooperation of a major money-center bank with at least an AA ranking; seldom are LOCs granted for longer than 10 years. A shortage of domestic banks with strong ratings has dramatically limited the attraction of these guarantees. This guarantee is not widely used: Only 5.9 percent of long-term issues (by dollar volume) were sold with LOC backing in 2004.[34]

The third, and most significant, bond guarantee is municipal-bond insurance. This insurance, purchased by the bond issuer, guarantees timely payment of principal and interest on that issue. Thus, a low-rated issue with insurance can sell at roughly the same interest rate as a higher-quality issue because the insurer adds its resources to insure payment of the issue's debt service.[35] A municipal-bond seller finds insurance attractive when the premium paid for insurance at time of issue is less than the discounted interest savings resulting from the greater market acceptance of the insured issue. Not all issues can be insured, and not all issues can profit from insurance.[36] The premium is paid when the bond is initially issued.

Five firms dominate the municipal bond insurance market: MBIA Insurance, Financial Security Assurance, Ambac Assurance Corporation, Financial Guaranty Insurance, and XL Capital Assurance. These are the only firms selling more than

---

[31]Ronald W. Forbes and John E. Petersen, "State Credit Assistance to Local Governments," in John E. Petersen and Wesley C. Hough, eds., *Creative Capital Financing for State and Local Governments* (Chicago: Municipal Finance Officers Association, 1983), 226.

[32]There is considerable doubt about the wisdom of such guarantees because they reduce the incentive for fiscal responsibility by the borrower. In no case should the guarantees be open-ended.

[33]Ibid., 22. Entities may also obtain a line of credit, with annual renewal, but this access can be terribly expensive.

[34]*Bond Buyer/Thomson Financial 2005 Yearbook* (New York: Source Media, 2005).

[35]An issue insured by a company whose guarantee produces a rating of AAA ordinarily sells for 25 to 30 basis points more than an actual AAA issue.

[36]Insurance may also be purchased by a bondholder to guarantee scheduled payments on his or her bond portfolio. That is not, however, the concern of an issuing municipality.

$10 billion and covering more than 150 issues in 2004.[37] Insurance coverage has quickly become common: The first insurance was sold in the early 1970s, and 3 percent of issues were insured in 1980. Insured issues now constitute more than half the new issue volume. It is a market with substantial demand because of considerable infrastructure financing and a desire to constrain lender risk.[38] At present, AAA ratings are given issues insured by the top four insurers; other programs provide ratings of at least AA. The insurance programs normally have quality limits for insurance and premiums, paid at time of issue, vary by quality, length, size, and issue type. Premiums range around 0.25 to 1.5 percent of the issue's total principal and interest. By pooling default risk, new-issue insurance should improve markets for small units and increase the market range for many borrowers.

Underwriting, Interest Rates, and Ownership

Bond issues are usually too large to be bought by a single investor, and the issuer cannot effectively market the issue to large numbers of individual investors.[39] Thus, bonds are typically sold to an underwriter, a firm that purchases the entire issue. The borrower receives the entire issue's proceeds quickly, without worrying about marketing. The underwriter hopes to resell the issue at a profit to investors. The gross profit (or underwriting spread) equals the difference between the price the firm pays for the bonds and the price the firm receives from their sale to investors. From that spread, the firm will pay all costs of distribution involved in the transaction. An increase in market interest rates can cause bond values to fall, so underwriters typically want to sell the bonds quickly.

Underwriting firms are selected either by negotiation or by competitive bid. In the former case, the underwriter is selected as the bond issue is being designed. An interest rate is negotiated between the borrowing unit and the underwriting firm. The underwriter will be engaged in presale marketing and will assist the borrower with such organizational services as preparing official statements, structuring the bond issue, and securing credit ratings. Negotiated bond sales dominate the revenue bond market (three-quarters of the issues by dollar volume) and competitive sales dominate the general obligation market (three-quarters of the issues by dollar volume). Unfortunately, noncompetitive selection opens the door for possible

[37]Congress established the for-profit firm, the College Construction Loan Insurance Association, with federal seed money in 1986 to insure low-rate issues (S&P's BBB or lower) from higher-education institutions. "Connie Lee" covered less than 1 percent of all insured issues in 1996—a poor fifth place among insurers. Some have argued for an extension of its role. Private insurers are not amused.

[38]Some public employee pension funds have considered insuring municipal issues, and Oregon has done so. See James A. White, "Pension Funds Consider Insuring Munis," *Wall Street Journal* (17 April 1992): C-1.

[39]"Minibonds" are sometimes sold directly to investors. Some municipalities have experimented with direct sales to investors via the Internet.

favoritism and bribes and eliminates market forces that reduce the spread.[40] Fifteen states have bond banks that underwrite and provide other services for municipal offerings; these sales are also negotiated.[41]

Two important documents must be prepared during the sale of bonds: the official statement and the legal opinion. The official statement, a requirement when the underwriter will be selected by competitive bid, contains two sections providing information prospective underwriters and investors need before committing funds to the borrower. One section provides information about the borrower's ability to repay its debt: a description of the community and its industries, its major taxpayers, debt currently outstanding, a record of tax collections and bond repayments in the past five years, and future borrowing plans. The other section describes the proposed bond issue: purpose, amount, and type of issue, its maturity structure and interest payment schedule, all provisions, date and place of bidding, whether a bond rating ahs been applied for, the name of the counsel preparing the legal opinion (described later), and where bonds will be delivered. The official statement will also indicate any maximum interest rate and discount. Most official statements will include a disclaimer indicating a right to refuse any and all bids, even though that right will seldom be used by units intending to maintain good relations with underwriters.[42]

The second document is the legal opinion prepared by a bond counsel, a certification that the bond issuer has complied with all federal, state, and local legal requirements governing municipal debt. Seldom will local law firms do this work; underwriters and large private investors require opinions from specialist law firms. The bond counsel ensures that the issuer has legal authority to borrow, that the revenue source for repayment is legal and irrevocable, and that the community is legally bound by provisions of the bond. The bond counsel also indicates whether interest paid on the debt will, in its opinion, be exempt from federal and state income tax. The bond counsel offers no judgment about the borrower's capacity to repay the debt; the bond counsel's concern is with how tightly the contract to repay

---

[40]The Public Securities Association recommended in 1993 a moratorium on political campaign contributions to candidates in states where public finance firms do bond business. This represents a major change in prior practice. Some scandals involving the selection of underwriters in that year produced that recommendation but similarly piqued the interest of the federal SEC. The SEC has historically provided little supervision of municipal securities, but, to prevent market abuses, it proposed in 1994 to pursue securities-fraud charges against state and local government officials if they (1) fail to disclose conflicts on interest, including the acceptance of political contributions from underwriters or financial advisors; (2) fail to issue annual financial statements and inform investors of significant financial developments; (3) fail to disclose terms and risks of bonds; or (4) make inaccurate statements of the finances of the jurisdiction. The idea, if fully implemented, would make municipal security-information requirements more consistent with those placed on private issuers.

[41]Bond banks reduce interest costs to local borrowers. See Martin T. Katzman, "Municipal Bond Banking: The Diffusion of a Public-Finance Innovation," *National Tax Journal* 33 (June 1980): 149–60; and David S. Kidwell and Robert J. Rogowski, "Bond Banks: A State Assistance Program That Helps Reduce New Issue Borrowing Costs," *Public Administration Review* 42 (March/April 1983): 108–12.

[42]SEC rules effective in 1990 have placed extra controls on municipal disclosure in the official statement. Although the rules are directed at underwriters, the statements to which they apply are those produced by municipal borrowers. See John E. Petersen, "The New SEC Rule on Municipal Disclosure: Implications for Issuers of Municipal Securities," *Government Finance Review* (October 1988): 17–20.

binds the borrower. Without a satisfactory opinion, the bond issue is virtually worthless on the tax-exempt market.

A competitive bid is the typical method of selecting underwriters for full-faith-and-credit bonds and for many revenue issues. In this method, the issuer selects the amount of principal to mature at various years through the issue's life, and underwriters bid on the interest rate the issuer would have to pay. The rates, of course, need not be the same for different maturities but would be the same for all bonds in a single maturity. The issuer chooses the underwriter bidding the lowest interest rate for the total issue. The winning underwriter bid determines what the interest cost will be to the issuer.

Two methods are used to compute interest cost when determining the lowest underwriter bid, net interest cost (*NIC*) and true interest cost (*TIC*). Both represent averages of the several coupon rates in the serial issue. The *NIC* method computes cost according to the formula

$$NIC = \frac{\text{Total interest (less premium or plus discount)}}{\text{Bond dollar years}}$$

and produces an average annual debt cost as a percentage of the outstanding principal of the debt. First, compute *N*, the total dollar cost of coupon payments over the life of the bond:

$$N = \sum_{i=1}^{n} (C_i \times A_i \times Y_i) + D$$

where

N = net dollar interest costs;
n = number of different maturities in issue;
C = coupon rate on each maturity;
A = par amount, or face value, in each maturity;
Y = number of years to maturity; and
D = bid discount (bid premium is a negative discount).

N equals the total interest paid through the life of the bond issue. The bond-dollar years (*BDY*) formula is

$$BDY = \sum_{i=1}^{n} (A_i \times Y_i)$$

BDY represents the amount borrowed and the time for which it is borrowed: $1 borrowed for 2 years equals 2 bond-dollar years, $2 borrowed for 5 years equals 10 bond-dollar years, and so on. Thus,

$$NIC = \frac{N}{BDY}$$

The *TIC*, or the Canadian interest cost, method is more complicated because it takes into account the time profile of interest-payment flows, but it is the norm in competitive bidding. If two bids have the same net interest cost, but one bid involves higher-interest payments in the early maturities of the issue and lower-interest payments in the later maturities (frontloading), then that bid would be less attractive: It requires the issuer to surrender resources earlier and thus to lose the return that could have been received from use of those resources. The second bid is, in present-value terms, lower than the first. True interest cost is the interest rate that equates the amount of dollars received by the bond issuer with the present value of the flow of principal and interest payments over the issue's life. The *TIC* formula is

$$B = \sum_{i=1}^{m} \frac{A_i}{(1+TIC)^i} + \sum_{i=1}^{m} \frac{I_i}{(1+TIC)^i}$$

where

B = aggregate dollar amount received by the issuer (the amount borrowed less discount or plus premium),
i = number of years until a cash payment occurs,
m = number of years to final maturity,
A_i = annual principal in dollars repaid in period i,
TIC = true interest cost, and
I_i = aggregate interest payment in period i (assuming one interest payment per year).

In a *TIC* computation for municipal-bond sale, the bid price or amount to be paid by the underwriter to the issuer (B) and the stream of debt-service payments (I_i) are specified by the bidder. The issuer defines the number of years to future payments (the maturities). The implied interest rate (*TIC*) is solved by iteration for successive approximation until the left and right sides of the equation balance.[43] Larger offerings require computer assistance for *TIC* calculation, but smaller issues can be handled using standard methods for approximating the internal rate of return. Table 15–5 illustrates *TIC* and *NIC* computation.

The successful underwriting firm or syndicate (a group of firms) then sells the bonds to investors. Underwriters cover their costs and make any profit from the difference between the price the underwriters pay the issuer and the price the underwriters receive from purchasers (the spread).[44] As the previously discussed bond-market mechanics demonstrated, an increase in market interest rates causes bond values to decline. If increases in market rates cause a substantial decline in the issue's value before the firm has sold the bonds, that spread can be negative.

[43]The internal-rate-of-return function on electronic spreadsheets quickly performs the calculations.

[44]In 2004, the average gross spread was $5.62 per $1,000 face value of bonds, averaging 5.53 for negotiated issues and $6.35 for competitive issues. The competitive spread typically is less than the negotiated spread, however. For comparison, the average spread was $8.10 in 1995. *The Bond Buyer Thomson Financial 2005 Yearbook*, (New York: Source Media, 2005): 61.

Table 15–5
A TIC and NIC Computation Worksheet

Bond Sold July 1, 2004, and Interest Payable on July 1 Thereafter (bid amount = $39,920)

Maturity Dates	Amounts ($)	Bid Interest Rate (coupon) (%)	Annual Interest Paid ($)	Bond Years	Bond Dollar Years
July 1, 2008	5,000	6.00	300	4	20,000
July 1, 2009	5,000	6.50	325	5	25,000
July 1, 2010	5,000	7.00	350	6	30,000
July 1, 2011	5,000	8.00	400	7	35,000
July 1, 2012	10,000	9.00	900	8	80,000
July 1, 2013	10,000	10.00	1,000	9	90,000
Total par value	40,000				

Schedule of Payments by Dates Paid

Maturity Dates	Interest ($)	Principal ($)	Total ($)
July 1, 2005	3,275	—	3,275
July 1, 2006	3,275	—	3,275
July 1, 2007	3,275	—	3,275
July 1, 2008	3,275	5,000	8,275
July 1, 2009	2,975	5,000	7,975
July 1, 2010	2,650	5,000	7,650
July 1, 2011	2,300	5,000	7,300
July 1, 2012	1,900	10,000	11,900
July 1, 2013	1,000	10,000	11,000
Total	23,925	40,000	63,925

NIC, Net interest cost; TIC, total interest cost.
Solving for *NIC:*

$$NIC = \frac{23,926 + 80}{280,000} = 8.573\%$$

Solving for *TIC:*

$$\$39,920 = \frac{3,275}{1+TIC} + \frac{3,275}{(1+TIC)^2} + \frac{3,275}{(1+TIC)^3} + \frac{8,275}{(1+TIC)^4} + \frac{7,795}{(1+TIC)^5}$$

$$+ \frac{7,650}{(1+TIC)^6} + \frac{7,600}{(1+TIC)^7} + \frac{11,900}{(1+TIC)^8} + \frac{11,000}{(1+TIC)^9}$$

TIC = 8.503%

(Sidebar 15–3 illustrates how much the several intermediaries to a bond issue receive in a typical transaction.)

Table 15–6 reports the type of entities holding municipal bonds. Ownership in any class is concentrated among units in higher tax brackets—those are the purchasers to whom the tax-exempt status of municipal-bond interest is especially attractive. Household holdings are higher than 30 years ago, although holdings

Sidebar 15–3
The Costs of Issuing Debt: Sacramento Regional Transit District Certificates of Participation

The several roles in borrowing must be compensated. These are the costs incurred when the Sacramento Regional Transit District borrowed $31 million through a COP to purchase buses:

Underwriting	$204,550
Bond counsel	$ 60,000
Financial advisor	$ 60,000
Lessor administration fee	$ 60,000
Printer	$ 22,000
Trustee	$ 9,300
Rating agency	$ 14,000

SOURCE: Public Financial Management, *Introduction to Public Finance and Public Transit* (Washington, D.C.: Federal Transit Administration, 1992), 52.

Table 15–6
Distribution of Municipal Debt by Holding Entity (End of Year)

	1985	1990	1995	2000	2004
Total outstanding	100.00%	100.00%	100.00%	100.00%	100.00%
Households	40.5	48.5	35.5	34.2	32.8
Money market funds	4.2	7.1	9.9	14.7	15.7
Mutual funds	4.1	9.5	16.3	14.7	14.5
Other insurance companies	10.3	11.6	12.4	12.8	12.4
Commercial banks	27	9.9	7.2	7.3	6.9
Bank personal trusts	5.6	6.8	8.4	6.7	4.9
Closed-end funds	0.1	1.2	4.6	4.6	4.4
Government-sponsored enterprises	0.2	0.3	0.3	0.2	2.7
Nonfinancial coroporate businesses	3	2.1	2.8	2.2	1.9
Brokers and dealers	2.3	0.7	1	0.7	1.6
Life insurance companies	1.1	1	0.9	1.3	1.4
Savings institutions	0.4	0.3	0.2	0.2	0.4
State and local general funds	0.9	1	0.4	0.1	0.2
State and local retirement funds	0.1	0	0.1	0.1	0

SOURCE: Federal Reserve Board, *Flow of Funds Accounts, Flows and Outstandings.*

have declined recently. The role of commercial-bank purchases has declined. Banks lost the ability to deduct from income for federal tax purposes the interest they paid on deposits used to purchase tax-exempt bonds in tax reforms in the 1980s; that loss pulled them from the market. Other shares have been rather stable, except for the development of mutual and money-market funds as an important financial intermediary. These holdings might properly be added to household holdings.

Lease-Purchase Finance and Certificates of Participation

Governments utilize two types of leases, operating leases and capital leases. From an accounting perspective, operating leases are treated like rentals. At the end of an operating lease, the leased equipment is returned to the lessor. If any one of the following conditions are met, then the lease is not an operating lease, but instead is considered a financing arrangement or capital lease.

- There is a bargain purchase option
- The lease transfers the title of the property to the lessee
- The term of the lease equals or exceeds the full life of the property
- The lease payments plus interest exceed the fair value of the property

Capital leases, or lease-purchase financing, resemble an installment purchase. A lessee, in this case a government, buys a property from the lessor through installment payments made over a given period of time. The capital lease is treated as debt instead of an expense in the government's accounts and unlike a operating lease, the government carries the equipment on its books as the owner.[45] Interest paid on a capital lease may be treated as debt from the accounting perspective; from the legal perspective it can be exempt from debt ceilings through the use of a nonappropriation clause, which subjects the lease to annual appropriations. Often nonappropriation clauses contain restrictions to protect the lessor from the replacement of equipment should the lease not be appropriated. For instance, a leased telecommunications system might have a covenant restricting the purchase or lease of a new system should the lease be terminated.[46]

On larger transactions, investors buy certificates of participation (COPs) that give them a share of lease payments made on that property; for smaller purchases, a bank or other financial intermediary may handle the entire transaction. The interest portion of these lease payments can also be exempt from federal taxation, if the standards for issuer and purpose are met; if certain state-specific conditions are met, the financial obligation is not subject to constitutional or other limits in regard to voter approval, capacity ceilings, and so on, because they are not strictly debt obligations. More issues have been raised in California than in any other state because of high infrastructure demand and strict controls on traditional finance there, but

---

[45]Federal lease-purchases generally are recognized as borrowing from the public in budget documents. See Office of Management and Budget, *Budget of the United States Government, Analytical Perspectives, Fiscal Year 2006* (Washington, D.C.: GPO, 2005), 251.

[46]Richard Baker, "Public Policy Implications of Tax Exempt Leasing in the United States," *International Journal of Public Policy,* 1(No. 1): 148.

Arizona, Colorado, Florida, Georgia, Illinois, New Jersey, New York, North Carolina, South Carolina, and Washington each issue high volumes.[47]

Figure 15–4 illustrates the flow of transactions in a COP. Suppose a government wants to acquire a new jail. It would arrange for the establishment of a nonprofit building corporation from which it would lease the new jail. The building corporation would borrow from private investors enough to build the jail, using the promised lease payments as the basis for prepayment of the loan.[48] A trustee, usually a bank, handles the distribution of lease payments, as they come from the government, to individual COP holders and manages any legal proceedings if lease payments do not arrive. The COP provides lenders less security than bonds, because funds normally must be appropriated on a year-to-year basis and politics may intervene. However, the requirement for annual appropriations, a nonappropriation clause, is legally critical to distinguish these transactions from debt subject to referenda, ceilings, and the like.

Figure 15–4
A Certificate-of-Participation Arrangement

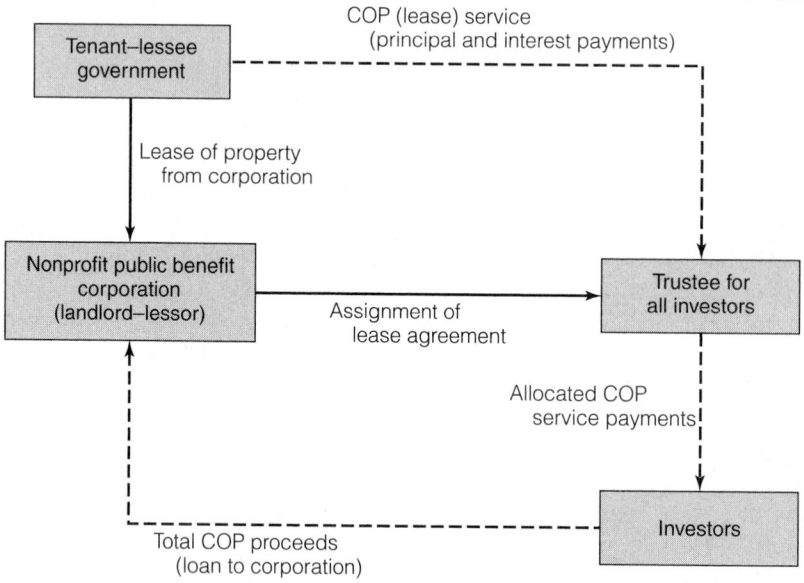

[47]Craig Johnson and John L. Mikesell, "Certificates of Participation and Capital Markets: Lessons from Brevard County and Richmond Unified School District," *Public Budgeting and Finance* 14 (Fall 1994): 42.
[48]There is another variety used to patch deficits: A government sells an existing facility to a holding corporation, uses the cash for government operations, then leases the facility back from the corporation. For a particularly unfortunate example, see Craig Johnson and John L. Mikesell, "The Richmond School District Default: COPs, Bankruptcy, Default, and State Intervention," in A. Khan and B. Hildreth, eds., *Case Studies in Public Budgeting and Financial Management* (Dubuque, Iowa: Kendall/Hunt, 1994).

Conclusion

Government debt exists because expenditure has exceeded revenue. Federal debt represents the accumulated effects of annual deficits; state and local government debt largely represents the outcome of capital-project financing. State and local government debt costs can be managed through care to maintain good creditworthiness (ratings), careful tailoring of maturities and timing of debt issues, use of the recently narrowed ability to issue federal tax-exempt debt, and use of available debt guarantees. Debt itself is not necessarily evidence of poor fiscal management.

CHAPTER 15 QUESTIONS AND EXERCISES

1. What restrictions are placed on state and local government debt in your state? What methods are used to avoid those limits? Is there a state bond bank?
2. Investigate the debt and debt-rating history for a large city of your selection. Have debt issues been full-faith and credit or limited liability? Have issues been insured?
3. Indicate which bond in the following pairs of bonds is likely to bear the higher interest rate (yield) and state why. If there is no general reason for a difference, indicate that they would be the same.
   a. A corporate bond rated Aaa or a municipal bond rated Aaa
   b. A municipal bond rated Baa or a municipal bond rated Aa
   c. A general-obligation bond issued by a city or a revenue bond issued by a city
   d. A general-obligation bond rated Aa issued by a city or a general obligation bond rated Aa issued by a county
   e. A municipal bond (term) with maturity in 5 years or a municipal bond (term) with maturity in 20 years
4. A city advertised for bids for the purchase of $2 million principal amount of Sewage Works Revenue Bonds. Bonds will be delivered on April 1, 2007; interest will be paid on April 1 of the following years. The bonds mature as follows:

Maturity	
Date	Amount ($)
April 1, 2012	50,000
April 1, 2013	50,000
April 1, 2014	50,000
April 1, 2015	100,000
April 1, 2016	100,000
April 1, 2017	100,000
April 1, 2018	150,000
April 1, 2019	150,000
April 1, 2020	150,000
April 1, 2021	550,000
April 1, 2022	550,000

Two bids were received:

From Five Points Securities:	Pay $2 million The interest rates for each maturity: 2012 through 2020, 5.50 percent 2021 through 2022, 6.25 percent
From Wellington-Nelson:	Pay $2 million The interest rates for each maturity: 2012 through 2014, 4.19 percent 2015 through 2020, 5.75 percent 2021 through 2022, 6.50 percent

For each bid, compute the net interest cost (*NIC*) and the true interest cost (*TIC*). Which bid is most advantageous to the city?

5. From tables in the *Wall Street Journal* or other papers that carry quotations on U.S. Treasury bonds, notes, and bills, determine the general shape of the term structure of interest rates. Trace the difference between short-term and long-term interest rates over the past year.

6. An Eminence Water Utility Revenue Bond matures in 15 years, pays a 5.5 percent coupon rate semiannually, and has a face value of $5,000. The market interest rate for similar risk and maturity municipal bonds is 4 percent. What is the current price of the bond? What would be its price if the market rate were 6 percent?

7. Publications like the *Wall Street Journal, Credit,* and *Capital Markets* often have advertisements by underwriters of municipal-bond issues they offer for sale (or of issues they have already placed). Locate such an advertisement and determine as many of these elements as you can about the issue: the face or par value, who borrowed the money, from whom the borrower received payment when the loan was made, from whom lenders will receive payment as they come due, what the rating of the issue is, whether the issue is insured and by whom, how much of the issue is term and how much is serial, what the borrower pledges for service of the loan, what the coupon rates are, and what total interest will be paid on a payment date five years in the future.

8. The Clinton administration proposed in the spring of 1993 to shorten the average maturity of the federal debt to reduce interest outlays in the budget. How would the administration do this, and what problems might this cause?

9. Solomon Keith, a bank janitor, won a large prize in the New York lottery in 1987. Unfortunately, Mr. Keith died before he could collect all of the twenty annual payments of $240,245 each to which he was entitled. To pay taxes and legal fees (as well as to distribute some of this estate to heirs), an auction was held in early July 1992 for rights to the 16 annual payments remaining in the prize (the first to be paid on July 15, 1992). Presidential Life Insurance Company was the winning bidder, paying $2.1 million for the prize. Suppose other

comparable investments of Presidential's funds could have earned about 5-percent annual interest. What do you think of the wisdom of their investment?

10. The property tax assessor for Wayne Township, Marion County, Indiana, wants new space. In June 1993, he was offered a lease-purchase arrangement for a 10,250-square-foot office building and accompanying tract of land. Using the data in Table A, compute *NIC* and *TIC* for the lease-payment schedule on the property.

Table A

Payment No.	Payment Date	Payment	Interest	Principal	Yearly Total	Principal Balance
1.	01/01/94	22,213.33	22,213.33	0.00		640,000.00
2.	07/01/94	22,040.00	19,040.00	3,000.00	44,253.33	640,000.00
3.	01/01/95	21,950.75	18,950.75	3,000.00		637,000.00
4.	07/01/95	21,861.50	18,861.50	3,000.00	43,812.25	634,000.00
5.	01/01/96	23,772.25	18,772.25	5,000.00		631,000.00
6.	07/01/96	23,623.50	18,623.50	5,000.00	47,395.75	626,000.00
7.	01/01/97	25,474.75	18,474.75	7,000.00		621,000.00
8.	07/01/97	25,266.50	18,266.50	7,000.00	50,741.25	614,000.00
9.	01/01/98	27,058.25	18,058.25	9,000.00		607,000.00
10.	07/01/98	26,790.50	17,790.50	9,000.00	53,848.75	598,000.00
11.	01/01/99	29,522.75	17,522.75	12,000.00		589,000.00
12.	07/01/99	29,165.75	17,165.75	12,000.00	58,688.50	577,000.00
13.	01/01/00	31,808.75	16,808.75	15,000.00		565,000.00
14.	07/01/00	31,362.50	16,362.50	15,000.00	63,171.25	550,000.00
15.	01/01/01	33,916.25	15,916.25	18,000.00		535,000.00
16.	07/01/01	33,380.75	15,380.75	18,000.00	67,297.00	517,000.00
17.	01/01/02	34,845.25	14,845.25	20,000.00		499,000.00
18.	07/01/02	34,250.25	14,250.00	20,000.00	69,095.50	479,000.00
19.	01/01/03	35,655.25	13,655.25	22,000.00		459,000.00
20.	07/01/03	35,000.75	13,000.75	22,000.00	70,656.00	437,000.00
21.	01/01/04	36,346.25	12,346.25	24,000.00		415,000.00
22.	07/01/04	35,632.25	11,632.25	24,000.00	71,978.50	391,000.00
23.	01/01/05	37,918.25	10,918.25	27,000.00		367,000.00
24.	07/01/05	37,115.00	10,115.00	27,000.00	75,033.25	340,000.00
25.	01/01/06	39,311.75	9,311.75	30,000.00		313,000.00
26.	07/01/06	38,419.25	8,419.25	30,000.00	77,731.00	283,000.00
27.	01/01/07	40,526.75	7,526.75	33,000.00		253,000.00
28.	07/01/07	39,545.00	6,545.00	33,000.00	80,071.75	220,000.00
29.	01/01/08	41,563.25	5,563.25	36,000.00		187,000.00
30.	07/01/08	40,492.25	4,492.25	36,000.00	82,055.50	151,000.00
31.	01/01/09	41,421.25	3,421.25	38,000.00		115,000.00
32.	07/01/09	40,290.75	2,290.75	38,000.00	81,712.00	77,000.00
33.	01/01/10	$1,040,160.25	$431,160.25	$639,000.00	40,160.25	39,000.00
TOTALS		$1,077,701.83	$437,701.83	$640,000.00		

Appendix 15–1

GENERAL PRINCIPLES OF STATE DEBT MANAGEMENT

The following principles outline the debt management policies endorsed by the Comptroller of the State of New York. They are consistent with the concept of fiscal sustainability and could serve as a reasonable model for any state or local government for guiding its use of debt.

General Principles of State Debt Management

1. Do not use refinancing to extend debt maturity.
2. Ensure present value and cash flow savings in every year
3. Maximize the economic benefits of debt refunding
4. Integrate the capital and financial planning process
5. Update both plans quarterly and provide realistic 4-year projections
6. Maximize the use of PAYGO financing
7. Target projects with low periods of probable usefulness
8. Maximize the use of surplus revenues to retire older and expensive debt
9. Use non-recurring revenues for capital spending/debt reduction
10. Long-term debt should be issued for capital purposes only
11. Issue no debt for operating expenses
12. Issue debt for capitalized interest only in extraordinary circumstances, such a pending construction of a revenue-producing facility
13. Keep debt to an affordable level
14. Limit outstanding debt and debt issuance
15. Minimize the costs of debt issuance
16. Limit the term of debt to maximize intergenerational equity
17. No debt issued beyond period of probable usefulness
18. Provide comprehensive and clear debt reporting
19. Continually strive toward superior disclosure practices.
20. Use competitive sales rather than negotiated sales.

SOURCE: New York State's Debt Policy, A Need for Reform (Office of New York State Comptroller Alan G. Hevesi, February 2005): 101.

CHAPTER 16

Managing Funds: Cash Management and Employee Retirement Funds

Why should governments have funds available to invest? Wouldn't those fund balances mean that people have been taxed for services not rendered? And why would we want taxes to be higher than is necessary to provide the governmental services our politicians have promised us? Shouldn't investable government funds be an immediate signal for tax cuts—so private resources can be in private hands for use in the private economy? In general, that would be true. But there are a couple of important reasons for government fund balances and, accordingly, for careful government fund management. One is the short-term handling of the working capital needed to maintain operations within the fiscal year. The other is the long-term management of pension-fund balances, accumulated to provide retirement benefits promised to employees.[1] Although forecasting, planning, and investing are required for each function, there are several critical differences in the rules of prudence for the two functions.

[1]Some governments and many nonprofit organizations have endowment funds to be managed over the long term for the benefit of certain defined activities. For instance, the Alaska Permanent Fund collects a portion of state oil revenue, invests the fund in a broad portfolio, and makes cash payments to Alaska citizens. (See Jonathan Anderson, "The Alaska Permanent Fund: Politics and Trust," *Public Budgeting & Finance* 22 (Summer 2002): 57–68.) Many principles of pension investment apply here, although there may be other provisions in regard to the endowment, including federal requirements in regard to distribution and donor requirements on use. There are other examples of governments establishing special funds to receive and manage natural resource revenues. Two examples are the Petroleum Fund of Norway and the National Oil Fund of Kazakhstan. An important purpose of each is to be a stabilizing buffer for national finances and to make some allowance for the fact that these are depleting resources.

The Cash Budget and Cash Management

Cash management encompasses the collection and disbursement of public money and the use of those funds between collection and disbursement in a manner consistent with the public interest. Treasury operations should (1) ensure the safety of public resources, (2) maintain liquidity when needed,[2] (3) increase the pool of funds available for investment, and (4) obtain the highest feasible yield on public funds. Simply put, cash management involves quickly getting use of money owed (*cash mobilization*), making payment as late as is economically reasonable (*disbursement control*), and doing something productive with the balances in between (*investment*). It should link with the tax collection system to provide information for taxpayer records and for the audit trail. To leave the resources to be used through the year in an account from which payment may be made immediately, for instance, would provide considerable safety and liquidity but negligible yield. Such a strategy would increase profits of the favored financial institution by providing it a low-cost source of short-run investable funds but would provide the government with no return.[3] The government fiscal officer must thus seek to invest these funds in money-market instruments to use this community resource.[4]

State and local governments have made considerable changes in their fund strategies over the past 50 years. As late as 1950, such governments held almost 40 percent of their financial assets in cash and checking accounts. By the mid-1970s, that percentage had fallen below 15 percent; by the 1980s, the percentage had fallen below 5 percent, and it has not increased.[5] Techniques of cash management—especially in cash-budget forecasting and ease of funds transfer—have made the changes possible; public demand for more economical use of government resources made the changes necessary.[6] The high interest rates of the 1980s (average yields for short-term federal securities above 10 percent from 1979 to 1982) made the potential returns from short-term investment particularly attractive to governments worried about providing services to a tax-resistant population; the techniques, once in place, were maintained even as interest rates declined. Because cash

---

[2]Liquidity is "the ease of converting an asset into money." Basil J. Moore, *An Introduction to the Theory of Finance* (New York: Free Press, 1968), 12. Some items may be valuable (land or antiques), but their value cannot be used directly to pay bills; they must be sold to obtain money before payment can be made (and market conditions may make it difficult to sell them quickly or at their normal value). Those items are illiquid.

[3]Idle deposits apparently neither keep down the loan cost in the community nor stimulate local economic activity. See Kerry S. Cooper, "The Economics of Idle Public Funds Policies: A Reconsideration," *National Tax Journal* 25 (March 1972): 97–99.

[4]Federal tax receipts are managed through the Treasury Tax and Loan Program, a joint operation of the Treasury and the Federal Reserve that is designed to manage receipts and to stabilize the supply of reserves in the banking system as a part of monetary policy. The system is described in Kenneth D. Garbade, John C. Partlan, and Paul J. Santoro, "Recent Innovations in Treasury Cash Management," *Current Issues in Economics and Finance, Federal Reserve Bank of New York* 10 (November 2004): 1–11.

[5]Board of Governors of the Federal Reserve System, *Flow of Funds Accounts, Financial Assets and Liabilities, Fourth Quarter, 1991: 2.1, Outstandings* (Washington, D.C.: Board of Governors, 1992).

[6]State and local governments were estimated to have lost $453 million in 1972 because of excess idle cash. George M. Blankenbeckler, "Excess Cash Management at the State and Local Levels," *State and Local Government Review* 10 (January 1978): 2–7. Governments have become more sophisticated in fund management since then.

management provides revenue without additional taxpayer burden, no government can afford to ignore its potential. The critical problem is the balance between yield, investment risk, and liquidity.

A public cash manager invests cash available from daily flows, not simply an annual surplus. The investment opportunity results because governments typically receive the largest revenue inflows in lump sums around tax-due days,[7] whereas expenditures occur in relatively smooth outflows. Figure 16–1 illustrates such a cash-balance pattern. The government in the figure receives major cash inflows at 2 days during the year, the start of April and the start of October. These may be property tax due dates, payment dates from vendors collecting a sales tax, receipt dates for intergovernmental assistance, or whatever. The government spends at a relatively constant rate throughout the year on payrolls, utilities, and so on. The budget-appropriation-disbursement process requirements make these outflows more or less predictable and controllable. (It should be apparent that, for the unit depicted in Figure 16–1, the first cash inflow is larger than the second and that spending exceeds receipts during the fiscal year shown here.) The cash manager invests available sums to as great a degree as possible. Thus, investment is of the daily surplus, not just annual surplus, for as many days as possible; any day that produces more inflow than outflow produces a potentially investable surplus.[8]

Figure 16–1
Cash Balance Through a Year for a Fund

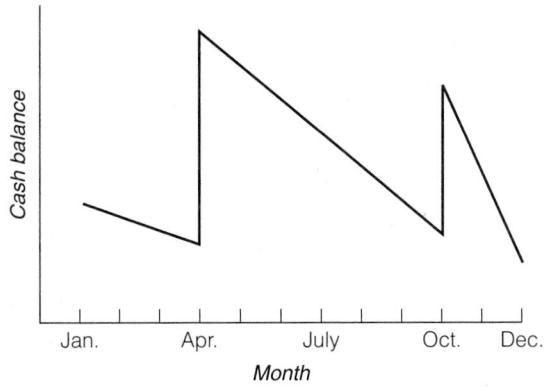

SOURCE: Philip Rosenberg, C. Wayne Stallings, and Charles K. Coe, *A Treasury Management Handbook for Small Cities and Other Government Units* (Chicago: Municipal Finance Officers Association, 1978), 56.

[7]Or tuition-due for colleges and universities. See Jon K. Speare and Margaret M. Cass, "Working Capital Management for Educational Institutions," *Journal of Cash Management* (May/June 1993): 49–51. Governments that sell services receive some day-to-day revenue from tolls, admissions, parking receipts, and so on. These flows are subject to greater daily variation than are tax collections.

[8]When cash flows do not follow the easily controllable patterns of tax due dates and paydays, they can be forecast using models of the type discussed in Chapter 13.

Elements of Cash Management

Governments need cash to bridge between daily disbursement outflows and revenue inflows because the two flows are seldom matched. Any cash held above that amount needed for the bridge means lost interest earnings. If the government, however, chooses to minimize those lost interest earnings and fails to hold adequate cash, it will not be able to pay its bills when due.[9] If cash flow could be perfectly forecast, managers would know how much cash would be available for how long, and investments could be made for exactly the period that cash would otherwise be idle. All flows are subject to forecast error, so the cash-management process is more complicated.

The balancing act involves dividing government resources between cash and short-term, marketable investments. Cash includes currency on hand and, predominantly, checkable deposits. These assets are liquid because they are immediately available for payment of bills. Unfortunately, they earn little or no interest. Short-term investments earn interest, but, because they are quickly marketable with little or no loss of value and low transaction cost, allow a liquidity cushion in case of cash emergencies. The balance is between the immediate liquidity that cash brings and the earnings produced by short-term investment.

The cash-management process includes three elements: (1) controlling the cash-collection and cash-disbursement process, (2) managing the available cash balances, and (3) investing those balances in short-term instruments. Recall from Chapter 12 that payments are stripped from tax returns early in the process of revenue administration. Payments follow the cash management process from the point of stripping. For a public manager, each portion of the process is governed by federal, state, or local laws that constrain the cash manager by "determining when monies can be collected, when obligations must be paid, where deposits can be placed and what securities can and cannot be purchased."[10] Although many of these limits reduce potential earnings from the cash-management program, most were introduced to prevent specific abuses of the public trust.

The cash manager seeks to control the largest fund pool for as long as possible by speeding collections, slowing outflows, and consolidating balances for productive use. That procedure maximizes the financial pool available for cash management. Figure 16–2 presents cash-control strategies used in the Department of the Interior, the collector of the largest amount of federal revenue outside the Treasury.

Accelerating Collections

The cash manager seeks to deposit all revenues owed to any part of the government as quickly as possible. That requires promptly billing any funds owed from goods or services sold or from taxes to be paid, rapidly processing remittances with

---

[9]Unless it borrows: Governments can borrow for short periods on the basis of anticipated revenue flows at extremely attractive rates.

[10]Frank M. Patitucci and Michael H. Lichtenstein, *Improving Cash Management in Local Governments* (Chicago: Municipal Finance Officers Association, 1977), 4.

Figure 16–2
Control for Cash Management: Receipts and Disbursement

Receipts and Deposits

Persons responsible for handling cash receipts should not participate in accounting or operating functions relative to controlling accounts receivable, preparing and mailing due statements, or approving credits for returns or adjustments of amounts due.

Receipts through the mail should be logged in the mailroom immediately, and receipts should be recorded within the day.

Large receipts ($1,000 federal threshold) should be deposited daily. All receipts should be deposited at least weekly.

Copies of cash receipts should be checked against the record of cash received by someone other than the person receiving the cash.

Wire transfers should be used for high-dollar cash receipts unless there are compelling reasons otherwise.

Receipt records should be maintained in a location separate from cash and checks.

Disbursements

Before vouchers are certified for payment, they should be reviewed for corrections of payee and payment amount, to verify correct delivery of purchased goods or service, and to check that payment is appropriate.

Transactions should be verified, using statistical sampling procedures when transactions are numerous and other arrangements of records permit.

Procedures should accommodate exploitation of discounts when economically warranted.

Wire transfer/electronic funds transfer should be used as frequently as feasible for better control, to ease recordkeeping, and to delay payment until actual due date.

The process should prevent duplicate payments on invoices.

Advances should be controlled, being used only when necessary. Excess travel advances should be collected promptly, managers should have periodic reports of outstanding travel advances, and systems should permit withholding of overdue travel advances from employee compensation.

SOURCE: Adapted from William L. Kendig, "Cash Management in the U.S. Department of the Interior," *Journal of Cash Management* (May/June 1985): 38–45.

an accurate accounting of funds to maintain fiscal records and control nonpayment, immediate deposit of funds into an account controlled by the cash manager, and encouraging the quickest collection possible (electronic funds transfer is normally the payment means of choice). Quick and sure control of funds, with proper accounting of source, is the primary concern.

Virtually all large transactions into government treasuries will be by electronic funds transfer. That procedure both speeds the collection and makes those funds immediately available for government use because there will be no lags associated with clearing checks and so on. States generally prefer Automated Clearing House

(ACH) transfers, but several provide for Federal Reserve wire transfers. These systems provide quick transfer of funds among banks on behalf of their customers. (Some governments also accept cashier's or certified checks, provided they arrive early enough for use of funds by the regular due date.) Payment into local treasuries are more likely to be on local banks, so electronic payment is less likely to be profitable, except for large payments from distant home offices of business taxpayers.[11] Newer direct electronic funds transfers allow individual bank customers, small businesses, and governments direct access to the bank's ACH system for online transfers, that is, the system that provides automatic teller machines (ATMs) and bank debit cards. Many states now use the system for food stamp and welfare payments, and it is reasonable to consider collections through it as well. Before electronic transfer, a favorite gimmick of some taxpayers would be to write their largest payment checks on distant banks and mail them from distant post offices to keep use of the funds for as long as possible.

Collection acceleration attempts to reduce the period between the time the taxpayer writes a check to the government and the time the government has use of those funds. This collection and deposit float consists of (1) mail time—the time it takes for the check to reach the government (most tax collection systems determine whether a return has been filed on time according to the postmark date, not the date when the return was received); (2) recordkeeping and processing time—the time it takes the revenue agency to process and deposit the check; and (3) clearance at the taxpayer's bank. (Electronic transfer slashes the process for the large, single transactions, but there remain many smaller checks totaling many dollars in aggregate.) Figure 16–3 outlines the flow. The government does not have full use of

Figure 16–3
Collection and Deposit Float

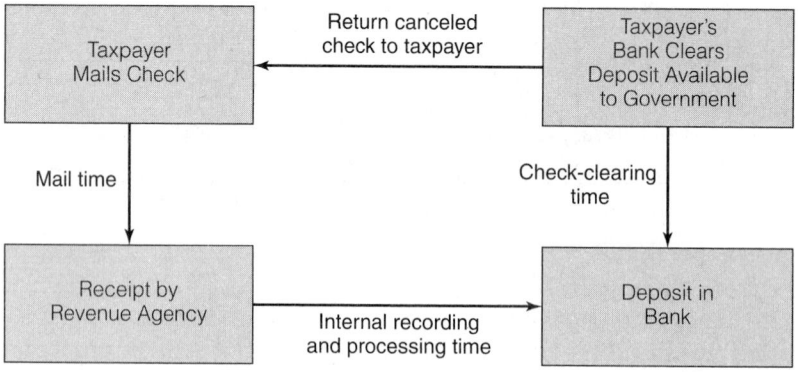

[11]At one time, cash managers in some large Texas cities flew to the state capital to pick up and immediately deposit the check for the state-collected city sales taxes. The interest for the extra few days more than covered the travel cost. Electronic funds transfer presumably has superseded this system.

Figure 16–4
A Postal Lockbox Collection System

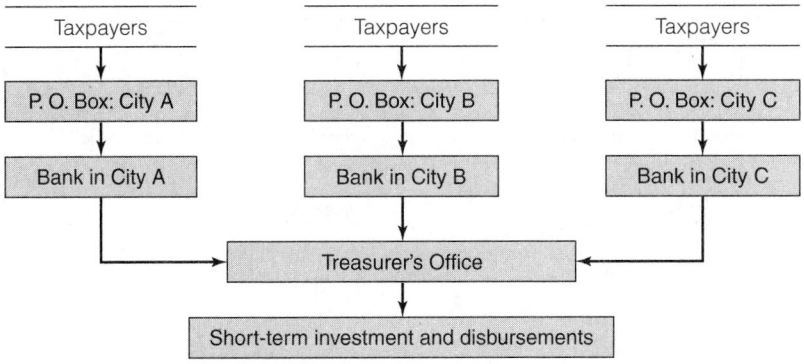

the check amount until the check has cleared the taxpayer's bank, so actions to reduce the length of any of these steps improves the cash pool.

Lockbox systems—an outsourcing of collections—offer one approach to speeding collections. Figure 16–4 diagrams such a system with regional banks acting as collection agents. Taxpayers mail payments to a local or nearby postal box. A bank in that city promptly empties the box, deposits checks, and transmits details to the government cash manager. Proximity to the taxpayer (and the taxpayer's bank) cuts both mail and clearing time. (Sidebar 16–1 shows the economic calculation of the value of a lockbox.) Furthermore, the bank may handle processing more quickly than a government mail-processing unit, but that depends on the specifics of the situation. Other governments use their own postal-box system to gain quick control over funds by reducing the need to sort revenue mail from other government mail.[12] The highest-quality systems have deposits made within 24 hours of receipt; internal recording and processing of returns often lags behind check deposits. Not only do quick collection and control provide longer investment pools, but rapid deposits also prevent questions that taxpayers rightly ask about the quality of any administration that leaves checks undeposited for extended periods. Lockbox systems are reputed to cut collection and deposit float by 1 to 4 days, depending on the environment.[13] They do cause some sacrifice of operational control by the government and of ability to quickly respond to citizen/taxpayer inquiries about the process.

[12]In some instances, banks may arrange to provide direct, over-the-counter collection of municipal utility payments, property taxes, or the like. The arrangement obviously reduces collection-deposit float.
[13]Collecting the apparently uncollectable, the long-time accounts receivable revenues, has always been difficult. One recent enterprise has been tried in Jersey City: Liens against delinquent taxpayers are bundled and sold at discount en masse to private investigators who collect whatever tax they can. To the extent these taxes are truly beyond the normal public grasp, the package will yield revenue. But most cities usually have low delinquency and relatively few hard-core noncollectables, so the transaction would be simply a short-term loan.

Sidebar 16–1
The Value of a Lockbox

Bank lockboxes allow quicker collection of payments not large enough to fall into an electronic funds transfer requirement. Lockbox services typically are charged on a per check-processed basis. Only those checks with interest potential large enough to cover that cost would merit diversion to the lockbox.

The computation mechanics are as follows:

Minimum Check Size 5 (Lockbox Charge × 365)/(Short-term Interest Rate × Days Saved Through Lockbox)

If the charge is 40 cents per check, the short-term interest rate is 3 percent, and the lockbox gets checks deposited 3 days earlier (as estimated by sampling), the minimum check for inclusion in the system is slightly less than $1,625. A similar computation would be applicable for testing the limits for electronic transfers. Lower short-term interest rates have made such systems less economically attractive, although all managers tend to feel more secure the quicker fund control is established.

Another way to accelerate collections is to accept credit cards for payment. Funds are quickly available without bad-check losses. Those gains have to be balanced against credit card company charges and bad-card fraud, but many government institutions (e.g., state universities), state tax departments, and enterprise activities accept them. Many governments use the Internet—with credit card payment—to collect utility payments, parking and traffic fines, business license charges, property taxes, and so on. Federal legislation passed in 1997 allows the Internal Revenue Service (IRS) to accept credit cards for tax liabilities; several states also accept credit card payment for certain taxes and user charges.[14]

Electronic transactions are faster and less costly than other exchange formats. This is the preferred and often required payment means for business tax remittances. The electronic transaction eliminates the float and makes bank location unimportant. To capitalize on their efficiency, governments need to also ensure their privacy, security, and verifiability (the audit trail). But hardcopy transactions are in certain decline and governments must adapt their collection (and disbursement) procedures to that environment.

[14]Federal individual income tax payments by credit card involve an intermediary. The intermediary makes payment and bills the credit card company for that payment plus a convenience charge sufficient to cover the card issuer's payment charge. This is typically the case for state and local governments as well.

Sidebar 16–2
Prompt-Payment Discounts

Should governments take advantage of prompt-payment discounts? The federal government drives small business wild with notorious slow payment, but not all governments have systems so restricted as to make dealings chronically late. To determine whether quick payment is worthwhile requires computation of the implicit interest rate it earns, for comparison with other rates available to the government:

Rate = [Amount saved by discount/Amount paid] × [365/Days paid early]

A common discount is 1 percent if paid within 10 days, with full amount due if not paid until the thirtieth day. If the original bill were $1,000, then

Rate = [10/990] × [365/20] = 18.4 percent

Waiting to pay the bill in 30 days rather than paying in 10 days is worthwhile if the agency can invest at an annual rate of 18 percent or higher for the 30-day period.

Most computerized accounts payable (A/P) systems have parameters that determine when payments are made. The system needs to have flexibility in payment dates, that the cash manager knows how the computerized system works, and that the manager actively monitors the payment system parameters and their performance.

Controlling Disbursements

The second important element is controlling disbursements, the other end of cash-management flow. Among the special features here, beyond the normal internal audit to verify claims before payment, are avoiding late-payment penalties and balancing early-payment discounts against the interest that could be earned from cash investment. Slow payment, as has been pointed out in an earlier chapter, can be a technique used to conceal budget imbalance. The objective here is not to conceal but to maximize return from a public resource.[15] Sidebar 16–2 shows the calculation for deciding whether early payment is attractive.

Disbursements fall into four categories: (1) payrolls—usually managed through a check-processing file with a single cash transfer made to cover all pay in the period; (2) debt service—a single paying agent (usually a bank) receives a single transfer (usually electronic) to cover principal and interest owed on a payment date and distributes individual payments to bondholders; (3) capital outlays (bond proceeds)—managed individually as the project flows toward completion; and

[15]Examples of these cash-management practices are reported in Executive Office of the President, Office of Management and Budget, *Report on Strengthening Federal Cash Management* (Washington, D.C.: GPO, 1980). Savings available there were estimated at $450 million per year.

(4) other purchases (supplies, equipment, contractual services, etc.)—usually processed in batch with payment dependent on vendors' discounts or on regular cycles. As service providers, not sellers of goods, governments usually have few opportunities to reduce cost and improve investable fund pools through tighter inventory management. They can, however, economize on funds by reducing lead times when supplies are restocked and by ensuring that stocks of supplies and consumables are no higher than absolutely necessary. Furthermore, savings can emerge by controlling the timing of major expenditures (large-ticket items) to coincide with periods of significant cash inflows. Good forecasting, careful information management, and stringent evaluation of the performance of suppliers can help with that. In all categories, the manager normally tries to maintain funds in cash-investment pools as long as possible because there will be minimal yield from a disbursing account.

Where the banking relationship permits, the government can gain substantial disbursement control through use of zero-balance accounts.[16] With such a system, each of the disbursement accounts would contain a zero balance; checks clearing on the account during a banking day would be covered by overdrafts. At the end of the day, sufficient funds would be transferred from the concentration account to cover the overdrafts in each zero-balance account and return the balance to zero. Transfers would occur only as the checks clear, not as checks are written. The zero-balance account eliminates disbursement float and makes the investment pool as large as possible for as long as possible. Unfortunately, local banks may not permit the arrangement, and laws may prohibit shopping outside the locality for the service.

Consolidating Balances

A third method used to improve cash-collection investment prospects is the concentration account. This approach produces a large investment pool without sacrificing the internal control available from maintaining separate accounts for each major expenditure area. Figure 16–5 illustrates such an arrangement. All revenues are received into a cash pool—the concentration account—rather than into the particular accounts from which checks will be written. As cash is needed for payroll, to pay vendors, to cover debt service, or whatever, it is transferred to that specific account. This central investment account retains any cash not needed to cover a specific disbursement. The concentration pool ensures longer availability of larger investable dollars, the key to higher interest earnings. The account would ideally receive collections from a receipt-generating funds of the government and would manage all account disbursements. The concentration account also reduces the potential impact of individual bad checks on the government balance needed to make disbursements.

---

[16]Banks have traditionally been compensated for their services through the use of funds in non-interest-bearing demand deposits. Therefore, banks require fees for service to operate a zero-balance account. Which avenue is superior for the government needs to be computed; see Margaret Kleusner, "Balances or Fees—How to Compensate the Bank," *Journal of Cash Management* (Jan./Feb. 1993): 34–37.

Figure 16–5
Application of a Concentration Account

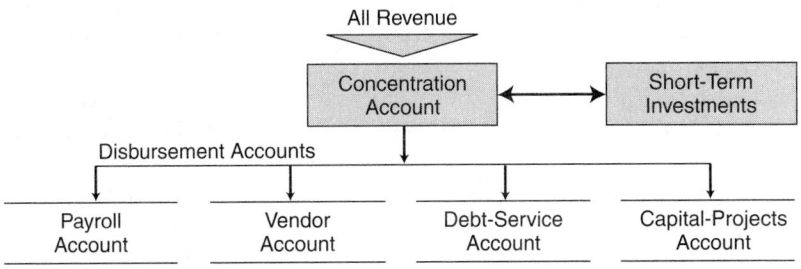

Financial institutions offer more attractive net yields for larger investments, and some transaction costs vary with the number of transactions, not the size of the transaction. Therefore, pooling funds to obtain the largest investment block available for the longest investment period possible should increase the net return from cash management. Pooling is not commingling of funds: Cash sources are recorded, and the invested money will be returned to the originating fund as the investment instruments mature. Interest from the investment pool may or may not be returned to the source fund, depending on state law and local investment orders. The simplest practice returns interest from the investment pool to the general fund for reapportionment by the legislative body.

Investing Idle Funds

Collection and disbursement control provides a pool for investment. Investable funds management seeks to determine the minimum cash balance required in the government checking account (possible the concentration account demand deposit), maintain that balance, and invest the rest. That balance may well be imposed through special constraints, like a compensating balance required by the bank as payment to it for services extended to the government. There may also be legal constraints or other contractual arrangements that dictate the balance. Such special controls then establish the cash level to be maintained.

If there is no required balance, then the manager is free to establish an optimal balance by evaluating the trade-off between the opportunity cost of holding too much cash (the interest earnings forgone) and the cost of being short of cash (the transaction costs involved in selling securities to obtain cash). The optimum cash-holding level has declined dramatically in recent years because computer technology has made quick and inexpensive security conversion feasible.[17] For

[17]Michael Dotsey, "An Investigation of Cash Management Practices and Their Effects on the Demand for Money," *Federal Reserve Bank of Richmond Economic Review* 70 (Sept./Oct. 1984): 3–5.

marketable-security portfolios, it is likely that external constraints will apply before cash levels decline to the otherwise optimal level.[18]

Investable-funds management requires the regular preparation of a cash budget to establish the amount available for investment. Although the largest units should operate on a daily-forecast basis, more governments forecast weekly or monthly. Both receipts and disbursements must be estimated on the basis of experience, administrative policy, and existing statutes. Some flows, both in and out, are easier to estimate than others, but all are uncertain. For most governments, the key elements for successful forecasting are the following:

Make errors on the side of conservatism.
Pay most attention to the major items.
Keep the forecast simple.
Maintain documentation of how the forecasts were prepared.[19]

That approach, carried over a number of investment periods, allows forecasting improvements and adjustments to refine the estimated investment pool.

Estimates must consider both what cash is available and for what periods of time that cash pool will be available. Money market conditions are often such that long-term interest rates are higher than short-term rates. When the 6-month Treasury bill rate is higher than the 3-month rate, cash available for 6 months can profitably be directed to the longer instrument. The manager can invest without fearing actual capital loss from interest-rate fluctuations if the manager matches the security term to the time that the cash will be available.[20] Matching is possible only if cash flows have been conservatively estimated through the fiscal year. Thus, forecasting revenue and expenditure flows is critical for a cash management program. Those forecasts will be keyed to recent fiscal years' experience and actions in the current year budget.

Suitable media for idle-cash investment provides a sound balance between a safe return on idle cash and the ability to respond to unexpected cash demands. Suitable instruments earn interest, are quickly salable at low cost, and are virtually without risk. Four standards for prudence are as follows:

1. **No default risk.** Commercial stocks and bonds should not be in the portfolio because of their default risk—the loss of principal because the investment fails or market estimates about the prospects of the activity change. Public pension funds may invest in such assets because of their long-term focus, but such investments remain inappropriate for cash management.

---

[18]Two models for determining optimal cash levels: William J. Baumol presents a deterministic model in "The Transactions Demand for Cash: An Inventory Theoretical Approach," *Quarterly Journal of Economics* 66 (November 1952): 545–56; and Merton H. Miller and Daniel Orr present a probabilistic model in "A Model of the Demand for Money by Firms," *Quarterly Journal of Economics* 80 (August 1966): 413–35. An application of the logic of each to Honolulu shows the probabilistic model suggested a much higher optimum balance. See Rita M. Maldonado and Lawrence S. Ritter, "Optimal Municipal Cash Management: A Case Study," *Review of Economic and Statistics* 47 (November 1971): 384–88.

[19]The logic of cash forecasting and some general guidelines are discussed in David A. Wismer, "Approach to Cash Flow Forecasting," *Journal of Cash Management* 5 (Jan./Feb. 1985): 12–16.

[20]Nathaniel B. Guild, ed., *The Public Money Manager's Handbook* (Chicago: Crain Books, 1981), 124.

2. **No credit market risk.** Long-term debt instruments should not be in the cash-investment portfolio because of credit-market risk—loss in the market value of a fixed-income asset that results when market interest rates rise.[21] Nobody can reliably forecast interest rates—and that would be required for prudent investment of short-term funds in long-term securities. Speculators do it—that is their business—but managers of public funds are not to be speculators.

3. **No artificially low rates of return.** State or local government debt would ordinarily be avoided because of its artificially low interest rates. (If rates on tax-exempt debt are sufficiently high to appear attractive to potential investors who do not pay income tax, they probably reflect a dangerously high risk to the principal.) Short-term taxable issues by governments may be considered, if they meet safety and liquidity investment criteria.

4. **No illiquid assets.** The funds have to be immediately available to cover bills that have to be paid. The manager cannot wait to find a buyer, for the market to recover, or for a security to mature to recover face value.

Beyond the constraints of sound financial management, cash managers must operate within the limits placed by federal, state, and local laws. Those controls can limit the places where deposits can be held, establish shares of total financial assets than may be placed with a particular depository, establish what securities and maturities can be purchased, define formulas for determining what interest rate will be paid on public fund deposits, limit the funds from which investment can be made, and so on.[22] Although the tendency has been toward greater freedom and expanded options, public cash managers are not likely to have all the options available to corporate cash managers because potential conflict-of-interest problems can emerge in the management of government resources. Besides, it is all other people's money and deserves to be treated with great care.

Controlling law normally allows a number of investment media for government fund managers.[23]

---

[21]Local governments in particular seem unable to grasp the principle that short-term funds ought never be placed in long-term investments. For instance, San Jose, California violated the principle in early 1984, losing $60 million on a $750 million investment pool and thereby imperiled the city's capacity to pay its bills. See Harold E. Boldt, "Do You Know the Way to San Jose? or Would You like to Invest City Funds in Long-Term Government Bonds?" *Missouri Municipal League* (September 1984): 17–19. Orange County, California repeated the mistake in the mid-1990s and had to file for bankruptcy protection. See Craig L. Johnson and John L. Mikesell, "The Orange County Debacle; Where Irresponsible Cash and Debt Management Practices Collide," *Municipal Finance Journal* 17 (Summer 1996): 1–15. They were not paying attention in Pennsylvania, either. Some small school districts there lost millions in similar transactions in the mid-1990s. Charles Gasparino and Michael Moss, "What Happened When a Small Town Trusted Local Financial Wizard," *Wall Street Journal* (December 26, 1997):A-1. Are they not paying attention?

[22]A list of state actions on how governments may manage idle cash appears in Advisory Commission on Intergovernmental Relations, *Understanding State and Local Cash Management* (Washington, D.C.: ACIR, 1977), 47–58.

[23]Federal government cash "investment" focuses on reducing the need to borrow, not on where to "park" investable funds.

Treasury Bills

Treasury bills (T-bills), short-term instruments issued by the U.S. government, are the most popular marketable security for cash managers. Federal Reserve Banks sell them in weekly auctions in 91-day, 182-day, and, in some auctions, 1-year maturities, as described in Sidebar 16–3. The secondary market is broad and lively, so T-bills can easily be liquidated if an unanticipated need for cash develops, or they can be purchased any time cash is available.

T-bill yields are typically the lowest of the marketable securities, but that disadvantage is compensated by their safety from default, short maturity, and easy marketability.

T-bills bear no interest in the ordinary sense, although they do yield a return to their holder. Because they are sold at a price less than their face value (i.e., at discount), the holder receives a yield equal to the difference between the purchase price and the price received when the bill matures (or is resold). Thus, the purchaser might pay $9,860 for a bill with a face value of $10,000; the return at maturity would be $140. The annualized rate of return or yield rate on a bill purchased through the discount mechanism may be computed according to the formula

$$\text{Investment Yield to Maturity } (Y) = [(100\,P) \times 365]/(P \times H)$$

where P = purchase price paid by the investor for each $100 of the bill's face value and H = the number of days to maturity.[24]

For example, if the auction price is $98.25 per $100 of face value ($9,825 for the $10,000 T-bill) for a 91-day bill, the effective yield would equal

$$Y = [(100 - 98.25) \times 365]/(98.25 \times 91) = 0.0714 \text{ or } 7.14\%.$$

The same approach can be applied to compute the effective yield for a bill purchased or sold on the secondary market, substituting for $100 the price per $100 of face value received on sale.[25]

Other Federal-Agency Issues

Federal agencies that make or guarantee loans issue their own securities. They include the National Mortgage Association, Federal National Mortgage Association, Bank for Cooperatives, Student Loan Marketing Association, Federal Home Loan Bank, Federal Land Bank, and others. These securities are not legal obligations of the U.S. government but have extremely low default risk. They normally sell at a yield between that of the Treasury issues and other money-market issues. The same dealers who trade in the Treasury market trade in these issues as well, so they are salable in a strong secondary market. Some state and local government

---

[24]Richard D.C. Trainer, *The Arithmetic of Interest Rates* (New York: Federal Reserve Bank of New York, 1982).

[25]The appropriate price of a bill, given a discount rate or desired investment yield, can be computed algebraically from the same formula. Pricing, however, is based on the 360-day financial year.

Sidebar 16–3
How Treasury Bills Are Auctioned Today

The federal government regularly must borrow to finance its deficit and to refinance prior debt that is retiring. Much of that financing is managed through auctions conducted by the Treasury. Here are the mechanics of bidding to purchase this debt.

Two different types of bids can be submitted in the T-bill auction: competitive and noncompetitive. Competitive bidders include money market banks, dealers, and other institutional investors who buy large quantities of T-bills. The tenders they submit indicate the amount of bills they wish to purchase and the price they are willing to pay. They are permitted to submit more than one tender. Noncompetitive bidders are usually small or inexperienced bidders who indicate the amount of bills they want to purchase (up to $1,000,000) and agree to pay the quantity weighted average of the accepted competitive bids.

After all bids are in, first the Treasury sets aside the amount of bills requested by the noncompetitive bidders. The remainder is allocated among the competitive bidders, beginning with those who bid the highest price, until the total amount is issued. The price paid by the noncompetitive bidders can then be calculated based on the competitive bids that were accepted.

SOURCE: Reprinted from Loretta J. Mester, "Going, Going, Gone: Setting Prices with Auctions," *Federal Reserve Bank of Philadelphia, Business Review* (Mar./Apr. 1988).

investment statutes are not clear about the legality of purchasing such issues, even though permitting investment in Treasury issues.

Negotiable Certificates of Deposit

A certificate of deposit (CD) is a time deposit with a commercial bank (or savings and loan association) issued for a specified period at a contracted interest rate. The issue is for a contracted period over which the stated interest rate holds, regardless of other rate changes in the period. The largest banks' issues are bought and sold by security dealers. CDs usually bear rates above those paid on federal securities and are marketable. Investment statutes often restrict state or local governments from acquiring CDs from out-of-state financial institutions, so some flexibility may be reduced. High-denomination CDs are usually not fully covered by federal insurance (negotiated rates typically begin with CDs of $100,000, and the current insurance limit and deposit insurance system policy no longer permits public depositors to break deposits into $100,000 chunks, each with a separate custodian name). Some states require banks to pledge particular assets (a collateralization) to guarantee the security of public funds: If the bank fails, those pledged assets would ensure that the public funds were not lost. Pledging is not popular with banks because it reduces profitability and the amount of credit a bank can extend.[26]

[26]James A. Verbugge, "The Effects of Pledging Regulations on Bank Asset Compositions," *Journal of Bank Research* 4 (August 1973): 168–76.

The unprecedented (for non-Depression times) level of bank and savings-and-loan-association failures in the late 1980s made public officials especially vigilant in safeguarding deposits. Collateralization is helpful and recommended[27] but does not guarantee protection if a failure should occur. Not only might the collateral not have a market value equal to its pledged value at the time of the collapse, but the troubled bank may have been sloppy about the collateral: misplacing agreements, pledging the collateral for more than one depositor, or even selling the collateral for cash needs. Some recommend custody of collateral with a third party. Therefore, the public depositor must pay attention to institution quality. That means some independent deposit-institution analysis: using financial institution reports to evaluate whether the institution is sufficiently capitalized to handle potential losses, whether it is generating sufficient profits, how dependent it is on large-denomination CDs that will be lost if competitiveness of its rates decline or if there are rumors of trouble, and the institution's extent of problem loans or leases (those on which interest is not being earned, those more than 90 days overdue, those renegotiated). Because statutes often limit deposits to local or regional institutions, the questioning may be embarrassing—but certainly less so than the loss of public deposits in a failure.[28]

Commercial Paper

Large corporations and finance companies sell commercial paper—short-term, unsecured promissory notes—directly to investors or through dealers. Maturities range up to 270 days. The secondary market is weak, but commercial paper from large corporate borrowers offers high rates. Higher risk and lower marketability reduce their attractiveness for most public cash-management programs. Furthermore, commercial paper offers substantially greater potential exposure to political problems than do other money-market instruments.[29]

Repurchase Agreements and Reverse Repurchase Agreements

A repurchase agreement (repo) is an agreement between a bank or security dealer and an investor in which the investor purchases a security, usually a U.S. Treasury security, with the commitment that the dealer will repurchase the security at a later date and a set price. A reverse repo involves sale of the security by the investor to the dealer at an agreed repurchase price. (Both are *derivatives,* instruments whose value is based on some other underlying security.) Maturity is short, 1 day to a few months, and flexible to meet the investor's requirements. The rate is slightly below the rate available on the security itself. The repo should be safe because a security

---

[27]Girard Miller and Michelle R. Saddler, "Collateralization: Protecting Public Deposits," *Government Finance Review* 3 (October 1987): 23–26.

[28]Robert L. Banks, "Assessing Bank Quality to Shield Public Funds," *City & State* (Sept. 1985): 24–25. There are a variety of bank and savings-and-local CD-rating services, including those from Standard & Poor's, Bank Safety, Inc., Sheshunoff Information Services, and others.

[29]Corporate bonds and stocks are to be avoided because of both default risk and credit-market risk. Because pension funds are more concerned with long-term investment, public pension funds do frequently acquire high-grade corporate stocks and bonds.

is available as full collateral on the transaction. Unfortunately, collapse of two large government security dealers in 1985 left many governments with large losses because collateral was missing. The market remains unregulated and uninsured.

State and Local Debt

Most public-investment statutes allow the purchase of state and local government bonds. Such purchases are made, but usually to support weak local bond markets and usually because of political pressure, not careful fiscal judgment. Normally, those acquisitions are unwise because the debt's term is too long for cash-management purposes and yields are too low. If the yield is sufficiently high to be attractive, default risk must be excessive. However, some municipal debt is now sold in taxable format and these yields may not be unattractive to tax-exempt purchasers.

State Investment Pools

A number of states—including California, Connecticut, Florida, Georgia, Illinois, Maryland, Massachusetts, Montana, New Jersey, North Carolina, Oklahoma, Oregon, Tennessee, Texas, Utah, Virginia, West Virginia, and Wisconsin—have formal local government investment pools to enable local governments to combine funds for short-term investment. The pools should offer professional management, wider markets for investment, and the return advantages of larger investment blocks. Overall, these pools should be most attractive for small governments; their use should grow with tight budgets and increased fiscal sophistication.[30] However, major losses in investment pools through poor management—the West Virginia consolidated-investment fund lost $279 million from a $1.3 billion fund in the late 1980s and the Orange County (California) Investment Pool lost $1.7 billion on its pool of $7.5 billion in 1994—raise cautions.[31] The problem is not the idea of the pool, but the capability and prudence of those operating them. The West Virginia fund put money in high-risk media; the Orange County pool invested funds available only for the short term in investments with credit-risk (i.e., their value was interest-rate sensitive) and borrowed to expand earnings from their client investment pool. Texas contracted operations of TexPool, its investment pool, to a private bank and financial adviser team in 1997 after the state assumed losses caused by ill-advised use of derivative securities under the system run by its state treasurer. Such contract privatization is likely to expand. To reduce client fears, some states have sought ratings for their pools, a high rating being dependent on an absence of leverage (borrowing new funds to boost earnings from funds invested by client governments) and keeping average maturity of holdings within guidelines from the regulated money market.

---

[30]Timothy Q. Cook and Jeremy G. Duffield, "Short-Term Investment Pools," *Economic Review of Federal Reserve Bank of Richmond* 66 (Sept./Oct. 1980): 6.

[31]Clare Ansberry, "West Virginia Weighs Lawsuit Against Brokers," *Wall Street Journal* (6 June 1989): 1, and California Senate Special Committee on Local Government Investments, *The Orange County Bankruptcy: Broad Repercussions, New Public Policy* (August 1995). The Orange County episode is examined in five articles in *Municipal Finance Journal* 17 (Summer 1996).

Money-Market Mutual Funds

Private money-market mutual funds provide a private-sector alternative to the state investment pools. They offer liquidity, considerable safety, and professional management. Seldom are these alternatives on the list of legal media for investment.

Keeping Score (Measuring Performance)

Cash management needs a rolling scorecard to evaluate the program's success and to improve the program's operation. At a minimum, score keeping should be done on a weekly basis, with the following noted:

Estimated total financial assets (cash and investments) held by unit (from the forecast)

Actual total financial assets held

Demand deposit and currency total

Interest received to date, this year

Interest received to date, last year

Six-month T-bill rate, this week

Six-month T-bill rate, same week last year

Comparing interest-rate profiles is important because substantial differences in investment income can occur from one year to the next from fluctuations in money-market conditions that have nothing to do with cash-management efforts. The data can provide feedback to improve forecasting models as well as to gauge the benefits from the program.

Managing Public Employee Retirement Funds

State and local government employee retirement funds had financial assets of more than $2 trillion at the end of 2005.[32] Table 16–1 lists the fifteen largest public pension funds, their assets, and their size rank among all pension funds. Public employee retirement funds are big money, both in total and among pension programs. Thirty-one of the top fifty pension funds, by amount of assets, are for public employees. These are considerable assets with considerable economic consequence. The funds represent payments during the employee's working life to defray the cost of pension promises made to those employees. Their prudent management is important for taxpayers and public employees alike, although exactly how depends on the nature of the retirement plan. If the public pension fund is not prudently managed, the requirements for payments to retired employees can have a troubling impact on the operations of the government and can violate the principles of intergenerational

[32]Board of Governors, *Flow of Funds Accounts*. The Federal government retirement funds also held over $1 trillion at the end of fiscal year 2004.

Table 16–1
Sponsors of the Fifteen Largest Public Employee Pension Funds, 2005

	Total Assets ($ Billions)	Overall Rank
California Public Employees	196.0	1
Federal Retirement Thrift	167.2	2
California State Teachers	134.0	3
New York State Common Retirement	131.9	4
Florida State Board of Administration	114.9	5
New York City Retirement	105.9	7
Texas Teachers	94.4	8
New York State Teachers	87.4	9
Wisconsin Investment Board	74.5	10
New Jersey Division of Investment	72.9	12
North Carolina Retirement System	69.5	14
Ohio Public Employees	67.6	16
Ohio State Teachers	62.0	17
Michigan Retirement	55.2	20
Pennsylvania School Employees	53.8	21

SOURCE: Pensions & Investments. Available online at www.pionline.com.

equity. Sound pension fund management is an important contributor to long-term fiscal sustainability.

Employers offer two types of retirement programs to their employees. In a *defined-contribution* plan, an employer regularly contributes money to an employee's retirement account but makes no guarantee about the size of benefits that will be paid on retirement. That payout depends on what has been put into the employee's account and on the investment choices made with the funds as they accumulate in the account. The amount to be placed into the employee's account is established as part of the employment agreement between employer and employee. Defined-contribution plans, by their nature, require that the government bear the cost of future retirement benefits at the time that the employee earns them; the employment agreement means that the contribution will be made when the contribution is earned. Retirement income depends on the amount of periodic contribution made by the employer, the success of the fund manager on earning a return on those contributions, and the length of time the fund can earn a return. The risk of managing fund resources to build enough resources to finance a pension is on the employee. Public employee retirement programs are seldom defined contribution; more than 90 percent are defined benefit.[33]

[33]Two large defined-contribution programs are as follows: Faculty at state universities may be in the TIAA/CREF program (its assets exceed $250 billion) and federal employees in the Federal Employee Retirement System Thrift Savings Plan (for those hired after 1983). In 1996, Michigan established a defined-contribution plan for all new state employees as their only retirement plan option, the first state to do so. West Virginia school employees were put in such a plan in 1991. See David Franecki, "Michigan Plan Should Bolster Mutual Funds," *Wall Street Journal* (23 December 1996): B-6.

In a *defined-benefit* plan, the employer guarantees what benefits will be paid at retirement.[34] A formula defines what benefits will be paid, with common arguments in that formula including years of service, age at retirement, and salary level at retirement. The benefit may be adjusted for cost-of-living changes, either automatically or as reflected in new wage and salary scales. The employer may make payments into a retirement fund and that fund will be invested, but the size of that fund does not determine the benefits paid to the retired employee. The retirement benefit must be paid, either from accumulations in the employee retirement fund (contributions made through the work years plus interest earned on those contributions) or, if they are not sufficient, from current payments into the retirement system. The risk of accumulating and managing the retirement fund is borne by the employing government and its taxpayers. Public employee pension funds typically have not accumulated sufficient reserves during employee work careers to cover the defined benefits to which plans entitle employees as part of their compensation. Thus, the government will have to pay, from its current revenue in later years, part of the compensation promised in earlier years. For example, in fiscal 2007, the government would pay the wages and salaries of its current workforce and 2007 pension payments to all prior employees whose work in earlier years entitled them to pensions. State and local retirement programs tend to be defined benefit in nature (forty-eight states by recent count), although a number also provide a defined contribution supplement but frequently without a contribution from the employer.[35] The Federal Employees Retirement System includes both defined benefit and defined contribution components.

For many years, governments and employees seemed content with this financing approach. Because governments do not go out of business (usually) and cannot be acquired by conglomerates, there appeared to be little danger of missed payments to employees. Payments can easily be made by raising taxes on the future tax base. Bernard Jump aptly summarizes the traditional view of state and local employee pensions:

> The pension, along with a degree of job security not generally associated with employment in the private sector, was assumed to be a fair offset for lower wages in public sector jobs. Commonly, public pension administration encountered few problems that required more than perfunctory attention from governments' top elected and professional officials. Each year, legislatures appropriated whatever was needed to cover the year's share of pension costs. In some jurisdictions, appropriations simply equaled the actual benefits to be paid during the year; in other instances, appropriations reflected at least nominally the actuarial cost of benefits accrued during the year by active employees. As long as work force size, benefit levels, and the number of retirees did not grow too

[34]In recent years, some private employers have developed "Cash Balance" pension plans. These defined-benefit plans express benefits as an "account balance" based on hypothetical pay credits (a percent of salary or total compensation) and hypothetical interest credits to employee accounts. Benefits are paid from commingled funds invested on behalf of all participants by plan trustees and employees do not own these "Accounts" nor make investment decisions about them. There are no known public employee cash-balance pension programs.

[35]U.S. Government Accounting Office, *State Pension Plans: Similarities and Differences Between Federal and State Designs,* GAO/GGD-99-45 (Washington, D.C.: U.S. GAO, 1999).

rapidly and the jurisdiction's financial condition remained stable, the fiscal implications of the pensions did not appear to be significant.[36]

That easy approach to pension was battered in the 1970s. Expenditures for employee retirement suddenly increased, absolutely and relative to current personnel cost, as many employees started drawing lucrative pensions. State and local governments began encountering impressive resistance to tax increases, including new constitutional restrictions against rate increases, and some governments teetered on the brink of default on contractual obligations in the midst of fiscal crisis. Credit-rating firms, bond underwriters, and investors all became aware of the risk associated with loans to governments whose sizable long-term pension liabilities could endanger repayment of debt. And possibly most important, investigators discovered an important incentive problem with traditional pension finance: Elected officials could seek public employee support with generous pension promises now, knowing that when the payments were made, those officials would not be part of the governing team required to raise those funds.

From those influences came a major effort to switch public pension finance from the traditional pay-as-you-go basis to an actuarial or full funding basis. A Government Accountability Office (GAO) report explains: "Although state and local governments rarely become insolvent or cease to operate, those with underfunded pension plans may face difficult budget choices in the future if they do not work toward full funding. Their future taxpayers will face a liability for benefits earned by current and former government workers, leaving these governments to choose between reducing future pension benefits or raising revenues."[37] Failure to fund a defined benefit pension program is not consistent with equity between the generations and is a problem for fiscal sustainability.[38]

Actuarial funding is "a procedure where the estimated cost—the actuarial present value—of pension benefits accruing to active employees is systematically paid by the employer into a fund (perhaps with a share paid in by the employee as well). In turn, the retirement fund makes payments to retirees and invests surplus funds."[39] Thus, the anticipated future cost of pension payments to an employee are handled while the employee is working. Pension payments on retirement comes from money set aside during the years of employment plus interest on that accumulation. Funding is based on estimates computed on several assumptions: (1) whether and when the employee will retire; (2) when the retired employee will die;

---

[36]Bernard Jump, Jr., "Public Employment, Collective Bargaining, and Employee Wages and Pensions," in *State and Local Government Finance and Financial Management: A Compendium of Current Research*, ed. Catherine Spain (Washington, D.C.: Government Finance Research Center, Municipal Finance Officers Association, 1978), 78.

[37]U.S. General Accounting Office, *State and Local Government Contributions to Underfunded Plans*, GAO/HEHS-96-56 (Washington, D.C.: General Accounting Office, 1997), 2.

[38]There is evidence that state and local government pension programs tend to be generous because their sponsoring governments are able to underfund them. See Richard W. Johnson, "Pension Underfunding and Liberal Retirement Benefits Among State and Local Government Workers," *National Tax Journal* 50 (March 1997): 113–142.

[39]Bernard Jump, Jr., *State and Local Employee Pension Plans: Watching for Problems* (Columbus, Ohio: Academy for Contemporary Problems, 1976), 9.

Table 16–2
National Summary of State and Local Government Employee Retirement System Finances: Fiscal Year 2001–2002 ($ thousands)

	Total	State	Local
Total receipts	−6,120,528	−8,448.868	2,328,340
Employee contributions	27,544,022	23,006,094	4,537,928
Government contributions	38,792,031	32,059,268	6,732,763
State governments' contributions	17,182,861	16,795,329	387,532
Local governments' contributions	21,309,170	15,263,939	6,345,231
Earnings on investments	−72,456,581	−63,514,230	−8,942,351
Total payments	121,980,231	98,225,642	23,754,589
Benefits	110,128,411	88,713,825	21,414,586
Withdrawals	4,079,492	3,257,640	821,852
Other payments	7,772,328	6,254,177	1,518,151

SOURCE: U.S. Bureau of Census, Governments Division.
NOTE: Detail may not add to total because of rounding.

(3) the progression of employee salary that will establish pension benefits; and (4) the rate of return earned on invested pension funds. None of those factors will be known; all must be reviewed and revised on a reasonable schedule if funding is to be meaningful.

For the pension system to avoid becoming a burden on future taxpayers and thereby threatening fiscal sustainability, the systems must accumulate assets adequate to meet the benefits promised during employee careers. Table 16–2 gives an idea of the extent to which the system functions. Receipts include contributions into the system by employers and employee and investment earnings on accumulated assets. When investment markets are down, as was the case in 2001–2002, the earnings may be negative (a capital loss). But in better economic conditions, the earnings will constitute a major share of receipts and will cover system benefits. Are fund accumulations large enough to cover the future costs of retirement benefits that have been earned? This is the question of actuarial funding and the results here are not so promising. The most recent data from Wiltshire Associates, a pension consultancy, survey of sixty-four state retirement systems shows a funding ratio (the percentage of pension liabilities that is covered by pension assets) of 83 percent in 2004 (compared with 77 percent in the same plans in 2003). In other words, the plans had 83 percent of the resources necessary to cover the pension promises made to current and previous employees. Their comparable data for city and county systems showed a funding ratio of 83 percent in 2003.[40] The funding ratios are lower than they were at the turn of the century, are lower than comparable ratios for private pension funds, and encompass wide variation in funding status between plans. The underfunded systems create a challenge for future operations

[40]Wilshire Research, *2005 Wilshire Report on State Retirement Systems: Funding Level and Asset Allocation* (March 10, 2005).

of their sponsoring governments. While the total assets of public pension funds are huge in the aggregate, they do not mean that the sponsoring government has made adequate accommodation for future liabilities.[41] (The federal Pension Benefit Guaranty Corporation does not cover government pension programs.)

The focus of these funds is long term, so they can direct their attention to yield over many years without special concern for short-term liquidity. In most cases, the fund managers have good forecasts of retirement points and can manage portfolios to accommodate necessary withdrawals, even with long average maturity for their investments.[42] Furthermore, the size of the pools allows the programs to accept higher risks on their investment strategies in the quest for better return. Almost all funds are permitted investment in less-liquid, higher-risk media, including corporate securities and, sometimes, direct equity participation.[43] All these factors work to move these funds away from deposits (demand and certificate) and toward investments. The funds are tax-exempt on their returns, so traditional state-local debt is not attractive. In general, the investment should be prudent. The Government Finance Officers Association defines prudent investments to be those meeting three tests:

1. **Creditworthiness:** Securities must meet credit standards as established by the retirement system's investment policy.
2. **Liquidity:** Investment maturities must be matched to the cash needs of the system.
3. **Market Rate of Return:** Investments must yield a rate of return commensurate with a recognized level of risk.[44]

Assets should be managed for the exclusive benefit of plan participants, but latitude and definitional flexibility create opportunities.

Table 16–3 shows the portfolio patterns from 1965 through 2004, reflecting changes in markets and opportunities for funds, along with the use of more professional and more aggressive managers. The data show a dramatically higher percentage of investment in corporate equity (stocks), some increase in holdings of U.S. government securities, but markedly lower percentages in corporate and foreign bonds. Holdings of tax-exempt securities have almost disappeared. In general, there

---

[41]Chronic underfunding of the public employee pension fund and poor investment performance, along with apparent financial irregularities city operations, brought a fiscal and political crisis to San Diego, California in 2005, including some discussion about filing for bankruptcy. The city promised benefits without making adequate allowance for their payment, and thereby created a significant additional burden of overall city finances. The outcome of the financial problems is not yet clear, but it is clear that pension mismanagement can intrude on operations of the rest of government.

[42]Fund managers can get surprised when inducements for early retirement have more takers than management forecast. Such episodes can create significant problems if long-term fixed-income securities must be sold before maturity when market yields are higher than coupons.

[43]The Washington State Investment Board experience shows the risk. Its move into venture capital from 1990 to early 1993 yielded around 1.6 percent per year, and its real estate assets fell below their purchase price. Savings accounts, let alone conservative portfolio media, would have done better. Not all hot investment ideas are so hot. See Randall Smith, "State's Gamble Shows Pitfalls of Investing," *Wall Street Journal* (20 May 1993): C-1. But the Board has time and values may recover.

[44]Approved GFOA executive Board, May 2, 1993. The Employee Retirement Income Security Act governs private pensions.

Table 16–3
Asset Distribution of State and Local Government Employee Retirement Funds (End of Selected Calendar Years)

	1965	1970	1975	1980	1985	1990	1995	2000	2004
Total financial assets	100.0%	100.0%	100.0%	100.0%	100.0%	100.0%	100.0%	100.0%	100.0%
Checkable deposits and currency	0.9%	0.7%	0.3%	0.3%	0.6%	0.6%	0.3%	0.4%	0.4%
Time and savings deposits	0.0%	0.3%	1.2%	1.9%	3.3%	1.0%	0.3%	0.0%	0.0%
Security repurchase agreements	0.0%	0.0%	0.0%	0.0%	1.3%	1.5%	2.4%	2.0%	2.0%
Credit market instruments	91.8%	82.3%	75.3%	74.9%	63.3%	50.2%	40.6%	34.8%	34.1%
Open market paper	0.0%	0.0%	0.0%	0.0%	1.3%	1.5%	2.4%	2.0%	2.4%
U.S. government securities	22.3%	10.9%	7.5%	20.3%	31.0%	28.9%	22.3%	17.7%	14.7%
Treasury	21.1%	8.5%	2.4%	10.6%	20.8%	18.0%	14.7%	9.0%	7.0%
Agency	14.7%	2.5%	5.1%	9.7%	10.2%	10.8%	7.6%	8.7%	7.7%
Municipal securities	7.6%	3.3%	1.8%	2.1%	0.3%	0.6%	0.1%	0.1%	0.0%
Corporate and foreign bonds	50.4%	58.2%	58.7%	46.9%	26.9%	17.7%	14.5%	14.1%	16.0%
Mortgages	10.9%	9.8%	7.2%	5.5%	3.8%	2.0%	1.2%	0.9%	1.0%
Corporate equities	7.3%	16.7%	23.4%	22.5%	30.1%	35.5%	52.1%	59.1%	58.0%
Miscellaneous assets	0.0%	0.0%	0.0%	4.1%	1.4%	11.1%	4.2%	3.7%	5.5%

SOURCE: Board of Governors of Federal Reserve System, *Flow of Funds Accounts of the United States* (Z1 release).

has been a movement away from credit-market instruments (fixed-income loans) toward equity. The change largely reflects a desire to obtain higher returns on the fund, thus reducing the need for payments by the government to achieve the benefits promised retirees. Managers of these funds have clearly moved toward a more professional approach to handling the resources that support employee pensions.

Critical Issues in Public Employee Retirement Fund Management

These fund balances create real opportunities for creativity and, unfortunately, a great target for scandal.[45] There are several particular issues. First, some governments have used employee pension funds as guaranteed markets for their own debt. The debt yields an artificially low rate of return because interest on most state and local debt is excluded from taxation—a benefit of no value to the public employee pension fund because its income is not subject to federal tax. Table 16–3 shows the share of funds in such debt to have declined dramatically, so progress has been made but the use still exists. Indeed, some national politicians have seen these funds as a natural source of money to finance state and local infrastructure, including some bond purchases as required elements of infrastructure-aid packages. Unless this debt is sold at rates equivalent to the market for comparable securities (two ways would be to make pension fund investment returns taxable or to make state-and-local-debt interest taxable), these investments would not represent prudent management of the portfolio.

Second, because pension-fund accumulations are large, even for funds that are not fully funded,[46] they are attractive to general government. Mayors and governors see these resources as public money, attractive to tap if the general government suffers difficult finances. Methods include forced loans as previously noted (but for operating rather than capital use), sale and lease back of government assets to the fund, and delayed or reduced current government contribution to the fund. The diversions increase the eventual tax payments needed to meet defined benefits. However, those problems almost certainly will hit when some other politician is in charge.

Third, pension fund (and smaller endowment-fund) management may be constrained to local firms in an effort to help the local firms and to build the local community. The firms frequently lack the expertise or scale for high-quality, low-cost management, although modern telecommunications allow local firms global-market access. The larger funds use many managers, both small and large, internal and external, to diversify investments for high return.

---

[45]Some of these issues were apparent long before the pools became so huge; see Louis M. Kohlmeier, *Conflicts of Interest: State and Local Pension Fund Asset Management* (New York: Twentieth Century Fund, 1976).

[46]A GAO report found, in a survey of 189 public funds from forty-seven states and Puerto Rico, that 68 percent were underfunded (42 percent of these had funding ratios below 75 percent). *Underfunded State and Local Pension Plans,* GAO/HRD-93-9R (Washington, D.C.: General Accounting Office, 1992). Since 1975 the plans have, however, made significant improvements in funding.

Fourth, public pension funds must consider the potential for social investing and economically targeted investing. Both bring objectives other than monetary return into the fund-management calculation. Social investing involves use of investment flows to encourage desirable and to discourage undesirable business firm activities. Among the concerns that have been addressed in the past have been how firms dealt with South Africa: their environmental behavior, their success in ending discrimination, attitudes toward employee rights, whether portfolios should include tobacco companies, and so on. If such investment management involves no loss of return or increased portfolio risk, neither taxpayers nor pension beneficiaries, present and prospective, are sacrificed for social purpose. But that is not often the case, and some trade-offs seem inevitable. The discussion continues, normally with politicians on one side and pension-fund managers on the other.[47]

Greater recent concern has been with the possibility of economically targeted investment (ETI), using the pension-fund dollars to increase economic development in the economy from which pension contributions were paid—that is, the state or the locality. Because stocks and bonds trade globally and business itself trades in international supply and product markets, investing in securities of "local" business would almost certainly have no particular impact. Any impact would probably have to come through small-business financing—that is, venture capital (limited partnerships usually) and private debt placement. Both tend toward high administrative cost and higher risk than with other prudent investments. If heavily targeted to the local area, furthermore, the pool loses geographic diversification that otherwise keeps the risk in the total portfolio down. ETI, though having some possible potential, obviously needs considerable checking against the basic purpose of the pension fund.[48]

Finally, the sheer size of the public employee pension funds creates an interesting problem. The largest funds have such large stock holdings in the companies they have selected that they cannot simply sell the stock of a poor performer. To do so would cause a major fall in the value of the stock as they sold, further reducing the value of their holding. Accordingly, the largest funds have to invest for the long haul and must take a proprietary interest in their selections. Indeed, the major public pension funds have been leaders in corporate governance reforms, especially those aimed at improving the accountability of corporate directors to the interests of shareholders and thus making the corporation more concerned with economic performance and less concerned with comfortable corporate executives. The pension funds amassed represent a dramatically different form of corporate ownership and, potentially, a structure of market capitalism requiring radical changes in theo-

---

[47]James A. White, "Pension Funds Issue Warning on Politics," *Wall Street Journal* (5 December 1989): C-1. However, two large and aggressive pension funds, the California Public Employees' Retirement System (Calpers) and the California Teachers' Retirement System (Calsters), have invested in programs of affordable housing lending (multifamily and low-income housing). See Michael J. Ybarra, "Two California Pension Funds Launch Initiative to Build Affordable Housing," *Wall Street Journal* (15 March 1994): A-81. Pension funds have historically been reluctant to make such investments, although both funds seem to have been attracted by satisfactory returns relative to investment risk in the venture.

[48]D. Jeanne Patterson, *The Use of Public Employee Retirement System Resources for Economic Development in the Great Lakes States* (Bloomington, Ind.: Institute for Development Strategies, 1993).

ries of economic and financial behavior. Calpers has been one of the most aggressive in working to improve corporate governance, transparency, and linkage between corporate chief executive pay and performance.[49]

Conclusion

Idle cash in public accounts should be invested at the highest yield consistent with principal safety and liquidity. Liquidity is important because the primary objective is to ensure that the government's bills get paid. Although many investment media are legally available to governments, U.S. T-bills, CDs, and repurchase agreements are the heart of most cash-management programs. Cash management involves four critical steps: forecasting daily cash balances, pooling available funds to maximize investable balances, investing in the most attractive instruments, and maintaining a scorecard for the program. Nationally, state and local governments have made great improvements in cash management over the past 30 years.

Public employee pension funds have become aggressive investors with large balances and professional managers. The funds are so large, although often insufficient to cover future benefits, that they are attractive pools for politicians to tap. They are also so large that some funds have become aggressive agents for reform of corporate governments and possibly for change in the nature of market capitalism.

CHAPTER 16 QUESTIONS AND EXERCISES

1. What controls are placed on state and local cash management in your state? What investment instruments are legal? Is there a state investment pool?
2. What charges do banks in your area apply for services rendered to governments?
3. What check size is the minimum for direction to the lockbox system if the lockbox costs 25 cents per check, the interest rate is 6 percent, and the lockbox saves one day in deposit time?
4. The Parks Board may receive 1-percent discount if it pays $1,000 bill for supplies within 10 days. Otherwise, it has 6 days to pay the net amount. The board can invest its cash at an 8.5-percent rate. Should it pay to receive the discount?
5. A 6-month (182 day) T-bill was auctioned at a price of $9,620 per $10,000 face value. What is the investment yield?

[49]As a result of these several factors, there is evidence that public pension funds earn a lower rate of return on their funds than do comparable private pension funds. Julia L. Coronado, Eric M. Engen, and Brian Knight, "Public Funds and Private Capital Markets; The Investment Practices and Performance of State and Local Pension Funds," *National Tax Journal* 51 (September 2003): 579–594. Because the public funds are predominantly defined benefit, this means promised benefits will require higher tax payments to support them.

6. What is the purchase price per $10,000 face value for a 3-month (91-day) T-bill for an 5.5-percent discount rate?
7. The city of Saratov has $895 million in its public employee pension fund, a defined benefit program that has only recently reached a fully funded status. The city council proposes to loan $95 million of that fund to a struggling bus manufacturer in the city as a part of the growth and development plan. The council chair supports the proposal as yielding a double dividend to the city. Not only will a high interest rate be earned on the investment but also the city will be stimulating growth of its tax base. As city finance officer you must prepare a position statement on the proposal. Do so.

CASES FOR DISCUSSION

CASE 16–1

Managing Cash for the Sheriff's Interest?

The ability to control how public funds are managed can be used to reward friends and allies without making any immediately apparent payment. That is why governments often create limits and controls on cash management and why oversight bodies are established to review management practices. The report that follows shows what can happen when controls are absent or do not function properly.

As you read the selection, identify what procedures should have been installed and operating to prevent the losses that may have occurred. In what proportion would you assign blame to the sheriff, the banking community, and public procedures, assuming the newspaper account is accurate?

Greene's Banking Cost Public at Least $600,000

By Kay Stewart

Jefferson County Sheriff Jim Greene cost the county's government and the public schools at least $600,000 by depositing tax money in bank accounts that earned no interest.

Greene said he deposited money in no-interest accounts from 1982 through 1989 because that was the way it was done before he became sheriff and he wanted to make this "concession" to past practices with the Louisville banks.

Although this was profitable for the banks, it was a loss to the taxpayers.

Greene refused to answer questions about whether his political interests influenced his decision on the deposits.

But he has sought favors from the banks that profited. Their executives or political action committees have given him political contributions, and some of the banks have also given him tickets to the Kentucky Derby and other sporting events.

In a secretly recorded conversation made public last month, Greene claimed that one bank executive refused his request for Derby tickets, adding that the executive explained that Greene hadn't put money in a no-interest account.

Greene's office is responsible for collecting tens of millions of dollars in property taxes. The money bypasses the sheriff's office and goes directly into a bank account. Greene has authority to invest money, usually for not more than 30 days, before it is disbursed to state and local governmental agencies.

All the money could have been placed in interest-earning accounts, but instead Greene put substantial portions in no-interest accounts.

His office's records show that from 1986 through 1989, Greene deposited about $86 million in no-interest accounts at six banks—approximately 12.5 percent of the roughly $674 million his office collected in those years. The result was lost interest totaling about $473,520.

Greene also put millions in taxes into no-interest accounts during his first term in office, from 1982 through 1985, but there was insufficient information in his records to accurately estimate the losses from those years. However, based on bank statements that were available, the newspaper calculated that at least another $130,000 could have been earned from those years.

County commissioners expressed dismay last week when they learned from a reporter that Greene hadn't earned a return on all deposits.

"That's just unheard of," said Commissioner Tom Eifler, a stockbroker. "It's unbelievable to let dollars sit."

Eifler noted that the interest money could have benefited many agencies, including the strapped library.

Officials of the banks either wouldn't comment or said they had merely followed the instructions of the sheriff's office in depositing the money.

Asked if his bank was obligated to advise Greene to put all deposits into interest-bearing accounts. Republic Bank President Scott Trager suggested that the sheriff knew what he was doing.

"It's not like an 80-year-old grandmother walking in with a million dollars."

In a written response to the newspaper, the only reason Greene gave for depositing a "small minority" of tax receipts in no-interest accounts was that it was in keeping with "past practices."

Before 1982, the law did not address whether sheriffs could invest tax money to earn interest, although a 1978 Kentucky attorney general's opinion said sheriffs could not. Greene claimed credit for persuading state legislators in 1982 to approve a new law, which allows—but does not require—sheriffs to see that collected taxes earn interest.

The law, however, states that fiscal courts can order sheriffs to invest the money—authority that members of Jefferson Fiscal Court, including County Judge-Executive Dave Armstrong, said last week they didn't realize they had.

Armstrong said he would ask Greene about his investment policies and would explore Fiscal Court's authority to oversee how Greene invests tax revenue.

Greene, a Democrat who is in his third term in office, refused to be interviewed about his bank dealings. He agreed to consider some written questions, but made only a brief response to some questions.

He has said that he has never received "anything of any value from any banks," but at least four of the banks have acknowledged giving him gifts, such as tickets to the Derby and to University of Kentucky basketball games. The bankers who acknowledged giving him tickets and political donations said the gifts were not related to banking transactions.

At the end of 1989, Greene stopped depositing tax money in the no-interest accounts, but he recently refused to say why. However, he addressed the issue last year in the secretly taped conversation with former deputy Randy Wells.

On the tape, which Wells released, Greene made vulgar, sexist and racist remarks and also talked about his attempts to get Derby tickets from banks.

At one point, Greene told Wells that he had asked a First National Bank vice president for Derby tickets but was told he wouldn't get any. Greene said the banker noted that the sheriff had not deposited any money that year in his "DDA"—a demand deposit account that did not earn interest.

Greene said he told the banker, "The paper's on my ass," adding that he had to deposit the money elsewhere. The banker, according to Greene, said, "That's the way we operate over here." Greene said he replied: "Well, goddamn it. You may get nothing next year."

Greene has said he wasn't certain it was his voice on the tape. The banker has denied that he linked Derby tickets with deposits, although he acknowledged that Greene had solicited Derby tickets.

Greene's decisions on the depositing of tax receipts adds another questionable element to his record.

In the last two years, new reports have documented that he hired a political friend to build a workout room for employees, loaded his payroll with relatives and supporters, bought guns and ammunition from a deputy at a huge markup, and gave employees large bonuses.

Last month, Greene was fined a record $21,600 for more than 200 violations of campaign-finance laws. In the last two weeks, five female deputies have charged in a lawsuit that they were sexually harassed by men in the sheriff's department. Three of the five said Greene himself had harassed them.

Several legislators and local officials called for his resignation, but Armstrong, Louisville Mayor Jerry Abramson and the executive committee of the local Democratic Party have not taken a public stand on his future.

The Accounts

The sheriff collects taxes on behalf of the state, the county, the county's public schools, and local sewer and volunteer fire districts.

The school system gets 14.45 percent of the interest earned on the tax money. The sheriff's office can spend the rest, but what is left must go to Jefferson Fiscal Court at the end of the sheriff's elected term.

Six banks—First National, Republic, Liberty, Bank of Louisville, Stock Yards and River City—received a total of about $86 million in no-interest deposits and nearly $272 million in interest-earning accounts from 1986 through 1989. The remaining money was in interest and no-interest accounts at Citizens Fidelity Bank and Trust Co.

The newspaper couldn't determine from sheriff's department records whether potential interest was also lost from the Citizens no-interest account. This account, which is where all the sheriff's tax receipts are initially deposited, operates differently from the other no-interest accounts.

Greene refused to comment on the Citizens account, and so did Rick Cook, a Citizens spokesman, saying such customer information is confidential.

To banks, no-interest deposits of the size Greene delivered are a boon. Banks can invest or lend that money without paying interest, increasing their profits.

Greene said in his written statement that he had no formula for dividing tax receipts among the banks, although the division was based primarily on their size. Nor was there a method in determining how much he divided between interest and no-interest accounts.

"It was simply my decision to maintain a small portion of the tax funds collected in non-interest-bearing accounts," he said.

Here are some results:

In December 1989, Greene kept an average of $5.4 million per day in a no-interest account at First National. If that money had been in the sheriff's department's money-market account at First National, it would have earned 5.25 percent interest that month—about $24,000.

For another 11 days in 1989, the sheriff had $7 million in a no-interest account at the Bank of Louisville—a loss of $11,075 at the 5.25 rate the bank was paying on the sheriff's money-market account.

At Republic Bank, Greene kept $4 million for 35 days in December 1988 and January 1989. That money could have earned more than $20,000 at 5.25 percent.

The Losers

Jefferson County government was the big loser because of Greene's practices.

Of the estimated $600,000 lost, the county would have received an additional $513,300—about $108,300 in 1986 and about $405,000 in 1990. The schools lost an estimated $86,700.

In early 1986, Greene transferred to county government about $833,000 his office didn't spend in his first term: in 1990, the amount was $1.2 million.

But with no effort, it could have been more.

The money could have helped the county through tough times in 1990, Armstrong said. At the time, Fiscal Court adopted a new tax on most insurance premiums to balance the budget.

Lauren Melton, spokeswoman for the school system, said it would not offer an opinion on the potential money that was lost.

Since 1982, Greene said, his office did invest most tax receipts, which earned nearly $7 million in interest for the schools and the county government, and to help pay for the operation of his office.

No Accountability

Greene's authority to invest tax receipts with little or no oversight is apparently unmatched in the state. Other sheriffs, under law, get their budgets approved by their respective fiscal courts.

But sheriffs in Jefferson and Fayette counties have for decades been required to submit only brief budget outlines to circuit court judges. In Fayette County, however, Sheriff Harold Buchignani said he turned over the job of collecting taxes to urban county government two years ago because it was better equipped to do the job.

Greene, however, "pretty much has a free rein to do what he wants" in determining how to invest tax receipts, said Assistant State Auditor Howard Kline. "Obviously . . . you hope he acts in the best interests of taxpayers."

Kline said most sheriffs solicit bids to obtain the highest interest rates—a practice Greene began only last year.

Citizens submitted the high bid—agreeing to pay 5.8 percent interest. In 1990, Greene did deposit tax receipts in interest-earning accounts but did not seek bids.

Most sheriffs, unlike Greene, also undergo an annual audit by the state auditor's office, which routinely checks on investment practices, Kline said. He said Greene has received permission from the auditor's office to hire a private firm to audit his office, although the state auditor remains responsible.

Greene has hired the firm of Deloitte & Touche, whose employees have given him political donations.

Kline said state auditors have reviewed the Deloitte & Touche reports, which contain no recommendations or concerns about Greene's investment practices. Greene said in his statement that "there have never been any major questions raised about the operation of this office and its tax-collecting function."

Joseph Blitzko, an accountant with the firm who was assigned to oversee audits of Greene's office, did not return several phone calls.

State Auditor Ben Chandler said his office will conduct the audit this year—not because of any concerns but because he wants his office to review all government agencies under his authority at least once during this term in office.

Greene's office has not been audited by the state for 10 years.

SOURCE: Louisville Courier Journal, 14 June 1992, A-1, A-10. Copyright © 1992. The Courier Journal. Reprinted by permission.

CASE 16–2

The Underfunded West Virginia Public Employees' Pension Fund

State and local governments have considerable freedom to manage the pension systems provided to their employees. That freedom has meant that some governments have limited funds available to pay benefits to their retired employees. West Virginia has made even less provision than most other governments. The following story describes the problem and some of the causes of the difficulty.

Consider These Questions

1. Was the prohibition of investment in stocks truly conservative investment policy?
2. Explain who bears the burden when pension systems are not actuarily funded.

"West Virginia's Pensioners Come Up Short"

by Jeff D. Opdyke

Charleston, W. Va.—Mary Alice Johnson, a 74-year-old retired clerk-typist for the state tax department, wishes she could afford an air conditioner. But the cost would bust her budget, because she hasn't seen an increase in her $318 monthly pension check since she retired in 1988.

The irony is that if Mrs. Johnson lived across the border—in Kentucky or Virginia, for example—she wouldn't have to shuffle electric fans around her row-house to try to cool off during the steamy summer months. That's because most public pension systems in other states are well-funded and can afford to pay steady cost-of-living increases to their retirees.

But not West Virginia, which has the most underfunded pension plan in the nation. How did it manage to accomplish this during one of the greatest bull markets in U.S. history, while many public pension plans elsewhere are flush with surplus assets?

West Virginia's woes, which are shared by a handful of public pension systems around the nation, are caused in part by outdated state laws, which until 1998 prohibited their pension funds from investing in stocks. But its problems have been compounded by the exemption of public pension plans from federal rules that require managers to fund plans adequately in the first place and to invest the assets prudently.

Limited Assets

As a result, West Virginia's state pension plans, with 41,400 retirees, have just 19.7% of the assets needed to pay accrued $4.3 billion in liabilities. Many retirees haven't seen a pension increase in 25 years. "Every chance the legislature gets, they give themselves a raise," Mrs. Johnson says. "But they don't care about retired people."

Now, West Virginia legislators are scrambling to find money to pay the looming pension bills. Lawmakers hope to float one of the largest municipal-bond offerings in U.S. history—$4 billion—in a taxpayer bailout of the system.

While acknowledging the shortcomings of public-worker pension plans in the state, West Virginia officials say the move to allow funds to buy stocks, together with the proposed bond issue, are designed to help the state overcome its pension funding problems over time.

"Our plan has never been in good shape," says Joseph Markus, who recently took a private sector job after serving as cabinet secretary in the state's Department of Administration, where he helped look into ways to address the pension issue. "Our big concern now is to make sure we're never in this situation again."

Corporate pension plans usually don't wind up in such sorry shape as some state plans because the Employee Retirement Income Security Act, a federal pension law, mandates prudent portfolio management. Erisa doesn't apply to state and municipal plans.

Century-Long Hiatus

Poor investment decisions can be one result. Skittishness about stock investments kept many public pension systems on the sidelines for years. After an 1880s shipping canal deal went sour, for example, Indiana stayed out of stocks until 1998. Today, its teachers' retirement plan has only about one-third the assets needed to meet $7.7 billion in expected liabilities.

Even though West Virginia finally began allowing its state and local pension plans to start investing in stocks two years ago, 30% of local plans still haven't waded into stocks, according to a state treasurer's survey last year. The state plans are moving into stocks slowly, and the hope with the bond issue is that West Virginia can invest the proceeds in the market and generate returns substantially above the interest it will be required to pay.

Still, cash, in the form of short-term money-market investments, is the favored asset in some plans. In the northern panhandle, the Moundsville policemen's plan had 60% of its assets in cash, while Fairmont's police plan, which is only 17% funded, had about 40% of its assets in certificates of deposit at the local bank.

In contrast, the state of Florida, which invested about three-quarters of its pension assets in stocks during the 1990s, has racked up average annual returns of roughly 14%. The assets nearly tripled to $100 billion, and the plan is now overfunded by $10 billion. Michigan's four state pension plans, thanks to 18% average annual returns for the past five years, are 100% funded, which has enabled the state to use some of the excess to pre-fund employee medical insurance premiums. Overall, most public plans have at least 75% of the funds necessary to meet future liabilities, a level many pension experts consider healthy.

A Lack of Money

But healthy isn't a word heard often in West Virginia. Poor investment performance has been compounded by the lack of money to actually invest. While federal pension law requires private pension plans to put enough money into pension plans to pay future obligations, the law doesn't apply to public plans.

Consequently, critics say, state lawmakers for decades have taken a pass-the-buck attitude toward local funding mandates. "Such large sums of money are involved that states see pension plans as a way to solve budgetary problems," says Steve Willborn, a law professor at the University of Nebraska, who has been working with the National Conference of Commissioners on Uniform State Laws to persuade legislatures to adopt uniform prudent portfolio-management principles.

In Oklahoma, lawmakers contributed the actuarially required amount to the state teachers' system only five times during the past 30 years. Today, that plan is $5 billion in the hole.

In West Virginia, 40 of the state's public plans have less than half the funding they need. In some cities, pensions for police and firefighters are so underfunded that "bankruptcy is a possibility [for the cities] if this isn't addressed soon." Jerry Simpson, the state's assistant treasurer.

Fire Department Plan

That's because there isn't enough money in the city coffers to pay the pension checks when the money in the pension plans runs out. For Huntington, the state's second-largest city with a population of about 54,000, that day could come soon: that city's fire department plan is just 2.3% funded. "This all scares the hell out of me," says Glenn White, the city's finance director.

Exacerbating the pension problem in West Virginia and elsewhere is the practice of recruiting trustees who are short on financial expertise but long on political obligations. Unlike the California Public Employees Retirement System, whose board includes the state treasurer, the state controller and appointed officials from the financial industries, typical trustees in West Virginia city pension plans include plan members and the mayor.

That helps explain why retired firefighters in some cities get steady cost-of-living increases—even as the pension plans are running out of money—while some retired state employees haven't seen an increase for a decade or more.

Scott Wilson, a 20-year veteran of Huntington's fire department, and a trustee of its plan, sees no problem with continued pension raises for retired firefighters, even if the city can't afford it. He concedes the trustees have no investment knowledge, but bristles at suggestions that outsiders should have any influences.

"It's our fund," he says. If public workers don't get the continued pension increases they're asking for, he says, they'll sue the city.

It's this kind of no-win loop that Rep. Robert Andrews (D., N.J.), is trying to close. He has introduced a bill that would extend some federal Erisa standards to state and local pension plans, including management by financial professionals rather than political appointees or plan members. Other provisions would make it tougher for local governments or politicians to fail to fund the plans or siphon off state contributions earmarked for the pension plans to pay for other things in the budget. Similar bills have been floated in years past, but either faded away or were shot down.

But in places such as West Virginia, pension reform will likely continue to be a hard sell. Few are willing to publicly suggest change. Police and firefighters "see that as a threat to their control," Mr. White says. "You might not make it home," he jokes.

SOURCE: The Wall Street Journal, 2 June 2000. Reprinted by permission of *The Wall Street Journal,* © 2000 Dow Jones & Company, Inc. All Rights Reserved Worldwide.

APPENDIX

Some Websites for Fiscal Administration Data and Information

A former editor of the *Journal of the American Medical Association* wrote: "The Internet is the biggest garbage pile of misinformation. Surfing the Internet for medical information or advice is no different than sitting in a local pub or cocktail party. There is lousy information and good information."[1] The same can be said for websites with information about government finances, budget policy, taxation, and so on. The Internet provides easy access to information—but there is no editorial screening of that information. Hence, anyone using the Internet as a reference tool must carefully weigh the provenance of the information. Some is the public finance equivalent of snake oil and, although the effect may not be quite as direct as bad medical advice, it can be hazardous to fiscal health.

Here are a number of websites that provide useful information for fiscal administration. Of course, websites and web addresses change without notice. But if the address listed here doesn't work, then check for the sponsoring organization with any good search engine.

Some Useful Government Websites:

Bureau of Labor Statistics Programs and Surveys:
www.bls.gov/bls/proghome.htm
Congressional Budget Office:
www.cbo.gov

[1]Jamie Talan, "The Net As a Partner in Health: An Unmatched Source of Medical Information, Support, and, Yes, Snake Oil," *Newsday* (17 September 1996): B21. George Lundberg, the editor, then established his own medical information website.

Congressional Research Service:
www.loc.gov/crsinfo/whatscrs.html
Department of Finance Canada:
www.fin.gc.ca/fin-eng.html
Federal Highway Administration, Highway Taxes and Fees:
www.fhwa.dot.gov/ohim/hwytaxes/taxpage.htm
Financial Management Service, U.S. Department of Treasury:
www.fms.treas.gov
"Fred:" Federal Reserve Bank of St. Louis database:
www.stls.frb.org/fred
Governments Division, U.S. Bureau of Census:
www.census.gov/ftp/pub/govs/www/index.html
HM Revenue & Customs (United Kingdom):
www.hmrc.gov.uk/home.htm
Individual Tax Statistics, Internal Revenue Service:
www.irs.gov/taxstats/indtaxstats/index.html
Internal Revenue Service:
www.irs.gov/index.html
MultiState Tax Commission:
www.mtc.gov
Office of Management and Budget:
www.whitehouse.gov/omb
U.S. Government Printing Office:
www.gpoaccess.gov

Some Organization Websites:

American Association for Budget and Program Analysis:
www.aabpa.org
American Enterprise Institute:
www.aei.org
Association for Budgeting and Financial Management:
www.abfm.org
Brookings Institution:
www.brookings.edu
Brookings/Urban Institute Tax Policy Center:
www.taxpolicycenter.org.

Center on Budget and Policy Priorities:
www.cbpp.org/info.html
Federation of Tax Administrators:
www.taxadmin.org
FinanceNet:
www.financenet.org
Government Finance Officers Association:
www.gfoa.org
Institute for Fiscal Studies:
www.ifs.org.uk
National Association of State Budget Officers:
www.nasbo.org
National Tax Association:
www.ntanet.org
Resources for the Future:
www.rff.org
Tax Analysts, Inc.:
www.taxanalysts.com
Tax Foundation
www.taxfoundation.org
Tax Policy Center (Urban Institute-Brookings)
www.taxpolicycenter.org
Urban Institute:
www.urban.org

Some Helpful Miscellaneous Websites:

Christiansen Capital Advisors (Gaming Data):
www.cca-i.com
Economics Working Paper Archive:
econwpa.wustl.edu
Fitch Investors Service:
www.fitchinv.com
Governing Magazine:
www.governing.com
Moody's Investor Service:
www.moodys.com/cust/default.asp

Standard and Poor's:

www.standardandpoors.com

Tax and Accounting Sites Directory (links to tax departments, U.S. and international):

www.taxsites.com

Tax History Project at Tax Analysts:

www.taxhistory.org

Websites of Some International Organizations

Asian Development Bank:

www.adb.org

European Bank for Reconstruction and Development:

www.ebrd.com

International Monetary Fund:

www.imf.org

Organisation for Economic Cooperation and Development (Washington Center):

www.oecdwash.org

Organisation for Economic Cooperation and Development on Budgeting, Management and Accountability:

www.oecd.org/department/0,2688,en_2649_34119_1_1_1_1_1,00.html

World Bank:

www.worldbank.org

World Bank Institute:

www.worldbank.org/wbi

World Bank: Tax Policy and Administration:

www1.worldbank.org/publicsector/tax

Glossary

The following terms are commonly used in public finance and budgeting. The General Accounting Office (GAO) provides a more complete listing of terms used in federal government financing in "A Glossary of Terms Used in the Federal Budget Process," GAO/AFMD-2.1-1 (Washington, D.C.: General Accounting Office, 1993). There are language differences from state to state, but the definitions try to cross as many state lines as possible.

ability to pay The principle that the tax burden should be distributed according to a person's affluence. It is based on the assumption that as a person's affluence increases, the person can and should contribute more to support government activities.

accounting system The procedures that record, classify, and report on the finances and operations of a business, government, individual, or other entity.

accrued interest Interest earned on a bond issue from its date or last coupon payment date to the date of delivery or settlement date to the purchaser.

activity A specific and distinguishable line of work performed by one or more organizational components of a government unit for the purpose of discharging a function or subfunction for which the government unit is responsible. For example, food inspection is an activity performed in the discharge of the health function.

ad valorem A tax computed from the value of the tax base.

advance appropriation Budget authority provided in an appropriation act to become available in a fiscal year, or beyond the fiscal year for which the appropriation act is passed. The amount is not included in the budget totals of the year in which the appropriation bill is enacted, but it is included in the budget totals for the fiscal year in which the amount will become available for obligation.

advance funding Budget authority provided in an appropriation act to obligate and disburse funds during a fiscal year from a succeeding year's appropriation. The funds so obligated increase the budget authority for the fiscal year in which they are obligated and reduce the budget authority for the succeeding fiscal year. Advance funding is a device for avoiding supplemental requests late in the fiscal year for certain entitlement programs should the appropriations for the current year prove to be too low.

advance refunding The refunding of an issue of securities prior to the date when the outstanding issue of securities can be redeemed. Thus, before redemption both the issue being refunded and the refunding issue are outstanding.

agency debt That portion of the federal debt incurred when a federal agency, other than the Treasury or the Federal Financing Bank, is authorized by law to borrow funds directly from the public or another fund or account. Agency debt may be incurred by agencies within the federal budget (such as the Tennessee Valley Authority) or by off-budget federal entities (such as the Postal Service). Debt of government-sponsored, privately owned enterprises (such as the Federal National Mortgage Association) is not included in the federal debt.

agency missions Responsibilities assigned to a specific agency for meeting national needs. Agency missions are expressed in terms of the purpose to be served by the programs authorized to carry out functions or subfunctions that, by law, are the responsibility of that agency and its component organizations. In contrast to national needs, generally described in the context of major functions, agency missions are generally described in the context of subfunctions.

allotment An authorization by the head (or other authorized employee) of an agency to his or her subordinates to incur obligations within a specified amount. An agency makes allotments pursuant to the requirements stated in the Office of Management and Budget (OMB) Circular no. A-34. The amount allotted by an agency cannot exceed the amount apportioned by the OMB.

amortization Paying the principal amount of an issue through periodic payments either directly to bondholders or to a sinking fund for later payment to bondholders. Amortization payments include interest and any payment on principal.

annual (one-year) authority A type of budget authority that is available for obligation only during a specified fiscal year and expires at the end of that time.

anticipation notes or warrants Short-term debt issued in anticipation of collection of taxes, the proceeds of a bond sale, or other revenue, and retirable from the collections they anticipate.

Anti-Deficiency Act Legislation enacted by Congress to prevent the incurring of obligations or the making of expenditures (outlays) in excess of amounts available in appropriations or funds; to fix responsibility within an agency for the creation of any obligation or the making of any expenditure in excess of an apportionment or reapportionment or in excess of other subdivisions established pursuant to 31 U.S.C. 665(g); and to assist in bringing about the most effective and economical use of appropriations and funds. The act is sometimes known as Section 3679 of the Revised Statutes, as amended.

apportionment A distribution made by the Office of Management and Budget of amounts available for obligation, including budgetary reserves established pursuant to law, in an appropriation or fund account. Apportionments divide amounts available for obligations by specific time periods (usually quarters), activities, projects, objects, or a combination thereof. The amounts so apportioned limit the amount of obligations that may be incurred. In apportioning any account, some funds may be reserved to provide for contingencies or to effect savings, pursuant to the Anti-Deficiency Act, or may be proposed for deferral or rescission pursuant to the Impoundment Control Act of 1974 (Title X of the Congressional Budget and Impoundment Control Act, P.L. 93-344, 31 U.S.C.1400, et seq.).

appropriation act A statute, under the jurisdiction of the House and Senate Committees on Appropriations, that generally provides authorization for federal agencies to incur obligations and to make payments out of the Treasury for specified purposes. An appropriation act, the most common means of providing budget authority, generally follows enactment of authorizing legislation unless the authorizing legislation itself provides the budget authority. Currently, there are thirteen regular federal appropriation acts enacted annually. From time to time, Congress also enacts supplemental appropriation acts. Similar relationships apply to state and local governments.

appropriation authority An authorization by an act of Congress that permits federal agencies to incur obligations and to make payments out of the Treasury for specified purposes. An appropriation usually follows enactment of authorizing legislation. An appropriation act is the most common means of providing budget authority, but in some cases the authorizing legislation itself provides the budget authority. (*See also* backdoor authority.) Appropriations do not represent cash actually set aside in the Treasury of purposes specified in the appropriations act; they represent limitations of amounts that agencies may obligate during the period of time specified in the respective appropriation acts. Several types of appropriations are not counted as budget authority because they do not provide authority to incur additional obligations. Examples of these include appropriations to liquidate contract authority—congressional action to provide funds to pay obligations incurred against contract authority; appropriations to reduce outstanding debt—congressional action to provide funds for debt retirement; and appropriations for refunds or receipts.

arbitrage Investing borrowed funds in higher rate-of-return investments.

ascending, or positive-yield, curve The interest-rate structure with long-term interest rates higher than short-term interest rates.

asked price The price at which dealers offer securities in the market.

assessed value The value placed on property, usually by a government employee, for the purpose of distributing property tax burden. That value may or may not be directly related to market value.

assets Property with economic value owned by an entity.

audit An examination of evidence, including records, facilities, inventories, systems, etc., to discover or verify desired information. A written report of findings normally results, and findings are normally based on investigation of a sample of agency operations.

authority A debt-issuing entity normally created by special act of a state legislature for the purpose of financing public facilities that have not been or cannot be financed by existing government bodies. Authorities usually lack taxing powers and do their financing with revenue bonds.

authorizing committee A standing committee of the House or Senate with legislative jurisdiction over the subject matter of those laws, or parts of laws, that set up or continue the legal operations of federal programs or agencies. An authorizing committee also has jurisdiction in those instances where backdoor authority is provided in the substantive legislation.

authorizing legislation Substantive legislation enacted by Congress that sets up or continues the legal operation of a federal program or agency either indefinitely or for a specific period of time or sanctions a particular type of obligation or expenditure within a program. Authorizing legislation is normally a prerequisite for appropriations. It may place a limit on the amount of budget authority to be included in appropriation of such sums as may be necessary. In some instances, authorizing legislation may provide authority to incur debts or to mandate payment to particular persons or political subdivisions of the country.

average life Measure equal to number of bond years divided by number of bonds ($1,000 increments).

backdoor authority Budget authority provided in legislation outside the normal (appropriation committees) appropriations process. The most common forms of backdoor authority are authority to borrow (also called *borrowing authority* or *authority to spend debt receipts*) and contract authority. In other cases (e.g., interest on the public debt), a permanent appropriation is provided that becomes available without any current action by Congress. Section 401 of the Congressional Budget and Impoundment Control Act of 1974 (31 U.S.C. 1351) specifies certain limits on the use of backdoor authority.

balance sheet A statement of the financial position of an entity that presents the value of its assets, liabilities, and equities on a specified date.

balances of budget authority Amounts of budget authority provided in previous years that have not been outlaid.

balloon maturity A bond issue with substantially more late maturities than early maturities. Some or all of the late maturities are often callable to allow for early redemption.

baseline An estimate of the receipts, outlays, and deficit that would result from continuing current law through the period covered by the budget.

basis point 1/100 of 1 percent. Ten basis points equal 1/10 of 1 percent.

bearer bond A security without owner identification, it is assumed that its bearer is the owner.

benefits received The principle that the tax burden should be distributed according to the benefits an individual receives from government. It is a logical extension of the exchange relationship of private markets.

benefits to former personnel Pensions, annuities, or other benefits due to former employees or their survivors, based (at least in part) on the length of their services to the government, other than benefits paid from funds financed from employer and/or employee contributions and premiums. These include federal payments to funds that provide benefits to former employees and excludes benefits provided in kind, such as hospital and medical care, and indemnities for disability or death of former employees.

bid discount Amount by which par value exceeds bid price.

bid price Price at which a prospective buyer offers to purchase securities.

block grant A type of grant given primarily to general-purpose government units in accordance with a statutory formula. Such grants can be used for a variety of activities within a broad functional area. Example of federal block-grant programs are Omnibus Crime Control and Safe Streets Act of 1968, Comprehensive Employment and Training Act of 1973, Housing and Community Development Act of 1974, and the 1974 Amendments to the Social Security Act of 1935 (Title XX).

bond A contract to pay a specified sum of money (the principal or face value) at a specified future date (maturity) plus interest paid at an agreed percentage of the principal. Maturity is usually longer than 1 year. Notes have shorter maturities and are issued with less formality.

bond bank A state institution that buys entire issue of municipal bonds from proceeds of state bonds.

bond discount The excess of the face value of a bond over its price (or underwriter bid).

bond insurance Insurance purchases to guarantee the timely payment of principal and interest to bondholders.

bond premium The excess of the bond price (or underwriter bid) over its face value (excluding any accrued interest).

bond year The number of 12-month intervals between the date of the bond and its maturity date, measured in $1,000. Thus, the bond year for a $5,000 bond dated April 1, 1985, and maturing June 1, 1986, is 5.830 (1.16667 [14 months divided by 12 months] 3 5 [number of $1,000 in $5,000 bond]).

borrowing authority Also called *authority to borrow* or *authority to spend debt receipts*, this statutory authority permits a federal agency to incur obligations and to make payments for specified purposes out of borrowed monies.

budget A financial plan, including proposed expenditures and estimated revenues, for a period in the future.

budget authority Authority provided by law to enter into obligations that will result in immediate or future outlays involving federal government funds, except that budget authority does not include authority to insure or guarantee the repayment of indebtedness incurred by another person or government. The basic forms of budget authority are appropriations, borrowing, and contract authority. Budget authority may be classified by the period of availability (1-year, multiple-year, no-year), by the timing of congressional action (current or permanent), or by the manner of determining the amount available (definite or indefinite).

budget calendar The timetable a government follows in budget preparation and adoption, either by law or by administrative regulation.

call The payment of principal before stated maturity, as provided for in the security contract.

callable bond A bond that permits the issuer to redeem it before maturity according to terms and price (the call price) stipulated in the bond agreement.

call premium The premium paid, stated as percentage of the principal amount called, for the exercise of a call provision.

Canadian interest cost *See* true interest cost.

cap A term commonly used to refer to legal limits on the budget authority and outlays for each fiscal year provided by discretionary appropriations. A sequester is required if an appropriation exceeds the cap.

capital assets Assets with a useful life of several years (also called *fixed assets*).

capital budget A plan for investment in capital assets separate from current or operating expenditures.

capital-improvement program A plan for future capital expenditures that identifies each capital project, its anticipated start and completion dates, the amount to be spent in each year, and the method of finance.

capitalized interest Funds reserved from an issue to pay interest on it for a period of time (often during construction of the project).

capital outlay Direct expenditure for acquisition of capital assets by contract or direct construction of buildings, roads, or other improvements and purchase of equipment, land, and existing structures. The work may be an addition, replacement, or major alteration, but not simple repair.

cash accounting system An accounting basis that records revenues when received in cash and expenditures when paid.

cash and security holdings Cash and deposits (including demand and time deposits) and governmental and private securities (bonds, notes, stocks, mortgages, etc.) held by a government.

cash budget An estimate of receipts and disbursements during a given period, usually as a cash-management guide. The projection usually covers a year with estimates made for periods within the year (month, week, day).

categorical grant A type of grant that can be used only for a specific program and is usually limited to a narrowly defined activity. Categorical grants consist of formula, project, and formula-project grants.

certificate of deposit A deposit with a financial institution for a contractual period at a contracted interest rate.

certificate of participation A security created as a part of a lease-purchase agreement. The lender, the holder of the certificate, owns a right to participate in periodic lease payments (interest and return of principal) as they are paid.

commercial paper Unsecured promissory obligations with a maturity of substantially less than 1 year to support current operations.

competitive bid A method of selling a new issue of municipal securities. Securities are awarded to underwriters presenting the best bid under criteria stipulated in the notice of sale. (*See also* negotiated sale.)

concentration account An account established to gather all cash available in separate accounts (payroll, vendor payment, debt service, etc.) from which checks will eventually be written. The concentration account serves as a pool from which interest-paying investments are made and from which cash is transferred to individual accounts as checks must be written.

concurrent resolution on the budget A resolution passed by both houses of Congress, but not requiring the signature of the president, setting forth, reaffirming, or revising the congressional budget for the U.S. government for a fiscal year.

congressional budget The budget as set forth by Congress in a concurrent resolution on the budget. By law the resolution includes (1) the appropriate level of total budget outlays and of total new budget authority; (2) an estimate of budget outlays and new budget authority for each major functional category, for undistributed intergovernmental transactions, and for such other matters relating to the budget as may be appropriate to carry out the purposes of the 1974 Congressional Budget and Impoundment Control Act; (3) the amount, if any, of the surplus or deficit in the budget; (4) the recommended level of federal receipts; and (5) the appropriate level of the public debt.

continuing resolution Legislation enacted by Congress to provide budget authority for federal agencies and/or specific activities to continue in operation until the regular appropriations are enacted. Continuing resolutions are enacted when action on appropriations is not completed by the beginning of a fiscal year. The continuing resolution usually specifies a maximum rate at which the obligations may be incurred, based on the rate of the prior year, the president's budget request, or an appropriation bill passed by either or both houses of the Congress.

contract authority Statutory authority that permits obligations to be incurred in advance of appropriations or in anticipation of receipts to be credited to a revolving fund or other account. By definition, contract authority is unfunded and must subsequently be funded by an appropriation to liquidate obligations incurred under the contract authority, or by the collection and use of receipts. (*See also* backdoor authority.)

controllability The ability of Congress and the president to increase and decrease budget outlays or budget authority in the year in question, generally the current or budget year. Relatively uncontrollable refers to spending that the federal government cannot increase or decrease without changing existing substantive law. For example, outlays in any one year are considered to be relatively uncontrollable when the program level is determined by existing statute or by contract or other obligations. Controllability, as exercised by Congress and the president, is determined by statute. In the case of Congress, all permanent budget authority is uncontrollable. For example, most trust fund appropriations are permanent, as are a number of federal fund appropriations and interest on the public debt, for which budget authority is automatically provided under a permanent appropriation enacted in 1847. In the case of the president, relatively uncontrollable spending is usually the result of open-ended programs and fixed costs (e.g., Social Security, medical care, veterans' benefits—outlays generally mandated by law), but also includes payments coming due resulting from budget authority enacted in a prior year, such as preexisting contracts.

corporation net income taxes Taxes on net income earned by business organized as a corporation. Net income is gross earnings less expenses.

cost-benefit analysis An analytical technique that compares the social costs and benefits of proposed programs or policy actions. All losses and gains experienced by society are included and measured in dollar terms. The net benefits created by an action are calculated by subtracting the losses incurred by some sectors of society from the gains that accrue to others. Alternative actions are compared, so as to choose one or more that yield the greatest net benefits, or ratio of benefits to costs. The inclusion of all gains and losses to society in cost-benefit analysis distinguishes it from cost-effectiveness analysis, which is a more limited view of costs and benefits.

cost-effectiveness analysis An analytical technique used to choose the most efficient method for achieving a program or policy goal. The costs of alternatives are measured by their requisite estimated dollar expenditures. Effectiveness is defined by the degree of goal attainment and may also (but not necessarily) be measured in dollars. Either the net effectiveness (effectiveness minus costs) or the cost-effectiveness ratios of alternatives are compared. The most cost-effective method chosen may involve one or more alternatives. The limited view of costs and effectiveness distinguishes this technique from cost-benefit analysis, which encompasses society-wide effects of alternatives.

coupon Detachable portions of a bond presented by its holder to bond issuer's paying agent to document interest due. The coupon rate is the rate of interest on the face value that the coupons reflect.

coupon rate Stated rate of interest payable on the principal amount.

coverage The number of times by which earnings of a revenue bond-financed project exceed debt service payable in a period. It gauges the margin of safety offered the bondholder.

crosswalk Any procedure for expressing the relationship between budgetary data from one set of classifications to another, such as between appropriation accounts and authorizing legislation or between the budget functional structure and the congressional committee spending jurisdictions.

current authority A type of budget authority enacted by Congress in or immediately preceding the fiscal year in which it becomes available.

current-charge revenue Amounts received from the public for performance of specific services benefiting the person charged and from sales of commodities and services, except liquor store sales. Includes fees, assessments, and other reimbursements for current services, rents, and sales derived from commodities or services furnished incident to the performance of particular functions, gross income of commercial activities, and the like. Current charges are distinguished from license taxes, which relate to privileges granted by the government or regulatory measures for the protection of the public.

current-services estimates Presidential estimates of budget authority and outlays for the ensuing fiscal year based on continuation of existing levels of service. These estimates reflect the anticipated costs of continuing federal programs and activities at present spending levels without policy changes—that is, ignoring all new initiatives, presidential or congressional, that are not yet law. These estimates of budget authority and outlays, accompanied by the underlying economic and programmatic assumptions upon which they are based (such as the rate of inflation, the rate of real economic growth, the unemployment rate, program caseloads, and pay increases) are required to be transmitted by the president to the Congress with the president's budget.

death and gift taxes Taxes imposed on transfer of property at death, in contemplation of death, or as a gift. The death tax may be either on the estate (the undivided holdings of the decedent) or on the inheritance (the share received by the heir).

debt Long-term credit obligations of the government and its agencies and all interest-bearing short-term (i.e., repayable within one year) credit obligations. Debt includes judgments, mortgages, and revenue bonds as well as general-obligation bonds, notes, and interest-bearing warrants. Noninterest-bearing short-term obligations, interfund obligations, amounts owed in a trust or agency capacity, advances and contingent loans from other governments, and rights of individuals to benefits from employee retirement funds are excluded. Nonguaranteed federal-agency debt is excluded from total long-term balances. Full-faith-and-credit debt is long-term debt for which the credit of government, implying the power of taxation, is unconditionally pledged. It includes debt payable initially from specific taxes or nontax sources, but representing a liability payable from any other available resources if the pledged sources are insufficient. For the federal government, this includes public debt (subject to Public Law 94-3 statutory limitations) and agency debt (issued outside the above federal statutory restrictions). Nonguaranteed debt consists of long-term debt payable solely from earnings of revenue-producing activities, from special assessments, or from specific nonproperty taxes. Net long-term debt is total long-term debt outstanding minus long-term debt offsets.

debt held by the public Part of the gross federal debt held by the public. The Federal Reserve System is included in "the public" for this purpose. Debt held by government trust funds (e.g., Social Security Trust Fund), revolving funds, and off-budget federal entities is excluded from debt held by the public.

debt limit The maximum debt a government unit may incur under constitutional, statutory, or charter requirements, either in total or as a percentage of assessed value. Limits typically encompass only full-faith-and-credit debt.

debt management Operations of the U.S. Treasury Department that determine the composition of the federal debt. Debt management involves determining the amounts, maturities, other terms and conditions, and schedule of offerings of federal debt securities and raising new cash to finance the government's operations. The objective of debt management is to raise the money necessary for the government's operations at the least cost to the taxpayer and in a manner that minimizes the effect of government operations on financial markets and on the economy.

debt outstanding All debt remaining unpaid on the date specified.

debt service Expenditure to pay interest and repay principal to owners of debt issued by an entity.

debt subject to statutory limit As defined by the Second Liberty Bond Act of 1917, as amended, it currently includes virtually all public debt. However, only a small portion of agency debt is included in this tabulation of federal debt. Under Public Law 96-78, approved September 29, 1979, an amendment to the Rules of the House of Representatives makes possible the establishment of the public debt limit as a part of the congressional budget process.

default Failure to pay a bond's principal and/or interest when due.

deferral of budget authority Any action or inaction by an officer or employee of the U.S. government that temporarily withholds, delays, or effectively precludes the obligation or expenditure of budget authority, including authority to obligate by contract in advance of appropriations as specifically authorized by law. Deferrals consist of (1) amounts reserved for contingencies pursuant to the Anti-Deficiency Act (31 U.S.C. 665) and (2) amounts temporarily withheld for other reasons pursuant to the Congressional Budget and Impoundment Control Act of 1974 (P.L. 93–344, 31 U.S.C. 1403). Deferrals may not extend beyond the end of the year in which the message reporting the deferral is transmitted and may be overturned by the passage of an impoundment resolution by either house of Congress.

deficiency apportionment A distribution by the Office of Management and Budget of available budgetary resources for the fiscal year that anticipates the need for supplemental budget authority. Such apportionments may only be made under certain specified conditions provided for by law (Anti-Deficiency Act, 31 U.S.C. 665[e]). In such instances, the need for additional budget authority is usually reflected by making the amount apportioned for the fourth quarter less than the amount that will actually be required. Approval of request for deficiency apportionment does not authorize agencies to exceed available resources within an account.

deficit The amount by which expenditures exceed revenues during an accounting period.

definite authority A type of budget authority that is stated as a specified sum at the time the authority is granted. This includes authority stated as "not to exceed" a specified amount.

demand deposit Checking account; claims against a bank (or similar financial institution) that may be transferred to another individual or firm by an order to pay (usually a check).

denomination The face amount of a note or bond.

deobligation A downward adjustment of previously recorded obligations. This may be attributable to the cancellation of a project or contract, price revisions, or corrections of estimates previously recorded as obligations.

derivative An investment instrument whose value is derived from the value of another asset. For instance, an option to purchase a financial instrument at some fixed future date would be a derivative instrument.

direct expenditure Payments to employees, suppliers, contractors, beneficiaries, and other final recipients of government payments (i.e., all expenditures other than intergovernmental expenditure).

direct loan Disbursement of funds by the government to a nonfederal borrower under a contract that requires the repayment of such funds with or without interest. The term includes the purchase of, or participation in, a loan made by another lender. The term also includes the sale of a government asset on credit terms of more than 90 days duration as well as financing arrangements for other transactions that defer payment for more than 90 days. It also includes loans financed by the Federal Financing Bank pursuant to agency loan guarantee authority. The term does not include the acquisition of a federally guaranteed loan in satisfaction of default or other guarantee claims or the price support loans of the Commodity Credit Corporation.

direct spending Direct spending, more commonly called mandatory spending, is a category of outlays from budget authority provided in law other than appropriations acts, entitlement authority, and the budget authority for the food stamp program. (*See also* discretionary appropriations.)

discretionary appropriations Discretionary appropriations is a category of budget authority that comprises budgetary resources (except those provided to fund direct-spending programs) provided in appropriations acts. (*See also* direct spending.)

discount The amount (stated in dollars or a percentage) by which the price of a security is less than its face amount.

document and stock transfer taxes Taxes on the recording, registering, and transfer of documents such as mortgages, deeds, and securities, except taxes on vehicle titles, which are classified elsewhere.

double-barreled bond A bond secured by the pledge of more than one source of repayment, often project revenue and taxing power.

emergency spending Spending that the president and the Congress have designated as an emergency requirement. Such spending is not subject to the limits on discretionary spending, if it is discretionary spending, or the pay-as-you-go rules, if it is direct spending.

encumbrances Purchase orders, contracts, or salary commitments that must be covered by an appropriation and for which part of the appropriation is reserved. When paid, they are no longer encumbrances.

entitlements Legislation that requires the payment of benefits (or entitlements) to any person or unit of government that meets the eligibility requirements established by such law. Authorizations for entitlements constitute a binding obligation on the part of the federal government, and eligible recipients have legal recourse if the obligation is not fulfilled. Budget authority for such payments is not necessarily provided in advance, and thus entitlement legislation requires the subsequent enactment of appropriations unless the existing appropriation is permanent. Examples of entitlement programs are Social Security benefits and veterans' compensation or pensions. Section 401(b) of the Congressional Budget and Impoundment Control Act of 1974 (P.L. 93-344, 31 U.S.C. 1351[b]) imposes certain limits on the use of entitlements.

expenditure (1) All amounts of money paid out by a government—net of recoveries and other correcting transactions—other than for retirement of debt, investment in securities, extension of credit, or as agency transactions. Note that expenditure includes only external transactions of a government and excludes noncash transactions such as the provision of prerequisites or other payment in kind. (2) The cost of goods received or services rendered whether cash payments have been made or not (accrual basis); payment of cost of goods received or services rendered (cash basis).

face amount The par value (i.e., principal or value on maturity) of a security.

failure of exclusion An element of nonappropriability; the inability to prevent people not paying for a service from receiving that service.

federal debt *See* gross federal debt, debt held by the public, and debt subject to statutory limit.

federal funds Federal funds are the monies collected and spent by the government other than those designated as trust funds. Federal funds include general, special, public enterprise, and intragovernmental funds. (*See also* trust funds.)

financial administration Activities involving finance and taxation. It includes central agencies for accounting, auditing, and budgeting; the supervision of local government finance; tax administration; collection, custody, and disbursement of funds; administration of employee-retirement systems; debt and investment administration; and the like.

financial advisor A consultant who advises a municipal securities issuer on matters relating to the issue: structure, timing, marketing, fairness of pricing, terms, bond ratings, and the like.

fiscal year The 12-month period at the end of which a government determines its financial condition and the results of its operations and closes its books. The following conventions are followed: (1) The budget year is the fiscal year for which the budget is being considered (the fiscal year following the current year). (2) The current year is the fiscal year in progress. (3) The prior year is the fiscal year immediately preceding the current year.

float Value of checks written but not yet presented for payment to the bank on which the check was written.

formula grants A type of grant that allocates federal funds to states or their subdivisions in accordance with a distribution formula prescribed by law or administrative regulation.

frontloading Providing higher coupon rates on the shorter maturity bonds or larger principal repayments in the early years of a serial bond issue.

full-faith-and-credit debt Long-term debt for which the credit of the government, implying the power of taxation, is unconditionally pledged. Includes debt payable initially from specific taxes or nontax sources, but representing a liability payable from any other available resources if the pledged sources are insufficient.

full funding Provides budgetary resources to cover the total cost of a program or project at the time it is undertaken. Full funding differs from incremental funding, where budget authority is provided or recorded for only a portion of total estimated obligations expected to be incurred during a single fiscal year. Full funding is generally discussed in terms of multiyear programs, whether or not obligations for the entire program are made in the first year. For further discussion of this term, see U.S. General Accounting Office, Further Implementation of Full Funding in the Federal Government, PAD-78-80, September 7, 1978.

functional classification A system of classifying budget resources by function so that budget authority and outlays of budget and off-budget federal entities, loan guarantees, and tax expenditures can be restated in terms of the national needs being addressed. Budget accounts are generally placed in the single budget function (e.g., national defense, health) that best reflects its major end purpose addressed to an important national need, regardless of the agency administering the program. A function may be divided into two or more subfunctions, depending on the complexity of the national need addressed by that function.

functions Public purposes served by government activities (education, highways, public welfare, etc.). Expenditure for each function includes amounts for all types of expenditure serving the purpose concerned.

fund An accounting device established to control receipt and disbursement of income from sources set aside to support specific activities or attain certain objectives. In the accounts of individual governments, each fund is treated as a distinct fiscal entity.

fund accounting The legal requirement for federal agencies to establish accounts for segregating revenues and other resources, together with all related liabilities, obligations, and reserves, for the purpose of carrying on specific activities or attaining certain objectives in accordance with special regulations, restrictions, or limitations. Fund accounting, in a broad sense, is required in the federal government to demonstrate agency compliance with requirements of existing legislation for which federal funds have been appropriated or otherwise authorized.

funding Issuance of bonds or other long-term debt in exchange for or to provide funds to retire outstanding short-term debt.

general fund The general fund consists of accounts for receipts not earmarked by law for a specific purpose, the proceeds of general borrowing, and the expenditure of these monies.

general obligation An instrument secured by a pledge of the issuer's full faith and credit.

general-obligation debt Long-term full-faith-and-credit obligations other than those payable initially from nontax revenue. Includes debt payable in the first instance from particular earmarked taxes, such as motor-fuel sales taxes or property taxes.

general revenue All revenue of government except utility revenue, liquor store revenue, and insurance-title revenue. All tax revenue and all intergovernmental revenue, even if designated for employee-retirement or local utility purposes, is classified as general revenue.

general revenue sharing Funds distributed to states and local general-purpose governments by the federal government under the State and Local Fiscal Assistance Act of 1972. The program is no longer in existence.

general sales or gross receipts taxes Sales or gross receipts taxes that are applicable with only specified exceptions to all types of goods, all types of goods and services, or all gross income, whether at a single rate or at classified rates. Taxes imposed distinctively on sales or gross receipts from selected commodities, services, or businesses are separate.

governmental receipts Collections from the public that result primarily from the exercise of the government's sovereign or governmental powers. Governmental receipts consist mostly of individual and corporation income taxes and social insurance taxes, but also include excise taxes, compulsory user charges, customs duties, court fines, certain license fees, and deposits of earnings by the Federal Reserve System. Gifts and donations are also counted as governmental receipts. They are compared with outlays in calculating a surplus or deficit. (*See also* offsetting collections.)

grant An assistance award in which substantial involvement is not anticipated between the federal government and the state or local government or other recipient during the performance of the contemplated activity.

gross federal debt Public debt and agency debt, including all public- and agency-debt issues outstanding.

impoundment Any action or inaction by an officer or employee of the U.S. government that precludes the obligation or expenditure of budget authority provided by Congress.

impoundment resolution A resolution by either the House of Representatives or the Senate that expresses disapproval of a proposed deferral of budget authority set forth in a special message transmitted by the president as required under Sec. 101 3(a) of the Impoundment Control Act of 1974 (P.L. 93-344, 31 U.S.C. 1403).

incremental funding The provision (or recording) of budgetary resources for a program or project based on obligations estimated to be incurred within a fiscal year when such budgetary resources will cover only a portion of the obligations to be incurred in completing the program or project as programmed. This differs from full funding, for which budgetary resources are provided or recorded for the total estimated obligations for a program or project in the initial year of funding. (For distinction, *see* full funding.)

indefinite authority Authority for which a specific sum is not stated but is determined by other factors, such as the receipts from a certain source or obligations incurred. (Authority to borrow that is limited to a specified amount that may be outstanding at any time—that is, revolving debt authority—is considered to be indefinite budget authority.)

indirect cost Any cost incurred for common objectives and that therefore cannot be directly charged to any single cost objective. These costs are allocated to the various classes of work in proportion to the benefit to each class. Indirect cost is also referred to as *overhead* or *burden cost*.

individual income tax A tax on individuals measured by net income, including distinctive taxes on income from interest, dividends, and the like.

industrial development bonds Municipal bonds that finance private industrial plant construction. Lease payments by the private firm service the bonds.

institutional investor or buyer A bank, financial institution, insurance company, mutual fund, or similar investment organization.

insurance trust system A government-administered program for employee retirement and social insurance protection relating to unemployment compensation; workmen's compensation; old-age, survivor's, disability, and health insurance and the like. Insurance trust revenue comprises amounts from contributions required of employers and employees for financing these social insurance programs and earnings on assets of such systems. Insurance trust expenditure corresponds with the character and object category, insurance benefits and repayments, and comprises only cash payments to beneficiaries (including withdrawal of contributions). These categories exclude costs of administering insurance trust systems, which are classed as general expenditure. Insurance trust revenue and expenditure do not include any contributions of a government to a system it administers. Any amounts paid by a government as employer contributions to an insurance trust system administered by another government are classed as general expenditure for current operation and as insurance trust revenue of the particular system and receiving government.

interest Price of borrowing money; rate measured by percentage of principal borrowed.

interest cost Dollar amount that a bond issuer pays over the life of the bond issue for use of the money that is borrowed. Premium is deducted from total to obtain net; discount is added to total to obtain net.

intergovernmental transactions Intergovernmental revenue and intergovernmental expenditure comprise, respectively, payments from one government to another as grants-in-aid, shared revenues, payments in lieu of taxes, or reimbursements for government services. They exclude amounts for the purchase of commodities, property, or utility services, any tax levied as such on facilities of the payer, and employer contributions by the government for social insurance (e.g., employee retirement and Old Age, Survivors, and Health Insurance [OASHI]).

internal control The system of methods and procedures within an organization that safeguard assets maintain reliability of financial and other data, promote operational efficiency, and induce adherence to the policies of the organization.

intragovernmental funds Intragovernmental funds are accounts for business-type or market-oriented activities conducted primarily within and between government agencies and financed by offsetting collections that are credited directly to the fund.

inverted or negative-yield curve The interest-rate structure with short-term interest rates lower than long-term rates.

investment Any asset purchased and held to generate interest, dividend, or rental income.

joint resolution A joint resolution requires the approval of both houses of Congress and the signature of the president, just as a bill does, and has the force of law if approved. There is no real difference between a bill and a joint resolution. The latter is generally used in dealing with limited matters, such as a single appropriation for a specific purpose.

lease-purchase financing A long-term lease sold publicly to finance capital equipment or real-property acquisitions.

lease revenue bond Tax exempt bond secured by lease-back by the local entity lessee. Lessee pledges operating revenues to lease payments. Title to the property reverts to the lessee when the bonds are paid off.

letter of credit (LOC) Agreement by a bank or other entity to honor drafts or other demands for payment of debt service.

level-debt service Serial maturities arranged so that the volume of maturing bonds increases at approximately the same rate as interest payments decline with reduced outstanding debt. Thus, total debt service remains almost constant, even as debt is retired.

license tax A tax enacted (either for revenue raising or for regulation) as a condition to the exercise of a business or nonbusiness privilege, at a flat rate or measured by such bases as capital stock, capital surplus, number of business units, or capacity. Excludes taxes measured directly by transactions, gross or net income, or value of property except those to which only nominal rates apply. "Licenses" based on these latter measures other than those at nominal rates are classified according to the measure concerned. Includes "fees" related to licensing activities—automobile inspection, gasoline and oil inspection, professional examinations and licenses, and so on—as well as license taxes producing substantial revenues.

limited-liability bond A bond that does not pledge the full faith and credit of the jurisdiction, but does usually dedicate a specific revenue source for repayment.

liquidity The ease with which an asset can be converted to money.

loan and loan-guarantee authority Statutory authorizations for a government pledge to pay all or part of the principal and interest to a lender if the borrower defaults.

long-term debt Debt payable more than 1 year after date of issue.

long-term debt issued The par value of long-term debt obligations incurred during the fiscal period concerned, including funding and refunding obligations. Debt obligations authorized but not actually incurred during the fiscal period are not included.

mandatory spending *See* direct spending.

maturity The date on which the debt principal is to be repaid.

maturity date The date on which all or a stated portion of the principal of a security is due and payable.

maturity schedule The schedule (dates and amounts) of principal maturities.

mil 1/10 of 1%.

millage Tax rate expressed in mils per dollar, normally in property taxation.

mission budgeting A budget approach that focuses on output rather than input and directs attention to how well an agency is meeting its responsibilities. By grouping programs and activities according to an agency's mission or end purposes, mission budgeting makes it easier to identify similar programs. Missions at the highest level in the budget structure then focus more sharply on the specific components of the mission and the programs needed to satisfy them. At the lowest levels are line items—that is, the supporting activities necessary to satisfy the missions. For further discussion of this term, see U.S. General Accounting Office, "A Mission Budget Structure for the Department of Agriculture—A Feasibility Study," PAD-80-08.

modified accrual system Accounting basis that records revenues when they are earned (whether or not cash is received then) and expenditures when goods and services are received (whether or not cash payments are made then).

moral-obligation bond Municipal bond not backed by full faith and credit, but law requires states to replenish its debt-service reserve if necessary.

mortgage revenue bond A tax-exempt security issued to make or purchase loans for single-family residences.

multiple-year authority A type of budget authority that is available for a specified period of time in excess of 1 fiscal year. This authority generally takes the form of 2-year, 3-year, etc., availability, but may cover periods that do not coincide with the start or end of a fiscal year. For example, the authority may be available from July 1 of one year through September 30 of the following fiscal year. This authority is sometimes referred to as *forward funding.*

multiyear-budget planning A budget-planning process designed to make sure that the long-range consequences of budget decisions are identified and reflected in the budget totals. Currently, multiyear-budget planning in the executive branch encompasses a policy review for a 3-year period beginning with the budget year, plus protections for the subsequent 2 years. This process provides a structure for the review and analysis of long-term program and tax-policy choices.

municipal bond A bond issued by a state or local government, including cities, towns, villages, counties, special districts, states, and state agencies.

negotiated sale Sale of a new issue of municipal securities through an exclusive agreement with an underwriter selected by the issuer. (*See also* competitive bid.)

net interest cost The percentage rate, from dividing the net interest cost in dollars by the amount borrowed.

nominal interest rate The contractual interest rate appearing on a bond and determining the amount of interest to be paid to a holder.

nonexhaustion An element of nonappropriability; one person's use of service does not preclude full concurrent use of that service by others.

nonguaranteed debt Long-term debt payable solely from pledged specific sources—for example, from earnings of revenue—producing activities (university and college dormitories, toll highways and bridges, electric power projects, public building and school building authorities, etc.) or from specific and limited taxes. It includes only debt that does not constitute an obligation against any other resources of the government if the pledged sources are insufficient.

nonrivalry *See* nonexhaustion.

no-year authority A type of budget authority that remains available for obligation for an indefinite period of time, usually until the objectives for which the authority was made available are attained.

object classification A uniform classification identifying the transactions of the government by the nature of the goods or services purchased (such as personnel compensation, supplies and materials, and equipment), without regard to the agency involved or the purpose of the programs for which they are used.

object-of-expenditure classification *See* object classification.

obligated balances Amounts of budget authority that have been obligated but not yet outlaid. Unobligated balances are amounts that have not been obligated and that remain available for obligation under law.

obligational authority The sum of (1) budget authority provided for a given fiscal year, (2) balances of amounts brought forward from prior years that remain available for obligation, and (3) amounts authorized to be credited to a specific fund or accounts during that year, including transfers between funds or accounts.

obligations Obligations are binding agreements that result in outlays, immediately or in the future. Budgetary resources must be available before obligations can be incurred legally.

off-budget federal entities Certain federally owned and controlled entities whose transactions (e.g., budget authority or outlays) have been excluded from budget totals under provisions of law. The fiscal activities of these entities, therefore, are not reflected in either budget authority or budget outlay totals. However, the outlays of off-budget federal entities are added to the budget deficit to derive the total government deficit that has to be financed by borrowing from the public or by other means.

offering price Price at which underwriters offer securities to investors.

offsetting collections Collections from the public that result from business-type or market-oriented activities and collections from other government accounts. These collections are deducted from gross disbursements in calculating outlays, rather than counted in governmental receipt totals. Some offsetting collections are credited directly to expenditure accounts; others, called offsetting receipts, are credited to receipt accounts.

operating budget A financial plan that presents proposed expenditures for a given period (typically a fiscal year) and estimates of revenue to finance them. Excludes expenditure for capital assets.

outlays Obligations are generally liquidated when checks are issued or cash disbursed. Such payments are called outlays. In lieu of issuing checks, obligations may also be liquidated (and outlays occur) by the maturing of interest coupons in the case of some bonds, or by the issuance of bonds or notes (or increases in the redemption value of bonds outstanding). Outlays during a fiscal year may be for payment of obligations incurred in prior years (prior-year outlays) or in the same year. Outlays, therefore, flow in part from unexpended balances of prior-year budget authority provided for the year in which the money is spent.

out-year estimates This term refers to estimates presented in the budget for years beyond the budget year (usually 4 years).

oversight committee The congressional committee charged with general oversight of the operation of an agency or program. In most cases, but not all, the oversight committee for an agency is also the authorizing committee for the agency's programs.

par value The face value of a security. For bonds, the amount that must be paid at maturity. A quotation of 100 means selling at par; below 100, at a discount (95 5 $950 for a $1,000 par value bond); above 100, at a premium (105 5 $1,050 for a $1,000 bond).

pay-as-you-go (PAYGO) Under BEA90, the requirement that revenue changes and entitlement changes carry a means of financing any change that would otherwise increase the federal deficit.

pay-as-you-go basis The financial policy of a government unit that finances capital outlays from current revenues rather than from borrowing.

pay-as-you-use basis The financial policy of a government unit that pays for the purchase of capital assets as the asset is used. Because assets have useful lives extending over several years, it normally means financing the asset by borrowing and repaying the debt over the life of the asset.

paying agent The bank, trust company, or other agent to which securities are presented for payment.

permanent authority A type of budget authority that becomes available as the result of previously enacted legislation (substantive legislation or prior appropriation act) and does not require current action by Congress. Authority created by such legislation is considered to be current in the first year in which it is provided and permanent in succeeding years.

personal services and benefits Amounts paid for compensation of officers and employees of the government. Consists of gross compensation before deductions for taxes, retirement plans, or other purposes.

personnel benefits Comprises cash allowances paid to civilian and military employees incident to their employment and payment to other funds for the benefit of employees. Prerequisites provided in kind, such as uniforms or quarters, and payments to veterans and former employees resulting from their employment are excluded. Personnel compensation comprises gross compensation (before deduction for taxes and other purposes) for services of individuals, including terminal leave payments. This classification covers all payments (salaries, wages, fees) for personal services rendered to the government by its officers or employees, either civil or military, and compensation for special services rendered by consultants or others.

point .1 percent.

poll taxes A capitation tax levied as a specific amount, uniform or graded, against persons, as ad valorem taxes on arbitrary valuation of polls.

premium Amount by which the price of security exceeds its par value.

prepayment provision Provision specifying at what time and on what terms repayment of the principal amount may be made before the stated maturity.

present value The sum that, when available now and invested at prevailing interest rates, will equal a given value at a defined date in the future.

price Security price generally quoted in terms of percent of par value (e.g., premium price 5 103, discount price 5 97) or in terms of annual yield to maturity (e.g., "yielding 10-3/8%").

price index A measure of the relative change occurring in a category of prices, compared with a base period. The base period is usually set to 100, and changes from that base represent percentage changes. Thus, if a composite price deflator with 1987 = 100 as a base rises to 105, then prices represented in the deflator have risen 5 percent since 1987.

principal amount Total face amount of all securities in the issue. (*See also* face amount.)

private placement The original placement of an issue in the private money market composed of different types of financial institutions (banks, life insurance companies, pension funds, REITs, etc.) with no public offering of the securities.

program Generally defined as an organized set of activities directed toward a common purpose, or goal, undertaken or proposed by an agency in order to carry out its responsibilities. In practice, however, the term program has many uses and thus does not have a well-defined, standard meaning in the legislative process. Program is used to describe an agency's mission, programs, functions, activities, services, projects, and processes. However, in some municipal usage, program refers to a service area, for example, police patrol, rather than to a purpose or goal.

program evaluation In general, the process of assessing program alternatives, including research and results, and the options for meeting program objectives and future expectations. Specifically, program evaluation is the process of appraising the manner and extent to which programs (1) achieve their stated objectives, (2) meet the performance perceptions and expectations of responsible federal officials and other interested groups, and (3) produce other significant effects of either a desirable or undesirable character.

progressive tax A tax with effective rates that are higher for families with high affluence than they are for families with low affluence.

project grant A grant that provides federal funding for fixed or known periods for specific projects or the delivery of specific services or products.

property tax A tax conditioned on ownership of property and measured by its assessed value. It includes general property taxes relating to property as a whole, real and personal, tangible or intangible, whether taxed at a single rate or at classified rates; and taxes on selected types of property, such as motor vehicles or certain or all intangibles.

proportional tax A tax with effective rates that do not change across families with different affluence levels.

public debt That portion of the federal debt incurred when the Treasury or the Federal Financing Bank (FFB) borrows funds directly from the public or another fund or account. To avoid double counting, borrowing from the Treasury is not included in the public debt. (The Treasury borrowing required to obtain the money to lend to the FFB is already part of the public debt.)

public employee-retirement system A government-administered contributory plan for financing retirement and associated benefits for government employees. Does not include noncontributory plans.

public enterprise funds Public enterprise funds are revolving accounts for business or market-oriented activities conducted primarily with the public and financed by offsetting collections that are credited directly to the fund.

public offering Sale by an underwriter to the public.

rating Grading by analysts or investors' services of quality (safety of principal and interest payment) of a bond.

reapportionment A revision by the Office of Management and Budget (OMB) of a previous apportionment of budgetary resources for an appropriation or fund account. Agency requests for reapportionment are usually submitted to the OMB as soon as a change in previous apportionment becomes necessary due to changes in amounts available, program requirements, or cost factors. A reapportionment would ordinarily cover the same period, project, or activity covered in the original apportionment.

reappropriations Congressional action to continue the obligation availability, whether for the same or different purposes, of all or part of the unobligated portion of budget authority that has expired or would otherwise expire. Reappropriations are counted as budget authority in the year for which the availability is extended.

reconciliation bill A bill, requiring enactment by both houses of Congress and approval by the president, making changes to legislation that has been enacted or enrolled.

reconciliation process A process used by Congress to reconcile amounts determined by tax, spending, and debt legislation for a given fiscal year with the ceilings enacted in the second required concurrent resolution on the budget for that year. Section 310 of the Congressional Budget and Impoundment Control Act of 1974 (P.L. 93-344, 31 U.S.C. 1331) provides that the second concurrent resolution on the budget, which sets binding totals for the budget, may direct committees to determine and recommend changes to laws, bills, and resolutions, as required to conform with the binding totals for budget authority, revenues, and the public debt. Such changes are incorporated into either a reconciliation resolution or a reconciliation bill. (*See also* concurrent resolution on the budget.)

reconciliation resolution A concurrent resolution, requiring passage by both houses of Congress but not the approval of the president, directing the clerk of the House or the secretary of the Senate to make specified changes in bills or resolutions that have not yet reached the stage of enrollment.

refunding The issuance of long-term debt in exchange for or to provide funds for the retirement of long-term debt already outstanding.

registered security A security registered by issuer as to ownership, the transfer of ownership of which must be registered with the issuer or trustee.

regressive tax A tax with effective rates that are lower for families with high affluence than they are for families with low affluence.

reoffering yields Interest rates at which underwriters resell individual bonds to investors.

rescission bill A bill or joint resolution that cancels, in whole or in part, budget authority previously granted by Congress.

revenue All amounts of money received by a government from external sources—net of refunds and other correcting transactions—other than from issue of debt, liquidation of investments, and as agency and private trust transactions. Note that revenue excludes noncash transactions such as receipt of services, commodities, or other "receipt in kind."

revenue-anticipation notes A short-term municipal-debt obligation with future revenues pledged for retirement of the notes at maturity.

revenue bond Limited liability bond whose debt-service requirements are paid only from the earnings of a public project.

revenue elasticity A coefficient measuring the percentage increase in revenue from a given source resulting from a 1-percent increase in economic activity.

roll over Issuance of new notes to retire outstanding notes.

sales and gross receipts taxes Taxes, including "licenses" at more than nominal rates, based on volume or value of transfers of goods or services, on gross receipts therefrom, or on gross income and related taxes based on use, storage, production (other than severance of natural resources), importation, or consumption of goods.

score keeping Procedures for tracking the status of congressional budgetary actions. Examples of score-keeping information include up-to-date tabulations and reports on congressional actions affecting budget authority, receipts, outlays, surplus or deficit, and the public-debt limit, as well as outlay and receipt estimates and reestimates.

securitization Borrrowing. For example, a number of states securitized future revenue from the tobacco settlement by selling bonds with future payments from tobacco companies pledged to service that debt.

selective sales and gross receipts taxes Sales and gross receipts taxes imposed on sales of particular commodities or services or gross receipts of particular businesses, separately and apart from the application of general sales and gross receipts taxes.

sequestration Reduction of federal spending according to Gramm-Rudman-Hollings formulas ordered by the president to cause deficit estimates to fall within deficit ceilings.

serial bond A bond in an issue that contains multiple maturities.

severance tax A tax imposed distinctively on removal of natural products—for example, oil, gas, other minerals, timber, fish—from land or water and measured by value or quantity of products removed or sold.

short-term debt Interest-bearing debt payable within 1 year from date of issue, such as bond-anticipation notes, bank loans, and tax-anticipation notes and warrants. Includes obligations having no fixed maturity date if payable from a tax levied for collection in the year of their issuance.

sinking fund Fund used to accumulate periodic payments toward redemption of bonds at maturity: Payments on schedule plus interest earnings will accumulate to par value of the bonds.

special-assessment bond Bond services from special assessments; a local tax against certain property to cover the cost of improvements giving special benefit to that property (e.g., sidewalks or street paving in an area). The bonds may be supported either by the special assessment alone or by full-faith and credit as well.

special funds Federal fund accounts for receipts earmarked for specific purposes and the associated expenditure of those receipts. (*See also* trust funds.)

specific tax A tax applied to physical units of a transaction.

spending authority As defined by Congressional Budget and Impoundment Control Act of 1974 (P.L. 93-344, 31 U.S.C. 1323), a collective designation for appropriations, borrowing authority, contract authority, and entitlement authority for which the budget authority is not provided in advance by appropriation acts. The latter three are also commonly referred to as *backdoor authority.*

spending committees The standing committees of the House and Senate with jurisdiction over legislation that permits the obligation of funds. For most programs, the House and Senate Appropriations Committees are the spending committees. For other programs, the authorizing legislation itself permits the obligation of funds (backdoor authority). When this is the case, the authorizing committees are then the committees with spending responsibility.

spending legislation (spending bill) A term used in the budget score keeping of the Congressional Budget Office to indicate legislation that directly provides budget authority or outlays. Spending legislation includes (1) appropriations legislation, (2) legislation that provides budget authority directly without the need for subsequent appropriations action, and (3) entitlement legislation that, while requiring subsequent appropriations action, essentially "locks in" budget authority at the time of authorization (except legislation that establishes conditional entitlements, where recipients are entitled to payments only to the extent that funds are made available in subsequent appropriations legislation).

spread A bond underwriter's gross profit: The price received by the underwriter on sale of the bonds less the price paid by the underwriter for those bonds.

substantive law Statutory public law other than appropriation law, sometimes referred to as *basic law*. Substantive law usually authorizes, in broad general terms, the executive branch to carry out a program of work.

supplemental appropriation An act appropriating funds in addition to those in an annual appropriation act. Supplemental appropriations provide additional budget authority beyond the original estimates for programs or activities (including new programs authorized after the date of the original appropriation act) in cases where the need for funds is too urgent to be postponed until enactment of the next regular appropriation bill. Supplementals may sometimes include items not appropriated in the regular bills for lack of timely authorizations.

supplemental summary of the budget (midyear or midseason review) A supplemental summary of the budget for the ensuing fiscal year transmitted to Congress by the president on or before July 15 of each year pursuant to the Budget and Accounting Act of 1921, as amended (31 U.S.C. II[b]). With respect to that ensuing fiscal year, the summary reflects (1) all substantial alterations in or reappraisals of the estimates of expenditures and receipts, (2) all substantial obligations imposed on that budget after its transmission to Congress, (3) the actual or proposed appropriations made during the fiscal year in progress, and (4) the estimated condition of the Treasury at the end of the fiscal year if the financial proposals contained in the budget are adopted. The summary also contains any information the president considers necessary or advisable to provide the Congress, and a complete and current estimate of the functions, obligations, requirements, and financial condition of the government for the ensuing fiscal year.

surplus A surplus is the amount by which receipts exceed outlays.

syndicate A group of underwriters.

tax A compulsory payment to a government based on holdings of a tax base.

tax credit A tax credit includes any special provisions of law that result in a dollar-for-dollar reduction in tax liabilities that would otherwise be due. In some cases, tax credits may be carried forward or backward from one tax year to another, whereas other tax credits lapse if not used in the year earned. Tax credits may result in a reduction of tax collections or an increase in the value of tax refunds.

tax-exempt bond A municipal bond whose interest is excluded from federal income tax and may or may not be similarly excluded from income or personal property tax in the jurisdiction where it was issued.

tax expenditure A revenue loss attributable to provisions of the federal income tax laws that allow a special exclusion, or deduction from gross income, or that provide a special credit, preferential tax rate, or deferral of tax liability.

tax-expenditures budget A list of legally sanctioned tax expenditures for each fiscal year that the 1974 Congressional Budget and Impoundment Act (P.L. 93-334, Sec. 601[e]) requires to be part of the president's budget submission to Congress.

tax-rate limit The maximum legal rate at which a government may levy a tax. The limit may apply to a single tax applied by a single government for a purpose, to a single tax applied by a single government, or class of governments, or to all taxes applied by any government or class of governments.

term bond A bond of an issue that has a single, deferred, stated maturity date.

Treasury bill The shortest-term federal security. Treasury bills have maturity dates normally varying from 3 to 12 months and are sold at a discount from face value rather than carrying an explicit rate of interest.

true interest cost A method of computing interest cost or rate that recognizes time value of money.

trust funds Trust funds are accounts, designated by law as trust funds, for receipts earmarked for specific purposes and the associated expenditure of those receipts. (*See also* special funds.)

underwriter Investment firm that buys an entire bond issue from an issuing government with the intention of reselling to the public.

underwriting Purchase of all bonds in a new issue and the marketing of them.

underwriting spread Difference between the offering price to the public and the price the underwriter pays the issuer.

unemployment compensation system A state-administered plan for compulsory unemployment insurance through accumulation of assets from contributions collected from employers or employees for use in making cash benefit payments to eligible unemployed persons. Does not include distinctive sickness or disability insurance plans carried out in conjunction with unemployment insurance programs by certain states. Unemployment insurance contributions collected by the state are deposited in the U.S. Treasury in a trust account maintained for the state; interest is credited by the U.S. Treasury on balances in state accounts; and funds are withdrawn by the state as needed to make unemployment compensation benefit payments.

unified budget The present form of the budget of the federal government adopted beginning with the 1969 budget, in which receipts and outlays from federal funds and trust funds are consolidated. When these fund groups are consolidated to display budget totals, transactions that are outlays of one fund group (i.e., interfund transactions) are deducted to avoid double counting. By law, budget authority and outlays of off-budget entities are excluded from the unified budget, but data relating to off-budget entities are displayed in the budget documents.

user fee This term refers to user, regulatory and other fees, charges, and assessments levied on a class directly availing itself of, or directly subject to a government service, program, or activity, but not on the general public, as measures to be utilized solely to support, usually subject to annual appropriations, the service, program, or activity.

virement Transfer of funds, as between items during budget execution.

warrant An order drawn by a government officer directing the treasurer of that government to pay a specified amount to the bearer after a specified date. Some state and local governments issue warrants rather than checks in order to strengthen internal expenditure control.

workers' compensation system A state-administered plan for compulsory accident and injury insurance of workers through accumulation of assets from contributions collected from employers for financing cash benefits to eligible injured workers.

zero-based budgeting A process emphasizing management's responsibility to plan, budget, and evaluate. Zero-based budgeting provides for analysis of alternative methods of operation and various levels of effort. It places new programs on an equal footing with existing programs by requiring that program priorities be ranked, thereby providing a systematic basis for allocating resources. Formally adopted at the federal level in 1977 and formally abandoned in 1981.

zero-coupon bond A bond that bears no interest but is marketed below face-value amount, to produce a substantial gain on maturity.

Selected Bibliography

The logic and practice of fiscal administration employs the knowledge of many disciplines, including economics, finance, political science, accounting, law, urban and regional planning, public affairs and administration, and sociology. Accordingly, publications associated with all those disciplines often contain ideas of value to the scholar and the practitioner in the field. However, academic journals and first-quality practitioner reviews concentrate on the works of fiscal administration as well: *National Tax Journal, Public Budgeting & Finance, Public Choice, Public Finance Review, Public Finance/Finances Publiques, Journal of Public Economics, Municipal Finance Journal, Journal of State Taxation, Publius, Government Accountants' Journal, Government Finance Review, Journal of Property Tax Assessment and Administration, Journal of Public Budgeting, Accounting, & Financial Management, OECD Journal on Budgeting, Tax Notes,* and *State Tax Notes*, to list only the best known and, arguably, the best. Not many articles from these publications appear in the bibliography that follows; as we tell our doctoral students, all of those articles are assigned.

Because fiscal administration is at the heart of government, it should not be surprising that the many talented people working in government finance offices prepare and publish remarkable studies that shape both theory and practice of fiscal administration; a reading list with nothing but reports from the General Accounting Office, Congressional Budget Office, Congressional Research Service, Joint Committee on Taxation, Office of Tax Analysis in the Treasury, and the Council of Economic Advisors would provide a graduate education in applied federal government finance, especially if supplemented with the monthly reviews published by the district banks of the Federal Reserve System. The documents of budget, revenue, legislative research, and finance departments of state and local governments can be excellent as well, but they tend to be less readily available. Documents from the International Monetary Fund, the World Bank, Organization for Economic Cooperation and Development, and the Asian Development Bank are also excellent and usually available through the Internet. All these materials represent the vital source documents for all students of fiscal administration, regardless of their age or experience. These documents are not included on the list; to be fair to all the quality sources would take more pages than are available here.

The bibliography that follows does not pretend to be exhaustive, but it does include many selections that are classics, are surprising or irritating, contain important arguments, or just simply should be familiar to anyone trying to specialize in fiscal administration.

Public Finance and Theories of the Public Sector

Arrow, Kenneth J., and Tibor Scitovsky, eds. *Readings in Welfare Economics*. Homewood, Ill.: Irwin, 1969.

Barr, Nicholas. "Economic Theory and the Welfare State: A Survey and Interpretations." *Journal of Economic Literature* 30 (June 1992): 741–803.

Baumol, William. "Macroeconomics of Unbalanced Growth: The Anatomy of the Urban Crisis." *American Economic Review* 62 (June 1967): 415–26.

Blinder, Alan S., and Robert M. Solow. "Does Fiscal Policy Matter?" *Journal of Public Economics* 1 (November 1973): 319–37.

Borcherding, Thomas E., ed. *Budgets and Bureaucrats, The Sources of Government Growth*. Durham, N.C.: Duke University Press, 1977.

Breton, Albert. *The Economic Theory of Representative Government*. Chicago: Aldine, 1974.

Buchanan, James M. *Fiscal Theory and Political Economy: Selected Essays by James M. Buchanan*. Chapel Hill, N.C.: University of North Carolina Press, 1960.

———. *Public Finance in Democratic Process*. Chapel Hill, N.C.: University of North Carolina Press, 1967.

———. *The Demand and Supply of Public Goods*. Chicago: Rand McNally, 1968.

Buchanan, James M., and Gordon Tullock. *The Calculus of Consent*. Ann Arbor: University of Michigan Press, 1962.

Burkhead, Jesse, and Jerry Miner. *Public Expenditure*. Chicago: Aldine Atherton, 1971.

Cropper, Maureen, and Wallace Oates. "Environmental Economics: A Survey." *Journal of Economic Literature* 30 (June 1992): 675–740.

Davis, Otto A., M. A. H. Dempster, and Aaron Wildavsky. "A Theory of the Budgetary Process." *American Political Science Review* 60 (September 1966): 529–47.

Downs, Anthony. *An Economic Theory of Democracy*. New York: Harper & Row, 1957.

———. "Why the Government Budget Is Too Small in a Democracy." *World Politics* 12 (1959–60): 541–63.

Harney, Donald F. *Service Contracting: A Local Government Guide*. Washington, D.C.: International City Management Association, 1992.

Hilke, John C. *Competition in Government-Financed Services*. New York: Quorum Books, 1992.

Kodrzycki, Yolanda. "Fiscal Pressures and the Privatization of Local Services." *New England Economic Review* (January/February 1998): 39–50.

Mankiw, Gregory. "A Quick Refresher Course in Macroeconomics." *Journal of Economic Literature* 28 (December 1990): 1645–60.

Megginson, William L., and Jeffry M. Netter, "From State to Market; A Survey of Empirical Studies on Privatization," *Journal of Economic Literature* 39 (June 2001): 321–89.

Mishan, E. J. *Welfare Economics: Ten Introductory Essays*, 2nd ed. New York: Random House, 1964.

Musgrave, Richard A. *The Theory of Public Finance*. New York: McGraw-Hill, 1959.

Musgrave, Richard A., and Alan T. Peacock. *Classics in the Theory of Public Finance*. New York: St. Martin's Press, 1967.
Niskanen, William A., Jr. *Bureaucracy and Representative Government*. Chicago: Aldine Atherton, 1971.
Olson, Mancur. *The Logic of Collective Action, Public Goods and the Theory of Groups*. Cambridge, Mass.: Harvard University Press, 1965.
Peacock, Alan T., and Jack Wiseman. *The Growth of Public Expenditure in the United Kingdom*. Princeton, N.J.: National Bureau of Economic Research and Princeton University Press, 1961.
Romer, Thomas. "Nobel Laureate: On James Buchanan's Contribution to Public Economics." *Journal of Economic Perspectives* 2 (Fall 1988): 165–79.
Rosen, Harvey, ed. *Studies in State and Local Finance*. Chicago: University of Chicago Press, 1986.
Rowley, Charles K., Friedrich Schneider, and Robert D. Tullison, eds. "The Next Twenty-Five Years of Public Choice." *Public Choice* 77 (September 1993): 1–7.
Samuelson, Paul A. "The Pure Theory of Public Expenditure." *Review of Economics and Statistics* 36 (November 1954): 387–89.
Sandmo, Agnar. "Buchanan on Political Economy." *Journal of Economic Literature* 28 (March 1990): 50–65.
Schultze, Charles L. *Memos to the President: A Guide Through Macroeconomics for the Busy Policymaker*. Washington, D.C.: Brookings Institution, 1992.
Tanzi, Vito, and Ludger Schuknecht. *Public Spending in the 20th Century: A Global Perspective*. Cambridge: Cambridge University Press, 2000.
Tiebout, Charles M. "The Pure Theory of Local Expenditure." *Journal of Political Economy* 64 (October 1956): 416–24.
Tullock, Gordon. *Private Wants, Public Means: An Economic Analysis of the Desirable Scope of Government*. New York: Basic Books, 1970.
Webber, Carolyn, and Aaron Wildavsky. *A History of Taxation and Expenditure in the Western World*. New York: Simon and Schuster, 1986.

Budget Theory

Bailey, John J., and Robert J. O'Connor. "Operationalizing Incrementalism: Measuring the Muddles." *Public Administration Review* 35 (Jan./Feb. 1975): 60–66.
Cleveland, Frederick A. "Evolution of the Budget Idea in the United States." *Annals of the American Academy of Political and Social Science* 62 (November 1915): 15–35.
Key, V. O. "The Lack of a Budgetary Theory." *American Political Science Review* 34, no. 6 (1940): 1137–44.
Koven, Steven G. *Ideological Budgeting: The Influence of Political Philosophy on Public Policy*. New York: Praeger, 1988.
Lee, Robert D., Jr., Ronald Johnson, and Philip G. Joyce *Public Budgeting Systems*, 7th ed. Boston: Jones and Bartlett, 2004.
LeLoup, Lance T. "The Myth of Incrementalism: Analytical Choices in Budgetary Theory." *Polity* 10 (Summer 1978): 488–509.
Lewis, Verne. "Toward a Theory of Budgeting." *Public Administration Review* 12, no. 1 (1952): 43–54.
Lindblom, Charles E. "The Science of 'Muddling Through'." *Public Administration Review* 9 (1959): 79–88.
McKinney, Jerome B. *Effective Financial Management in Public and Nonprofit Agencies*. New York: Quorum Books, 1986.
Meyers, Roy T., ed. *Handbook of Government Budgeting*. San Francisco: Jossey-Bass, 1998.
Meyers, Roy T. *Strategic Budgeting*. Ann Arbor, Mich.: University of Michigan Press, 1996.
Pitsvada, Bernard T. "The Executive Budget—An Idea Whose Times Has Passed." *Public Budgeting & Finance* 6 (Spring 1988): 85–94.
Premchand, A. *Controlling Government Spending, The Ethos, Ethics, and Economics of Expenditure Management*. Noidar, India: Oxford Press India, 2005.
Rubin, Irene S., ed. *New Directions in Budget Theory*. Albany: State University of New York Press, 1988.
———. "Budget Theory and Budget Practice: How Good the Fit?" *Public Administration Review* (March/April 1990): 179–89.
Schick, Allen, "The Road to PPB: The Stages of Budget Reform." *Public Administration Review* 26, no. 4 (December 1966): 243–58.
Thompson, Fred. "Mission-Driven, Results-Oriented Budgeting: Financial Administration and the New Public Management." *Public Budgeting & Finance* 14 (Fall 1994): 90–105.
Webber, Carolyn, and Aaron Wildavsky. *A History of Taxation and Expenditure in the Western World*. New York: Simon & Schuster, 1986.
Wildavsky, Aaron. *A Comparative Theory of Budgeting Process*, 2nd ed. Boston: Little, Brown, 1986.

Budgetary Politics

Alvarez, R. M., and J. L.Saving, "Congressional Committees and the Political Economy of Federal Outlays," *Public Choice*, 92 (July 1997): 55–73.
Gosling, James J. *Budgetary Politics in American Governments*. New York: Longman, 1992.
Greider, William. "The Education of David Stockman." *The Atlantic Monthly* (December 1981): 27–54.
LeLoup, Lance. *Budgetary Politics*, 4th ed. Brunswick, Ohio: King's Court, 1988.
Rauch, Jonathan. *Demosclerosis: The Silent Killer of American Government*. New York: Times Books, 1995.

Rubin, Irene S. *The Politics of Public Budgeting*, 4th ed. New York: Seven Bridges Press, 2000.
Sharkansky, Ira. *The Politics of Taxing and Spending*. Indianapolis: Bobbs-Merrill, 1969.
Wildavsky, Aaron. *The Politics of the Budgetary Process*. Boston: Little, Brown, 1964.
———. *The New Politics of the Budgetary Process*, 2nd ed. New York: Harper Collins, 1992.
Wildavsky, Aaron, and Naomi Caiden. *The New Politics of the Budgetary Process*, 3rd ed. New York: Longman, 1997.

Budget Methods and Issues

Anthony, Robert. "Games Government Accountants Play." *Harvard Business Review* 63 (Sept./Oct. 1985): 161–70.
Brecher, Charles *et al.* "Follow the Money: Using Expenditure Analysis as an Evaluation Tool," *American Journal of Evaluation* 26 (June 2005): 166–88.
Brown, Richard E., Thomas P. Gallagher, and Meredith C. Williams. *Auditing Performance in Government: Concepts and Cases*. New York: Wiley, 1982.
Burkhead, Jesse. *Government Budgeting*. New York: Wiley, 1956.
Carpenter, Frances H., and Florence C. Sharp. *Popular Reporting: Local Government Financial Reports to the Citizenry*. Norwalk, Conn.: Governmental Accounting Standards Board, 1992.
Clynch, Edward J. "Zero-Base Budgeting in Practice: An Assessment." *International Journal of Public Administration* 1 (Spring 1979): 43–64.
Coombs, H. M., and D. E. Jenkins. *Public Sector Financial Management*. London: Chapman and Hall, 1991.
Cothran, Dan A. "Entrepreneurial Budgeting: An Emerging Reform?" *Public Administration Review* 53 (Sept./Oct. 1993): 445–54.
Duquette, Dennis J., and Alexis Stowe. "Enter the Era of Performance Measurement Reporting." *Government Accountants' Journal* 41 (Summer 1992): 19–28.
Forsythe, Dall W. "Financial Management and the Reinvention of Government." *Public Productivity and Management Review* 16 (Summer 1993): 415–23.
Garner, C. William. *Accounting and Budgeting in Public and Nonprofit Organizations, A Manager's Guide*. San Francisco: Jossey-Bass, 1991.
Golembiewski, Robert T., and Jack Rabin. *Public Budgeting and Finance, Behavioral, Theoretical, and Technical Perspectives*, rev. and exp., 3rd ed. New York: Dekker, 1983.
Grifel, Stuart S. "Performance Measurement and Budgetary Decisionmaking." *Public Productivity and Management Review* 16 (Summer 1993): 403–7.
Grizzle, Gloria. "Does Budget Format Govern Actions of Budgetmakers?" *Public Budgeting & Finance* 6 (Spring 1986): 60–70.
Harr, David J. "How Activity Accounting Works in Government." *Management Accounting* 72 (September 1990): 36–40.
Haveman, Robert H., and Julius Margolis. *Public Expenditures and Policy Analysis*, 3rd ed. Boston: Houghton Mifflin, 1983.
Hyde, Albert C., ed. *Government Budgeting: Theory, Process, and Politics*, 2nd ed. Pacific Grove, Calif.: Brooks/Cole, 1992.
Jones, Peter. *Combating Fraud and Corruption in the Public Sector*. London: Chapman and Hall, 1993.
Miller, Gerald J. *Government Financial Management Theory*. New York: Dekker, 1991.
———. *Financial Management Handbook for Local Governments*. Chicago: Government Finance Officers Association, 1986.
Novick, David, ed. *Program Budgeting*, 2nd ed. New York: Holt, Rinehart & Winston, 1969.
Organization for Economic Cooperation and Development. *Budgeting for Results: Perspectives on Public Expenditure Management*. Paris: OECD, 1995.
Premchand, A. *Government Budgeting and Expenditure Controls*. Washington, D.C.: International Monetary Fund, 1983.
———, ed. *Government Financial Management: Issues and Country Studies*. Washington, D.C.: International Monetary Fund, 1990.
———. *Public Expenditure Management*. Washington, D.C.: International Monetary Fund, 1993.
Pyhrr, Peter A. "The Zero-Base Approach to Government Budgeting." *Public Administration Review* 37 (Jan./Feb. 1977): 1–8.
Rabin, Jack, ed. *Handbook of Public Budgeting*. New York: Dekker, 1992.
Steiss, Alan Walter. *Financial Management in Public Organizations*. Pacific Grove, Calif: Brooks/Cole, 1989.

Federal Budgeting—Process, Institutions, and Analysis

Axelrod, Donald. *Budgeting for Modern Government*. New York: St. Martin's Press, 1988.
———. *A Budget Quartet*. New York: St. Martin's Press, 1989.
Benda, Peter M., and Charles H. Levine. "OMB and the Central Management Problem: Is Another Reorganization the Answer?" *Public Administration Review* (September/October 1986): 379–91.
Bennett, James T., and Thomas J. DiLorenzo. *Underground Government: The Off-Budget Public Sector*. Washington, D.C.: Cato Institute, 1983.
Berman, Larry. "The Office of Management and Budget That Almost Wasn't." *Political Science Quarterly* 92 (Summer 1977): 283–89.
———. *The Office of Management and Budget and the Presidency, 1921–1979*. Princeton, N.J.: Princeton University Press, 1979.
Caiden, Naomi. "Problems in Implementing Government Expenditure Limitations." Appendix C in Aaron Wildavsky, ed., *How to Limit Government Spending*. Berkeley: University of California Press, 1980, pp. 143–62.

Capital Budget Symposium. *Public Budgeting & Finance* 18, no. 3 (Fall 1998), entire issue.
Cheek, Logan M. *Zero-Base Budgeting Comes of Age*. New York: AMACOM, 1977.
Cogan, John F. *et al. The Budget Puzzle, Understanding Federal Spending*. Stanford, Calif.: Stanford University Press, 1994.
Collender, Stanley E. *The Guide to the Federal Budget,* FY (various years). New York: The Urban Institute Press and/or The Century Foundation Press, 1986–2000.
Cranford, John. *Budgeting for America,* 2nd ed. Washington, D.C.: Congressional Quarterly, 1989.
Cuny, Thomas J. "Federal Budget Concepts—Bright Lights or Black Holes?" *Public Budgeting & Finance* (Summer 1998): 94–132.
Doyle, Richard. "Congress, the Deficit, and Budget Reconciliation." *Public Budgeting & Finance* 16 (Winter 1996): 59–81.
Eisner, Robert. *The Great Deficit Scares: The Federal Budget, Trade, and Social Security*. New York: The Century Fund, 1997.
Fenno, Richard. *The Power of the Purse*. Boston: Little, Brown, 1966.
Finley, James J. "The 1974 Congressional Initiative in Budget Making." *Public Administration Review* (May/June 1975): 270–78.
Fisher, Louis. *Presidential Spending Power*. Princeton University Press, 1975.
Franklin, Daniel P. *Making Ends Meet: Congressional Budgeting in the Age of Deficits*. Washington, D.C.: CQ Press, 1993.
Gramlich, Edward M. "Different Approaches for Dealing with Social Security." *Journal of Economic Perspectives* 10 (Summer 1996): 55–66.
Gross, Bertram. "The New Systems Budgeting." *Public Administration Review* (March/April 1969): 113–37.
Haveman, Robert. "Should Generational Accounts Replace Public Budgets and Deficits?" *Journal of Economic Perspectives* 8 (Winter 1994): 95–112.
Heclo, Hugh. "OMB and the Presidency—The Problem of 'Neutral Competence'." *The Public Interest*, no. 38 (Winter 1975): 80–98.
Hogan, Joseph J. "Ten Years After: The US Congressional Budget and Impoundment Control Act of 1974." *Public Administration* 63 (Summer 1985): 133–49.
Ippolito, Dennis S. *Hidden Spending: The Politics of Federal Credit Programs*. Chapel Hill, N.C.: University of North Carolina Press, 1984.
Jones, L. R. and Jerry L. McCaffery, *Budgeting and Financial Management in the Federal Government*. Greenwich, Conn.: Information Age Publishing, 2001.
———. "Implementing the Chief Financial Officers Act and the Government Performance and Results Act in the Federal Government." *Public Budgeting & Finance* 17 (Spring 1997): 35–55.
———. "Reform of the Planning, Programming, Budgeting System, and Management Control in the U.S. Department of Defense: Insights from Budgeting Theory," *Public Budgeting & Finance*, 25 (Fall 2005): 119.
Joyce, Philip G. "Congressional Budget Reform: The Unanticipated Implications of Federal Policy Making." *Public Administration Review* 56 (July/August 1996): 317–25.
Kelly, Brian. *Adventures in Porkland: How Washington Wastes Your Money and Why They Won't Stop*. New York: Villard, 1992.
King, Ronald F. *Budgeting Entitlements: The Politics of Food Stamps*. Washington, D.C.: George Washington University Press, 2000.
Kravchuk, Robert S., and Ronald W. Schak. "Designing Effective Performance Measurement Systems under the Government Performance and Results Act of 1993." *Public Administration Review* 56 (July/August 1996): 348–58.
LeLoup, Lance T. "Appropriations Politics in Congress: The House Appropriations Committee and Executive Branch Agencies." *Public Budgeting & Finance* 4 (Winter 1984): 78–99.
Light, Paul C. *Monitoring Government: Inspectors General and the Search for Accountability*. Washington, D.C.: Brookings Institution, 1993.
Lynch, Thomas D. *Federal Budget and Financial Management Reform*. New York: Quorum Books, 1991.
McCaffery, Jerry L., and L. R. Jones. *Budgeting and Financial Management for National Defense*. Greenwich, Conn: Information Age Publishing, 2004.
Merewitz, Leonard, and Stephen H. Sosnick. *The Budget's New Clothes*. Chicago: Markham, 1971.
Morstein Marx, Fritz. "The Bureau of the Budget: Its Evolution and Present Role." *American Political Science Review* 39 (1945): 653–84, 869–98.
Mosher, Frederick C. *The GAO: The Quest for Accountability in American Government*. Boulder, Colo: Westview Press, 1979.
———. *A Tale of Two Agencies: A Comparative Analysis of the General Accounting Office and the Office of Management and Budget*. Baton Rouge: Louisiana State University Press, 1984.
Munson, Richard. *The Cardinals of Capitol Hill*. New York: Grove Press, 1993.
Musgrave, Richard A. "The Nature of Budgetary Balance and the Case for the Capital Budget." *American Economic Review* (1939) vol. XXIX, 2. June.
———. "Should We Have a Capital Budget?" *Review of Economics and Statistics* 45 (1963): 21.
Myers, Roy T. "Biennial Budgeting by the U.S. Congress." *Public Budgeting & Finance* (Summer 1988): 21–32.
Novick, David (ed.). *Program Budgeting: Program Analysis and The Federal Budget*. Washington, D.C.: U.S. Government Printing Office, 1964, 1965.
Payne, James L. *The Culture of Spending: Why Congress Lives Beyond Our Means*. San Francisco: Institute for Contemporary Studies Press, 1991.

Penner, Rudolph G., and Alan J. Abramson. *Broken Purse Strings: Congressional Budgeting, 1974–88*. Ann Arbor and Washington, D.C.: Gerald R. Ford Foundation and the Urban Institute Press, 1988.
Pyhrr, Peter A. *Zero-Base Budgeting*. New York: John A. Wiley & Sons, 1973.
Radin, Beryl. "The Government Performance and Results Act (GPRA): Hydra-Headed Monster or Flexible Management Tool?" *Public Administration Review* (July/August 1998): 307–316.
Reischauer, Robert D., ed. *Setting National Priorities, Budget Choices for the Next Century*. Washington, D.C.: Brookings Institution, 1997.
Report of the President's Commission to Study Capital Budgeting. Washington, D.C.: Government Printing Office, 1999.
Rivlin, Alice, and Isabel Sawhill, ed. *Restoring Fiscal Sanity: How to Balance the Budget*. Washington, D.C.: Brookings Institution, 2004.
Rubin, Irene S. *Balancing the Federal Budget*. New York: Chatham House, 2002.
Sample, V. Alaric. "Resource Planning and Budgeting for National Forest Management." *Public Administration Review* 52 (July/Aug. 1992): 339–46.
Savage, James D. *Balanced Budgets and American Politics*. Ithaca, N.Y.: Cornell University Press, 1988.
Schick, Allen. *The Federal Budget: Politics, Policy, Process*, 2nd ed. Washington, D.C.: The Brookings Institution, 2000.
———. "Is Budget Innovation Possible?" Ch. 7 in *Budget Innovation in the States*. Washington, D.C.: The Brookings Institution, 1971, pp. 192–218.
———. "A Death in the Bureaucracy: The Demise of Federal PPB." *Public Administration Review* (March/April 1973): 146–56.
———. "The Budget Bureau That Was: Thoughts on the Rise, Decline, and Future of a Presidential Agency." *Law and Contemporary Problems* 35, no. 3 (1970): 519–39.
———. "The Road to PPB: The Stages of Budget Reform." *Public Administration Review* 26, no. 4 (December 1966): 243–58.
———. "The Road from ZBB." *Public Administration Review* 38 (Mar./Apr. 1978): 177–80.
———. *Congress and Money, Budgeting, Spending, and Taxing*. Washington, D.C.: Urban Institute Press, 1980.
———. "Micro-Budgetary Adaptations to Fiscal Stress in Industrialized Democracies." *Public Administration Review* 48 (Jan./Feb. 1988): 523–33.
———. *The Capacity to Budget*. Washington, D.C.: Urban Institute Press, 1990.
Schier, Steven E. *A Decade of Deficits: Congressional Thought and Fiscal Action*. Albany, N.Y.: State University of New York Press, 1992.
Schlesinger, Arthur F., Jr. *The Imperial Presidency*. New York: Houghton Mifflin, 1973.
Schultze, Charles L. *The Politics and Economics of Public Spending*. Washington, D.C., 1968.
Seckler-Hudson, Catheryn. "Performance Budgeting in Government." *Advanced Management* (March 1953): 5–9, 30–32.
Shuman, Howard E. *Politics and the Budget*, 3rd ed. Englewood Cliffs, N.J.: Prentice Hall, 1992.
Stockman, David. *The Triumph of Politics: Why the Reagan Revolution Failed*. New York: Harper & Row, 1986.
The Century Fund. *Balancing the Budget: The Basics*. New York:
Thelwell, Raphael. "Gramm-Rudman-Hollings Four Years Later: A Dangerous Illusion." *Public Administration Review* (March/April 1990): 190–98.
Tomkin, Shelley Lynn. *Inside OMB: Politics and Process in the President's Budget Office*. Armonk, N.Y.: M. E. Sharpe, 1998.
United States, Budget and Accounting Act of 1921, 42 Stat. 18 (1921).
United States, Congress, House of Representatives, Commission on Economy and Efficiency in Government, Final Report, "The Need for a National Budget." H. Doc. 854, 62nd Congress, 2d session, 1912, pp. 7–12. (June 19, 1912.)
United States, The Commission on Organization of the Executive Branch of Government, A Report to the Congress, "Budget and Accounting Recommendations" (First Hoover Commission Report, February 1949).
United States, Executive Office of the President, Bureau of the Budget, "Planning-Programming-Budgeting," Bulletin No. 66–3, October 12, 1965.
Wildavsky, Aaron. "The Political Economy of Efficiency: Cost-Benefit Analysis, Systems Analysis, and Program Budgeting." *Public Administration Review* (December 1966): 292–310.
———. *How to Limit Government Spending*. Berkeley: University of California Press, 1980.
Wildavsky, Aaron, and Naomi Caiden. *The New Politics of the Budgetary Process*, 3rd ed. New York: Longman, 1997.

State and Local Budgeting: Process, Institutions, and Analysis

Abney, Glenn, and Thomas P. Lauth. "The Line-Item Veto in the States: An Instrument for Fiscal Restraint or an Instrument of Partisanship?" *Public Administration Review* 45 (May/June 1985): 372–77.
Aronson, J. Richard, and Eli Schwartz, ed. *Management Policies in Local Government Finance*. Fifth Edition. Washington, D.C.: International City/County Management Association, 2004.
Albritton, Robert, and Ellen Dran. "Balanced Budgets and State Surpluses: The Politics of Budgeting in Illinois." *Public Administration Review* 47 (Mar./Apr. 1987): 143–52.
Bland, Robert, and Irene Rubin. *Budgeting, A Guide for Local Governments*. Washington, D.C.: International City/County Management Association, 1997.
Briffault, Richard. *Balancing Acts: The Reality Behind State Balanced Budget Requirements*. New York: Century Foundation, 1996.
Clark, Terry Nichols, and Lorna Crowley Ferguson. *City Money*. New York: Columbia University Press, 1983.

Clynch, Edward J. and Thomas P. Lauth, eds. *Governors, Legislatures, and Budgets, Diversity Across the American States*. New York: Greenwood Press, 1991.

Duncombe, H. Sydney, *et al.* "Zero-Base Budgeting in Idaho—An Evaluation After Five Years." *Government Accountants' Journal* 30 (Summer 1981): 25–26.

Fisher, Louis. "Line Item Veto Act of 1996: Heads-up from the States." *Public Budgeting & Finance* 17 (Summer 1997): 3–17.

Fisher, Peter. "Grading Places: What Do the Business Climate Ratings Really Tell Us?" *State Tax Notes* (September 5, 2005): 739–43.

Forsythe, Dall W. *Memos to the Governor, An Introduction to State Budgeting*. Washington, D.C.: Georgetown University Press, 1997.

Gosling, James J. "Patterns of Influence and Choice in the Wisconsin Budgetary Process." *Legislative Studies Quarterly* 10 (November 1985): 457–82.

———. "The State Budget Office and Policy Making." *Public Budgeting & Finance* 7 (Spring 1987): 51–65.

Hanushek, Eric. "The Economics of Schooling." *Journal of Economic Literature* 14 (Sept. 1986): 1141–77.

Howard, Marcia A. "State Tax and Expenditure Limitations: There is No Story." *Public Budgeting & Finance* (Summer 1989): 83–90.

Hutchison, Tony, and Kathy James. *Legislative Budget Procedures in the 50 States: A Guide to Appropriations and Budget Processes*. Denver: National Conference of State Legislatures, 1988.

Joyce, Philip G., and Daniel R. Mullins. "The Changing Fiscal Structure of the State and Local Public Sector: The Impact of Tax and Expenditure Limitations." *Public Administration Review* (May/June 1991): 240–53.

Kelly, Janet M., and Rivenbark, William C. *Performance Budgeting for State and Local Government*. Armonk, New York: M. E. Sharp, 2003.

Laffer, Arthur B., and Jan P. Seymour, eds. *The Economics of the Tax Revolt: A Reader*. New York: Harcourt Brace Jovanovich, 1979.

Lauth, Thomas P. "Zero-Base Budgeting in Georgia State Government: Myth and Reality." *Public Administration Review* 38 (Sept./Oct. 1978): 420–30.

———. "Performance Evaluation in the Georgia Budgetary Process." *Public Budgeting & Finance* 5 (Spring 1985): 67–82.

Melkers, Julia, and Katherine Willoughby. "The State of the States: Performance-Based Budgeting Requirements in 47 out of 50." *Public Administration Review* 58 (January/February 1998): 66–73.

Mullins, Daniel, and Philip G. Joyce. "Tax and Expenditure Limitations and State and Local Fiscal Structure: An Empirical Assessment." *Public Budgeting & Finance* 16 (Spring 1996): 75–101.

Pagano, Michael A., and Richard J. T. Moore. *Cities and Fiscal Choices: A New Model of Urban Public Investment*. Durham, N.C.: Duke University Press, 1985.

Schick, Allen. *Budget Innovation in the States*. Washington, D.C.: Brookings Institution, 1970.

Sjoquist, David L., ed. *State and Local Finances Under Pressure*. Cheltenham, U.K.: Edward Elgar, 2003.

Sokolow, Alvin D., and Beth Walter Honadle. "How Rural Local Governments Budget: The Alternatives to Executive Preparation." *Public Administration Review* 44 (Sept./Oct. 1984): 373–83.

Thurmaier, Kurt M. and Katherine G. Willoughby. *Policy and Politics in State Budgeting*. Armonk, N.Y.: M. E. Sharpe, 2001.

International Government Finances

Chu, Ke-young, and Richard Hemming, eds. *Public Expenditure Handbook: A Guide to Public Policy Issues in Developing Countries*. Washington, D.C.: International Monetary Fund, 1991.

Evans, Lewis, *et al.* "Economic Reform in New Zealand 1984–95: The Pursuit of Efficiency." *Journal of Economic Literature* 34 (December 1996): 1856–902.

Heller, Peter S. *Who Will Pay?* Washington, D.C.: International Monetary Fund, 2003.

Jones, L. R., and Jerry L. McCaffery. *Government Response to Financial Constraints: Budgetary Control in Canada*. Westport, Conn.: Greenwood Press, 1989.

Mikesell, John L., and Daniel Mullins, "Reforming Budget Systems in Countries of the Former Soviet Union," *Public Administration Review*, 61 (September/October 2001).

Public Revenues: General

Aaron, Henry, and Michael J. Boskin, eds. *The Economics of Taxation*. Washington, D.C.: Brookings Institution, 1980.

Aaron, Henry, and William, G. Gale, eds. *The Economic Effects of Fundamental Tax Reform*. Washington, D.C.: Brookings Institution, 1996.

Aaron, Henry, and Harvey Galper. *Assessing Tax Reform*. Washington, D.C.: Brookings Institution, 1985.

Aaron, Henry, and Joseph A. Pechman, eds. *How Taxes Affect Economic Behavior*. Washington, D.C.: Brookings Institution, 1981.

Bahl, Roy W., and Johannes F. Linn. *Urban Public Finance in Developing Countries*. New York: Oxford University Press, 1992.

Bell, Michael, and Ronald Fisher. "State Limitations on Local Taxing and Spending Powers." *National Tax Journal* 32 (Dec. 1978): 391–96.

Bird, Richard M. *Tax Policy and Economic Development*. Baltimore: Johns Hopkins University Press, 1992.
Blum, Walter J., and Harry Kalven, Jr. *The Uneasy Case for Progressive Taxation*. Chicago: University of Chicago Press, 1953.
Boskin, Michael. "Tax Policy and Economic Growth: Lessons from the 1980s." *Journal of Economic Perspectives* 2 (Fall 1988): 71–97.
Bosworth, Barry P. *Tax Incentives and Economic Growth*. Washington, D.C.: Brookings Institution, 1984.
Brunori, David. *State Tax Policy, A Political Perspective*. Washington, D.C.: Urban Institute Press, 2001.
———. *Local Tax Policy: A Federalist Perspective*. Washington, D.C.: Urban Institute Press, 2003.
Burgess, Robin, and Nicholas Stern. "Taxation and Development." *Journal of Economic Literature* 31 (June 1993): 762–830.
Fisher, Ronald C. *State and Local Public Finance*. Glenview, Ill.: Scott, Foresman, 1988.
Fullerton, Don. "On the Possibility of an Inverse Relationship Between Tax Rates and Government Revenues." *Journal of Public Economics* 19, no. 1 (1982): 3–22.
———. "The Use of Effective Tax Rates in Tax Policy." *National Tax Journal* 39 (September 1986): 285–92.
Fullerton, Don and Diane Lim Rogers. *Who Bears the Lifetime Tax Burden?* Washington, D.C.: Brookings Institution, 1993.
Gold, Steven D., ed. *Reforming State Tax Systems*. Denver: National Conference of State Legislatures, 1986.
———., ed. *The Unfinished Agenda for State Tax Reform*. Washington, D.C.: National Conference of State Legislatures, 1988.
Kotlikoff, Lawrence. "Taxation and Savings: A Neoclassical Perspective." *Journal of Economic Literature* 22 (Dec. 1984): 1576–629.
Lewis, Alan. *The Psychology of Taxation*. New York: St. Martin's Press, 1982.
Messere, Ken, Flip de Kam, and Christopher Heady. *Tax Policy: Theory and Practice in OECD Countries*. Oxford, U.K.: Oxford University Press, 2003.
Musgrave, Richard A. *Fiscal Systems*. New Haven, Conn.: Yale University Press, 1969.
———., ed. *Broad-Based Taxes: New Options and Sources*. Baltimore: Johns Hopkins University Press, 1973.
Musgrave, Richard A., and Carl S. Shoup, eds. *Readings in the Economics of Taxation*. Homewood, Ill.: Irwin, 1959.
Pechman, Joseph A., ed. *What Should Be Taxed: Income or Expenditure?* Washington, D.C.: Brookings Institution, 1980.
———. *Who Paid the Taxes, 1966–85?* Washington, D.C.: Brookings Institution, 1985.
Peters, B. Guy. *The Politics of Taxation: A Comparative Perspective*. Cambridge, Mass.: Blackwell, 1991.
Shome, Parthasarathi, ed. *Tax Policy Handbook*. Washington, D.C.: International Monetary Fund, 1995.
Slemrod, Joel, ed. *Do Taxes Matter? The Impact of the Tax Reform Act of 1986*. Cambridge, Mass.: MIT Press, 1990.
———. "Optimal Taxation and Optimal Tax Systems." *Journal of Economic Perspectives* 4 (Winter 1990): 157–78.
———, ed. *Why People Pay Taxes: Tax Compliance and Enforcement*. Ann Arbor: University of Michigan Press, 1992.
Slemrod, Joel, and Jon Bakija. *Taxing Ourselves: A Citizen's Guide to the Great Debate Over Tax Reform*. Cambridge, Mass.: MIT Press, 1996.
Steurle, C. Eugene. *Contemporary U.S. Tax Policy*. Washington, D.C.: Urban Institute Press, 2004.
———. *The Tax Decade: How Taxes Came to Dominate the Public Agenda*. Washington, D.C.: Urban Institute Press, 1992.
Tanzi, Vito. *Taxation in an Integrating World*. Washington, D.C.: Brookings Institution, 1995.
Wassmer, Robert W., and Ronald C. Fisher. "An Evaluation of the Recent Move to Centralize the Finance of Public Schools in Michigan." *Public Budgeting & Finance* 16 (Fall 1996): 90–112.

Public Revenues: Property Taxes

Aaron, Henry. *Who Pays the Property Tax? A New View*. Washington, D.C.: Brookings Institution, 1975.
Bahl, Roy W., ed. *The Taxation of Urban Property in Less Developed Countries*. Madison: University of Wisconsin Press, 1979.
Bahl, Roy W., and Paul Smoke, ed. *Restructuring Local Government Finance in Developing Countries: Lessons from South Africa*. Cheltanham, U.K.: Edward Elgar, 2003.
Bird, Richard, and Enid Slack, ed. *International Handbook of Land and Property Taxation*. Cheltanham, U.K.: Edward Elgar, 2004.
Bowman, John H., and John L. Mikesell. "Assessment Uniformity: The Standard and Its Attainment." *Property Tax Journal* 9 (December 1990): 219–34.
Eckert, Joseph D., ed. *Property Appraisal and Assessment Administration*. Chicago: International Association of Assessing Officers, 1990.
Fisher, Glenn W. *The Worst Tax? A History of the Property Tax in America*. Lawrence, Kan.: University Press of Kansas, 1996.
Lynn, Arthur D., Jr., ed. *The Property Tax and Its Administration*. Madison, Wis.: University of Wisconsin Press, 1967.
Midwinter, Arthur, and Claire Monaghan. *From Rates to the Poll Tax*. Edinburgh, Scotland: Edinburgh University Press, 1993.
Mieszkowski, Peter M. "The Property Tax: An Excise Tax or a Profits Tax?" *Journal of Public Economics* 1, no. 1 (1972): 73–96.
Mieszkowski, Peter M., and Zodrow, George. "Taxation and the Tiebout Model." *Journal of Economic Literature* 27 (September 1989): 1098–146.
Mikesell, John L. "Patterns of Exclusion of Personal Property from American Property Tax Systems." *Public Finance Quarterly* 20 (Oct. 1992): 528–42.
Netzer, Dick. *Economics of the Property Tax*. Washington, D.C.: Brookings Institution, 1965.
Organization for Economic Cooperation and Development. *Taxes on Immovable Property*. Paris: Organization for Economic Cooperation and Development, 1983.

Public Revenues: Goods and Services Taxes

Aaron, Henry, ed. *The Value-Added Tax: Lessons from Europe*. Washington, D.C.: Brookings Institution, 1981.

Barthold, Thomas A. "Issues in the Design of Environmental Excise Taxes." *Journal of Economic Perspectives* 8 (Winter 1994): 133–52.

Cline, Robert, John L. Mikesell, Thomas Neubig, and Andrew Phillips, "Sales Taxation of Business Inputs: Existing Tax Distortions and the Consequences of Extending the Sales Tax to Business Services," *State Tax Notes*, XXXV (February 14, 2005): 457–70.

Cnossen, Sijbren. *Excise Systems: A Global Study of the Selective Taxation of Goods and Services*. Baltimore: Johns Hopkins University Press, 1977.

———, ed. *Theory and Practice of Excise Taxation*. Oxford, U.K.: Oxford University Press, 2005.

Due, John F. *Sales Taxation*. Urbana: University of Illinois Press, 1957.

———. *Indirect Taxation in Developing Countries*. Baltimore: Johns Hopkins University Press, 1970.

Due, John F., and John L. Mikesell. *Sales Taxation: State and Local Structure and Administration*, 2nd ed. Washington, D.C.: Urban Institute Press, 1994.

Fields, Robert J. *Understanding and Managing Sales and Use Tax*. Chicago: Commerce Clearing House, 1991.

Fox, William F., ed. *Sales Taxation: Critical Issues in Policy and Administration*. Westport, Conn.: Praeger, 1992.

Kaldor, Nicholas. *An Expenditure Tax*. London: George Allen and Unwin, 1955.

Metcalf, Gilbert. "Value-Added Taxation: A Tax Whose Time Has Come?" *Journal of Economic Perspectives* 9 (Winter 1995): 121–40.

Mikesell, John L. "State Sales Tax Policy in a Changing Economy." *Public Budgeting & Finance* 12 (Spring 1992): 83–91.

———. "A Quality Index for State Sales Tax Structure—Measuring the States Against an Ideal Standard," *State Tax Notes*, XXXV (January 10, 2005): 129–36.

Organization for Economic Cooperation and Development. *Taxing Consumption*. Paris: Organization for Economic Cooperation and Development, 1988.

———. *Taxation and the Environment: Complementary Policies*. Paris: Organization for Economic Cooperation and Development, 1993.

Ring, Raymond J., Jr. "Consumers' Share and Producers' Share of the General Sales Tax," *National Tax Journal* 52 (March 1999): 79–90.

Schenk, Alan, and Oliver Oldman. *Value Added Tax: A Comprehensive Approach in Theory and Practice*. Ardsley, N.Y.: Transnational Publishers, 2001.

Seidman, Lawrence. *The USA Tax: A Progressive Consumption Tax*. Cambridge, Mass.: MIT Press, 1997.

Sullivan, Clara. *The Tax on Value Added*. New York: Columbia University Press, 1965.

Tait, Alan A. *Value Added Tax: International Practice and Problems*. Washington, D.C.: International Monetary Fund, 1988.

U.S. Advisory Commission on Intergovernmental Relations. *The Michigan Single Business Tax: A Different Approach to State Business Taxation*. Washington, D.C.: Advisory Commission on Intergovernmental Relations, 1978.

Public Revenues: Income Taxation

Auerbach, Alan J., and Kevin A. Hassett, ed. *Toward Fundamental Tax Reform*. Washington, D.C.: American Enterprise Institute, 2005.

Auerbach, Alan J., and Joel Slemrod. "The Economic Effects of the Tax Reform Act of 1986." *Journal of Economic Literature* 35 (June 1997): 589–632.

Birnbaum, Jeffery H., and Alan S. Murray. *Showdown at Gucci Gulch*. New York: Vintage Books, 1987.

Bradford, David F. *Untangling the Income Tax*. Cambridge, Mass.: Harvard University Press, 1986.

Brownlee, W. Ellliot. *Federal Taxation in America: A Short History*. New edition. Cambridge, U.K.: Cambridge University Press, 2004.

Conlon, Timothy J., Margaret T. Wrightson, and David R. Beam. *Taxing Choices, The Politics of Tax Reform*. Washington, D.C.: CQ Press, 1990.

Goode, Richard. *The Individual Income Tax*, rev. ed. Washington, D.C.: Brookings Institution, 1976.

Hufbauer, Gary Clyde. *U.S. Taxation of International Income: Blueprint for Reform*. Washington, D.C.: Institute for International Economics, 1992.

Penniman, Clara. *State Income Taxation*. Baltimore: Johns Hopkins University Press, 1980.

U.S. Department of Treasury. *Blueprints for Basic Tax Reform*. Washington, D.C.: Government Printing Office, 1977.

Public Revenues: Charges, Etc.

Altshuler, Alan A., and Jose A. Gomez-Ibanez, with Arnold M. Howitt. *Regulation for Revenue: The Political Economy of Land Use Extractions*. Washington, D.C./Cambridge, Mass: Brookings Institution/Lincoln Institute for Land Policy, 1993.

Cutler, David and Grant Miller. "Water, Water Everywhere: Municipal Finance and Water Supply in American Cities," National Bureau of Economic Research Working Paper 11096 (January 2005).

Clotfelter, Charles T., and Philip J. Cook. *Selling Hope: State Lotteries in America*. Cambridge, Mass.: Harvard University Press, 1989.
Mikesell, John L. "Lotteries in State Revenue Systems: Gauging a Popular Revenue Source After 35 Years." *State and Local Government Review* 33 (Spring 2001): 86–100.
Shoup, Donald C. "The Ideal Source of Local Public Revenue," *Regional Science and Urban Economics* 34 (2004): 753–84.

Public Revenues: Forecasting, Estimating, and Tax Expenditures

Auerbach, Alan J. "Dynamic Revenue Estimation." *Journal of Economic Perspectives* 10 (Winter 1996): 141–58.
Mikesell, John L. "Tax Expenditure Budgets, Budget Policy, and Tax Policy: Confusion in the States," *Public Budgeting & Finance*, XXII (Winter 2002): 34–51.
Surrey, Stanley. *Pathways to Tax Reform*. Cambridge, Mass.: Harvard University Press, 1973.

Public Revenues: Administration and Compliance

Aaron, Henry J. and Joel Slemrod. *The Crisis in Tax Administration*. Washington, D.C.: Brookings Institution, 2004.
Bird, Richard M., and Milka Casanegra de Jantscher, eds. *Improving Tax Administration in Developing Countries*. Washington, D.C.: International Monetary Fund, 1992.
Cowell, Frank A. *Cheating the Government: The Economics of Evasion*. Cambridge, Mass.: MIT Press, 1990.
Johnson, David C. *Perfectly Legal*. New York: Portfolio, 2003.
Payne, James L. *Costly Returns: The Burdens of the U.S. Tax System*. San Francisco: Institute for Contemporary Studies, 1993.
Steuerle, C. Eugene. *Who Should Pay for Collecting Taxes? Financing the IRS*. Washington, D.C.: American Enterprise Institute, 1986.

Intergovernmental Fiscal Relationships

Agranoff, Robert, and Michael McGuire. "A Jurisdiction-Based Model of Intergovernmental Management in U.S. Cities." *Publius: The Journal of Federalism* 28, no. 4 (Fall 1988): 1–20.
Break, George F. *Financing Government in a Federal System*. Washington, D.C.: Brookings Institution, 1980.
Oates, Wallace E. *Fiscal Federalism*. New York: Harcourt Brace Jovanovich, 1972.
Rivlin, Alice M. *Reviving the American Dream*. Washington, D.C.: The Brookings Institution, 1992.
Tannenwald, Robert. "Come the Devolution, Will the States Be Able to Respond?" *New England Economic Review* (May/June 1998): 53–83.
Tannenwald, Robert, and Nicholas Turner. "Interstate Fiscal Disparity in State Fiscal Year 1999," Federal Reserve Bank of Boston Public Policy Discussion Papers No. 04-9 (December 2004).

Public Debt, Working Capital, and Pension Funds

Afonso, Antonio. "Understanding the Determinants of Sovereign Debt Ratings: Evidence for the Two Leading Agencies," *Journal of Economics and Finance* 27 (Spring 2003): 56–74.
Aronson, J. Richard. "The Idle Balances of State and Local Governments: An Economic Analysis of National Concern." *Journal of Finance* 23 (June 1968): 499–508.
Aronson, J. Richard, and Eli Schwartz. *Management Policies in Local Government Finance*, 3rd ed. Washington, D.C.: International City Management Association, 1987.
Berne, Robert, and Richard Schramm. *The Financial Analysis of Governments*. Englewood Cliffs, N.J.: Prentice Hall, 1986.
Bland, Robert L. "The Interest Cost Savings from Municipal Bond Insurance: The Implications for Privatization." *Journal of Policy Analysis and Management* 6, no. 2 (1987): 207–19.
Capeci, John. "Credit Risk, Credit Ratings, and Municipal Bond Yields: A Panel Study." *National Tax Journal* 44 (December 1991, pt. 1): 41–56.
Epstein, R. Mark, and Timothy A. Rattigan. "Pay-as-You-Go vs. Bond Financing: An Overview of Project Funding Methods." *Municipal Finance Journal* 10, no. 4 (1989): 289–303.
Fabozzi, Frank J. *The Municipal Bond Handbook*, 2 vol. Homewood, Ill.: Dow Jones–Irwin, 1983.
Feenberg, Daniel R., and James M. Poterba. "Which Households Own Municipal Bonds? Evidence from Tax Returns." *National Tax Journal* 44 (December 1991, pt. 1): 93–104.
Garbade, Kenneth. "Origins of the Federal Reserve Book-Entry System," *Federal Reserve Bank of New York Policy Review* (December 2004): 33–50.
Giertz, J. Fred. "The Impact of Pension Funding on State Government Finances," *State Tax Notes* (August 18, 2003): 507–13.
Hackbart, Merl M., and James Leigland. "State Debt Management Policy: A National Survey." *Public Budgeting & Finance* (Spring 1990): 37–54.
Heins, A. James. *Constitutional Restrictions Against State Debt*. Madison: University of Wisconsin Press, 1963.

Hildreth, W. Bartley. "The Changing Roles of Municipal Market Participants." *Public Administration Quarterly* 11, no. 3 (1987): 314–41.

Hushbeck, Clare. *Public Employee Pension Funds: Retirement Security for Plan Participants or Cash Cow for State Governments?* American Association of Retired Persons Public Policy Institute Report 9301. Washington, D.C.: American Association of Retired Persons, 1993.

Kenyon, Daphne A. "Effects of Federal Volume Caps on State and Local Borrowing." *National Tax Journal* 44 (December 1991, pt. 1): 81–92.

Lamb, Robert, and Stephen P. Rappaport. *Municipal Bonds: The Comprehensive Review of Tax-Exempt Securities and Public Finance*. New York: McGraw-Hill, 1980.

Lehmann, Michael B. *The Dow Jones–Irwin Guide to Using the Wall Street Journal.* Homewood, Ill.: Dow Jones–Irwin, 1987.

Leigland, James, and Robert Lamb. *WPP$$: Who Is to Blame for the WPPSS Disaster?* Cambridge, Mass.: Ballinger, 1986.

Loveley, Mary E., and Michael J. Wasylenko. "State Taxation of Interest Income and Municipal Borrowing Costs." *National Tax Journal* 45 (March 1992): 37–52.

Marlin, George J., and Joe Mysak. *The Guide to Municipal Bonds: The History, the Industry, the Mechanics*. New York: American Banker/Bond Buyer, 1991.

Miller, Girard. *A Public Investor's Guide to Money Market Instruments*. Chicago: Municipal Finance Officers Association, 1982.

Nathans, Eli. "Municipal Bond Insurance: The Economics of the Market." *Municipal Finance Journal* 13, no. 2 (Summer 1992): 1–20.

Peng, Jun. "Public Pension Funds and Operating Budgets: A Tale of Three States," *Public Budgeting & Finance* 24 (Summer 2004): 59–73.

Petersen, John E. "Managing and Investing Public Money." *Governing* 6 (March 1993): 43–54.

Petersen, John E., and Dennis R Strachota, eds. *Local Government Finance: Concepts and Practices*. Chicago: Government Finance Officers Association, 1991.

Quigley, John E., and Daniel L. Rubinfeld. "Private Guarantees for Municipal Bonds: Evidence from the Aftermarket." *National Tax Journal* 44 (December 1991, pt. 1): 29–40.

Ramsey, Jim, and Merl Hackbart. "Municipal Bond Sales in Foreign Markets: Experience and Results," *Public Budgeting & Finance* 16 (Fall 1996): 3–12.

Simonsen, William, and Mark D. Robbins. "Does It Make Any Difference Anymore? Competitive versus Negotiated Municipal Bond Issuance." *Public Administration Review* 56 (Jan./Feb. 1996): 57–63.

Steiss, Alan Walter. *Strategic Facilities Planning: Capital Budgeting and Debt Administration.* Lanham, Maryland: Lexington Books, 2005.

Zehner, Andrew L., and George A. Valais. *Linked Deposits: Leveraging for Economic Development.* Chicago: Government Finance Officers Association, 1990.

Zimmerman, Dennis. *The Private Use of Tax-Exempt Bonds*. Washington, D.C.: Urban Institute Press, 1991.

Zorn, Paul. *Survey of State and Local Government Employee Retirement Systems*. Washington, D.C.: Public Pension Coordinating Council, 1991.

Index

Note: Page numbers followed by letters indicate the following: f indicates figures, n indicates notes, s indicates sidebars, and t indicates tables.

A

AAA corporate debt, yield of Aaa municipal and, 591f
Aaa municipal and AAA corporate debt, yield of, 591f
Aaron, Henry J., 406n, 534n
Abken, Peter A., 590n
Abuses sought by auditors, some errors or, 168t
Accelerating collections, 614–619
Account, concentration, 621f
Accounting and financial reporting, governmental, 56–60
Accounting for time, 258–263
Act, first general appropriation, 91s
Activities or outcomes, 217–218t
Activity-based costing (ABC), 199, 200–201s
Adjusted gross income (AGI), 340, 342–345
Administration, debt, 575–610
Administrative-cost estimates for major taxes, 507t
Advisory Commission on Intergovernmental Relations (ACIR), 559
Agency and function, federal spending by, 211f
Agency budget requests, preparation of, 141–151
    budget justification, 142–145
    elements of cost estimation, 145–151
Agreements, repurchase, 626–627
Ahlbrandt, Jr., Roger S., 5n
Aid, school, 561–563
Aid to Families with Dependent Children (AFDC), 559
All families
    effective tax rates for, 306–307t
    federal tax distributions for, 306–307t
    tax rates by income quintiles for, 337t
Alm, James, 493n
Almy, Richard R., 417n, 436n
Alternate minimum tax (AMT), 344n, 357, 359–360s
Alternative classifications, expenditure in, 213
Altshuler, Alan A., 468n
Analyses
    break-even, 149–150s
    cost-benefit, 263–280
    payback, 276t
Anderson, Jonathan, 611n
Ansberry, Clare, 627n
Anthony, Robert N., 65n
Appeals, frivolous, 504s
Appropriability. *See* Nonappropriability
Appropriation act, first general, 91s
Appropriations subcommittees from 109th congress, 90t
Arithmetic of rates, levies, and assessed value, 420–431
Army Corps of Engineers, 197
Aronson, J. Richard, 295, 475n, 579n
Assessed value, arithmetic of, 420–431
Assessment ratios, property classifications by statutory rates and, 437t
Assessments, doing
    approaches, 427–429
    cycles, 426–427
    managing parcel data, 429–431
    standards, 423–426
Audit and evaluation, 167–170
Audit coverage by Internal Revenue Service (IRS) by type of return, 502t
Auditors, some errors or abuses sought by, 168t
Auten, Gerald E., 311n
Automated Clearing House (ACH), 615–616
Automatic teller machine (ATM), 616

B

Bad taxes, good or, 418–420
Bahl, Roy W., 545n, 583n
Baker, Bruce, 130n
Baker, Richard, 605n
Balance, phantom, 156–161
Balances, consolidating, 620–621
Baldwin, John A., 496n
Banks, Robert L., 626n
Barr, Paul G., 180n
Barro, Robert J., 311n
Barta, Patrick, 423n
Bartlett, Bruce, 342n
Bator, Francis M., 3n
Baumol, William J., 273n, 622n
Bean, David R., 58n
Beard, Charles A., 294, 294n
Belongia, Michael T., 156n
Benefit-base excises, 382
Benefits, individual, 17t, 18t
Berman, Larry, 84n
Betting, lotteries and offtrack, 479–483
Biemiller, Lawrence, 160n
Bierman, Jr., Harold, 276n
Bills, treasury, 624
Birnbaum, Jeffrey H., 21n
Bish, Robert, 14n
Blackley, Paul R., 156n
Blair, John P., 22n
Bland, Robert L., 123n, 584n
Blankenbeckler, George M., 612n
Blind, Texas Commission for the, 220f
Block grants, 558–559
Blondal, Jon. R, 60n
Blum, Walter J., 304n
Blumenthal, Marsha, 338n
Boardman, Anthony, 280n
Boldt, Harold E., 623n
Bond values, mechanics of, 586–588
Bonds
    inflation-indexed, 580–581s
    municipal, 584–585
Border patrol, 229f
Borg, Mary O., 483n
Borrowing, 130f
Boskin, Michael J., 534n
Botner, Stanley B., 238n
Bowman, John H., 382n, 418n, 424n, 442n
Bracket rates, lowest and highest, 348–349t
Bradbury, J. C., 9n
Bradbury, Katherine L., 311n, 562n
Break-even analysis, 149–150s
Break, George F., 298n, 550n
Briffault, Richard, 156n
Brown, Jr., John Y., 5n
Brundage, Percival Flack, 84n
Brunori, David, 314n
Buchanan, James M., 19n
Budget. *See also* On-budget/off-budget
    cash, 612–628
    executive, 154–161
    federal, 79–118
    illustration of new performance, 220f
    intra-year cash, 166–167
Budget and Performance Integration (BPI), 226
Budget authority, relationship to outlays, 53f
Budget classifications, alternative, 193–201
Budget classifications and reform, 192–243
    alternative budget classifications, 193–201
    expenditure in alternative classifications, 213
    new performance budgeting, 214–232
    performance budgets, 201–205
    program budgets, 205–212
    provision of government services, 193–201
    results/outcomes, 214–232

Budget cycles, 48–56
audit and evaluation, 54–56
execution, 52–54
executive preparation, 49–51
legislative consideration, 51
phases of, 49f
state, 126t
Budget execution, managing, 161–167
internal controls, 165–167
Budget for fire department, Tempe, Arizona, line-item, 43–44f
Budget formats and associated features, alternative, 197t
Budget illustration, Salt Lake City performance, 203–204f
Budget justification, 142–145
checklist for, 144t
Budget methods and practices, 141–191
audit and evaluation, 167–170
executive budget, 154–161
managing budget execution, 161–167
preparation of agency budget requests, 141–151
review of budgets, 151–154
Budget process
federal, 82–108, 83t, 86–87t
functions of, 46–48
Budget process, logic of, 31–78
budget cycle, 48–56
budget process and logic, 38–48
budgets and political strategies, 61–69
governmental accounting and financial reporting, 56–60
size and growth of government expenditure, 32–38
Budget request, capital, 255t
Budget requests, preparation of agency, 141–151
budget justification, 142–145
elements of cost estimation, 145–151
Budget-status report, 164f
Budget structures and institutions, 79–140
federal and state-local, 79–140
federal budget, 79–118
state and local budgets, 118–130
Budget structures, program, 206–207t
Budget timetable, congressional, 89t
Budgeting
capital, 244
capital improvement programming and, 251f
challenges for new performance, 221–225
federal integration of performance and, 226–232
government, 200–201s
new performance, 214–232
problems in capital, 256–257
Budgeting process, capital, 249–256
Budgets
capital, 246–249
performance, 201–205
program, 205–212
review of, 151–154
salary classification in miscellaneous, 213f
state and local, 118–130
tax expenditure, 514, 530–534
traditional, 196–201
Budgets and political strategies, 61–69
incrementalist insight, 61–62
roles, visions, and incentives, 62–64
strategies, 64–69
Bunamo, Michael, 264n
Burgess, Robin, 315n
Burkhead, Jesse, 248n

C

Caiden, 64n
Caiden, Naomi, 61, 62n
Calculation, coefficient of dispersion, 441t
California's ReadyReturn pilot, 496s
Calmes, Jackie, 95n
Campbell, David, 352n
Campos, Ed, 48n
Cantor, Jeffrey A., 576n
Cantor, Richard, 594n
Capital asset inventory, 250
Capital budget request, selected questions for, 255t
Capital budgeting, 244
problems in, 256–257
process, 249–256
Capital budgets
executing, 256
implementation of, 253–256
reasons for having, 246–249
Capital improvement plan (CIP), 250–252
Capital improvement programming and budgeting, 251f
Capital project, net present value (NPV) and evaluating, 275s
Carlino, Gerald, 267n
Carlton, Jim, 530n
Caro, Robert, 583n
Carr, Jennifer, 561n
Cash balance through year, 613f
Cash budget, 612–628
Cash budget, intra-year, 166–167
Cash management, 611, 612–628
Cash management, control for, 615f
Cash management, elements of, 614–621
accelerating collections, 614–619
consolidating balances, 620–621
controlling disbursements, 619–620
Cass, Margaret M., 613n
Castelazo, Moly D., 61n
Categorical grants, 555–558
CBO, 515
Certificate of participation (COP), arrangement, 606f
Certificate, suspending sales tax by, 392f
Certificates of deposit (CDs), negotiable, 625–626
Certificates of participation (COP), 605–606
Sacramento Regional Transit District, 604s
Chaloupka, Frank J., 380n
Chan, James L., 58n
Chang, S., 571n
Chang, Yee Ching Lillian, 274n
Charge guidelines, 474–477
Charge receipts, federal user, 465t
Charges, user, 461, 468–477
Charging fees, federal system, 467s
Chase, Samuel B., 278n
Chen, Li-Khan, 584n
Chrystal, Alec, 112n
Chua, Dale, 360n
Cilke, James M., 522n
Cirre, Richard J., 269n
Clark, Colin, 40n
Classifications
budget, 192–243
expenditure in alternative, 213
property, 437t
Classifications of functions of government (COFOG), 210
Cline, Robert, 389n
Clotfelter, Charles, 482
Clotfelter, Charles T., 483n
Clynch, Edward J., 122n
Cnossen, Sijbren, 373n, 379n, 383n, 384n, 464n, 507n
Coase, Ronald, 8n
Coe, Charles K., 613
Coefficient of dispersion (CD), 440
and property tax bills, 443s
Cogan, John F., 85n, 141n
Colbert, Jean-Baptiste, 298
Collectability, 314
Collecting taxes, 492–513
Collection and deposit float, 616f
Collection system, postal lockbox, 617f
Collections, accelerating, 614–619
Commerce, sales taxes and Internet, 396–399
Commercial paper, 626
Commodity exemptions, 394–395
Competition, failure of, 8–10
Compounding, 259f
Compounding, discounting and, 258–263

Comprehensive income measures, two more, 343s
Computation
income tax, 358t
tax, 357
Computation worksheet, TIC and NIC, 603t
Concentration account, application of, 621f
Congress, appropriations subcommittees from 109th, 90t
Congressional Budget Office (CBO), 82, 244
approach to individual income tax, 523s
Congressional budget timetable, 89t
Conrad, James, 505n
Contingent-valuation method (CVM), 270s
Contributions, social insurance, 335t
Cook, Philip J., 482, 483n
Cook, Timothy Q., 627n
Cooper, Kerry S., 612n
Coronado, Julia L., 637n
Corporate debt, yield of Aaa municipal and AAA, 591f
Corporate income taxation, 357–365
dividing base, 361–362
integration with individual tax, 362–364
international harmonization, 364–365
Corporate income taxes, individual and, 335t
Correspondence and subsidiarity, 542–544
Cost-benefit analysis, 263–280
decision criteria, 273–277
elements in, 265–271
selecting discounted rates, 271–273
special problems of, 277–280
special problems of cost-benefit analysis, 277–280
Cost-benefit analysis, elements in
benefit estimation and evaluation, 266–269
estimating project costs, 269–271
project objectives, 265–266
Cost-benefit analysis, special problems of
cost-benefit analysis and politics, 279–280
multiple objectives, 277–278
valuing projects that save lives, 278–279
Cost estimation, elements of, 145–151
nonpersonnel costs, 147–148
paying staff, 146–147
personnel costs, 146–147
screening for errors, 148–151
Costs
of issuing debt, 604s
nonpersonnel, 147–148
personnel, 146–147
Coulson, N. Edward, 267n
Council of Economic Advisers on externalities and environment, 323s
Council of Economic Advisors, 7s, 85n
Countries around world, value-added tax (VAT) rate in, 405t
Countries, government in selected industrialized, 39t
Credit
earned income tax, 355s
enhancements, 597–599
Credit ratings by Mergent, Standard & Poor's, and Fitch, 596–597t
Credits, 354
Criteria conflict, projects with ranking, 277t
Criteria, decision, 273–277
Cropper, Maureen L., 279n
Curve, tax revenue, 310f
Cycles
budget, 48–56, 49f
state budget, 126t

D

Darby, Julia, 542n
Darlington, Lord, 192
Das, Jishnu, 12n
Davie, Bruce F., 585n
DeBoer, Larry, 156n, 505n
Debt
costs of issuing, 604s
distribution of municipal, 604t
federal, 575–579, 578t
municipal, 579–606
state and local, 627
state and local government, 579–606
U.S. federal, 577f
yield of Aaa municipal and AAA corporate, 591f
Debt administration, 575–610
federal debt, 575–579
municipal debt, 579–606
state and local government debt, 579–606
Debt policy, appropriate, 585–586
Debt structure and design, 588–591
Decision criteria, 273–277
Deductions, personal, 345–347
Defense, program-budget structure in U.S. Department of, 209t
Deficit reduction, 156–161
Deficits
federal, 109–116
and surpluses of federal government, 110–111t
Deflating-dividing between real and price change, 36s
Department of Defense, program-budget structure in U.S., 209t
Deposit float, collection and, 616f
Development, economic, 318–321
Di Leo, Luca, 13n
Diaz-Gimenez, Javier, 417n
Dillon, John F., 24, 24n
Disbursements
controlling, 619–620
receipts and, 615f
Discount rate to use, 272s
Discounted rates, selecting, 271–273
Discounting and compounding, 258–263
Discounts, prompt-payment, 619s
Discretionary federal outlays, 105f
Discretionary federal spending, mandatory and, 104t
Discretionary relationships. *See* Mandatory/discretionary relationships
Disparity, fiscal, 545–547
Dispersion and property tax bills, coefficient of, 443s
Dispersion calculation, coefficient of, 441t
Distortion, measuring value of economic, 317s
Distribution, flow of production and, 377f
Dobbs, Michael, 225n
Dolan, Julie, 199n
Doran, John J., 158n
Dotsey, Michael, 112n, 621n
Downs, Anthony, 19n
Doyle, Richard, 115n
Drinen, D. J., 9n
Drucker, Peter F., 153n, 153s, 476n
Due, John F., 387n, 501n, 507n
Duffield, Jeremy G., 627n

E

Earned income tax credit (EITC), 338, 355s
Eckert, Joe, 423n
Eckert, Joseph K., 421n
Eckstein, Otto, 277n, 278, 278n
Economic advantage from bigness, 544–545
Economic development, 318–321
Economic distortion, measuring value of, 317s
Economic effects, 315–318
Economic equivalence of RST and VAT, 401s
Economic income, family, 343s
Economically targeted investment (ETI), 636
Edsall, Thomas B., 101n
Edwards, Kimberly K., 427n

Effective tax rates, 354–356
for all families, 306–307t
Effects, economic, 315–318
Eisner, Robert, 112n
Employee retirement fund management, public, 635–637
Employee retirement funds, 611
distribution of state and local government, 634t
Employee retirement system finances, state and local government, 632t
Engen, Eric M., 637n
English, William B., 591n
Engstrom, John H., 58n
Enterprises
government, 102–103s
government gambling, 479–483
Environment, externalities and, 323s
Environmental excises, regulatory and, 383
Equity, 300–309
business and individual shares, 308
horizontal and vertical, 302
question, 378–379
those who pay, 304
Errors or abuses sought by auditors, 168t
Estimating, revenue, 514, 527–530
Evaluation
audit and, 167–170
project, 244
Excess burden of tax, 317s
Excise taxation, selective, 379
Excises
benefit-base, 382
luxury, 379–380
miscellaneous, 383
regulatory and environmental, 383
sumptuary, 380–381
Exclusion of producers' goods, 389–393
Executive budget, 154–161
phantom balance and deficit reduction, 156–161
plan and balancing, 154–161
Exemptions
commodity, 394–395
on families of three, 356t
federal individual income tax, 348–349t
personal, 347–349
Expanded income, 343s
Expenditure budgets, tax, 514
Expenditure/public revenue process, public, 40–42
Expenditures
in alternative classifications, 213
size and growth of government, 32–38
state and local government, 120–121t
Externalities, 6–8
and environment, 323s
taxes and, 322–324

F

Failure, market, 2–10
Families
effective tax rates for all, 306–307t
exemptions on, 356t
federal tax distributions for all, 306–307t
tax rates by income quintiles for all, 337t
Family economic income, 343s
Farhi, Paul, 64n
Farney, Dennis, 125n
Faucheux, Ron, 20n
Federal-agency issues, miscellaneous, 624–625
Federal aid to state and local governments, 554t
Federal budget, 79–118
Federal budget process, 82–108
major acts establishing, 83t
major events in, 86–87t
Federal debt, 575–579, 577f, 578t
Federal deficits, fighting, 109–116
Federal fiscal policy, 116–118
Federal funds/trust funds, 102–103s
Federal government
deficits and surpluses of, 110–111t
spending by, 80–81
Federal income tax
largest tax expenditures in, 534t
payments, 337t
Federal individual income tax
exemptions, 348–349t
structure, 341f
Federal integration of performance and budgeting, 226–232
Federal outlays
discretionary, 105f
by function, 81t
Federal spending
by agency and function, 211f
mandatory and discretionary, 104t
Federal tax distributions for all families, 306–307t
Federal tax table, portion of, 351f
Federal taxes on goods and services, 374t
Federal user charge receipts, 465t
Fees
charging, 467s
user, 461, 466–468
Fessenden, Ford, 225n
Field, Thomas F., 517n
Filers, single, 350f
Finance, lease-purchase, 605–606
Finance, public, 1–27
market failure and functions of government, 2–10
privatization, 11–24
Finances, government, 592–593s
Finances, property taxes in U.S. government, 416t
Finances, state and local government employee retirement system, 632t
Financial Accounting Standards Board (FASB), 56
Financial analysis, financing plan/long-term, 252–253
Financial information for management, 53f
Financial reporting, governmental accounting and, 56–60
Financing plan/long-term financial analysis, 252–253
Fire department, Tempe, Arizona, line-item budget for, 43–44f
Fiscal assistance, general-purpose, 560–561
Fiscal disparity, 545–547
Fiscal policy, federal, 116–118
Fiscal relations, intergovernmental, 541–571
Fisher, Glenn W., 415n
Fisher, Louis, 95n, 125n
Fisher, Ronald C., 319n
Fishing rights, government creates market for, 7s
Flat-rate income tax, 356t
Fleenor, Patrick, 356n
Forbes, Ronald W., 598n
Forbus, P. R., 571n
Forecasting, alternative methods for, 518–524
deterministic modeling, 519–520
econometric models, 521–522
microdata models, 522–524
multiple regression, 520–521
univariate projections and extrapolations, 518–519
Forecasting, steps in revenue, 522t
Forecasts, revenue, 514
Format, object-of-expenditure (or input), 42–45
Forrester, John P., 125n
Forsythe, Dall W., 51n, 63n, 155n, 415n
Fortune, Peter, 584n
Fox, W., 406n
Franchise Tax Board (FTB), 496s
Franecki, David, 629n
Frankel, Glenn, 491n
Friel, Brian, 222n
Frivolous appeals, 504s
Fuller, Jeffrey J., 147n
Fullerton, Donald, 307n, 311n
Function, federal spending by agency and, 211f

Fund management, public employee retirement, 635–637
Funds
distribution of state and local government employee retirement, 634t
employee retirement, 611
federal funds/trust, 102–103s
fifteen largest public employee pension, 629t
investing idle, 621–628
managing, 611
managing public employee retirement, 628–637
money-market mutual, 628
public school district revenues by source of, 562t

G

Gaddy, Clifford G., 353n
Gaebler, Ted, 215n
Gale, William G., 353n
Gambling enterprises, 477
government, 479–483
Garbade, Kenneth D., 579n, 612n
Garrett, Thomas A., 61n
Gasparino, Charles, 623n
General-purpose fiscal assistance, 560–561
General taxes on goods and services, 384–387
Generally accepted accounting principles (GAAP), 58
Gesalman, Anne Beilli, 457n
Glaeser, Edward L., 11n
Goertz, Robert K., 238n
Gold, Steven D., 433n, 434n
Gomez-Ibanez, Jose A., 468n
Good or bad taxes, 418–420
Good, Richard, 333n
Goods
exclusion of producers', 389–393
nonmarket, 270s
public, 3–6
Goods and services
federal taxes on, 374t
general taxes on, 384–387
state and local taxes on, 375t
Goods and services, taxes on, 372–414
benefit-base excises, 382
equity question, 378–379
general taxes on goods and services, 384–387
luxury excises, 379–380
miscellaneous excises, 383
regulatory and environmental excises, 383
retail sales, 384–387
retail sales taxes, 387–399
selective excise taxation, 379
sumptuary excises, 380–381
value-added taxes (VATs), 384–387, 400–407
Goodsell, Charles T., 215n
Goolsbee, Austan, 362n
Government
budgeting, 200–201s
creates market for fishing rights, 7s
enterprises, 102–103s
gambling enterprises, 479–483
revenue by source and level, 293t
revenue from tax collected by level of, 549t
in selected industrialized countries, 39t
utilities, 477–478
Government Accountability Office (GAO), 54, 210, 249n, 631
Government Accounting Standards Board (GASB), 56
Government debt, state and local, 579–606
Government expenditures
size and growth of, 32–38
state and local, 120–121t
Government finances
property taxes in U.S., 416t
when they go horribly wrong, 592–593s
Government, market failure and functions of, 2–10
externalities, 6–8
failure of competition, 8–10
public goods, 3–6
Government performance and results act (GPRA) of 1993, 216s
Government sales revenues, state and local, 462–463t
Government services
amenable to public pricing, 474t
provision of, 193–201
Government spending
in national income, 34t
as percentage of GDP, 35f
Governmental accounting and financial reporting, 56–60
Governments
federal aid to state and local, 554t
spending by state and local, 119–130
Graetz, Michael J., 417n
Graham, Cecil, 192
Gramlich, Edward M., 263n
Grant proposals, guides for writing, 557s
Grants
block, 558–559
categorical, 555–558
coordination and assistance, 551–561
Grieson, Ronald, 311n
Griffith, Cara, 561n
Gross domestic product (GDP), 32, 296, 334, 519, 576
tax revenue as percentage of, 297t
U.S. federal debt relative to, 577f
Grossman, Michael, 380n
Groves, Harold M., 332n
Growth rates and simple projections, 38s
Guidelines, charge, 474–477
Guild, Nathaniel B., 622n

H

Haig, Robert M., 341n
Hammer, Jeffrey, 12n
Hamovitch, William, 311n
Hansen, David E., 424n
Hanushek, Eric A., 232n
Harmonization, international, 364–365
Harper, Lucinda, 117n
Harris, Lee, 420n
Hart, Ariel, 473n
Hatry, Harry P., 254n
Haveman, Robert H., 273n
Haynes, William Warren, 269n
Head, J. G., 277n
Health Care Financing Administration, 218n
Heard, Jacquelyn, 180n
Heeschen, Paul E., 165n
Hildreth, B., 606n
Hildreth, W. Bartley, 308n, 515n
Hilke, John C., 15n
Hillhouse, Albert, 246n, 252n
Hilton, Rita M., 225n
Hitt, Greg, 95n
Hodge, Scott, 356n
Hoffer, George E., 418n
Holding entity, distribution of municipal debt by, 604t
Homeland Security, performance goals from Department of, 231f
Horizontal and vertical equity, 302
Hough, Wesley C., 598n
Hovey, Harold A., 267, 267n
Howard, Kenneth, 247n, 256, 256n, 257
Howitt, Arnold M., 468n
Hubbard, Kin, 470
Hubbard, R. Glenn, 363n
Hutchison, Tony, 123n, 125n

I

Idle funds, investing, 621–628
Illustrations
of new performance budget, 220f
PART performance measurement scoring, 229f
Salt Lake City performance budget, 203–204f
of tax return processing flow, 499f
Impact, shifting and incidence, 305f
Incidence, impact, shifting and, 305f

Income
argument about taxing, 336–340
defining, 340–342
expanded, 343s
family economic, 343s
Income measures, two more comprehensive, 343s
Income quintiles for all families, tax rates by, 337t
Income tax
computation, 358t
Congressional Budget Office (CBO) approach to individual, 523s
flat-rate, 356t
largest tax expenditures in federal, 534t
Income tax credit, earned, 355s
Income tax exemptions, federal individual, 348–349t
Income tax payments, distribution of federal, 337t
Income tax structure, federal individual, 341f
Income, taxable, 349–350
Income taxation, corporate, 357–365
dividing base, 361–362
integration with individual tax, 362–364
international harmonization, 364–365
Income taxation, individual, 340–357
adjusted gross income (AGI), 342–345
credits, 354
defining income, 340–342
effective tax rates, 354–356
indexation, 356–357
personal deductions, 345–347
personal exemptions, 347–349
tax computation, 357
tax rates, 350–353
taxable income, 349–350
Income taxes, 331–371
argument about taxing income, 336–340
background, 332–335
corporate income taxation, 357–365
individual and corporate, 335t
individual income taxation, 340–357
payroll taxation, 365–366
Indebtedness, summary of state and local, 582t
Indexation, 356–357
Individual and corporate income taxes, 335t
Individual benefits from project, 17t, 18t
Individual income tax, CBO approach to, 523s
Individual income tax exemptions, federal, 348–349t
Individual income tax structure, federal, 341f
Individual income taxation, 340–357
adjusted gross income (AGI), 342–345
credits, 354
defining income, 340–342
effective tax rates, 354–356
indexation, 356–357
personal deductions, 345–347
personal exemptions, 347–349
tax computation, 357
tax rates, 350–353
taxable income, 349–350
Individual tax, integration with, 362–364
Individuals filing jointly, married, 350f
Industrialized countries, government in selected, 39t
Inflation-indexed bonds, 580–581s
Information, financial, 53f
Infrastructure investment, public, 244
Ingber, Jeffrey F., 579n
Inman, Robert P., 310n
Interest rates, 599–605
Intergovernmental fiscal relations, 541–571
coordination and assistance, 547–551
correspondence and subsidiarity, 542–544
diversity and coordination, 541–571
economic advantage from bigness, 544–545
fiscal disparity, 545–547
grants coordination - and assistance, 551–561
mandates, coordination and assistance, 563–566
states and school aid, 561–563
tax systems, 547–551
Intergovernmental revenue, sources of, 553t
Internal Revenue Service (IRS), 222, 461n, 494, 618
Internal Revenue Service (IRS) by type of return, audit coverage by, 502t
International harmonization, 364–365
International Organization of Supreme Audit Institutions (ITOSAI), 54n
Internet commerce, sales taxes and, 396–399
Intra-year cash budget, 166–167
Inventory, capital asset, 250
Investing idle funds, 621–628
Investment pools, state, 627
Investment, public infrastructure, 244

J

James, Kathy, 123n, 125n
Johnson, Craig L., 438n, 606n, 623n
Johnson, David S., 118n
Johnson, James A., 476n
Johnson, Keith, 13n
Johnston, David Cay, 339n
Joyce, Philip G., 128n, 225n
Jump, Jr., Bernard, 631n

K

Kahn, Alfred E., 476n
Kaldor, Nicholas, 302n, 384n
Kalvern, Jr., Harry, 304n
Kattelus, Susan C., 58n
Katzman, Martin T., 600n
Kearns, Paula, 125n
Keeping score, 628
Kelly, Brian, 92n
Kendig, William L., 615n
Key, Jr., V. O., 31n
Keynes, John Maynard, 117n, 311, 311n
Khan, A., 606n
Kidwell, David S., 600n
Kiefer, Donald W., 117n
Kleusner, Margaret, 620n
Knight, Brian, 637n
Kohlmeier, Louis M., 635n
Kolbert, Elizabeth, 157n
Kolman, Erasmus H., 84n
Kravchuk, Robert S., 58n
Krutilla, John V., 278, 278n, 280n

L

Lady Windermere's Fan, 192, 192n
Laffer, Arthur, 311
Laixuthai, Adit, 380n
Landers, Jim, 479n
Lauth, Thomas P., 122n
Lease-purchase finance, 605–606
Lee, Connie, 599n
Lee, Jr., Robert D., 122n
Lehan, Edward A., 197n
Lemov, Penelope, 485n
Lending, state and local net, 130f
Letter of credit (LOC), 598
Levenson, Albert, 311n
Levies, arithmetic of, 420–431
Levy control, rate computations for, 446t
Licenses, user fees and, 466–468
Lichtenstein, Michael H., 614n
Liebschutz, David S., 434n
Light, Paul C., 47n
Lindholm, Richard W., 440n
Liquor stores, 477, 478
Little, Jane Sneddon, 119n
Livingston, Robert L., 21n
Local budgets, state and, 118–130
Local debt, state and, 627
Local government debt, state and, 579–606

Local government employee retirement funds, distribution of state and, 634t
Local government employee retirement system finances, state and, 632t
Local government sales revenues, state and, 462–463t
Local governments
federal aid to state and, 554t
spending by state and, 119–130
Local indebtedness, summary of state and, 582t
Local taxes on goods and services, state and, 375t
Local taxes, state and, 318–321
Localities, tax sources levied by states and, 295t
Lockbox collection system, postal, 617f
Lockboxes, value of, 618s
Long-term financial analysis. *See* Financing plan/long-term financial analysis
Long-term tax base elasticities, selected, 313t
Longman, Phillip, 12n
Lotteries and offtrack betting, 479–483
Lottery performance, state, 481t
Luxury excises, 379–380

M

MacManus, Susan A., 147n
Madhusudhan, Ranjana C., 479n
Maggs, John, 14n
Maier, Henry W., 155n
Major tax structures, 372–414
Major taxes
administrative-cost estimates for, 507t
tax revenue as percentage from, 297t
Maldonado, Rita M., 622n
Man, Joyce Y., 438n
Management
cash, 611, 612–628
financial information for, 53f
public employee retirement fund, 635–637
Management by Objective (MBO), 225
Managing funds, 611
Mandates, coordination and assistance, 563–566
Mandatory and discretionary federal spending, 104t
Mandatory/discretionary relationships, 102–103s
Mankiw, N. Gregory, 117n
Mansfield, Edwin, 544n
Mantell, Nancy, 515n
Manvel, Allen, 424n
Manwaring, Robert L., 561n
Margolis, Julius, 273n
Market failure and functions of government, 2–10
externalities, 6–8
failure of competition, 8–10
public goods, 3–6
Market for fishing rights, government creates, 7s
Marks, T. H., 522n
Married individuals filing jointly, 350f
Marshall, John, 344n
Martinez-Vasquez, Jorge, 543n
Mason, Paul M., 483n
Matson, Morris C., 245n
Maydew, Edward L., 362n
Mayer, Christopher J., 427n
McCaffery, Jerry, 65n, 115n, 238n
McCartner, Scott, 457n
McCarty, T. N., 522n
McDaniel, Paul R., 534, 534n
McKean, Roland, 278, 278n
McLure, Jr., Charles E., 373n
McNees, Stephen K., 527n
Measurement scoring illustration, PART performance, 229f
Medicare, Social Security and, 107–108s
Medium-term expenditure frameworks (MTEF), 46n
Megginson, William L., 12n, 13n
Melkers, 220n
Meltsner, Arnold J., 152n
Mencken, H. L., 298n
Mergent Municipal Rating Group, yield by, 595t
Mihm, J. Christopher, 222n
Mikesell, John L., 22n, 295, 311n, 313n, 382n, 387n, 389n, 393n, 394n, 396n, 397n, 406n, 418n, 424n, 442n, 482n, 492n, 501n, 507n, 532n, 606n, 623n
Miller, Girard, 626n
Miller, Merton H., 622n
Minimum tax, alternate, 359–360s
Moak, Lennox, 246n, 252n
Money-market mutual funds, 628
Monopolies, revenue from sales by public, 461
Monopoly revenue, public, 477–483
government gambling enterprises, 479–483
government utilities, 477–478
liquor stores, 478
lotteries and offtrack betting, 479–483
Moore, Basil J., 612n
Moore, Thomas, 179n
Morgan, Jr., Daniel C., 389n
Morgenstern, Richard, 311n
Morris, Timothy J., 85n
Mosher, Frederick, 84n
Moss, Michael, 623n
Mullins, Daniel R., 125n, 128n, 444n
Multiple regression, steps in revenue forecasting by, 522t
Municipal and AAA corporate debt, yield of Aaa, 591f
Municipal bonds and Tax Reform Act of 1986, 584–585
Municipal debt, 579–606
Municipal debt by holding entity, distribution of, 604t
Municipal Rating Group, yield by Mergent, 595t
Muris, Timothy J., 141n
Murray, Alan, 158n
Murray, Matthew, 406n, 494n
Murray, Shailagh, 64n
Musgrave, Richard A., 268f, 294, 294n, 305n
Mushkin, Selma J., 472n, 474, 474n
Mutual funds, money-market, 628

N

Nachimaias, David, 22n
National Aeronautics and Space Administration (NASA), 64–65
National Endowment for the Arts (NEA), 223
National Football League (NFL), 267n
Negotiable certificates of deposit (CDs), 625–626
Nester, Howard, 522n
Net interest cost (NIC), 601
Net lending, state and local, 130f
Net present value (NPV), 244n
and evaluating capital project, 275s
Netter, Jeffry M., 12n
Neubig, Tom, 389n
New performance budget, illustration of, 220f
New performance budgeting, 214–232, 221–225
New Zealand Value-Added Tax (VAT) Return, 404f
NIC computation worksheet, TIC and, 603t
Niskanen, Jr., William A., 199n
Nonappropriability, elements of, 4f
Nonmarket goods, measuring value of, 270s
Nonpersonnel costs, 147–148
Nowak, Norman D., 501n

O

Oates, Wallace E., 419n, 420n, 542n
Object-of-expenditure (or input) format, 42–45
Office of Management and Budget (OMB), 82, 156n, 228, 265n, 515
Offtrack betting, lotteries and, 479–483
O'Leary, Rosemary, 23n
O'Lessker, Karl, 88n

Olsen, Nina E., 338n
On-budget/off-budget, 102–103s
Opschoor, J. B., 322n
Organization for Economic Cooperation and Development (OECD), 296, 297n, 364n, 385
Orr, Daniel, 622n
Osborne, David, 198n, 215n
Outcomes. *See* Results/outcomes
Outcomes, activities or, 217–218t
Outlays
  discretionary federal, 105f
  federal, 81t
  relationship of budget authority to, 53f
Owens, Cynthia, 67n
Ownership, 599–605

P

Packer, Frank, 594n
Pagano, Michael A., 246n
Paper, commercial, 626
Parcel record card for residential real property, 430–431f
Pareto, Vilfredo, 16n
Parisi, Michael, 352n
Park, individual demand for, 268f
Parker, Jonathan A., 118n
Parker, Robert P., 33n
Parsons, Christi, 20n
PART performance measurement scoring illustration, 229f
PART (Program Assessment Rating Tool), 226
Partlan, John C., 612n
Patitucci, Frank M., 614n
Patrol, border, 229f
Patterson, D. Jeanne, 636n
Patton, Terry K., 58n
Pay-as-you-go (PAYGO), 115, 527
Payback analysis, 276t
Paying staff, 146–147
Payments, distribution of federal income tax, 337t
Payroll taxation, 365–366
Pearson, Rick, 20n
Pechman, Joseph A., 298n
Pension Benefit Guaranty Corporation (PBGC), 109n
Pension funds, fifteen largest public employee, 629t
Performance
  government, 216s
  measuring, 628
Performance and budgeting, federal integration of, 226–232
Performance budget illustration
  new, 220f
  Salt Lake City, 203–204f
Performance budgeting
  challenges for new, 221–225
  new, 214–232
Performance budgets, 201–205
Performance goals from Department of Homeland Security, 231f
Personal deductions, 345–347
Personal exemptions, 347–349
Personnel costs, 146–147. *See also* Nonpersonnel costs
Peters, B. Guy, 225n
Peters, J. L., 515n
Petersen, John E., 427n, 598n, 600n
Peterson, George E., 417n, 583n
Phantom balance, 156–161
Phantom balance and deficit reduction, 156–161
Phillips, Andrew, 389n
Pierre, Jon, 225n
Pigou, A. C., 322n
Pilot, California's ReadyReturn, 496s
Planning process
  revenue systems as separate, 41f
  service delivery as separate, 41f
Planning Programming Budget Execution System (PPBES), 209–210
Pogue, Thomas F., 308n
Policy, debt, 585–586
Policy, tax, 298–318
Political strategies, budgets and, 61–69
Politics, cost-benefit analysis and, 279–280
Pollock, Richard, 127n
Portney, Paul R., 273n, 279n
Postal lockbox collection system, 617f
Pounian, Charles A., 147n
Pozo, Susan, 493n
Pradhan, Sanjay, 48n
Pratt, Michael D., 418n
President's Management Agenda (PMA), 226
Price change, deflating-dividing between real and, 36s
Price, Willard, 472n
Pricing, public, 474t
Pricing, tax-exclusive and tax-inclusive, 386s
Privatization, 11–24
  building social decisions from private preferences, 15–19
  layers of government, 22–24
  politics, representation, and government finance, 19–22
Producers' goods, exclusion of, 389–393
Production and distribution, flow of, 377f
Production, revenue, 309–313
Program Assessment Rating Tool (PART), 226
Program budget structure, 206–207t
  in U.S. Department of Defense, 209t
Program budgets, 205–212
Project, capital, 275s
Project evaluation, 244
Project, individual benefits from, 17t, 18t
Projections, growth rates and simple, 38s
Prompt-payment discounts, 619s
Property classifications by statutory rates and assessment ratios, 437t
Property tax bills, coefficient of dispersion and, 443s
Property tax control structures and impacts, 444t
Property tax relief mechanisms, 431–448
  circuit-breakers, 434–436
  classification, 436–437
  deferrals, 436
  exemptions and abatements, 432–434
  fractional assessment and assessment disparity, 439–443
  limits and controls, 443–448
  tax increment financing (TIF), 437–438
Property taxation notification, truth in, 447f
Property taxes, 415–460
  arithmetic of rates, levies, and assessed value, 420–431
  good or bad taxes, 418–420
  property tax relief mechanisms, 431–448
  in U.S. government finances, 416t
Proposals, guides for writing grant, 557s
Provision, flow of public-service, 194f
Public employee pension funds, fifteen largest, 629t
Public employee retirement fund management, 628–637, 635–637
Public expenditure/public revenue process, 40–42
Public finance, principles of, 1–27
  market failure and functions of government, 2–10
  privatization, 11–24
Public goods, 3–6
Public infrastructure investment, 244
Public monopolies, revenue from sales by, 461
Public monopoly revenue, 477–483
  government gambling enterprises, 479–483
  government utilities, 477–478
  liquor stores, 478
  lotteries and offtrack betting, 479–483
Public pricing, government services amenable to, 474t
Public revenue process. *See* Public expenditure/public revenue process
Public school district revenues by source of funds, 562t

Public-service provision, flow of, 194f
Putka, Gary, 14n
Pyramiding, retail sales tax, 378t, 390f

Q

Question, equity, 378–379

R

Rados, David L., 476n
Rafool, Mandy, 128n
Ranking criteria conflict, projects with, 277t
Ratchford, B. U., 583n
Rate computations for levy control, 446t
Rates
  arithmetic of, 420–431
  discount, 272s
  discounted, 271–273
  effective tax, 354–356
  interest, 599–605
  tax, 350–353
Rating Group, yield by Mergent Municipal, 595t
Ratings, 591–597
  credit, 596–597t
Ratios and shares, 153s
Real property, parcel record card for residential, 430–431f
Receipts
  and disbursements, 615f
  federal user charge, 465t
Reduction, deficit, 156–161
Reed, Steven R., 457n
Reel, Monte, 68n
Reese, Thomas J., 298n
Regression, steps in revenue forecasting by multiple, 522t
Regulatory and environmental excises, 383
Relationships, mandatory/discretionary, 102–103s
Remote vendors and use taxes, 396–399
Reports, budget-status, 164f
Repurchase agreements, 626–627
Residential real property, parcel record card for, 430–431f
Results/outcomes, 214–232
Retail sales, 384–387
Retail sales tax (RST), 376
  pyramiding, 378t, 390f
  value-added tax (VAT) versus, 406–407
Retail sales taxes, 387–399
  commodity exemptions, 394–395
  exclusion of producers' goods, 389–393
  remote vendors and use taxes, 396–399
  sales taxes and Internet commerce, 396–399
  taxation of services, 393–394
  variation in state sales taxes, 395–396
Retail Sales, Virginia, 388f
Retirement fund management, public employee, 635–637
Retirement funds
  distribution of state and local government employee, 634t
  employee, 611
  managing public employee, 628–637
Retirement system finances, state and local government employee, 632t
Returns
  audit coverage by Internal Revenue Service (IRS) by type of, 502t
  New Zealand Value-Added Tax (VAT), 404f
Revenue curve, tax, 310f
Revenue, estimating, 514, 527–530
Revenue forecast (or baseline), 515–527
  alternative methods for forecasting, 518–524
  choosing method, 524–525
  forecasts for long term, 526–527
  general guides for, 516–518
  wrong forecasts, 527
Revenue forecasting, steps in, 522t
Revenue forecasts, 514
Revenue options, criteria for evaluating, 291–330
Revenue process, public expenditure/public, 40–42
Revenue production, adequacy of, 309–313
Revenue, public monopoly, 477–483
  government gambling enterprises, 479–483
  government utilities, 477–478
  liquor stores, 478
  lotteries and offtrack betting, 479–483
Revenues
  government, 293t
  intergovernmental, 553t
  public school district, 562t
  from sales by public monopolies, 461
  sharing, 560–561
  state and local government sales, 462–463t
  systems as separate planning process, 41f
  from tax collected by level of government, 549t
  from user charges, 461
  from user fees, 461
Reverse repurchase agreements, 626–627
Rhyne, Charles S., 466n
Richardson, James A., 308n, 515n
Ring, Jr., Raymond J., 389n
Riordon, William L., 169n
Ritter, Lawrence S., 622n
Robb, Edward H., 311n
Robinson, Roland I., 579n
Rogers, David, 570n
Rogers, Diane Lim, 307n
Rogowski, Robert J., 600n
Rosenberg, Philip, 613
Rousmaniere, Peter F., 54n, 168n
Rowland, Mary, 353n
RST and VAT, economic equivalence of, 401s
RST (retail sales tax), 376
  pyramiding, 378t, 390f
  value-added tax (VAT) versus, 406–407
Rubin, Irene S., 64n, 123n
Rubin, Marilyn Marks, 515n

S

Sack, Kevin, 159n
Sacramento Regional Transit District Certificates of Participation (COP), 604s
Saddler, Michelle R., 626n
Saffer, Henry, 380n
Salary classification in miscellaneous budgets, 213f
Sales by public monopolies, revenue from, 461
Sales, retail, 384–387
Sales revenues, state and local government, 462–463t
Sales tax by certificate, suspending, 392f
Sales taxes and Internet commerce, 396–399
Sales taxes, retail, 378t, 387–399, 390f
  commodity exemptions, 394–395
  exclusion of producers' goods, 389–393
  remote vendors and use taxes, 396–399
  sales taxes and Internet commerce, 396–399
  taxation of services, 393–394
  variation in state sales taxes, 395–396
Sales taxes, variation in state, 395–396
Sales, Virginia Retail, 388f
Salt Lake City performance budget illustration, 203–204f
Sanford, C., 384n
Sanford, Cedric, 507n
Santoro, Paul J., 612n
Sawyer, Lawrence B., 165n
Schemo, Diana Jean, 225n
Schenker, Eric, 264n
Schick, Allen, 209n
School aid, states and, 561–563
Schultze, Charles L., 117n

Schwab, Robert M., 420n
Schwartz, Eli, 295, 475n, 579n
Schwartz, S. I., 424n
Score, keeping, 628
Securities and Exchange Commission (SEC), 594n
Seidman, Laurence S., 384n
Selective excise taxation, 379
Separate planning process
  revenue systems as, 41f
  service delivery as, 41f
Separation, tax-source, 549t
Service delivery as separate planning process, 41f
Services
  federal taxes on goods and, 374t
  general taxes on goods and, 384–387
  provision of government, 193–201
  state and local taxes on goods and, 375t
  taxation of, 393–394
Services, taxes on goods and, 372–414
  benefit-base excises, 382
  equity question, 378–379
  general taxes on goods and services, 384–387
  luxury excises, 379–380
  miscellaneous excises, 383
  regulatory and environmental excises, 383
  retail sales, 384–387
  retail sales taxes, 387–399
  selective excise taxation, 379
  sumptuary excises, 380–381
  value-added taxes (VATs), 384–387, 400–407
Shannon, John, 440, 440n, 552, 552n
Shapiro, Ian, 417n
Shares, ratios and, 153s
Sharing, revenue, 560–561
Sheffrin, Steven M., 561n
Shifting and incidence, impact, 305f
Shome, Parthasarathi, 360n, 519n
Shoup, Carl S., 495n
Simons, Henry C., 341n
Single filers, 350f
Slemrod, Joel, 337n, 338n, 494n, 508n
Slobodzian, Joseph A., 177n
Smidt, Seymour, 276n
Smith, Adam, 299n, 309n
Smith, Randall, 633n
Snell, Ronald K., 126n
Social insurance contributions, 335t
Social Security and Medicare, 107–108s
Sorum, Nikki, 508n
Souleles, Nicholas S., 118n
Speare, Jon K., 613n
Spending
  government, 34t, 35f
  mandatory and discretionary
  federal, 104t
  by state and local governments, 119–130
Stabile, Donald R., 576n
Staff, paying, 146–147
Stallings, C. Wayne, 613
State and local budgets, 118–130
State and local debt, 627
State and local government
  debt, 579–606
  expenditures, 120–121t
  sales revenues, 462–463t
State and local government employee retirement funds, distribution of, 634t
State and local government employee retirement system finances, 632t
State and local governments
  federal aid to, 554t
  spending by, 119–130
State and local indebtedness, summary of, 582t
State and local net lending, 130f
State and local taxes, 318–321
  on goods and services, 375t
State budget cycles, 126t
State investment pools, 627
State lottery performance, 481t
State sales taxes, variation in, 395–396
States and localities, tax sources levied by, 295t
States and school aid, 561–563
Statutory rates and assessment ratios, property classifications by, 437t
Steiss, Alan Walter, 252n
Stern, Nicholas, 315n
Steuerle, Eugene, 531, 531n
Stiglitz, Joseph E., 114, 114n, 305n
Stocker, Frederick D., 475, 475n, 480n
Stockman, David A., 161n
Stoke, Charles B., 266n
Stores, liquor, 477, 478
Stout, David, 160n
Straussman, Jeffrey D., 23n
Streamlined Sales Tax Project (SSTP), 399
Streeter, Sandy, 88n
Subsidiarity, correspondence and, 542–544
Sumptuary excises, 380–381
Sunley, Emil M., 528n
Surpluses of federal government, deficits and, 110–111t
Surrey, Stanley S., 534, 534n
Suyderhoud, Jack P., 127n
Systems, tax, 303t, 547–551

T

Table, portion of federal tax, 351f
Tait, Alan A., 400n
Tannenwald, Robert, 546n
Tanzi, Vito, 298n, 519n
Tatom, John A., 112n, 379n
Tax
  alternate minimum, 359–360s
  computation, 357
  excess burden of, 317s
  flat-rate income, 356t
  integration with individual, 362–364
Tax base elasticities, selected long-term, 313t
Tax bills, coefficient of dispersion and property, 443s
Tax collected by level of government, revenue from, 549t
Tax collection, core functions of, 496–505
  appeal or protest, 503–504
  audit, 501–503
  declaration or assessment, 498
  delinquency control, compliance, and collections, 500–501
  enforcement, 505
  revenue and taxpayer accounting, 498–500
  taxpayer registration/service, 497
Tax credit, earned income, 355s
Tax distributions for all families, federal, 306–307t
Tax-exclusive and tax-inclusive pricing, 386s
Tax exemptions, federal individual income, 348–349t
Tax expenditures
  budgets, 514, 530–534
  estimates, 533s
  in federal income tax, 534t
Tax-inclusive pricing, tax-exclusive and, 386s
Tax increment financing (TIF), 437–438, 438t
Tax payments, distribution of federal income, 337t
Tax policy, standards for, 298–318
  adequacy of revenue production, 309–313
  collectability, 314
  economic effects, 315–318
  equity, 300–309
Tax pyramiding, retail sales, 378t, 390f
Tax rate and tax revenue, relationships between, 310f
Tax rates, 350–353
  effective, 354–356
  by income quintiles for all families, 337t
Tax Reform Act of 1986, municipal bonds and, 584–585
Tax relief mechanisms, property, 431–448

Tax return processing flow, illustration of, 499f
Tax Return, Virginia Retail Sales and Use, 388f
Tax revenue
curve, 310f
as percentage from major taxes, 297t
as percentage of gross domestic product (GDP), 297t
relationships between tax rate and, 310f
Tax-source separation, 549t
Tax sources levied by states and localities, 295t
Tax structures, 415–460
arithmetic of rates, levies, and assessed value, 420–431
federal individual income, 341f
good or bad taxes, 418–420
property tax relief mechanisms, 431–448
property taxes, 415–460
Tax structures, major, 331–371, 372–414
argument about taxing income, 336–340
background, 332–335
benefit-base excises, 382
corporate income taxation, 357–365
equity question, 378–379
general taxes on goods and services, 384–387
individual income taxation, 340–357
payroll taxation, 365–366
regulatory and environmental excises, 383
retail sales, 384–387
retail sales taxes, 387–399
sumptuary excises, 380–381
value-added taxes (VATs), 384–387, 400–407
Tax systems, 547–551
regressivity, proportionally, and progressivity in, 303t
Tax table, portion of federal, 351f
Taxable income, 349–350
Taxation, 291–330
corporate income, 357–365
criteria for evaluating revenue options, 291–330
economic development, 318–321
individual income, 340–357
payroll, 365–366
selective excise, 379
of services, 393–394
standards for tax policy, 298–318
state and local taxes, 318–321
taxes and externalities, 322–324
in United States, 292–298
Taxation notification, truth in property, 447f
Taxes
administrative-cost estimates for major, 507t
and externalities, 322–324
good or bad, 418–420
income, 331–371
individual and corporate income, 335t
property, 415–460
remote vendors and use, 396–399
sales, 396–399
state and local, 318–321, 375t
tax revenue as percentage from major, 297t
variation in state sales, 395–396
Taxes, collecting, 492–513
core functions of tax collection, 496–505
people and businesses paying taxes they owe, 492–494
taxpayer active or passive, 494–496
total collection cost, 505–508
Taxes on goods and services, 372–414
benefit-base excises, 382
equity question, 378–379
general, 384–387
general taxes on goods and services, 384–387
luxury excises, 379–380
miscellaneous excises, 383
regulatory and environmental excises, 383
retail sales, 384–387
retail sales taxes, 387–399
selective excise taxation, 379
sumptuary excises, 380–381
value-added taxes (VATs), 384–387, 400–407
Taxes, retail sales, 387–399
commodity exemptions, 394–395
exclusion of producers' goods, 389–393
remote vendors and use taxes, 396–399
sales taxes and Internet commerce, 396–399
taxation of services, 393–394
variation in state sales taxes, 395–396
Taxing income, argument about, 336–340
Tempe, Arizona, line-item budget for fire department, 43–44f
Ter-Minassian, Teresa, 543n
Texas Commission for the Blind, 220f
Thornton, Daniel L., 112n
Thurmaier, Kurt, 23n
TIC and NIC computation worksheet, 603t
Tidrick, Donald E., 58n
Time, accounting for, 258–263
Timetable, congressional budget, 89t
Traditional budgets, 196–201
Trainer, Richard D. C., 624n
Transparency, 320–321
Treasury bills (t-bills), 624
auctioning of, 625s
Treasury yield curve, U.S., 590f
Triplett, Jack E., 33n
True interest cost (TIC), 601
Trust funds. *See* Federal funds/trust funds
Tullock, Gordon, 19n, 199n
Turner, Nicholas, 546n

U

Underwriting, 599–605
Unfunded Mandates Reform Act of 1995 (UMRA), 565
U.S.
Department of Agriculture (USDA), 210
federal debt relative to GDP, 577f
government spending in, 35f
taxation in, 292–298
treasury yield curve, 590f
U.S. government finances, property taxes in, 416t
Use Tax Return, Virginia Retail Sales and, 388f
Use taxes, remote vendors and, 396–399
User charge receipts, federal, 465t
User charges, 461, 468–477
advantages of, 470–472
limitations of, 472–474
User fees
and licenses, 466–468
revenue from, 461
Utilities, government, 477–478
Utt, Ronald D., 92n

V

Vaillancourt, Francois, 508n
Value-Added Tax (VAT) Return, New Zealand, 404f
Value-added taxes (VATs), 376, 384–387, 400–407, 519
economic equivalence of RSTs and, 401s
features, 403–406
rate in countries around world, 405t
versus retail sales taxes (RSTs), 406–407
Van der Hoek, M. Peter, 60n
Vehorn, Charles L., 472n
Vendors, remote, 396–399
Verbugge, James A., 625n

Vertical equity, horizontal and, 302
Vickers, John, 11n
Vining, Aidan, 280n
Virginia Retail Sales and Use Tax Return, 388f
Viscusi, W.K., 279n
Vogt, Walter, 545n
Voorhees, William R., 58n
Vos, H. B., 322n

W

Wagner, Gary A., 127n
Walden, Michael L., 310n
Wallich, Christine I., 543n
Wallin, Bruce, 444n
Wasi, Nada, 426n
Wasylenko, Michael, 319n
Waters, W. G., 280n
Weisbrod, Burton A., 278, 278n
Weiss, Edmond H., 197n
Weiss, Randall D., 528n
Welch, Ronald B., 506n
Weyant, John P., 273n
White, James A., 599n, 636n
White, Michelle J., 426n
Widow(er)s, qualifying, 350f
Wildavsky, Aaron, 61, 62n, 64n, 65n
Wilde, Oscar, 192, 192n
Willoughby, 220n
Wilson, Earl R., 58n
Wise, Charles R., 23n
Wismer, David A., 622n
Worksheet, TIC and NIC computation, 603t
World, value-added tax (VAT) rate in countries around, 405t
Writing grant proposals, guides for, 557s
Wyscarver, Roy A., 522n

Y

Yarrow, George, 11n
Ybarra, Michael J., 636n
Yield curve, U.S. treasury, 590f
Young, David W., 65n

Z

Zee, Howell H., 298n
Zero-based budget (ZBB), 225
Zimmerman, Dennis, 585n
Zodrow, George R., 419n
Zorn, C. Kurt, 311n, 522n